Percentage distribution of GDP, 1993												
Agriculture	Industry	Services and other	Government purchases as percentage of GDP, 1993	Exports as a percentage of GDP, 1993	Gross domestic saving as a percentage of GDP, 1993	Central government surplus/deficit (−) as percentage of GDP	Annual inflation rate, 1980–1993	Energy consumption per capita, 1993 (kg of oil equivalent)	Life expectancy at birth, 1993 (years)	Infant mortality rate, 1993 (per 1,000 live births)	Under-5 mortality rate, 1993 (per 1,000 live births)	Country
33	12	55	17	21	−11	na	42.3	43	46	146	282	Mozambique
56	14	30	9	31	10	na	24.3	35	52	84	167	Tanzania
53	12	35	14	5	−2	na	na	21	45	114	185	Uganda
31	27	41	11	11	24	−4.8	8.7	242	61	80	122	India
30	18	52	14	12	8	na	8.6	59	56	106	122	Bangladesh
29	18	54	13	42	21	−3.8	9.9	99	58	61	94	Kenya
34	43	24	18	36	19	na	20.6	141	51	83	191	Nigeria
25	25	50	14	16	12	−7.4	7.4	209	62	88	137	Pakistan
19	48	33	9	24	40	−2.3	7.0	623	69	30	54	China
23	36	41	22	na	34	na	24.5	2,033	69	40	66	Uzbekistan
22	33	45	9	32	16	−1.5	13.6	328	67	42	59	Philippines
21	40	40	12	23	22	−4.7	22.4	1,765	70	23	29	Romania
19	39	42	10	28	31	0.7	8.5	321	63	56	111	Indonesia
18	22	60	14	25	6	−4.1	13.6	539	64	64	86	Egypt
15	30	55	13	14	22	−7.0	53.5	983	67	62	84	Turkey
35	47	18	13	17	7	na	37.2	3,960	69	16	26	Ukraine
6	39	55	22	19	13	na	69.3	2,390	71	15	17	Poland
9	51	39	15	39	32	na	35.4	4,438	65	21	31	Russia
11	37	52	na	8	21	−1.0	423.4	666	67	57	63	Brazil
13	43	43	17	22	28	na	13.2	955	67	53	68	Algeria
24	29	47	15	24	30	−1.4	17.1	1,235	68	35	54	Iran
16	35	50	12	17	18	na	24.9	694	70	36	44	Colombia
10	39	51	10	37	36	2.1	4.3	678	69	36	45	Thailand
8	28	63	9	13	16	na	57.9	1,439	71	35	43	Mexico
na	na	na	13	80	38	1.7	2.2	1,529	71	13	17	Malaysia
6	31	63	na	6	na	na	374.3	1,351	72	24	27	Argentina
7	43	50	11	29	35	0.6	6.3	2,863	71	11	12	Korea
na	na	na	18	19	19	−3.7	8.4	2,373	78	7	9	Spain
1	38	61	20	22	22	−2.4	2.8	4,170	76	6	7	Germany
2	33	65	22	25	14	−5.1	5.6	3,718	76	7	8	United Kingdom
3	32	65	18	23	20	−10.1	8.8	2,697	78	8	9	Italy
3	29	67	18	19	19	−2.3	6.1	5,316	78	7	8	Australia
3	29	69	19	23	20	−3.8	5.1	4,031	77	7	9	France
na	na	na	22	30	18	−3.8	3.9	7,821	78	7	8	Canada
2	41	57	10	9	33	na	1.5	3,642	80	4	6	Japan
na	na	na	17	10	15	−4.0	3.8	7,918	76	9	10	United States
				21	22		19.6	1,421	66	48	75	World

Economics

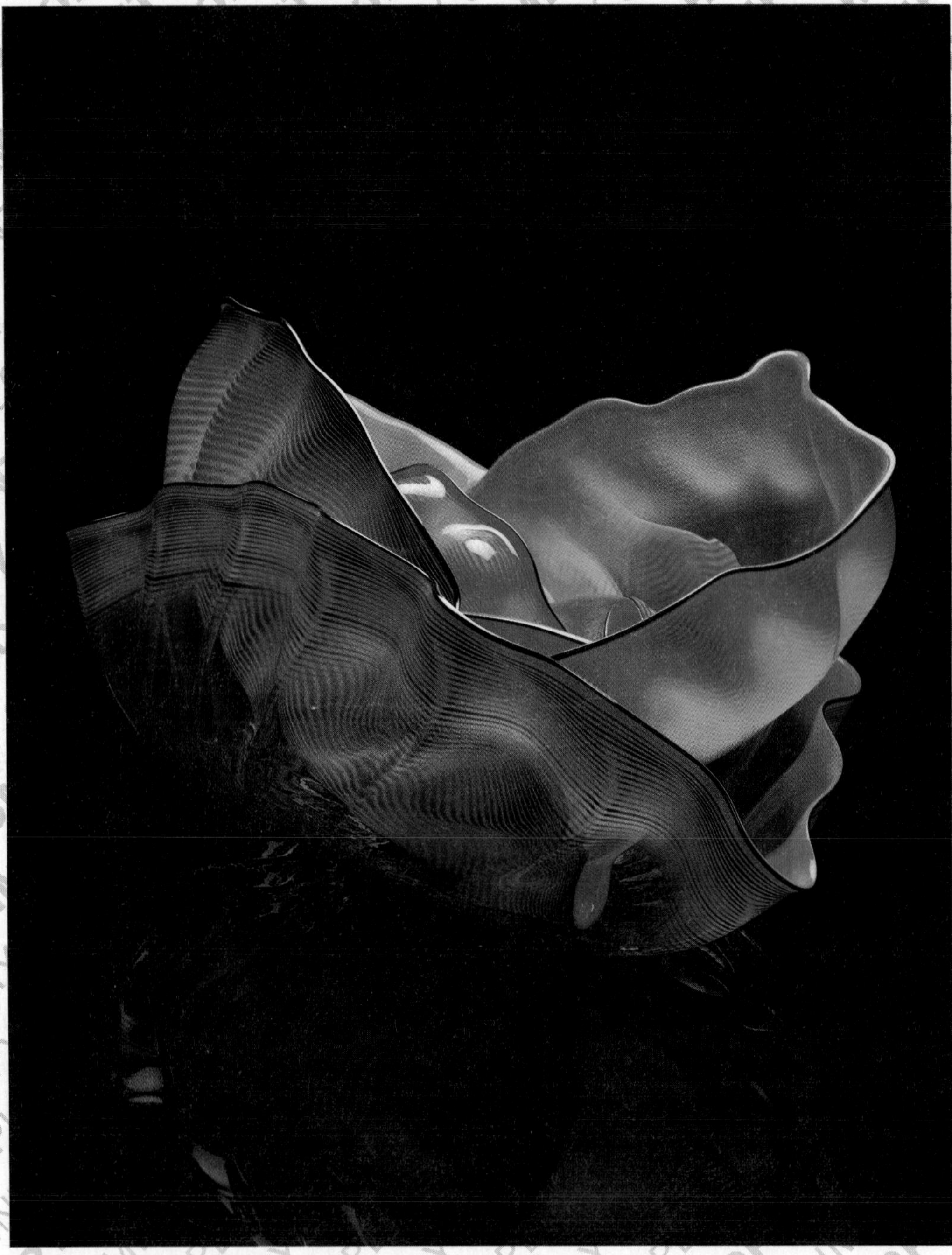

Photo by Roger Schreiber

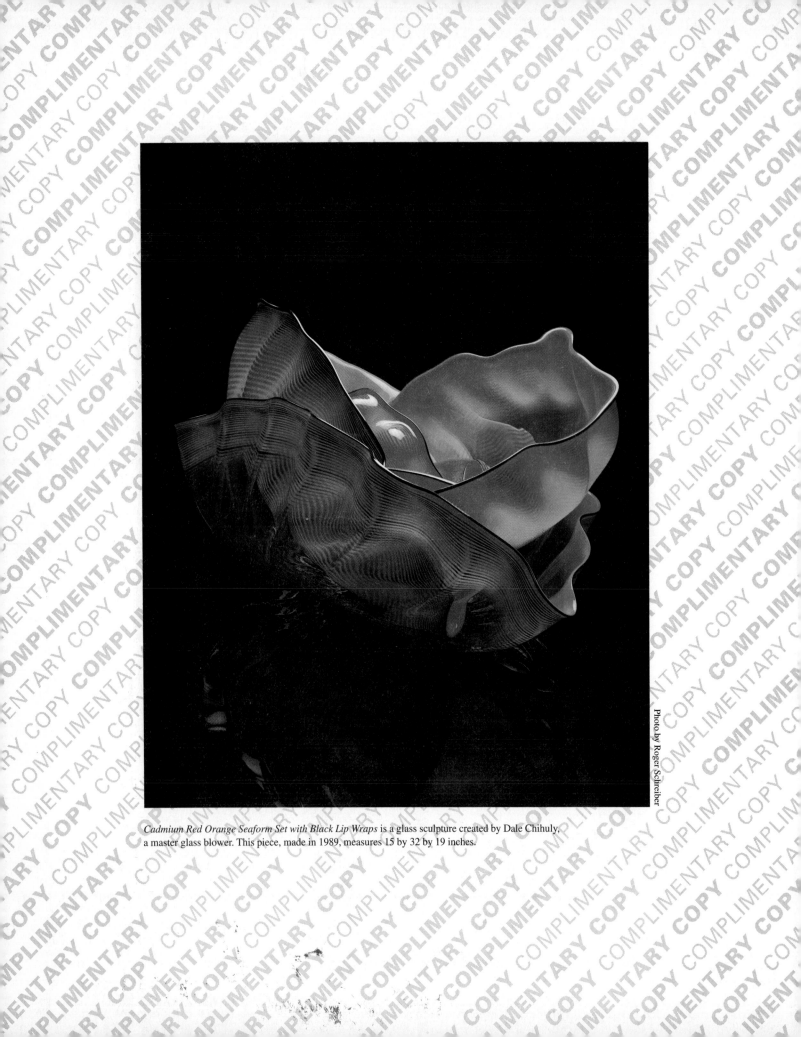

Cadmium Red Orange Seaform Set with Black Lip Wraps is a glass sculpture created by Dale Chihuly, a master glass blower. This piece, made in 1989, measures 15 by 32 by 19 inches.

Economics

Timothy Tregarthen

University of Colorado, Colorado Springs

WORTH PUBLISHERS

For Suzanne, Doran, and Brittany, with love

Economics

Printed in the United States of America
Library of Congress Card Catalog No. 95-061217
ISBN: 1-57259-093-9
Printing: 1 2 3 4—99 98 97 96

Development Editor: Elisa Adams
Design: Malcolm Grear Designers
Art Director: George Toulomes
Production Editors: Elizabeth Mastalski and Margaret Comaskey
Production Supervisor: Stacey B. Alexander
Layout: Heriberto Lugo
Picture Editor: Lana Berkovich
Line Art: Demetrios Zangos
Composition and Separations: Progressive Information Technologies
Printing and Binding: Von Hoffmann Press, Inc.

Cover: *Cadmium Red Orange Seaform Set with Black Lip Wraps* 1989.
(Detail) Glass sculpture by Dale Chihuly. 15 × 32 × 19″.
Photo by Roger Schreiber
Illustration credits begin on page IC-1 and constitute an extension of the copyright page.

Value-Pak bundled items with corresponding ISBN numbers:

1-57259-172-2
Tregarthen: Economics with Mogab/McClung: Study Guide
t/a Economics

1-57259-173-0
Tregarthen: Microeconomics with Mogab/McClung: Study Guide
t/a Microeconomics

1-57259-174-9
Tregarthen: Macroeconomics with Mogab/McClung: Study Guide
t/a Macroeconomics

1-57259-201-X
Tregarthen: Economics with Alston/Chi: Visual Microeconomics and Alston/Chi: Visual Macroeconomics

1-57259-202-8
Tregarthen: Microeconomics with Alston/Chi: Visual Microeconomics

1-57259-203-6
Tregarthen: Macroeconomics with Alston/Chi: Visual Macroeconomics

1-57259-176-5
Alston/Chi: Visual Microeconomics with Alston/Chi: Visual Macroeconomics

Worth Publishers

33 Irving Place
New York, NY 10003

About the Author

Timothy Tregarthen is Professor of Economics at the University of Colorado at Colorado Springs (UCCS). He has taught at the University since 1971, and has served as Chairman of the Department of Economics from 1974 to 1985. He has received two outstanding teaching awards at the university and in 1987 he received the Chancellor's Award as the university's outstanding professor.

Dr. Tregarthen completed his graduate work in economics at the University of California at Davis, where he was a Woodrow Wilson National Fellow and a Regents Fellow. He received his M.A. in economics in 1970 and his Ph.D. in 1972. He was student body president at California State University at Chico and received his B.A. in economics *magna cum laude* from that institution in 1967.

He was Executive Editor of *The Margin* magazine from 1985 to 1994. He founded the freshman seminar program at UCCS in 1991 and served as director of the program until 1995. He has been a visiting professor at The Colorado College and for the Semester at Sea program.

He is the author of hundreds of articles on a wide range of economic issues. He has written two books and a nationally syndicated humor column on economics from 1980 to 1985.

Dr. Tregarthen has long been active in community affairs in Colorado Springs. He was Chairman of the El Paso County Planning Commission. He also chaired the board of the National Multiple Sclerosis Society, Southeast Colorado Chapter. He is currently a Stephen Minister at Calvary United Methodist Church, a peer counselor for the Colorado Springs Multiple Sclerosis Society, and a member of Centennial Sertoma Club.

Contents in Brief

Contents

List of Cases in Point

Preface

Three developments in this decade will shape all our lives in the next century:

- New trade agreements have brought international trade to the forefront of daily life to a greater degree than ever before.
- The shift to market-based economic systems all over the world has transformed the challenges of economic development and of international relations.
- Communications technology, which has advanced dramatically over the past 150 years, has taken even more rapid leaps in the last five. It will change the way we live, the way we play, and the way we learn.

As if all these changes were not enough, developments in the works over the last two decades provide a backdrop of change that renders these current developments all the more breathtaking. The integration of computer technology into virtually all aspects of production has revolutionized the workplace and the demands it places on all of us. The slowing pace of economic growth has made choices in economic policy even more difficult. The emergence of a persistent federal budget deficit, and the struggle to bring it down, have helped set the stage for a fundamental debate over the appropriate role of government in a market economy.

The changes that are sweeping our world have important implications for introductory courses in economics—and the texts designed for them. They do not, of course, change the essential content of the course. Much of the power of economics lies in the fact that its basic principles help us to understand our world—regardless of how much that world might have changed. Indeed, the dizzying pace of change that we see all about us makes the mastery of these basic principles all the more important. I believe that a textbook that will help usher in the next century must

- make clear to students just what the essential principles of economics are,
- establish strong links between theoretical principles and real-world experience,
- incorporate a clear and consistent international focus from beginning to end, and
- give students a sense of the intellectual excitement of the field and an appreciation for the gains it has achieved and the challenges that lie ahead.

I have written *Economics* because I believe that these goals are important and that they are achievable. *Economics* achieves them by offering students a book that is relevant, organized in a way that stresses basic concepts, and offers a clear framework for understanding essential ideas.

Relevance

Economics as a field has enjoyed enormous success because of its relevance to the issues, big and small, that we all face. I've tried very hard to bring that sense of relevance to my writing of *Economics.* Each chapter begins with a *What's Ahead* essay that presents some issue relevant to the chapter. As analytical tools and concepts are introduced, they're applied in a series of lively, provocative *Case in Point* essays.

In these essays, readers will see how economic forces have influenced real issues and real people. Many of the *What's Ahead* and *Case in Point* essays are based on stories of people who are grappling with the forces examined in the text. When students read about the impact of exchange rates, they'll meet a business executive whose firm was clobbered by the fall of the peso in 1994 and 1995. When they read about the effects of inflation, they'll find out how Ferdinand Porsche, the automobile engineer, ended up selling one of the grandest cars in the world for enough money for a half-dozen rides on the local streetcar system. When they read about shutdown points for a firm, they'll meet a vintner who shut down a vineyard in the face of falling prices for red grapes.

The sense of relevance brought by the *What's Ahead* and *Case in Point* essays is reinforced in the discussion questions at the end of the chapter. These questions include not only general review questions to test basic understanding but examples drawn from the news and, again, from interviews with people in the marketplace. These questions not only suggest the relevance of economic analysis but they strengthen students' critical thinking skills as they apply economics to real situations.

Students will get a big dose of relevance in the first chapter of *Economics.* As I was getting the manuscript ready to go to press in 1995, I picked a single day in February and selected events from that day, drawn from newspapers all over the country. The chapter presents those events with a discussion of how economics applies to them. Students will see how stories ranging from the finding of a red wolf cub in Bull's Island in North Carolina to a move by the Fed to raise interest rates relate to economics and to the material they'll be studying in the course.

Textbooks have a three-year life span, and over that period new events will unfold and new issues will emerge. I will be writing new *Case in Point* essays throughout the next three years and making those essays available to readers over the Internet and through distribution to instructors.

Organization

Economics breaks new ground in its organization. The basic set of topics presented in all introductory courses in economics has evolved because it works; *Economics* doesn't tamper with that. But it does present those topics in a way that I think represents an important step forward in teaching the principles of economics.

The first organizational choice in writing an introductory text is whether to present microeconomics or macroeconomics first. I've chosen to begin with microeconomics. In my view, this has always been the right choice; students learn tools in microeconomics that they can apply in macroeconomics. Recent developments in the profession have made that ordering even more appropriate; much of the most exciting work in macroeconomics has come as economists have built the theory on a more solid microeconomic foundation.

I recognize, however, that there are legitimate arguments for a macro-first approach. Where the macroeconomics portion of *Economics* relies on microeconomic principles, they are developed in sufficient detail for a student starting with that portion of the book to be able to master the analysis.

Microeconomics

Within the microeconomics portion of the text, three organizational innovations stand out. To my knowledge, they are not available in other texts.

First, the theories of consumer behavior (Chapter 6) and of production and cost (Chapter 7) are preceded by a chapter that develops a general rule for maximizing behavior. The marginal decision rule is developed in an intuitive manner and then is applied as an integrating device *throughout* the book's discussion of microeconomics. Instead of a hodgepodge of rules applied under different market conditions, students learn a single rule they can apply within any market setting. The chapter also investigates conditions under which maximizing choices will—and will not—lead to desirable outcomes. This chapter provides a solid perspective on the strengths and the limitations of markets, as well as the role of government in the economy.

Second, the text is organized in a way that emphasizes the difference between the price-taking behavior of models of perfect competition and the price-setting behavior found in models of imperfect competition. Part Three introduces the price-taking choices of the model of perfect competition. Price-taking choices in product markets are introduced first (Chapter 8), followed by price taking in labor markets (Chapter 9), in capital and natural resource markets (Chapter 10), and in international markets (Chapter 11).

Part Four introduces market settings in which firms are not price takers but are price setters. The marginal decision rule continues to apply, but the fact that buyers or sellers can choose their price changes the outcome of maximizing choices.

A student's ability to use the marginal decision rule in the context of price-setting choices is reinforced through applications to monopoly choices (Chapter 12), monopolistic and oligopolistic market choices (Chapter 13), and choices in imperfectly competitive factor markets (Chapter 14).

A third organizational innovation appears in the treatment of the microeconomic aspects of international trade. The concept of comparative advantage emerges in Chapter 2 with an innovative approach to the derivation of the production possibilities curve. An entire chapter in the section of the book devoted to perfect competition develops basic trade theory within the context of the model of perfectly competitive markets. The new theory of international trade, with its implications for strategic trade policy, is presented within the context of Chapter 13's discussion of monopolistic competition and oligopoly. This important development in economic thought is an outgrowth of theories of imperfect competition. *Economics* is the first text to achieve that integration of new developments of trade theory with theories of imperfect competition.

Part Five, Microeconomic Applications, offers instructors a potpourri of applications of microeconomic theory to domestic policy issues. Professors may choose among chapters on agriculture (Chapter 16), antitrust policy and regulation (Chapter 17), pollution (Chapter 18), poverty and discrimination (Chapter 19), and health care (Chapter 20). From the Justice Department's investigations of Microsoft to the Supreme Court's 1995 ruling limiting affirmative action programs, students will appreciate the chance to see microeconomic principles applied in greater depth to specific problems. Instructors may also wish to incorporate Part Ten, which examines the economic systems of different countries and which explores the problems facing former Soviet-bloc nations undergoing the transition to market systems.

Macroeconomics

Organizational innovations continue in the macroeconomics portion of *Economics.* International implications of macroeconomic policy are built into the discussion from the beginning. Just as the microeconomics half of the text is organized around the integrating principle of the marginal decision rule, the macroeconomics half is organized around the model of aggregate demand and aggregate supply (AD-AS).

Macroeconomic principles are introduced from the beginning, as the circular flow model is built step by step in introducing issues in measuring GDP (Chapter 21). Chapter 22 deals with problems of inflation, unemployment, and the business cycle and introduces the labor market.

Chapter 23 offers yet another innovative feature of *Economics.* The chapter explains how the model of demand and supply that was introduced in Chapter 3 is applied in the study of macroeconomics. Students are introduced to markets they will encounter again and again: the markets for bonds and foreign exchange. In addition, the chapter introduces the AD-AS model. In this chapter and in the next two, students have an opportunity to begin working with the model, which is developed more rigorously in Part Seven.

The student's introduction to macroeconomics is completed with chapters on money, banking, and the Federal Reserve (Chapter 24) and on money and the economy (Chapter 25). One payoff from the introduction of bond and foreign exchange markets in Chapter 23 comes here. The analysis of the impact of Federal Reserve actions includes bond market effects of monetary policy from the beginning.

The inclusion of chapters on money in the introductory portion of the macroeconomics section serves three purposes. First, it reinforces the discussion of bond and foreign exchange markets and the AD-AS model in Chapter 23. Second, it allows full treatment of the Keynes effect in the detailed derivation of the aggregate demand curve that will come in Chapter 26. The final advantage is one of relevance. Monetary policy is likely to be in the news as the course is taught; introducing the concepts and tools relevant to this policy allows major news events to be brought into the classroom early in the course.

Part Seven develops models central to economic analysis. First, the AD-AS model is developed in detail in Chapter 26. The short-run and long-run aggregate supply curves are derived from a production function for the economy and from a supply curve for labor. Flexible prices in the long run produce a vertical long-run aggregate supply curve; sticky prices in the short run produce an upward-sloping short-run aggregate supply curve. Instructors who do not wish to take time for this more rigorous presentation of the AD-AS model may choose to skip this chapter; the development of the model in Chapter 23 will be sufficient to take students through the applications that follow.

Chapter 27 presents consumption theory and introduces the aggregate expenditures model. This model is used to develop the concept of multiplier effects; the AD-AS model remains the basic model used in the text.

The remaining chapters in Part Seven present an analysis of investment (Chapter 28) and of net exports (Chapter 29). The latter chapter provides an introduction to the theory of international finance and is integrated into the development of the AD-AS model.

Part Eight focuses on policy choices in the short run. It begins with monetary policy (Chapter 30) and then turns to fiscal policy (Chapter 31). By this time, students have worked through the complete AD-AS model several times, and will be quite familiar with it.

Chapter 32 again breaks new ground. *Economics* is the only introductory text on the market that explicitly applies the AD-AS model to the phases of inflation and unemployment we have observed in the United States since 1961. It is the only text that uses the AD-AS model to show how inflation and unemployment can both fall in the face of rising aggregate demand.

Chapter 33 serves as a capstone to the analysis of the macroeconomy in the short run. It applies the AD-AS model to actual data for the 1930s, 1960s, 1970s, 1980s, and 1990s. It shows how the curves have been shifted by events and by the monetary and fiscal policies applied during these periods. At the same time, a history of macroeconomic thought is woven into the discussion. Students will see Keynesian economics developing in the 1930s, then winning a central role in macroeconomic policy in the 1960s. They will see difficulties coming from the supply side in the 1970s and the role these developments played in the growing acceptance of monetarist and new classical schools. They'll also see how new Keynesian thought emerged in response to the challenges mounted by the monetarist and new classical schools. Finally, they will see how monetary policy took center stage in the 1980s and 1990s. The text is organized so that instructors who wish to do so can go directly from Chapters 26 and 27 to Chapters 32 and 33.

The discussion turns to the long run in Part Nine. This discussion begins with another innovative chapter on contemporary issues that are long run in nature (Chapter 34). These include the deficit, the issue of U.S. competitiveness, and growing concerns about fairness. The investment–saving identity is developed to show the potential relationships between the government and trade deficits. This analysis is then applied to the emergence of large and persistent trade deficits in the 1980s and the resultant concern about U.S. competitiveness.

The problem of economic growth is presented in Chapter 35. Because the AD-AS model has by now become so familiar to students, it's easy to show the significance, and the sources, of economic growth.

Chapter 36 addresses the challenge of economic development, incorporating the latest data available on the world's economies from the *World Development Report 1995.* The international focus is continued in Part Ten, which examines economic systems. Chapter 37 discusses market economies and Chapter 38 looks at socialist economies and the problems and successes that have been encountered by those nations undergoing the transition to a market economy.

The organization of *Economics* is different, and it is a difference with a purpose. It is a difference aimed at helping students to understand, integrate, and apply economic principles.

Clarity

Economics brings clarity in part through its writing style. But it also brings clarity through several pedagogical features that are integral components of the text.

The *What's Ahead* essay at the beginning of each chapter presents an issue or event that seeks to capture the reader's imagination and motivate his or her study of the material that follows. The short essay also provides an introduction to the material that will follow. That's accompanied by a list of *Chapter Objectives* that spell out for the student what mastery of the material in the chapter implies.

Definitions of key terms are highlighted in the margin as they're introduced, for easy review. A *Checklist* at the conclusion of each major section reviews the key points covered in that section. At the conclusion of each chapter, *A Look Back—And a Look Ahead* reviews the material covered in the chapter and gives the student a preview of what's coming in subsequent chapters.

Scattered throughout the text are *Reader's Advisories.* These flags warn students of common errors that can be made and show how to avoid them.

The *For Discussion* questions at the end of each chapter are intended for just that purpose: to promote discussion of the issues raised in the chapter and to engage students in critical thinking about the material. They also serve as tests of student understanding. The *Problems* provide numerical exercises as a further test of understanding.

Economics provides students with a resource that enhances their learning experience with its organization, relevance, and clarity. But it doesn't stop there. It's one part of a package that has been carefully designed to help students make the economic way of thinking their own.

Supplements for the Student

Study Guide

The *Study Guide,* by John Mogab and Bruce A. McClung of Southwest Texas State University, will help students at all levels of ability to review, learn, reinforce their understanding, and master the material in each chapter.

Each *Study Guide* chapter provides a key point review, which is a thorough overview of chapter content, and learning objectives, which are keyed to questions in the study guide chapter and to page numbers in the textbook. There is a matching exercise to help students verify and reinforce their understanding of the key terms used in the chapter, as well as a set of objective test questions, which are true-false and multiple-choice questions covering all important points in the chapter.

In addition, there are problems and applications designed to challenge students to apply quantitative and conceptual reasoning to their knowledge. This section contains tables to complete, graphs to draw and interpret, and exercises that help students consolidate their understanding of key ideas. There are also questions to think about, which encourage students to think critically about material they have learned.

Answers to key terms, questions, and problems and applications are provided.

Visual Microeconomics and Visual Macroeconomics

Visual Microeconomics and *Visual Macroeconomics,* by Richard Alston and Wan Fu Chi of Weber State University, are software packages consisting of fourteen programs designed to utilize and reinforce concepts that are presented in Tregarthen's *Economics* and further developed in the software. These programs are not "black box" simulations that do little more than encourage students to guess and play games. Rather, in the microeconomic simulation, strategic decisionmaking is rewarded and punished in accordance with economic theory. In the macroeconomic simulation, goals and outcomes are carefully explicated, eliminating the occurrence of unexplained "surprises." Emphasis is placed on the difficulty of designing credible fiscal and monetary policies in light of both short- and long-run market responses to government intervention in the economy. Each simulation builds upon the material contained in earlier programs. The programs take full advantage of the multiple-access capabilities provided by Microsoft Windows. On-screen multiple-choice and data entry quizzes reinforce basic economic concepts, test comprehension, and provide immediate feedback. In addition to these fourteen programs, *Visual Microeconomics* and *Visual Macroeconomics* contain an inclusive hypertextualized glossary of the key terms found in the textbook. A subset of this glossary, customized to include definitions for additional terms not found in the textbook, is incorporated into each of the programs. The fourteen programs include the following:

Program 1 Working with Graphs and Algebra for Economic Analysis (Chapter 1)

Program 2 Confronting Scarcity: Choices in Production (Chapter 2)

Program 3 Demand and Supply (Chapter 3)

Program 4 Elasticity: A Measure of Response (Chapter 4)

Program 5 The Analysis of Consumer Choice (Chapter 6)

Program 6 Behind the Supply Curve: Production and Cost (Chapter 7)

Program 7 Competitive Markets for Goods and Services (Chapter 8)

Program 8 International Trade and Finance (Chapters 11 and 29)

Program 9 Monopoly and the World of Imperfect Competition (Chapters 12 and 13)

Program 10 Measuring the Economy's Output (Chapter 21)

Program 11 Demand and Supply in the Macroeconomy (Chapter 23)

Program 12 Money and the Economy (Chapters 10, 24, and 25)

Program 13 Aggregate Demand and Aggregate Supply (Chapter 26)

Program 14 Consumption, Investment, New Exports (Chapters 27, 28, and 29)

Supplements for the Instructor

The Instructor's Resource Manual

Authors Virginia Lee Owen of Illinois State University and Sarah Tinkler of Weber State University have prepared a comprehensive set of teaching resources, containing chapter summaries, chapter outlines, and suggested answers to questions and problems in the textbook. These include learning objectives aimed at students in survey courses as well as those specializing in economics.

The *Instructor's Resource Manual* includes suggestions for active learning, such as topics for microessays (very short writing assignments) and for group activities (simulations, role playing, mock trials, discussions, and debates).

Another complement to the manual are the lecture supplements. These contain *Economics in the News* (summaries of current news events with commentaries on their economic implications), *Lecture Extensions* (suggested topics illustrating or extending the concepts), and *Theory in Focus* (full reproductions of relevant news articles).

There is a section on common student difficulties, in which concepts difficult for students to comprehend are identified, common student mistakes are explained, and suggestions for overcoming these problems are provided.

Additional materials include a bibliography of readings, audiovisual materials, and computer software. Also included in each chapter is a reprint of a relevant article from *The Margin.*

Test Bank

The *Test Bank* to accompany Tregarthen's *Economics* by Orley Amos of Oklahoma State University is divided into two separate volumes, one for microeconomic topics and the other for macroeconomic topics. In total, there are approximately 4000 multiple-choice and true-false questions. The questions range in difficulty to test comprehension, interpretation, analysis, and synthesis. All major topics are covered. The *Test Bank* questions are also available in test-generation systems for the Windows, Macintosh, and PC operating environments.

Transparencies

Full color acetate transparency sets for macroeconomics and microeconomics include key graphs, charts, and diagrams, enlarged for effective projection.

Acknowledgments

I have, over the years, read many text prefaces and their offers of heartfelt thanks to large numbers of people who participated in some fashion in the production of the book. I never realized, though, the degree to which a text is truly the joint product of the efforts of literally hundreds of people. I have been humbled and gratified by the enormous contributions of my colleagues and of the staffers at Worth Publishers that have made this book possible. I am the author, but I am delighted to acknowledge my enormous debt to their efforts.

First, I would like to thank Richard Alston of Weber State University. Dick has been involved in this project from its inception. He and I developed the plan for this book; his ideas are fundamental to its approach. In addition to offering a wealth of invaluable suggestions at every stage of the preparation of the text, he has directed the development of the outstanding computer tutorial that is available with the text. His contributions and ideas have enriched this book greatly.

I would also like to thank my colleagues in the Department of Economics at the University of Colorado at Colorado Springs. Paul Ballantyne has been my mentor, friend, and colleague for 25 years. He and Dale DeBoer, Larry Eubanks, and Daphne Greenwood have been there with help and advice whenever I have needed it; I appreciate their help and their friendship deeply.

The economists who have reviewed the manuscript at various stages are listed here. Their contributions have been tremendously important. They have saved me from many errors and have helped me with their critiques and with their wisdom. *Economics* is a far better book because of their experience and their help.

Jack E. Adams
University of Arkansas, Little Rock

James Q. Aylsworth
Lakeland Community College

Andrew H. Barnett
Auburn University

Peter S. Barth
University of Connecticut

Kari Battaglia
University of North Texas

Herbert Bernstein
Drexel University

Bruce Bolnick
Northeastern University

M. Neil Browne
Bowling Green State University

Michael R. Butler
Texas Christian University

Charles Capone
Baylor University

Shirley Cassing
University of Pittsburgh

Steven L. Cobb
University of North Texas

Mary Cookingham
Michigan State University

Lawrence A. Daellenbach
University of Wisconsin at La Crosse

John P. Dahlquist
College of Alameda

Smile Dube
California State University, Sacramento

Donald H. Dutkowsky
Syracuse University

Kathie S. Gilbert
Western New Mexico University

Lynn G. Gillette
Hardin-Simmons University

Otis W. Gilley
Louisiana Tech University

Robert Harris
University of Indianapolis

Daniel Himarios
University of Texas at Arlington

Jim Holcomb
University of Texas at El Paso

Solomon Honig
Montclair State University

Nancy A. Jianakoplos
Colorado State University

Walter Johnson
University of Missouri

Bill Kerby
California State University, Sacramento

Walter Kemmsies
Memphis State University

Michael Kupilik
University of Montana

Patrick Lenihan
Eastern Illinois State University

Jane Lillydahl
University of Colorado at Boulder

Roger Mack
DeAnza College

Michael Magura
University of Toledo

Henry N. McCarl
University of Alabama at Birmingham

Judith A. McDonald
Lehigh University

David Molina
University of N. Texas

W. Douglas Morgan
University of California, Santa Barbara

Richard Moss
Ricks College

James Nordyke
New Mexico State University

John G. Pomery
Purdue University

Tom Potiowsky
Portland State University

Edward Price
Oklahoma State University

W. Gregory Rhodus
Bentley College

Malcolm Robinson
University of North Carolina, Greensboro

Greg S. Rose
Sacramento City College

Terri A. Sexton
California State University, Sacramento

Alden Shiers
California Polytechnic State University, San Luis Obispo

John L. Solow
University of Iowa

John Somers
Portland Community College

Gary W. Sorenson
Oregon State University

Michael K. Taussig
Rutgers University

Steven G. Ullman
University of Miami

Donald A. Wells
University of Arizona

Louise B. Wolitz
University of Texas at Austin

I would like to thank the many people whose efforts have brought this project to fruition. Paul Shensa, the executive economics editor at Worth Publishers, had the original vision for this project and has seen it through to completion. He has been a good friend and a gentle taskmaster.

Bob Worth, who founded the company and led it for 28 years, retired during the period in which the manuscript for *Economics* was completed. His vision and inspiration have left their mark. Bob's successor at Worth, Mike Needham, has been a continuing source of encouragement and strength.

Elisa Adams has been a thorough and conscientious development editor. Her suggestions and comments have been insightful and helpful.

Production editors Barbara Toniolo, Betsy Mastalski, and Margaret Comaskey have succeeded in pulling together the manuscript, features, and art into their final form. George Toulomes and Demetrios Zangos are responsible for creating a wonderful design. Stacey Alexander has masterminded the production of the final product.

I have been assisted by three able research assistants, Charles Gale, Meari Prinster, and Deborah Nordland. They worked with dedication and great skill. I have also benefited from the able assistance of the research librarians at the University of Colorado at Colorado Springs. Their help in tracking down information has been invaluable.

Finally, I want to thank my family. My children, Doran and Brittany, have lived with this book most of their lives. My wife Suzanne, who has been a colleague and collaborator in many projects, has been a constant source of encouragement and advice. They have all put up cheerfully with the somewhat imperialistic nature of a project such as this one; parts of it have invaded virtually every room in the house. This book would not have been possible without them, and I am profoundly grateful for their love and for their support. It is to them that this effort is dedicated.

Timothy Tregarthen

Colorado Springs, Colorado
December, 1995
E-mail: tregarthen @ aol • com

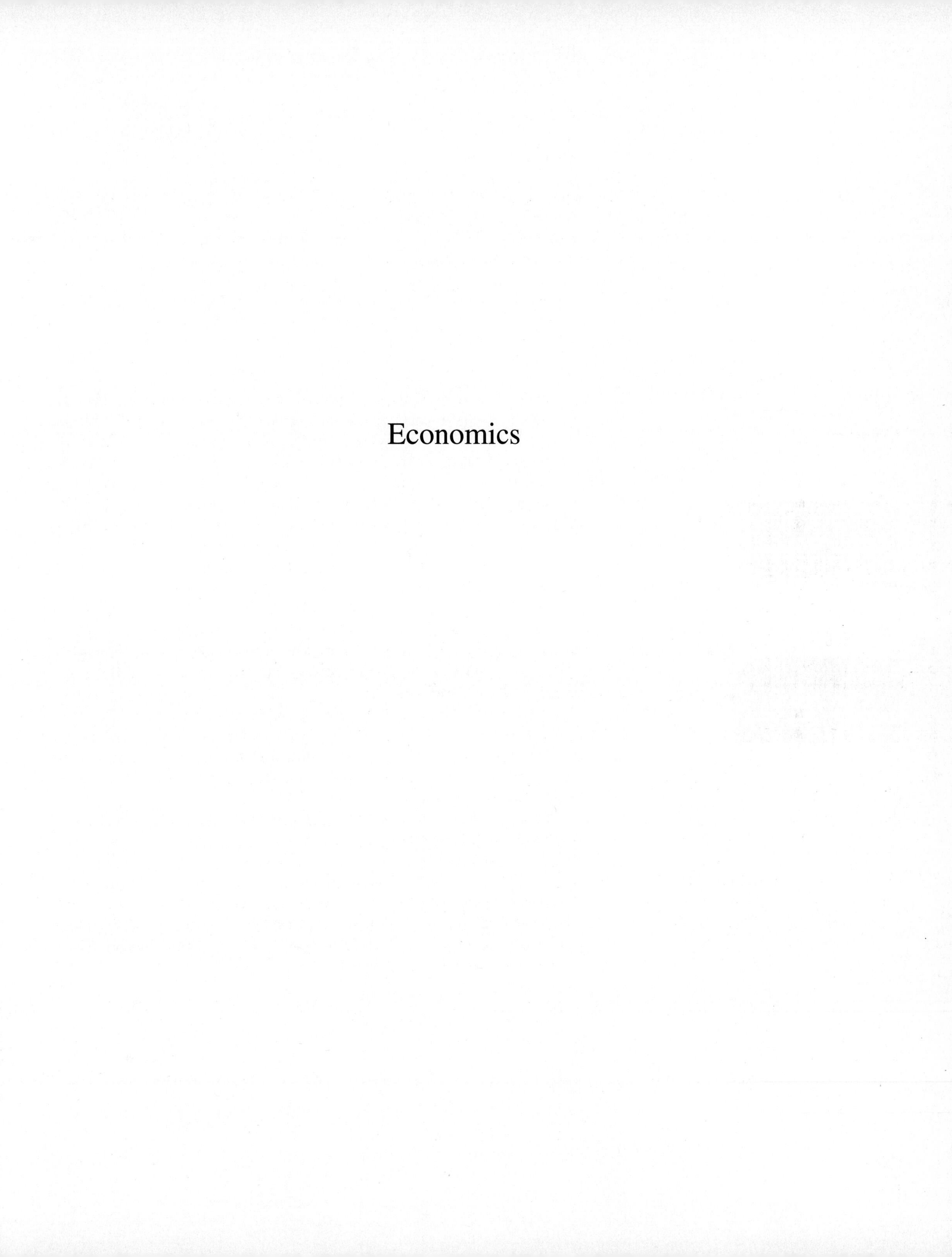

Economics

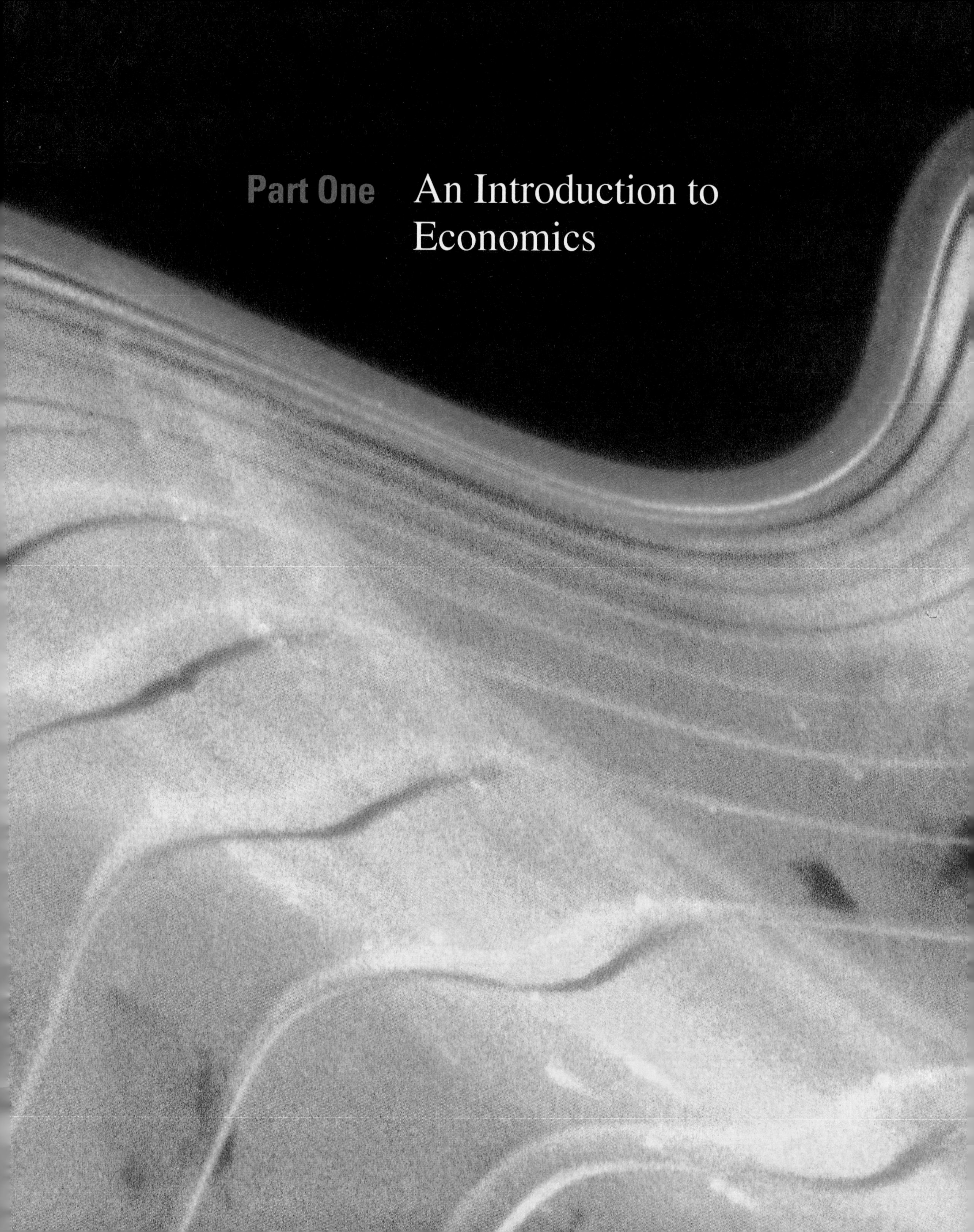

Part One An Introduction to Economics

1

Economics: The Study of Choice

Chapter Objectives

After mastering the material in this chapter, you will be able to:

1. Explain how the concepts of scarcity and cost relate to choice in economics.
2. Explain the aspects of the economic approach to problems that distinguishes economics from other sciences.
3. Explain the role of models in economic analysis.
4. Explain how the scientific method is applied in economics and the limitations inherent in putting this method to work.

The difficulty in life is the choice.
George Moore, *The Bending of the Bough,* Act IV

What's Ahead

The prospect of a course in economics can be rather intimidating. It needn't be. Chances are, you've been an amateur economist for years!

Every time you've made a choice, you've participated in the activity economists study. Every time you've asked why you made the choice you did, you've done what economists do.

This chapter addresses the question: What is economics? Here's the answer: Economics is the study of the choices people make.

Economists investigate a firm's choices concerning how much steel or cotton to produce, an individual's choice of how many hours to work, a nation's choice of how much to spend on defense.

Because choices range over every imaginable aspect of human experience, so does economics. Economics is defined not by the topics economists investigate but by the way in which economists investigate them. Although economists use certain types of investigative tools and procedures common to all scientific analysis, the basic perspective with which economists approach problems is unique. This chapter discusses the elements of economics that distinguish it from other sciences as well as the characteristics it has in common with other sciences.

What Is Economics?

Economics is the study of how people choose among the alternatives available to them. It's the study of little choices ("Should I take the chocolate or the strawberry?") and big choices ("Should we require a reduction in energy consumption in order to protect the environment?"). It's the study of individual choices, choices by firms, and choices by governments. Life presents each of us with a wide range of alternative uses of our time and other resources; economists examine how we choose among those alternatives.

Economics is the study of how people choose among the alternatives available to them.

The Scope of Economics: A Day in the Life of the Nation

If economics is about making choices, it must be relevant to the whole range of human behavior. To illustrate that relevance, let's examine, from an economic perspective, some of what was happening on a single day. I've chosen February 2, 1995 because it was one of the last days before the manuscript for this chapter had to go to the compositor to prepare it for printing. Here's an economist's-eye view of some events on that day.

> *Item:* **The Federal Reserve, commonly referred to as "the Fed," increased interest rates. It was the seventh time in the last year the Fed had moved to boost rates.**

Economic Perspective: The Fed's action was the lead story in most of the two-dozen papers I reviewed. It was intended to slow down the rate at which the economy had been expanding. But slowing down the economy meant eliminating jobs. Raising interest rates meant people would pay more to borrow money to buy cars and houses. It meant that many credit card customers would face higher interest charges. Why would the Fed do that? *How* would the Fed do that? The second half of this book will help you to understand the answers to these questions.

> *Item:* **Financial aid for students attending California's newest school, California State University, Monterey Bay, was approved by a committee of the California State Senate.[1]**

Economic Perspective: The measure was on the legislature's fast track because of the urgency attached to it. The school, which was to open its doors in the fall of 1995, was too new to qualify for any federal aid programs—the state package would be the only government scholarship help available for the 1,000 students expected to enroll.

The real significance of this story, though, lies not in financial aid but in the school itself. It sits on a former military base, Fort Ord. As the nation has scaled back defense spending following the end of the Cold War, it has faced the challenge of finding new uses for resources once used for military production—not just the military bases themselves but also the military and civilian workers whose defense jobs were eliminated. The problem of shifting resources from one activity to another is one to which we'll turn again and again in this book.

> *Item:* **The manager of the Cape Romain National Wildlife Refuge in North Carolina announced that a red wolf pup had been born on Bull's Island. It was the first pup born in the wild since the species became extinct in the area 140 years ago.[2]**

Economic Perspective: Species preservation has become a hot topic in recent years. Choices to hunt the wolf had eliminated it from the area over a century ago—the species had been maintained in zoos since. Now, in response to an increased interest in making wilderness areas more like they were before Europeans arrived in North America, wolves are being reintroduced. The effort to reintroduce wolves is a particularly controversial one, since many people view wolves as dangerous.

[1] "State Aid Proposed for CSU Campus," *San Jose Mercury News,* February 2, 1995, B1.

[2] Lynne Langley, "Red Wolf Pup Born in Wilds of Bull's Island," *The Post and Courier,* February 2, 1995, 11-A.

The red wolf was the first to be reintroduced to the wild under the federal program. Shortly before the announcement that the pup had survived on Bull's Island, authorities had begun releasing wolves into Yellowstone National Park.

Should species be protected? What if they pose a potential threat to people—or to the livestock people raise? What if protecting species means giving up other activities, such as logging or the development of housing projects? We'll return in subsequent chapters to an examination of the issues involved in species preservation.

***Item:* A nationwide group of amphitheaters announced it would begin selling tickets independently later in the year, putting it in competition with Ticketmaster, a firm that provides telephone ticket sales for concerts and sporting events throughout the nation.[3]**

Economic Perspective: Rock group Pearl Jam had filed an antitrust suit against Ticketmaster the previous year, arguing the firm had monopolized ticket sales and was adding too high a service charge for these sales. The new venture would put a major chain of theaters, jointly owned by Sony Music, Blockbuster, and Pace Entertainment, in competition with Ticketmaster. Questions of market power, competition, and their effects on prices are central to the first half of this book. Another issue is raised here: Sony is a Japanese firm. How do foreign-owned firms affect a domestic economy? We'll examine that issue in the second half of this book.

***Item:* A Rand Corporation study of the American family used U.S. Census data to compare the status of families in 1990 to that of families in 1960. Among its findings: (1) The poverty rate among families is up, in large part because of a tripling in the number of households headed by women—almost half of those households get by at or below the poverty line. The median income of a married couple with children under the age of 18 was $43,000. For a household with children that was headed solely by the mother, it was $13,000. (2) A tripling in the divorce rate has left its mark—only half the children with divorced parents had seen their father at least one time within the last year, and only one in three of those fathers sends full child support. (3) Even among two-parent households, parents spend a lot less time with their children than they once did—the average parent spends seven hours per week with a child. That's only a third of the average amount of time spent in 1960.[4]**

Economic Perspective: The authors of the study, M. Omar Rahman of Harvard University and Julie DaVanzo of Rand, listed several forces at work in these rather dismal results. First, they note that rising incomes for men and women have made it easier for men and women to live apart. Those same higher incomes have made it relatively more "costly" for parents to spend time with their kids! Higher incomes aren't the only cause of higher divorce rates, the authors note. In 1960, half of all survey respondents said parents should stay together for the sake of the children; just 20 percent expressed this view in 1990. The authors argue that rising divorce rates may be one reason fewer mothers marry in the first place—with divorce an increasingly likely prospect, the benefits of marriage fall. Finally, the authors note that government aid programs such as Aid to Families with Dependent Children tend to reduce the economic benefits of marriage for low-income people.

[3] Neill Strauss, "The Pop Life," *The New York Times,* February 2, 1995, p. C16.
[4] Joseph Hanania, "Beaver's Grave New World," *The Dallas Morning News,* February 2, 1995, p. 1C.

As a footnote to this story, I should note that the *Dallas Morning News* report was continued to a page that also featured Ann Landers's advice column. The headline on that column was: "Stepmother Wants Compensation for Child-Care Duties."

There was, of course, a lot more going on February 2, 1995 than this brief survey reveals. The point is that virtually everything that happened that day was the outcome of a set of choices. Those choices are the stuff of economics. We can use economic analysis to study any choice that people make.

The Economic Problem: Making Choices

When the nation chose to turn Fort Ord into California State University, Monterey Bay, it was choosing to produce more education—and less defense. The study of the family suggests that parents are spending more time earning incomes—and less time raising their children. The Fed's decision to raise interest rates was one factor in a subsequent decline in housing construction—the economy lost jobs and housing. The reintroduction of the red wolf to Cape Romaine is one aspect of a bigger choice—to preserve the area as wilderness rather than making it a housing development or a research center. Pearl Jam's action had cost the group revenue; for a while it refused to book concerts in halls having contracts with Ticketmaster.

All choices mean that one alternative is selected over another. The central concepts of economics are defined in terms of the alternatives involved in any choice.

Scarcity

Our resources are limited. At any one time, we have only so much land, so many trees, so much oil, so many people. But our wants, our desires for the things we can produce with those resources, are unlimited. We would always like more and better housing, more and better education—more and better of virtually everything.

If our resources were unlimited, we could say yes to each of our wants—and there would be no economics. Because our resources *are* limited, we *can't* say yes to everything. To say yes to one thing requires that we say *no* to another. We must make choices among the alternatives we face.

Our unlimited wants are continually crashing up against our limited resources, forcing us to choose among alternatives. **Scarcity** is the situation created when we are forced to choose among alternatives. A **scarce good** is one for which the choice of one alternative requires that another alternative be given up.

Land is an example of a scarce good. A parcel of land presents us with several alternative uses. We could build a house on it. We could put a gas station or a convenience store on it. We could create a small park on it. We could leave the land vacant in order to be able to make a decision later as to how it should be used.

Suppose we've decided the land should be used for a house. Should it be a large and expensive house or a modest one? Suppose it is to be a modest single-family house. Who should live in the house on that parcel of land? If the Lees live in it, the Fongs cannot. There are alternative uses of the land both in the sense of the type of use and also in the sense of who gets to use it. The fact that land is scarce means that society must make choices concerning its use.

- **Scarcity** is a situation in which we are forced to choose among alternatives.
- A **scarce good** is one for which the choice of one alternative requires that another be given up.

Case in Point: Searching for Grizzlies

Jim Tolisano is looking for a few big bears.

Specifically, he's looking for grizzly bears in Colorado's San Juan Mountains. A lot of loggers and developers hope he fails.

Grizzlies are generally thought to have disappeared from Colorado decades ago. If Mr. Tolisano is able to prove that they continue to roam in Colorado's high country, a great many things will change.

The federal government is required by the Endangered Species Act of 1973 to list plant and animal species that are threatened with extinction and to implement measures to save them. The grizzly is on the government's list of endangered species. If Mr. Tolisano and his associates can prove that grizzlies live in Colorado, the government will be required to protect them.

That protection would certainly mean a ban on bear hunting in the region where the grizzly might roam. It would be likely to mean putting a halt to proposed federal timber sales in the Rio Grande and San Juan national forests. Logging operations already under way might be forced to shut down. Protection of grizzlies would probably end development of the East Fork Ski Area, a huge resort proposed in the region.

Given the presumption that there aren't any grizzlies in the region, the Forest Service has already decided that expanded logging operations should be permitted and has issued a special use permit for the ski area. If Mr. Tolisano finds evidence that grizzlies still live in the San Juans, however, the Endangered Species Act would require the choice of another alternative: preserving the habitat of the bears.

The threat to logging and development is not an idle one. Designation of the spotted owl as an endangered species forced the cancellation of logging operations covering 11.6 million acres in the Pacific Northwest, a cancellation expected to eliminate as many as 100,000 jobs.

Colorado's undeveloped mountain regions are a scarce resource. They can be left in their natural state to preserve the habitat for wildlife. An alternative is to subject them to increased logging and development, which means reducing the habitat for wildlife. One set of alternatives, logging and development, has already been chosen. If Mr. Tolisano finds the bears he's looking for, that choice will change.

Source: Barry Noreen, "Species Preservation: At What Cost?" *The Margin* 7 (Spring 1992): 34–35.

Virtually everything is scarce. Consider air, which is available in huge quantity at no charge to us. The test of whether air is scarce is whether it has alternative uses. What uses can we make of the air? One is to breathe it. Another is to dump garbage into it—to pollute it. We dump garbage into the air when we drive our cars, burn wood in our fireplaces, or operate our factories. Most productive activities involve the dumping of some quantity of garbage into the air. We certainly need the air to breathe. But just as certainly, we need to dump garbage into it. Those two uses are clearly alternatives to each other. If we dump more garbage, the air will be less desirable to breathe. If we decide we want to breathe cleaner air, we must dump less garbage. Air is thus a scarce good. Goods that are scarce force us to make choices. Not all goods, however, force such choices. Goods for which one use does not require that we give up another are called **free goods.**

A **free good** is one that does not pose the problem of scarcity; one use of the good is not an alternative to another.

There aren't many free goods. Conflicts are already arising over the allocation of orbital slots for satellites in outer space—this means that parts of outer space are scarce. Court battles have been fought for centuries over the right to sunshine, making sunshine a scarce resource in some settings. Scarcity characterizes virtually everything with which we must deal. Because nearly everything is scarce, the scope of economics is wide indeed.

Scarcity and the Fundamental Economic Questions

Economists examine the choices forced on us by scarcity within three broad categories. Every economy must answer the following questions:

1. **What Should Be Produced?** Producing one thing requires giving up another. Producing better education, for example, may require cutting back on other services, such as health care. A decision to preserve a wilderness area requires giving up other uses of the land. Every society must decide *what* it will produce with its scarce resources.
2. **How Should Goods and Services Be Produced?** There are many ways to produce goods and services. Tomatoes, for example, can be produced using a great deal of labor and some hoes—or they can be produced with just a few people using massive machines that plough the land, plant the plants, irrigate the soil, and even pick and sort the tomatoes. Just as society makes a decision about what to produce, it must also determine *how* to produce it.
3. **For Whom Should Goods and Services Be Produced?** If a good or service is produced, a decision must be made about who will get it. A decision to have one person receive a good or service usually means it won't be available to someone else. Representatives of the poorest nations on earth often complain, for example, that the United States, with its 250 million people, consumes more than twice as much energy as do the 3 billion people in the world's 41 poorest countries. They argue that the world's energy should be more evenly allocated. Should it? That's a *"for whom"* question.

Every economy is forced by scarcity to determine *what* should be produced, *how* it should be produced, and *for whom* it should be produced. We shall be returning to these questions again and again in our investigation of economics.

Cost

It is within the context of scarcity that economists define what is perhaps the most important concept in all of economics, the concept of cost. The **cost** of any choice is the value of the best opportunity forgone in making it.

The cost to you of reading the remainder of this chapter will be the value of the best other use to which you could have put your time. If the most valuable alternative use of the land for California State at Monterey Bay was its old use as a military base, then the cost of education produced there will include the value of the land's contribution to forgone defense services. If you choose to spend $10 on a potted plant, you have simultaneously chosen to forgo the benefits of spending the $10 on a pizza or a paperback book. If the book is the most valuable of those alternatives, then the cost of the plant is the value of the enjoyment you would have gotten from the book.

The concepts of scarcity, choice, and cost are at the heart of economics. A good is scarce if it has alternative uses. The existence of alternative uses forces us to make choices. The cost of any choice is the value of the best alternative forgone in making it.

The **cost** of any choice is the value of the best opportunity forgone when the choice is made.

The Economic Way of Thinking

The choices people make are widely studied. Anthropologists may study the choices of primitive peoples; political scientists may study the choices of legislatures; psychologists may study how people choose a mate; and sociologists may study the forces that have led to the rise in single-parent households. Economists study such questions as well. What is it about the study of choices by economists that makes economics different from these other disciplines?

These features distinguish the economic approach to choice:

1. Economists give special attention to the cost involved in any choice.
2. Economists assume that individuals make choices that seek to maximize the value of some objective.
3. Economists place special emphasis on the consequences that occur as a result of a choice to do a little more or a little less of something.

Each of these features that characterize the economic way of thinking is examined below in greater detail.

1. Costs Are Important

If doing one thing requires giving up another, then the expected benefits of the alternatives we face will affect the ones we choose. If Russia had declared that the destruction of the United States remained its primary objective, Fort Ord might not have become a university campus. We've already seen that rising incomes have boosted the cost to parents of spending time with their children—and reduced the time they spend with them. Economists argue that an understanding of cost is crucial to the examination of choices.

2. Individuals Maximize

What motivates people as they make choices? Perhaps more than anything else, it is the economist's answer to this question that distinguishes economics from other fields. Economists assume that individuals **maximize;** that is, they make choices that they expect will create the maximum value of some objective, given the constraints they face.

Economists assume, for example, that the owners of business firms seek to maximize profit. Given the assumed goal of profit maximization, economists can predict how firms in an industry will respond to changes in the markets in which they operate.

Similarly, economists assume that maximizing behavior is at work when they examine the behavior of consumers. The satisfaction people receive from consuming goods and services is called **utility**. In studying consumers, economists assume that individual consumers make choices aimed at maximizing utility.

As the set of available alternatives changes, we expect that the choices individuals make will change. A rainy day could change the cost of reading a good book; we might expect more reading to get done in bad than in good weather. A high income can make it very costly to take a day off; we might expect highly paid individuals to work more hours than those who aren't paid as well. If individuals are maximizing utility and firms are maximizing profits, then a change in the set of alternatives they face may affect their choices in a predictable way.

- To **maximize** is to make a choice that is expected to achieve the maximum value possible for some objective.
- **Utility** is the satisfaction people receive from consuming goods and services or engaging in some activities.

Case in Point — Did the Persian Gulf War Turn a Profit?

The United States won an impressive victory in its 1990 war with Iraq. Was the operation a financial success as well?

U.S. allies pledged to pay the United States $54.6 billion to support the war effort. The Department of Defense spent about $60 billion to fight the war. That suggests that the war might have generated a financial loss of about $5.4 billion.

But Heritage Foundation defense policy analyst Baker Spring suggests there is a difficulty in interpreting the total cost figure. "That cost figure includes the cost of all the soldiers, all the matériel—all the American military force that General Schwarzkopf used to prosecute the war," he says. "A lot of those costs would have been incurred anyway. We would have been paying the soldiers, operating the ships, and flying the planes whether there had been a war or not."

Mr. Spring's observation suggests that the costs of the war be considered at the margin: What costs did the United States incur by fighting the war that it would not have incurred otherwise? What was the marginal cost of having one more war?

"Consider, for example, a soldier who was already on active duty before the war started," says Mr. Baker. "You wouldn't count that soldier's salary in the marginal cost of the war—the soldier would have been paid anyway. But soldiers in combat receive hazardous duty pay—you would count that extra cost. In general, the marginal cost of the war is the amount by which spending increased as a direct result of the war effort."

The federal government's Office of Management and Budget (OMB) has estimated what it calls the "incremental" cost of the war, a concept equivalent to Mr. Baker's notion of marginal cost. That estimate suggests that the marginal cost of the war was $36.1 billion—far less than the payments the United States received from its allies.

U.S. casualties in the war, another cost, were remarkably low. In fact, some analysts argue that the war effort may actually have saved U.S. lives. The leading cause of deaths among U.S. soldiers has traditionally been highway accidents. The war separated 400,000 soldiers from their cars for several months; the death toll from military highway accidents dropped dramatically during Operation Desert Shield and Operation Desert Storm.

Of course, most of the cost of the war was not borne by the United States. Iraq and Kuwait suffered the brunt of war damage to people and to resources. For the people of those countries, the cost of the war was huge. For the United States, however, an analysis of the war's cost at the margin suggests that the effort generated an impressive profit.

Source: "Did Desert Storm Turn a Profit?" *The Margin* 7 (Fall 1991): 13.

3. Choices Are Made at the Margin

Economists argue that most choices are made "at the margin." To make a choice at the **margin** is to decide whether to do a little more or a little less of something.

Consider the problem of curtailing water consumption when supplies are limited. Economists frequently argue that one way to induce people to conserve water is to raise its price. A common response to this recommendation is that a higher price would have no effect on water consumption, because water is a necessity. Faced with a higher price, some critics argue, people will continue to consume as much water as before; higher prices will not induce greater conservation.

But choices in water consumption, like virtually all choices, are made at the margin. Individuals don't make choices about whether they should or should not consume water. Rather, they decide whether to consume a little more or a little less water. Household water consumption in the United States was 167 gallons per person per day in 1985. Could a higher price cause people to reduce their use, say, to 166 gallons per person per day? To 165? When we examine the choice to consume water at the margin, the notion that a higher price would affect consumption seems much more plausible. A recent study of responses by households to higher prices for residential water found that a 10 percent increase in the price of water would lead to a reduction in demand of between about 4 and

A choice made at the **margin** is a choice whether to do a little more or a little less of something.

9 percent, depending on how the price increase was structured.[5] Other studies by economists of water demand have yielded similar results. Prices affect our consumption of water because choices in water consumption, like other choices, are made at the margin.

The concept of considering choices at the margin has proved to be an enormously useful one for economic analysis. It can, however, be a dangerous one as well. It focuses our analytical lenses on small changes and can thus result in our ignoring large consequences. For example, an economist is more likely to consider whether automobile production will expand or contract, or whether people will drive a little more or a little less, than a larger question: Should we have cars at all? Many critics of economic analysis say that by focusing on small changes, economists ignore the possibility of big ones. Economists respond that small changes are the ones we generally make, and that a study of them is more useful than speculation about the consequences of large changes that aren't likely to occur.

Microeconomics and Macroeconomics

The study of economics is generally divided into two broad branches. One focuses on individual components of economic activity; the other looks at the total of all economic activity. To understand this division, we must start with the goods and services that are produced and exchanged in the economy. A **good** is a tangible commodity, such as a chair or a watermelon, that people value. A **service** is an intangible commodity, such as the activity of a teacher or a waiter, that people value. A set of arrangements through which a particular good or service is produced and exchanged is called a **market.** An **economy** is a system of institutions that provides for the production and exchange of goods and services. An economy may include markets, but there may be other institutions, such as government agencies, that produce or distribute goods and services. The economy can have whatever geographical designation we care to give it. We may speak of the economy of a city, a nation, or a region.

Everyone who participates in the consumption or production of goods and services is part of the economy. Since all of us satisfy at least the first criterion, we are all part of the economy. Markets can take all sorts of forms. When economists speak of the market for food, for example, they are talking about an enormously complex mix of farmers, distributors, retail stores, government agencies, and consumers who interact to produce and exchange food. They may confine their analysis to the market for food in a small town or speak of the global market for food. Instead of focusing on food in general, an economist might speak of the market for veal, or for almonds, or for broccoli.

- A **good** is a tangible commodity that people value.
- A **service** is an intangible commodity that people value.
- A **market** is a set of arrangements through which a particular good or service, or a group of goods or services, is produced and exchanged.
- An **economy** is a system of institutions through which goods and services are produced and exchanged.
- **Microeconomics** is a branch of economics that examines the choices of consumers and firms and the impacts of those choices on particular markets.
- **Macroeconomics** is a branch of economics that examines the impact of choices on the total level of economic activity.

The two broad branches of economics are microeconomics and macroeconomics. Your economics course, for example, may be designated as a "micro" or as a "macro" course. **Microeconomics** is a branch of economics that focuses on the choices made by consumers and firms and the impacts those choices have on specific markets. **Macroeconomics** is a branch of economics that focuses on the impact of choices on the total level of economic activity. It deals particularly with the determination of total output, level of employment, and price level.

[5] Michael L. Nieswiadomy and David J. Molina, "Comparing Residential Water Demand Estimates under Decreasing and Increasing Block Rates Using Household Data," *Land Economics* 65 (3) (August 1989): 280–289.

How does the weather in Argentina affect the producers and consumers of eggs in Oregon? Why do women end up doing most of the housework? Why do senior citizens get discounts on public transit systems? Why do we seem to make so little progress in the war on drugs? These questions are generally regarded as microeconomic because they focus on individual units or markets in the economy.

Is the total level of economic activity rising or falling? Is the rate of inflation increasing or decreasing? What's happening to the unemployment rate? These are questions that deal with aggregates, or totals, in the economy; they are problems of macroeconomics. The question about the level of economic activity, for example, refers to the total value of all production in the economy. Inflation is a measure of the rate of change in the average price level for the entire economy; it is a macroeconomic problem. The total levels of employment and unemployment in the economy represent the aggregate of all labor markets; unemployment is thus a topic of macroeconomics.

Both microeconomics and macroeconomics give attention to individual markets. But in microeconomics that attention is an end in itself; in macroeconomics it is aimed at explaining the movement of major economic aggregates—the level of total output, the level of employment, and the price level.

Why Study Economics?

There are many reasons for studying economics. One is the desire to discover explanations for the things we observe. Why, for example, do professional baseball players earn far more, on average, than professional football players? Why do airlines charge lower prices to customers who book flights two weeks in advance than they charge to customers who book flights two days in advance? Why is unemployment, on average, much higher in Germany than in the United States?

Another reason for studying economics is a concern that the choices we make might not be appropriate ones. Why do some groups suffer from discrimination in the marketplace? Why are our highways often heavily congested? Why do we choose to dump so much pollution in the air and water? Understanding why the choices we make are not always good ones may help us to find ways to correct the problems that grow out of inappropriate choices.

A third reason for studying economics is to predict the outcomes of those choices. How will a proposed tax measure affect interest rates? How will the expanded use of robots in manufacturing affect employment? Will decreased federal spending for education promote or hinder economic growth?

A fourth reason for studying economics is that we may gain insights that will allow us to do a better job in managing a firm or some other organization. Many firms, foundations, and government agencies employ economists because these organizations have found that the insights economists offer can help them to achieve their goals.

Economists at Work

Whatever one's intellectual interest in economics, an obvious question is: What could I do if I were to seek work as an economist? This section profiles three economists to suggest the range of employment opportunities available to economists.

Cases in Point: Three Economists: In Business, in Government, and in Academe

Sally Millar Reilly: A Business Economist

How often will bank customers use ATM machines? What will be the volume of those transactions? These are questions that are important to a bank. Boston's BayBank turns to its product manager, economist Sally Millar Reilly, for the answers.

Ms. Reilly, who earned a bachelor's degree in economics from Boston University and a master's degree in business economics at Bentley College, has forecast demand for the bank's main consumer products: home improvement loans, personal loans, and revolving credit loans. She's now forecasting ATM transactions by the bank's customers. The bank uses her forecasts in budgeting decisions and in determining the number of ATMs to deploy. Ms. Reilly says that the thing she likes best about her work is the opportunity to communicate with people at all levels of management.

Ms. Reilly is one of about 23,000 business economists in the United States. These economists interpret and forecast economic conditions relevant to a firm's market and use the tools of economic analysis to help their firms operate more efficiently. The median annual base salary for business economists in 1994, according to a survey by the National Association of Business Economists, was $80,000 for economists with a Ph.D., $62,000 for those with a master's degree, and $60,500 for those with a bachelor's degree. Most business economists also earn additional income from writing, consulting, or lecturing; this income averaged about $10,000 per year in 1994.

Steve Haugen: A Government Economist

We hear about Steve Haugen's work every month when the national statistics for unemployment are released. Mr. Haugen is an economist for the U.S. Bureau of Labor Statistics, the agency that compiles the official monthly estimate of the nation's unemployment rate.

Mr. Haugen is involved in other efforts for the Bureau as well. One recent project was to estimate the impact of an increase in the minimum wage on the distribution of hourly earnings. He says that the thing he likes best about his job is that it allows him to conduct research in "a totally objective and apolitical environment."

Mr. Haugen received his bachelor's degree in economics and in history at Harvard University and his M.B.A. at Massachusetts Institute of Technology.

The federal government is the largest single employer of U.S. economists, but many economists work for state and local governments as well. The average salary for economists working for the federal government was $47,523 in 1991.

Maria Muniagurria: An Economist in Academe

Economic growth came virtually to a halt in the early 1990s. Did that indicate a general slowdown that would persist through the rest of the century, or was it a temporary phenomenon? Can the world's economies continue to grow in the next century? These are some of the questions that fascinate Maria Muniagurria, an economist at the University of Wisconsin at Madison. Ms. Muniagurria's research focuses on technological change and its role in generating economic growth.

Ms. Muniagurria, who received her bachelor's degree in economics at Purdue University and her master's and Ph.D. degrees at the University of Minnesota, is one of about 23,000 academic economists in the United States. Economists at colleges and universities conduct research and teach graduate and undergraduate courses. Ms. Muniagurria teaches courses in macroeconomics and growth theory.

Although economists in every arena are engaged in research, it is in academe that people have the most freedom to define their own projects. Ms. Muniagurria reports that it is that freedom to do what she wants in terms of research, along with the challenge of her work, that she values most in her career.

The *Chronicle Higher Education* reports that average salaries for university economics professors in the 1994–1995 academic year were as follows:

Institution	Professor	Associate Professor	Assistant Professor	New Assistant Professor
Public	$64,350	$49,940	$43,340	$40,741
Private	72,152	49,078	43,006	41,885

Source: *Chronicle of Higher Education,* 28 April 1995, A46.

Checklist ✓

- Economics is the study of human choices; it therefore touches on virtually every aspect of human behavior.
- Scarcity is defined by the fact that a choice to pursue one alternative requires that we give up another.
- Given scarcity, a society must make choices about what to produce, how to produce it, and for whom it should be produced.
- All choices have costs. These costs affect the choices people make.
- Economists generally assume that choices are made in a way that maximizes the value of some objective.
- Economists focus on choices made at the margin; they thus assess the marginal consequences of choices.
- Economics is generally divided between two broad categories, microeconomics and macroeconomics.
- We study economics for its intellectual interest, for the insight it gives us into economic problems, for purposes of forecasting, and to help organizations operate more efficiently.
- About two-thirds of all economists work for business firms, or for government agencies, and the remaining third teach economics.

Although many economists are involved in teaching, most work for business firms or government agencies. About two-thirds of the nation's 70,000 economists work for business firms and government agencies; the remainder teach or do research at colleges and universities.

In the past, a career in teaching economics almost certainly meant teaching at the college or university level. But more and more schools are offering economics instruction earlier. Roughly half the nation's high school students are required to take an economics course in order to graduate from high school. In many districts economics is taught even earlier. The ideas of scarcity, choice, and cost, for example, are incorporated today in many kindergarten curricula! Even more of the basic concepts of economics can be introduced by the third grade. A career in teaching economics may thus involve teaching at any grade level.

Economics as a Science

Economics differs from other fields because of its emphasis on cost, the assumption of maximization, and the analysis of choices at the margin. But certainly much of the basic methodology of economics and many of its difficulties are common to every science. This section explores the nature of scientific research and examines how economic research relates to it.

Scientists examine relationships between variables. A **variable** is something whose value can change. A **constant** is something whose value doesn't change. The speed at which a car is traveling is an example of a variable. The number of feet in a mile and the number of minutes in an hour are examples of constants.

- A **variable** is anything whose value can change.
- A **constant** is something whose value does not change.

The Scientific Method

In all science, research proceeds within a framework called the **scientific method,** a systematic set of procedures through which knowledge is created. In the scientific method, hypotheses are suggested and then tested. A **hypothesis** is an assertion of a relationship between two or more variables that could be proven to be false. A statement is not a hypothesis if no conceivable test could show it to be false. The statement "Plants like sunshine" is not a hypothesis; there is no way to test whether plants like sunshine or not, so it is impossible to prove the statement false. The statement "Increased solar radiation increases the rate of plant growth" is a hypothesis; experiments could be done to show the relationship between solar radiation and plant growth. If solar radiation were shown to be unrelated to plant growth or to retard plant growth, then the hypothesis would be demonstrated to be false.

- The **scientific method** is a set of procedures through which knowledge is created.
- A **hypothesis** is a testable proposition about the relationship between two or more variables.
- A **theory** is a hypothesis that has been tested extensively without being rejected and that has won widespread acceptance.
- A **law** is a theory that has won virtually universal acceptance.

If a test reveals that a particular hypothesis is false, then the hypothesis is rejected or modified. In the case of the hypothesis about solar radiation and plant growth, we would probably find that more sunlight increases plant growth over some range but that too much can actually retard plant growth. Such results would lead us to modify our hypothesis about the relationship between solar radiation and plant growth.

If the tests of a hypothesis yield results consistent with it, then further tests are conducted. A hypothesis that has not been rejected after widespread testing and that wins widespread acceptance is generally called a **theory.** A theory that has been subjected to even more testing and that has won virtually universal acceptance is called a **law.**

Consider Charles Darwin's work on evolution in the nineteenth century. Darwin, inspired by the work of economists on the problem of scarcity, suggested a hypothesis that species develop their characteristic traits through a process of natural selection. As the implications of this hypothesis were subjected to testing that failed to reject it, Darwin's idea came to be known as the theory of evolution. Acceptance of this theory, however, has not yet become so widespread that we refer to the "law" of evolution.

Sir Isaac Newton's hypothesis about the nature of the gravitational force between two objects has passed from the status of theory to the status of law: we speak of the law of gravity. The elevation of Newton's hypothesis to the status of a law does not, however, mean that the hypothesis has been proved. No hypothesis, theory, or law is ever "proved" to be correct. Scientists can only fail to demonstrate that a proposition is false; they cannot prove it to be true. Thus, we cannot prove the law of gravity; we can only fail to reject it. We might have tremendous confidence in the proposition, but our acceptance must always be provisional. That's because we don't have the ability to observe every detail about the universe. We can't be certain that someone, sometime, won't come along and find an example that suggests that the law of gravity does not always hold.

The Scientific Method in Economics

Many economists regard economics as a science because they try to follow the scientific method. Hypotheses are proposed and tested; those that survive repeated tests gain recognition as theories. Some hypotheses or theories in economics have won sufficiently wide acceptance that they are now considered laws. Sometimes, however, economists don't observe the distinction made in other fields between a hypothesis and a theory. They often refer to a newly stated hypothesis as a theory even before it has been subjected to testing.

Some economists reject the notion that their discipline qualifies as a science. They argue, in part, that problems inherent in the testing of hypotheses in economics are so great that the scientific method cannot be meaningfully applied. Further, they assert that many important propositions in economics are in principle not testable. These challenges to the applicability of the scientific method to economics are examined later in this chapter.

Models in Economics

All scientific thought involves simplifications of reality. The real world is too complex for the human mind—or the most powerful computer—to consider. Scientists thus construct **models,** or simplified representations, of some aspect of the real world. Models are always based on assumed conditions that are simpler than those of the real world, assumptions that are necessarily false. A model of the real world cannot be the real world.

Suppose we wish to predict with great accuracy how long it would take for an iron ball, dropped from the top of a very tall building, to hit the sidewalk below. We want to do this without actually dropping the ball. We might use Newton's law of gravitational acceleration as our model of the problem. This law states that the rate at which the ball travels increases with the square of the time it has traveled. Using this model, we could compute the rate at which the ball will accelerate and thus estimate quite precisely how long it will take to hit the sidewalk. But this model assumes that the universe consists of only three

A **model** is a simplified representation of a particular problem.

things: the ball, the sidewalk, and the earth itself. Lots of other things could affect the ball's progress, including the friction of the air, the gravitational pull on the ball exerted by the planet Pluto or by the crowd that might gather to watch the actual experiment, and so on. We assume those influences away, however, because we expect them to be trivial and because including them would unnecessarily complicate our problem.

Economists make extensive use of models. We'll encounter our first model in Chapter 2; it simplifies by assuming that the economy produces only two goods. The second model we'll explore, the model of demand and supply, is introduced in Chapter 3. It assumes that all goods in a particular market are identical and that no one firm has any ability to control its own price. These assumptions represent sharp departures from reality. The economy can produce far more than two goods, and most firms have a degree of control over the prices they charge. These models help us to understand the real world; they do not describe it.

Models serve two functions in economics. First, they help us to understand how the economy works. By expressing a problem in terms of a simplified model, we may gain a deeper understanding of some essential aspects of that problem. The model that assumes the economy can produce only two goods, for example, will suggest some important aspects of choices in producing goods and services. Second, models can be used to generate hypotheses about the economy. For example, the model of demand and supply predicts that if the supply of a good or service decreases, its price will rise and the quantity demanded will fall. That is a hypothesis that can be tested. This particular hypothesis has won such widespread acceptance that it is considered a law, one that we will encounter in Chapter 3.

Testing Hypotheses in Economics

Suppose we want to test the hypothesis that a reduction in the supply of gasoline will increase the price of gasoline and reduce the quantity consumers demand. To test this hypothesis, we could find a case in which the supply of gasoline has fallen and then see what has happened to price and to the quantity demanded.

In August 1990, for example, Iraqi troops invaded Kuwait. That invasion, and the global response to it, created fears of a wider war. One result was that suppliers reduced the quantity of gasoline they supplied. Our hypothesis suggests that this reduction in supply should have increased the price and reduced the quantity demanded. The average retail price of regular unleaded gasoline rose from $1.08 in July to $1.19 in August. The quantity of gasoline consumed fell by 11 percent the following month.

Although the increase in price and the reduction in gasoline consumption were consistent with the hypothesis that a reduced supply will lead to a higher price and will reduce the quantity consumers demand, caution must be exercised in assessing this evidence. Two problems exist in interpreting any set of economic data. One problem is that several things may be changing at once; a second is that the initial event may be unrelated to the event that follows. The next two sections examine these problems in detail.

The All-Other-Things-Unchanged Problem

The hypothesis that a reduction in the supply of gasoline produces a higher price and reduces the quantity consumers demand carries with it the assumption that no other changes occur that might also affect demand. Indeed, a better statement of the hypothesis would be: A reduction in the supply of gasoline will increase its price and will reduce the quantity of gasoline demanded, ceteris paribus. **Ceteris paribus** is a Latin phrase that means "all other things unchanged."

Consider gasoline demand in September 1990. Demand was affected not just by the gasoline price increase but by the fact that it was September. Gasoline consumption always falls in September because people return from their summer vacations and go back to work. A second factor affecting demand was the recession that began in July 1990. The recession acted to reduce gasoline use in two ways. It put downward pressure on incomes, so that people didn't buy as much. Second, it reduced employment, so that not as many people were driving to work.

The events in the late summer of 1990 did not, in short, offer a conclusive test of the hypothesis that a reduction in the supply of gasoline would lead to an increase in its price and a reduction in the quantity demanded. Other things did change, and they affected price and demand. Such problems are likely to affect any analysis of economic events. We can't ask the world to stand still while we conduct experiments in economic phenomena. Economists employ a variety of statistical methods to allow them to isolate the impact of single events such as price changes, but they can never be certain that they have accurately isolated the impact of a single event in a world in which virtually everything is changing all the time.

In laboratory sciences, it is relatively easy to conduct experiments in which only selected things change and all other factors are held constant. The economists' laboratory is the real world; economists don't generally have the luxury of conducting controlled experiments.

The Fallacy of False Cause

Hypotheses in economics typically specify a relationship in which a change in one variable causes another to change. We call the variable that responds to the change the **dependent variable;** the variable that induces a change is called the **independent variable.** Sometimes the fact that two variables move together can suggest the false conclusion that one of the variables has acted as an independent variable that has caused the change we observe in the dependent variable.

Consider the following hypothesis: Stock prices, as measured by the Dow Jones Industrial Index, will rise in years in which a team from the National Football Conference (NFC) wins the Super Bowl and will fall when a team from the American Football Conference (AFC) wins.[6] This hypothesis seems preposterous. Yet the evidence is largely consistent with it. From 1967, when the Super Bowl was first played, to 1994, there have been only three years in which the Super Bowl rule has failed to predict the direction of stock prices.

Despite impressive evidence consistent with the hypothesis, it has won no support as an explanation of stock market prices. That's because there isn't any reason to believe that there should be a relationship between the team that wins the Super Bowl and stock prices. In general, economists first look to see whether a hypothesis is consistent with a model that makes sense and then examine the evidence that either lends support to or refutes the hypothesis. The simple fact that a hypothesis is consistent with a body of evidence is seldom sufficient to

- **Ceteris paribus** means "all other things unchanged."
- A **dependent variable** is one that changes in response to a change in another variable.
- An **independent variable** is a variable that induces a change in a dependent variable.

[6] The actual hypothesis has an exception: If an AFC team that was part of the old National Football League (NFL) before it merged with the American Football League wins, stock prices will rise. The Pittsburgh Steelers, for example, play in the AFC but were part of the NFL. If they play in the Super Bowl, the hypothesis predicts that stock prices are certain to rise!

Case in Point — Smoking, Health, and Murder

It is well established that smoking contributes to cancer, heart disease, and a host of other ailments. But does smoking make a person more likely to be murdered?

The evidence suggests that it may. People who smoke two packs per day are twice as likely to be murdered than are non-smokers, according to three medical researchers. Smoking is closely associated with being murdered.

The researchers are not, however, asserting that smoking will get you killed. Their research, reported in the *Lancet,* is an effort to illustrate the fallacy of false cause. The fact that two series of numbers tend to move together does not prove that one causes the other. There is simply no reason to believe that smoking makes it more likely that a person will be the target of a murder attempt. And it certainly would be awkward to conclude that being murdered causes a person to smoke!

A more likely explanation for the fact that smokers are more likely to be murdered than nonsmokers lies in income levels. People with lower incomes are more likely to be victims of murder than people with higher incomes. And smoking is much more common among low-income individuals than among high-income individuals.

Source: George Davy Smith, Andrew N. Phillips, and James D. Neaton, "Smoking as an 'Independent Risk Factor' for Suicide: Illustration of an Artifact from Observational Epidemiology?" *Lancet* 340 (8821) (19 September 1992): 709–712.

cause economists to believe it. In the case of the gasoline price increase in August 1990 for example, a widely used economic model predicted that consumers would be likely to respond by reducing the quantity of gasoline demanded. That gives economists greater confidence in the hypothesis and thus lends greater credibility to evidence consistent with the hypothesis.

Sometimes there is a logical reason to expect two events to be related, but an error is made in deciding that one causes the other. We observe, for example, that more people walk under umbrellas when it's raining than when it isn't. It would be incorrect to infer from this that people cause rain by opening their umbrellas.

Reaching the incorrect conclusion that one event causes another because the two events tend to occur together is called the **fallacy of false cause.** Here's a case of what some economists consider an example of the fallacy of false cause: The quantity of money and the level of economic activity in an economy generally tend to move together; increases in the quantity of money occur with increases in the level of economic activity, and vice versa. Many economists argue that changes in the quantity of money cause changes in the level of economic activity. Other economists reply that this is an example of the fallacy of false cause; they contend that it is changes in the level of economic activity that cause changes in the quantity of money.

Because of the danger of the fallacy of false cause, economists use special statistical tests to determine whether changes in one thing actually do cause changes observed in another. Given the inability to perform controlled economics experiments, however, these tests do not always offer convincing evidence that persuades all economists that one thing does, in fact, cause changes in another.

- The **fallacy of false cause** is the incorrect presumption that because two events tend to occur together, one must cause the other.
- **Experimental economics** employs controlled experiments using human or animal subjects to test economic hypotheses.

Economics in the Laboratory

Although economists rely most often on observations of the real world to test their hypotheses, some tests are conducted in the laboratory. This approach to economic research is called **experimental economics.** It uses controlled experiments that rely on human or animal subjects to test hypotheses.

One experiment, for example, subjected rats to varying "prices" for two soft drinks to see whether their responses to changing prices were consistent with hypotheses drawn from the model of demand and supply (they were). Other experiments have used human subjects. These experiments typically involve a form of game in which the strategies chosen by players can be studied to see whether they are consistent with some hypothesis. The advantage of an experimental approach is that experiments can be controlled; the disadvantage is that the experiment cannot be the real world. Hypotheses that are shown to be consistent with both experimental and real-world evidence, though, are likely to win greater support among economists.

Normative and Positive Statements

Two kinds of assertions in economics can be subjected to testing. We've already examined one, the hypothesis. Another testable assertion is a statement of fact, such as "It will rain tomorrow" or "The average income earned in the United States possesses, on average, greater purchasing power than does the average income in any other country." Like hypotheses, such assertions can be demonstrated to be false. Unlike hypotheses, they can also be shown to be correct. Statements of fact and hypotheses are called **positive statements.**

Although people often disagree about positive statements, such disagreements can ultimately be resolved through investigation. There is another category of assertions, however, for which investigation can never resolve differences. **Normative statements** are those that make a value judgment. Such judgments are the opinions of the speaker; no one can "prove" that the statement is or is not correct. Here are some examples of normative statements in economics: "We ought to do more to help the poor." "People should be paid according to the amount of work they do." "Corporate profits are too high." The statements are based on the values of the person who makes them. They can't be proved false.

Because people have different values, normative statements often provoke disagreement. An economist whose values lead him or her to conclude that we should provide more help for the poor will disagree with one whose values lead to a conclusion that we should not. Because no test exists for these values, these two economists will continue to disagree, unless one persuades the other to adopt a different set of values. Many of the disagreements among economists are based on such differences in values and therefore are unlikely to be resolved.

A Confusion of Economists?

We have names for groups of things. A group of fish is called a *school.* A group of peacocks is called an *ostentation.* A group of larks is called an *exultation.* What might we call a group of economists?

Some people, bewildered by the conflicting arguments they often hear from economists, would no doubt say that a group of economists should be called a *confusion!* George Bernard Shaw, the late British author and playwright, once observed that if all the economists in the world were laid out end to end, they would not reach a conclusion. An anonymous wag has added that if all the economists in the world were laid out end to end, it would be a good thing!

But it's easy to overstate the significance of disagreement among economists. There is, for example, broad agreement on the basic approach that economists take to questions: the importance of costs, a focus on individual decisions

- A **positive statement** is a statement of fact or a hypothesis.
- A **normative statement** is one that makes a value judgment.

and maximizing behavior, and the need to analyze choices at the margin. Economists generally agree about the impact of price changes on the behavior of firms and of consumers. They generally agree about how specific events will affect market prices. Indeed, the ideas presented in this book are ideas that have won general agreement among economists. Where there is substantial disagreement, this text will note it.

Disagreements among economists can be frustrating. It might be nice if economists agreed on everything. Economists might then achieve what the great British economist John Maynard Keynes suggested in a 1933 essay:

> If economists could manage to get themselves thought of as humble, competent people, on a level with dentists, that would be splendid!

But the disagreements that occur among economists may be a good thing. Disagreement sparks intellectual inquiry; it is through disagreement that much scientific progress is achieved. And it is disagreement that gives excitement and challenge to a field. There is much that we don't know about the economy. That means there is much left to discover.

Checklist ✓

- Economists try to employ the scientific method in their research.
- Scientists cannot prove a hypothesis to be true, they can only fail to prove it false.
- Economists, like other scientists, use models to assist them in their analyses.
- Two problems inherent in tests of hypotheses in economics are the all-other-things-unchanged problem and the fallacy of false cause.
- Experimental economics uses controlled experiments to test hypotheses in economics.
- Many statements made by economists are normative; such statements cannot be tested. Positive statements can be tested.
- Although disagreements among economists are common, economists generally agree about how economic questions should be approached and agree on a wide range of behavioral relationships.

A Look Back—And a Look Ahead

Choices are forced on us by scarcity; economists study the choices that people make. Some key choices assessed by economists include what to produce, how to produce it, and for whom it should be produced. Economics is distinguished from other academic disciplines that also study choices by the approach economists take to those issues. The distinguishing features of economic analysis are an insistence on the central importance of costs in evaluating choices, the assumption of maximizing behavior on the part of individual decisionmakers, and an emphasis on evaluating choices at the margin.

Economic analyses may be aimed at explaining individual choice or choices in an individual market; such investigations are largely the province of microeconomics. The analysis of the aggregated impact of those individual choices on total output, level of employment, and the price level is the province of macroeconomics.

Economists work within the framework of the scientific method. Hypotheses are formulated and then tested. These tests can only refute a hypothesis; hypotheses in science cannot be proved. A hypothesis that has been widely tested often comes to be regarded as a theory; one that has won virtually universal acceptance is a law.

Because of the complexity of the real world, economists rely on models that rest on a series of simplifying assumptions. The models are used to generate hypotheses about the economy that can be tested using real-world data. These empirical tests are most often based on statistical examinations of real-world data and observations. Empirical tests can also be applied to statements of fact. Statements of fact and hypotheses are positive statements. To a limited degree, economists are beginning to develop experimental approaches to economic questions; these approaches make use of both human and nonhuman subjects. Given the difficulties of conducting statistical and experimental tests, many empirical investigations by economists fall short of providing definitive tests of hypotheses. Economists may thus disagree about whether a particular hypothesis has been refuted by empirical testing. Normative statements, unlike positive statements, can't be tested and thus provide a further source for potential disagreement. Economists disagree about many issues, but they nevertheless share broad agreement about the basic perspective from which they approach problems.

The remaining chapters in Part One continue the discussion of the study of choices in economics. Chapter 2 examines choices in production; Chapter 3 explores the nature of market choices. The Chapter 1 Appendix reviews an important mathematical tool that is used throughout this text: the graph.

Terms and Concepts for Review

Ceteris paribus
Constant
Cost
Dependent variable
Economics
Economy
Experimental economics
Fallacy of false cause
Free good
Good
Hypothesis
Independent variable
Law
Macroeconomics
Margin
Market
Maximize
Microeconomics
Model
Normative statement
Positive statement
Scarce good
Scarcity
Scientific method
Service
Theory
Utility
Variable

For Discussion

1. Which of the following are scarce? Why or why not?
   a. air
   b. water
   c. land
   d. leisure time
   e. money
2. Comment on the following statement: "Scarcity doesn't exist in socialist systems because production choices are made by the government."
3. Determine whether each of the following raises a "what," "how," or "for whom" issue. Are the statements normative or positive?
   a. We must expand our efforts in space exploration.
   b. The federal government doesn't spend enough for children.
   c. We need to devote more police resources to the inner city.
   d. We should resist automation because it destroys jobs.
   e. We must protect the environment, even at the cost of producing goods and services.
   f. We should emulate Japanese management practices.
   g. Access to health care should not be limited by income.
4. Your time is a scarce resource. What if the quantity of time were increased, say to 48 hours per day, and everyone still lived as many days as before. Would time still be scarce? Think about the last time you told your Aunt Martha that you would have written to her but that you didn't have time. Why was that a meaningless statement?
5. When you registered for this course in economics, what objective did you have in mind? What costs were involved? Carefully estimate the cost of your choice. Does your behavior in this instance fit the economists' model of maximizing choice? Can you think of any choices that you make that are not aimed at maximizing the value of some objective?
6. Most college students are under age 25. Give two explanations for this—one based on the benefits people of different ages are likely to receive from higher education and one based on the costs (in the economic sense) of a college education to students of different ages.
7. David Lucas, a developer in South Carolina, purchased two undeveloped beachfront lots in 1986 for $975,000. He planned to build a house on each. He intended to sell one of the houses and keep the other for his family. The two lots were the only ones in the immediate area on which houses had not already been built. After he purchased the lots but before he began construction, the

South Carolina Coastal Commission, a state agency, banned all further development of beachfront property in the area. Mr. Lucas now had two lots that he couldn't use. He sued, demanding that the state compensate him for his loss.

The state argued that it should not be required to compensate landowners for the impact of its regulations and that such a requirement would be too costly. The Supreme Court ruled in 1992 that Mr. Lucas should be compensated.

How does a requirement that landowners such as Mr. Lucas be compensated affect the cost of regulations like the South Carolina restriction?

8. Suppose Jim Tolisano finds the grizzlies he's looking for in Southern Colorado (see the Case in Point on page 6). How will this discovery affect the cost of timber sales in the San Juans? The cost of the proposed ski area?

9. The July 1995 issue of *Working Woman* magazine lists the job of a pharmacoeconomist as one of the ten "Best of the Best" careers for women. Pharmacoeconomists work for hospital chains, government agencies, insurance companies, and HMOs. They are, according to the magazine, paid salaries ranging from $60,000 to $200,000 per year. What do you suppose they do?

10. Using the principle of marginal analysis, think about your behavior the next time you are at a hamburger stand. Why might an economist expect that you would be more likely to order one hamburger, one order of French fries, and one soft drink rather than three hamburgers?

11. Suppose the government were considering a military action that was expected to require the use of force roughly on the scale required by Operation Desert Storm (see the Case in Point on page 9). Would it make sense to use the experience of Desert Storm in evaluating whether to commit U.S. troops? Which measure of the cost of Desert Storm would be most relevant? What other considerations would be relevant? Would a willingness of U.S. allies to pay for part of the proposed military action affect the cost?

12. Many models in physics and in chemistry assume the existence of a perfect vacuum. Yet we know that a perfect vacuum doesn't exist. Are such models valid? Why would they be based on assumptions that are essentially incorrect?

13. Categorize each of the following statements as a normative statement or as a positive statement. If the statement is positive, how might you test it?

a. What this city needs is a good deli.

b. Reducing the supply of heroin will increase total spending on heroin.

c. A stitch in time saves nine.

d. A job worth doing is worth doing well.

e. Early to bed, early to rise, makes a man healthy, wealthy, and wise.

f. Higher incomes make people happy.

g. Poverty must be eliminated.

h. Americans are too materialistic.

i. Government deficits cause inflation.

j. The rich get richer and the poor get poorer.

14. Suppose you were asked to test the proposition that government deficits cause inflation. What evidence might you want to consider? In what ways would the problem of carrying out controlled experiments make your analysis difficult?

15. The text offers one explanation for the fact that smokers are more likely to be murdered than nonsmokers. Can you suggest some others?

1 Appendix Graphs in Economics

A glance through the pages of this book should convince you that there are a lot of graphs in economics. The language of graphs is one means through which economic ideas are presented. If you're already familiar with graphs, you'll have no difficulty with this aspect of your study. If you've never used graphs or haven't used them in some time, this appendix will help you feel comfortable with the graphs you'll encounter in this text.

Imagine a primer written in Greek for children. If you were unfamiliar with the language, the book would appear complex: "τον ποταμον διαβαινει" looks rather formidable. Written in English, however, "He crossed the river" is quite simple. The Greek primer presents much the same problem as graphs. The ideas presented graphically in this text are straightforward. But if you're unfamiliar with the language, they can seem confusing.

This appendix is a primer in the language of graphs and in the way graphs are used in economics. The language is an easy one to learn, and once you learn it, you'll find economics much easier to understand.

Constructing and Interpreting Graphs

The key to understanding graphs is to understand the rules that apply to their construction and interpretation. This section defines those rules and suggests some ways in which graphs are used in economics.

Graphs and Variables

Much of the analysis in economics deals with relationships between variables. A variable is simply a quantity whose value can change. Examples of variables include a person's annual income, the population of China, and per capita coffee consumption in the United States. A **graph** is a pictorial representation of a relationship between two or more variables.

To illustrate the use of a graph in economics, let's examine the relationship between the number of bakers employed per day and the number of loaves of bread produced per day in a small bakery. The manager of the bakery, Felicia Alvarez, has recorded her daily output of bread and the number of bakers she hires. Her findings are presented in the table in Exhibit 1A-1; they suggest that output increases as she adds more bakers. Adding the first baker increases output from 0 to 400 loaves of bread per day. We would say that bread production increases as more bakers are hired, *ceteris paribus*.

A **graph** is a pictorial representation of a relationship between two or more variables.

Each additional baker increases the bakery's output, but by smaller and smaller amounts. The second baker, for example, increases output by 300 loaves per day, the sixth by only 50. The tendency of output to rise by less and less as more workers are added is a phenomenon that is widely observed in economic analysis. In the bakery case, we assume that the size of the bakery itself, the number of ovens, and the amount of other equipment remain constant as Ms. Alvarez adds more bakers. That's an important assumption we typically make when we draw a graph. Because we're showing how bread output varies with the number of bakers, we hold all other variables, save for the ones shown in the graph, constant in constructing a table and/or drawing the curve.

The information in the table is also presented in a graph in Exhibit 1A-1. Each variable is assigned to one of the two axes in the graph. In this case, the number of bakers per day is reported on the horizontal axis, and the output of bread is reported on the vertical axis. The curve that relates output to the number of bakers is called a *total product curve.* Notice that the letters on the curve correspond to the pair of values given in the table.

EXHIBIT 1A-1

Drawing a Graph

To draw a graph, we assign one variable to each of the two axes. All other factors are assumed to be unchanged. In the case shown here, the number of bakers is shown on the horizontal axis, and the number of loaves of bread produced per day is shown on the vertical axis. We plot the values given in the table and connect the points, obtaining a total product curve that shows the relationship between the number of workers (number of bakers) and output (loaves of bread produced in a day).

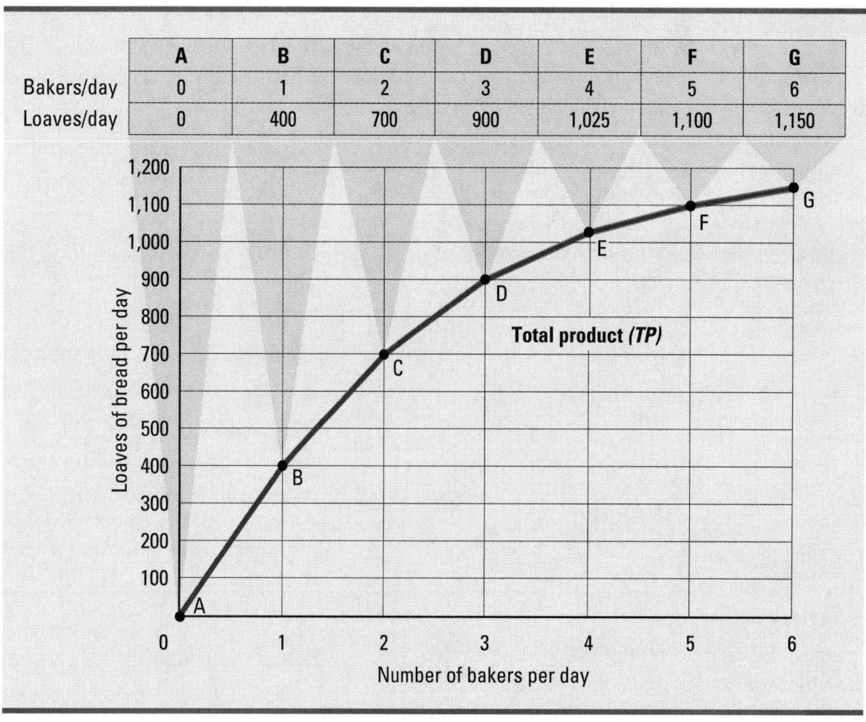

	A	B	C	D	E	F	G
Bakers/day	0	1	2	3	4	5	6
Loaves/day	0	400	700	900	1,025	1,100	1,150

Positive and Negative Relationships

The curve in Exhibit 1A-1 slopes upward, suggesting that an increase in the quantity of labor causes an increase in total output. A decrease in the quantity of labor would result in a reduction in output. When two variables move in the same direction, there is a **positive relationship** between the two variables. A positive relationship is implied by an upward-sloping curve in a graph. If two variables move in opposite directions, they have a **negative relationship.** Such a relationship would be depicted by a downward-sloping curve in a graph.

- A **positive relationship** between two variables is one in which both variables move in the same direction.
- A **negative relationship** is one in which two variables move in opposite directions.

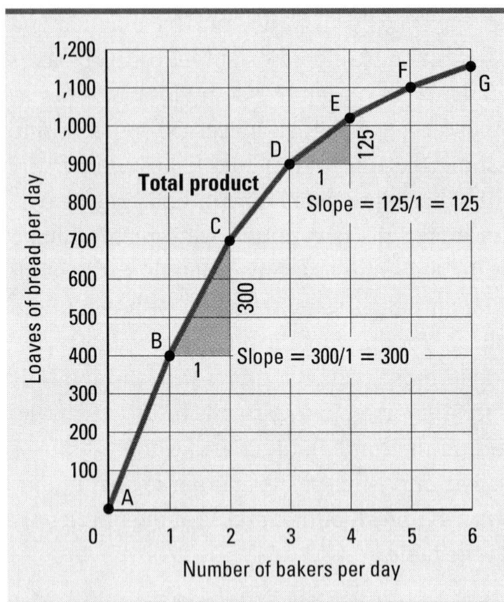

EXHIBIT 1A-2

Computing the Slope of a Curve

We can calculate the slope of a curve by dividing the change in the variable on the vertical axis by the change in the variable on the horizontal axis, measured between two points on the curve. For example, the slope of the curve between points B and C is 300. Here, the slope declines as the number of bakers increases.

Slopes of Curves

Although the total product curve in Exhibit 1A-1 is upward sloping, it becomes less and less steep as the number of bakers is increased. That's because each additional baker adds less to the total number of loaves the bakery produces each day. The rate at which one variable changes in response to changes in another is measured as the **slope** of a curve; it is measured by dividing the change in the variable on the vertical axis by the change in the variable on the horizontal axis between two points on the curve. Exhibit 1A-2 shows the same curve that was shown in Exhibit 1A-1, with the slope calculated between two pairs of points. The slope between B and C, for example is 300, the increase in number of loaves that occurs with the second worker. The slope between D and E is 125; the slope continues to decline as we travel to the right along the curve. A curve whose slope changes as we travel along it shows a **nonlinear relationship.** A **linear relationship** is one shown by a curve whose slope is constant—a straight line.

Shifts in Curves

The total product curve shown in Exhibits 1A-1 and 1A-2 is based on a given oven capacity and stock of other kitchen tools. It shows the quantity of bread produced with varying numbers of bakers, ceteris paribus. Suppose Ms. Alvarez installs more ovens and purchases additional tools. That change should result in greater output with any number of bakers. Such a change shifts the total output curve, as shown in Exhibit 1A-3.

Exhibit 1A-3 illustrates a fundamental point about graphical relationships. Suppose we begin at point C on the original total product curve, TP_1. Two bakers are employed; they produce 700 loaves of bread per day. An increase in the number of bakers to, say, three moves us along the total product curve to a new point, D, at which 900 loaves per day are produced. But a change in the quantity of kitchen equipment, or in any other independent variable, produces a shift in the curve to TP_2. In general, a change in one of the variables shown in the graph causes a movement *along* the curve; a change in another variable that had been held constant *shifts* the curve. Learning to determine when an event causes a movement along a curve versus a shift in it is one of the keys to understanding economic relationships.

EXHIBIT 1A-3

A Shift in a Curve

A graph illustrates a relationship between two variables; other variables that affect the relationship are assumed constant. A change in one of those other variables will result in a shift in the curve. Here, an increase in the quantity of kitchen equipment available causes the curve showing total output to shift upward from TP_1 to TP_2.

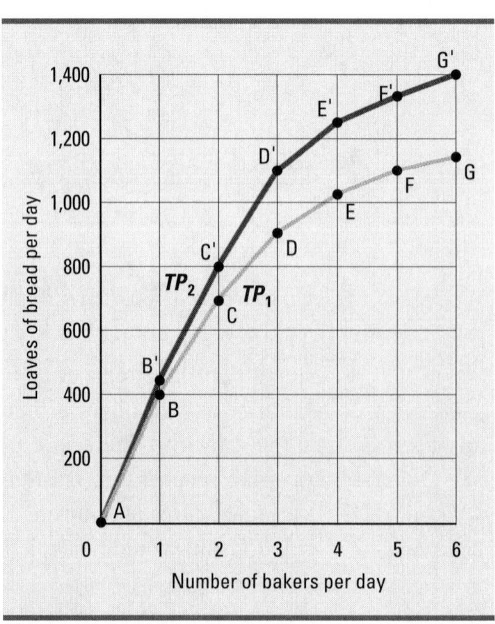

Checklist

A graph shows a relationship between two variables. An upward-sloping curve suggests a positive relationship between the two variables. As we travel from A to B, for example, an increase in variable 2 leads to an increase in variable 1.

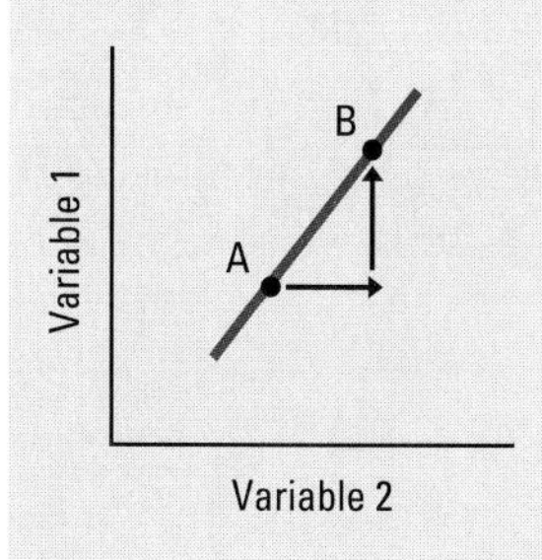

Here there is a negative relationship between the two variables. As we travel from C to D, an increase in variable 2 causes a reduction in variable 1.

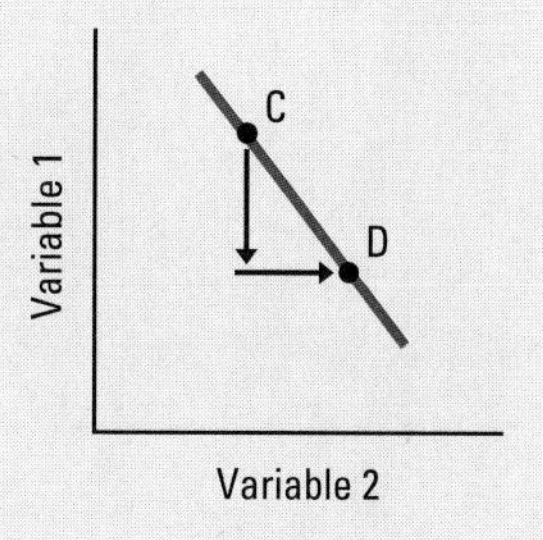

The slope of a curve is the ratio of the vertical change to the horizontal change between two points on the curve. Here, the curve is linear; its slope is the same between any two points. Notice also that this line suggests a negative relationship; its slope will be a negative value.

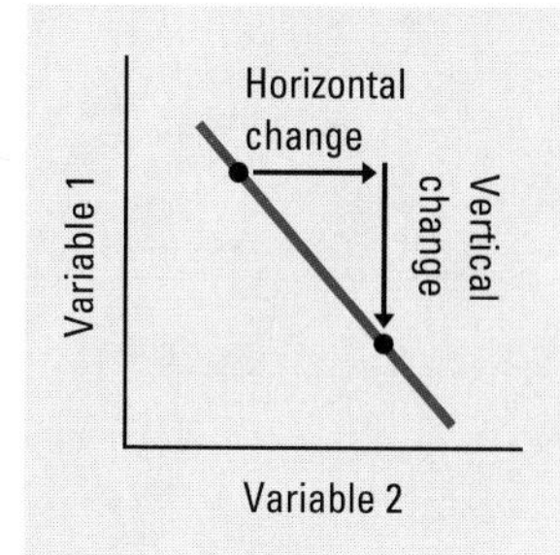

A nonlinear curve is one whose slope changes as we travel along it. Curve A shows a positive relationship in which the slope is decreasing. Curve B shows a positive relationship in which the slope is increasing.

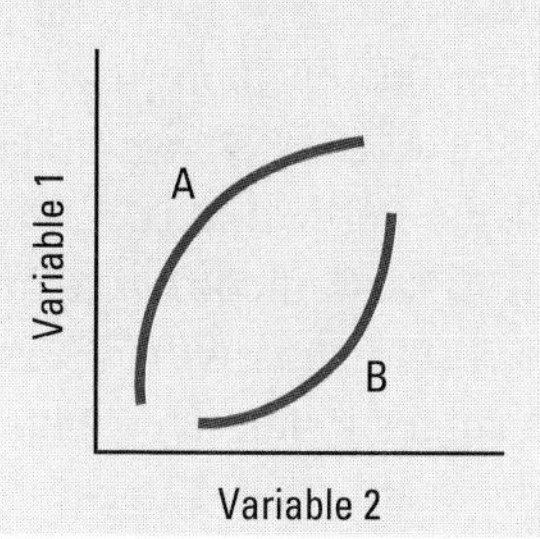

A change in a variable shown on the graph produces a movement along the curve such as the movement from A to B along curve D_1. A change in one of the variables held constant in drawing curve D_1 shifts the curve. Here, it shifts to D_2.

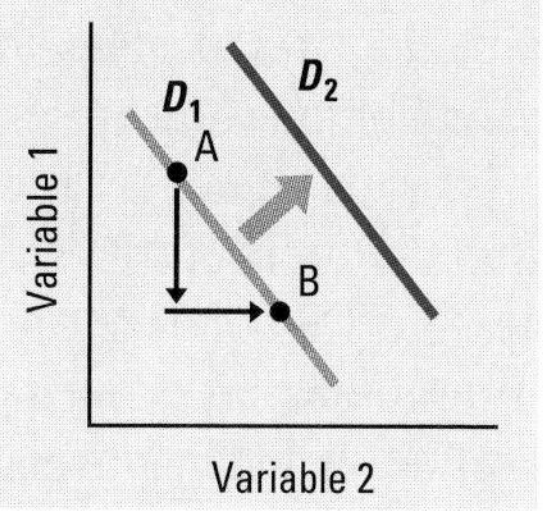

Time-Series Graphs

One of the most common types of graphs used in economics shows how the value of a particular variable or variables has changed over some period. Such a graph is called a **time-series graph,** which is a graph that shows how one or more variables has changed over some period of time. One of the variables in a time-series graph is time itself. The other can be any variable whose value changes over time.

Exhibit 1A-4 shows a time-series graph of monthly unemployment rates in the United States from 1980 to 1995. Time is shown as a variable on the horizontal axis; unemployment rates are shown on the vertical axis. The graph is constructed by plotting points showing the unemployment rate for each month and then connecting these points with a line. The line shows that unemployment generally rose from 1980 to 1983, then fell, then rose again in the early 1990s. It has been declining since.

- The **slope** of a curve is the ratio of the change in the variable on the vertical axis to the change in the variable on the horizontal axis, measured between two points on the curve.
- A **nonlinear relationship** is shown by a curve whose slope is changing.
- A **linear relationship** implies a curve of constant slope—a straight line.
- A **time-series graph** depicts how the value of a variable changes over time.

EXHIBIT 1A-4

A Time-Series Graph of U.S. Unemployment

The curve shows the monthly unemployment rate in the United States from 1980 through June of 1995.

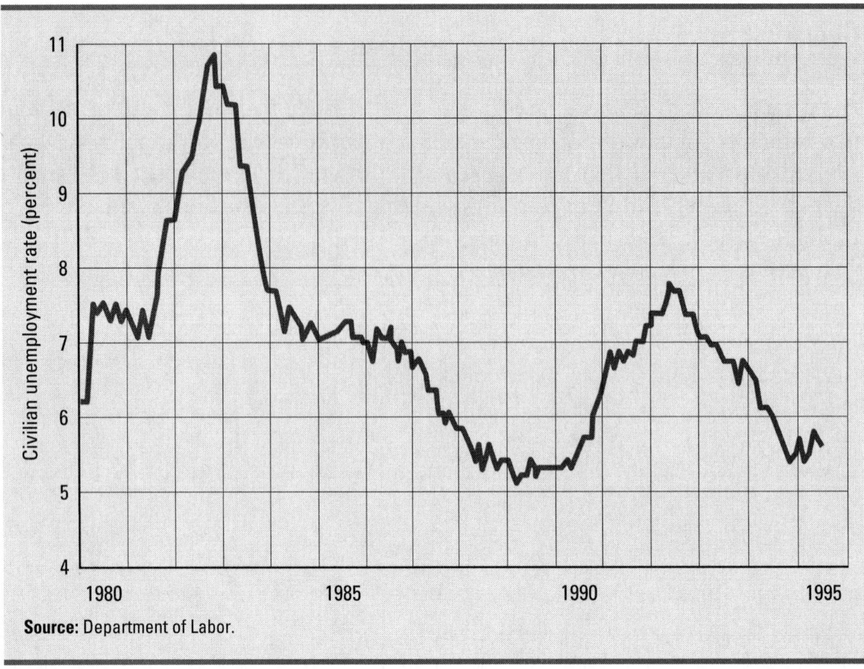

Source: Department of Labor.

Graphs: A Consumer Advisory

Notice that the vertical axis of the graph in Exhibit 1A-4 begins at 4 percent, not at zero. That's done to show changes in the unemployment rate more clearly. The 1980s were a period in which the unemployment rate rose to its highest level since the Great Depression of the 1930s and then fell by more than half. The scaling of the vertical axis appropriately depicts these large swings in the rate.

But one can play tricks with the scaling of the vertical axis. Consider the 1993 debate about President Clinton's proposal to raise income tax rates. The measure was intended to boost federal revenues and thus reduce the deficit. Critics of the president's proposal argued that changes in tax rates have little or no effect on federal revenues. Higher tax rates, they said, would cause some people to scale back their income-earning efforts and thus produce only a small gain—or even a loss—in revenues. Op-ed essays in *The Wall Street Journal,* for example, often show a graph very much like that presented in Panel (a) of Exhibit 1A-5. It shows federal revenues as a percentage of gross domestic product (GDP), a measure of total income in the economy, since 1960. Various tax reduction and tax increase measures were enacted during that period, but Panel (a) appears to show they had little effect on federal revenues relative to total income.

Laura Tyson, President Clinton's chief economic adviser, charges that those graphs are misleading. In a *Wall Street Journal* piece, she noted the scaling of the vertical axis used by the President's critics. She argued that a more reasonable scaling of the axis shows that federal revenues tend to increase relative to total income in the economy and that cuts in taxes reduce the federal government's share. Her alternative version of these events does, indeed, suggest that federal receipts have tended to rise and fall with changes in tax policy, as shown in Panel (b) of Exhibit 1A-5.[7]

[7] Laura Tyson, "Higher Taxes Do So Raise Money," *The Wall Street Journal,* 3 August 1993, A14.

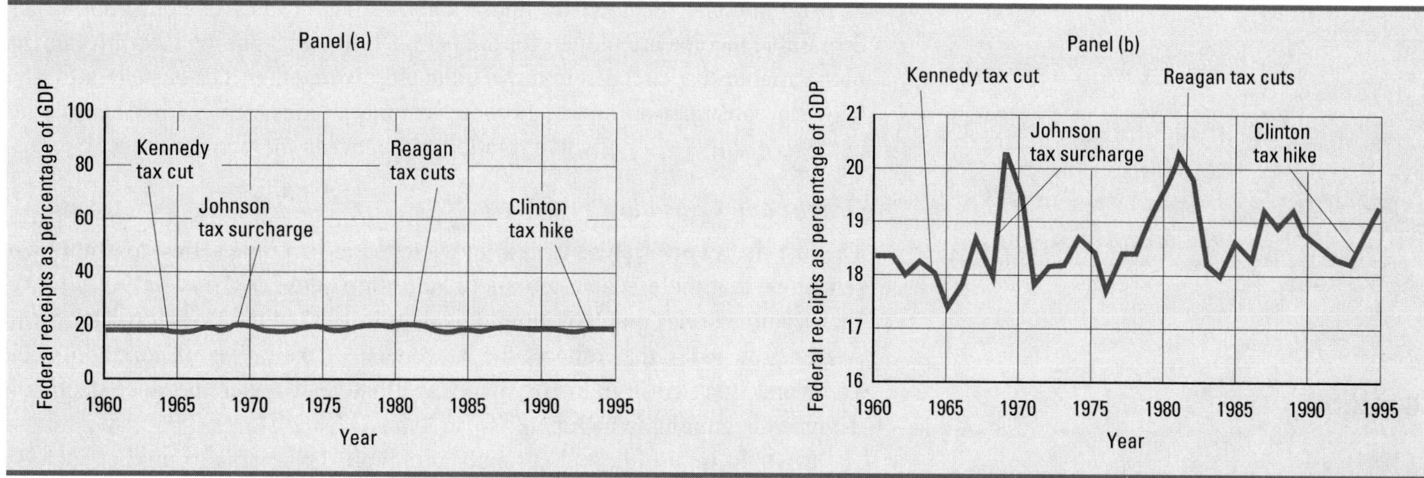

EXHIBIT 1A-5

Two Tales of Taxes and Income

A graph of federal revenues as a percentage of GDP emphasizes the stability of the relationship when plotted with the vertical axis scaled from 0 to 100, as in Panel (a). Scaling the vertical axis from 16 to 24 percent, as in Panel (b), stresses the short-term variability of the percentage and suggests that major tax rate changes have affected federal revenues.

Which version is correct? Both are. Both graphs show the same data. It's certainly true that federal revenues have, relative to economic activity, been remarkably stable over the past several decades, as emphasized by the scaling in Panel (a). But it is also true that the federal share has varied between about 17 and 20 percent. And a small change in the federal share translates into a large amount of money. A 1-percentage-point change in the federal share of total income in today's economy equals more than $60 billion.

It's easy to be misled by time-series graphs. Large changes can be made to appear trivial and trivial changes to appear large through an artful scaling of the axes. The best advice for a careful consumer of graphical information is to note carefully the range of values shown and then to decide whether the changes are really significant.

Testing Hypotheses with Time-Series Graphs

John Maynard Keynes, one of the most famous economists ever, proposed in 1936 a hypothesis about total spending for consumer goods in the economy. He suggested that this spending was positively related to the income households receive. One way to test such a hypothesis is to draw a time-series graph of both variables to see whether they do, in fact, tend to move together. Exhibit 1A-6 shows the values of consumption spending and *disposable income,* which is

EXHIBIT 1A-6

A Time-Series Graph of Disposable Income and Consumption

Plotted in a time-series graph, disposable income and consumption appear to move together. This is consistent with the hypothesis that the two are directly related. The two variables moved apart during World War II, when the availability of many consumer goods was restricted by government policy in order to free resources for the war effort.

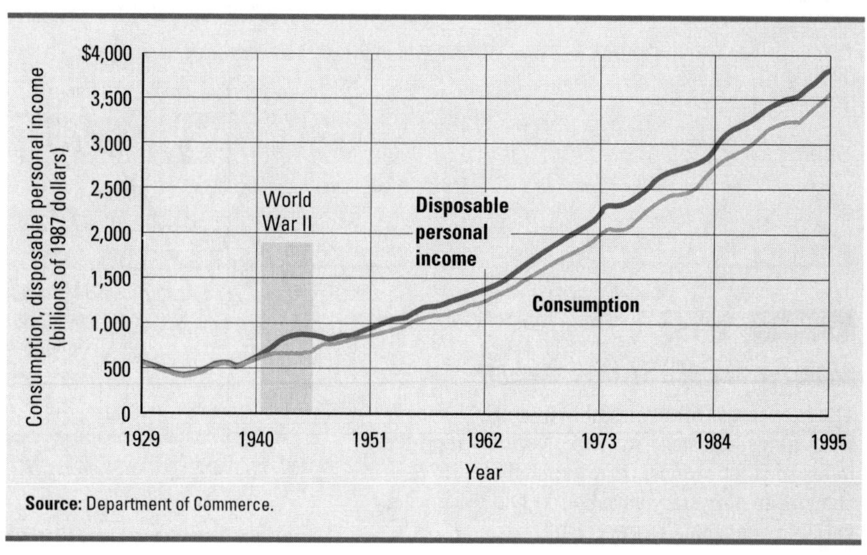

Source: Department of Commerce.

after-tax income received by households. Annual values of consumption and disposable income are plotted for the period 1929–first half of 1995. Notice that both variables have tended to move quite closely together. The close relationship between consumption and disposable income is consistent with Keynes's hypothesis that there is a positive relationship between the two variables.

Graphs and Causation

The fact that two variables tend to move together in a time series does not by itself prove that there is a systematic relationship between the two. Exhibit 1A-7 shows a time-series graph of monthly values in 1987 of the Dow Jones Industrial Average, an index that reflects the movement of the prices of common stock. The worst stock crash in history happened that year; notice the steep decline in the index beginning in October.

It would be useful, and certainly profitable, to be able to predict such declines. Exhibit 1A-7 also shows the movement of monthly values of a "mystery variable," *X,* for the same period. The mystery variable and stock prices appear to move closely together. Was the plunge in the mystery variable in October responsible for the stock crash? The answer is: Not likely. The mystery value is monthly average temperatures in San Juan, Puerto Rico. Attributing the stock crash in 1987 to the weather in San Juan would be an example of the fallacy of false cause.

Notice that Exhibit 1A-7 has two vertical axes. The left-hand axis shows values of temperature; the right-hand axis shows values for the Dow Jones Industrial Average. Two axes are used here because the two variables, San Juan temperature and the Dow Jones Industrial Average, are scaled in different units.

Checklist

- The slope of a linear curve is constant. The slope of a nonlinear curve changes at different points.
- A change in one of the variables assumed as given in drawing a curve produces a shift in the curve.
- A time-series graph shows changes in a variable over time; one axis is always measured in units of time.
- One use of time-series graphs is to plot the movement of two or more variables together to see if they tend to move together.

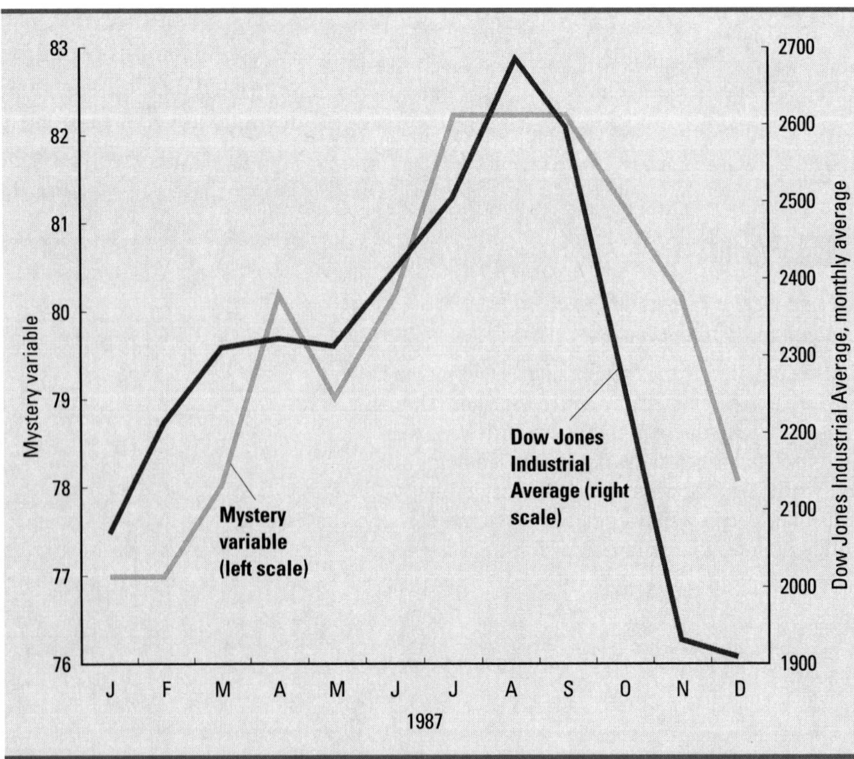

EXHIBIT 1A-7

Stock Prices and a Mystery Variable

The movement of the monthly average of the Dow Jones Industrial Average, a widely reported index of stock values, corresponded closely to changes in a mystery variable, *X.* Did the mystery variable contribute to the crash?

Terms and Concepts for Review

Graph
Linear relationship
Negative relationship
Nonlinear relationship
Positive relationship
Slope
Time-series graph

Problems

1. Panel (a) shows a graph of a positive relationship; panel (b) shows a graph of a negative relationship. Decide whether each proposition below is demonstrating a positive or negative relationship, and decide which graph you would expect to illustrate each proposition.

Panel (a)

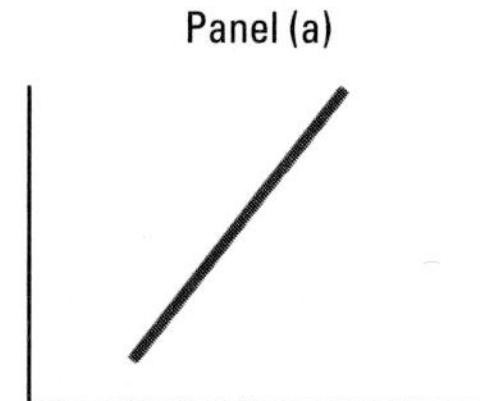

Panel (b)

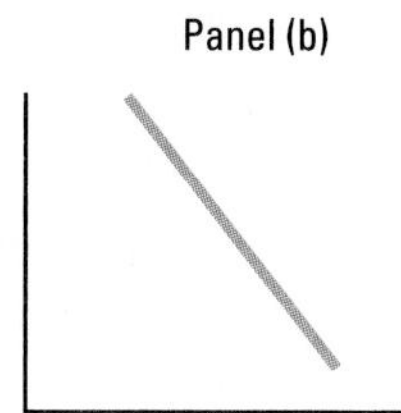

   a. An increase in national income in any one year increases the number of people killed in highway accidents.
   b. An increase in the poverty rate causes an increase in the crime rate.
   c. As the income received by households rises, they purchase fewer beans.
   d. As the income received by households rises, they spend more on home entertainment equipment.
   e. The warmer the day, the less soup people consume.

2. Suppose you have a graph showing the results of a survey asking people how many left and right shoes they owned. The results suggest that people with one left shoe had, on average, one right shoe. People with seven left shoes had, on average, seven right shoes. Put left shoes on the vertical axis and right shoes on the horizontal axis; plot the following observations:

Left shoes	1	2	3	4	5	6	7
Right shoes	1	2	3	4	5	6	7

   Is this relationship positive or negative? What is the slope of the curve?

3. Suppose your assistant inadvertently reversed the order of numbers for right shoe ownership in the survey above. You thus have the following table of observations:

Left shoes	1	2	3	4	5	6	7
Right shoes	7	6	5	4	3	2	1

   Is the relationship between these numbers positive or negative? What's implausable about that?

4. Suppose some of Ms. Alvarez's kitchen equipment breaks down. The following table gives the values of bread output that were shown in Exhibit 1A-1. It also gives the new levels of bread output that will occur because of the breakdown. Plot the two curves, labeling the first curve TP_1 and the second TP_2. What has happened?

	A	B	C	D	E	F	G
Bakers/day	0	1	2	3	4	5	6
Loaves/day	0	400	700	900	1,025	1,100	1,150
Loaves/day after breakdown	0	380	670	860	975	1,025	1,050

5. Steven Magee has suggested that there is a relationship between the number of lawyers per capita in a country and the country's rate of economic growth. The relationship is described with the following Magee curve.

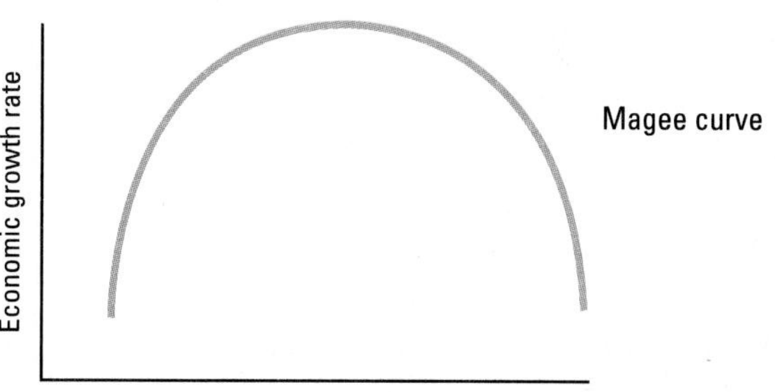

   What do you think is the argument made by the curve? What kinds of countries do you think are on the upward-sloping region of the curve? Where would you guess the United States is? Japan? Does the Magee curve seem plausible to you?

6. Look at the Case in Point on page 17. Draw a graph with the number of packs of cigarettes smoked per day on the horizontal axis and the probability that a person will be murdered on the vertical axis. Show a positive relationship between these variables. Do you agree with the relationship implied in the graph? Why or why not?

7. Draw graphs showing the likely relationship between each of the following pairs of variables. In each case, put the first variable mentioned on the horizontal axis and the second on the vertical axis.
   a. The amount of time a student spends studying economics and the grade he or she receives in the course
   b. Per capita income and total expenditures on health care
   c. Alcohol consumption by teenagers and academic performance
   d. Birth rates and income levels

2

Confronting Scarcity: Choices in Production

Chapter Objectives

After mastering the material in this chapter, you will be able to:

1. Describe the factors of production that are used to produce an economy's goods and services.
2. Show graphically the combinations of goods an economy is capable of producing.
3. Explain the basis for the transfer of factors of production from one activity to another and discuss how such transfers affect production costs.
4. Explain what it means for an economy to use its factors of production fully and efficiently.
5. Discuss the nature and causes of economic growth.
6. Explain the role of economic freedom in achieving an efficient allocation of goods and services.

Costs merely register competing attractions.
Frank H. Knight, 1921

What's Ahead

For more than four decades, Americans had sacrificed to provide a defense they regarded as adequate to meet the challenge posed by the Soviet Union. Trillions of dollars were spent to build the nation's military might. The resources used were scarce; producing all that defense came at a cost of fewer schools, hospitals, tennis rackets, sweaters, haircuts—the list of consumer goods and services given up was virtually endless. In terms of the classic metaphor, the United States gave up butter—civilian goods and services—to produce more guns—defense.

Then, with a swiftness that no cold warrior could have anticipated, the challenge evaporated. The Soviet Union collapsed in December 1991. The world suddenly seemed far less dangerous than it had been. That meant the United States could produce a lot fewer guns—and a lot more butter.

But what sort of butter should it produce? Should the United States transfer the resources that were used for defense to the production of better health care? Better schools? Better maintenance of our bridges and roads? A cleaner environment? Or should the opportunity to cut defense spending be used to reduce the federal deficit? Questions about what to do with the so-called peace dividend have held center stage in the public policy debates of the last several years.

The question of what an economic system should produce is not just a question that confronts the United States in the face of the collapse of the Soviet

Crock—By Bill Rechin and Brant Parker

Union. Every economic system must always make choices about what to produce. In this chapter we use the production possibilities model to examine the nature of such choices. As its name suggests, this model shows the goods and services that an economy is capable of producing—its possibilities—given the resources it has available. The model specifies what it means to use resources fully and efficiently and suggests some important implications for international trade. We can also use the model to explain the nature and causes of economic growth, a process that expands the set of production possibilities available to an economy.

We then turn to an examination of the institutional setting, or economic system, in which choices are made. Different economic systems result in different sets of choices; this fact helps to explain the dramatic shift from government-dominated to market-dominated economic systems that has been occurring throughout the world in recent years. We conclude with an examination of the role of government in an economy that relies chiefly on markets to allocate goods and services.

Factors of Production

This chapter examines choices in the production of goods and services. Choices concerning what goods and services to produce are choices about an economy's use of its **factors of production,** the resources available to it for the production of goods and services. The choices people make in using their factors of production determine their standard of living, the manner in which incomes will be distributed, and the rate at which incomes grow.

The factors of production in an economy are its capital, labor, and natural resources. **Capital** includes everything that has been produced for use in the production of other goods and services. It includes factors such as office buildings, machinery, and tools. **Labor** is the human effort applied to the production of goods and services. **Natural resources** are the resources of the natural environment that can be used for the production of goods and services.

Capital

Take yourself back a few million years to the time the first human beings walked the earth. They produced food by picking leaves or fruit off a plant or by catching an animal and eating it. We know that very early on, however, they began shaping stones into tools, apparently for use in butchering animals. Those first tools were the first capital because they were produced for use in producing other goods—food and clothing.

Capital in the modern economy is conceptually no different than those first stone tools. Its actual composition, of course, is far more complex.

Modern versions of the first stone tools include such things as saws, meat cleavers, hooks, and grinders; all are used in butchering animals. Tools such as hammers, screwdrivers, and wrenches are also capital. Transportation equipment, such as cars and trucks, is capital. Facilities such as roads, bridges, ports, and airports are capital. Buildings, too, are capital; they help us to produce goods and services.

- **Factors of production** are the resources the economy has available to produce goods and services.
- **Capital** is a factor of production that has been produced for use in the production of other goods and services.
- **Labor** is the human effort applied to the production of goods and services.
- **Natural resources** are the resources of the natural environment that can be used for the production of goods and services.

Capital does not consist solely of physical objects. A discovery of a new manufacturing technique is capital. It is an intellectual resource that has been produced for use in the production of other goods and services. The score for a new symphony is capital because it will be used to produce concerts. Computer software used by business firms or government agencies to produce goods and services is capital. Capital may thus include physical goods and intellectual discoveries.

Any resource is capital if it satisfies two criteria:

1. The resource must have been produced.
2. The resource can be used to produce other goods and services.

One form of capital that plays a particularly important role in the economy is **technology,** the knowledge that can be applied to the production of goods and services. Technology is what we know about using what we have to produce goods and services. Gains in technology, whether from the discovery of new production methods, new products, or new materials, add to the capital available to the economy and thus to its ability to produce goods and services.

Labor

Labor is human effort applied to production. People who work to repair tires, to pilot airplanes, to teach children, or to enforce laws are all part of the economy's labor.

In some contexts, it is useful to distinguish two forms of labor. The first is the human equivalent of a natural resource. It is the natural ability an untrained, uneducated person brings to a particular production process. But most workers bring far more. The skills and abilities a worker has as a result of education, training, or experience that can be used in production are called **human capital.** Students who are attending a college or university are acquiring human capital. Workers who are gaining skills through experience or through training are acquiring human capital. Children who are learning to read are acquiring human capital.

The amount of labor available to an economy can be increased in two ways. One is to increase the total number of people available to work. The other is to increase their human capital. In the United States and in most other countries, it is increases in human capital that have played the most important role in expanding the economy's ability to produce goods and services.

Natural Resources

There are two essential characteristics of natural resources. The first is that they be natural—that no human effort has been used to make or alter them. The second is that they be available for the production of goods and services.

Consider oil. Oil in the ground is a natural resource because it is found in the environment (not manufactured) and can be used to produce goods and services. Two hundred years ago, however, oil was a nuisance, not a natural resource. Pennsylvania farmers in the eighteenth century who found oil oozing up through their soil were dismayed, not delighted. No one knew what could be done with the oil. It wasn't until the mid-nineteenth century that a method was found for refining oil, transforming it into a natural resource.

- **Technology** is knowledge that can be applied to the production of goods and services.
- **Human capital** is the set of acquired skills and abilities that workers bring to the production of goods and services.

Case in Point — Medical Discovery Transforms Trash Tree to Treasure

Fifteen years ago, the Pacific yew tree would not have been on anyone's list of the natural resources of the Pacific Northwest. It isn't big enough to provide useful lumber. The scraggly tree isn't exactly gorgeous; it's difficult to imagine anyone going to see a Pacific yew. In the past, the homely yew has been routinely regarded as a weed, ending up in trash piles as a result of clearing operations.

Early in the 1980s, however, researchers at the National Cancer Institute (NCI) began examining the cancer-treating potential of taxol, a chemical that can be extracted from the bark of the yew. Preliminary tests suggested that taxol could save the lives of many women with ovarian cancer for whom all other treatments had failed. In 1991, the NCI harvested 150,000 yew trees to obtain enough taxol to treat 12,000 women in a large-scale experiment. Bristol-Myers, a major pharmaceutical firm, has been given the exclusive right to market the drug for the treatment of ovarian cancer.

The discovery transformed the lowly yew into a natural resource—and a topic of debate. Environmentalists worried that harvesting yew trees for their bark would destroy some of the ancient forests of the Pacific Northwest in which the yew grows. Although the demand for yew bark for treatment of ovarian cancer isn't likely to be large enough to endanger the species, environmentalists predicted that taxol would prove to be an effective treatment for other cancers as well. Wendell Wood, spokesperson for the Oregon Natural Resources Council, said in 1991, "There are more than 150,000 cases of [breast and lung] cancers this year. Roughly 15 times the demand is going to be on us immediately. There isn't going to be enough taxol to meet the demand."

The problem of preserving the yew may be solved through developing alternative sources of taxol. Some researchers have shown that taxol can be extracted from the tree's needles, a process that doesn't require killing the tree. It may also be possible to create artificial taxol in the laboratory. Other researchers have discovered that taxol can be extracted from trees that are common in India. Whatever the course of future technological developments, however, one thing is clear. The lowly yew has become a valuable natural resource.

Source: Cindy Kelly and Suzanne Tregarthen, "Discovery Turns Tree from Trash to Treasure," *The Margin* 7 (Fall 1991): 43.

Checklist

- An economy's factors of production include capital, labor, and natural resources.
- Capital includes physical and intellectual capital.
- Labor can be increased by increasing the number of workers or by increasing their human capital.
- The economy's stock of natural resources can be increased by increasing the quantity of these resources or by discovering new uses for known resources.

Once oil has been pumped out of the ground, it is no longer a natural resource. It is now capital, something that has been produced that can be used to produce other goods, such as gasoline or plastic or drugs.

Because something is a natural resource only if it can be used to produce goods and services, one might conclude that the environment is something to be plundered—that a tree has value only for its wood or that a mountain has value only for its minerals. But the concept of a natural resource as something that can be used to produce goods and services must be understood in terms of the meaning of a good or service. We saw in Chapter 1 that a good or service is a tangible or intangible thing from which people gain utility. If people gain utility from the existence of an unspoiled wilderness, then that wilderness is producing a service by providing esthetic pleasure. The wilderness is thus a natural resource.

The natural resources available to us can be expanded in two ways. One is the discovery of new natural resources, such as the discovery of a deposit of uranium. The other is the discovery of new uses for resources, as happened when new techniques allowed oil to be put to productive use or sand to be used in manufacturing computer chips.

The Production Possibilities Curve

An economy's factors of production are scarce; they cannot produce an unlimited quantity of goods and services. The **production possibilities curve** illustrates graphically the alternative combinations of goods and services an economy can produce with its limited factors of production. It thus serves as a model of production choices. In drawing the graph of a production possibilities curve, we assume that an economy can produce only two goods and that the quantities of the factors of production available to the economy are given.

Deriving a Production Possibilities Curve

Our derivation of a production possibilities curve will begin with the case of a single farmer. Suppose that Sam MacDonald, who operates his farm by himself, can grow two goods, cabbages and potatoes. Mr. MacDonald has three fields on which these goods can be grown. The factors of production available for field 1 are assumed to be fixed; they include Mr. MacDonald's labor, the size and quality of the field, and any farm equipment Mr. MacDonald has available for the field. Suppose that field 1 can produce the combinations of cabbages and potatoes shown in the table in Exhibit 2-1. If field 1 were devoted exclusively to cabbage production, it could produce 200 pounds of cabbage per year (combination A in the table). Devoted exclusively to potatoes, it could produce 100 pounds of potatoes per year (combination C). Assume that Mr. MacDonald could produce any combination that lies on a straight line between point A and point C; he could, for example, produce 100 pounds of cabbages and 50 pounds of potatoes per year (point B). We can think of field 1 as a tiny economy and draw a production possibilities curve showing these combinations of output; this curve is shown in Exhibit 2-1 also.

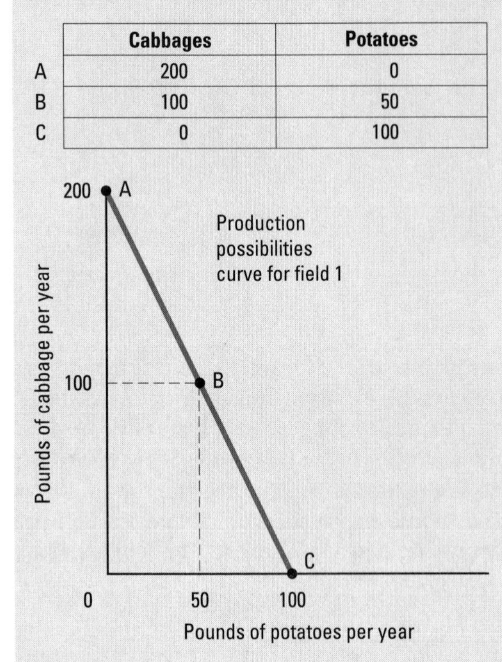

	Cabbages	Potatoes
A	200	0
B	100	50
C	0	100

EXHIBIT 2-1

A Production Possibilities Curve

The table above shows the combinations of cabbages and potatoes farmer MacDonald's field 1 is capable of producing each year. The combinations of cabbages and potatoes field 1 is capable of producing are also illustrated with a production possibilities curve. Notice that this curve is linear.

The production possibilities curve in Exhibit 2-1 is downward sloping, suggesting a negative relationship between production of cabbage and potatoes on field 1. That, in turn, suggests that field 1 is a scarce resource. Using it to produce more of one good means producing less of another. Production possibilities curves slope downward because of scarcity.

Because the production possibilities curve in Exhibit 2-1 is linear, its slope is constant. Between points A and B, for example, the slope is -2. This slope measures the rate at which Mr. MacDonald must give up cabbage production in order to produce additional potatoes. To see this more clearly, examine Exhibit 2-2. Suppose Mr. MacDonald is producing 100 pounds of cabbage and 50 pounds of potatoes per year at point B. Now consider what would happen if he decided to produce 1 more pound of potatoes. The segment of the curve around point B is magnified in Exhibit 2-2. The slope between points B and B′ is -2 (it equals -2 pounds/1 pound). Producing 1 additional pound of potatoes at point B′ requires giving up 2 pounds of cabbage. More generally, we can conclude that the absolute value of the slope of a production possibilities curve shows the amount of the good on the vertical axis that must be given up to produce an additional unit of the good on the horizontal axis.

Recall that Farmer MacDonald has three fields. The factors of production for all three fields are assumed to be fixed. Exhibit 2-3 shows production possibilities curves for each field. In this example, each of the fields, if devoted entirely to potatoes, could produce 100 pounds of potatoes. The fields differ, however, in their ability to produce cabbages. Those differences result in different slopes for each curve. We can use the slopes to compare the amounts of cab-

The **production possibilities curve** illustrates graphically the alternative combinations of goods and services an economy can produce with its scarce factors of production.

EXHIBIT 2-2

The Slope of a Production Possibilities Curve

The slope of the linear production possibilities curve in Exhibit 2-1 is constant; it is − 2. In the magnified section of the curve shown here, the slope is calculated between points B and B′. Expanding potato production to 51 pounds per year from 50 pounds requires a reduction in cabbage production to 98 pounds from 100 pounds per year. To shift from B′ to B″, Mr. MacDonald must give up 2 more pounds of cabbage. The slope of a production possibilities curve measures the quantity of the good on the vertical axis that must be given up in order to produce an additional unit of the good on the horizontal axis. The negative slope of the curve is an implication of scarcity.

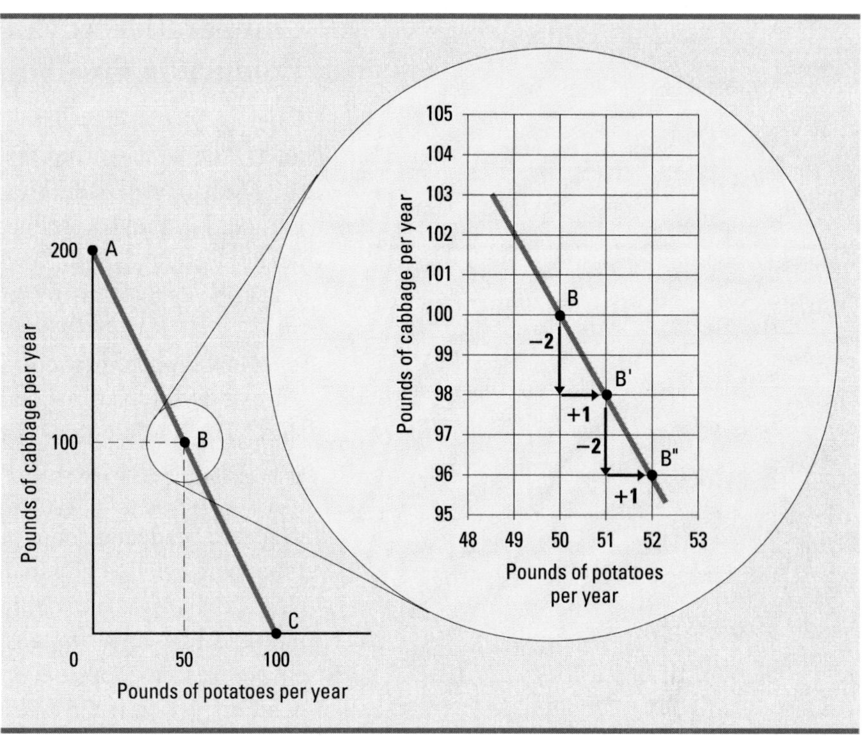

bage that must be given up to produce an additional pound of potatoes. The cost of producing an additional unit of any good is the value of what must be given up to produce it. It is, in the words of economist Frank H. Knight that opened this chapter, the "competing attraction." The greater the absolute value of the slope of the production possibilities curve, the greater that cost will be. The field for which the cost of an additional pound of potatoes is greatest is thus the field with the steepest production possibilities curve; the field for which the cost is lowest is the field with the flattest production possibilities curve. The field with the lowest cost of producing potatoes is field 3; its slope of − 0.5 means that Mr. MacDonald must give up half a pound of cabbage on that field to produce an additional pound of potatoes. On field 2, he must give up 1 pound of cabbage. We've already seen that an additional pound of potatoes requires giving up 2 pounds of cabbage on field 1.

EXHIBIT 2-3

Production Possibilities on Three Fields

The slopes of the production possibilities curves for each field differ. The steeper a production possibilities curve, the greater the cost of an additional unit of potatoes. The field with the lowest cost of producing additional potatoes is field 3. The field with the highest cost is field 1.

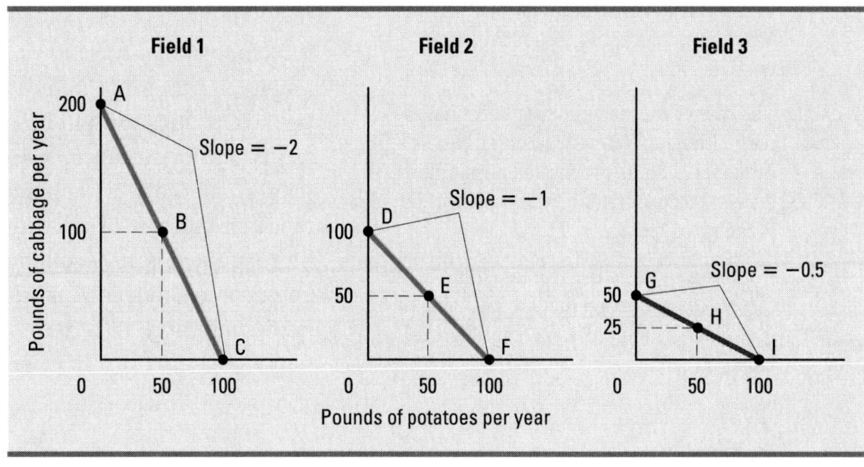

Comparative Advantage and the Production Possibilities Curve

Suppose Mr. MacDonald is producing nothing but cabbage on each of his three fields. To find the quantity he produces, we add up the values at the points where the production possibilities curves for the fields intersect the vertical axes in Exhibit 2-3. Field 1 produces 200 pounds of cabbage; field 2, 100 pounds; and field 3, 50 pounds. Mr. MacDonald can thus produce 350 pounds of cabbage per year if he devotes his resources exclusively to that crop. He produces no potatoes.

Now suppose he wants to produce 100 pounds of potatoes. That will require shifting one of his fields out of cabbage production. Which one will he choose to shift? The sensible thing for him to do is to choose the field on which potatoes cost the least—field 3. It has an advantage not because it is particularly well suited to potato production (all the fields in this example are equally well suited to potato production) but because it is the least productive field for cabbages. Producing a pound of potatoes on field 3 requires giving up just half a pound of cabbage. Field 3 has a comparative advantage in potato production because it is the field for which the cost of additional potatoes is lowest. More generally, economists say that an economy has a **comparative advantage** in producing a good or service if the cost of producing that good or service is lower for that economy than for any other. To put this in terms of the production possibilities curve, field 3 has a comparative advantage in potato production (the good on the horizontal axis) because its production possibilities curve is flattest.

If Mr. MacDonald wanted to produce more than 100 pounds of potatoes, he would turn next to field 2, which has the next-lowest cost for potatoes. To produce even more, he would turn finally to field 1. His choices for the three fields combined are shown in a production possibilities curve for all three fields in Exhibit 2-4. Notice that this production possibilities curve, which is made up of linear segments from each field, has a bowed-out shape; the absolute value of its slope increases as Mr. MacDonald produces more and more potatoes. This is a result of transferring resources from the production of one good to another according to comparative advantage. We shall examine the significance of the bowed-out shape of the curve in the next section.

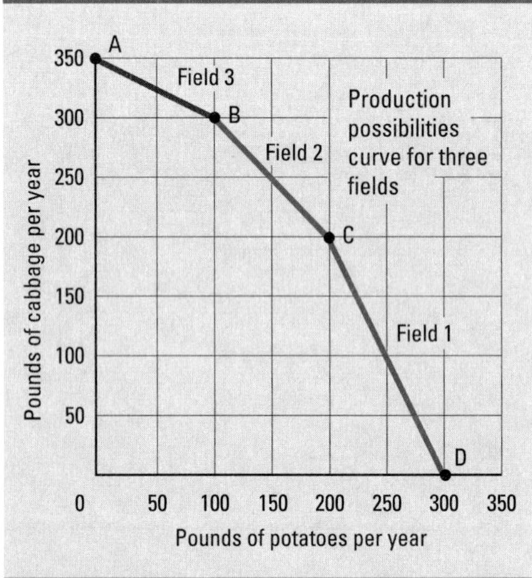

EXHIBIT 2-4

A Production Possibilities Curve for All Three Fields

The curve shown combines the respective production possibilities curves for each of Mr. MacDonald's three fields into a single production possibilities curve. At point A, Mr. MacDonald is producing 350 pounds of cabbage per year and no potatoes. If he wished to expand potato production, he would use field 3, which has a comparative advantage in potatoes.

The Law of Increasing Cost

Suppose Mr. MacDonald is operating at point A in Exhibit 2-4. All three of his fields are devoted to cabbage production. If he decides to switch to potato production, the first 100 pounds of potatoes will be grown on field 3, the field with the comparative advantage in potatoes. For each of those first 100 pounds of potatoes, Mr. MacDonald gives up half a pound of cabbage. The next 100 pounds of potatoes will be produced on field 2, at a cost of 1 pound of cabbage per pound of potatoes. The final 100 pounds of potatoes will be produced on field 1, at a cost of 2 pounds of cabbage per pound of potatoes produced. The fact that the cost of additional potatoes increases as Mr. MacDonald produces more of them is a reflection of the **law of increasing cost.** This law holds that as an economy moves along its production possibilities curve in the direction of producing more of a particular good, the cost of additional units of that good will increase.

- An economy has a **comparative advantage** in producing a particular good if it has the lowest cost for producing that good.
- The **law of increasing cost** states that as output increases for one good in an economy that is on its production possibilities curve, the cost of additional units will be greater and greater.
- **Full employment** means that all the factors of production that are available for use under current market conditions are being utilized.

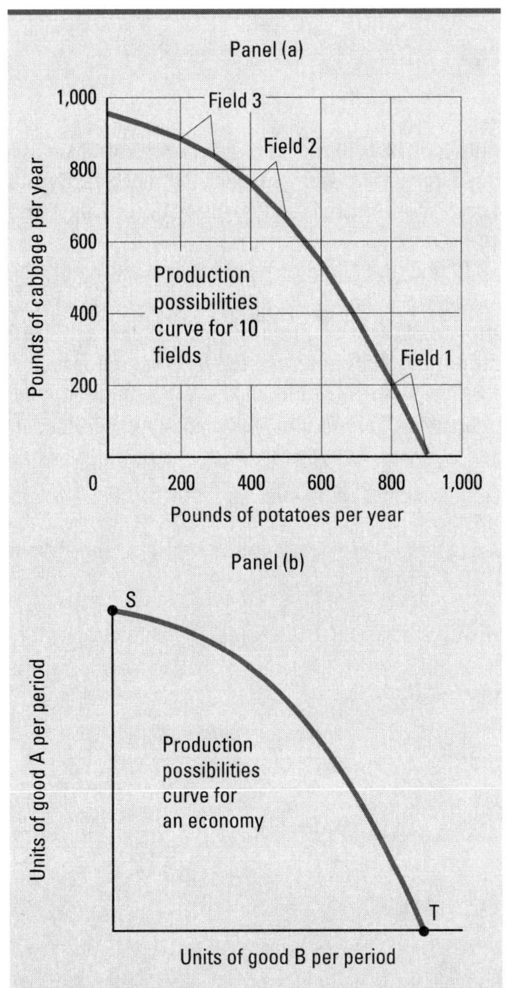

EXHIBIT 2-5

Production Possibilities Curves with More Factors of Production

The production possibilities curve in Panel (a) is based on linear production possibilities curves for individual fields, as in Exhibit 2-3. This time, however, the curves for 10 fields are combined; they include the 3 fields we've already discussed. Once again, the combined curve transfers fields from cabbage to potato production based on comparative advantage. The result is a bowed-out production possibilities curve showing that the cost of additional potatoes rises as more of them are produced.

The curve for an economy with far more resources can be drawn as a smooth curve, as shown in Panel (b). This production possibilities curve shows combinations of two goods, A and B, that can be produced.

In order to examine the roles of increasing cost and comparative advantage in an economy, we must first investigate the shape of a production possibilities curve for an economy rather than for Mr. MacDonald's three fields. As we increase the number of different resources available, the shape of the production possibilities curve will begin to resemble a smooth, bowed-out curve. Panel (a) of Exhibit 2-5, for example, shows a production possibilities curve for 10 fields, including the 3 fields we have already examined. Even though each field has a linear production possibilities curve, the combination of these linear segments resembles a smooth curve rather than a series of straight lines.

An economy with millions of workers, millions of fields, and millions of firms can be described by a smooth production possibilities curve, as in Panel (b) of Exhibit 2-5. The curve suggests the production choices available to an economy that produces two goods, A and B. The concepts of comparative advantage and increasing cost explain the bowed-out shape of this curve. At point S, the economy is producing only good A; no units of good B are produced. Moving to the right along the production possibilities curve, we see that the first units of good B are produced using factors of production that have a comparative advantage in producing good B. That means the cost of those initial units is relatively low; the production possibilities curve is relatively flat. As more of good B is produced, however, factors of production that are relatively better suited to producing good A must be used, increasing the cost of producing additional units of good B. The production possibilities curve accordingly becomes steeper and steeper.

Resource Allocation and the Production Possibilities Curve

Economists generally argue that it is better for an economy to operate on its production possibilities curve than to operate within it. An economy that is operating within its production possibilities curve could, by moving onto it, produce more of the goods and services that provide people value, such as food, housing, education, medical care, and music. Having more of these goods available to people would improve their standard of living. Economists conclude that it's better to be on the production possibilities curve rather than inside it.

Two things could leave an economy operating at a point inside its production possibilities curve. First, it might fail to use the resources it has available to it. Second, it might not allocate resources on the basis of comparative advantage. In either case, production within the production possibilities curve implies the economy could improve its performance.

Idle Factors of Production

Suppose an economy fails to put all its factors of production to work. Some workers are without jobs, some buildings are without occupants, some fields are without crops. Because an economy's production possibilities curve assumes the full use of the factors of production available to it, the failure to use some factors results in a level of production that lies inside the production possibilities curve.

If all the factors of production that are available for use under current market conditions are being utilized, the economy is experiencing **full employment.**

Case in Point: The Cost of the Great Depression

The U.S. economy looked very healthy in the beginning of 1929. It had enjoyed 7 years of dramatic growth and unprecedented prosperity. Its resources were fully employed; it was operating quite close to its production possibilities curve.

By summer, however, things started going wrong. Production and employment fell. They continued to fall for the next several years. By 1933, more than 25 percent of the nation's workers had lost their jobs. Production had plummeted by almost 30 percent. The economy had moved well within its production possibilities curve.

Output began to grow after 1933, but the economy continued to have vast numbers of idle workers, idle factories, and idle farms. These resources were not put back to work fully until 1942, when World War II demanded mobilization of the economy's factors of production.

Between 1929 and 1942, the economy produced 25 percent fewer goods and services than it would have if its resources had been fully employed. That was a loss, measured in today's dollars, of \$2.6 trillion. In material terms, the forgone output represented a greater cost than it would ultimately require to fight World War II. The Great Depression was a costly experience indeed.

An economy can't operate on its production possibilities curve unless it has full employment.

Exhibit 2-6 shows an economy that can produce food and clothing. If it chooses to produce at point A, for example, it can produce F_A units of food and C_A units of clothing. Now suppose that a large fraction of the economy's workers lose their jobs, so the economy no longer has full employment. Less food and clothing will be produced, moving the economy to point B, where the economy produces less food (F_B) and less clothing (C_B) than at point A. We often think of the loss of jobs in terms of the workers; they've lost a chance to work and to earn income. But the production possibilities model points to another loss—goods and services the economy could have produced aren't being produced.

- An economy that is operating on its production possibilities curve is engaged in **efficient production.**
- An economy that is using the resources it has available but producing at a point inside its production possibilities curve is engaging in **inefficient production.**

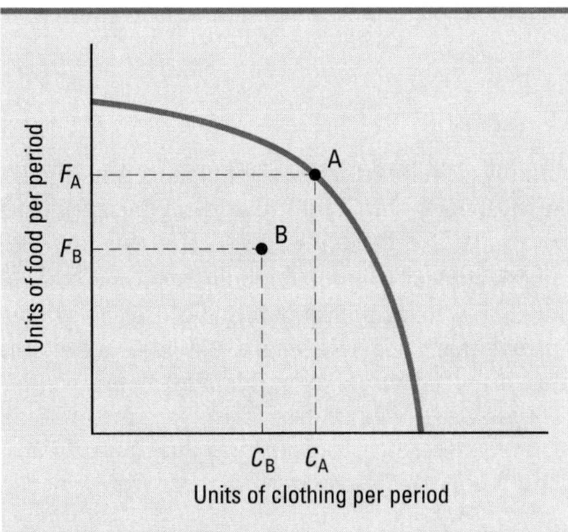

EXHIBIT 2-6

Idle Factors and Production

When an economy fails to put its available factors of production to work, it loses output. Here, an economy is capable of producing food and clothing at point A. If many of the economy's workers lose their jobs, the economy will produce less food and less clothing and will move to point B, which lies within the production possibilities curve.

Inefficient Production

An economy achieves a point on its production possibilities curve only if it allocates its factors of production on the basis of comparative advantage. If it fails to do that, it will operate inside the curve.

Suppose that, as before, Mr. MacDonald has been producing only cabbage and then starts producing potatoes. This time, however, he switches fields from one crop to the other in numerical order: field 1 first, field 2 second, and then field 3. Exhibit 2-7 illustrates the result. Instead of the bowed-out production possibilities curve ABCD, we get a bowed-in curve, AB′C′D. Suppose that Mr. MacDonald is producing 100 pounds of potatoes and 150 pounds of cabbage at point B′. Had he based his production choices on comparative advantage, he would have switched field 3 to potatoes and then field 2, so he would have operated at point C. He would be producing more potatoes and more cabbage—and he would not be working any harder or using any more resources than he is at B′. When an economy is operating on its production possibilities curve, we say that it is engaging in **efficient production.** If it is using the same quantity of resources but is operating inside its production possibilities curve, it is engaging in **inefficient production.** Inefficient production implies that the economy could be producing more goods without using additional resources.

Points on the production possibilities curve thus satisfy two conditions: the economy is at full employment, and it is making efficient use of its factors of production. If there are idle or inefficiently allocated factors of production, the economy will operate inside the production possibilities curve. Thus, the production possibilities curve not only shows what can be produced; it provides insight into how goods and services should be produced. It suggests that in order to obtain efficiency in production, factors of production should be allocated on the basis of comparative advantage. Further, full employment must be achieved if the economy is to produce the goods and services it is capable of producing.

EXHIBIT 2-7

Inefficient Production

When factors of production are allocated on a basis other than comparative advantage, the result is inefficient production. Curve AB′C′D shows the combinations possible to Mr. MacDonald if he transfers his fields from cabbage to potato production in numerical order: field 1, then field 2, and so on. The selection of fields on any basis other than comparative advantage will yield a solution inside the production possibilities curve ABCD.

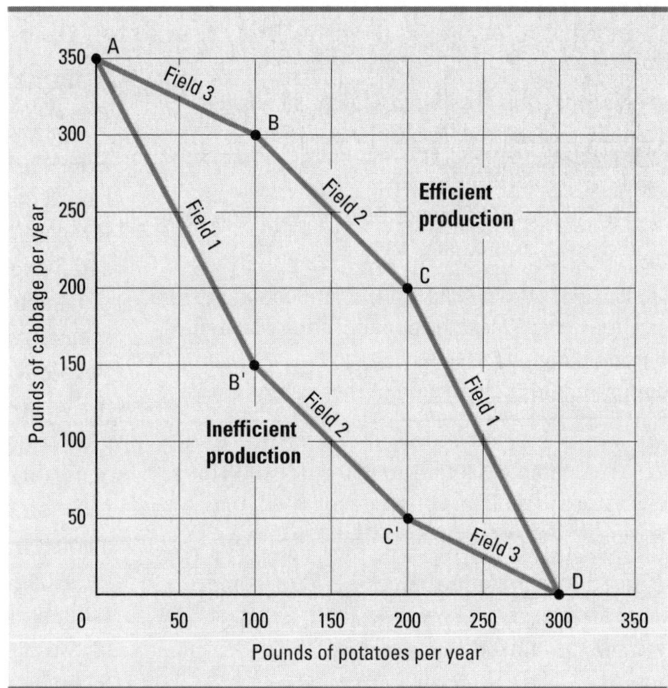

Case in Point: Specialization in the American Colonies

Very early in the development of the American colonies, a pronounced degree of regional specialization was evident. The Southern colonies specialized in agricultural activities, particularly the production of tobacco. The New England colonies, most notably Massachusetts, specialized in shipbuilding and other manufacturing activities.

Why build ships in New England? The South boasted a generous endowment of timber; indeed, much of the lumber used in shipbuilding came from the South. The South also boasted good harbors. Shipbuilding developed in New England primarily because the region was poorly suited for growing crops; it thus had a comparative advantage in building ships. Resources in the South that were perfectly suitable for shipbuilding could be used even more productively in agricultural activities. This regional specialization meant that as a whole, the colonies were able to produce more ships—and more agricultural goods—than would otherwise have been possible.

Eighteenth-century engravings of a New England shipyard and a farm near Salem, North Carolina.

Checklist

- A production possibilities curve shows the combinations of two goods the economy is capable of producing.
- The downward slope of the production possibilities curve is an implication of scarcity.
- The bowed-out shape of the production possibilities curve results from allocating resources based on comparative advantage. Such an allocation implies that the law of increasing cost will hold.
- An economy that fails to make full and efficient use of its factors of production will operate inside its production possibilities curve.
- An allocation of resources based on comparative advantage is likely to result in a high degree of specialization.

Specialization

The production possibilities model implies that specialization will occur. For efficiency, factors of production must be employed in specific uses in which they have a comparative advantage. If Mr. MacDonald selects point C in Exhibit 2-7, for example, he will assign field 1 exclusively to cabbage production and fields 2 and 3 exclusively to potato production.

Such specialization is typical in an economic system. Workers, for example, specialize in particular fields in which they have a comparative advantage. People work and use the income they earn to buy goods and services from people who have a comparative advantage in doing other things. The result is a far greater quantity of goods and services than would be available without this specialization.

Nations specialize as well. Much of the land in the United States clearly has a comparative advantage in agricultural production and is devoted to that activity. Hong Kong, with its huge population and tiny endowment of land, allocates virtually none of its land to agricultural use; that option would be too costly. Its land is devoted largely to manufacturing and the provision of housing for manufacturing workers.

Applications of the Production Possibilities Model

The production possibilities curve is a model of an economy. The model provides powerful insights about the real world, insights that help us to answer some important questions: How does trade between two countries affect the quantities of goods available to people? What determines the rate at which production will increase over time? What is the role of economic freedom in the economy? In this section we explore applications of the model to questions of international trade, economic growth, and the choice of an economic system.

Comparative Advantage and International Trade

One of the most powerful implications of the concepts of comparative advantage and the production possibilities curve relates to international trade. We can think of different nations as being equivalent to Mr. MacDonald's fields. Each will have a comparative advantage in certain activities, and efficient world production requires that each nation specialize in those activities in which it has a comparative advantage. A failure to allocate resources in this way means that world production falls inside the production possibilities curve; more of each good could be produced by relying on comparative advantage.

If nations specialize, then they must rely on each other. They will sell the goods in which they specialize and purchase other goods from other nations. Suppose, for example, that the world consists of three countries: Russia, the United States, and Japan. Suppose they can produce computers and wheat according to the table in Exhibit 2-8. Like Mr. MacDonald's fields, each country has a separate production possibilities curve; the three have been combined to illustrate a world production possibilities curve in Exhibit 2-8.

If production is allocated according to comparative advantage, the three countries together will have the production possibilities curve shown in Exhibit 2-8. At point B, for example, Russia specializes in wheat, while the United States and Japan produce only computers. At point C, Russia and the United

EXHIBIT 2-8

Comparative Advantage and International Trade

Three countries can produce computers and wheat according to the schedules listed in the table; we assume each has a linear production possibilities curve. Taken together, the three nations have the combined curve shown. Failure to allocate world resources according to comparative advantage will result in a solution such as Q, where less of both goods is produced than would be possible with efficient production.

World Production

Point on curve	Computers	Wheat
A	1,000	0
B	900	400
C	400	900
D	0	1,000

Russia		United States		Japan	
Computers	Wheat	Computers	Wheat	Computers	Wheat
100	0	500	0	400	0
50	200	250	250	200	50
0	400	0	500	0	100

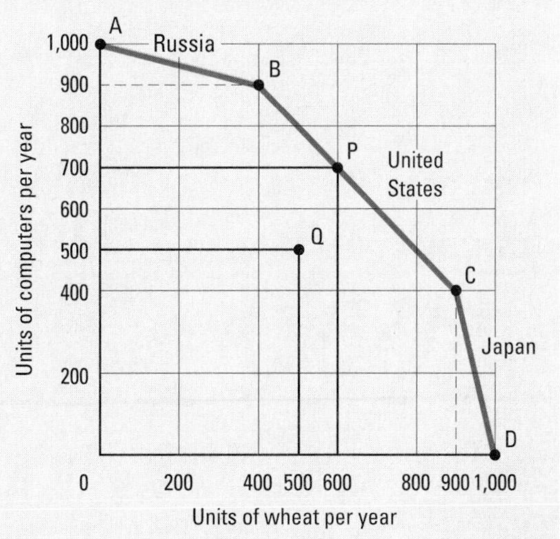

Case in Point: The Expansion of Free Trade

We've already discussed specialization of economic activity in the American colonies. This specialization was enhanced with the ratification of the U.S. Constitution, which contained an important provision for free trade. The Constitution expressly prohibits efforts by states to restrict goods and services from other states. This provision allows goods and services to flow freely across state lines. Kansas can't try to block wheat from South Dakota; Massachusetts can't keep out computers made in Texas.

The success of the United States as a free trade zone has not been lost on the rest of the world. A free trade agreement between the United States and Canada was signed in 1987; it allows virtually unrestricted movement of goods and services between the two countries. The North American Free Trade Agreement (NAFTA), ratified in 1993, added Mexico to a free trade zone that incorporated all of North America. Preliminary discussions are under way to extend the concept throughout the western hemisphere. By the beginning of 1993, members of the European Community (EC) had taken a giant step toward creating the same situation in Europe as they removed restrictions limiting the flow of goods and services among member countries. However, substantial restrictions still limit imports of goods and services from countries outside the EC. In 1994, nations of the Pacific rim, including the United States, Japan, and China, agreed to create a free trade zone for the Pacific rim early in the next century.

Even among countries that restrict trade, the barriers have been coming down. Countries all over the world are moving in the direction of free trade—trade that will allow the world to move closer to its production possibilities curve.

States combine to produce 900 units of wheat, while Japan produces 400 computers. They could also operate at point P, producing 700 units of computers and 600 units of wheat. To do this, Russia will produce only wheat, Japan will produce only computers, and the United States will produce 300 units of computers and 200 units of wheat. Presumably, Russia could trade some of its wheat for some of Japan's computers.

But suppose the countries refuse to trade; each insists on producing its own computers and wheat. Suppose further that each chooses to produce at the midpoint of its own production possibilities curve—Russia produces 50 units of computers and 200 units of wheat, the United States produces 250 units of each, and Japan produces 200 units of computers and 50 units of wheat. World production thus totals 500 units of computers and 500 units of wheat, point Q in Exhibit 2-8. If the three countries were willing to move from isolation to trade, they would achieve a gain in the production of both goods. Producing at a point such as P requires no more resources, no more effort than production at Q. It does, however, require that the world's resources be allocated on the basis of comparative advantage.

Nearly all economists agree that largely unrestricted trade between countries is desirable; restrictions on trade generally force the world to operate inside its production possibilities curve. In some cases restrictions on trade could be desirable, but in the main, free trade promotes greater production of goods and services for the world's people. The role of international trade is explored in greater detail in subsequent chapters of this book.

Economic growth is the process through which an economy's production possibilities curve is shifted outward.

Economic Growth

An increase in either the physical quantity or the quality of factors of production available to an economy will allow the economy to produce more goods and services; it will shift the economy's production possibilities curve outward. The process through which an economy achieves an outward shift in its production possibilities curve is called **economic growth.** An outward shift in a production possibilities curve is illustrated in Exhibit 2-9.

Sources of Economic Growth

Economic growth implies an outward shift in an economy's production possibilities curve. Its source, then, is straightforward: anything that increases the factors of production available to the economy contributes to economic growth.

One way to achieve an increase in factors of production is to have more of them. The United States, for example, produces a total output of goods and services that is approximately 35 times greater than the total output of Switzerland, in large part because of the greater quantity of factors of production in the United States. The United States has, for example, approximately 39 times as many workers and 227 times as much land.

Although an economy can increase its factors of production by increasing their quantity, it can also increase their quality. The primary ways it does so are through increases in human capital and improvements in technology.

Workers today possess, on average, more human capital than they did 100 years ago. In 1890, just 3.5 percent of workers had completed a high school education. In 1990, 86 percent had graduated from high school. Fewer than 1 percent of the workers in 1890 had graduated from college; as late as 1940 only 4.6 percent had graduated from college. By 1990, more than 20 percent had graduated from college. In addition to being better educated, today's workers have received more and better training on the job. They bring far more skills to their work than did workers 100 years ago.

Consider the technological changes that have occurred within the past 100 years. Automated production has become commonplace. Innovations in transportation (automobiles, trucks, and airplanes) have made the movement of goods and people far cheaper and far faster. Computers have transformed the workplace. A dizzying array of new materials is available for manufacturing.

EXHIBIT 2-9

Economic Growth and the Production Possibilities Curve

An economy capable of producing two goods, A and B, is initially operating at point M on production possibilities curve QMR in Panel (a). Given this production possibilities curve, the economy could not produce a combination such as that shown by point N, which lies outside the curve. An increase in the factors of production available to the economy would shift the curve outward, as shown in Panel (b). The curve shifts to SNT, allowing the choice of a point such as N, at which more of both goods will be produced.

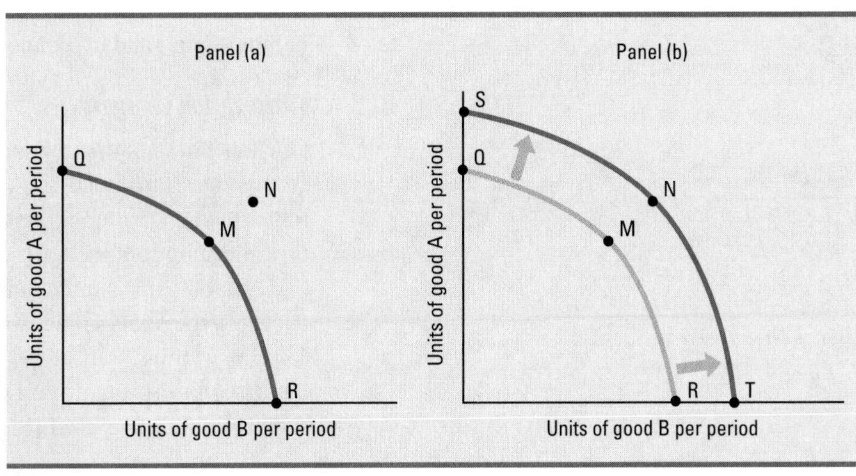

EXHIBIT 2-10

Sources of U.S. Economic Growth, 1909–2000

Total output during the period shown will have increased 13-fold by the end of the century. The chart shows the percentage of this increase accounted for by increases in the quantity of labor and of capital and by increases in human capital and improvements in technology. In the first half of the century, gains in the quantities of these inputs were most important. In the second half of the century, qualitative changes have dominated.

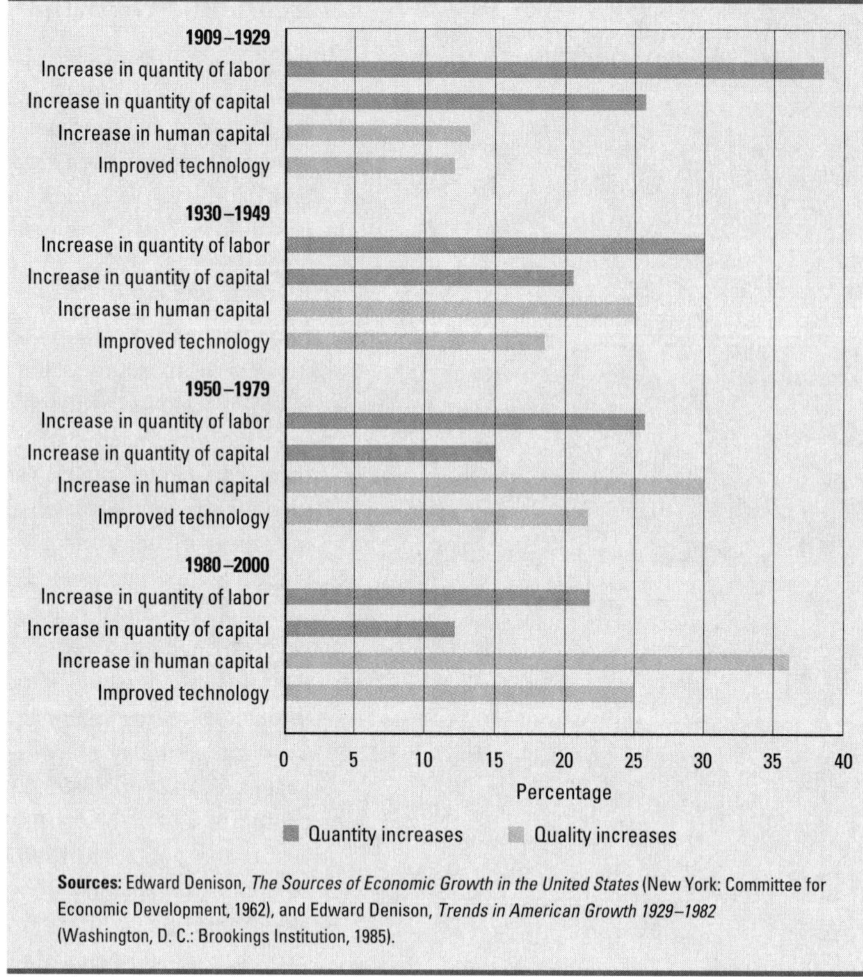

Sources: Edward Denison, *The Sources of Economic Growth in the United States* (New York: Committee for Economic Development, 1962), and Edward Denison, *Trends in American Growth 1929–1982* (Washington, D. C.: Brookings Institution, 1985).

Exhibit 2-10 summarizes the primary sources of economic growth in the United States during most of the twentieth century, as estimated by the late Edward Denison, who was one of the world's leading experts on economic growth. By 2000, the economy's total output of goods and services will have increased by roughly 13-fold. In the first part of the period, increases in the quantities of labor and capital played a dominant role in expanding output; in the second half of the century, though, it has been qualitative improvements in human capital and in technology that have been most important.

Waiting for Growth

One essential feature of economic growth is the concept of waiting. When Stone Age people fashioned the first tools, they had to spend time building capital rather than engaging in consumption. They did this in order to enhance their future consumption; the tools they made would make them more productive.

Exhibit 2-10 shows that more than 70 percent of the increased output expected in the final two decades of the twentieth century will be the result of some form of waiting. Part of the growth will be the result of gains in capital—both increases in the quantity of capital and improvements in technology. Resources society could have used to produce consumer goods are being used to produce

Case in Point: Guns, Butter, and Economic Growth

The former Fort Ord sign on Highway 1 now announces the entrance to California State University at Monterey Bay.

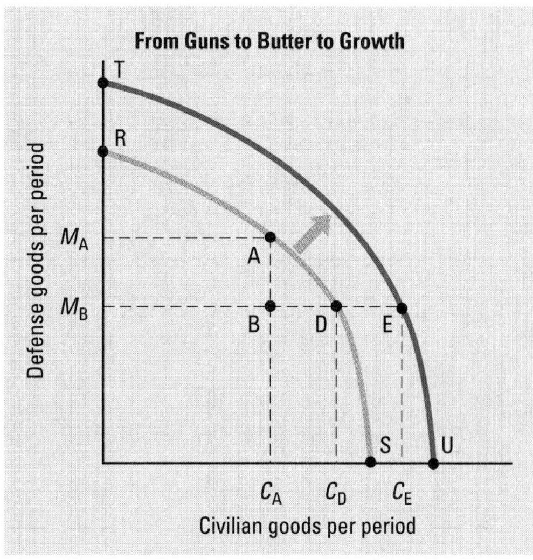

The United States has charted a course to produce fewer guns and more butter. Over the period 1991–1997, federal defense spending will have been cut by nearly $300 billion. The Congressional Budget Office (CBO), in a 1992 report, predicts that the results of those cuts could be not just a greater abundance of civilian goods but more economic growth.

One immediate mechanism through which defense cuts can lead to increased civilian goods is the closing of military bases. The Department of Defense designated 39 major bases for closing in 1993 alone. The facilities of those bases will be available for civilian use. In the past, closed bases have been converted into industrial parks, municipal airports, prisons, shopping centers, training facilities, local government offices, parks, and medical centers.

Private firms that once produced defense goods are making the shift to civilian goods production. Shipyards that produced destroyers and submarines are now making cruise vessels and cargo ships. Martin Marietta, a leading defense contractor, was producing missiles for the Department of Defense in the 1980s. Now it produces rockets for use in launching communications satellites.

The shift from defense production to civilian production is not always an easy one. Workers and production facilities can't be shifted from bullets to bowling balls overnight. One reason for the sluggish economic performance of the early 1990s is that cuts in defense don't shift the economy directly from point A to point D on production possibilities curve RS; the economy shifts first to a point such as B. Military production has dropped from M_A to M_B, but civilian production has not moved from C_A to C_D. The economy makes fewer guns, but it hasn't completed the transition to producing more butter. Only as factories are retooled and workers retrained can the economy complete the transition from guns to butter.

The CBO report stresses that the shift toward civilian production need not merely imply a shift along the production possibilities curve. To the extent that increased civilian production is focused on new capital goods, it could shift the curve outward as well, say to the new curve TU. That could increase total production by as much as $50 billion by the year 2000 (point E).

Source: Congressional Budget Office, "The Economic Effects of Reduced Defense Spending" (Washington, D.C.: Government Printing Office, 1992).

new goods and new knowledge for production instead—all to enhance future production. Part of the growth will come from increased human capital. Increases in human capital often require the postponement of consumption. If you're a college student, you're engaged in precisely this effort. You are devoting time to study that could have been spent working, earning money, and thus engaging in a higher level of consumption. If you're like most students, you're making this choice to postpone consumption because you expect it will allow you to earn more income, and thus enjoy greater consumption, in the future.

Think of an economy as being able to produce two goods, capital and consumer goods (those destined for immediate use by consumers). By focusing on the production of consumer goods, the people in the economy will be able to enjoy a higher standard of living today. If they reduce their consumption—and their standard of living—today in order to produce more capital, they will be able to shift their production possibilities curve outward in the future. That may allow them to produce even more consumer goods. A decision for greater growth typically involves the sacrifice of present consumption.

Arenas for Choice: A Comparison of Economic Systems

Under what circumstances will a nation achieve efficiency in the use of its factors of production? The discussion above suggested that Mr. MacDonald would have an incentive to allocate his fields efficiently because by doing so he could achieve greater output of cabbages and potatoes than would be possible from inefficient production. But why would he want to produce more of these two goods—or of any goods? Why would decisionmakers throughout the economy want to achieve such efficiency?

Economists assume that privately owned firms seek to maximize their profits. The drive to maximize profits will lead firms such as Mr. MacDonald's to allocate resources efficiently to gain as much production as possible from their factors of production. But whether firms will seek to maximize profits depends on the nature of the economic system. An **economic system** is the set of rules that define how an economy's resources are to be owned and how decisions about their use are to be made.

Classifying Economic Systems

Most of the world's economies operate under one of four types of economic systems. In a **market capitalist economy,** resources are generally owned by private individuals who have the power to make decisions about their use. A market capitalist system is often referred to as a free enterprise economic system. In a **command capitalist economy,** resources are generally privately owned, but the government has broad powers to dictate their use. In a **command socialist economy,** the government is the primary owner of resources such as capital and natural resources and has broad power to allocate the use of the economy's resources. A fourth type of economic system is a **market socialist economy.** Under market socialism, the government is the primary owner of capital and natural resources, but decisions about the use of these factors are made primarily by individuals who operate firms.

- An **economic system** is the set of rules that define how an economy's resources are to be owned and how decisions about their use are to be made.
- In a **market capitalist economy,** resources are generally owned by private individuals who have the power to make decisions concerning their use.
- In a **command capitalist economy,** resources are generally owned by private individuals, but the government exercises broad power to determine their use.
- In a **command socialist economy,** the government owns most of the capital and natural resources and has broad power to determine how the economy's resources will be allocated.
- In a **market socialist economy,** the government owns most of the capital and natural resources but allows the individuals who operate firms to make choices about the use of these factors.

The United States is a market capitalist economy. Other market economies include those of Western Europe, Japan, South Korea, Taiwan, Hong Kong, and Singapore.

Command capitalist economic systems have long been dominant in Latin America, where extensive government controls dictate the use of privately owned resources. Many Latin American economies are in the process of removing controls in an effort to transform their economies into market capitalist economies. Countries making this transition include Argentina, Bolivia, Chile, Costa Rica, El Salvador, and Mexico. Most of the economies of the Middle East and Africa are command capitalist economies.

The former Soviet Union and China were once the primary examples of command socialist economies. China, however, began a process of transformation to a market capitalist system in 1979. Nations such as Poland, Hungary, and the former East Germany, which were part of the Soviet empire and had command socialist systems, are now moving toward market capitalist economies. Russia has maintained government ownership of most capital and natural resources, but it has shifted power over the use of these resources to the operators of individual firms. It is thus an example of a market socialist economy, although its leaders have indicated that they are seeking a transition to a market capitalist economy. Today, Cuba and North Korea are the primary examples of command socialist economic systems.

The dramatic global shift toward market capitalist economic systems that has occurred in the 1980s and 1990s is in large part the result of two important features of such economies. First, their emphasis on individual ownership and decisionmaking power has almost always yielded greater individual freedom than has been available under command capitalist or socialist systems. People seeking political, religious, and economic freedom have thus gravitated toward market capitalist systems. Second, market economies are more likely than other systems to allocate resources on the basis of comparative advantage.

Suppose Mr. MacDonald had the same three fields we considered earlier in this chapter but was operating in a command capitalist economic system. In such a system, he might be prohibited by government regulation from transferring resources from one use to another to achieve the gains possible from comparative advantage. If he were operating under a command socialist system, he wouldn't be the owner of his fields and thus would be unlikely to profit from their efficient use. Even under market socialism, the fact that the farm was not his could reduce his incentive to use it efficiently—he might not profit directly from making it more profitable. Generally speaking, it is market capitalist economies that offer the greatest inducement for resources to be allocated on the basis of comparative advantage. Market economies thus tend to be more productive and to deliver higher material standards of living than do command capitalist or socialist economies.

An important advantage of a market capitalist economy is that it creates opportunities for **entrepreneurs,** people who seek greater profits by finding new ways to combine capital, labor, and natural resources. Entrepreneurs may create new products, as Steve Jobs did when he invented the personal computer, or find new ways of producing existing products, as Henry Ford did when he applied the use of standardized parts and mass production methods to the manufacture of automobiles.

Market capitalist economic systems encourage entrepreneurship in two ways. First, because capital is privately owned, entrepreneurs have the opportunity to earn profits. Second, because choices about the use of factors of production are made by individuals, entrepreneurs who think they can find more profitable ways of combining factors have the opportunity to try new methods. Entrepreneurs take a risk—they may profit handsomely if they succeed, or lose everything if they fail. Their willingness to try out new ideas gives us new products and improved ways of producing old ones. Such discoveries help push the production possibilities curve outward, thus enhancing our standard of living.

Entrepreneurs are people who seek greater profits by finding new ways to combine capital, labor, and natural resources.

Government in a Market Economy

The production possibilities model provides a menu of choices among alternative combinations of goods and services. Given those choices, which combinations shall be produced?

In a market economy, this question is answered in large part through the interaction of individual buyers and sellers. (This interaction is the topic of Chapter 3.) As we have already seen, government plays a role as well. It may seek to encourage greater consumption of some goods and discourage consumption of others. In the United States, for example, tax policies encourage the purchase of housing and discourage the consumption of alcohol and tobacco. Government may try to stop the production and consumption of some goods altogether, as many governments do with drugs such as heroin and cocaine. Government may supplement the private consumption of some goods by producing more of them itself, as many U.S. cities do with golf courses and tennis courts. In other cases, there may be no private market for a good or service at all. In the guns versus butter choice outlined at the beginning of this chapter, the U.S. government is virtually the sole provider of guns—national defense.

Many of the most important debates in economics center on determining the precise role of government in a market economy. These debates will occupy us over and over again in subsequent chapters of this book. How forceful a role should government play in protecting the environment? Should the government take over the health care system? Should the government give up the war on drugs? Reaching a conclusion that a market economy produces better economic performance than a command capitalist or socialist one does not preclude debate on economic issues.

The specific role of government varies from country to country. In the United States, it varies from city to city. Generally, however, government serves the following roles in most market economies.

1. ***Enforcement of a Legal System.*** Some entity must determine and enforce a system of laws. Without government playing such a role, a market could not function. It is government that protects the property rights of people such as Mr. MacDonald. It also provides protection of individuals and their liberties. One widely acknowledged role of government is to protect people from potential abuses in the market, such as fraud.

2. ***Provision of Certain Goods and Services.*** Most people agree that the market's provision of many goods and services would be inadequate. They thus turn to government to increase the provision of goods and services such as national defense, education, parks, highways, and a host of others. Chapters 5 and 15 examine the government provision of goods and services in greater detail.

3. ***Redistribution of Income.*** A market economy distributes income according to the value it places on the factors of production people own. That distribution may not accord with everybody's views of what is fair; they thus turn to government to transfer income or wealth from some people to others.

4. ***Expanding Production and Economic Growth.*** An economy may fall short of full employment, or it may use its factors of production inefficiently. In either case, the economy will sacrifice goods and services it is capable of producing.

Checklist

- The ideas of comparative advantage and specialization suggest that restrictions on international trade are likely to be inefficient.
- Economic growth is the result of increasing the quantity or quality of an economy's factors of production.
- Policies to encourage growth generally involve postponing consumption in order to increase capital and human capital.
- Market capitalist economies have generally proved more productive than command capitalist, command socialist, or market socialist economies.
- One important advantage of a market capitalist economy is that it encourages entrepreneurial activity.
- Government plays a crucial role in any market economy.

Government may employ policies aimed at achieving full and efficient utilization of the resources it has available. Government policy may also seek to increase the rate of growth of the economy, thus expanding the range of choices offered by its production possibilities curve.

A Look Back—And a Look Ahead

In Chapter 1 we saw that economics deals with choices. In Chapter 2 we have examined more carefully the range of choices in production that must be made in any economy. In particular, we looked at choices involving the allocation of an economy's factors of production: capital, natural resources, and labor.

The production possibilities model is a device to assist us in thinking about many of these choices. The model assumes that the economy has factors of production (labor, natural resources, and capital) that are fixed in both quantity and quality. When illustrated graphically, the production possibilities model limits its analysis to two goods. Given the economy's factors of production, the economy can produce various combinations of the two goods. If it uses its factors of production efficiently and has full employment, it will be operating on the production possibilities curve.

Two characteristics of the production possibilities curve are particularly important. First, it is downward sloping. This reflects the scarcity of the factors of production available to the economy; producing more of one good requires giving up some of the other. Second, the curve is bowed out. Another way of saying this is to say that the curve gets steeper as we move from left to right; the absolute value of its slope is increasing. Producing each additional unit of the good on the horizontal axis requires a greater sacrifice of the good on the vertical axis than did the previous units produced. This fact, called the law of increasing cost, is the inevitable result of efficient choices in production—choices based on comparative advantage.

Efficient use of factors of production implies a considerable degree of specialization. It also implies that restrictions on trade, whether domestic or international, are likely to be inefficient.

Increasing the quantity or quality of factors of production will shift the production possibilities curve outward. This process is called economic growth. Economic growth in the United States has, in recent years, relied chiefly on improvements in the quality of capital and labor. Whatever the source of economic growth, it is likely to involve an element of waiting; society's scarce resources must be devoted to activities that will enhance future productivity rather than present consumption.

Choices concerning the use of scarce resources take place within the context of a set of institutional arrangements that define an economic system. The principal distinctions between systems lie in the degree to which ownership of capital and natural resources and decisionmaking authority over scarce resources are held by government or by private individuals. The basic systems reviewed include market capitalist, command capitalist, command socialist, and market socialist economies. An increasing body of evidence suggests that market capitalist economies tend to be most productive; many socialist and command capitalist economies are moving in the direction of market capitalist systems. One advantage of a market capitalist economy is that it encourages entrepreneurial activity.

The presumption in favor of market-based systems does not preclude a role for government. Government is required to provide the system of laws on which market systems are founded. It may also be used to provide certain goods and services, to help individuals in need, and to protect individuals in the marketplace.

The production possibilities model suggests the set of answers to the "what to produce" question. It also provides insights into how goods and services should be produced. Chapter 3 suggests how the "what" and "for whom" questions are answered in a market economy.

Terms and Concepts for Review

Capital

Command capitalist economy

Command socialist economy

Comparative advantage

Economic growth

Economic system

Entrepreneur

Efficient production

Factors of production

Full employment

Human capital

Inefficient production

Labor

Law of increasing cost

Market capitalist economy

Market socialist economy

Natural resources

Production possibilities curve

Technology

For Discussion

1. Draw a production possibilities curve based on the assumption that the economy has only one factor of production, labor, and that all workers are identical in terms of their ability to produce goods and services. The economy is capable of producing two goods, legal services and personal counseling.
2. Identify the following as land, capital, or labor:
   - **a.** An unemployed factory worker
   - **b.** A college professor
   - **c.** The library building on your campus
   - **d.** The Rocky Mountains
   - **e.** Oil
   - **f.** The White House
   - **g.** The local power plant
3. Suppose an economy can produce two goods, A or B. It is now operating at point E on production possibilities curve RT. An improvement in the technology available to produce good A shifts the curve to ST, and the economy selects point E′. How does this change affect the cost of producing an additional unit of good B?

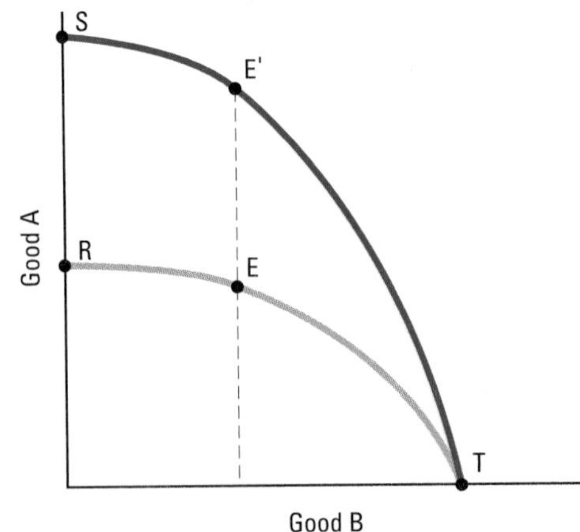

4. Could a nation's production possibilities curve ever shift inward? Explain what such a shift would mean, and discuss events that might cause such a shift to occur.
5. Suppose blue-eyed people were banned from working. How would this affect a nation's production possibilities curve?

6. Evaluate this statement: "The U.S. economy could achieve greater growth by devoting fewer resources to consumption and more to investment; it follows that such a shift would be desirable."
7. Two countries, Sportsland and Foodland, have similar total quantities of capital, labor, and natural resources. Both can produce two goods, figs and footballs. Sportsland's resources are particularly well suited to the production of footballs but are not very productive in producing figs. Foodland's resources are very productive when used for figs but aren't capable of producing many footballs. With figs on the vertical axis and footballs on the horizontal, draw the production possibilities curves for each country. In which country is the cost of additional footballs generally greater? Explain.
8. Suppose a country is committed to using its resources based on the reverse of comparative advantage doctrine: it first transfers those resources for which the cost is greatest, not lowest. Describe this country's production possibilities curve.
9. Suppose each state in the United States had been instructed by the Constitution to restrict its imports from other states. How would this have affected U.S. production of goods and services?
10. As of the beginning of 1993, nations in the European Community have eliminated all barriers to the flow of goods, services, labor, and capital across their borders. Even such things as consumer protection laws and the types of plugs required to plug in appliances have been standardized to ensure that there will be no barriers to trade. The EC estimates that the achievement of free trade will boost output in member countries by 4.3 to 6.4 percent. How does the elimination of trade barriers increase output?
11. How did the discovery of taxol, described in the Case in Point on page 33, affect the production possibilities curve for the United States?
12. The tiny Bruneau Hot Springs snail, about the size of the tip of a pencil, was added to the federal government's Endangered Species List in 1993. With a mandate to take measures necessary to save the snail, which lives in parts of the Snake River in Idaho, the U.S. Fish and Wildlife Service took action to restrict the water rights of 59 farms and ranches in an effort to preserve the water levels thought necessary to ensure the snail's survival. The firms affected account for half the economic activity in the Bruneau area, and they protested vigorously. What is the scarce resource here? Should the government act to protect it? Why or why not?

Problems

1. The nation of Leisureland can produce two goods, bicycles and bowling balls. The western region of Leisureland can, if it devotes all its resources to bicycle production, produce 100 bicycles per month. Alternatively, it could devote all its resources to bowling balls and produce 400 per month—or it could produce any combination of bicycles and bowling balls lying on a straight line between these two extremes. Draw a production possibilities curve for Western Leisureland (with bicycles on the vertical axis). What does it cost to produce an additional bowling ball in Western Leisureland?
2. Suppose that Eastern Leisureland can, if it devotes all its resources to the production of bicycles, produce 400. If it devotes all its resources to bowling ball production, though, it can produce only 100. Draw the production possibilities curve for Eastern Leisureland. How much does it cost to produce an additional bowling ball in Eastern Leisureland? Explain the difference in cost between Western and Eastern Leisureland. Which region has a comparative advantage in producing bowling balls? Bicycles?
3. Draw the production possibilities curve for Leisureland, one that combines the curves for Western and Eastern Leisureland. Suppose it is determined that 400 bicycles must be produced. How many bowling balls can be produced? Where will these goods be produced?
4. The Case in Point on page 38 comments on the cost, measured as forgone production of goods and services, of the Great Depression. Output in the United States also fell below its full employment level when the economy slipped into a recession late in 1990. The following data show actual production versus production the economy could have achieved if it had operated at full employment in every year from 1990, when it last achieved full employment, to the first half of 1995, when it returned approximately to full employment. Compute the cost of this period, measured as forgone output, both as a dollar figure and as a percentage of full employment output lost.

Year	Actual Output ($ billions)	Full Employment Output ($ billions)
1990	$4,897	$4,936
1991	4,868	5,042
1992	4,979	5,148
1993	5,135	5,251
1994	5,342	5,363
1995	5,473	5,474

3

Demand and Supply

Chapter Objectives

After mastering the material in this chapter, you will be able to:

1. Explain how the price and quantity of a good are determined by the interaction of demand and supply.
2. Explain factors that can change demand or supply and show how such changes affect the price and quantity of a good in the market.
3. Explain how the equilibrium price achieves a balance between the quantity demanded and the quantity supplied.
4. Explain conditions under which persistent shortages or surpluses can occur.
5. Discuss ways in which the predictions of the model of demand and supply are consistent with what we observe in the real world, and comment on the limitations of the model.
6. Use the model of demand and supply to predict how markets will respond to particular events.

The level of the sea is not more surely kept, than is the equilibrium of value in society, by the demand and supply . . . .

Ralph Waldo Emerson, 1860

What's Ahead

For Dennis Archuleta, the California flood of March 1995 meant higher broccoli prices.

"Things went pretty wild," says Mr. Archuleta, a produce distributor for Federal Foods in Colorado. "I had guys calling me in a panic who couldn't get broccoli for their stores or restaurants. I was able to get it for them, but the price had gone up to $25 a case. It was $12 before the flood."

Broccoli wasn't the only crop affected by the flooding, which was the worst in the state's history. Artichokes, cauliflower and lettuce crops were all hit hard. In the Salinas Valley, known as the nation's salad bowl, 30,000 acres were under water by mid-March.

"The situation is drastic," Dole Vegetable Products Co. vice-president Richard Bascou told The Wall Street Journal. *"Supply will go way down, and that will certainly drive up prices."*

The California flood sharply reduced the availability of many crops. But grocery shoppers could still find plenty of lettuce, plenty of broccoli, plenty of cauliflower. They did, however, have to pay a lot more to get these vegetables.

The marketplace is always responding to events such as the California flood that affect the price and output of particular goods. The demand for some goods increases, while the demand for others falls. The supply of some goods rises, while the supply of others falls. As such events unfold, prices adjust to keep markets in balance. This chapter explains how the forces of demand and supply interact to determine market prices. We'll see how prices adjust to changes in demand and supply, and we'll also see how changes in prices affect buyers and sellers.

The model of demand and supply that we shall develop in this chapter is one of the most powerful tools in all of economic analysis. You'll be using it throughout your study of economics.

Think for a moment about the purchases you've made in, say, the last month. You've certainly purchased food. You may also have bought some clothing, gotten a haircut, gone to a concert, purchased a book, or attended a movie. Why were those goods and services available to you? Why did they cost what they did?

Think now of the entire United States, with its millions of consumers and millions of different goods and services. Why do those goods and services get produced? Who arranges to produce those goods and services in quantities that match the quantities consumers want to buy?

The answer to all these questions lies, for the most part, in two simple words: demand and supply. These words suggest market forces of extraordinary power and scope. These forces determine what you pay for most of the goods and services you consume—and what you'll earn from the labor and other factors of production you may supply.

The production possibilities model lays out a menu of the alternatives available to a society. We're now ready to examine a second model, one that helps to explain which combinations on that menu will be selected. The model of demand and supply suggests the forces that move markets—forces that drive prices up or down, that increase or decrease quantities produced and consumed, and that achieve a balance between quantities demanded and supplied. We'll look first at the variables that influence demand. Then we'll turn to supply, and finally we'll put demand and supply together as we explore the operation of the model of demand and supply.

Demand

How many pizzas will be demanded this year? How many people will visit their doctors? How much housing will people purchase?

Each good or service has its own special characteristics that determine the quantity people wish to consume. One is the price of the good or service itself. Other independent variables that are important determinants of demand include consumer preferences, prices of related goods and services, income, demographic characteristics such as population size and consumer expectations. The number of pizzas people will purchase, for example, depends very much on whether they like pizza. It also depends on the prices for alternatives such as hamburgers or spaghetti. The number of doctor visits is likely to vary with income—people with higher incomes are likely to see a doctor more often than people with lower incomes. The demands for pizza, for doctor visits, and for housing are certainly affected by population.

While different variables play different roles in influencing the demands for different goods and services, economists pay special attention to one: the price of the good or service. Given the values of all the other variables that affect demand, a higher price tends to reduce the quantity people demand, and a lower price tends to increase it. A medium pizza typically sells for \$5 to \$10. Suppose the price were \$30. Chances are, you'd buy a lot fewer pizzas at that price than you do now. Suppose pizzas typically sold for \$2 each. At that price, people would be likely to eat more pizzas than they do now.

The Demand Curve and the Law of Demand

Because people will purchase different quantities of a good or service at different prices, economists must be careful when speaking of the "demand" for something. Economists have therefore developed some specific terms for expressing the general concept of demand.

- The **quantity demanded** of a good or service is the quantity consumers are willing to buy at a particular price during a particular period, ceteris paribus.
- A **demand schedule** is a table that shows the quantities of a good or service demanded at different prices during a particular period, ceteris paribus.
- A **demand curve** is a graphical representation of a demand schedule. It shows the relationship between the price and quantity demanded of a good or service during a particular period, ceteris paribus.

The **quantity demanded** of a good or service is the quantity consumers will be willing to buy at a particular price during a particular period, ceteris paribus. Suppose, for example, that 100,000 movie tickets are sold each month in a particular town at a price of $6 per ticket. That quantity, 100,000, is the quantity of movie admissions demanded per month at a price of $6. If the price were $8, we would expect the quantity demanded to be less. If it were $4, we would expect the quantity demanded to be greater.

A **demand schedule** is a table that shows the quantities of a good or service demanded during a particular period at different prices, assuming the values of other variables that affect the quantity demanded remain constant. To introduce the concept of a demand schedule, let's consider the demand for eggs in the United States. The table in Exhibit 3-1 shows quantities of eggs that will be demanded each month at prices ranging from 90 cents to 40 cents per dozen; the table is a demand schedule. We see that the higher the price, the lower the quantity demanded.

The information given by a demand schedule can be presented with a **demand curve,** which is a graphical representation of a demand schedule. A demand curve thus shows the relationship between the price and quantity demanded of a good or service during a particular period, assuming the values of other variables that affect the quantity demanded remain constant. The demand curve in Exhibit 3-1 shows the prices and quantities of eggs demanded that are given in the demand schedule. At point A, for example, we see that 500 million dozen eggs per month are demanded at a price of 60 cents per dozen.

Price alone does not determine the quantity of eggs people consume. Egg consumption will be affected by such variables as income and population. Preferences will play a role—per capita egg consumption in the United States has fallen by about one-third since World War II, in large part because people want to reduce their consumption of cholesterol. We also expect other prices to

EXHIBIT 3-1

A Demand Schedule and a Demand Curve

The table is a demand schedule; it shows quantities of eggs demanded per month in the United States at particular prices, ceteris paribus. These data are then plotted on the demand curve. At point A on the curve, 500 million dozen eggs per month are demanded at a price of 60 cents per dozen. At point B, 600 million dozen eggs per month are demanded at a price of 50 cents per dozen.

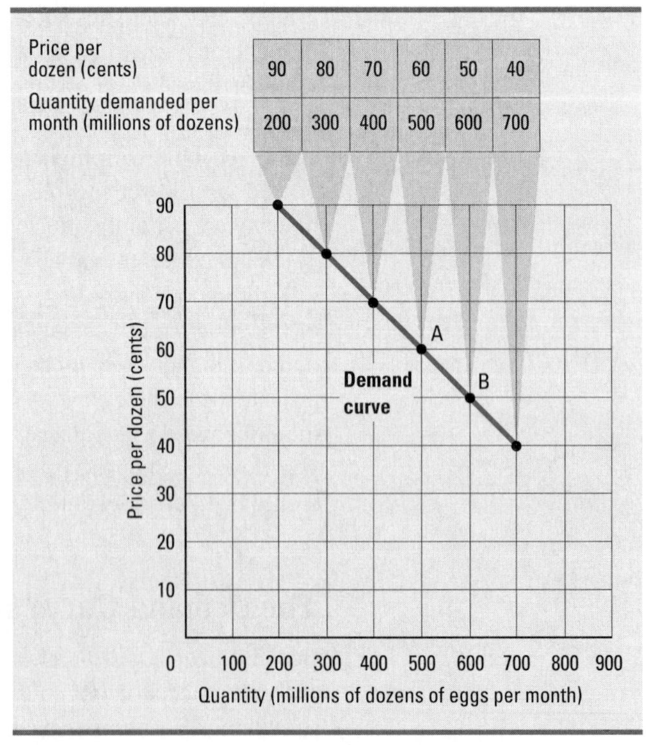

Price per dozen (cents)	90	80	70	60	50	40
Quantity demanded per month (millions of dozens)	200	300	400	500	600	700

A **change in quantity demanded** is a movement along the demand curve; it results from a change in the price of a good or service.

The **law of demand** holds that, for virtually all goods and services, there is a negative relationship between price and quantity demanded, ceteris paribus.

A **change in demand** is a shift in the demand curve.

affect egg consumption. People often eat bacon with their eggs, so a reduction in the price of bacon might induce people to eat more eggs. An alternative to eggs is cereal, so a reduction in the price of cereal might result in the consumption of more cereal and fewer eggs. Changes in other variables that affect demand can thus change the quantity demanded at each price. To isolate the effect of changes in price on the quantity of a good or service demanded, we show the quantity demanded at each price, assuming those other variables remain unchanged. That's the same thing we do in drawing a graph of any relationship between two variables; we assume that the values of other variables that may affect the variables shown in the graph remain unchanged for the period under consideration.

A change in price, with no change in any of the other variables that affect demand, results in a movement along the demand curve. For example, if the price of eggs falls from 60 cents to 50 cents per dozen, consumption rises from 500 million dozen to 600 million dozen eggs per month. That's a movement from point A to point B along the demand curve in Exhibit 3-1. A movement along a demand curve, which results from a change in price, is called a **change in quantity demanded.** Note that a change in quantity demanded is not a change in the demand curve; it is a movement *along* the demand curve.

The Law of Demand

The negative slope of the demand curve in Exhibit 3-1 suggests a key behavioral relationship of economics. The **law of demand** holds that, for virtually all goods and services, there is a negative relationship between price and quantity demanded, given the values of other determinants of demand. A higher price induces a reduction in quantity demanded. A lower price induces an increase in quantity demanded.

The law of demand is called a law because of the wide range of studies whose results are consistent with it. You've observed one manifestation of the law—when a store finds itself with an overstock of some item and needs to sell these items quickly, what does it do? It typically has a sale, expecting that a lower price will increase the quantity demanded.

There may be a handful of exceptions to the law of demand. If people judge the quality of a good based on its price, for example, a higher price could induce an increase in the quantity demanded. Another possible exception could come if a good has "snob appeal"—if part of the attraction of purchasing a good lies in the fact that most other people can't afford it. Some economists argue, for example, that part of the appeal of a Rolls Royce lies in the fact that its price is far higher than the price of other luxury cars. In general, however, we expect the law of demand to hold. Given the values of other variables that influence demand, a higher price reduces the quantity demanded. A lower price increases the quantity demanded. Demand curves, in short, slope downward.

Changes in Demand

A change in one of the variables held constant in constructing a demand schedule will change the quantities demanded at each price. The result will be a shift in the demand curve. A shift in a demand curve is called a **change in demand.**

Suppose, for example, that something happens to increase the quantity of eggs demanded at each price. Several events could produce such a change: an increase in incomes, an increase in population, an increase in the price of cereal,

Price	Old quantity demanded	New quantity demanded
90¢	200	400
80	300	500
70	400	600
60	500	700
50	600	800
40	700	900

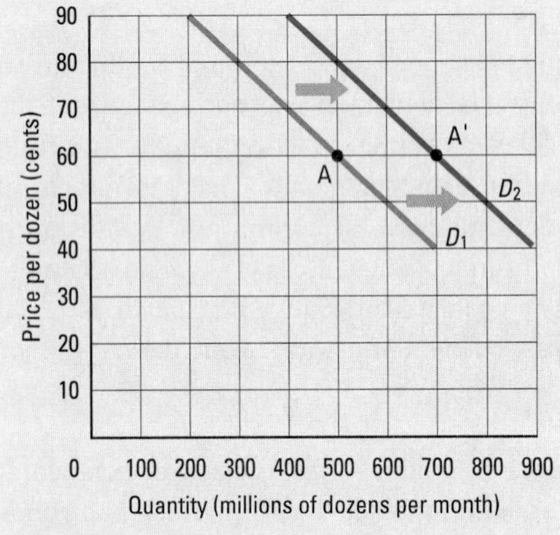

EXHIBIT 3-2

An Increase in Demand

An increase in the quantity of a good or service demanded at each price is shown as an increase in demand. Here, the original demand curve D_1 shifts to D_2. Point A on D_1 corresponds to a price of 60 cents per dozen and a quantity demanded of 500 million dozen eggs per month. On the new demand curve D_2, the quantity demanded at this price rises to 700 million dozen eggs per month (point A′).

or a discovery that the cholesterol in eggs isn't harmful to health would all be likely to increase the quantity of eggs demanded at each price. Such a change thus produces a new demand schedule. Exhibit 3-2 shows such a change in the demand schedule for eggs. We see that the quantity of eggs demanded per month is greater at each price than before. These new values in the demand schedule produce a new demand curve. The original curve, labeled D_1, shifts to the right to D_2. At a price of 60 cents per dozen, for example, the quantity demanded rises from 500 million dozen eggs per month (point A) to 700 million dozen per month (point A′).

Just as demand can increase, it can fall. In the case of eggs, demand might fall as a result of events such as a reduction in population, a reduction in the price of cereal, or a change in preferences. A discovery that the cholesterol in eggs contributes not only to heart disease but to cancer as well, for example, would change preferences and reduce the demand for eggs.

A reduction in the demand for eggs is illustrated in Exhibit 3-3. The demand schedule shows that fewer eggs are demanded at each price than in Exhibit 3-1. The result is a shift in demand from the original curve D_1 to D_3. The quantity of eggs demanded at a price of 60 cents per dozen falls from 500 million dozen per month (point A) to 300 million dozen eggs per month (point A″).

A variable that can change the quantity of a good or service demanded at each price is called a **demand shifter.** While different goods and services will have different demand shifters, the demand shifters are likely to include consumer preferences, the prices of related goods and services, income, demographic characteristics, and consumer expectations. Each of these is examined briefly below.

Consumer Preferences

Changes in consumer preferences can have important consequences for demand. We've already seen that concern about cholesterol has led to a reduced demand for eggs. Similar concern has increased the demand for chicken and has reduced the demand for beef.

A change in consumer preferences that makes one good or service more popular will shift the demand curve to the right. A change that makes it less popular will shift the demand curve to the left.

EXHIBIT 3-3

A Reduction in Demand

A reduction in demand occurs when the quantities of a good or service demanded fall at each price. Here, the demand schedule shows a lower quantity of eggs demanded at each price than we had in Exhibit 3-1. The reduction shifts the demand curve for eggs to D_3 from D_1. The quantity demanded at a price of 60 cents per dozen, for example, falls from 500 million dozen per month (point A) to 300 million dozen eggs per month (point A″).

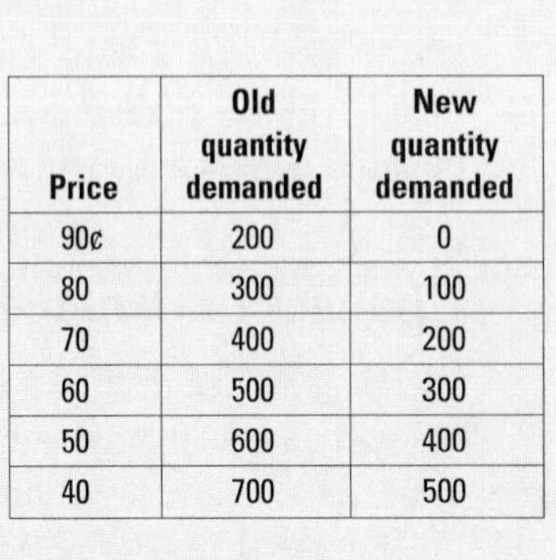

Price	Old quantity demanded	New quantity demanded
90¢	200	0
80	300	100
70	400	200
60	500	300
50	600	400
40	700	500

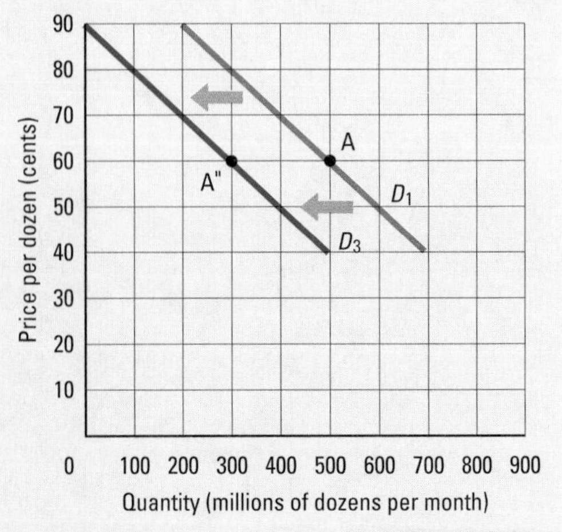

Case in Point: Cheaper Skies and Safer Streets

Airline fares, relative to other consumer prices, fell sharply in the first half of the 1980s. Although they edged up slightly in the second half of the decade, they were still substantially lower at the end of the decade than they had been at the beginning. According to economists Richard McKenzie of the University of California at Irvine and John Warner of Clemson University, those lower airfares saved lives.

The economists reasoned that air travel and car travel are substitutes for trips such as long vacations. A reduction in the price of air travel should therefore reduce the demand for car travel. The economists argued that because air travel is about 100 times safer per passenger mile than car travel, a switch from cars to planes would save lives.

The economists' first step in testing their hypothesis was to estimate the demand curve for passenger car driving in the United States. They found that the total number of passenger miles driven depends on the price of driving (measured as the average cost per mile of driving a car relative to other consumer prices), population, income, the average speed at which cars travel (a measure of the convenience of car travel), and the price of air travel relative to car travel. The statistical results were consistent with their hypothesis. A higher price of car travel reduces the quantity demanded. Demand for car travel is increased by greater population, higher income, and greater average speed. The economists also found that lower airfares reduce the demand for travel by car; air and car travel appear to be substitutes.

The next step was to relate travel by car to highway deaths. Total passenger miles driven is the most important determinant of highway deaths; other important factors include alcohol consumption per capita and the percentage of female drivers (greater alcohol consumption increases highway deaths; a greater percentage of female drivers reduces them). Given their estimate of the relationship between passenger miles driven and highway deaths and their estimate of the relationship between airline ticket prices and car travel, the economists were able to relate lower airline fares to reduced highway deaths. They concluded that lower fares have saved more than 1,000 lives per year on the nation's highways.

Sources: Timothy Tregarthen,"Do Cheaper Skies Save Lives?" *The Margin* 3(5) (January 1988): 9.

- A **demand shifter** is a variable that can change the quantity of a good or service demanded at each price.
- If a reduction in the price of one good increases the demand for the other, the two goods are **complements.**
- If a reduction in the price of one good reduces the demand for the other, the two goods are **substitutes.**

Prices of Other Goods and Services

Suppose the price of bacon were to fall. People who eat eggs often enjoy eating them along with bacon; the lower price of bacon might therefore increase the demand for eggs, shifting the demand curve for eggs to the right. A lower price for a breakfast cereal, however, would be likely to reduce egg demand, shifting the demand curve for eggs to the left.

In general, if a reduction in the price of one good increases the demand for another, the two goods are called **complements.** If a reduction in the price of one good reduces the demand for another, the two goods are called **substitutes.** These definitions hold in the reverse as well: Two goods are complements if an increase in the price of one reduces the demand for the other, and they are substitutes if an increase in the price of one increases the demand for the other. Bacon and eggs are complements; breakfast cereal and eggs are substitutes.

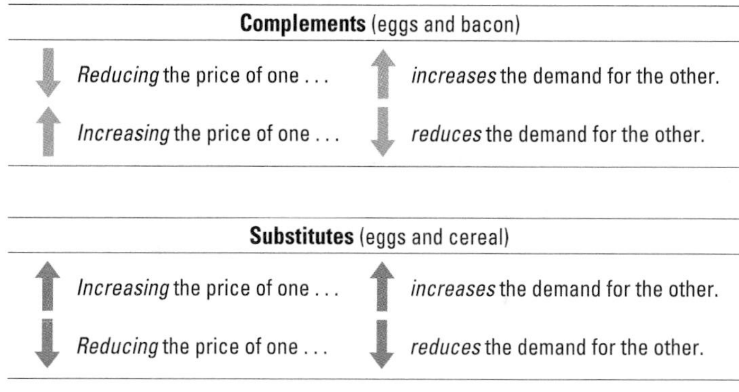

Complements (eggs and bacon)
Reducing the price of one . . .
increases the demand for the other.
Increasing the price of one . . .
reduces the demand for the other.
Substitutes (eggs and cereal)
Increasing the price of one . . .
increases the demand for the other.
Reducing the price of one . . .
reduces the demand for the other.

A **normal good** is one whose demand is increased by increased income.

An **inferior good** is one whose demand is reduced by increased income.

Complementary goods are goods used in conjunction with one another. Tennis rackets and tennis balls, coffee and cream, and stationery and postage stamps are complementary goods. Substitute goods are goods used instead of one another. Volleyballs, for example, are likely to be substitutes for tennis rackets. Tea is a substitute for coffee, and a fax machine is a substitute for using postage stamps.

Income

As incomes rise, people increase their consumption of many goods and services, and as incomes fall, their consumption of these goods and services falls. For example, an increase in income is likely to raise the demand for ski trips, new cars, and jewelry. There are, however, goods and services for which consumption falls as income rises—and rises as income falls. As incomes rise, for example, people tend to consume more steak but less hamburger, more fresh fruit but fewer beans.

A good for which demand increases when income increases is called a **normal good.** A good for which demand decreases when income increases is called an **inferior good.** An increase in income shifts the demand curve for steak (a normal good) to the right; it shifts the demand curve for hamburger (an inferior good) to the left.

Demographic Characteristics

The number of consumers affects the total quantity of a good or service that will be consumed; in general, the greater the population, the greater the demand. Other demographic characteristics can affect demand as well. As the share of the population over age 65 increases, the demand for medical services, ocean cruises, and motor homes increases. The birth rate in the United States fell sharply between 1955 and 1975 but has gradually increased since then. That increase has raised the demand for such things as infant supplies, elementary

Reader's Advisory !

It's crucial to distinguish between a change in quantity demanded, which is a movement along the demand curve caused by a change in price, and a change in demand, which implies a shift of the demand curve itself. A change in demand is caused by a change in a demand shifter. This drawing of a demand curve highlights the difference.

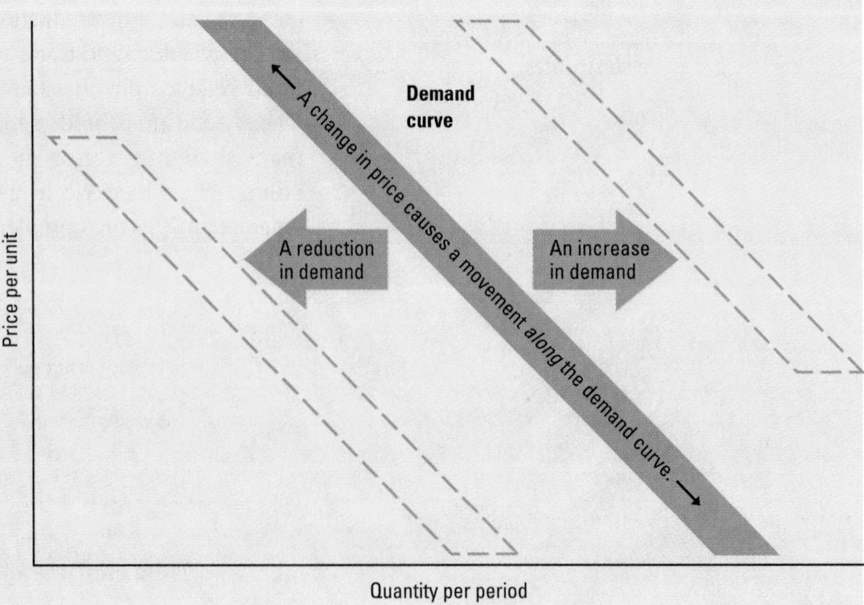

school teachers, soccer coaches, and roller blades. It is likely to increase the demand for higher education in the second half of the 1990s. Demand can thus shift as a result of changes in both the number and characteristics of consumers.

Consumer Expectations

The consumption of goods that can be easily stored, or whose consumption can be postponed, is strongly affected by consumer expectations. If people expect gasoline prices to rise tomorrow, for example, they'll fill up their tanks today to try to beat the price increase. The same will be true for goods such as automobiles and washing machines: an expectation of higher prices in the future will lead to greater consumption today. If the price of a good is expected to fall, however, people are likely to reduce their purchases today and await tomorrow's lower prices. The expectation that computer prices will fall, for example, can reduce current demand.

Checklist

- The quantity demanded of a good or service is the quantity consumers are willing to buy at a particular price during a particular period, ceteris paribus.
- A demand schedule is a table that shows the quantities of a good or service demanded at different prices during a particular period, ceteris paribus.
- A demand curve shows graphically the quantities demanded in a particular period at different prices, ceteris paribus.
- A change in the price of a good or service causes a change in the quantity demanded—a movement *along* the demand curve.
- A change in a demand shifter causes a change in demand, which is shown as a *shift* of the demand curve. Demand shifters include consumer preferences, the prices of related goods, income, demographic characteristics of consumers, and consumer expectations.
- Two goods are substitutes if an increase in the price of one causes an increase in the demand for the other. Two goods are complements if an increase in the price of one causes a decrease in the demand for the other.
- A good or service is a normal good if an increase in consumer income causes an increase in demand. A good or service is an inferior good if an increase in income causes a decrease in demand.

Supply

What determines the quantity of a good or service producers are willing to offer for sale? Price is one; a higher price is likely, ceteris paribus, to induce suppliers to offer a greater quantity of a good or service. Production cost is another determinant of supply. Variables that affect production cost include the prices of factors used to produce the good or service, returns from related activities, technology, the number of sellers of the good or service, the expectations of sellers, and natural events such as weather changes. Still another factor affecting the quantity of a good that will be offered for sale is the number of suppliers—the greater the number of firms supplying a particular good or service, the greater will be the quantity offered.

Price and the Supply Curve

The **quantity supplied** of a good or service is the quantity sellers are willing to sell at a particular price during a particular period, ceteris paribus. Given a seller's production costs, the receipt of a higher price increases profits. That will induce sellers to increase the quantity they supply.

There is no law of supply to correspond to the law of demand. There are many cases in which a higher price will not induce an increase in quantity supplied. Goods that can't be produced, such as land, are fixed in supply—a higher price can't induce an increase in the quantity supplied. There are even cases, which we investigate in microeconomic analysis, in which a higher price induces a reduction in the quantity supplied.

Generally speaking, however, an increase in price results in a greater quantity supplied. The relationship between price and quantity supplied is suggested in a **supply schedule,** a table that shows quantities supplied at different prices over particular periods of time, given the values of other variables that affect the quantity supplied. Exhibit 3-4 gives a supply schedule for the quantities of eggs that will be supplied at various prices, given the values of other variables that affect supply. At a price of 40 cents per dozen, for example, producers will be willing to supply 300 million dozen eggs per month. A higher price, say 60 cents per dozen, induces a greater quantity supplied—500 million dozen eggs per month.

- The **quantity supplied** of a good or service is the quantity sellers are willing to sell at a particular price during a particular period, ceteris paribus.
- A **supply schedule** is a table that shows the quantities of a good or service supplied at different prices during a particular period, ceteris paribus.

EXHIBIT 3-4

A Supply Schedule and a Supply Curve

The supply schedule shows the quantity of eggs that will be supplied in the United States each month at particular prices, ceteris paribus. The same information is given graphically in the supply curve. The values given here suggest a positive relationship between price and quantity supplied.

Price per dozen (cents)	40	50	60	70	80	90
Quantity supplied per month (millions of dozens)	300	400	500	600	700	800

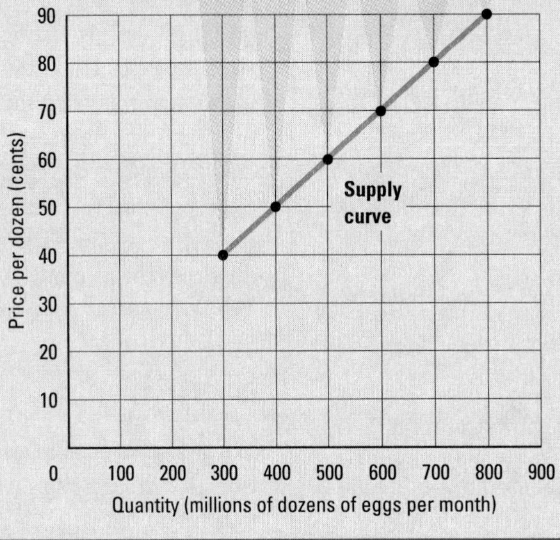

A **supply curve** is a graphical representation of a supply schedule. It shows the relationship between price and quantity supplied, assuming the other variables that affect the quantity supplied remain unchanged. Because the relationship between price and quantity supplied is, in general, positive, supply curves are generally upward sloping. The supply curve for eggs in Exhibit 3-4 shows graphically the values given in the supply schedule.

A change in price causes a movement along the supply curve; such a movement is called a **change in quantity supplied.** As was the case with a change in quantity demanded, a change in quantity supplied does not shift the supply curve. By definition, it is a movement along the supply curve.

Changes in Supply

When we draw a supply curve, we assume that other variables that affect the willingness of sellers to supply a good or service are unchanged. It follows that a change in any of those variables will cause a **change in supply,** which is a shift in the supply curve.

A change that increases the quantity of a good or service supplied at each price shifts the supply curve to the right. Suppose, for example, that the price of chicken feed falls. That will reduce the cost of producing eggs and thus increase the quantity of eggs producers will offer for sale at each price. The supply schedule in Exhibit 3-5 shows an increase in the quantity of eggs supplied at each price—and that causes a shift in the supply curve to S_2, as shown. We see that the quantity supplied at each price increases by 200 million dozen eggs per month. At point A on the original supply curve S_1, for example, 500 million dozen eggs per month are supplied at a price of 60 cents per dozen. After the increase in supply, 700 million dozen eggs per month are supplied at the same price (point A′ on curve S_2).

- A **supply curve** is a graphical representation of a supply schedule. It shows the relationship between the price and quantity supplied of a good or service during a particular period, ceteris paribus.
- A **change in quantity supplied** is a movement along the supply curve; it results from a change in the price of a good or service.
- A **change in supply** is a shift in the supply curve.
- A **supply shifter** is a variable that can change the quantity of a good or service supplied at each price.

EXHIBIT 3-5

An Increase in Supply

If there is a change in supply that increases the quantity supplied at each price, as is the case in the supply schedule here, the supply curve shifts to the right. At a price of 60 cents per dozen, for example, the quantity supplied rises from the previous level of 500 million dozen per month on supply curve S_1 (point A) to 700 million dozen per month on supply curve S_2 (point A′).

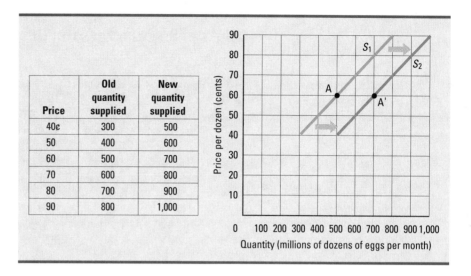

Price	Old quantity supplied	New quantity supplied
40¢	300	500
50	400	600
60	500	700
70	600	800
80	700	900
90	800	1,000

An event that reduces the quantity supplied at each price shifts the supply curve to the left. An increase in production costs and a widespread disease that reduces the ability of chickens to lay eggs are examples of events that might reduce supply. Exhibit 3-6 shows a reduction in the supply of eggs. We see in the supply schedule that the quantity of eggs supplied falls by 200 million dozen eggs per month at each price. The supply curve thus shifts from S_1 to S_3.

A variable that can change the quantity of a good or service supplied at each price is called a **supply shifter.** Supply shifters include variables that change production costs, such as changes in the prices of factors of production, changes in returns from alternative activities, changes in technology, changes in producer expectations, and natural events. Another potential supply shifter is a change in the number of sellers. Each of these supply shifters is discussed briefly below.

Prices of Factors of Production

A change in the price of labor or some other factor of production will change the cost of producing any given quantity of the good or service. This change in the cost of production will change the quantity of output that suppliers are willing to offer at any price. An increase in factor prices should reduce the quantity suppliers will offer at any price, shifting the supply curve to the left. A reduction in factor prices increases the quantity suppliers will offer at any price, shifting the supply curve to the right.

Suppose farmers must pay a higher price for the water they use to irrigate their crops. That increase in production cost will cause them to produce a smaller quantity at each price, shifting the supply curves for the affected crops to the left. An increase in wages or in the cost of chicken feed shifts the supply curve for eggs to the left. A reduction in any of these costs would shift the supply curve to the right.

Returns from Alternative Activities

To produce one good or service means forgoing the production of another. The concept of cost in economics suggests that the value of the activity forgone is a cost of the activity chosen; this cost should affect supply. One cost of producing eggs, for example, is not selling the chickens. An increase in the price people are willing to pay for fresh chicken would make it more profitable to sell chickens

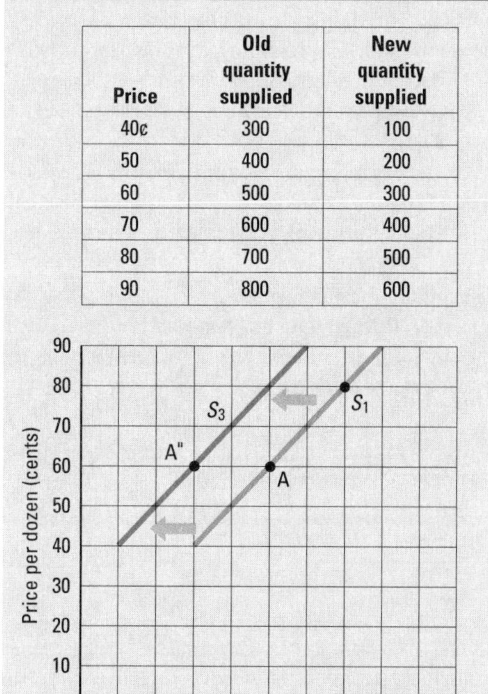

Price	Old quantity supplied	New quantity supplied
40¢	300	100
50	400	200
60	500	300
70	600	400
80	700	500
90	800	600

EXHIBIT 3-6

A Reduction in Supply

A change in supply that reduces the quantity supplied at each price shifts the supply curve to the left. At a price of 60 cents per dozen, for example, the original quantity supplied was 500 million dozen eggs per month (point A). With a new supply curve S_3, the quantity supplied at that price falls to 300 million dozen eggs per month (point A″).

Case in Point The Monks of St. Benedict's Get Out of the Egg Business

Ultimately, it was cookies that lured the monks of St. Benedict's out of the egg business.

St. Benedict's is a Benedictine monastery, nestled on a ranch high in the Colorado Rockies, about 20 miles down the road from Aspen.

The monastery's 17 monks operate the ranch to support themselves and to provide help for poor people in the area. They graze cattle—about 800 head—and produce hay and cookies. They used to produce eggs.

Attracted by potential profits and the peaceful nature of the work, the monks went into the egg business in 1967. The monks had 10,000 chickens producing their Monastery Eggs brand.

Charlie Albanese (left) working with Brother Jeffrey Briggs and Brother John Collins (in black hat) on St. Benedict's "Monastery Cookies."

For a while, business was good. Very good. Then, in the late 1970s, the price of chicken feed started to rise rapidly.

"When we started in the business, we were paying $60 to $80 a ton for feed—delivered," recalls the monastery's abbot, Father Joseph Boyle. "By the late 1970s, our cost had more than doubled. We were paying $160 to $200 a ton. That really hurt, because feed represents a large part of the cost of producing eggs."

The monks adjusted to the blow. "When grain prices were lower, we'd pull a hen off for a few weeks to molt, then return her to laying. After grain prices went up, it was 12 months of laying and into the soup pot," Father Joseph says.

Grain prices continued to rise in the 1980s. Demand fell at the same time, as Americans worried about the cholesterol in eggs. Times got tougher in the egg business.

"We were still making money in the financial sense," Father Joseph says. "After all, we didn't have to pay for our labor. But we tried an experiment in 1985 producing cookies, and it was a success. We finally decided that devoting our time and energy to the cookies would pay off better than the egg business, so we quit the egg business in 1986."

The cookie business has been good to the monks. They sold 200,000 ounces of Monastery Cookies in 1987. The monks' calculation that they would earn a higher return on their labor in cookies than in eggs has proved correct.

And there is another advantage as well.

"The chickens didn't stop laying eggs on Sunday," Fr. Joseph chuckles. "But now we can take Sundays off. We're not hemmed in in the way we were with the chickens."

Source: Timothy Tregarthen, "The Monks of St. Benedict's: Getting Out of the Egg Business," *The Margin* 4(1) (September/October 1988): 14–15.

and would thus increase the cost of producing eggs. It would shift the supply curve for eggs to the left.

Technology

A change in technology alters the combinations of inputs or the types of inputs required in the production process. An improvement in technology usually means that fewer and/or less costly inputs are needed. If the cost of production is lower, the profits available at a given price will increase, and producers will produce more. With more produced at every price, the supply curve will shift to the right.

Impressive technological changes have affected the computer industry in recent years. Computers are much smaller and are far more powerful than they were only a few years ago—and they are much cheaper to produce. The result has been a huge increase in the supply of computers, shifting the supply curve to the right.

Producer Expectations

All supply curves are based in part on suppliers' *expectations* about future market conditions. After all, production decisions are typically made long before a product is ready for sale. Those decisions necessarily depend on expectations. Changes in producer expectations can have important effects on price and output.

Consider, for example, the owners of oil deposits. Oil pumped out of the ground and used today will be unavailable in the future. If a change in the international political climate leads many owners to expect that oil prices will rise in the future, they may decide to leave their oil in the ground, planning to sell it later when the price is higher. Thus, the original supply curve for oil will shift to the left.

Reader's Advisory

There are two special things to note about dealing with supply curves. The first is similar to the reader's advisory on demand curves—it's important to distinguish carefully between changes in supply and changes in quantity supplied. A change in supply results from a change in a supply shifter and implies a shift of the supply curve to the right or left. A change in price produces a change in quantity supplied and induces a movement along the supply curve. A change in price does not shift the supply curve.

The second caution relates to the interpretation of increases and decreases in supply. Notice that in Exhibit 3-5 an increase in supply is shown as a shift of the supply curve to the right; the curve shifts in the direction of increasing quantity with respect to the horizontal axis. In Exhibit 3-6 a reduction in supply is shown as a shift of the supply curve to the left; the curve shifts in the direction of decreasing quantity with respect to the horizontal axis.

Because the supply curve is upward sloping, a shift to the right produces a new curve that lies below the original curve. Students sometimes make the mistake of thinking of such a shift as a shift "down" and therefore as a reduction in supply. Similarly, it's easy to make the mistake of showing an increase in supply with a new curve that lies above the original curve. But that's a *reduction* in supply!

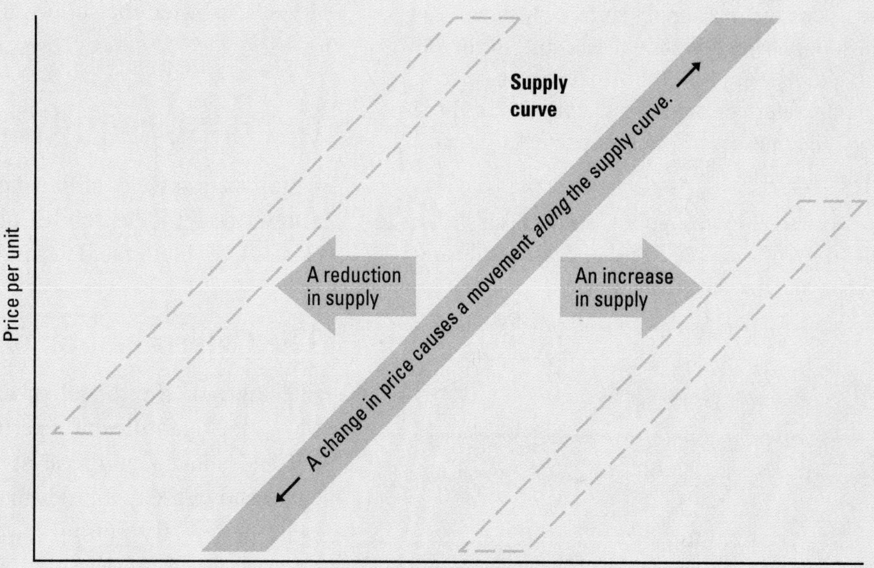

To avoid such errors, focus on the fact that an increase in supply is an increase in the quantity supplied at each price, and the supply curve shifts in the direction of increased quantity on the horizontal axis. Similarly, a reduction in supply is a reduction in the quantity supplied at each price, and the supply curve shifts in the direction of a lower quantity on the horizontal axis.

Natural Events

Storms, insect infestations, and drought all affect agricultural production and thus the supply of agricultural goods. If something destroys a substantial part of an agricultural crop, the supply curve will shift to the left. If there is an unusually good harvest, the supply curve will shift to the right. In the introduction to this chapter we discussed the impact on the vegetable market of the 1995

Checklist

- The quantity supplied of a good or service is the quantity sellers are willing to sell at a particular price during a particular period, ceteris paribus.
- A supply schedule shows the quantities supplied at different prices, ceteris paribus. A supply curve shows this same information graphically.
- A change in the price of a good or service causes a change in the quantity supplied—a movement *along* the supply curve.
- A change in a supply shifter causes a change in supply, which is shown as a shift of the supply curve. Supply shifters include the price of inputs, returns from related activities, technology, the number of firms, expectations, and natural events.
- An increase in supply is shown as a shift to the right of a supply curve; a decrease in supply is shown as a shift to the left.

floods in California, which shifted the supply curve for many vegetables to the left.

The Number of Sellers

The supply curve for an industry, such as that for eggs, includes all the firms in the industry. A change in the number of firms in an industry would change the output of the industry at each price and would thus change supply. An increase in the number of firms producing a good or service shifts the supply curve to the right; a reduction in the number of firms shifts the supply curve to the left.

The rental market for home videos has been affected dramatically by an increase in the number of firms. When the market first emerged in the early 1980s, a few specialty shops rented home videos. During the past few years, the number of firms renting these products has exploded. Grocery stores, drug stores, and convenience stores have jumped into the market. The addition of these new firms has shifted the supply curve for home video rentals to the right.

Demand, Supply, and Equilibrium

In this section we combine the demand and supply curves we've just studied into a new model. The **model of demand and supply** uses demand and supply curves to explain the determination of price and output in individual markets.

The Determination of Price and Output

The logic of the model of demand and supply is simple. The demand curve shows the quantities of a particular good or service that consumers will be willing and able to purchase at each price during a specified period. The supply curve shows the quantities that sellers will offer for sale at each price during that same period. By putting the two curves together, we should be able to find a price at which the quantity buyers want to purchase equals the quantity sellers will offer for sale.

Exhibit 3-7 combines the demand and supply data introduced in Exhibits 3-1 and 3-4. Notice that the two curves intersect at a price of 60 cents per dozen—at this price the quantity demanded and supplied are equal. Consumers want to purchase, and sellers are willing to offer for sale, 500 million dozen eggs per month. The market for eggs is in equilibrium. Unless the demand or supply curve shifts, there will be no tendency for price to change. The **equilibrium price** in any market is the price at which quantity demanded equals quantity supplied. The equilibrium price in the market for eggs is thus 60 cents per dozen. The **equilibrium output** is the output that will be demanded and supplied at the equilibrium price.

Notice that with an upward-sloping supply curve and a downward-sloping demand curve, there is only a single price at which the two curves intersect. This means there is only one price at which equilibrium is achieved. It follows that at any price other than the equilibrium price, the market will not be in equilibrium. Let's examine what happens at prices other than the equilibrium price.

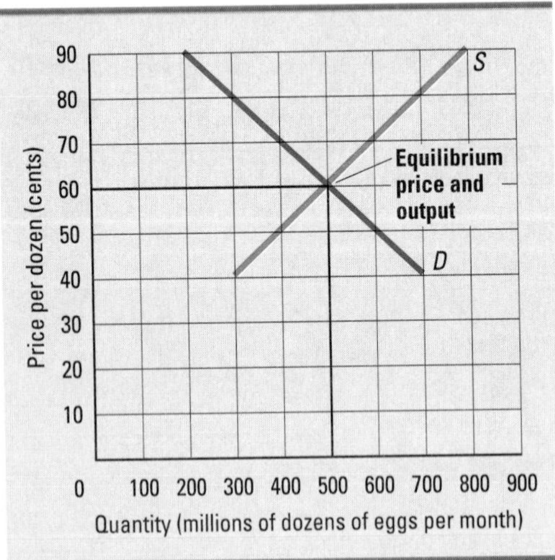

EXHIBIT 3-7

The Determination of Equilibrium Price and Output

When we combine the demand and supply curves for a good in a single graph, the point at which they intersect is called the equilibrium price. Here, the equilibrium price is $0.60 per dozen. Consumers demand, and suppliers supply, 500 million dozen eggs per month at this price.

Surpluses

Exhibit 3-8 shows the same demand and supply curves we have just examined, but this time the initial price is $0.80 per dozen eggs. Because this price is not the equilibrium price, we no longer have a balance between quantity demanded and quantity supplied. At a price of $0.80, we read over to the demand curve to determine the quantity of eggs consumers will be willing to buy—300 million dozen per month. The supply curve tells us what sellers will offer for sale—700 million dozen per month. The difference, 400 million dozen eggs per month, is called a surplus. More generally, a **surplus** is the amount by which the quantity supplied exceeds the quantity demanded at the current price. There is, of course, no surplus at the equilibrium price; a surplus occurs only if the current price exceeds the equilibrium price.

EXHIBIT 3-8

A Surplus in the Market for Eggs

At a price of $0.80, the quantity supplied is 700 million dozen eggs per month and the quantity demanded is 300 million dozen per month; there is a surplus of 400 million dozen eggs per month. Given a surplus, the price will fall quickly toward the equilibrium level of $0.60.

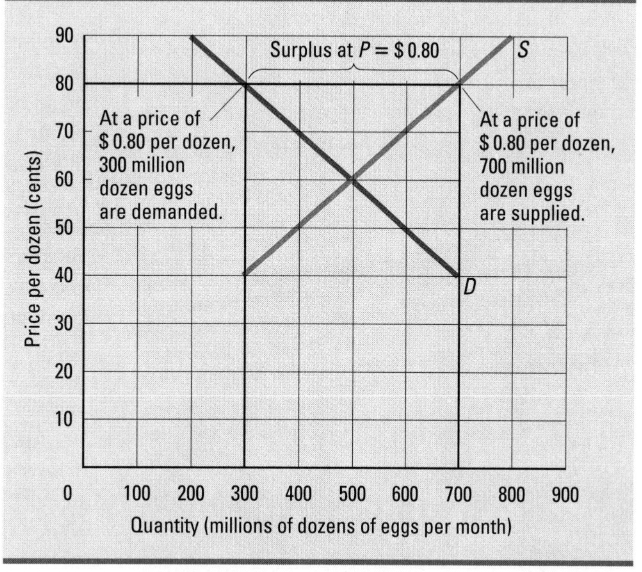

A surplus in the market for eggs won't last long. With unsold eggs on the market, sellers will begin to reduce their prices to clear out unsold eggs. As the price of eggs begins to fall, the quantity of eggs supplied begins to decline. At the same time, the quantity of eggs demanded begins to rise. Remember that the reduction in quantity supplied is a movement *along* the supply curve—the curve itself doesn't shift in response to a reduction in price. Similarly, the increase in quantity demanded is a movement *along* the demand curve—the demand curve doesn't shift in response to a reduction in price. Price will continue to fall until it reaches its equilibrium level, at which the demand and supply curves intersect. At that point, there will be no tendency for price to fall further.

In general, surpluses in the marketplace are short-lived. The prices of most goods and services adjust quickly, eliminating the surplus. In our investigation of labor markets later in this book, however, we shall see that labor surpluses (which are called unemployment in the labor market) can be sustained over long periods. One reason is that wages don't adjust quickly to imbalances in demand and supply. There can, as a result, be persistent surpluses in the labor market.

Another source of persistent surpluses is price controls imposed by government agencies. A **price floor** is a minimum price set above the equilibrium price. By definition, a price floor creates a surplus. Governments often seek to assist farmers by setting the prices of their products above equilibrium levels, and this creates surpluses in many agricultural markets.

- The **model of demand and supply** combines demand and supply curves to explain the determination of price and output in a market.
- The **equilibrium price** is the price at which the quantity demanded equals the quantity supplied.
- The **equilibrium output** is the output demanded and supplied at the equilibrium price.
- A **surplus** exists if the quantity of a good or service supplied exceeds the quantity demanded at the current price.
- A **price floor** is a minimum price set above the equilibrium price.

Case in Point Dairy Floor Milks Consumers, Boosts Producers

Every year, the federal government goes to the market to buy milk, butter, and cheese—a *lot* of milk, butter, and cheese. In a typical year, the government snaps up about $3 billion worth of these dairy products.

The government's spending spree isn't a result of a particular enthusiasm for dairy products on the part of Washington bureaucrats. In fact, most of the milk, butter, and cheese the government buys won't be used. Although some of it is distributed to low-income people, most sits unused in government warehouses. The government in 1994 had more than 5 billion pounds of milk, butter, and cheese in storage.

The government's purchase program is part of an effort to prop up dairy prices. The government sets a minimum price for raw milk; it's illegal for a dairy to pay dairy farmers less. Because the price floor exceeds the equilibrium price, the program produces a surplus. By itself, such a program might not be particularly helpful to dairy farmers; it raises the price they receive but lowers the quantity they sell. However, the federal government guarantees that it will purchase any surplus the program creates, thus assuring producers not only of a higher price but of a greater quantity sold as well.

The specific dairy products the government purchases are called manufactured milk products. The milk, for example, isn't fresh but powdered nonfat milk. Butter and cheese, of course, are manufactured from raw milk. By buying these manufactured products in sufficient quantity the government boosts the prices of all milk products, including fresh milk.

The federal program affects consumers in two ways. As taxpayers, they pay to buy and store surplus milk, butter, and cheese. The more important cost, however, is the higher prices consumers face. University of Maryland economist Bruce Gardner estimates that the program boosts the prices consumers pay by about 30 percent—for example, a gallon of milk that sells for $3 would sell for about $2.30 in the absence of federal intervention.

Mr. Gardner, for one, doesn't think much of the government's effort. "I see no justification whatever for government support of the industry," he says. But many dairy farmers, to whom the federal support may make the difference between making money and losing it, feel quite differently: "Without the dairy program, I'd lose money, and that means I'd get out of the business," says Wisconsin dairy farmer Bob Henshaw. "If you want milk, you've got to pay for it."

Source: Personal interviews.

Shortages

Just as a price above the equilibrium price will cause a surplus, a price below equilibrium will cause a shortage. A **shortage** occurs if the quantity demanded exceeds the quantity supplied at the current price for a good or service.

Exhibit 3-9 shows a shortage in the market for eggs. Suppose the price is 40 cents per dozen. At that price, 300 million dozen eggs would be supplied per month and 700 million dozen would be demanded per month. When more eggs are demanded than supplied, there is a shortage.

A **shortage** exists if the quantity of a good or service demanded exceeds the quantity supplied at the current price.

In the face of a shortage, sellers are likely to begin to raise their prices. As the price rises, there will be an increase in the quantity supplied (but not a change in supply) and a reduction in the quantity demanded (but not a change in demand) until the equilibrium price is achieved.

EXHIBIT 3-9

A Shortage in the Market for Eggs

At a price of $0.40 per dozen, the quantity of eggs demanded is 700 million dozen per month and the quantity supplied is 300 million dozen per month. The result is a shortage of 400 million dozen eggs per month.

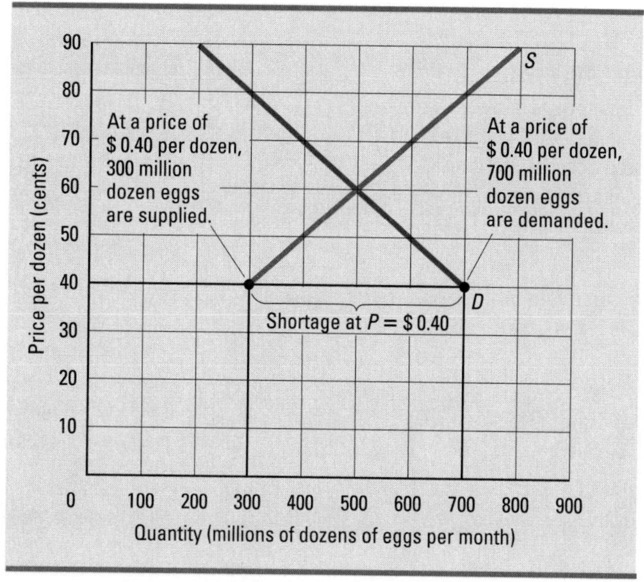

Shortages will be persistent if a government agency imposes a **price ceiling,** a maximum price set below the equilibrium price. Government price ceilings typically make it illegal to sell a good or service for a price above the ceiling price. One of the most common forms of price ceiling is rent controls, which restrict the rents property owners may charge. To the degree that such controls are successful in holding rents below the equilibrium level, they inevitably create housing shortages.

Shifts in Demand and Supply

A change in one of the variables (shifters) held constant in any model of demand and supply will create a change in demand or supply. A shift in a demand or supply curve changes the equilibrium price for a good or service. Exhibit 3-10 combines the information about changes in the demand and supply of eggs presented in Exhibits 3-2, 3-3, 3-5, and 3-6. In each case, the original solution is at an equilibrium price of 60 cents per dozen and the corresponding quantity of 500 million dozen eggs per month. Exhibit 3-10 shows what happens with an increase in demand, a reduction in demand, an increase in supply, and a reduction in supply. Each of these possibilities is discussed in turn below.

An Increase in Demand

An increase in demand for eggs shifts the demand curve to the right, as shown in Panel (a) of Exhibit 3-10. The equilibrium price rises to 70 cents per dozen. As the price rises to the new equilibrium level, the quantity supplied increases to 600 million dozen eggs per month.

Demand shifters that could cause an increase in demand include a shift in consumer preferences that leads to greater egg consumption; a lower price for a complement to eggs, such as ham or bacon; a higher price for a substitute for eggs, such as cereal; an increase in income; and an increase in population. Because eggs can't be stored for very long periods of time, however, it's unlikely that changes in consumer expectations would produce changes in demand.

A **price ceiling** is a maximum price set below the equilibrium price.

EXHIBIT 3-10

Changes in Demand and Supply

A change in demand or in supply changes the equilibrium solution in the model. Panels (a) and (b) show an increase and a decrease in demand, respectively; Panels (c) and (d) show an increase and a decrease in supply, respectively.

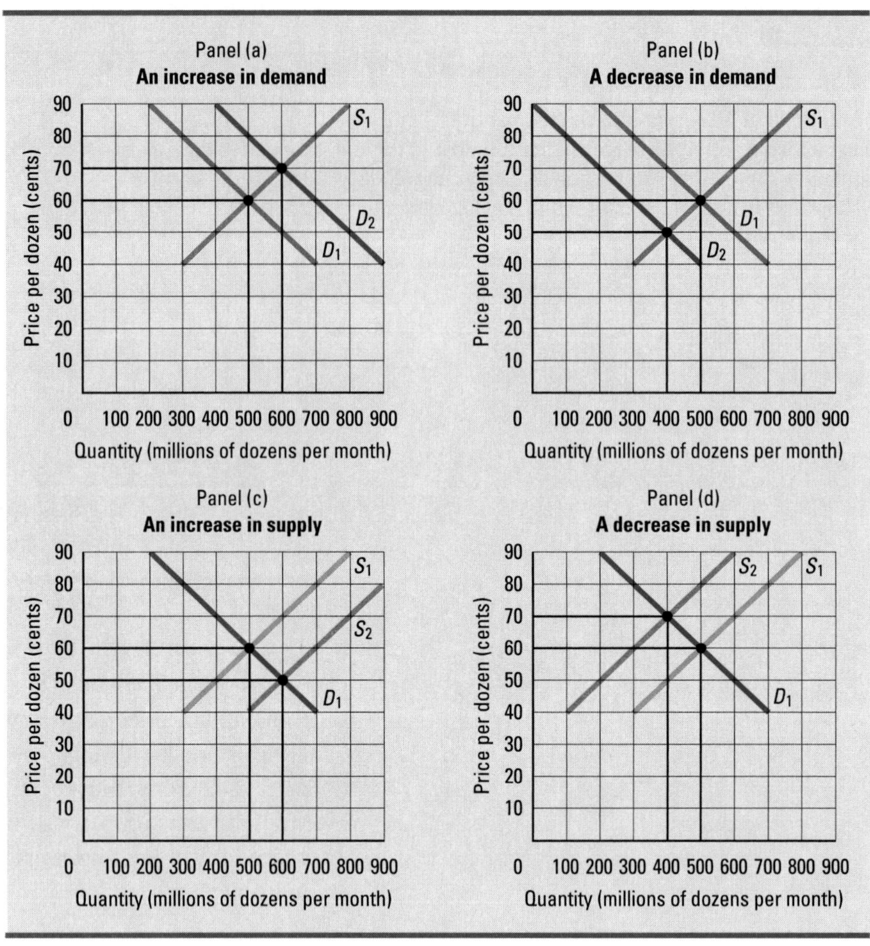

A Decrease in Demand

Panel (b) of Exhibit 3-10 shows that a decrease in demand shifts the demand curve to the left. The equilibrium price falls to 50 cents per dozen. As the price falls to the new equilibrium level, the quantity supplied decreases to 400 million dozen eggs per month.

Demand shifters that could reduce the demand for eggs include a shift in consumer preferences that makes people want to consume fewer eggs; an increase in the price of a complement, such as ham or bacon; a reduction in the price of a substitute, such as cereal; a reduction in income; and a reduction in population.

An Increase in Supply

An increase in the supply of eggs shifts the supply curve to the right, as shown in Panel (c) of Exhibit 3-10. The equilibrium price falls to 50 cents per dozen. As the price falls to the new equilibrium level, the quantity of eggs demanded increases to 600 million dozen eggs per month.

The supply shifters that could increase supply include a reduction in the prices of inputs such as chicken feed and labor, a decline in the returns available from alternative uses of the inputs that produce eggs, an improvement in the technology of egg production, and an increase in the number of egg-producing firms.

Cases in Point — Shifts in Demand and Supply of Four Products

Health Concerns Boost Yogurt Demand

The perception of yogurt as a healthful food helped push its demand to record levels early in the 1990s. *The Wall Street Journal* reported that sales jumped 10 percent to $1.39 billion for the 12 months that ended in the summer of 1993.

The sharp gains were fueled primarily by the introduction of low-fat and nonfat yogurt products. A further boost came in 1992, when a study sponsored by the National Yogurt Association reported a link between yogurt consumption and a stronger immune system. Yogurt has also been cited as a factor in preventing cancer and heart disease.

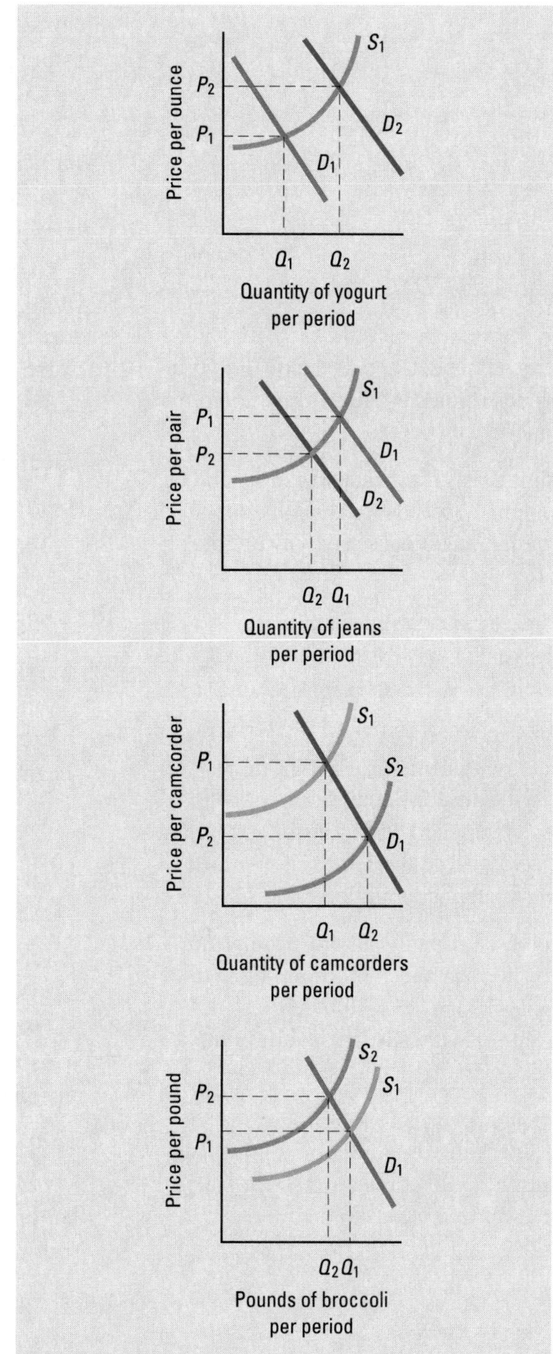

Market for Blue Jeans Shrinks

The population age 15 to 25 in the United States plunged by more than 2 million in the last decade. That was bad news for makers of jeans. People in that age group purchase more jeans than anyone else—an average of four to six pairs per year.

The nation's jeans makers took another blow as younger consumers appeared to change their preferences. "Today, these kids have more choices," says Levi Strauss & Co. marketing manager Dan Chew. "They opt for sweats, jams, and bicycle shorts instead of jeans."

Sales of jeans fell more than 20 percent in the 1980s.

Camcorder Makers Cut Costs, Prices

Camcorders, which were once a toy few people could afford, have become a common fixture at family gatherings. When the devices were first introduced in 1985, they typically cost well over $1,000. By 1995 their price had fallen below $500.

The plunge in price came as new firms entered the market and as manufacturers found cheaper methods of making the devices.

Flood Boosts Broccoli Prices

The introduction to this chapter discussed the impact of the 1995 floods in California on vegetable prices. The floods destroyed crops, shifting the supply curves for those crops to the left and raising their prices. Here, the supply curve for broccoli shifts to the left, increasing the equilibrium price and reducing the equilibrium quantity.

A Decrease in Supply

Panel (d) of Exhibit 3-10 shows that a decrease in supply shifts the supply curve to the left. The equilibrium price rises to 70 cents per dozen. As the price rises to the new equilibrium level, the quantity demanded decreases to 400 million dozen eggs per month.

The supply shifters that could reduce supply include an increase in the prices of inputs used in the production of eggs, an increase in the returns available from alternative uses of these inputs, a decline in production because of problems in technology (perhaps caused by a restriction on drugs used to induce chickens to lay eggs), a reduction in the number of egg-producing firms, or a natural event such as a disease that kills a substantial proportion of the egg industry's hens.

The Cases in Point on page 69 describe some recent events that illustrate shifts in demand and supply. As demand and supply curves shift, prices adjust to maintain a balance between the quantity of a good demanded and the quantity supplied. If prices did not adjust, this balance could not be maintained.

The supply curve for eggs that we have examined in this chapter is linear. Often, however, supply curves are nonlinear, as we see in the supply curves drawn in the Cases in Point. Notice that these supply curves, like the ones we've already examined, are upward sloping.

Checklist ✓

- The equilibrium price is the price at which the quantity demanded equals the quantity supplied. It is determined by the intersection of the demand and supply curves.
- A surplus exists if the quantity of a good or service supplied exceeds the quantity demanded at the current price; it causes downward pressure on price.
- A shortage exists if the quantity of a good or service demanded exceeds the quantity supplied at the current price; it causes upward pressure on price.
- An increase in demand, all other things unchanged, will cause the equilibrium price to rise; quantity supplied will increase. A decrease in demand will cause the equilibrium price to fall; quantity supplied will decrease.
- An increase in supply, all other things unchanged, will cause the equilibrium price to fall; quantity demanded will increase. A decrease in supply will cause the equilibrium price to rise; quantity demanded will decrease.
- Government-imposed minimum prices may create a surplus. Government-imposed maximum prices may create a shortage.

The Model of Demand and Supply: An Assessment

How useful is the model of demand and supply? Its implications are broadly consistent with what we generally observe in the real world.

1. Quantities demanded and supplied are generally in balance in most markets. Shortages or surpluses are the exception, not the rule, in a market economy.
2. Markets respond appropriately to changes in demand and supply. When demand for a good or service changes, we generally observe the responses predicted by the model: The price of the good or service is bid up or down, and firms respond by changing the quantity supplied. When medical studies suggested that oat bran was good for the heart, for example, consumer demand increased sharply. The price of oats shot up, and farmers responded with an increase in the quantity supplied. When the supply of broccoli fell after the 1995 flooding in California, the price of broccoli shot up and broccoli consumption fell.
3. When prices are set above or below the equilibrium price, responses are generally consistent with the model. Courses in microeconomics present some exceptions, but in most markets, price floors create surpluses and price ceilings create shortages.

The model of demand and supply is one of the most widely used tools of economic analysis. That widespread use is no accident. The model yields results that are, in fact, broadly consistent with what we observe in the marketplace. Your mastery of this model will pay big dividends in your study of economics.

A Look Back—And a Look Ahead

In this chapter we have examined the model of demand and supply. We found that a demand curve shows the quantity demanded at each price, all other things unchanged. The law of demand asserts that this relationship is always negative: an increase in price reduces the quantity demanded, ceteris paribus. The supply curve shows the quantity of a good or service that sellers will offer at various prices, ceteris paribus. Supply curves are generally upward sloping.

The equilibrium price occurs where the demand and supply curves intersect. At this price, the quantity demanded equals the quantity supplied. A price higher than the equilibrium price increases the quantity supplied and reduces the quantity demanded, causing a surplus. A price lower than the equilibrium price increases the quantity demanded and reduces the quantity supplied, causing a shortage. Changes in demand or supply, caused by changes in the determinants of demand and supply otherwise held constant in the analysis, change the equilibrium price and output.

This chapter completes a general introduction to economics. If you're studying microeconomic theory, you'll turn next to an examination of some basic tools of microeconomic analysis. If you're studying macroeconomics, you'll look at some basic macroeconomic problems and issues. Whatever your field of inquiry, it will make extensive use of the model of demand and supply.

Terms and Concepts for Review

Change in demand
Change in quantity demanded
Change in quantity supplied
Change in supply
Complements
Demand curve
Demand schedule
Demand shifter
Equilibrium output
Equilibrium price
Inferior good
Law of demand
Model of demand and supply
Normal good
Price ceiling
Price floor
Quantity demanded
Quantity supplied
Shortage
Substitutes
Supply curve
Supply schedule
Supply shifter
Surplus

For Discussion

In answering these questions, assume that the number of firms in each industry remains unchanged.

1. What do you think happens to the demand for pizzas during the Super Bowl?
2. Which of the following goods are likely to be classified as normal goods or services? Inferior?
   - **a.** Beans
   - **b.** Tuxedos
   - **c.** Used cars
   - **d.** Used clothing
   - **e.** Computers
   - **f.** Books reviewed in *The New York Times*
   - **g.** Macaroni and cheese
   - **h.** Calculators
   - **i.** Cigarettes
   - **j.** Caviar
   - **k.** Legal services
3. Which of the following pairs of goods are likely to be classified as substitutes? Complements?
   - **a.** Peanut butter and jelly
   - **b.** Right shoes and left shoes
   - **c.** Nike brand and Reebok brand sneakers
   - **d.** IBM and Apple Macintosh brand computers
   - **e.** Dress shirts and ties
   - **f.** Airline tickets and hotels
   - **g.** Gasoline and tires
   - **h.** Beer and wine
   - **i.** Faxes and first-class mail
   - **j.** Cereal and milk
   - **k.** Cereal and eggs
4. The Case in Point on page 57 asserts that lower airfares have led to reduced traffic fatalities. Using the logic suggested by that case, suggest how each of the following events would affect the number of highway fatalities in any one year.
   - **a.** An increase in the price of gasoline
   - **b.** A large reduction in rental rates for passenger vans
   - **c.** An increase in airfares

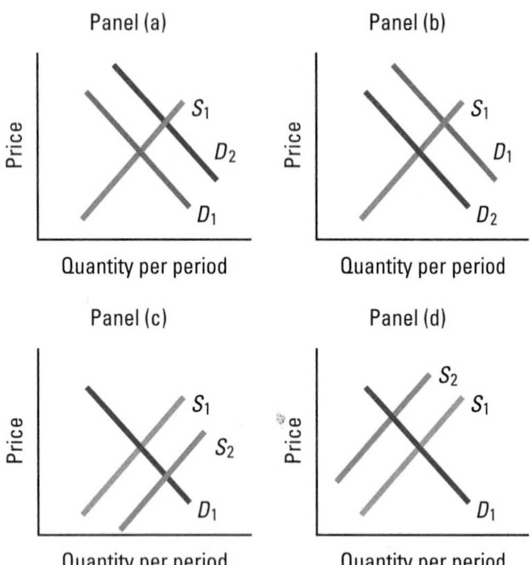

5. The graphs above show four possible shifts in demand or in supply. Relate each of the events described below to one of them.
   - **a.** How did the 1995 floods in California affect the market for broccoli?
   - **b.** The Surgeon General decides french fries aren't bad for your health after all and issues a report endorsing their use. What happens to the demand for french fries?
   - **c.** How do you think rising incomes affect the market for ski vacations?
   - **d.** A new technique is discovered for manufacturing computers that greatly lowers their production cost. What happens to the market for computers?
   - **e.** How would a ban on smoking in public affect the market for cigarettes?
   - **f.** A severe frost in Brazil in 1994 destroyed about one-quarter of the coffee crop. How should this have affected the market for coffee?
6. Children under age 2 are now allowed to fly free on U.S. airlines; they usually sit in their parents' laps. Some safety advocates have urged that they be required to be strapped in infant seats, which would mean their parents would have to purchase tickets for them. Some economists have argued that such a measure would actually increase infant fatalities. Can you say why?
7. Suppose egg prices rise sharply and most people expect them to remain high. How might this affect the monks' supply of cookies? (See the Case in Point on page 62.)
8. Gasoline prices typically rise in Colorado during the summer, a time of heavy tourist traffic. A "street talk" feature on a radio station in Colorado Springs sought consumer reaction to higher gasoline prices in 1992. Here was one response: "I don't like 'em [the higher prices] much. I think the gas companies just use any excuse to jack up prices, and they're doing it again now." How does this consumer's perspective differ from that of economists who use the model of demand and supply?
9. A Conference Board report in 1993 predicted that the 1990s would see a sharp increase in the number of high-income households. It predicted, for example, that the number of households earning $100,000 or more would double by the year 2000. Much of the boom in high-income households, the organization said, would be the result of gains in income for women, who entered the ranks of professional workers in large numbers in the 1980s and 1990s.

   Name some goods and services for which this development is likely to increase demand. Are there any for which it will reduce demand?
10. Gary Jacobson, a stock analyst for Kidder Peabody, has some bad news for manufacturers of fitness products. "We're all a bunch of lazy slobs," he told *The Wall Street Journal* in 1993. In somewhat more analytical terms, he said that "the market for fitness products is flattening." The *Journal* reported evidence that backs Mr. Jacobson's claim. American Sports Data reported that the number of "frequent fitness participants" declined 4.8 percent in 1991 and 2.7 percent in 1992. The firm reported that for every person who exercises regularly, there are three couch potatoes who don't.

    Show what all this means for the market for fitness products.
11. For more than a century, milk producers have produced skim milk, which contains virtually no fat, along with regular milk, which contains 4 percent fat. But a century ago, skim milk accounted for only about 1 percent of total production, and much of it was fed to hogs. Today, skim and other reduced-fat milks make up the bulk of milk sales. What curve shifted, and what factor shifted it?

Problems

The following problems are based on the model of demand and supply for eggs as shown in Exhibit 3-7 on page 64. You can graph the initial demand and supply curves by using the following values, with all quantities in millions of dozens of eggs per month:

Price	Quantity demanded	Quantity supplied
$.40	700	300
.50	600	400
.60	500	500
.70	400	600
.80	300	700
.90	200	800

Reader's Advisory !

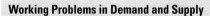

Working Problems in Demand and Supply

You're likely to be given problems in which you'll have to shift a demand or supply curve. Suppose you are told that an invasion of pod-crunching insects has gobbled up half the crop of fresh peas, and you are asked to use demand and supply analysis to predict what will happen to the price and quantity of peas demanded and supplied. Here are some suggestions.

Put the quantity of the good you're asked to analyze on the horizontal axis and its price on the vertical axis. Draw a downward-sloping line for demand and an upward-sloping line for supply. The equilibrium price is determined by the intersection of the two curves. Label the equilibrium solution. You may find it helpful to use a number for the equilibrium price instead of the letter "P." Pick a price that seems plausible, say, 79 cents per pound. Don't worry about the precise positions of the demand and supply curves; you can't be expected to know what they are.

Step 2 can be the most difficult step; the problem is to decide which curve to shift. The key is to remember the difference between a change in demand or supply and a change in quantity demanded or supplied. At each price, ask yourself whether the given event would change the quantity demanded. Would the fact that fewer peas are available change the quantity demanded at a price of say, 79 cents per pound? Clearly not; none of the demand shifters has changed. The event would, however, reduce the quantity supplied at this price, and the supply curve would shift to the left. There is a change in supply and a reduction in the quantity demanded. There is no change in demand.

Next check to see whether the result you've obtained makes sense. The graph in step 2 makes sense; it shows price rising and quantity demanded falling.

It's easy to make a mistake such as the one shown below. One might, for example, reason that when fewer peas are available, fewer will be demanded, and therefore the demand curve will shift to the left. This suggests the price of peas will fall—but that doesn't make sense. If only half as many fresh peas were available, their price would surely rise. The error here lies in confusing a change in quantity demanded with a change in demand. Yes, consumers will end up consuming fewer peas. But no, they won't demand fewer peas at each price than before; the demand curve does not shift.

1. Set up the graph.

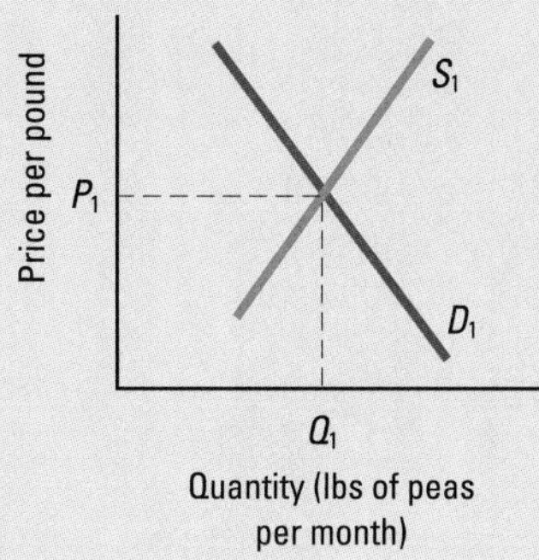

2. Shift the curve.

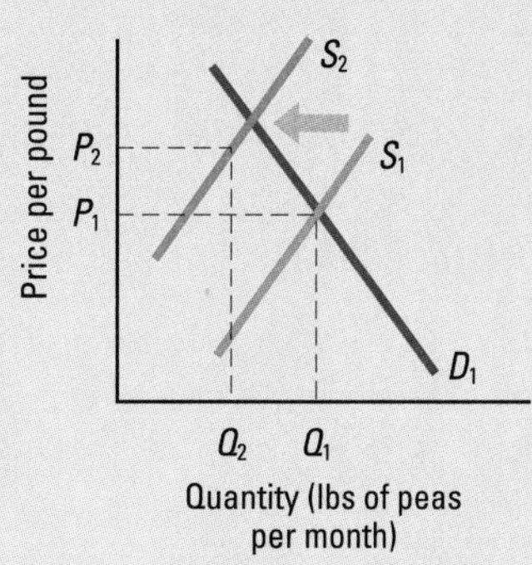

3. Troubleshoot.

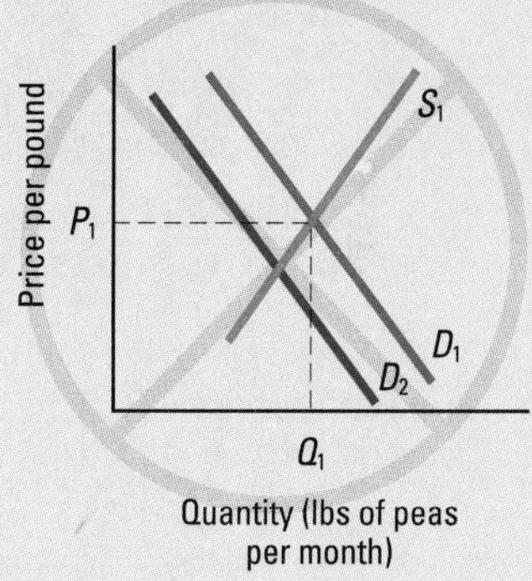

1. Suppose the quantity demanded rises by 400 million dozen eggs per month at each price. Draw the initial demand and supply curves as given in the table on page 72, draw the new demand curve given by this change, and show the new equilibrium price and output.
2. Suppose the quantity demanded falls, relative to the values given in the table on page 72, by 400 million dozen eggs per month at prices between 40 and 70 cents per dozen; at prices of 80 and 90 cents per dozen, the quantity demanded becomes zero. Draw the new demand curve and show the new equilibrium price and output.
3. Suppose the quantity supplied rises by 400 million dozen eggs per month at each price, while the quantities demanded retain the values shown in the table on page 72. Draw the new supply curve and show the new equilibrium price and output.
4. Suppose the quantity supplied falls, relative to the values given in the table on page 72, by 400 million dozen eggs per month at prices of 50 cents and above; at a price of 40 cents per dozen, the quantity supplied becomes zero. Draw the new supply curve and show the new equilibrium price and output.

Part Two Basic Tools of Microeconomics

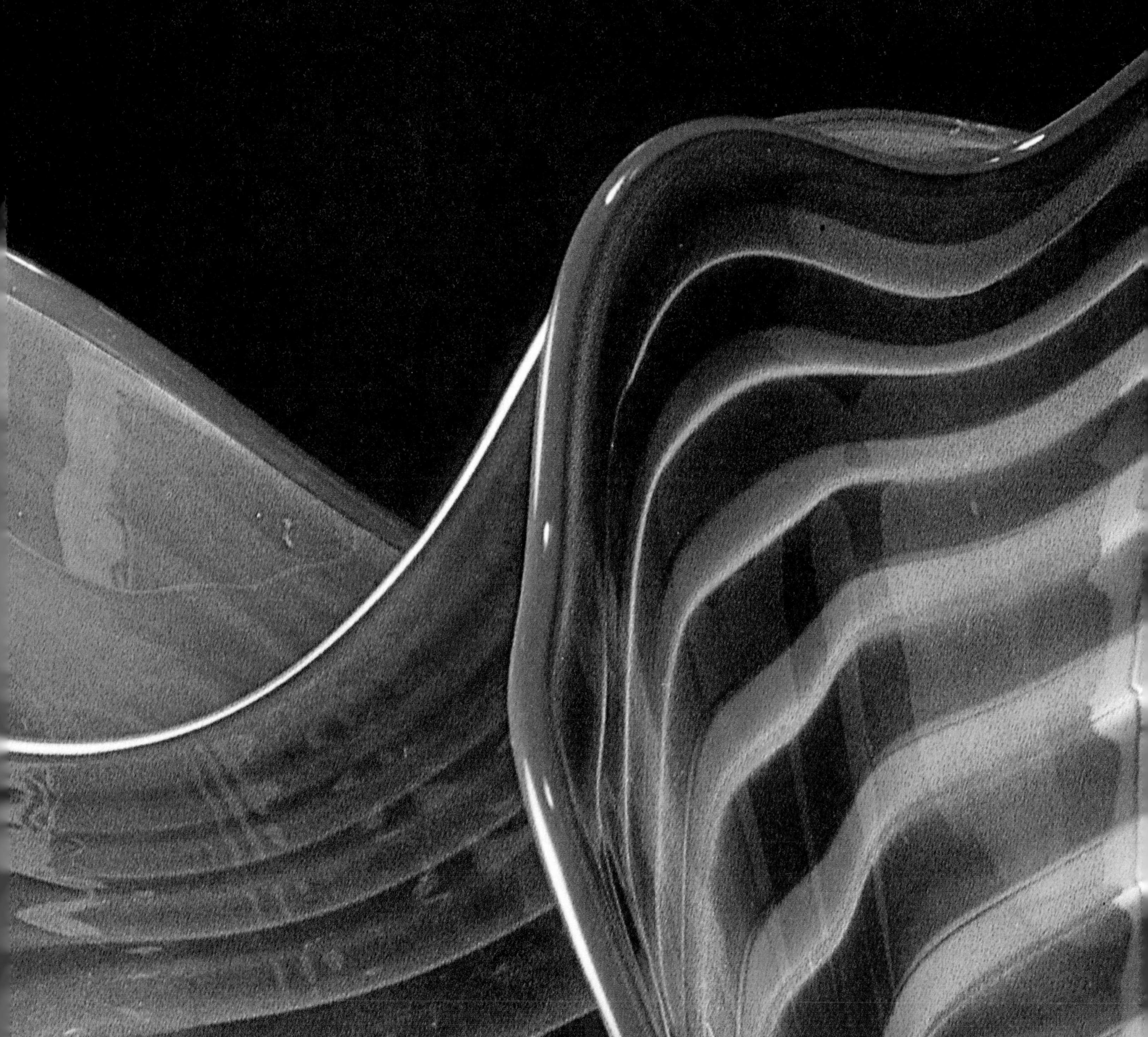

4

Chapter Objectives

After mastering the material in this chapter, you will be able to:

1. Define and explain the general approach economists use to assess how responsive one variable is to changes in another.
2. List the factors that affect the responsiveness of quantity demanded to changes in price.
3. Explain the relationship between the responsiveness of quantity demanded to changes in price and the way in which total spending on a good or service is affected by changes in price.
4. Show the way economists measure how demand for a good or service is affected by changes in income and by changes in the prices of other goods and services.

Elasticity: A Measure of Response

The *elasticity* (or *responsiveness*) *of demand* in a market is great or small according as the amount demanded increases much or little for a given fall in price, and diminishes much or little for a given rise in price.

Alfred Marshall
Principles of Economics, 1890

What's Ahead

Imagine that you're the manager of the public transportation system for a large metropolitan area. Operating costs for the system have soared in the last few years, and you're under pressure to boost revenues. What do you do?

An obvious choice would be to raise fares. That will make your customers angry, but at least it will generate the extra revenue you need—or will it? The law of demand says that raising fares will reduce the number of passengers riding on your system. What if the number of passengers falls by so much that your higher fares actually reduce your revenues? If that happens, you'll have made your customers mad and your financial problem worse!

Of course, the law of demand only tells us that the higher fares will reduce ridership—it doesn't tell us by how much. If the number of passengers falls only a little, then the higher fares that your remaining passengers are paying might produce the higher revenues you need. The challenge for you is to determine how much the number of passengers will fall as a result of your fare increase. If it plunges a great deal, your higher fares could reduce revenues for your system. If it falls only a little, your higher fares will succeed in creating more revenue.

The law of demand tells us the direction of the response of quantity demanded to a price change. It tells us that higher fares, for example, will reduce the number of passengers using the system. But you need to know how much of a reduction you'll have. You need to know just how responsive the quantity demanded is to a price change.

This chapter introduces a measure of response, a measure that suggests how much a response we can expect in one variable as a result of a change in another. We saw in the last chapter that the quantity of a good or service demanded changes in response to a change in its price, to changes in prices of related goods and services, and to changes in income. In this chapter we'll see how economists measure the strength of such responses.

Elasticity is the ratio of the percentage change in a dependent variable to the percentage change in an independent variable, ceteris paribus.

Before we begin our discussion of the responsiveness of demand to changes in various independent variables, let's start with another type of response: the relationship between skin cancer and the thickness of the earth's ozone layer. In doing so, we'll see how the concept of *elasticity* can be used to measure the responsiveness of one variable to changes in another. Then we'll put the concept to work on demand.

The earth is wrapped in a layer of ozone high up in the stratosphere. This ozone layer protects us by filtering the sun's ultraviolet rays. Scientists generally agree that the ozone layer is getting thinner. This thinning of the ozone allows more ultraviolet light to penetrate the atmosphere; those ultraviolet rays contribute to skin cancer. Many scientists believe that less ozone in the stratosphere means more skin cancer on the earth. How much more? Scientists calculate that a 1 percent reduction in the thickness of the ozone layer produces a 3 percent increase in the number of skin cancer cases reported.

The skin cancer/ozone case illustrates how one variable can respond to another. A 1 percent change in an independent variable, the thickness of the ozone layer, appears to lead to a 3 percent change in the dependent variable, the number of cases of skin cancer.

Economists measure the responsiveness of one variable to a change in another in terms of **elasticity,** which is the ratio of the percentage change in a dependent variable to the percentage change in an independent variable. In the case of skin cancer and ozone, for example, we would say that the elasticity of skin cancer cases with respect to the thickness of the ozone layer is 3.

In equation form, elasticity (e) is measured as

$$e = \frac{\text{percentage change in dependent variable}}{\text{percentage change in independent variable}} \quad \textbf{(1)}$$

The elasticity of the number of cases of skin cancer with respect to the thickness of the ozone layer is thus calculated as

$$e = \frac{3\%}{1\%} = 3$$

Elasticity measures responsiveness. It reports one variable's percentage change as a response to a percentage change in another variable. We'll investigate several different elasticities in this chapter, but they'll share a common structure: a change in an independent variable causes a change in a dependent variable. Elasticity is the ratio of the percentage change in a dependent variable to the percentage change in an independent variable.

We'll begin our analysis of elasticity by examining responsiveness of quantity demanded to a price change. This measure of response plays a key role in economic analysis.

The Price Elasticity of Demand

We know from the law of demand how the quantity demanded will respond to a price change: it will change in the opposite direction. But how *much* will it change? It seems reasonable to expect, for example, that a 10 percent change in the price charged for a visit to the doctor would yield a different change in quantity demanded than a change in the price of an Oldsmobile. But how *much* is this difference?

Price elasticity of demand (e_p) is the ratio of the percentage change in the quantity demanded to the percentage change in price, ceteris paribus.

To show the strength of the responsiveness of quantity demanded to a change in price, we need to apply the concept of elasticity. The **price elasticity of demand** for a good or service, e_p, is the ratio of the percentage change in quantity demanded to the percentage change in the price of the good or service, ceteris paribus. Because it reports the responsiveness of quantity demanded to a price change, with all other independent variables in the demand function unchanged, the price elasticity of demand reflects movements along a demand curve.

Thus

$$e_p = \frac{\text{percentage change in quantity demanded}}{\text{percentage change in price}} \qquad \textbf{(2)}$$

Because price and quantity demanded always move in opposite directions, the price elasticity of demand is always negative. A positive percentage change in price implies a negative percentage change in quantity demanded, and vice versa.

Computing the Price Elasticity of Demand

Intuitively, the computation of the price elasticity of demand would seem to be quite simple: find two points on a demand curve, and determine the percentage changes in price and output between those points. That's precisely what we do, but there's a small wrinkle in the process.

Exhibit 4-1 shows a typical demand curve, a demand curve for sweaters. Suppose the initial price is $80 and the quantity demanded is 40 sweaters per year; we are at point A on the curve. Now suppose the price falls to $70 and we want to report the responsiveness of the quantity demanded. We see that at the new price, the quantity demanded rises to 60 sweaters per year (point B). To compute the elasticity, we need to compute the percentage changes in price and in quantity demanded between points A and B.

The standard method for computing the percentage change in a variable is to compute the change relative to the original value of the variable. We divide the change in the variable by the value of the variable before the change. For example, a person who earns $30,000 per year and receives a $3,000 raise is said to have a 10 percent gain in income: $3,000/$30,000 = 0.10, or 10 percent.

EXHIBIT 4-1

Responsiveness and Demand

A demand curve such as the one shown here shows how changes in price lead to changes in the quantity demanded. A movement from point A to point B, for example, shows how a $10 reduction in price increases the number of units demanded by 20. A movement from B to A is a $10 increase in price, which reduces quantity demanded by 20 units.

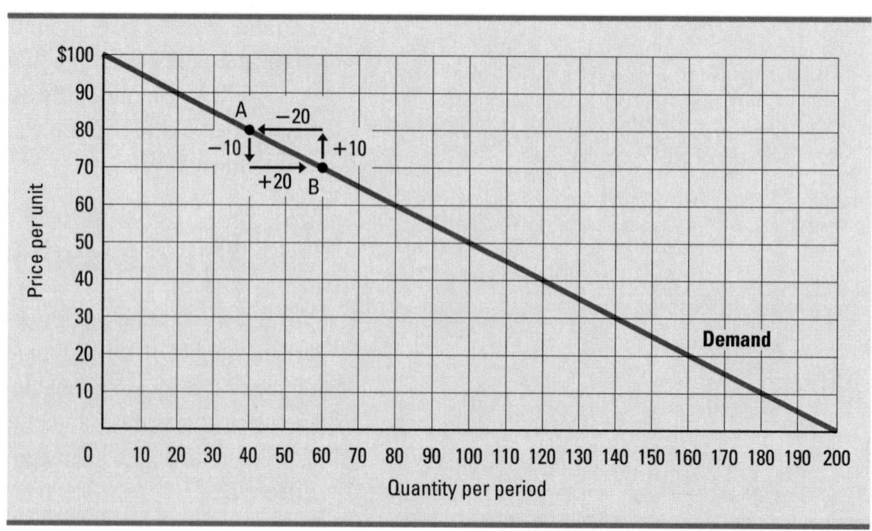

Using the standard method, the percentage change in quantity demanded between points A and B would thus be 20/40, or 50 percent. The percentage change in price would be −10/80, or −12.5 percent. The price elasticity of demand would then be reported as 50/−12.5 = −4.

The difficulty with the method of computing percentage changes from the original values of the variables is that we get a different set of percentage changes depending on where we start. For example, if we start at point B and then move to point A, we get a quite different estimate of elasticity. The price and quantity at point B are $70 and 60 sweaters. In moving to point A, the price rises to $80 and the quantity demanded falls to 40 units. Computing percentage changes from point B gives a change in quantity demanded of −33.3 percent (or −20/60) and a change in price of 14.3 percent (or 10/70). The price elasticity of demand now seems to be −33.3/14.3 = −2.3.

If elasticity is to be a measure of response, it doesn't seem very satisfactory for it to yield different values between the same two points! We can solve this problem by measuring the percentage change between two points as the change in the variable divided by the *average* value of the variable between the two points. Thus, the percentage change in quantity between point A and point B in Exhibit 4-1 is computed relative to the average values at points A and B: (60 + 40)/2 = 50. The percentage change in quantity is thus 20/50, or 40 percent. The percentage change in price is considered relative to the average of the two prices: ($80 + 70)/2 = $75. We thus have a percentage change of −10/75, or −13.3 percent. The price elasticity of demand between points A and B is thus 40/−13.3 = −3.

This measure of elasticity, which is based on percentage changes relative to the average value of each variable between two points, is called **arc elasticity.** It is the method we shall use in computing elasticities of demand.

Using the arc elasticity method, the price elasticity of demand is computed using the average value of price, $\hat{P}$, and the average value of quantity demanded, $\hat{Q}$. We shall use the Greek letter Δ to mean "change in," so the change in quantity between two points is ΔQ and the change in price is ΔP. We can thus write the formula for the price elasticity of demand as

$$e_p = \frac{\frac{\Delta Q}{\hat{Q}}}{\frac{\Delta P}{\hat{P}}} \tag{3}$$

The price elasticity of demand between points A and B is thus

$$e_p = \frac{\frac{20}{50}}{\frac{-10}{75}} = -3$$

Now the elasticity value is the same no matter which direction we move on the demand curve in Exhibit 4-1. If we start at point B and move to point A, we have

$$e_p = \frac{\frac{-20}{50}}{\frac{10}{75}} = -3$$

Arc elasticity is computed by calculating percentage changes relative to the average value of each variable between two points.

The arc elasticity method gives us an estimate of elasticity. It gives the average value of elasticity over a large range of change, such as the movement between points A and B. For a precise computation of elasticity, we would need to consider the response of a dependent variable to an extremely small change in an independent variable; we would then solve for elasticity using calculus. The fact that arc elasticities are approximate suggests an important practical rule in calculating elasticities: we should consider only small changes in dependent variables. We can't apply the concept of elasticity to large changes with any great confidence.

Another argument for considering only small changes in computing price elasticities of demand will become evident in the next section. We'll investigate what happens to price elasticities as we travel along a linear demand curve.

Price Elasticities Along the Demand Curve

What happens to the price elasticity of demand when we travel along the demand curve? The answer depends on the nature of the demand curve itself. On a linear demand curve, such as the one in Exhibit 4-2, elasticity becomes smaller (in absolute value) as we travel downward and to the right. On certain nonlinear demand curves, however, elasticity is the same everywhere. Let's begin with the case of linear demand.

Changing Elasticities and Linear Demand

Exhibit 4-2 shows the same demand curve we saw in Exhibit 4-1. We've already calculated the price elasticity of demand between points A and B; it equals −3. Notice, however, that when we use the same method to compute the price elasticity of demand between other sets of points, our answer varies. For each of the pairs of points shown, the changes in price and quantity are the same (−$10 and 20 units, respectively). But at the high prices and low quantities on the upper part of the demand curve, the percentage change in quantity is relatively large while the percentage change in price is relatively small. The absolute value of

EXHIBIT 4-2

Computing Price Elasticities of Demand for a Linear Demand Curve

The price elasticity of demand varies between different pairs of points along a linear demand curve. The higher the price and the lower the quantity demanded, the greater the absolute value of the price elasticity of demand.

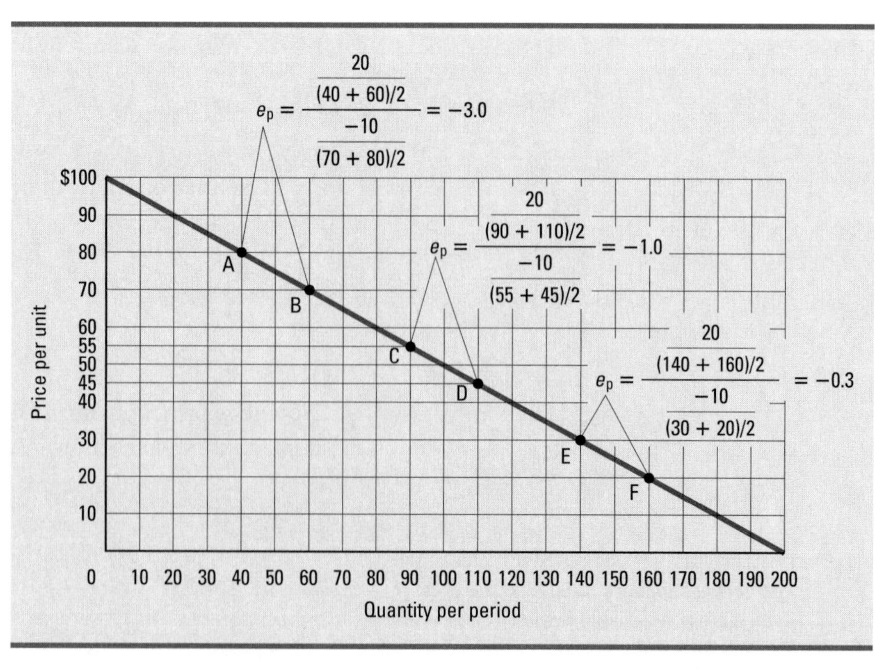

A constant price elasticity of demand curve is one whose price elasticity of demand is the same at every point on the curve.

the price elasticity of demand is thus relatively large. As we travel down the demand curve, equal changes in quantity represent smaller and smaller percentage changes while equal changes in price represent larger and larger percentage changes, and the absolute value of the elasticity measure declines. Between points C and D, for example, the price elasticity of demand is -1, and between points E and F the price elasticity of demand is -0.3. For any linear demand curve, the absolute value of the price elasticity of demand will fall as we travel down and to the right along the curve.

A Constant Price Elasticity Demand Curve

Exhibit 4-3 illustrates a nonlinear demand curve. The curve is based on Equation (4):

$$Q = \frac{10}{P} \qquad \textbf{(4)}$$

The values for P and Q given in the table in Exhibit 4-3 are based on this demand function as well.

Just as we did in Exhibit 4-2, we can compute the price elasticity of demand between various sets of points on the demand curve. Notice that all three of the price elasticities computed equal -1.0. Any demand curve given by $Q = K/P$, where K is some constant, will have a price elasticity of -1 throughout its range.

The demand curve in Exhibit 4-3 is a **constant price elasticity of demand curve;** its elasticity is the same at every point. Many of the empirical estimates that economists make of elasticity are consistent with a demand curve of this type.

EXHIBIT 4-3

The Price Elasticity of Demand

The demand curve is given by the equation $Q = 10/P$. The equation yields the combinations of prices and quantities shown in the table. The price elasticity of demand can be calculated between two points on the curve; the values shown equal -1.0. This demand curve exhibits constant elasticity of demand.

Point	A	B	C	D	E	F	G	H	I	J
Price	$10.00	$9.00	$8.00	$7.00	$6.00	$5.00	$4.00	$3.00	$2.00	$1.00
Quantity	1.00	1.11	1.25	1.43	1.67	2.00	2.50	3.33	5.00	10.00

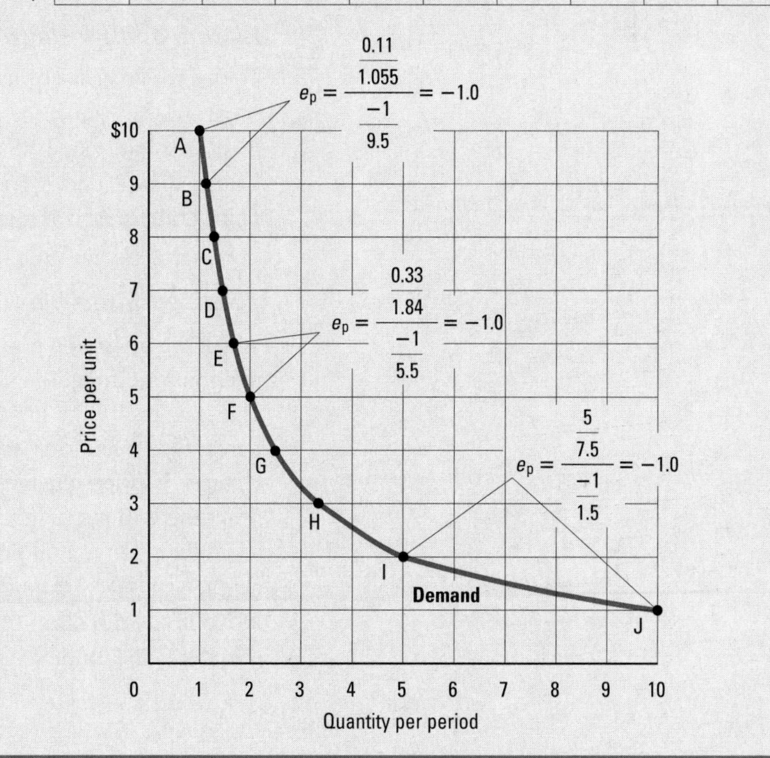

- If the absolute value of the price elasticity of demand is greater than 1, demand is **price elastic.**
- If the absolute value of the price elasticity of demand is equal to 1, demand is **unit price elastic.**
- If the absolute value of the price elasticity of demand is less than 1, demand is **price inelastic.**

The Price Elasticity of Demand and Changes in Total Spending

Suppose the price of gasoline increases. Will consumers' total spending on gasoline go up or down? The question is an important one. Oil companies will certainly want to know whether a price increase would cause spending to rise or fall. To assess the impact of the gasoline price increase on consumers, we need to know whether their spending on gasoline will rise or fall. In fact, determining the impact of a price change on total spending is crucial to the analysis of many problems in economics.

The problem in assessing the impact of a price change on total spending on a good or service is that a change in price always changes the quantity demanded in the opposite direction. An increase in price reduces the quantity demanded, and a reduction in price increases the quantity demanded. Because total spending is found by multiplying the price per unit times the quantity demanded, it isn't clear whether a change in price will cause total spending to rise or fall.

Suppose, for example, that 1,000 gallons of gasoline per day are demanded at a price of $1.25 per gallon. Total spending for gasoline thus equals $1,250 per day. If an increase in the price of gasoline to $1.40 reduces the quantity demanded to 950 gallons per day, total spending rises to $1,330 per day.

Now consider another price increase. Suppose 1,000 cans of frozen orange juice per month are demanded at a price of $1 per can. Total spending for orange juice equals $1,000 per month. If an increase in the price of orange juice to $1.10 reduces quantity demanded to 880 cans per month, total expenditures for orange juice fall to $968 per month.

In our first example, an increase in price increased spending on a good. In the second, a price hike reduced spending. Can we find a rule to determine how a price change will affect total spending? We can, and the key to the rule is the price elasticity of demand.

Elastic, Unit Elastic, and Inelastic Demand

To determine how a price change will affect total spending on a good or service, economists place price elasticities of demand into three categories, based on their absolute value. If the absolute value of the price elasticity of demand is greater than 1, demand is termed **price elastic.** If it is equal to 1, demand is **unit price elastic.** And if it is less than 1, demand is **price inelastic.**

Relating Elasticity to Total Spending

When the price of a good or service changes, the quantity demanded changes in the opposite direction. Total spending will move in the direction of the variable that changes by the larger percentage. If quantity demanded changes by a larger percentage than price, total spending will change in the direction of the quantity change. If price changes by a larger percentage than quantity demanded, total spending will move in the direction of the price change.

When demand is price inelastic, a change in price results in a smaller percentage change in quantity demanded. That implies that total spending will move in the direction of the price change: a reduction in price will reduce total spending, and an increase in price will increase it.

Case in Point

Drought Boosts Farm Revenue

Wheat farmers suffered in 1988 from the worst drought since the Great Depression—and had a record year for total wheat sales.

In terms of the model of demand and supply, the drought reduced supply. It shifted the supply curve to S_2, raising the equilibrium price to P_2 and reducing the quantity of wheat demanded to Q_2.

The demand for wheat is inelastic. Estimates of the price elasticity of demand for wheat range between -0.3 and -0.7. When demand is inelastic and price rises, total spending rises. Total spending by consumers equals total revenue for producers; an increase in price thus boosts farm revenues.

The drought shifted the supply curve for wheat to the left. Wheat production plunged 14 percent in 1988. Inelastic demand meant prices rose by an even greater percentage; the average price per bushel of wheat soared from $2.57 in 1987 to $3.72 in 1988, an increase of 45 percent. The larger percentage increase in prices raised total revenues for wheat farmers.

Producers of other grains generally had a similar experience. The prices of agricultural goods rose, and equilibrium quantities fell. The demand for most farm products is inelastic—higher prices and smaller quantities mean greater revenues.

Of course, farmers whose crops were wiped out by the 1988 drought didn't have a good year. But for farmers taken as a group, a bad year for production meant a good year for farm revenues.

Source: Department of Agriculture data.

A farmer and his son examine their drought-stricken wheat field.

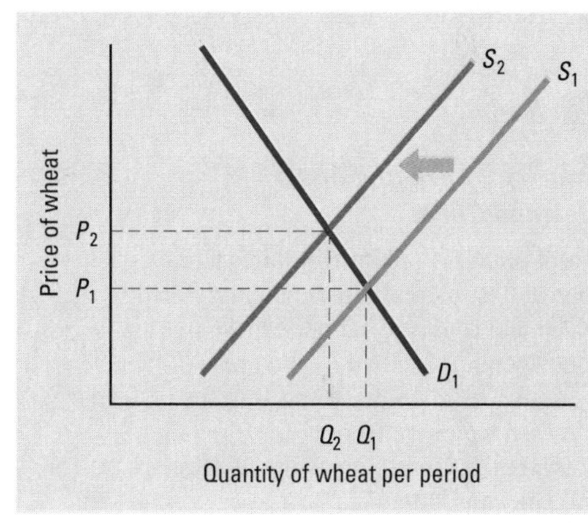

Consider the price elasticity of demand for gasoline. We calculate this value for the price and quantity changes already given:

$$e_p = \frac{\frac{-50}{975}}{\frac{0.15}{1.325}} = \frac{-5.13\%}{11.32\%} = -0.45$$

The demand for gasoline is price inelastic, and total spending moves in the direction of the price change. When price rises, total spending rises.

When demand is price elastic, a change in price results in a larger percentage change in quantity demanded. That implies that total spending will move in the direction of the quantity change: a reduction in price will increase total spending, and an increase in price will reduce it.

Now consider the case of orange juice. We can compute the price elasticity of demand for orange juice as

$$e_p = \frac{\frac{-120}{940}}{\frac{0.10}{1.05}} = \frac{-12.77\%}{9.52\%} = -1.3$$

Demand is price elastic, and total spending moves in the direction of the quantity change. Quantity demanded and total spending fall.

A demand curve can also be used to show changes in total spending. Exhibit 4-4 shows the demand curve from Exhibits 4-1 and 4-2. At point A, total spending for sweaters is given by the area of a rectangle drawn with point A in the upper right-hand corner and the origin in the lower left-hand corner. The height of the rectangle is price; its width is quantity. When we reduce the price and move to point B, the rectangle showing total spending becomes shorter and wider. Notice that the area gained in moving to the rectangle at B is greater than the area lost; total spending rises. Recall from Exhibit 4-2 that demand is elastic between points A and B. In general, demand is elastic in the upper half of any linear demand curve, so total spending moves in the direction of the quantity change.

EXHIBIT 4-4

Changes in Total Spending and a Linear Demand Curve

Moving from point A to point B implies a reduction in price and an increase in the quantity demanded. Demand is elastic between these two points. Total spending, shown by the areas of the rectangles drawn from points A and B to the origin, rises. When we move from point E to point F, which is in the inelastic region of the demand curve, total spending falls.

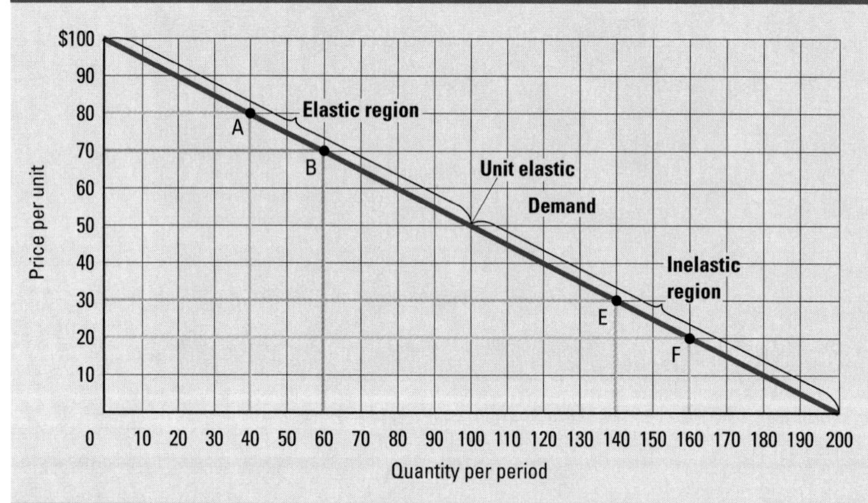

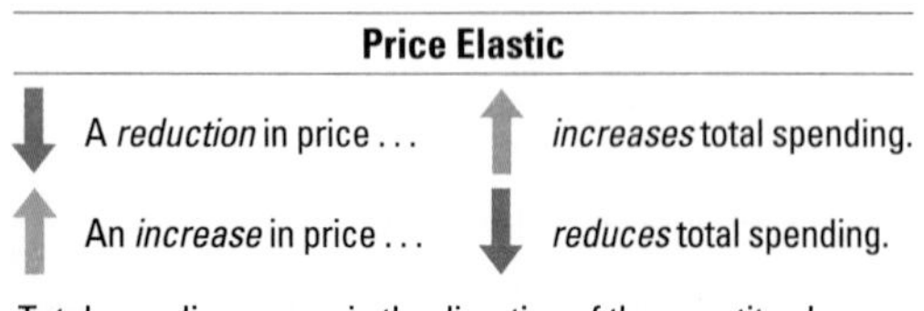

Price Inelastic

An *increase* in price . . . *increases* total spending.

A *reduction* in price . . . *reduces* total spending.

Total spending moves in the direction of the price change.

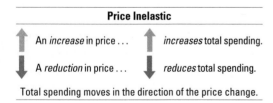

A movement from point E to point F also shows a reduction in price and an increase in quantity demanded. This time, however, we are in an inelastic region of the demand curve. Total spending now moves in the direction of the price change—it falls. Notice that the rectangle drawn from point F is smaller in area than the rectangle drawn from point E.

We've noted the reason a linear demand curve is likely to be more elastic in its upper half, where prices are relatively high and quantities relatively low, than in its lower half, where prices are relatively low and quantities relatively high. We can be even more specific. For any linear demand curve, demand will be price elastic in the upper half of the curve and price inelastic in its lower half.

But what happens to total spending in response to a price change when demand is unit price elastic? In such a case, the percentage change in quantity demanded offsets the percentage change in price, and total spending remains unchanged. Exhibit 4-5 shows the demand curve for which the price elasticity of demand was computed in Exhibit 4-3. Recall that the price elasticity of demand

EXHIBIT 4-5

Total Spending and Unit Price Elastic Demand

Here is the same demand curve we encountered in Exhibit 4-3. It shows a constant elasticity of demand and is unit price elastic. Notice that total spending (*TS*), as given by the areas of rectangles drawn from points A, F, and J, is always the same. Indeed, the area of a rectangle drawn from any point on the demand curve will equal $10. A change in price does not affect total spending when demand is unit price elastic.

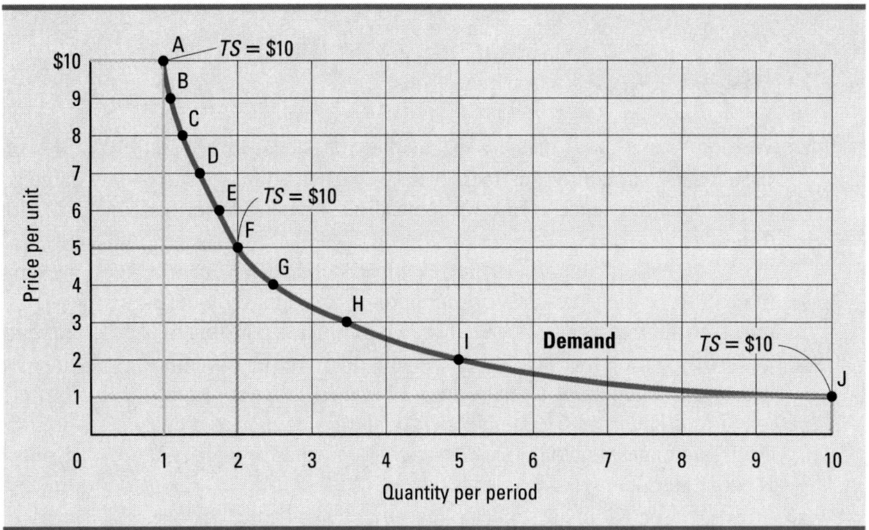

was −1 between various pairs of points. This demand curve shows a constant elasticity of demand; it is also unit price elastic. Total spending *(TS)* is the same at every point on the demand curve (i.e., *TS*=$10 at each point). A linear demand curve is unit price elastic at its midpoint.

Determinants of the Price Elasticity of Demand

The greater the absolute value of the price elasticity of demand, the greater the responsiveness of quantity demanded to a price change. Depending on whether demand is elastic, unit elastic, or inelastic, total spending may rise, remain unchanged, or fall in response to a price change. What determines whether demand is more or less elastic? The most important determinants of the price elasticity of demand for a good or service are the availability of substitutes, the importance of the item in household budgets, and time.

Availability of Substitutes

The price elasticity of demand for a good or service will be greater in absolute value if many close substitutes are available for it. If there are lots of substitutes for a particular good or service, then it's easy for consumers to switch to those substitutes when there is a price increase for that good or service. Suppose, for example, that the price of Ford automobiles goes up. There are many close substitutes for Fords—Chevrolets, Chryslers, Toyotas, and so on. The availability of close substitutes tends to make the demand for Fords more elastic.

If a good has no close substitutes, its demand is likely to be somewhat less elastic. There are no close substitutes for water, for example. The price elasticity of demand for water is generally estimated to be about −0.5. It is inelastic.

Importance in Household Budgets

One reason price changes affect quantity demanded is that they change how much a consumer can buy; a change in the price of a good or service affects the purchasing power of a consumer's income and thus affects the amount of a good the consumer will buy. This effect is stronger when a good or service is important in a typical household's budget.

A change in the price of clothing, for example, is more important in a household budget than a change in the price of straight pins. The clothing price change

Case in Point: Elasticity and the Drug War

We don't have good data on the market for illegal drugs, but economists who study this market have reached some tentative conclusions about the nature of demand elasticities for various drugs.

In the case of marijuana, for example, demand is generally thought to be inelastic. This presumption is based partly on estimates of the impact of price changes on marijuana consumption and partly on the fact that the drug's low price makes it a minor item in the budgets of casual users. Harvard University economist Mark Kleiman, a leading expert on the economics of illegal drugs, estimates that the price elasticity of demand for marijuana is no greater than −0.4.

Professor Kleiman suggests that the elasticity for cocaine, however, is much greater. Part of the reason for that greater elasticity is the drug's higher price; a "hit" of cocaine costs about 5 times as much as a hit of marijuana. Expenditures on cocaine thus make up a bigger share of consumer budgets than expenditures on marijuana. Kleiman estimates that the demand for cocaine is unit price elastic, or −1.

Professor Kleiman thinks the different elasticities suggest very different strategies for enforcement efforts aimed at restricting the supply of the two drugs. If law enforcement officials succeed in reducing the supply of a drug, it will shift the supply curve to the left, raising price. That would increase total expenditures on marijuana, increasing the revenues earned by dealers. Unit elastic demand for cocaine, however, means total expenditures would be unchanged. Since the enforcement efforts would also increase the costs to cocaine dealers, their profits would fall. Professor Kleiman concludes that enforcement efforts aimed at restricting marijuana sales should be reduced, whereas those aimed at cocaine should be increased.

Source: Timothy Tregarthen, "The Drug War: Battling Supply and Demand," *The Margin* 5(3) (January/February 1990):17–22.

therefore produces a stronger income effect, and a stronger impact on quantity demanded, than a change in the price of pins. We can thus conclude that the greater the importance of an item in household budgets, the greater the absolute value of the price elasticity of demand is likely to be.

Time

Suppose the price of electricity rises tomorrow morning. What will happen to the quantity demanded?

The answer depends in large part on how much time we allow for a response. If we're interested in the reduction in quantity demanded by tomorrow afternoon, we can expect that the response will be very small. But if we give consumers a year to respond to the price change, we can expect the response to be much greater. Some will switch fuels, for example, from electricity to gas for appliances such as stoves and heaters. We therefore expect that the absolute value of the price elasticity of demand will be greater when more time is allowed for consumer responses.

Consider the price elasticity of gasoline demand. Economists James M. Griffin of Texas A&M University and Henry B. Steele of the University of Houston estimate that the price elasticity of demand for gasoline is −0.1 when consumers are given no more than a month to respond to a price change. Demand is very inelastic because a short period of time doesn't give consumers much of a chance to respond. Over longer periods, they may switch to more fuel-efficient cars and make greater use of public transit systems. Over very long periods, many people may even move. If gasoline is getting cheaper, consumers may move further from work to escape city congestion; if gasoline prices are rising, they may move closer to work to economize on gasoline. Professors Griffin and Steele estimate that over a period of several years, the demand for gasoline becomes elastic, with a price elasticity of −1.5.[1]

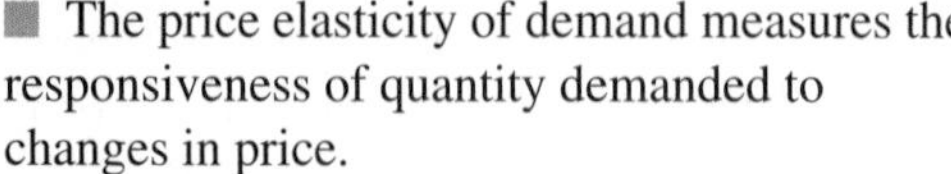

- The price elasticity of demand measures the responsiveness of quantity demanded to changes in price.
- The price elasticity of demand is calculated by dividing the percentage change in quantity demanded by the percentage change in price. It is always negative.
- Demand is inelastic if the absolute value of the price elasticity of demand is less than 1; it is unit elastic if the absolute value is equal to 1; and it is elastic if the absolute value is greater than 1.
- When demand is price inelastic, total spending moves in the direction of the price change. When demand is unit price elastic, total spending doesn't change in response to a price change. When demand is price elastic, total spending moves in the direction of the quantity change.
- The absolute value of the price elasticity of demand is greater when substitutes are available, when the good is important in household budgets, and when buyers have more time to adjust to changes in the price of the good.

[1] See James M. Griffin and Henry B. Steele, *Energy Economics and Policy* (New York: Academic Press, 1980), p. 232.

Case in Point: Commuter Rail Elasticities Rise with Time

The introduction to this chapter asked you to imagine you are the director of a commuter rail system serving a large city, and your finance officer has just advised you that the system faces a deficit. Your board doesn't want you to cut service, which means that you can't cut costs. Your only hope is to increase revenue.

Would a fare increase boost revenue? Higher fares will mean higher revenues, but only if the demand for rail transit is inelastic. A study of demand for the Southeastern Pennsylvania Transportation Authority by economist Richard Voith, of the Federal Reserve Bank of Philadelphia, suggests it is—but only for a few months.

Mr. Voith calculates that a 25-cent increase in fares would produce an immediate increase of $9,500 per day in total revenues of the system. That increase in total revenue suggests inelastic demand; Mr. Voith estimates that the elasticity of demand, computed immediately after a price change, is −0.62. But as consumers have more time to adjust, they make other arrangements. Some organize car pools. Ultimately, some will move. As consumers adjust to the fare increase, the quantity demanded will fall further, and the revenue gains produced by the fare increase will dwindle. Mr. Voith says that within a year of the fare increase, revenues will have fallen—demand will have become elastic. Mr. Voith estimates that, given several years to adjust, the price elasticity of demand for the Pennsylvania system, which serves Philadelphia, is −1.59.

The fact that demand is inelastic over short periods and elastic over longer ones, Mr. Voith says, explains a common problem for transit systems. Faced with budget difficulties, managers raise fares. For a brief time, that increases revenue. But eventually demand becomes elastic and the fare increase pushes total revenue down.

Source: Richard Voith, "The Long-Run Elasticity of Demand for Commuter Rail Transportation," *Journal of Urban Economics* 30 (November 1991): 360–372, and personal interview.

Other Measures of the Responsiveness of Demand

Although the response of quantity demanded to changes in price is the most widely used measure of elasticity, economists are interested in the response to changes in other determinants of demand as well. Two of the most important measures show how demand responds to changes in income and to changes in the prices of other goods and services.

Income Elasticity of Demand

One of the key determinants of the demand for any good or service is the level of consumer income. We measure the **income elasticity of demand,** e_y, as the percentage change in quantity demanded at a given price divided by the percentage change in income that produced the demand change, ceteris paribus.

$$e_y = \frac{\text{percentage change in } Q}{\text{percentage change in } y}$$

The **income elasticity of demand** (e_y) is the percentage change in quantity demanded divided by the percentage change in income, ceteris paribus.

Here y stands for consumer income. A positive income elasticity of demand means that income and demand move in the same direction—an increase in income increases demand, and a reduction in income reduces demand. As we

Case in Point Beer Taxes and Teen Deaths

Automobile accidents are the leading cause of death for people under age 35 in the United States, and alcohol consumption is involved in more than half of fatal highway accidents.

Economists Michael Grossman of the City University of New York and Henry Saffer of Kean College of New Jersey estimated the relationship between beer prices and highway death rates for young people by linking two elasticities. First they estimated the price elasticity of beer consumption by young people; then they estimated the elasticity of the highway death rate with respect to beer consumption. Combining these two elasticities, they concluded that for people age 18 to 24, the elasticity of the death rate with respect to an increase in the price of beer is −1.3. There is thus a negative relationship between the two variables. On the basis of this estimate of elasticity, we could predict that a 10 percent increase in the price of beer would lead to a 13 percent reduction in the highway death rate for young people. But what if young people merely shifted their consumption of alcohol to other types of beverages?

The economists used another cross price elasticity to rule out the possibility that higher beer taxes would lead young people to drink more wine or distilled liquor. They estimated the cross price elasticities of demand for wine and for distilled liquor by young people with respect to the price of beer and found these values are zero. For young people taken as a group, beer appears not to be a substitute for other alcoholic beverages. The economists concluded that higher beer prices would not lead young people to consume more wine or distilled liquor. It thus appears that higher taxes on beer would significantly reduce highway deaths among this age group.

Source: Michael Grossman and Henry Saffer, "Beer Taxes, the Legal Drinking Age, and Youth Motor Vehicle Fatalities," *Journal of Legal Studies* 16(2) (June 1987); 351–374.

saw in Chapter 3, a good whose demand rises as income rises is called a normal good.

Most goods and services are normal, and thus their income elasticities are positive. Goods and services for which demand is likely to move in the same direction as income include housing, seafood, rock concerts, and medical services.

In an examination of the demand for state colleges in New York, New Jersey, and Pennsylvania, for example, four economists found a strong link between family income and the number of students seeking to attend school. The economists, Rajindar Koshal and Manjulika Koshal of Ohio University, Jules Levine of Long Island University, and Daniel Lindley, who is now practicing law, estimated that the income elasticity of demand for enrollment in public colleges and universities in the three states was 1.67. That means that a 10 percent increase in incomes could be expected to increase the demand for public institutions of higher education in the three states by 16.7 percent.[2] The positive income elasticity implies that a college education is a normal good.

If a good or service is inferior, then an increase in income reduces demand for the good. That implies a negative income elasticity of demand. Cigarette consumption falls as income rises; cigarettes are thus an example of an inferior good. Other goods and services for which the income elasticity of demand is likely to be negative include used clothing, beans, and intercity bus service.

When we compute the income elasticity of demand, we are looking at the change in the quantity demanded at a specific price. We are thus dealing with a change that shifts the demand curve. An increase in income shifts the demand for a normal good to the right; it shifts the demand for an inferior good to the left.

[2] "The Demand for Higher Education in Three Mid-Atlantic States," *New York Economic Review* 18 (Fall 1988): 3–20.

The **cross price elasticity of demand** for one good or service equals the percentage change in quantity demanded for that good or service divided by the percentage change in price of a related good or service.

Checklist

- The income elasticity of demand reflects the responsiveness of demand to changes in income. It is the percentage change in quantity demanded divided by the percentage change in income, ceteris paribus.
- Income elasticity is positive for normal goods and negative for inferior goods.
- The cross price elasticity of demand measures the way demand for one good or service responds to changes in the price of another. It is the percentage change in the quantity demanded of one good or service at a specific price divided by the percentage change in the price of a related good or service, ceteris paribus.
- Cross price elasticity is positive for substitutes, negative for complements, and zero for goods or services whose demands are unre-

Cross Price Elasticity of Demand

We saw in Chapter 3 that the demand for a good or service is affected by the prices of related goods or services. A reduction in the price of stereo speakers, for example, would increase the demand for CD players, suggesting that speakers are a complement of CD players. A reduction in the price of CD players, however, would reduce the demand for cassette players, suggesting that CD players are a substitute for cassette players.

The measure economists use to describe the responsiveness of demand for a good or service to changes in other prices is called the **cross price elasticity of demand,** e_{cp}. It equals the ratio of the percentage change in the quantity demanded of one good or service at a specific price to the percentage change in the price of a related good or service. We are varying the price of a related good when we consider the cross price elasticity of demand, so the response of quantity demanded is shown as a shift in the demand curve.

The cross price elasticity of the demand for good A with respect to the price of good B is given by

$$e_{cp} = \frac{\text{percentage change in } Q_A}{\text{percentage change in } P_B}$$

Cross price elasticities of demand define whether two goods are substitutes, complements, or unrelated. If two goods are substitutes, an increase in the price of one will lead to an increase in the demand for the other—the cross price elasticity of demand is positive. If two goods are complements, an increase in the price of one will lead to a reduction in the demand for the other—the cross price elasticity of demand is negative. If two goods are unrelated, a change in the price of one will not affect the demand for the other—the cross price elasticity of demand is zero.

A Look Back—And a Look Ahead

This chapter introduced a new tool: the concept of elasticity. Elasticity is a measure of the degree to which one variable, a dependent variable, responds to a change in an independent variable. It is the ratio of the percentage change in a dependent variable to the percentage change in an independent variable, ceteris paribus.

Elasticity measures are particularly useful in working with demand. The most widely used elasticity measure is the price elasticity of demand, which reflects the responsiveness of quantity demanded to price changes. Demand is said to be elastic if the absolute value of the price elasticity of demand is greater than 1, unit elastic if it is equal to 1, and inelastic if it is less than 1. The price elasticity of demand is useful in forecasting the response of quantity demanded to price changes; it is also useful for predicting the impact a price change will have on total spending. Total spending moves in the direction of the quantity change if demand is price elastic, it moves in the direction of the price change if demand is price inelastic, and it does not change if demand is unit price elastic.

Two other elasticity measures commonly used in conjunction with demand are income elasticity and cross price elasticity. The signs of these elasticity measures play important roles. A positive income elasticity tells us that a good is normal; a negative income elasticity tells us the good is inferior. A positive cross price elasticity tells us that two goods are substitutes; a negative cross price elasticity tells us they are complements.

This chapter is the first in a series in Part Two on basic tools of microeconomic analysis. In Chapter 5, we'll examine the nature of maximizing behavior and explore its relationship to economic efficiency. Then in Chapters 6 and 7 we'll turn to the theory of consumer behavior and the theory of production and cost. Later, we'll apply the tools introduced in Part Two to various types of markets in the economy.

Terms and Concepts for Review

Arc elasticity

Constant price elasticity of demand curve

Cross price elasticity of demand

Elasticity

Income elasticity of demand

Price elastic

Price elasticity of demand

Price inelastic

Unit price elastic

For Discussion

1. Explain why the price elasticity of demand is always a negative number.
2. Economists Dale Heien and Cathy Roheim Wessells reported in the May 1988 issue of the *American Journal of Agricultural Economics* that the price elasticity of demand for fresh milk is −0.63 and the price elasticity of demand for cottage cheese is −1.1. Why do you think the elasticity estimates differ?
3. The price elasticity of demand for health care has been estimated to be −0.2. Characterize this demand as elastic, unit elastic, or inelastic. The text argues that the greater the importance of an item in consumer budgets, the greater its elasticity. Health care costs account for a relatively large share of household budgets. How could the price elasticity of demand for health care be such a small number?
4. Suppose you are able to organize an alliance that includes all farmers. They agree to follow the group's instructions with respect to the quantity of agricultural products they produce. What might the group seek to do? Why?
5. Suppose you're the chief executive officer of a firm, and you have been planning to reduce your prices. Your marketing manager reports that the price elasticity of demand for your product is −0.65. How will this news affect your plans?
6. Suppose the price elasticity of demand for wheat is −0.7 and that farmers have an unusually good year—the wheat harvest is higher than ever. What will happen to the total revenues received by wheat farmers?
7. Suppose the income elasticity of the demand for beans is −0.8. Interpret this number.
8. Transportation economists generally agree that the cross price elasticity of demand for automobile use with respect to the price of bus fares is about zero. Explain what this number means.
9. The Case in Point on beer taxes and highway deaths suggests that a higher tax on beer would save the lives of young people. Should taxes therefore be raised?
10. Suppose the Southeastern Pennsylvania Transportation Authority (described in the Case in Point about commuter rail) lowers its fares. What will happen to its total revenues in the next few weeks? In the next few years? Explain.

Problems

1. Compute the price elasticity of demand between points B and C and between points D and E in Exhibit 4-2. What happens?
2. Consider the following quote from the July 8, 1993 issue of *The Wall Street Journal:* "A bumper crop of oranges in Florida last year drove down orange prices. As juice marketers' costs fell, they cut prices by as much as 15%. That was enough to tempt some value-oriented customers: unit volume of frozen juices actually rose about 6% during the quarter." Given these numbers, and assuming there were no changes in demand shifters for frozen orange juice, what was the price elasticity of demand for frozen orange juice? What do you think happened to total spending on frozen orange juice? Why?

3. Suppose you are the manager of a restaurant that serves an average of 400 meals per day at an average price per meal of $20. On the basis of a survey, you've determined that reducing the price of an average meal to $18 would increase the quantity demanded to 450 per day. Compute the price elasticity of demand between these two points. Would you expect total revenues to rise or fall? Explain.

4. The text notes that, for any linear demand curve, demand is price elastic in the upper half and price inelastic in the lower half. Consider the following demand curves:

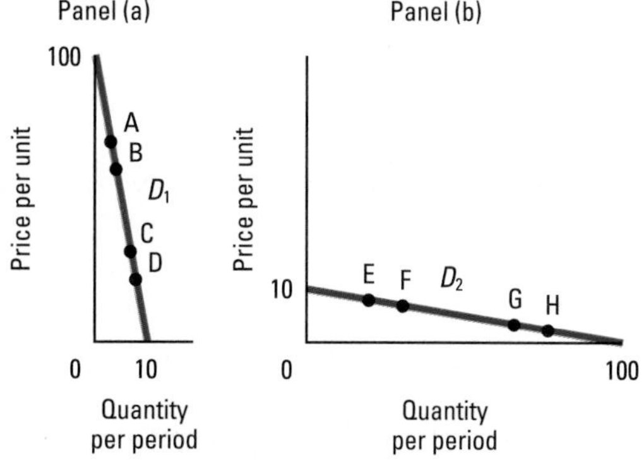

The tables below give the prices and quantities corresponding to each of the points shown on the two demand curves:

	Demand curve D_1 [Panel (a)]			Demand curve D_2 [Panel (b)]	
	Price	Quantity		Price	Quantity
A	80	2	E	8	20
B	70	3	F	7	30
C	30	7	G	3	70
D	20	8	H	2	80

a. Compute the price elasticity of demand between points A and B and between points C and D. Are your results consistent with the notion that a linear demand curve is price elastic in its upper half and price inelastic in its lower half?

b. Compute the price elasticity of demand between points E and F and between points G and H. Are your results consistent with the notion that a linear demand curve is price elastic in its upper half and price inelastic in its lower half?

5. a. Compare total spending at points A and B on D_1 in Panel (a) of Problem 4. Is your result consistent with your finding about the price elasticity of demand between those two points?

b. Compare total spending at points C and D on D_1 in Panel (a) of Problem 4. Is your result consistent with your finding about the price elasticity of demand between those two points?

c. Compare total spending at points E and F on D_2 in Panel (b) of Problem 4. Is your result consistent with your finding about the price elasticity of demand between those two points?

d. Compare total spending at points G and H on D_2 in Panel (b) of Problem 4. Is your result consistent with your finding about the price elasticity of demand between those two points?

5

Markets, Maximizers, and Efficiency

Chapter Objectives

After mastering the material in this chapter, you will be able to:

1. Explain the approach through which decisionmakers can obtain the maximum value from an objective.
2. Show how competitive markets guide the maximizing choices made by consumers and firms.
3. Explain the role of property rights in market exchange and the two characteristics property rights must have if exchange is to occur.
4. Explain why the forces of demand and supply are not likely to lead to the allocation of some resources to their best uses.
5. Explain the potential role of government in seeking to correct the misallocation of resources in the marketplace.

That which is every bodies business, is no bodies business.

Izaak Walton
The Compleat Angler
1653

What's Ahead

The marketplace can in some cases achieve wondrous results. In a world with billions of people, it can guide the allocation of resources to produce the goods and services people demand. As individuals and firms seek to maximize their respective utilities and profits, resources can be allocated in a way that not only serves the purpose of increasing individual welfare but improves social welfare as well.

But if the market has the potential to work all these wonders, why must we rely on the government to provide services such as national defense and police protection? Why does the market allow the pollution of our air and water? Why does it lead to the extinction of whole species and threaten the extinction of others? Why does the market work well in some cases but not in others?

We will discover the answers to these questions by pursuing three major themes. First, we will examine in more detail the nature of maximizing behavior. As we saw in Chapter 1, the assumption of maximizing behavior is one of the things that distinguishes the economic approach to the analysis of human behavior from other social sciences. In this chapter we'll first develop a rule for maximizing, one that we'll apply throughout our inquiry in microeconomic analysis. Second, we will examine conditions under which the individual pursuit of maximization produces a result that maximizes the welfare of society as a whole. Third, we'll examine cases in which it does not. We will find that government intervention may improve the efficiency of resource allocation in cases in which individual maximization does not serve social interests.

The Logic of Maximizing Behavior

To say that individuals maximize is to say that they pick some objective and then seek to maximize its value. A sprinter might want to maximize his or her speed; a television evangelist might seek to maximize the size of his or her viewing audience. Economists place special attention on two groups of maximizers: consumers and firms. We assume that consumers seek to maximize utility, the satisfaction they derive from their consumption of goods and services and from other activities they pursue. We assume that firms seek to maximize **profit,** which is the difference between their total revenues and their total costs. The costs involved in this concept of profit are computed in the economic sense—as the value of the best opportunity forgone.

The assumption of maximizing behavior lies at the heart of economic analysis. As we explore its implications, however, we must keep in mind the distinction between models and the real world. Our model assumes that individuals make choices in a way that achieves a maximum value for some clearly defined objective. As we'll see, this assumption gives us a set of underlying principles we can use to make predictions about the choices people make.

A model based on maximization uses the concept to simplify the analysis of choice. In using such a model, economists don't assume that people actually go through the calculations we will describe. What economists do argue is that people's behavior is broadly consistent with such a model. People may not consciously seek to maximize anything, but they behave as if they do.

We owe the insight of maximization to a nineteenth-century British economist, Jeremy Bentham. Bentham was seeking a scientific explanation for human behavior, one that would put the study of human choices on the same rational footing that discoveries in the natural sciences were giving to physics, chemistry, and biology. He proposed a theory that stated individuals make choices in order to promote pleasure and to avoid pain. In particular, he argued that we make our choices in a way that *maximizes*—Bentham invented the word—the degree of satisfaction we gain from our activities.

Adam Smith had already established the proposition that individuals act in their self-interest—and had shown how the marketplace can guide self-interest to the service of the public interest. But Bentham's pinpointing of the specific notion of maximizing suggested an even more fruitful approach to the general idea of choices based on self-interest. Economists of the nineteenth century were quick to apply mathematics to Bentham's idea of maximization, discovering in the process simple rules that govern all types of maximizing behavior.

In this chapter we will develop a rule of maximization for consumers' and firms' choices. Once we have established this rule, we will have a framework of analysis that will serve us throughout our exploration of microeconomic theory. Economists typically use the assumption of maximizing behavior in developing hypotheses about the ways in which people are likely to respond to changes in the economic environment.

The Analysis of Maximizing Behavior

The activities of consumers and firms have benefits, and they also have costs. We assume that given these benefits and costs, consumers and firms will make choices that maximize the **net benefit** of each activity—the total benefit of the activity minus the total cost. The specific measures of benefit and cost vary with the kind of choice being made. In the case of a firm's choices in production, for example, the total benefit of production is the revenue a firm receives from the product; the total cost is the cost the firm incurs by producing it. The net benefit is thus total revenue minus total cost, or profit.

- **Profit** is the difference between a firm's total revenue and its total economic costs.
- The **net benefit** of any activity is its total benefit minus its total cost.

- The **marginal benefit** of an activity is the amount by which an additional unit of the activity increases total benefit.
- The **marginal cost** of an activity is the amount by which an additional unit of the activity increases total cost.
- To maximize net benefit, apply the **marginal decision rule:** If the marginal benefit of an additional unit of an activity exceeds the marginal cost, the level of the activity should be increased. If the marginal benefit is less than the marginal cost, the level should be reduced. Net benefit is maximized at the quantity of the activity at which marginal benefit equals marginal cost.
- A **constraint** is a boundary that limits the range of choices an individual or a firm can make.

Economists argue that in order to maximize net benefit, consumers and firms evaluate each activity at the margin—they consider the marginal benefit and the marginal cost of the activity. The **marginal benefit** is the amount by which an additional unit of an activity increases its total benefit. The **marginal cost** is the amount by which an additional unit of an activity increases its total cost. To determine the quantity of any activity that will maximize its net benefit, we apply the **marginal decision rule:** If the marginal benefit of an additional unit of an activity exceeds the marginal cost, the quantity of the activity should be increased. If the marginal benefit is less than the marginal cost, the quantity should be reduced. Net benefit is maximized at the point at which marginal benefit equals marginal cost.

Maximizing choices must be made within the parameters imposed by some **constraint,** which is a boundary that limits the range of choices that can be made. A consumer may seek the greatest satisfaction possible—but must do so within the limits of his or her income. A firm can't produce beyond the limits of its production capacity. Economists assume that people maximize, but they do so within the limits imposed by the constraints they face.

The marginal decision rule forms the foundation for the structure economists use to analyze all choices. At first glance, it may seem that a consumer seeking satisfaction from, say, jelly beans has little in common with an entrepreneur seeking profit from the production of custom-designed semiconductors. But maximizing choices always follow the marginal decision rule—and that rule holds regardless of what is being maximized or who is doing the maximizing. To understand this rule, and to see how its application derives the maximum net benefit from an activity, we shall examine an effort by a student to maximize her test scores. After completing our analysis of this problem, we shall extend the marginal decision rule to other choices in the economy.

A Problem in Maximization

Suppose a college student, Laurie Phan, is faced with two midterms tomorrow, one in economics and another in accounting. She has already decided to spend 10 hours studying for the two examinations. This decision imposes a constraint on the problem. We'll consider how she might have chosen such a constraint later.

Ms. Phan has some notion of how study time in each subject will influence her score on each exam. Her objective is to allocate her 10 hours of study in such a way that she will achieve the highest combined score for the two exams, each of which will count 500 points. Exhibit 5-1 shows Ms. Phan's estimate of the relationship between study time and her final score.

EXHIBIT 5-1

Study Time and Estimated Exam Scores

Laurie Phan has estimated the relationship between the amount of time she studies for each of her upcoming exams and the scores she will receive. In each course, she expects that each additional hour of study time will add less to her total score than did the previous hour.

Expected Midterm Scores

	Hours Studying for Each Exam										
Course	0	1	2	3	4	5	6	7	8	9	10
Economics	249	289	328	365	399	429	453	470	479	480	473
Accounting	262	316	358	390	414	430	440	446	449	450	450

Two features of the table of expected exam scores shown in Exhibit 5-1 are particularly important. First, Ms. Phan's expected scores in economics and accounting generally increase, the more hours she devotes to each subject. Second, additional hours of study add less and less to her expected score in each subject. The first hour spent studying accounting adds 54 points to her expected score, the second adds 42, and the third adds 32. The tenth hour adds nothing to her expected accounting score. In economics, her score also rises by less and less with each additional hour of study. She apparently expects that a tenth hour of studying economics would be counterproductive; it reduces her expected score.

Ms. Phan has already decided to spend 10 hours studying for the two exams, so we can present the data in Exhibit 5-1 in a slightly different form. The top row in the table in Exhibit 5-2 shows Ms. Phan's expected score from studying economics, as before. The second row shows her expected score in accounting if she devotes the remaining time to studying accounting. (Each hour spent studying economics is an hour *not* spent studying accounting.) If she spends 1 hour studying economics (for an expected score of 289), she has 9 hours left to study accounting (for an expected score of 450). If she spends 10 hours studying economics (for an expected score of 473), she will have no time to study accounting (and will receive a score of 262). Because the table in Exhibit 5-2 shows her scores in the two courses for each possible study combination, we can add the total scores from each combination to determine how Ms. Phan should divide her time between the two courses. The table shows that she will receive the highest total score by spending 6 hours studying economics and 4 hours studying accounting.

EXHIBIT 5-2

Laurie Phan's Score-Maximizing Solution

Ms. Phan achieves the maximum expected total score by spending 6 hours studying economics and 4 hours studying accounting.

	Hours Studying Economics										
Course	0	1	2	3	4	5	**6**	7	8	9	10
Economics	249	289	328	365	399	429	**453**	470	479	480	473
Accounting	450	450	449	446	440	430	**414**	390	358	316	262
Total score	699	739	777	811	839	859	**867**	860	837	796	735

Calculating Total Benefits and Total Costs

Laurie Phan's problem has now been solved; she has determined the number of hours she should spend studying for each exam if she wishes to maximize her total score. Our purpose, however, is to show how the marginal decision rule applies to problems in maximization. Our next step is to recast the expected exam scores in Exhibit 5-2 in terms of the total benefits and total costs of Ms. Phan's study choices.

We measure the total benefit of studying economics as the amount by which Ms. Phan's expected score in economics exceeds what she would get if she didn't study at all. If she studies economics for one hour, she expects a score of 289—40 points higher than if she didn't study. The total benefit of studying for 1 hour is thus 40 points. If she studies for 2 hours, she expects a score of 328—79 points higher than if she didn't study at all. The total benefits of studying economics are recorded in the first row of Exhibit 5-3. The values given are her

EXHIBIT 5-3

The Benefits and Costs of Studying Economics

The table shows the total benefit and total cost of time Laurie Phan spends studying economics. Panel (a) shows that Ms. Phan's net benefit of economics study is maximized where total benefit exceeds total cost by the greatest amount—at 6 hours studying economics. The net benefit curve in Panel (b) shows the difference between total benefit and total cost at each level of economics study.

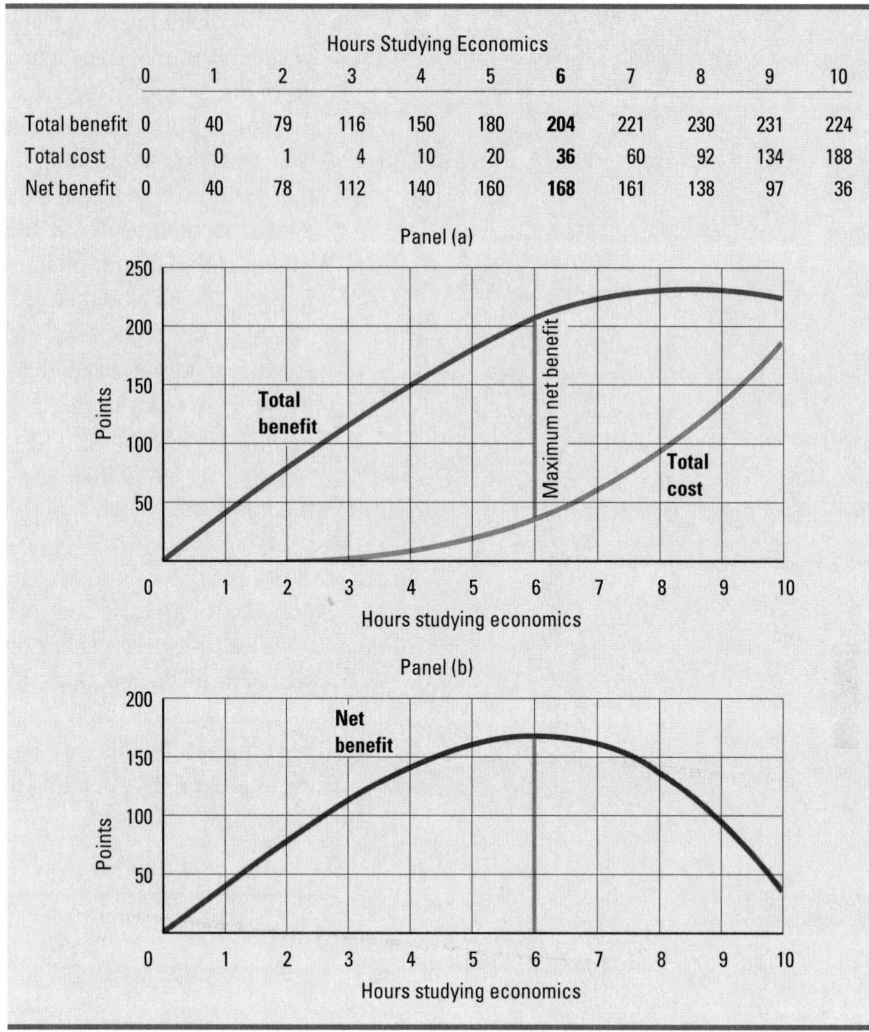

	Hours Studying Economics										
	0	1	2	3	4	5	6	7	8	9	10
Total benefit	0	40	79	116	150	180	**204**	221	230	231	224
Total cost	0	0	1	4	10	20	**36**	60	92	134	188
Net benefit	0	40	78	112	140	160	**168**	161	138	97	36

expected economics scores minus the 249 points she would expect to get if she didn't study. The values for total benefits are plotted in the same exhibit; notice that the total benefit of studying economics reaches a maximum value at 9 hours of study.

What is the cost to Ms. Phan of studying economics? Given that she has decided to spend 10 hours studying either economics or accounting, the cost of studying economics is the amount by which it reduces her potential score in accounting. We can determine that cost by reading the second row of the table in Exhibit 5-2. The first hour spent studying economics won't reduce her expected accounting score at all; it remains 450. From the point of view of her expected accounting score, the first hour of economics study is free! The second hour studying economics reduces her expected accounting score to 449—it has a total cost of 1 point. To complete the computation of total costs, we look at the expected accounting score associated with the time spent studying economics and see how many points Ms. Phan loses in accounting. If she studies economics for 5 hours, for example, she expects an accounting score of 430—20 points less than if she didn't study economics at all. The total cost of studying economics for five hours is thus a sacrifice of 20 points in her accounting score. Ms. Phan's estimates of total costs are reported and graphed in Exhibit 5-3.

The net benefit of studying economics—her total benefit minus her total cost—is reported in the third row of Exhibit 5-3. It is also the vertical distance between the total benefit and total cost curves in Exhibit 5-3. Ms. Phan's net benefit is maximized when she studies economics for 6 hours. Recall that 6 hours studying economics and 4 hours studying accounting was the solution that maximized her total score.

Maximizing at the Margin

We are now ready to apply the marginal decision rule. In terms of Laurie Phan's problem, this requires that we consider the marginal benefit and the marginal cost of studying economics. The marginal benefit of spending an additional hour studying economics is the increase in her expected economics score that comes with that hour of study. The marginal cost is the reduction in her expected accounting score associated with an additional hour of studying economics.

Exhibit 5-4 shows how marginal benefits and marginal costs can be computed from the total benefit and total cost figures of Exhibit 5-3. Notice that the marginal benefits and costs are listed *between* the columns for total benefit and total cost. That's because the marginal benefit or cost of a particular hour of study is the change in total cost as we go from one value to the next. When Ms. Phan increases her study time in economics from 4 hours to 5, for example, her total benefit increases by 30 points, so the marginal benefit of devoting the fifth

EXHIBIT 5-4

Marginal Benefits and Marginal Costs

The values for total benefit and total cost given in Exhibit 5-3 are reported again here. The marginal benefit (MB) and marginal cost (MC) of each increase in study time are also reported. Ms. Phan maximizes her possible score by studying economics up to the point that the marginal benefit of an additional hour of study equals the marginal cost.

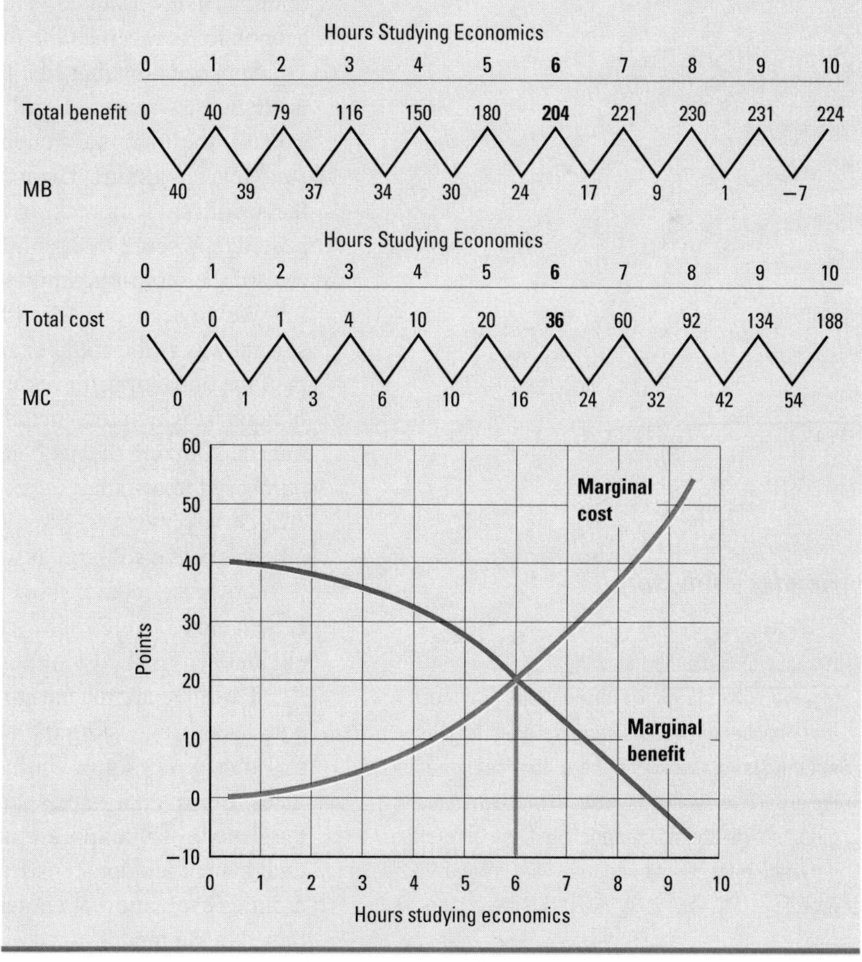

Hours Studying Economics	0	1	2	3	4	5	**6**	7	8	9	10
Total benefit	0	40	79	116	150	180	**204**	221	230	231	224
MB		40	39	37	34	30	24	17	9	1	−7

Hours Studying Economics	0	1	2	3	4	5	**6**	7	8	9	10
Total cost	0	0	1	4	10	20	**36**	60	92	134	188
MC		0	1	3	6	10	16	24	32	42	54

hour to studying economics is 30. The increase in total cost as she goes from 4 hours studying economics to 5 hours is the 10 points by which the extra hour of studying economics reduces her expected accounting score; that is the marginal cost of devoting the fifth hour to economics. The values for marginal benefit and marginal cost are plotted midway between the hour values on the graph in Exhibit 5-4. For example, the marginal benefit of increasing economics study from 4 hours to 5 hours, or 30 points, is plotted midway between 4 and 5 hours in the graph. That's because marginal benefit and cost occur as the quantity of an activity increases by 1 unit; it is the increase from 4 hours to 5 that generates the additional benefit and cost.

Exhibit 5-4 shows that by moving to the point at which the marginal benefit and marginal cost curves intersect, Ms. Phan achieves the allocation of study time—6 hours of economics and 4 of accounting—that maximizes her total score. To see more clearly why this is so, imagine that she had initially decided to spend 3 hours studying economics and 7 studying accounting. At 3 hours of studying economics, the marginal benefit of another hour of studying exceeds the marginal cost. An additional hour of economics study adds more to her economics score than it subtracts from her accounting score. That means she should spend a fourth hour on economics. At 4 hours, the marginal benefit of studying economics still exceeds the marginal cost, so it makes sense for her to spend the next hour studying economics. As long as the marginal benefit of another hour of studying economics exceeds the marginal cost, Ms. Phan should spend that hour on economics. Once the two curves intersect at 6 hours, further study of economics isn't warranted. The marginal benefit of the seventh hour of studying economics is less than the marginal cost.

Suppose now that Ms. Phan had initially decided to spend 8 hours studying economics. We see in Exhibit 5-4 that at this number of hours, the marginal cost exceeds the marginal benefit. That means that she is spending too much time studying economics. The marginal benefit of studying economics doesn't justify the sacrifice she is making in her accounting score. She could increase her expected total score by spending less time studying economics—and thus moving toward the score-maximizing solution of 6 hours of economics study.

We've seen that Ms. Phan could derive the score-maximizing solution in several ways. She could examine all the possible combinations of study time and pick the one that achieves the maximum total score. She could pick the number of hours at which total benefit exceeds total cost by the greatest possible amount, thus maximizing the net benefit of her study time. And finally, she could pick the number of hours studying economics at which the marginal benefit and marginal cost curves intersect. Most important, all these approaches are equivalent; they all achieve the solution at which her total expected score is maximized. Exhibit 5-5 shows the relationships among the total benefit and total cost curves, the net benefit curve (which shows total benefit minus total cost), and the marginal benefit and marginal cost curves.

The three approaches to Ms. Phan's problem in allocating her study time are equivalent, suggesting the importance of the marginal decision rule. A decision-maker may not know the nature of the total benefit and cost curves he or she faces. But it's not unreasonable to expect that he or she can determine whether the benefit of one more unit of an activity exceeds its cost. And, provided the total benefit and total cost curves have the same basic shapes as those in Exhibit 5-5, this evaluation of choices at the margin achieves the maximizing result predicted in the model.

Reader's Advisory !

It's easy to make the following mistake in thinking about the marginal decision rule: "Because *marginal* benefit equals *marginal* cost, *total* benefit equals *total* cost and there is no net benefit." It's crucial to avoid this error. In fact, when marginal benefit equals marginal cost, the difference between total benefit and total cost is maximized.

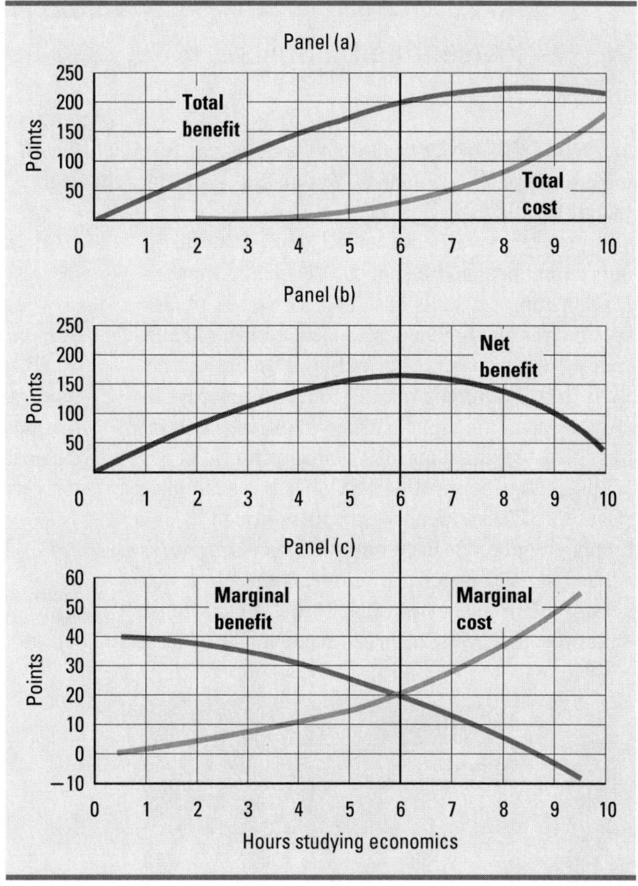

EXHIBIT 5-5

Maximizing Net Benefit

The total benefit of economics study exceeds total cost by the greatest amount, thus maximizing net benefit, at the same number of hours at which the marginal benefit and marginal cost curves intersect.

Decisions and Maximization: The General Rule

The arguments that apply to Laurie Phan's problem of maximization of her expected total exam score apply to all the maximization problems we will study in this text. We assume that in carrying out an activity aimed at achieving a particular objective, a decisionmaker will pursue additional units of the activity as long as the marginal benefit exceeds the marginal cost. If marginal cost exceeds marginal benefit, the decisionmaker should cut back on the activity. At the point where marginal benefit equals marginal cost, the net benefit of the activity is maximized (see Exhibit 5-5).

The marginal decision rule explains why consumers and firms pick the levels of the activities they pursue. Economists argue that the levels of economic activity we observe are not values chosen by accident. They emerge from maximizing choices. Given this perspective, we can predict how these choices will change when there is a change in the benefits and costs people confront in the market.

Case in Point: Preventing Oil Spills

Do we have enough oil spills in our oceans and waterways? It is a question that perhaps only economists would ask—and as economists we should ask it.

There is, of course, no virtue in an oil spill. It destroys wildlife, and fouls shorelines, and cleanup costs can be tremendous. However, preventing oil spills has costs as well—greater enforcement expenditures and higher costs to shippers of oil, and therefore higher costs to consumers. The only way to prevent oil spills completely is to stop shipping oil; that is a cost few people would accept. But what is the right balance between environmental protection and satisfying consumer demands for oil?

Vanderbilt University economist Mark Cohen has examined the U.S. Coast Guard's efforts to reduce oil spills through its enforcement of shipping regulations in coastal waters and on rivers. He focused on the costs and benefits of enforcement efforts in 1981. On the basis of the frequency of oil spills before the Coast Guard began its enforcement, Mr. Cohen estimated that the Coast Guard prevented 1,159,352 gallons of oil from being spilled in 1981.

A total of 824,921 gallons of oil were actually spilled in 1981; should the Coast Guard have attempted to prevent even more spillage? Mr. Cohen estimated that the marginal benefit of preventing one more gallon from being spilled was \$7.27 (\$3.42 in avoided cleanup cost, \$3 less in environmental damage, and \$0.85 worth of oil saved). The marginal cost of preventing one more gallon from being spilled was \$5.50. Mr. Cohen suggests that because the marginal benefit of more vigorous enforcement exceeded the marginal cost, even more vigorous Coast Guard efforts would have been justified.

Source: Mark A. Cohen, "The Costs and Benefits of Oil Spill Prevention and Enforcement," *Journal of Environmental Economics and Management* 13(2) (June 1986): 167–188.

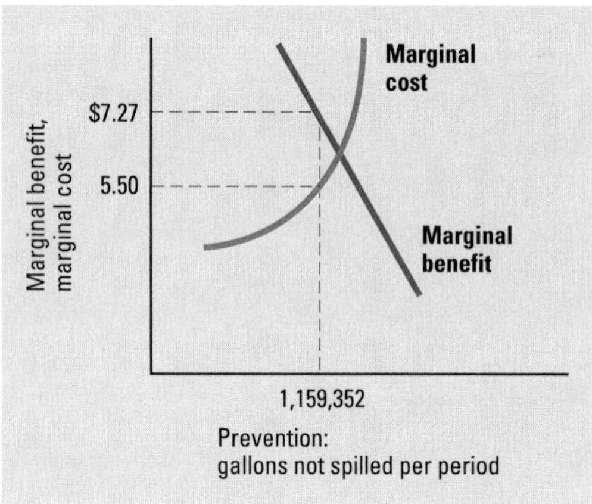

Consider Ms. Phan's problem of allocating her study time. We began that problem with the assumption that she was committed to spending 10 hours studying for her exams. But why 10 hours? The utility maximization assumption says that individuals allocate their time in a way that achieves the maximum utility possible. Suppose that Ms. Phan's most valuable alternative to study is training for a marathon next month, and that she has just learned that her chances of winning are quite good. That news increases the marginal benefit of training and thus increases the marginal cost of study time. The marginal decision rule predicts that she'll study less and train more.

We can also use the marginal decision rule in questions of public policy. How much police protection should we have? How much should we spend on education? How clean should we make our air? The answer in each case, assuming that we seek to maximize net benefit, is that each activity should be expanded up to the point at which the marginal benefit of an additional unit equals the marginal cost.

Checklist ✓

- Economists assume that decisionmakers make choices in a way that maximizes the value of some objective.
- Maximization involves determining the change in total benefit and the change in total cost associated with each unit of an activity. These changes are called marginal benefit and marginal cost, respectively.
- If the marginal benefit of an activity exceeds the marginal cost, the decisionmaker will gain by increasing the activity.
- If the marginal cost of an activity exceeds the marginal benefit, the decisionmaker will gain by reducing the activity.
- The net gain from an activity is maximized at the point at which the marginal benefit of the activity equals the marginal cost.

Maximizing and Efficiency in the Marketplace

Decisionmakers who apply the marginal decision rule achieve the greatest net benefit from an activity for themselves. But how about society? Does a world of individual maximizers achieve the maximum net benefit for society? The answer to that question is a qualified yes. Under some conditions, individuals who maximize their own net benefits achieve an allocation of resources that maximizes the net benefits of economic activity to society.

When the net benefits of all economic activities are maximized, economists say the allocation of resources is **efficient.** If net benefits are not maximized, the allocation of resources is **inefficient.** An inefficient allocation of resources means that society is not getting all that it could from the scarce resources at its command.

We saw in Chapter 2 that efficiency in production requires that resources be allocated according to the principle of comparative advantage. If resources are not allocated on this basis, it will be possible to reallocate them in a way that increases the production of all goods and services. Such a change would clearly follow the marginal decision rule—its benefits would exceed its costs. An inefficient allocation, as defined here, thus includes inefficiency in production. We'll see in this chapter that there can be other sources of inefficiency as well.

Achieving Efficiency

Suppose you have gone to the grocery store to purchase tomatoes. We've already learned something remarkable about that decision: you can be confident that you'll find tomatoes available once you get there. That's because the price of tomatoes is likely to move quickly to the equilibrium price. The equilibrium price of tomatoes is determined by the intersection of demand and supply and thus ensures that the quantity supplied will match the quantity demanded. One effect of the equilibrium price of tomatoes, then, is that there will be neither surpluses nor shortages of tomatoes.

- An **efficient** allocation of resources is one that achieves the maximum net benefit from all activities.
- An **inefficient** allocation of resources is one that does not achieve the maximum net benefit from one or more activities.

The equilibrium price of tomatoes contains information. Suppose you find that the price of tomatoes is 69 cents per pound. Assuming that the price is determined by demand and supply in a competitive market as shown by Panel (a) in Exhibit 5-6, the price tells you that the marginal cost of making a pound of tomatoes available to you at that time and at that price was 69 cents. This marginal

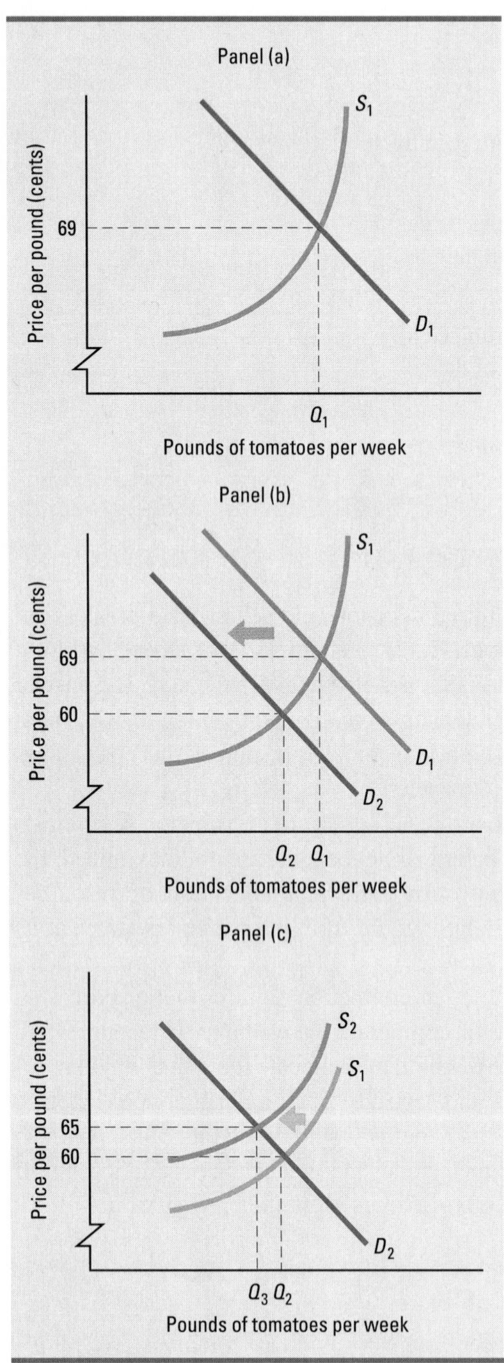

cost is considered in the economic sense—the price of 69 cents informs you that 69 cents' worth of other goods and services didn't get produced in order to make an additional pound of tomatoes available to you.

On what basis can we presume that the price of a pound of tomatoes equals its marginal cost? The answer lies in our marginal decision rule. Profit-maximizing tomato producers will produce more tomatoes as long as their marginal benefit exceeds their marginal cost. What is the marginal benefit to a producer of an extra pound of tomatoes? It is the price that the producer will receive. What is the marginal cost? It is the value of what must be given up to produce an extra pound of tomatoes. Producers maximize profit by expanding production up to the point at which their marginal cost of producing tomatoes equals their marginal benefit, which is the market price. The price of 69 cents thus reflects the marginal cost to society of making an additional pound of tomatoes available.

As a consumer, then, you face a price of tomatoes that signals their marginal cost. You will purchase tomatoes as long as your marginal benefit exceeds your own marginal cost—the 69 cents you must pay for the tomatoes. Your decision to purchase the tomatoes thus sends a signal of its own—to producers. You are telling them that your benefit from the tomatoes exceeded the value of what had to be given up to produce them. Your purchase ratifies the decisions of producers to forgo producing other goods and services in order to produce tomatoes.

At the equilibrium price and output of tomatoes, then, the marginal benefit of tomatoes to consumers, as reflected by the price they are willing to pay, equals the marginal cost of producing tomatoes. Where marginal benefit equals marginal cost, net benefit is maximized. The equilibrium quantity of tomatoes, as determined by demand and supply, is efficient.

But what if you, and a lot of other consumers, decide that you don't like tomatoes so much? That change in consumer preferences will reduce the demand for tomatoes, as shown in Panel (b) of Exhibit 5-6. The quantity of tomatoes demanded will be less than the quantity supplied at a price of 69 cents. The surplus of tomatoes will force the price down. As it falls, some producers will find that their marginal benefit of producing tomatoes has slipped below their marginal cost, and they will cut back on tomato production. As they produce fewer tomatoes, they will free resources for the production of other goods and services whose value at the margin now exceeds that of tomatoes. In this case, consumers have sent a signal to producers that tomatoes have become less valuable to them; producers respond by shifting production to other, more valuable goods and services. The price of tomatoes will continue to fall until the marginal benefit of tomatoes is again at least as great as the marginal cost—the value at the margin of the goods and services given up to produce tomatoes. In the case

EXHIBIT 5-6

Price Signals and Maximizing Behavior

In Panel (a) we see that market equilibrium generates a price that equates the quantity demanded to the quantity supplied. It also results in a price at which the marginal benefit of a pound of tomatoes equals its marginal cost. The price of 69 cents signals consumers that 69 cents' worth of other goods and services were given up to produce the last pound of tomatoes. Panel (b) shows that a change in preferences could reduce the demand for tomatoes from D_1 to D_2, reflecting a reduction in the marginal benefit of the good. Producers will reduce their production to Q_2, freeing resources for the production of other goods and services that are now more valuable at the margin. The falling price signals producers that the benefit of tomato production has fallen. Panel (c) shows that a higher price of fertilizer increases the marginal cost of producing tomatoes, shifting the supply curve from S_1 to S_2. That will increase the price of tomatoes, signaling consumers to reduce their consumption. In the case shown, the price rises to 65 cents per pound.

shown, the equilibrium price falls to 60 cents. At that new price, an efficient solution is again achieved.

Now suppose that the price of fertilizer rises, increasing the marginal cost of tomato production. Producers will respond by cutting their production of tomatoes further, shifting the supply curve for tomatoes to the left. The price of tomatoes will begin to rise. The rising price sends a signal to consumers that the marginal cost of producing tomatoes has risen. Utility maximization meant that tomatoes had been consumed up to the point that marginal benefit equaled marginal cost. With the marginal cost (the price) to consumers higher, consumers cut back on their consumption. Panel (c) of Exhibit 5-6 shows this change.

The marketplace can be thought of as a kind of gigantic signaling mechanism. Prices convey information to producers about the benefits consumers receive from goods and services—and give information to consumers about the costs of producing those goods and services. Given our assumptions that producers are maximizing profits and consumers are maximizing utility, we can predict how they will respond to changes in those signals. We can also infer that as firms and consumers respond to changing price signals, they will achieve the efficient solution in the marketplace—provided that prices confront decision-makers with the marginal costs and the marginal benefits of their choices. We shall refer to this requirement as the **efficiency condition.**

Efficiency and Equity

As people make their choices in the marketplace, they are revealing not just their preferences but their wealth. Demand, after all, reflects ability as well as willingness to pay for goods and services. The market will be far more responsive to the preferences of a wealthy person than to those of a poor one.

An efficient allocation of resources emerges from a particular distribution of wealth. If 1 percent of the population controls virtually all the wealth, then the market will efficiently allocate virtually all its production to those same people. An efficient allocation may not be one that everyone would regard as being equitable.

If the distribution of income and wealth is inequitable, then the market's distribution of goods and services will be inequitable as well. But what is an inequitable distribution of income and wealth? What is an equitable distribution? Should everyone have the same income? The same wealth? Is the current distribution fair? Should the rich have less and the poor have more? Should the middle class have more? Equity is very much in the mind of the observer. What may seem equitable to one person may seem inequitable to another. There is, however, no test we can apply to determine whether the distribution of income and wealth is or is not equitable. That question requires a normative judgment.

Determining whether the allocation of resources is or is not efficient is thus not the only task facing society. It must also determine whether the distribution of income and wealth is equitable. Whatever distribution society chooses, an efficient allocation of resources is still preferred to an inefficient one. Because an efficient allocation maximizes net benefits, the gain in net benefits could be distributed in a way that leaves all people better off than they would be at any inefficient allocation. If an efficient allocation of resources seems inequitable, it must be because the distribution of income and wealth is inequitable. We shall explore questions of equity in more detail in subsequent chapters.

The **efficiency condition** requires that prices in the marketplace confront decisionmakers with the marginal benefits and marginal costs of their decisions. If the efficiency condition is met, the allocation of resources will be efficient.

Case in Point: Saving the Elephant Through Exchange

The African elephant, the world's largest land mammal, is in danger of disappearing. The elephant population of Central and East Africa, which numbered more than 1 million in 1980, fell below 500,000 by the end of the decade. Kenya's elephant population fell most precipitously, from 140,000 at the beginning of the 1980s to fewer than 20,000 in 1990.

Elephants are killed chiefly for their ivory. The tusks from a single elephant can fetch more than $2,000 in the black market—almost twice the annual per capita income of Kenya.

To combat the slaughter, the Central African countries of Kenya, Zambia, Tanzania, and Somalia have imposed bans on killing elephants. Government patrols trained in guerrilla warfare roam the countryside with orders to shoot poachers on sight. But the elephants continue to be slaughtered at a rate of 200 per day. Bans on the export of ivory and international bans on trade in ivory have failed to stop the massacre.

The basic problem is that no one in Central Africa owns property rights in elephants. There is thus no one who can profit from efforts to preserve or expand the population of elephants. Indeed, from the standpoint of many villagers, elephants are a nuisance. A few elephants can destroy a village and ruin crops. Poachers killing elephants thus meet with little resistance from local people in Central Africa, who have nothing to gain financially from blocking the poachers; the poachers may even be doing them a service.

Although prospects are not encouraging in the central part of the continent, there is good news to the south. Elephant populations in Botswana, Namibia, South Africa, and Zimbabwe increased during the 1980s. Botswana's herd, for example, increased from 20,000 at the beginning of the decade to more than 50,000 by the end of the decade. What's the secret of countries in which herds are increasing?

Each of the four countries of southern Africa has established exclusive, transferable licenses to hunt elephants. Each license allows a hunter to kill a single elephant. The licenses are typically granted to villages or regional parks, which can sell them to hunters. A village or park that succeeds in increasing its own herd qualifies for additional licenses. The village of Masoka, in Zimbabwe, earns about $40,000 a year by selling licenses.

Villages and parks that own licenses have a vital stake in making sure that poachers don't slaughter their elephants. They also have a stake in trying to increase the sizes of their herds. They are thus constantly on guard to protect their rights—and to increase their herds.

Sources: Denise Barton, "Conservationists vs. the African Elephant," *The Margin* 5(3) (January/February 1990): 24–25, and Lisa Grainger, "Are They Safe in Our Hands?" *The Times of London* (16 July 1994):18.

The Role of Property Rights

Markets such as the market for tomatoes achieve an efficient allocation of resources as producers offer tomatoes for sale to consumers. That interaction, in turn, requires that producers possess property rights to the tomatoes they produce. **Property rights** are a set of rules that specify the ways in which an owner can use a resource. The owner of a tomato may own the right to slice it, to store it, and to eat it but does not have the right to hurl the tomato at passersby.

A system of property rights forms the basis for all market exchange. Before exchange can begin, there must be a clear specification of who owns what. The system of property rights must also show what purchasers are acquiring when they buy rights to particular resources. Because property rights must exist if exchange is to occur, and because exchange is the process through which economic efficiency is achieved, a system of property rights is essential to the efficient allocation of resources.

Property rights are a set of rules that specify the ways in which the resources for which they are defined may be used.

Although property rights vary for different resources, two characteristics are required if the marketplace is to achieve an efficient allocation of resources:

1. Property rights must be exclusive. An **exclusive property right** is one that allows its owner to prevent others from using the resource. The owner of a house, for example, has the right to exclude others from the use of the house. If this right did not exist, ownership would have little value; it isn't likely that the property could be exchanged in a market. It's difficult to imagine that people would buy resources they were free to use anyway—and from which they would have no power to exclude others.
2. Property rights must be transferable. A **transferable property right** is one that allows the owner of a resource to sell or lease it to someone else. In the absence of transferability, no exchange could occur. Because exchange is essential to achieve an efficient allocation of resources in the marketplace, the transferability of property rights is essential to economic efficiency.

Checklist

- In a competitive system in which prices are determined by supply and demand, prices generally send signals that reflect the marginal cost and marginal benefit of alternative activities.
- An efficient allocation of resources is one that maximizes the net benefits of each activity.
- An inefficient allocation of resources is one that does not maximize the net benefits of each activity.
- An inequitable allocation of resources implies that the distribution of wealth is inequitable. Judgments about equity in the distribution of income and wealth are normative judgments.
- Market efficiency requires that property rights be exclusive and transferable.
- When price signals reflect the marginal benefits and marginal costs of choices, we expect that the allocation of resources will be efficient.

Market Failure: Sources of Inefficiency

Private decisions in the marketplace may not be consistent with the maximization of the net benefit of a particular activity. The failure to achieve an efficient allocation of scarce resources is called **market failure.** Market failure will occur whenever decisionmakers aren't faced with the full costs and benefits of their choices.

When market failure occurs, it is because one of the conditions that lead to an efficient allocation of resources does not hold. Price may not be determined by the interaction of demand and supply, or exclusive, transferable property rights may not exist. Whenever one of the conditions that yield an efficient allocation of resources is absent, the net benefits of an activity will not be maximized. Thus, an alternative allocation exists that would increase net benefits, increasing the welfare of society.

Noncompetitive Markets

The model of demand and supply assumes that markets are competitive. No one in these markets has any power over the equilibrium price; each consumer and producer takes the market price as given and responds to it. Under such conditions, price is determined by the intersection of demand and supply. At this equilibrium solution, price and marginal cost are equal.

In some markets, however, individual buyers or sellers are powerful enough to influence the market price. Sellers with such power are likely to set a price greater than marginal cost. Buyers with such power are likely to set a price below marginal cost. In Part Four, we will study cases in which producers or consumers are in a position to determine the prices they charge or must pay, respectively. We shall find that when individual firms or consumers have power over the market price, the price signal we require for market efficiency will be distorted—it will not equal marginal cost.

- An **exclusive property right** is one that allows its owner to prevent others from using a resource.
- A **transferable property right** is one that can be sold or leased to someone else.
- **Market failure** occurs when private decisions do not result in an efficient allocation of scarce resources.

Public Goods

Some goods are unlikely to be produced and exchanged in a market because of special characteristics of the goods themselves. The benefits of these goods are such that exclusion is not feasible. Once they are produced, anyone can enjoy

Reader's Advisory !

Note that the definitions of public and private goods are based on characteristics of the goods themselves—*not* on whether they are provided by the public or the private sector. Postal services are a private good provided by the public sector. Farmers and ranchers provide open space, which is a public good.

them; there is no practical way to exclude people who haven't paid for them from consuming them. Furthermore, the marginal cost of adding one more consumer is zero. A good for which exclusion cannot be applied and for which the marginal cost of an additional user is zero is a **public good.** A good for which exclusion is possible and for which the marginal cost of another user is positive is a **private good.**

National defense is a public good. Once defense is provided, it is not possible to exclude people who haven't paid for it from its consumption. Further, the cost of an additional user is zero—an army doesn't cost any more if there is one more person to be protected. Other examples of public goods include law enforcement, fire protection, and efforts to preserve species threatened with extinction.

Free Riders

Suppose a private firm, Star Wars, Inc., develops a completely reliable system to intercept any missiles that might be launched toward the United States from anywhere in the world. This service is a public good. Once it is provided, no one can be excluded from the system's protection on grounds he or she hasn't paid for it, and the cost of adding one more person to the group protected is zero. Suppose that the system, by eliminating a potential threat to U.S. security, makes the average person in the United States better off; the benefit to each household from the added security is worth $40 per month. There are roughly 100 million households in the United States, so the total benefit of the system is $4 billion per month. Assume that it will cost Star Wars $1 billion per month to operate. The benefits of the system far outweigh the cost.

Suppose that Star Wars installs its system and sends a bill to each household for $20 for the first month of service—an amount equal to half of each household's benefit. If each household pays its bill, Star Wars will enjoy a tidy profit; it will receive revenues of $2 billion per month.

But will each household pay? Once the system is in place, each household would recognize that it enjoys the benefits of the security provided by Star Wars whether it pays its bill or not. Although some households will voluntarily pay their bills, it seems unlikely that very many will. Recognizing the opportunity to consume the good, most would be free riders. **Free riders** are people or firms that consume a public good without paying for it. Even though the total benefit of the system is $4 billion, Star Wars won't be faced by the marketplace with a signal that suggests that the system is worthwhile. It's unlikely that it will recover its cost of $1 billion per month.

The bill for $20 from Star Wars sends the wrong signal, too. An efficient market requires a price equal to marginal cost. But the marginal cost of protecting one more household is zero; adding one more household adds nothing to the cost of the system. A household that decides not to pay Star Wars anything for its service is paying a price equal to its marginal cost.

Because no household can be excluded and because the cost of an extra household is zero, the efficiency condition will not be met in a private market. What is true of Star Wars, Inc., is true of public goods in general; they simply do not lend themselves to private market provision.

- A **public good** is a good or service for which exclusion cannot be applied and for which the marginal cost of an additional user is zero.
- A **private good** is one for which exclusion is possible and for which the marginal cost of an additional user is positive.
- **Free riders** are people or firms that consume a public good without paying for it.

Public Goods and the Government

Because individuals are unlikely to fully reveal their demand for public goods, private firms will produce a smaller quantity of public goods than is efficient. In

A **quasi-public good** is one for which some benefits are public while others are private.

An **external cost** is imposed when an action imposes costs on others outside the context of market exchange.

such cases, it may be desirable for government agencies to step in. Government can supply a greater quantity of the good by direct provision, by purchasing the public good from a private agency, or by subsidizing consumption. In any case, the cost is financed through taxation and thus avoids the free rider problem.

Most public goods are provided directly by government agencies. Governments produce national defense and law enforcement, for example. Some public goods are produced by private firms under contract with government agencies. Park maintenance and fire services are public goods that are sometimes produced by private firms. In other cases, the government promotes consumption by subsidizing some activities. Private charitable contributions often support activities that are public goods; federal and state governments subsidize these by allowing taxpayers to reduce their tax payments by a fraction of the amount they contribute.

Quasi-Public Goods

Some private goods have some attributes of public goods. Goods for which some benefits are private while others are public are called **quasi-public goods.** Consider, for example, a magnificently landscaped front yard. It's a private good—the owner can exclude others from walking on it, and having additional people occupy it would certainly impose a cost. But the aesthetic benefits of the yard are largely public. Neighbors can't easily be excluded from admiring it, and the cost of having a neighbor admire it is probably zero.

Some of the benefits of a quasi-public good spill over to other people. The result is that individuals making choices such as landscaping a yard don't confront all the benefits of their choices. Economic theory predicts that front yards won't be as pretty as would be economically efficient! It also explains efforts to overcome this problem through such devices as neighborhood associations, peer pressure, and even covenants requiring property owners to maintain their yards in certain ways.

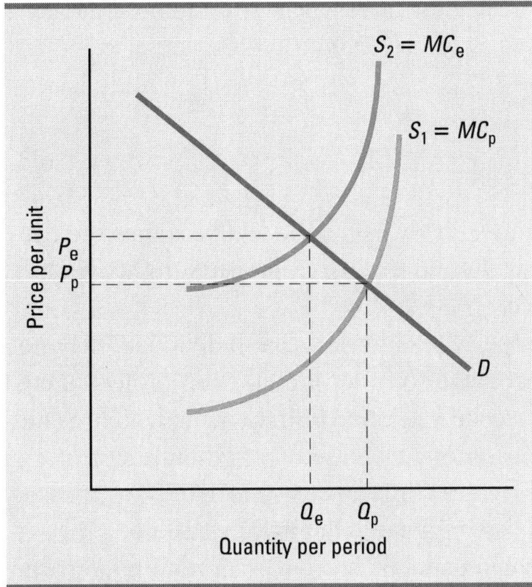

EXHIBIT 5-7

External Costs

When firms in an industry generate external costs, the supply curve S_1 reflects only their private marginal cost, MC_p. Forcing firms to pay the external costs they impose shifts the supply curve to S_2, which reflects the full marginal cost of the firms' production at equilibrium, MC_e. Output is reduced and price goes up.

External Costs

Suppose that in the course of production, the firms in a particular industry generate air pollution. These firms thus impose costs on others, but they do so outside the context of any market exchange—no agreement has been made between the firms and the people affected by the pollution. The firms thus won't be faced with the costs of their action. Any action that imposes costs on others outside of any market exchange imposes an **external cost.**

Actions taken by an agent can also impose benefits on others, again in the absence of any market agreement. Such cases often occur when benefits are nonexclusive; they are thus associated with public goods, which we have just examined.

External Costs and Efficiency

The case of the polluting firms is illustrated in Exhibit 5-7. The industry supply curve S_1 reflects private marginal costs, MC_p. The market price is P_p for a quantity Q_p. If the external costs generated by the pollution were added, the new supply curve S_2 would reflect higher marginal costs, MC_e. Faced with those costs, the market would generate a lower equilibrium quantity, Q_e. That quantity would command a higher price, P_e. The failure to confront producers with the cost of their pollution means that consumers do not pay the full cost of the good

A **common property resource** is one for which no exclusive property rights exist.

they are purchasing. The level of output is therefore higher than would be economically efficient. If a way could be found to confront producers with the full cost of their choices, then consumers would be faced with a higher cost as well. Exhibit 5-7 shows that consumption would be reduced to the efficient level, Q_e, at which demand and the full marginal cost curve (MC_e) intersect.

External Costs and Government Intervention

If an activity generates external costs, the decisionmakers generating the activity will not be faced with its full costs. As a result, they will carry out an excessive quantity of the activity. In such cases, government may try to intervene to reduce the level of the activity toward the efficient quantity. In the case shown in Exhibit 5-7, for example, firms generating an external cost have a supply curve S_1 that reflects their marginal costs, MC_p. These costs, however, do not include the external costs the firms generate. A fee imposed on the firms would increase their marginal costs to MC_e, thus shifting the supply curve to S_2. Output falls to Q_e and price rises to P_e. Taxes or other restrictions may be imposed on the activity that generates the external cost in an effort to confront decisionmakers with the costs that they are imposing. In many areas, firms and consumers that pollute rivers and lakes are required to pay fees based on the amount they pollute. Firms in many areas are required to purchase permits in order to pollute the air; the permits serve to confront the firms with the costs of their choices.

Another approach to dealing with problems of external costs is direct regulation. For example, a firm may be ordered to reduce its pollution. A person who turns his or her front yard into a garbage dump may be ordered to clean it up. Participants at a raucous party may be told to be quiet. Zoning restrictions typically prohibit industrial activities in residential areas in an effort to limit the generation of external costs. Alternative ways of dealing with external costs are discussed in more detail in Chapter 18.

Checklist

- A competitive market is necessary if price is to equal marginal cost.
- Property rights must be exclusive and transferable if the allocation of resources is to be efficient.
- Public sector intervention to increase the level of provision of public and quasi-public goods may improve the efficiency of resource allocation by overcoming the problem of free riders.
- A common property resource is unlikely to be allocated efficiently in the marketplace.
- Activities that generate external costs are likely to be carried out at levels that exceed those that would be efficient; public sector intervention that seeks to confront decisionmakers with the full costs of their choices may be appropriate.

Common Property Resources

Exclusive, transferable property rights give owners an incentive to use their resources efficiently. A resource for which no exclusive property rights exist is called a **common property resource.**

The difficulty with common property resources is that individuals may not have adequate incentives to engage in efforts to preserve or protect them. Consider, for example, the relative fates of cattle and buffalo in the United States in the nineteenth century. Cattle populations increased throughout the century; the buffalo nearly became extinct. The chief difference between the two animals was that exclusive property rights existed for cattle but not for buffalo.

Owners of cattle had an incentive to maintain herd sizes. A cattle owner who slaughtered all of his or her cattle without providing for replacement of the herd wouldn't have a source of future income. Cattle owners not only maintained their herds, but engaged in extensive efforts to breed high-quality livestock. They invested time and effort in the efficient management of the resource on which their livelihoods depended.

Buffalo hunters surely had similar concerns about the maintenance of buffalo herds, but they had no individual stake in doing anything about them—the animals were a common property resource. Thousands of individuals hunted buffalo for a living. Anyone who cut back on hunting in order to help to preserve the herd would lose income—and face the likelihood that other hunters would

Case in Point — Externalities, Cigarettes, and Alcohol

Smokers and heavy drinkers impose substantial costs on themselves. Do they impose external costs as well? A 1989 Rand Corporation study, directed by University of Michigan economist Willard G. Manning, suggests that they do. The Rand study concluded that smokers more than pay for their external costs through taxes they pay, but heavy drinkers do not.

The private costs of smoking are huge. Health experts estimate that each pack of cigarettes smoked reduces a smoker's life expectancy by more than 2 hours. Smoking-related illnesses kill more than 300,000 people per year in the United States alone. The Rand study estimates that the value of life expectancy lost is about $5 per pack smoked. But that is a private cost—a cost smokers impose on themselves.

Smokers generate external costs in three ways. First, they impose costs on others by forcing health care costs up and thus raising health insurance premiums. They also cause fires that destroy more than $300 million worth of property each year. Finally, smokers may kill nonsmokers with their smoke. An estimated 2,400 people die each year from so-called passive smoking. The Rand researchers estimate that the total value of external costs generated by smokers is 53 cents per pack.

In an important way, however, smokers also generate external benefits. Smokers contribute to retirement programs and to Social Security, then die sooner than nonsmokers. They thus subsidize the retirement costs of the rest of the population. According to the Rand study, that produces a benefit of 24 cents per pack. The net external cost of smoking is thus 29 cents per pack. Given that state and federal excise taxes averaged 37 cents per pack in 1989, the Rand researchers concluded that smokers more than pay their own way.

The Rand study defined heavy drinking as alcohol consumed in excess of an equivalent of two drinks per day. Heavy drinking, like smoking, increases health insurance costs for the rest of the population. Heavy drinkers also account for a large number of highway fatalities. In 1985, for example, 22,400 people died in alcohol-related highway accidents. Of those, only 7,400 had not been drinking.

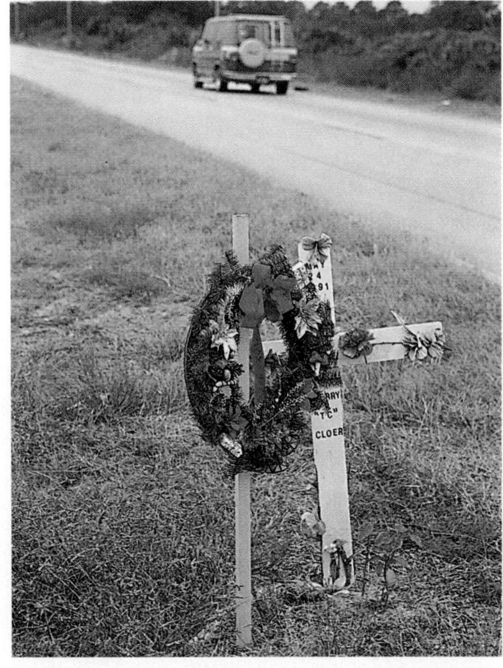

Like smokers, heavy drinkers die earlier than those in the rest of the population. But unlike smokers, they also leave the work force earlier, so drinkers don't yield the same retirement benefits to society that smokers do.

The Rand researchers estimated that the total external cost of alcohol consumption is $1.19 per excess ounce consumed. The average of federal, state, and local excise taxes per ounce of alcohol was $0.23 per ounce in 1985. The study concluded that increases in alcohol taxes were justified on grounds of external costs.

Source: Willard G. Manning, Emmett B. Keeler, Joseph P. Newhouse, Elizabeth M. Sloss, and Jeffrey Wasserman, "The Taxes of Sin: Do Smokers and Drinkers Pay Their Way?" *Journal of the American Medical Association* 261 (March 17, 1989):1604–1609.

go on hunting at the same rate as before. A profit-maximizing hunter would thus be likely to go on killing buffalo, even with the knowledge that this killing could destroy the species.

Today, exclusive rights to buffalo have been widely established. The demand for buffalo meat, which is lower in fat than beef, has been increasing, but the number of buffalo in the United States is rising rapidly. If buffalo were still a common property resource, that increased demand would, in the absence of other restrictions on hunting of the animals, surely result in the elimination of the animal.

Case in Point: Common Property, Grass, and Cattle in the Old West

Nineteenth-century settlers on the Great Plains saw immediately the profits that could be made from grazing cattle. But there was one big problem: they didn't have an effective way to establish exclusive property rights. The federal government owned the land and stood ready to sell it for $1.25 per acre, but that price was prohibitive. An alternative was to homestead the land, but that meant acquiring only 160 acres. The arid landscape would support only a few cattle on an area that size, hardly enough to keep a family going.

An early photograph of cattle in the West.

Undaunted by their inability to establish property rights, these settlers simply started grazing cattle on the federal land. In doing so, they faced the problem of a common property resource—no one exercised exclusive property rights to the land. As more and more cattle owners started grazing their animals in a particular area, the prairies on which the cattle fed were being overgrazed. Because no individual held exclusive rights to the grassland, no one had an incentive to act to preserve it.

Early ranchers were quick to observe the problem. They banded together in cattlemen's associations. These associations staked out claims to specific regions and then sought to limit grazing in areas that they claimed. A cattlemen's association in Montana published its claim to a grazing area in the *Helena Daily Herald* in 1883 and ordered all others to stay out: "We, the undersigned stock owners . . . hereby give notice that we consider said range already overstocked; therefore we positively decline allowing any outside parties . . . locating herds upon this range the use of our corrals, nor will they be permitted to join us in any roundup on said range from and after this date."

Notice the association couldn't deny use of the range—it didn't own the land. But denying participation in the roundup proved an effective device because it was much cheaper to round up cattle in cooperation with other ranchers than it was to do it individually. The cattlemen's associations thus presented an effective solution to the problem of the common property resource in the Old West by imposing a form of exclusion that limited grazing.

When a species is threatened with extinction, it is likely that no one has exclusive property rights to it. Whales, condors, grizzly bears—whatever the animal that is threatened—are common property resources. In such cases a government agency may impose limits on the killing of the animal or destructtion of its habitat. Such limits can prevent the excessive private use of a common property resource. Alternatively, as was done in the case of the buffalo, private rights can be established, giving resource owners the task of preservation.

A Look Back—And a Look Ahead

Economists insist that individuals do not make choices willy-nilly. Rather, they assume that individuals make those choices in a purposeful way, one that seeks the maximum value for some objective. Economists assume that consumers seek to maximize utility and that firms seek to maximize profits.

Whatever is being maximized, choices are based on the marginal decision rule. Following the marginal decision rule results in an allocation that achieves the greatest degree of individual utility or profit possible.

If utility and profit maximizing choices are made in the context of a price system that confronts decisionmakers with all the costs and all the benefits of their choices, the allocation of resources in the economy is efficient. An efficient allocation is one that maximizes the net benefit of an activity. Equity is a separate issue, one that calls for a normative evaluation of the fairness of the distribution of income and wealth.

The allocation of resources will be inefficient in the absence of competitive markets. It will also be inefficient if property rights are not exclusive and transferable. These two conditions break down when there are public goods, common property resources, or external costs. In each of those cases, public sector intervention may improve the efficiency of resource allocation.

We shall apply the marginal decision rule throughout the remainder of Part Two and in Parts Three through Five. We shall assume in Parts Three and Four that prices are confronting decisionmakers with the costs and benefits of their choices. In Part Five, we shall explore cases in which they do not.

Terms and Concepts for Review

Common property resource	Marginal decision rule
Constraint	Market failure
Efficiency condition	Net benefit
Efficient	Private good
Exclusive property right	Profit
External cost	Property rights
Free riders	Public good
Inefficient	Quasi-public good
Marginal benefit	Transferable property right
Marginal cost	

For Discussion

1. Suppose you are a discus hurler and your goal is to maximize the distance you achieve. You "produce" discus hurls by practicing. The total benefit of practice is distance achieved, and input that achieves this distance is hours of practice. Describe the total benefit curve of practice. What point on the curve would you select?
2. This chapter argues that consumers maximize utility and firms maximize profits. What do you suppose each of the following might be presumed to maximize?
   a. A minister or rabbi
   b. A United States Senator
   c. The manager of a major league baseball team
   d. The owner of a major league baseball team
   e. The director of a charitable organization
3. Suppose Laurie Phan is still facing midterms in accounting and economics, but an Achilles tendon injury is going to keep her out of the marathon for which she had been training. How might this affect the total amount of study time she chooses? How will it affect her expected grades?
4. The discussion of economic efficiency in Chapter 2 noted that an economy that fails to allocate resources according to comparative advantage will operate within, rather than on, its production possibilities curve. We asserted that a reallocation of resources that moves the economy to the curve will generate marginal benefits in excess of marginal costs, thus satisfying the marginal decision rule. Why is that true?
5. Assess each of the following statements from the standpoint of marginal analysis.
   a. A job worth doing is worth doing well.
   b. Early to bed, early to rise, makes a man healthy, wealthy, and wise.
   c. Never leave to tomorrow what you can do today.
6. Comment on the following statement: "Most people never go to college. Of the ones that do, most don't take economics. The notion that everyone follows the marginal decision rule is absurd—most people haven't heard of it, and if they heard of it, they wouldn't understand it."
7. "Economic efficiency is a nice concept for technicians and accountants, but what's valuable in life can't be toted up on a calculator and plotted on a graph. Ultimately, it's people and their preferences that matter." Comment.

8. For each of the following goods, indicate whether exclusive, transferable property rights exist and whether the good poses a problem for public policy. If it does, does the problem relate to a problem of property rights?
   a. Clean air
   b. Tomatoes
   c. Housing
   d. Blue whales
9. The dry-cleaning industry is a major source of air pollution. What can you conclude about the price and output of dry-cleaning services?
10. Economists often recommend that polluters such as dry-cleaning establishments be charged fees for the pollution they emit. Critics of this idea respond that the establishments would simply respond by passing these charges on to their customers. Comment on this objection.
11. Government agencies often require that children be inoculated against communicable diseases such as polio and measles. Is there any justification for such a requirement?
12. Which of the following goods or services are public?
   a. Libraries
   b. Fire protection
   c. Television programs
   d. Health care
   e. Water for household consumption
13. Notice that the discussion of quasi-public goods focused on front yards, not backyards. Why? In what sense might each of the following be considered a quasi-public good?
   a. Preservation of an architectural landmark
   b. A rancher's production of beef
   c. The planting of grasses, trees, and shrubs by owners of hillside property
14. If a village in Botswana is granted several licenses to kill elephants, how does this give it an incentive to preserve elephants and increase the size of the herd? How does the international ban on ivory sales affect the incentive in Botswana to preserve the elephant?
15. The number of fish caught in the ocean has fallen in recent years despite more intensive fishing efforts and the use of more sophisticated equipment. Explain why this is happening. How do you think this drop in the catch affects the price of seafood?

Problems

1. Joe Higgins is thinking about how much time to spend studying for an exam tomorrow in biology. Using "utility units" he measures the benefits and costs of study; his calculations are shown in the following table.

Hours spent studying	Total benefit	Total cost
0	0	0
1	100	50
2	180	100
3	240	150
4	280	200
5	300	250
6	300	350

   a. In three separate graphs, lined up vertically as in Exhibit 5-5, show the total benefit and total cost curves, the net benefit curve, and the marginal benefit and marginal cost curves. (*Hint:* Remember that marginal values are plotted at the midpoints of the corresponding intervals on the horizontal axis.)
   b. In each graph, find the solution that maximizes the net benefit of time spent studying. Confirm that all three approaches yield the same solution.
2. Now suppose some friends of Joe's call to say they're having a party tonight. Joe calculates that the party is now his best alternative to study, and he increases his estimate of the cost of each hour of study by 20 units of utility. One hour of study now costs 70; two hours cost 140; three hours 210, and so on. Draw the new set of total benefit, total cost, net benefit, marginal benefit and marginal cost curves as in Problem (1), and compute the new solution that maximizes the net benefit of study time.
3. The local gasoline market in a particular community has demand and supply curves given by the following data. (All quantities are in millions of gallons per month.)

Price per gallon	Quantity demanded	Quantity supplied
$0.50	6	0
.75	5	1
1.00	4	2
1.25	3	3
1.50	2	4
1.75	1	5
2.00	0	6

   a. Plot the demand and supply curves, and determine the equilibrium price and quantity.
   b. Now suppose that the community determines that each gallon of gasoline consumed imposes 50 cents in pollution costs. Accordingly, a 50 cents-per-gallon tax is imposed. The tax is imposed on sellers of gasoline, and it has the effect of increasing by 50 cents the price required to induce the quantities supplied in the table. Plot the new supply curve, and determine the new equilibrium price and output.

6

The Analysis of Consumer Choice

Chapter Objectives

After mastering the material in this chapter, you will be able to:

1. Explain the relationship between total utility and marginal utility.
2. Explain the use of the marginal decision rule in utility maximization.
3. Explain how price changes affect the combination of goods and services a utility-maximizing consumer will select.
4. Use the concept of utility maximization to distinguish between the substitution and income effects of a price change.
5. Use a demand curve to show how price changes affect consumer welfare.
6. Explain how the concept of utility can be applied to the analysis of equity in the distribution of income and in the tax system.

Utility is what goes up when you feel better.

—Kenneth Boulding

What's Ahead

Price rises. The quantity demanded falls. Price falls. The quantity demanded rises. These basic relationships are given by the law of demand.

The law of demand is at the bedrock of economic analysis; it is one of the most reliable relationships in all of economics. But why does it hold? What is there about the preferences of consumers that makes it so?

In this chapter, we'll look behind the demand curve to see how utility-maximizing consumers can be expected to respond to price changes. We'll apply the marginal decision rule to the problem of utility maximization. In doing so, we'll find that the law of demand is an implication of utility maximization for most goods and services. We'll also find, however, that it is possible in theory for the demand curves for some goods and services to slope upward! The universality of the law of demand is thus not purely theoretical but is a result based on the observation of actual behavior in the marketplace.

We can approach the analysis of utility maximization in two ways. The chapter covers one, the material in the Chapter 6 Appendix another. An alternative is to examine both approaches and to compare them.

The Concept of Utility

Why do you buy the goods and services you do? It must be because they provide you with satisfaction—you feel better off because you have purchased them. Economists call this satisfaction *utility.*

The concept of utility, however, is an elusive one. A person who consumes a good such as peaches gains utility from eating the peaches. But we can't measure this utility the same way we can measure a peach's weight or calorie content. There is no scale we can use to determine the quantity of utility a peach generates.

Francis Edgeworth, one of the most important contributors to the theory of consumer behavior, imagined a device he called a hedonimeter (after hedonism, the pursuit of pleasure):

> . . . let there be granted to the science of pleasure what is granted to the science of energy; to imagine an ideally perfect instrument, a psychophysical machine, continually registering the height of pleasure experienced by an individual. . . . From moment to moment the hedonimeter varies; the delicate index now flickering with the flutter of passions, now steadied by intellectual activity, now sunk whole hours in the neighborhood of zero, or momentarily springing up towards infinity.[1]

Perhaps some day a hedonimeter will be invented. The utility it measures will not be a characteristic of particular goods, but rather of each consumer's reactions to those goods. The utility of a peach exists not in the peach itself, but in the preferences of the individual consuming the peach. One consumer may wax ecstatic about a peach; another may say it tastes OK. Again, utility is the satisfaction each person derives from his or her consumption of goods and services. It is not a characteristic of the goods and services themselves.

When we speak of maximizing utility, then, we are speaking of the maximization of something we can't measure. We assume, however, that each consumer acts as if he or she can measure utility and arranges consumption so that the utility gained is as high as possible.

Total Utility

If we could measure utility, **total utility** would be the number of units of utility that a consumer gains from consuming a given quantity of a good, service, or activity during a particular time period. The higher a consumer's total utility, the greater that consumer's level of satisfaction. Total utility is the measure economists use to describe the total benefit a consumer derives from consumption of a good, service, or activity.

Panel (a) of Exhibit 6-1 shows the total utility Henry Higgins obtains from attending movies. In drawing his total utility curve, we are imagining that we can measure his total utility. The total utility curve shows that when Mr. Higgins attends no movies during a month, his total utility from attending movies is zero. As he increases the number of movies he sees, his total utility rises. When he consumes 1 movie, he obtains 36 units of utility. When he consumes 4 movies, his total utility is 101. He achieves the maximum level of utility possible, 115, by seeing 6 movies per month. Seeing a seventh movie adds nothing to his total utility.

Mr. Higgins's total utility rises at a decreasing rate. The rate of increase is given by the slope of the total utility curve, which is reported in Panel (a) as well. The slope of the curve between 0 movies and 1 movie is 36. It is 28 between 1 and 2 movies, 22 between 2 and 3, and so on. The slope between 6 and 7 movies is zero; the total utility curve between these two quantities is horizontal.

Total utility is a conceptual measure of the number of units of utility a person obtains by consuming a given quantity of a good, service, or activity during a given time period.

Marginal utility is the amount by which an additional unit of a good, service, or activity increases a consumer's total utility, ceteris paribus.

Marginal Utility

The amount by which total utility rises with consumption of an additional unit of a good, service, or activity, ceteris paribus, is **marginal utility.** The first movie Mr. Higgins sees increases his total utility by 36 units. Hence, the marginal util-

[1] Francis Y. Edgeworth, *Mathematical Psychics: An Essay on the Application of Mathematics to the Moral Sciences* (New York: Augustus M. Kelley, 1967), p. 101. First published 1881.

EXHIBIT 6-1

Total Utility and Marginal Utility Curves

Panel (a) shows Henry Higgins's total utility curve for attending movies. It rises as the number of movies increases, reaching a maximum of 115 units of utility at 6 movies per month. Marginal utility is shown in Panel (b); it is the slope of the total utility curve. Because the slope of the total utility curve declines as the number of movies increases, the marginal utility curve is downward sloping.

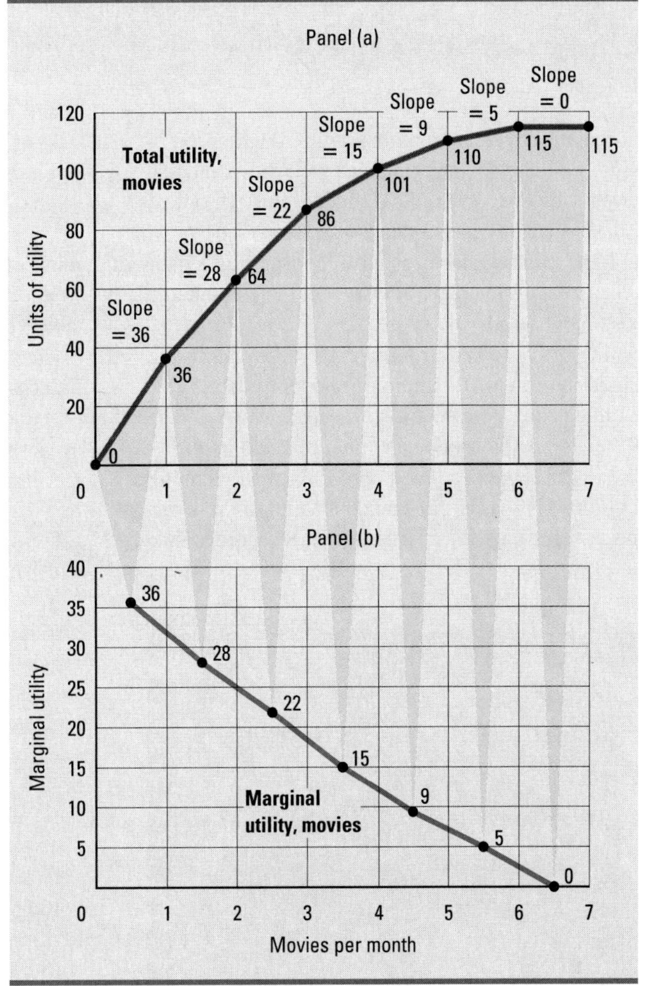

ity of the first movie is 36. The second increases his total utility by 28 units; its marginal utility is 28. The seventh movie does not increase his total utility; its marginal utility is zero. Mr. Higgins's marginal utility curve is plotted in Panel (b) of Exhibit 6-1; it is downward sloping. The curve shows that Mr. Higgins's marginal utility for movies declines as he consumes more of them.

Mr. Higgins's marginal utility from movies is typical of all goods and services. Suppose that you're *really* thirsty and you decide to consume a soft drink. Consuming the drink increases your utility, probably by a lot. Suppose now you have another. That second drink probably increases your utility by less than the first. A third would increase your utility by still less. This tendency of marginal utility to decline beyond some level of consumption during a period is called the **law of diminishing marginal utility.** This law suggests that all goods and services will have downward-sloping marginal utility curves.

The **law of diminishing marginal utility** states that, beyond some level of consumption, the marginal utility of any good or service will decline as the quantity consumed increases during a given time period.

One way to think about this effect is to remember the last time you ate at an "all you can eat" cafeteria-style restaurant. Did you eat only one type of food? Did you consume food without limit? No, because of the law of diminishing marginal utility. As you consumed more of one kind of food, its marginal utility fell. You reached a point at which the marginal utility of another dish was greater, and you switched to that. Eventually, there was no food whose marginal utility was great enough to make it worth eating, and you stopped.

Case in Point: Channel Zapping

Zenith Corporation introduced the remote control to television in 1956. The device, called Space Command, enjoyed a modest success. It allowed viewers to turn their sets on and off, adjust the volume, and select from among the available offerings of ABC, CBS, and NBC. Some cities boasted a handful of independent stations, but it was rare that a viewer couldn't count the available options on one hand.

The blossoming of cable systems and cable networks in the late 1980s changed the role of the remote. Suddenly there were scores, even hundreds, of channels available to viewers. The wider range of choice has spawned a new phenomenon in television viewers: the channel zapper. The popularity of the remote, which not only allows viewers to zap one channel in favor of another but to make selections on a videocassette recorder, has soared.

As recently as 1985, fewer than 20 percent of U.S. households with television sets owned remote control devices. By 1995, 85 percent did.

Channel zappers sit down at the television not to watch a particular program but to browse. They switch from one channel to another when their interest fades. It can fade quickly; a 1992 study by the Cable Television Administration and Marketing Society found that particularly active zappers change channels an average of once every 30 seconds. The study classed 23 percent of cable system viewers as "restless viewers" who routinely zap one program in favor of another.

Because they now need not only to attract viewers but to hold them, broadcasters have changed the way they deliver programming. In 1968, for example, television news programs ran excerpts ("sound bites") of the statements of political leaders that were 42.5 seconds long, on average. By 1992, the average bite was just 7.3 seconds long—newscasters try to cut to something else before the zappers do.

Zapping (also known as channel surfing, grazing, or prowling) has a straightforward economic explanation. Zappers, like everyone else, experience diminishing marginal utility. For them, however, utility doesn't just taper off slowly—it collapses. With more alternatives, the probability of obtaining greater marginal utility somewhere else is high. Is the marginal utility of the news declining? *Zap!* Is MTV growing stale? *Zap!* Is the football game getting dull? *Zap!* The remote control allows viewers to respond to diminishing marginal utility with the squeeze of a thumb. And squeeze they do. *Zap!*

Source: "The Zapper! All About the Remote Control," *TV Guide* 40(33) (August 15, 1992):8–13.

What would life be like in a world of constant or increasing marginal utility? Let's go back to the cafeteria and imagine that your favorite food is creamed spinach. You start with that because its marginal utility is highest of all the choices before you in the cafeteria. As you eat more, however, its marginal utility doesn't fall; it remains higher than the marginal utility of any other option. Unless eating more creamed spinach somehow increases your marginal utility for some other food, you will eat only creamed spinach. And until you've reached the limit of your body's capacity (or the restaurant manager's patience), you won't stop. Failure of marginal utility to diminish would thus lead to extraordinary levels of consumption of a single good to the exclusion of all others.

- The utility of a good or service is determined by how much satisfaction a particular consumer obtains from it. Utility is not a quality inherent in the good or service itself.
- Total utility is a conceptual measure of the number of units of utility a consumer gains from consuming a good, service, or activity.
- Marginal utility is the increase in total utility obtained by consuming one more unit of a good, service, or activity.
- As a consumer consumes more and more of a good or service, its marginal utility falls.

Maximizing Utility

Economists assume that consumers behave in a manner consistent with the maximization of utility. To see how consumers do that, we'll put the marginal decision rule to work. First, however, we must reckon with the fact that the ability of consumers to purchase goods and services is limited by their budgets.

A **budget constraint** restricts a consumer's spending to the total budget available to the consumer.

The Budget Constraint

The total utility curve in Exhibit 6-1 shows that Mr. Higgins achieves the maximum total utility possible from movies when he sees six of them each month. It's likely that his total utility curves for other goods and services will have much the same shape, reaching a maximum at some level of consumption. We assume that the goal of each consumer is to maximize utility. Does that mean a person will consume each good at a level that yields the maximum utility possible?

The answer, in general, is no. Our consumption choices are constrained by the income available to us and by the prices we must pay. Suppose, for example, that Mr. Higgins can spend just $25 per month for entertainment and that the price of going to see a movie is $5. To achieve the maximum total utility from movies, Mr. Higgins would have to exceed his entertainment budget. Mr. Higgins must arrange his consumption so that his total expenditures do not exceed his **budget constraint;** his total spending cannot exceed the budget he has available.

Algebraically, we can write the budget constraint for two goods X and Y as

$$P_X Q_X + P_Y Q_Y \leq B \tag{1}$$

where P_X and P_Y are the prices of goods X and Y and Q_X and Q_Y are the quantities of goods X and Y chosen. The total income available to spend on the two goods is *B,* the consumer's budget. Equation (1) states that total expenditures on goods X and Y (the left-hand side of the equation) cannot exceed *B.*

Suppose that in addition to movies, Mr. Higgins enjoys concerts, and the average price of a concert ticket is $10. He must select the number of movies he sees (Q_M) and concerts he attends (Q_C) so that his monthly spending on the two goods satisfies his budget constraint:

$$\$5Q_M + \$10Q_C \leq \$25$$

We assume that consumers cannot spend more than their budget constraints allow. They could spend less, but that would result in lower levels of utility. A utility-maximizing consumer, then, will spend up to the limit of his or her budget constraint.

Individuals may, of course, choose to save or to borrow. When we allow this possibility, we write the budget constraint not just for a single period of time but for several periods. For example, economists often examine budget constraints over a consumer's lifetime. A consumer may in some years save for future consumption and in other years borrow on future income for present consumption. Whatever the time period, a consumer's spending will be constrained by his or her budget.

To simplify our analysis, we shall assume that a consumer's spending in any one period is based on the budget available in that period. In this analysis consumers neither save nor borrow. We could extend the analysis to cover several periods to generate the same basic results that we shall establish using a single period.

Applying the Marginal Decision Rule

Because consumers can be expected to spend the budget they have, utility maximization is a matter of arranging that spending to achieve the highest total utility possible. If a consumer decides to spend more on one good, he or she must necessarily spend less on another in order to satisfy the budget constraint.

The marginal decision rule states that an activity should be expanded if its marginal benefit exceeds its marginal cost. For a consumer seeking to maximize utility, the activity is spending more on a particular good. The marginal benefit of this activity is the utility gained by spending an additional $1 on the good. The marginal cost is the utility lost by spending $1 less on another good.

How much utility is gained by spending another $1 on a good? It is the marginal utility of the good divided by its price. The utility gained by spending an additional dollar on good A, for example, is

$$\frac{MU_A}{P_A}$$

This additional utility is the *marginal benefit* of spending another $1 on the good.

Suppose that the marginal utility of good A is 4 and that its price is $2. Then an extra $1 spent on A buys 2 units of additional utility ($MU_A/P_A = 4/2 = 2$). If the marginal utility of good A is 1 and its price is $2, then an extra $1 spent on A buys 0.5 additional units of utility ($MU_A/P_A = 1/2$).

The loss in utility from spending $1 less on another good or service is calculated the same way: as the marginal utility divided by the price. The *marginal cost* to the consumer of spending $1 less on a good is the loss of the additional utility that could have been gained from spending that $1 on the good.

Suppose a consumer derives more utility by spending an additional $1 on good A rather than on good B:

$$\frac{MU_A}{P_A} > \frac{MU_B}{P_B} \tag{2}$$

The marginal benefit of shifting $1 from good B to the consumption of good A exceeds the marginal cost. In terms of utility, the gain from spending an additional $1 on good A exceeds the loss in utility from spending $1 less on good B. The consumer can increase utility by shifting spending from B to A.

As the consumer buys more of good A and less of good B, however, the marginal utilities of the two goods will change. The law of diminishing marginal utility tells us that the marginal utility of good A will fall as the consumer consumes more of it; the marginal utility of good B will rise as the consumer consumes less of it. The result is that the value of the left-hand side of Equation (2) will fall and the value of the right-hand side will rise as the consumer shifts spending from B to A. When the two sides are equal, total utility will be maximized. In terms of the marginal decision rule, the consumer will have achieved a solution at which the marginal benefit of the activity (spending more on good A) is equal to the marginal cost:

$$\frac{MU_A}{P_A} = \frac{MU_B}{P_B} \tag{3}$$

We can extend this result to all goods and services a consumer uses. Utility maximization requires that the ratio of marginal utility to price be equal for all of them, as suggested in Equation (4).

$$\frac{MU_a}{P_a} = \frac{MU_b}{P_b} = \frac{MU_c}{P_c} = \cdots \tag{4}$$

Equation (4) states the **utility-maximizing condition:** Utility is maximized for a given budget when total outlays equal the budget and when the ratios of marginal utilities to prices are equal for all goods and services.

The **utility-maximizing condition** requires that total outlays equal the budget and that the ratio of marginal utility to price is equal for all goods and services.

The utility-maximizing condition is a straightforward application of the marginal decision rule. If the marginal utility per $1 spent on good A exceeds that of good B, then the marginal benefit of spending $1 more on good A exceeds the marginal cost of spending $1 less on good B. Total utility rises. As more money is transferred from good B to good A, the marginal utility of good A falls, and the marginal utility of good B rises. Eventually the ratios of marginal utility to price will be equal, and no further gains in utility can be achieved by rearranging spending. A consumer who satisfies Equation (4) achieves the maximum total utility possible from a given level of expenditures.

The Problem of Divisibility

If we are to apply the marginal decision rule to utility maximization, goods must be divisible. The notion of spending an additional $1 to increase the quantity of, say, apples consumed seems plausible enough, but what about spending another $1 on a house or a car? Can a consumer buy a little more house or a little more car in the same way he or she buys another apple?

The problem is whether a particular good or service is *divisible.* A good is divisible if it can be purchased in any quantity. Strictly speaking, few goods are completely divisible. Even apples fail the strict test; grocers generally frown on requests to purchase one-third of an apple. But in applying the marginal decision rule, we must assume that goods are, indeed, divisible. Otherwise we can't meaningfully speak of spending $1 more or $1 less on them.

In the case of a house or a car, we can think of the quantity as depending on characteristics of the house or car itself. Thus, a house with three bedrooms could be considered as containing a larger quantity of "house" than another with two bedrooms. A car with a compact disc player could be regarded as containing "more car" than one that has only a cassette player.

Stretching the concept of quantity in this manner doesn't entirely solve the problem. It's still difficult to imagine that one could purchase "more house" by spending $1 more on housing. Remember, however, that we are dealing with a model. When we use a model, we often assign characteristics that may not fit the real world precisely. Here we assume that all goods and services are divisible.

- A budget constraint limits what a consumer can spend.
- Utility maximization requires seeking the greatest total utility from a given budget.
- Utility is maximized when total outlays equal the budget available and when the ratios of marginal utility to price are equal for all goods and services a consumer consumes; this is the utility-maximizing condition.
- We assume that all goods and services are divisible.

Applications of Utility Theory

Utility theory is at the foundation of the economic theory of consumer behavior. In this section we will see how it applies to the analysis of demand and to the problem of equity in income distribution.

Utility Maximization and Demand

Does the proposition that consumers maximize utility imply that market demand curves will be downward sloping? We will see in this section that the answer is a qualified yes. In most cases, utility-maximizing behavior implies that the demand curve will be downward sloping. We shall see, however, that there are cases in which this is not so.

Deriving an Individual's Demand Curve

Suppose, for simplicity, that Felicia Andrews consumes only apples and oranges. Apples cost $2 per pound and oranges cost $1 per pound, and her budget allows her to spend \$20 per week on the two goods. We assume that Ms. Andrews will adjust her consumption so that the utility-maximizing condition given in Equation (3) holds for the two goods: the ratio of marginal utility to price is the same for apples and oranges. That is,

$$\frac{MU_A}{\$2} = \frac{MU_O}{\$1} \tag{5}$$

Here MU_A and MU_O are the marginal utilities of apples and oranges, respectively, and Q_A and Q_O are their quantities. Suppose that at this solution, she is purchasing 5 pounds of apples and 10 pounds of oranges per week. Her spending equals her budget of \$20 per week.

$$\$2Q_A + \$1Q_O = \$20 \tag{6}$$

Now suppose that an unusually large harvest of apples lowers their price to \$1 per pound. The lower price of apples increases the marginal utility of each \$1 Ms. Andrews spends on apples, so that

$$\frac{MU_A}{\$1} > \frac{MU_O}{\$1} \tag{7}$$

Ms. Andrews will respond by purchasing more apples. As she does so, the marginal utility she receives from apples will decline. If she regards apples and oranges as substitutes, she will also buy fewer oranges. That will cause the marginal utility of oranges to rise. She will continue to adjust her spending until the marginal utility per \$1 spent is equal for both goods:

$$\frac{MU_A}{\$1} = \frac{MU_O}{\$1} \tag{8}$$

Suppose that at this new solution, she purchases 12 pounds of apples and 8 pounds of oranges. She is still spending all of her budget of \$20 on the two goods.

It is through a consumer's reaction to different prices that we trace the consumer's demand curve for a good. When the price of apples was \$2 per pound, Ms. Andrews maximized her utility by purchasing 5 pounds of apples, as illustrated in Exhibit 6-2. When the price of apples fell, she increased the quantity of apples she purchased to 12 pounds.

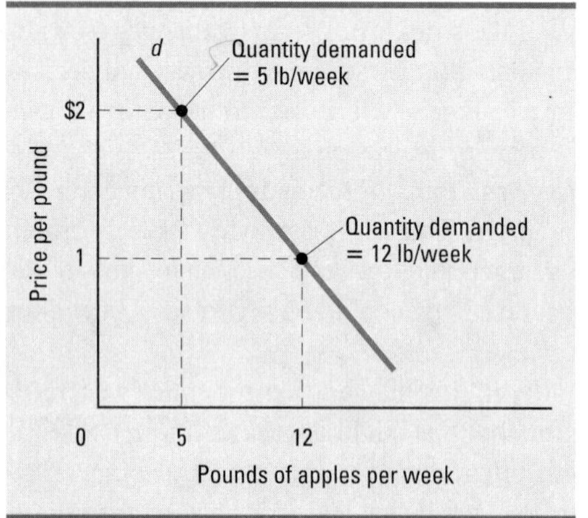

EXHIBIT 6-2

Utility Maximization and an Individual's Demand Curve

Felicia Andrews's demand curve for apples, *d*, can be derived by determining the quantities of apples she will buy at each price. Those quantities are determined by the application of the marginal decision rule to utility maximization. At a price of \$2 per pound, Ms. Andrews maximizes utility by purchasing 5 pounds of apples per week. When the price of apples falls to \$1 per pound, the quantity of apples at which she maximizes utility increases to 12 pounds per week.

From Individual Demand to Market Demand

The market demand curves we studied in Chapters 3 and 4 are derived from individual demand curves such as the one depicted in Exhibit 6-2. Suppose that in addition to Ms. Andrews, there are two other consumers in our particular market—Ellen Smith and Koy Keino. The quantities each consumes at various prices are given in Exhibit 6-3, along with the quantities for Ms. Andrews. The demand curves for each are shown in Panel (a). The market demand curve for all three consumers is then found by adding the quantities demanded at each price. At a price of \$2 per pound, for example, Ms. Andrews demands 5 pounds of apples per week, Ms. Smith demands 3, and Mr. Keino demands 8. A total of 16 pounds of apples are demanded per week at this price. Adding the individual quantities demanded at \$1 per pound yields market demand of 40 pounds per week.

Individual demand curves, then, reflect utility-maximizing adjustments by consumers to various market prices. Market demand curves are found by sum-

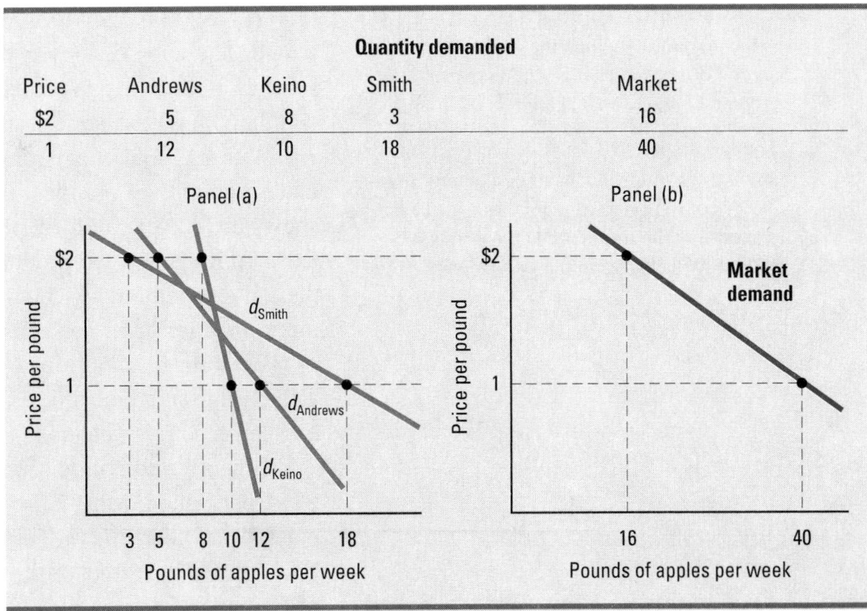

Price	Andrews	Keino	Smith	Market
		Quantity demanded		
$2	5	8	3	16
1	12	10	18	40

EXHIBIT 6-3

Deriving a Market Demand Curve

The demand schedules for Felicia Andrews, Ellen Smith, and Koy Keino are given in the table. Their individual demand curves are plotted in Panel (a). The market demand curve for all three is shown in Panel (b).

ming those individual demands. A market demand curve thus shows the utility-maximizing quantities that will be purchased by consumers in the market at each price.

Substitution and Income Effects

In the last section, we saw that when the price of apples fell from $2 to $1 per pound, Felicia Andrews increased the quantity of apples she demanded. Behind that adjustment, however, lie two distinct effects. It's important to distinguish these effects because they can have quite different implications for the shape of the demand curve.

First, the reduction in the price of apples made them cheaper relative to oranges. Before the price change, it cost the same amount of money to buy 2 pounds of oranges or 1 pound of apples. After the price change, it cost the same amount to buy 1 pound of either oranges or apples. In effect, 2 pounds of oranges would exchange for 1 pound of apples before the price change, and 1 pound of oranges would exchange for 1 pound of apples after the price change.

Second, the price reduction made consumers of apples richer. Before the price change, Ms. Andrews was purchasing 5 pounds of apples and 10 of oranges at a total cost to her of $20. At the new lower price of apples, she could purchase this same combination for $15. In effect, the price reduction for apples gave Ms. Andrews $5 in additional purchasing power. It was equivalent to handing her a $5 bill.

To distinguish these two effects, economists consider first the impact of a price change with no change in purchasing power. An **income-compensated price change** is an imaginary exercise in which we assume that when the price of a good or service changes, the consumer's income is adjusted so that he or she has just enough to purchase the same combination of goods and services at the new set of prices. Ms. Andrews was purchasing 5 pounds of apples and 10 pounds of oranges before the price change. Buying that same combination after the price change would cost $15. The income-compensated price change thus

An **income-compensated price change** is one in which we imagine that a consumer's income is adjusted at the same instant a price changes, so the consumer has just enough to buy the same goods and services at the new price.

- The **substitution effect** of a price change is the amount by which the consumption of a good or service changes in response to an income-compensated change in its price.
- The **income effect** of a price change is the amount by which a consumer changes his or her consumption of a good or service in response to the implicit change in income caused by a change in the good's price.

requires us to take $5 from Ms. Andrews when the price of apples falls to $1 per pound. She can still buy 5 pounds of apples and 10 pounds of oranges. If the price of apples increased, we would give Ms. Andrews more money so that she could purchase the same combination of goods.

With $15 and cheaper apples, Ms. Andrews *could* buy 5 pounds of apples and 10 pounds of oranges. But would she? The answer lies in Equation (7). It shows that the extra utility per $1 she could obtain from apples now exceeds the extra utility per $1 from oranges. She will thus increase her consumption of apples. If she had only $15, any increase in her consumption of apples would require a reduction in her consumption of oranges. In effect, she responds to the income-compensated price change for apples by substituting apples for oranges. The change in a consumer's consumption of a good in response to an income-compensated price change is called the **substitution effect**.

Suppose that with an income-compensated reduction in the price of apples to $1 per pound, Ms. Andrews would increase her consumption of apples to 9 pounds per week and reduce her consumption of oranges to 6 pounds per week. The substitution effect of the price reduction is an increase in apple consumption of 4 pounds per week.

The substitution effect always involves a change in consumption in a direction opposite that of the price change. When a consumer is maximizing utility, the ratio of marginal utility to price is the same for all goods. An income-compensated price reduction increases the extra utility per dollar available from the good whose price has fallen; a consumer will thus purchase more of it. An income-compensated price increase reduces the utility per dollar from the good; the consumer will purchase less of it.

To complete our analysis of the impact of the price change, we must now consider the $5 in additional purchasing power that Ms. Andrews effectively gained from it. After the price reduction, it cost her just $15 to buy what cost her $20 before. She has, in effect, $5 more than she did before. Her additional income may have an effect on the number of apples she consumes. The change in consumption of a good resulting from the implicit change in income because of a price change is called the **income effect** of a price change. We calculate the amount of this implicit change in income by multiplying the quantity of the good purchased before the price change times the change in its price. When the price of a good rises, there is an implicit reduction in income. When the price of a good falls, there is an implicit increase. When the price of apples fell, Ms. Andrews (who was consuming 5 pounds of apples per month) received an implicit increase in income of $5.

Suppose Ms. Andrews uses her implicit increase in income to purchase 3 more pounds of apples and 2 more pounds of oranges per week. She has already increased her apple consumption to 9 pounds per week because of the substitution effect, so the added 3 pounds bring her consumption level to 12 pounds per week. That's precisely what we observed when we derived her demand curve; it's the change we would observe in the marketplace. We see now, however, that her increase in quantity demanded consists of a substitution effect and an income effect. Exhibit 6-4 shows the combined effects of the price change.

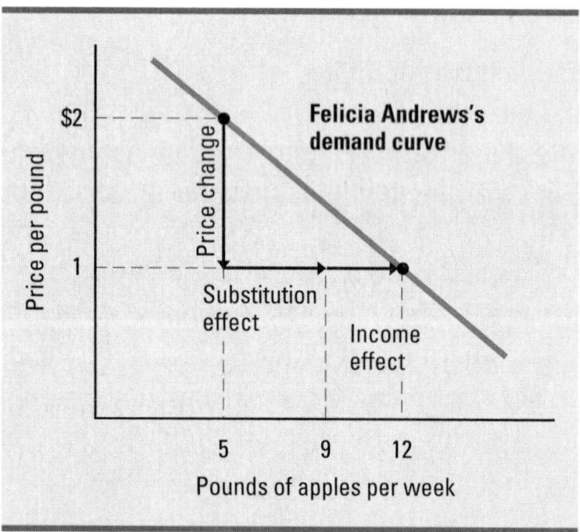

EXHIBIT 6-4

The Substitution and Income Effects of a Price Change

This demand curve for Ms. Andrews was presented in Exhibit 6-3. It shows that a reduction in the price of apples from $2 to $1 per pound increases the quantity Ms. Andrews demands from 5 pounds of apples to 12. This graph shows that this change consists of a substitution effect and an income effect. The substitution effect increases the quantity demanded by 4 pounds, the income effect by 3, for a total increase in quantity demanded of 7 pounds.

The size of the substitution effect depends on the rate at which the marginal utilities of goods change as the consumer adjusts consumption to a price change. As Ms. Andrews increases her consumption of apples and reduces her consumption of oranges, the marginal utility of apples will fall and the marginal utility of oranges will rise. If relatively small changes in quantities consumed produce large changes in marginal utilities, the substitution effect required to restore the equality of marginal-utility-to-price ratios will be small. If much larger changes in quantities consumed are needed to produce equivalent changes in marginal utilities, then the substitution effect will be large.

The magnitude of the income effect of a price change depends on how responsive the demand for a good is to a change in income and on how important the good is in a consumer's budget. When the price changes for a good that makes up a substantial fraction of a consumer's budget, the change in the consumer's purchasing power is substantial. A change in the price of a good that makes up a trivial fraction of a consumer's budget, however, has little effect on his or her purchasing power; the income effect of such a price change is small.

Because each consumer's response to a price change depends on the sizes of the substitution and income effects, these effects play a role in determining the price elasticity of demand. The larger the substitution effect, the greater the absolute value of the price elasticity of demand. When the income effect moves in the same direction as the substitution effect, a greater income effect contributes to a greater price elasticity of demand as well. There are, however, cases in which the substitution and income effects move in opposite directions. We shall explore these ideas in the next section.

Normal and Inferior Goods

The nature of the income effect of a price change depends on whether the good is normal or inferior. The income effect reinforces the substitution effect in the case of normal goods; it works in the opposite direction for inferior goods.

Normal Goods. We saw in Chapter 3 that a normal good is one whose consumption increases with an increase in income. When the price of a normal good falls, there are two effects:

1. The substitution effect contributes to an increase in the quantity demanded because consumers substitute more of the good for other goods.
2. The reduction in price increases the consumer's purchasing power. Because the good is normal, this increase in purchasing power further increases the quantity of the good demanded through the income effect.

In the case of a normal good, then, the substitution and income effects reinforce each other. Ms. Andrews's response to a price reduction for apples is a typical response to a lower price for a normal good.

An increase in the price of a normal good works in an equivalent fashion. The higher price causes consumers to substitute more of other goods, whose prices are now relatively lower. The substitution effect thus reduces quantity demanded. The higher price also reduces purchasing power, causing each consumer to reduce consumption of the good via the income effect.

Inferior Goods. We saw in Chapter 3 that an inferior good is one for which demand falls when income rises. It is likely to be a cheap good that people don't really like very much. When incomes are low, people consume the inferior good because it's what they can afford. As their incomes rise and they can afford something they like better, they consume less of the inferior good. Hamburger and beans are examples of inferior goods. Both are relatively inexpensive sources of protein. As incomes rise, people tend to substitute more expensive sources of protein and to purchase smaller quantities of hamburger and beans.

When the price of an inferior good falls, two things happen:

1. Consumers will substitute more of the inferior good for other goods because its price has fallen relative to those goods. The quantity demanded increases as a result of the substitution effect.
2. The lower price increases purchasing power. But, because the good is inferior, this reduces quantity demanded.

The case of inferior goods is thus quite different from that of normal goods. The income effect works in a direction *opposite* to that of the substitution effect in the case of an inferior good, whereas it reinforces the substitution effect in the case of a normal good.

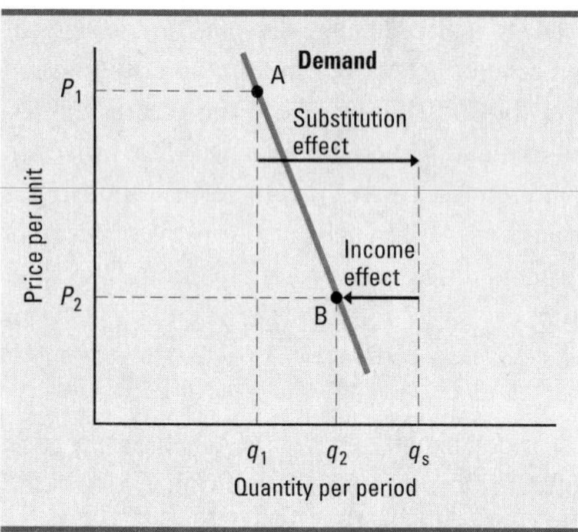

EXHIBIT 6-5

Substitution and Income Effects for Inferior Goods

The substitution and income effects work against each other in the case of inferior goods. The consumer begins at point A, consuming q_1 units of the good at a price P_1. When the price falls to P_2, the consumer moves to point B, increasing quantity demanded to q_2. The substitution effect increases quantity demanded to q_s, but the income effect reduces it from q_s to q_2.

Exhibit 6-5 illustrates the substitution and income effects of a price reduction for an inferior good. When the price falls from P_1 to P_2, the quantity demanded by a consumer increases from q_1 to q_2. The substitution effect increases quantity demanded from q_1 to q_s. But the income effect reduces quantity demanded from q_s to q_2; the substitution effect is stronger than the income effect. The result is consistent with the law of demand: A reduction in price increases the quantity demanded. The quantity demanded is smaller, however, than it would be if the good were normal. Inferior goods are therefore likely to have less elastic demand than normal goods.

The fact that income and substitution effects move in opposite directions in the case of inferior goods raises a tantalizing possibility: What if the income effect were the *stronger* of the two? Could demand curves be upward sloping?

The answer, from a theoretical point of view, is yes. If the income effect in Exhibit 6-5 were larger than the substitution effect, it would lower quantity demanded below q_1. The result would be a reduction in quantity demanded in response to a reduction in price. The demand curve would be upward sloping!

The suggestion that a good could have an upward-sloping demand curve is generally attributed to Robert Giffen, a British journalist who wrote widely on economic matters late in the nineteenth century. Such goods are thus called **Giffen goods.** To qualify as a Giffen good, a good must be inferior and must have an income effect strong enough to overcome the substitution effect.

Although Giffen goods are a theoretical possibility, no one has ever found one—at least for humans. But the fact that the possibility exists illustrates an important point about economic theory: purely theoretical investigations sometimes turn up ideas that might not occur to us intuitively. The fact that utility-maximizing behavior is theoretically consistent with the existence of a Giffen good reminds us that the law of demand is an empirical proposition. We can have confidence in the law of demand because virtually all real-world experience is consistent with it. One sometimes hears people say that the law of demand is fine in theory but is not valid in the real world. The facts show quite the opposite: the law of demand can be easily violated in theory, but it is confirmed by our real-world experience.

Consumer Surplus

Consumers buy goods and services to increase their utility. If such purchases did not increase utility, they would not be made. Consumers receive benefits from their purchases that exceed the value of what they give up for them.

A consumer purchases additional units of a good or service as long as the dollar value of the marginal utility gained exceeds the price of the item. As more

Case in Point: Found! A Giffen Good

Some thirsty little Texas rats have blazed their way into the annals of economic history. They have an upward-sloping demand curve for quinine water.

Researchers at Texas A&M University and at the University of Houston have led the way in conducting economic experiments using laboratory animals. In one set of experiments, they have used rats to test the propositions of the theory of consumer behavior.

In the experiment, rats were given all the water they wanted, plus soft drinks (root beer and collins mix). The water was free, but they had to "pay" for root beer and collins mix by pushing two levers. Pushing the root beer lever earned a rat a squirt of root beer; pushing the collins mix lever earned a squirt of collins mix. The "prices" of root beer and collins mix were set by adjusting the quantity of each drink the rats received for a single push. A reduction in the quantity per push was equivalent to a price increase. The rats were put on a budget; they got only so many lever pushes per day. The number of pushes was, in effect, the rat's income.

Once rats were confronted with an income and prices, they quickly settled into their own equilibrium solutions for the two soft drinks. When prices or the rats' incomes were changed, the animals adjusted their consumption in ways that were consistent with economic theory. For example, the researchers were able to confront the rats with income-compensated price changes and confirm that the substitution effect always changed consumption in a direction opposite to that of a price change.

In another experiment, the researchers tried to create a Giffen good. They reasoned that the good would have to be inferior and would have to loom large in the rats' budgets. That meant the rats had to be poor and the good cheap. It also had to be something the rats weren't crazy about. The researchers tried quinine water. Rats hate quinine water.

A group of rats were given slightly less than the minimum quantity of water that rats require. They could supplement their fluid intake with root beer or quinine water, each of which required pushes on a lever. After several adjustments of prices and budgets, the researchers found a combination of a low income, a relatively high price for root beer, and a very low price for quinine water at which the rats were willing to spend much of their incomes on quinine water.

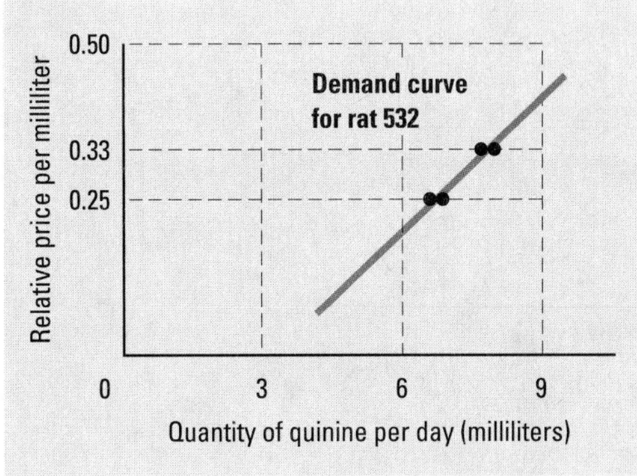

The researchers then reduced the price of quinine water. That effectively made the rats richer—and they responded by consuming less quinine water. A Giffen good had been found! The accompanying graph shows how one rat responded to the price change. The points show actual values of rat 532's consumption at relative quinine water prices of 0.33 and 0.25. When the relative price of quinine water was lowered from 0.33 to 0.25, rat 532 consumed less quinine water. The demand curve for rat 532 is drawn so that it roughly corresponds to the four observations.

The experiments illustrate one approach often used in experimental economics—the use of laboratory animals to demonstrate propositions in economic theory. The researchers who did the study concluded that their demonstration of the existence of a Giffen good suggests that economists should look more carefully for similar cases in the world of human behavior.

Source: Raymond Battalio, John H. Kagel, and Carl A. Kogut, "Experimental Confirmation of the Existence of a Giffen Good," American Economic Review 81(4) (September 1991): 961–970, and Timothy Tregarthen, "Found! A Giffen Good," *The Margin* 3(2) (October 1987): 8–10.

is consumed, however, marginal utility declines; when the dollar value of the utility gained equals the price, no more units will be purchased. The value of the marginal utility gained from all the units of a good purchased up to the last must therefore be greater than the market price. Consumers thus receive utility whose value exceeds what must be given up to purchase goods and services.

The benefits a consumer receives from goods and services are measured in terms of the maximum amount he or she would be willing to pay for them. The surplus of benefits a consumer receives from purchasing any good or service is the difference between the consumer's willingness to pay and what the consumer actually pays for the good or service. This difference is called **consumer surplus.**

- A **Giffen good** is a good for which the demand curve is upward sloping.
- **Consumer surplus** is the difference between what a consumer would be willing to pay for a good or service and the price the consumer must pay to obtain that good or service.

Exhibit 6-6 illustrates the concept of consumer surplus. Han Kim is a baseball fan; his demand curve for attending baseball games is shown here. His demand curve shows that he would be willing to pay $29 to see one game per year. He would be willing to pay $28 to see a second, $27 to see a third, and so on. At a price of $20 per game, his quantity demanded is 10 games per season; he spends $200 for the 10 games. But adding his willingness to pay for each of those games, we find that his total benefit is $245 ($29 + 28 + 27 + · · · + 21 + 20). He thus receives a consumer surplus of $45.

EXHIBIT 6-6

Consumer Surplus

Consumer surplus is the difference between what a consumer is willing to pay and what he or she actually must pay to obtain a good or service. Here, Han Kim would be willing to pay an amount equal to the area OABCE, or $250, to see 10 baseball games per year; that is his total benefit from consuming 10 games. He pays $20 per game, requiring total expenditures of OACE, or $200. The difference, ABC, is his consumer surplus; it equals $50.

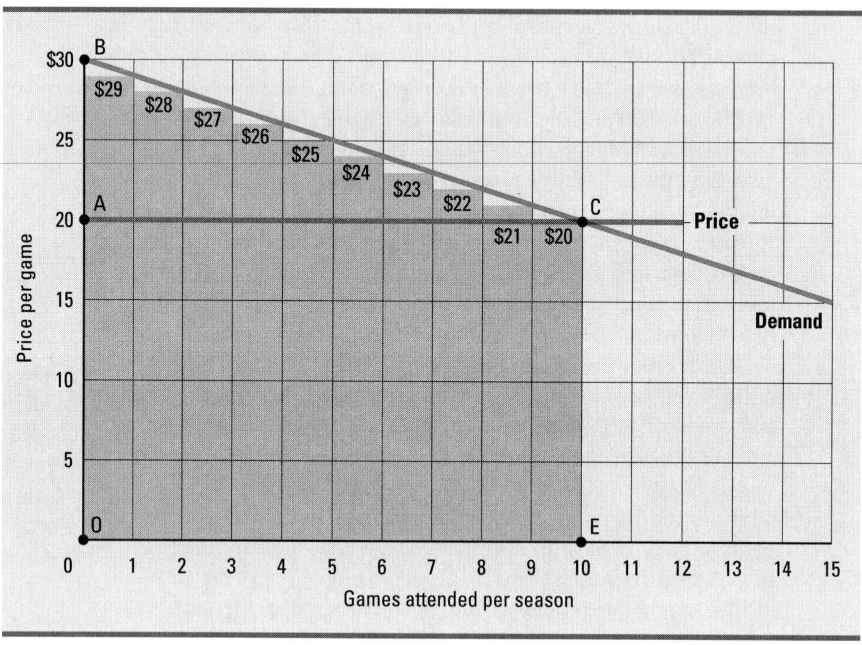

Mr. Kim's total benefit from one baseball game, $29, is shown in Exhibit 6-6 as the shaded area bounded by zero and 1 game and a price of $29. The benefit of the second game is the shaded area bounded by 1 and 2 games and a price of $28. His total willingness to pay, or total benefit, from consuming 10 games is thus the sum of the shaded areas in Exhibit 6-6; it equals his willingness to pay of $245. This shaded area is *approximately* the area under the demand curve between 0 and 10 games per season, the area OABCE. It isn't quite equal to that area; the shaded bars leave out the small triangles between the tops of the bars and the demand curve. The actual area under the demand curve between 0 and 10 games is $250; it is found by summing the areas of the rectangle OACE and the triangle ABC.

The area under the demand curve over the range of the quantity a consumer purchases is thus an approximation of willingness to pay. By making the units on the horizontal axis smaller, we bring the shaded bars that show willingness to pay closer to equaling the full area under the demand curve. For example, if Mr. Kim could purchase tickets for single innings instead of whole baseball games, each of the shaded rectangles in Exhibit 6-6 would be one-ninth as wide, and the shaded area would more closely approximate the area under the demand curve.

Case in Point: Estimating the Value of Recreation

One common application of the concept of consumer surplus is the estimation of the total benefits of activities that are given away for no charge. Consumers are often charged no fee for using state or national recreational areas, for example, yet they clearly benefit from using the resource. It's important to know whether those benefits justify continued use of the land for recreational purposes rather than for some alternative.

Economists use the concept of consumer surplus in measuring such benefits. They first make a statistical estimate of the demand curve for the resource. Sometimes demand curves are based on information about the travel costs consumers have incurred to use the resource; sometimes they are based on surveys that reveal consumers' willingness to pay for the resource.

One research effort estimated the value to deer hunters of two adjacent recreational areas in Louisiana, the Sherburne Wildlife Management Area and the Atchafalaya National Wildlife Refuge. Economists E. Jane Luzar, James E. Hotvedt, and Christopher Gan estimated the demand curve for hunting in the two areas, using travel cost information collected from hunters during the 1987–1988 deer hunting season. Notice that the demand curve they estimated was nonlinear, as shown here. The total benefit (the area under the demand curve shown) equaled $472,508 per season. Because the price charged was zero, the entire area under this demand curve was also consumer surplus.

The economists note that the total benefit worked out to a consumer surplus of $24.70 per visit per hunter. This is somewhat lower than estimates of consumer surplus for hunting in Idaho, where the daily consumer surplus per hunter for elk hunting was estimated at $63.17 and deer hunting yielded a value of $43.74.

Source: E. Jane Luzar, James E. Hotvedt, and Christopher Gan, "Economic Valuation of Deer Hunting on Louisiana Public Land: A Travel Cost Analysis," *Journal of Leisure Research* 24(3) (Second Quarter 1992): 99–113.

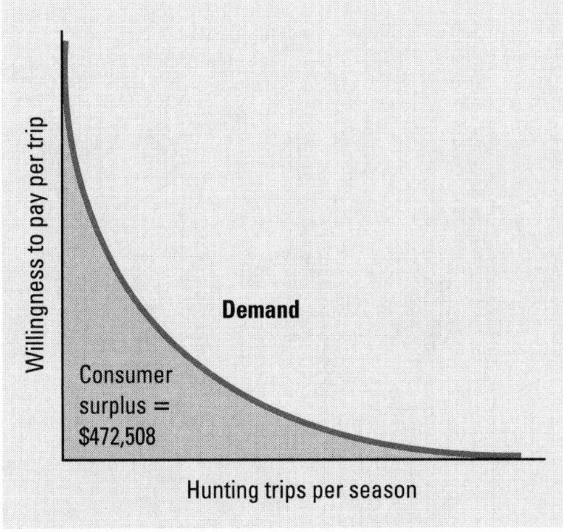

Given our assumption of divisibility, we can make the units measured on the horizontal axis as small as we wish, so that willingness to pay can be considered equal to the area under the demand curve.

Utility and Equity

We can't measure utility the same way we can measure such variables as height and weight. This fact suggests one reason the question of equity in the allocation of goods and services is so difficult to resolve. To see the difficulty, let's imagine that it doesn't exist.

Suppose that we can determine how much utility each person obtains from particular goods or services. Utilities can be compared and added just as weight can. If one consumer receives 14 units of utility and another 12, *total utility* for the two consumers is 26.

Now suppose that we have made the normative judgment that a given stock of goods and services should be allocated among consumers in a way that achieves the maximum total utility possible. How do we maximize total utility? We must ensure that for each good or service, every consumer has the same marginal utility. Suppose Henry Garcia's marginal utility for pears is 6 and Josef Mohammed's is 3. If we take a pear from Mr. Mohammed, he will lose 3 units of utility. If we give it to Mr. Garcia, he will gain 6 units of utility and the total utility of society will be increased by 3 units. As we take pears from Mr. Mohammed, the law of diminishing marginal utility suggests that his marginal utility will rise. As we give them to Mr. Garcia, his marginal utility will fall. At the point at which the marginal utilities of the two consumers are equal, we will have maximized their total utility from pear consumption.

Alternatively, we could redistribute income instead of goods. Suppose we determine that Mr. Garcia's marginal utility from additional income is greater than Mr. Mohammed's. We could then increase society's total utility by transferring income from Mr. Mohammed to Mr. Garcia. We could maximize utility by continuing to transfer income until the marginal utility of $1 in income is equal for all consumers.

One difficulty with all this social engineering, of course, is that we don't know how to measure utility. Even if we could measure utility, how can we presume that one person's utility can be added to another's to obtain a measure of society's total utility? Would Mr. Garcia's gain of 6 units of utility really compensate for Mr. Mohammed's loss of 3? Before we take from one person to give to another, we should determine whether one person's gain in utility has a greater or lower value to society than another person's loss.

Despite the difficulties inherent in comparing one person's utility with another, some economists argue that the law of diminishing marginal utility establishes a basis on which income can be redistributed. Given the diminishing marginal utility of income, the first $1 of income to a person during a particular period is more important than the ten-thousandth. It follows, they argue, that taking a $1 from a rich person and giving it to a poor person increases society's utility, since the marginal utility of $1 to the rich person is low while the marginal utility of $1 to the poor person is high.

If we use the diminishing marginal utility of income to justify a transfer of income, we accept the logic that the marginal utility of $1 to a poor person exceeds the marginal utility of $1 to a rich person. That conclusion, however, is not a necessary result of the law of diminishing marginal utility. Although each additional $1 in income may add less and less to the utility of a particular person, it doesn't follow that the marginal utility of $1 to that person is more or less than the marginal utility of $1 to some other person. Once again, we need a way to compare the significance of additional utility to different people.

Again, if we use the concept of utility as a guide to increasing social welfare, we are making the normative judgment that we should seek the maximum degree of utility possible. Such an effort could conflict with other normative judgments we might make. Suppose, for example, we have decided that people

Case in Point — Do the Rich Pay Enough Taxes?

The call for the rich to pay their "fair share" of income taxes is often heard. But what should that fair share be?

Consider the top 5 percent of income earners in the United States. They earned 27 percent of total income in 1991. How much of the tax burden should they shoulder?

Given the law of diminishing marginal utility, many economists would argue that the richest 5 percent of taxpayers should certainly pay more than 5 percent of the taxes. If everyone paid the same percentage of their income in taxes, for example, the rich would have paid 27 percent of total income taxes in 1991. But the U.S. income tax system is structured so that people pay a higher percentage of their income in taxes as their income rises. The richest 5 percent of taxpayers actually paid 43 percent of total income taxes in 1991.

To determine whether the share of total taxes paid by the rich is too high or too low, we must make a normative judgment. During the 1980s, the share of total taxes paid by the superrich generally increased. In 1979, the richest 5 percent of taxpayers paid 37.6 percent of income taxes collected. The highest 10 percent of income earners paid 49.5 percent of taxes collected in 1979; that share rose to 54.5 percent in 1989.

The share of total taxes paid by lower income earners fell during the 1980s. The lowest 50 percent of income earners contributed 6.8 percent of income taxes collected in 1979. Their share fell to 6.1 percent in 1989.

Obviously, not all people agree about whether a particular distribution of tax burdens is fair. Some people insist that the burden on rich taxpayers is too great; others insist it's too light. Fairness and equity are normative issues and people often have clashing views on normative issues.

Source: Internal Revenue Service *SOI Bulletin* 13(2) (Fall 1993): table 1.

Checklist

- The law of demand suggests that the price effect will be negative: a change in price changes quantity demanded in an opposite direction.
- The substitution effect of a price change changes consumption in a direction opposite to the price change.
- The income effect of a price change reinforces the substitution effect if the good is normal; it moves consumption in the opposite direction if the good is inferior.
- If a good is inferior and the income effect is stronger than the substitution effect, the demand curve is upward sloping.
- Consumer surplus is given by the area under the demand curve and above the market price over the range of consumption of a good or service.
- The law of diminishing marginal utility is often used to justify programs of income redistribution and taxes based on income.

should be able to keep what they have earned. Mr. Mohammed may have earned the money to purchase his pears; should we now take the pears from him in an effort to increase society's utility, or should we instead take money from him to give to Mr. Garcia?

In this hypothetical case, the objective was to distribute a given stock of goods and services in a way that maximizes total utility. But what about the mechanisms through which goods and services are produced? It is likely that establishing a system of distributing goods and services will affect the incentives that lead people to produce them. If the distribution system destroys the incentives that induce people to produce goods and services, then it could make everyone in the economy poorer.

It is thus difficult to use the concepts of utility and diminishing marginal utility to design a program for income redistribution. To say that a problem is difficult, however, is not to say that we cannot grapple with it. Virtually every country in the world makes some effort to redistribute income from rich to poor. One basis for those efforts is the presumption that society's total utility is increased as a result. The argument of diminishing marginal utility has been a major element in arguments that justify such redistribution efforts.

The concept of diminishing marginal utility is also applied to tax policy. If the marginal utility of $1 of income is lower for a rich person than for a poor person, then it follows that less utility is sacrificed by taxing the rich than by taxing the poor. It is largely on this basis that rich people are generally taxed far more heavily than poor people.

Taxes paid in the United States generally rise with income. The federal income tax, for example, rises as income increases. Other taxes that are not based on income tend nonetheless to rise with income. Sales taxes, for example, rise as income rises because people with higher incomes tend to spend more than people with lower incomes.

A Look Back—And a Look Ahead

In this chapter we've examined the nature of utility-maximizing behavior. Economists assume that consumers make choices consistent with the objective of achieving the maximum total utility possible for a given budget constraint.

Utility is a conceptual measure of satisfaction; it is not actually measurable. The theory of utility maximization allows us to ask how a utility-maximizing consumer would respond to a particular event.

By following the marginal decision rule, consumers will achieve the utility maximizing condition: expenditures equal consumers' budgets, and ratios of marginal utility to price are equal for all pairs of goods and services. Thus, consumption is arranged so that the extra utility per dollar spent is equal for all goods and services. The marginal utility from a particular good or service diminishes as consumers consume more of it during a period of time.

Utility maximization underlies consumer demand. The amount by which the quantity demanded changes in response to a change in price consists of a substitution effect and an income effect. The substitution effect always changes quantity demanded in a manner consistent with the law of demand. The income effect of a price change reinforces the substitution effect in the case of normal goods, but it affects consumption in an opposite direction in the case of inferior goods. If the income effect for an inferior good is stronger than the substitution effect, the demand curve will be upward sloping. A good with an upward-sloping demand curve is called a Giffen good.

The law of diminishing marginal utility suggests that the amount a consumer will pay for the first unit of a good is greater than what he or she will pay for subsequent units. This implies that the value of the total utility a consumer gains from consuming a good or service exceeds what the consumer is required to pay. This consumer surplus is measured as the area under the demand curve and above the market price over the range of consumption of the good or service.

Utility theory suggests a rationale for efforts to redistribute income. The law of diminishing marginal utility, when applied to income, suggests that each additional $1 of income a person receives adds less and less to total utility. Many economists argue that this implies that taking $1 from a rich person and giving it to a poor person will increase society's total utility. Although such redistribution efforts affect incentives for production, and conceptual problems of measurement and in comparison of total utility are involved, most societies engage in such redistribution. The law of diminishing marginal utility is also an important conceptual foundation for taxation based on income.

The Chapter 6 Appendix presents an alternative approach to utility maximization. It does not rely on the concept of marginal utility, and it gives us a graphical representation of the utility-maximizing condition.

In this chapter we looked at the consumer behavior that underlies the demand curve. In Chapter 7 we'll examine the production theory that underlies the supply curve. We'll see how a firm can minimize the cost of producing a given level of output—or achieve the maximum output possible for a given level of cost.

Terms and Concepts for Review

Budget constraint

Consumer surplus

Giffen good

Income effect

Income-compensated price change

Marginal utility

Law of diminishing marginal utility

Substitution effect

Total utility

Utility-maximizing condition

For Discussion

1. Suppose you really, *really* like ice cream. You *adore* ice cream. Does the law of diminishing marginal utility apply to your ice cream consumption?
2. If two commodities that you purchase on a regular basis carry the same price, does that mean they both provide the same total utility? Marginal utility?
3. If a person goes to the bowling alley planning to spend $15 but comes away with $5, what, if anything, can you conclude about the marginal utility of the alternatives (e.g., bowl another line, have a soda or a sandwich) available to the person at the time he or she leaves?
4. Which do you like more—going to the movies or watching rented tapes on the VCR? If you engage in both activities during the same period, say a week, explain why.
5. Name five examples of things that you normally consume that might yield negative satisfaction if you consume them to excess. What might the phrase "consume them to excess" mean?
6. At many major athletic events, ticket scalpers are able to sell tickets at the gate for prices that are three, four, even five times more than the official price. Why do some people pay such high prices? What role might the concept of consumer surplus play in your answer?
7. Do you tend to eat more at a fixed price buffet or when ordering from an *á la carte* menu? Explain, using the marginal decision rule that guides your behavior.
8. Explain why being an inferior good is a necessary but not sufficient condition for status as a Giffen good.
9. Disneyland once charged a relatively small admission fee and also charged for each ride. Now the Disney theme parks charge a much higher admission fee and there is no charge for individual rides. Draw an individual's demand curve for any one ride, and show the effective price and quantity demanded. Why are consumers willing to pay such a large admission fee?
10. Do you think an extra $1 of income has the same marginal utility to, say, Madonna as to a poor person? If Madonna's marginal utility is lower, does that justify taking $1 from her and giving it to the poor person?

Problems

1. Suppose the marginal utility of good A is 20 and its price is $4, and the marginal utility of good B is 50 and its price is $5. The individual to whom this information applies is spending $20 on each good. Is he or she maximizing satisfaction? If not, what should the individual do to increase total satisfaction? On the basis of this information can you pick an optimum combination? Why or why not?
2. John and Marie settle down to watch the evening news. Marie is content to watch the entire program, while John continually zaps it in favor of possible alternatives. Draw the likely marginal utility curves for the two individuals.
3. Li, a very careful maximizer of utility, consumes two services, going to the movies and bowling. She has arranged her consumption of the two activities so that the marginal utility of going to a movie is 20 and the marginal utility of going bowling is 10. The price of going to a movie is $10, and the price of going bowling is $5. Show that she is satisfying the requirement for utility maximization. Now show what happens when the price of going bowling rises to $10.
4. The campus Property Maintenance Department has determined that the demand curve for water from campus drinking fountains is given by the following:

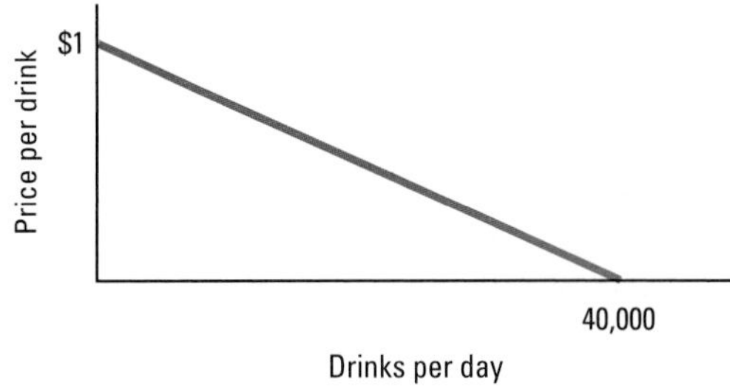

What is the total benefit of the campus's provision of drinking fountains?

5. Suppose we determine that all individuals have the same marginal utility of income curve and that our goal is to ensure that the marginal utility of income is the same for all individuals. Show that this requires that all individuals have the same income.

6 Appendix

Consumer Choice: The Indifference Curve Approach

This appendix presents an alternative way of looking at the problem of utility maximization, one that avoids the concept of marginal utility. (The marginal utility approach lends useful insights, but it suffers from our inability to measure utility.) The alternative we explore here requires only that we be able to observe the rates at which consumers exchange one good for another.

We'll begin our analysis with a graphical presentation of the budget constraint. We'll then examine a new concept that allows us to draw a map of a consumer's preferences. Then we can draw some conclusions about the choices a utility-maximizing consumer could be expected to make.

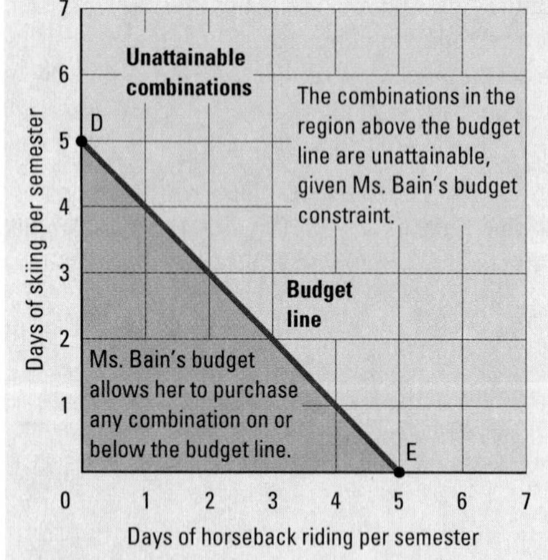

EXHIBIT 6A-1

The Budget Line

The budget line shows combinations of skiing and horseback riding Janet Bain could consume if the price of each activity is $50 and she has $250 available for them each semester. The slope of this budget line is −1, the negative of the price of horseback riding divided by the price of skiing.

A **budget line** shows graphically the combinations of two goods a consumer can buy with a given budget.

The Budget Line

We saw that a consumer's choices are limited by the budget available. Total spending for goods and services can fall short of the budget constraint but may not exceed it.

For a consumer who buys only two goods, the budget constraint can be shown graphically with a **budget line.** A budget line shows graphically the combinations of two goods a consumer can buy with a given budget.

Suppose a college student, Janet Bain, enjoys skiing and horseback riding. A day spent pursuing either activity costs $50. Suppose she has $250 available to spend on these two activities each semester. Ms. Bain's budget line is illustrated in Exhibit 6A-1.

The budget line shows all the combinations of skiing and horseback riding Ms. Bain can purchase with her budget of $250. She could also spend less than $250, purchasing combinations that lie below and to the left of the budget line in Exhibit 6A-1. Combinations above and to the right of the budget line are beyond the reach of her budget.

The vertical intercept of the budget line (point D) is given by the number of days of skiing per month that Ms. Bain could enjoy if she devoted all of her money to skiing and none to horseback riding. She has $250, and the price of a day of skiing is $50. If she spent the entire amount on skiing, she could ski five days per semester. The horizontal intercept of the budget line (point E) is the number of days she could spend horseback riding if she devoted her $250 entirely to that sport. She could purchase five days of either skiing or horseback riding per semester.

Because the budget line is linear, we can compute its slope between any two points. Between points D and E the vertical change is −5 days of skiing; the hor-

An **indifference curve** shows combinations of two goods that yield the same level of utility.

izontal change is 5 days of horseback riding. The slope is thus $-5/5 = -1$. More generally, we find the slope of the budget line by finding the vertical and horizontal intercepts and then computing the slope between those two points. The vertical intercept of the budget line is found by dividing Ms. Bain's budget, B, by the price of skiing, the good on the vertical axis (P_s). The horizontal intercept is found by dividing B by the price of the horseback riding, the good on the horizontal axis, (P_h). The slope is thus

$$\text{Slope} = -\frac{\frac{B}{P_s}}{\frac{B}{P_h}} \qquad \textbf{(1)}$$

Multiplying the numerator and denominator by the negative of the denominator, P_h/B, we have

$$\text{Slope} = -\frac{\frac{B}{P_s}}{\frac{B}{P_h}} \times \frac{\frac{P_h}{B}}{\frac{P_h}{B}}$$

$$= -\frac{P_h}{P_s} \qquad \textbf{(2)}$$

Equation 2 shows that the slope of a budget line is the inverse of the price of the good on the horizontal axis divided by the price of the good on the vertical axis.

Indifference Curves

Suppose Ms. Bain spends two days skiing and three days horseback riding per semester. She will derive some level of total utility from that combination of the two activities. There are other combinations of the two activities that would yield the same level of total utility. Combinations of two goods that yield equal levels of utility are shown on an **indifference curve.**[1] Because all points along an indifference curve generate the same level of utility, economists say that a consumer is *indifferent* between them.

Exhibit 6A-2 shows an indifference curve for combinations of skiing and horseback riding that yield the same level of total utility. Point X marks Ms. Bain's initial combination of two days skiing and three days horseback riding per semester. The indifference curve shows that she could obtain the same level of utility by moving to point W, skiing for seven days and going horseback riding for one day. She could also get the same level of utility at point Y, skiing just one day and spending five days horseback riding. Ms. Bain is indifferent among combinations W, X, and Y. We assume that the two goods are divisible, so she is indifferent between *any* two points along an indifference curve.

Look at point T in Exhibit 6A-2. It has the same amount of skiing as point X, but fewer days are spent horseback riding. Ms. Bain would thus prefer point X to point T. Similarly, she prefers X to U. What about a choice between the combinations at point W and point T? Because combinations X and W are equally satisfactory, and because Ms. Bain prefers X to T, she must prefer W to T. In general, any combination of two goods that lies below and to the left of an indifference curve for those goods yields less utility than any combination on the

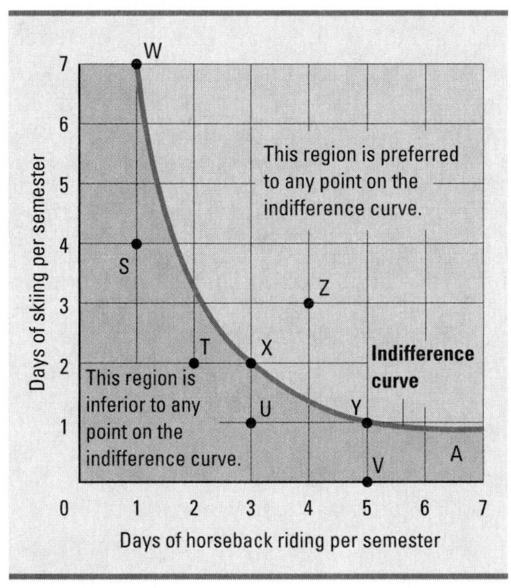

EXHIBIT 6A-2

An Indifference Curve

The indifference curve A shown here gives combinations of skiing and horseback riding that produce the same level of utility. Janet Bain is thus indifferent as to which point on the curve she selects. Any point below and to the left of the indifference curve would produce a lower level of utility; any point above and to the right of the indifference curve would produce a higher level of utility.

[1] Limiting the situation to two goods allows us to show the problem graphically. By stating the problem of utility maximization with equations, we could extend the analysis to any number of goods and services.

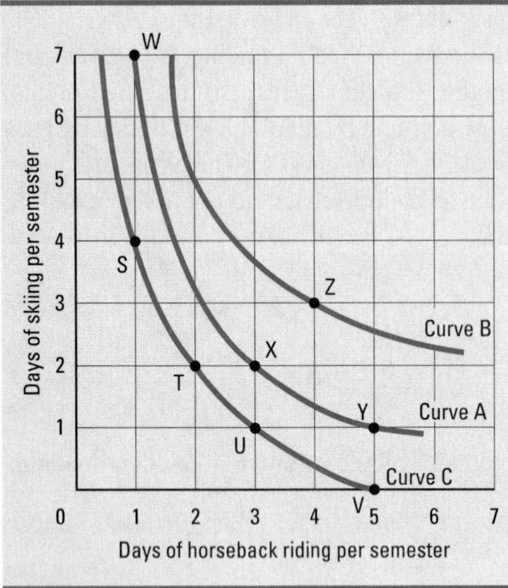

EXHIBIT 6A-3

Indifference Curves

Each indifference curve suggests combinations among which the consumer is indifferent. Curves that are higher and to the right are preferred to those that are lower and to the left. Here, indifference curve B is preferred to curve A, which is preferred to curve C.

indifference curve. Such combinations are *inferior* to combinations on the indifference curve.

Point Z, with three days of skiing and four days of horseback riding, provides more of both activities than point X; Z therefore yields a higher level of utility. It is also superior to point W. In general, any combination that lies above and to the right of an indifference curve is preferred to any point on the indifference curve.

We can draw an indifference curve through any combination of two goods. Exhibit 6A-3 shows indifference curves drawn through each of the points we have discussed. Indifference curve A from Exhibit 6A-2 is inferior to indifference curve B. Ms. Bain prefers all the combinations on indifference curve B to those on curve A, and she regards each of the combinations on indifference curve C as inferior to those on curves A and B.

Although only three indifference curves are shown in Exhibit 6A-3, in principle an infinite number could be drawn. The collection of indifference curves for a consumer constitutes a kind of map illustrating a consumer's preferences. Different consumers will have different maps. We'll see later in this appendix that we have good reason to expect the indifference curves for all consumers to have the same basic shape as those shown here: they slope downward, and they become less steep as we travel down and to the right along them.

Compare points X and S in Exhibit 6A-3. Note that point X (on curve A) includes more horseback riding but less skiing than S (on curve C). Which combination is better? X lies on a higher indifference curve; it therefore generates a higher level of utility. A consumer would always prefer to be on a higher than a lower indifference curve. Every point on indifference curve B is thus preferred to every point on indifference curve A. Every point on indifference curve A or curve B is preferred to every point on curve C.

The slope of an indifference curve shows the rate at which two goods can be exchanged without affecting the consumer's utility. Exhibit 6A-4 shows indifference curve C from Exhibit 6A-3. Suppose Ms. Bain is at point S, consuming four days of skiing and one day of horseback riding per semester. Suppose she spends another day horseback riding. This additional day of horseback riding does not affect her utility if she gives up two days of skiing, moving to point T.

EXHIBIT 6A-4

The Marginal Rate of Substitution

The marginal rate of substitution is equal to the absolute value of the slope of an indifference curve. It is the maximum amount of one good a consumer is willing to give up to obtain an additional unit of another. Here, it is the number of days of skiing Janet Bain would be willing to give up to obtain an additional day of horseback riding. Notice that the marginal rate of substitution (MRS) declines as she consumes more and more days of horseback riding.

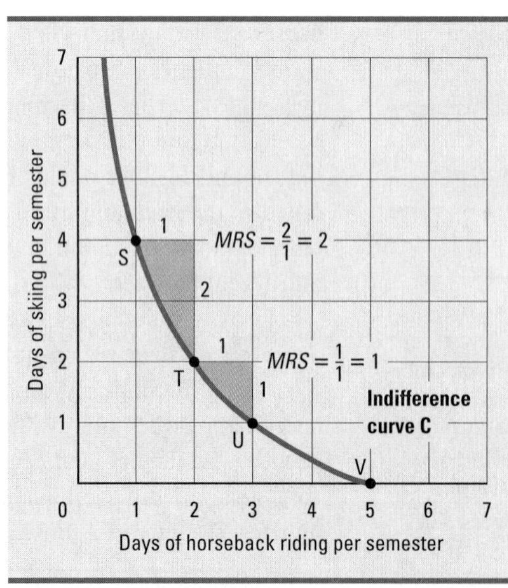

The **marginal rate of substitution** is the maximum amount of one good that a consumer will give up to obtain an additional unit of another.

She is thus willing to give up two days of skiing for a second day of horseback riding. The curve shows, however, that she would be willing to give up at most one day of skiing to obtain a third day of horseback riding (shown by point U).

The maximum amount of one good a consumer would be willing to give up in order to obtain an additional unit of another is called the **marginal rate of substitution,** which is equal to the absolute value of the slope of the indifference curve between two points. Exhibit 6A-4 shows that as Ms. Bain devotes more and more time to horseback riding, the rate at which she is willing to give up days of skiing for additional days of horseback riding—her marginal rate of substitution—diminishes.

The Utility-Maximizing Solution

We assume that each consumer seeks the highest indifference curve possible. The budget line gives the combinations of two goods that the consumer can purchase with a given budget. Utility maximization is therefore a matter of selecting a combination of two goods that satisfies two conditions:

1. The point at which utility is maximized must be within the attainable region defined by the budget line.
2. The point at which utility is maximized must be on the highest indifference curve consistent with condition 1.

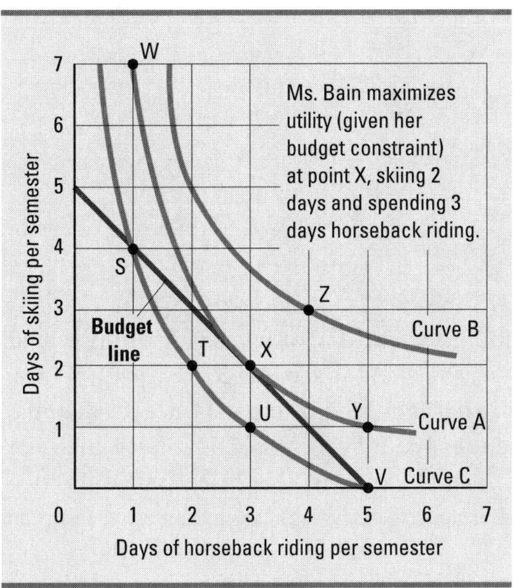

EXHIBIT 6A-5

The Utility-Maximizing Solution

Combining Janet Bain's budget line and indifference curves from Exhibits 6A-1 and 6A-3, we find a point that (1) satisfies the budget constraint and (2) is on the highest indifference curve possible. That occurs for Ms. Bain at point X.

Exhibit 6A-5 combines Janet Bain's budget line from Exhibit 6A-1 with her indifference curves from Exhibit 6A-3. Our two conditions for utility maximization are satisfied at point X, where she skis two days per semester and spends three days horseback riding.

The highest indifference curve possible for a given budget line is tangent to the line; the indifference curve and budget line have the same slope at that point. The slope of the indifference curve shows the marginal rate of substitution (*MRS*) between two goods. The slope of the budget line gives the price ratio between the two goods; it is the rate at which one good exchanges for another in the market. At the point of utility maximization, then, the rate at which the consumer is willing to exchange one good for another equals the rate at which the goods can be exchanged in the market. For any two goods A and B, with good B on the horizontal axis and good A on the vertical axis,

$$MRS_{A,B} = \frac{P_B}{P_A} \quad \textbf{(3)}$$

Problem 3 at the end of this appendix asks you to confirm that the solution at X in Exhibit 6A-5 suggests why we can be confident that indifference curves have the bowed-in shape given here. Suppose Ms. Bain's indifference curves were linear and that they had the same slope as the budget line, −1. Then the highest indifference curve she could select would coincide with her budget line, and she would be indifferent between any combinations on it. Ms. Bain would never be able to choose whether to ski or to ride. We observe that real consumers aren't constantly in such a quandary. You can confirm for yourself that if Ms. Bain's indifference curves were linear but had a slope unequal to the slope of the budget line, or if her indifference curves were bowed out like the production possibilities curve, then she would devote her entire budget to a single activity. (Remember that consumers want to choose the highest indifference curve possible.) We observe that real consumers consume lots of different things; this is consistent with bowed-in curves.

Utility Maximization and the Marginal Decision Rule

How does the achievement of the utility maximizing solution in Exhibit 6A-5 correspond to the marginal decision rule? That rule says that additional units of an activity should be pursued if the marginal benefit of the activity exceeds the marginal cost. The observation of that rule would lead a consumer to the highest indifference curve possible for a given budget.

Suppose Ms. Bain has chosen a combination of skiing and horseback riding at point S in Exhibit 6A-6. She's now on indifference curve C. She's also on her budget line; she's just spending all of the budget, $250, available for the purchase of the two goods.

EXHIBIT **6A-6**

Applying the Marginal Decision Rule

Suppose Ms. Bain is initially at point S. She is spending all of her budget, but she isn't maximizing utility. Because her marginal rate of substitution exceeds the rate at which the market asks her to give up skiing for horseback riding, she can increase her satisfaction by moving to point D. Now she's on a higher indifference curve E. She'll continue exchanging skiing for horseback riding until she reaches point X, at which she's on curve A, the highest indifference curve possible.

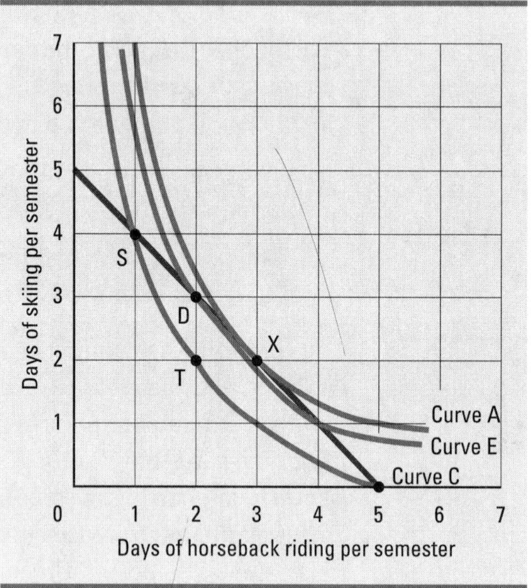

An exchange of two days of skiing for one day of horseback riding would leave her at point T, and she would be as well off as she is at S. Her marginal rate of substitution between S and T is 2; her indifference curve is steeper than the budget line at point S. The fact that her indifference curve is steeper than her budget line tells us that the rate at which she is *willing* to exchange the two goods differs from the rate the market asks. She would be willing to give up as many as two days of skiing to gain an extra day of horseback riding; the market demands that she give up only one. The marginal decision rule says that if an additional unit of an activity yields greater benefit than its cost, it should be pursued. If the benefit to Ms. Bain of one more day of horseback riding equals the benefit of two days of skiing, yet she can get it by giving up only one day of skiing, then the benefit of that extra day of horseback riding is clearly greater than the cost.

Because the market asks that she give up less than she is willing to give up for an additional day of horseback riding, she'll make the exchange. Beginning at point S, she'll exchange a day of skiing for a day of horseback riding. That moves her along her budget line to point D. Recall that we can draw an indifference curve through any point; she's now on indifference curve E. It's above and to the right of indifference curve C, so Ms. Bain is clearly better off. And that should come as no surprise. When she was at point S, she was willing to give up two days of skiing to get an extra day of horseback riding. The market asked her to give up only one; she got her extra day of riding at a bargain! Her move along her budget line from point S to point D suggests a very important principle. If a consumer's indifference curve intersects the budget line, then it will always be possible for the consumer to make exchanges along the budget line that move to a higher indifference curve. Ms. Bain's new indifference curve at point D also intersects her budget line; she's still willing to give up more skiing than the market asks for additional riding. She'll make another exchange and move along her budget line to point X, at which she attains the highest indifference curve possible with her budget. Point X is on indifference curve A, which is tangent to the budget line.

Having reached point X, Ms. Bain clearly wouldn't give up still more days of skiing for additional days of riding. Beyond point X, her indifference curve is flatter than the budget line—her marginal rate of substitution is less than the absolute value of the slope of the budget line. That means that the rate at which she'd be willing to exchange skiing for horseback riding is less than the market asks. She can't make herself better off than she is at point X by further rearranging her consumption. Point X, where the rate at which she's willing to exchange one good for another equals the rate the market asks, gives her the maximum utility possible.

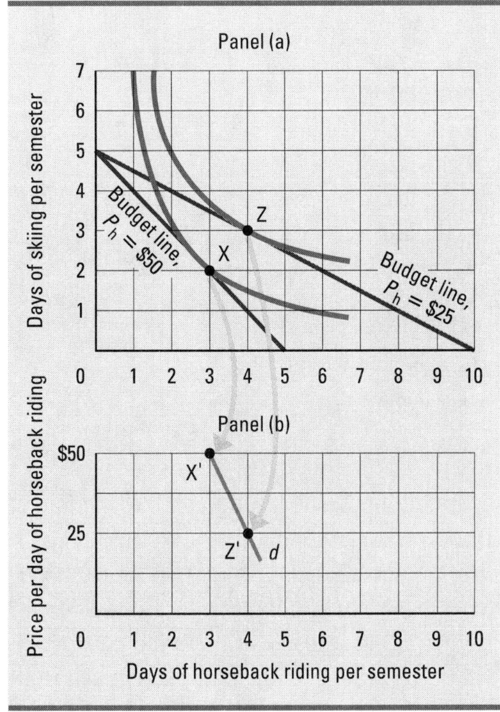

EXHIBIT 6A-7

Utility Maximization and Demand

By observing a consumer's response to a change in price, we can derive the consumer's demand curve for a good. Panel (a) shows that at a price for horseback riding of $50 per day, Janet Bain chose to spend three days horseback riding per semester. Panel (b) shows that a reduction in the price to $25 increases her quantity demanded to four days per semester. Points X and Z, at which Ms. Bain maximizes utility at horseback riding prices of $50 and $25, respectively, become points X′ and Z′ on her demand curve, *d*, for horseback riding in Panel (b).

Utility Maximization and Demand

Exhibit 6A-6 showed Janet Bain's utility-maximizing solution for skiing and horseback riding. She achieved it by selecting a point at which an indifference curve was tangent to her budget line. A change in the price of one of the goods, however, will shift her budget line. By observing what happens to the quantity of the good demanded, we can derive Ms. Bain's demand curve.

Panel (a) of exhibit 6A-7 shows the original solution at point X, where Ms. Bain has $250 to spend and the price of a day of either skiing or horseback riding is $50. Now suppose the price of horseback riding falls by half, to $25. That changes the horizontal intercept of the budget line; if she spends all of her money on horseback riding she can now ride 10 days per semester. Another way to think about the new budget line is to remember that its slope is equal to the negative of the price of the good on the horizontal axis divided by the price of the good on the vertical axis. When the price of horseback riding (the good on the horizontal axis) goes down, the budget line becomes flatter. Ms. Bain picks a new utility-maximizing solution at point Z.

The solution at Z involves an increase in the number of days Ms. Bain spends horseback riding. Notice that only the price of horseback riding has changed; all other features of the utility-maximizing solution remain the same. Ms. Bain's budget and the price of skiing are unchanged; this is reflected in the fact that the vertical intercept of the budget line remains fixed. (Recall that the vertical intercept was determined by dividing the budget by the price of a day's skiing.) Ms. Bain's preferences are unchanged; they are reflected by her indifference curves. Because all other factors in the solution are unchanged, we can determine two points on Ms. Bain's demand curve for horseback riding from her indifference curve diagram. At a price of $50, she maximized utility at point X, spending three days horseback riding per semester. When the price falls to $25, she maximizes utility at point Z, riding four days per semester. Those points are plotted as points X′ and Z′on her demand curve for horseback riding in Panel (b) of Exhibit 6A-7.

Substitution and Income Effects

We can use indifference curve analysis to illustrate the substitution and income effects of a price change. Recall that the substitution effect is the change in consumption that results from an income-compensated change in a good's price.

Suppose that Bill Jensen, a friend of Ms. Bain's, also enjoys skiing and horseback riding. He also has a budget of $250 per semester to spend on the two activities, and he faces the same prices as Ms. Bain faced: $50 for a day of skiing and $50 for a day of horseback riding.

Mr. Jensen's preferences differ from Ms. Bain's, so his indifference curves are different. In Exhibit 6A-8, he faces the budget line UV. He maximizes utility at point R on indifference curve A. If the price of a day of horseback riding falls to $25, his budget line shifts to UW, and he maximizes utility at point S on indifference curve B.

EXHIBIT 6A-8

The Substitution and Income Effects of a Price Change

Bill Jensen faces budget line UV and maximizes utility at point R, with 4 days of skiing and 1 day of horseback riding each semester. A reduction in the price of horseback riding to $25 shifts his budget line to UW. The substitution effect of the price change is the change from point R to point T. The income effect is the change from point T to point S.

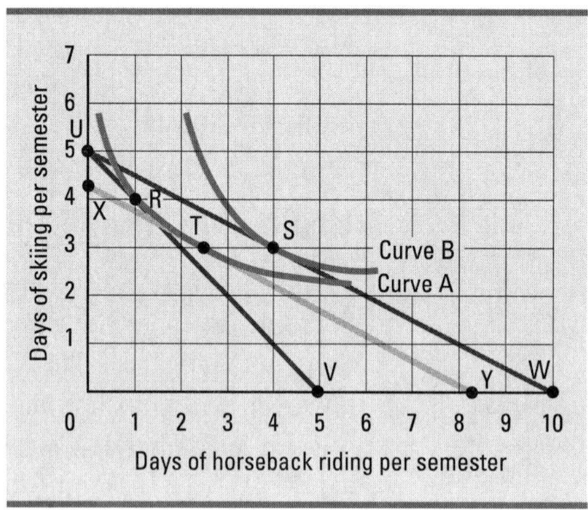

The shift from R to S can be separated into a substitution and an income effect. To compute the substitution effect, we imagine that the consumer's income was changed at the same time as the price was changed, so that the consumer remains on the original indifference curve. We construct a budget line XY that is parallel to the budget line UW that emerged as a result of the price change. We then look to see where this imaginary budget line is tangent to the original indifference curve. In this case, the tangency occurs at T. The shift from R to T is the substitution effect of the price change. Notice that it results in an increase in days of horseback riding.

The income effect of the price change results from the movement from the imaginary budget line XY to the final budget line UW. Mr. Jensen's consumption shifts from point T to point S. This is the income effect of the price change.

The estimation of the substitution and income effects using indifference curve analysis thus involves three steps:

1. We draw the new budget line that results from the price change. In the case we've considered, the new budget line is UW.
2. We sketch another budget line whose slope equals the slope of the new budget line and that is tangent to the original indifference curve. This is the line XY, tangent to indifference curve A. The tangency occurs at point T. The movement from R to T is the substitution effect.

3. The movement from the tangency on the imaginary budget line to the tangency on the budget line created by the price change is called the income effect. Here, the income effect is the change from point T to point S.

It's important to remember that the separation of the change in consumption resulting from a price change into a substitution and income effect is a conceptual exercise. We would observe Mr. Jensen moving from point R to point S in Exhibit 6A-8. The reason for separating the change from R to S into a substitution and income effect lies in the potential difference in the two responses.

The substitution effect will always lead the consumption of a good in a direction opposite that of the price change. The change produced by the income effect depends on whether the good is normal or inferior. In Mr. Jensen's case, the reduction in the price of horseback riding produced an implicit increase in income, which increased his consumption of the activity: horseback riding is for him a normal good.

Exhibit 6A-9 illustrates what could happen in the case of an inferior good. Suppose the Smith family consumes steak and hamburger. Its budget for the two goods is $25 per week. Suppose steak costs $5 per pound and hamburger costs $2.50. In the case shown, the family faces a budget line UV and maximizes utility by consuming 3 pounds of steak and 4 pounds of hamburger per week.

EXHIBIT 6A-9

Substitution and Income Effects, or an Inferior Good

The Smith family has a budget of $25 per week to spend on steak and hamburger. With a price of steak of $5 per pound and a price of hamburger of $2.50 per pound, it faces the budget constraint UV. It maximizes utility by selecting point R on indifference curve A and consuming 3 pounds of steak and 4 pounds of hamburger per week. An increase in the price of hamburger to $5 per pound rotates the budget line to UW; the family now selects 2 pounds of steak and 3 pounds of hamburger at point S. The change from R to S comprises a substitution effect from R to T and an income effect from T to S. In this case, hamburger is an inferior good and the income effect changes consumption in a direction opposite to the substitution effect.

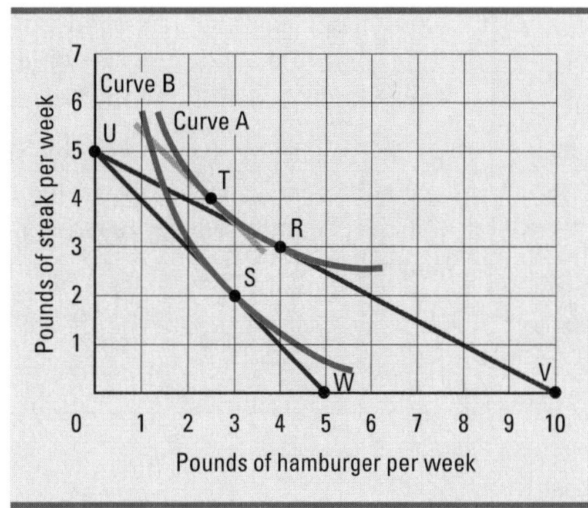

Now suppose the price of hamburger rises to $5. The budget line rotates downward to UW. It slope now equals −1, the new ratio of the price of hamburger to the price of steak. The family now maximizes utility at point S, consuming less steak (2 pounds) and less hamburger (3 pounds) than before. We can separate the family's response to the price change into a substitution and income effect by constructing a line whose slope is −1 that is tangent to the original indifference curve A. This is the light maroon line in Exhibit 6A-9. The tangency occurs at point T; the substitution effect is the movement from R to T. The change in consumption of hamburger due to the substitution effect is the reduction from 4 pounds to 2.5 pounds per week.

The higher price of hamburger implies an implicit reduction in the family's income; this is the shift in the imaginary budget line to the new budget line UW. The result of this shift is a movement from point T to point S. The family's consumption of hamburger is increased by a reduction in income, so hamburger is an inferior good.

With an inferior good, the substitution and income effects pull in opposite directions. The substitution effect of the price increase reduces hamburger consumption, and the income effect increases it. In this case, the Smith family's income effect increases hamburger consumption from 2.5 pounds to 3 pounds per week. Because the substitution effect reduced consumption by 1.5 pounds, the net result of the two forces was a reduction in consumption by 1 pound per week—the movement from R to S. If the income effect were stronger than the substitution effect, the higher price of hamburger would result in an increase in consumption. That would be the Giffen case discussed in the chapter.

Indifference curve analysis gives us the same results as does the marginal utility approach employed in the main chapter. The indifference curve has a firmer conceptual footing, however, because it does not require that we assume the measurement of utility—which we can't measure. The use of indifference curve analysis requires only that we be able to observe the rate at which consumers are willing to exchange one good for another.

Checklist

- A budget line shows combinations of two goods a consumer is able to consume, given a budget constraint.
- An indifference curve shows combinations of two goods that yield equal satisfaction.
- To maximize utility, a consumer chooses a combination of two goods at which an indifference curve is tangent to the budget line.
- At the utility-maximizing solution, the consumer's marginal rate of substitution (the slope of the indifference curve) is equal to the price ratio of the two goods.
- We can derive a demand curve from an indifference map by observing the quantity of the good consumed at different prices.
- The substitution effect of a price change is found by constructing an imaginary budget line whose slope equals the slope of the budget line produced by the price change and that is tangent to the original indifference curve. The income effect is the movement from the substitution effect solution to the final tangency on the new budget line.

Terms and Concepts for Review

Budget line

Indifference curve

Marginal rate of substitution

For Discussion

1. How does an increase in income affect a consumer's budget line? His or her total utility?
2. Joe Kassel loves to smoke and to eat the greasiest hamburgers imaginable. Both activities appear to be bad for him. What do his indifference curves for these two goods look like?
3. Suppose Ms. Bain is now consuming at point V in Exhibit 6A-5. Use the marginal decision rule to explain why a shift to X would increase her utility.
4. Suppose that you are a utility maximizer and so is your economics instructor. What can you conclude about your respective marginal rates of substitution for movies and concerts?
5. How does a reduction in price affect total utility? Does your answer change if a good is inferior?
6. Relate the derivation of Ms. Bain's demand curve for horseback riding in Exhibit 6A-7 to the ceteris paribus assumption in the law of demand.

Problems

Sid is a commuter student at his college. During the day, he snacks on cartons of yogurt and the "house special" sandwiches at the Student Center cafeteria. A carton of yogurt costs $1.20; the Student Center often offers specials on the sandwiches, so their price varies a great deal. Sid has a budget of $36 per week for food at the Center.

Five of Sid's indifference curves are given by the following schedule; the points listed in the tables correspond to the points shown in the graph.

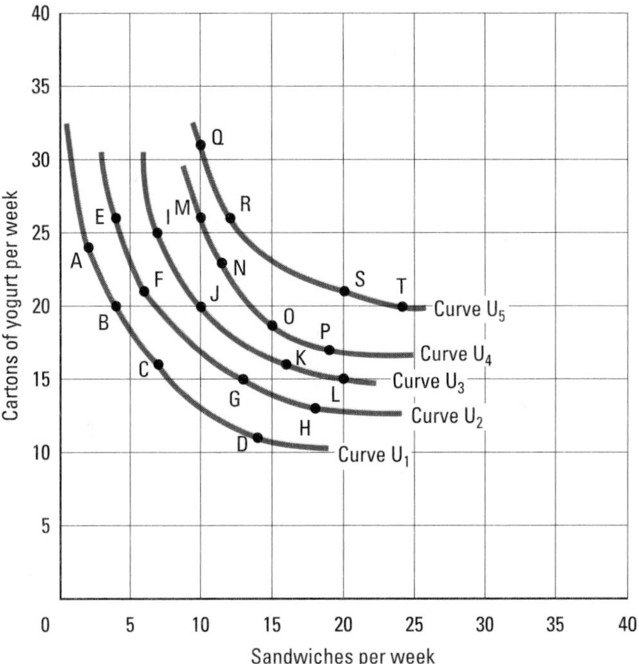

1. Use the above set of Sid's indifference curves as a guide in drawing your own graph grid. Draw Sid's indifference curves and budget line, assuming sandwiches cost $3.60. Identify the point at which he maximizes utility. How many sandwiches will he consume? How many cartons of yogurt? (*Hint:* All of the answers in this exercise occur at one of the combinations given in the tables at the right.)

2. Now suppose the price of sandwiches is cut to $1.20. Draw the new budget line. Identify the point at which Sid maximizes utility. How many sandwiches will he consume? How many cartons of yogurt?

3. Identify the substitution and income effects of the price change in (Problem 2). The substitution effect takes him from Point _____ to Point _____. The income effect takes him from Point _____ to Point _____. Explain carefully what the substitution and income effects mean. Are sandwiches a normal good or an inferior good? Why?

4. Now draw the budget lines implied by a price of yogurt of $1.20 and sandwich prices of $0.90 and $1.80. With the observations you've already made for sandwich prices of $3.60 and $1.20, draw the demand curve. Are yogurt and sandwiches substitutes or complements? Explain how this demand curve illustrates the law of demand.

Curve U_1

Point on Curve	Sandwiches	Yogurt
A	2	24
B	4	20
C	7	16
D	14	11

Curve U_2

Point on Curve	Sandwiches	Yogurt
E	4	26
F	6	21
G	13	15
H	18	13

Curve U_3

Point on Curve	Sandwiches	Yogurt
I	7	25
J	10	20
K	16	16
L	20	15

Curve U_4

Point on Curve	Sandwiches	Yogurt
M	10	26
N	12	23
O	15	18
P	19	17

Curve U_5

Point on Curve	Sandwiches	Yogurt
Q	10	31
R	12	26
S	20	21
T	24	20

7

Production and Cost

Chapter Objectives

After mastering the material in this chapter, you will be able to:

1. Show how a firm's output varies as it uses more or less of a single factor of production, with all other factors fixed.
2. Explain how the relationship between a firm's cost and its output is affected by the relationship between its use of factors of production and its output.
3. Describe the primary measures economists use of the production costs facing firms, and discuss the significance of each.
4. Contrast the alternatives available to firms when making choices over long versus short periods of time.
5. Show how a firm can choose a combination of factors of production that minimizes the total cost of producing a given level of output.

The essential requisites of production are three—labour, capital, and natural agents

—John Stuart Mill

What's Ahead

It is dawn in Beijing, China. Already thousands of Chinese are out cleaning the city's streets. They are using brooms.

On the other side of the world night falls in Washington, D.C., where the streets are also being cleaned—by a handful of giant street-sweeping machines driven by a handful of workers.

The difference in method is not the result of a greater knowledge of modern technology in the United States—the Chinese know perfectly well how to build street-sweeping machines. It is a production decision based on costs in the two countries. In China, where wages are relatively low, an army of workers armed with brooms is the least expensive way to produce clean streets. In Washington, where labor costs are high, it makes sense to use more machinery and less labor.

All types of production efforts require choices in the use of factors of production. This chapter examines such choices. Should a good or service be produced using relatively more labor and less capital? Or should relatively more capital and less labor be used? What about the use of natural resources?

In this chapter we'll also look carefully at the nature of production processes and the costs those processes imply for the production of goods and services. We'll see why firms make the production choices they do and how their costs affect their choices. We'll apply the marginal decision rule to the production process and see how this rule ensures that production is carried out at the lowest cost possible.

Just as we examined the nature of consumer behavior (in Chapter 6) in order to build a better understanding of demand, so in this chapter we examine the nature of production and costs in order to gain a better understanding of

In this chapter we shift our focus to **firms,** organizations that produce goods and services. In producing goods and services, firms combine the factors of production we discussed in Chapter 2—labor, capital, and natural resources—to produce various products.

Firms are organizations that produce goods and services.

We'll put the marginal decision rule to work in our analysis; we'll assume that firms engage in production in order to earn a profit and that they seek to make this profit as large as possible. That is, they seek to maximize their profits.

Whether we consider the operator of a shoeshine stand at an airport or the firm that produces airplanes, we'll find there are basic relationships between the use of factors of production and output levels, and between output levels and costs, that apply to all production. Just as the material in Chapter 6 was at the foundation of demand, the material in this chapter is at the foundation of supply.

Production Choices and Costs: The Short Run

Our analysis of production and cost begins with a period economists call the **short run.** The short run is a planning period over which the managers of a firm must consider some of their factors of production as fixed in quantity. For example, a restaurant may regard its building as a fixed factor over a period of at least the next year. It would take at least that much time to find a new building or to expand or reduce the size of its present facility. Decisions concerning the operation of the restaurant during the next year must assume the building will remain unchanged. Other factors of production could be changed during the year, but the size of the building must be regarded as a constant.

A factor of production whose quantity can be changed during a particular period is called a **variable factor of production.** When the quantity of a factor of production cannot be changed during a particular period, it is called a **fixed factor of production.** For the restaurant, its building is a fixed factor for at least a year; factors such as labor and food, however, can be variable over the year.

While the managers of the restaurant are making choices concerning its operation over the next year, they are also planning for longer periods. Over those periods, managers may contemplate alternatives such as modifying the building, building a new facility, or selling the building and leaving the restaurant business. The planning period over which a firm can consider all factors of production as variable is called the **long run.**

At any one time, a firm may be making both short-run and long-run choices. The managers may be planning what to do for the next few days and for the next few years. Their decisions over the next few days are likely to be short-run choices. Decisions that will affect operations over the next few years may be long-run choices, in which managers can consider changing every aspect of their operations. Our analysis in this section focuses on the short run. We'll examine long-run choices later in this chapter.

- The **short run** is a planning period over which at least one of a firm's factors of production is fixed in quantity.
- A **variable factor of production** is one whose quantity can be changed during a particular period.
- A **fixed factor of production** is one whose quantity cannot be changed during a particular period.
- The **long run** is a planning period during which all of a firm's factors of production are variable.
- The **total product curve** of a variable factor relates output to the quantity of the variable factor used in a period, given the levels of all other factors of production.

Production in the Short Run

A firm uses factors of production to produce a product. Our first task is to explore the relationship between factors of production and the output of a firm.

Consider a hypothetical firm, Acme Box Company, a manufacturer of wooden storage boxes. Suppose that Acme has a lease on its building and equipment. During the period of the lease, Acme's capital stock is its fixed factor of production. Acme's variable factors of production include things such as labor, lumber, and electricity. In the analysis that follows, we shall simplify by assuming that labor is Acme's *only* variable factor of production.

Total and Marginal Products

Exhibit 7-1 shows the quantities of boxes Acme can obtain from various quantities of labor and its given level of capital. A **total product curve** shows the

EXHIBIT 7-1

Acme Box Company's Total Product Curve

The table gives output levels per day for Acme Box Company at various quantities of labor per day, assuming the firm's capital stock is fixed. These values are then plotted graphically as a total product curve.

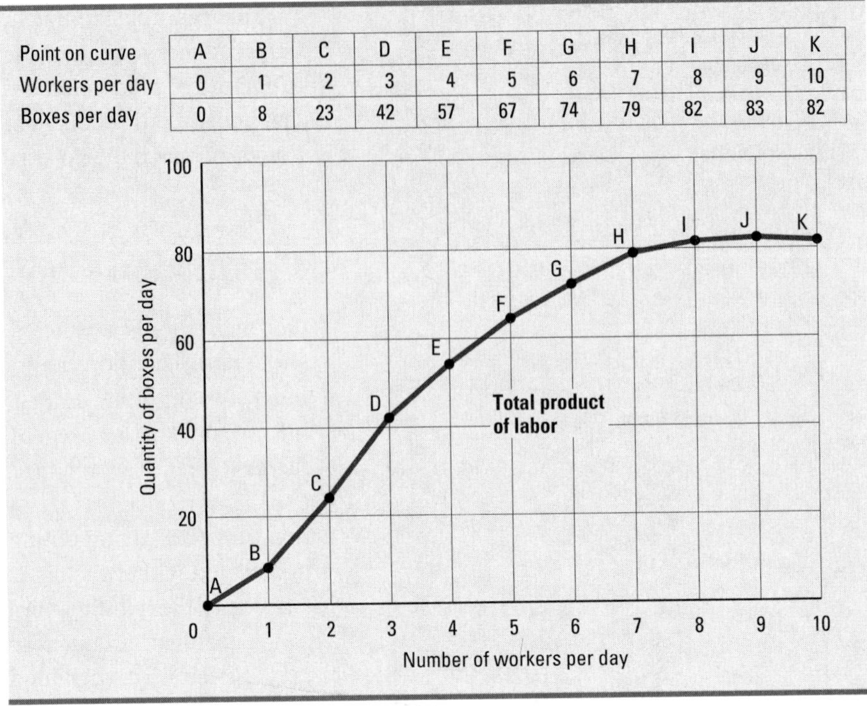

Point on curve	A	B	C	D	E	F	G	H	I	J	K
Workers per day	0	1	2	3	4	5	6	7	8	9	10
Boxes per day	0	8	23	42	57	67	74	79	82	83	82

quantities of output that can be obtained from different quantities of a variable factor of production, assuming other factors of production are fixed.

Notice what happens to the slope of the total product curve in Exhibit 7-1. Between 0 and 3 units of labor, the curve becomes steeper. Between 3 and 9 units of labor, the curve continues to slope upward, but its slope diminishes. Beyond 9 units of labor, production begins to decline and the curve slopes downward.

We measure the slope of any curve as the vertical change between two points divided by the horizontal change between the same two points. The slope of the total product curve for labor equals the change in output (ΔQ) divided by the change in units of labor (ΔL):

$$\text{Slope of the total product curve for labor} = \frac{\Delta Q}{\Delta L}$$

The slope of a total product curve for any variable factor is a measure of the additional output associated with an additional unit of the variable factor, with the quantities of all other factors held constant. We call this additional output the **marginal product** of the variable factor. The marginal product of labor, for example, is the increase in output that results from an additional unit of labor, ceteris paribus. It is measured as the slope of the total product curve for labor. Exhibit 7-2 shows the calculation of marginal product as changes in total product and relates the slope of the total product and marginal product curves. The total product curve in Panel (a) is repeated from Exhibit 7-1. Notice that marginal product rises as the slope of the total product curve increases, falls as the slope of the total product curve declines, reaches zero when the total product curve achieves its maximum value, and becomes negative as the total product curve slopes downward. Note further that marginal products are plotted at the midpoint of each interval. The marginal product of the fifth unit of labor, for example, is plotted between 4 and 5 units of labor.

The **marginal product** of a factor of production is the change in total output resulting from a 1-unit increase in the quantity of the factor used, holding the quantities of all other factors constant.

EXHIBIT 7-2

The Marginal Product of Labor

The table gives the same values for quantities of labor and total product that we had in Exhibit 7-1. Marginal product is the change in output resulting from a one-unit increase in labor. Panel (a) shows the total product curve. The slope of the total product curve is marginal product, which is plotted in Panel (b). Values for marginal product are plotted at the midpoint of the respective intervals.

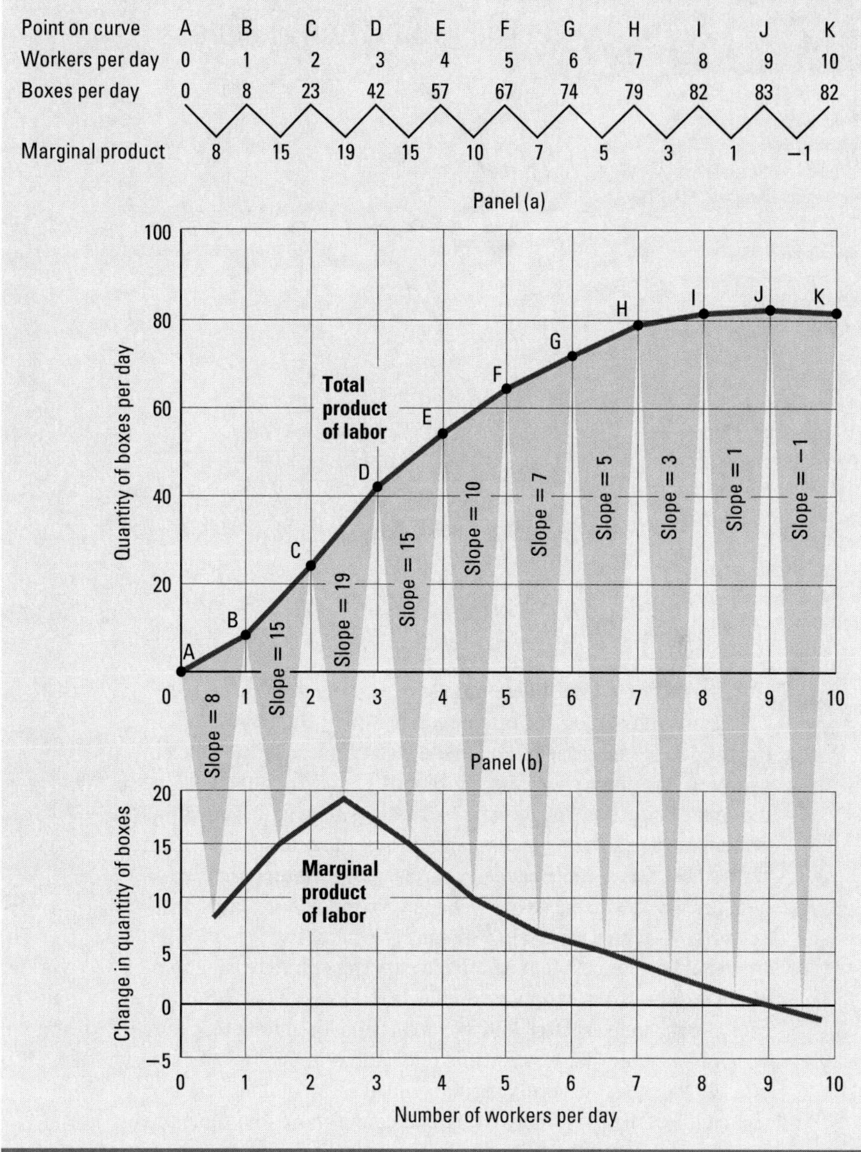

Increasing, Diminishing, and Negative Marginal Returns

Adding the first worker increases Acme's output from 0 to 8 storage boxes per day. The second worker adds 15 units to total output; the third adds 19. The marginal product goes up because when there are more workers, each one can specialize to a degree. One worker might do the sawing, another the assembling, and another the sanding and finishing. Their increasing marginal products are reflected by the increasing slope of the total product curve over the first 3 units of labor and by the upward slope of the marginal product curve over the same range. The range over which marginal products are increasing is called the range of **increasing marginal returns.** Increasing marginal returns exist in the context of a total product curve for labor, so we are holding the quantities of other factors constant. Increasing marginal returns may occur for any variable factor.

Increasing marginal returns to a factor of production occur when the marginal product of the factor is rising as more of it is used, given a constant level of all other factors.

A fourth worker adds less to total output than the third; the marginal product of the fourth worker is 15 boxes. The data in Exhibit 7-2 show that marginal product continues to decline after the fourth worker as more and more workers

Case in Point The Production of Fitness

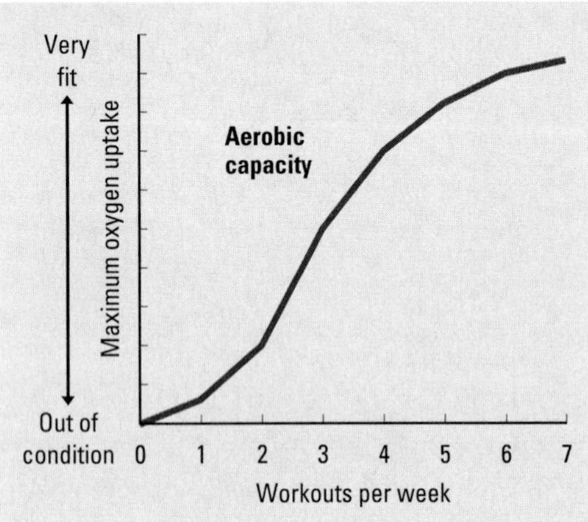

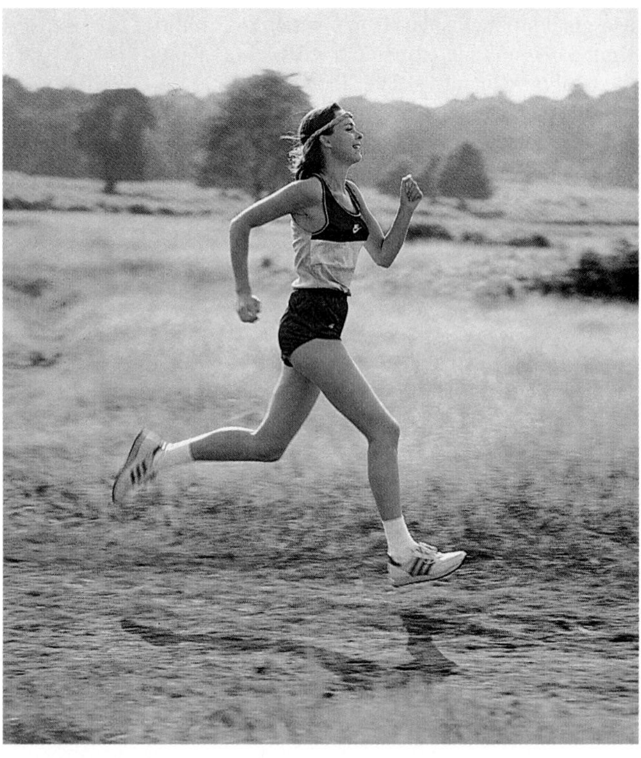

How much should an athlete train?

Sports physiologists often measure the "total product" of training as the increase in an athlete's aerobic capacity—the capacity to absorb oxygen into the bloodstream. An athlete can be thought of as producing aerobic capacity using a fixed factor (his or her natural capacity) and a variable input (exercise). The chart shows how this aerobic capacity varies with the number of workouts per week. The curve has a shape very much like a total product curve—which, after all, is precisely what it is.

The data suggest that an athlete experiences increasing marginal returns from exercise for the first three days of training each week; indeed, over half the total gain in aerobic capacity possible is achieved. It is for this reason that three days of exercise per week are generally recommended for nonathletes. A person can become even more fit by exercising more, but the gains become smaller with each added day of training. The law of diminishing marginal returns applies to training.

The increase in fitness that results from the sixth and seventh workouts each week is small. Studies also show that the costs of daily training, in terms of increased likelihood of injury, are high. Many trainers and coaches now recommend that athletes—at all levels of competition—take a day or two off each week.

Source: Jeff Galloway, *Galloway's Book on Running* (Bolinas, Calif.: Shelter Publications, 1984), p. 73. Reprinted by permission.

are hired. The additional workers allow even greater opportunities for specialization, but because they are operating with a fixed stock of capital, each new worker adds less to total output. The ninth worker adds only a single box to total output. When each additional unit of a variable factor adds less to total output, the firm is experiencing **diminishing marginal returns.** Over the region of diminishing marginal returns, the marginal product of the variable factor is positive but falling. Once again, we assume the quantities of all other factors of production are fixed. Diminishing marginal returns may occur for any variable factor. Panel (b) shows that Acme Box experiences diminishing marginal returns between the third and ninth workers, or between 42 and 83 boxes per day.

Diminishing marginal returns occur when additional units of a variable factor add less and less to total output, given constant quantities of all other factors.

After the ninth worker, Acme's fixed plant becomes so crowded that adding another worker actually reduces output. When additional units of a variable factor reduce total output, given constant quantities of all other factors, the company experiences **negative marginal returns.** Now the total product curve is downward sloping, and the marginal product curve falls below zero.

Negative marginal returns can occur for any variable factor. When labor is fixed in quantity, for example, additional equipment might get in the way of the workers and cause output to fall. Clearly, a firm will never intentionally add so much of a variable factor of production that it enters a region of negative marginal returns.

The idea that the marginal product of a variable factor declines over some range is important enough, and general enough, that economists state it as a law. The **law of diminishing marginal returns** holds that the marginal product of any variable factor of production will eventually decline, assuming the quantities of other factors of production are given.

To see the logic of the law of diminishing marginal returns, imagine a case in which it does not hold. Say that you have a small plot of land for a vegetable garden, 10 feet by 10 feet in size. The plot itself is a fixed factor in the production of vegetables. Suppose you are able to hold constant all other factors—water, sunshine, temperature, fertilizer, and seed—and vary the amount of labor devoted to the garden. How much food could the garden produce? If the law of diminishing marginal returns did not hold, the answer is that you could grow an *unlimited* quantity of food on your small plot—enough to feed the entire world! You could add an unlimited number of workers to your plot and still increase output. If you didn't get enough output with, say, 500 workers, you could use 5 million; the five-millionth worker would add at least as much to total output as the first. If diminishing marginal returns to labor did not occur, the total product curve would slope upward at a constant or increasing rate—food production in your garden could always be increased by adding more labor.

Reader's Advisory !

It is easy to confuse the concept of diminishing marginal returns with the concept of negative marginal returns. To say a firm is experiencing diminishing marginal returns is *not* to say its output is falling. Diminishing marginal returns mean the value of the *marginal product* of a variable factor is declining. Output is still increasing, but at a decreasing rate—an additional unit of input increases output by a smaller amount than the previous unit of input.

Costs in the Short Run

A firm's costs of production depend on the quantities and prices of its factors of production. Suppose, for example, that capital is a firm's only variable factor of production and that 10 units of capital are required to produce 100 units of output. Suppose further that capital costs $50 per unit. Then the capital cost of producing 100 units of output is $500.

The concept of marginal product can be used in examining what happens to a firm's costs as it produces more units. The marginal product of a factor tells us how much more output the firm obtains when it uses one more unit of the factor. The cost of that additional output is simply the price of the additional unit of the factor.

Variable, Fixed, and Total Costs

The costs associated with the use of variable factors of production are called **variable costs.** The costs associated with the use of fixed factors are called **fixed costs.** The sum of fixed and variable costs is **total cost.**

Any cost that varies with the level of output is a variable cost. For most firms, variable costs include costs for raw materials, salaries of production workers, and utilities.

Fixed costs do not vary with output. The salaries of top management may be fixed costs; any charges set by contract over a period of time are likely to be fixed costs. A term commonly used for fixed costs is *overhead.*

- **Negative marginal returns** occur when additional units of a variable factor of production reduce total output, given constant quantities of all other factors.
- The **law of diminishing marginal returns** holds that if the quantity of a variable factor of production is increased, with the quantities of all other factors given, the marginal product of the variable factor will eventually decline.
- **Variable costs** are the costs incurred by a firm in its use of variable factors of production.
- **Fixed costs** are the costs associated with fixed factors of production.
- **Total cost** is the sum of fixed and variable costs.

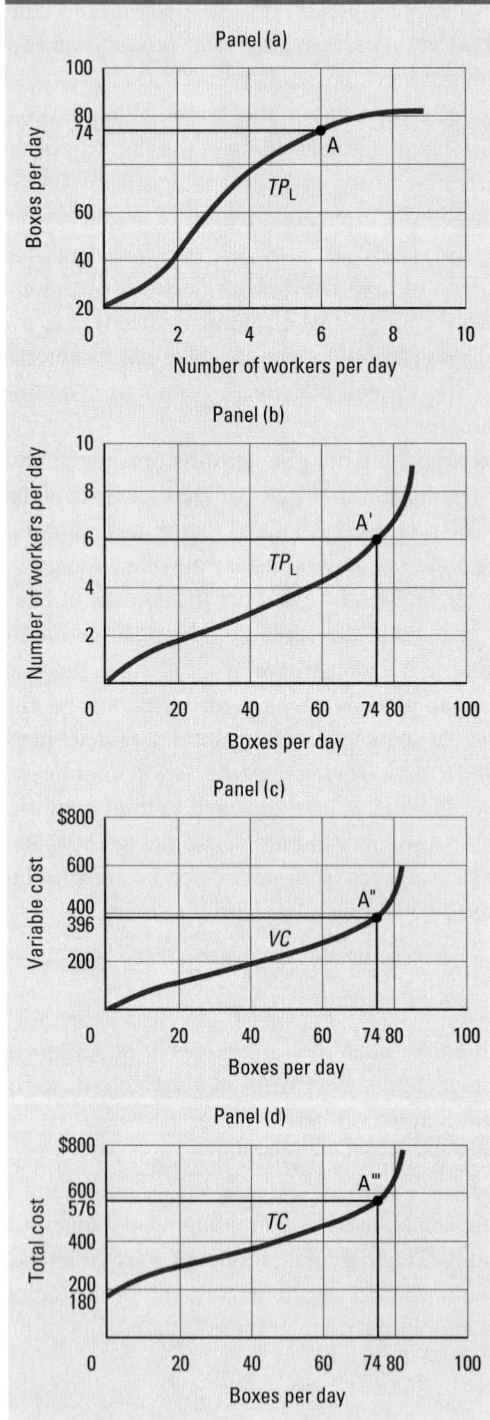

EXHIBIT 7-3

Deriving the Total Cost Curve

The total product curve TP_L in Panel (a) was derived in Exhibit 7-1 for Acme Box Company. (The downward-sloping portion of the curve has been omitted.) At point A, the firm uses 6 units of labor and produces 74 boxes per day.

The total product curve TP_L in Panel (b) is the same as in Panel (a), except that the axes have been reversed. The vertical axis shows the number of workers, and the horizontal axis shows output. Point A′ corresponds to point A in Panel (a).

We get to Panel (c) by multiplying each unit of labor by the wage ($66 per day). That converts the vertical axis from units of labor to dollars spent on labor—Acme's variable cost curve *VC*. The variable cost of 74 boxes is $396 (point A″).

Finally, in Panel (d), we add the firm's fixed cost of $180 per day to its variable cost curve to obtain its total cost curve *TC*. The total cost of producing 74 boxes, for example, is the variable cost of $396 plus $180, or $576 (point A‴).

From Total Product to Total Cost

Let's illustrate the relationship between Acme Box Company's total product curve and its variable and total costs. Acme can vary the quantity of labor it uses each day, so the cost of this labor is a variable cost. We assume capital is a fixed factor of production, so its cost is a fixed cost in the short run.

Suppose that Acme pays a wage of $66 per worker per day. If labor is the only variable factor, Acme's variable costs per day amount to $66 times the number of workers it employs.

Suppose the price of capital to Acme is $15 per unit per day and that its present plant is the equivalent of 12 units of capital. Acme's 12 units of capital cost $180 per day. In the short run, Acme can't increase or decrease its quantity of capital—it must pay the $180 per day no matter what it does. Even if the firm cuts production to zero, it must still pay $180 per day in the short run.

Acme's total cost is its fixed cost of $180 plus its variable cost, which will depend on the quantity of labor it employs. A total cost curve shows the firm's total cost at each level of output. Such a curve can be derived from a total product curve as illustrated in Exhibit 7-3.

Panel (a) shows the total product curve introduced in Exhibit 7-1. At point A, for example, the firm employs 6 workers and produces 74 boxes per day. We want a total cost curve with output on the horizontal axis, so we reverse the axes of the total product curve to place output on the horizontal axis and labor on the vertical axis. The new total product curve for labor is shown in Panel (b). Point A′ corresponds to point A in Panel (a). Next we convert units of labor (on the vertical axis) to a variable cost. To do this, we multiply each quantity of labor by its price, thus obtaining the variable cost associated with each level of output. Multiplying 6 units of labor by a price of $66 per worker, for example, gives us a variable cost of $396 at point A″ in Panel (c). Finally, we add the fixed cost of $180 to obtain a total cost of $576 for 74 units of output; this is shown as point A‴ in Panel (d). Repeating this exercise for each point on the total product curve yields the total cost curve in Panel (d).

Notice the relationship between the shapes of the total product curve in Panel (a) and the total cost curve in Panel (d). The total product curve becomes steeper over the range of increasing marginal returns—from 0 to 3 units of labor, or from 0 to 42 boxes. Over that range of production the total cost curve is becoming flatter; costs are rising at a decreasing rate. Acme experiences diminishing marginal returns beyond the third unit of labor, or the forty-second box. Each new worker adds less to total output, yet Acme pays the same wage to each worker. As a result, costs rise faster and faster. The total product curve rises at a decreasing rate, but the total cost curve rises at an increasing rate.

When the firm has increasing marginal returns to its variable factor, it takes less additional labor—and less additional cost—to produce each additional unit

EXHIBIT 7-7

Marginal Cost, Average Total Cost, and Average Variable Cost in the Short Run

Total cost figures for Outdoor Gear are taken from Exhibit 7-5. The other values are derived from these. Average total cost equals total cost divided by quantity produced, marginal cost is the change in total cost with each additional unit of output, and average variable cost is variable cost (equals total cost minus fixed cost) divided by quantity produced. Minimum values for average total cost *(ATC)* and average variable cost *(AVC)* are highlighted in the table. The marginal cost *(MC)* curve (from Exhibit 7-6) intersects the *ATC* and *AVC* curves at these points, the lowest on both curves.

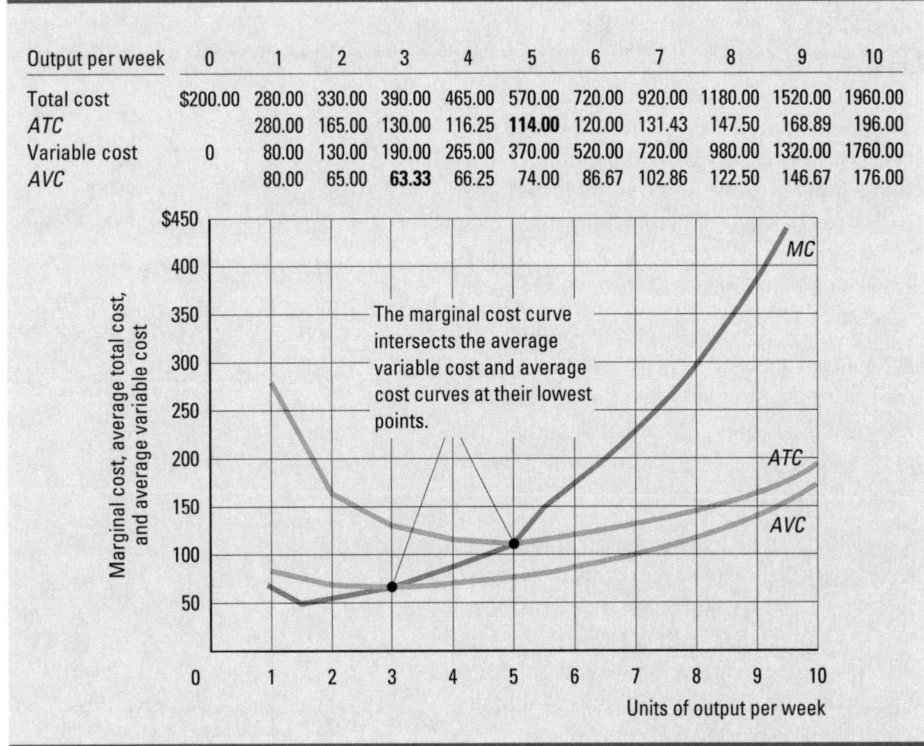

Output per week	0	1	2	3	4	5	6	7	8	9	10
Total cost	$200.00	280.00	330.00	390.00	465.00	570.00	720.00	920.00	1180.00	1520.00	1960.00
ATC		280.00	165.00	130.00	116.25	**114.00**	120.00	131.43	147.50	168.89	196.00
Variable cost	0	80.00	130.00	190.00	265.00	370.00	520.00	720.00	980.00	1320.00	1760.00
AVC		80.00	65.00	**63.33**	66.25	74.00	86.67	102.86	122.50	146.67	176.00

Exhibit 7-7 shows the computation of short-run average total cost and average variable cost for Outdoor Gear and graphs of these values. Notice that the curves for short-run average total cost and average variable cost fall, then rise. We say that these cost curves are U-shaped.

Exhibit 7-7 includes the marginal cost curve from Exhibit 7-6. It intersects the average total cost and average variable cost curves at their lowest points. When marginal cost is below average total cost or average variable cost in the short run, the average curves slope downward. When marginal cost is greater than short-run average total cost or average variable cost, the average values rise.

We shall see in the next chapter that the marginal cost curve is the foundation for the supply curve. We'll learn that the portion of the marginal cost curve that lies above average variable cost is the supply curve for the firm.

You've experienced a relationship equivalent to the one between marginal and average values during your career as a student. Your grade point average (GPA) represents the average grade you've earned in your course work so far. When you take an additional course, your grade in that course represents the marginal grade. What happens to your GPA when you get a grade that's lower than your previous average? It falls. What happens to your GPA when you get a grade that's higher than your previous average? It rises.

The checklist summarizes what we have learned so far about the relationship between the firm's short-run production function and its short-run cost curves. We'll put our analysis of cost curves in the short run to work in subsequent chapters as we examine production choices by firms. We turn next to an examination of production and cost in the long run, a planning period in which the firm can consider changing the quantities of all factors.

Checklist

- In Panel (a), the total product curve for a variable input in the short run shows that the firm experiences increasing marginal returns from zero to F_a units of the variable factor (zero to Q_a units of output), diminishing marginal returns from F_a to F_b (Q_a to Q_b units of output), and negative marginal returns beyond F_b units of input.
- Panel (b) shows that marginal product rises over the range of increasing marginal returns, falls over the range of diminishing marginal returns, and becomes negative over the range of negative marginal returns.
- In Panel (a), increasing marginal returns occurred over the range of output from zero to Q_a. In Panel (c), total cost rises at a decreasing rate over that range, then rises at an increasing rate beyond Q_a, the range of diminishing marginal returns. The total cost at zero units of output (the vertical axis) is fixed cost (*FC*).
- Panel (d) shows that marginal cost falls over the range of increasing marginal returns, then rises over the range of diminishing marginal returns. The marginal cost curve intersects the average total cost and average variable cost curves at their lowest points.

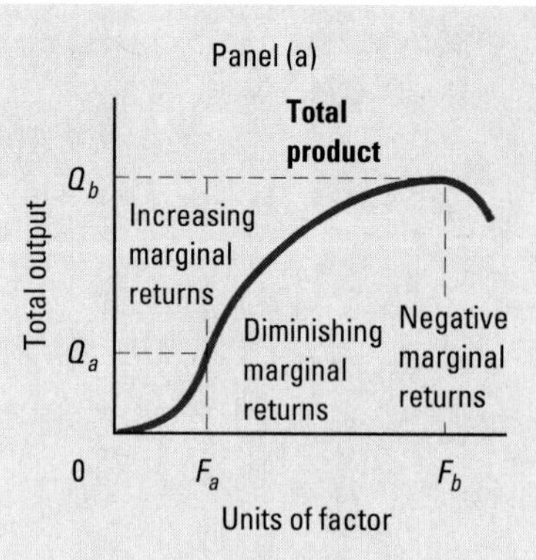

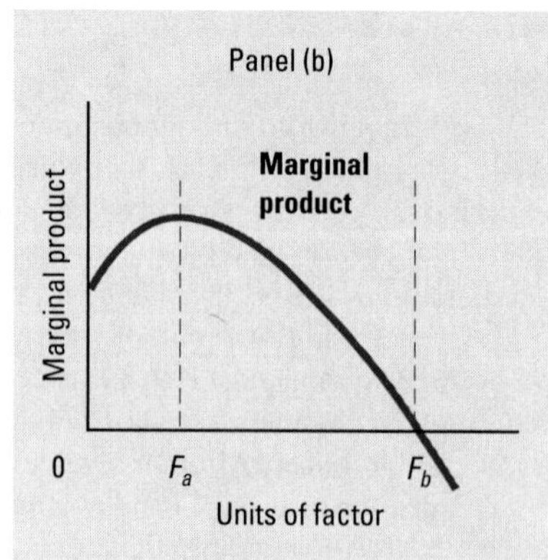

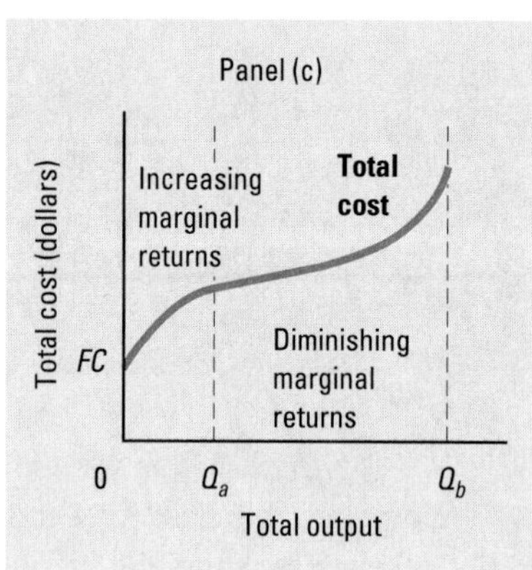

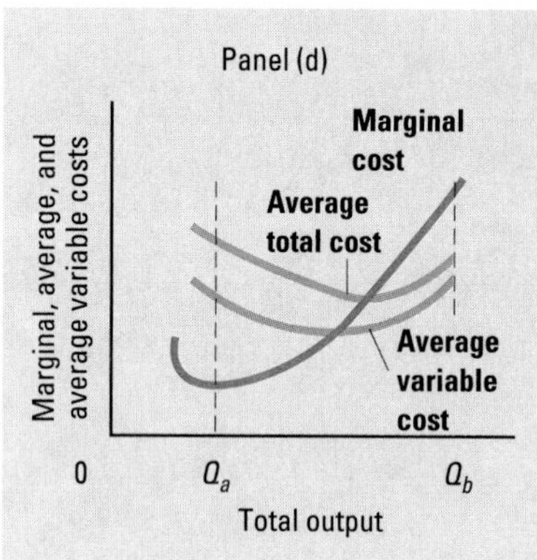

Production Choices and Costs: The Long Run

In a long-run planning perspective, a firm can consider changing the quantities of all its factors of production. That gives the firm two opportunities it does not have in the short run. First, the firm can select the mix of factors it wishes to use. Should it choose a production process with lots of labor and not much capital, like the street sweepers in China? Or should it select a process that uses a great deal of capital and relatively little labor, like street sweepers in the United States? The second thing the firm can select is the scale of its operations. In the short run, a firm can increase output only by increasing its use of a variable factor. But in the long run, all factors are variable, so the firm can expand the use of all of its factors of production. The question facing the firm in the long run is: How much of an expansion or contraction in the scale of its operations should it undertake?

In its long-run planning, the firm not only regards all factors as variable—it regards all costs as variable as well. There are no fixed costs in the long run. Because all factors are variable, production choices for the long run are more complex. And because all costs are variable, the structure of costs in the long run differs somewhat from what we saw in the short run.

Choosing the Factor Mix

How shall a firm decide what mix of capital, labor, and other factors to use? We can apply the marginal decision rule to answer this question.

Suppose a firm uses capital and labor to produce a particular good. It must determine how to produce the good and the quantity it should produce. We'll address the question of how much the firm should produce in subsequent chapters, but certainly the firm will want to produce whatever quantity it chooses at as low a cost as possible. Another way of putting that goal is to say that the firm seeks, at every level of total cost, the maximum output possible.

At any level of total cost, the firm can vary its factor mix. It could, for example, substitute labor for capital in a way that leaves its total cost unchanged. In terms of the marginal decision rule, we can think of the firm as considering whether to spend an additional $1 on one factor, hence $1 less on another. The marginal decision rule says that a firm will shift spending among factors as long as the marginal benefit of such a shift exceeds the marginal cost.

What is the marginal benefit, say, of an additional $1 spent on capital? An additional unit of capital produces the marginal product of capital. To determine the marginal benefit of $1 spent on capital, we divide capital's marginal product by its price: MP_K/P_K. The price of capital is the "rent" paid for the use of a unit of capital for a given period. If the firm already owns the capital, then this rent is a kind of implicit cost; it represents the return the firm could get by renting the capital or by selling it and earning interest on the money thus gained.

Suppose, for example, that the price of capital is $2 per unit and the marginal product of capital is 4 (1 more unit of capital adds 4 units of output). Dividing that marginal product by the price of capital gives a marginal product per additional $1 spent on capital of 2. To put it another way, $1 buys 0.5 units of capital, and if 1 unit of capital adds 4 units of output, then 0.5 units should add half as much, or 2 units of output.

If capital and labor are the only factors, then spending an additional $1 on capital while holding total cost constant means taking $1 out of labor. The cost of that action will be the output lost from cutting back $1 worth of labor. That cost equals the ratio of the marginal product of labor to the price of labor, MP_L/P_L, where the price of labor is the wage.

Suppose that a firm's marginal product of labor is 15 and the price of labor is $5 per unit; the firm gains 3 units of output by spending an additional $1 on labor. Suppose further that the marginal product of capital is 50 and the price of capital is $50 per unit, so the firm would lose 1 unit of output by spending $1 less on capital. Thus,

$$\frac{MP_L}{P_L} > \frac{MP_K}{P_K}$$

$$\frac{15}{5} > \frac{50}{50}$$

The firm can gain 2 units of output, without any change in cost, by transferring $1 from capital to labor. It will continue to transfer funds from capital to labor as long as it gains more from additional labor than it loses from reductions in capital. As the firm shifts spending in this fashion, however, the marginal product of labor will fall and the marginal product of capital will rise. At some point, the ratios of marginal product to price will be equal for the two factors. At this point, the firm will obtain the maximum output possible for a given total cost:

$$\frac{MP_L}{P_L} = \frac{MP_K}{P_K} \tag{1}$$

Suppose that a firm that uses capital and labor is satisfying Equation (1) when suddenly the price of labor rises. A higher price of labor lowers the ratio of the marginal product of labor to the price of labor:

$$\frac{MP_L}{P_L} < \frac{MP_K}{P_K}$$

The firm will shift funds out of labor into capital. It will continue to shift from labor to capital until the ratios of marginal product to price are equal for the two factors. In general, a profit-maximizing firm will seek a combination of factors such that

$$\frac{MP_1}{P_1} = \frac{MP_2}{P_2} = \cdots = \frac{MP_n}{P_n} \tag{2}$$

When a firm satisfies the condition given in Equation (2) for efficient use, it produces the greatest possible output for a given cost. To put it another way, the firm achieves the lowest possible cost for a given level of output.

As the price of labor rises, the firm will shift to a factor mix that uses relatively more capital and relatively less labor. As a firm increases its ratio of capital to labor, we say it is becoming more **capital intensive.** A lower price for labor will lead the firm to use relatively more labor and less capital, reducing its ratio of capital to labor. As a firm reduces its ratio of capital to labor, we say it is becoming more **labor intensive.** The notions of labor-intensive and capital-intensive production are purely relative; they imply only that a firm has a higher or lower ratio of capital to labor. Sometimes economists speak of labor-intensive versus capital-intensive countries in the same manner.

Now that we understand how to apply the marginal decision rule to the problem of choosing the mix of factors, we can answer the question that began this chapter: Why does the United States employ a capital-intensive production process to clean streets while China chooses a labor-intensive process? To answer this, suppose for a moment that the prices of labor and capital are the same in China and the United States. In that case, China and the United States can be expected to use the same method to clean streets. But the price of labor relative to the price of capital is, in fact, far lower in China than in the United States. A lower relative price for labor increases the ratio of the marginal product of labor to its price, making it efficient to substitute labor for capital. China thus finds it cheaper to clean streets with lots of people using brooms, while the United States finds it efficient to clean streets with large machines and relatively less labor.

The marginal decision rule is applied to the choice of a factor mix much as it is in the theory of consumer behavior. (In Chapter 6 we explored how a consumer determines what mix of goods and services to consume.) There are, however, several differences between a firm's choice of a factor mix and a consumer's selection of goods and services. First, a consumer seeks to maximize utility, but a firm does not seek to maximize output. Instead, the firm seeks to maximize its output at a given level of total cost—or, equivalently, to minimize the cost of producing a given level of output. Second, the firm does not have a

- A firm becomes more **capital intensive** when it increases the ratio of capital to labor that it uses.

- A firm becomes more **labor intensive** when it reduces the ratio of capital to labor that it uses.

Case in Point: The Maquiladoras

One implication of the marginal decision rule for factor use is that firms in countries where labor is relatively expensive, such as the United States, will use capital-intensive production methods. Less developed countries, where labor is relatively cheap, will use labor-intensive methods.

Some U.S. firms are getting it both ways. They complete part of the production process in the United States, using capital-intensive methods. They then ship the unfinished goods to *maquiladoras,* plants in Mexico where further processing is done using low-cost workers and labor-intensive methods.

RCA, for example, produces the basic materials for electronic components at its plants in the United States, then ships them to its maquiladora in Juarez for final assembly. Baxter Travenol Laboratories, a major U.S. manufacturer of hospital supplies, manufactures latex in the United States and ships it to its plant in Mexico for fabrication into surgical gloves.

Many U.S. clothing manufacturers produce cloth at U.S. plants using large high-speed looms. They then ship the cloth to Mexico, where it is fashioned into clothing by workers using sewing machines. The resulting clothing items are shipped back to the United States, labeled "Assembled in Mexico from U.S. materials."

The maquiladora program permits U.S. firms to operate plants in Mexico that carry out a portion of the manufacturing process. Partly finished goods from the United States are not taxed; import duties are imposed on the goods as they return to the United States, but only on the value added by the processing in Mexico. More than 1,000 U.S. firms operate maquiladoras. These enterprises constitute the third-largest source of employment in Mexico, behind oil production and tourism.

The maquiladoras have been a boon to workers in Mexico, who enjoy a higher demand for their services and receive higher wages as a result. The system also benefits the U.S. firms that participate and U.S. consumers who obtain cheaper goods than they would otherwise. It works because different factor prices imply different mixes of labor and capital. Companies are able to carry out the capital-intensive side of the production process in the United States and the labor-intensive side in Mexico.

Source: "Mexico's Maquiladoro Industries," *The Margin* 4(2) (November/December 1988): 28.

budget constraint. Firms determine their production levels on the basis of expectations concerning their sales and profits, not how much money they have available. And finally, marginal product is a measurable variable, but marginal utility is not. The marginal decision rule is, as a result, more directly applicable to the analysis of real-world problems. For example, many firms use the ideas we have explored here in determining what mix of factors to use.

Costs in the Long Run

As in the short run, costs in the long run depend on the firm's level of output, the costs of factors, and the quantities of factors needed for each level of output. The chief difference between long- and short-run costs is there are no fixed factors in the long run. There are thus no fixed costs. All costs are variable, so we do not distinguish between variable cost and total cost in the long run: total cost *is* variable cost.

The most important measure of cost in the long run is the **long-run average cost (LRAC) curve.** The LRAC shows the firm's cost per unit at each level of output, assuming that all factors of production are variable. The LRAC curve assumes that the firm has chosen the optimal factor mix, as described in the previous section, for producing any level of output. The costs it shows are, therefore, the lowest costs possible for each level of output.

EXHIBIT 7-8

The Long-Run Average Cost Curve

The LRAC curve is found by taking the lowest average total cost curve at each level of output. Here, average total cost curves for quantities of capital of 20, 30, 40, and 50 units are shown for the Lifetime Disc Co. At a production level of 10,000 CDs per week, Lifetime minimizes its cost per CD by producing with 20 units of capital (point A). At 20,000 CDs per week, an expansion to a plant size associated with 30 units of capital minimizes cost per unit (point B). The lowest cost per unit is achieved with production of 30,000 CDs per week using 40 units of capital (point C). If Lifetime chooses to produce 40,000 CDs per week, it will do so most cheaply with 50 units of capital (point D).

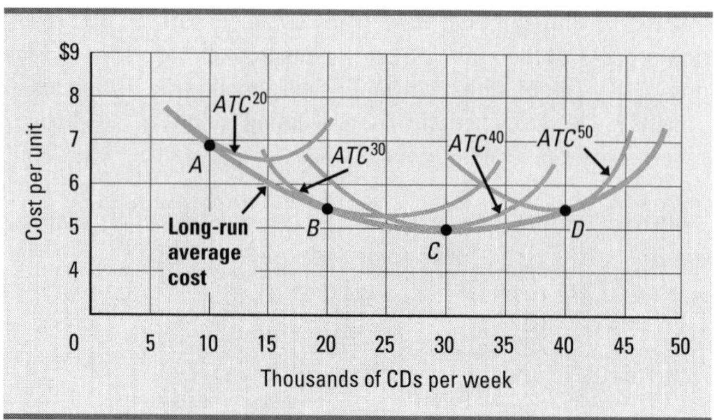

Exhibit 7-8 shows how a firm's LRAC curve is derived. Suppose Lifetime Disc Co. produces compact discs (CDs) using capital and labor. We have already seen how a firm's average total cost curve can be drawn in the short run for a given quantity of a particular factor of production, such as capital. In the short run, Lifetime Disc might be limited to operating with a given capital stock; it would face one of the average total cost curves shown in Exhibit 7-8. If it has 30 units of capital, for example, its average total cost curve is ATC^{30}. In the long run the firm can examine the average total cost curves associated with varying levels of capital. Average total cost curves for Lifetime Disc are shown in Exhibit 7-8 for quantities of capital from 20 to 50 units. The firm determines its LRAC curve from this set of short-run curves by finding the lowest average total cost associated with each level of output.

- The **long-run average cost (LRAC) curve** shows the lowest cost per unit at each level of output, assuming all factors of production are variable.
- A question of **returns to scale** asks how output will be affected by a given percentage change in the quantities of all factors used by a firm.
- **Increasing returns to scale** (also called **economies of scale**) imply that when a firm increases all of its factors by a certain percentage, output increases by a larger percentage.
- If an increase in all factors by a given percentage results in an increase in output by the same percentage, the firm is experiencing **constant returns to scale.**
- A firm whose output rises by a smaller percentage than the increase in all its factors is experiencing **decreasing returns to scale,** or **diseconomies of scale.**

Returns to Scale

Suppose a firm doubles all of its factors of production. What will happen to its output? This is a question of **returns to scale.** It asks how output is affected when every factor is changed by a given percentage—how output is affected when the scale of a firm's operations is changed.

When an increase in all of a firm's factors by a certain percentage increases its output by a larger percentage, a firm is experiencing **increasing returns to scale,** or **economies of scale.** Because output increases by a larger proportion than does the firm's use of factors, its cost per unit falls. Economies of scale thus imply a downward-sloping LRAC curve.

One source of increasing returns to scale is gains from specialization. As the scale of a firm's operation expands, it is able to use its factors in more specialized ways, increasing their productivity. Another source of increasing returns to scale lies in the economies that can be gained from mass production methods. As the scale of a firm's operation expands, the company can begin to utilize large-scale machines and production systems that can substantially reduce cost per unit.

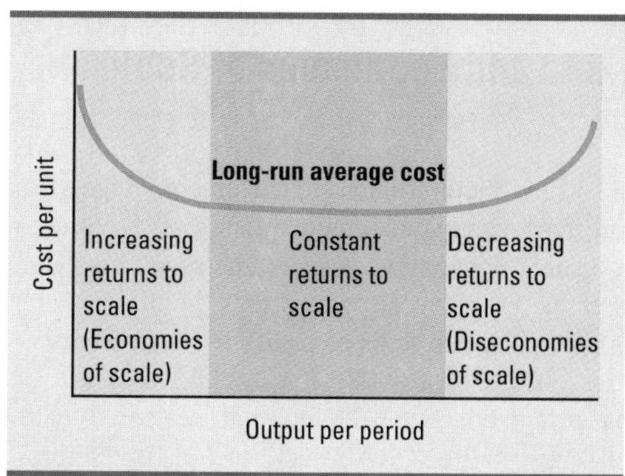

EXHIBIT 7-9

Returns to Scale and Long-Run Average Cost

The downward-sloping region of the firm's LRAC curve is associated with increasing returns to scale. There may be a horizontal range associated with constant returns to scale. The upward-sloping range of the curve implies decreasing returns to scale.

Checklist

- A firm chooses its factor mix in the long run on the basis of the marginal decision rule; it seeks to equate the ratio of marginal product to price for all factors of production. By doing so, it minimizes the cost of producing a given level of output.
- The long-run average cost (LRAC) curve is derived from the average total cost curves associated with different quantities of the factor that is fixed in the short run. The LRAC curve shows the lowest cost per unit at which each output can be produced.
- A firm may experience increasing returns to scale, constant returns to scale, or decreasing returns to scale.
- Increasing returns to scale imply a downward-sloping LRAC curve. Constant returns to scale imply a horizontal LRAC curve. Decreasing returns to scale imply an upward-sloping LRAC curve.
- A firm's ability to exploit increasing returns to scale is limited by the extent of market demand for its products.
- The range of output over which firms experience increasing, constant, or decreasing returns to scale is an important determinant of how many firms will survive in a particular market.

Alternatively, a firm may find that increasing all of its factors by some percentage increases its output by the same percentage. When the firm's output changes by the same percentage as the change in all factors, it is experiencing **constant returns to scale.** If output is rising by the same percentage as a firm's factors, then its cost per unit remains constant; the LRAC curve is horizontal.

Finally, a firm may find that increasing all its factors of production by an equal percentage increases its output by a smaller percentage. Such a case is called **decreasing returns to scale,** or **diseconomies of scale.** Decreasing returns to scale mean that costs per unit will rise as the firm increases its use of factors, so the LRAC curve slopes upward.

Why would a firm experience decreasing returns to scale? At first glance, it might seem that the answer lies in the law of diminishing marginal returns, but this is not the case. The law of diminishing marginal returns, after all, tells us how output changes as a single factor is increased, with all other factors of production held constant. With decreasing returns to scale, all factors are changed by an equal percentage. Decreasing returns are generally thought to be caused by management problems. As the scale of a firm's operations expands, it becomes harder and harder for management to coordinate and guide the activities of individual units of the firm. Eventually, the diseconomies of management overwhelm any gains the firm might be achieving by operating with a larger scale of plant, and long-run average costs begin rising.

Firms are likely to experience all three types of returns to scale, as shown in Exhibit 7-9. At very low levels of output, the firm is likely to experience increasing returns to scale as it expands the scale of its operations. There may follow a range of output over which the firm experiences constant returns to scale—empirical studies suggest that the range over which firms experience constant returns to scale is often very large. And certainly there must be some range of output over which decreasing returns to scale occur; this phenomenon is one factor that limits the size of firms. A firm operating on the upward-sloping part of its LRAC curve is likely to be undercut in the market by smaller firms operating with lower costs per unit of output.

Returns to Scale and the Size Distribution of Firms

The nature of returns to scale has a powerful effect on the sizes of firms that will operate in any market. Suppose firms in a particular industry experience decreasing returns to scale at relatively low levels of output. That industry will be characterized by a large number of small firms. The restaurant market appears to be such an industry. Barbers and beauticians are another example.

If firms in an industry experience increasing returns to scale over a very wide range of output, firms that expand to take advantage of lower cost will force out smaller firms that have higher costs. Such industries are likely to have a few large firms instead of a great many small ones. In the refrigerator industry, for example, the size of firm necessary to achieve the lowest possible cost per unit is large enough to limit the market to only a few firms. In most cities, increasing returns to scale seem to leave room for only a single newspaper.

One factor that can limit the achievement of economies of scale is the demand facing an individual firm. The scale of output required to achieve the lowest unit costs possible may require sales that exceed the demand facing a firm. A grocery store, for example, could minimize unit costs with a large store and a large volume of sales. But the demand for groceries in a small, isolated community may not be able to sustain such a volume of sales. The firm is thus limited to a small scale of operation even though this might involve higher unit costs.

Case in Point: Wal-Mart: Taking Advantage of Small Markets and Economies of Scale

When Sam Walton, the founder of Wal-Mart, died in 1992, he was the richest man in America. What did he know that other discount store owners didn't?

Discount retail chains appear to exhibit economies of scale. As they increase the size and number of retail stores in the chain, they enjoy substantial cost savings through high product turnover, low inventory, and more efficient management. Huge volume discounts on their merchandise reduce factor costs. So extensive are the apparent economies of scale that many discount retailers have taken the view that discount stores should locate in cities of over 100,000 people in order to justify the scale of operation.

Sam Walton disagreed. He believed that he could take advantage of Wal-Mart's falling LRAC curve by locating in relatively small communities. There, small Mom-and-Pop stores and medium-sized stores faced costs so high that he could easily undersell them, thereby attracting much of the retail business to Wal-Mart. But why didn't other retail chains follow in his path? The answer, which Sam Walton knew all along, was that many small communities were too small to support *two* big discount stores. There would not be enough business to justify such a large operation if the market were shared by more than one discount store. Sam Walton gambled that if he could beat the other retailers to the punch, he would prevent them from entering the market. By 1995, Wal-Mart had over 2,000 stores in operation and had emerged as the leading retail firm in the United States. Sam Walton gambled on his negatively sloped LRAC curve—and won!

A Look Back—And a Look Ahead

In this chapter we have concentrated on the production and cost relationships facing firms in the short run and in the long run.

In the short run, a firm has at least one factor of production that it cannot vary. This fixed factor limits the firm's range of factor choices. As a firm uses more and more of a variable factor (with a fixed quantity of other factors of production), it is likely to experience at first increasing, then diminishing, then negative marginal returns. Thus, the short-run total cost curve has a positive value at a zero level of output (the firm's fixed cost), then slopes upward at a decreasing rate (the range of increasing marginal returns), and then slopes upward at an increasing rate (the range of diminishing marginal returns).

In addition to short-run total product and total cost curves, we derived a firm's marginal product, average total cost, average variable cost, and marginal cost curves.

If the firm is to maximize profit in the long run, it must select the cost-minimizing combination of factors for its chosen level of output. Thus, the firm must try to hire factors of production in accordance with the marginal decision rule. That is, it will hire factors so that the ratio of marginal product to factor price is equal for all factors of production.

A firm's long-run average cost (LRAC) curve includes a region of increasing returns to scale, over which the curve slopes downward, and a region of decreasing returns to scale, over which the curve slopes upward. There may be an intervening range of output over which the firm experiences constant returns to scale; its LRAC curve will be horizontal over this range. The size of operations necessary to reach the lowest point on the LRAC curve has a great deal to do with determining the relative sizes of firms in an industry.

The Chapter 7 Appendix suggests a graphical approach to the firm's problem of choosing the input mix. This approach is similar in many ways to the graphical analysis of consumer choice presented in the Chapter 6 Appendix.

This chapter concludes Part Two, our discussion of basic tools of microeconomics. We'll put our analyses of utility maximization and of production and cost to work in Parts Three and Four. We'll consider how firms and consumers interact in a variety of market contexts. That interaction depends greatly on the behavior of consumers and on the relationships between production and cost.

Terms and Concepts for Review

Average total cost
Average variable cost
Capital intensive
Constant returns to scale
Decreasing returns to scale
Diminishing marginal returns
Diseconomies of scale
Economies of scale
Firms
Fixed costs
Fixed factor of production
Increasing marginal returns
Increasing returns to scale
Labor intensive
Law of diminishing marginal returns
Long run
Long-run average cost (LRAC) curve
Marginal product
Negative marginal returns
Returns to scale
Short run
Total cost
Total product curve
Variable costs
Variable factor of production

For Discussion

1. Which of the following would be considered long-run choices? Which are short-run choices?
   - **a.** A dentist hires a new part-time dental hygienist.
   - **b.** The local oil refinery plans a complete restructuring of its production processes, including relocating the plant.
   - **c.** A farmer increases the quantity of water applied to his or her fields.
   - **d.** A law partnership signs a 3-year lease for an office complex.
   - **e.** The university hires a new football coach with a 3-year contract.
2. "There are no fixed costs in the long run." Explain.
3. The local McDonald's restaurant is swamped with business. It is contemplating adding a new grill and french fry machine. But the day supervisor suggests simply hiring more workers. How should the manager decide which alternative to pursue?
4. Suppose that the average age of students in your economics class is 23.7 years. If a new 19-year-old student enrolls in the class, will the average age in the class rise or fall? Explain.
5. Suppose a firm is operating at the minimum point of its short-run average total cost curve, so that marginal cost equals average total cost. Under what circumstances would it choose to alter the size of its plant? Explain.
6. What happens to the difference between average total cost and average variable cost as a firm's output expands? Explain.
7. How would each of the following affect average total cost, average variable cost, and marginal cost?
   - **a.** An increase in the cost of the lease of the firm's building
   - **b.** A reduction in the price of electricity
   - **c.** A reduction in wages
   - **d.** A change in the salary of the president of the company

8. Consider the following types of firms. For each one, the long-run average cost curve eventually exhibits decreasing returns to scale. For which firms would you expect decreasing returns to set in at relatively low levels of output?
   a. A copy shop
   b. A hardware store
   c. A dairy
   d. A newspaper
   e. An automobile manufacturer
   f. A restaurant
9. As car manufacturers incorporate more sophisticated computer technology, auto repair shops require computerized testing equipment, which is quite expensive, in order to repair newer cars. How is this likely to affect the shape of these firms' long-run average total cost curves? How is it likely to affect the number of auto repair firms in any market?

Problems

1. Suppose a firm is producing 1,000 units of output. Its fixed costs per unit are $100. Its average variable costs are $50. What is the total cost of producing 1,000 units of output?
2. The director of a nonprofit foundation that sponsors 8-week summer institutes for graduate students analyzed the costs and expected revenues for the next summer institute and recommended that the session be canceled. In her analysis she included a share of the foundation's overhead—the salaries of the director and staff and costs of maintaining the office—to the program. She estimated costs and revenues as follows:

Projected revenues (from tuition and fees):	$300,000
Projected costs:	
Overhead	50,000
Room and board for students	100,000
Costs for faculty and miscellaneous	175,000
Total costs	$325,000

   What was the error in the director's recommendation?
3. The cost for printing 10,000 copies of an issue of a magazine is 45 cents per copy. For 20,000, the cost is 35 cents per copy; for 30,000, the cost is 30 cents per copy. The cost continues to decline slightly over every level of output that the publishers of the magazine have considered. Sketch the approximate shapes of the average and marginal cost curves. What are some variable costs of publishing magazines? Some fixed costs?
4. A firm is currently operating with 40 units of capital and 120 units of labor. Given these quantities, the marginal product of labor is 20 and the marginal product of capital is 4. Suppose the price of labor is $10 and the price of capital is $30. The firm wishes to leave its total cost unchanged. What should it do?
5. Suppose a firm finds that the marginal product of capital is 60 and the marginal product of labor is 20. If the price of capital is $6 and the price of labor is $2.50, how should the firm adjust its mix of capital and labor? What will be the result?

7 Appendix

A Graphical Approach to Choosing the Factor Mix

We saw in this chapter that a firm minimizes the cost of producing a given level of output by combining factors of production in a way that satisfies the marginal decision rule. As applied to factor choice, the rule requires that a firm choose a factor combination at which the ratio of marginal product to input price is equal for all inputs. In this appendix we shall examine a graphical approach to determining the optimal combination of factors of production.

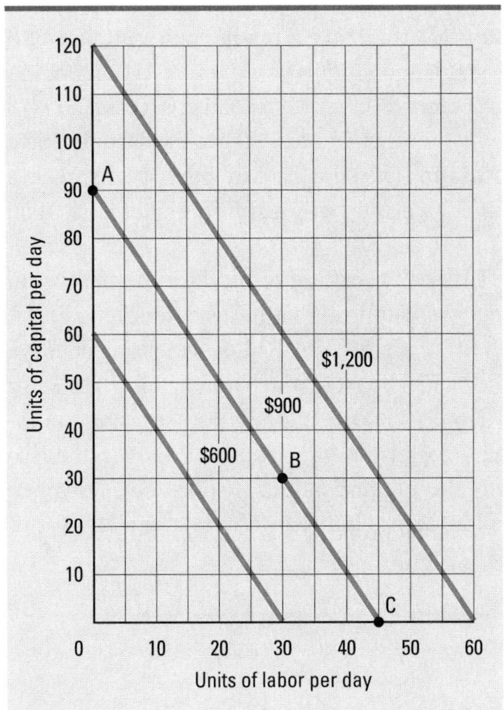

EXHIBIT 7A-1

Isocost Curves

An isocost curve shows combinations of two factors (here, capital and labor) that result in the same total cost. The isocost curves drawn here are based on costs of capital and labor of $10 and $20 per unit, respectively. Higher isocost curves show higher total costs.

- An **isocost curve** shows combinations of two factors that result in the same total cost for a firm.
- An **isoquant curve** shows combinations of two factors that yield the same level of output.

Cost and Output Consequences of Factor Use

Suppose Timely Watch Company produces watches using two factors, capital and labor. The price of a unit of capital is $10, and the price of a unit of labor is $20. We assume that Timely is considering its use of capital and labor over the long run, so both factors are variable.

Given the factor prices Timely faces, several combinations of capital and labor will result in the same level of total cost. Timely could, for example, use 45 units of labor and no capital; the total cost of this combination would be $900 (45 × $20). This is shown as point C in Exhibit 7A-1. Alternatively, it could use 90 units of capital and no labor, again with a total cost of $900 (90 × $10). This is point A. Or it could use 30 units of labor and 30 units of capital (point B), again generating a total cost of $900 [(30 × $20) + (30 × $10) = $900]. The straight line ABC shows all the combinations of capital and labor that yield a total cost of $900. Any curve that shows combinations of two factors that result in the same total cost to the firm is called an **isocost curve.** The prefix *iso* means "equal," hence the term *isocost.* Different total costs correspond to different isocost curves; isocost curves for $600 and for $1,200 are also shown in the exhibit. In general, the further up and to the right an isocost curve, the greater the total cost associated with it.

Just as we can show different combinations of capital and labor that have the same total cost, we can show different combinations of capital and labor for the same level of total output. Timely Watch, for example, could produce watches using a variety of combinations of labor and capital. If it reduces the amount of capital, Timely must increase its use of labor to achieve the same level of output as before. The curve that shows combinations of two factors that achieve the same quantity of total output is called an **isoquant curve.** The term *isoquant* is derived from the prefix *iso,* meaning "equal," and *quantity.* Exhibit 7A-2 shows isoquant curves for Timely Watch for various quantities of watches per day. The isoquant curve labeled "20," for example, shows combinations of capital and labor that will produce 20 watches per day. The higher the isoquant curve, the greater the quantity produced.

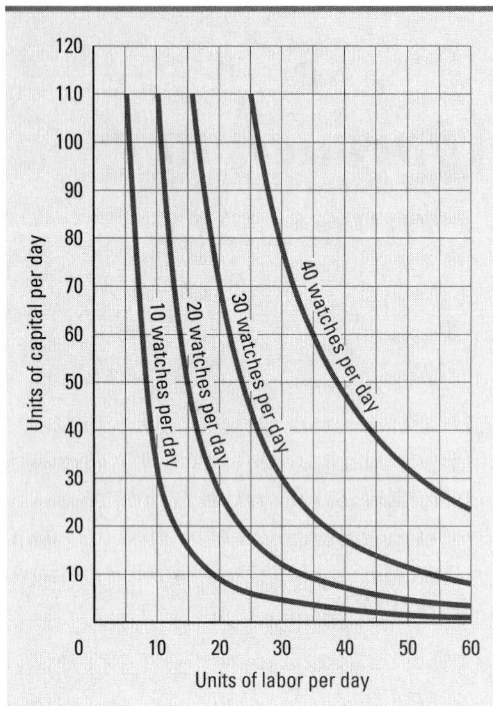

EXHIBIT 7A-2

Isoquant Curves

An isoquant curve shows combinations of two factors that achieve the same level of output (here, watches per day). The isoquants shown are for Timely Watch Company.

Minimizing Cost, Maximizing Output

We can put our isocost and isoquant curves to work by putting them together. This allows us to find the lowest cost at which a given level of output can be produced or, equivalently, to find the maximum output consistent with a given cost.

Suppose Timely Watch has decided to produce 30 watches per day, as cheaply as possible. Panel (a) of Exhibit 7A-3 shows the three isocost curves from Exhibit 7A-1 and the isoquant curve for 30 watches per day from Exhibit 7A-2. To minimize cost, Timely will seek the lowest isocost curve that is consistent with producing 30 watches per day. At point B, the isocost curve for $900 just touches the isoquant curve for 30 watches (the two curves are *tangent* at B; they have the same slope). The firm could achieve even lower costs by moving to, say, the $600 isocost curve, but no point on this curve has enough capital and labor to produce 30 watches per day. Alternatively, Timely could produce at a point such as E, where the isocost and isoquant curves *intersect*. At this point, the firm uses 8 units of capital and 56 units of labor for a total cost of $1,200 [(8 × $10) + (56 × $20)]. This is clearly inefficient; the 30 watches could have been produced for only $900 by operating at point B. Any other isocost curve that intersects the isoquant curve for 30 watches will result in higher costs than $900.

Alternatively, we can think of Timely as seeking to produce the maximum output possible for a particular total cost. Suppose that it has determined that it will incur a total cost of $900. Panel (b) of Exhibit 7A-3 shows the isocost curve for $900 from Exhibit 7A-1, together with the isoquants from Exhibit 7A-2. To obtain the highest output possible, Timely chooses the highest isoquant consistent with a total cost of $900. Notice that of the four isoquants shown, the isoquant for 40 watches per day yields the highest output. It does not, however, touch the isocost curve; Timely could not produce 40 watches at a total cost of

EXHIBIT 7A-3

Minimizing Cost and Maximizing Output

In Panel (a), we see that $900 is the lowest cost at which 30 units of output can be produced. In Panel (b), we see that the maximum quantity of watches that can be produced with $900 is 30. These solutions are achieved at point B in each case, where the slopes of the isoquant and isocost curves are equal. Notice that points E and D are inefficient; the isoquant and isocost curves intersect at these points but are not tangent.

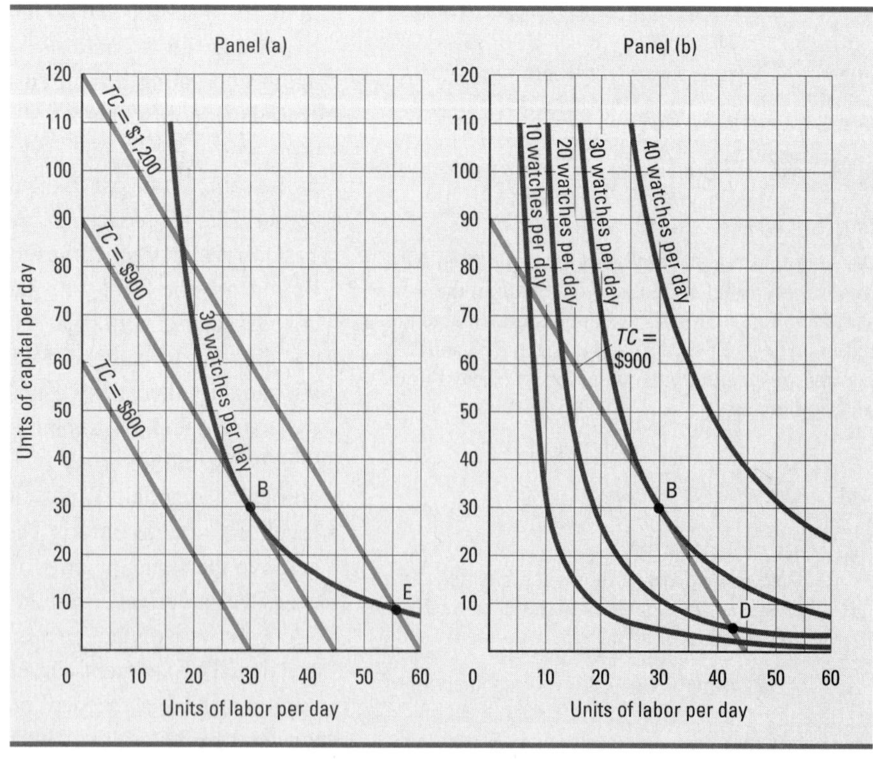

$900. The maximum number of watches Timely can produce and still limit its total costs to $900 is 30. The isoquant curve for 30 watches just touches the isocost curve for $900 at Point (b)—the two curves are tangent and thus have the same slope at that point. To produce the maximum number of watches for $900, Timely should use 30 units of capital and 30 units of labor.

Compare points B and D in panel (b) of Exhibit 7A-3. At point D, Timely is spending $900 per day, using 5 units of capital and 42.5 units of labor. But the isoquant curve that intersects the isocost curve at point D is for only 20 watches per day. Point D, and all points at which isoquant curves intersect the isocost curves, is inefficient. To achieve the greatest possible output for a given level of total cost, we find a point at which the isocost and isoquant curves are tangent and thus have the same slope (such as point B).

Slopes of Isocost and Isoquant Curves

Efficient production occurs at a point on an isocost-isoquant graph at which the slopes of the two curves are equal. To learn more about such a solution, we shall solve for the slopes of those two curves.

The slope of any curve is given by the change in the value on the vertical axis divided by the change in the value on the horizontal axis between two points. Because capital is the variable on the vertical axis and labor is the variable on the horizontal axis for both kinds of curves, the slope of an isocost or isoquant curve will be given by the change in capital divided by the change in labor, $\Delta K/\Delta L$, between two points on the respective curves.

Consider a movement from point A to point B on the isocost curve in Panel (a) of Exhibit 7A-4. The firm has reduced its capital by 20 units and increased its labor by 10 units; the slope is thus $-20/10 = -2$. To derive a more general expression for the slope of an isocost curve, we can ask the following question:

EXHIBIT 7A-4

The Slopes of Isocost and Isoquant Curves

The slopes of the isocost curve in Panel (a) and the isoquant curve in Panel (b) are given by the ratios of the change in capital divided by the change in labor between points A and B and between C and D, respectively. In both cases, the slope is -2.

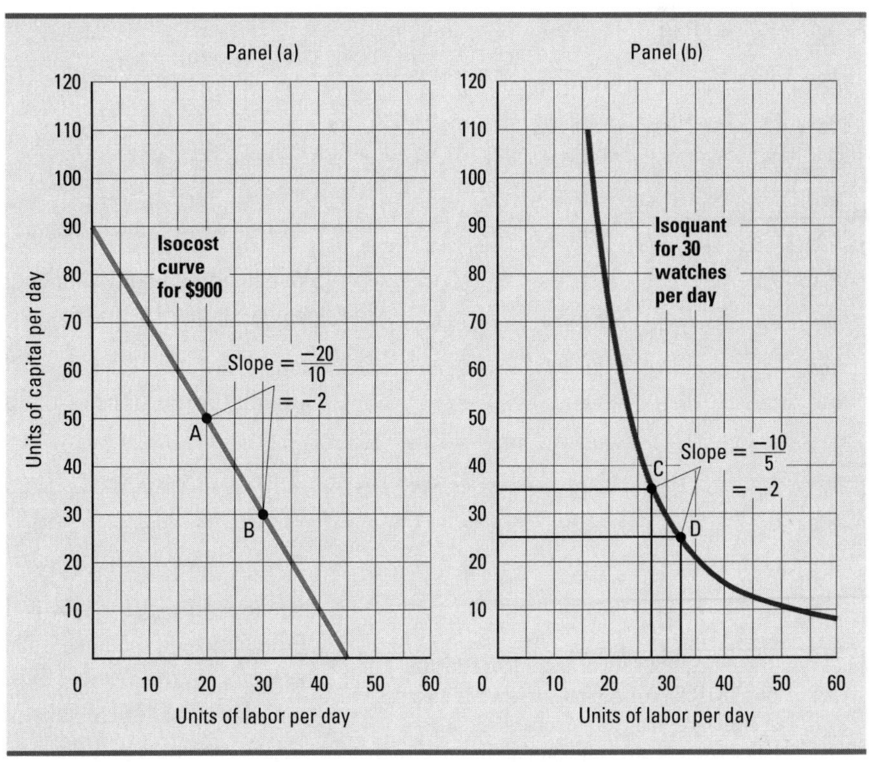

What happens to the firm's total cost when it moves between two points on an isocost curve? We know the answer to this question already: by definition, the change in total cost in moving between two points on an isocost curve is zero. But it is instructive to pursue the question anyway. The change in cost resulting from the change in capital used equals the change in capital times the price of capital ($\Delta K \times P_K$). The change in cost resulting from the change in labor used equals the change in labor times the price of labor ($\Delta L \times P_L$). The sum of these changes is zero:

$$(\Delta K)P_K + (\Delta L)P_L = 0 \quad \textbf{(1)}$$

Solving for the slope of the isocost curve, $\Delta K/\Delta L$, we have

$$(\Delta K)P_K = -(\Delta L)P_L$$

$$\frac{\Delta K}{\Delta L} = -\frac{P_L}{P_K} \quad \textbf{(2)}$$

The slope of the isocost curve is thus the negative of the ratio of the price of the factor on the horizontal axis (in this case, labor) to the price of the factor on the vertical axis (in this case, capital).

As the firm moves to higher isocost curves, it faces higher total costs; however, the slopes of these isocost curves are the same.

In moving between points C and D on the isoquant for 30 watches per day in Panel (b) of Exhibit 7A-4, the firm reduces capital by 10 units and increases labor by 5 units, leaving output unchanged. The slope over this range of the curve is thus $-10/5 = -2$. We call this slope the **marginal rate of technical substitution (MRTS)** of capital for labor; it is the rate at which the firm can substitute capital for labor without affecting the quantity produced.

Following a strategy similar to the one we used with the isocost curve, we can ask: What is the change in output as we move along an isoquant curve? Once again, the answer is zero. The change in output (ΔQ) resulting from the change in capital (ΔK) can be derived from the definition of the marginal product of capital:

$$MP_K = \frac{\Delta Q}{\Delta K} \quad \textbf{(3)}$$

Or

$$\Delta Q = (\Delta K)MP_K \quad \textbf{(4)}$$

We can add an equivalent expression for the change in output resulting from the change in labor:

$$(\Delta K)MP_K + (\Delta L)MP_L = 0 \quad \textbf{(5)}$$

Solving for the slope of the isoquant, $\Delta K/\Delta L$, we have

$$(\Delta K)MP_K = -(\Delta L)MP_L$$

$$\frac{\Delta K}{\Delta L} = -\frac{MP_L}{MP_K} = MRTS \quad \textbf{(6)}$$

The slope of the isoquant is thus the negative of the ratio of the marginal product of the factor on the horizontal axis (in this case, labor) to the marginal product of the factor on the vertical axis (in this case, capital). This slope, again, is the marginal rate of technical substitution of capital for labor.

The **marginal rate of technical substitution (MRTS)** of capital for labor is the rate at which capital can be substituted for labor without affecting output; it is the negative of the slope of the isoquant curve.

We now see why an isoquant becomes flatter as we travel down and to the right along it. As we move down and to the right, the firm is substituting labor

Case in Point The Maquiladoras Revisited

We can use isocost-isoquant analysis to see more clearly the advantages of the maquiladora program discussed in the earlier Case in Point. The maroon line in Panel (a) is an isoquant showing initial production of cloth; the isoquant in Panel (b) shows the assembly of cloth into clothing. The red lines are isocost curves for the United States and Mexico. The isocost curves for the United States are steeper than those for Mexico because U.S. prices of labor relative to capital are much higher. Suppose that the isocost curves drawn in both panels show the same level of total cost for both countries. Given that total cost, a firm will seek to produce the greatest quantity possible.

Of course, U.S. firms aren't required to participate in the maquiladora program. And if they do, they can choose which part of the production process should take place in the United States and which part should take place in Mexico. A firm facing the curves shown will engage in the initial manufacturing in the United States—production in Mexico would put the firm on a lower isoquant at the same total cost. The firm will assemble the goods in Mexico—assembly in the United States would put the firm on a lower isoquant at the same total cost.

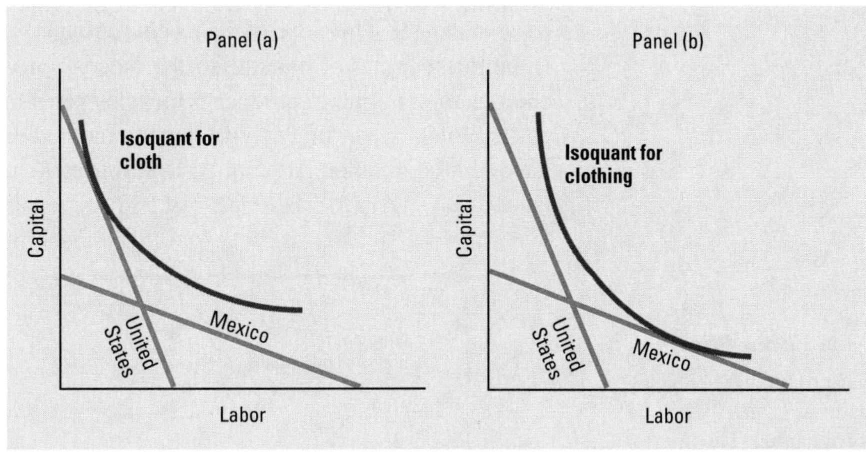

for capital. As the firm uses more labor and less capital, the marginal product of labor falls. The movement down and to the right thus reduces the numerator in Equation (6). Further, as the firm uses less capital and more labor, the marginal product of capital goes up. Increasing the firm's use of labor further increases the marginal product of capital. The denominator in Equation (6) thus gets larger. The absolute value of the ratio of marginal products in Equation (6) thus declines as the firm moves down and to the right along the isoquant; the curve becomes flatter.

Combining Factors of Production: The Cost-Minimizing Solution

We have established that a firm can produce a given output at the lowest possible cost by operating where the isoquant curve for that level of output is tangent to the isocost curve. We have also solved for the slope of each curve. The slope of the isoquant curve is given by the negative of the marginal rate of technical substitution ($-MP_L/MP_K$), and the slope of the isocost curve is given by the negative of the price ratio of the two factors ($-P_L/P_K$). At the point of tangency, the slopes of the two curves are equal, so

$$-\frac{MP_L}{MP_K} = -\frac{P_L}{P_K} \tag{7}$$

The firm achieves the lowest-cost factor combination by selecting its factors so that the marginal rate of technical substitution is equal to the price ratio for the two factors. Dividing both sides by the negative of the price of labor and multiplying both sides by the marginal product of capital, we have

$$\frac{MP_L}{P_L} = \frac{MP_K}{P_K} \tag{8}$$

Equation (8) gives the same result we developed for the marginal decision rule of factor use in this chapter: A firm should combine factors in such a way that the marginal contribution to output of $1 spent on each factor is equal.

Exhibit 7A-5 shows the case of a firm that uses capital and labor to produce custom mountain bicycles. The isoquant curve gives combinations of capital and labor that yield 5 bicycles per month. At the original isocost curve, Uphill Mountain Bikes minimizes its cost at point A by using K_a units of capital and L_a units of labor per period. Now suppose the price of labor rises relative to the price of capital. The slope of the isocost curve is given by the ratio of the price of labor to the price of capital, so the isocost curve becomes steeper. If Uphill chooses to continue to produce 5 bicycles per month, it will achieve the lowest cost possible by shifting to a production method that relies more heavily on capital and less on labor. At point B, Uphill uses K_b units of capital and L_b units of labor.

EXHIBIT 7A-5

Responding to a Change in Factor Prices

Uphill Mountain Bikes was producing 5 bicycles per month, operating at point A. It was using L_a units of labor and K_a units of capital. The price of labor rose relative to the price of capital, making the isocost curve steeper. If Uphill continues to produce 5 bikes per month, it should do so at point B, using less labor (L_b) and more capital (K_b).

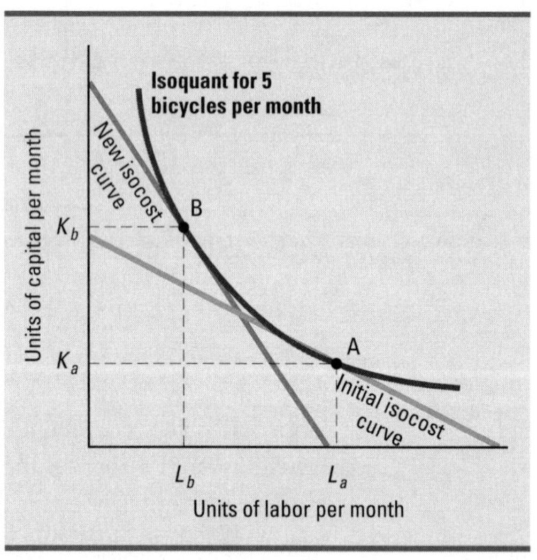

Maximizing Output Versus Maximizing Utility

If you studied the Appendix to Chapter 6, you probably noticed a close similarity between that analysis and the one in this appendix. The graphical tools are, indeed, closely related. A budget line shows combinations of two goods that have the same cost; an isocost curve shows combinations of two factors that have the same cost. An indifference curve shows combinations of two goods that generate the same level of total utility; an isoquant curve shows combinations of two factors that generate the same level of output. A consumer obtains the greatest utility possible from a given budget by choosing a combination of goods at which an indifference curve is tangent to the budget line; a firm obtains the greatest output possible for a given level of total cost by choosing a combination of factors at which an isoquant curve is tangent to the isocost curve for that total cost. The consumer maximizes utility where the marginal rate of substitution between two goods equals their price ratio; the firm produces the maximum output for a given total cost where the marginal rate of technical substitution between two factors equals their price ratio. The marginal rate of substitution is given by the ratio of marginal utilities; the marginal rate of technical substitution is given by the ratio of marginal products.

Despite all these similarities, there are three important differences:

1. Although consumers seek to maximize utility, firms do not seek to maximize output. What firms seek to maximize is profit, not output. We can say that firms seek the maximum output for a given level of total cost.
2. Consumers have budget constraints; firms do not. A firm can pick any total cost it chooses, based on its own expectations of its ability to sell what it produces. We shall examine how firms pick their outputs and total costs in subsequent chapters.
3. Production is measurable; utility is not.

These differences are important to keep in mind, but the similarities between the two types of analysis are quite pronounced. Noting them will help you to understand both approaches better.

Checklist

- An isocost curve shows combinations of two factors that generate the same total cost.
- An isoquant curve shows combinations of two factors that generate the same total output.
- A firm produces a given output at the lowest possible cost by operating where an isocost curve is tangent to the isoquant curve for that level of output.
- The slope of an isocost curve is the negative of the price ratio between the two factors.
- The slope of an isoquant curve is the negative of the marginal rate of technical substitution between the two factors.
- At the efficient solution, the price ratio between the two factors equals the marginal rate of technical substitution.

Terms and Concepts for Review

Isocost curve

Isoquant curve

Marginal rate of technical substitution

Problems

1. Suppose there are two cities, one in the United States and one in China, with an equal amount of street sweeping to produce. Using a graph of isocost and isoquant curves, compare the relative amounts of capital and labor that would be used in the two cities.

2. Suppose the United States and China produce food using two factors, land and labor. Suppose land is cheap relative to labor in the United States while it is more expensive relative to labor in China. Draw an isocost-isoquant curve analysis for the two countries with land and labor as the factors. Assume both countries produce the same quantity of food. Compare the combinations of labor and land used. In which country would you expect output per worker to be greater? In which country would you expect output per unit of land to be greater?

3. People from England often comment on the "flimsy" nature of modern U.S. houses. They note that British houses are generally built with stone or brick while U.S. houses contain a great deal of wood. Use isocost-isoquant curve analysis to try to explain why U.S. builders tend to use more wood while the British tend to use more stone. (*Hint:* Draw an isoquant for a single house, and show the least-cost solution for the two countries.)

Part Three The Competitive Economy

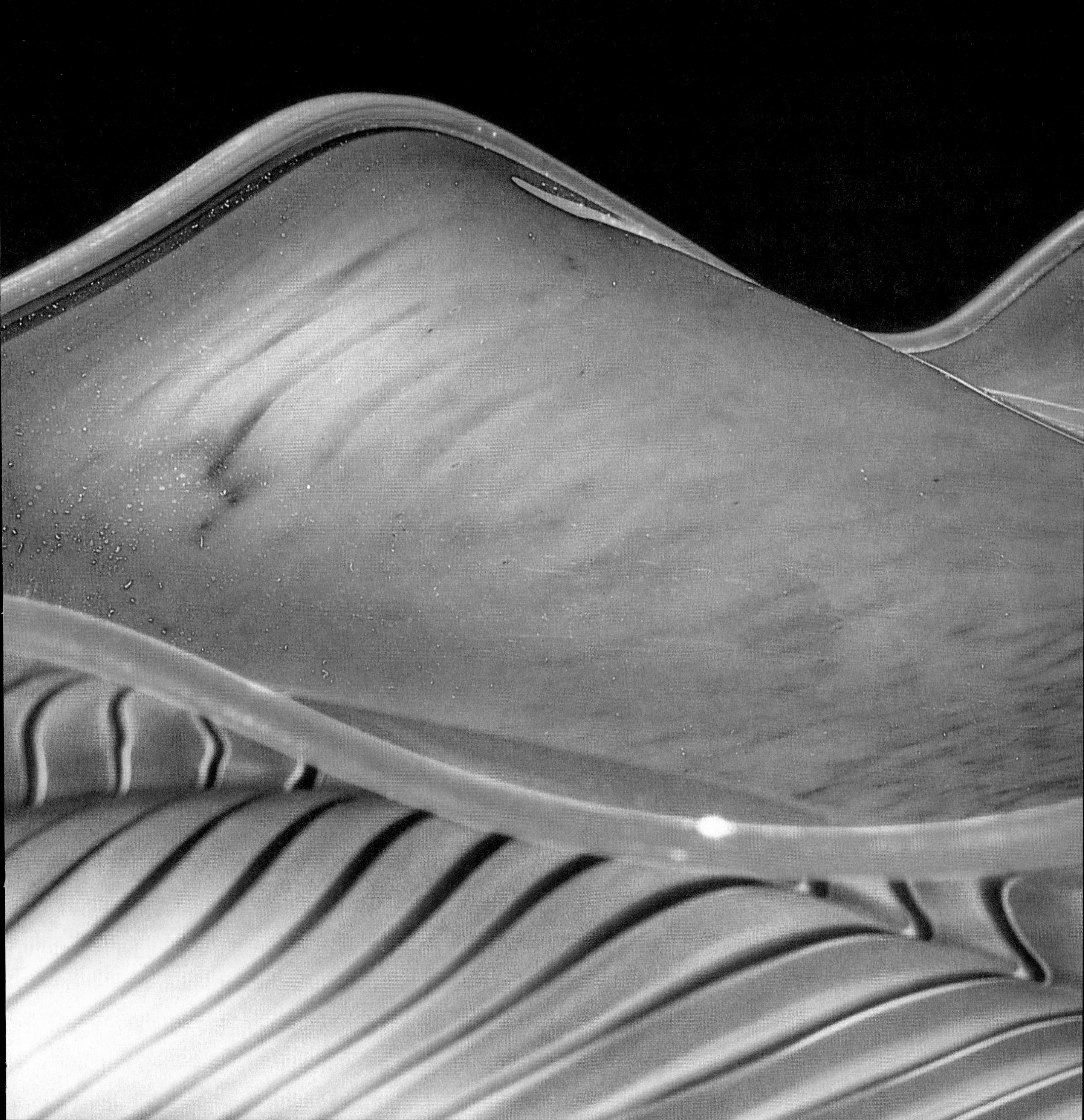

8

Competitive Markets for Goods and Services

Chapter Objectives

After mastering the material in this chapter, you will be able to:

1. Explain what it means for a firm to take the market price as given.
2. Explain how a perfectly competitive firm determines its profit-maximizing output and how this relates to the determination of supply.
3. Explain the role of profit in determining long-run equilibrium in perfect competition.
4. Explain the reasons a firm might shut down in the short run or leave the industry in the long run.
5. Explain why price equals marginal cost in perfect competition.
6. Explain how a perfectly competitive market responds in the short run and in the long run to changes in demand, technology, and factor costs.

We should worry much less about whether competition in a given case is perfect and worry much more whether there is competition at all.
Friedrich A. von Hayek

What's Ahead

They produce a commodity that is essential to our daily lives, one for which the demand is virtually assured. And yet many seem to live on the margin of failure—thousands are driven out of business each year. We provide billions of dollars in aid for them, but still we hear of the hardships they face. Their plight stirs our concern—many of us even attend concerts given on their behalf. They are our nation's farmers.

What is it about farmers, and farming, that arouses our concern? Much of the answer probably lies in our sense that, somehow, farming is fundamental to the American way of life. Our country was built, in large part, by independent men and women who made their living from the soil. Many of us perceive their plight as our plight. But part of the answer lies in the fact that farmers do, in fact, face a difficult economic environment. Most of them operate in highly competitive markets, markets that tolerate few mistakes and offer small rewards. Perhaps finally our concern is stirred by our recognition that the farmers' plight is our blessing. The low prices that make life difficult for farmers are the low prices we enjoy as consumers of food.

But what keeps farm prices so low? What holds farmers in a situation where many of them always seem to be just getting by? We shall see in this chapter that prices barely high enough to keep farmers in business are precisely what we would expect to prevail in a competitive market. In this chapter we'll examine a model of how competitive markets work. This model will help to explain the situation facing farmers, but it will also help us to understand the determination of price and output in a wide range of markets.

We'll put the concepts of marginal cost, average variable cost, and average total cost we developed in the last chapter to work to see how firms in a competitive market respond to market forces. We'll see how firms adjust to changes in demand and supply in the short run and in the long run. This is the first of many chapters that will examine how firms respond to a particular structure of market and how that response affects the market.

- **Perfect competition** is a model of the market that assumes that there are a large number of firms and buyers, that the firms produce identical products, that it is easy for new firms to enter and for existing firms to leave the market, and that buyers and sellers have complete information about market conditions.
- **Price takers** are individuals in a market—buyers or sellers—who have no ability to affect the price of the good in the market.

Perfect Competition: A Model

Virtually all firms in a market economy face competition from other firms. We'll be exploring a variety of competitive environments in subsequent chapters. In this chapter, and in the next three, we'll be working with a model of a highly idealized form of competition. It is competition economists call "perfect."

Perfect competition is a model of the market based on the assumption that a large number of firms produce identical goods and face a large number of buyers. The model of perfect competition also assumes that it's easy for new firms to enter the market and for existing ones to leave. And finally, it assumes that buyers and sellers have complete information about market conditions.

Assumptions of the Model

The assumptions of the model of perfect competition, taken together, imply that individual buyers and sellers in a perfectly competitive market accept the market price as given and respond to it. No one buyer or seller has any influence over that price. Individuals who must take the market price as given are called **price takers.** A consumer or firm that takes the market price as given has no ability to influence that price. A price-taking firm or consumer is like an individual who's buying or selling stocks. He or she looks up the current price and buys or sells at that price. The price is determined by demand and supply in the market—not by individual buyers or sellers. In a perfectly competitive market, each firm and each consumer is a price taker.

To see how the assumptions of the model of perfect competition imply price-taking behavior, let us examine each of them in turn.

Identical Goods

In a perfectly competitive market for a good or service, one unit of the good or service cannot be differentiated from any other on any basis. Graded no. 1 hard red winter wheat being sold in the grain market in Chicago is an example. No buyer can identify which farm a particular bushel of wheat came from, nor would he or she care to know. One bushel of wheat is as good as another. There are no brand preferences or customer loyalty; there are no locational preferences and no quality differences among individual producers.

The assumption that goods are identical is necessary if firms are to be price takers. If one grower's wheat were perceived as having special properties that distinguish it from the wheat grown by others, then the grower of the special wheat would have some power over its price. By assuming that all goods and services produced by firms in a perfectly competitive market are identical, we establish a necessary condition for price-taking behavior.

A Large Number of Buyers and Sellers

How many buyers and sellers are in our market? The answer rests on our presumption of price-taking behavior. There are so many buyers and sellers that none of the buyers or sellers has any influence on the market price regardless of how much they purchase or sell. A firm in a perfectly competitive market can react to prices but cannot affect the prices it pays for the factors of production or the prices it receives for its output.

Ease of Entry and Exit

The assumption that it's easy for other firms to enter a perfectly competitive market implies an even greater degree of competition. Firms in a market must deal not only with the large number of competing firms but with the possibility that still more firms might enter the market.

The concept of easy entry is a relative one. For example, the lawn maintenance industry is certainly easy to enter. One needs a mower, an edger, and perhaps an ad in the newspaper, and the business is launched. In contrast, the industry that supplies natural gas to homes is relatively difficult to enter. Homes in virtually every community are supplied with natural gas by a single firm, either a regulated monopoly or a government-operated enterprise. In either case, it's hard to imagine additional firms being able to install the underground pipes that would deliver a competing supply of natural gas.

Entry is thus far easier in the lawn maintenance industry than in the residential natural gas industry. But what of the cases in between? The best way to gauge ease of entry is to see how often it occurs. If we see that new firms frequently appear in a particular market, then we can conclude that entry is relatively easy. The restaurant industry in most communities, for example, must be relatively easy to enter—new firms enter often. Later in this chapter, we'll see how ease of entry is related to the sustainability of profits. If entry is easy, then the promise of high profits will quickly attract new firms. If entry is difficult, it won't.

The model of perfect competition assumes easy exit as well as easy entry. The assumption of easy exit strengthens the assumption of easy entry.

Suppose a firm is considering entering a particular market. Entry may be easy, but suppose that getting out is difficult. For example, suppliers of factors of production to firms in the industry might be happy to accommodate new firms but might require that they sign on for long-term contracts. Such contracts could make leaving the market difficult and costly. If that were the case, a firm might be hesitant to enter in the first place. Easy exit helps make entry easier. Ease of exit also plays a role in the achievement of long-run equilibrium in perfect competition. We thus assume that it is both easy to enter and to exit a market.

Complete Information

We assume that all sellers have complete information about prices, technology, and all other knowledge relevant to the operation of the market. No one seller has any information about production methods that isn't available to all other sellers. If one seller had an advantage over other sellers, perhaps special information about a lower-cost production method, then that seller could exert some control over market price—the seller would no longer be a price taker.

We assume also that buyers know the prices offered by every seller. If buyers didn't know about prices offered by different firms in the market, then a firm might be able to sell a good or service for a price other than the market price and thus could avoid being a price taker.

The availability of information that is assumed in the model of perfect competition implies that information can be obtained at low cost. If consumers and firms can obtain information at low cost, they're likely to do so. Information about the marketplace may come over a computer modem, over the airways in a television commercial, or over a cup of coffee with a friend. Whatever its source, we assume that its low cost ensures that consumers and firms have enough of it so that everyone buys or sells goods and services at market prices determined by the intersection of demand and supply curves.

Case in Point — A Price Taker's Lament

Bill Adams can tell you what life for a price-taking firm is like. He runs one.

Mr. Adams is president of Associated Sales, a Phoenix firm that sells household appliances to builders of custom homes. The firm is a small one, with $2 million in annual sales.

After more than 20 years in business, Mr. Adams knows exactly how his prices are set. "The market tells us what we can sell a product for," he says. "Our customers want to know two things: the price and whether you can get the merchandise to them on time. And the primary factor is the price."

As president of his own company, Mr. Adams can charge any price he wants. But he has lots of competitors from which his customers can choose. If his prices drift above those of his rivals, he won't make sales. The items he sells, such as top-of-the-line refrigerators and stoves, are typically quite expensive. But even the smallest deviation of his price from the market's can doom him.

"If I could raise the price of every item I sold by $10, I'd be in good shape. But I can't," he says.

Of course, Mr. Adams could charge a lower price than his rivals. But he says that he's barely making a profit now—a lower price would create sales, but he'd be losing money.

As long as Mr. Adams's firm charges the market price for the items he sells, he can compete with his rivals and make sales. The highly competitive marketplace for his product makes him a price taker.

Source: Personal interview.

The assumptions of the perfectly competitive model ensure that each agent is a price taker. It is the market that determines price in the model of perfect competition, not individual firms. No individual has enough power in a perfectly competitive market to have any impact on that price.

Perfect Competition and the Real World

Are there any markets whose conditions correspond precisely to those of the perfectly competitive model? The assumptions of identical products, a large number of buyers, easy entry and exit, and perfect information are, after all, rather strong. The notion that firms must sit back and let the market determine price seems to fly in the face of what we know about most real firms—in which managers customarily *do* set prices.

Some agricultural markets conform to the assumptions of the perfectly competitive model—farmers produce identical goods and take market prices as given. Markets for various financial instruments, such as stocks, are often perfectly competitive. One share of General Motors common stock, for example, is identical to every other share of General Motors common stock. There are a large number of buyers and sellers, a seller can enter or exit the market at any time, and information about price is instantly available.

But the number of markets that precisely match the assumptions of perfect competition is small. And yet the model of perfect competition is one of the most widely used models in economics. How can a model that fits so little explain so much?

The answer lies in our analysis in Chapter 1 of the basic role of models. Recall that a model in economics is a set of assumptions that abstract from conditions of the real world. The result is that *no* model's assumptions are completely realistic. A model's usefulness comes not from its ability to describe the real world but from the insights it gives us in analyzing that world. How will the market respond to a change in demand? How will it respond to a change in production cost? We'll see that answers to these questions that are based on the model of perfect competition correspond closely to the actual responses of a wide range of actual markets. It is because of its insights into the responses of actual markets that the model of perfect competition has proved so useful a tool.

We might ask some questions about markets that the model of perfect competition can't help us answer. If we want, for example, to assess how the managers of specific hotels determine the prices they charge, the model of perfect competition won't be any help—it assumes that managers have no control over prices. If we want to understand the directions in which price and output in the hotel industry move, however, the model of perfect competition gives us a powerful tool for analysis.

We'll examine other market models in subsequent chapters, models that directly address problems such as price setting. But for now, we will assume price-taking behavior and the conditions that ensure that behavior will occur. Making these assumptions gives us an analytical tool, the model of perfect competition, that has tremendous power in assessing the behavior of markets.

Checklist ✓

- The central characteristic of the model of perfect competition is the fact that price is determined by demand and supply; buyers and sellers are price takers.
- The model assumes a large number of firms producing identical goods or services, a large number of buyers, easy entry and exit in the industry, and complete information about prices in the market.
- Although few real-world markets correspond to the conditions of perfect competition, the model remains useful in analyzing the forces that influence price and output even in markets that do not seem to match the assumptions of perfect competition.

Output Determination in the Short Run

Our goal in this section is to see how a firm in a perfectly competitive market determines its output level in the short run—a period in which at least one factor is fixed. We shall see that the firm can maximize profit by applying the marginal decision rule. It will increase output up to the point that the marginal benefit of an additional unit of output is just equal to the marginal cost. This fact has an important implication: over a wide range of output, the firm's marginal cost curve is its supply curve.

Price and Revenue

Each firm in a perfectly competitive market is a price taker; the equilibrium price and industry output are determined by demand and supply. Exhibit 8-1 shows how demand and supply in the market for radishes, which we shall assume are produced under conditions of perfect competition, determine total output and price. The equilibrium price is 40 cents per pound; the equilibrium quantity is 10 million pounds per month. Notice that the supply curve is not linear, we'll see later that its shape is determined by the marginal cost curve.

Each firm in the radish industry, because it is a price taker, assumes it can sell all the radishes it wants at a price of 40 cents per pound. No matter how many or how few radishes it produces, the firm expects to sell them all for 40¢ a pound.

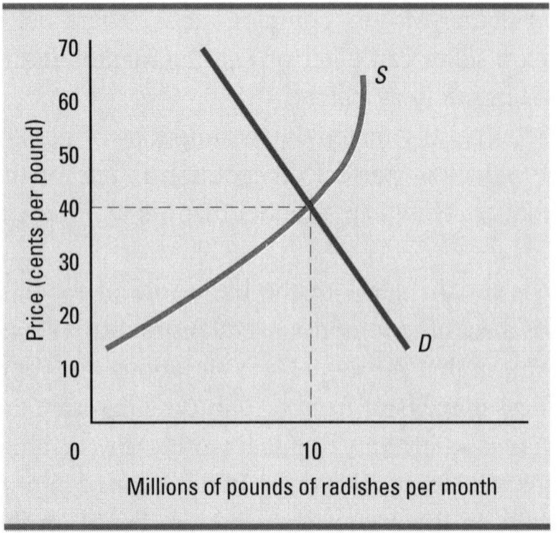

EXHIBIT 8-1

The Market for Radishes

Price and output in a competitive market are determined by demand and supply. In the market for radishes, the equilibrium price is 40 cents per pound; 10 million pounds per month are produced and purchased at this price.

Total revenue is equal to a firm's total output times the price at which it sells that output.

The assumption that the firm expects to sell all the radishes it wants at the market price is crucial. If a firm didn't expect to sell all of its radishes at the market price—if it would have to lower the price to sell some quantities—the firm wouldn't be a price taker. And price-taking behavior is central to the model of perfect competition.

The firm expects to sell all it wants at the market price, but it can't sell anything at any price higher than the market price. The assumption of complete information ensures that every buyer knows the market price of radishes. Buyers are price takers as well; they can buy all the radishes they want at the market price. Given the assumption that all radishes are identical, no buyer is willing to purchase radishes from any seller at any price higher than the market price.

Radish growers thus have no reason to charge a price lower than the market price and are unable to charge a price higher than the market price. For radish growers, the price is very much like the weather. They may complain about it, but in perfect competition there isn't anything any of them can *do* about it.[1]

Total Revenue

A firm in a perfectly competitive market responds to that market by selecting the output it will produce. In determining the quantity of that output, one important consideration is the revenue the firm will gain by producing it.

A firm's **total revenue** is found by multiplying its output by the price at which it sells that output. For a perfectly competitive firm, total revenue is the market price times the quantity the firm produces.

Exhibit 8-2 shows total revenue curves for a radish grower for three possible market prices: 20, 40, and 60 cents per pound. Each total revenue curve is a linear, upward-sloping line. At any price, the greater the quantity a perfectly competitive firm sells, the greater its total revenue.

[1] Although there is nothing a perfectly competitive firm can do individually about the price it faces, firms may organize and seek political changes. Some farmers, for example, have won government intervention that has raised the prices they receive. We'll explore such possibilities in subsequent chapters.

EXHIBIT 8-2

Total Revenue and Marginal Revenue

Panel (a) shows different total revenue curves for each market price in perfect competition. A total revenue curve is a straight line coming out of the origin. The slope of a total revenue curve is marginal revenue; it equals the market price in perfect competition. Marginal revenue is thus a horizontal line at the market price, as shown in Panel (b).

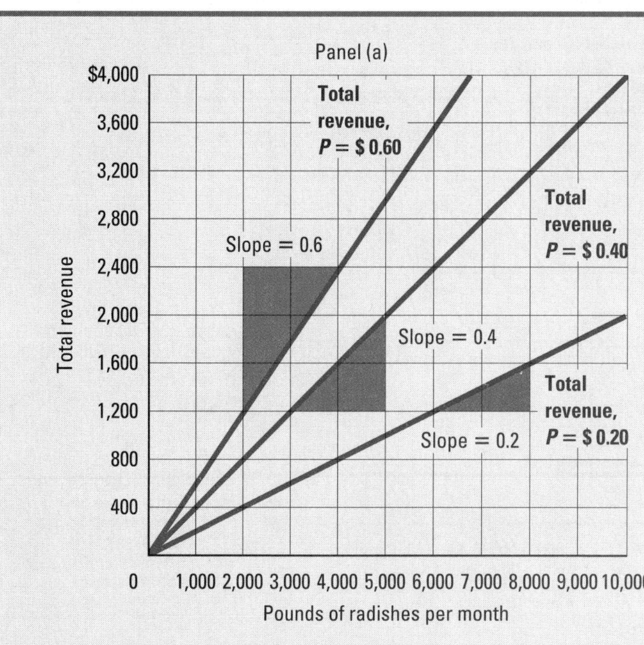

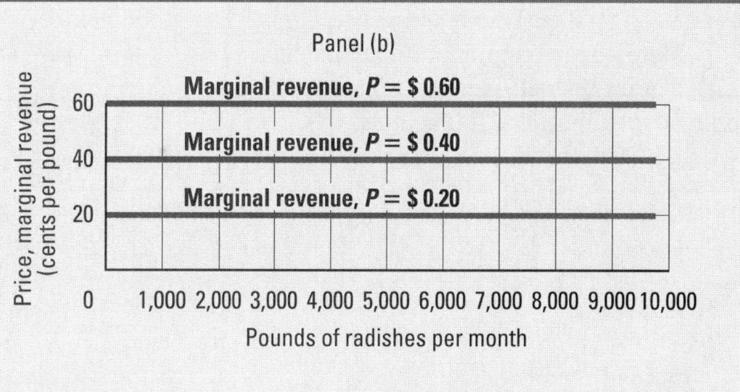

Marginal revenue is the increase in a firm's total revenue when it sells an additional unit of output. It is measured as the slope of the total revenue curve ($\Delta TR/\Delta Q$).

Marginal Revenue

The slope of a total revenue curve is particularly important. It equals the change in the vertical axis (total revenue) divided by the change in the horizontal axis (quantity) between any two points. The slope measures the rate at which total revenue increases as output increases. We can think of it as the increase in total revenue associated with a 1-unit increase in output. We call this increase **marginal revenue.** Marginal revenue is thus the slope of the total revenue curve. How much additional revenue does a radish producer gain from selling one more pound of radishes? The answer, of course, is the market price for one pound. Because the firm can sell any quantity at the market price, the marginal revenue equals the market price. If the market price of a pound of radishes is 40 cents, then the marginal revenue is 40 cents. Marginal revenue curves for prices of 20, 40, and 60 cents are given in Panel (b) of Exhibit 8-2.

The market price in a perfectly competitive market provides half the information required to apply the marginal decision rule to the question of how much output a firm should produce. The marginal benefit of producing one more unit is the additional revenue—the marginal revenue—that unit will generate. For a perfectly competitive firm, that marginal revenue is given by the market price.

Revenue, Cost, and Profit

A firm's profit is the difference between total revenue and total cost. We found in Chapter 7 that a firm's total cost curve in the short run intersects the vertical axis at some positive value equal to the firm's fixed costs. Total cost then rises at a decreasing rate over the range of increasing returns to the firm's variable factors. It rises at an increasing rate over the range of diminishing returns. Exhibit 8-3 shows the total cost curve for a typical radish grower, Tom Chen, as well as the total revenue curve for a price of 40 cents per pound. His fixed cost is $400 per

EXHIBIT 8-3

Total Revenue, Total Cost, and Profit

Profit is the vertical distance between the total revenue and total cost curves (revenue minus costs). Here, the maximum profit attainable by Tom Chen for his radish production is $938 per month at an output of 6,700 pounds.

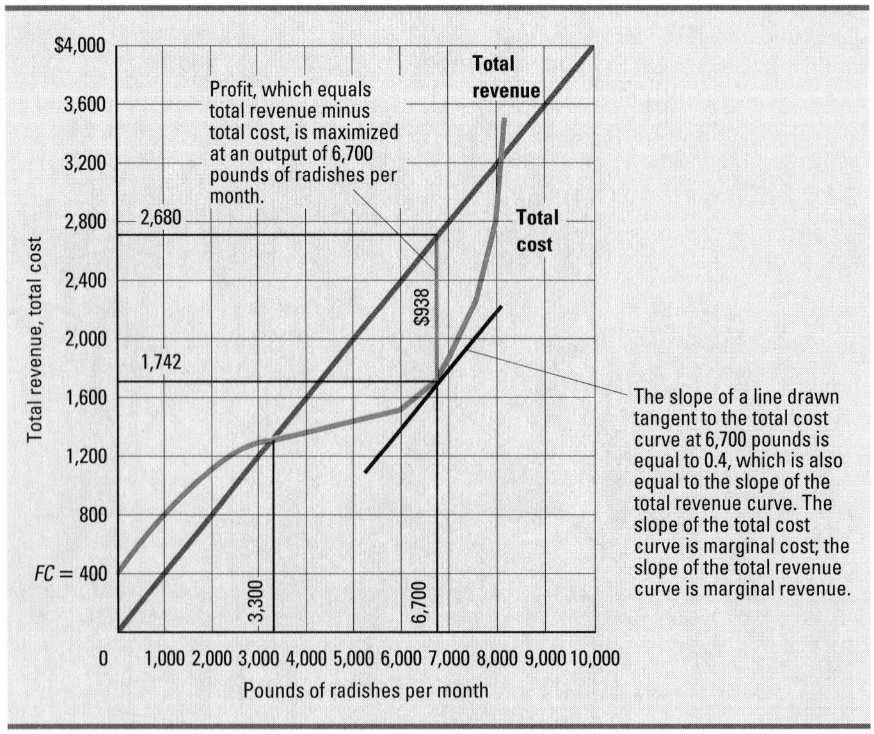

month. Mr. Chen's profit is the vertical distance between the total revenue curve and the total cost curve.

Let's examine the total revenue and total cost curves in Exhibit 8-3 more carefully. At zero units of output, Mr. Chen's total cost is $400 (his fixed cost); total revenue is zero. Total cost continues to exceed total revenue up to an output of 3,300 pounds per month, at which point the two curves intersect. At this point, profit equals zero. As Mr. Chen expands output above 3,300 pounds per month, total revenue becomes greater than total cost. We see that at a quantity of 3,300 pounds per month, the total revenue curve is steeper than the total cost curve. Because revenues are rising faster than costs, profits rise with increased output. As long as the total revenue curve is steeper than the total cost curve, profit increases as the firm increases its output.

The total revenue curve's slope doesn't change as the firm increases its output. But the total cost curve becomes steeper and steeper as diminishing returns set in. Eventually, the total cost and total revenue curves will have the same slope. That happens in Exhibit 8-3 at an output of 6,700 pounds of radishes per month. Notice that a line drawn tangent to the total cost curve at that quantity has the same slope as the total revenue curve.

As output increases beyond 6,700 pounds, the total cost curve continues to become steeper. It thus becomes steeper than the total revenue curve. Profits fall as costs rise faster than revenues. *The firm maximizes profit at the output level at which the total revenue curve and the total cost curve have the same slope.*

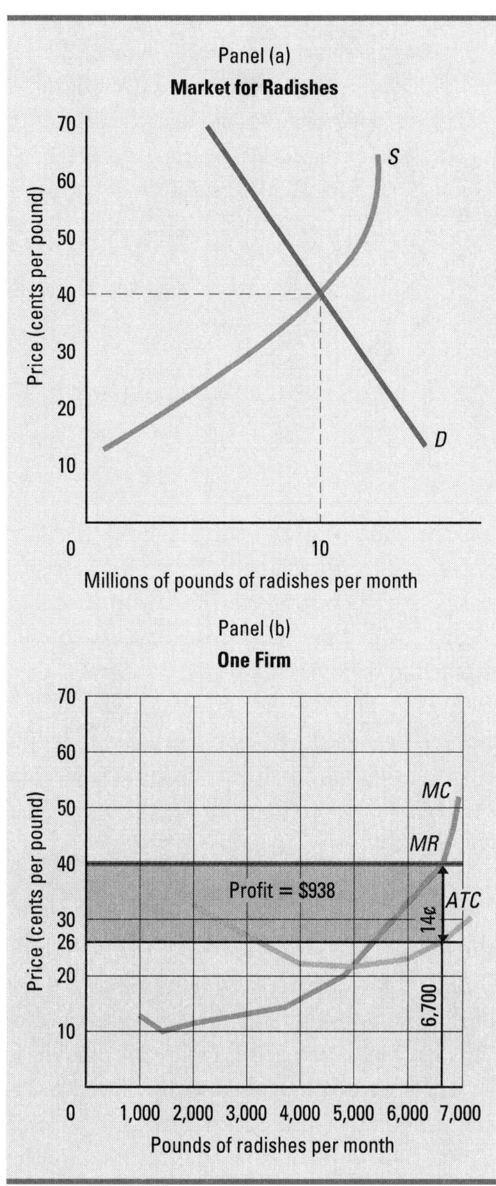

EXHIBIT 8-4

Maximizing Profit: Marginal Revenue and Marginal Cost

The market price is determined by the intersection of demand and supply. The firm takes the market price, 40 cents per pound, as given and maximizes profits by selecting an output at which marginal revenue *(MR)* equals marginal cost *(MC)*. Profit per unit is the difference between average total cost *(ATC)* and price (here, 14 cents per pound); profit is profit per unit times the quantity produced ($0.14 × 6,700 = $938).

Maximizing at the Margin

The slope of the total revenue curve is marginal revenue; the slope of the total cost curve is marginal cost. Profit, the difference between total revenue and total cost, is maximized where marginal revenue equals marginal cost. This is consistent with the marginal decision rule, which holds that a profit-maximizing firm should increase output until the marginal benefit of an additional unit equals the marginal cost. For a firm, the marginal benefit of selling an additional unit is measured as marginal revenue. Finding the output at which marginal revenue equals marginal cost is thus an application of our marginal decision rule.

Exhibit 8-4 shows how a firm can use the marginal decision rule to determine its profit-maximizing output. In Panel (b), its marginal revenue curve is a horizontal line *(MR)* at the market price, which is determined by demand and supply. The firm's marginal cost *(MC)* curve intersects the marginal revenue curve at the point where profit is maximized. Mr. Chen maximizes profits by producing 6,700 pounds of radishes per month. That is, of course, the result we obtained in Exhibit 8-3, where we saw that the firm's total revenue and total cost curves differ by the greatest amount at the point at which the slopes of the curves, which equal marginal revenue and marginal cost, respectively, are equal.

We can use the graph in Exhibit 8-4 to compute Mr. Chen's profit. Profit per unit is the difference between price and average total cost. At the profit-maximizing output of 6,700 pounds of radishes per month, average total cost *(ATC)* is 26 cents per pound, as shown in Exhibit 8-4. Price is 40 cents per pound, so profit per unit is 14 cents. Profit is found by multiplying profit per unit by the number of units produced; the firm's profit is thus $938 ($0.14 × 6,700). It is shown graphically by the area of the shaded rectangle in Exhibit 8-4, which equals the vertical distance between total revenue and total cost at an output of 6,700 pounds of radishes in Exhibit 8-3.

Reader's Advisory !

Look carefully at the rectangle that shows total profit in Panel (b) of Exhibit 8-4. It is found by taking the profit-maximizing quantity, 6,700 pounds, then reading up to the av-erage total cost *(ATC)* curve and the marginal revenue *(MR)* curve at the market price. Profit per unit equals price minus average total cost *(MR − ATC)*. The firm's total profit equals profit per unit times the quantity produced. It is found by extending horizontal lines from the *ATC* and *MR* curves to the vertical axis and taking the area of the rectangle formed. There is no reason for the profit-maximizing quantity to correspond to the lowest point on the *ATC* curve; it does not in this case. Students sometimes make the mistake of calculating profit per unit as the distance between the *MR* curve and the lowest point on the *ATC* curve. Profit per unit is actually the distance between the *MR* curve and the *ATC* curve at the quantity determined by the intersection of marginal cost *(MC)* and marginal revenue *(MR)* in Panel (b) of Exhibit 8-4.

Losses in the Short Run

In the short run, a firm has one or more inputs whose quantities are fixed. That means that in the short run the firm can't leave its industry. Even if it is losing money, going entirely out of business is not an option in the short run. The firm may close its doors, but it must continue to pay the fixed costs associated with those doors—and any other fixed inputs the firm may have.

A firm that is losing money—whose profits have become negative—in the short run may either continue to produce or shut down its operations, reducing its output to zero. It will choose the option that minimizes its losses. The crucial test of whether to operate or shut down lies in the relationship between price and average variable cost.

Producing to Minimize Loss

Suppose the demand for radishes falls to D_2, as shown in Panel (a) of Exhibit 8-5. The market price for radishes plunges to 18 cents per pound. That price is below average total cost; Mr. Chen loses money. Although the new market price falls short of average total cost, it still exceeds average variable cost, shown in Panel (b) as *AVC.* Mr. Chen should therefore continue to produce an output at which marginal cost equals marginal revenue. These curves (labeled *MC* and MR_2) intersect in Panel (b) at an output of 4,444 pounds of radishes per month.

When producing 4,444 pounds of radishes per month, Mr. Chen faces an average total cost of 23 cents per pound. At a price of 18 cents per pound, he loses a nickel on each pound produced. Total losses at an output of 4,444 pounds per month are thus $222.20 per month.

No producer likes to lose money, but the money-losing solution shown in Exhibit 8-5 is the best Mr. Chen can attain. Any level of production other than the one at which marginal cost equals marginal revenue would produce even greater losses.

Suppose Mr. Chen were to shut down and produce no radishes. That would reduce variable costs to zero, but he would still face fixed costs of $400 per month (recall that $400 was the vertical intercept of the total cost curve in Exhibit 8-3). By shutting down, Mr. Chen would lose $400 per month. By continuing to produce, he loses $222.20.

The firm's **shutdown point** is the minimum value of average variable cost.

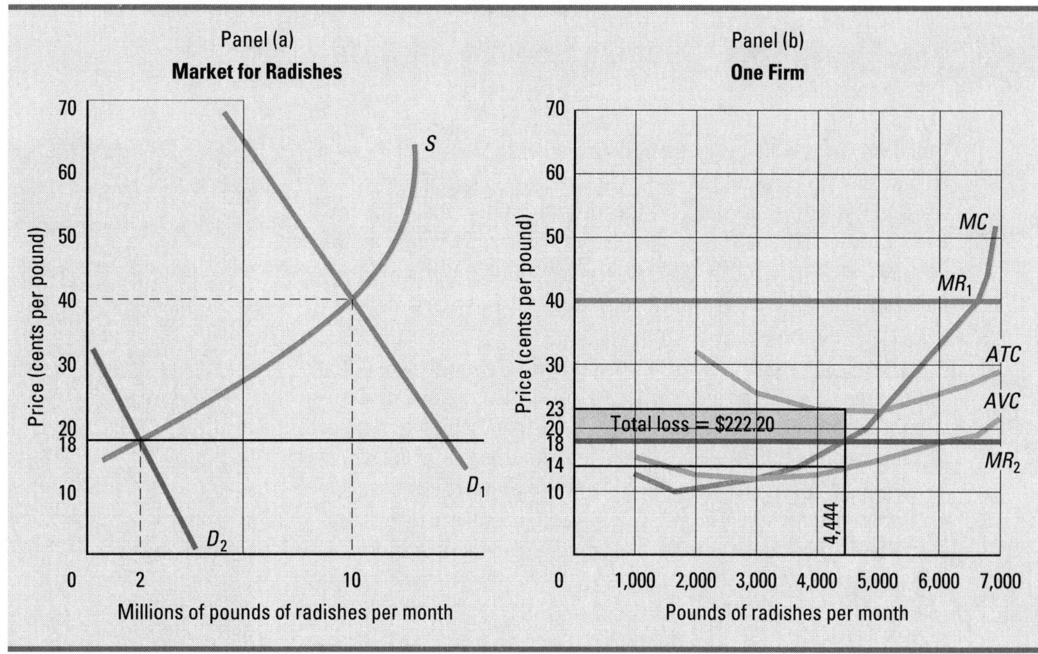

EXHIBIT 8-5

Losing Money in the Short Run

Tom Chen loses money when price drops below average total cost *(ATC)*, as it does in Panel (b) as a result of a reduction in demand. If price is above average variable cost *(AVC)*, however, he can minimize his losses by producing where marginal cost *(MC)* equals marginal revenue (MR_2). Here, that occurs at an output of 4,444 pounds of radishes per month. The price is 18 cents per pound, and average total cost is 23 cents per pound. He loses 5 cents per pound, or $222.20 per month.

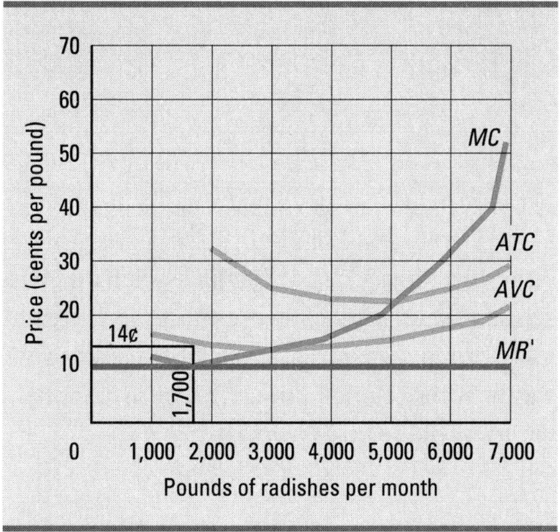

EXHIBIT 8-6

Shutting Down

The market price of radishes drops to 10 cents per pound, so marginal revenue *(MR')* is below Mr. Chen's average variable cost *(AVC)*. He would thus lose more money by continuing to operate than by shutting down. Whenever price falls below average variable cost, the firm will shut down, reducing its production to zero.

Mr. Chen is better off producing where marginal cost equals marginal revenue because at that output price exceeds average variable cost. Average variable cost is 14 cents per pound, so by continuing to produce, he covers his variable costs, with 4 cents per pound left over to apply to fixed costs. Whenever price is greater than average variable cost, the firm maximizes profit (or minimizes loss) by producing the output level at which marginal revenue and marginal cost intersect.

Shutting Down to Minimize Loss

Suppose price drops below a firm's average variable cost. Now the best strategy for the firm is to shut down, reducing its output to zero. The minimum level of average variable cost, which occurs at the intersection of the marginal cost curve and the average variable cost curve, is called the **shutdown point.** Any price below the minimum value of average variable cost will cause the firm to shut down. If the firm were to continue producing, it would not only lose its fixed costs but would face an additional loss by not covering its variable costs.

Exhibit 8-6 shows what Mr. Chen will do if the price of radishes drops to 10 cents per pound. Price is less than average variable cost, so he would not only lose his fixed cost but would incur additional losses by producing. Suppose, for example, he decided to operate where marginal cost equals marginal revenue, producing 1,700 pounds of radishes per month. Average variable cost equals 14 cents per pound, so he'd lose 4 cents on each pound he produces, plus the loss of his fixed costs. If he shut down, he'd lose only his fixed cost. Because the price of 10 cents falls below his average variable cost, his best course is to shut down.

Case in Point: Shutting Down a Vineyard

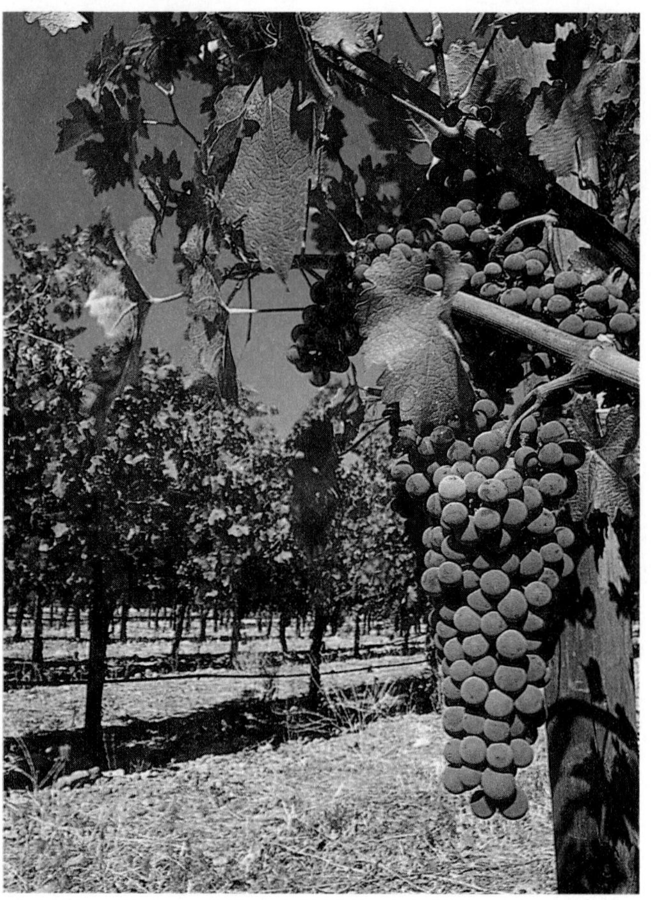

Business firms can close their doors to shut down, but can a farmer shut down a field?

Many California vintners, faced with falling prices for red-wine grapes, did just that in the early 1980s. They simply chose to let their grapes rot in the fields rather than pick them. They kept their vines alive to produce in subsequent years, but they didn't harvest their current crops.

During the expansion of the California wine industry in the 1960s and 1970s, growers had to make a crucial choice—whether to plant grapes such as Zinfandel from which red wines are made or to plant grapes such as Chardonnay from which white wines are made. Leaning toward the preferences of growers and consumers in Europe, where red wines have long dominated the wine industry, most California vintners opted to grow red-wine grapes.

Early in the 1980s, however, consumer preferences in the United States shifted strongly toward white wine and away from red wine. The result was higher prices for white-wine grapes and lower prices for red-wine grapes. And that spelled trouble for growers of red-wine grapes.

Growers found prices had fallen not just below their average total cost curves, which meant they were losing money, but below their average variable cost curves. Grower Phil Johnson recalls the situation: "When the price fell below the cost of harvesting and hauling the grapes, many growers left their grapes on the vine."

Sean James was one of those growers. "The price fell below our variable cost, and we simply didn't pick the grapes," he said. "We kept our grapes alive because we expected a recovery, which we eventually got. But when prices were down, we didn't harvest."

Shutting down is not the same thing as going out of business. A firm shuts down by closing its doors; it can reopen them whenever it expects to cover its variable costs. We can even think of a firm's decision to close at the end of the day as a kind of shutdown point; the firm makes this choice because it doesn't anticipate that it will be able to cover its variable cost overnight.

Marginal Cost and Supply

In the model of perfect competition, we assume that a firm determines its output by finding the point where market price, which is marginal revenue, intersects the marginal cost curve. Provided that price exceeds average variable cost, the firm produces the quantity determined by the intersection of the marginal revenue and marginal cost curves.

A supply curve tells us the quantity that will be produced at each price, and that's what the firm's marginal cost curve tells us. The firm's supply curve in the short run is thus its marginal cost curve for prices above the minimum value of average variable cost. At prices below average variable cost, the firm's output drops to zero.

Panel (a) of Exhibit 8-7 shows the average variable cost and marginal cost curves for a hypothetical astrologer, Madame LaFarge, who is in the business of providing astrological consultations over the telephone. We shall assume that this industry is perfectly competitive. At any price below $10 per call, Madame LaFarge would shut down. If the price is $10 or greater, however, she produces an output at which price equals marginal cost. The marginal cost curve is thus her supply curve at all prices greater than $10.

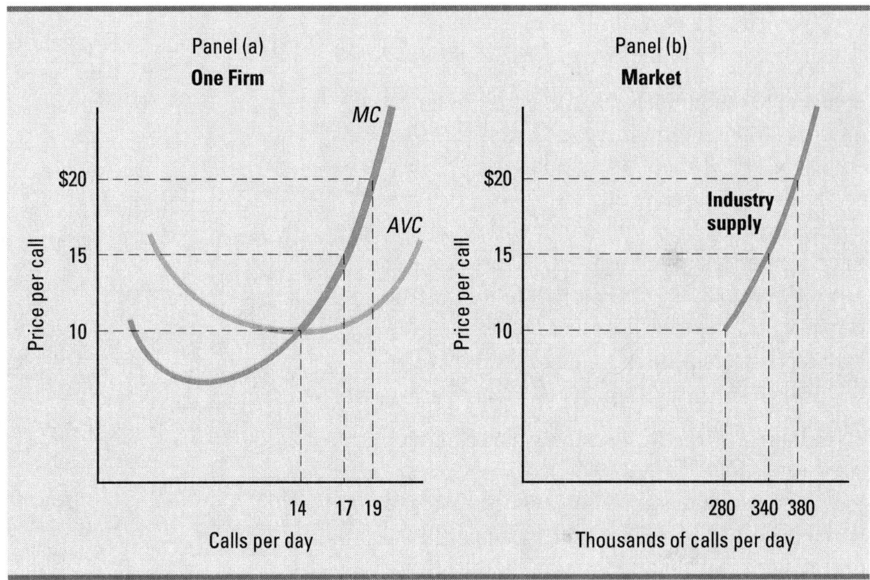

EXHIBIT 8-7

Marginal Cost and Supply

The supply curve for a firm is that portion of its marginal cost *(MC)* curve that lies above the average variable cost *(AVC)* curve, shown in Panel (a). To obtain the supply curve for the industry, we add the outputs of each firm at each price. The supply curve in Panel (b) assumes that there are 20,000 identical firms in the astrological call industry.

Suppose now that the astrological forecast industry consists of Madame LaFarge and 19,999 other firms identical to hers. The industry supply curve is found by adding the outputs of each firm at each price, as shown in Panel (b) of Exhibit 8-7. At a price of $15 per call, for example, Madame LaFarge will supply 17 calls per day. Multiplying that quantity times 20,000, we find that the industry will supply 340,000 calls per day at a price of $15 per call. The supply curve found by summing the supply curves for individual firms in the short run is called the **short-run supply curve.**

The **short-run supply curve** is a supply curve found by summing the supply curves of individual firms in the short run.

Checklist

- Price (P) and industry output (Q) in a competitive market are determined by demand and supply. In Panel (a) Q is industry output. In Panels (b) through (d) the output of a single firm is shown as q. We can think of q as being a trivially small fraction of industry output Q.
- In Panel (b), the total revenue curve for a firm (TR) is a straight line whose slope is the market price. The total cost (TC) curve in the short run has a vertical intercept equal to fixed cost (FC). Profit is the difference between total revenue and total cost. Profit is maximized where the slopes of the two curves are equal.
- Panel (c) shows that the profit-maximizing output is found where marginal revenue (MR) equals marginal cost (MC), so long as price exceeds average variable cost (AVC). If price falls below AVC, the firm will shut down. Profit is the difference between price and short-run average total cost (ATC) times the quantity the firm produces. The shaded area that represents profit here has the same dollar value as the vertical line that shows profit in Panel (b).
- In Panel (d), the firm's supply curve in the short run is its marginal cost (MC) curve over the range where marginal cost exceeds average variable cost (AVC). The short-run supply curve for the market is found by summing the supply curves of individual firms.

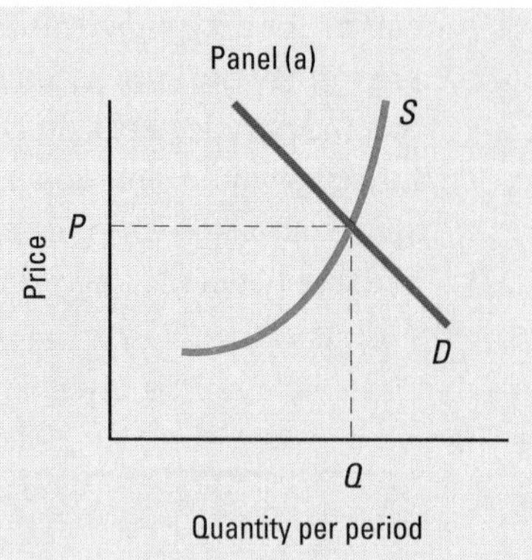

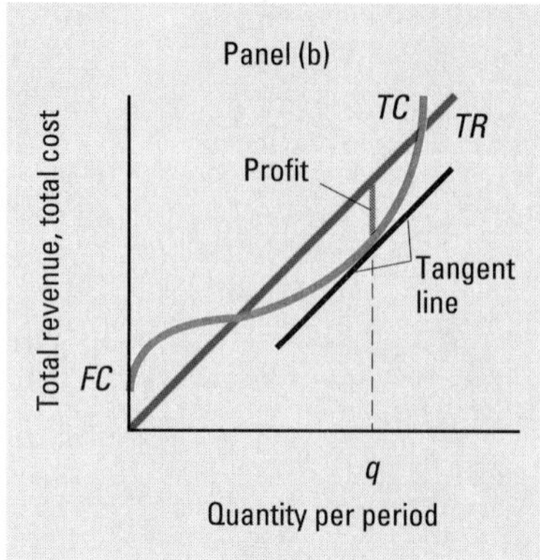

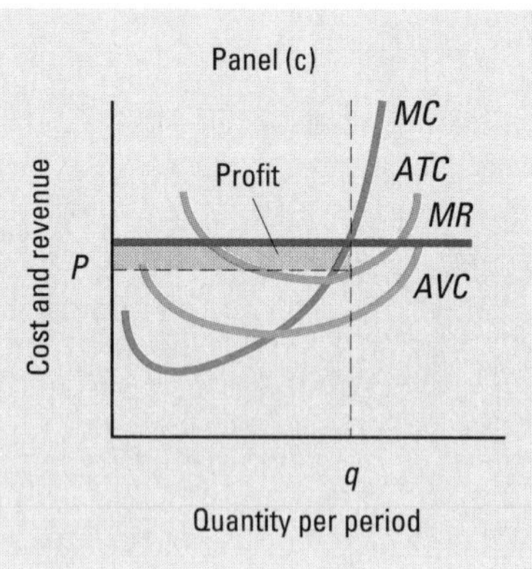

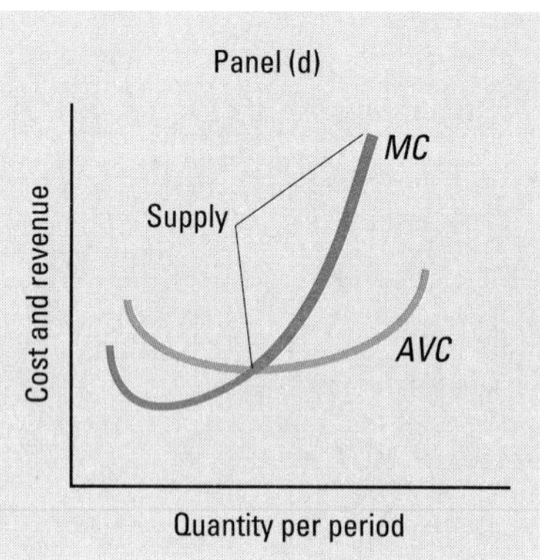

Perfect Competition in the Long Run

In the long run, a firm is free to adjust all of its inputs. New firms can enter any market; existing firms can leave their respective markets. We shall see in this section that the model of perfect competition predicts that at a long-run equilibrium production takes place at the lowest possible cost per unit and that all economic profits and losses are eliminated.

Profit and Loss

Profits and losses play a crucial role in the model of perfect competition. The existence of profits in a particular industry attracts new firms to the industry in the long run. As new firms enter, the supply curve shifts to the right, price falls, and profits fall. Firms continue to enter the industry until profits fall to zero. If firms in an industry are experiencing losses, some will leave. The supply curve shifts to the left, increasing price and reducing losses. Firms continue to leave until the remaining firms are no longer losing money—until profits are zero.

Before examining the mechanism through which entry and exit eliminate profits and losses, we shall examine an important key to understanding it: the difference between the accounting and economic concepts of profit and loss.

Economic Versus Accounting Concepts of Profit and Loss

Profit equals total revenue minus total cost. A loss (negative profit) is incurred if total cost exceeds total revenue. When economists speak of profit, however, they have in mind a very different concept than that used by accountants in computing the profits of business firms.

Accountants include only **explicit costs** in their computation of total cost. Explicit costs include charges that must be paid for factors of production such as labor and capital, together with an estimate of depreciation. Profit computed using explicit costs is called **accounting profit.** Panel (a) of Exhibit 8-8 shows the computation of accounting profit for Tom Chen, the radish farmer. Mr. Chen earns total revenue of $2,680 and has explicit costs totaling $942, for an accounting profit of $1,738 per month.

EXHIBIT 8-8

Accounting Versus Economic Profits

Panel (a) shows a profit and loss statement for Tom Chen's radish farm for a typical month. It reports only explicit costs and is thus an estimate of accounting profit.

Suppose that the best alternative use of the effort and land Mr. Chen uses to grow radishes is carrot production, and that Mr. Chen estimates he would earn accounting profits of $250 per month producing carrots. In addition, he estimates that his time is worth $550 per month. These amounts represent implicit costs of producing radishes. Mr. Chen's economic profit and loss statement might be reported as shown in Panel (b).

Panel (a)

Monthly Profit and Loss Statement: Accounting Profit

Tom Chen

Revenue			
Sale of 6,700 pounds of radishes @ $0.40/pound			$2,680.00
Cost of goods sold (explicit costs)			
Variable factors			
Labor	$400.00		
Equipment rental	300.00		
Supplies (seed, etc.)	92.00		
Explicit variable cost		$792.00	
Fixed factors			
Property tax	150.00		
Explicit fixed cost		150.00	
Total explicit cost			942.00
Accounting profit			$1,738.00

Panel (b)

Monthly Profit and Loss Statement: Economic Profit

Tom Chen

Revenue			
Sale of 6,700 pounds of radishes @ $0.40/pound			$2,680.00
Cost of goods sold (explicit costs)			
Variable factors			
Labor	$400.00		
Value of owner's.labor	550.00		
Equipment rental	300.00		
Supplies (seed, etc.)	92.00		
Total variable cost		$1,342.00	
Fixed factors			
Property tax	150.00		
Forgone return on carrots	250.00		
Total fixed cost		400.00	
Total explicit plus implicit cost			1,742.00
Profit			$938.00

Economists recognize costs in addition to the explicit costs listed by accountants. If Mr. Chen were not growing radishes, he could be doing something else with the land and with his own efforts. Suppose the most valuable alternative use of his land would be to produce carrots, from which Mr. Chen could earn $250 per month in accounting profits. The income he forgoes by not producing carrots is a cost, viewed in the economic sense, of producing radishes. Suppose further that Mr. Chen could be working for another farmer instead of for himself, and that the farmer would be willing to pay him $550 per month. The returns he could get from alternative uses of his labor and his land are part of the economic concept of cost. These costs are not explicit; they would not appear on conventional accounting statements. A cost that is included in the economic concept of cost but that is not an explicit cost is called an **implicit cost.**

- **Explicit costs** are charges that must be paid for the use of factors of production such as labor and capital, together with estimated depreciation costs.
- **Accounting profit** is profit computed using explicit costs as the only measure of cost.
- A cost that is included in the economic concept of cost but that is not an explicit cost is called an **implicit cost.**

Case in Point — Easy Entry and Videocassette Rentals

Michelle Sedlak remembers the good old days in the video rental business.

"When I started in the business, we were charging $8 for a 24-hour rental for the first tape, $4 for the second," she says.

That was in 1982. Videocassette recorders (VCRs) had just been introduced, and there weren't many video rental outlets. "In 1982 you had to *look* for a video store. The nearest competition was likely to be several miles away. Now there's a video store on practically every block. The competition has really driven the price down."

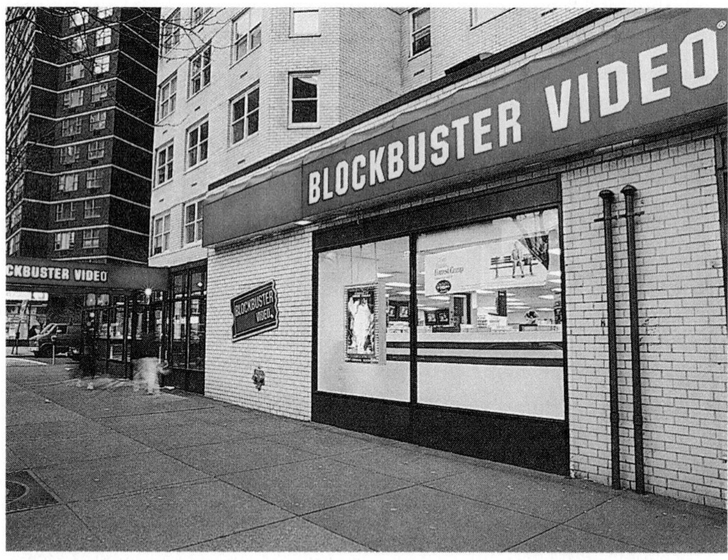

How much? By 1990 Ms. Sedlak was a store manager for Budget Video, a small chain in Baltimore, Maryland. She was charging $1.99 per night for new releases and $0.99 to $1.50 for other titles.

The price reduction Ms. Sedlak cites has been typical of the entire industry. Says Paul Eisele, president of the Fairfield Group, a video industry consulting firm in Connecticut, "Basically, prices vary with the ebb and flow of stores in the industry. As the number of stores increases, prices fall."

Mr. Eisele notes that high initial profits and the promise of rapid growth attracted firms to the industry in the first place. The industry is also easy to enter. The number of video stores in the United States increased from 5,000 in 1981 to 25,000 in 1990, he says.

Rapid entry and falling prices had produced sharply lower accounting profits by 1990. "Several years ago, our profits were as high as 80 percent of sales," Ms. Sedlak recalls. "That fell pretty quickly to 50 percent. Now, we're lucky to get 10 percent. The business has gotten a lot tougher."

Source: Timothy Tregarthen, "Supply, demand and videotape," *The Margin* 6(1) (September/October 1990): 29.

Whenever economists speak of costs or total costs, they generally have in mind a measure that includes both explicit and implicit costs. In this text, all references to cost will be to measures that include implicit as well as explicit costs. The term *profit* thus means total revenue minus implicit as well as explicit costs.

Panel (b) of Exhibit 8-8 shows the computation of Mr. Chen's profits based on the economic assessment of costs. All the explicit costs reported in the accounting statement are listed. His implicit costs, the return he could be getting by using his field to grow carrots instead of radishes and the value of his labor are included as well. His economic profit of $938 thus represents the return he gains in excess of what he could earn in the best alternative use of his resources.

Suppose Mr. Chen's experience is typical of radish growers. They are all earning more than they could have earned in the next-best activity, which we shall assume is carrot production. If firms in the radish market are making a return greater than the return available from growing carrots, then some carrot producers could probably be earning more by producing radishes than they are earning from carrots. When they subtract the implicit cost of the return they're forgoing from radish production, they'll find that they are suffering a loss in the economic sense. More generally, the existence of profits in one industry always implies that losses *must* be occurring in other industries.

If carrot producers can earn a higher return producing radishes, we expect that some of them will exit the carrot industry and enter the radish industry. Carrot producers will enter the radish industry as long as there are profits to be made from radish production.

As firms enter the radish market, the supply of radishes will increase, lowering the price and profitability of producing radishes. As firms leave the carrot market, the supply of carrots will fall, increasing the price and profitability of carrot production. Firms will continue to enter the radish market as long as there are profits to be made. Their entry, however, lowers profits. Prices will continue to drop until profits in the radish industry are zero. Profits from carrot production, which were negative when there were profits to be earned from producing radishes, will rise to zero. That suggests an important long-run result: *Profits in a system of perfectly competitive markets will, in the long run, be driven to zero in all industries.*

The process through which entry will eliminate profits in the long run is illustrated in Exhibit 8-9, using the initial situation that was presented in Exhibit 8-4. The price of radishes is 40 cents per pound. Mr. Chen's average total cost at an output of 6,700 pounds of radishes per month is 26 cents per pound. Mr. Chen thus earns a profit of $938 per month.

Profits in the radish industry attract entry in the long run. Panel (a) shows that as firms enter, the supply curve shifts to the right and the price of radishes falls. New firms enter as long as there are profits to be made—as long as price exceeds average total cost *(ATC)* in Panel (b). As price falls, marginal revenue falls to MR_2 and the firm reduces the quantity it supplies, moving along the marginal cost *(MC)* curve to the lowest point on the *ATC* curve, at 22 cents per pound and an output of 5,000 pounds per month. Although the output of individual firms falls in response to falling prices, there are now more firms, so industry output rises to 13 million pounds per month in Panel (a).

EXHIBIT 8-9

Eliminating Profits in the Long Run

If firms in an industry are making a profit, entry will occur in the long run. Entry continues until firms in the industry are operating at the lowest point on their respective long-run average cost curves and profits fall to zero.

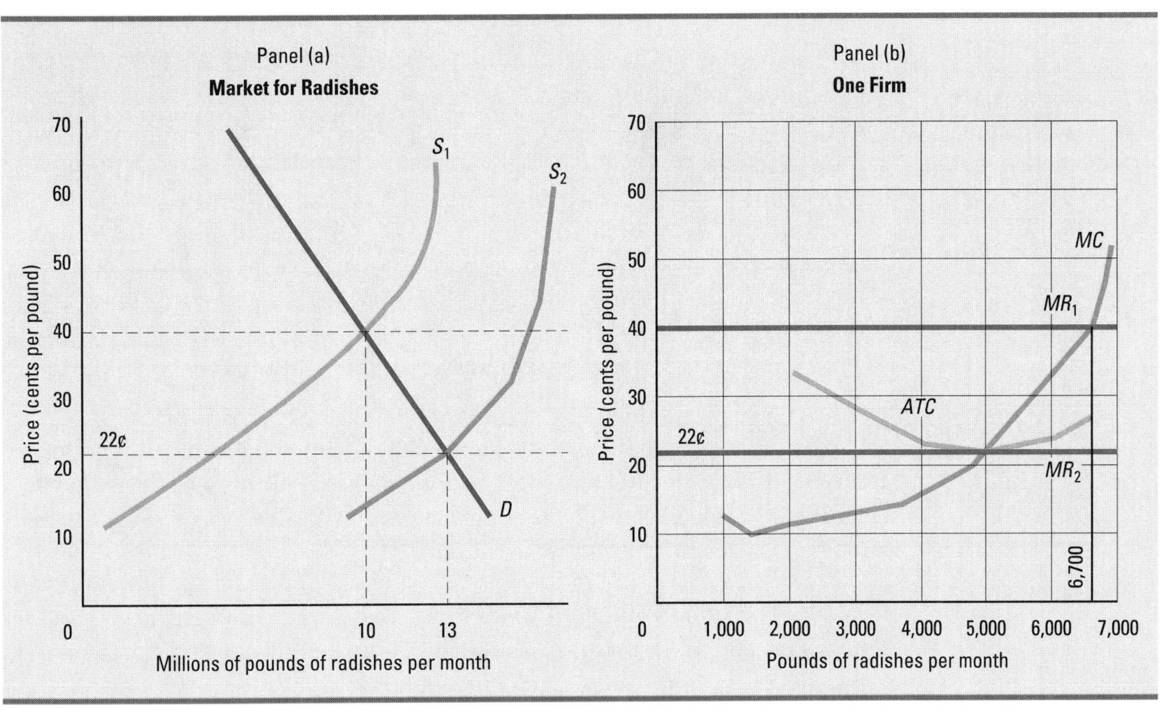

The ease of entry in perfectly competitive markets helps to explain why many producers in them seem to earn such low returns. If the long-run equilibrium solution is a price at which typical firms in the industry just cover their costs, we should expect that some firms will fall short of that mark. Those firms will suffer losses and be driven from the industry. The firms that survive will barely do so. If firms in a competitive market enjoy profits, the pleasure will be fleeting. New firms will enter, driving profits back down to zero.

The perennial difficulties of America's farmers are much easier to understand when we recognize that they compete in markets that can, for the most part, be characterized as perfectly competitive. The model of perfect competition predicts that farmers will earn zero profit in long-run equilibrium. That means that some are always operating on the knife edge of being forced from the industry. The zero-profit solution, of course, means that farmers can expect to earn a level of accounting profit that's just enough to keep them in business. But that leaves very little margin for error.

Eliminating Losses: The Role of Exit

Just as entry eliminates profits in the long run, exit eliminates losses. In Exhibit 8-10, Panel (a) shows the case of an industry in which the market price is initially below *ATC*. In Panel (b), at price P_1 a single firm produces a quantity q_1, assuming it is at least covering its average variable cost. The firm's losses are shown by the shaded rectangle bounded by its average total cost C_1 and price P_1 and by output q_1.

EXHIBIT 8-10

Eliminating Losses in the Long Run

Panel (b) shows that at the initial price P_1, firms in the industry cannot cover average total cost (MR_1 is below *ATC*). That induces some firms to leave the industry, shifting the supply curve in Panel (a) to S_2, reducing industry output to Q_2 and raising price to P_2. At that price (MR_2), firms earn zero profit, and exit from the industry ceases. Panel (b) shows that the firm increases output from q_1 to q_2; total output in the market falls in Panel (a) because there are fewer firms.

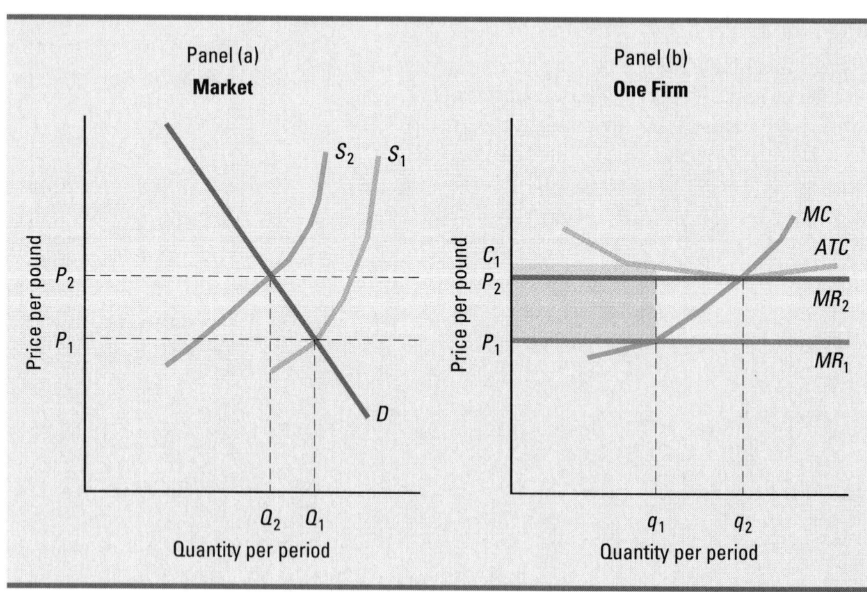

Because firms in the industry are losing money, some will exit. The supply curve in Panel (a) shifts to the left, and it continues shifting as long as firms are suffering losses. Eventually the supply curve shifts all the way to S_2, price rises to P_2, and economic profits return to zero.

Entry, Exit, and Production Costs

In our examination of entry and exit in response to profit or loss in a perfectly competitive industry, we assumed that the *ATC* curve of a single firm does not

A **long-run supply curve** shows the quantity of a good or service supplied at various prices after all long-run adjustments to a price change have been completed.

shift as new firms enter or existing firms leave the industry. That is the case when expansion or contraction doesn't affect price in the markets for the inputs the industry uses. But in some cases, entry or exit does affect input costs.

As new firms enter, they demand the inputs used by the industry. If the industry is a significant user of those inputs, that increase in demand could push up the market price of inputs for all firms in the industry. If that occurs, then entry into an industry that is enjoying profits will boost average costs at the same time as it puts downward pressure on price. Long-run equilibrium will still occur at a zero level of profit and with firms operating on the lowest point on the *ATC* curve, but that cost curve will be somewhat higher than before entry occurred.

Similarly, if firms leave an industry in response to losses, smaller quantities of inputs used in the industry will be demanded. If the industry is a significant enough factor in the market for those inputs, input prices will fall. Costs in the industry will fall while prices are rising as firms leave. The final solution, once again, will be one in which the remaining firms in the industry earn zero profit, with somewhat lower costs than existed before exit occurred.

The behavior of production costs as firms in an industry expand or reduce their output has important implications for the **long-run supply curve,** a curve that relates the price of a good or service to the quantity produced after all long-run adjustments to a price change have been completed. Every point on a long-run supply curve therefore shows a price and quantity supplied at which firms in the industry are earning zero profit. Unlike the short-run supply curve, the long-run curve does not hold factor costs and the number of firms constant.

Exhibit 8-11 shows three supply curves. S_A is a short-run supply curve for a particular good. If expanded production and the entry of new firms leave production costs in the industry unchanged, as was the case in Exhibits 8-9 and 8-10, then the long-run supply curve will be a horizontal line, like supply curve S_B. Because the long-run equilibrium price moves to the lowest point on the *ATC* curve, price is unaffected by the expansion or contraction of the industry. Finally, if industry expansion tends to increase production costs and contraction reduces them, then the long-run supply curve will be upward sloping, like supply curve S_C. Notice that the long-run supply curve S_C is still flatter than the short-run curve S_A. That's because entry or exit occur in the long run, increasing the responsiveness of quantity supplied to a price change.

EXHIBIT 8-11

Short-Run Versus Long-Run Supply

S_A is a typical short-run supply curve; it is found by summing the marginal cost curves for firms in a market. For an industry with constant production costs, the long-run supply curve is a horizontal line like S_B. For an industry in which production costs vary as output rises or falls, the long-run supply curve is upward sloping but flatter than the short-run curve, as suggested by curve S_C.

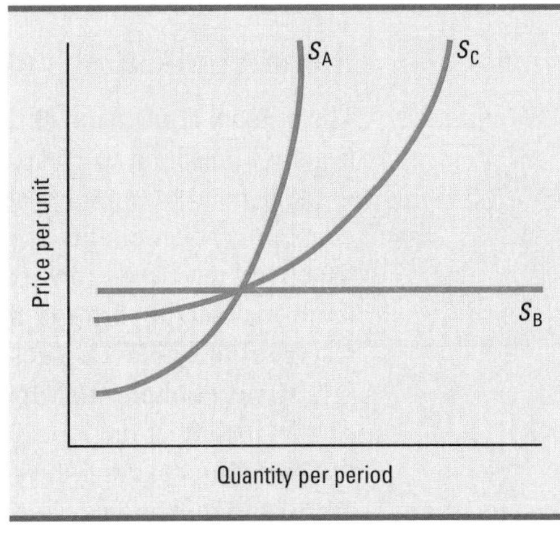

Checklist

- The economic concept of profit differs from accounting profit. The accounting concept deals only with explicit costs, while the economic concept of profit incorporates explicit and implicit costs.
- The existence of profits attracts entry; losses lead to exit.
- In long-run equilibrium, firms in a perfectly competitive industry will earn zero profit.
- The long-run supply curve in an industry with constant production costs is a horizontal line. The supply curve for an industry in which production costs increase as output rises is upward-sloping.
- Perfect competition results in the production of goods and services at the lowest cost possible in the long run.
- Perfect competition generates prices equal to marginal cost, a necessary condition for an efficient allocation of resources.

Profits and Efficiency in the Long Run

We see that profits induce entry and losses induce exit. Entry or exit in an industry continue until profits return to zero. When profits are zero, it means that firms in an industry are doing only as well as they could do operating in other markets—no better, no worse. There is thus no incentive for firms outside the industry to enter and no incentive for firms in the industry to exit. Equilibrium is achieved in perfect competition only when profits have fallen to zero throughout the system.

This process of eliminating profits or losses ensures that firms will end up operating at the lowest point on their LRAC curves. Production thus occurs at the lowest cost possible, a necessary condition for an efficient market. A perfectly competitive market thus provides consumers with goods and services that are produced at the lowest possible cost.

We saw in Chapter 5 that a necessary condition for economic efficiency is a price equal to marginal cost. Perfect competition achieves this result. That's because the market supply curve is the sum of the supply curves of individual firms—which are, in turn, nothing more than the firms' marginal cost curves (where marginal cost exceeds average variable cost). The price that emerges in a perfectly competitive market is thus the price that guides the economy's resources to their highest-valued uses.

Some Applications of the Model of Perfect Competition

The primary application of the model of perfect competition is in predicting how firms will respond to changes in demand and in production costs. To see how firms respond to a particular change, we determine how the change affects demand or cost conditions and then see how the profit-maximizing solution is affected in the short run and in the long run. Having determined how the profit-maximizing firms of the model would respond, we can then predict firms' responses to similar changes in the real world.

In the examples that follow, we shall assume, for simplicity, that entry or exit do not affect the input prices facing firms in the industry. We shall assume that firms are covering their average variable costs, so we can ignore the possibility of shutting down.

Changes in Demand

Changes in demand can occur for any of the reasons we discussed in Chapter 3. There may be a change in preferences, incomes, the price of a related good, population, or consumer expectations. A change in demand causes a change in the market price, thus shifting the marginal revenue curves of firms in the industry.

Let's consider the impact of a change in demand for oats. Suppose new evidence suggests that eating oats is good for your health and that this increases the demand for oats. To assess the impact of this change, we assume that the industry is perfectly competitive and that it is initially in long-run equilibrium at a price of $1.70 per bushel. Profits, considered in the economic sense, are zero.

The initial situation is depicted in Exhibit 8-12. Panel (a) shows that at a price of $1.70, industry output is Q_1 (point A). Panel (b) shows that the market price constitutes the marginal revenue, MR_1, facing a single firm in the industry. The firm responds to that price by finding the output level at which the marginal cost (MC) and MR_1 curves intersect. That implies a level of output q_1 at point A′.

EXHIBIT 8-12

An Increase in Demand

The oat industry begins in equilibrium at a price of $1.70 per bushel with an output of Q_1 bushels of oats per period [point A in Panel (a)]. A single firm produces q_1 units per period [point A′ in Panel (b)]. Demand increases, raising the price to $2.30 per bushel. Firms in the market respond by increasing their output—a single firm boosts output to q_2 at point B′ in Panel (b). Industry output rises to Q_2 at point B in Panel (a). The short-run solution leaves firms with a profit; this profit induces long-run entry. New entry shifts the supply curve to the right until profits are eliminated. That occurs here with supply curve S_2, the original price of $1.70 per bushel, and industry output Q_3 at point C in Panel (a). The single firm returns to its original output level q_1 at point A′ in Panel (b).

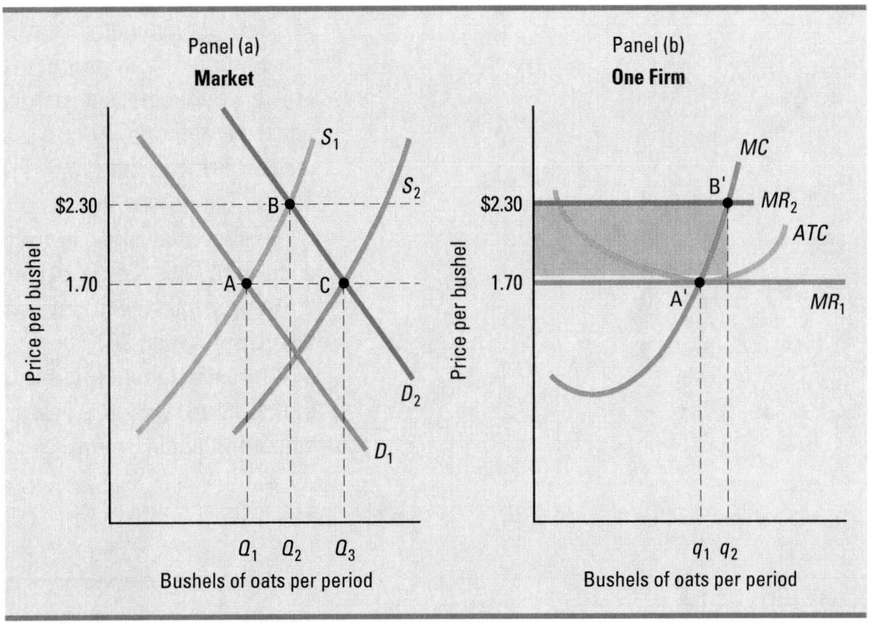

The new medical evidence causes demand to increase to D_2 in Panel (a). That increases the market price to $2.30 (point B), so the marginal revenue curve for a single firm rises to MR_2 in Panel (b). The firm responds by increasing its output to q_2 in the short run (point B′). Notice that the firm's average total cost is slightly higher than its original level of $1.70; that's because of the U shape of the curve. The firm is making a profit shown by the shaded rectangle in Panel (b). Other firms in the industry will earn a profit as well; that profit will, in the long run, attract entry by new firms. New entry will shift the supply curve to the right; entry will continue as long as firms are making a profit. The supply curve in Panel (a) shifts to S_2, driving the price down in the long run to the original level of $1.70 per bushel and returning firms to a zero-profit equilibrium. A single firm will return to its original level of output, q_1 (point A′) in Panel (b), but because there are more firms in the industry, industry output rises to Q_3 (point C) in Panel (a).

A reduction in demand would lead to a reduction in price, shifting each firm's marginal revenue curve downward. Firms would experience losses, thus causing exit in the long run and shifting the supply curve to the left. Eventually, the price would rise back to its original level, assuming changes in industry output did not lead to changes in input prices. There would be fewer firms in the industry, but each firm would end up producing the same output as before.

Changes in Production Cost

A firm's costs change if the costs of its inputs change. They also change if the firm is able to take advantage of a change in technology. Changes in production cost shift the *ATC* curve. If a firm's variable costs are affected, its marginal cost curves will shift as well. Any change in marginal cost produces a similar change in industry supply, since it is found by adding up marginal cost curves for individual firms.

Suppose a reduction in the price of oil reduces the cost of producing oil changes for automobiles. We shall assume that the oil-change industry is perfectly competitive and that it is initially in long-run equilibrium at a price of $27 per oil change, as shown in Panel (a) of Exhibit 8-13. Suppose that the reduction in oil prices reduces the cost of an oil change by $3.

A reduction in production cost shifts the firm's cost curves down. The firm's average total cost and marginal cost curves shift down, as shown in Panel (b). In Panel (a) the supply curve shifts from S_1 to S_2. The industry supply curve is made up of the marginal cost curves of individual firms; because each of them has shifted downward by $3, the industry supply curve shifts downward by $3.

Notice that price in the short run falls to $26; it does not fall by the $3 reduction in cost. That's because the supply and demand curves are sloped. While the supply curve shifts downward by $3, its intersection with the demand curve falls by less than $3. The firm in Panel (b) responds to the lower price and lower cost by increasing output to q_2, where MC_2 and MR_2 intersect. That leaves firms in the industry with a profit; the profit for the firm is shown by the shaded rectangle in Panel (b). Profits attract entry in the long run, shifting the supply curve

EXHIBIT 8-13

A Reduction in Production Cost

In Panel (a), the market for oil changes is initially in equilibrium at a price of $27. Industry output equals Q_1. That price defines a firm's marginal revenue curve, MR_1 in Panel (b). It produces q_1 oil changes and earns zero profits, the maximum possible. A reduction in the price of oil that reduces the cost of producing an oil change by $3 shifts the firm's marginal cost curve to MC_2 and its *ATC* curve to ATC_2; the shift in *MC* shifts the supply curve in Panel (a) to S_2. Price falls to $26. The firm increases its output to q_2 and earns a profit given by the shaded area. In the long run, profits attract entry, shifting the supply curve to S_3, reducing the price to $24, and returning the firm's output to its original level, q_1.

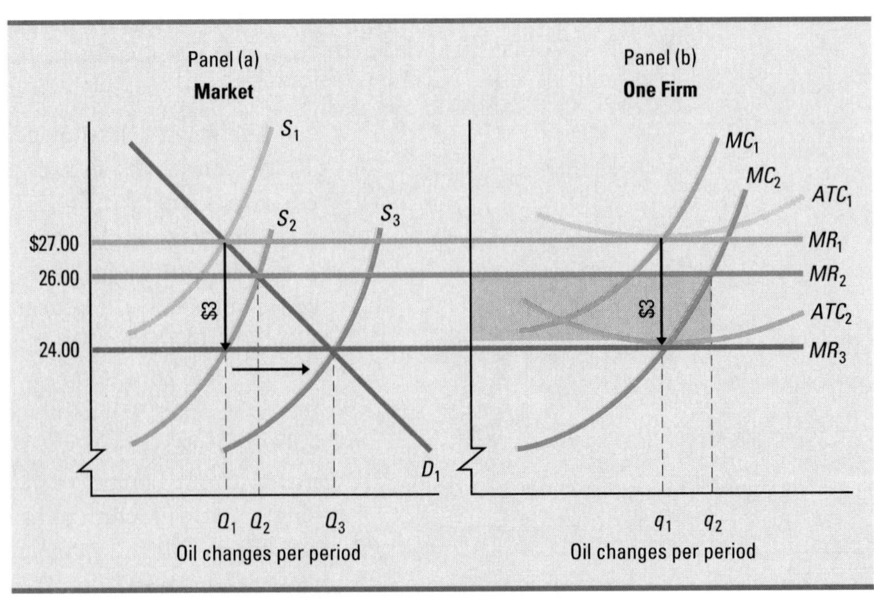

to the right to S_3. Entry will continue as long as firms are making a profit—it will thus continue until the price falls by the full amount of the $3 reduction in cost. The price falls to $24, industry output rises to Q_3, and the firm's output returns to its original level, q_1.

An increase in variable costs would shift the average total, average variable, and marginal cost curves upward. It would shift the industry supply curve upward by the same amount. The result in the short run would be an increase in price, but by less than the increase in cost per unit. Firms would experience losses, causing exit in the long run. Eventually, price would increase by the full amount of the increase in production cost.

Some cost increases will not affect marginal cost. Suppose, for example, that an annual license fee of $5,000 is imposed on firms in a particular industry. The fee is a fixed cost; it does not affect marginal cost. Imposing such a fee shifts the average total cost curve upward but causes no change in marginal cost. There is no change in price or output in the short run. Because firms are losing money, there will be exit in the long run. Prices ultimately rise by enough to cover the cost of the fee, leaving the remaining firms in the industry with zero profit.

Price will change to reflect whatever change we observe in production cost. A change in variable cost causes price to change in the short run. In the long run, any change in average total cost changes price by an equal amount.

Checklist

- The long-run equilibrium solution for a perfectly competitive industry is a price, determined by demand and supply, at which firms in the industry are earning zero profit.
- The long-run solution may be altered by a change in demand or by a change in production cost.
- Firms in the industry respond to any short-run change in demand or in supply by producing where price, which is marginal revenue, equals marginal cost, provided price exceeds average variable cost.
- In the long run, entry or exit will eliminate any profits or losses.
- When production costs change, price will change by less than the change in production cost in the short run. Price will adjust to fully reflect the change in production cost in the long run.
- A change in fixed cost will have no effect on price or output in the short run. It will induce entry or exit in the long run so that price will change by enough to leave firms earning zero profit.

A Look Back—And a Look Ahead

The assumptions of the model of perfect competition ensure that every decision-maker is a price taker—demand and supply in the market determine price. Although most firms in real markets have some control over their prices, the model of perfect competition suggests how changes in demand or in production cost will affect price and output in a wide range of real-world cases.

A firm in perfect competition maximizes profit in the short run by producing an output level at which marginal revenue equals marginal cost, provided marginal revenue is at least as great as the minimum value of average variable cost. For a perfectly competitive firm, marginal revenue equals price. This implies that the firm's marginal cost curve is its short-run supply curve for values greater than average variable cost. If price drops below average variable cost, the firm shuts down.

If firms in an industry are earning a profit, entry by new firms will drive price down until profit achieves its long-run equilibrium value of zero. If firms are suffering a loss, exit by existing firms will continue until price rises to eliminate the loss and profits are zero. A long-run equilibrium may be changed by a change in demand or in production cost, which would affect supply. The adjustment to the change in the short run is likely to result in profits or losses; these will be eliminated in the long run by entry or by exit.

This chapter is the first in which we examine the model of perfect competition. We shall continue to use the model in the next three chapters. In Chapters 9 and 10, we'll examine perfectly competitive markets for factors of production. Then in Chapter 11, we'll explore the model in the context of international trade.

Terms and Concepts for Review

Accounting profit	Perfect competition
Explicit costs	Price taker
Implicit costs	Short-run supply curve
Long-run supply curve	Shutdown point
Marginal revenue	Total revenue

For Discussion

1. Explain how each of the assumptions of perfect competition contributes to the fact that all decisionmakers in perfect competition are price takers.
2. Consider the following goods and services. Which are the most likely to be produced in a perfectly competitive industry? Which are not? Explain why you made the choices you did, relating your answer to the assumptions of the model of perfect competition.
   a. Coca-Cola and Pepsi
   b. Potatoes
   c. Private physicians in your local community
   d. Government bonds and corporate stocks
   e. Taxicabs in Lima, Peru—a city that does not restrict entry or the prices drivers can charge
   f. Oats
3. Explain why an economic profit of zero is acceptable to a firm.
4. Explain why a perfectly competitive firm whose average total cost exceeds the market price may continue to operate in the short run. What about the long run?
5. You've decided to major in biology rather than economics. A news report suggests that the salaries of business and economics majors are increasing. How does this affect the cost of your choice?
6. Explain how each of the following events would affect the marginal cost curves of firms and thus the supply curve in a perfectly competitive market in the short run.
   a. An increase in labor prices
   b. A tax of $1 per unit imposed on the seller
   c. The introduction of cost-cutting technology
   d. The imposition of an annual license fee of $1,000
7. In a perfectly competitive market, who benefits from an event that lowers production costs for firms?
8. We've assumed that as production in an industry expands or contracts, input prices do not change. Suppose, however, that they do. Suppose that having more firms enter an industry causes some input prices to rise. How would this affect your analysis of the effect of an increase in demand?
9. Dry cleaning establishments generate a considerable amount of air pollution in producing cleaning services. Suppose these firms are allowed to pollute without restriction and that reducing their pollution would add significantly to their production costs. Who benefits from the fact that they pollute the air? Now suppose the government requires them to reduce their pollution. Who will pay for the cleanup? (Assume dry cleaning is a perfectly competitive industry, and answer these questions from a long-run perspective.)
10. In Exhibit 8-11, why doesn't the long-run supply curve S_C go as low as the short-run supply curve S_A?

Problems

1. Suppose rocking-chair manufacturing is a perfectly competitive industry in which there are 1,000 identical firms. Each firm's total cost is related to output per day as follows:

Quantity	Total cost
0	$500.00
1	$1,000.00
2	$1,300.00
3	$1,500.00
4	$1,800.00
5	$2,200.00
6	$2,700.00
7	$3,300.00
8	$4,000.00

   a. Prepare a table that shows total cost, variable cost, average total cost, and marginal cost at each level of output.
   b. Plot the average total cost, average variable cost, and marginal cost curves for a single firm (remember that values for marginal cost are plotted at the midpoint of the respective intervals). What is the firm's supply curve? How many chairs would the firm produce at prices of $350, $450, $550, and $650? (In computing quantities, assume that a firm produces a certain number of completed chairs each day; it does not produce fractions of a chair on any one day.)

c. Suppose the demand curve in the market for rocking chairs is given by the following:

Price	Quantity of chairs demanded/day
$650	5,000
550	6,000
450	7,000
350	8,000

Plot the market demand curve for chairs. Compute and plot the market supply curve, using the information you obtained for a single firm in part (b). What is the equilibrium price? The equilibrium quantity?

d. Given your solution in part (c), plot the total revenue and total cost curves for a single firm. Does your graph correspond to your solution in part (b)? Explain.

2. The following table shows the total output, total revenue, total variable cost, and fixed cost of a firm. What level of output should the firm produce? Should it shut down? Should it exit the industry? Explain.

Output	Total Revenue	Variable Cost	Fixed Cost
1	$1,000	$1,500	$500
2	2,000	2,000	500
3	3,000	2,600	500
4	4,000	3,900	500
5	5,000	5,000	500

3. Suppose a rise in fuel costs increases the cost of producing oats by 50 cents per bushel. Illustrate graphically how this change will affect the oat market and a single firm in the market in the short run and in the long run.

4. Suppose the demand for car washes in Collegetown falls as a result of a cutback in college enrollment. Show graphically how the price and output for the market and for a single firm will be affected in the short run and in the long run. Assume the market is perfectly competitive and that it is initially in long-run equilibrium at a price of $12 per car wash. Assume also that input prices don't change as the market responds to the change in demand.

9

Wages and Employment in Perfect Competition

Chapter Objectives

After mastering the material in this chapter, you will be able to:

1. Show how markets for factors of production in general and labor markets in particular are linked to markets for goods and services.
2. Explain why firms demand labor, and relate the demand for labor to its contribution to the revenues received by firms.
3. Relate the quantity of labor a firm will demand to the marginal decision rule.
4. Explain how the demand for labor will be affected by a change in labor's marginal product or by a change in the price of the good or service the labor produces.
5. Relate the quantity of labor supplied to the demand for leisure, and explain why the supply curve for labor could be backward bending.
6. Discuss alternative responses to low wages and discriminatory wages for some workers.

Country-wide high wages spell country-wide prosperity, provided, however, the higher wages are paid for in higher production.

Henry Ford

What's Ahead

College pays; workers with a college education generally earn more than workers with a high school education. One way of measuring the payoff from college is to compare the degree to which the wages of college-trained workers exceed the wages of high-school-trained workers. Viewed in that context, the payoff from college soared in the 1980s and early 1990s.

In 1979, young male college graduates (those with 5 years of experience) earned 27 percent more than young male high school graduates. By 1993 the gap had more than doubled—young male college graduates earned a stunning 66 percent more than young male high school graduates. Female college graduates gained as well. Young female college graduates earned 35 percent more than their high-school-educated counterparts in 1979; that gap increased to 69 percent by 1993. Women's wages also rose relative to men's during the period.

The dramatic widening of the wage gap between workers with different levels of education, and the narrowing of the wage gap between men and women, reflected the operation of demand and supply in the market for labor. For reasons we'll explore in this chapter, the demand for college graduates was increasing while the demand for high school graduates—particularly male high school graduates—was slumping.

But why would the demand curves for different kinds of labor shift? What determines the demand for labor? What about the supply? How do changes in demand and supply affect wages and employment? In this chapter we'll apply what we've learned so far about production, profit maximization, and utility maximization to answer those questions in the context of a perfectly competitive market for labor.

We'll also examine two problems for public policy suggested by competitive labor markets. They generate very low incomes for some workers, and they may produce discriminatory results.

This is the first of two chapters about perfectly competitive markets for factors of production. Chapter 10 examines markets for capital and for natural resources. We'll begin our analysis with a brief overview of the role of factor markets in the economy.

Labor Markets: An Overview

A great deal of economic activity can be thought of as a process of exchange between households and firms. Firms produce goods and services for households. Households purchase these goods and services from firms. Households supply factors of production—labor, land, and capital—that firms require. The payments firms make in exchange for these factor services represent the incomes households earn.

The Circular Flow Model of the Economy

The flow of goods and services, factors of production, and the payments they generate is illustrated in Exhibit 9-1. This **circular flow model** of the economy shows the interaction of households and firms as they exchange goods and services and factors of production. The model here shows only the private domestic economy; it omits the government and foreign sectors.

EXHIBIT 9-1

The Circular Flow of Economic Activity

The circular flow model shows flows of spending between households and firms through product and factor markets. The inner arrows show goods and services flowing from firms to households and factors of production flowing from households to firms. The outer flows show the payments for goods, services, and factors of production.

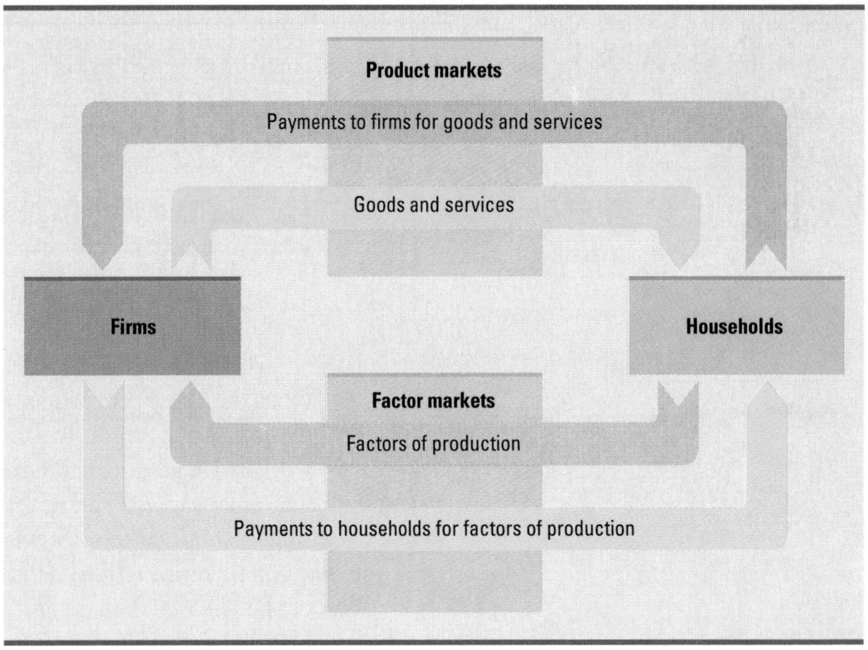

- A **circular flow model** shows how households and firms interact.
- **Product markets** are markets in which firms supply goods and services demanded by households.
- **Factor markets** are markets in which households supply factors of production demanded by firms.

The circular flow model shows that goods and services are supplied by firms and demanded by households in a set of **product markets.** We examined how these markets operate under conditions of perfect competition in the preceding chapter. Now we turn to the **factor markets** in which households supply factors of production—labor, capital, and natural resources—to firms in exchange for money payments. Our model is called a circular flow model because households use the money they receive from their supply of factors of production to buy goods and services from firms. Firms, in turn, use the money they receive from households to pay for their factors of production.

The lower portion of the circular flow model in Exhibit 9-1 includes markets for all the factors of production used by firms in the economy. Our focus in this chapter is on labor markets. We'll examine markets for capital and for natural resources in the next chapter.

Labor Markets

The circular flow model suggests that households earn income from firms by supplying factors of production to them. The total income earned by households thus equals the total income earned by the labor, capital, and natural resources supplied to firms.

Labor generates considerably more income in the economy than all other factors of production combined. Exhibit 9-2 shows the share of total income earned annually by workers in the United States since 1959. Labor accounts for roughly 80 percent of the income earned in the U.S. economy. The rest is generated by owners of capital and of natural resources.

EXHIBIT 9-2

Labor's Share of U.S. Income, 1959–1994

Workers have accounted for roughly 80 percent of all the income earned in the United States since 1959. The remaining income was generated by capital and natural resources.

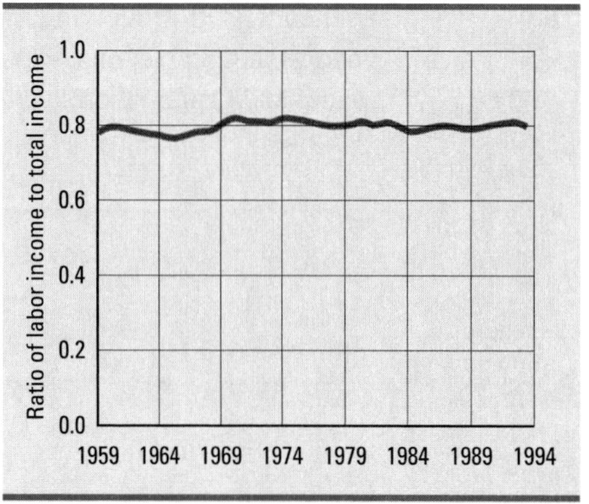

We calculate the total income earned by workers by multiplying their wage times the number of workers employed. We can view the labor market as a single market, as suggested in Panel (a) of Exhibit 9-3. Here we assume that all workers are identical, that there is a single market for them, and that they all earn the same wage, W; the level of employment is L. Although the assumption of a single labor market flies wildly in the face of reality, economists often use it to highlight broad trends in the market. For example, if we wish to show the impact of an increased demand for labor throughout the economy, we can show labor as a single market in which the increase in demand raises wages and employment.

But we can also use demand and supply analysis to focus on the market for a particular group of workers. We might examine the market for plumbers or for beauticians. We might even want to focus on the market for, say, clerical workers in the Boston area. In such cases, we would examine the demand for and the supply of a particular segment of workers, as suggested by the graphs in Panel (b) of Exhibit 9-3.

Macroeconomic analysis typically makes use of the highly aggregated approach to labor market analysis illustrated in Panel (a), where labor is viewed as a single market. Microeconomic analysis typically assesses particular markets for labor, as suggested in Panel (b).

EXHIBIT 9-3

Alternative Views of the Labor Market

One way to analyze the labor market is to assume that it is a single market with identical workers, as in Panel (a). Alternatively, we could examine specific pieces of the market, focusing on particular job categories or even on job categories in particular regions, as the graphs in Panel (b) suggest.

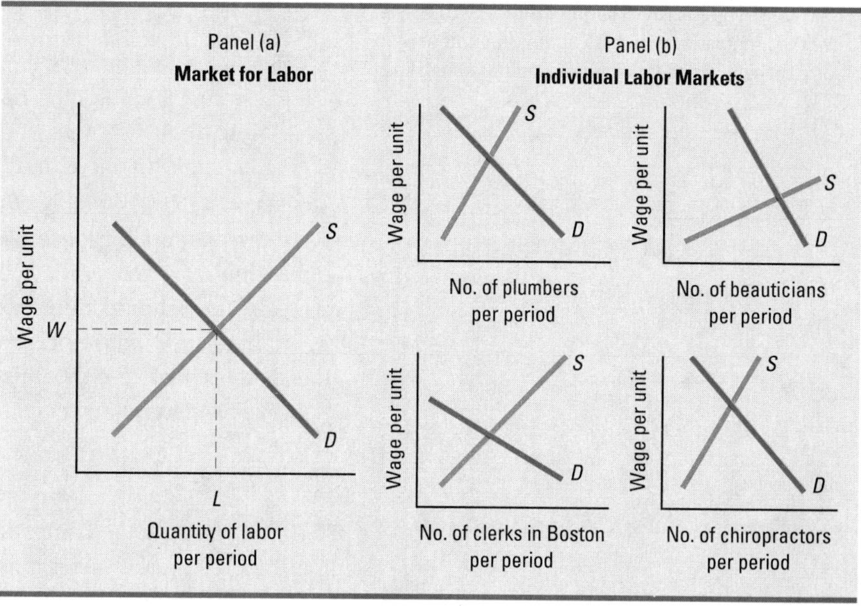

Checklist

- The circular flow model suggests the linkage between factor markets and product markets.
- In terms of total income earned, labor is the most important factor of production.
- We can use demand and supply analysis to interpret developments in the market for labor as a whole or to focus on particular job categories and/or geographical areas.
- In using the model of demand and supply to examine labor markets, we assume that perfect competition exists—that all workers and employers are price takers.

Our use of the model of demand and supply to analyze the determination of wages and employment implies an important assumption. We are assuming that market forces, not individuals, determine wages in the economy. The model says that equilibrium wages are determined by the intersection of the demand and supply curves for labor in a particular market. Workers and firms in the market are thus price takers; they take the market-determined wage as given and respond to it. We are, in short, assuming that perfect competition prevails in the labor market. Just as there are some situations in the analysis of markets for goods and services for which such an assumption is inappropriate, so there are some cases in which the assumption is inappropriate for labor markets. We'll turn to such cases in Chapter 13. We'll find in this chapter, however, that the assumption of perfect competition can give us important insights into the forces that determine wage and employment levels for workers.

We'll begin our analysis of labor markets in the next section by looking at the forces that influence the demand for labor. In the following section we'll turn to supply.

The Demand for Labor

A firm must have labor to produce goods and services. But how much labor will the firm employ? A profit-maximizing firm will base its decision to hire additional units of labor on the marginal decision rule: If the extra output that is produced by hiring one more unit of labor adds more to total revenue than it adds to total cost, the firm will increase profit by increasing its use of labor. It will continue to hire more and more labor up to the point that the extra revenue generated by the additional labor no longer exceeds the extra cost of the labor.

For example, if a computer software company could increase its annual total revenue by $40,000 by hiring a programmer at a cost of $39,000 per year, the marginal decision rule says that it should do so. Since the programmer will add $39,000 to total cost and $40,000 to total revenue, hiring the programmer will increase the company's profit by $1,000. If still another programmer would increase annual total revenue by $38,000 but would also add $39,000 to the firm's total cost, that programmer should not be hired. He or she would add less to total revenue than to total cost and would reduce profit.

Marginal revenue product (MRP) is the amount by which an additional unit of a factor increases a firm's total revenue during a period.

Marginal Revenue Product and Marginal Factor Cost

The amount that an additional unit of a factor adds to a firm's total revenue during a period is called the **marginal revenue product (MRP)** of the factor. An additional unit of a factor of production adds to a firm's revenue in a two-step process: First, it increases the firm's output. Second, the increased output increases the firm's total revenue. We find marginal revenue product by multiplying the marginal product (MP) of the factor by the marginal revenue (MR). The marginal revenue product of labor (MRP_L) is the marginal product of labor (MP_L) times the marginal revenue the firm obtains from additional units of output. If an additional worker adds 4 units of output per day to a firm's production, and if each of those 4 units brings in an additional \$20 in revenue, then the worker's marginal revenue product is \$80 per day.

$$MRP = MP \times MR \quad \textbf{(1)}$$

In a perfectly competitive market the marginal revenue a firm receives equals the market-determined price P. Therefore, for firms in perfect competition, we can use Equation (2) to express marginal revenue product:

$$\text{In perfect competition, } MRP = MP(P) \quad \textbf{(2)}$$

The marginal revenue product for labor, MRP_L, equals the marginal product of labor, MP_L, times the price, P, of the good or service the labor produces:

$$MRP_L = MP_L(P) \quad \textbf{(3)}$$

The law of diminishing marginal returns tells us that if the quantity of a factor is increased while other inputs are held constant, its marginal product will eventually decline. If marginal product is falling, marginal revenue product must be falling as well.

Suppose that an accountant, Stephanie Lancaster, has started an evening call-in tax advice service. Between the hours of 7 and 10 P.M., customers can call in and get advice on their income taxes. Ms. Lancaster's firm, TeleTax, is one of several firms offering similar advice; the going market price is \$10 per call. Ms. Lancaster's business has expanded, and now she hires other accountants to handle the calls. She must determine how many accountants to hire.

As Ms. Lancaster adds accountants, her service is able to take more calls. Exhibit 9-4 gives the relationship between the number of accountants available to answer calls each evening and the number of calls TeleTax handles. Panel (a) shows the increase in the number of calls handled by each additional accountant—that accountant's marginal product. The first accountant can handle 13 calls per evening. Adding a second accountant increases the number of calls handled by 20. With two accountants, a degree of specialization is possible if each accountant takes calls dealing with questions about which he or she has particular expertise. Hiring the third accountant increases TeleTax's output per evening by 23 calls.

Suppose the accountants share a fixed facility for screening and routing calls. They also share a stock of reference materials to use in answering calls. As more accountants are added, the firm will begin to experience diminishing marginal returns. The fourth accountant increases output by 20 calls. The marginal product of additional accountants continues to decline after that. The marginal product curve shown in Panel (a) of Exhibit 9-4 thus rises and then falls.

EXHIBIT 9-4

Marginal Product and Marginal Revenue Product

The table gives the relationship between the number of accountants employed by TeleTax each evening and the total number of calls handled. From these values we derive the marginal product and marginal revenue product curves.

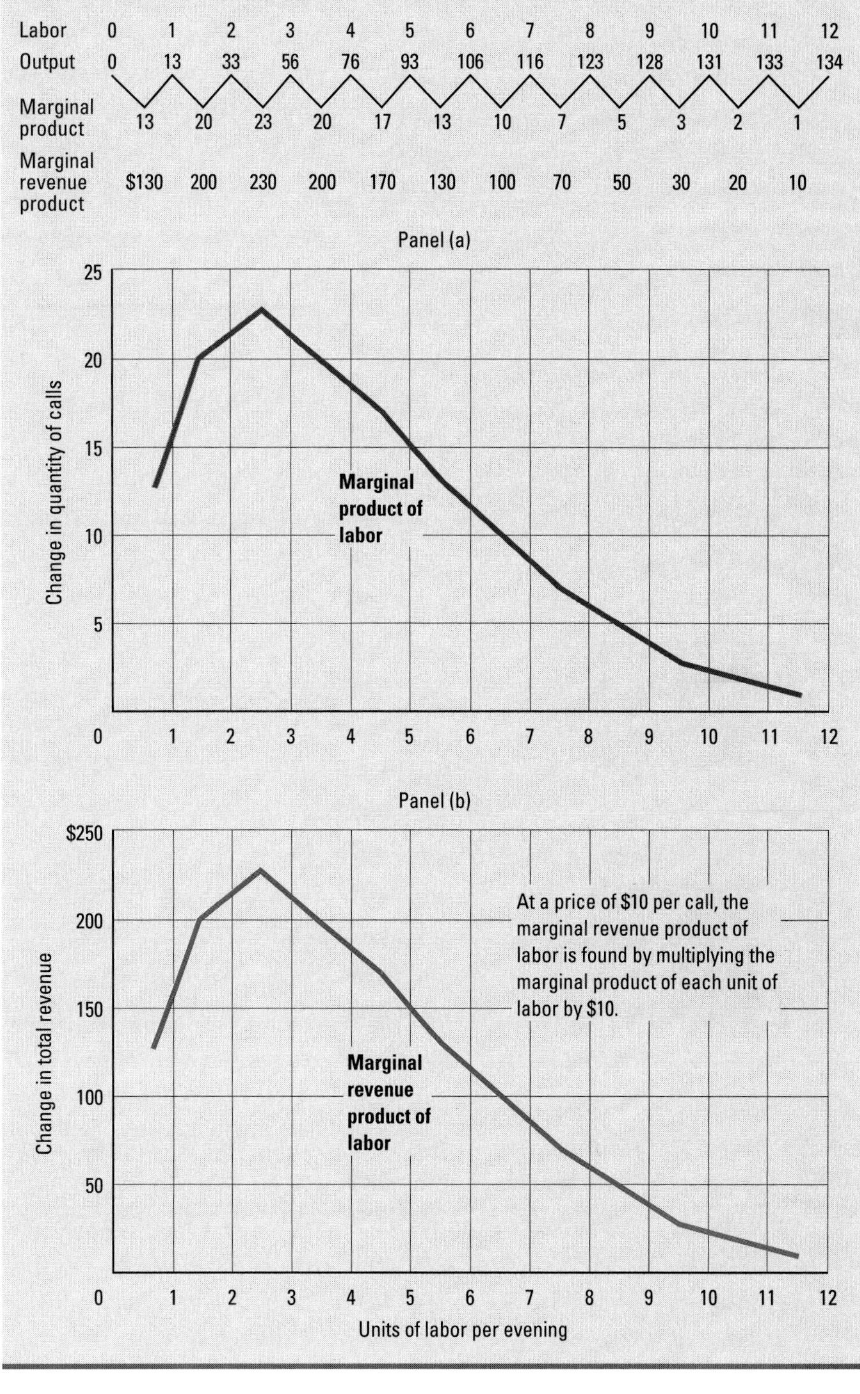

Labor	Output	Marginal product	Marginal revenue product
0	0		
		13	$130
1	13		
		20	200
2	33		
		23	230
3	56		
		20	200
4	76		
		17	170
5	93		
		13	130
6	106		
		10	100
7	116		
		7	70
8	123		
		5	50
9	128		
		3	30
10	131		
		2	20
11	133		
		1	10
12	134		

Each call TeleTax handles increases the firm's revenues by $10. To obtain marginal revenue product, we multiply the marginal product of each accountant by $10; the marginal revenue product curve is shown in Panel (b) of Exhibit 9-4.

We can use Ms. Lancaster's marginal revenue product curve to determine the quantity of labor she will hire. Suppose accountants in her area are available to offer tax advice for a nightly fee of $150. Each additional accountant Ms. Lancaster hires thus adds $150 per night to her total cost. The amount a factor adds to a firm's total cost per period is called its **marginal factor cost (MFC).** In

Marginal factor cost (MFC) is the change in total cost when one more unit of a factor of production is added.

Equation 4, marginal factor cost (MFC) is the change in total cost (ΔTC) divided by the change in the quantity of the factor (ΔF). The marginal factor cost to TeleTax of additional accountants, \$150 per night, is shown as a horizontal line in Exhibit 9-5. It is simply the market wage.

$$MFC = \frac{\Delta TC}{\Delta F} \tag{4}$$

EXHIBIT 9-5

Marginal Revenue Product and Demand

The downward-sloping portion of a firm's marginal revenue product curve is its demand curve for a variable factor. At a marginal factor cost of \$150, TeleTax hires the services of 5 accountants.

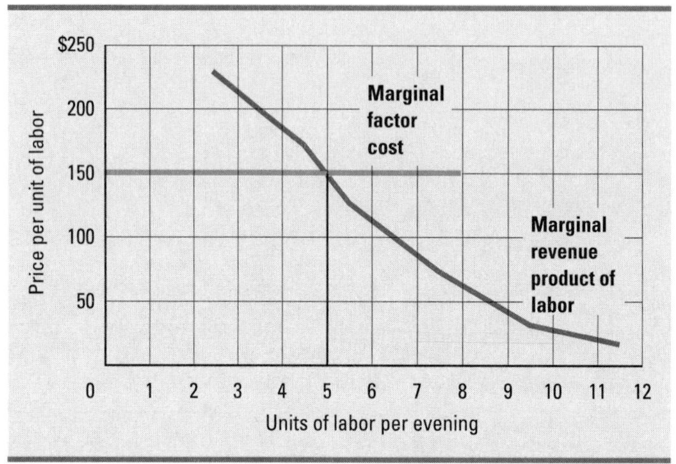

TeleTax will maximize profit by hiring additional units of labor up to the point where the marginal revenue product curve intersects the marginal factor cost curve; we see in Exhibit 9-5 that it will hire 5 accountants. Based on the information given in Exhibit 9-4, we know that the 5 accountants will handle a total of 93 calls per evening; TeleTax will earn a total revenue of \$930 per evening. The firm pays \$750 for the services of the 5 accountants—that leaves \$180 to apply to the fixed cost associated with the tax advice service, including the implicit cost of Stephanie Lancaster's effort in organizing the service.

If TeleTax had to pay a higher price for accountants, it would face a higher marginal factor cost curve and would hire fewer accountants. If the price were lower, TeleTax would hire more accountants. TeleTax's marginal revenue product curve shows the number of accountants it will hire at each price for accountants; it is thus the firm's demand curve for accountants. Notice, however, that Exhibit 9-5 shows only the downward-sloping portion of the marginal revenue product curve derived in Exhibit 9-4. That is the portion of the curve that exhibits diminishing returns, and a firm will always seek to operate in the range of diminishing returns to the factors it uses. In general, we may interpret the downward-sloping portion of a firm's marginal revenue product curve for a factor as its demand curve for that factor.

A firm's demand curve for labor is thus the downward-sloping portion of its marginal revenue product curve. We find the market demand for labor by adding the demand curves for individual firms, just as we added demand curves for individual consumers to obtain a market demand curve for a good or service.

Shifts in Labor Demand

The fact that a firm's demand curve for labor is given by its *MRP* curve provides a guide to the factors that will shift the curve. In perfect competition, marginal revenue product is equal to marginal product times price; anything that changes either of those two variables will shift the curve. The marginal revenue product of labor will change when there is a change in the quantities of other factors employed. It will also change as a result of a change in technology, a change in the price of the good labor produces, or a change in the number of firms hiring the labor.

Changes in the Use of Other Factors of Production

As a firm changes the quantities of different factors of production it uses, the marginal product of labor may change. Having more tools, for example, is likely to make additional carpenters more productive—it will increase their marginal product. That increase in their marginal product would increase the demand for carpenters. When an increase in the use of one factor of production increases the demand for another, the two factors are **complementary factors of production.**

One important complement of labor is human capital. When workers gain additional human capital, their marginal product rises. The demand for them by firms thus increases.

Other inputs may be regarded as substitutes for each other. A robot, for example, may substitute for some kinds of assembly-line labor. Two factors are **substitute factors of production** if the increased use of one lowers the demand for the other.

- Two factors are **complementary factors of production** if an increase in the use of one increases the demand for the other.
- Two factors are **substitute factors of production** if the increased use of one lowers the demand for the other.

Changes in Technology

Technological changes can increase the demand for some workers and reduce the demand for others. The production of a more powerful computer chip, for example, may increase the demand for software engineers. It may also allow other production processes to be computerized and thus reduce the demand for workers who had been employed in those processes.

Technological changes have been among the most important sources of increases in output in the economy over the past century. The application of sophisticated technologies to production processes has boosted the marginal products of workers who have the skills these processes require. That has increased the demand for them. The same technologies have been a substitute for less skilled workers, and the demand for them has fallen.

Changes in Product Demand

A change in demand for a final product changes its price, at least in the short run. An increase in the demand for a product increases its price and shifts the demand for factors that produce the product to the right. A reduction in demand for a product reduces its price and reduces the demand for the factors used in producing it.

Suppose, for example, that the demand for computers increases. The price and quantity of computers available will go up. A higher price for computers increases the *MRP* of computer assembly workers and thus increases the demand for these workers.

A Change in the Number of Firms

We can determine the demand curve for any factor by adding the demand for that factor by each of the firms using it. If more firms employ the factor, the demand curve shifts to the right. A reduction in the number of firms shifts the demand curve to the left.

If the number of restaurants in an area increases, for example, the demand for waiters and waitresses in the area goes up. We expect to see local wages rise as a result.

Price Elasticity of the Demand for Labor

Could an increase in the wage lower the incomes of workers?

Any question about how a price change affects total spending on a good is an elasticity question. If the demand for a certain type of labor is elastic, an increase in its price—its wage—will, all other things unchanged, reduce the quantity demanded by a greater percentage than the increase in the price, and total spending on that type of labor will fall. Total spending on labor by firms is the income workers receive, so the answer to the above question is yes—if the demand for workers is elastic.

The elasticity of demand for labor is important. Not only can we predict whether a price change will increase or decrease the income earned by workers; we can also predict how much the quantity of labor demanded will change in response to a change in its price.

Several things affect the elasticity of demand for labor. They are similar in character to the things that affect the demand for a good or service. They include the availability of substitutes for labor, the price elasticity of demand for the good the labor produces, and the time period.

The Availability of Substitutes

If other factors of production can easily be substituted for labor, then the demand for labor will tend to be relatively elastic. Workers whose tasks could easily be performed by machines, for example, face more elastic demand than workers who perform tasks requiring judgment that would be difficult for a machine to perform.

- A firm's demand for a factor is the marginal revenue product of the factor.
- The market demand for labor is found by adding the demand curves for labor of individual firms.
- The market demand for labor will change as a result of a change in the use of a complementary input or a substitute input, a change in technology, a change in the price of the good produced by labor, or a change in the number of firms that employ the labor.
- The price elasticity of demand for labor in a particular market depends on the availability of substitutes for the factor, the price elasticity of demand for the good the labor produces, and the time period over which employers can adjust for price changes.

The Price Elasticity of Demand for the Product

The price elasticity of demand for labor is closely linked to the price elasticity of demand for the good or service the labor produces. A change in the price of labor leads to a change in the price of the good produced by the labor. If the demand for that good is highly elastic, the quantity demanded will change substantially. That will, in turn, lead to a relatively large change in the use of the inputs that produce the good. The more elastic the demand for the good or service, the greater the price elasticity of demand for labor.

The Time Period

The longer the time period, the greater the elasticity of demand for any factor of production. As time passes, firms have more opportunity to alter their production technology, undertake research to find substitute inputs, and alter the quantities of inputs that were fixed in the short run.

Suppose, for example, that a reduced supply of university professors raises their wages. At first, universities face a choice of either paying the higher wage

Case in Point: Minimum Wages and Worker Incomes

Minimum wages are intended to help lower-paid workers increase their incomes. Do they?

A minimum wage boosts the wage employers must pay for unskilled workers above the equilibrium wage. If the equilibrium wage is $4 per hour, a minimum wage of $5 per hour reduces the quantity of labor demanded. If the demand for unskilled labor is elastic, then the higher wage reduces not only employment opportunities but the total income of unskilled workers as a group. (The higher minimum raises the incomes of those workers who keep their jobs, of course, but it cuts the incomes of workers who lose their jobs to zero. With elastic demand, this latter effect dominates, and the total income earned by unskilled workers falls.)

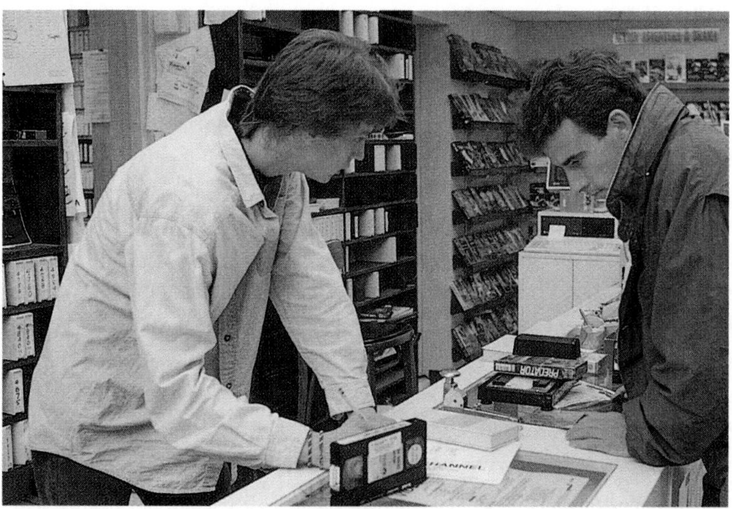

If, however, the demand for unskilled workers is inelastic, then a higher minimum wage will increase the incomes of unskilled workers. It will still reduce their employment, but because their wage rises by a greater percentage than employment falls, total incomes rise.

Evidence on this important point is mixed. Studies that look at the impact of higher minimum wages on particular demographic groups, such as teenagers, generally show that increases in minimum wages tend to increase incomes, suggesting inelastic demand. A study of higher minimum wages by Peter Linneman of the University of Pennsylvania, however, looked at the impact of higher minimum wages on those workers whose wages would be affected when the minimum was increased. For those workers, Mr. Linneman found the demand to be elastic, so the higher minimum wage lowered their incomes.

Sources: Peter Linneman, "The Economic Impacts of Minimum Wage Laws: A New Look at an Old Question," *Journal of Political Economy* 90(3) (June 1982): 443–469.

or cutting back on the number of students (a result that would accompany higher tuition). Over longer periods, however, universities might shift to such substitutes as computers and televised courses to substitute for the labor professors provide, making the demand for professors more elastic in the long run than in the short run.

The Supply of Labor

The demand curve for labor is one determinant of the equilibrium wage and quantity of labor in a perfectly competitive market. The supply curve, of course, is the other.

Economists think of the supply of labor as a problem in which individuals choose how to allocate their time. Everyone has 24 hours in a day. There are lots of uses to which we can put our time: we can raise children, work, study, play, participate in volunteer efforts, and so on. To simplify our analysis, let us assume that there are two ways in which an individual may spend his or her time: in work or in leisure. Leisure is a type of consumption good; individuals gain utility directly from it. Work provides income which, in turn, can be used to purchase goods and services that generate utility.

The more work a person does, the greater his or her income, but the smaller the amount of leisure time available. An individual who chooses more leisure time will earn less income than would otherwise be possible. There is thus a tradeoff between leisure and the income that can be earned from work. We can think of the supply of labor as the flip side of the demand for leisure. The more leisure people demand, the less labor they supply.

Two aspects of the demand for leisure play a key role in understanding the supply of labor. First, leisure is a normal good. All other things unchanged, an increase in income will increase the demand for leisure. Second, the "price" of leisure is the wage an individual can earn. A worker who can earn \$10 per hour gives up \$10 in income by consuming an extra hour of leisure. The \$10 wage is thus the price of an hour of leisure. A worker who can earn \$20 an hour faces a higher price of leisure.

Income and Substitution Effects

Suppose wages rise. The higher wage increases the price of leisure. We saw in Chapter 6 that consumers substitute more of other goods for a good whose price has risen. The substitution effect of a higher wage causes the consumer to substitute labor for leisure. To put it another way, the higher wage induces the individual to supply a greater quantity of labor.

We can see the logic of this substitution effect in terms of the marginal decision rule. Suppose an individual is considering a choice between extra leisure and the additional income from more work. Let MU_{Le} equal the marginal utility of an extra hour of leisure. What is the price of an extra hour of leisure? It is the wage W that the individual forgoes by not working for an hour. The extra utility of \$1 worth of leisure is thus given by MU_{Le}/W.

Suppose, for example, that the marginal utility of an extra hour of leisure is 20 and the wage is \$10 per hour. Then MU_{Le}/W equals 20/10, or 2. That means that the individual gains 2 units of utility by spending an additional \$1 worth of time on leisure. For a person facing a wage of \$10 per hour, \$1 worth of leisure would be the equivalent of 6 minutes of leisure time.

Let MU_Y be the marginal utility of an additional \$1 of income (Y is the abbreviation economists generally assign to income). The price of \$1 of income is just \$1, so the price of income P_Y is always \$1. Utility is maximized by allocating time between work and leisure so that

$$\frac{MU_Y}{P_Y} = \frac{MU_{\text{Le}}}{W} \tag{5}$$

Now suppose the wage rises to W'. That reduces the marginal utility of \$1 worth of leisure, MU_{Le}/W', so that the extra utility of earning \$1 will now be greater than the extra utility of \$1 worth of leisure:

$$\frac{MU_Y}{P_Y} > \frac{MU_{\text{Le}}}{W} \tag{6}$$

Faced with the inequality in Equation 6, an individual will give up some leisure time and spend more time working. As the individual does so, however, the marginal utility of the remaining leisure time rises and the marginal utility of the income earned will fall. The individual will continue to make the substitution until the two sides of the equation are again equal. For a worker with a given income, the substitution effect of a wage increase always reduces the amount of leisure time consumed and increases the amount of time spent working. A higher wage thus produces a positive substitution effect on labor supply.

But the higher wage also has an income effect. An increased wage means a higher income, and if leisure is a normal good, the quantity of leisure demanded will go up. And that means a *reduction* in the quantity of labor supplied.

For labor supply problems, then, the substitution effect is always positive; a higher wage induces a greater quantity of labor supplied. But the income effect is always negative; a higher wage implies a higher income, and a higher income implies a greater demand for leisure. With the substitution and income effects working in opposite directions, it isn't clear whether a wage increase will increase or decrease the quantity of labor supplied—or leave it unchanged!

Exhibit 9-6 illustrates the opposite pull of the substitution and income effects of a wage change facing an individual worker. A locksmith, Meredith Wilson, earns $10 per hour. She now works 42 hours per week, on average, earning $420.

EXHIBIT 9-6

The Substitution and Income Effects of a Wage Change

The substitution and income effects influence Meredith Wilson's supply of labor when she gets a pay raise. At a wage of $10 per hour, she supplies 42 hours of work per week (point A). At $15 per hour, the substitution effect pulls in the direction of an increased quantity of labor supplied, and the income effect pulls in the opposite direction.

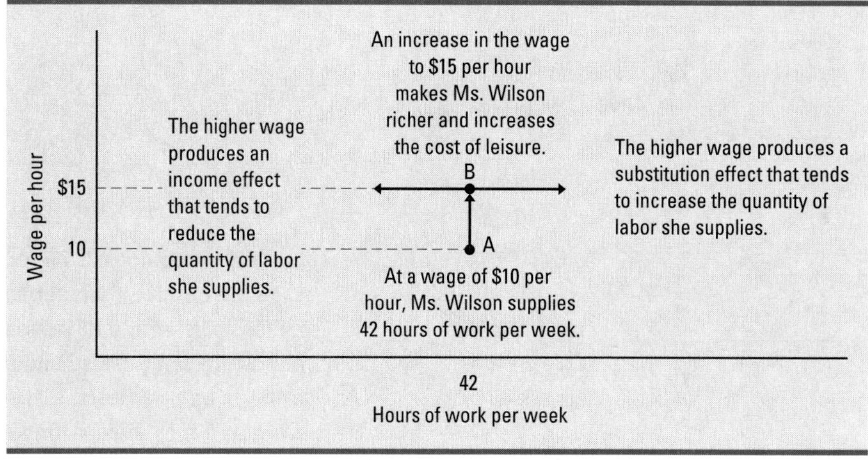

Now suppose Ms. Wilson receives a $5 raise to $15 per hour. As shown in Exhibit 9-6, the substitution effect of the wage change induces her to increase the quantity of labor she supplies; she substitutes some of her leisure time for additional hours of work. But she's richer now; she can afford more leisure. At a wage of $10 per hour, she was earning $420 per week. She could earn that same amount at the higher wage in just 28 hours. With her higher income, she can certainly afford more leisure time. The income effect of the wage change is thus negative; the quantity of labor supplied falls. The effect of the wage increase on the quantity of labor Ms. Wilson supplies depends on the relative strength of the substitution and income effects of the wage change. We'll see what Ms. Wilson decides to do in the next section.

Wage Changes and the Slope of the Supply Curve

What would any one individual's supply curve for labor look like? One possibility is that over some range of labor hours supplied, the substitution effect will dominate. Because the marginal utility of leisure is relatively low when little labor is supplied (i.e., when most time is devoted to leisure), it takes only a small increase in wages to induce the individual to substitute more labor for less leisure. Further, because few hours are worked, the income effect of those wage changes will be small.

Exhibit 9-7 shows Meredith Wilson's supply curve for labor. At a wage of $10 per hour, she supplies 42 hours of work per week (point A). An increase in her wage to $15 per hour boosts her quantity supplied to 48 hours per week (point B). The substitution effect thus dominates the income effect of a higher wage.

EXHIBIT 9-7

A Backward-Bending Supply Curve for Labor

As the wage rate increases from $10 to $15 per hour, the quantity of labor Meredith Wilson supplies increases from 42 to 48 hours per week. Between points A and B, the positive substitution effect of the wage increase outweighs the negative income effect. As the wage rises above $15, the negative income effect just offsets the substitution effect, and Ms. Wilson's supply curve becomes a vertical line between points B and C. As the wage rises above $20, the income effect becomes stronger than the substitution effect, and the supply curve bends backward between points C and D.

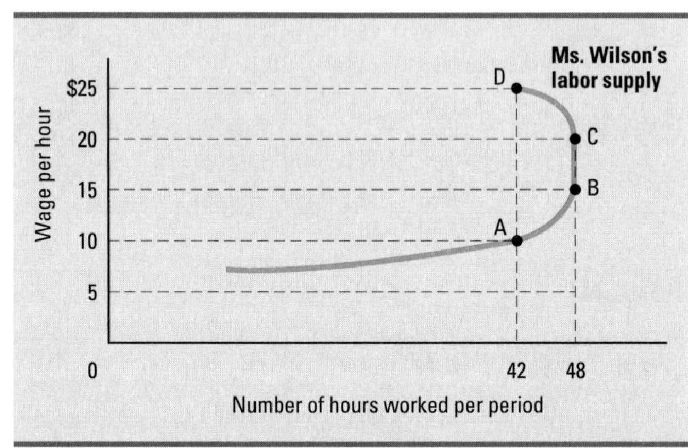

It is possible that beyond some wage rate, the negative income effect of a wage increase could just offset the positive substitution effect; over that range, a higher wage would have no effect on the quantity of labor supplied. That's illustrated between points B and C on the supply curve in Exhibit 9-7; Ms. Wilson's supply curve is vertical over that range. As wages continue to rise, the income effect becomes even stronger, and further increases in the wage reduce the quantity of labor she supplies! The supply curve illustrated here bends backward beyond point C and thus assumes a negative slope. The supply curve for labor can thus slope upward over part of its range, become vertical, and then bend backward as the income effect of higher wages begins to dominate the substitution effect.

It is quite likely that some individuals have backward-bending supply curves for labor—beyond some point, a higher wage induces that individual to work less, not more. In analyses of the labor market, economists often assume that the income and substitution effects just cancel each other, producing a vertical supply curve for labor. We shall see some applications of vertical supply curves for labor in subsequent chapters of this book.

Although the supply curve for labor may be vertical in the aggregate, it is likely that supply curves for labor in individual labor markets are upward sloping. As wages in one industry rise relative to wages in other industries, workers shift their labor to the relatively high-wage one. An increased quantity of labor is supplied in that industry; the degree to which wages in that industry rise is thus moderated. Thus, the mobility of labor between competitive labor markets is likely to prevent the total number of hours worked from falling as the wage rate increases. We shall thus assume that supply curves for labor in particular markets are upward sloping.

Case in Point — Celebrities Supply Check-Cashing Effort

It wasn't exactly a study of labor supply, and it certainly wasn't serious, but *Spy* magazine's July 1990 investigation of the willingness of big celebrities to cash small checks suggests some of the same issues that are involved in conventional estimates of supply.

The magazine set up a corporation that sent letters to 58 rich and famous people explaining that, due to a computer error, they had been overcharged for a recent purchase. A refund check of $1.11 was enclosed with each letter. A decision to cash a check required giving up some time and effort on the part of the celebrity or an assistant in exchange for a little extra money. Within 2 months, 26 rich and famous people had cashed their checks. Michael Douglas and Faye Dunaway were among the celebrities who snapped up the money. For the rest, the chance to pick up $1.11 wasn't worth the effort.

The magazine then sent refund checks for $2 to the 32 holdouts. At this higher price, 6 of the previous holdouts were willing to make the effort to cash their checks—they included Richard Gere and Candice Bergen. The magazine then offered a refund check of a whopping $3.47 to the 26 rich and famous people who had ignored the $2 offer. Two more rich and famous people—designer Halston and opera star Beverly Sills—snapped up the bait.

The magazine's experiment then turned to the 26 celebrities who had cashed their checks for $1.11 to see how much lower they would be willing to go. Those celebrities got checks for $0.64. Offered a lower reward, just 13 made the effort to cash their checks—Cher was among them. These 13 were then sent checks for $0.13. That was enough of a reward to attract just 2 rich and famous people: developer Donald Trump and arms dealer Adnan Khashoggi.

Putting *Spy's* results together, we obtain a supply curve for celebrity check-cashing effort. At $0.13, the magazine had just 2 takers. When the offer went up to $0.64, more celebrities were willing to cash their checks. As the reward went higher, the quantity of check-cashing effort went higher. Finally, at the highest refund check offered, a majority of the original group of 58 couldn't resist. The payments were too small to reflect much of an income effect; they suggest that the higher the "wage" offered, the greater the willingness of rich and famous people to deposit a check.

Sources: Julius Lowenthal, *Spy,* July 1990; and Cindy Kelly, "Celebrities and Supply," *The Margin* 6(3) (January-February 1991): 18–19.

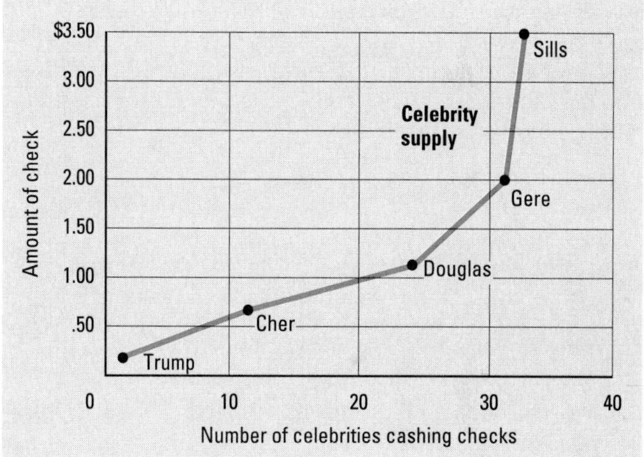

Donald Trump *Cher* *Michael Douglas* *Richard Gere* *Beverly Sills*

Shifts in Labor Supply

What events shift the supply curve for labor? People supply labor in order to increase their utility—just as they demand goods and services in order to increase their utility. The supply curve for labor will shift in response to changes in the same set of factors that shift demand curves for goods and services.

Changes in Preferences

A change in attitudes toward work and leisure can shift the supply curve for labor. If people decide they value leisure more highly, the supply curve for labor will shift to the left. If they decide they want more goods and services, the supply curve is likely to shift to the right.

Changes in Income

An increase in income will increase the demand for leisure, reducing the supply of labor. We must be careful here to distinguish movements along the supply curve from shifts of the supply curve itself. An income change resulting from a change in wages is shown by a movement along the curve; it produces the income and substitution effects we already discussed. But suppose income is from some other source—people receive grants from the government or win a lottery. Those nonlabor increases in income are likely to shift the supply curve for labor of the recipients to the left.

Changes in the Prices of Related Goods and Services

Several goods and services are complements of labor. If transportation costs fall, for example, it becomes cheaper for workers to go to work, and the supply of labor tends to increase. If recreational activities (which are a substitute for work effort) become much cheaper, individuals might choose to consume more leisure time and supply less labor.

Changes in Population

A population increase increases the supply of labor; a reduction lowers it. Labor organizations have generally opposed increases in immigration because their leaders fear that the increased number of workers will shift the supply curve for labor to the right and put downward pressure on wages.

Changes in Expectations

One change in expectations that could have an effect on labor supply is life expectancy. Another is confidence in the availability of Social Security. Suppose, for example, that people expect to live longer yet become less optimistic about their likely benefits from Social Security. That could induce an increase in labor supply.

Labor Supply in Specific Markets

The supply of labor in particular markets could be affected by changes in any of the variables we've already examined—changes in preferences, incomes, prices of related goods and services, population, and expectations. In addition to these variables that affect the supply of labor in general, there are changes that could affect supply in specific labor markets.

A change in wages in related occupations could affect supply in another. A sharp reduction in the wages of surgeons, for example, could induce more physicians to specialize in, say, family practice, increasing the supply of doctors in

Checklist

- A higher wage increases the price of leisure and increases worker incomes. The effects of these two changes pull the quantity of labor supplied in opposite directions.
- A wage increase raises the quantity of labor supplied through the substitution effect, but it reduces the quantity supplied through the income effect. The supply curve of labor may thus be positively or negatively sloped, or both.
- Economists often assume that the supply curve for labor, taken in the aggregate, is vertical; that implies that the substitution and income effects just offset each other. The supply curves for individual labor markets, however, are likely to be upward sloping.
- The supply curve for labor will shift as a result of a change in worker preferences, a change in nonlabor income, a change in the prices of related goods and services, or a change in expectations.
- The supply of labor in particular markets could shift because of changes in wages in related markets or changes in entry requirements.

Case in Point: Child Care Costs and Labor Supply

Mothers typically face a big hurdle if they choose to work: finding care for their children. Economists Laura Duberstein of the University of Michigan and Karen Oppenheim Mason of the University of Hawaii have examined the relationship between child care costs and women's willingness to work. Their research also sheds light on the roles of wages and preferences in the supply of labor.

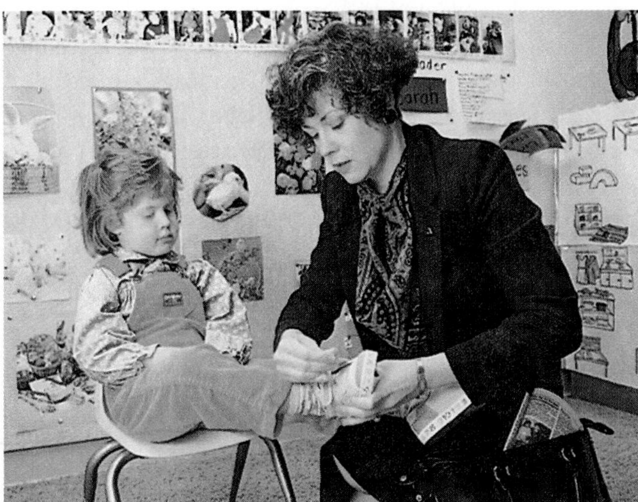

The two economists used data from a 1986 survey of 1,383 mothers with preschool-aged children in the Detroit metropolitan area. The survey asked about child care costs faced by each respondent and whether the woman planned to participate in the work force within the next year. It also asked several questions designed to elicit information about attitudes toward work and about the efficacy of child care.

The survey results suggested that women's plans to participate in the labor force were positively related to wages, suggesting an upward-sloping supply curve. Changes in preferences and child care costs, however, could shift the supply curve. Respondents were less likely to supply their labor if they preferred a traditional family structure with a husband as the primary breadwinner. They were also less likely to supply their labor if they felt that care provided by others was strongly inferior to a mother's care. Finally, they were less likely to supply their labor if child care costs were higher.

Source: Laura Duberstein and Karen Oppenheim Mason, "Do Child Care Costs Influence Women's Work Plans? Analysis for a Metropolitan Area," Research Report, Population Studies Center, University of Michigan, July 1991.

that area. Improved job opportunities for women in other fields appear to have shifted the supply curve for nurses to the left.

The supply of labor in a particular market could also shift because of a change in entry requirements. Most states, for example, require barbers and beauticians to obtain extensive training before entering the profession. Elimination of such requirements would increase the supply of these workers. Financial planners have, in recent years, sought the introduction of tougher licensing requirements, which would reduce the supply of financial planners.

Worker preferences regarding specific occupations can also affect labor supply. A reduction in willingness to take risks could lower the supply of labor available for risky occupations such as farm work (the most dangerous work in the United States), law enforcement, and fire fighting. An increased desire to work with children could raise the supply of child care workers, elementary school teachers, and pediatricians.

Labor Markets at Work

We've seen that a firm's demand for labor depends on the marginal product of labor and the price of the good the firm produces. We add the demand curves of individual firms to obtain the market demand curve for labor. The supply curve for labor depends on variables such as population and worker preferences. Supply in a particular market depends on variables such as worker preferences, the skills and training a job requires, and wages available in alternative occupations. Wages are determined by the intersection of demand and supply.

Once the wage in a particular market is determined, individual firms in perfect competition take it as given. Because the firm is a price taker, it faces a horizontal supply curve for labor at the market wage. For one firm, changing the quantity of labor it hires does not change the wage. We'll consider cases in which an individual firm's choices do affect the wage it pays in Chapter 14. In the context of the model of perfect competition, however, buyers and sellers are price takers. That means that the choices of a firm in hiring labor do not affect the wage.

The operation of labor markets in perfect competition is illustrated in Exhibit 9-8. The wage W_1 is determined by the intersection of demand and supply in Panel (a). Employment equals L_1. An individual firm takes that wage as given; it is the supply curve s_1 facing the firm. This wage also equals the firm's marginal factor cost. The firm hires l_1 units of labor, a quantity determined by the intersection of its marginal revenue product curve for labor MRP_1 and the supply curve s_1. As we did in the last chapter, we use lowercase letters to show quantity for a single firm and uppercase letters to show quantity in the market; we do the same with supply.

EXHIBIT 9-8

Wage Determination and Employment in Perfect Competition

Wages in perfect competition are determined by the intersection of demand and supply in Panel (a). An individual firm takes the wage W_1 as given. It faces a horizontal supply curve for labor at the market wage, as shown in Panel (b). This supply curve s_1 is also the marginal factor cost curve for labor. The firm responds to the wage by employing l_1 units of labor, a quantity determined by the intersection of its marginal revenue product curve MRP_1 and its supply curve s_1.

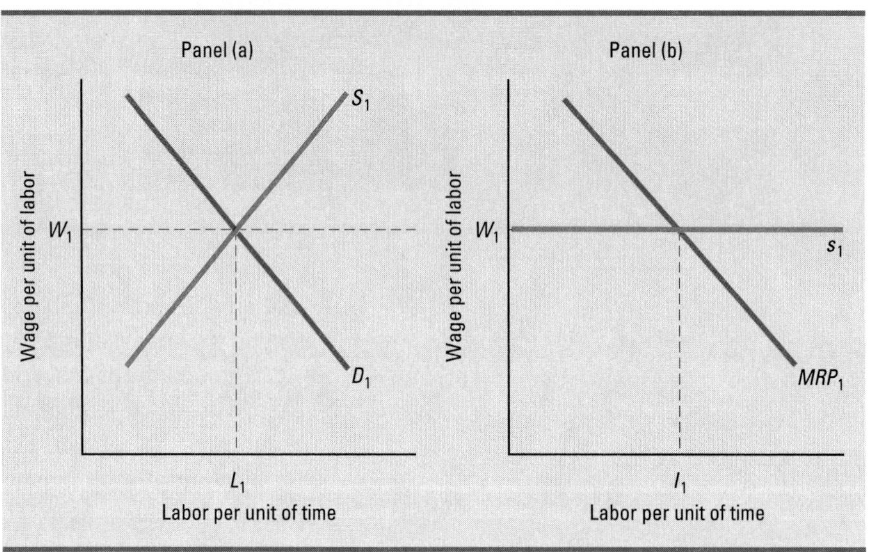

Changes in Demand and Supply

If wages are determined by demand and supply, then changes in demand and supply should affect wages. An increase in demand or a reduction in supply will raise wages; an increase in supply or a reduction in demand will lower them.

Panel (a) of Exhibit 9-9 shows how an increase in the demand for labor affects wages and employment. The shift in demand to D_2 pushes the wage to W_2 and boosts employment to L_2. Such an increase implies that the marginal product of labor has increased, that the number of firms has risen, or that the price of the good the labor produces has gone up. As we've seen, the marginal product of labor could rise because of an increase in the use of other factors of production, an improvement in technology, or an increase in human capital.

Clearly, a rising demand for labor has been the dominant trend in the market for U.S. labor through most of the history of the nation. Wages and employment have generally risen as the availability of capital and other factors of production

EXHIBIT 9-9

Changes in the Demand and Supply for Labor

Panel (a) shows an increase in demand for labor; the wage rises to W_2 and employment rises to L_2. A reduction in labor demand, shown in Panel (b), reduces employment and the wage level. An increase in the supply of labor, shown in Panel (c), reduces the wage to W_2 and increases employment to L_2. Panel (d) shows the effect of a reduction in the supply of labor; wages rise and employment falls.

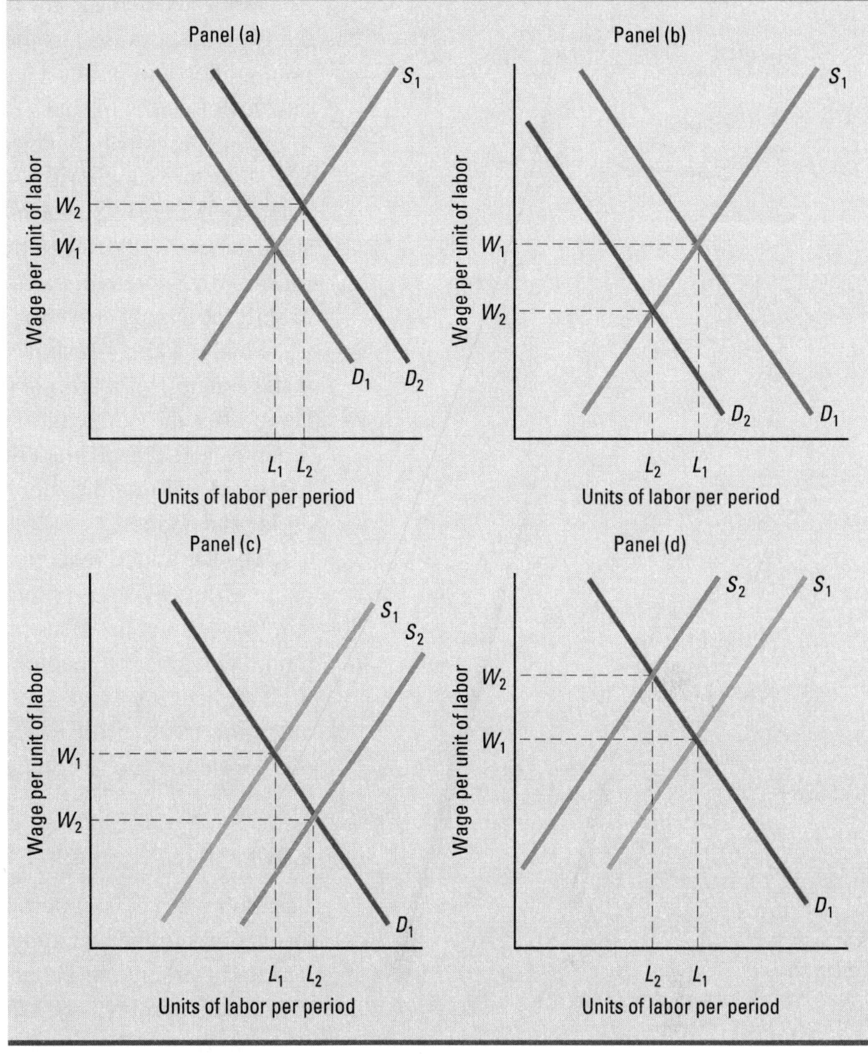

have increased, as technology has advanced, and as human capital has increased. All have increased the productivity of labor, and all have acted to increase wages.

Panel (b) shows a reduction in the demand for labor to D_2. Wages and employment both fall. Given that the demand for labor in the aggregate is generally increasing, reduced labor demand is most often found in specific labor markets. A slump in construction activity in a particular community, for example, can lower the demand for construction workers. Technological changes can reduce as well as increase demand. The Case in Point on wages and technology (page 213) suggests that technological changes since the late 1970s have tended to reduce the demand for workers with only a high school education while increasing the demand for those with a college education.

Panel (c) shows the impact of an increase in the supply of labor. The supply curve shifts to S_2, pushing employment to L_2 and cutting the wage to W_2. For labor markets as a whole, such a supply increase could occur because of an increase in population or an increase in the amount of work people are willing to do. For individual labor markets, supply will increase as people move into a particular market.

Just as the demand for labor has increased throughout much of the history of the United States, so has the supply of labor. Population has risen both through immigration and through natural increases. Such increases tend, all other determinants of wages unchanged, to reduce wages. The fact that wages have tended to rise suggests that demand has, in general, increased more rapidly than supply. Still, the more supply rises, the smaller the increase in wages will be, even if demand is rising. U.S. wages have, for example, increased much more slowly since the early 1970s than they did during the previous two decades. One reason for this was increased participation in the labor force by women, which tended to shift the supply curve for labor to the right.

Finally, Panel (d) shows the impact of a reduction in labor supply. One dramatic example of a drop in the labor supply was caused by a reduction in population after the outbreak of bubonic plague in Europe in 1348—the so-called Black Death. The plague killed about one-third of the people of Europe within a few years, shifting the supply curve for labor sharply to the left. Wages doubled during the period.[1]

The fact that a reduction in the supply of labor tends to increase wages explains efforts by some employee groups to reduce labor supply. Members of certain professions have successfully promoted strict licensing requirements that limit the number of people who can enter the profession—U.S. physicians have been particularly successful in this effort. Unions often seek restrictions in immigration in an effort to reduce the supply of labor and thereby boost wages. We'll examine such efforts to restrict supply more carefully in Chapter 14.

Labor Markets and Public Policy

The labor market is important partly because labor accounts for the bulk of factor incomes in the economy. But its primary importance stems from the simple fact that workers are people. Changes in wages affect the incomes of people. Changes in employment affect whether people have jobs. In this section, we'll examine two problems of labor markets. First, because the market assigns a wage equal to marginal revenue product, people whose marginal revenue product is low will receive low incomes. Second, labor markets can generate results that may be discriminatory. Women and members of some minority groups may, because of their gender or race or their ethnicity, receive lower wages than others.

This section introduces some of the economic issues involved in these two problems. They are examined in greater detail in Chapter 19.

Labor Markets and Poverty

The Case in Point on technology and the wage gap (page 213) suggests an extremely important social problem. As changes in technology boost the demand for highly educated workers and reduce the demand for less educated ones, the gap between the earnings of these two groups widens. It appears that the modern workplace will continue to seek out workers with strong intellectual skills. In such a world, what will happen to people who lack the opportunity to develop these skills?

[1] Carlo M. Cipolla, *Before the Industrial Revolution: European Society and Economy, 1000–1700,* 2nd ed. (New York: Norton, 1980), pp. 200–202. The doubling in wages was a doubling in real terms, meaning that the purchasing power of an average worker's wage doubled.

Case in Point

Technology, Capital, and the Wage Gap

The introduction to this chapter noted the startling change in relative wages of college-educated versus high-school-educated workers in the 1980s. Adjusted for inflation, the wages of workers with a college education rose while the wages of workers with only a high school education fell, widening the gap between the wages of the two groups. The 1980s also saw a sharp increase in the wages of women relative to men.

Economists John Bound and George Johnson of the University of Michigan have examined explanations for the increased educational wage gap. One possible explanation lies on the supply side. If the supply of high-school-educated workers increased more than the supply of college-educated workers during the period, that would account for the gap. But the reverse was true: the supply of college-educated workers increased more than the supply of high-school-educated workers. The explanation of the increased gap had to lie in changes in demand.

One reason factor demand might change is that product demand can change. In the 1980s, for example, the demand for U.S.-produced manufactured goods fell as a result of a recession and increased use of imported manufactured goods. That reduced the demand for labor in manufacturing, in which high-school-educated workers made up a relatively large share of the work force. But Mssrs. Bound and Johnson found that other product demand shifts during the period tended to hurt college-educated workers more than their high-school-educated counterparts. On balance, they concluded that changes in product demand had actually tended to lower the wages of college-educated relative to high-school-educated workers.

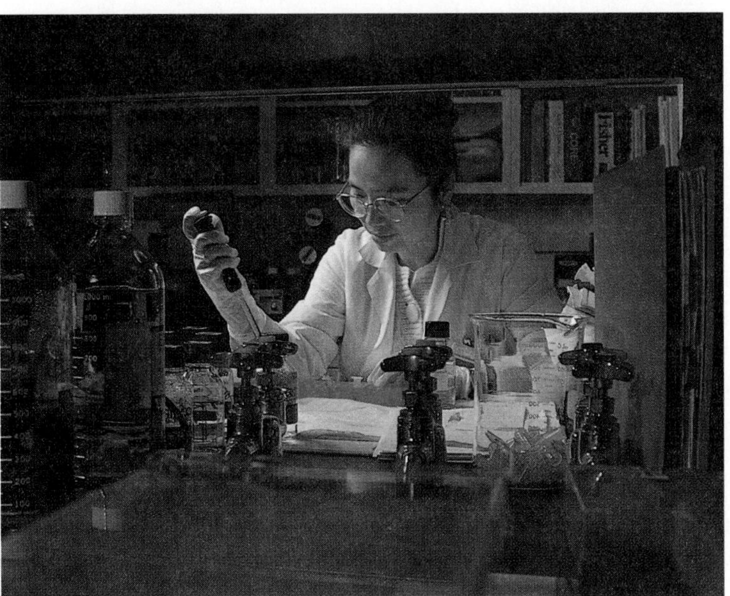

The economists also examined the possibility that a shift by some firms to the use of foreign workers had increased the gap. U.S. firms in some industries shifted a substantial share of their manufacturing activity to foreign plants during the 1980s, reducing the demand for U.S. labor. Because those shifts involved primarily unskilled workers, they contributed to the widening wage gap. But Mr. Bound says that it can't fully explain that gap: "The wage gap widened in a broad range of industries, including the service sector, and that can't be explained by a shift in international trade," he says. "For example, the gap between wages of high-school-educated and college-educated workers widened in hospitals, and they aren't affected by foreign production."

Having ruled out other factors, the economists concluded that technological changes accounted for the widened wage gap. The primary source of that change, they argue, has been the computer revolution. "It's not just computers sitting on someone's desk," Mr. Bound says. "It's the use of computer applications in all phases of production." As computers are integrated into more and more production processes, firms require relatively more workers with higher education—and relatively fewer workers with less education.

The use of other forms of "high-tech" capital has also had an effect on wages. Economists Ernst Berndt, Catherine Morrison, and Larry Rosenblum of the Massachusetts Institute of Technology reported in a 1992 study that the share of all capital represented by high-tech equipment such as computers, communications equipment, and technical instruments more than doubled during the late 1970s and early 1980s.

Increases in the use of high-tech capital, the Michigan economists argue, have increased the demand for college-educated workers. They have also increased the demand for women relative to men, since women tend to be concentrated in occupations requiring greater intellectual skills while men tend to be concentrated in occupations that emphasize physical skills. Thus, the shift to more sophisticated production not only widened the high school–college wage gap—it narrowed the male-female wage gap. Bound and Johnson found that the average wage gap between men and women fell from 30 percent in 1979 to 24 percent in 1988.

Source: John Bound and George Johnson, "What Are the Causes of Rising Wage Inequality in the United States?" *Economic Policy Review,* Federal Reserve Bank of New York, 1(1) (January 1995): 9–17; Ernst Berndt, Catherine Morrison, and Larry Rosenblum, "HighTech Capital Formation and Labor Composition in U.S. Manufacturing Industries: An Exploratory Analysis," National Bureau of Economic Research Working Paper no. 4010, 1992; and personal interview.

The government could respond to declining wages for some workers by ordering that wages be higher—by imposing minimum wages above current equilibrium levels. Such a strategy is suggested in Panel (a) of Exhibit 9-10. Suppose the current equilibrium wage of unskilled workers is W_1, determined by the intersection of the demand and supply curves of these workers. The government determines that this wage is too low and orders that it be increased to W_m, a minimum wage. This strategy reduces employment from L_1 to L_2, but it raises the incomes of those who continue to work. The higher wage also increases the quantity of labor supplied to L_2'. The gap between the quantity of labor supplied and the quantity demanded, $L_2' - L_2$, is a surplus—a surplus that increases unemployment.

EXHIBIT 9-10

Alternative Responses to Low Wages

Government can respond to a low wage by imposing a minimum wage of W_m in Panel (a). This increases the quantity of labor supplied and reduces the quantity demanded. It does, however, increase the income of those who keep their jobs. Another way the government can boost wages is by raising the demand for labor in Panel (b). Both wages and employment rise.

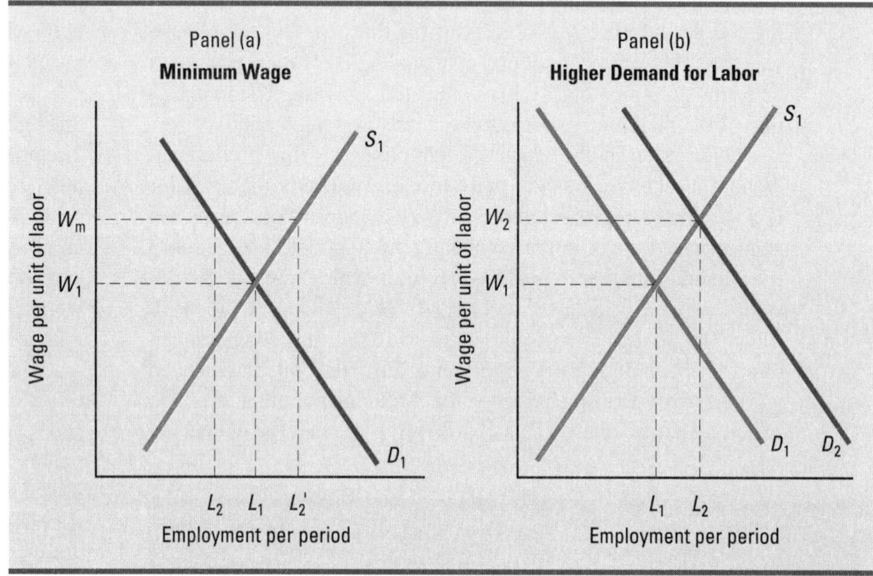

Some economists oppose increases in the minimum wage on grounds that such increases boost unemployment. Other economists argue that because the demand for labor is relatively inelastic, a higher minimum wage boosts the incomes of unskilled workers as a group. That gain, they say, justifies the policy, even if it increases unemployment. We'll see in Chapter 14 that one can make an even stronger case for minimum wages in labor markets that are not perfectly competitive.

An alternative approach to imposing a legal minimum is to try to boost the demand for labor. Such an approach is illustrated in Panel (b). An increase in demand to D_2 pushes the wage to W_2 and at the same time increases employment to L_2. Public sector training programs that seek to increase human capital are examples of this policy.

Another alternative is to subsidize the wages of workers whose incomes fall below a certain level. People who lack the skills—and the ability to acquire the skills—needed to earn a higher wage can earn more without the loss of jobs implied by a higher minimum wage. Such a program could be costly. It would also reduce the incentive for low-skilled workers to develop the skills that are in greater demand in the marketplace.

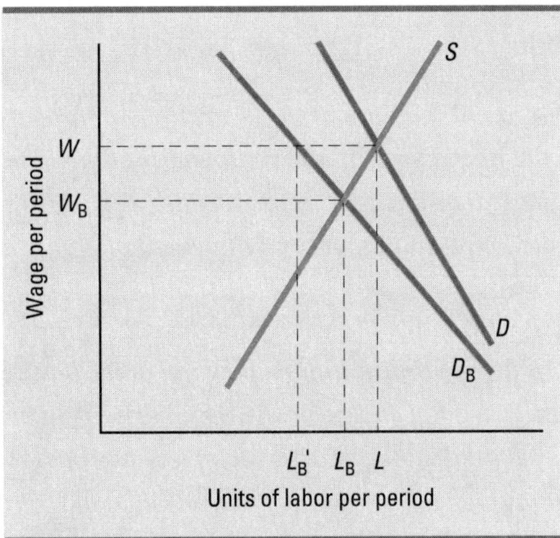

EXHIBIT 9-11

Discrimination in the Labor Market

The demand curve D and the supply curve S are identical for black and for white workers. Both groups of workers receive a wage W and experience an employment level of L. If employers have racist preferences, however, they will perceive the productivity of black workers to be lower than for other workers. The result will be a lower wage W_B and a lower level of employment L_B for black workers.

Discrimination

Workers in a competitive market receive a wage equal to their marginal revenue product. But a worker's marginal revenue product doesn't come stamped on his or her forehead; it must be estimated by employers. What if employer estimates of a worker's productivity are influenced by that worker's ethnicity or sex?

Suppose, for example, that all workers are identical, except that half are black and half are white. In Exhibit 9-11, we assume for simplicity that the supply curves of black and white workers are identical and are given by S. If all workers are identical, the demand curves for black workers and for white workers are also identical. Suppose this demand curve is D, producing a wage W for all workers and employment of L black workers and L white workers. If, however, employers perceive black workers as being less productive than other workers, their demand curve for black workers might be D_B instead of D. That would produce a wage for black workers of W_B, below the wage for white workers. Employment for black workers would also be curtailed to L_B.

The problem suggested by Exhibit 9-11 appears to exist for many groups of workers in the economy. Black male workers, for example, earn about 15 percent less than white males who are similar in terms of education, age, experience, and other variables. Hispanic workers and women also appear to suffer from discrimination.

Our discussion thus far has suggested the existence of racist attitudes on the part of employers. But suppose that not all employers have such attitudes. Profit-maximizing nonracist firms would hire black workers because they are cheaper. As firms take advantage of cheaper black labor, the demand curve for this labor will shift to the right, and the wage gap will be eliminated. Competition among profit-maximizing firms would eliminate racism and sexism from the market.

But competition hasn't eliminated wage gaps between white and minority workers or between men and women. Another explanation for this fact might be that racism exists not among employers but among customers. If a firm's customers prefer not to deal with women or with members of minority groups, then the marginal revenue product of female or minority workers will be reduced, reducing their wage.

Whatever the source of discrimination, its effects are difficult to eliminate. Suppose firms are not allowed to pay lower wages to black workers. In Exhibit 9-11, the wage must be W for all workers. Given that black workers face a lower demand than other workers, requiring that they be paid a wage of W lowers their employment to L_B'. If the demand for these workers is elastic, an equal pay requirement would actually lower their income.

Another strategy is to require firms to hire more black workers in an effort to shift the demand curve to the right. This is the affirmative action approach.

Despite the use of both equal-pay requirements and affirmative action, there has been no tendency over the last two decades for wage gaps attributable to discrimination to diminish.

The competitive model of labor markets suggests that workers will receive a wage that reflects the market value at the margin of their contribution to output. We've seen two problems with this process of wage determination. First, it may generate wages for some workers that do not allow what is generally regarded as an adequate standard of living. Second, the market's assessment of a worker's value may reflect discriminatory judgments that unfairly lower the worker's wage.

Checklist

- Wages in a competitive market are determined by demand and supply.
- An increase in demand or a reduction in supply will increase the equilibrium wage.
- A reduction in demand or an increase in supply will reduce the equilibrium wage.
- The government may respond to low wages for some workers by imposing the minimum wage or by attempting to increase the demand for those workers.
- Discrimination can reduce the perceived marginal revenue product of some groups of workers and thus lower their wage.

A Look Back—And a Look Ahead

In this chapter we have extended our understanding of the operation of perfectly competitive markets by looking at the market for labor. We found that the common sense embodied in the marginal decision rule is alive and well. A firm should hire additional labor up to the point that the marginal benefit of doing so equals the marginal cost.

The demand curve for labor is given by the marginal revenue product (MRP) of labor. A profit-maximizing firm will hire labor up to the point that its marginal revenue product equals its marginal factor cost (MFC). The demand for labor shifts whenever there is a change in (1) related factors of production, including investment in human capital; (2) technology; (3) product demand; and (4) the number of firms.

The quantity of labor supplied is closely linked to the demand for leisure. As more hours are worked, income goes up, but the marginal cost of work measured in terms of forgone leisure also increases. We saw that the substitution effect of a wage increase always increases the quantity supplied. But the income effect of a wage increase tends to reduce the quantity of labor supplied. It is possible that above some wage, the income effect more than offsets the substitution effect. At or above that wage, an individual's supply curve for labor is backward bending. Supply curves for labor in individual markets, however, are likely to be upward sloping.

Because competitive labor markets generate wages equal to marginal revenue product, workers who add little to the value of a firm's output will receive low wages. The public sector may require a higher minimum wage, seek to improve these workers' human capital, or subsidize their wages. We also saw that competitive markets may generate wages based on incorrect perceptions of the marginal products of minority workers and women.

In Chapter 10, we'll examine competitive markets for two other factors of production—capital and natural resources.

Terms and Concepts for Review

Circular flow model

Complementary factors of production

Factor markets

Marginal factor cost (MFC)

Marginal revenue product (MRP)

Product markets

Substitute factors of production

For Discussion

1. Suppose firms in the economy were to produce fewer goods and services. How do you think this would affect household spending on goods and services? (*Hint:* Use the circular flow model to analyze this question.)
2. Explain the difference between the marginal product of a factor and the marginal revenue product of a factor.
3. In perfectly competitive input markets, the factor price and the marginal factor cost are the same. True or false? Explain.

4. Many high school vocational education programs are beginning to shift from an emphasis on training students to perform specific tasks to training students to learn new tasks. Students are taught, for example, how to read computer manuals so that they can more easily learn new systems. Why has this change occurred? Do you think the change is desirable?

5. How would an increase in the prices of so-called truck crops, crops of fresh produce that must be brought immediately to market, affect the wages of workers who harvest those crops?

6. If individual labor supply curves of all individuals are backward bending, does this mean that a market supply curve for labor in a particular industry will also be backward bending?

7. There was an unprecedented wave of immigration to the United States during the latter third of the nineteenth century. Wages, however, rose at a rapid rate throughout the period. Why was the increase in wages surprising in light of rising immigration, and what probably caused it?

8. Suppose you were the economic advisor to the president of a small underdeveloped country. What advice would you give him or her with respect to how the country could raise the productivity of its labor force? (*Hint:* What factors increase labor productivity?)

9. The text argues that the effect of a minimum wage on the incomes of unskilled workers depends on whether the demand for their services is elastic or inelastic. Explain why, and comment on the evidence concerning this elasticity.

10. How would a successful effort to increase the human capital of unskilled workers affect their wage? Why?

Problems

1. Felicia Alvarez, the bakery manager introduced in the appendix to Chapter 1, faces the following total product curve, which gives the relationship between the number of bakers she hires each day and the number of loaves of bread she produces, assuming all other factors of production are given.

Number of bakers per day	Loaves of bread per day
0	0
1	400
2	700
3	900
4	1,025
5	1,100
6	1,150

Assume that bakers in the area receive a wage of $100 per day. Plot the bakery's marginal revenue product and marginal factor cost curves (remember that marginal values are plotted at the midpoints of the respective intervals). How many bakers will Ms. Alvarez employ per day?

2. Suppose that wooden boxes are produced under conditions of perfect competition and that the price of a box is $10. The demand and supply curves for the workers who make these boxes are given by the following:

Wage per day	Workers demanded	Workers supplied
$100	6,000	12,000
80	7,000	10,000
60	8,000	8,000
40	9,000	6,000
20	10,000	4,000

a. Plot the demand and supply curves for labor, and determine the equilibrium wage for box makers.

b. Using the data presented for Acme Box in Exhibit 7-2, compute Acme's marginal revenue product curve for box makers. How many of these workers will Acme employ?

3. Assume that the market for nurses is perfectly competitive. Illustrate graphically how each of the following events will affect the demand or supply for nurses. State the impact on wages and on the number of nurses employed.

a. New hospital instruments reduce the amount of time physicians must spend with patients in intensive care and increase the care that nurses can provide.

b. The number of doctors increases.

c. Changes in the labor market lead to greater demand for the services of women in a wide range of occupations. The demand for nurses, however, does not change.

d. New legislation establishes primary care facilities in which nurses care for patients with minor medical problems. No supervision by physicians is required in the facilities.

e. The wage for nurses rises.

4. Plot the supply curves for labor implied by each of the following statements.

a. "I'm sorry, kids, but now that I'm earning more, I just can't afford to come home early in the afternoon, so I won't be there when you get home from school."

b. "They can pay me a lot or they can pay me a little. I'll still put in my 8 hours a day."

c. "Wow! With the raise the boss just gave me, I can afford to knock off early each day."

9 Appendix Indifference Curve Analysis of Labor Supply

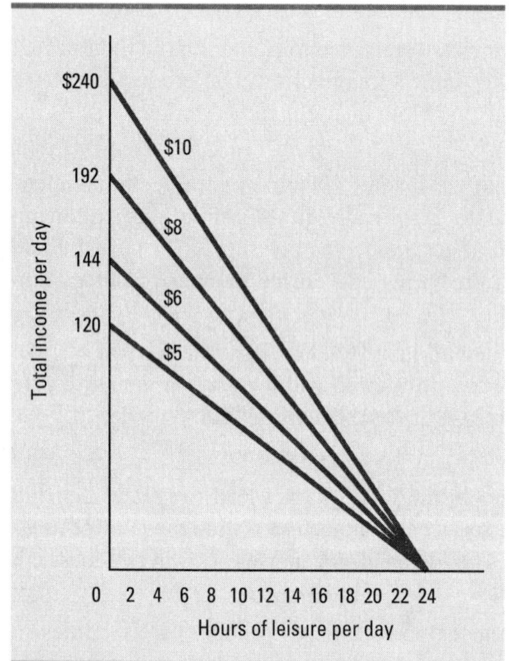

EXHIBIT 9A-1

Wages and Budget Lines

Sylvia Roggi can either consume her time as leisure or supply it in exchange for income. At a wage of $6 per hour, she could, if she did nothing but work, earn $144 per day. At a wage of $8 per hour, she could earn $192 per day. If she consumes some of her time as leisure, she will earn less income. The budget lines show the combinations of leisure and income she could consume at each wage.

In this appendix we apply the indifference curve analysis we developed in the appendix to Chapter 6 to the problem of an individual's supply of labor.

An individual has 24 hours per day. The individual can either consume this time as leisure or supply it to a firm in exchange for income—a wage. Individuals gain utility by consuming more leisure, but they also gain utility by enjoying higher incomes. We can think of income and leisure as two goods that consumers enjoy, and we can use indifference curves to assess how individuals choose how much of each good to consume. The supply curve for labor emerges from such choices.

Budget Lines

A budget line shows combinations of two goods a consumer can select with a given budget and with a given set of prices. Budget lines for income-leisure choices are constrained by the number of hours in a day and by the wage a worker can earn.

Suppose Sylvia Roggi, a clerk, can work as many hours as she wishes at a wage of $5 per hour. That means that if she were to work 24 hours per day, she could earn $120 per day. Working 24 hours per day would mean consuming no leisure. If she consumes 24 hours of leisure per day, she does no work and earns no money. The budget line for a wage of $5 per hour in Exhibit 9A-1 illustrates the combinations of income and leisure that Ms. Roggi has available.

The end points of the budget line for a wage of $5 per hour show the two extremes available to Ms. Roggi: an income of $120 and no leisure, or an income of $0 and 24 hours of leisure. The slope of the line between those points is −$120/24, or −$5 per hour; it is the negative of the wage. The slope of the budget line, the wage, is the rate at which Ms. Roggi must give up income if she is to consume additional leisure. The wage is thus the price of leisure.

Budget lines for wages of $6, $8, and $10 per hour are also shown in the exhibit. As the wage rises, the maximum amount Ms. Roggi could earn rises. The slope of each budget line is the negative of the wage per hour associated with that budget line.

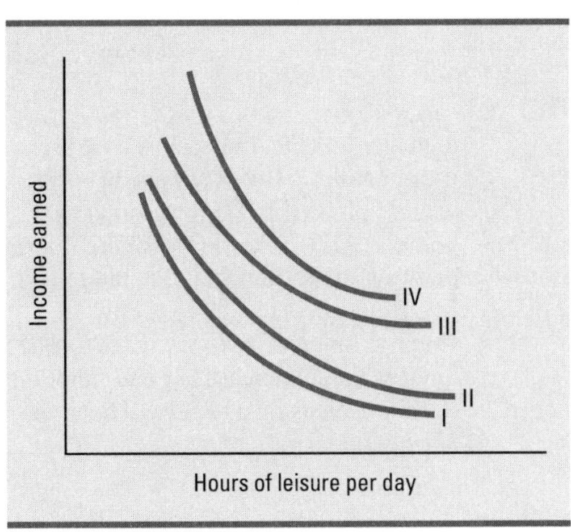

EXHIBIT 9A-2

Indifference Curves for Income and Leisure

Four of Sylvia Roggi's indifference curves for income and leisure are shown here. Curves I, II, III, and IV show successively higher levels of total utility.

Indifference Curves

An indifference curve for income and leisure shows the combinations of these two goods that yield a given level of total utility. A utility-maximizing individual will seek the highest indifference curve possible.

Exhibit 9A-2 shows four of Sylvia Roggi's indifference curves for income and leisure. Their shapes are typical of indifference curves; they suggest that her marginal rate of substitution, the rate at which she is willing to give up income to obtain additional leisure, declines as she consumes more leisure. This shape is consistent with common sense: if Ms. Roggi is working a great deal, earning a substantial amount each day and consuming very little leisure, she will be willing to give up a relatively large amount of income to obtain an additional hour of leisure. But as she travels down and to the right along an indifference curve, she is willing to give up less income to obtain an additional unit of leisure.

Labor Supply and Income-Leisure Choice

Suppose the wage is $5 per hour. To determine how much labor Ms. Roggi will supply at this wage, we combine in Exhibit 9A-3 the budget line for a wage of $5 with the indifference curves for income and leisure from Exhibit 9A-2. She will seek the highest indifference curve possible.

At a wage of $5 per hour, the highest indifference curve Ms. Roggi can attain is indifference curve I. She maximizes utility at point A where the indifference curve is tangent to the budget line for a wage of $5. At this point she consumes 18 hours of leisure per day, which means she supplies 6 hours of labor. That quantity of labor yields her an income of $30 per day.

At the utility-maximizing solution at point A, the slopes of the budget line and of indifference curve I are equal. Now the rate at which Ms. Roggi can exchange income for leisure in the market, the slope of the budget line, is equal to the rate at which she is willing to exchange income for leisure, the slope of her indifference curve.

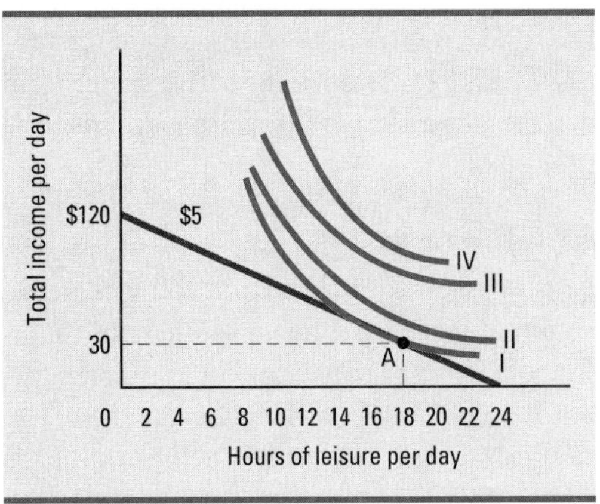

EXHIBIT 9A-3

Utility Maximization

At a wage of $5 per hour, Ms. Roggi selects point A on budget line I. Higher indifference curves would yield greater utility, but they are unattainable at a wage of $5. At point A, the slopes of her budget line and of indifference curve I are equal.

Responding to Wage Changes

At different wages Ms. Roggi faces different budget lines. The market wage affects the quantity of leisure she consumes and the income she is able to earn. Panel (a) of Exhibit 9A-4 combines the budget lines for wages of $5, $6, $8, and $10 per hour with the four indifference curves from Exhibit 9A-2.

Point A on indifference curve I gives Ms. Roggi's utility-maximizing solution for a wage of $5, which we have already examined. At this point she consumes 18 hours of leisure, supplying the other 6 hours as labor. At a wage of $5 per hour, she earns $30 per day.

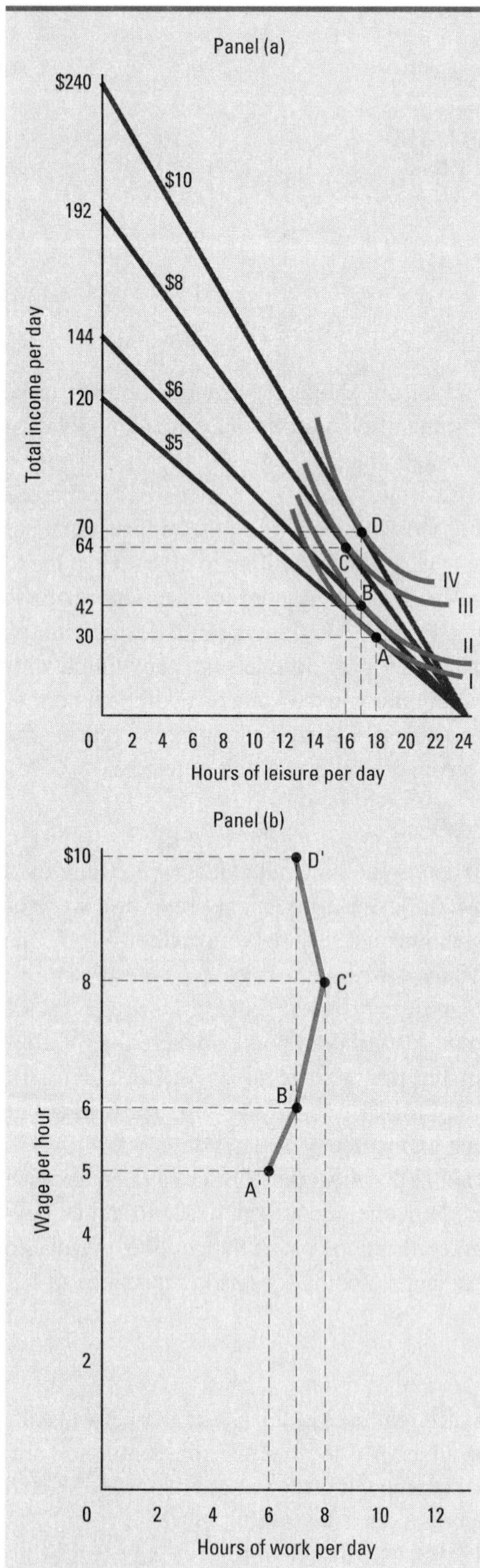

EXHIBIT 9A-4

Wage Changes and the Supply Curve

As the wage increases from $5 per hour to $6, then $8, Ms. Roggi's utility-maximizing combinations of income and leisure in Panel (a) move in the direction of greater income and less consumption of leisure, hence greater quantities of labor supplied. When the wage rises to $10, however, Ms. Roggi responds by moving to point D, consuming more leisure than at point C but still achieving a greater income. In Panel (b), we see the quantities of labor supplied at each wage. Points A′ to D′ correspond to points A to D in Panel (a). We see that as the wage rises from $5 to $6, then to $8, Ms. Roggi's supply curve is upward sloping. An increase in the wage to $10 induces her to increase her consumption of leisure, causing a backward bend in her supply curve.

If the wage were to rise to $6 per hour, Ms. Roggi could attain point B on indifference curve II. At this point she consumes 17 hours of leisure, supplies 7 hours of labor, and earns a daily income of $42. An increase in the wage to $8 per hour would allow Ms. Roggi to move to point C on indifference curve III. At this point she consumes 16 hours of leisure, supplies 8 hours of labor, and earns an income of $64 per day.

If the wage were to rise still further, to $10 per hour, Ms. Roggi would move to point D on indifference curve IV. At this point she consumes 17 hours of leisure, supplies 7 hours of labor, and earns an income of $70 per day. She is able to supply less labor than she did at a wage of $8 per hour and still earns more income.

The combinations of income and leisure at which Ms. Roggi maximizes utility at different wages can be used to derive her supply curve for labor. Panel (b) of Exhibit 9A-4 shows hourly wages and the quantity of labor she supplies at each wage. Points A′, B′, C′, and D′ on her supply curve correspond to the utility-maximizing combinations A, B, C, and D, respectively. The increase in leisure consumed by Ms. Roggi when the wage rises to $10 per hour produces a backward bend in her supply curve for labor.

Substitution and Income Effects of a Wage Change

We can use indifference curve analysis to assess the substitution and income effects of wage changes. The examination of these two effects will help us to understand more clearly the shapes of labor supply curves.

Suppose a hospital orderly, Matt Jensen, earns a wage of $6 per hour. The budget line implied by this wage is illustrated in Exhibit 9A-5. He maximizes utility at point A, consuming 16 hours of leisure per day, working 8 hours and receiving an income of $48 per day. Now suppose his wage is increased to $12 per hour, rotating the budget line upward as shown. He now maximizes utility at point B, where he again consumes 16 hours of leisure and supplies 8 hours of work per day. His income rises to $96 per day.

Mr. Jensen's response to the wage increase can be divided into a substitution effect and an income effect. To estimate the substitution effect, we construct an imaginary budget line with a slope equal to the new wage, tangent to the original indifference curve at point C. The substitution effect is the shift from point A to point C; it implies a reduction in the consumption of leisure and therefore an increase in the quantity of labor supplied. This substitution effect is Mr. Jensen's

EXHIBIT 9A-5

Substitution and Income Effects of a Wage Change

At a wage of $6 per hour, hospital orderly Matt Jensen maximizes utility at point A, consuming 16 hours of leisure and thus working 8 hours per day. An increase in his wage to $12 rotates his budget line upward. He now maximizes utility at point B. The substitution effect of the wage change (sub) is shown by the change from point A to point C; the income effect (inc) is the change from point C to point B.

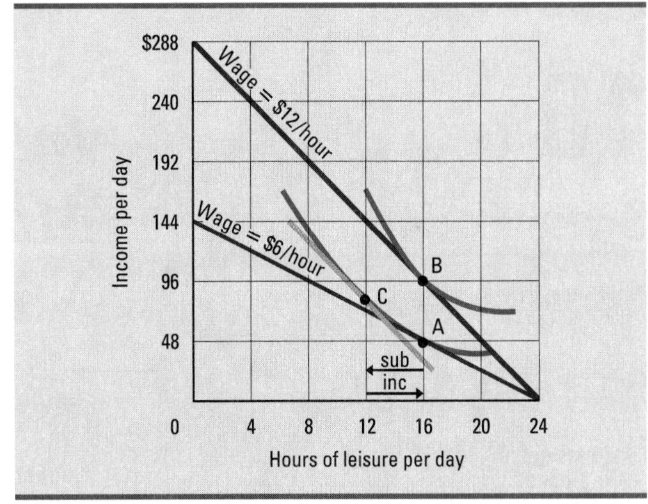

response to the fact that his leisure is now more costly. The higher wage also increases Mr. Jensen's income. The income effect of the wage change is the movement from point C to point B; it is the movement resulting from the shift in the imaginary budget line, shown as a lighter line, to the new budget line for a wage of $12. Because leisure is a normal good, the income effect of a higher wage is an increase in the consumption of leisure, and thus a reduction in the quantity of labor supplied.

In Mr. Jensen's case, the income effect offsets the substitution effect; he supplies the same quantity of labor at a wage of $12 as he did at a wage of $6. Because the income and substitution effects of a wage change always pull in opposite directions, we can't be sure whether an increase in the wage will increase or decrease the quantity of labor supplied—or leave it unchanged.

For Discussion

1. In 1860, the average work week in the United States for nonfarm employment was about 75 hours. By 1920 it had fallen to 50 hours. Wages during this period increased dramatically. What do you think accounted for the decline in hours worked? What does it suggest about the relative strengths of the substitution and income effects of higher wages during the period?
2. The percentage of women who are members of the labor force has risen steadily in the last four decades, a period in which wages have risen. In 1950, 33.1 percent of women were in the labor force. By 1994 that percentage had increased to 58.8 percent. What do you think happened?
3. Laid-back Lance values his leisure highly and doesn't place a high premium on income. Workaholic Wanda has virtually no outside interests and places a low value on additional leisure. Compare the likely shapes of their indifference curves.

Problems

1. Jessie earns $15 per hour in her job as a tester of semiconductors. Allen earns $12.50 per hour in his job as a fry cook. On a single graph, plot their budget lines for income and leisure. Which individual faces the higher cost of leisure? Why?
2. Suppose the wage is $10 per hour and all adults are given a basic living allowance of $120 per day. Show graphically how this would affect the budget line of any one worker.
3. Draw three sets of indifference curves and budget lines showing the responses of three workers to an increase in wages from $5 to $10 per hour. Worker A has a downward-sloping supply curve for labor, worker B has an upward-sloping supply curve, and worker C has a vertical supply curve.

10

Interest Rates and the Markets for Capital and Natural Resources

Chapter Objectives

After mastering the material in this chapter, you'll be able to:

1. Show how interest rates link the values of events that happen at different times.
2. Explain how interest rates are determined in financial markets.
3. Describe the forces at work in determining the values of stocks and bonds.
4. List and interpret the forces that influence firms' demand for capital.
5. Describe the relationship between interest rates and saving.
6. Show how the demands of future generations affect the present markets for renewable and exhaustible resources, and explain how the interest rate affects the relationship between future demands and current usage of natural resources.
7. Review how natural resource markets have functioned in the past, and discuss how they're likely to affect economic activity in the future.

A nation's capital is increased by parsimony and diminished by neglect.
Adam Smith, 1776

What's Ahead

MCI Corporation announced in 1993 that it was launching one of the most ambitious capital investment projects ever undertaken. It will spend more than $100 billion over the next 10 years in a project that will allow it to provide local telephone service in 10 major U.S. metropolitan areas.

The plan puts MCI in head-to-head competition with regional telephone companies that have, in the past, had monopolies in providing local telephone service. To install the millions of miles of fiber-optic cable and other equipment it needs to compete in local markets, MCI will have to raise money. Lots of money. To do that, it must convince people to give up funds they could use for consumption or for other financial investments and make those funds available to MCI's project. The people who provide the funds will be betting that MCI's investment will pay off with big profits.

The venture is an enormously risky one. Ever since Alexander Graham Bell invented the telephone, local telephone service in virtually every part of the country has been provided by monopoly firms. Those firms are well entrenched; competing with them will be a daunting task. As it launched its venture, officials at MCI could not even be sure that the state and local regulatory agencies that govern local telephone service would permit the kind of competition it seeks to provide. Even if the project is successful, the rewards to the company and to the individuals that put their money into the venture will be a long time in coming. MCI expects that installation of the equipment and lines won't be completed until early in the next century.

MCI's venture is bigger than most capital projects, but it shares some basic characteristics with all acquisition of capital by firms. As we saw in Chapter 2, the production of capital goods—the goods used in producing other goods and services—requires that consumption be sacrificed. The returns to capital will be spread over the period in which the capital is used. The choice to acquire capital is thus a choice to give up consumption today in hopes of returns in the future.

And those returns are far from certain; the choice to acquire capital is inevitably a risky one.

For all its special characteristics, however, capital is a factor of production. As we investigate the market for capital, we'll find that the ideas of marginal revenue product and marginal factor cost that we developed in the last chapter will continue to serve us. The big difference will come in contending with the fact that the benefits and costs of holding capital are distributed over time.

We'll also examine markets for natural resources in this chapter. Like decisions involving capital, choices in the allocation of natural resources have effects that will be felt over long periods of time. For exhaustible natural resources such as oil, the effects of those choices will be felt forever.

The analysis of capital and natural resources shifts us from the examination of outcomes in the current period to the analysis of outcomes distributed over many periods. Interest rates, which link the values of payments that occur at different times, take center stage when we analyze capital and the use of natural resources. Accordingly, much of our attention will be devoted to an examination of interest rates and their interpretation.

Time and Interest Rates

Time, the saying goes, is nature's way of keeping everything from happening all at once. And the fact that everything doesn't happen at once introduces an important complication in economic analysis.

MCI has decided to use funds now to install capital that won't begin to produce income for several years, so it needs a way to compare the significance of funds spent now versus income earned later. It must find a way to compensate investors who give up the use of their funds for several years, until the project can begin to pay off. How can payments that are distributed across time be linked to one another? Interest rates are the linkage mechanism; we shall investigate how they achieve that linkage in this section.

The Nature of Interest Rates

Let's consider a delightful problem of choice. Your Aunt Carmen offers to give you $10,000 now or $10,000 in one year. Which would you pick?

Most people would choose to take the money now. One reason for that choice is that prices are likely to rise over the next year. The purchasing power of $10,000 today is thus greater than the purchasing power of $10,000 a year hence. There's also a question of whether you can count on the money. If you take it now, you've got it. If you wait a year, who knows what will happen?

Let's eliminate both of these problems. Suppose that you're confident that prices won't change during the year, and you're absolutely certain that if you choose to wait for the money, you and it will both be available.

Will you take the money now or wait?

Chances are, you'd *still* want to take the money now. Perhaps there are some things you'd like to purchase with the money, and you'd like them sooner rather than later. Moreover, if you wait a year to get the money, you won't be able to use it while you're waiting. If you take it now, you'll always have a choice of whether to spend now or wait.

Case in Point: Waiting, AIDS, and Life Insurance

It is a tale of the 1990s that has become all too familiar.

Call him Roger Johnson. He has AIDS, a disease that will almost certainly kill him. Mr. Johnson is unable to work and his financial burdens compound his tragic medical situation. He's mortgaged his house and sold his other assets in a desperate effort to get his hands on the cash he needs for care, for food, and for shelter. He has a life insurance policy, but it will pay off only when he dies. If only he could get some of the money sooner . . .

The problem has spawned a market solution—investors who buy the life insurance policies of the terminally ill. Mr. Johnson can sell his policy to one of these investors and collect the purchase price. The investor takes over his premium payments. When Mr. Johnson dies, the investor will collect the proceeds of the policy.

The new industry is called the viatical industry. It provides the terminally ill with access to quick cash while they're alive; it provides investors a healthy interest premium on their investment.

It's grisly business. Potential buyers pore over patients' medical histories, studying T-cell counts and other indicators of how soon the patient will die. From the buyer's point of view, a speedy death is desirable. A patient with a life expectancy of less than 6 months can typically sell his or her life insurance policy for 90 percent of its face value; a $200,000 policy would thus fetch $180,000. A person with a better prognosis will collect less. Patients expected to live 2 years, for example, typically get only 60 percent of the face value of their policies.

Life Partners, Inc., in Waco, Texas, is one of the leaders in the viatical settlements industry. It claims it is arranging purchases of more than $100 million in policies per year—and that the number is growing fast. The firm says that its clients earn an interest return of 25 percent per year on their investments.

Kim D. Orr, an agent for the firm, says that the firm's activities make for a win-win situation. "Six years ago I had a cousin who died of AIDS. He was, at the end, destitute, and had to rely totally on his family for support. Today, there's a broad market, with lots of investors, and a patient can realize a high fraction of the face value of a policy on selling it. The market helps investors and patients alike."

Many life insurance companies now offer terminally ill policy holders an option to selling their policies to another person. Policyholders can simply accept early payment of the proceeds of their policies. The payments, of course, are only a fraction of the value of the policy.

Source: Personal interview.

Now suppose Aunt Carmen wants to induce you to wait for the money and changes the terms of her gift. She offers you $10,000 now or $11,000 in one year. In effect, she's offering you a $1,000 bonus if you'll wait a year for the money. If you agree to wait a year to receive Aunt Carmen's payment, you'll be accepting her promise to provide funds instead of the funds themselves. Either will increase your **wealth,** which is the sum of all your assets less all your liabilities. **Assets** are anything you have that is of value; **liabilities** are obligations to make future payments. The alternative to holding wealth is to consume it. You could, for example, take Aunt Carmen's $10,000 and spend it for a trip to Europe, thus reducing your wealth. Aunt Carmen's promise to pay you money also has value; it is an asset. By making a better offer—$11,000 instead of $10,000—she's trying to induce you to accept an asset you won't be able to consume during the year.

- **Wealth** is the total of assets less liabilities.
- **Assets** are anything that is of value.
- **Liabilities** are obligations to make future payments.
- **Interest** is a premium paid to people who agree to postpone their use of wealth.
- An **interest rate** is equal to the premium paid to postpone the use of wealth divided by the amount of wealth whose use is postponed.
- The **present value** of a specific future value is the amount that would, if deposited today at some interest rate, equal the future value.

The $1,000 bonus Aunt Carmen is offering if you'll wait a year for her payment is interest. In general, **interest** is a premium paid to people who agree to postpone their use of wealth. The **interest rate** is the premium paid, expressed as a percentage of the amount of wealth whose use is postponed. Aunt Carmen is offering you a $1,000 premium if you'll pass up the $10,000 today. She's thus offering you an interest rate of 10 percent ($1,000/$10,000 = 0.1 = 10%).

Suppose you tell Aunt Carmen that, given the two options, you'd still rather have the $10,000 today. She now offers you $11,500 if you'll wait a year for the payment—an interest rate of 15 percent. The greater the premium she pays for waiting, the higher the interest rate.

You are probably familiar with the role of interest rates in loans. In a loan, the borrower obtains a sum of money now in exchange for promising to repay the loan in the future. The lender thus must postpone his or her use of wealth until the time of repayment. To induce lenders to be willing to postpone their use of their wealth, borrowers offer interest. Borrowers are willing to pay interest because it allows them the use of money now rather than having to wait for it. And lenders require interest payments to compensate them for postponing their own use of their wealth.

Interest Rates and Present Value

We saw in the previous section that people generally prefer to receive a $1 payment today rather than wait to receive it later. We may conclude that the value today of a payment in the future is less than the dollar value of the future payment. An important application of interest rates is to show the relationship between the current and future values of a particular payment.

To see how we can calculate the current value of a future payment, let's consider an example similar to Aunt Carmen's offer. This time you have $1,000 and you deposit it in a bank, where it earns interest at the rate of 10 percent per year.

How much will you have in your bank account at the end of 1 year? You'll have the original $1,000 plus 10 percent of $1,000, or $1,100:

$$\$1{,}000 + (0.10)(\$1{,}000) = \$1{,}100$$

More generally, if we let P_0 equal the amount you deposit today, r the percentage rate of interest, and P_1 the balance of your deposit at the end of 1 year, then we can write

$$P_0 + rP_0 = P_1 \qquad \textbf{(1)}$$

Factoring out the P_0 term on the left-hand side of Equation 1 we have

$$P_0(1 + r) = P_1 \qquad \textbf{(2)}$$

We can now ask what P_1, a sum that will be available 1 year from now, is worth today. We solve for this by dividing both sides of Equation 2 by $(1 + r)$ to obtain

$$P_0 = \frac{P_1}{1 + r} \qquad \textbf{(3)}$$

Equation 3 suggests how we can compute the value today, P_0, of an amount P_1 that will be paid a year hence. An amount that would equal a particular future value if deposited today at a specific interest rate is called the **present value** of that future value.

More generally, the present value of any payment to be received n periods from now is

$$P_0 = \frac{P_n}{(1 + r)^n} \qquad \textbf{(4)}$$

Suppose, for example, that your Aunt Carmen offers you the option of $1,000 now or $15,000 in 30 years. We can use Equation 4 to help you decide which sum to take. The present value of $15,000 to be received in 30 years, assuming an interest rate of 10 percent, is

$$P_0 = \frac{P_{30}}{(1 + r)^{30}} = \frac{\$15{,}000}{(1 + 0.10)^{30}} = \$859.63$$

Assuming that you could earn that 10 percent return with certainty, you'd be better off taking Aunt Carmen's $1,000 now; it's greater than the present value, at an interest rate of 10 percent, of the $15,000 she would give you in 30 years.

The present value of some future payment depends on three things. First, it depends on the size of the payment itself. The bigger the future payment, the greater its present value. Second, the present value depends on how long a period will elapse before the payment is made. The present value, at an interest rate of 10 percent, of $15,000 in 30 years is $859.63. But that same sum, if paid in 20 years, has a present value of $2,229.65. And if paid in 10 years, its present value is more than twice as great: $5,783.15. The longer the time period before a payment is to be made, the lower its present value. Finally, present values depend on interest rates. The present value of a payment of $15,000 to be made in 20 years is $2,229.65 if the interest rate is 10 percent; it rises to $5,653.34 at an interest rate of 5 percent. The lower the interest rate, the higher the present value of a future payment. Exhibit 10-1 gives present values of a payment of $15,000 at various interest rates and for various time periods.

EXHIBIT 10-1

Time, Interest Rates, and Present Value

The higher the interest rate and the longer the time until the payment is made, the lower the present value of a future payment. The table shows the present value of a future payment of $15,000 under different conditions. The present value of $15,000 to be paid in 5 years is $11,752.89 if the interest rate is 5 percent. Its present value is just $391.26 if it is to be paid in 20 years and the interest rate is 20 percent.

Present Value of $15,000

	Time until payment			
Interest rate (%)	5 years	10 years	15 years	20 years
5	$11,752.89	$9,208.70	$7,215.26	$5,653.34
10	9,313.82	5,783.15	3,590.88	2,229.65
15	7,457.65	3,707.77	1,843.42	916.50
20	6,028.16	2,422.58	973.58	391.26

The concept of present value can also be applied to a series of future payments. Suppose you've been promised $1,000 at the end of each of the next 5 years. Because each payment will occur at a different time, we calculate the present value of the series of payments by taking the value of each payment separately. At an interest rate of 10 percent, the present value P_0 is

$$P_0 = \frac{\$1{,}000}{1.10} + \frac{\$1{,}000}{1.10^2} + \frac{\$1{,}000}{1.10^3} + \frac{\$1{,}000}{1.10^4} + \frac{\$1{,}000}{1.10^5} = \$3{,}790.78$$

Interest rates can thus be used to compare the values of payments that will occur at different times. Choices concerning capital and natural resources require such comparisons, so you'll find applications of the concept of present value throughout this chapter. The next section examines the role interest rates play in saving.

Interest Rates and Saving

Just as interest rates link the values of payments at different times, they link the consequences of choices in the timing of consumption. In our examination of consumption choices in Chapter 6, consumers ignored the future. Their consumption choices in a particular period were constrained by their incomes in that period—they neither saved nor borrowed. Now that we've added interest rates to our arsenal, we can extend the analysis of consumption choices to choices across many periods.

Saving is income not spent on consumption.

Dissaving is negative saving; it occurs when consumption during a period exceeds income during the period.

Consumption, Saving, and Income

In examining consumption choices across time, economists think of consumers as having an expected stream of income over their lifetimes. It is that expected income that defines their consumption possibilities. The problem for consumers is to determine when to consume this income. They can spend less of their projected income now and thus have more available in the future. Alternatively, they can boost their current spending by borrowing against their future income.

Saving is income not spent on consumption. If Y_t and C_t equal a consumer's income and consumption during a particular period, respectively, then saving during that period, S_t, equals $Y_t - C_t$ (we shall ignore taxes in this analysis). **Dissaving** occurs when consumption exceeds income during a period. A consumer is dissaving if C_t is greater than Y_t; saving is negative. Dissaving can be financed either by borrowing or by using past savings. Many people, for example, save in preparation for retirement and then dissave during their retirement years.

Saving adds to a household's wealth. Dissaving reduces it. Indeed, a household's wealth is the sum of all past saving less all past dissaving.

Saving plays an important role in the theory of capital. If an economy is to increase its stock of capital, it must devote more of its resources to the production of capital goods and less to the production of consumption goods. That requires consumers to devote less of their income to consumption—they must increase their saving.

We can think of saving as a choice to postpone consumption. Because interest rates are a premium paid to people who postpone their use of wealth, interest rates are a kind of reward paid to savers. Will higher interest rates encourage the behavior they reward? The answer is a resounding maybe. Just as higher wages might not increase the quantity of labor supplied, higher interest rates might not increase saving. The problem, once again, lies in the fact that the income and substitution effects of a change in interest rates will pull in opposite directions.

Income and Substitution Effects

Consider a hypothetical consumer, Elaine Bouvier. Let us simplify the analysis of Ms. Bouvier's choices concerning the timing of consumption by assuming that there are only two periods: the present period is period 0, and the next is period 1. Suppose the interest rate is 8 percent and her income in both periods is expected to be $30,000.

Ms. Bouvier could, of course, spend $30,000 in period 0 and $30,000 in period 1. In that case, her saving equals zero in both periods. But she has alternatives. She could, for example, spend more than $30,000 in period 0 by borrowing against her income for period 1. Alternatively, she could spend less than $30,000 in period 0 and use her saving—and the interest she earns on that saving—to boost her consumption in period 1. If, for example, she spends $20,000 in period 0, her saving in period 0 equals $10,000. She'll earn $800 interest on that saving, so she'll have $40,800 to spend in the next period.

For each $1, Ms. Bouvier saves in period 0, she'll have $1.08 in period 1. To put it another way, for each $1 she spends in period 0, she won't have $1.08 in period 1. More generally, the price of $1 spent on consumption in one period is equal to $1 plus the market rate of interest in the next period.

Suppose the interest rate rises to 10 percent. Now Ms. Bouvier gives up $1.10 in consumption in period 1 for every $1 she spends in period 0—the increase in the interest rate has boosted the price of current consumption. A higher price produces a substitution effect that reduces an activity—Ms. Bouvier will spend less in the current period due to the substitution effect. The substitution effect of a higher interest rate thus boosts saving. But the higher interest rate also means that she earns more income on her saving. Consumption in the current period is a normal good, so an increase in income can be expected to increase current consumption. But an increase in current consumption implies a reduction in saving. The income effect of a higher interest rate thus tends to reduce saving. Whether Ms. Bouvier's saving will rise or fall depends on the relative strengths of the substitution and income effects.

To see how an increase in interest rates might reduce saving, imagine that Ms. Bouvier has decided that her goal is to have $40,800 to spend in period 1. At an interest rate of 8 percent, she achieves that goal by saving $10,000 in period 0. At an interest rate of 10 percent, she could achieve her goal with less saving. Let x equal the amount she saves in period 0; in period 1 she wants to have an additional $10,800 to use for consumption. We can thus solve for x:

$$x(1 + 0.10) = \$10,800$$
$$x = \$9,818.18$$

She can thus reduce her saving and still achieve her goal of having $40,800 to spend in the next period. The increase in the interest rate has reduced her saving.

Because changes in interest rates produce substitution and income effects that pull saving in opposite directions, we can't be sure what will happen to saving if interest rates change. There have been times when higher interest rates have appeared to increase saving and times when they appear to have reduced it.

Checklist

- People generally prefer to receive money now rather than to wait and receive it later.
- Interest is a payment made to people who agree to postpone their use of wealth.
- We compute the present value, P_0, of a sum to be received in n years, P_n, as $P_0 = P_n/(1 + r)^n$.
- The present value of a future payment will be greater the larger the payment, the sooner it is due, and the lower the rate of interest.
- The substitution and income effects of a change in interest rates pull saving in opposite directions, so there is no clear relationship between interest rates and the level of saving.

The Bond Market and Interest Rate Determination

When we read that interest rates shoot up on news of trouble in the Middle East or fall after government forecasters predict a slowing in economic growth, we're reading about the interaction of demand and supply in a global marketplace in which money is borrowed and lent. This section examines the operation of the market for bonds, an important market in which interest rates are determined.

When corporations, government agencies, or other organizations wish to borrow large sums of money, they often issue bonds. Your college or university may have issued a bond to finance a construction project. When the expenditures of the U.S. government exceed its revenues, it makes up the difference by selling bonds.

A **bond** is a promise to pay back a certain amount of money at a certain time. It's an IOU. The market for bonds is an enormously important one; it's essential to have a solid understanding of how it works.

Bond Basics

Two key characteristics of a bond are its face value and its maturity date. The **face value** is the sum the issuer promises to pay the holder of the bond when the bond matures. The **maturity date** is the date on which the face value must be paid.

Suppose Mega Corporation decides to build a new manufacturing plant; the cost of the plant is expected to be $25 million. Suppose it finances the project by

MEGA CORP. BOND

$10,000

Payable one year from date of issue

EXHIBIT 10-2

Mega Corporation's One-Year, $10,000 Bond

A bond always includes the face value and the maturity date. This bond matures in one year and has a face value of $10,000.

issuing bonds of the type shown in Exhibit 10-2. The face value of this bond is $10,000; its maturity date is 1 year from the date on which it is issued.

Most corporate bonds are issued for periods much longer than a year. Longer-term bonds typically feature a **coupon rate,** which specifies the percentage of the face value that will be paid periodically to the holder of the bond. Suppose, for example, that Mega issues a 20-year $10,000 bond with a 6 percent annual coupon rate. This bond promises to pay the holder $600 per year (6 percent of $10,000) for 20 years, with the $10,000 face value being paid at the end of the 20-year period. A bond that doesn't carry a coupon rate, and thus pays only the face value when it matures, is called a **zero-coupon bond.**

Whether a bond carries a coupon or not, whatever the period until it matures, and whatever the face value of the bond may be, its issuer will attempt to sell the bond at the highest possible price. Buyers of bonds will seek the lowest prices they can obtain. Newly issued bonds are generally sold in auctions. Potential buyers bid for the bonds, which are sold to the highest bidders. If Mega Corporation has 2,700 bonds to sell, they will go to the buyers who offer the best prices.

Bond Prices and Interest Rates

We already learned how to compute the present value of a future payment, given the interest rate. The face value of a zero-coupon bond gives us the future payment P_n; the price paid for the bond gives us its present value P_0. We know that the relationship between the future payment and present value is given by Equation 4:

$$P_0 = \frac{P_n}{(1 + r)^n}$$

We can solve this equation for r by first multiplying both sides by $(1 + r)^n$ and then rearranging terms:

$$P_0(1 + r)^n = P_n$$

$$(1 + r)^n = \frac{P_n}{P_0}$$

Raising both sides to the power $1/n$, we have

$$1 + r = \left(\frac{P_n}{P_0}\right)^{1/n}$$

We subtract 1 from both sides to obtain Equation 5, which expresses the interest rate as a function of the face value of the bond (P_n), the price of the bond (P_0), and the number of years until the bond matures (n):

$$r = \left(\frac{P_n}{P_0}\right)^{1/n} - 1 \qquad (5)$$

Equation 5 tells us that the interest rate on a bond will be higher the lower is its price. Consider, for example, the relationship between the price at which Mega Corporation's 1-year ($n = 1$), $10,000 zero-coupon bonds sell and their interest rate. At a price of $9,000, we have

$$r = \frac{\$10{,}000}{\$9{,}000} - 1 = 0.111 = 11.1\%$$

- A **bond** is a promise to pay back a certain amount of money at a certain time.
- The **face value** of a bond is the sum the issuer promises to pay when the bond matures.
- The **maturity date** of a bond is the date on which the issuer promises to pay the face value.
- A **coupon rate** is a percentage of the face value of a bond that will be paid periodically to its owner.
- A **zero-coupon bond** is a bond that does not carry a coupon rate.

If the bonds sell at a lower price, say $8,000, we have

$$r = \frac{\$10,000}{\$8,000} - 1 = 0.25 = 25\%$$

The relationship between bond prices and interest rates is equivalent to the relationship we established in the previous section between interest rates and present value: the higher the interest rate, the lower the present value. Because the price paid for a bond *is* its present value, it follows that a lower bond price implies a higher interest rate.

For bonds with a given face value and maturity date, it is their price that determines their interest rates. Higher prices for bonds mean lower interest rates; lower bond prices mean higher interest rates. The explanation of interest rates thus lies in the explanation of bond prices. We shall see in the next section how bond prices are determined by demand and supply.

Demand and Supply in the Market for Bonds

Once a bond has been issued, it may change hands many times before it matures. If you buy Mega Corporation's bond on the day it's issued, you can sell it at any time up to its maturity date. In fact, it could be bought and sold any number of times before that date. Whoever owns the bond when it matures receives the $10,000.

Bonds are traded in the bond market, an international marketplace in which bonds are always being bought and sold. Bond transactions are typically recorded on computer networks, so traders know instantly the prices at which bonds are being traded all over the world. It's a huge market; more than $100 billion worth of U.S. government bonds alone are traded every day.

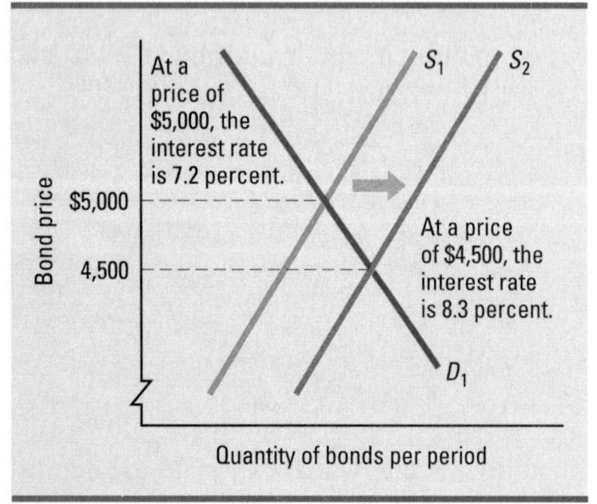

EXHIBIT 10-3

Demand and Supply for Bonds

Consider 10-year zero-coupon bonds with a face value of $10,000. The price of bonds is determined by the intersection of demand and supply. Here, the initial price of bonds is $5,000. An increase in supply to S_2 lowers the price to $4,500. That raises the interest rate on these bonds from 7.2 to 8.3 percent.

The Determination of Bond Prices

To simplify our analysis of the bond market, let us assume that all bonds, regardless of the issuer, are identical. They all carry the same face value, coupon rate, and maturity date. In particular, let us assume that all bonds are 10-year zero-coupon bonds with a face value of $10,000.

Exhibit 10-3 shows how bond prices are determined. The demand curve and supply curve intersect at a price of $5,000. Using Equation 5, we find that this price implies an interest rate of 7.2 percent.

Bonds are supplied initially by firms, governments, and other institutions that wish to borrow money. A higher price for bonds means that these institutions will raise more money for the obligations they issue. To put it another way, a higher price reduces the cost to these institutions of borrowing money—which is likely to increase the amount they'll want to borrow. It is thus plausible that the supply curve for bonds should be upward sloping.

We know that the holders of bonds may sell them at any time. The higher the price, the greater the proceeds from the sale of a bond and the greater the likelihood that holders of bonds will sell them. Higher prices are thus likely to induce a greater quantity supplied of both newly issued and previously issued bonds.

Bonds may be purchased by individuals, firms, government agencies, or other institutions. A family saving money for college educations might buy bonds that mature when the college expenses are expected to come due. A local government that has a surplus in its budget may buy bonds in order to earn extra revenue from the funds. A corporation's pension fund may buy bonds in order to earn more money to meet future retirement expenses. The lower the price of a bond, the greater the interest return from holding it. We therefore expect that the quantity of bonds demanded will be greater when their price is lower.

A change in bond prices changes the wealth of bond owners. Indeed, some purchasers buy bonds in anticipation that bond prices will rise, thus producing a gain in wealth. Another reason the demand curve for bonds slopes downward in Exhibit 10-3 is that many people expect that lower prices are more likely to rise than to fall. Similarly, another reason the supply curve slopes upward is that higher prices may cause many bond owners to anticipate a fall in prices.

When the supply of bonds increases (perhaps because the federal government increases its borrowing and thus sells more bonds or because corporations are raising more money to finance acquisitions of capital), the supply curve for bonds shifts to the right. A shift to S_2, for example, reduces the price to $4,500. The interest rate thus rises to 8.3 percent.

Checklist

- A bond is a promise by the issuer to pay the face value to the holder when the bond matures. Interest rates in the economy are determined in the bond market.
- Bonds have different face values and maturity dates. Some bonds carry periodic payments based on the coupon rate.
- For all bonds, the interest return is determined by the relationship between the price of the bond, its face value, and its coupon rate.
- Bond prices are determined by the intersection of the demand and supply curves for bonds. An increase in the demand or a reduction in the supply will increase bond prices and lower interest rates. A reduction in demand or an increase in supply will lower bond prices and increase interest rates.

Interest Rates and Capital

The quantity of capital firms employ in their production of goods and services has enormously important implications for economic activity and for the standard of living people in the economy enjoy. Increases in capital increase the marginal product of labor and boost wages at the same time they boost total output. An increase in the stock of capital therefore tends to raise incomes and improve the standard of living in the economy.

Capital is often a fixed factor of production in the short run. A firm can quickly add a new computer or a new fax machine, but it can't quickly retool an assembly line or add a new office building. Determining the quantity of capital a firm will use is likely to involve long-run choices.

The Demand for Capital

A firm uses additional units of a factor until marginal revenue product equals marginal factor cost. Capital is no different, save for the fact that the revenues and costs it generates are distributed over time. As the first step in assessing a firm's demand for capital, then, we determine the present value of marginal revenue products and marginal factor costs.

Capital and Net Present Value

Suppose Carol Stein is considering the purchase of a new $95,000 tractor for her farm. Ms. Stein expects to use the tractor for 5 years and then sell it; she expects that it will sell for $20,000 at the end of the 5-year period. She has the $95,000 on hand now; her alternative to purchasing the tractor is to purchase a 5-year bond yielding 7 percent annual interest.

Ms. Stein expects that the tractor will bring in additional revenue of $40,000 but will cost $20,000 per year to operate, for a net revenue of $20,000 annually. For simplicity, we shall suppose that this net revenue accrues at the end of each year.

The **net present value (NPV)** of an asset equals the present value of the revenues minus the present value of the costs associated with the asset.

Investment is an addition to capital stock.

Should she buy the tractor? We can answer this question by computing the tractor's **net present value (NPV),** which is equal to the present value of all the revenues minus the present value of all the costs associated with it. We thus measure the difference between the present value of marginal revenue products and the present value of marginal factor costs. If NPV is greater than zero, purchase of the asset will increase the profitability of the firm. A negative NPV implies that the funds for the asset would yield a higher return if used to purchase a bond. A firm will maximize profits by acquiring additional capital up to the point that the present value of capital's marginal revenue product equals the present value of marginal factor cost.

If the revenues generated by an asset in period t equal R_t and the costs in period t equal C_t, then the net present value NPV_0 of an asset expected to last for n years is

$$NPV_0 = R_0 - C_0 + \frac{R_1 - C_1}{1 + r} + \cdots + \frac{R_n - C_n}{(1 + r)^n} \quad \textbf{(6)}$$

To purchase the tractor, Ms. Stein pays \$95,000. She will receive revenues of \$40,000 per year, less the operating cost of \$20,000, plus the \$20,000 she expects to get by selling the tractor at the end of 5 years. The net present value of the tractor, NPV_0, is thus given by

$$NPV_0 = -\$95{,}000 + \frac{\$20{,}000}{1.07} + \frac{\$20{,}000}{1.07^2} + \frac{\$20{,}000}{1.07^3} + \frac{\$20{,}000}{1.07^4} + \frac{\$40{,}000}{1.07^5} = \$1{,}264$$

Given the cost of the tractor, the returns Ms. Stein projects, and an interest rate of 7 percent, Ms. Stein will increase her profits by purchasing the tractor. The tractor will yield a return whose present value is \$1,264 greater than the return that could be obtained by purchasing a bond.

Ms. Stein's acquisition of the tractor is called investment. Economists define **investment** as an addition to capital stock. Any acquisition of new capital goods therefore qualifies as investment.

The Demand Curve for Capital

Our analysis of Carol Stein's decision whether to purchase a new tractor suggests the forces at work in determining the economy's demand for capital. In deciding to purchase the tractor, Ms. Stein evaluated the price she would have to pay to obtain the tractor, the costs of operating it, the marginal revenue product she would receive by owning it, and the price she could get by selling the tractor when she expects to be done with it. Notice that with the exception of the purchase price of the tractor, *all* those figures were projections. Her decision to purchase the tractor depends almost entirely on the costs and benefits she *expects* will be associated with its use.

Finally, Ms. Stein converted all those figures to an NPV based on the interest rate prevailing at the time she made her choice. A positive NPV means that her profits will be increased by purchasing the tractor. That result, of course, depends on the prevailing interest rate. At an interest rate of 7 percent, the NPV is positive. At an interest rate of 8 percent, the NPV would be negative. At that interest rate, Ms. Stein would do better to purchase the bond.

Case in Point: The Net Present Value of an MBA

An investment in human capital differs little from an investment in capital—one acquires an asset that will produce additional income over the life of the asset. One's education produces—or it can be expected to produce—additional income over one's working career.

Ronald Yeaple, a professor at the University of Rochester business school, has estimated the net present value (NPV) of an MBA obtained from each of 20 top business schools. The costs of attending each school include tuition and forgone income. To estimate the marginal revenue products of a degree, Mr. Yeaple started with survey data showing what graduates of each school were earning 5 years after obtaining their MBAs. He then estimated what students with the savvy to attend those schools would have been earning without an MBA. The estimated marginal revenue product for each year is the difference between the salary students earned with a degree versus what they would have earned without it. The NPV is then computed using Equation 6.

The estimates given here show the NPV of an MBA over the first 7 years of work after receiving the degree. They suggest that an MBA from 15 of the schools ranked is a good investment—but that a degree at the other schools might not be. Mr. Yeaple says that extending income projections beyond 7 years wouldn't significantly affect the analysis, because present values of projected income differentials with and without an MBA become very small.

	Net Present Value, First 7 Years of Work
Harvard	$148,378
Chicago	106.847
Stanford	97,462
MIT	85,736
Yale	83,775
Wharton	59,486
UCLA	55,088
Berkeley	54,101
Northwestern	53,562
Cornell	30,874
Virginia	30,046
Dartmouth	22,509
Michigan	21,502
Carnegie-Mellon	18,679
Texas	17,459
Rochester	− 307
Indiana	− 3,315
NYU	− 3,749
North Carolina	− 4,565
Duke	− 17,631

Source: "The MBA Cost-Benefit Analysis," *The Economist* (Aug. 6 1994): 58.

At any one time, millions of choices like that of Ms. Stein concerning the acquisition of capital will be under consideration. Each decision will hinge on the price of a particular piece of capital, the expected cost of its use, its expected marginal revenue product, its expected scrap value, and the interest rate. Firms will not only be considering the acquisition of new capital; they will be considering retaining existing capital as well. Ms. Stein, for example, may have other tractors. Should she continue to use them, or should she sell them? If she keeps them, she'll experience a stream of revenues and costs over the next several periods; if she sells them, she'll have money now that she could use for something else. To decide whether a firm should keep the capital it already has, we need an estimate of the NPV of each unit of capital. Such decisions are always affected by the interest rate. At higher rates of interest, it makes sense to sell some capital rather than hold it. At lower rates of interest, the NPV of holding capital will rise.

Depreciation is a reduction in the value of capital due to wearing out or to the passage of time.

Net investment equals investment minus depreciation during a particular period.

The **demand curve for capital** shows the quantity of capital firms intend to hold at each interest rate.

A firm's stock of capital is always declining due to **depreciation,** which is a reduction in the value of capital due to wearing out or to the passage of time. A tractor, for example, depreciates with use and with time—that's why Ms. Stein expects to sell her tractor at the end of 5 years for a price much lower than the price she must pay to buy it. Just as investment adds to the stock of capital, depreciation reduces it. **Net investment** equals investment minus depreciation; it is the amount by which the capital stock changes from one period to another.

Firms can, to a degree, control the rate of depreciation by devoting additional resources to the maintenance of capital. That's another choice that is affected by the interest rate. Efforts to maintain the existing stock of capital will have a greater NPV at low interest rates than at high interest rates. Just as a higher interest rate could induce a firm to reduce its capital by selling some of it, so a higher interest rate can induce a firm to reduce capital by allowing it to depreciate more rapidly.

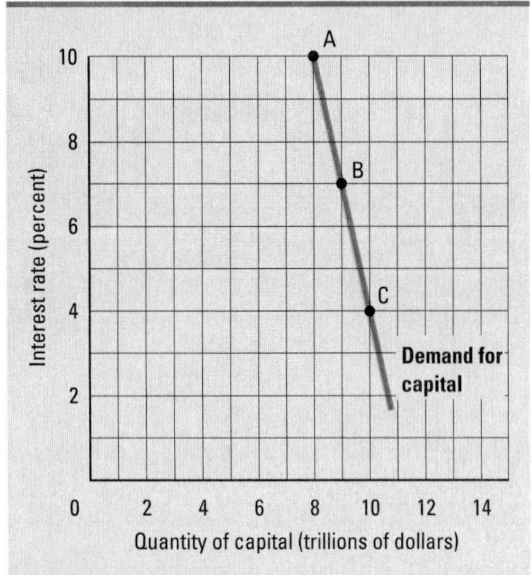

EXHIBIT 10-4

The Demand Curve for Capital

The quantity of capital firms will want to hold depends on the interest rate. The higher the interest rate, the less capital firms demand. Here, firms demand a capital stock of $8 trillion at an interest rate of 10 percent (point A), $9 trillion at 7 percent (point B), and $10 trillion at 4 percent (point C).

Because firms' choices to acquire new capital and to hold existing capital depend on the interest rate, the **demand curve for capital** in Exhibit 10-4, which shows the quantity of capital firms intend to hold at each interest rate, is downward sloping. At point A, we see that at an interest rate of 10 percent, $8 trillion worth of capital is demanded in the economy. At point B, a reduction in the interest rate to 7 percent increases the quantity of capital demanded to $9 trillion. At point C, at an interest rate of 4 percent, the quantity of capital demanded is $10 trillion. A reduction in the interest rate increases the quantity of capital demanded.

The demand curve for capital for the economy is found by summing the demand curves of all holders of capital. Ms. Stein's demand curve, for example, might show that at an interest rate of 8 percent, she'll demand the capital she already has—suppose it's $600,000 worth of equipment. If the interest rate drops to 7 percent, she'll add the tractor; the quantity of capital she demands rises to $695,000. At interest rates greater than 8 percent, she might decide to reduce her maintenance efforts for some of the capital she already has; the quantity of capital she demands would fall below $600,000. As with the demand for capital in the economy, we can expect individual firms to demand a smaller quantity of capital when the interest rate is higher.

Changes in the interest rate do not immediately produce changes in the actual quantity of capital. Suppose, for example, that the interest rate is 7 percent and firms have a capital stock of $9 trillion (point B in Exhibit 10-4). A reduction in the interest rate to 4 percent increases the quantity of capital firms demand to $10 trillion. Firms expand their investment to reach this goal, and net investment becomes positive, but the new capital won't appear instantly. Some time will elapse before the new equilibrium at point C is achieved. Similarly, if firms are at point B and the interest rate rises to 10 percent, the quantity of capital demanded will fall to $8 trillion at point A. But $1 trillion in capital won't suddenly disappear. Firms with more capital than they wish to hold will cut back their maintenance efforts and will certainly stop buying new capital. Net investment is likely to become negative until the capital stock falls to the desired level of $8 trillion.

Shifts in the Demand for Capital

Why might the demand for capital change? Because the demand for capital reflects the marginal revenue product of capital, anything that changes the marginal revenue product of capital will shift the demand for capital. Our search for demand shifters must thus focus on factors that change the marginal product of capital, the prices of the goods capital produces, and the costs of acquiring and holding capital. Let's discuss some factors that could affect these variables and thus shift the demand for capital.

Expectations. Choices concerning capital are always based on expectations. NPV is computed from the expected revenues and costs over the expected life of an asset. If firms' expectations change, their demand for capital will change. If something causes firms to revise their sales expectations upward, it is likely to increase their demand for capital. Similarly, an event that dampens firms' expectations is likely to reduce their demand for capital.

Technological Change. Technological changes can boost the marginal product of capital and thus boost the demand for capital. The discovery of new ways to integrate computers into production processes, for example, has dramatically increased the demand for capital in the last few years. Many universities are adding new classroom buildings or renovating old ones so they can better use computers in instruction, and businesses use computers in nearly every facet of operations.

Changing Demand for Goods and Services. Ultimately, the source of demand for factors of production is the demand for the goods and services produced by those factors. As population and incomes expand, we can expect more demand for goods and services, and this will boost the demand for capital.

Changes in Relative Factor Prices. Firms achieve the greatest possible output for a given total cost by operating where the ratios of marginal product to factor price are equal for all factors of production. For a firm that uses capital and labor, for example, this requires that $MP_L/P_L = MP_K/P_K$. Suppose these equalities hold and the price of labor rises. The ratio of the marginal product of labor to its price goes down, and the firm substitutes capital for labor.

Similarly, an increase in the price of capital goods would, ceteris paribus, cause firms to substitute other factors of production for capital. The demand for capital would, therefore, fall.

Capital and the Bond Market

If the quantity of capital demanded varies inversely with the interest rate, and if the interest rate is determined in the bond market, then it follows that the capital and bond markets are interrelated. Because the acquisition of new capital is generally financed by issuing bonds, a change in the demand for capital leads to a change in the supply of bonds—and that affects the interest rate. A change in the interest rate, in turn, affects the quantity of capital demanded on any demand curve.

The relationship between the demand for capital and the bond market thus goes both ways. Changes in the demand for capital affect the bond market, and changes in the bond market can affect the quantity of capital demanded.

Changes in the Demand for Capital and the Bond Market

When a firm decides to expand its capital stock, it can finance its purchase of capital in several ways. It may already have the funds on hand. It may borrow the money for the capital from a bank. Still another way for firms to raise money is to sell shares of stock or to sell bonds. When a firm sells stock, it is selling shares in the ownership of the firm. When it sells bonds, of course, it accepts a liability—it must make payments on the bonds as they come due.

We shall focus on the relationship between the bond market and firms' demand for capital. Because banks can always purchase bonds rather than making loans, the interest rates at which firms can borrow is influenced by the bond market. We shall see later in this chapter that the prices at which firms can sell their stock are also influenced by the bond market. Firms make much greater use of the bond market than the stock market to raise funds.

Exhibit 10-5 suggests how an increased demand for capital by firms will affect the bond market, and thus the quantity of capital firms will demand. In Panel (a) the initial price for bonds is P_1. This price implies an interest rate of r_1 in Panel (b), at which K_1 units of capital are demanded (on curve D_1). Now suppose an improvement in technology increases the marginal product of capital, shifting the demand curve for capital in Panel (b) to the right to D_2. Firms can be expected to finance the increased acquisition of capital by supplying additional bonds, shifting the supply curve for bonds to S_2 in Panel (a). The price of bonds drops to P_2. A lower price for bonds implies a higher interest rate r_2 in Panel (b). The final solution in the market for capital is thus a greater demand for capital and a higher interest rate; the new quantity of capital demanded is K_2 on demand curve D_2.

EXHIBIT 10-5

Bond and Capital Markets

The interest rate is determined in the bond market and the quantity of capital demanded varies with the interest rate, so events in the bond and capital markets are interrelated. If the demand for capital increases to D_2 in Panel (b), the supply of bonds is likely to increase as firms finance their acquisitions of capital by selling bonds. Panel (a) shows the result in the bond market, a shift in the supply curve for bonds to S_2 and a reduction in the price of bonds to P_2. That raises the interest rate to r_2, and the quantity of capital demanded will be K_2 on demand curve D_2 in Panel (b).

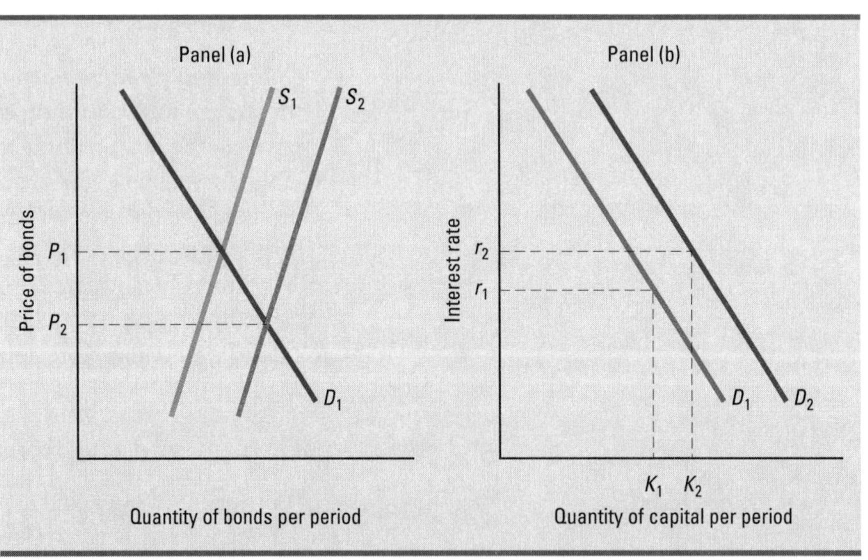

Bond Market Changes and the Demand for Capital

Events in the bond market can also affect the quantity of capital firms will hold. We've seen, for example, that government agencies borrow money by selling bonds; a change in government borrowing therefore implies a change in the supply of bonds. That will change bond prices and interest rates. It will, as a result, affect the quantity of capital demanded.

Suppose government agencies decide to increase their borrowing. They sell more bonds, shifting the supply curve for bonds in Panel (a) of Exhibit 10-6 to S_2. The price of bonds falls to P_2, raising the interest rate to r_2. If there is no change in the demand for capital, the quantity of capital firms demand falls to K_2 in Panel (b).

EXHIBIT 10-6

A Change in the Bond Market Affects the Capital Market

A change that begins in the bond market can affect the quantity of capital firms demand. Here, an increase in government borrowing raises the supply of bonds to S_2 in Panel (a). Assuming there is no change in the demand for capital, the quantity of capital demanded falls to K_2 in Panel (b).

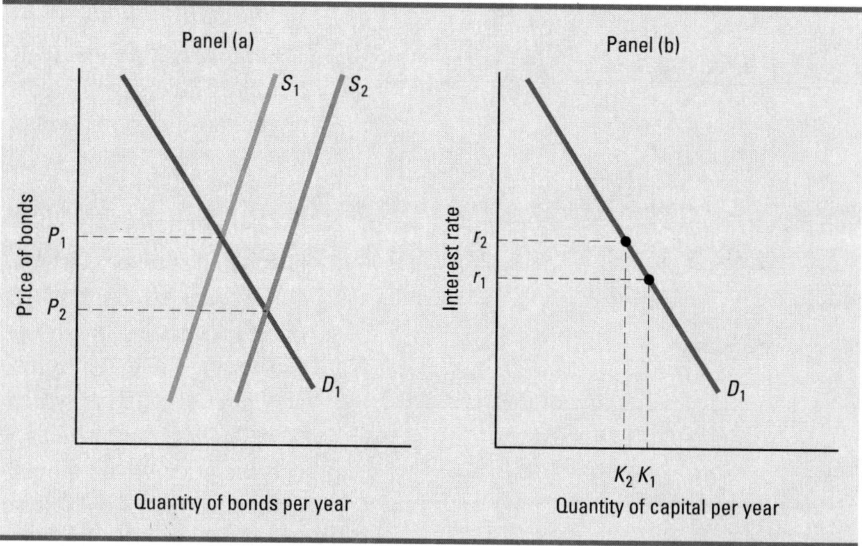

Our model of the market for capital thus assumes that the interest rate is determined in the bond market. Given the demand curve for capital, that interest rate then determines the quantity of capital firms demand.

The Ownership of Capital and the Stock Market

The circular flow model introduced in Chapter 9 suggests that capital, like other factors of production, is supplied by households to firms. Firms, in turn, pay income to those households for the use of their capital. Generally speaking, however, capital is actually owned by firms themselves. General Motors owns its assembly plants, and Wal-Mart owns its stores; these firms therefore own their capital. But the firms, in turn, are owned by people—and those people, of course, live in households. It is through their ownership of firms that households own capital.[1]

A firm may be owned by one individual (a sole proprietorship), by several individuals (a partnership), or by owners of shares in the firm (a corporation). Although most firms are sole proprietorships or partnerships, the bulk of the nation's total output is accomplished by corporations. Corporations own most of the capital stock as well. This section describes how the prices of shares of stock in corporations are determined. Ultimately, the same forces that determine the value of a firm's stock determine the value of a sole proprietorship or partnership.

Shares of stock are exchanged in the **stock market,** which is the set of institutions in which shares of stock are bought and sold. The New York Stock Exchange (NYSE) is one such institution. There are many others all over the world. Members of the NYSE buy and sell stocks on the floor of the exchange, on their own behalf and on behalf of clients and firms they represent. To purchase a share of stock, you place an order with a stockbroker who relays your order to one of the traders at the NYSE or at some other exchange.

The **stock market** is the set of institutions in which shares of stock are bought and sold.

[1] Some capital is owned by government agencies and by nonprofit institutions. In addition, owner-occupied homes are considered part of the capital stock. Our focus here is on the capital used by private firms.

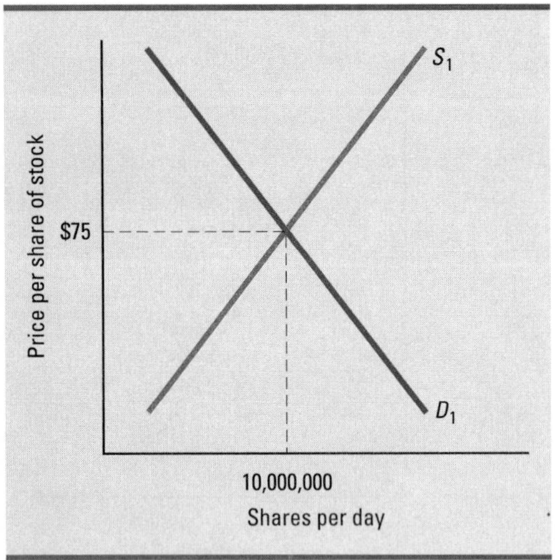

EXHIBIT 10-7

Demand and Supply in the Stock Market

The equilibrium price of stock shares in Intel Corporation is initially $75, determined by the intersection of demand and supply curves D_1 and S_1, at which 10 million shares trade each day.

Demand and Supply in the Stock Market

The process through which shares of stock are bought and sold can seem chaotic. Traders with orders from customers who want to buy stock shout out the prices those customers are willing to pay. Traders with orders from customers who want to sell shout out offers of prices at which their customers are willing to sell. If the price someone is willing to pay matches the price at which someone else is willing to sell, the trade is made. The most recent price at which a stock has traded is reported throughout the world.

Exhibit 10-7 applies the model of demand and supply to the determination of stock prices. Suppose the demand curve for shares of stock in Intel Corporation is given by D_1 and the supply by S_1 and that these curves intersect at a price of $75, at which 10 million shares are traded each day. If the price were higher, more shares would be offered for sale than would be demanded, and the price would quickly fall. If the price were lower, more shares would be demanded than would be supplied, and the price would quickly rise. In general, we can expect the price of shares of stock to move quickly to their equilibrium levels.

Demand, Supply, and Present Value

The intersection of the demand and supply curves for shares of stock in a particular company determines the equilibrium price for the stock. But what determines the demand and supply for shares of a company's stock? What forces might shift the curves? The concept of present value helps us answer these questions.

The owner of a share of a company's stock owns a share of the company. If a corporation has 10 shares outstanding and you own 1 of them, you own one-tenth of the company. You are, therefore, entitled to one-tenth of the profits. Because a share of stock gives its owner a share of a company's future profits, it follows that the expected level of future profits plays a role in determining the value of its stock.

Let's consider a highly simplified case. Corporation XYZ has 100,000 shares of stock outstanding and will earn $1.1 million in profit in 1 year, all of which will be distributed as dividends to stockholders. Dividends thus equal $11 per share. After a year, the firm will be sold and the proceeds of the sale will be distributed to the firm's creditors—stockholders will receive no further returns.

A share of XYZ stock will command a price equal to the present value of the $11 due in a year. At an interest rate of 10 percent, the present value is $10 (= $11/1.1). We can therefore expect the demand and supply curves for this stock to intersect at a price of $10.

The real world, of course, is not so simple. First, not all profits are returned to stockholders as dividends; some may be retained and reinvested in the firm. Such investments, however, are likely to increase the future profitability of a firm. It makes little difference whether stockholders are rewarded with dividends or with shares that have become more valuable because the firm is expected to be more profitable. A more important complication is that there is, in principle, no limit to a corporation's life. Rather than anticipating a single dividend payment, stockholders can anticipate a stream of such payments that continues indefinitely. Most important, the future profits of a firm cannot be known with certainty; investors can only predict what they might be.

Case in Point: A Stock Market in Election Outcomes

The 1992 presidential campaign was a tough one for public opinion polls to predict, as the strong third-party campaign of Ross Perot upset the usual relationships between opinion polls and election results. Surveys done the night before the election were quite wide of the mark in predicting the final vote—particularly the vote for Perot.

A group of college students, however, predicted the actual vote for all three candidates with astonishing accuracy, coming within 1 percentage point of the actual results. The students were participants in the Iowa Political Stock Market (IPSM), a market created by three University of Iowa economists to test ideas about the determination of stock prices—and to give students a chance to participate in a real market.

Participants in the market could invest as little as $5 or as much as $500. They bought and sold "stock" in each candidate. After the election, owners of stock received a payment equal to the final percentage of votes cast for each candidate. Bill Clinton, for example, won 43 percent of the total vote; 1 share of Clinton stock thus paid 43 cents. Participation in the market was open to anyone with $5 and access to a computer; most of the 1,002 participants were students at colleges all over the nation.

Ross Perot.

The market was conducted on the Internet. An investor willing to pay 40 cents per share for 3 shares of stock in candidate George Bush, for example, placed the order via computer. That order went into a queue with all the other orders to buy Bush stock, ranked according to price. Offers to sell Bush shares were handled the same way. Then buy and sell transactions were made. Suppose, for example, that 40 cents per share was the highest bid in the queue to buy Bush stock but 41 cents per share was the lowest price at which anyone was willing to sell. In that case, no sale would be made. The moment someone entered the market with an offer to sell at 40 cents, however, the trade would be completed.

Investors in the market had a financial incentive in predicting the outcome of the election accurately. If 1 share of Perot stock, for example, was selling at 15 cents and some participants were convinced he would get 18 percent of the vote, they'd be quick to bid his stock up. In effect, the market combined the wisdom of all participants. That combined wisdom proved more than a match for major opinion polls. The table below lists the market's forecast versus the forecasts issued by major opinion surveys conducted the night before the election.

		Forecast of Election (Percentages)			
	Actual	**IPSM**	**Harris**	***Los Angeles Times***	**Gallup**
Clinton	43	43	44	44	41
Bush	38	38	38	34	39
Perot	19	19	17	18	14

The IPSM offers markets in elections all over the world. Your instructor has the information necessary for you to participate. Even if you don't choose to invest, you can observe the buying and selling. All that's required is a computer with a modem and access to the Internet.

Source: Iowa Political Stock Market, University of Iowa.

Stock prices in the real world thus reflect the present value of profits projected into the future. The greater a firm's expected future profits, the greater the value of its stock. Stock prices will also reflect uncertainty. The more uncertain a firm's future prospects, the lower the value of its stock. Each individual is likely to have a different assessment of what a firm's profits are likely to be and how uncertain those profits are.

Look again at the demand and supply curves for Intel shares given in Exhibit 10-7. The downward slope of the demand curve suggests that at lower prices for the stock, more people calculate that the present value of the firm's earnings justifies the stock's purchase. The upward slope of the supply curve tells us that as the price of the stock rises, more people conclude that the firm's future earnings don't justify holding the stock and therefore sell it. At the equilibrium price, the number of shares supplied by people who think holding the stock no longer makes sense just balances the number of shares demanded by people who think it does.

The relationship between present value and the price of a stock suggests an important conclusion about the nature of stock prices. The equilibrium price of a share of stock in a company strikes a balance between those who think the stock is worth more and those who think it's worth less than the current price. It can thus be thought of as the market's best guess as to the present value of the company's future profits. A change in a company's expected profitability will therefore affect the value of its stock.

Because the value of shares depends on the present value of future profits, we can expect interest rates to affect stock prices. An increase in interest rates will, ceteris paribus, reduce the present value of future profits. Increases in interest rates therefore tend to reduce stock prices; reductions in interest rates tend to increase them.

Checklist ✓

- The demand curve for capital shows that firms demand a greater quantity of capital at lower interest rates.
- Among the forces that can shift the demand curve for capital are changes in technology, changes in the demands for goods and services, changes in relative factor prices, and changes in expectations.
- An increase in the demand for capital is likely to induce an increase in the supply of bonds. The new quantity of capital demanded will be on a new demand curve for capital at a higher interest rate.
- Events in the bond market can affect the quantity of capital demanded. With no change in the demand curve for capital, a change in the interest rate will change the quantity of capital demanded.
- Stock prices are determined by demand and supply. Among the determinants of demand and supply are a firm's expected profits and the interest rate.
- The price of a share of stock reflects the market's estimate of the present value of a company's future profitability.

Natural Resources and Conservation

Natural resources are the gifts of nature. They include everything from oil to fish in the sea to magnificent scenic vistas. The stock of a natural resource is the quantity of the resource with which the earth is endowed. For example, a certain amount of oil lies in the earth, a certain population of fish live in the sea, and a certain number of acres make up an area such as Yellowstone National Park. These stocks of natural resources, in turn, can be used to produce a flow of goods and services. Each year, we can extract a certain quantity of oil, harvest a certain quantity of fish, and enjoy a certain number of visits to Yellowstone.

As with capital, we examine the allocation of natural resources among alternative uses across time. By definition, natural resources cannot be produced. Our consumption of the services of natural resources in one period can affect their availability in future periods. We must thus consider the extent to which the expected needs of future generations should be taken into account when we allocate natural resources.

Natural resources often present problems of property rights in their allocation. We saw in Chapter 5 that a resource for which exclusive property rights have not been defined will be allocated as a common property resource. In such a case, we expect that the marketplace will not generate incentives to use the resource efficiently; natural resources that are common property may, in the absence of government intervention, be destroyed. In this chapter, we shall consider natural resources for which exclusive property rights have been defined. The public sector's role in the allocation of common property resources is investigated in Chapter 15.

We can distinguish two categories of natural resources, those that are renewable and those that are not. A **renewable natural resource** is one whose services can be used in one period without reducing the stock of the resource that will be available in subsequent periods. The fact that they *can* be used in such a manner does not mean that they will be; renewable natural resources can be depleted. Wilderness areas, land, and water are renewable natural resources. The consumption of the services of an **exhaustible natural resource,** on the other hand, necessarily reduces the stock of the resource. Oil and coal are exhaustible natural resources.

- A **renewable natural resource** is one whose services can be consumed without reducing the stock of the resource.
- An **exhaustible natural resource** is one for which consumption of its services necessarily reduces the stock of the resource.

Future Generations and Exhaustible Natural Resources

Owners of exhaustible natural resources can be expected to take the interests of future as well as current consumers into account in their extraction decisions. The greater the expected future demand for an exhaustible natural resource, the greater will be the quantity preserved for future use.

Hotelling's principle asserts that the expected price of an exhaustible natural resource will rise at a rate equal to the market rate of interest.

Expectations and Resource Extraction

Suppose you are the exclusive owner of a deposit of oil in Wyoming. You know that any oil you pump from this deposit and sell cannot be replaced.You are aware that this is true of all the world's oil; the consumption of oil inevitably reduces the stock of this resource.

If the quantity of oil in the earth is declining and the demand for this oil is increasing, then it's likely that the price of oil will rise in the future. Suppose you expect the price of oil to increase at an annual rate of 15 percent.

Given your expectation, should you pump some of your oil out of the ground and sell it? To answer that question, you need to know the interest rate. If the interest rate is 10 percent, then your best alternative is to leave your oil in the ground. With oil prices expected to rise 15 percent per year, the dollar value of your oil will increase faster if you leave it in the ground than if you pump it out, sell it, and purchase an interest-earning asset. If the market interest rate were greater than 15 percent, however, it would make sense to pump the oil and sell it now and to purchase an interest-bearing asset. The return from the asset would exceed the rate at which you expect the value of your oil to increase. Higher interest rates thus reduce the willingness of resource owners to preserve these resources for future use.

The supply for an exhaustible resource such as oil is thus governed by its current price, its expected future price, and the interest rate. An increase in the expected future price—or a reduction in the interest rate—reduces the supply of oil today, preserving more for future use. If owners of oil expect lower prices in the future, or if the interest rate rises, they will supply more oil today and conserve less for future use.

Exhibit 10-8 illustrates how expectations about future demand for an exhaustible resource affect current consumption. The current demand D for these services is given by their marginal revenue product *MRP.* Suppose MC_C measures the current marginal cost of extracting the resource. Current extraction reduces future stocks, so we can add to this marginal cost a sum reflecting the value of the resource to future consumers. Adding the present value of the value we expect future consumers to place on the resource gives us MC_T, which measures the total marginal cost of current consumption. The equilibrium quantity of the resource consumed is therefore Q, determined by the intersection of the demand and MC_T curves. If future demand for the resource is expected to rise, the present value of future demands increases and shifts MC_T to MC'_T, reducing current consumption to Q'.

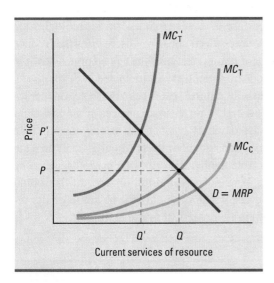

EXHIBIT 10-8

Future Generations and Exhaustible Resources

The current demand D for the services of an exhaustible resource is given by its marginal revenue product *(MRP).* While MC_C measures the current marginal cost of extraction, MC_T adds the present value of the cost to future consumers of a reduction in the stock of the resource. The efficient level of current consumption is thus at Q. An increase in expected demands increases this cost to MC'_T and reduces current consumption to Q'.

Hotelling's Principle and Resource Prices

Because owners of exhaustible natural resources take expected prices into account in their extraction choices, the expected price will rise over time. A hypothesis known as **Hotelling's principle**[2] predicts that the expected price of an

[2] Harold Hotelling, "Economics of Exhaustible Resources," *Journal of Political Economy* 39 (April 1931): 137–175.

exhaustible resource will rise at the market rate of interest. To see why, imagine what would happen if the price of a resource remained unchanged. Owners of the resource would increase current extraction, but that would lower the current price relative to the expected price. The current price would continue to fall until the price of the resource was expected to increase at the rate of interest. The market would be in equilibrium, and no further changes in current supply would occur.

Although Hotelling's principle suggests that exhaustible natural resources will become more expensive, over the past century actual prices of some exhaustible natural resources have fallen! Exhibit 10-9 shows the prices of four major natural resources over the past century. Prices have been adjusted for inflation to reflect the prices of these resources relative to other prices. If there is inflation, Hotelling's principle implies that the expected prices of exhaustible natural resources, corrected for inflation, will rise. The fact that actual prices of zinc and copper have been falling means not only that expectations about prices have been wrong but that they have been consistently wrong for the last century!

How could price expectations be so consistently wrong? In setting their expectations, people in the marketplace must anticipate not only future demand but future supply as well. Demand in future periods could fall short of expectations if new technologies produce goods and services using less of a natural resource. That has clearly happened. The quantity of energy—which is generally produced using exhaustible fossil fuels—used to produce a unit of output has fallen by more than half in the last two decades. Supply increases when previously unknown deposits of natural resources are discovered and when technologies are developed to extract and refine resources more cheaply. Discoveries that reduce the demand and increase the supply of natural resources can push prices down in a way that people in previous periods might not have anticipated.

Will we ever run out of exhaustible natural resources? Past experience, together with Hotelling's principle, suggests a provisional answer. If no new technologies or discoveries that reduce demand or increase supply occur, then resource prices will rise. As they rise, consumers of these resources will demand lower quantities of these resources. Eventually, the price of a particular resource could rise so high that the quantity demanded would fall to zero. At that point, no more of the resource would be used. There would still be some of the resource in the earth—it simply wouldn't be practical to use more of it.

EXHIBIT 10-9

Natural Resource Prices, 1890–1992

The chart shows changes in the prices of four exhaustible resources—oil, coal, copper, and zinc—from 1890 to 1992. Here, all prices have been adjusted for inflation; for example, if the inflation rate in a particular period is 5 percent and the price of a natural resource rises 6 percent, then the price increase recorded here is 1 percent. All prices have been converted to index numbers by setting them equal to 100 in 1890. We see that the inflation-adjusted prices of oil and coal are about the same as they were a century ago, while the prices of zinc and copper have fallen by about half.

Sources: Data on mineral prices from U.S. Bureau of the Census, *Historical Statistics of the United States: Colonial Times to the Present,* Part I (Washington, D.C.: U.S. Government Printing Office, 1975); U.S. Bureau of the Census, *Statistical Abstract of the United States,* various volumes; and Louis M. Irwin, *Economic Indicators of Mineral Scarcity: A Time Series Analysis of Mineral Prices* (Boulder: University of Colorado, 1989) (Master's Thesis). All price data are adjusted by the GDP deflator; values from 1890 to 1928 are from Robert J. Gordon, *Macroeconomics,* 6th edition (New York: Harper Collins 1993), table A-1; data from 1929 to 1992 are from U.S. Council of Economic Advisers, *Economic Report of the President 1995* (Washington, D.C.: U.S. Government Printing Office, 1995), table B-3.

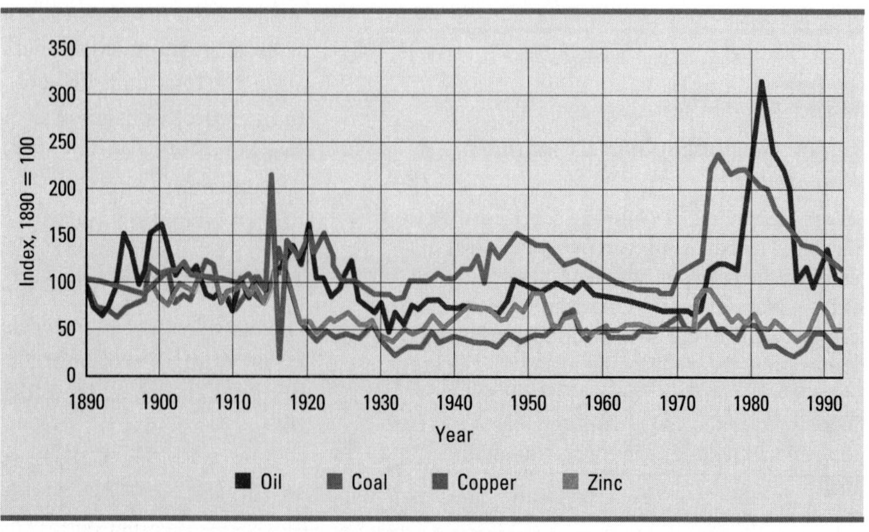

Case in Point The Doomsday Bet

Virtually everything we produce—and thus everything we consume—requires the use of some exhaustible natural resource. There's only so much oil, so much coal, so much copper, so much molybdenum—so much of any of a host of resources vital to economic activity. Our continued use of these resources must therefore mean that we're running out of them.

If our activities require natural resources, and if we inevitably have less and less of them, then it would seem that we must be headed for trouble. And trouble is just what many scientists think inevitably awaits us. An influential study, *Limits to Growth,* predicted in 1971 that, barring major discoveries or changes in policy, the earth was likely to run out of copper, gold, lead, mercury, natural gas, petroleum, silver, tin, and zinc by the end of the century. The authors of *Limits* argued that resource scarcity would make economic activity increasingly difficult and that even under the most optimistic assumptions, massive starvation and global depression would set in by the middle of the next century.

Economists, armed with a theoretical framework that suggests that rising prices of some factors will lead firms to make substitutions and to seek new technologies, have generally argued against the doomsday view. Indeed, the constant effort to cut current and expected costs by reducing resource use can reduce natural resource prices. The history of the last century suggests that factor substitution, technological change, and discoveries of additional resource deposits have combined to make resources *less* scarce.

Economist Julian Simon, impressed by the evidence that resources have become relatively less scarce over the past century, issued an open challenge to doomsayers in 1981. He told them to pick any ten exhaustible natural resources. If their average price, adjusted for inflation, rose over the next decade, Simon would pay $1,000. If their price fell, however, Mr. Simon would get the $1,000.

Only one of the doomsayers, biologist Paul Ehrlich of Stanford University, took Mr. Simon up on his offer. Mr. Ehrlich, the author of a 1968 book that argued resource scarcity would lead to the starvation of hundreds of millions of people by 1990, is one of the leading proponents of the view that humankind faces a grim future.

The average inflation-adjusted price of the ten resources Mr. Ehrlich chose fell during the 1980s—just as did the prices of exhaustible resources generally. Mr. Ehrlich paid the $1,000.

Source: Personal interviews with Paul Ehrlich and Julian Simon.

New technologies and the discovery of additional deposits of exhaustible resources tend to pull resource prices down. They prolong the life of natural resources and pull prices in a direction opposite to that predicted by Hotelling's principle. Over the last century, discoveries and new technologies have dominated in this tug-of-war, and resource prices have fallen.

Renewable Natural Resources

As is the case with exhaustible natural resources, our consumption of the services of renewable natural resources can affect future generations. Unlike exhaustible resources, however, renewable resources can be consumed in a way that does not diminish their stocks.

The **carrying capacity** of a resource is the quantity of its services that can be consumed in one period without reducing the stock of the resource in subsequent periods.

The quantity of a renewable natural resource that can be consumed in any period without reducing the stock of the resource available to the next period is its **carrying capacity.** Suppose, for example, that a school of 10 million fish increases by 1 million fish each year. The carrying capacity of the school is therefore 1 million fish per year—the harvest of 1 million fish each year will leave

Economic rent is the amount by which the current price of a resource exceeds the minimum price necessary to make the resource available.

the size of the population unchanged. Harvests that exceed a resource's carrying capacity reduce the stock of the resource; harvests that fall short of it increase that stock.

Just as is the case with exhaustible natural resources, future generations have a stake in current consumption of a renewable resource. Exhibit 10-10 shows the efficient level of consumption of such a resource. Suppose Q_{cap} is the carrying capacity of a particular resource and MC_C is the current marginal cost of utilizing the resource, including costs for the labor and capital required to make its services available. To adjust current marginal cost to reflect the value of the resource to future generations, we add a charge representing the present value of future consumption of the resource, just as we did for exhaustible resources in Exhibit 10-8. MC_T reflects the addition of such a charge; the efficient level of consumption in the current period is found at point E, at the intersection of the current period's demand and MC_T. Notice that in the case shown, current consumption at Q_E is less than the carrying capacity of the resource. A larger stock of this resource will be available in subsequent periods than is available now.

Now suppose interest rates increase. That reduces the present value of future demands on the resource and thus shifts MC_T down to MC'_T. The result is an increase in current consumption to Q'_E. Now consumption exceeds the carrying capacity, and the stock of the resource available to future generations will be reduced.

The model of Exhibit 10-10 applies as well in the case of a scenic resource. The carrying capacity of the resource is the maximum number of visits per period that do not reduce the quality of the resource. Incorporating future generations' benefits from the resource produces a total marginal cost curve that coincides with the current marginal cost curve up to the carrying capacity of the resource; it then rises above the current cost curve beyond that number of visits.

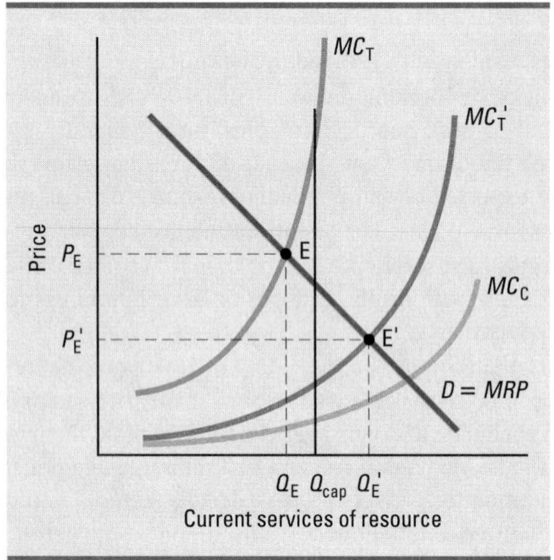

EXHIBIT 10-10

Future Generations and Renewable Resources

The efficient quantity of services to consume is determined by the intersection of the marginal cost curve MC_T and the demand curve D. It occurs at point E, at a quantity of Q_E. This lies below the carrying capacity of the resource, Q_{cap}. An increase in interest rates, however, reduces MC_T to MC'_T. The efficient level of current consumption rises to Q'_E, which now exceeds the carrying capacity of the resource.

Rent and the Market for Land

We turn finally to the case of land that is used solely for the space it affords for other activities—parks, buildings, golf courses, or whatever. We shall assume that the carrying capacity of such land equals its quantity.

The supply of land is a vertical line. No matter what happens to the price of land in a particular area, its quantity cannot change. Suppose, for example, that the price of a 1-acre parcel of land is zero. At that price, there is still 1 acre of land; quantity is unaffected by price. As the price rises, there is still only 1 acre in the parcel. That means that the price of the parcel exceeds the minimum price—zero—at which the land would be available. The amount by which any price exceeds the minimum price necessary to make a resource available is called **economic rent.** If our 1-acre parcel in Exhibit 10-11 commands a price P per acre, the entire amount is economic rent.

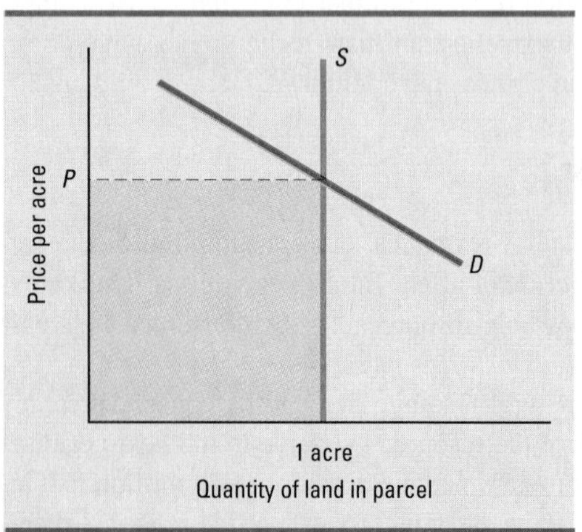

EXHIBIT 10-11

The Market for Land

The price of a parcel of land is determined by the intersection of a vertical supply curve and the demand for a parcel. The sum paid for the parcel, shown by the shaded area, is economic rent.

The demand for land by firms is determined by their expectations of the future marginal revenue product of any parcel. Because land ownership offers returns in the future, the price firms are willing to pay equals the NPV of future uses of the land. The highest bid will come from the buyer whose NPV is highest.

The rent land earns is affected by interest rates. When interest rates are high, the NPV of land is relatively low. As interest rates fall, the NPV rises.

Checklist

- The demand for the services of a natural resource in any period is given by the marginal revenue product of those services.
- Natural resources are either renewable or exhaustible.
- Owners of natural resources have an incentive to take expected future demands for them into account in making choices about resource supply; Hotelling's principle suggests that the expected price of an exhaustible natural resource will rise at the rate of interest.
- The services of a renewable natural resource may be consumed at levels that are below or greater than the carrying capacity of the resource.
- The payment for land (or any resource fixed in supply) is economic rent.

A Look Back—And a Look Ahead

Time is the complicating factor when we analyze capital and natural resources. Because current choices affect the future stocks of both resources, we must take those future consequences into account. And because a payment in the future is worth less than an equal payment today, we need to convert the dollar value of future consequences to present value.

Interest rates link the dollar consequences of events that occur at different times. We determine the present value of a future payment by dividing the amount of that payment by $(1 + r)^n$, *where r is the interest rate and n is the number of years until the payment will occur. The present value of a given future value is smaller at higher values of n and at higher interest rates.*

Interest rates reward those who postpone their use of money. Although interest rates are the reward for saving, higher interest rates may not boost saving. That's because the substitution and income effects of an increase in the interest rate pull saving in opposite directions.

Interest rates are determined in the bond market. The higher the price of bonds, the lower the interest rate. The lower the price of bonds, the higher the interest rate.

We assume that firms determine whether to acquire an additional unit of capital by examining the net present value (NPV) of the asset. When NPV equals zero, the present value of capital's marginal revenue product equals the present value of its marginal factor cost. The demand curve for capital shows the quantity of capital demanded at each interest rate. Among the factors that shift the demand curve for capital are changes in expectations, new technology, change in demands for goods and services, and change in relative factor prices.

Most of the capital owned by households is in the form of shares of stock in corporations. The prices of these shares represent the stock market's assessment of the present value of the issuing firms' profitability.

Markets for natural resources are distinguished according to whether the resources are renewable or exhaustible. Owners of natural resources have an incentive to consider future as well as present demands for these resources. Land, because it has a vertical supply curve, generates a return that consists entirely of rent.

In the next chapter, we shall extend our analysis of perfect competition to the international arena. We'll examine why international trade occurs and explore its impact on domestic economies.

Terms and Concepts for Review

Asset
Bond
Carrying capacity
Coupon rate
Demand curve for capital
Depreciation
Dissaving
Economic rent
Exhaustible natural resource
Face value (of a bond)
Hotelling's principle
Interest
Interest rate
Investment
Liability
Maturity date (of a bond)
Net investment
Net present value (NPV)
Present value
Renewable natural resource
Saving
Stock market
Wealth
Zero-coupon bond

For Discussion

1. The charging of interest rates is often viewed with contempt. Do interest rates serve any useful purpose?
2. How does an increase in interest rates affect the present value of a future payment?
3. Two payments of $1,000 are to be made one year from today and two years from today. Which has the greater present value? Why?
4. The Case in Point on the viatical settlements industry suggests that investors pay only 90 percent of the face value of a life insurance policy that's expected to be paid off in 6 months. Why? Wouldn't it be more fair if investors paid the full value?
5. How would each of the following events affect the demand curve for capital?
   a. A prospective cut in taxes imposed on business firms
   b. A reduction in the price of labor
   c. An improvement in technology that increases capital's marginal product
   d. An increase in interest rates
6. If developed and made practical, cold fusion technology would allow the production of virtually unlimited quantities of cheap, pollution-free energy, using a natural resource as ubiquitous as ocean water. Some scientists predict that the technology for cold fusion will be developed within the next few decades. How does the expectation that cold fusion will be developed affect the market for oil today?
7. Suppose interest rates rise. What will happen to the price of land?
8. Is the rent paid for an apartment economic rent? Explain.
9. Suppose you own a ranch out in the country, and that commercial and residential development start to take place around your ranch. How will this affect the value of your property? What will happen to the quantity of land? What kind of return will you earn?
10. Explain why higher interest rates tend to increase the current use of natural resources.

Problems

Use the tables on page 247 to answer problems 1–4. Table (a) gives the present value of $1 at the end of different time periods, given different interest rates. For example, at an interest rate of 10 percent, the present value of $1 to be paid in 20 years is $0.149. At 10 percent interest, the present value of $1,000 to be paid in 20 years equals $1,000 times $0.149, or $149, Table (b) gives the present value of a stream of payments of $1 to be made at the end of each period for a given number of periods. For example, at 10 percent interest, the present value of a series of $1 payments, made at the end of each year for the next 10 years, is $6.145. Using that same interest rate, the present value of a series of 10 payments of $1,000 each is $1,000 times $6.145, or $6,145.

1. Your Uncle Arthur, not to be outdone by Aunt Carmen, offers you a choice. You can have $10,000 now or $30,000 in 15 years. If you took the money now, you could put it in a bond fund earning 8 percent interest. Use present value analysis to determine which alternative is better.
2. Remember Carol Stein's tractor? We saw that at an interest rate of 7 percent, a decision to purchase the tractor would pay off; its net present value is positive. Suppose the tractor is still expected to yield $20,000 in net revenue per year for each of the next 5 years and to sell at the end of 5 years for $20,000; and the purchase price of the tractor still equals $95,000. Use Tables (a) and (b) to compute the net present value of the tractor at an interest rate of 8 percent.
3. Mabel Jones is thinking about going to college. If she goes, she'll earn nothing for the next 4 years and, in addition, will have to pay tuition and fees totaling $10,000 per year. She also wouldn't earn the $25,000 per year she could make by working full time during the next four years. After her four years of college, she expects that her income, both while working and in retirement, will be $20,000 per year more, over the next 50 years, than it would have been had she not attended college. Should she go to college? Assume that the interest rate is 6 percent

and that each payment for college and dollar of income earned occur at the end of the years in which they occur. Ignore possible income taxes in making your calculations.

4. A bond with a face value of $10,000 matures in 10 years and pays a coupon rate of 6 percent. You want to assure an 8 percent rate of return. How much would you offer for the bond? (*Hint:* You need to compute the present value of the future payments the bond offers.)

5. You own several barrels of wine; over the years, the value of this wine has risen at an average rate of 10 percent per year. It is expected to continue to rise in value, but at a slower and slower rate. Assuming your goal is to maximize your revenue from the wine, at what point will you sell it?

Table (a)

Present Value of $1 to Be Received at the End of a Given Number of Periods

	Percent									
Period	2%	4%	6%	8%	10%	12%	14%	16%	18%	20%
1	0.980	0.962	0.943	0.926	0.909	0.893	0.877	0.862	0.847	0.833
2	0.961	0.925	0.890	0.857	0.826	0.797	0.769	0.743	0.718	0.694
3	0.942	0.889	0.840	0.794	0.751	0.712	0.675	0.641	0.609	0.579
4	0.924	0.855	0.792	0.735	0.683	0.636	0.592	0.552	0.515	0.842
5	0.906	0.822	0.747	0.681	0.621	0.567	0.519	0.476	0.437	0.402
10	0.820	0.676	0.558	0.463	0.386	0.322	0.270	0.227	0.191	0.162
15	0.743	0.555	0.417	0.315	0.239	0.183	0.140	0.180	0.084	0.065
20	0.673	0.456	0.312	0.215	0.149	0.104	0.073	0.051	0.037	0.026
25	0.610	0.375	0.233	0.146	0.092	0.059	0.038	0.024	0.016	0.010
30	0.552	0.308	0.174	0.099	0.057	0.033	0.020	0.012	0.007	0.004
40	0.453	0.208	0.097	0.046	0.022	0.011	0.005	0.003	0.001	0.001
50	0.372	0.141	0.054	0.021	0.009	0.003	0.001	0.001	0	0

Table (b)

Present Value of $1 to Be Received at the End of Each Period for a Given Number of Periods

	Percent									
Period	2%	4%	6%	8%	10%	12%	14%	16%	18%	20%
1	0.980	0.962	0.943	0.926	0.909	0.893	0.877	0.862	0.847	0.833
2	1.942	1.886	1.833	1.783	1.736	1.690	1.647	1.605	1.566	1.528
3	2.884	2.775	2.673	2.577	2.487	2.402	2.322	2.246	2.174	2.106
4	3.808	3.630	3.465	3.312	3.170	3.037	2.322	2.246	2.174	2.106
5	4.713	4.452	4.212	3.993	3.791	3.605	3.433	3.274	3.127	2.991
10	8.983	8.111	7.360	6.710	6.145	5.650	5.216	4.833	4.494	4.192
15	12.849	11.118	9.712	8.559	7.606	6.811	6.142	5.575	5.092	4.675
20	16.351	13.590	11.470	9.818	8.514	7.469	6.623	5.929	5.353	4.870
25	19.523	15.622	12.783	10.675	9.077	7.843	6.873	6.097	5.467	4.948
30	22.396	17.292	13.765	11.258	9.427	8.055	7.003	6.177	5.517	4.979
40	27.355	19.793	15.046	11.925	9.779	8.244	7.105	6.233	5.548	4.997
50	31.424	21.482	15.762	12.233	9.915	8.304	7.133	6.246	5.554	4.999

11

Competitive Markets and International Trade

Chapter Objectives

After mastering the material in this chapter, you will be able to:

1. Understand why a country will choose to import many goods and services that it is capable of producing itself.
2. Explain how market prices guide an economy to a specific point on its production possibilities curve.
3. Recognize why economists argue that trade allows a higher level of consumption of goods and services worldwide than would be the case in the absence of trade.
4. Show the impact of tariffs and quotas on the equilibrium price and quantity of goods traded in perfectly competitive markets.
5. Evaluate the arguments presented by proponents of restrictions on trade and explain who are the winners and losers when an industry is protected from foreign competi-

It is impossible to move toward a market economy while the country is isolated from the world economy.

Nikolai Ryzhkov, Minister of Economic Affairs in the former Soviet Union

What's Ahead

The winds of international trade have blown generally freer in the 1990s. Nations all over the world have dramatically lowered the barriers they impose on the products of other countries.

One region that was once closed to virtually all trade but is now open is Eastern Europe and the countries that made up the former Soviet Union. A key part of these countries' struggle to create market capitalist economic systems has been the opening of their borders to international trade.

In Western Europe, the members of the European Community (EC) had by the beginning of 1993 eliminated virtually every restriction on the free flow of goods and services among them. A truckload of electronic equipment from Italy could pass through France on its way to Spain with no more restrictions than would be encountered by a truck delivering goods from Michigan to Illinois.

In 1993 Canada, Mexico, and the United States approved the North American Free Trade Agreement (NAFTA), which will create a similar free trade area. The 18 member nations of the Asian-Pacific Economic Cooperation organization (APEC) agreed in 1994 to forge a free-trade area among industrialized nations such as the United States and Japan by 2010. Other member nations such as Mexico and China agreed to participate by 2020. The 115 member nations in GATT, the General Agreement on Tariffs and Trade, have slashed trade restraints among themselves.

Why are so many countries moving to make trade freer? What are the effects of free trade? Why do such efforts meet with resistance? Why do some nations continue to impose high barriers against foreign goods and services? How do such barriers affect the economy?

This chapter will answer those questions by exploring international trade within the context of the model of perfect competition. The model predicts that free international trade will benefit the countries that participate in it. It will not, however, benefit everyone in those countries. Generally speaking, most people benefit from free trade, but some are hurt. The unequal distribution of benefits and burdens of free trade is one reason nations tend to raise barriers against it.

The chapter examines other justifications for restricting trade and explores the impacts of those restrictions.

It seems that everywhere we look these days, the products we use have foreign labels attached to either them or their components. This book was written on a Macintosh computer, which is a product of Apple Computer, a California-based firm. But the computer itself was not produced in the United States. It was assembled in Mexico from components made in Singapore, South Korea, Taiwan, Hong Kong, and a dozen or more other countries at far-flung corners of the world.

Consultations between the author in Colorado and the publisher in New York took place over a telecommunication system owned by an American company, AT&T. But the calls were made using telephones produced in Taiwan and Guatemala. Manuscripts were taken to the Federal Express office in a car made in Japan. The paper on which the manuscript was printed was produced from trees grown in Canada, and the powdered ink used by the laser printer was imported from Brazil. The U.S. company that actually printed the book did so on a printing press made in Germany. About the only thing that was purely an American input into the production process came from the labor in writing and editing it. This textbook is, in many respects, foreign-made.

The production of this textbook was not unusual. In 1994, for example, the United States imported $818 billion worth of goods and services from abroad. That represented more than 12 percent of all goods and services purchased in the United States that year. U.S. imports included automobiles, a wide range of consumer goods, and agricultural commodities. The flow of foreign-made goods is a two-way street—foreigners are large buyers of American-made products. In 1994, $716 billion worth of U.S. production was exported. Included among these American exports were mainframe computers, aircraft, power generation equipment, machinery and factory supplies, motor vehicles and parts, military hardware, and agricultural commodities.

Why does all this trade occur? To answer this question, we shall first examine what a country can produce and consume in isolation. Then we'll see how a country's consumption possibilities are expanded through international trade.

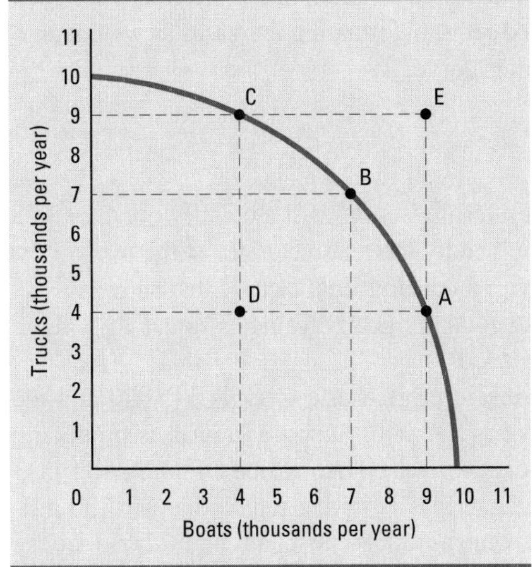

EXHIBIT 11-1

Taiwan's Production Possibilities Curve

The production possibilities curve for Taiwan shows the maximum quantities of trucks and boats that it can produce, given the factors of production and technology available to it. To maximize the value of total production, Taiwan must operate somewhere along this curve. Production at point D implies that Taiwan is failing to use its resources fully and efficiently; production at point E is unattainable.

Production and Consumption Without International Trade

Suppose the country of Taiwan is completely isolated from the rest of the world. It neither exports nor imports goods and services. We shall use the production possibilities model to analyze Taiwan's ability to produce goods and services.

The Production Possibilities Curve

A production possibilities curve illustrates the production choices available to an economy. Recall from Chapter 2 that the production possibilities curve for a particular country is determined by the factors of production and the technology available to it. Exhibit 11-1 shows a production possibilities curve for Taiwan, which produces only two goods—trucks and boats. We shall use this production possibilities curve to locate the combination of goods that will maximize the total value of Taiwan's output of goods and services.

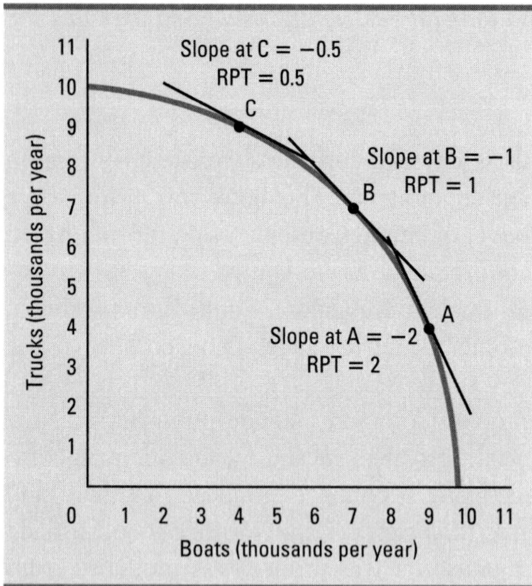

EXHIBIT 11-2

Taiwan's Rates of Product Transformation

The slope of the production possibilities curve at any point is equal to the slope of a line tangent to the curve at that point. The absolute value of that slope equals the rate of product transformation (RPT).

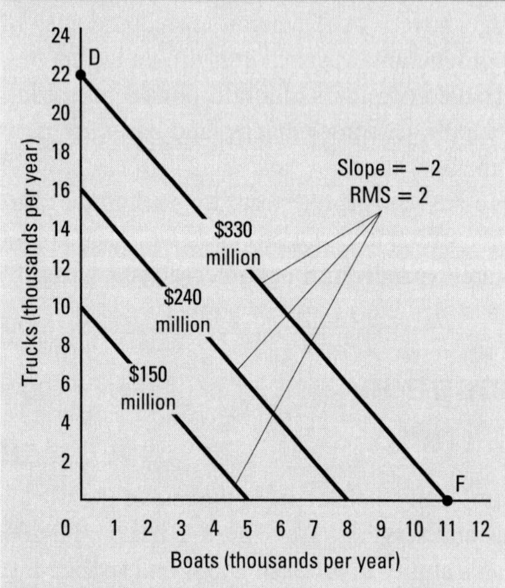

EXHIBIT 11-3

Trading Lines

Given the prices of two goods, a trading line can be drawn for any level of total production. Here, the price of a truck is $15,000 and the price of a boat is $30,000. The rate of market substitution (RMS) is 2. Trading lines are drawn for levels of production of $150 million, $240 million, and $330 million.

In order to maximize the value of its output, Taiwan must be operating somewhere on its production possibilities curve. If instead it were operating inside the curve at a point such as D, then another combination on the curve, such as B, would provide more of both goods (Taiwan produces 3,000 more trucks and 3,000 more boats per year at B than at D). At any point inside the curve, Taiwan would not be maximizing the value of its output. Point E suggests an even higher level of output than points A, B, or C, but because point E lies outside Taiwan's production possibilities curve, it cannot be attained.

Different points on a production possibilities curve, though, yield different values of total output. In this section we'll learn how to find the point that maximizes that value, and we'll see why a perfectly competitive market achieves that point.

We saw in Chapter 2 that the absolute value of the slope of a production possibilities curve at any point gives the quantity of the good on the vertical axis that must be given up to produce an additional unit of the good on the horizontal axis. The rate at which units of one good can be transformed into another is called the **rate of product transformation (RPT).**

Exhibit 11-2 gives rates of product transformation at points A, B, and C on Taiwan's production possibilities curve. Recall that the slope of the curve at any point is equal to the slope of a line drawn tangent to the curve at that point. The absolute value of that slope equals the rate of product transformation. The slope of a line tangent to the production possibilities curve at point B, for example, is −1. The rate of product transformation is thus 1; at point B, one truck must be given up to produce an additional boat. As the law of increasing costs predicts, as Taiwan produces more boats, it must give up more and more trucks for each additional boat. Taiwan's rate of product transformation increases as we travel to the right on its production possibilities curve.

The Trading Line

At what point on the production possibilities curve will a country operate? In a market economy, that will be determined by the relative prices of the two goods. We illustrate these relative prices with a **trading line,** a curve that shows all the combinations of two goods whose total monetary value is equal to a fixed amount, given the prices of the two goods.

Suppose that the long-run equilibrium price of a truck is $15,000 and the long-run equilibrium price of a boat is $30,000. Suppose Taiwan is producing $330 million worth of trucks and boats per year. Trading line DF in Exhibit 11-3 shows all the combinations of trucks and boats with a total value of $330 million. At point D, for example, Taiwan produces no boats and 22,000 trucks ($15,000 × 22,000 = $330 million). Taiwan could also produce an output combination worth $330 million at point F by producing 11,000 boats and no trucks. Every other point on trading line DF shows a combination of trucks and boats with a total value of $330 million.

Exhibit 11-3 also shows trading lines for total output values of $240 million and $150 million. A trading line can be drawn for any total value of output. Note that the higher up and to the right the trading line, the greater the value of output combinations on that line.

The slope of a trading line plays a key role. Let's calculate the slope of the trading line that represents total production of $330 million between points D and F in Exhibit 11-3. In going from D to F, the vertical change is a reduction of 22,000 trucks, and the horizontal change is an increase of 11,000 boats. The

- The **rate of product transformation (RPT)** is the rate at which units of one good can be transformed into another.
- A **trading line** is a line that shows all the combinations of two goods whose total monetary value equals some fixed amount.
- The **rate of market substitution (RMS)** is the rate at which units of one good can be exchanged for another in the marketplace.

slope is thus $-22{,}000/11{,}000 = -2$. To obtain a more general expression for the slope, consider that the quantity of 22,000 trucks at point D is found by taking the \$330 million total value for that trading line and dividing by the price of a truck (\$330,000,000/\$15,000 = 22,000). The quantity of boats at point F is determined the same way. Letting P_T equal the price of a truck and P_B the price of a boat, we find the slope of the trading line DF:

$$\frac{-\dfrac{\$330{,}000{,}000}{P_T}}{\dfrac{\$330{,}000{,}000}{P_B}} = \frac{P_B}{-P_T} = \frac{\$30{,}000}{-\$15{,}000} = -2 \qquad (1)$$

No matter what value we select for a trading line, the absolute value of its slope will be equal to the ratio of the price of the good on the horizontal axis to the price of the good on the vertical axis. Trading lines for different total values of production but for the same set of prices will all have the same slope, as in Exhibit 11-3.

We can use the slope of a trading line to determine the rate at which units of one good can be exchanged for another in the marketplace. This rate, expressed as the *negative* of the slope, is called the **rate of market substitution (RMS).** It is typically reported as the rate at which the good on the vertical axis can be exchanged for a unit of the good on the horizontal axis. It equals the absolute value of the slope of the trading line. If a truck costs \$15,000 and a boat costs \$30,000, then two trucks in Taiwan exchange for one boat. The rate of market substitution of trucks for boats is 2.

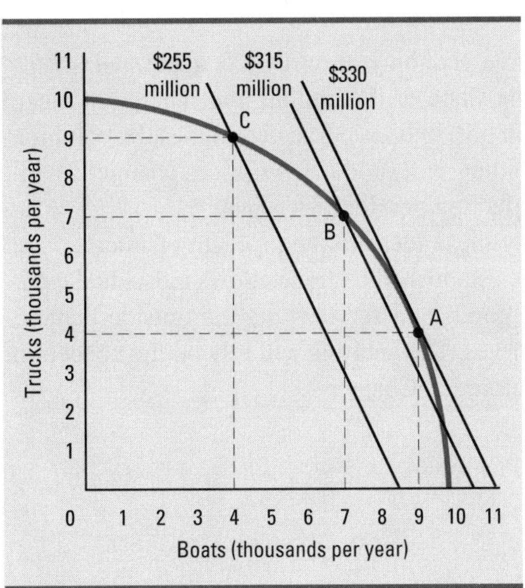

EXHIBIT 11-4

Maximizing the Total Value of Domestic Production

The most highly valued combination of outputs on the production possibilities curve is found where the curve is tangent to a trading line. This occurs at point A; total output will be \$330 million per year. At that point the rate of market substitution equals the rate of product transformation (RMS = RPT).

Combining the Production Possibilities Curve and the Trading Line

A production possibilities curve shows the combinations of goods and services an economy is capable of producing. A trading line shows combinations of two goods that have the same value. To find the highest value of production possible for the economy, we select the highest trading line consistent with its production possibilities curve.

Exhibit 11-4 combines Taiwan's production possibilities curve from Exhibit 11-1 with trading lines for several values of output. We continue to assume that the price of a truck is \$15,000 and the price of a boat is \$30,000. The combination at point A reaches the highest possible trading line, and it therefore has the highest total value of all possible combinations. All other combinations of trucks and boats that Taiwan could produce result in a lower total value. At point A, the trading line is tangent to the production possibilities curve. This means the rate of market substitution and the rate of product transformation at that point are equal. The rate at which trucks can be transformed into boats in production (the RPT) equals the rate at which they can be exchanged in the market.

A remarkable fact about perfect competition is that the process of profit maximization will achieve the output with the highest value of production. To see that this is so, suppose Taiwan is now operating at point B, producing 7,000 trucks and 7,000 boats per year. The prices of trucks and boats remain \$15,000 and \$30,000, respectively. The total value of output is \$315 million. We saw in Exhibit 11-2 that the rate of product transformation at this point is 1. By shifting enough resources out of truck production to produce one truck, the economy can produce one more boat. But a boat is worth twice as much as a truck. Clearly, private firms will profit by making such transfers. As they transfer resources out of truck production to produce boats, firms will move Taiwan's combination of goods produced toward point A. They will profit from such transfers as long as the rate of product transformation differs from the rate of market substitution. At point A these two rates are equal, no further transfers will be profitable.

The process through which resources in a perfectly competitive economy are guided to their highest-valued use involves a combination of two models we've already studied: production possibilities and demand and supply. The production possibilities model lays out the alternatives available to a particular economy. Demand and supply determine prices and thus the slope of the trading line. Those prices guide price-taking firms to the most valuable combination of goods the economy is capable of producing.

Exhibit 11-5 illustrates how changes in demand affect the combination of goods and services an economy will produce. Suppose an economy produces two goods, A and B. The demand and supply curves in Panels (a) and (b) show an initial price of \$20 for good A and \$10 for good B. That implies a trading line whose slope is ½; such a curve is tangent to the production possibilities curve at point R in Panel (c). Notice that the quantities of the two goods at R (A = 2,000, B = 1,000) correspond to the initial equilibrium values on the demand and supply curves.

Now suppose consumers demand more of good B and reduce their demand for good A. The price of good B rises to \$20 while the price of good A falls to \$10. The rate of market substitution rises to 2, and the corresponding trading line is now tangent to the production possibilities curve at point S in Panel (c). Production of good B has increased to 2,000 units while production of good A has fallen to 1,000 units.

Prices in a perfectly competitive economy are set by demand and supply. These prices, in turn, determine the slope of the trading line. The point where that line is tangent to the production possibilities curve determines the combination of goods and services the economy will produce. As prices change, so will the combination chosen on the production possibilities curve.

In the next section, we'll apply these ideas to the problem of international trade. We'll see that the trading line established by trade allows individual countries to consume combinations of goods and services that lie outside their respective production possibilities curves. The analysis will rely on the concept of comparative advantage that we explored in Chapter 2.

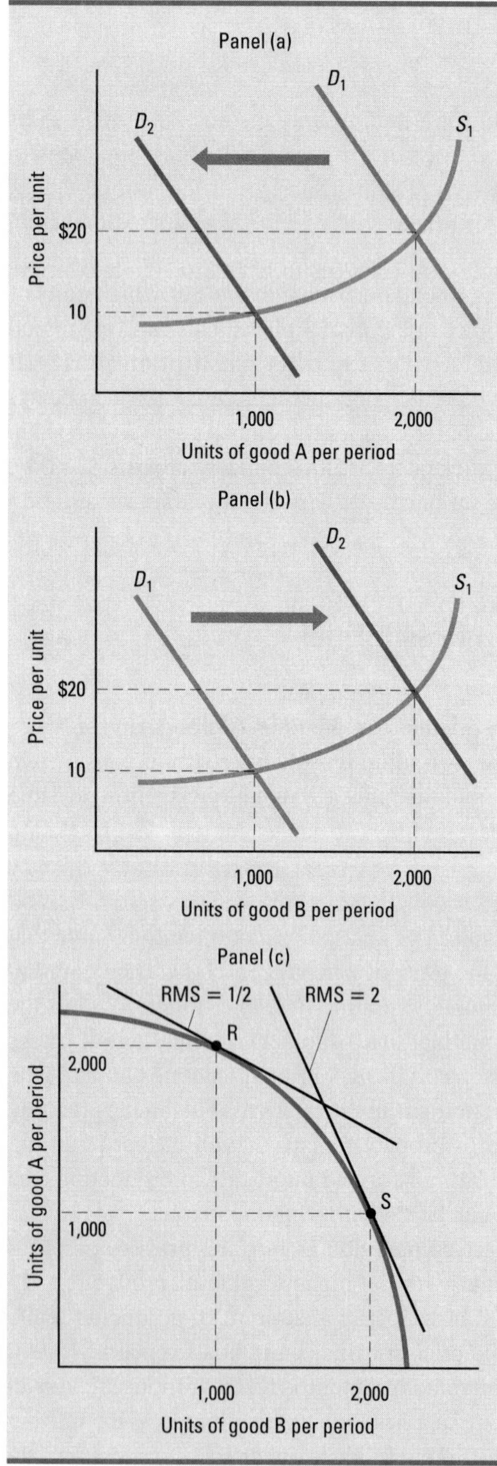

EXHIBIT 11-5

A Change in Demand Produces a Movement Along the Production Possibilities Curve

Panel (a) shows the initial equilibrium price and output for good A, \$20 and 2,000 units; Panel (b) shows the equilibrium price and output for good B, \$10 and 1,000 units. The corresponding point on the production possibilities curve is point R in Panel (c). The price ratio of good B to good A is ½; a trading line with this slope is tangent to the production possibilities curve at R. We can conclude that the rate of product transformation equals ½ also.

Now suppose that the demand for good A falls while the demand for good B rises. The change in prices increases the slope of the trading line, moving the economy along the production possibilities curve to point S in Panel (c).

Checklist

- In order to maximize the value of its output, a country must be producing a combination of goods and services that lies on its production possibilities curve.
- The rate of product transformation (RPT) is the rate at which a country can reduce the output of one good in order to increase the output of another. It is equal to the absolute value of the slope of the production possibilities curve at any point.
- A trading line shows all the combinations of two goods that have the same total value.
- The rate of market substitution (RMS) gives the rate at which people are willing to exchange goods as determined by supply and demand. It is the absolute value of the slope of the trading line.
- The most highly valued combination of goods and services is found where the rate of product transformation equals the rate of market substitution (RPT = RMS). That combination occurs where the production possibilities curve is tangent to a trading line.

The Gains from Trade

People participate in international trade because they make themselves better off by doing so. In this section we use the trading lines and production possibilities curves for two countries to see why. We'll find that countries that participate in international trade are able to consume more of all goods and services than they were able to consume while producing in isolation from the rest of the world.

Comparative Advantage

Let's use our example again. Taiwan and Hong Kong each produce two goods, boats and trucks. The boat and truck industries are perfectly competitive in both countries. Suppose no trade occurs between the two countries. Their respective equilibrium solutions are illustrated in Exhibit 11-6. Taiwan's combination of trucks and boats is at point A on its production possibilities curve in Panel (a); that is the solution we derived in the last section. Suppose Hong Kong has a different production possibilities curve and a different trading line; the price of a boat in Hong Kong is one-fifth the price of a truck. Hong Kong maximizes the value of its production with the combination at point A′ in Panel (b), producing 4,750 trucks and 2,000 boats per year.

The two countries differ in their respective abilities to produce trucks and boats. As we can see by looking at the intersection of the production possibilities curves with the vertical axes in Exhibit 11-6, Taiwan is able to produce more trucks than Hong Kong. If Taiwan concentrated all of its resources on the production of trucks, it could produce 10,000 trucks per year. Hong Kong could produce only 5,000. Now look at the intersection of the production possibilities curves with the horizontal axes. If Taiwan concentrated all of its resources on the production of boats, it could produce 10,000 boats. Hong Kong could produce only 7,000 boats. Because it is capable of producing more of both goods, we may infer that Taiwan is a country with more resources or a higher level of technology than Hong Kong.

EXHIBIT 11-6

Production Possibilities in Taiwan and Hong Kong Before Trade

Taiwan's long-run equilibrium before trade is shown at point A in Panel (a), where Taiwan produces and consumes 4,000 trucks and 9,000 boats per year. Hong Kong maximizes the value of its total output by producing at point A′ in Panel (b), at 4,750 trucks and 2,000 boats per year. At equilibrium, the rate of product transformation (RPT) equals the rate of market substitution (RMS).

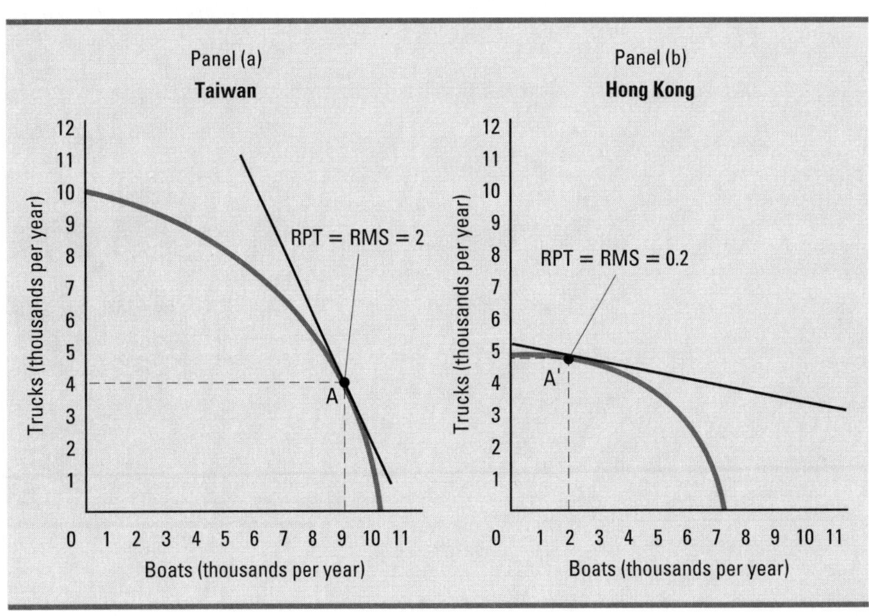

— The **terms of trade** give the rate at which a country can trade domestic products for imported products.

Despite Taiwan's greater ability to produce both goods, it can still gain from trade with Hong Kong—and Hong Kong can gain from trade with Taiwan. The key lies in an examination of the relative costs of the two goods in the two countries. The country with a lower relative cost for a particular good or service has a comparative advantage in producing it and will export it to other countries.

We can determine relative costs in the two countries by comparing the slopes of their respective production possibilities curves in Exhibit 11-6. At point A, 1 additional boat costs 2 trucks in Taiwan; that is its rate of product transformation. At point A′, 1 additional boat in Hong Kong costs only 0.2 trucks. Alternatively, we can ask about the cost of an additional truck. In Taiwan, an additional truck costs ½ boat. In Hong Kong, it costs 5 boats. Taiwan thus has a comparative advantage in producing trucks; Hong Kong has a comparative advantage in producing boats. This situation is suggested pictorially in Exhibit 11-7.

EXHIBIT 11-7

Comparative Advantage in Taiwan and Hong Kong

Because their rates of product transformation differ, Hong Kong and Taiwan have a comparative advantage in producing different goods.

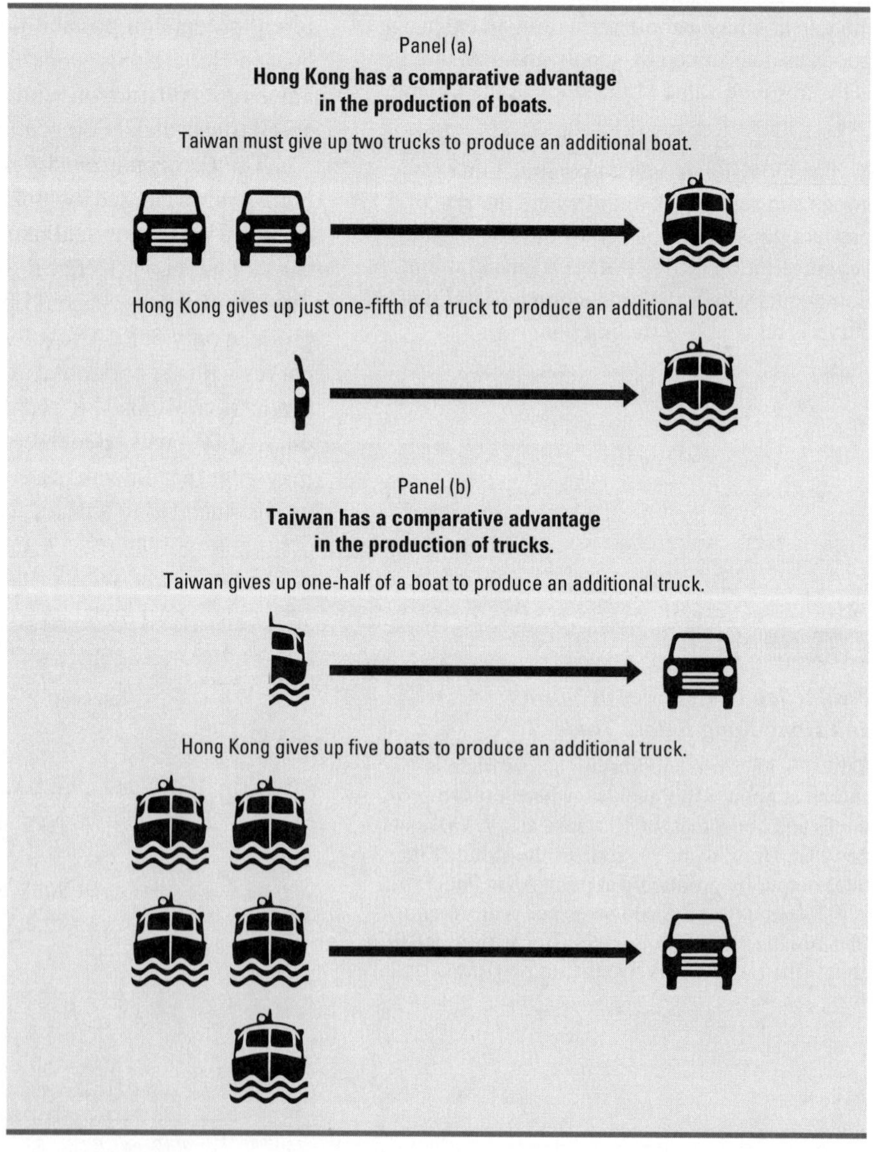

Panel (a)
Hong Kong has a comparative advantage in the production of boats.
Taiwan must give up two trucks to produce an additional boat.
Hong Kong gives up just one-fifth of a truck to produce an additional boat.
Panel (b)
Taiwan has a comparative advantage in the production of trucks.
Taiwan gives up one-half of a boat to produce an additional truck.
Hong Kong gives up five boats to produce an additional truck.

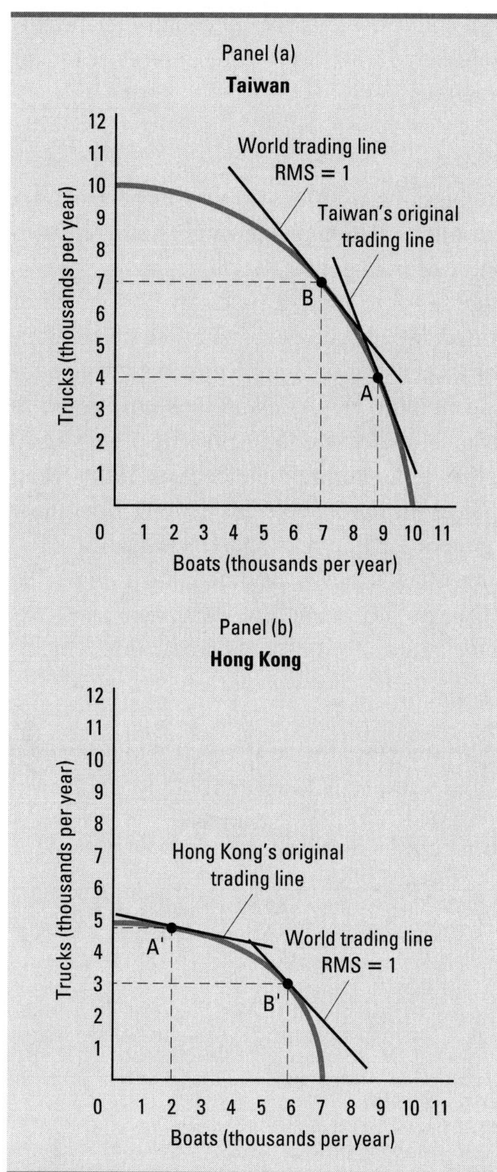

EXHIBIT 11-8

International Trade Induces Greater Specialization

The most highly valued domestic output and consumption level available to Taiwan prior to trade is found at point A in Panel (a). With the shift to the world trading line, Taiwan produces more trucks and fewer boats at point B. Hong Kong shifts from A′ to B′ in Panel (b), producing more boats and fewer trucks. Trade leads each country to a greater degree of specialization in the good in which it has a comparative advantage.

Specialization and the Gains from Trade

We have so far assumed that no trade occurs between Taiwan and Hong Kong. Now let us assume that trade opens up. The fact that the rates of product transformation and market substitution differ between the two countries suggests the possibility for mutually advantageous trade. The opportunities created by trade will induce a greater degree of specialization in both countries, specialization that reflects comparative advantage.

Trade and Specialization

Before trade, truck producers in Taiwan could exchange a truck for half a boat. In Hong Kong, however, a truck could be exchanged for 5 boats. Once trade is opened between the two countries, truck producers in Taiwan will rush to export trucks to Hong Kong.

Boat producers in Hong Kong enjoy a similar bonanza. Before trade, one of their boats could exchange for one-fifth of a truck. By shipping their boats to Taiwan, they can get 2 trucks for each boat. Boat producers in Hong Kong will rush to export boats to Taiwan.

As Taiwan's trucks pour into Hong Kong, however, the price of trucks there will fall; Hong Kong's trading line will become steeper. At the same time, the fact that so many boats from Hong Kong are arriving in Taiwan will cause their price to fall; Taiwan's trading line will become flatter.

Where will all this end? We started with a boat exchanging for a fraction of a truck in Hong Kong and for 2 trucks in Taiwan. The final rate will be somewhere between those two extremes. Suppose that the final exchange rate is 1 boat for 1 truck. That will be a much higher rate than what Hong Kong's boat producers received before trade. Taiwan's truck producers will now get 1 boat per truck—a far better exchange than was available to them before trade. The new rate of market exchange gives a single trading line for the two countries; its slope is -1.

The **terms of trade** give the rate at which a country can trade domestic products for imported products. In our example with trade between Hong Kong and Taiwan, the terms of trade between the two countries are such that 1 truck exchanges for 1 boat.

Because Taiwan and Hong Kong face the same relative prices of trucks and boats, they have the same rate of market substitution: it now equals 1. Recall that a trading line can be drawn for any value of total output. A new set of trading lines with a slope of -1 is drawn in Exhibit 11-8. Taiwan's original combination of trucks and boats, point A, no longer generates the maximum value of the two goods possible. Taiwanese manufacturers will move to produce more trucks and fewer boats until they reach the point on their production possibilities curve at which the rate of product transformation equals the new rate of market substitution. That occurs at point B in Panel (a); Taiwan now produces 7,000 trucks and 7,000 boats per year.

In Panel (b), the new trading line means that the original solution at A′ no longer maximizes the value of Hong Kong's output. Producers will shift resources out of truck production and into boat production. The value of production is maximized at point B′; Hong Kong produces 3,000 trucks and 6,000 boats per year.

We see that trade between the two countries causes each country to specialize in the good in which it has a comparative advantage. Taiwan produces more trucks, and Hong Kong produces more boats.

Gaining from Trade

As a result of trade, Taiwan now produces more trucks and fewer boats. Hong Kong produces more boats and fewer trucks. Through exchange, however, both countries could end up consuming more of *both* goods.

We can't use the model in Exhibit 11-8 to predict precisely how much of each good will be exported and imported. We can, however, show some possibilities. Suppose Taiwan ships 2,500 trucks per year to Hong Kong in exchange for 2,500 boats, as shown in the table in Exhibit 11-9. Taiwan thus emerges with 4,500 trucks (the 7,000 it produces at B minus the 2,500 it ships) and 9,500 boats. It has 500 more of each good than it did before trade because Hong Kong ships 2,500 boats to Taiwan in exchange for the 2,500 trucks. Hong Kong now has 5,500 trucks and 3,500 boats, a gain of 1,250 trucks and 1,500 boats.

The trading lines for the two countries have been combined into a single line in the graph in Exhibit 11-9; trade occurs along this line, with one truck exchanging for one boat. As Taiwan trades trucks for boats, its production remains

EXHIBIT 11-9

The Mutual Benefits of Trade

Taiwan and Hong Kong each consume more of both goods when there is trade between them. The table shows values of production and consumption for each country before trade (BT) and after trade (AT). Here, the final terms of trade allow 1 truck to exchange for 1 boat (the rate of market substitution, RMS, equals 1). Taiwan exports 2,500 trucks to Hong Kong in exchange for 2,500 boats and ends up at point C on the world trading line; Hong Kong ends up at point C′. Notice that this world curve has the same slope as the trading lines in Exhibit 11-8; it has been redrawn here as a single line, with the graphs for the two countries moved so that both production possibilities curves are tangent to the world trading line.

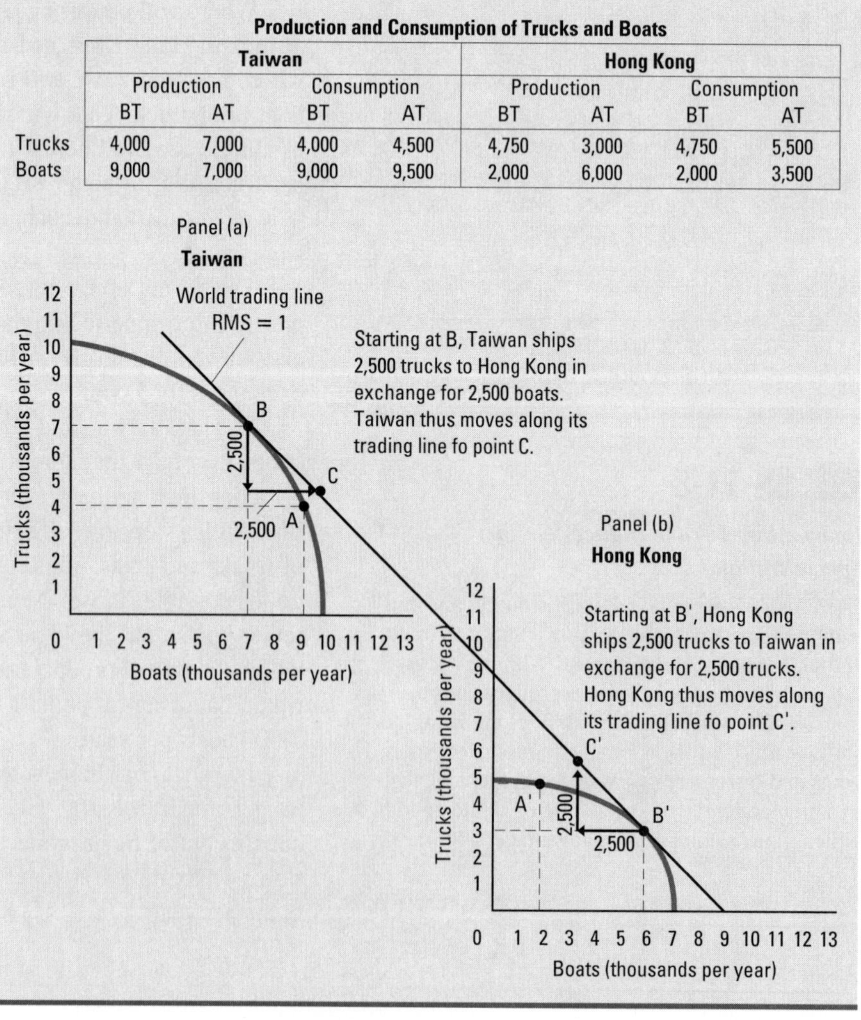

Production and Consumption of Trucks and Boats

	Taiwan				Hong Kong			
	Production		Consumption		Production		Consumption	
	BT	AT	BT	AT	BT	AT	BT	AT
Trucks	4,000	7,000	4,000	4,500	4,750	3,000	4,750	5,500
Boats	9,000	7,000	9,000	9,500	2,000	6,000	2,000	3,500

Case in Point: America's Shifting Comparative Advantage

What is America's comparative advantage? A look at the country from an airplane on a cross-country flight suggests a traditional answer. Its vast open spaces give it a comparative advantage in the production of agricultural products. But the traditional answer is outdated—agricultural goods account for only a small share of U.S. exports. Doomsayers about the U.S. role in the twenty-first century suggest that our comparative advantage will instead lie in flipping hamburgers and sweeping the floors around Japanese computers. The doomsayers' answer makes for good jokes, but it hardly squares with the facts. America's comparative advantage now lies largely in its production of high-tech capital equipment.

C-COR Electronics in Pennsylvania uses high-tech capital equipment it purchases from Hewlett-Packard, a leading U.S. manufacturer

In 1960, only 20 percent of the capital goods produced in the United States were exported; by 1990 nearly half were. U.S. exports of capital goods accounted for just 1.4 percent of total output in 1960; by 1990 that share had more than tripled. Capital goods now account for more than 40 percent of U.S. exports.

Tom Saponas, a plant manager for Hewlett-Packard, which manufactures electronic capital goods, suggests that the source of the U.S. advantage lies in what might be called a climate of innovation. "The Japanese are generally superior to us in high-volume production," he says. "Where we excell is in producing difficult-to-make, low-volume things—the kinds of capital firms often need. I think that's a result of a greater emphasis here on entrepreneurial effort and problem solving. It fosters more flexibility and an ability to respond more quickly to technological change."

The emergence of the United States as a world leader in capital goods production puts it atop two rising global tides. First, the world is becoming more capital-intensive generally. In the last 20 years, the share of world output devoted to capital goods has risen to 26 percent from 22 percent. Second, as pointed out in a Case in Point essay in Chapter 9, firms all over the world are demanding more and more high-tech capital, a segment of the capital goods sector in which the United States is particularly dominant. The effort of other countries to acquire more capital—and especially more high-tech capital—has become a bonanza for the United States. Economist Lawrence Lindsey, a member of the Board of Governors of the United States Federal Reserve System, says that each 1 percent rise in world investment spending translates into a 1.5 percent boost in U.S. exports of capital goods.

Sources: Lawrence B. Lindsey, "America's Growing Lead," *The Wall Street Journal,* 7 February 1992; and personal interview with Tom Saponas.

at point B. But it now consumes combination C; it has more of both goods than it had at A, the solution before trade. As Hong Kong sends boats to Taiwan in exchange for trucks, it moves along the trading line to point C′, where it has more trucks and more boats than it had before trade.

Both countries end up with more of both goods as a result of trade. This is the same lesson we learned in Chapter 2, when we saw that world production could be increased by allowing countries to specialize in the goods in which they have a comparative advantage. Trade allows each country to consume a larger quantity of both goods than it can produce.

Whenever two countries have different rates of product transformation and market substitution, trade can expand the consumption of both goods in both countries if each increases production of the good or service in which it has a comparative advantage. This result is analogous to what we learned in Chapter 2 in our discussion of Mr. MacDonald's farm. We found that when he allocated his

Case in Point

U.S. Broom Makers Struggle with New Competition

France Broom Company, a manufacturer of corn-straw brooms in Illinois, was cited in a September 1993 *New York Times* article as one that would probably be adversely affected by passage of NAFTA. The United States then imposed a 32 percent tariff on imported brooms. Under the terms of NAFTA, 30 percent of that tariff was to be eliminated immediately; another 20 percent would be eliminated in 1999 and the rest in 2005. Stan Koschnick, the company manager, was quoted in the article as saying that passage of NAFTA would badly hurt it: "I'm sure I'm biased, but I think NAFTA's a bad deal," he said at that time.

In the spring of 1995, more than a year after NAFTA had gone into effect, Mr. Koschnick was still unhappy about NAFTA. "I still think it's a bad deal. We haven't been strongly affected by it yet, but I'm sure we will be," he said.

Sources: Barnaby J. Feder, "Tiny Industry Fears NAFTA's Reach," *The New York Times,* 24 September 1993, p. D1; and personal interview.

fields according to the principle of comparative advantage, he was able to produce more cabbages and more potatoes than if he used each field to produce both goods. Here, Taiwan and Hong Kong are similar to Mr. MacDonald's fields. Whenever resources are allocated on the basis of comparative advantage, the production those resources achieve is increased.

Although all countries can increase their consumption through trade, not everyone in those countries will be happy with the result. In the case of Taiwan and Hong Kong, for example, some boat producers in Taiwan will be displaced as cheaper boats arrive from Hong Kong. Some truck producers in Hong Kong will be displaced as cheaper trucks arrive from Taiwan. The production possibilities model suggests that the resources displaced will ultimately find more productive uses. They will produce trucks in Taiwan and boats in Hong Kong. But there will be a period of painful transition as workers and owners of capital and natural resources move from one activity to another.

Despite the transitional problems affecting some factors of production, the potential benefits from free trade are large. For this reason, most economists are strongly in favor of opening markets and extending international trade throughout the world. The economic case has been a powerful force in moving the world toward freer trade, but substantial barriers remain. In the next section, we shall look at the various ways in which trade is limited or restricted. We shall see how such restrictions affect the prices we pay for goods and services. We also explore the arguments offered in favor of and against such restrictions on international trade.

Checklist

- If the rate of product transformation differs between two countries, there is an opportunity for mutually advantageous trade.
- The terms of trade give the rate at which a country can trade domestic products for imported products.
- International trade leads countries toward specialization in the production of goods for which they have a comparative advantage.
- Free international trade can increase the availability of all goods and services in all the countries that participate in it.

Restrictions on International Trade

In spite of the strong theoretical case that can be made for free international trade, virtually every country in the world has erected at least some barriers to trade. This section examines the impacts of those restrictions.

A **protectionist policy** is one in which a country restricts the importation of goods and services produced in foreign countries. Such policies are designed to protect companies and workers in the home economy from competition by foreign firms. Protection often takes the form of either a tariff or a quota, but it can also come in the form of voluntary export restrictions and nontariff barriers. Each of these is discussed below.

Protectionist policies are restrictions on free international trade designed to protect domestic industries from competitive market forces that originate beyond the borders of the country.

A **tariff** is a tax imposed by a government on imported goods or services.

Tariffs

A **tariff** is a tax on imported goods and services. The average tariff on dutiable imports in the United States (i.e., those imports on which a tariff is imposed) is about 5 percent. Some imports have much higher tariffs. For example, the U.S. tariff on imported orange juice is 35 cents per gallon (which amounts to about 40 percent of value). The tariff on imported canned tuna fish is 35 percent, and the tariff on imported shoes ranges between 20 and 40 percent.

A tariff affects the equilibrium price and output of a good or service in the country that imposes the tariff. Panel (a) of Exhibit 11-10 shows the situation before the imposition of a tariff. Demand is shown by the curve labeled "Domestic demand." The supply available from domestic companies is labeled "Domestic supply." If no foreign suppliers were allowed to sell in the domestic economy, the equilibrium price and quantity, determined by the intersection of domestic supply and domestic demand, would be P_D and Q_D. Suppose that foreign suppliers of the good have a cost advantage that allows them to sell any quantity at a lower price than domestic producers. The foreign supply curve is thus below the

EXHIBIT 11-10

The Impact of a Tariff

Panel (a) shows that without a tariff the domestic economy consumes Q_T units at a price P_W. Domestic firms supply quantity Q_{DS}; foreign firms supply Q_{FS}. Panel (b) shows the impact of imposing a tariff that completely eliminates the cost advantage of foreign firms. The tariff raises the domestic price to P'_W and reduces the total quantity consumed to Q'_T. The quantity supplied by domestic firms rises to Q'_{DS}; the quantity supplied by foreign firms falls to Q'_{FS}.

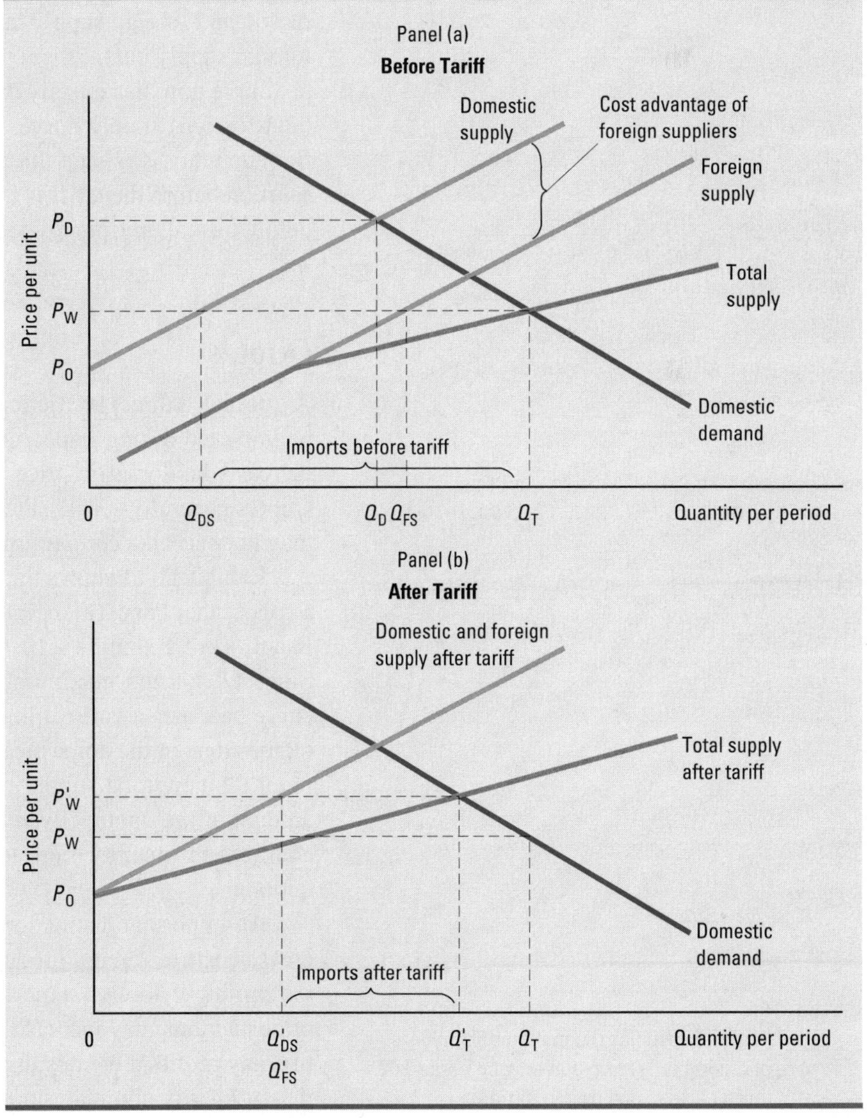

domestic supply curve in Panel (a). We find the total supply curve by adding the quantity supplied by foreign suppliers to the quantity supplied by domestic suppliers at each price. Thus, the total supply curve is identical to the foreign supply curve up to P_O, the price at which domestic suppliers enter the market. Above that price, the total supply curve is the sum of the quantities offered by domestic and foreign suppliers at each price.

The equilibrium price and quantity in Panel (a) are found at the intersection of the domestic demand and total supply curves. Domestic consumers purchase a total quantity of Q_T units at price P_W. The quantity Q_T is the sum of the quantity supplied by domestic suppliers (Q_{DS}) plus the quantity supplied by foreign suppliers (Q_{FS}). Imports equal total consumption (Q_T) minus domestic production (Q_{DS}). By allowing free trade, consumers in the domestic economy obtain a substantially larger quantity of the good at a substantially lower price than would be the case if they relied on domestic suppliers alone.

Now suppose a tariff exactly equal to the cost advantage of foreign suppliers is imposed on imported goods. The impact of such a tariff is shown in Panel (b) of Exhibit 11-10. The tariff raises the marginal cost of goods obtained from foreign suppliers. The foreign supply curve shifts upward and becomes the same as that of domestic suppliers. (Had a larger or smaller tariff been imposed, the domestic and foreign supply curves would not be identical.) Given the shift of the foreign supply curve, the total supply curve is also changed. The new total supply curve now lies exactly twice as far to the right at each price as the domestic (and foreign) supply curve. After the imposition of the tariff, the new equilibrium quantity is Q'_T and the equilibrium price is P'_W. Comparing the equilibrium solution before the tariff is imposed with the solution after the tariff, we see that output has fallen from Q_T to Q'_T while the price has risen from P_W to P'_W.

Quotas

A **quota** is a direct restriction on the total quantity of a good or service that may be imported during a specified period. Quotas restrict total supply and therefore increase the domestic price of the good or service on which they are imposed. Quotas generally specify that an exporting country's share of a domestic market may not exceed a certain limit.

Exhibit 11-11 shows the situation before and after the imposition of a quota. Suppose that Panel (a), before the quota, shows the same situation that existed in Panel (a) of Exhibit 11-10. The new quota limits imports to Q'_{FS} in Panel (b). Since Q'_{FS} is the maximum amount that can be imported, the foreign supply curve becomes a vertical line at that quantity. The new total supply curve takes on the slope of the domestic supply curve once the quota is reached. Beyond that point the new total supply curve is simply the domestic supply curve plus the amount of the quota. Given the quota, the equilibrium price rises to P'_W and the equilibrium quantity falls to Q'_T. Imports fall to the quantity allowed by the quota.

An important distinction between quotas and tariffs is that quotas don't increase costs to foreign producers; tariffs do. In the short run, a tariff will reduce the profits of foreign exporters of a good or service. A quota, however, raises price and thus may increase profits. Because the quota imposes a limit on quantity, any profits it creates in other countries won't induce the entry of new firms that ordinarily eliminates profits in perfect competition.

A **quota** specifies the maximum amount of a good or service that may be imported during a specified period of time.

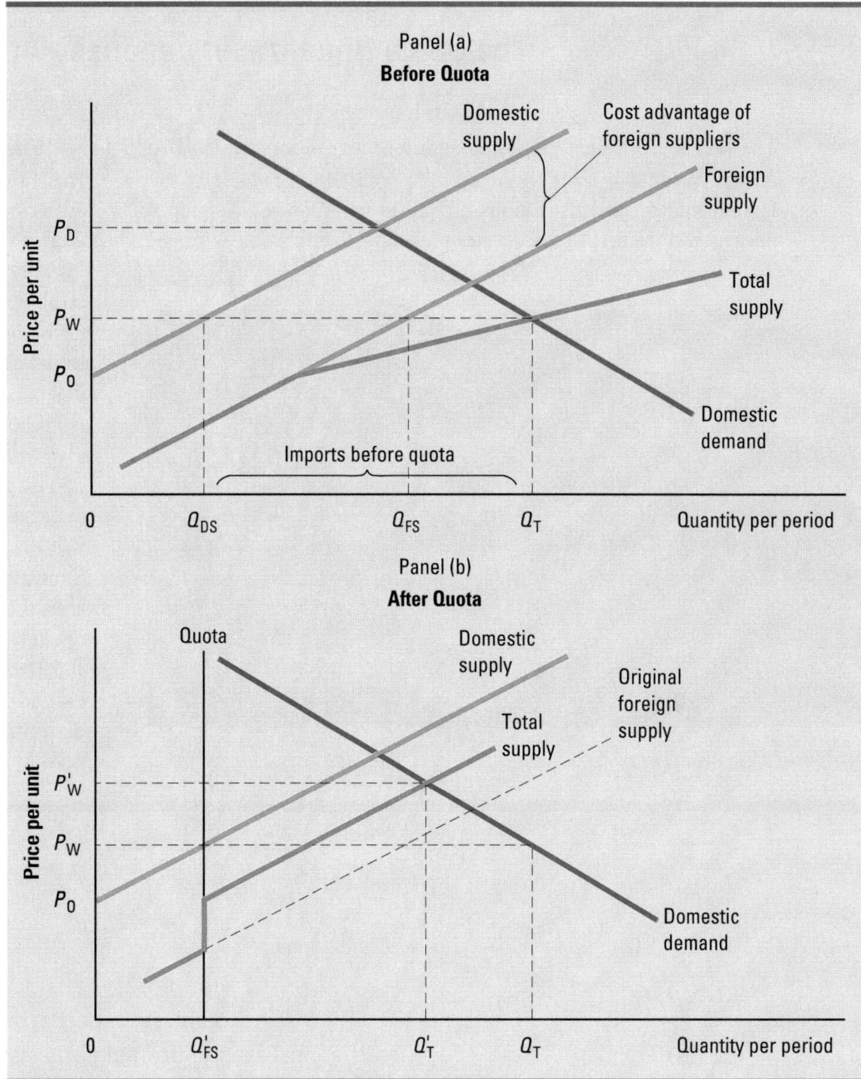

EXHIBIT 11-11

The Impact of a Quota

The imposition of a quota of Q'_{FS} limits the quantity of a good that can be imported into the domestic economy from foreign suppliers. In Panel (b), the quota raises the domestic price and reduces the quantity consumed.

Voluntary Export Restrictions

Voluntary export restrictions are a form of trade barrier by which foreign firms agree to limit the quantity of goods exported to a particular country. They came to prominence in the United States in the 1980s. The U.S. government persuaded foreign exporters of automobiles and steel to agree to limit their exports to the United States.

A **voluntary export restriction** is a trade barrier by which foreign firms agree to limit the quantity of exports to a particular country.

Although such restrictions are called voluntary, they typically are agreed to only after pressure is applied by the country whose industries they protect. The United States, for example, has succeeded in pressuring many other countries to accept quotas limiting their exports of goods ranging from sweaters to steel.

Case in Point: The Quota Bonanza for Japanese Automakers

The U.S. government pressured Japanese automakers in 1981 to accept voluntary restrictions on their exports of cars to the United States. The restrictions proved to be a bonanza for Japanese as well as for American automakers.

Worker at Japanese Toyota factory in Kentucky.

The restriction shifted the supply curve of foreign cars to the left. Prices of Japanese cars rose by about $2,500. The prices of American cars rose by about the same amount. But higher prices weren't the only result of the export restriction.

The agreement set a limit on the *number* of vehicles Japan could export to the United States. When it was imposed, virtually all of Japan's export autos were compact cars. But Japanese automakers have begun shifting to production of midsize and luxury cars like the Lexus, for which their accounting profit per car is higher.

Although the restrictions boosted profits for Japanese companies, each individual company had an incentive to raise profits even more by finding ways to avoid the restriction. The easiest way to do that was to establish production plants in the United States. Cars built in the United States by Japanese-owned firms aren't counted as Japanese exports. Honda Motor Company opened the first of these "transplants" in the United States in 1982. By 1993 there were 10 Japanese assembly plants in the United States. Japanese automakers operate more U.S. plants than Chrysler. The export limitation agreement has played an important role in shifting Japanese production to the United States.

A voluntary export restriction works precisely like an ordinary quota. It raises prices for the domestic product and reduces the quantity consumed of the good or service affected by the quota. It can also increase the profits of the firms that agree to the quota, since it raises the price they receive for their products.

Nontariff Barriers

A **nontariff barrier** is a government policy that restricts imports without imposing tariffs or quotas. Safety standards, labeling requirements, pollution controls, and quality restrictions all may have the effect of restricting imports.

Many restrictions aimed at protecting consumers in the domestic market create barriers as a purely unintended, and probably desirable, side effect. For example, limitations on the insecticides that may be present in foods are often more stringent in the United States than in other countries. These standards tend to discourage the import of foreign goods, but their primary purpose appears to be to protect consumers from harmful chemicals, not to restrict trade. But other nontariff barriers seem to serve no purpose other than to keep foreign goods out. Tomatoes produced in Mexico, for example, compete with those produced in the United States. But Mexican tomatoes tend to be smaller than U.S. tomatoes. The United States has long imposed size restrictions to "protect" U.S. consumers from small tomatoes. The result is a highly effective trade barrier that protects U.S. producers and raises U.S. tomato prices.

A **nontariff barrier** is a regulation that restricts imports without imposing a quota or tariff.

Case in Point — Japan's Papa-Mamas: Trade Barrier or Cultural Tradition?

Japan's retail sales are dominated by small shops, called "papa-mama" stores. These shops account for more than half of all retail sales in Japan. By contrast, small "mom-and-pop" stores account for only 3 percent of retail sales in the United States.

Japan's papa-mamas are protected by law. No retailer in Japan can open a store with more than 5,382 square feet (about 10 percent of the size of a small U.S. department store) in any city without obtaining permission from other retailers in that city. Although there are provisions for large firms to bypass this barrier (Toys 'Я' Us has opened large stores in Japan), it generally takes 8 to 10 years to gain the necessary permits.

The system makes it much more difficult for U.S. firms to enter the Japanese market than it is for Japanese firms to enter the U.S. market. A Japanese firm can gain access to a major share of the U.S. market by striking a deal with a few firms such as Wal-Mart, K-Mart, and Sears. U.S. firms seeking entrée to the Japanese market, however, must negotiate within a labyrinth of tiny, individually owned shops. One result is that less than a quarter of the U.S. goods exported to Japan consists of consumer goods.

U.S. firms complain that the restrictions preserving papa-mamas constitute an unfair trade practice. Japanese officials defend them as a vital part of their culture. Are the papa-mamas a trade barrier or a cultural icon? The answer is that they are both. They clearly make it more difficult for foreigners to export goods and services to Japan, and they are clearly a valued institution in Japan. The cost of this institution is borne primarily by Japanese consumers, who must pay the higher prices associated with small stores. Trade barrier or not, the papa-mamas are beginning to lose ground to large chain discounters. As Japanese consumers turn to larger outlets, entry into the Japanese market will become easier.

Justifications for Trade Restriction: An Evaluation

The conceptual justification for free trade is one of the oldest arguments in economics; there is no disputing the logic of the argument itself. But critics stress that the argument is a theoretical one. In the real world, they say, there are several arguments that can be made to justify protectionist measures.

Infant Industries

One argument for trade barriers is to serve as a kind of buffer to protect domestic industries that are just getting started. Initially, firms in a new industry may be too small to achieve significant economies of scale. Fledgling firms could be clobbered by established firms in other countries. A new domestic industry with potential economies of scale is called an **infant industry.**

Consider the situation where firms in a country are attempting to enter a new industry in which many large firms already exist in the international arena. The foreign firms have taken advantage of economies of scale and have therefore achieved relatively low levels of cost of production. New firms, facing low levels of output and higher average costs, may find it difficult to compete. The infant industry argument suggests that by offering protection during an industry's formative years, a tariff or quota may allow the new industry to develop and prosper.

An **infant industry** is a new domestic industry with a potential for economies of scale.

EXHIBIT 11-12

Average U.S. Tariff Rates, 1820–1993

The average U.S. tariff on dutiable (taxable) imports was high early in the nineteenth century; then it fell. It rose again during the Civil War and the Great Depression. Tariff rates have fallen quite sharply since 1930.

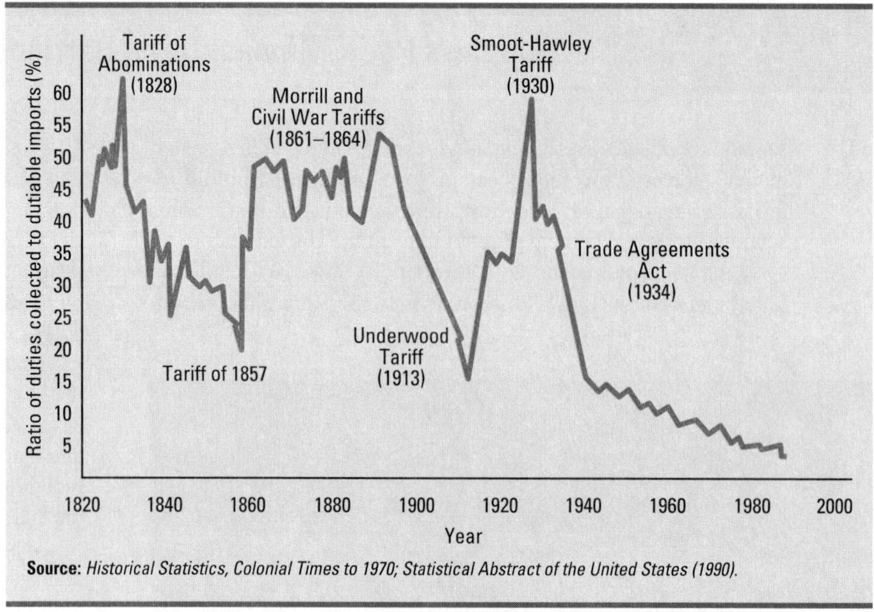

Source: *Historical Statistics, Colonial Times to 1970; Statistical Abstract of the United States (1990).*

The infant industry argument played a major role in tariff policy in the early years of this country's development. Exhibit 11-12 shows average tariff rates on dutiable imports in the United States since 1820. The high tariffs of the early nineteenth century were typically justified as being necessary to allow U.S. firms to gain a competitive foothold in the world economy. As domestic industries became established, tariff rates fell. Subsequent increases in tariffs were a response in part to internal crises: the Civil War and the Great Depression. Tariff rates have fallen dramatically since 1930; they now average about 3 percent.

A new version of the infant industry argument has been used in the past few years as technological developments have spawned whole new industries and transformed existing ones. The new version of the infant industry argument assumes an imperfectly competitive market. We shall examine this idea in Part Four, which considers departures from perfect competition. International trade in imperfectly competitive models is considered in Chapter 13.

Critics of the infant industry argument say that once protection is in place, it may be very difficult to remove. Inefficient firms may be able to survive for long periods under the umbrella of infant industry protection.

National Security

It is sometimes argued that the security of the United States would be threatened if this country depended on foreign powers as the primary source of strategic materials. In time of war, the United States might be cut off from sources of foreign supply and lose some of the materials upon which U.S. industry depends.

One area where the national security argument is applied is the oil industry. Given the volatility of the political situation in the Middle East, some people say, the United States should protect the domestic oil industry in order to ensure adequate production capability in the event Middle Eastern supplies are cut off.

An alternative to tariff protection of strategic commodities is to stockpile those commodities for use in time of crisis. The United States maintains a strategic petroleum reserve, for example, for use in case of a cutoff in foreign supplies.

Job Protection

The desire to maintain existing jobs threatened by foreign competition is probably the single most important source of today's protectionist policies. Some industries that at one time had a comparative advantage are no longer among the world's lowest-cost producers; they struggle to stay afloat. Cost cutting leads to layoffs, and layoffs lead to demands for protection.

The model of international trade in perfect competition suggests that trade will threaten some industries. As countries specialize in activities in which they have a comparative advantage, sectors in which they don't have this advantage will shrink. Maintaining those sectors through trade barriers blocks a nation from enjoying the gains possible from free trade.

A further difficulty with using trade barriers to shore up employment in a particular sector is that it can be an enormously expensive strategy. Suppose enough of a foreign good is kept out of the United States to save one U.S. job. That shifts the supply curve slightly to the left, raising prices for U.S. consumers. The loss to consumers is the cost per job saved. Estimates of the cost of saving *one* job in the steel industry through restrictions on steel imports, for example, go as high as $750,000 per year.

Cheap Foreign Labor

One reason often given for the perceived need to protect American workers against free international trade is that workers must be protected against cheap foreign labor. From a theoretical point of view, of course, if foreign countries can produce a good at lower cost than we can, it is in our collective interest to obtain it from them. But workers counter by saying that the low wages of foreign workers means that foreign workers are exploited. To compete with foreign workers, American workers would have to submit themselves to similar exploitation. This objection, however, fails to recognize that differences in wage rates generally reflect differences in worker productivity.

Consider the following example: U.S. workers in the widget industry earn $20 per hour while Indonesian workers in the widget industry earn only $2 per hour. If we assume that we are dealing with competitive industries, then the wages in both countries are based on the marginal revenue product of the workers. The higher wage of U.S. workers must mean that they have a higher marginal product—they are more productive. The higher wage of U.S. workers need not imply that labor costs are higher in the United States than in Indonesia.

Exhibit 11-13 illustrates the point. It takes only 1 hour of labor in the U.S. to produce a widget, whereas it takes 10 hours of labor in Indonesia. To find the labor cost per widget in the two countries, we multiply the hours of labor by the wage rate. We see that the labor cost per widget is the same in the two countries. The lower wage in Indonesia therefore does not represent a threat to U.S. workers.

EXHIBIT 11-13

Labor Costs per Widget Reflect Both Wages and Productivity

Although the wage rate is higher in the United States than in Indonesia, the labor costs per widget in the two countries are the same. The difference in wage rates reflects the higher level of productivity of U.S. workers in the widget industry.

Country	Hours of Labor per Widget	Labor Cost per Hour (Wage Rate)	Labor Cost per Widget
United States	1	$20	$20
Indonesia	10	$2	$20

Dumping occurs when an exporter sells a good to a country at a price below its own production cost.

Retaliation Against Dumping

Foreign producers of goods and services are often accused of "dumping" their goods in the U.S. market. An exporter is said to be engaged in **dumping** if it sells goods in a foreign market at a price below its own production cost.

In the United States, domestic firms may file charges with the Commerce Department, accusing foreign competitors with dumping. If Commerce finds that foreign firms have sold goods in U.S. markets below their cost of production, it imposes higher tariffs against the countries in which the firms are located. In 1993, for example, the U.S. Commerce Department slapped duties of up to 73 percent on steel produced by 19 different nations whose firms were found guilty of dumping steel in the United States.

The Commerce Department evaluates charges of dumping by estimating the actual cost a foreign firm incurs in producing goods. In estimating these costs, Commerce assumes that the firm "should" earn a certain profit rate. In the steel ruling, for example, it assumed that foreign firms should earn a profit rate equal to 8 percent of total sales—about double the actual rate earned by U.S. corporations. Imposing this rule often results in a finding that foreign firms are selling below cost.

One difficulty with tariffs imposed in retaliation against dumping, then, is that the charge is often based on an arbitrary assessment of a firm's costs. Another objection, of course, is that the retaliation imposes high costs on U.S. consumers of the goods and services affected.

Differences in Environmental Standards

Another justification for protectionist measures is that free trade is unfair if it pits domestic firms against foreign rivals who do not have to adhere to the same regulatory standards. In the debate over NAFTA, for example, critics argued that Mexican firms, facing relatively lax pollution control standards, would have an unfair advantage over U.S. firms if restraints on trade between the two countries were removed.

Economic theory suggests, however, that differences in pollution control policies can be an important source of comparative advantage. In general, the demand for environmental quality is positively related to income. People in higher-income countries demand higher environmental quality than do people in lower-income countries. That means that pollution has a lower cost in poorer than in richer countries. If an industry generates a great deal of pollution, it may be more efficient to locate it in a poor country than in a rich country. In effect, a poor country's lower demand for environmental quality gives it a comparative advantage in production of goods that generate a great deal of pollution.

Suppose that a good can be produced for the same cost in a rich or in a poor country, but that the cost does not include an estimate of pollution cost. Suppose that the people in the poor country do not regard the pollution generated as a significant cost. People in the United States, with their greater demand for environmental quality, do. Provided the benefits exceed the costs in the poor country, with the costs computed based on the preferences and incomes of people in that country, it makes sense for more of the good to be produced in the poor country and less in the rich country. Such an allocation leaves people in both countries better off than they would be otherwise.

Do economists support *any* restriction on free international trade? In the context of competitive industries, it seems safe to say that, for nearly all economists, the answer is no. The gains from trade are so large, and the costs of restraining it so high, that it's hard to find any satisfactory reason to limit trade in a competitive environment. In cases of imperfectly competitive markets, which we examine in the next four chapters, some economists argue that a case for protectionism can be made. But there is virtually no support among economists for trade restrictions in competitive industries.

Checklist

- Protectionist policies restrict the importation of goods and services produced in foreign countries.
- Tariffs are taxes on imported goods and services. Quotas are limitations on the quantity that can be imported. Both tariffs and quotas decrease the equilibrium quantity and raise the equilibrium price of the goods and services on which they are imposed.
- Voluntary export restrictions have the same economic effect as quotas.
- Nontariff barriers restrict trade through government policies other than tariffs or quotas.
- Arguments in favor of protectionist policies include the infant industry argument, the national security argument, the job protection argument, the cheap foreign labor argument, the retaliation against dumping argument, and the environmental standards argument. Economists generally agree that in competitive markets, none of these arguments justifies protectionist measures.

A Look Back—And a Look Ahead

In this chapter we have seen how international trade makes it possible for countries to improve upon their domestic production possibilities. In order to show why this is true, we established as a baseline the combination of domestic outputs that maximized the total value of production.

A country maximizes the value of its production by operating at a point on its production possibilities curve at which the rate of product transformation equals the rate of market substitution (RPT=RMS). This solution is found graphically at the point where a trading line is tangent to the production possibilities curve.

A country that is maximizing the value of its domestic production can obtain more of all goods by opening its markets to free international trade. Free trade allows both nations to reach beyond their domestic production possibilities curves. If nations specialize in the production of goods and services in which they have a comparative advantage, total output is increased. Free trade enhances production possibilities on a worldwide scale. It does not, however, benefit everyone. Some workers and owners of other factors of production will be hurt by free trade, at least in the short run.

The imposition of a tariff, quota, or voluntary export restriction raises the equilibrium price and reduces the equilibrium quantity of the good on which the restriction is imposed. Although there are many arguments in favor of such restrictions on free trade, economists generally agree that none of them justifies protectionist measures in competitive international markets.

In the next four chapters we move from the model of perfect competition to the examination of models of imperfect competition. The distinguishing characteristic of all these models is the assumption that rather than being price takers, firms in imperfectly competitive markets can set their own prices. Armed with the model of perfect competition, we will be in a better position to assess the social and economic implications of resource allocation under conditions of imperfect competition.

Terms and Concepts for Review

Dumping

Infant industry

Nontariff barrier

Protectionist policy

Quota

Rate of market substitution (RMS)

Rate of product transformation (RPT)

Tariff

Terms of trade

Trading line

Voluntary export restriction

For Discussion

1. Explain how consumer preferences help to determine the point on a country's production possibilities curve at which it will operate.
2. Each point on a production possibilities curve reflects fully employed resources and resources that are allocated efficiently in production. On what basis, then, can an economist say that a move from one point to another on the curve is an improvement?
3. Suppose a country that does not engage in trade with other countries produces two goods, apples and jogging shoes. Now suppose that a fitness craze sweeps the country and increases the demand for jogging shoes. How will this affect the relative prices of the two goods? How will it affect the slope of the trading line? How will it affect production of the two goods?
4. The text suggests that the United States may have a comparative advantage over other countries in the production of high-tech capital goods. What do you think might be the sources of this advantage?
5. "I know a lawyer who can type 100 words per minute but pays a secretary $10 per hour to type court briefs. But the secretary can only type 50 words per minute. I have told my lawyer friend a hundred times she'd be better off doing the typing herself, but she just won't listen." Who has the better part of this disagreement, the lawyer or the friend? Explain.
6. Which individuals in the United States might benefit from a tariff placed on the importation of shoes? Which might lose?
7. Explain why economists argue that protectionist policies lead to the misallocation of resources in the domestic economy.
8. Tomatoes grow well in Kansas. Why do the people of Kansas buy most of their tomatoes from Florida, Mexico, and California?
9. Suppose the United States imposes a quota on the import of copper. Who might be helped? Who might be hurt?
10. Some people argue that international trade is fine, but that firms in different countries should play on a "level playing field." They argue that if a good can be produced more cheaply abroad than at home, tariffs should be imposed on the good so that the costs of producing it are the same everywhere. What do you think of this argument?

Problems

1. Suppose the following table presents four points on the linear production possibilities curves for two countries (Argentina and Chile) that are currently not trading with one another. Argentina is currently producing at combination C and Chile is producing at combination B′. What is the opportunity cost of clothing in Argentina? What is the opportunity cost of clothing in Chile? Which country has a comparative advantage in food production? Which country has a comparative advantage in clothing production?

Argentina			Chile		
Point	**Food**	**Clothing**	**Point**	**Food**	**Clothing**
A	90	0	A′	15	0
B	60	15	B′	10	5
C	30	30	C′	5	10
D	0	45	D′	0	15

2. Show how both countries in Problem 1 could be made better off if they specialized according to comparative advantage and engaged in trade.
3. Argentina and New Zealand each produce wheat and mutton, as shown on the accompanying production possibilities curves.

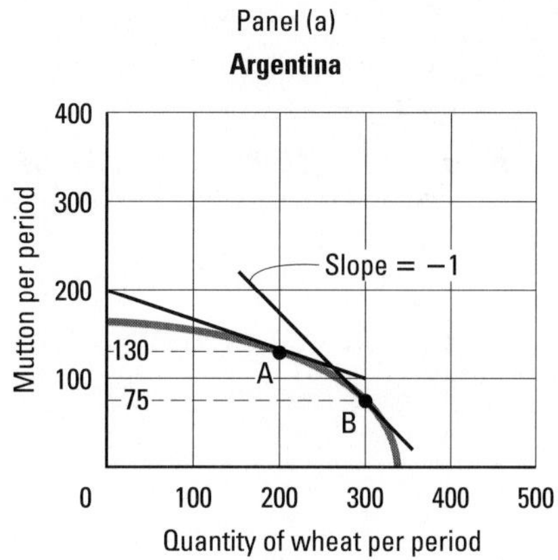

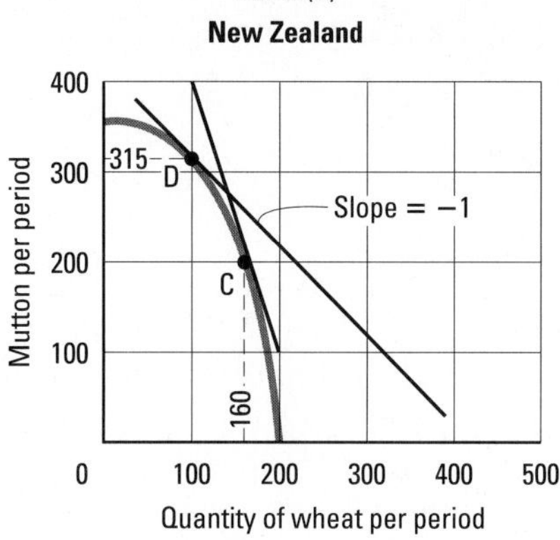

Assume there is no trade between the two countries, and that Argentina is now producing at A and New Zealand at C. Given the trading lines shown at each of these points, compute the rate of product transformation in each country. Which country has a comparative advantage in which good? Explain.

4. Assume that trade opens between Argentina and New Zealand and that, with trade, a unit of mutton exchanges for a unit of wheat. Before trade, Argentina produced at A and New Zealand produced at C. Argentina moves to point B while New Zealand moves to point D. Calculate and illustrate graphically an exchange between Argentina and New Zealand that would leave both countries with more of both goods than they had before trade.

5. The U.S. demand and supply for stem roses are given by the following table, with all quantities in millions of dozens:

Price per Dozen	Quantity Demanded per Month	Quantity Supplied per Month
$30	1.0	3.0
20	2.0	2.0
10	3.0	1.0

Suppose that at any price below $10 per dozen, the quantity supplied by U.S. producers drops to zero.

a. Draw the demand and supply curves and compute the equilibrium price and output of roses, assuming the United States does not engage in international trade in roses.

b. The United States now begins international trade in roses, and foreign suppliers are able to export roses to the U.S. market according to the following supply schedule:

Price per Dozen	Foreign Supply per Month
$30	6.0
20	4.0
10	2.0
5	1.0

Suppose foreign suppliers will supply no roses to the U.S. market at any price below $5 per dozen. Draw the foreign supply and total supply (domestic plus foreign) curves for roses in the United States. What will be the price and output of roses now that imported roses are permitted?

c. Suppose a quota of 1 million roses per month is placed on foreign producers. How will this affect the price and output of roses in the United States?

Part Four Departures from Perfect Competition

12

Monopoly

Chapter Objectives

After mastering the material in this chapter, you will be able to:

1. Explain the differences between monopoly and perfect competition.
2. Explain the sources of monopoly power and the meaning of the term "natural monopoly."
3. Explain the relationship between demand, total revenue, and marginal revenue.
4. Use demand, marginal revenue, and marginal cost curves to show how a monopolist chooses its profit-maximizing level of output and price.
5. Explain why a monopolist doesn't have a supply curve.
6. Explain why the monopoly solution is likely to be inefficient.
7. Explain why a monopolist may want to charge different prices to different buyers.
8. Discuss the pros and cons of monopoly in the real world.

Businessmen praise competition and love monopoly.
Leonard Silk

What's Ahead

If your college or university is like most, you spend a lot of time, and money, dealing with firms that face very little competition. Your campus bookstore is likely to be the only firm selling the texts that professors require you to read. Your school may have granted an exclusive franchise to a firm for providing food service. You face a single supplier of local telephone service. Your utilities—electricity, natural gas, and water—are probably provided by a single firm.

Up to this point, we've assumed that individual firms operate in a competitive market, taking the price, which is determined by demand and supply, as given. In this chapter we investigate the behavior of firms that have a particular market all to themselves. As the only supplier of a particular good or service, they face the market demand curve alone.

We'll find that firms that have their respective markets all to themselves behave in a manner that is in many respects quite different from the behavior of firms in perfect competition. Such firms continue to use the marginal decision rule in maximizing profits, but their freedom to select the price they charge affects the ways in which this rule is applied.

A monopoly firm is likely to produce less, and charge more for what it produces, than firms in a competitive industry. We'll find that, as a result, a monopoly solution is likely to be inefficient. We'll also learn why some firms charge different prices to different consumers. Finally, we'll explore the policy alternatives available to government agencies in dealing with monopoly firms.

The Nature of Monopoly

A **monopoly** is at the opposite end of the spectrum from a perfectly competitive firm. A monopoly firm has no rivals. It is the only firm in its industry, and there are no close substitutes for the good or service it produces. A monopoly firm not only has the market to itself; it need not worry about other firms entering. In the monopoly case, entry by potential rivals is prohibitively difficult.

A monopoly does not take the market price as given; it determines its own price. It selects from its demand curve a price that yields the maximum profit

- A **monopoly** is a firm that is the only producer of a good or service for which there are no close substitutes and for which entry by potential rivals is prohibitively difficult.
- **Barriers to entry** are market conditions that prevent the entry of new firms in a monopoly market.
- A **natural monopoly** exists whenever a single firm confronts economies of scale over the entire range of production that is relevant to its market.

possible. A monopoly's ability to select its price allows it to earn profit; the entry of new firms (which eliminates profit in the long run in a competitive market) cannot occur in monopoly. We shall see in this chapter that a monopoly firm charges a higher price and produces a smaller output than would an otherwise identical competitive firm. A market economy with monopoly firms will not achieve an efficient allocation of resources. In the case of monopoly, government intervention may improve allocative efficiency.

Sources of Monopoly

Why are some markets dominated by single firms? What are the sources of monopoly power? Economists have identified five factors which, individually or in combination, may lead to domination of a market by a single firm and create barriers to entry that prevent the entry of new firms. **Barriers to entry** are characteristics of a particular market that block new firms from entering it. They include economies of scale, special advantages of location, the importance of sunk cost, a dominant position in the ownership of some inputs required for the production of the good, and government restrictions. Although these conditions may allow one firm to gain and to hold monopoly control over a market, there are often forces at work that can erode this control.

Economies of Scale

Scale economies and diseconomies define the shape of a firm's long-run average cost (LRAC) curve as it increases its output. If a firm can increase its output proportionately more than it increases the quantities of its factors of production, it is said to experience economies of scale—long-run average cost declines as the level of production increases.

A firm that confronts economies of scale over the entire range of outputs demanded in the industry is a **natural monopoly.** In a natural monopoly, the LRAC of any one firm intersects the market demand curve where long-run average costs are falling or are at a minimum. If this is the case, one firm in the industry will expand to exploit the economies of scale available to it. Because this firm will have lower unit costs than its rivals, it can drive them out of the market and gain monopoly control over the industry.

Suppose there are 12 firms, each operating with the scale of plant shown by $SRAC_1$ in Exhibit 12-1. A firm that expanded its scale of operation to achieve an average cost curve such as $SRAC_2$ could produce 240 units of output at a lower

EXHIBIT 12-1

Economies of Scale Lead to Natural Monopoly

A firm with falling long-run average cost (*LRAC*) throughout the range of outputs relevant to existing demand (*D*) will monopolize the industry. Here, one firm operating with a large plant ($SRAC_2$) produces 240 units of output at a lower cost than the $7 cost per unit of 12 firms operating at a smaller scale ($SRAC_1$), each producing 20 units of output.

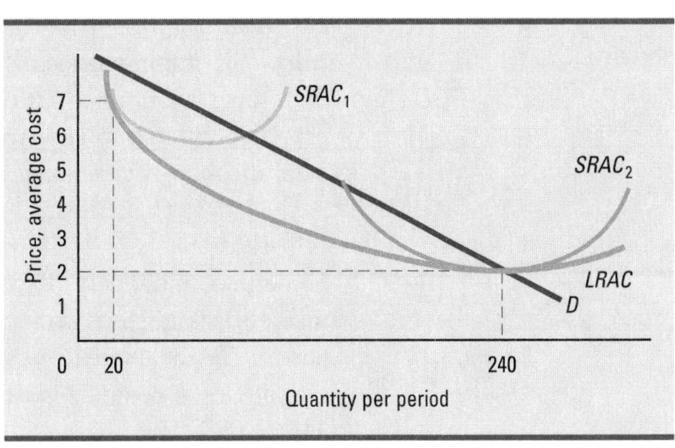

Case in Point: The Stirrup and the Rise and Fall of the Roman Empire

Did the invention of the stirrup bring on the collapse of the Roman Empire?

By the first century A.D., the Roman Empire encompassed most of Europe, the Middle East, and northern Africa. Its success, argues economic historian Leonard Dudley of the University of Montreal, rested in large part on its ability to produce military force at a lower cost than its adversaries.

Up to the first century A.D., military operations were conducted by foot soldiers. In general, the larger the number of soldiers, the more powerful the army. The Roman army used a strategy in which its legions of soldiers stood side by side holding large shields, forming a virtually invincible wall. Each additional soldier increased military force by providing greater protection to the other soldiers. The advantages of large numbers meant that the cost per unit of producing military force fell as the quantity of force increased.

Just as remarkable as the rise of the Roman Empire was its fall. From the first century to the ninth, Rome succumbed to a series of foreign invasions and civil wars.

Historians attribute Rome's success largely to its ability to establish and maintain military control. Explanations of its failure range from moral laxity to high taxes to lead in the water pipes that served its ruling class—more than 400 factors have been cited to explain the fall of the greatest empire in human history. Mr. Dudley links Rome's rise—and fall—to its long-run average cost curve for the production of military force.

Mr. Dudley suggests that, during the period of Rome's expansion, there were significant economies of scale throughout its range of production of military services. That gave Rome an advantage over the peoples it conquered; it could maintain an army at a lower cost per unit of military force than could its rivals. In effect, it emerged as a natural monopolist in the "market" for military control over most of the Western world.

But economies of scale depend crucially on the nature of the technology available. Mr. Dudley argues that the introduction of the saddle in the first century and the subsequent introduction of the stirrup greatly increased the effectiveness of mounted soldiers in combat. Smaller cavalry units could now defeat much larger armies of foot soldiers. Mounted soldiers fought for the most part as individuals; they didn't rely on their fellow soldiers for protection, Mr. Dudley says. He suggests that cavalry units could produce military force at a lower cost per unit than foot soldiers. The new technology didn't generate economies of scale; if anything, Rome lost its cost advantage in military production. The result, Mr. Dudley says, was that smaller states could compete effectively with Rome, and the Empire vanished.

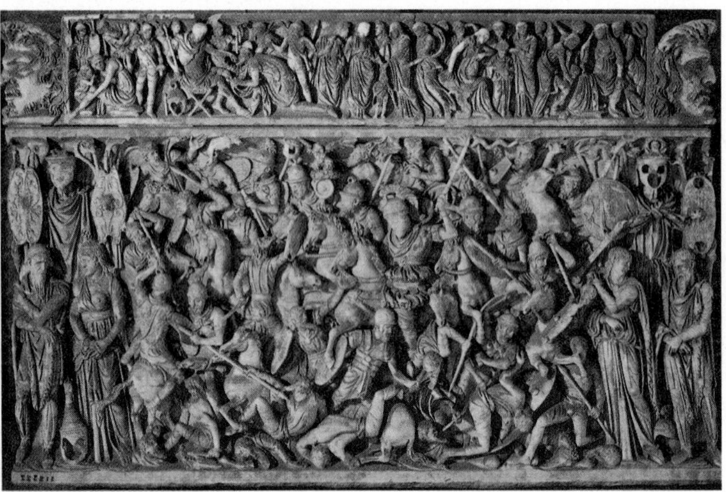

The second-century sarcophagus of a general in the army of the Roman emperor Marcus Aurelius.

Source: Leonard Dudley, "Structural Change in Interdependent Bureaucracies: Was Rome's Failure Economic or Military?" *Explorations in Economic History* 27 (June 1990): 232–248.

cost than could the smaller firms producing 20 units each. By cutting its price below the minimum average cost of the smaller plants, the larger firm could drive the smaller ones out of business. In this situation, the industry demand is not large enough to support more than one firm. If another firm attempted to enter the industry, the natural monopolist would always be able to undersell it.

Location

Sometimes monopoly power is the result of location. For example, sellers in markets isolated by distance from their nearest rivals have a degree of monopoly power. The local movie theater in a small town has a monopoly in showing first-run movies. Doctors, dentists, and mechanics in isolated towns may also be monopolists.

A **sunk cost** is an expenditure that has already been made that cannot be recovered.

Sunk Costs

Entry into an industry will be more difficult the greater the cost of establishing a new business in that industry. That cost will, in turn, be greater if the outlays required to start a business are unlikely to be recovered if the business should fail.

Suppose, for example, entry into a particular industry requires extensive advertising to make consumers aware of the new brand. Should the effort fail, there is no way to recover the expenditures for such advertising. Entry into an industry will require expenditures that won't be recoverable if the venture fails. An expenditure that has already been made and that cannot be recovered is called a **sunk cost.**

If a substantial fraction of a firm's initial outlays will be lost upon exit from the industry, exit will be costly. Difficulty of exit can make for difficulty of entry. The more firms have to lose from an unsuccessful effort to penetrate a particular market, the less likely they are to try. The potential for high sunk costs could thus contribute to the monopoly power of an established firm by making entry more difficult.

Restricted Ownership of Raw Materials and Inputs

In a very few cases the source of monopoly power is the ownership of strategic inputs. If a particular firm owns all of an input required for the production of a particular good or service, then it may emerge as the only producer of that good or service.

The Aluminum Company of America (ALCOA) gained monopoly power through its ownership of virtually all the bauxite mines in the world (bauxite is the source of aluminum). The International Nickel Company of Canada at one time owned virtually all the world's nickel. De Beers has acquired rights to nearly all the world's diamond production, giving it enormous power in the market for diamonds. This power may decline, however, if Russia, which has huge diamond reserves, begins to develop this resource and sell it independently of De Beers.

Government Restrictions

Another important basis for monopoly power consists of special privileges granted to some business firms by government agencies. State and local governments commonly assign exclusive franchises—rights to conduct business in a specific market—to cab and bus companies, to cable television companies, and to providers of telephone services, electricity, natural gas, and water. They may also regulate entry into an industry or a profession through licensing and certification requirements. Governments also provide patent protection to inventors of new products or production methods; these patents may afford their holders a degree of monopoly power during the 17-year life of the patent.

The Fragility of Monopoly Power

Monopoly power can be a fleeting thing. Firms constantly seek out the market power that monopoly offers. When conditions are right to achieve this power, firms that succeed in carving out monopoly positions are often able to enjoy substantial profits, for reasons explained in the next section. But those profits invite continuing attempts to break down the barriers to entry that insulate monopolies from competition.

Case in Point A Monopoly to Fight AIDS

A single firm, Burroughs Wellcome, produces azidothymidine (AZT), the leading drug for the treatment of AIDS. AIDS activists have accused the firm of unfairly exploiting its monopoly position in its pricing of the drug, whose wholesale price is more than $2,000 per year per person.

Although AZT was developed by government scientists, the Food and Drug Administration granted Burroughs Wellcome the exclusive right to market the drug. The FDA often gives private firms exclusive rights to manufacture and distribute drugs the government has developed. Burroughs Wellcome will maintain its monopoly position until 2005, when its exclusive franchise expires.

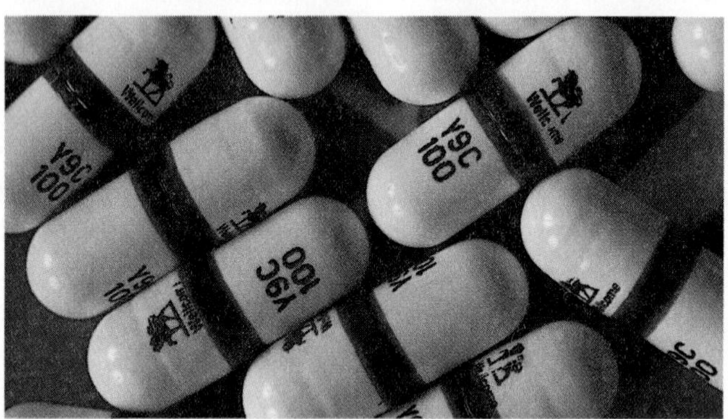

Two firms, Barr Laboratories and Novopharm Ltd., have sought permission to produce a generic version of the drug. They predicted that their version would cost about half as much as the Burroughs Wellcome product. The company sued, charging that the generic products would infringe on its patent. In a 1993 ruling, a federal judge sided with Burroughs Wellcome, allowing the firm's monopoly position to stand.

Reaction to the ruling was mixed. Evan Wilder, a spokesman for the New York chapter of Act-Up, an organization representing AIDS victims, called the ruling a "major disappointment." Paul Holcombe, a spokesman for Burroughs Wellcome, hailed the ruling: "The point here . . . is whether generic companies which spend little money or effort on basic research should have the ability to come in and profit from our discovery before the patents we legally own expire. New medicines don't come from generic pharmaceutical companies."

Stock in Wellcome PLC, the British company that owns Burroughs Wellcome, jumped 37½ cents per share the day the ruling was announced.

Source: Edward Felsenthal, "Wellcome's AZT Monopoly Faces Test," *The Wall Street Journal*, 28 June 1993, B1.

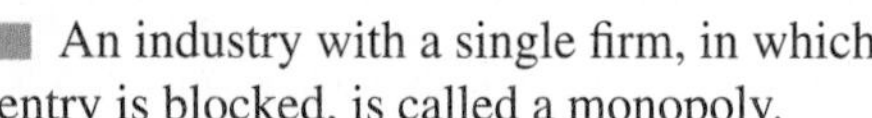

Checklist

- An industry with a single firm, in which entry is blocked, is called a monopoly.
- The sources of monopoly power include economies of scale, locational advantages, high sunk costs associated with entry, restricted ownership of key inputs, and government restrictions.
- The sources of monopoly may be eroded by technological advances or other changes in the economy.

Technological change and the pursuit of profits chip constantly at the entrenched power of monopolies. Whether it be companies such as Sprint and MCI challenging AT&T's old monopoly in long-distance telephone service, catalog companies challenging the monopoly positions of some retailers, or Federal Express taking on the U.S. Postal Service, the assaults on monopoly power are continuous.

Indeed, the barriers to entry that help define monopoly are falling so rapidly that one can reasonably ask whether the model is useful. The narrow response to this challenge is to note that many monopoly firms continue to exist, particularly those whose monopoly power is the result of government policy. The broader answer, however, is that the monopoly model can be used to explain many choices by firms, even those firms that don't satisfy the strict definition of monopoly. That model, which is developed in the next two sections, can be used to examine the pricing choices of any firm facing a downward-sloping demand curve.

The Monopoly Model

Analyzing choices is a more complex challenge for a monopoly firm than for a perfectly competitive firm. After all, a competitive firm takes the market price as given and determines its output. Because a monopoly has its market all to itself,

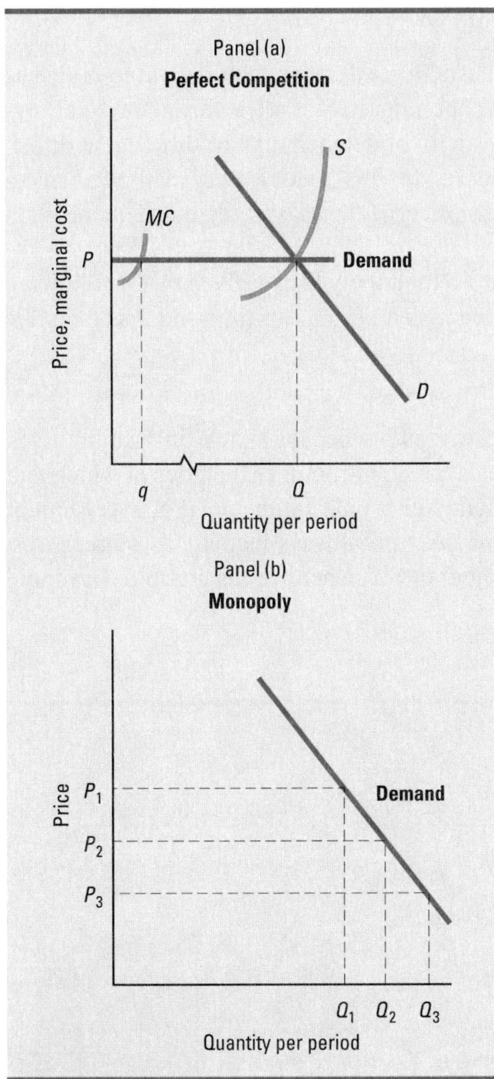

EXHIBIT 12-2

Perfect Competition Versus Monopoly

Panel (a) shows the determination of equilibrium price and output in a perfectly competitive market. A typical firm with marginal cost curve *MC* is a price taker, choosing to produce quantity *q* at the equilibrium price *P*. In Panel (b) a monopoly faces a downward-sloping market demand curve. As a price setter, it can charge any price it wishes on this demand curve. Once it sets a price, however, the quantity demanded is found from the demand curve. The monopoly firm can sell additional units only by lowering price. The perfectly competitive firm, by contrast, can sell any quantity it wishes at the market price.

- A **price setter** is a firm that faces a downward-sloping demand curve.
- The power a firm has to set its own price is called **monopoly power.**

it can determine not only its output but its price as well. What kinds of price and output choices will such a firm make?

We will answer that question in the context of the marginal decision rule: A firm will produce additional units of a good until marginal revenue equals marginal cost. To apply that rule to a monopoly firm, we must investigate the special relationship that exists in monopoly between demand and marginal revenue.

Monopoly and Market Demand

Because a monopoly firm has its market all to itself, it faces the market demand curve. Unlike a perfectly competitive firm, the monopoly firm can pick any price it wants on its demand curve.

Exhibit 12-2 compares the demand situations faced by a monopoly and a perfectly competitive firm. In Panel (a), the equilibrium price for a perfectly competitive firm is determined by the intersection of the demand and supply curves. The supply curve is found by summing the supply curves of individual firms. Those, in turn, consist of the portions of marginal cost curves that lie above average variable cost. The marginal cost curve *MC* for a single firm is illustrated; the market supply curve is the horizontal summation of all the firms' marginal cost curves. Notice the break in the horizontal axis; the quantity produced by a single firm is a trivially small fraction of the whole. In the perfectly competitive model, one firm has *nothing* to do with the determination of the market price. Each firm in a perfectly competitive industry faces a horizontal demand curve defined by the market price.

Contrast the situation shown in Panel (a) with the one faced by the monopoly firm in Panel (b). Because it is the only supplier in the industry, the monopolist faces the downward-sloping market demand curve. It may choose to produce any quantity. But, unlike the perfectly competitive firm, which can sell all it wants at the going market price, a monopolist can sell a greater quantity only by cutting its price.

Suppose, for example, that a monopoly firm can sell Q_1 units at a price P_1 in Panel (b). If it wishes to increase its output to Q_2 units—and sell that quantity—it must reduce its price to P_2. To sell quantity Q_3 it would have to reduce the price to P_3. The monopoly firm may choose its price and output, but it is restricted to a combination of price and output that lie on the demand curve. It could not, for example, charge price P_1 and sell quantity Q_3. A firm that faces a downward-sloping demand curve is called a **price setter.**

Because monopoly firms are price setters, the concept of a supply curve has no meaning in monopoly. A supply curve shows the quantity a firm will produce in response to each market price; supply curves thus exist only for price takers.

A firm that acts as a price setter is often said to possess **monopoly power**—it can set its own price. The degree of monopoly power is often assessed in terms of the price elasticity of demand facing a firm. A perfectly competitive firm faces perfectly elastic demand and has no monopoly power. A firm that faces both a downward-sloping demand curve and competition from other firms faces demand that is highly elastic, because its rivals produce close substitutes for its product. That firm's demand, however, will be less elastic than that of a perfectly competitive firm; it has a degree of monopoly power. The demand faced by a monopoly firm is likely to be still less elastic, because there are no rival firms producing close substitutes. A monopoly firm thus has the highest degree of monopoly power possible.

Total Revenue and Elasticity

We saw in Chapter 4 that a firm's elasticity of demand with respect to price has important implications for assessing the impact of a price change on total revenue. We also saw that the price elasticity of demand may be different at different points on a firm's demand curve. In this section, we shall see why a monopoly firm will always select a price in the elastic region of its demand curve.

Suppose the demand curve facing a monopoly firm is given by the following equation, where Q is the quantity demanded per unit of time and P is the price per unit:

$$Q = 10 - P \tag{1}$$

This demand equation implies the demand schedule shown in Exhibit 12-3. Total revenue for each quantity equals the quantity times the price at which that quantity is demanded. Because a monopolist must cut the price of every unit in order to increase sales, total revenue does not always increase as output rises. Here, total revenue reaches a maximum of $25 when 5 units are sold. Beyond 5 units, total revenue begins to decline.

EXHIBIT 12-3

Demand, Elasticity, and Total Revenue

Suppose a monopolist faces the downward-sloping demand curve shown in Panel (a). In order to increase the quantity sold, it must cut the price. Total revenue is found by multiplying the price and quantity sold at each price. Total revenue, plotted in Panel (b), is maximized at $25, when the quantity sold is 5 units and the price is $5. At that point on the demand curve, the price elasticity of demand equals −1.

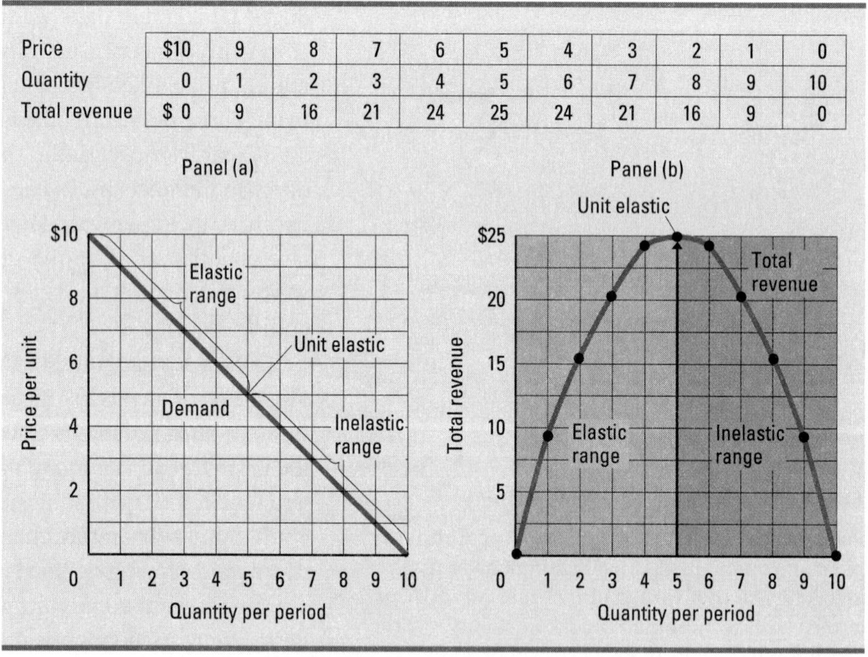

Price	$10	9	8	7	6	5	4	3	2	1	0
Quantity	0	1	2	3	4	5	6	7	8	9	10
Total revenue	$ 0	9	16	21	24	25	24	21	16	9	0

The demand curve in Panel (a) shows ranges of values of the price elasticity of demand. We saw in Chapter 4 that elasticity varies along a linear demand curve in a special way: demand is elastic at points in the upper half of the demand curve and inelastic in the lower half of the demand curve. The relationship between demand, elasticity, and total spending corresponds closely to the relationship between demand, elasticity, and total revenue.

If demand is elastic, a price reduction increases total revenue. To sell an additional unit, a monopoly firm must lower its price. The sale of one more unit will thus increase revenue if demand is elastic. The elastic range of the demand curve corresponds to the range over which the total revenue curve is rising in Panel (b) of Exhibit 12-3.

If demand is inelastic, a price reduction reduces total revenue. Because the firm must lower its price in order to sell an additional unit, total revenue falls as the firm sells additional units over the inelastic range of the demand curve. The downward-sloping portion of the total revenue curve in Panel (b) thus corresponds to the inelastic range of the demand curve.

Finally, recall that the midpoint of a linear demand curve is the point at which demand becomes unit elastic. That point on the total revenue curve in Panel (b) corresponds to the point at which total revenue reaches a maximum.

The relationship between elasticity, demand, and total revenue has an important implication for the selection of the profit-maximizing price and output: a monopoly firm will not choose a price and output in the inelastic range of the demand curve. Suppose, for example, that the monopoly firm in Exhibit 12-3 is charging $3 and selling 7 units. Its total revenue is thus $21. Because this combination is in the inelastic portion of the demand curve, the firm could increase its total revenue by raising its price. It could, at the same time, reduce its total cost. Raising price means reducing output; a reduction in output would reduce total cost. If the firm is operating in the inelastic range of its demand curve, then, it is not maximizing profits. The firm could earn a higher profit by raising price and reducing output. It will continue to raise its price until it is in the elastic portion of its demand curve. A profit-maximizing monopoly firm will therefore select a price and output combination in the elastic range of its demand curve.

The firm could, of course, choose a point at which demand is unit elastic. At that point, total revenue is maximized. But the firm seeks to maximize profit, not total revenue. A solution that maximizes total revenue will not maximize profit unless marginal cost is zero.

Demand and Marginal Revenue

In the perfectly competitive case, the additional revenue a firm gains from selling an additional unit—its marginal revenue—is equal to the market price. The firm's demand curve, which is a horizontal line at the market price, is also its marginal revenue curve. But a monopoly firm can sell an additional unit only by lowering the price. That fact complicates the relationship between the monopoly's demand curve and its marginal revenue.

Suppose the firm in Exhibit 12-3 sells 2 units at a price of $8 per unit. Its total revenue is $16. Now it wishes to sell a third unit and wants to know the marginal revenue of that unit. To sell 3 units rather than 2, the firm must lower its price to $7 per unit. Total revenue rises to $21. The marginal revenue of the third unit is thus $5. But the *price* at which the firm sells the third unit is $7. Marginal revenue is less than price.

To see why the marginal revenue of the third unit is less than its price, let's examine more carefully how the sale of that unit affects the firm's revenues. The firm brings in $7 from the sale of the third unit. But selling the third unit required the firm to charge a price of $7 instead of the $8 the firm was charging for 2 units. Now the firm receives less for the first 2 units. The marginal revenue of the third unit is the $7 the firm receives for that unit *minus* the $1 reduction in revenue for each of the first two units. The marginal revenue of the third unit is thus $5.

EXHIBIT 12-4

Demand and Marginal Revenue

The marginal revenue curve for the monopoly firm lies below its demand curve. It shows the additional revenue gained from selling an additional unit. Notice that, as always, marginal values are plotted at the midpoints of the respective intervals.

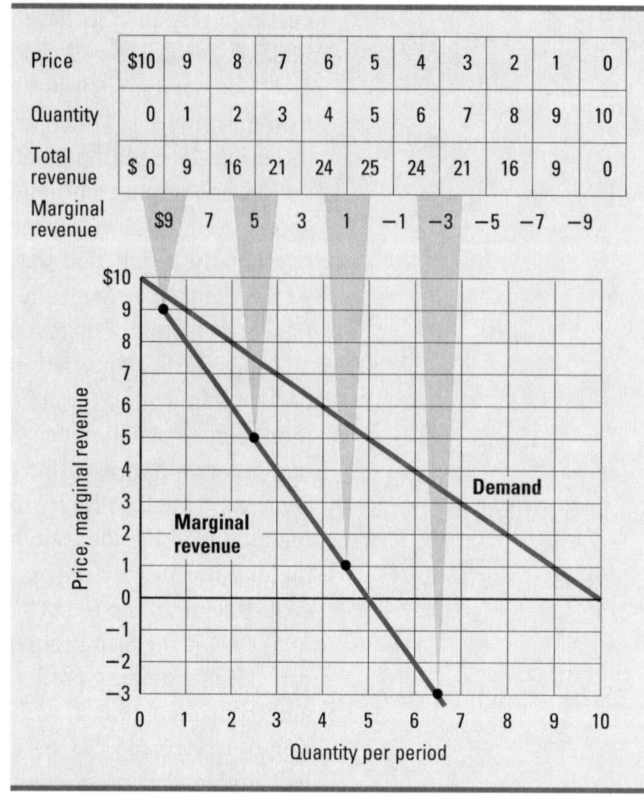

Price	$10	9	8	7	6	5	4	3	2	1	0
Quantity	0	1	2	3	4	5	6	7	8	9	10
Total revenue	$ 0	9	16	21	24	25	24	21	16	9	0

Marginal revenue: $9 7 5 3 1 −1 −3 −5 −7 −9

Marginal revenue is always less than price for the monopoly firm. Exhibit 12-4 shows the relationship between demand and marginal revenue, based on the demand curve introduced in Exhibit 12-3.

When the demand curve is linear, as in Exhibit 12-4, the marginal revenue curve can be placed according to the following rules:

1. The marginal revenue curve is always below the demand curve.
2. The marginal revenue curve will bisect any horizontal line drawn between the vertical axis and the demand curve.[1]

The marginal revenue and demand curves in Exhibit 12-4 follow these two rules. The marginal revenue curve lies below the demand curve, and it bisects any horizontal line drawn from the vertical axis to the demand curve. At a price of $6, for example, the quantity demanded is 4. The marginal revenue curve passes through 2 units at this price. At a price of 0, the quantity demanded is 10; the marginal revenue curve passes through 5 units at this point.

Just as there is a relationship between the firm's demand curve and the price elasticity of demand, there is a relationship between its marginal revenue curve and elasticity. Where marginal revenue is positive, demand is elastic. Where marginal revenue is negative, demand is inelastic. Where marginal revenue is zero, demand is unit elastic. A firm wouldn't produce an additional unit of output with negative marginal revenue. And, assuming that the production of an additional unit has some cost, a firm won't produce the extra unit if it has zero marginal revenue. Because a monopoly firm will generally operate where marginal revenue is positive, we see once again that it will operate in the elastic range of its demand curve.

Checklist

- A monopoly firm is a price setter; the concept of a supply curve is meaningless in monopoly.
- If the firm faces a downward-sloping demand curve, marginal revenue is less than price.
- Marginal revenue is positive in the elastic range of a demand curve, negative in the inelastic range, and zero where demand is unit elastic.
- A monopoly firm will never operate in the inelastic range of the demand curve.
- If a monopoly firm faces a linear demand curve, its marginal revenue curve is also linear. The marginal revenue curve lies below the demand curve and bisects any horizontal line drawn from the vertical axis to the demand curve.

[1] To put it another way, the marginal revenue curve will be twice as steep as the demand curve. The demand curve in Exhibit 12-4 is given by the equation $Q = 10 - P$, which can be written $P = 10 - Q$. The marginal revenue curve is given by $P = 10 - 2Q$.

Case in Point — Profit-Maximizing Hockey Teams

Professional hockey teams set admission prices at levels that maximize their profits, according to four economists at the University of Vancouver. The economists, who argue that hockey teams can be regarded as monopoly firms, use the monopoly model to examine the teams' behavior.

The economists, Donald G. Ferguson, Kenneth G. Stewart, John Colin H. Jones, and Andre Le Dressay, used data from the 1981 to 1983 seasons to estimate demand and marginal revenue curves facing each team in the National Hockey League. They found that demand for a team's tickets is affected by population and income in the team's home city, the team's standing in the National Hockey League, and the number of superstars on the team.

Because a sports team's costs don't vary significantly with the number of fans who attend a given game, the economists assumed that marginal cost is zero. The profit-maximizing number of seats sold per game is thus the quantity at which marginal revenue is zero, provided a team's stadium is large enough to hold that quantity of fans. This unconstrained quantity is labeled Q_u, with a corresponding price P_u, in the graph.

Stadium size and the demand curve facing a team may prevent the team from selling the profit-maximizing quantity of tickets. If its stadium holds only Q_c fans, for example, the team will sell that many tickets at price P_c; its marginal revenue is positive at that quantity. Economic theory thus predicts that the marginal revenue for teams that consistently sell out their games will be positive, and the marginal revenue for other teams will be zero.

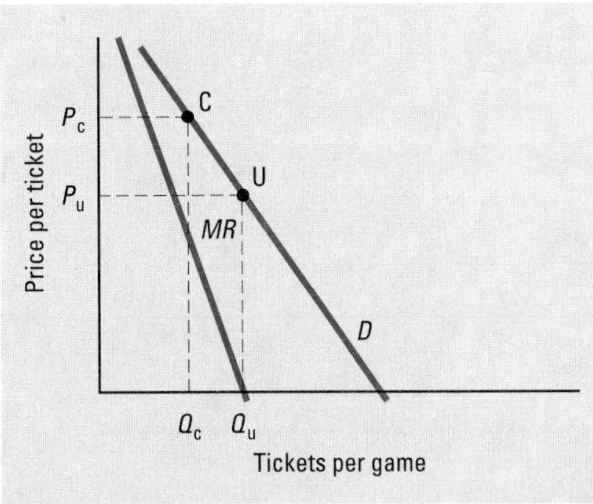

The economists' statistical results were consistent with the theory. They found that teams that don't typically sell out their games operate at a quantity at which marginal revenue is about zero, and that teams with sell-outs have positive marginal revenue. "It's clear that these teams are very sophisticated in their use of pricing to maximize profits," Mr. Ferguson concludes.

Source: Timothy Tregarthen, "Are Profits the Goal of Hockey Team Owners?" *The Margin* 7 (Spring 1992): 49.

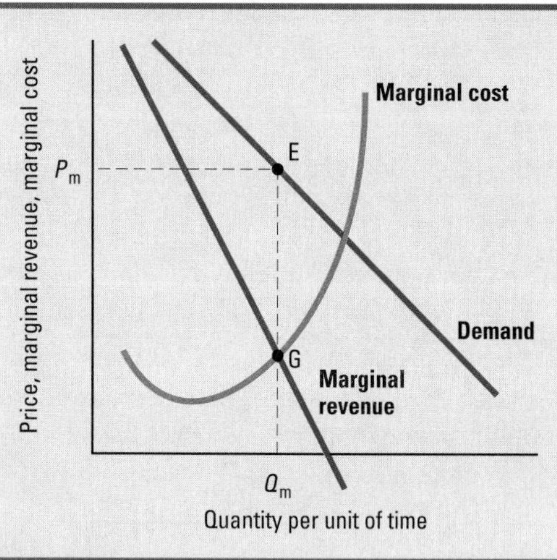

EXHIBIT 12-5

The Monopoly Solution

The monopoly firm maximizes profit by producing an output Q_m at point G, where the marginal revenue and marginal cost curves intersect. It sells this output at price P_m.

Profit Maximization

Profit-maximizing behavior is always based on the marginal decision rule presented in Chapter 5: Additional units of a good should be produced as long as the marginal revenue of an additional unit exceeds the marginal cost. The maximizing solution occurs where marginal revenue equals marginal cost.

Monopoly Equilibrium: Applying the Marginal Decision Rule

Exhibit 12-5 shows a demand curve and an associated marginal revenue curve facing a monopoly firm. The marginal cost curve is like those we derived in Chapter 7; it falls over the range of output in which the firm experiences increasing returns, then rises as the firm experiences diminishing returns.

To determine the profit-maximizing output, we note the quantity at which the firm's marginal revenue and marginal cost curves intersect (Q_m in Exhibit 12-5). We read up from Q_m to the demand curve to find the price P_m at which the firm can sell Q_m units. The profit-maximizing price and output are given by point E on the demand curve.

We thus can determine a monopoly firm's profit-maximizing price and output by following three steps:

1. Determine the demand, marginal revenue, and marginal cost curves.
2. Select the output level at which the marginal revenue and marginal cost curves intersect.
3. Determine from the demand curve the price at which that output can be sold.

Once we have determined the monopoly firm's price and output, we can determine its profit by adding the firm's average total cost curve to the graph showing demand, marginal revenue, and marginal cost, as shown in Exhibit 12-6. The average total cost at an output of Q_m units is ATC_m. The firm's profit per unit is thus $P_m - ATC_m$. Total profit is found by multiplying the firm's output, Q_m, by profit per unit, so total profit equals $Q_m(P_m - ATC_m)$, the area of the shaded rectangle in Exhibit 12-6.

EXHIBIT 12-6

Computing Monopoly Profit

A monopoly firm's profit per unit is the difference between price and average total cost. Total profit equals profit per unit times the quantity produced. Total profit is given by the area of the shaded rectangle.

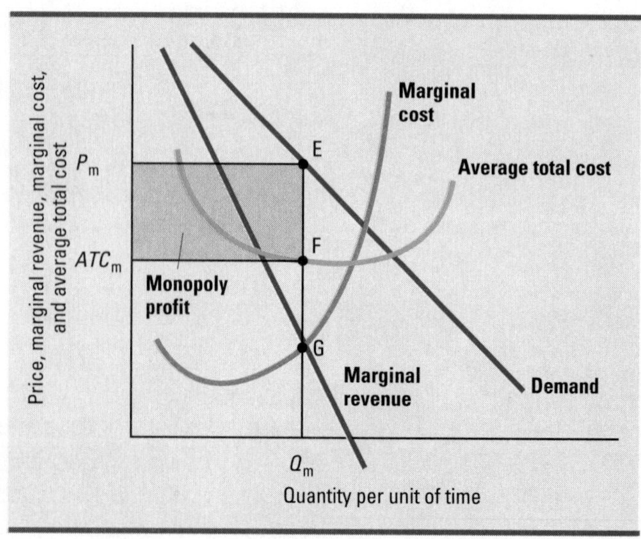

A Case Study of Profit Maximization

Let's apply what we have learned about profit maximization in monopoly to a hypothetical case study. We shall see that by following the steps outlined in the previous section, we can find the output level that yields the maximum profit possible for a monopoly firm.

Suppose a firm, Hercules Medcorp, produces a special wheelchair with a seat that rises to allow users to stand. Because it was able to obtain and enforce a patent on its design and production process, Hercules Medcorp has a monopoly on this type of wheelchair.

We shall follow the steps outlined above to determine the output and price at which Hercules will maximize its profit.

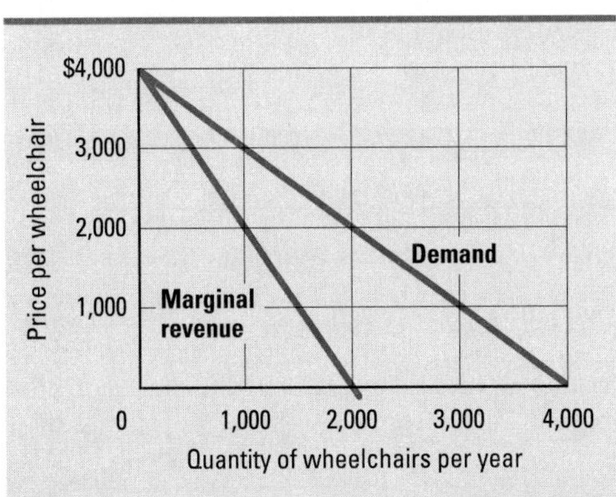

EXHIBIT 12-7

Hercules Medcorp: Demand and Marginal Revenue

Hercules Medcorp's demand is given by the equation $Q = 4{,}000 - P$. That implies the demand and marginal revenue curves shown.

Step 1: *Define Demand, Marginal Revenue, and Marginal Cost*

Suppose the demand curve facing Hercules Medcorp for its wheelchairs is given by the equation

$$Q = 4{,}000 - P \quad (2)$$

We can rewrite this equation with price as the dependent variable:

$$P = 4{,}000 - Q \quad (3)$$

Exhibit 12-7 shows this demand curve. Because the demand curve is linear, the marginal revenue curve is also linear; it lies below the demand curve and bisects any horizontal line drawn from the vertical axis to the demand curve. Its equation is

$$MR = 4{,}000 - 2Q \quad (4)$$

Exhibit 12-8 gives Hercules Medcorp's marginal and average total cost curves. Notice that these curves have the characteristics described in Chapter 7: the average total cost curve is U-shaped, and at its lowest point it crosses the marginal cost curve.

EXHIBIT 12-8

Average and Marginal Cost

The average total cost curve *ATC* and marginal cost curve *MC* for Hercules Medcorp exhibit the familiar shapes developed in Chapter 7.

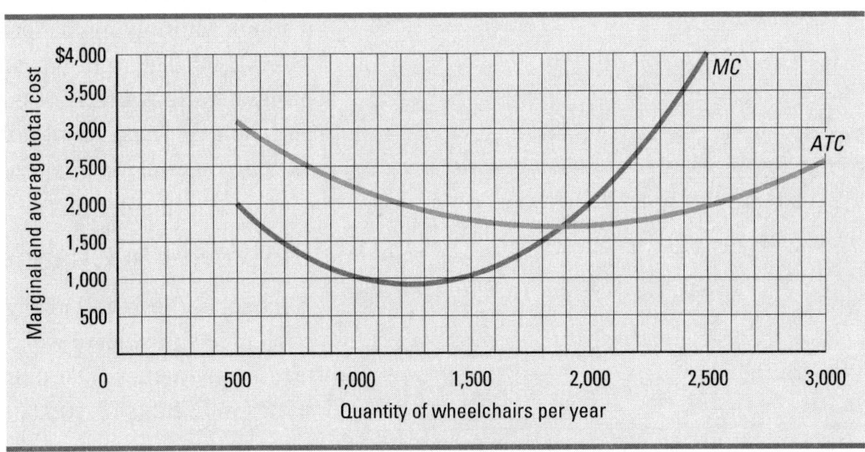

Step 2: *Determine the Profit-Maximizing Output*

To determine the profit-maximizing output, we combine the curves we've derived so far for Hercules Medcorp. The profit-maximizing output occurs where marginal cost equals marginal revenue. We see in Exhibit 12-9 that these curves intersect at an output of 1,500 wheelchairs per year, point G.

EXHIBIT 12-9

Maximizing Profit: The Monopoly Case

The table provides cost and revenue information for selected prices and levels of output. The graph shows that profit is maximized at point G, where marginal revenue (*MR*) equals marginal cost (*MC*). We read up from point G to the demand curve *D*, where point E shows the profit-maximizing price. Profit per unit is the difference between price and average total cost ($2,500 at point E minus $1,833⅓ at point F on the average total cost curve *ATC*), or $666⅔. Multiplying by the output, 1,500 units, we find the company's total profit is $1 million per year.

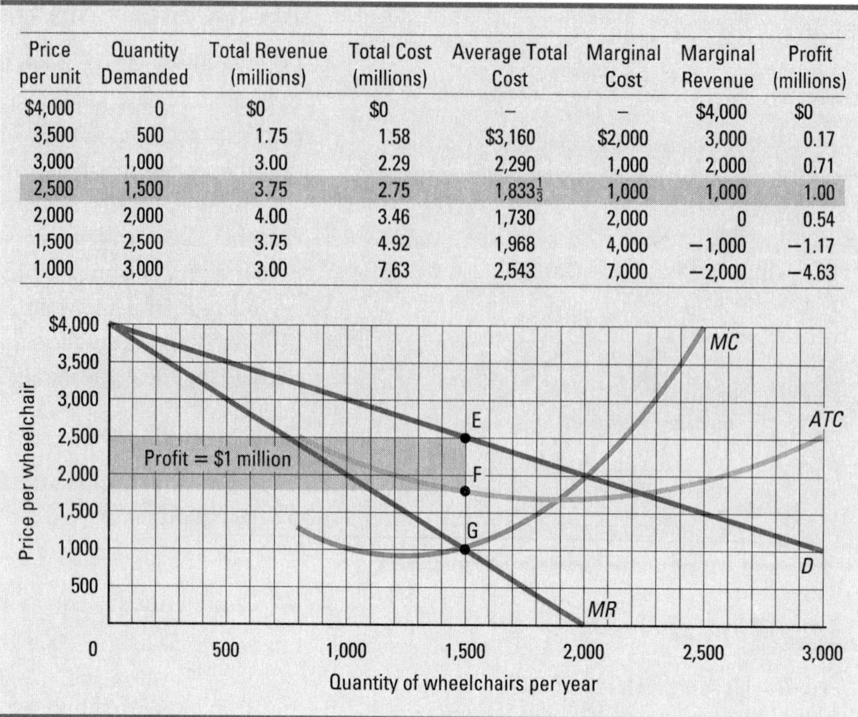

Price per unit	Quantity Demanded	Total Revenue (millions)	Total Cost (millions)	Average Total Cost	Marginal Cost	Marginal Revenue	Profit (millions)
$4,000	0	$0	$0	–	–	$4,000	$0
3,500	500	1.75	1.58	$3,160	$2,000	3,000	0.17
3,000	1,000	3.00	2.29	2,290	1,000	2,000	0.71
2,500	1,500	3.75	2.75	1,833⅓	1,000	1,000	1.00
2,000	2,000	4.00	3.46	1,730	2,000	0	0.54
1,500	2,500	3.75	4.92	1,968	4,000	−1,000	−1.17
1,000	3,000	3.00	7.63	2,543	7,000	−2,000	−4.63

Step 3: *Determine the Profit-Maximizing Price*

Having identified its profit-maximizing quantity, we look to the demand curve in Exhibit 12-9 to determine the price at which Hercules can sell 1,500 wheelchairs: $2,500 per unit. If the company attempted to charge a higher price, the quantity demanded would fall and some of the output would go unsold.

Hercules Medcorp maximizes profits by producing 1,500 wheelchairs per year and selling them at a price of $2,500 per unit. The average total cost at that level of production at point F is $1,833⅓. The firm thus earns a profit of $666⅔ per unit. Multiplying that profit by 1,500 units of output gives an annual profit of $1,000,000. The right-hand column in the table in Exhibit 12-9 shows the firm's profit at various levels of output. The profit associated with 1,500 units of output, the maximum profit possible, is shown by the shaded rectangle in Exhibit 12-9.

Responses to Changes in Demand or Costs

A monopoly firm will change its price and output when its demand or marginal cost curve shifts. Here we review three types of changes a monopoly firm might face in its market. The monopoly firm's response to each of these changes is shown in Exhibit 12-10.

Changes in Demand

A shift in the demand curve facing a monopoly firm shifts the associated marginal revenue curve as well. That changes the profit-maximizing output; the firm determines the profit-maximizing price using the new market demand curve. A shift in demand can occur as a result of any of the demand shifters outlined in Chapter 3: a change in preferences, a change in income, a change in the prices of related goods and services, a change in population, or a change in consumer expectations.

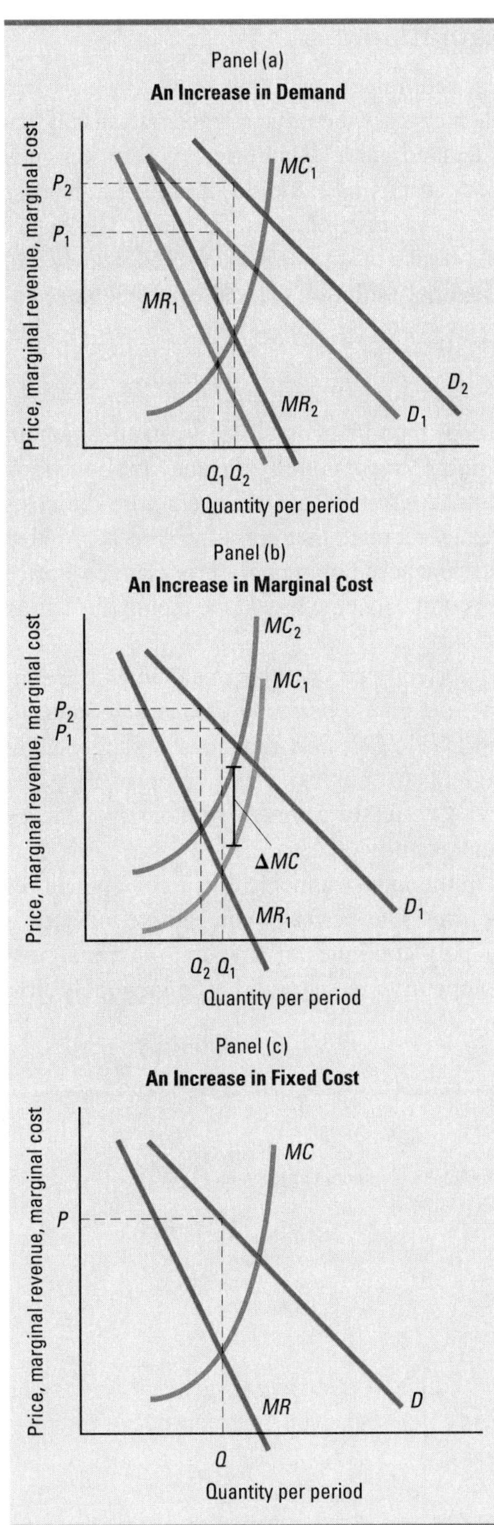

EXHIBIT 12-10

Responses to Market Changes

Panel (a) shows that an increase in demand shifts the demand curve from D_1 to D_2. This shifts the associated marginal revenue curve from MR_1 to MR_2. The monopoly firm increases its output to Q_2 and increases its price to P_2.

Suppose that in Panel (b) marginal cost increases by an amount ΔMC, shifting MC_1 to MC_2. The firm chooses a new output Q_2 where the new marginal cost curve MC_2 intersects marginal revenue MR_1. The firm raises its price to P_2. Notice that price does not rise as much as the increase in marginal cost ΔMC.

An increase in fixed cost does not affect demand; it therefore does not affect marginal revenue. It also does not affect marginal cost and therefore does not affect the firm's price or output in the short run. If the increase in fixed cost raises average cost above the demand curve D, the firm will leave the industry in the long run. Otherwise price and output will remain at P and Q in Panel (c).

Panel (a) of Exhibit 12-10 shows a firm producing Q_1 units at price P_1. An increase in demand means that the demand curve D_1 and marginal revenue curve MR_1 shift to the right, to D_2 and MR_2, respectively. The firm responds by increasing its price to P_2 and output to Q_2.

A reduction in demand would mean that the demand and marginal revenue curves shift to the left, so the firm would respond by reducing price and output.

Changes in Marginal Cost

A shift of the marginal cost curve changes the monopoly firm's profit-maximizing price and output. A change in marginal cost could occur as a result of a change in technology, a change in factor prices, or a tax imposed on each unit of output.

Panel (b) of Exhibit 12-10 shows an increase in marginal cost from MC_1 to MC_2; the curve shifts up by ΔMC. That reduces the profit-maximizing output from Q_1 to Q_2; the monopoly firm raises its price from P_1 to P_2. Price does not, however, rise by the full amount of the increase in marginal cost. If the firm were to raise its price by the full increase in cost, it would sell fewer than Q_2 units and would not be maximizing its profit.

Similarly, if marginal cost were to fall, the marginal cost curve would shift downward. The result would be a reduction in price and an increase in output, but price would not fall by as much as the reduction in marginal cost.

Changes in Fixed Cost

A firm's fixed cost is affected by a change in the cost associated with a fixed factor, a change in returns from a related activity, or a tax such as an annual license fee imposed on the firm. Because a change in fixed cost does not affect demand, it does not affect marginal revenue. A change in fixed cost does not affect marginal cost either. As a result it affects neither price nor output in the short run, as shown in Panel (c) of Exhibit 12-10. A change in fixed cost does change average total cost and thus affects the firm's profits. It does not change average variable cost and therefore would not affect the firm's decision about whether to continue to operate in the short run. If the firm continues to earn a profit, price and output remain unchanged in the long run as well. If the change raises average total cost above the demand curve, the firm leaves the industry in the long run.

Efficiency, Equity, and Regulation

We have seen that a monopoly firm determines its output by setting marginal cost equal to marginal revenue. It then charges the price at which it can sell that output, a price determined by the demand curve. That price exceeds marginal revenue; it therefore exceeds marginal cost as well. That contrasts with the case in perfect competition, in which price and marginal cost are equal. The higher price charged by a monopoly firm allows it a profit—a profit earned in large part at the expense of consumers. The monopoly solution thus raises problems of equity as well as of efficiency.

Monopoly and Efficiency

The fact that price in monopoly exceeds marginal cost suggests that the monopoly solution violates the basic condition for economic efficiency introduced in Chapter 5, that the price system must confront decisionmakers with the costs and benefits of their choices. Efficiency requires that consumers be confronted with prices that equal marginal costs. Because a monopoly firm charges a price greater than marginal cost, consumers will consume less of the monopoly's good or service than is economically efficient.

To contrast the efficiency of the perfectly competitive outcome with the inefficiency of the monopoly outcome, imagine a perfectly competitive industry whose solution is depicted in Exhibit 12-11. The short-run industry supply curve is the summation of individual marginal cost curves; it may be regarded as the marginal cost curve for the industry. A perfectly competitive industry achieves equilibrium at point C, at price P_c and quantity Q_c.

Now suppose that all the firms in the industry merge and a government restriction prohibits entry by any new firms. Our perfectly competitive industry is now a monopoly. Assume the monopoly continues to have the same marginal cost and demand curves that the competitive industry did. The monopoly firm

EXHIBIT 12-11

Perfect Competition, Monopoly, and Efficiency

Given market demand and marginal revenue, we can compare the behavior of a monopoly to that of a perfectly competitive industry. The marginal cost curve may be viewed as the supply curve of a perfectly competitive industry. The perfectly competitive industry produces quantity Q_c and sells the output at price P_c. The monopolist restricts output to Q_m and raises the price to P_m.

Reorganizing a perfectly competitive industry as a monopoly results in a net loss to society given by the shaded area GMC. It also transfers a portion of the consumer surplus earned in the competitive case to the monopoly firm.

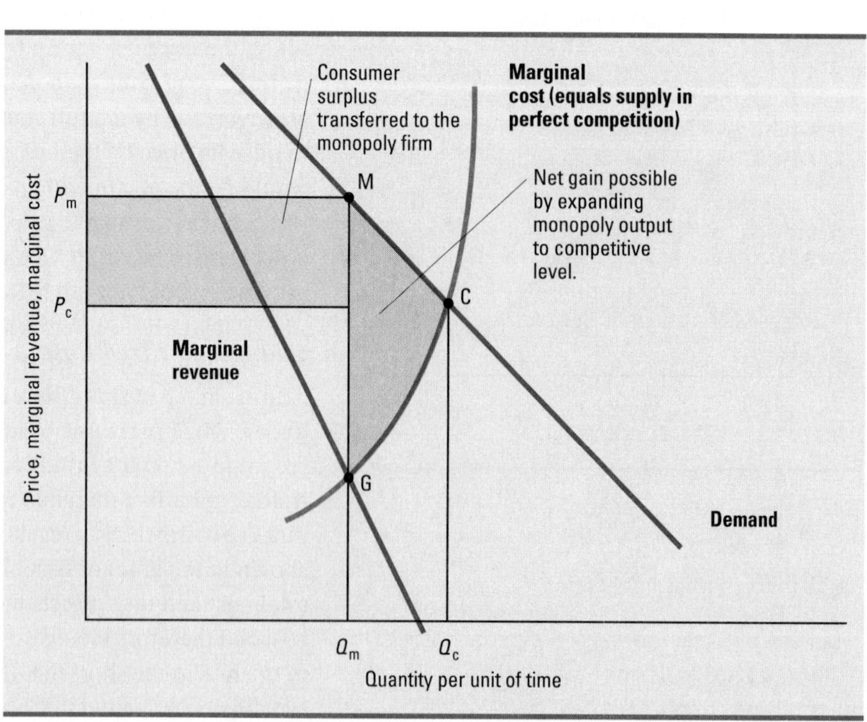

faces the same market demand curve, from which it derives its marginal revenue curve. It maximizes profit at output Q_m and charges price P_m. Output is lower and price higher than in the competitive solution.

Society would gain by moving from the monopoly solution at Q_m to the competitive solution at Q_c. The benefit to consumers would be given by the area under the demand curve between Q_m and Q_c; it is the area Q_mMCQ_c. An increase in output, of course, has a cost. Because the marginal cost curve measures the cost of each additional unit, we can think of the area under the marginal cost curve over some range of output as measuring the total cost of that output. Thus, the total cost of increasing output from Q_m to Q_c is the area under the marginal cost curve over that range—the area Q_mGCQ_c. Subtracting this cost from the benefit gives us the net gain of moving from the monopoly to the competitive solution; it is the shaded area GMC. That is the potential gain from moving to the efficient solution. Alternatively, it can be thought of as a net loss, the cost of converting the industry to a monopoly.

Monopoly and Equity

The monopoly solution raises issues not just of efficiency but of equity. Exhibit 12-11 shows that the monopolist charges price P_m rather than the competitive price P_c; the higher price charged by the monopoly firm reduces consumer surplus. Part of the reduction in consumer surplus is the area under the demand curve between Q_c and Q_m; it is contained in the "net loss" area GMC. But consumers also lose the area of the rectangle bounded by the competitive and monopoly prices and by the monopoly output; this lost consumer surplus is transferred to the monopolist.

The fact that society suffers a net loss due to monopoly is an efficiency problem. But the transfer of a portion of consumer surplus to the monopolist is an equity issue. Is such a transfer legitimate? After all, the monopoly firm enjoys a privileged position, protected by barriers to entry from competition. Should it be allowed to extract these gains from consumers? We'll see in the next section that public policy suggests that the answer is no. Regulatory efforts imposed in monopoly cases seek to reduce the degree to which monopoly firms extract consumer surplus from consumers.

- To maximize profit, a monopoly firm determines its demand, marginal revenue, and marginal cost curves and produces an output at which marginal cost equals marginal revenue.
- The firm's profit-maximizing price is given by the point on the demand curve for the profit-maximizing quantity.
- A monopoly firm produces an output that is less than the efficient level. The result is a net loss to society, given by the area between the demand and marginal cost curves over the range of output between the output chosen by the monopoly firm and the efficient level, where marginal cost equals demand.

Regulation of Monopoly Firms

Public policy toward monopoly generally recognizes two important dimensions of the monopoly problem. On the one hand, the combination of competing firms into a monopoly creates an inefficient and, to many, inequitable solution. On the other hand, some industries are characterized as natural monopolies; production by a single firm allows economies of scale that result in lower costs.

Combinations of competing firms into a monopoly firm are generally forbidden. The United States bans most efforts to create a monopoly by combining several firms or by unfairly driving competitors out of business. Regulatory efforts to prevent monopoly fall under the purview of the nation's antitrust laws. Such efforts are examined in Chapter 17.

Where a natural monopoly exists, the price charged by the firm may be subject to regulation. Public utilities such as electricity or natural gas, for example, are often provided by a monopoly firm at prices regulated by a state or local government agency. Typically, such agencies seek to force the firm to charge lower prices, and to make less profit, than it would otherwise seek. Price regulation in the case of natural monopoly is also examined in Chapter 17.

Case in Point: The Topsy-Turvy World of Telecommunications

By the time you read this book, local telephone service may have become a hotly contested market in California. And the rest of the nation may be moving in the same direction.

California's Public Utilities Commission (PUC) voted in 1995 to open most of the state to competition in local telephone service on January 1, 1996. On that date, companies with their own transmission lines and switching systems could begin operating local services in competition with companies such as Pacific Bell and GTE, which had once operated as monopoly suppliers of local telephone service in specific areas of the state. Companies without their own equipment were to be permitted to offer services using the facilities of local telephone companies by March 1, 1996.

Several long distance companies, such as MCI and Sprint, already have lines for their large business customers' long distance calls. MCI launched a project in 1994 to install the lines that would be needed to provide local service in several metropolitan areas throughout the United States. The PUC's action will allow those companies to use those facilities to provide local services.

Cable television companies may also enter the market for local telephone service in California. The companies already have hookups with their subscribers for video transmission; the PUC's ruling will allow them to develop telephone services among subscribers as well.

The PUC's action came as Congress was debating legislation that would deregulate most telecommunications services throughout the United States. As *Economics* went to press in 1995, it seemed likely that Congress would approve legislation that would deregulate cable and telephone services and allow cable companies to provide telephone services and telephone companies to provide cable television services.

It's impossible to say where the brave new world of telecommunications is heading. But one thing is certain: just as the old days of a single company providing long distance telephone service are long gone, so the days of monopoly local phone service are numbered.

Sources: Leslie Cauley, "California Issues Phone-Market Rules Giving Rival Firms Very Wide Access," *The Wall Street Journal,* 25 July 1995, B6; and Barbara Grady, "California Regulators Set Timetable for Opening Market," Reuters, America On Line, 24 July 1995.

Price Discrimination

In the examples above, the monopoly firm sold all units of output at the same price. In some cases, however, firms can charge different prices to different consumers. If such an opportunity exists, the monopolist can increase profits further.

When a firm charges different prices for the same good or service to different consumers, even though there is no difference in the cost to the firm of supplying these consumers, the firm is engaging in **price discrimination.**

The potential for price discrimination exists whether a firm has a monopoly or not. As long as a firm faces a downward-sloping demand curve, we can use the monopoly model to assess whether it will engage in price discrimination.

Examples of price discrimination abound. Senior citizens and students are often offered discount fares on city buses. Children receive discount prices for movie theater tickets, entrance fees at zoos and theme parks, and airline and train fares. Faculty and staff at colleges and universities may receive discounts at the campus bookstore. Airlines give discount prices to customers who are willing to stay over a Saturday night. Physicians may charge wealthy patients more than poor ones. In all these cases a firm charges different prices to different customers for what is essentially the same product.

Not every instance of firms charging different prices to different customers constitutes price discrimination. Differences in prices may reflect different costs associated with providing the product. One buyer may require special billing practices, another may require delivery on a particular day of the week, and yet another may require special packaging. Price differentials based on differences in production costs are not examples of price discrimination.

Price discrimination means charging different prices to different customers for the same good or service even though the cost of supplying those customers is the same.

Elasticity and Price Discrimination

Why would a firm charge different prices to different consumers? The answer can be found in the marginal decision rule and in the relationship between marginal revenue and elasticity.

Suppose an airline has found that its long-run profit-maximizing solution for a flight between Minneapolis and Miami is to carry 300 passengers, all of whom pay $200 per ticket. The airline has a degree of monopoly power, so it faces a downward-sloping demand curve. The airline has noticed that there are essentially two groups of customers on each flight—people who are traveling for business reasons and people who are traveling for personal reasons (visiting family or friends or taking a vacation). We'll call this latter group tourists.

It seems likely that the price elasticities of demand of these two groups for a particular flight will differ. Tourists may have a wide range of substitutes—they could take their trips at a different time, they could vacation in a different area, or they could easily choose not to go at all. Business travelers, however, may be attending meetings or conferences at a particular time and in a particular city. They have options, of course, but the range of options is likely to be more limited than the range of options facing tourists. Given all this, tourists are likely to have more elastic demand than business travelers for a particular flight.

The difference in elasticities suggests the airline could increase its profit by adjusting its pricing. It has already determined that 300 passengers is its profit-maximizing quantity. It could, however, profit by changing its mix of tourist and business passengers. Suppose the airline wants to add one tourist and subtract one business traveler on each flight. To attract one more tourist it must reduce the price charged to tourists; to eliminate a business traveler it must raise the price to business travelers. Because tourist demand is more elastic, a relatively small reduction in price will attract another tourist. Because business demand is less elastic, it will take a relatively large increase in price to discourage one business traveler from making the trip.

With a small reduction in price to tourists and a large increase in price to business travelers—and no change in the total number of passengers—the firm will increase its profits. It will continue to reduce its price to tourists and raise its price to business travelers as long as it gains revenue from the exchange. If the airline can find a way to charge tourists a lower price than business travelers, it will increase its profits.

Of course, the airline can impose a discriminatory fare structure only if it can distinguish tourists from business travelers. Airlines typically do this by looking at the travel plans of their customers. Trips that involve a stay over a weekend, for example, are more likely to be tourist-related, whereas trips that begin and end during the work week are likely to be business trips. Thus, airlines charge much lower fares for trips that extend through a weekend than for trips that begin and end on weekdays.

In general, price discrimination strategies are based on differences in elasticity among groups of customers and the differences in marginal revenue that result. A firm will seek a price structure that offers customers with more elastic demand a lower price and offers customers with relatively less elastic demand a higher price.

It is always in the interest of a firm to discriminate. Rearranging sales among groups of customers increases total revenue without increasing total cost. Yet most of the goods and services that we buy are not offered on a discriminatory basis. A grocery store doesn't charge a higher price for vegetables to vegetarians, whose demand is likely to be less elastic than that of its omnivorous customers. An audio store doesn't charge a different price for Pearl Jam's compact disks to collectors seeking a complete collection than it charges to casual fans who could easily substitute a disk from another performer.

In order for the firm to charge different customers different prices, three conditions must be met.

1. ***A Price-Setting Firm.*** The firm must have some degree of monopoly power—it must be a price setter. A price-taking firm can only take the market price as given—it isn't in a position to make price choices of any kind.
2. ***Distinguishable Customers.*** The market must be capable of being segmented—separated so that customers with different elasticities of demand can be identified and treated differently. Airlines, for example, must have a mechanism for determining whether a customer is traveling for business or for personal reasons.
3. ***Prevention of Resale.*** The various market segments must be isolated in some way from one another to prevent customers who are offered a lower price from selling to customers who are charged a higher price. If consumers can easily resell a product, then discrimination is unlikely to be successful. It is for this reason that airlines try to prevent customers from reselling tickets.

Price Discrimination at Work

Price discrimination crops up in a wide range of market settings. Because of the profits at stake, firms have proved to be quite ingenious at finding ways to segment their markets and to exploit differences in elasticity. The examples here suggest the variety of discriminatory techniques that exist in the marketplace. Whenever different groups are charged different prices, we should expect to find that the group with the greater elasticity of demand is charged the lower price.

Senior Citizen Discounts

Senior citizens are often offered discounts for travel and entertainment. They are an easy group to identify and are likely to have more elastic demand than other consumers for a wide range of goods and services. One source of that greater elasticity is that they are more likely than the general population to be traveling as tourists than for business purposes. A second is that their time may be less costly, so their cost of seeking out information about alternatives to a given good or service is lower than for the rest of the population. Special discounts are thus likely to generate more response from older groups than from the rest of the population.

Coupons

When a firm issues coupons that offer a lower price for a given good or service, it is discriminating—buyers who don't have a coupon pay a higher price. Coupons allow the firm to make a distinction among buyers; some people are more price-conscious and are more willing to take time to seek out bargains than others are. That's likely to be expressed in a willingness to collect and use coupons. Such customers are likely to have more elastic demand for a store's goods or services than other customers; using coupons allows the seller to charge a lower price to the buyers whose demand is more elastic.

Checklist

- A firm that charges different prices to different customers for a good or service that has the same cost to each one is engaging in price discrimination.
- A discriminating firm charges lower prices to customers whose demand is more elastic and higher prices to customers whose demand is less elastic.
- In order to engage in price discrimination, a firm must be a price setter, must be able to identify consumers whose elasticities differ, and must be able to prevent resale of the good or service among consumers.
- The firm will adjust its prices so that customers with more elastic demand pay lower prices than customers with less elastic demand.

Tuition and Scholarships

Your college or university almost certainly practices price discrimination. Having set a specific tuition level for all students, it offers price reductions, in the form of scholarships or other financial aid, to some. The lower prices typically go to students with the best academic records or to students with special athletic, musical, or other skills. Those are the students that other colleges and universities are competing for—they thus have more options and more elastic demand.

Bargaining

For most goods, a price is posted by the seller; the buyer can take it or leave it. But for other goods, prices are determined through bargaining, in which the seller offers a different price to each buyer. Bargaining allows sellers the greatest degree of price discrimination possible; instead of charging different prices to different groups of buyers, the seller charges a different price to *each* buyer. Bargaining is a costly process because it takes time. But where the stakes are sufficiently great, as for high-priced items like cars or houses, we observe that bargaining takes place. In countries where low income produces a low cost of time, bargaining is much more common.

Assessing Monopoly and the Monopoly Model

Monopoly firms leave us much to criticize. On grounds of economic efficiency, we may object that they produce too little and charge too much, reducing economic welfare. Nor is a monopoly solution an efficient solution. And the high prices and persistent profits earned by monopoly firms strike many as inequitable.

But the objections to monopoly run much deeper than worries over economic efficiency and high prices. Because it enjoys barriers that block potential rivals, a monopoly firm wields considerable market power. For many people, that concentration of power is objectionable. A decentralized, competitive market constantly tests the ability of firms to satisfy consumers, pushes them to find new products and new and better production methods, and whittles away excessive profits. Firms that operate in the shelter of monopoly may be largely immune to such pressures. Consumers are left with fewer choices, higher costs, and lower quality.

In weighing the negative results of monopoly, we must be careful to avoid the mistake of simply assuming that competition is the alternative to monopoly, that every monopoly can and should be replaced by a competitive market. One key source of monopoly power, after all, is economies of scale. In the case of natural monopoly, the alternative to a single firm is many small, high-cost producers. We may not like having only one local provider of electricity, but we might like even less having dozens of providers whose costs—and prices—are higher. Where monopolies exist because economies of scale prevail over the entire range of market demand, they may serve a useful economic role. We may wish to regulate their production and pricing choices, but we may not want to give up their cost advantages.

Although economists are hesitant to levy blanket condemnations of monopoly, they are generally sharply critical of monopoly power where no natural

Checklist

Characteristics of Perfect Competition and Monopoly

Characteristic or Event	Perfect Competition	Monopoly
Market	Large number of sellers and buyers producing a homogeneous good or service; easy entry.	Large number of buyers, one seller. Entry is blocked.
Demand and marginal revenue curves	The firm's demand and marginal revenue curve is a horizontal line at the market price.	The firm faces the market demand curve; marginal revenue is below market demand.
Price	Determined by demand and supply; each firm is a price taker.	The monopoly firm determines price; it is a price setter.
Profit maximization	Firms produce where marginal cost equals marginal revenue.	Firms produce where marginal cost equals marginal revenue and charge the corresponding price on the demand curve.
Price	Price equals marginal cost.	Price is greater than marginal cost.
Profit	Entry forces profit to zero in the long run.	Because entry is blocked, a monopoly firm can sustain a profit in the long run.
Efficiency	The equilibrium solution is efficient because price equals marginal cost.	The equilibrium solution is inefficient because price is greater than marginal cost.
Effect of an increase in marginal cost	Price rises by less than the increase in marginal cost in the short run; it rises by the full amount of the increase in long run.	Price rises by less than the increase in marginal cost.
Effect of an increase in fixed cost	No change in price or output in the short run; price rises to cover the increase in cost in the long run.	No change in price or output in the short or long run, provided the firm is still able to cover its average total cost.

monopoly exists. When firms have substantial monopoly power only as the result of government policies that block entry, there may be little defense for their monopoly positions. In those cases, it may be appropriate for government policy to address the removal of the barriers that insulate the monopoly firm from competition.

Public policy toward monopoly aims generally to strike the balance implied by economic analysis. Where natural monopoly situations exist, such as in the provision of residential electricity, monopolies are permitted—and their prices are regulated. In other cases, monopoly is prohibited outright. Monopolies are not likely to be tolerated if they don't appear to offer cost or other technological advantages.

A Look Back—And a Look Ahead

This chapter has examined the profit-maximizing behavior of monopoly firms. Monopoly occurs if an industry consists of a single firm and entry into that industry is blocked.

Potential sources of monopoly power include the existence of economies of scale over the range of market demand, locational advantages, high sunk costs associated with entry, restricted ownership of raw materials and inputs, and government restrictions such as licenses or patents.

Because the demand curve faced by the monopolist is downward sloping, the firm is a price setter. It will maximize profits by producing the quantity of output at which marginal cost equals marginal revenue. The profit-maximizing price is then found on the demand curve for that quantity.

Where conditions permit, a firm can increase its profits to a level even greater than that implied by simple profit maximization. It can reallocate sales of the profit-maximizing output among consumers so that sales to consumers with more elastic demand are increased and sales to consumers with less elastic demand are reduced. To do this, the firm must discriminate on the basis of price, charging lower prices to consumers with greater elasticities of demand. In order to engage in price discrimination, a firm must be able to identify which consumers have greater elasticity and must be able to prevent resale markets among its consumers.

Because a typical monopolist holds market price above marginal cost, the major impact of monopoly is a reduction in efficiency. Compared to a competitive market, the monopoly suggests more centralized power, higher profits, and less pressure to be responsive to consumer preferences. The following checklist summarizes the differences between the model of perfect competition and monopoly.

We've now examined the choices of firms in two market settings, perfect competition and monopoly. These two settings represent extremes on the competitive spectrum; Chapter 13 examines cases in between these two extremes.

Terms and Concepts for Review

Barriers to entry
Monopoly
Monopoly power
Natural monopoly
Price discrimination
Price setter
Sunk cost

For Discussion

1. What are the necessary conditions for a monopoly position in the market to be established?

2. Suppose the government were to impose an annual license fee on a monopolist equal to its monopoly profits. How would such a fee affect price and output? Do you think that such a fee would be appropriate? Why or why not?

3. Name one monopoly firm you deal with. What is the source of its monopoly power? Do you think it seeks to maximize its profits?

4. "A monopolist will never produce so much output as to operate in the inelastic portion of the demand curve." Explain.

5. Here is an ad taken from the classified section of the Colorado Springs *Gazette-Telegraph:*

1-WAY TCKT to Hawaii, male, $300. 635-0786

Your own newspaper probably has a similar section in which people advertise airplane tickets for sale. How does this secondary market for tickets affect the ability of airlines to engage in price discrimination? Why do you suppose the ad notes that the ticket is "male"?

6. "A monopoly is not efficient, and its pricing behavior leads to losses." What does this statement mean?

7. What conditions are necessary for a monopolist to be able to practice price discrimination?

8. What is a natural monopoly?

9. Restaurants typically charge much higher prices for dinner than for lunch, despite the fact that the cost of serving these meals is about the same. Why do you think this is the case? (*Hint:* Think about the primary consumers of these meals and their respective elasticities.)

10. Suppose a 50 percent tax is imposed on a monopoly firm's profits. What happens to its price and output? (*Hint:* Be careful—focus on marginal revenue, marginal cost, and demand.)

Problems

1. A university football team estimates that it faces the following demand schedule for tickets for each game it

Price per Ticket	Tickets per Game
$30	0
20	20,000
10	40,000
0	60,000

The team plays in a stadium that holds 60,000 fans. It estimates that its marginal cost of attendance, and thus for tickets sold, is zero.

a. Draw the demand and marginal revenue curves. Compute the team's profit-maximizing price and the number of tickets it will sell at that price.

b. Determine the price elasticity of demand at the price you determined in part (a).

2. Now suppose the city in which the university in Problem 1 is located imposes a $10,000 annual license fee on all suppliers of sporting events, including the University. How does this affect the price of tickets?

3. Suppose the city in Problem 2 now imposes a tax of $10 per ticket sold. Using the demand and marginal revenue curves you drew in Problem 1, draw the new marginal cost curve and determine the profit-maximizing price and output.

13

The World of Imperfect Competition

Chapter Objectives

After mastering the material in this chapter, you will be able to:

1. Explain what happens to the model of perfect competition when the assumption of homogeneous products is replaced by the assumption that each firm in an industry produces a good or service that's different in some respect from its competitors' products.
2. Understand the difficulties created for economic analysis when a market is dominated not by one firm but by a few firms.
3. Interpret alternative measures of the concentration of monopoly power.
4. Explain how a firm's choices are affected when it can't be sure how its competitors will respond to those choices.
5. Understand why firms may try to collude and why such collusion is difficult.
6. Discuss the economic effects of advertising.
7. Explain the implications of imperfect competition for the theory of international trade.

Coke is it!

Pepsi—the choice of a new generation.

What's Ahead

Coca-Cola and Pepsi Co battle for greater shares of the soft drink market. Chrysler, Ford, and General Motors fight each other while struggling to regain ground lost to foreign car imports. United Parcel Service attempts to muscle Federal Express aside as the leader in the overnight delivery industry. Apple Computer and IBM join forces in an effort to gain market share and to throttle Microsoft's dominance of the market for computer operating software.

This is not the aloof world of perfect competition where consumers are indifferent about which firm has produced a particular product, where each firm knows it can sell all it wants at the going market price, where all firms settle for zero profit in the long run. Nor is it the stable world of monopoly where a single firm maximizes its profits, secure in the knowledge that barriers to entry will keep any would-be competitors away. This is the world of imperfect competition, one that lies between the idealized extremes of perfect competition and monopoly. It is a world in which firms battle over market shares, in which profits may persist, in which rivals try to outguess each other with their pricing, advertising, and product development strategies.

Unlike the chapters on perfect competition and monopoly, this chapter does not provide a single, consistent theory of firms' behavior. There are too many variations on an uncertain theme for a single theory to explain the behavior of firms in the complex world of imperfect competition. Rather, the chapter provides an overview of some of the many different theories and explanations advanced by economists. The analytical tools you have learned in the course of studying competitive and monopoly markets will be very much in evidence.

The spectrum of business enterprise ranges from perfectly competitive firms to monopoly. Between these extremes lies the business landscape in which the vast majority of firms—those in the world of imperfect competition—actually operate. **Imperfect competition** is a market structure with more than one firm in an industry in which at least one firm is a price setter. An imperfectly competitive

- **Imperfect competition** exists in an industry with more than one firm and in which at least one firm is a price setter.
- **Monopolistic competition** is characterized by many firms producing differentiated products in a market with easy entry and exit.

firm has a degree of monopoly power. This power may be based on product differentiation that leads to a downward-sloping demand curve, or it may result from the interaction of rival firms in an industry with only a few firms.

There are two broad categories of imperfectly competitive markets. The first is one in which many firms compete, each offering a slightly different product. The second is one in which the industry is dominated by a few firms. An important feature of both kinds of markets is advertising, which we shall examine later in this chapter. Finally, we shall explore the implications of imperfectly competitive markets for international trade.

Reader's Advisory !

The term "monopolistic competition" is easy to confuse with the term "monopoly." Remember, however, that the two models are characterized by quite different market conditions. A monopoly is a single firm with high barriers to entry. Monopolistic competition implies an industry with many firms, differentiated products, and easy entry and exit.

Monopolistic Competition: Competition Among the Many

The first model of an imperfectly competitive industry that we shall investigate has conditions quite similar to those of perfect competition. The model of monopolistic competition assumes a large number of firms. It also assumes easy entry and exit. This model differs from the model of perfect competition in one key respect: it assumes that the goods and services produced by firms are differentiated. This differentiation may occur by virtue of advertising, convenience of location, product quality, reputation of the seller, or other factors. **Monopolistic competition** is therefore a model characterized by many firms producing similar but differentiated products in a market with easy entry and exit.

Restaurants are a monopolistically competitive sector: in most areas there are many firms, each is different, and entry and exit are very easy. Each restaurant has many close substitutes—these may include other restaurants, fast-food outlets, and the deli and frozen food sections at local supermarkets. Other industries that engage in monopolistic competition are retail stores, barber and beauty shops, auto repair shops, service stations, banks, and law and accounting firms.

Profit Maximization

Suppose a restaurant raises its prices slightly above those of similar restaurants with which it competes. Will it have any customers? The answer is likely to be yes. Because the restaurant is different from other restaurants, some people will continue to patronize it. The restaurant thus can set its price; it doesn't take the market price as given.

Because products in a monopolistically competitive industry are differentiated, firms face downward-sloping demand curves. As we saw in Chapter 12, whenever a firm faces a downward-sloping demand curve, the graphical framework for monopoly can be used. An important distinction in monopolistic competition, however, emerges from the assumption of easy entry. In monopolistic competition, entry will eliminate any profits in the long run. We begin with an analysis of the short run, a period in which the model of monopolistic competition looks exactly like the model of monopoly.

The Short Run

Because a monopolistically competitive firm faces a downward-sloping demand curve, its marginal revenue curve is a downward-sloping line that lies below the demand curve, as in the monopoly model.

Exhibit 13-1 shows the demand, marginal revenue, marginal cost, and average total cost curves facing a monopolistically competitive firm, Mama's Pizza. Mama's competes with several other similar firms in a market in which entry and exit are relatively easy. Mama's demand curve *D* is downward sloping; even if Mama's raises its prices above those of its competitors, it will still have some customers. Given the downward-sloping demand curve, Mama's marginal revenue curve *MR* lies below demand. To sell more pizzas, Mama's must lower its price, and that means its marginal revenue from additional pizzas will be less than price.

EXHIBIT 13-1

Short-Run Equilibrium in Monopolistic Competition

Looking at the intersection of the marginal revenue curve *MR* and the marginal cost curve *MC*, we see the profit-maximizing quantity is 2,150 units per week. Reading up to the average total cost curve *ATC*, we see the cost per unit equals $9.20. Price, given on the demand curve *D*, is $10.40, so the profit per unit is $1.20. Total profit per week equals $1.20 times 2,150, or $2,580; it is shown by the shaded rectangle.

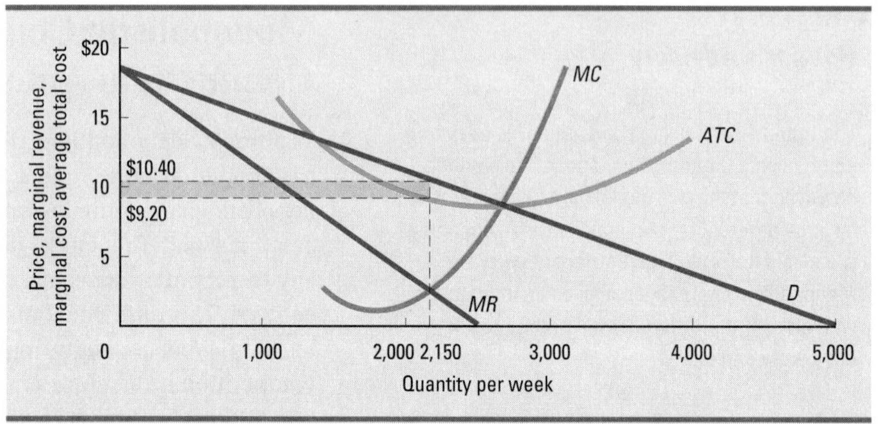

Given the marginal revenue curve *MR* and marginal cost curve *MC*, Mama's will maximize profits by selling 2,150 pizzas per week. Mama's demand curve tells us that it can sell that quantity at a price of $10.40. Looking at the average total cost curve *ATC,* we see that the firm's cost per unit is $9.20. Its profit per unit is thus $1.20. Total profit, shown by the shaded rectangle, is $2,580 per week.

Notice that, as was the case in monopoly, we do not use the demand and supply model to illustrate monopolistic competition. A supply curve assumes that firms are price takers. A monopolistically competitive firm is a price setter; the concept of a supply curve has no meaning in monopolistic competition.

The Long Run

We see in Exhibit 13-1 that Mama's Pizza is earning a profit. If Mama's experience is typical, then other firms in the market are also earning returns that exceed, by $2,580 per week, what their owners could be earning in some related activity. And that means, of course, that firms in related activities—perhaps pizza sales in other towns—aren't doing as well as they could be doing in the market in which Mama's competes. Some of them will exit the markets in which they now compete and enter Mama's market.

As new firms enter, the availability of substitutes for Mama's pizzas will increase, which will reduce the demand facing Mama's Pizza. Its demand curve will shift to the left. Any shift in a demand curve shifts the marginal revenue curve as well. New firms will continue to enter, shifting the demand curves for existing firms to the left, until pizza firms such as Mama's no longer make a profit. The zero-profit solution occurs where Mama's demand curve is tangent to

Excess capacity exists when the profit-maximizing level of output is less than the output associated with the minimum possible average total cost of production.

its average total cost curve—at point A in Exhibit 13-2. Mama's price will fall to $10 per pizza and its output will fall to 2,000 pizzas per week. Mama's will just cover its cost. It will earn a normal accounting profit, hence zero profit. At any other price, the firm's cost per unit would be greater than the price at which a pizza could be sold, and the firm would sustain a loss. Thus, the firm and the industry are in long-run equilibrium. There is no incentive for firms to either enter or leave the industry.

EXHIBIT 13-2

Monopolistic Competition in the Long Run

The existence of profits in a monopolistically competitive industry will induce entry in the long run. As new firms enter, the demand curve *D* and marginal revenue curve *MR* facing a typical firm will shift to the left, to *D*′ and *MR*′. Eventually this produces a profit-maximizing solution at zero profit where *D*′ is tangent to the average total cost curve *ATC* (point A). The long-run equilibrium solution here is an output of 2,000 units per week at a price of $10 per unit.

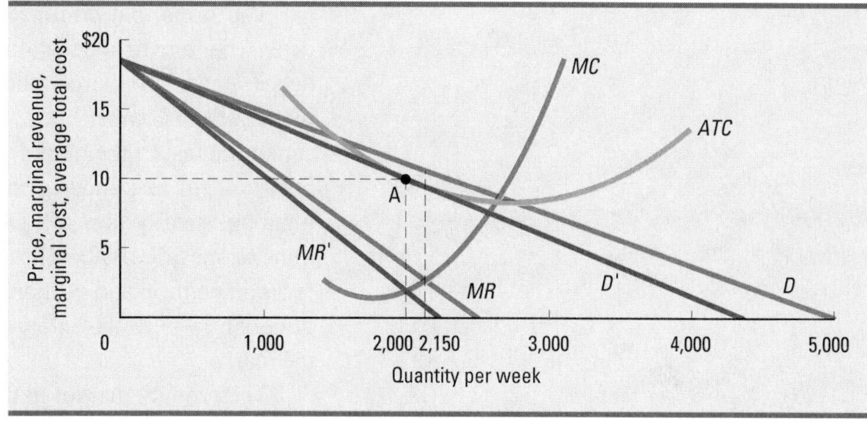

Excess Capacity: The Price of Variety

The long-run equilibrium solution in monopolistic competition always produces zero profit, at a point to the left of the minimum of the average total cost curve. The firm thus produces less than the output at which it would minimize average total cost. The firm has **excess capacity.**

Because monopolistically competitive firms charge prices that exceed marginal cost, monopolistic competition is inefficient. The marginal benefit people receive from an additional unit of the good is given by its price. Since the benefit of an additional unit of output is greater than the marginal cost, people would be better off if output were expanded. Furthermore, an expansion of output would lower cost. But monopolistically competitive firms will not voluntarily increase output since that would entail a loss.

One can thus criticize a monopolistically competitive industry for falling short of the efficiency standards of perfect competition. But monopolistic competition is inefficient because of product differentiation. Think about a monopolistically competitive activity in your area. Would consumers be better off if all the firms in this industry produced identical products so that they could match the assumptions of perfect competition? If identical products are impossible, would consumers be better off if some of the firms were ordered to shut down on grounds the model predicts there will be "too many" firms? The inefficiency of monopolistic competition may be a small price to pay for the wide range of product choices it offers.

Furthermore, remember that perfect competition is merely a model. It isn't a goal toward which an economy might strive as an alternative to monopolistic competition.

Checklist ✓

- A monopolistically competitive industry features some of the same characteristics as perfect competition: a large number of firms and easy entry and exit.
- The characteristic that distinguishes monopolistic competition from perfect competition is differentiated products; each firm is a price setter and thus faces a downward-sloping demand curve.
- Short-run equilibrium for a monopolistically competitive firm is identical to that of a monopoly firm. The firm produces an output at which marginal revenue equals marginal cost and sets its price according to its demand curve.
- In the long run any profits or losses will be eliminated by entry or by exit, leaving firms with zero profit.
- A monopolistically competitive industry will have some excess capacity; this may be viewed as the cost of the product diversity that this market structure produces.

Oligopoly: Competition Among the Few

A new marketing strategy introduced by General Motors is likely to affect Toyota; Toyota is likely to respond. Toyota's response will affect the outcome of the new GM strategy. A decision by Procter & Gamble to lower the price of Crest toothpaste may elicit a response from Colgate-Palmolive, and that response will affect sales of Crest. In an **oligopoly,** the market is dominated by a few firms, each of which recognizes that its own actions will produce a response from its rivals and that those responses will affect it.

The firms that dominate an oligopoly recognize that they are interdependent: what one firm does affects each of the others. This recognized interdependence stands in sharp contrast to the models of perfect competition and of monopolistic competition, where we assume that each firm is so small that it assumes the rest of the market will, in effect, ignore what it does. A perfectly competitive firm responds to the market, not to the actions of any other firm. A monopolistically competitive firm responds to its own demand, not to the actions of specific rivals. These presumptions greatly simplify the analysis of perfect competition and of monopolistic competition. We do not have that luxury in oligopoly, where the interdependence of firms is the defining characteristic of the market.

The product market in oligopoly can vary anywhere from standardized, homogeneous goods to highly differentiated products produced for custom orders. Some oligopoly industries make standardized products: steel, aluminum, wire, and industrial tools. Other oligopoly industries make differentiated products: cigarettes, automobiles, computers, ready-to-eat breakfast cereal, and soft drinks.

Measuring Concentration in Oligopoly

Oligopoly means that a few firms dominate an industry. But how many is "a few," and how large a share of industry output does it take to "dominate" the industry?

Compare, for example, the ready-to-eat breakfast cereal industry and the ice cream industry. The cereal market is dominated by two firms, Kellogg's and General Mills, which together captured 66 percent of market sales in 1991. Four other firms, Post, Quaker Oats, Ralston Purina, and Nabisco, added another 28 percent, leaving only 6 percent to all other firms in the industry.[1] This oligopoly has a high degree of concentration of market power. Power is much less concentrated in the production of ice cream, where the four largest firms accounted for just 26 percent of output in 1987.

One way to measure the degree to which output in an industry is concentrated among a few firms is to use a **concentration ratio,** which reports the percentage of output accounted for by the largest firms in an industry. The higher the concentration ratio, the more the firms in the industry take account of their rivals' behavior. The lower the concentration ratio, the more the industry reflects the characteristics of monopolistic competition or perfect competition.

Concentration ratios are reported by the U.S. Census Bureau, based on surveys it conducts of manufacturing firms every 5 years. These surveys show con-

- An **oligopoly** is a market dominated by a few firms; each of those firms recognizes that its own choices will affect the choices of its rivals and that its rivals' choices will affect it.
- A **concentration ratio** reports the percentage of total industry output accounted for by the largest firms in the industry.
- A **Herfindahl index** is an alternative measure of concentration, found by squaring the percentage share of each firm in an industry, then summing these squared market shares.

[1] Richard Gibson, "Cereal Giants Battle Over Market Share," *The Wall Street Journal,* 16 December 1991, B1.

EXHIBIT 13-3

Concentration Ratios and Herfindahl Indexes

Two measures of concentration are reported by the Census Bureau: it gives concentration ratios and the Herfindahl index for various industries.

Percentage of 1987 Industry Shipments

Industry	Largest 4 firms	Largest 8 firms	Largest 20 firms	Largest 50 firms	Herfindahl Index
Ice cream	26	34	46	61	222
Breakfast cereal	87	99	99+	100	2,207
Chewing gum	96	100			D*
Malt beverages (beer)	64	95	100		1,349
Cigarettes	92	D	D	100	D
Men's and boys' shirts	22	32	50	69	194
Women's, misses', and juniors' blouses and shirts	12	21	34	50	80
Motor vehicles and auto bodies	90	95	99	99+	D
Sporting and athletic goods	13	21	35	57	94

*D, data withheld by the government to avoid revealing information about specific firms.
Source: *U.S. Bureau of the Census, 1987 Census of Manufacturing, MC87-5-6, Concentration Ratios in Manufacturing* (Washington, D.C.: U.S. Government Printing Office, February, 1992), table 4.

centration ratios for the largest 4, 8, 20, and 50 firms in each industry category. Some concentration ratios from the 1987 survey are reported in Exhibit 13-3.

An alternative measure of concentration is found by squaring the percentage share of each firm in an industry, then summing these squared market shares to derive a **Herfindahl index.** The largest Herfindahl index possible is the case of monopoly, where one firm has 100 percent of the market; the index is 100^2, or 10,000. An industry with two firms, each with 50 percent of total output, has a Herfindahl index of 5,000 ($50^2 + 50^2$). In an industry with 10,000 firms that each have .01 percent of the market, the Herfindahl index is 1. Herfindahl indexes reported by the Census Bureau are also given in Exhibit 13-3.

The census data sometimes understate the degree to which a few firms dominate the market. One problem is that the industries given are sometimes too broad to capture significant cases of industry dominance. The sporting goods industry, for example, appears to be highly competitive if we just look at measures of concentration, but markets for individual goods, such as golf clubs, running shoes, and tennis rackets, tend to be dominated by a few firms. Further, the data reflect shares of the national market. A tendency for regional domination doesn't show up in the data. For example, the cement industry appears to be highly competitive. But cement is produced in local markets—it's too expensive to ship it very far—and many of these local markets are dominated by a handful of firms.

The census data can also overstate the degree of actual concentration. The "motor vehicles and auto bodies" category, for example, has a 4-firm concentration ratio that suggests the industry is strongly dominated by four large firms (in fact, U.S. production is dominated by three: General Motors, Ford, and Chrysler). But those firms hardly account for all car sales in the United States; foreign producers have captured a large portion of the domestic market. Including those foreign competitors suggests a far less concentrated industry than the census data imply.

Profit Maximization in Oligopoly

There is no single model of oligopoly behavior that corresponds to economists' models of perfect competition, monopoly, and monopolistic competition. Uncertainty about the interaction of rival firms makes specification of a single

Case in Point — IBM Battles to Regain Market Share

To speak of computers in the 1960s was to speak of IBM. The company controlled over 90 percent of the industry, and big, expensive computers were the rule. Then Apple Computer introduced its first personal computer in 1976 and turned the old world upside down, leaving the old leader struggling to catch up. The personal computer quickly emerged as the industry standard—IBM's lead in mainframe machines didn't matter to small businesses and to ordinary people who wanted a computer they could use at home.

IBM didn't even get around to introducing a personal computer until 1981, but though the company ranked only fifth in personal computer shipments that year, it had reestablished itself as the industry leader by 1985. Still, that leadership didn't pack the punch that IBM had enjoyed in the old days—its reemergence as the industry leader brought it just over one-fourth of the market. Even that leadership proved fleeting; the emergence of dozens of new companies kept chipping away at the shares of the leaders. By 1992, IBM's share had dwindled to less than half its 1985 level, and the company had fallen behind Apple.

The company has fought back, and hard. It reorganized, giving its PC division independent control over product development, pricing, and marketing. IBM has been aggressive in introducing new models and in slashing its costs and prices. The result has been gains in market share—IBM recaptured the industry lead again in 1993. The old days of dominance, however, are clearly over. The top eight firms in the industry accounted for less than half of all personal computers manufactured in 1994.

Source: Stefan Fatsis, "Transformed IBM Reacts to Changes in Computer Market," *Colorado Springs Gazette Telegraph* (30 May 1993):F1.

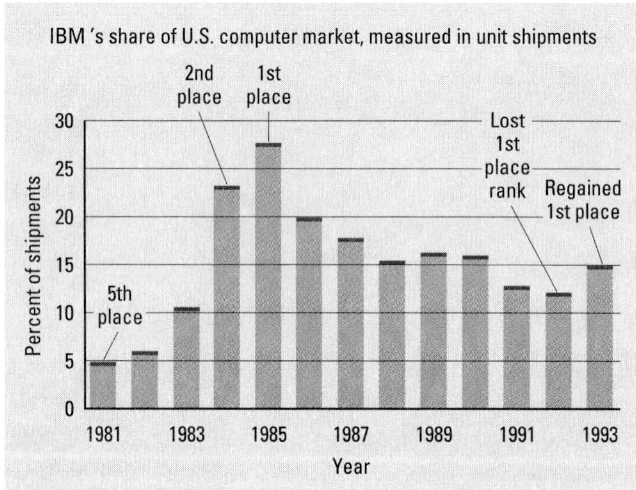

model of oligopoly impossible. Instead, economists have devised a variety of models that deal with the uncertain nature of rivals' responses in different ways. In this section we review two types of oligopoly models, the kinked demand curve and collusion models. After examining these traditional approaches to the analysis of oligopoly behavior, we shall turn to another method of examining oligopolistic interaction: game theory.

The Kinked Demand Curve Model

An oligopoly firm knows that its actions will affect its rivals, and that the reactions of its rivals will affect it. But the firm isn't likely to know what those reactions will be—and this fact can make it very difficult for a firm to predict the outcome of its decisions.

Consider pricing choices. If a firm's rivals match its price changes, then a change in price will produce certain effects. Say that Coca-Cola raises its price.

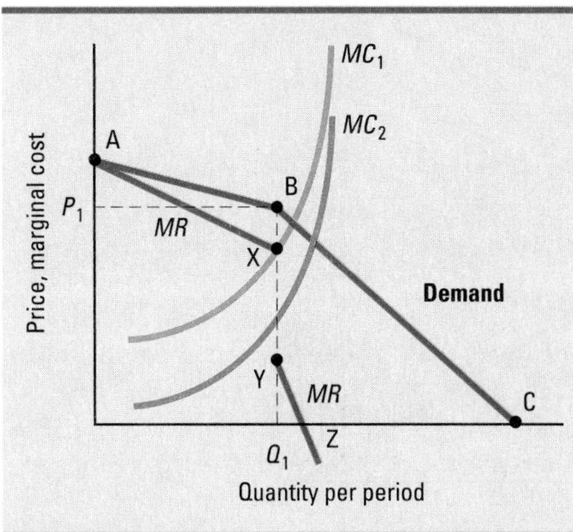

EXHIBIT 13-4

The Kinked Demand Curve Model

The initial price is at P_1 and the initial quantity is at Q_1. If the firm believes that rivals will not respond to price increases but will match price reductions, then the demand curve it faces will have two segments, AB for prices above P_1 and BC for prices below P_1. That implies two distinct marginal revenue segments, AX and YZ. If the marginal cost curve passes through the region where there is a break in the two segments, there will be no change in output. The kinked demand curve model thus predicts that prices will be relatively stable.

A **kinked demand curve model** assumes that rival firms will not change their prices if another firm raises its price but that they will match any price reduction.

If Pepsi and other soft drink manufacturers do the same, the price change may have only modest effects on the quantity Coca-Cola sells. But if Coca-Cola raises its price and its rivals do not, Coca-Cola may see a very large reduction in the quantity it sells. Because the response of its rivals will affect the market's response to a price change, a firm can't know what will happen when it changes its price.

One way of dealing with the uncertainty faced by an oligopoly firm is to assume that rival firms will respond in a particular way to its price changes: they will not change their prices if a firm raises its prices, but they will reduce their prices to match any price reduction. A model that assumes this behavior is a **kinked demand curve model.** It implies that the demand curve faced by a firm will have two distinct segments.

A firm that believes its rivals will not change their prices if it increases its prices but will match any price reduction assumes the kinked-demand response. The firm faces a relatively elastic demand curve for price increases and a less elastic demand curve for price reductions. Exhibit 13-4 shows such a situation. At point B, the firm is charging a price P_1 and selling Q_1 units of output. If it raises its price above P_1, rivals won't respond and its quantity demanded will decline along section AB of its demand curve. If it lowers its price below P_1, its rivals do respond, limiting the increase in quantity demanded to points along section BC of its demand curve.

Different marginal revenue curves are associated with each section of the demand curve. The marginal revenue curve associated with AB is labeled "AX" in Exhibit 13-4; the marginal revenue curve associated with BC is labeled "YZ." The marginal revenue curve thus has two segments, AX and YZ, with a break in between. Marginal cost equals marginal revenue at *X*; the firm is maximizing profit.

Now suppose the firm's production costs fall, shifting its marginal cost curve to MC_2. There is no reason for the firm to change its output as a result, because there is no new intersection with the marginal revenue curve. Indeed, marginal cost could shift up or down anywhere between marginal revenue segments AX and YZ without changing the firm's price or output.

One testable implication of the kinked demand curve model is that prices will be less likely to change in response to a change in production cost in oligopoly industries than in more competitive industries or in unregulated monopolies. The evidence, however, is inconsistent with this hypothesis; prices charged by oligopoly firms don't change less frequently than those of other firms. Still more elaborate versions of the model have been used successfully to explain pricing choices in some industries. One survey of small business firms found that the percentage of firms that expected their rivals to match a price reduction was somewhat greater than the percentage that expected rivals to match a price increase, a result consistent with the model's assumptions.[2]

Collusion in Oligopoly

Firms in any industry could achieve the maximum profit attainable if they all agreed to select the monopoly price and output and to share the profits. One approach to the analysis of oligopoly is to assume that firms in the industry collude, selecting the monopoly solution.

[2] See V. Bhaskar, S. Machin, and G. Reid, "Testing a Model of the Kinked Demand Curve," *Journal of Industrial Economics* 39(3) (March 1991): 241–254.

EXHIBIT 13-5

Monopoly Through Collusion

Two identical firms have the same horizontal marginal cost curve *MC*. Their demand curve $D_{combined}$ and marginal revenue curves, $MR_{one\ firm}$ and $MR_{combined}$, are also identical. The profits of the two firms are maximized if each produces the monopoly output ½ Q_m at point A. Industry output at point B is thus Q_m and the price is P_m. At point C, the efficient solution, output would be Q_c and the price would equal marginal cost.

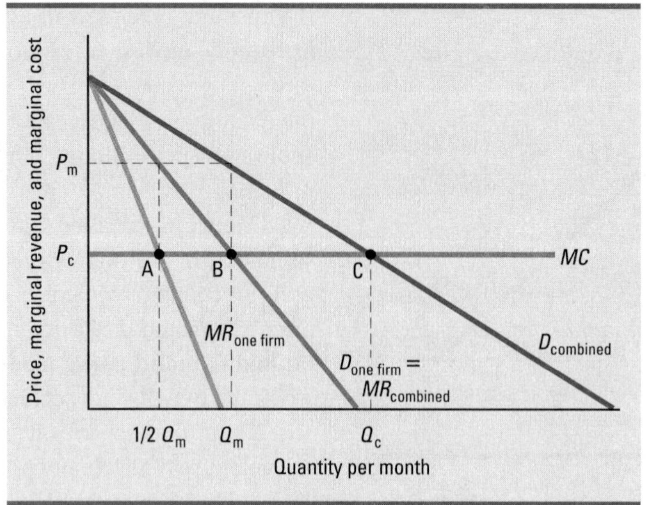

Suppose an industry is a **duopoly,** an industry with two firms. Exhibit 13-5 shows a case in which the two firms are identical. To simplify the analysis, let's assume that each has a horizontal marginal cost curve *MC*. The demand and marginal revenue curves are the same for both firms. We find the combined demand curve for the two firms, $D_{combined}$, by adding the individual demand curves together. Because one firm's demand curve, $D_{one\ firm}$, represents one-half of market demand, it is the same as the combined marginal revenue curve for the two firms, $MR_{combined}$. If these two firms act as a monopoly, together they produce Q_m and charge a price P_m. This result is achieved if each firm selects its profit-maximizing output, which equals ½ Q_m. This solution is inefficient; the efficient solution is price P_c and output Q_c, found where the combined market demand curve $D_{combined}$ and the marginal cost curve *MC* intersect.

Overt Collusion. In the simplest form of collusion, **overt collusion,** firms openly agree on price, output, and other decisions aimed at achieving monopoly profits. Firms that coordinate their activities through overt collusion and by forming collusive coordinating mechanisms are participating in a **cartel.**

Firms form a cartel to gain monopoly power. A successful cartel can earn large profits, but there are several problems with forming and maintaining one. First, in many countries, including the United States, cartels are generally illegal. (They are banned because their purpose is to raise prices and restrict output.) Second, the cartel may not succeed in inducing all firms in the industry to join. Firms that remain outside the cartel can compete by lowering price, and thus they prevent the cartel from achieving the monopoly solution. Third, there is always an incentive for individual members to cheat on cartel agreements. Suppose the members of a cartel have agreed to impose the monopoly price in their market and to limit their output accordingly. Any one firm might calculate that it could charge slightly less than the cartel price and thus capture a larger share of the market for itself. Cheating firms expand output and drive prices down below the level originally chosen.

- A **duopoly** is an industry that consists of two firms.
- **Overt collusion** means that firms agree openly on price, output, and other decisions aimed at achieving monopoly profits.
- A **cartel** is a group of firms engaged in overt collusion.

The Organization of Petroleum Exporting Countries (OPEC), perhaps the best-known cartel, is made up of 13 oil-producing countries. In the 1970s OPEC successfully acted like a monopoly by restricting output and raising prices. By the mid-1980s, however, the monopoly power of the cartel had been weakened by expansion of output by nonmember producers such as Mexico and Venezuela

Case in Point — The Matzo Fix

The three conspirators spoke guardedly at Ratner's Restaurant on Manhattan's Lower East Side. Millions of dollars were at stake in their negotiations, and stiff fines or even a jail sentence awaited them if they were caught.

They met each fall at Ratner's to fix the price of matzo, a flat, unleavened bread eaten primarily by Jews at Passover. The conspirators came from the nation's biggest Matzo producers: Manischewitz, Aron Streit, and Horowitz. The Manischewitz executive would tell the representatives of the other two firms about its plans for price and output for the next Passover; Aron Streit and Horowitz would agree to charge the same price.

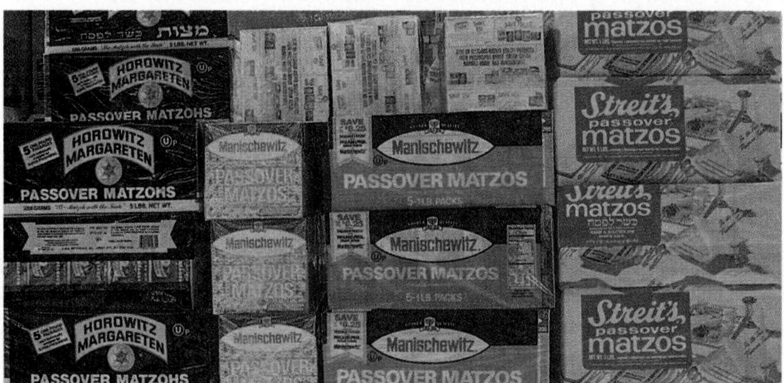

Federal prosecutors indicted Manischewitz in 1990 for violating the Sherman Antitrust Act, a federal statute that prohibits such conspiracies. The other two firms were named as unindicted coconspirators. Manischewitz pleaded no contest to the charges and was slapped with a $1 million fine. Federal Judge Harold Ackerman, in levying the fine, said that he hoped it would "send a message to the business community that a United States court, faced with conduct of this nature, will not tolerate what it perceives to be an egregious assault on a free competition society."

In addition to the fine, Manischewitz was sued by many of its major customers, who charged they had been harmed by the monopoly price. The firm settled one suit by paying $500,000 and agreeing to provide $2.5 million worth of kosher food to a charity.

In the end, however, Manischewitz was able to continue its market dominance in a different guise—it purchased Horowitz. The combination of the two firms left Manischewitz with 90 percent of the matzo market.

Source: Timothy Tregarthen, "The Great Matzo Conspiracy," *The Margin* 7 (Fall 1991): 52.

and by cheating among the cartel members. Whether the cartel can successfully restrict output and raise prices in the future remains an open question.

Tacit Collusion. An alternative to overt collusion is **tacit collusion,** an unwritten, unspoken understanding through which firms agree to limit their competition. Firms may, for example, begin following the price leadership of a particular firm, raising or lowering their prices when the leader makes such a change. The price leader may be the largest firm in the industry, or it may be a firm that has been particularly good at assessing changes in demand or cost.

Tacit collusion has been alleged to occur in a wide range of industries. The former U.S. Steel Corporation, now USX, was considered a price leader early in this century. General Motors was regarded as a price leader in the automobile industry before foreign firms increased the competitiveness of the industry. A Federal Trade Commission (FTC) investigation of tacit collusion through price leadership in the breakfast cereal industry found that in 15 cases of industrywide price increases between 1965 and 1970, Kellogg's had led 12. Post followed in 10 of these increases; General Mills followed in 9. Only once did neither of Kellogg's main rivals fail to follow the leader. The FTC charged that industry leaders had monopolized the industry through tacit collusion and price leadership, but the suit was ultimately dismissed in court. The charge against major cereal producers was the first attempt by the government to prosecute tacit collusion as an illegal conspiracy.

Tacit collusion is an unwritten, unspoken agreement through which firms limit competition among themselves.

It is difficult to know how common tacit collusion is. The fact that one firm changes its price shortly after another one does cannot prove that a tacit conspiracy exists. After all, we expect to see the prices of all firms in a perfectly competitive industry moving together in response to changes in demand or production costs.

Game Theory and Oligopoly Behavior

Oligopoly presents a problem in which decisionmakers must select strategies taking into account the uncertain responses of their rivals. A choice based on the recognition that the actions of others will affect the outcome of the choice and that takes these possible actions into account is called a **strategic choice. Game theory** is an analytical approach through which strategic choices can be assessed.

Among the strategic choices available to an oligopoly firm are pricing choices, marketing strategies, and product development efforts. An airline's decision to raise or lower its fares—or to leave them unchanged—is a strategic choice. The other airlines' decision to match or ignore their rival's price change is also a strategic choice. Wendy's used its former chief executive officer, Dave Thomas, as a spokesperson; this was a strategic marketing decision. IBM boosted its share in the highly competitive personal computer market, in large part because a strategic product development strategy accelerated the firm's introduction of new products.

Once a firm implements a strategic decision, there will be an outcome. The outcome of a strategic decision is called a **payoff.** In general, the payoff in an oligopoly game is the change in profit to each firm. The firm's payoff depends partly on the strategic choice it makes and partly on the strategic choices of its rivals. Firms in the airline industry, for example, raised their fares in 1993, expecting to enjoy increased profits as a result. They changed their strategic choices when Northwest chose to slash its fares, and all firms ended up with a payoff of lower profits.

We shall use two applications to examine the basic concepts of game theory. The first examines a classic game theory problem called the prisoners' dilemma. The second deals with strategic choices by two firms in a duopoly.

The Prisoners' Dilemma

Suppose a local district attorney is certain that two individuals, Frankie and Johnny, have committed a burglary, but she has no evidence that would be admissible in court.

The DA arrests the two. On being searched, each is discovered to have a substantial amount of marijuana. The DA now has a sure conviction on a possession of marijuana charge, but she will get a conviction on the burglary charge only if at least one of the prisoners confesses and implicates the other.

The DA decides on a strategy designed to elicit confessions. She separates the two prisoners and then offers each the following deal: "If you confess and your partner doesn't, you'll get the minimum sentence of 1 year in jail on the possession and burglary charges. If you both confess, your sentence will be 3 years in jail. If your partner confesses and you don't, the plea bargain is off and you'll get 6 years in prison. If neither of you confess, you'll each get 2 years in prison on the drug charge."

The two prisoners each face a dilemma; they can choose to confess or not confess. Because the prisoners are separated, they can't plot a joint strategy. Each must make a strategic choice in isolation.

- A **strategic choice** is based on the recognition that the actions of others will affect the outcome of the choice, and it takes these actions into account.
- **Game theory** is an analytical framework used in the analysis of strategic choices.
- The outcome of a strategic choice is a **payoff.**
- A **dominant strategy** is one that is the same regardless of the action of the other player in a game.
- A game has a **dominant strategy equilibrium** if every player has a dominant strategy.
- A **Nash equilibrium** occurs when each player makes the best strategic choice, given the choice expected of the other player.

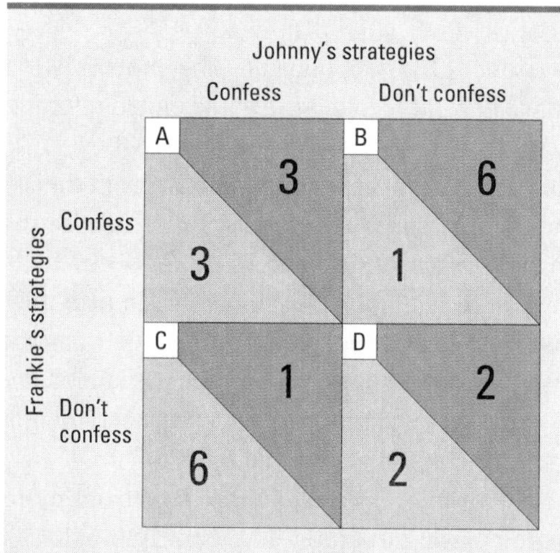

EXHIBIT 13-6

Payoff Matrix for the Prisoners' Dilemma

The four cells represent each of the possible outcomes of the prisoners' game. Within each cell, the payoff to Frankie is given by the jail sentence in the lower left portion of the cell; Johnny's payoff is the sentence in the shaded portion in the upper right. The goal of each player is to achieve the lowest sentence.

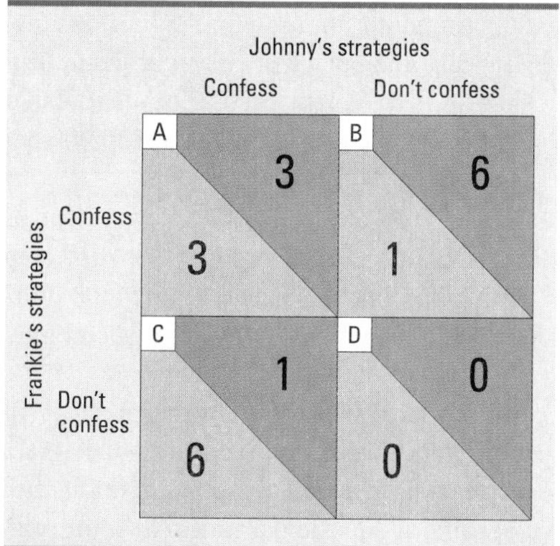

EXHIBIT 13-7

A Revised Payoff Matrix

With the payoff matrix changed so that both players go free if neither confesses (cell D), the prisoners' dilemma game no longer has a dominant strategy equilibrium. Each player selects the best strategy, given the choice expected of the other player. The result is a Nash equilibrium for each player.

The outcomes of these strategic choices, as outlined by the DA, depend on the strategic choice made by the other prisoner. The payoff matrix for this game is given in Exhibit 13-6. The two rows represent Frankie's strategic choices; she may confess or not confess. The two columns represent Johnny's strategic choices; he may confess or not confess. There are four possible outcomes: Frankie and Johnny both confess (cell A), Frankie confesses but Johnny doesn't (cell B), Frankie doesn't confess but Johnny does (cell C), and neither Frankie nor Johnny confesses (cell D). The portion at the lower left in each cell shows Frankie's payoff; the shaded portion at the upper right shows Johnny's payoff.

If Johnny confesses, Frankie's best choice is to confess—she'll get a 3-year sentence rather than the 6-year sentence she'd get if she didn't confess. If Johnny does not confess, Frankie's best strategy is still to confess—she'll get a 1-year rather than a 2-year sentence. In this game, Frankie's best strategy is to confess, regardless of what Johnny does. When a player's best strategy is the same regardless of the action of the other player, that strategy is said to be a **dominant strategy.** Frankie's dominant strategy is to confess to the burglary.

For Johnny, the best strategy to follow if Frankie confesses is to confess. The best strategy to follow if Frankie doesn't confess is also to confess. Confessing is a dominant strategy for Johnny as well. A game in which there is a dominant strategy for each player is called a **dominant strategy equilibrium.** Here, the dominant strategy equilibrium is for both prisoners to confess; the payoff will be given by cell A in the payoff matrix.

From the point of view of the two prisoners together, a payoff in cell D would have been preferable. Had they both denied participation in the robbery, their combined sentence would have been 4 years in prison—2 years each. Indeed, cell D offers the lowest combined prison time of any of the outcomes in the payoff matrix. But because the prisoners can't communicate, each is likely to make a strategic choice that results in a more costly outcome.

Of course, the outcome of the game depends on the way the payoff matrix is structured. Suppose neither prisoner possessed any drugs, and they know they'll go free on the burglary charge if neither confesses. If both prisoners deny the burglary charge, the payoff in cell D is now zero prison time. With the revised payoff matrix shown in Exhibit 13-7, no dominant strategy exists. If Johnny confesses, the best strategy for Frankie is to confess. But if Johnny doesn't confess, the best strategy is not to confess. Frankie's choice depends on her expectation of what Johnny will do. Johnny, meanwhile, faces the same problem. If Frankie confesses, his best strategy is to confess; if she doesn't, his best strategy is to deny the burglary charge. A **Nash equilibrium** occurs when each player makes the best strategic choice, given the choice expected of the other player. The Nash equilibrium is named in honor of John Nash, the mathematician who developed the concept—and who shared the 1994 Nobel Prize in economics for his work.

Both versions of the prisoners' dilemma described here have had a Nash equilibrium. If a player's Nash equilibrium is the same regardless of the strategy chosen by the other player, then the equilibrium can be said to be a dominant strategy. And if both players have a dominant strategy, then the game has a dominant strategy equilibrium. In a game with a dominant strategy equilibrium, we can predict the outcome. In a game with a Nash equilibrium but no dominant strategy equilibrium, we can't. The strategy chosen by each player depends on what that player expects the other player, or players, to do.

- A **tit-for-tat strategy** is one in which a firm responds to cheating by a rival by cheating and to cooperation by a rival by cooperating.
- A **trigger strategy** is a threat to respond to a rival's cheating by permanently revoking an agreement.

Repeated Oligopoly Games

The prisoners' dilemma was played once, by two players. The players were given a payoff matrix; each could make one choice, and the game ended after the first round of choices.

The real world of oligopoly has as many players as there are firms in the industry. They play round after round: a firm raises its price, another firm introduces a new product, the first firm cuts its price, and so on. An oligopoly game is a bit like a baseball game with an unlimited number of innings—one firm may come out ahead after one round, but another will emerge on top another day. In the computer industry game, the introduction of personal computers changed the rules. IBM, which had won the old game quite handily, struggles to keep up in a world in which rivals continue to slash prices and improve quality.

Oligopoly games may have more than two players, so the games are more complex, but this doesn't change their basic structure. The concepts of Nash equilibrium and dominant strategies remain. The fact that the games are repeated introduces new strategic considerations. A player must consider not just the ways in which its choices will affect its rivals now but how its choices will affect them in the future as well.

To keep the game simple, let's consider a duopoly game. The two firms have colluded, either tacitly or covertly, to create a monopoly solution. As long as each player upholds the agreement, the two firms will earn the maximum profit possible in the enterprise.

There will, however, be a powerful incentive for each firm to cheat. The monopoly solution may generate the maximum profit possible for the two firms combined, but what if one firm captures some of the other firm's profit? Suppose, for example, that two equipment rental firms, Quick Rent and Speedy Rent, operate in a community. Given the economies of scale in the business and the size of the community, it isn't likely that another firm will enter. Each firm has about half the market, and they have agreed to charge the prices that would be chosen if the two combined as a single firm. Each earns profits of $20,000 per month.

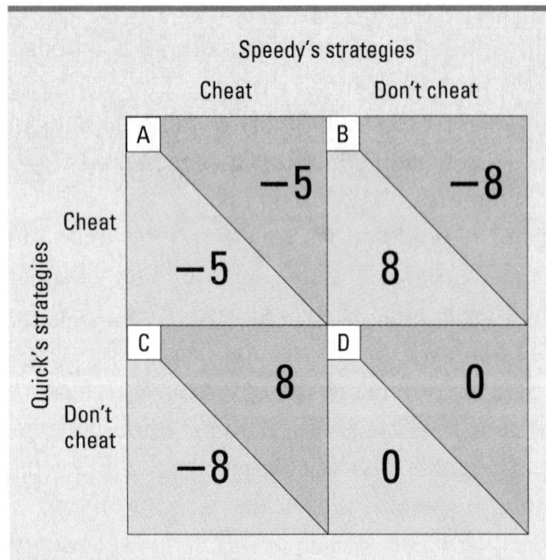

EXHIBIT 13-8

To Cheat or Not To Cheat: Game Theory in Oligopoly

Two rental firms, Quick Rent and Speedy Rent, operate in a duopoly market. They have colluded in the past, achieving a monopoly solution. Cutting prices means cheating on the arrangement; not cheating means maintaining current prices. The payoffs are changes in monthly profits, in thousands of dollars. If neither firm cheats, then neither firm's profits will change. In this game, cheating is a dominant strategy equilibrium.

Quick and Speedy could cheat on their arrangement in several ways. One of the firms could slash prices, introduce a new line of rental products, or launch an advertising blitz. Such an approach wouldn't be likely to increase the total profitability of the two firms, but if one firm could take the other by surprise, it might profit at the expense of its rival.

Let's focus on the strategy of cutting prices, which we'll call a strategy of cheating on the duopoly agreement. The alternative is not to cheat on the agreement. Cheating increases a firm's profits *if* its rival doesn't respond. Exhibit 13-8 shows the payoff matrix facing the two firms at a particular time. As in the prisoners' dilemma matrix, the four cells list the payoffs for the two firms. If neither firm cheats (cell D), profits remain unchanged.

This game has a dominant strategy equilibrium. Quick's preferred strategy, regardless of what Speedy does, is to cheat. Speedy's best strategy, regardless of what Quick does, is to cheat. The result is that the two firms will select a strategy that lowers their combined profits!

Quick Rent and Speedy Rent face an unhappy dilemma. They both want to maximize profit, yet each is likely to choose a strategy inconsistent with that goal. If they continue the game as it now exists, each will continue to cut prices, eventually driving prices down to the point where price equals average total cost (presumably, the price-cutting will stop there). But that would leave the two firms with zero profits.

Case in Point — MAD—The Ultimate Trigger

It was the most chilling acronym of the cold war: MAD stood for *m*utually *a*ssured *d*estruction. The United States and the Soviet Union had enough nuclear weapons to destroy the other several times over, and each threatened to launch sufficient nuclear weapons to destroy the other country if the other country launched a nuclear attack against it or any of its allies. Since the launching of such an attack would evoke a similar response from the other country, the acronym was apt: complete destruction would be mutually assured.

When the United States discovered that the Soviet Union was placing nuclear missiles in Cuba in 1962, its response was swift and unequivocal: President John F. Kennedy announced that any attack from Cuba against the United States would be viewed as an attack by the Soviet Union, and that the Soviet Union would be destroyed as a result. A naval blockade was imposed on Cuba until the missiles were removed. The Soviet Union backed down from the nuclear standoff, and the missiles were withdrawn.

On its face, the MAD doctrine seemed ludicrous. It was, after all, a commitment by each nation to respond to any nuclear attack with a counterattack that many scientists expected would end human life on earth. As crazy as it seemed, however, it worked. For 40 years, the two nations did not go to war. The collapse of the Soviet Union in 1991 ended the need for a MAD doctrine. But during the time that the United States and the Soviet Union were rivals, MAD was a very effective trigger indeed.

Made in 1963 at the height of the Cold War, Stanley Kubrick's classic film Dr. Strangelove *presented a darkly comic view of the Doomsday Machine, the movie's version of MAD. Peter Sellers (far right) portrayed the President.*

Checklist

- The key characteristics of oligopoly are a recognition that the actions of one firm will produce a response from rivals and that these responses will affect it. Each firm is uncertain what its rivals' responses might be.
- The degree to which a few firms dominate an industry can be measured using a concentration ratio or a Herfindahl index.
- The kinked demand curve model predicts that oligopoly prices will be relatively stable.
- One way to avoid the uncertainty firms face in oligopoly is through collusion. Collusion may be overt, as in the case of a cartel, or tacit, as in the case of price leadership.
- Game theory is a tool that can be used to understand strategic choices by firms. Firms can use tit-for-tat and trigger strategies to encourage cooperative behavior by rivals.

Both firms have an interest in maintaining the status quo of their collusive agreement. Overt collusion is one device through which the monopoly outcome may be maintained, but that is illegal. One way for the firms to encourage each other not to cheat is to use a **tit-for-tat strategy.** In this strategy a firm responds to cheating by cheating, and it responds to cooperative behavior by cooperating. As each firm learns that its rival will respond to cheating by cheating, and to cooperation by cooperating, cheating on agreements becomes less and less likely.

Still another way firms may seek to force rivals to behave cooperatively rather than competitively is to use a **trigger strategy,** in which a firm makes clear that it will respond to cheating by permanently revoking an agreement. A firm might, for example, threaten to cut prices down to the level of average total cost—and leave them there—in response to any price-cutting by a rival. A trigger strategy is calculated to impose huge costs on any firm that cheats—and on the firm that threatens to invoke the trigger. A firm might threaten to invoke a trigger in hopes that the threat will forestall any cheating by its rivals.

Game theory has proved to be an enormously fruitful approach to the analysis of a wide range of problems. Corporations use it to map out strategies and to anticipate rivals' responses. Governments use it in developing foreign policy strategies. Military leaders play war games on computers using the basic ideas of game theory. Any situation in which rivals make strategic choices to which competitors will respond can be assessed using game theory analysis.

Extensions of Imperfect Competition: Advertising and International Trade

The analysis of imperfectly competitive markets has produced dramatic advances in two areas in the last few decades. One is the understanding of the role of advertising. The second is a new perspective on international trade. We'll examine each of these important areas of economic research in this section.

Advertising

One important aspect of imperfect competition is advertising. Firms in monopolistic competition and oligopoly use advertising when they expect it to increase their profits. We see the results of these expenditures in a daily barrage of advertising on television, radio, newspapers, magazines, billboards, passing buses, park benches, the mail, home telephones—in virtually every medium imaginable. Is all this advertising good for the economy?

We've already seen that a perfectly competitive economy with fully defined and easily transferable property rights will achieve an efficient allocation of resources. There is no role for advertising in such an economy, because everyone knows that firms in each industry produce identical products. Furthermore, buyers already have complete information about the alternatives available to them in the market.

But perfect competition contrasts sharply with imperfect competition. Imperfect competition can lead to a price greater than marginal cost and thus generate an inefficient allocation of resources. Firms in an imperfectly competitive market may advertise heavily. Is this advertising a cause of the problem of inefficiency, or is it part of the solution? Does advertising insulate imperfectly competitive firms from competition and allow them to raise their prices even higher, or does it encourage greater competition and push prices down?

There are two ways in which advertising could lead to higher prices to consumers. First, the advertising itself costs money; in 1985, U.S. firms spent $95 billion on advertising, an amount equal to 2.4 percent of the value of all goods and services produced that year. By pushing up production costs, advertising may push up prices. If the advertising serves no socially useful purpose, these costs represent a waste of resources in the economy. Second, firms may be able to use advertising to manipulate demand and create barriers to entry. If a few firms in a particular market have developed intense brand loyalty, it may be difficult for new firms to enter—the advertising creates a kind of barrier to entry. By maintaining barriers to entry, firms may be able to sustain high prices.

But advertising has its defenders. They argue that advertising provides consumers with useful information and encourages price competition. Without advertising, these defenders argue, it would be impossible for new firms to enter an industry. Advertising, they say, raises competition and thus lowers prices and encourages a greater range of choice for consumers.

Advertising, like all other economic phenomena, has benefits as well as costs. To assess those benefits and costs, let's examine the impact of advertising on the economy.

Advertising and Information

Advertising does inform us about products and their prices. Even critics of advertising generally agree that when advertising advises consumers about the availability of new products, or when it provides price information, it serves a useful function. But much of the information provided by advertising appears to be of limited value. Hearing that "Pepsi is the right one, baby" or "Coors is the right one now" may not be among the most edifying lessons consumers could learn.

Some economists argue, however, that even advertising that seems to tell us nothing may provide useful information. They note that a consumer is unlikely to make a repeat purchase of a product that turns out to be a dud. Advertising an inferior product is likely to have little payoff; people who do try it aren't likely to try it again. It isn't likely a firm could make money by going to great expense to launch a product that produced only unhappy consumers. Thus, if a product is heavily advertised, its producer is likely to be confident that many consumers will be satisfied with it and make repeat purchases. If this is the case, then the fact that the product is advertised, regardless of the content of that advertising, signals consumers that at least its producer is confident that the product will satisfy them.

Advertising and Competition

If advertising creates consumer loyalty to a particular brand, then that loyalty may serve as a barrier to entry to other firms. Some brands of household products, such as laundry detergents, for example, are so well established they may make it difficult for other firms to enter the market.

In general, there is a positive relationship between the degree of concentration of market power and the fraction of total costs devoted to advertising. This relationship, critics argue, is a causal one; the high expenditures on advertising are the cause of the concentration. To the extent that advertising increases industry concentration, it is likely to result in higher prices to consumers and lower levels of output. The higher prices associated with advertising are not simply the result of passing on the cost of the advertising itself to consumers; they also derive from the monopoly power the advertising creates.

But advertising may encourage competition as well. By providing information to consumers about prices, for example, it may encourage price competition. Suppose a firm in a world of no advertising wants to increase its sales. One way to do that is to lower price. But with no advertising, it is extremely difficult to inform potential customers of this new policy. The likely result is that there would be little response, and the price experiment will probably fail. Price competition would thus be discouraged in a world without advertising.

Empirical studies of markets in which advertising is not allowed have confirmed that advertising encourages price competition. One of the most famous studies of the effects of advertising looked at pricing for prescription eyeglasses. In the early 1970s, about half the states in the United States banned advertising by firms making prescription eyeglasses; the other half allowed it. A comparison of prices in the two groups of states by economist Lee Benham showed that the cost of prescription eyeglasses was far lower in states that allowed advertising than in states that banned it.[3] Mr. Benham's research proved quite influential—virtually all states have since revoked their bans on such advertising.

Advertising may also allow more entry by new firms. When Kia entered the U.S. market in 1994 to sell low-price compact cars, it flooded the airwaves with advertising. Suppose, however, that such advertising had not been possible.

[3] Lee Benham, "The Effect of Advertising on the Price of Eyeglasses," *Journal of Law and Economics* 15(2) (1972): 337–352.

Case in Point: The Ban on Cigarette Advertising

Cigarettes were once one of the most heavily advertised products on television, but radio and television advertising of the product was banned by the federal government in 1970 because of health concerns associated with smoking. The ban provided a partial test of how advertising restrictions might affect the market for a widely promoted consumer good.

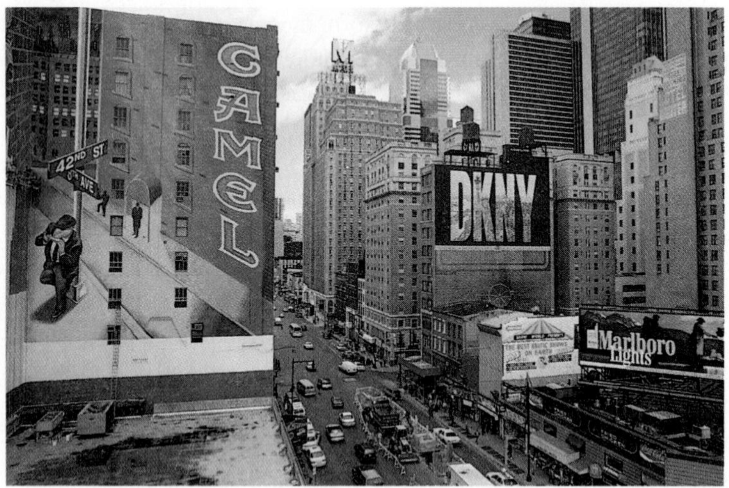

A Street in Midtown Manhattan.

The ban does not appear to have had any particular effect on cigarette sales. Indeed, per capita cigarette consumption had been falling before the ban was imposed; it rose after the ban!

Economist Woodrow Eckard of the University of Colorado at Denver has examined the impact of the ban on television and radio advertising on the competitiveness of the cigarette industry. If advertising makes industries less competitive, then limiting advertising should have made the cigarette industry more competitive. If advertising encourages competition, then a ban on a major form of advertising should have reduced competition. That would tend to boost profits of cigarette firms.

Mr. Eckard's findings were consistent with the hypothesis that advertising encourages competition. He found that the market shares of the leading cigarette producers had been declining but stabilized or increased after the ban was imposed. New brand entry virtually stopped for four years after the ban. Profit margins of tobacco companies increased.

Tobacco industry spokespersons howled in 1995 when President Clinton proposed new restrictions on cigarette advertising. But privately, some industry executives said that the restrictions might boost the profits of leading firms. "Whenever you put on competitive restraints, the bigger get bigger and the smaller players get knocked out," a Philip Morris executive told *The Wall Street Journal.*

Sources: Woodrow Eckard, "Competition and the Cigarette TV Advertising Ban," *Economic Inquiry* 29(1) (January 1991): 119–133; and Suein L. Hwang, "Clinton Ad Ban Could Strengthen Philip Morris," *The Wall Street Journal,* 21 August 1995, B1.

Could Kia have entered the market in the United States? It seems highly unlikely that *any* new product could be launched without advertising. The absence of advertising would thus be a barrier to entry that would increase the degree of monopoly power in the economy. A greater degree of monopoly power would, over time, translate into higher prices and reduced output.

Advertising is thus a two-edged sword. On the one hand, the existence of established and heavily advertised rivals may make it difficult for a new firm to enter a market. On the other hand, entry into most industries would be virtually impossible without advertising.

Economists don't agree on whether advertising helps or hurts competition in particular markets, but one general observation can safely be made—a world with advertising is more competitive than a world without advertising would be. The important policy question is more limited—and more difficult: would a world with *less* advertising be more competitive than a world with more?

Imperfect Competition and the New International Economics

The model of international trade under conditions of perfect competition presented in Chapter 11 predicts that trade flows will be based on comparative ad-

- The **new international economics** is a body of thought that applies theories of imperfect competition to the analysis of international trade.
- **Two-way trade** occurs when a country both imports and exports the product of a particular industry.
- **One-way trade** occurs when a country is, in its trade with another country, either an importer or an exporter of the goods and services of a particular industry; it is not both.

vantage. In particular, it suggests that countries will tend to specialize in the production of goods in which they have a comparative advantage and will export those goods. They will import goods in which other countries have a comparative advantage.

Many markets, however, don't come close to meeting the conditions of perfect competition. Economists have discovered that models of imperfect competition suggest predictions that match much of what we observe about trade among nations today. This approach, called the **new international economics,** not only yields different predictions about the nature of trade than does the perfectly competitive model—it suggests some startlingly different policy conclusions as well.

Two-Way Trade

American car buyers can choose Chevrolets, Fords, and Chryslers. They can also choose imported cars such as Toyotas. Japanese car buyers may choose to purchase Toyotas—or imported cars such as Chevrolets, Fords, and Chryslers. The United States imports cars from Japan and exports cars to it. Japan, conversely, imports cars from the United States and exports cars to it. International exchanges in which countries both import and export the same good are called **two-way trade.**

In a perfectly competitive world, such as the one we examined in Chapter 11, two-way trade would not occur. Countries would be either exporters or importers of a good; they would not be both. Such trade is called **one-way trade.** Exhibit 13-9 shows two-way trade as a percentage of total trade for several countries. The table shows that 60.7 percent of total U.S. trade in 1980 was two-way trade—trade that cannot be explained in terms of comparative advantage within the context of the model of perfect competition.

The explanation of two-way trade lies in a key feature of monopolistic competition and of some cases of oligopoly: product differentiation. Suppose two countries have similar endowments of factors of production, but their products are differentiated—clocks produced by different manufacturers, for example, are different. Consumers in the United States buy some clocks produced in Switzerland, just as consumers in Switzerland purchase some clocks produced

EXHIBIT 13-9

Two-Way Trade as a Percentage of Total Trade

Two-way trade accounts for the bulk of trade conducted by most developed countries. Their trade with less developed countries is more likely to be one-way trade. The figures here are estimates for 1980.

Two-way Trade (percentage)

Country	World	Latin America	All less developed countries	All developed countries
Belgium	79.7%	11.4%	40.1%	77.6%
Canada	58.5	25.0	33.0	79.2
France	80.4	16.3	44.2	79.2
Germany	65.4	13.0	34.6	74.1
Italy	65.4	19.8	44.3	59.8
Japan	28.8	10.6	17.6	33.6
Netherlands	74.2	17.7	45.5	70.3
Sweden	66.5	7.6	17.4	72.5
United Kingdom	79.1	24.0	44.2	77.5
United States	60.7	29.6	35.0	66.7

Source: Claudy Culem and Lars Lundberg, "The Product Pattern of Two-way Trade: Stability Among Countries over Time," *Weltwirtschaftliches Archiv* 122(1) (1986):113–130.

in the United States. Indeed, if two countries are similar in their relative endowments of factors of production, two-way trade based on product differentiation is likely to be more important than one-way trade based on comparative advantage.

The data in Exhibit 13-9 confirm the tendency for two-way trade to dominate among similar countries. All the countries named in the table are "developed" economies—economies with high incomes and high ratios of capital to labor. With the exception of Japan, these countries engage primarily in two-way trade with other developed countries; 77.6 percent of Belgium's trade with other developed countries, for example, is two-way trade. When these same countries trade with less developed countries—countries with low incomes and low ratios of capital to labor—two-way trade is much less important. Just 17.4 percent of Sweden's trade with less developed countries, for example, is two-way trade. Thus, when developed countries trade with less developed countries, the flow of goods and services is much more likely to go one way, as predicted by traditional theory, with countries exporting the goods in which they have a comparative advantage.

Among the developed nations shown in Exhibit 13-9, Japan stands out as an exception to the general rule. Although its trade is more likely to be two-way with developed than with less developed countries, two-way trade remains much less important for Japan than for other developed economies. Perhaps this is because Japan depends on other countries for raw materials and dominates many markets for finished products. Its trade thus tends to be one-way rather than two-way. The situation may also reflect the impact of nontariff barriers in limiting Japanese consumption of imported goods and services that are also produced in Japan.

Strategic Trade Policy

The new international economics has implications for public policy that are anathema to the traditional theory of international trade. The theory suggests that it may be possible for countries to increase economic welfare by intervening in international markets to subsidize particular export sectors and protect some industries from foreign competition. In perfect competition such measures would reduce the goods and services available to the country that imposes them, but when imposed on trade in an imperfectly competitive world they may actually increase income.

Suppose technological change has spawned a new industry. Given the economies of scale in this industry, only a few firms are likely to dominate it worldwide—it will emerge as an oligopoly. The firms that dominate it are likely to earn economic profits. Furthermore, because there will be only a few firms, they will be located in only a few countries.

Some proponents of the new international economics regard such firms as a kind of prize for which different countries will compete. The countries that "win" these prizes will be home to firms that earn profits by supplying goods to the rest of the world. Their governments could conceivably impose taxes on these profits that would enhance economic welfare within the country. The potential for such gains may justify government efforts to assist firms seeking to acquire a dominant position in the new industry. Government aid could take the form of protectionist trade policies aimed at allowing these firms to expand in the face of foreign competition, assistance with research and development efforts, programs to provide workers with special skills needed by the industry, or

Strategic trade policy is the use of government intervention to promote the development of a particular industry that will increase domestic welfare through its trade with the rest of the world.

subsidies in the form of direct payments or special tax treatment. Any such policy aimed at promoting the development of key industries within a country that may increase domestic welfare through trade with the rest of the world is known as a **strategic trade policy.**

Proponents of strategic trade policy often cite the development of the semiconductor industry in Japan as a successful application of the approach. Semiconductors are the "brains" of modern computers. The market for semiconductors was dominated by a few U.S. firms in the 1970s when the Japanese government, in conjunction with several Japanese firms, selected this industry as one in which Japan would seek dominance. The government helped to finance research and development efforts and encouraged banks to make money available to the industry. The government also imposed protective tariffs to insulate these Japanese firms from foreign competition. By the mid-1980s, Japanese firms had won dominance of the semiconductor industry. The United States had dominated this market at the beginning of the decade, but it held only a 5 percent share by the end.

The U.S. government responded with a strategic trade initiative of its own. It organized and helped fund Sematech, a research consortium of semiconductor manufacturers. The United States also won concessions from Japan to limit its exports of semiconductors to the United States. By 1995, the U.S. share of world semiconductor production remained small—and Korean firms were beginning to push Japanese firms aside in the struggle for market dominance. The fact remains that the U.S. government launched a program based on the ideas of the new international economics.

Although strategic trade policy suggests a conceptually positive role for government in international trade, proponents of the approach note that it has dangers. Firms might use the strategic trade argument even if their development were unlikely to offer the gains specified in the theory. The successful application of the approach requires that the government correctly identify industries in which a country can, in fact, gain dominance—something that may not be possible to do. Finally, those firms whose success the policy promotes might block the taxes that would redistribute the gains of the policies to the population in general.

Checklist

- If advertising reduces competition, it tends to raise prices and reduce quantities produced. If it enhances competition, it tends to lower prices and increase quantities produced.
- Product differentiation may create two-way trade between countries, particularly those with similar relative factor endowments.
- Strategic trade policy seeks to expand domestic welfare by providing protection for specific industries.

A Look Back—And a Look Ahead

This chapter has examined the world of imperfect competition that exists between the polar extremes of perfect competition and monopoly. Imperfectly competitive markets exist whenever more than one seller exists in a market and each seller has some degree of control over price. Firms in imperfectly competitive markets are price setters.

This chapter examined two general market types: monopolistic competition and oligopoly. Monopolistic competition is characterized by many firms producing similar but differentiated goods and services in a market with easy entry. Oligopoly is characterized by a relatively few firms producing either standardized or differentiated products. There may be substantial barriers to entry.

In the short run, a monopolistically competitive firm's pricing and output decisions are the same as those of a monopoly. In the long run, profits will be whittled away by the entry of new firms and new products that increase the number of close substitutes. The demand curve facing a typical firm will eventually fall and become tangent to the average total cost curve, resulting in zero profit. The monopolistically competitive firm will operate with excess capacity, a sign of inefficient resource allocation, but such inefficiency is the price people appear willing to pay for the highly diversified products available from these imperfectly competitive firms.

An industry dominated by a few firms is an oligopoly. The degree to which a few firms dominate can be measured using concentration ratios and Herfindahl indexes. Each oligopolist is aware of its interdependence with other firms in the industry and is constantly aware of the behavior of its rivals. Oligopolists engage in strategic decisionmaking in order to determine their best output and pricing strategies as well as the best forms of nonprice competition.

We examined two traditional models of oligopoly behavior. The kinked demand curve model predicts that sometimes oligopoly firms will not change their prices in response to a change in cost. The collusion model suggests that firms in an industry will find a way to behave as if they were a single monopoly firm, extracting the maximum profit possible from a market. They may accomplish this through overt collusion in a cartel or tacit collusion with price leadership.

We also examined game theory models. In these models firms make strategic choices based on a payoff matrix. If each firm has a dominant strategy, the game has a dominant strategy equilibrium. Even if a game lacks a dominant strategy equilibrium, it may have a Nash equilibrium. Firms may use tit-for-tat or trigger strategies to induce rivals to engage in cooperative behavior.

Advertising is likely to occur in imperfectly competitive markets. Advertising can increase the degree of competitiveness by encouraging price competition and promoting entry. It can also decrease competition by establishing brand loyalty and thus creating barriers to entry.

Incorporating theories of imperfect competition into the analysis of international trade helps to explain the phenomenon of two-way trade. It also suggests a possible justification for government intervention in the form of strategic trade policy to promote the domestic development of new export industries.

This chapter examined the implications of imperfect competition in product markets. Chapter 14 focuses on imperfect competition in markets for factors of production.

Terms and Concepts for Review

Cartel
Concentration ratio
Dominant strategy
Dominant strategy equilibrium
Duopoly
Excess capacity
Game theory
Herfindahl index
Imperfect competition
Kinked demand curve model
Monopolistic competition
Nash equilibrium
New international economics
Oligopoly
One-way trade
Overt collusion
Payoff
Strategic choice
Strategic trade policy
Tacit collusion
Tit-for-tat strategy
Trigger strategy
Two-way trade

For Discussion

1. What are the major distinctions between a monopolistically competitive industry and an oligopolistic industry?
2. What is the difference between a price taker and a price setter?
3. Suppose a city experiences substantial population growth. What is likely to happen to profits in the market for haircuts, a monopolistically competitive market?
4. Economists have observed that the price of candy bars (supplied in an oligopolistic industry) is generally the same for different brands and that changes in price are quite rare. Can you offer any explanations for this price rigidity?
5. We saw that a change in marginal cost may not change a firm's profit-maximizing output or price in the kinked demand curve model. Would price also be unlikely to change in response to a change in demand?
6. Some professors grade students on the basis of an absolute percentage of the highest score earned on each test given during the semester. All students who get within a certain percentage of the highest score earned get an A. Why don't these professors worry that the students will get together and collude in such a way as to keep the high score in the class equal to a very low total?
7. Under what circumstances will a country both export and import the products of the same industry?
8. Which of the following goods are more likely to be involved in two-way than in one-way trade?
   a. tires
   b. lumber
   c. shoes
   d. computers
   e. wheat
9. Your mother probably told you to avoid tit-for-tat behavior. Why does it make sense for firms to do it?
10. Here's a question that's mostly for fun. Which of the following cars is produced in the United States? Can you match each car to the country in which it was primarily produced? What does all this say about the nature of international trade?

1. Pontiac LeMans	A. Canada
2. Chevrolet Lumina	B. Korea
3. Mercury Capri	C. Mexico
4. Honda Accord Coupe	D. United States
5. Dodge Stealth	E. Japan
6. Mercury Tracer	F. Australia
7. Plymouth Voyager	

Problems

1. Suppose the monopolistically competitive barber shop industry in a community is in long-run equilibrium. Incomes rise. Illustrate the short-run and long-run effects of the change on the price and output of a typical firm in the market.
2. Consider the same industry as in Problem 1. Suppose the market is in long-run equilibrium and that an annual license fee is imposed on firms. How does this affect price and output in the short run and in the long run?
3. Industry A consists of four firms, each of which has an equal share of the market. Industry B consists of two firms, each of which has an equal share of the market. Compare the 4-firm concentration ratios and the Herfindahl indexes for the two industries.
4. Given the payoff matrix below for a duopoly in which each firm is considering an expanded advertising campaign, determine whether each firm has a dominant strategy. Is there a dominant strategy equilibrium? All figures in the payoff matrix reflect changes in annual profits (in millions of dollars).

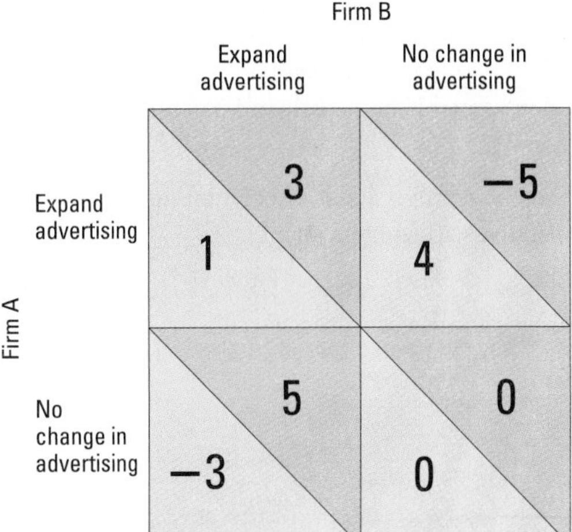

14

Imperfectly Competitive Markets for Factors of Production

Chapter Objectives

After mastering the material in this chapter, you will be able to:

1. Describe the difference between the computations of marginal revenue product for firms that are price takers and those that are price setters in their product markets.
2. Explain why firms that are price setters in their product markets have lower input demand curves than otherwise identical price-taking firms.
3. Discuss what happens when a single firm is the only buyer of a factor.
4. Relate the nature, role, and history of labor unions in the United States.
5. Explain how input supply is affected by monopoly power, and explain the range of solutions possible in the case of bilateral monopoly.
6. Explain how professional associations and cooperatives affect input supply.

The workmen desire to get as much, the masters to give as little as possible. The former are disposed to combine in order to raise, the latter in order to lower the wages of labor.
Adam Smith, 1776

What's Ahead

The two sides certainly seemed determined to live up to Adam Smith's dictum.

Major league baseball players, whose salaries averaged more than $1 million per year in 1994, walked off their jobs and shut down the 1994 season. They were protesting a plan by their employers, the owners of baseball teams, to impose a limit on how much each team spent on player salaries. As Economics *went to press in 1995, baseball players were back at work, but no agreement had been reached. The possibility of another strike continued to cloud the future of major league baseball.*

Some people thought the players were simply being greedy. They were already the highest-paid players of any sport, but there seemed to be no limit to their desire for more money. Other people believed it was the owners who were the bad guys. After all, the owners of other types of firms don't band together to limit their payrolls. There's no salary cap on computer programmers or carpenters. Why should the owners be allowed to "combine . . . in order to lower the wages of labor"?

For economists, greed is not the issue. All individuals act in their own self-interest. The showdown between players and owners represented an intriguing battle over the rules of the game in salary determination. It took place in an arena in which revolutionary changes in the rules have occurred in the last three decades. Those changes have produced a textbook example of the economic forces at work in the determination of wages in imperfectly competitive markets.

Markets for labor and for other factors of production can diverge from the conditions of perfect competition in several ways, all of which involve price-setting behavior. Firms that purchase inputs may be price setters in the markets in which they sell their products, or they may be price setters in the markets in which they purchase their inputs. Suppliers of inputs may have market power as well: a firm may have monopoly control over some key input, or input suppliers may band together to achieve market power. Workers may organize a union. Suppliers of services, such as physicians or hairdressers, may band together in associations that exert power in the marketplace. Individual firms may join in a producers' cooperative that seeks to influence market prices.

This chapter puts the marginal decision rule to work in the analysis of imperfectly competitive markets for labor and for other factors of production. Imperfect competition in these markets generally results in a reduction in the quantity of an input used, relative to the competitive equilibrium. The price of the input, however, may be higher or lower than in perfect competition, depending on the nature of the market structure involved.

The Demand for Factors of Production

What determines how much an accounting firm will be willing to pay for the services of a secretary? A professional basketball team for a center? A hospital for the services of a nurse or physician?

We examined questions such as these in the context of perfectly competitive markets in Chapter 9. Because many of the principles that apply to firms' choices in perfectly competitive markets apply also to imperfectly competitive markets, it will be helpful to begin by reviewing what we've learned about firms' demands for factors of production in perfect competition. Then we'll turn to the case of imperfectly competitive markets.

Factor Demand in Perfect Competition: A Review

A perfectly competitive firm faces a market-determined price for each factor of production and then decides how much of each factor to use. To maximize profits, it hires additional units of the factor up to the point that the factor's marginal revenue product (*MRP*) equals its marginal factor cost (*MFC*).

The firm's *MRP* curve is its demand curve for the factor. We find the *MRP* curve by multiplying the factor's marginal product by the price of the good or service the firm produces. The price is determined in the market; the firm takes it as given. Market demand is the aggregate of individual demands, so the market demand for a factor of production is also determined by the factor's *MRP*. In a perfectly competitive market, the price of a factor of production equals the *MRP* of the factor. It also equals *MFC*.

The maximizing rule for perfectly competitive firms applies to imperfectly competitive firms as well. To maximize profits, a firm will add more units of a factor as long as the factor's *MRP* exceeds its *MFC*. Equilibrium will be reached where the *MRP* and *MFC* curves intersect. As was the case with imperfectly competitive product markets, the differences created in imperfect markets stem from the fact that firms in these markets are price setters, not price takers.

Factor Demand in Imperfectly Competitive Product Markets

An essential characteristic of imperfect competition, whether it be monopoly, monopolistic competition, or oligopoly, is that individual firms face downward-sloping demand curves. A downward-sloping demand curve means that mar-

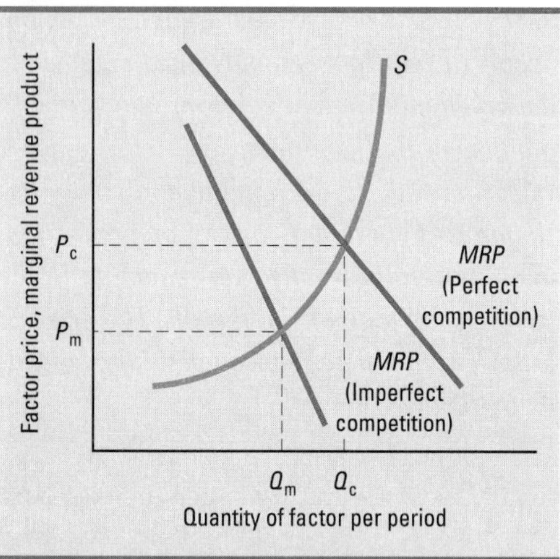

EXHIBIT 14-1

Factor Demand: Perfect Versus Imperfect Competition

Given a factor supply curve *S*, firms in a perfectly competitive product market demand Q_c of an input, paying a price of P_c per unit. If the same market were imperfectly competitive, firms would demand only Q_m of the input and pay P_m per unit. The marginal revenue product (*MRP*) curve for imperfectly competitive firms lies below the *MRP* curve for perfect competition.

ginal revenue will be less than price. And that means that an imperfectly competitive firm's *MRP* curve for a factor will be lower than that of a perfectly competitive firm charging the same price and getting the same marginal product. For the perfectly competitive firm, *MRP* is marginal product multiplied by price. For an imperfectly competitive firm, *MRP* is marginal product multiplied by marginal revenue, which is less than price.

Suppose, for example, that the price of a good produced in a perfectly competitive market is $10, and the marginal product of an additional worker for one week is 20 units of output. The *MRP* of labor will be $200—hiring an additional worker for 1 week adds $200 to the firm's revenues. Suppose that, by coincidence, a monopoly firm charges $10 for its product as well, and the marginal product of one more worker for one week is also 20 units of output. To calculate the *MRP* of the worker, we multiply marginal product by marginal revenue. Because marginal revenue for a monopoly—and for any price setter—is less than price, *MRP* will be *less* than $200. If marginal revenue is, say, $7 then marginal revenue product will be $140—not the $200 that we had for the perfectly competitive firm. Even though labor is just as productive, the demand by an imperfectly competitive firm will be less than the demand by a perfectly competitive firm.

We've already seen that firms in imperfectly competitive product markets are likely to produce less than would otherwise similar firms in perfectly competitive markets. It should come as no surprise, then, that imperfectly competitive firms will demand smaller quantities of factors of production as well.

With lower demand for factors, an imperfectly competitive market faces lower factor prices than would an otherwise equivalent perfectly competitive market. Exhibit 14-1 illustrates the contrast between the two market types. Given the factor supply curve *S*, firms in a perfectly competitive market demand Q_c units of the input and pay a price of P_c per unit. If firms were imperfectly competitive but all other determinants of input demand were the same, only Q_m units of the input would be demanded and the price would be P_m.

The relationship between input demand and market structure suggests that suppliers of inputs have an interest in the degree of competitiveness of product markets. In general, the more closely a product market resembles the conditions of perfect competition, the closer marginal revenue will be to price, and the greater *MRP* will be. Competitive output markets are therefore in the best interest of suppliers of inputs as well as consumers.

Checklist

- The demand for any factor depends on its marginal product and on the marginal revenue that marginal product brings to firms.
- Because marginal revenue is less than price for price-setting firms, marginal revenue product (*MRP*) is lower in imperfect competition than in perfect competition, all other things the same.
- Because *MRP* is lower in imperfect competition than in perfect competition, imperfect product markets result in smaller input quantities and lower input prices than perfectly competitive product markets.

Price-Setting Buyers: The Case of Monopsony

We have seen that market power in product markets exists when firms have the ability to set the prices they charge. Firms may also have the power to set the prices they pay in factor markets.

A firm can set price in a factor market if instead of a market-determined price it faces an upward-sloping supply curve for the factor. This fact creates a fundamental difference between price-taking and price-setting firms in factor markets. A price-taking firm can hire any amount of the factor at the market price; it faces a horizontal supply curve for the factor at the market-determined price, as shown in Panel (a) of Exhibit 14-2. A price-setting firm facing supply curve *S* in Panel (b) obtains Q_1 units of the factor when it sets the price P_1. To obtain a larger quantity, such as Q_2, it must offer a higher price, P_2.

Monopsony is a market in which there is a single buyer of a good, service, or factor of production.

EXHIBIT 14-2

Factor Market Price Setters and Price Takers

A price-taking firm faces the market-determined price, P, for the factor in Panel (a) and can purchase any quantity it wants at that price. A price-setting firm faces an upward-sloping supply curve S in Panel (b). The price-setting firm sets the price consistent with the quantity of the factor it wishes to obtain. Here, the firm can obtain Q_1 units at a price P_1, but it must pay a higher price per unit, P_2, to obtain Q_2 units.

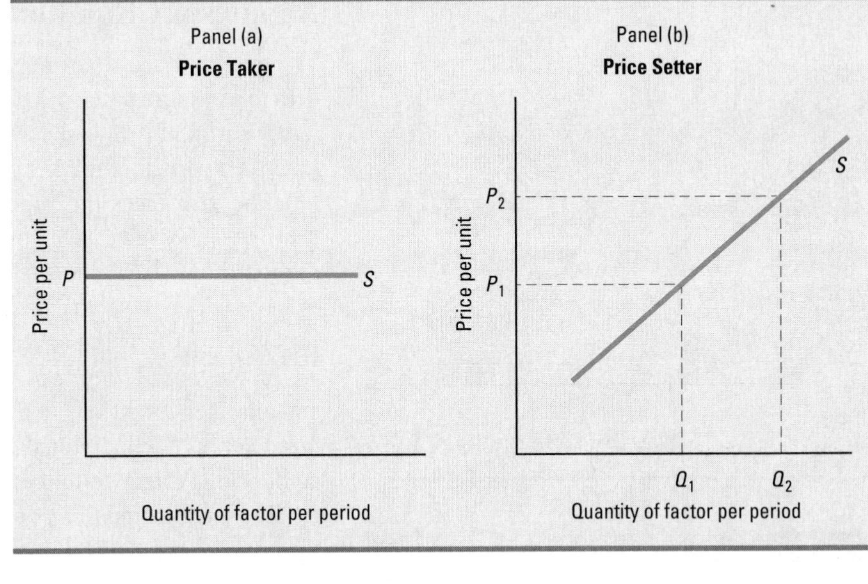

Consider a situation in which one firm is the only buyer of a particular factor. A market in which there is a single buyer of a good, service, or factor of production is called a **monopsony.** Monopsony is the buyer's counterpart of monopoly. Monopoly implies a single seller; monopsony implies a single buyer.

Assume that the suppliers of a factor in a monopsony market are price takers; there is perfect competition in factor supply. But a single firm constitutes the entire market for the factor. That means that the monopsony firm faces the market supply curve for the factor. Such a case is illustrated in Exhibit 14-3, where the price and quantity combinations on the supply curve for the factor are given in the table.

Suppose the monopsony firm is now using 3 units of the factor at a price of \$6 per unit. Its total factor cost for this factor is \$18. Now suppose the firm is considering adding 1 unit of the factor. Given the supply curve, the only way the firm can obtain 4 units of the factor rather than 3 is to set a higher price: \$8. That would increase the firm's total factor cost from \$18 to \$32. The marginal factor cost of the fourth unit of the factor is thus \$14. It includes the \$8 the firm pays for the fourth unit plus an additional \$2 for each of the 3 units the firm was already using, since it has increased the price to \$8 from \$6. The marginal factor cost (*MFC*) thus exceeds the price of the factor. We can plot the *MFC* for each increase in the quantity of the factor the firm uses; notice in Exhibit 14-3 that the *MFC* curve lies above the supply curve. As always in plotting marginal values, we plot the \$14 midway between units 3 and 4 because it is the increase in factor cost as the firm goes from 3 to 4 units.

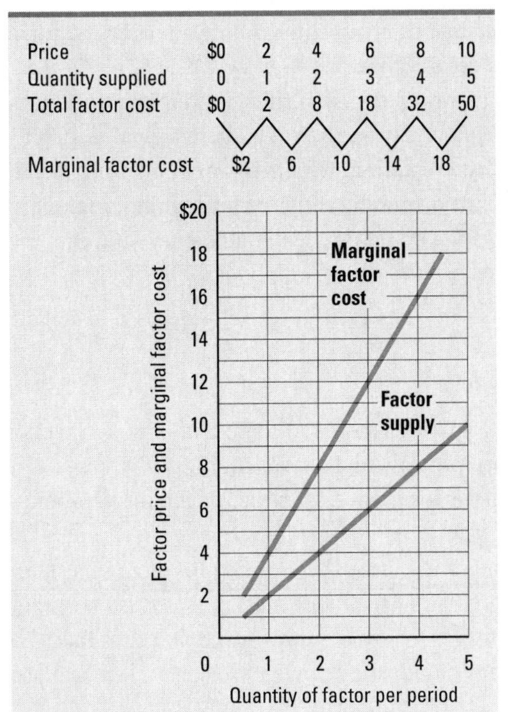

Price	\$0	2	4	6	8	10
Quantity supplied	0	1	2	3	4	5
Total factor cost	\$0	2	8	18	32	50
Marginal factor cost	\$2	6	10	14	18	

EXHIBIT 14-3

Supply and Marginal Factor Cost

The table gives prices and quantities for the factor supply curve plotted in the graph. Based on those observations, values for total and marginal factor cost are computed. Notice that the marginal factor cost curve lies above the supply curve and has a slope that is twice as great.

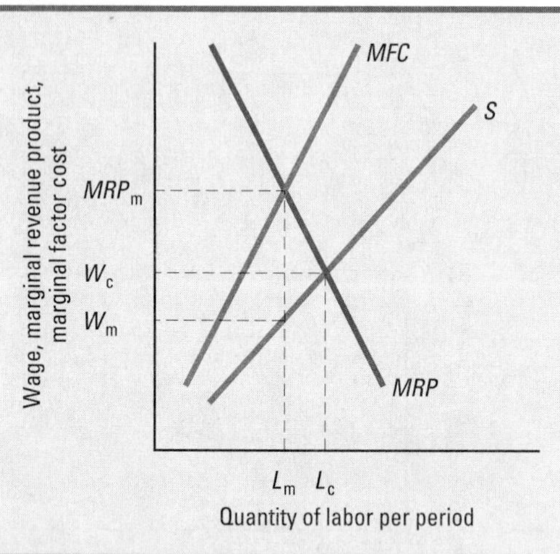

EXHIBIT 14-4

Monopsony Equilibrium

Given the supply curve for labor *S* and the marginal factor cost curve *MFC,* the monopsony firm will select the quantity of labor at which the *MRP* of labor equals its *MFC.* It thus uses L_m units of labor (determined by the intersection of *MRP* and *MFC*) and pays a wage of W_m per unit (the wage, taken from the supply curve, at which L_m units of labor are available). The quantity of labor used by the monopsony firm is less than would be used in a competitive market (L_c), and the wage paid by the monopsony firm is less than the competitive wage (W_c).

Monopsony Equilibrium

The marginal decision rule, as it applies to a firm's use of factors, calls for the firm to add more units of a factor up to the point that the factor's *MRP* is equal to its *MFC.* Exhibit 14-4 illustrates this solution for a firm that is the only buyer of labor in a particular market.

The firm faces the supply curve for labor *S* and the marginal factor cost curve for labor *MFC.* The profit-maximizing quantity is determined by the intersection of the *MRP* and *MFC* curves—the firm will hire L_m units of labor. The wage at which the firm can obtain L_m units of labor is given by the supply curve for labor; it is W_m. Labor receives a wage that is less than its *MRP.*

If the monopsony firm were broken up into a large number of small firms and all other conditions in the market remained unchanged, then the sum of the *MRP* curves for individual firms would be the market demand for labor. The equilibrium wage would be W_c, and the quantity of labor demanded would be L_c. Thus, compared to a competitive market, a monopsony solution generates a lower factor price and a smaller quantity of the factor demanded.

Monopoly and Monopsony: A Comparison

There is a close relationship between the models of monopoly and monopsony. A clear understanding of this relationship will help to clarify both models.

Exhibit 14-5 compares the monopoly and monopsony equilibrium solutions. Both types of firms are price setters: the monopoly is a price setter in its product market, and the monopsony is a price setter in the factor market in which it has monopsony power. Both firms must change price to change quantity: the monopoly must lower its product price to sell an additional unit of output, and the monopsony must pay more to hire an additional unit of the factor. Because both types of firms must adjust prices to change quantities, the marginal consequences of their choices are not given by the prices they charge (for products) or pay (for factors). For a monopoly, marginal revenue is less than price; for a monopsony, marginal factor cost is greater than price.

Both types of firms follow the marginal decision rule: a monopoly produces a quantity of product at which marginal revenue *MR* equals marginal cost *MC,* and a monopsony employs a quantity of factor at which *MRP* equals *MFC.* Both firms set prices at which they can sell or purchase the profit-maximizing quantity. The monopoly sets its product price based on the demand curve it faces; the monopsony sets its factor price based on the factor supply curve it faces.

Monopsony in the Real World

Although pure cases of monopsony are rare, there are many situations in which buyers have a degree of **monopsony power.** A buyer has monopsony power if it faces an upward-sloping supply curve for a good, service, or factor of production.

For example, a firm that accounts for a large share of employment in a small community may be large enough relative to the labor market that it is no longer a price taker. Instead, it must raise wages to attract more workers. It thus faces an upward-sloping supply curve and has monopsony power. We can expect it to use that power to pay a wage below the *MRP* of labor.

A buyer has **monopsony power** if it faces an upward-sloping supply curve for a good, service, or factor of production.

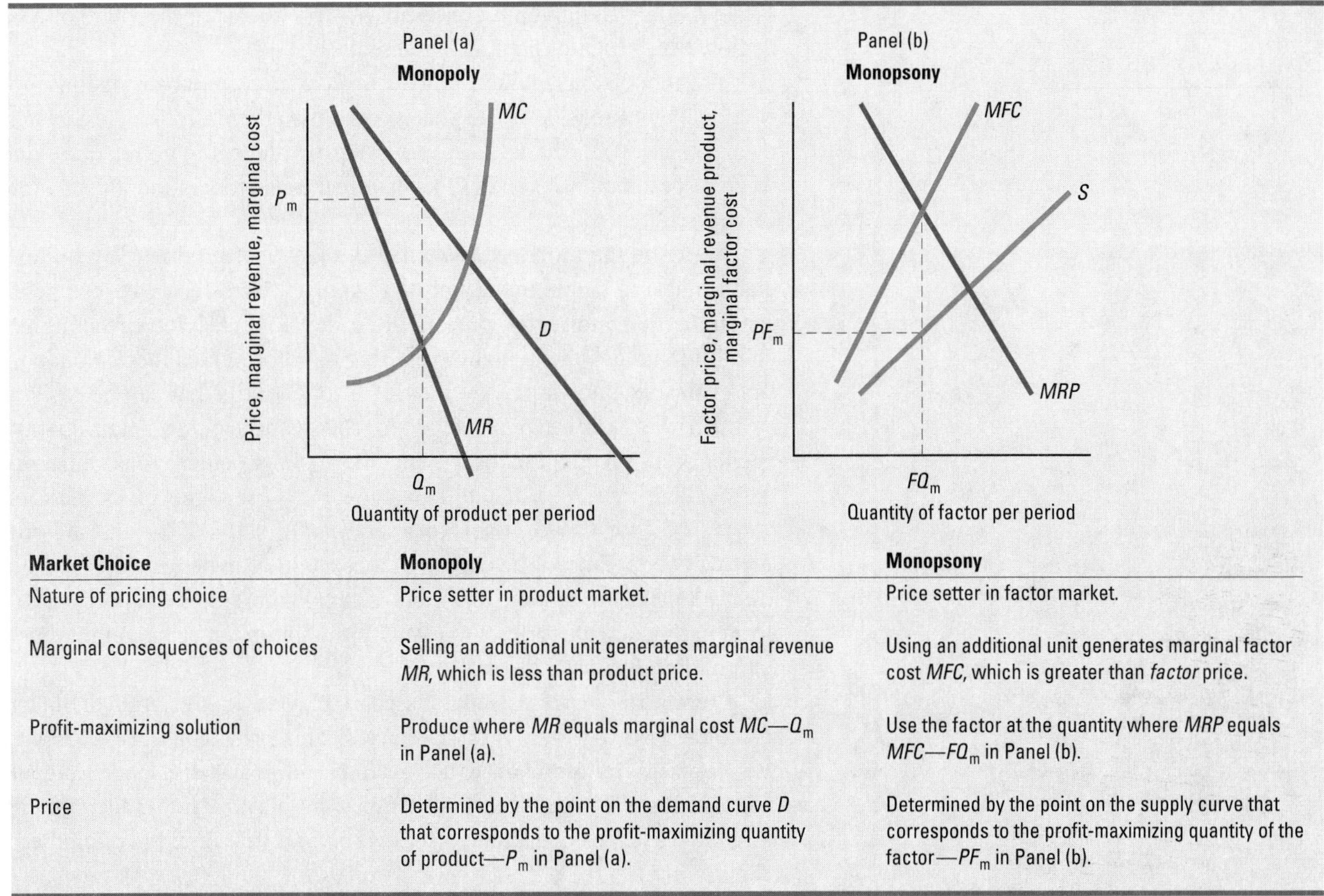

Market Choice	Monopoly	Monopsony
Nature of pricing choice	Price setter in product market.	Price setter in factor market.
Marginal consequences of choices	Selling an additional unit generates marginal revenue *MR*, which is less than product price.	Using an additional unit generates marginal factor cost *MFC*, which is greater than *factor* price.
Profit-maximizing solution	Produce where *MR* equals marginal cost *MC*—Q_m in Panel (a).	Use the factor at the quantity where *MRP* equals *MFC*—FQ_m in Panel (b).
Price	Determined by the point on the demand curve *D* that corresponds to the profit-maximizing quantity of product—P_m in Panel (a).	Determined by the point on the supply curve that corresponds to the profit-maximizing quantity of the factor—PF_m in Panel (b).

EXHIBIT 14-5

Monopoly and Monopsony

The table summarizes the information firms can derive from the graphs in Panels (a) and (b).

Monopsony power is much more likely to emerge in factor markets than in product markets. Firms are the buyers of factors of production, and firms often grow to sufficient size to acquire a degree of monopsony power in the market for a particular factor. Cases in which an individual consumer dominates a particular market are probably rare. A very wealthy collector of handcrafted goods from a particular region might acquire some monopsony power. This consumer would purchase an increased quantity of the goods up to the point at which his or her demand curve intersects the upward-sloping *MFC* curve. Price would be determined on the supply curve at that quantity—which would be less than *MFC*.

One of the most widely studied cases of monopsony is the case of professional sports. The next section reviews some of the major issues in such markets.

Monopsonies in Sports

Professional sports provide almost a laboratory experiment in which economists can test the implications of their theories of wage determination in competitive versus monopsony labor markets. In their analyses, economists assume professional teams are profit-maximizing firms that hire labor (athletes and other workers) to produce a product: fans who watch games. Fans influence revenues directly by purchasing tickets and indirectly by generating the ratings that determine television and radio advertising revenues from broadcasts of games.

In a competitive system, a player should receive a wage equal to his *MRP*—the increase in team revenues the player is able to produce. As New York Yankee owner George Steinbrenner once put it, "You measure the value of a ballplayer by how many fannies he puts in the seats."

The monopsony model, however, predicts that players facing monopsony employers will receive wages that are less than their *MRP*s. A test of monopsony theory, then, would be to determine whether players in competitive markets receive wages equal to their *MRP*s and whether players in monopsony markets receive less.

Applying the monopsony model to a factor of production requires not only that we have a single buyer but that supply for the factor be competitive. One can argue that individual players often develop a degree of name recognition that differentiates their product and that therefore gives them monopoly power. But even well-known players provide a set of skills that can be easily provided by other well-known players. A baseball team seeking a top-quality starting pitcher or a basketball team seeking an excellent center would have several options. There may be a handful of athletes whose fame gives them monopoly power, but it seems reasonable to assert that the skills of the vast majority of athletes can be replaced. The supply of these skills can be regarded as competitive. We shall therefore assume that there is an upward-sloping supply curve for players in particular categories. Given this assumption, let us examine wage determination in professional baseball.

Before 1977, professional baseball players in the United States labored under the terms of the "reserve clause." This provision specified that a player was "owned" by his team. Once a team had acquired a player's contract, the team could sell, trade, retain, or dismiss the player. Unless the team dismissed him, the player was unable to offer his services for competitive bidding by other teams.

Players entered major league baseball through a draft that was structured so that only one team had the right to bid for any one player. Throughout a player's career, there was always only one team that could bid on him—each player faced a monopsony purchaser for his services to major league baseball.

Gerald Scully, an economist at the University of Texas at Dallas, estimated the impact of the reserve clause on player salaries. He sought to demonstrate whether player salaries fell short of *MRP*. Scully estimated the *MRP* of players in a two-step process. First, he studied the determinants of team attendance. He found that in addition to factors such as population and income in a team's home city, the team's win-loss record had a strong effect on attendance. Second, he examined the player characteristics that determined win-loss records. He found that for hitters, batting average was the variable most closely associated with a team's winning percentage. For pitchers, it was the earned-run average—the number of earned runs allowed by a pitcher per nine innings pitched.

With equations that predicted a team's attendance and its win-loss record, Scully was able to take a particular player, describe him by his statistics, and compute his *MRP*. Scully then subtracted costs associated with each player for such things as transportation, lodging, meals, and uniforms to obtain the player's net *MRP*. He then compared players' net *MRP*s to their wages.

Scully's results, shown in Exhibit 14-6, show net *MRP* and salary, estimated on a career basis, for players he classified as mediocre, average, and star-quality, based on their individual statistics. To compute career values, Scully used statistics for the 1968 and 1969 seasons, then assumed career lengths of 4 years for mediocre players, 7 years for average players, and 10 years for star players. For average and star-quality players, salaries fell far below net *MRP*, just as the theory of monopsony suggests.

	Career Net *MRP*	Career Salary	Salary as Percentage of Net *MRP*
Hitters			
Mediocre	−$129,300	$60,800	
Average	906,700	196,200	22
Star	3,139,100	477,200	15
Pitchers			
Mediocre	−$53,600	$54,800	
Average	1,119,200	222,500	20
Star	3,969,600	612,500	15

Source: Gerald Scully, "Pay and Performance in Major League Baseball," *American Economic Review* 64(2) (December 1974): 915–930.

EXHIBIT 14-6

The Impact of the Reserve Clause: Net Marginal Revenue Product and Wages

Based on data for the 1968 and 1969 major league baseball seasons, economist George Scully estimated the following values for career net marginal revenue product (*MRP*) and salaries for hitters and pitchers of various ability levels. His results show that average and star-quality players received salaries that were a small fraction of their *MRP*s.

The fact that mediocre players with negative net *MRP*s received salaries presents something of a puzzle. One explanation could be that when they were signed to contracts, these players were expected to perform well, so their salaries reflected their expected contributions to team revenues. Their actual performance fell short, so their wages exceeded their *MRP*s. Another explanation could be that teams paid young players more than they were expected to contribute to revenues early in their careers. In any event, Scully found that the costs of mediocre players exceeded their estimated contribution to team revenues, giving them negative net *MRP*s.

A further test of the monopsony argument was provided in 1977, when the reserve clause arrangement was changed. Players were given the right to become "free agents" after 6 years. At that point, they could offer their services to other teams.

The results were striking. Economists Paul Sommers and Noel Quinton of Middlebury College, using an approach similar to Scully's, estimated the *MRP*s and salaries of 14 players who became available as free agents in 1977. They found that hitters' salaries increased to about half of their net *MRP*s. Pitchers' salaries rose to a level roughly equal to their estimated net *MRP*s, as shown in Exhibit 14-7. Subsequent estimates of the relationship between salaries of baseball players and their net *MRP*s suggest that the gap between the salaries and net *MRP*s of hitters has continued to close as the monopsony power of baseball teams has weakened.

Pitcher	Net *MRP*	1977 Salary
Doyle Alexander	$166,203	$166,677
Bill Campbell	205,639	210,000
Rollie Fingers	303,511	332,000
Wayne Garland	282,091	230,000
Don Gullett	340,846	349,333

Source: Based on Paul Sommers and Noel Quinton, "Pay and Performance in Major League Baseball: The Case of the First Family of Free Agents," *Journal of Human Resources* 17(3) (Summer 1982): 426–436. Reprinted by permission of the University of Wisconsin Press.

EXHIBIT 14-7

Free Agent Pitchers in 1977: Salary Versus Net Marginal Revenue Product

Basketball and football players have had much the same experience. Basketball players won a limited degree of free agency in 1976 and an expanded form in 1981. Average annual player salaries rose from $109,000 in 1976 to $925,000 in 1990. Football players worked under an almost pure form of monopsony up to 1989, when a few players were allowed free agency status each year. Then, in 1993, 484 players were released to the market as free agents. Those players received pay increases averaging more than 100 percent that year.

Given the dramatic impact on player salaries of more competitive markets for athletes, events such as the 1994–1995 strike in major league baseball should come as no surprise. Under the reserve clause, teams were able to obtain the services of players at wages equal to less than 25 percent of the players' *MRP*s. With free agency and a more competitive market, player salaries appear to be roughly equal to *MRP*s. The proposal by the owners in 1994 to put a ceiling on the total payroll of each team was an attempt to reinstate some of the old monopsony power of the owners. Players had a huge financial stake in resisting such attempts. While players went back to work in 1995, the issue of a salary cap remained unresolved. The battle between owners and players over how salaries will be determined will continue.

Monopsony in Other Labor Markets

A firm that has a dominant position in a local labor market may have monopsony power in that market. Even if a firm does not dominate the total labor market, it may have monopsony power over certain types of labor. For example, a hospital may be the only large employer of nurses in a local market, and it may impose monopsony power over them.

Colleges and universities generally pay part-time instructors considerably less for teaching a particular course than they pay full-time instructors. In part, the difference reflects the fact that full-time faculty members are expected to have more training and are expected to contribute far more in other areas. But part of the explanation may lie in the monopsony model.

Case in Point — Nurses and Hospital Monopsonies

Individual hospitals have a substantial monopsony hold over nurses in the short run but much less in the long run, says Northwestern University economist Daniel Sullivan.

Using data from the American Hospital Association's annual survey of hospitals, Mr. Sullivan looked at how nurses responded to a wage change by an individual hospital. Mr. Sullivan found that if a hospital lowered its wages for nurses by 10 percent, 14 percent fewer nurses would be willing to work for it a year later. (A perfectly competitive employer would lose all of its workers if it cut the wage it paid.) "If a hospital lowered wages, not all of its employees would leave immediately, which indicates monopsony power," Mr. Sullivan explains. "The hospital can pay below the marginal revenue product."

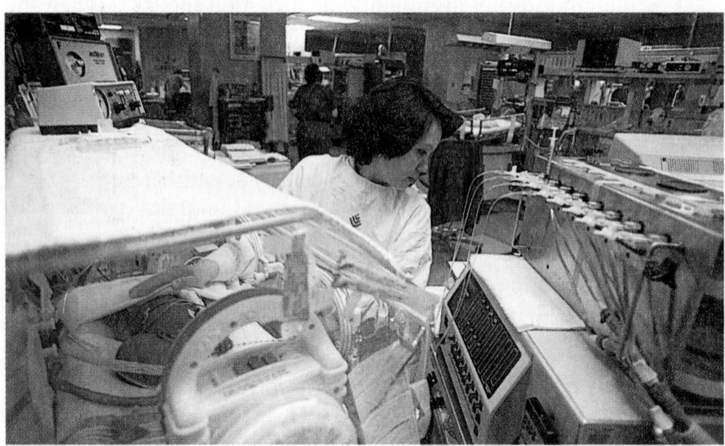

Mr. Sullivan found that over a longer period, the quantity supplied was much more responsive, suggesting a flatter supply curve and a reduced degree of monopsony power. A 10 percent increase in the wage offered by a hospital would produce a 40 percent increase in the number of nurses willing to work for it over a 4-year period.

Mr. Sullivan says that one reason for the greater short-run monopsony power is that nurses are reluctant to change hospitals because they might lose seniority. They also face search costs in applying for new work. The longer a wage change by one hospital persists, however, the more likely nurses are to respond to it.

Source: Cindy Kelley, "Monopsony in the Market for Nurses," *The Margin* 7(Fall 1991):45.

The men and women hired as part-time instructors are likely to have other regular employment. A university hiring a local accountant to teach a section of accounting doesn't have to worry that that person is going to go to another state for a better offer as a part-time instructor. For part-time teaching, then, the university may be the only employer in town—and thus able to exert monopsony power to drive the part-time instructor's wage below the instructor's *MRP.*

Monopsony in Other Factor Markets

Monopsony power may emerge in markets for factors other than labor. The U.S. Department of Defense, for example, has considerable monopsony power in the market for military goods. Major retailers often have some monopsony power with respect to some of their suppliers.

Monopsony power is most likely to emerge for factors that are highly specialized or for factors that are costly to ship. Farmers have often faced single buyers or markets in which only a handful of food-processing firms dominate the local market. Del Monte, for example, is a dominant firm in the purchase of California produce. Sunkist exercises a degree of monopsony power over citrus growers. Fishing boat owners in California have charged that canneries there exert monopsony power in the market for tuna. Milk markets were once characterized as monopsonies because often a single dairy was the only purchaser of raw milk from individual dairy farms. Falling transportation costs have since given dairy farmers the option of shipping their milk over a wider range, weakening the monopsony power of dairies considerably.

Whatever the source of monopsony power, the expected result is the same. Buyers with monopsony power are likely to pay a lower price and to buy a smaller quantity of a particular factor than buyers who operate in a more competitive environment.

Monopsony and the Minimum Wage

We've seen that wages will be lower in monopsony than in otherwise similar competitive labor markets. In a competitive market, workers receive wages equal to their marginal revenue products. Workers employed by monopsony firms receive wages that are less than marginal revenue product. This fact suggests sharply different conclusions for the analysis of minimum wages and competitive versus monopsony conditions.

In a competitive market, the imposition of a minimum wage above the equilibrium wage necessarily reduces employment, as we learned in Chapter 9. In a monopsony market, however, a minimum wage above the equilibrium wage could increase employment at the same time it boosts wages.

Exhibit 14-8 shows a monopsony employer that faces a supply curve *S*, from which we derive the marginal factor cost curve *MFC*. The firm maximizes profit by employing L_m units of labor and paying a wage of $4 per hour. The wage is below the firm's marginal revenue product.

Now suppose the government imposes a minimum wage of $5 per hour; it is illegal for firms to pay less. At this minimum wage, L_c units of labor are supplied. To obtain any smaller quantity of labor, the firm must pay the minimum wage. That means that the section of the supply curve showing quantities of labor supplied at wages below $5 is irrelevant; the firm can't pay those wages. Notice that the section of the supply curve below $5 is shown as a cross-hatched line. If the firm wants to hire more than L_c units of labor it must pay wages given by the supply curve.

Marginal factor cost is affected by the minimum wage. To hire additional units of labor up to L_c, the firm pays the minimum wage. The additional cost of labor beyond L_c continues to be given by the original *MFC* curve. The marginal factor cost curve thus has two segments, a horizontal segment at the minimum wage for quantities up to L_c and the solid portion of the *MFC* curve for quantities beyond that.

The firm will still employ labor up to the point that *MFC* equals *MRP*. In the case shown in Exhibit 14-8, that occurs at L_c. The firm thus increases its employment of labor in response to the minimum wage.

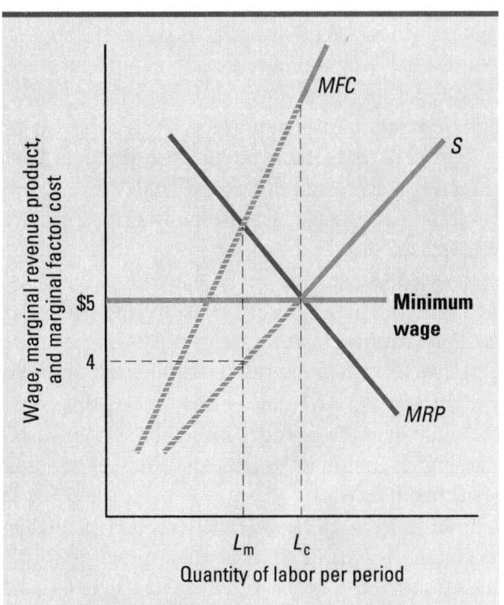

EXHIBIT 14-8

Minimum Wages and Monopsony

A monopsony employer faces a supply curve *S*, a marginal factor cost curve *MFC*, and a marginal revenue product curve *MRP*. It maximizes profit by employing L_m units of labor and paying a wage of $4 per hour. The imposition of a minimum wage of $5 per hour makes the cross-hatched sections of the supply and *MFC* curves irrelevant. The marginal factor cost curve is thus a horizontal line at $5 up to L_c units of labor. *MRP* and *MFC* now intersect at L_c, so that employment increases.

Checklist

- A monopsony is a price setter in the factor market in which it has monopsony power.
- The monopsony buyer selects a profit-maximizing solution by employing the quantity of factor at which marginal factor cost (*MFC*) equals marginal revenue product (*MRP*) and paying the price on the factor supply curve corresponding to that quantity.
- Monopsony equilibrium is analogous to monopoly equilibrium.
- Where monopsony power has existed in professional sports, wages for players have been well below competitive levels. Introducing a more competitive structure to markets for athletes has boosted player salaries dramatically.
- A degree of monopsony power exists whenever a firm faces an upward-sloping supply curve for a factor.
- A minimum wage could increase employment in a monopsony labor market.

Case in Point: Higher Minimum Wages and Fast Food Jobs in New Jersey

The fast food industry is a major employer of unskilled labor. How would a higher minimum wage affect employment in the industry?

A higher minimum wage would tend to reduce employment in the industry if the labor market is competitive. It would increase employment if fast food firms have a degree of monopsony power—if they face upward-sloping supply curves for labor.

New Jersey provided a test case in 1992 when it raised its minimum wage to $5.05 per hour—well above the federal minimum then of $4.25. Princeton University economists David Card and Alan B. Krueger surveyed 410 fast food restaurants in New Jersey and in eastern Pennsylvania before and after the New Jersey increase to learn the impact of the higher minimum. The restaurants in eastern Pennsylvania were included as a comparison group; they faced the federal minimum of $4.25. Firms were interviewed a month before and eight months after the effective date of the higher New Jersey minimum wage.

The survey showed that employment rose among New Jersey fast food outlets while it fell in Pennsylvania. New Jersey firms also increased the percentage of full-time workers after the minimum wage increase.

The results, the authors note, are consistent with the monopsony model. The higher minimum forced firms in New Jersey to pay higher wages. The average starting wage in New Jersey rose from $4.61 before the law was imposed to $5.08 after. Average starting salaries among Pennsylvania firms, meanwhile, remained about the same over the period. The authors also investigated whether the higher minimum wage reduced other benefits for workers; they found it did not.

Higher minimum wages in New Jersey resulted in higher prices at the restaurants surveyed. The average price of a full meal in New Jersey jumped 6 cents; it remained unchanged in eastern Pennsylvania.

The Card-Krueger study found its way almost immediately into the public debate; the Clinton administration cited it in 1995 in calling for a higher minimum wage.

Source: David Card and Alan B. Krueger, "Minimum Wages and Employment: A Case Study of the Fast Food Industry in New Jersey and Pennsylvania," *American Economic Review* 84(4) (September 1994): 772–793.

Price Setters on the Supply Side

Buyers aren't the only agents capable of exercising market power in factor-pricing choices. Suppliers of factor services can exercise market power and act as price setters themselves, in two ways. First, a supplier may be a monopoly, or have a degree of monopoly power, in the supply of a factor. In that case, economists analyze the firm's choices as they would analyze those of any other imperfectly competitive firm. Second, individual suppliers of a factor of production may band together in an association to gain clout in the marketplace. Farmers, for example, often join forces to offset what they perceive as unfair market power on the part of buyers of their products. Each case is discussed below.

Monopoly Suppliers

A firm with monopoly power over a particular factor can be expected to behave like any other monopoly. It will set marginal revenue equal to marginal cost and charge a price taken from its demand curve.

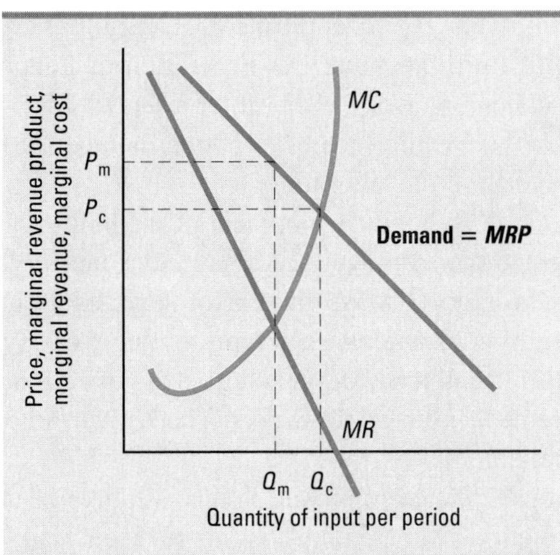

EXHIBIT 14-9

Monopoly Supply and Competitive Demand

A monopoly supplier of a factor maximizes profit just like any other monopolist. It selects an output at which marginal revenue *MR* equals marginal cost *MC* and charges a price determined by its demand curve. Since the demand curve is marginal revenue product (*MRP*), the monopoly factor supplier receives a price equal to *MRP*. Relative to the perfectly competitive solution—a price of P_c and a quantity of Q_c—a monopoly supplier restricts output to Q_m and raises price to P_m.

De Beers has a virtual monopoly in the diamond market; it sells these diamonds as factors to jewelers and to industrial users of diamonds. Intel produces virtually all the microprocessors, and Microsoft produces most of the operating software, used in personal computers.

A monopoly supplier of a factor faces a demand curve that represents the *MRP* of the factor. This situation is illustrated in Exhibit 14-9. The firm will charge a price P_m and sell Q_m units of the factor, receiving a price equal to the *MRP* of the factor.

Unions

Workers in a competitive market receive a wage equal to their *MRP.* If they face monopsony power, they get less. Regardless of the market structure, workers are likely to seek higher wages and better working conditions. One way they can try to improve their economic status is to organize into a **labor union,** an association of workers that seeks to raise wages and to improve working conditions. Unions represent their members in **collective bargaining,** a process of negotiation of worker contracts between unions and employers. To strengthen its position, a union may threaten a strike—a refusal by union members to work—unless its demands are met.

- A **labor union** is an association of workers that seeks to increase wages and to improve working conditions for its members.
- **Collective bargaining** is the representation of workers by a union during contract negotiations.
- A **closed shop** is a firm in which workers must belong to a union before they can gain employment.

A Brief History of Unions in the United States

Workers have banded together in associations aimed at bettering their lot at least since the medieval period, when the first professional guilds were formed. The first unions in the United States were the "workingmen's societies" that sprang up late in the eighteenth century in Philadelphia, Boston, and New York. These organizations, which were partly social and partly economic, sought to increase wages, shorten working hours, and regulate the terms and conditions of apprenticeship. They were generally short-lived; only the Philadelphia Cordwainers (shoemakers) lasted as long as 12 years. The early union movement in the United States was met with enormous hostility from the courts, which generally held union efforts to be an illegal attempt to restrain trade.

In the nineteenth century, skilled workers, especially shoemakers and printers, continued efforts to organize. One goal they consistently sought was a **closed shop,** a work rule that requires workers in a particular firm to belong to a union—an arrangement that gives unions monopoly power in the supply of labor. A second objective was to gain greater political and economic strength by banding associations of different crafts together. In 1827 the Mechanics' Union of Trade Associations was formed; it was a federation of several individual associations. Union federations followed quickly in New York and in other major cities. While the growth of unions was impressive, union members still represented a tiny fraction of the work force; by 1860, only 0.1 percent of all workers in the United States were unionized.

Early labor leaders recognized that any success in improving working conditions in one city could cause employers to move to another. To counter that problem, unions began an effort to merge local craft unions—unions representing workers in a particular trade—into national craft unions. By 1872 there were 41 national craft unions representing more than 300,000 workers.

The trend toward centralization of union organization continued in 1881, when six national craft unions, representing printers, glassworkers, iron and steelworkers, molders, and cigar makers, joined forces as the Federation of

Organized Trades and Labor Unions. This organization merged in 1886 with unions in another labor federation to form the American Federation of Labor (AFL). The AFL grew quickly; by the end of World War I it represented 4 million workers, or roughly 80 percent of all union members. Union membership had risen to slightly more than 10 percent of the labor force.

Another form of centralization came with the development of the industrial union, a form of union that represented the employees of a particular industry, regardless of craft. The United Mine Workers (UMW) was one of the first industrial unions. Rather than a collection of craft unions, each representing workers with specific skills, the UMW represented all mine workers regardless of craft in reaching collective bargaining agreements with mine owners. The United Auto Workers (UAW) is another industrial union.

The legal climate in which unions operated improved in the twentieth century, with unions winning legal recognition as bargaining agents for their members. Closed-shop arrangements have been declared illegal, but many states permit **union-shop** arrangements, in which a firm is allowed to hire nonunion workers who are required to join the union within a specified period. In 20 states union shops are illegal; each firm must be an **open shop,** where jobs are open to union as well as nonunion members.

In 1955, the AFL merged with another national labor organization, the Congress of Industrial Organizations, to form the AFL-CIO. This largest of all labor organizations remains an important economic and political force today; however, the goal of a single national organization representing all workers has not been reached. The Teamsters Union, one of the most aggressive and rapidly growing unions, remains outside the AFL-CIO; the UAW left the AFL-CIO in 1968 and has remained independent since.

But the biggest disappointment to labor organizers must have been the failure to recruit a large fraction of the labor force to union ranks. The strength of organized labor, measured as the fraction of the labor force it represents, peaked in 1960, when unions accounted for just over 31 percent of the labor force. Union strength has fallen since; in 1995 just 15 percent of U.S. workers belonged to unions. In the private sector, only 11 percent of workers were union members. Part of the reason for the failure of unions to represent a larger share of workers lies in the market forces that govern wages. As the *MRP*s of workers rose throughout the economy, their wages increased as well—whether they belonged to a union or not. Because of the impressive wage gains of workers throughout the economy during the last two centuries, the attraction of unions has remained weak.

Wages and other Union Goals

Higher wages once dominated the list of union objectives, but more recent agreements have focused on nonwage issues as well. Unions seek job security, improved nonwage benefits such as health insurance and provision of child care, and better job safety. Unions such as the UAW have negotiated contracts under which members who are laid off will continue to receive payments nearly equal to the wages they earned while on the job. Unions have also pushed hard for benefits such as health insurance and retirement pensions and for greater worker involvement in management decisions.

Union efforts to obtain higher wages have different effects on workers depending on the nature of the labor market. When unions confront an employer with monopsony power, their task is clear: they seek a wage closer to *MRP* than

A **union shop** is a firm that can hire union as well as nonunion workers, but nonunion workers are required to join the union within a specified period of time.

An **open shop** is a firm that can hire and retain union as well as nonunion members.

A **bilateral monopoly** is a situation in which a monopsony buyer faces a monopoly seller.

the employer is now paying. If the labor market is a competitive one in which wages are determined by demand and supply, the union's task is more difficult. Increasing the wage requires either increasing the demand for labor or reducing the supply. If the union merely achieves a higher wage in the absence of an increase in demand or a reduction in supply, then the higher wage will create a surplus of labor, or unemployment.

Increasing Demand. The demand for labor in a competitive market is found by summing the *MRP* curves of individual firms. Increasing demand thus requires increasing the marginal product of labor or raising the price of the good produced by labor.

One way that unions can increase the marginal product of their members is by encouraging investment in their human capital. Unions may seek to achieve this by pressuring firms to implement training programs. Some unions conduct training efforts themselves.

Another way to increase the *MRP* of a factor is to reduce the use by firms of substitute factors. Unions generally represent skilled workers, and they are vigorous proponents of minimum wage laws that make unskilled workers more expensive. A higher minimum wage induces firms to substitute skilled for unskilled labor and thus increases the demand for the skilled workers unions represent.

Still another way to increase the *MRP* of labor is to increase the demand for the products labor produces. This form of union activity has generally been concentrated in the promotion of "Made in the U.S.A." goods. Unions have also promoted restrictive trade legislation aimed at reducing the supply of foreign goods and thus increasing the demand for domestic ones.

Reducing Supply. Unions can restrict the supply of labor in two ways. First, they can seek to slow the growth of the labor force; unions from the earliest times have aggressively opposed immigration. Union efforts to promote Social Security also cut the labor supply by encouraging workers to retire early. Second, unions can promote policies that make it difficult for workers to enter a particular craft. Unions representing plumbers and electrical workers, for example, have restricted the number of people who can enter these crafts in some areas by requiring that workers belong to a union but limiting the union's membership.

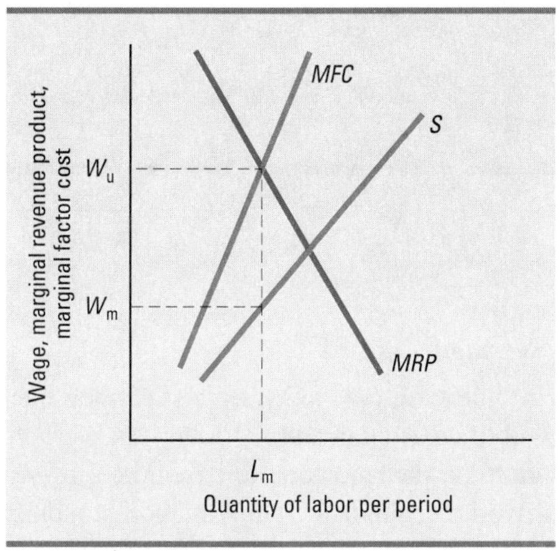

EXHIBIT 14-10

Bilateral Monopoly

If a union has monopoly power over the supply of labor and faces a monopsony purchaser of this labor, the wage negotiated between the two will be indeterminate. The employer wants a wage W_m on the supply curve *S*. The union will seek a wage close to the maximum the employer would be willing to pay for this quantity, W_u, at the intersection of the marginal revenue product (*MRP*) and marginal factor cost (*MFC*) curves. The actual wage is likely to be somewhere between these two amounts.

Bilateral Monopoly

Suppose a union has negotiated a closed-shop arrangement with an employer that possesses monopsony power in its labor market. The union has a kind of monopoly in the supply of labor. A situation in which a monopsony buyer faces a monopoly seller is called **bilateral monopoly.** Wages in such a model are indeterminate.

Exhibit 14-10 shows the same monopsony situation in a labor market that was shown in Exhibit 14-4. The employer will seek to pay a wage W_m for a quantity of labor L_m. The union will seek W_u, the highest wage the employer would be willing to pay for that quantity of labor. This wage is found on the *MRP* curve. The model of bilateral monopoly does not tell us the wage that will emerge. Whether the final wage will be closer to what the union seeks or closer to what the employer seeks will depend on the bargaining strength of the union and of the employer.

Case in Point: Unions and the Airline Industry

Unions that represent pilots and other airline workers have successfully maintained high wages and excellent working conditions, but they may have threatened their employers—and thus, in the long run, their jobs—with extinction.

Major airlines face competition not just with each other but with so-called low-cost carriers, airlines that operate with substantially lower costs, and offer their passengers lower prices, than the major airlines. Part of the secret of low-cost operations has been to operate with nonunion employees.

Frank J. Dooley, an economist at North Dakota State University, has compared average labor cost for Southwest Airlines, one of the low-cost carriers, with those of major airlines such as American Airlines and United Airlines. He estimates that Southwest has labor costs that are 38 percent lower than those of the major airlines.

Southwest's labor cost advantage, Mr. Dooley says, comes from union work rules that keep the productivity of the major carriers well below that achieved by Southwest, whose employees don't belong to unions. Southwest's pilots, for example, fly for an average of 63.7 hours per month, versus 48.3 hours for pilots at the major airlines. He says that productivity differences give low-cost carriers a sharp advantage. For the 620-mile flight between Baltimore and Chicago, for example, average labor costs for major airlines are a whopping $1,200 per flight higher than for low-cost carriers.

Some airlines are swapping union concessions about pay and work rules for a share in the company. United's employees, for example, accepted pay cuts and changes in work rules as part of a deal that won them a majority interest in the company. Those concessions were valued at $5 billion. But Dooley says that unions and the major airlines will have to go even further to compete effectively.

Source: Frank J. Dooley, "Deja Vu for Airline Industrial Relations," *Journal of Labor Research* 15(2) (Spring 1994): 169–191.

Unions and the Economy: An Assessment

Where unions operate effectively in otherwise competitive markets, they may reduce economic efficiency. Efforts to increase demand for American workers through restricting imports, or to increase demand for skilled workers by restricting opportunities for unskilled workers, almost certainly reduce economic efficiency. Artificial restrictions on the supply of labor reduce efficiency as well. In each case, the wage gain will increase the cost of producing a good or service and thus shift its supply curve to the left. Such efforts, if successful, increase the earnings of union members by creating higher prices and smaller quantities for consumers. They may also reduce the profitability of their employers.

Other attempts by unions to increase their wages through increasing the demand for their members are not likely to create inefficiency. For example, union efforts to increase worker productivity or to encourage consumers to buy products made by union members do not reduce economic efficiency.

When unions seek a greater share of market power for workers to offset wage-setting power by the firms that employ them, these efforts are unlikely to contribute further to economic efficiency. In the case of bilateral monopoly, the amount of labor employed is restricted by the monopsony firm to a quantity that falls short of the efficient level. The labor union seeks merely to offset the monopsony firm's ability to restrict the wage. The efficiency damage has, in effect, already been done.

Are unions successful in their primary goal of increasing wages? Wages for union members in 1992 were on average 32 percent higher than nonunion wages. This figure by itself tends to overstate the impact of unions, however, because unions generally represent workers who are more highly skilled than other workers. After we adjust for the effects of differences in skills and other factors, unions appear to raise wages for their members by 10 to 25 percent.

Other Suppliers and Monopoly Power

Just as workers may organize into unions to gain a degree of monopoly power in the marketplace, so other suppliers may organize with a similar goal. Two of the most important types of organizations aimed at garnering market power are professional associations and producers' cooperatives.

Professional Associations

Professional people generally belong to organizations that represent their interests. Physicians in the United States, for example, belong to the American Medical Association (AMA), and lawyers belong to the American Bar Association. Both organizations work vigorously to advance the economic interests of their members.

Professional organizations often lobby for legislation that protects their members. They may seek to restrict competition by limiting the number of individuals who can be licensed to practice a particular profession. The AMA, for example, has been very successful in limiting the number of physicians, thus maintaining higher salaries than would otherwise exist. The American Bar Association has fought legal reforms aimed at limiting awards to plaintiffs who win damage suits; such reforms would be likely to reduce the incomes of lawyers.

Producers' Cooperatives

Independent producers sometimes band together into a cooperative for purposes of selling their products. The cooperative sets the price and assigns individual firms production quotas. In effect, a cooperative acts as a legal cartel.

Because they violate the provisions of the laws that outlaw such arrangements in most industries, producers' cooperatives must be authorized by Congress. Farmers have sometimes been given such rights when they are confronted by monopsony buyers. For example, Congress granted dairy farmers the right to form cooperatives in the 1920s because they faced monopsony buyers. High transportation costs for fresh milk, together with economies of scale in processing milk, generally left only one dairy processor to buy raw milk from dairy farmers in a particular area. By forming a cooperative, farmers could counter the monopsony power of a processor with monopoly power of their own, creating a bilateral monopoly.

- A firm that has monopoly power in the supply of a factor makes choices in the same manner as any other monopoly firm; it maximizes profit by selecting a level of output at which marginal revenue equals marginal cost and selling that output at a price determined by the demand curve.
- Unions have traditionally sought to raise wages and to improve working conditions by exerting market power over the supply of labor.
- U.S. unions gained considerably in importance during the first half of this century, but they now represent only about 15 percent of the labor force.
- Professional associations often seek market power through their influence on government policy.
- Producers' cooperatives, a form of legal cartel, have been organized in some agricultural markets in an effort to offset the perceived monopsony power of some buyers of agricultural products.

A Look Back—And a Look Ahead

Factor markets diverge from perfect competition whenever buyers and/or sellers are price setters rather than price takers. In general, price setters will use less of a factor than would be used if all participants in the market were price takers.

Some firms that demand factors are price setters in their product markets. A firm considering how much of a factor to use examines the marginal consequences of additional units of the factor—it considers the factor's marginal revenue product (MRP) and marginal factor cost (MFC). The MRP is found by multiplying the factor's marginal product by the marginal revenue of the additional output. But that marginal revenue is less than the market price, so the price-setting firm obtains a lower MRP than would an otherwise identical price-taking firm. The power to set price in a product market therefore reduces the demand for the factors used in producing the product.

Another source of price-setting power may occur in factor markets. A firm that is the sole purchaser of a factor is a monopsony. The distinguishing feature of the application of the marginal decision rule to monopsony is that the MFC of the factor exceeds its price. Less of the factor is used than would be the case if the factor were demanded by many firms. The price paid by the monopsony firm is determined from the factor supply curve; it is less than the competitive price would be. The lower quantity and lower price that occur in a monopsony factor market arise from features of the market that are directly analogous to the higher product price and lower product quantity chosen in monopoly markets. A price floor (e.g., a minimum wage) can induce a monopsony to increase its use of a factor.

Sellers can also exercise power to set price. A factor may be sold by a monopoly firm, which is likely to behave in a way that corresponds to the monopoly model discussed in Chapter 12.

When there are a large number of sellers, they may band together in an organization that seeks to exert a degree of market power on their behalf. Workers (sellers of labor), for example, have organized unions to seek better wages and working conditions. This can be accomplished by restricting the available supply or by increasing the demand for labor. When a union represents all of a monopsony firm's workers, the situation is called bilateral monopoly. This results in a kind of price setters' standoff, in which the firm seeks a low wage and the union a high one.

Professional associations may seek to improve the economic position of their members by supporting legislation that reduces supply or raises demand. Some agricultural producers join producers' cooperatives to exert some power over price and output. These agricultural cooperatives must be authorized by Congress; they would otherwise violate laws against collusion in the marketplace.

In the next chapter we shall turn from the examination of the choices of individuals in the marketplace to the choices of individuals in the political arena. We shall explore the role of the public sector in a market economy and investigate the kinds of choices made in it.

Terms and Concepts for Review

Bilateral monopoly	Monopsony
Closed shop	Monopsony power
Collective bargaining	Open shop
Labor union	Union shop

For Discussion

1. Suppose all the producers of soft drinks merged into a single firm. What would happen to the industry's demand for sugar?
2. Are unions likely to support government efforts to promote competition among U.S. firms? Why?
3. Although unions have an interest in maintaining the competitiveness of U.S. industry, they have generally advocated restrictions on foreign competition. Why?
4. There is a growing tendency in the United States for hospitals to merge, reducing competition in local markets. How are such mergers likely to affect the market for nurses?
5. When a town has a single university, the university may have monopsony power in the hiring of part-time faculty. But what about the hiring of full-time faculty? (*Hint:* The market for full-time faculty is a national one.)
6. David Letterman earns more than $10 million per year from CBS. Why do you suppose he earns so much? Is there any reason to believe he is underpaid?
7. Nursing is primarily a women's profession; advertising is primarily a men's profession. Why is monopsony power more likely in nursing than in advertising?
8. Suppose a union obtains a closed-shop agreement with firms in a particular industry. Is there any limit to the wages the union can achieve for its workers?
9. It is illegal for firms in most industries to join together in a producers' cooperative. Yet such arrangements are common in agriculture. Why?
10. In proposing an increase in the minimum wage in 1995, the Clinton administration noted that in some markets, a higher minimum wage could actually increase employment for unskilled workers. How could this happen?

Problems

Suppose a firm faces the following supply curve for labor by unskilled workers:

Wage per Day	Number of Workers
$80	10
72	9
64	8
56	7
48	6
40	5
32	4
24	3
16	2
8	1
0	0

1. In terms of its demand for labor, what sort of firm is this? Explain. Prepare a table of values for the firm's marginal factor cost curve and the values for the supply curve for labor.
2. Plot the supply and marginal factor cost curves for this firm. Remember to plot marginal values at the midpoints of the intervals.
3. Suppose the firm faces the following total product schedule for labor:

Number of Workers	Output per Day
0	0
1	92
2	176
3	252
4	320
5	380
6	432
7	476
8	512
9	540
10	560

   Compute the schedules for the firm's marginal product and marginal revenue product curves, assuming the price of the good the firm produces is $1 and that the firm operates in a perfectly competitive product market.
4. Add the marginal revenue product curve from Problem 3 to your graph in Problem 2, and determine the number of workers the firm will employ and the wage it will pay.
5. Now suppose the firm is required to pay a minimum wage of $48 per day. Show what will happen to the quantity of labor the firm will hire and the wage it will pay.

15

Public Finance and Public Choice

Chapter Objectives

After mastering the material in this chapter, you will be able to:

1. Explain how government intervention has the potential to correct problems of market failure, and explain its role in intervening when no market failure is present.
2. Explain government's role in the redistribution of income.
3. Discuss how the scope and scale of government activity have changed during the past two centuries.
4. Describe the major types of taxes in the United States and assess them in terms of the criteria economists use to evaluate taxes.
5. Explain why the people who pay taxes may not be the ones who bear the burden of taxes.
6. Contrast the public interest and public choice perspectives on decisionmaking in the public sector.
7. Explain the approaches economists use in estimating demand and marginal cost curves to find efficient solutions to problems of market failure.
8. Explain why most eligible voters typically abstain from voting.
9. Discuss the reasons special interests are likely to play such an important role in public sector choices.

The State is a machine for the oppression of one class by another.
V. I. Lenin

What's Ahead

You pay sales taxes on most of the goods you purchase. If you smoke or drink or drive a car, you pay special taxes levied on cigarettes, alcohol, or gasoline. If you work, you may pay income and payroll taxes.

But government is far more than an institution that collects taxes. If you go to a state school, you are a consumer of public sector services. You consume the services of the public sector when you drive on a street or go to a park. You consume public sector services because you are protected by law enforcement agencies and by the armed forces. And the production of everything you consume is affected by regulations imposed by state, local, or federal government agencies.

The public sector is a crucially important part of the economy. It's important partly for its sheer size. Government agencies either produce or purchase nearly one-fifth of all goods and services; the federal government is the largest purchaser of goods and services in the world. Government agencies in the United States are also involved in income redistribution and in the regulation of private sector activities. This chapter examines the role of government in a market economy and the ways in which the taxes that support the government affect economic behavior.

This chapter also examines the efforts of economists to explain how and why choices in the public sector are made. Economists put the notions of self-interest and the marginal decision rule to work in the analysis of choices made by people in the public sector—voters, government employees, interest groups, and politicians.

This chapter examines two broad areas of the economic analysis of government. The first is **public finance,** which is the study of government expenditure and tax policy and its impact on the economy. The study of public finance includes such topics as the determination of the efficient level of public goods provision and the analysis of the effect of a particular tax on prices and outputs. The second area we will examine is the analysis of how public sector choices are made.

Public finance is the study of government expenditure and tax policy and the impacts of these policies on the economy.

- **Government expenditures** include all spending by government agencies.
- **Government purchases** occur when a government agency purchases or produces a good or service.
- **Transfer payments** are government payments to individuals in the form of grants rather than as payments for labor or other services.

The Demand for Government Services

What is it we want from our government? An easy answer is, "A great deal." The role of government has expanded dramatically in the last 75 years. In 1929, government expenditures at all levels (state, local, and federal) were less than 10 percent of the nation's total output, or gross domestic product (GDP). By 1995, that share had tripled. Total government spending per capita, adjusted for inflation, has increased more than sixfold since 1929.

Exhibit 15-1 shows total government expenditures and revenues as a percentage of GDP over this period. All levels of government—state, local, and federal—are included. **Government expenditures** include all spending by government agencies. The primary component of government revenues is taxes; revenue also includes miscellaneous revenues from fees, fines, and other sources.

Exhibit 15-1 also shows government purchases as a percentage of GDP. **Government purchases** occur when a government agency purchases or produces a good or service. When a public school produces education, for example, its spending is counted as a government purchase. A city police department's purchase of new cars is also a government purchase.

Government expenditures and government purchases aren't equal, because much spending by governments is not for the purchase of goods and services. The primary source of the gap between government expenditures and purchases is **transfer payments,** payments made by governments to individuals as grants rather than in return for labor or other services. They thus represent government expenditures but not government purchases. Governments engage in transfer payments in order to redistribute income from one group to another. Welfare programs such as Aid to Families with Dependent Children (AFDC) and food stamps are transfer payments. Social Security is the largest transfer payment program in the United States. Interest payments on government debt, which are also a form of expenditure, are another example of an expenditure that is not counted as a government purchase.

EXHIBIT 15-1

Government Revenues, Expenditures, and Purchases as a Percentage of GDP, 1929–1995

The chart shows total expenditures, revenues, and purchases for all levels of government as a percentage of the economy's total output, as measured by gross domestic product (GDP). The shaded bars mark periods of war.

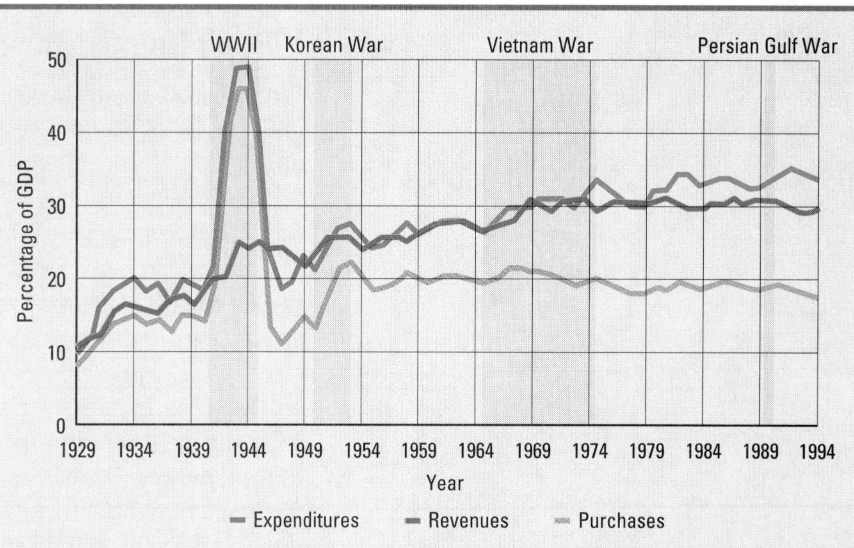

Source: U.S. Council of Economic Advisers, *Economic Report of the President 1995* (Washington, D.C.: U.S. Government Printing Office, February 1995), tables B-1, B-84, and B-116. Data prior to 1959 are taken from earlier issues of the report.

Several points about Exhibit 15-1 bear special attention. Note first the path of government purchases. Government purchases rose dramatically during World War II, then dropped back to about their prewar level almost immediately afterward. Government purchases rose again, though less sharply, during the Korean War. This time, however, they didn't drop back very far after the war. It was during this period that military spending rose to meet the challenge posed by the Soviet Union and other communist states. Government purchases have been close to 20 percent of GDP ever since. Neither the Vietnam War nor the Persian Gulf War had the dramatic impact on spending that characterized the two earlier wars. A second development, the widening gap between expenditures and purchases, has occurred since the 1960s. This reflects the growth of federal transfer programs, principally Social Security and programs to help people pay for health care costs. We will discuss these programs later in this chapter. Finally, note the relationship between expenditures and receipts. Prior to 1980, receipts roughly matched expenditures for the public sector as a whole, except during World War II. But expenditures have remained consistently higher than revenues since 1980. This reflects the federal government's deficit, a phenomenon that seems to have become a permanent fixture in recent years.

The evidence presented in Exhibit 15-1 doesn't fully capture the rise in demand for public sector services. In addition to a government that spends more, people in the United States have clearly chosen a government that does more. The scope of regulatory activity conducted by governments at all levels has risen sharply in the last several decades. Regulations designed to protect consumers, to prevent discrimination, and to protect the environment are all part of the response to a rising demand for public services.

To understand the expanded demand for government activities, it will be useful to distinguish three broad types of government involvement in economic activity. First, the government attempts to respond when the market fails to allocate resources efficiently. Second, government agencies act to encourage or discourage the consumption of certain goods and services. And third, the government redistributes income.

Responding to Market Failure

When resources are allocated efficiently, people obtain the maximum degree of utility possible from the resources available to the economy, given the distribution of income. An efficient allocation of resources is achieved if decisionmakers are confronted by all the costs and all the benefits of their decisions. This condition would be met in a world of perfect competition in which exclusive and fully transferable property rights were defined for all resources. One implication of perfect competition is that prices equal marginal costs, a necessary condition for an efficient allocation of resources.

The real world, however, is dominated by imperfect competition. Prices that emerge from monopoly, monopolistic, or oligopoly markets generally do not equal marginal costs, so individuals are not confronted by the costs and benefits of their choices. Further, some resources, by their very nature, do not fall under the property rights structure that would allow for their efficient allocation, even if the markets that provided them were perfectly competitive.

Markets may therefore fail to achieve an efficient allocation of resources. We shall review each of the major sources of market failure and then show how public sector intervention could achieve an efficient allocation of goods and services.

Case in Point: Providing Education: Should Government Buy It or Produce It?

The provision of a free education is a well-established role for government, one that few people question. More and more people, however, are questioning whether the government should produce education.

Traditionally, local school districts have provided education by producing it; schools are owned and operated by the public sector. But some school districts are now beginning to experiment with private sector production of education.

The school board in Hartford, Connecticut decided in 1994 that the public schools weren't working. It signed a contract with a private firm that took over all aspects of the operation of local schools. The company hires the teachers and administrators of the district. It remains accountable to the school board for what it does.

An alternative advocated by some economists is the provision of vouchers similar to food stamps. An annual voucher good for, say, $3,000 would be provided for each child. Parents could then choose to send their children to private schools or to public schools; the schools would get the vouchers and cash them in with the government agency that issued them. In 1995, voucher systems were operating in a handful of school districts in the United States.

Another approach to the production of education is charter schools. A charter school is organized privately and then contracts with a local school district to provide education for children in the area who want it. The charter school receives a certain amount of money from the school district, not the parents, for each pupil.

The goal of such alternatives is to provide parents with more choices in selecting the types of education their children will receive. The theory is that if parents have more choices, schools will be more responsive to the parents' preferences. Critics of such alternatives argue that parents may not make wise choices and that providing choice weakens public schools.

Public Goods

We saw in Chapter 5 that a public good is a good or service for which exclusion is prohibitively costly and for which the marginal cost of adding another consumer is zero. Goods and services such as national defense and the enforcement of laws are public goods.

The difficulty posed by public goods is that once they are provided, they are freely available to everyone. No consumer can be excluded from consumption of the good on grounds that he or she hasn't paid for it. Each consumer thus has an incentive to be a free rider in consuming the good. The result is that firms providing a public good don't get a signal from consumers that reflects their benefit of consuming the good. Faced with all of the costs of producing the good but only a fraction of the benefits, firms can be expected to produce less of a public good than is economically efficient.

If the benefits of a public good exceed its costs, the government can employ taxes to require that people pay for the good, then improve economic welfare by providing it. The fact that the market does not produce a particular public good may not mean that people don't value the good; it could simply reflect the free rider phenomenon. One role for government, then, is the provision of public goods. Government agencies may either produce the good themselves, as do local police departments, or pay private firms to produce them, as is the case with many government-sponsored research efforts.

External Costs

External costs are imposed when an action by one agent harms another, outside of any market agreement. The lack of a market agreement means that the agent responsible for the external cost doesn't face that cost. As a result, the activity that produces the cost will be carried out at a higher level than is economically efficient.

Take the case of a coal-burning power plant that generates pollutants. In the absence of government intervention, the plant may have no reason to consider the cost of this pollution in making its production decisions. The firm would thus have no reason to incorporate the pollution cost in the prices it charges, so consumers aren't faced with prices that reflect the full cost of the firm's production. Government agencies may seek to limit the firm's emissions of pollution through regulation. Other government regulations prohibit lead in gasoline and limit the production of chlorofluorocarbons—the gases thought to damage the ozone layer—in order to limit activities that generate external costs.

Imperfect Competition

In a market with perfect competition, price equals marginal cost. If competition is imperfect, however, individual firms face downward-sloping demand curves and will charge prices greater than marginal cost. Consumers in such markets will be faced by prices that exceed marginal cost, and the allocation of resources will be inefficient.

An imperfectly competitive private market will therefore produce less of a good than is efficient. As we saw in Chapter 12, government agencies seek to prohibit monopoly in most markets and to regulate the prices charged by those monopolies that are permitted.

Assessing Government Responses to Market Failure

When prices fail to confront decisionmakers with all the costs and all the benefits of their choices, government intervention may improve the allocation of resources by changing the signals decisionmakers receive. In every case of market failure, it is possible that the benefits of government participation in the marketplace will exceed the costs.

To see the potential benefits from government intervention, we shall use the procedure we adopted in Chapter 12. The total benefit of a good over some range of quantities is given by the area under the demand curve over that range. The cost is the area under the marginal cost curve over the same range of quantities.

Exhibit 15-2 illustrates how the government can intervene in cases of market failure. Panels (a) and (c) show the cases of public goods and imperfect competition, respectively; the output at market equilibrium is less than the efficient output. The benefit of moving toward the efficient solution is given by the area under the demand curve *D* between the original output *W* and the efficient output *R*. The cost is given by the area under the marginal cost curve *MC* over the same range. Panel (b) shows the case of external costs, where the output at market equilibrium is higher than the efficient solution. The benefit of a reduction in output is given by the area under the *MC′* curve from the original to the efficient output—it is the cost avoided by producing less of the good. The cost is the benefit lost—the area under the demand curve over this same range. The net gain achieved in each case by moving to the efficient output is given by the shaded triangles in Exhibit 15-2. These potential gains represent an important argument for government participation in a market economy.

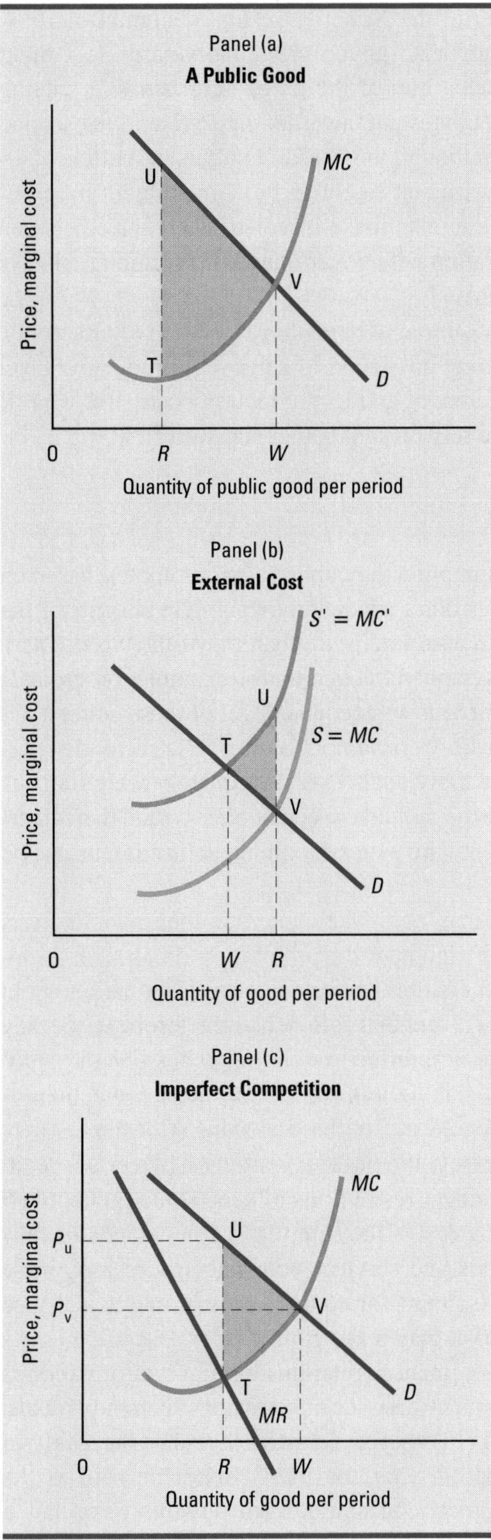

EXHIBIT 15-2

Correcting Market Failure

In Panel (a), a private market produces *R* units of a public good. By imposing taxes to finance an increase in provision of the public good to the efficient level *W*, the government generates increased benefits of *R*UV*W*. The total cost is *R*TV*W*. The net gain, produced as a result of the public sector's intervention, is the shaded area TUV.

Panel (b) shows that if the production of a good generates an external cost, the supply curve *S* reflects only the private marginal cost *MC*. If the public sector forces firms generating this externality to face the external cost, then the supply curve shifts up to *MC′*; it now reflects both private marginal cost and the cost of the externality. Output falls from *R* to *W*. The reduction in cost is *W*TU*R*, the reduction in benefit is *W*TV*R*, and the net gain is the shaded area TUV.

In Panel (c), an imperfectly competitive firm produces *R* units and charges price P_U. If the firm could be induced to expand its output to *W*, the efficient level, the gain would be the area under the demand curve *D*, between *R* and *W*, *R*UV*W*. The cost would be *R*TV*W*, and the net gain would be the shaded region TUV.

How can government intervention move the economy toward the efficient output? In the case of a public good, the government can collect taxes and pay firms to provide the public good, as it does when it pays private firms to conduct basic scientific research. Alternatively, it can collect taxes and produce the public good itself, as it generally does with police services and national defense. In the case of external costs, a government agency may ban certain activities or place other limits on them. Zoning regulations, for example, ban industrial activities in residential neighborhoods. The federal Environmental Protection Agency (EPA) regulates the amount of pollution emitted by new cars. Such regulations may move market solutions closer to efficient levels. Finally, the government can also regulate the prices charged by monopoly firms to move them closer to the efficient levels. The regulation of prices charged by public utilities is an example of such intervention.

Although the models of market failure suggest that government intervention *may* improve the efficiency of resource allocation, this result cannot be assumed. Government officials may lack the information they need to select the efficient solution. Even if they have the information, they may have goals other than the achievement of an efficient allocation of resources. Each instance of government intervention involves an interaction with utility-maximizing consumers and profit-maximizing firms, none of whom can be assumed to be passive participants in the process. Producers of public goods may lobby for excessive consumption by the government of their goods. Firms generating external costs may try to block measures that would force them to bear these costs. Some consumers seek special measures to protect their interests. Firms that impose prices greater than marginal cost are likely to fight any effort to force them to accept lower prices. So, while the potential exists for improved resource allocation in cases of market failure, government intervention may not always achieve it. Suppose, for example, that in an effort to make a firm face the consequences of an external cost it is imposing, a government agency levies too large a fee on the firm. The firm might then go from producing too much of a good or service to producing too little of it.

The late George Stigler, winner of the Nobel Prize for economics in 1982, once remarked that people who advocate government intervention to correct every case of market failure reminded him of the judge at an amateur singing contest who, upon hearing the first contestant, awarded first prize to the second singer. Stigler's point was that even though the market is often an inefficient allocator of resources, so is the government likely to be. Government may improve on what the market does; it can also make it worse. The choice between the market's allocation and an allocation with government intervention is always a choice between imperfect alternatives.

We turn next to a very different source of demand for public sector activity. Market failure implies that the market has failed to achieve a production level that corresponds to consumer preferences and to production costs. But what if we reject consumer preferences and rely on some other standard?

Merit and Demerit Goods

Merit goods are goods whose consumption the public sector promotes, based on a presumption that many individuals don't adequately weigh the benefits of the good and should thus be induced to consume more than they otherwise would. Many local governments support symphony concerts, for example, on grounds that the private market would not provide an adequate level of these cultural activities. **Demerit goods** are goods whose consumption the public sector discourages, based on a presumption that individuals don't adequately weigh all the costs of these goods and should thus be induced to consume less than they otherwise would. Taxes imposed on alcohol are generally aimed at limiting its use on grounds that it is a demerit good.

Left to themselves, consumers may not make choices in their own interests because they lack information. One argument for prohibiting drugs such as cocaine and heroin holds that consumers don't have adequate information about the consequences of using these drugs and that if they had the information, they wouldn't use the drugs. A prohibition, in effect, might help consumers by protecting at least some of them from making a mistake. Consumer protection efforts by government agencies are based on similar reasoning. Consumers may not have adequate information to assess the hazards presented by certain products; thus, they benefit from government restrictions to keep some products off the market. Such regulations carry a cost—the safety and other standards they impose raise the prices of the goods and services consumers purchase. Some goods deemed too risky or otherwise unfit for consumer use could actually be useful; keeping them out of the market may make consumers worse off.

The issue in promulgating government regulations based on information is whether government agencies are in fact wiser decisionmakers than individuals. The Food and Drug Administration (FDA), for example, regulates the safety of prescription drugs—drugs not approved by the FDA cannot be sold in the United States. Such regulation protects consumers from possible risks, but it also denies them access to drugs that could be beneficial.

- **Merit goods** are goods whose consumption the public sector encourages on grounds that individuals don't adequately weigh their benefits.
- **Demerit goods** are goods whose consumption the public sector discourages on grounds that individuals don't adequately weigh their costs.

Government provision of some merit goods appears to have nothing to do with a presumption of inadequate consumer information. Indeed, government provision of some merit goods is difficult to explain. Why, for example, do many local governments provide tennis courts but not bowling alleys, golf courses but not auto racetracks, symphony halls but not movie theaters? One possible explanation is that some consumers—those with a fondness for tennis, golf, and classical music—have been more successful than others in persuading their fellow citizens to assist in funding their consumption activities.

Income Redistribution

The proposition that a private market will achieve an efficient allocation of resources if there is perfect competition and a system of well-defined, transferable property rights always comes with a qualification. The allocation of resources will be efficient *given* the initial distribution of income. If 5 percent of the people receive 95 percent of the income, it might be efficient to allocate roughly 95 percent of the goods and services produced to them—but many people might argue that such a distribution of income is undesirable and that the allocation of resources that emerges from it is undesirable as well.

There are several reasons to believe that the distribution of income generated by a private economy might not be satisfactory. For example, the incomes people can earn are in large measure due to luck. Talent is distributed in unequal measure. Many people suffer handicaps that limit their earning potential. Changes in demand and supply can produce huge changes in the values—and the incomes—the market assigns to particular skills. Much income results from inherited wealth and thus depends on the family into which one happens to have been born. Given all this, many people argue that incomes should not be determined solely by the marketplace.

A more fundamental reason for concern about income distribution is that people care about the welfare of others. People with higher incomes often have a desire to help people with lower incomes. This preference is demonstrated in voluntary contributions to charity and in support of government programs to redistribute income.

A public goods argument can be made for government programs that redistribute income. Suppose that people of all income levels feel better off knowing that financial assistance is being provided to the poor and that they experience this sense of well-being whether or not they are the ones who provide the assistance. In this case, helping the poor is a public good. When the poor are helped, other people feel better off; this benefit is nonexclusive. One could thus argue that leaving private charity to the marketplace is inefficient and that the government should participate in income distribution.

Government efforts to redistribute income are measured in terms of the volume of transfer payments. These payments are typically divided into two categories. A **means-tested transfer payment** is one for which the recipient qualifies on the basis of income; means-tested programs transfer income from people who have more to people who have less. The largest means-tested program in the United States is Medicaid, which provides health care to the poor. Other means-tested programs include Aid to Families with Dependent Children and food stamps. A **non-means-tested transfer payment** is one for which income is not a qualifying factor. Social Security, a program that taxes workers and their employers and transfers this money to retired workers, is the largest non-means-tested transfer program. Indeed, it is the largest transfer program in the United States. Other non-means-tested transfer programs include Medicare, unemployment compensation, and programs that aid farmers.

A **means-tested transfer payment** is a transfer payment for which recipients qualify on the basis of income.

A **non-means-tested transfer payment** is one for which income is not a qualifying factor.

EXHIBIT 15-3

Federal Transfer Payment Spending

This chart shows federal means-tested and non-means-tested transfer payment spending as a percentage of GDP in the United States since 1962.

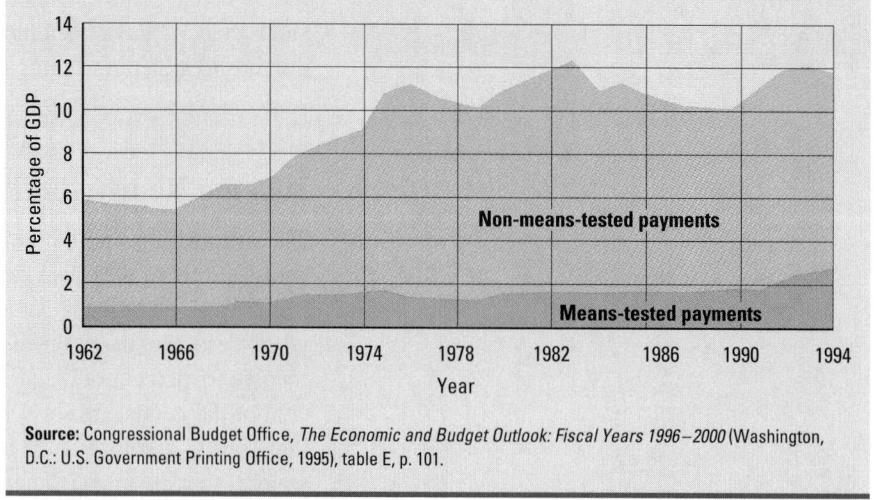

Source: Congressional Budget Office, *The Economic and Budget Outlook: Fiscal Years 1996–2000* (Washington, D.C.: U.S. Government Printing Office, 1995), table E, p. 101.

Checklist

- Government's role in the economy has expanded dramatically during the past 65 years.
- One role of government is to correct problems of market failure associated with public goods, externality costs, and imperfect competition.
- Government intervention to correct market failure problems always has the potential to increase the economic welfare of all parties.
- Governments may seek to alter the level of provision of private goods, based on a judgment that the private market will provide too much or too little of the goods. Private goods for which such judgments have been made are called merit or demerit goods.
- Governments often act to redistribute income. Such redistribution often goes from people with higher incomes to people with lower incomes, but other transfer payments go to people who are relatively better off.

Transfer payments are considered unearned income in the sense that they aren't payments in exchange for the supply of labor, capital, or natural resources. Exhibit 15-3 shows federal spending on means-tested and non-means-tested programs as a percentage of gross domestic product (GDP), the total value of output, since 1962. As the chart suggests, the bulk of income redistribution efforts in the United States are non-means-tested programs.

The fact that most transfer payments in the United States are not means-tested leads to something of a paradox: many transfer payments go from people whose incomes are relatively low to people whose incomes are relatively high. Social Security, for example, transfers income from people who are working to people who have retired. But retired people enjoy higher incomes, on average, than working people in the United States. Aid to farmers, another form of non-means-tested payments, transfers income to farmers, who on average are wealthier than the rest of the population. These situations have come about because of policy decisions, which we discuss later in the chapter.

Financing Government

If government services are to be provided, they must be paid for. The primary source of government revenue is taxes. In this section we examine the principles on which taxes are based, compare alternative types of taxes, and consider the problem of determining who actually bears the burden of taxes.

In addition to imposing taxes, governments obtain revenue by charging **user fees,** which are charges levied on consumers of government-provided services. The tuition and other fees charged by public universities and colleges are user fees, as are visitor charges at national parks. Finally, government agencies may obtain revenue by selling assets or by holding bonds on which they earn interest.

User fees are charges levied on consumers of government-provided services.

Principles of Taxation

Taxes are the most important source of government revenue. Virtually anything can be taxed, but what *should* be taxed? Are there principles that can guide us in choosing a system of taxes?

Case in Point — Do the Rich Pay Their Fair Share?

Most Americans don't think the rich pay enough taxes. A *Wall Street Journal* poll in February 1993 found that 77 percent of respondents didn't think the rich paid their fair share.

President Clinton stressed the need to boost taxes for the rich when he introduced sharply higher rates for the nation's highest income earners. "I will ask the economic elite who made more money and paid less in taxes [during the Reagan and Bush administrations] to pay their fair share," Mr. Clinton said in a White House speech early in his term.

But what *is* a fair share for the rich? According to the Internal Revenue Service (IRS), the 5 percent of households who had the highest incomes in the United States in 1991 received 27 percent of adjusted gross income (adjusted gross income is total income less personal exemptions). They paid 43 percent of all income taxes collected. Whether that 43 percent share is fair is a normative judgment. President Clinton has clearly concluded that it is too small.

If the share of total income taxes now paid by the richest 5 percent is too small, then an obvious response is to raise taxes for the rich. But raising tax rates for the rich may not boost their share of taxes paid. In 1980, the richest 5 percent of taxpayers paid 37 percent of all income taxes collected. The highest tax rate then was 70 percent. By 1991 the top rate had fallen to 28 percent, but the share of income taxes paid by the richest 5 percent had risen to 43 percent. When tax rates imposed on the rich went down, they responded by earning more money and ended up paying a larger share of total taxes.

Source: Internal Revenue Service, *SOI Bulletin* 13(2) (Fall 1993): table 1.

Jean-Baptiste Colbert, who served as minister of finance in France in the seventeenth century, is generally credited with one of the most famous principles of taxation:

> The art of taxation consists in so plucking the goose as to obtain the largest possible amount of feathers with the smallest possible amount of hissing.

Economists, who don't generally deal with geese, cite two criteria for selecting a tax system. The first is based on the ability of people to pay taxes, and the second focuses on the benefits they receive from government services.

Ability to Pay

The **ability-to-pay principle** implies that people with more income should pay more taxes. As income rises, the doctrine asserts, people are able to pay more for public services; a tax system should therefore be constructed so that taxes rise too.

The ability-to-pay doctrine lies at the heart of tax systems that link taxes paid to income received. The relationship between taxes and income may take one of three forms: taxes can be regressive, proportional, or progressive.

- The **ability-to-pay principle** suggests that people with more money should pay more taxes.
- A **regressive tax** is one that takes a lower percentage of income as income rises.

Regressive Tax. A **regressive tax** is one that takes a lower percentage of income as income rises. Taxes on cigarettes, for example, are regressive. Cigarettes are an inferior good—their consumption falls as incomes rise. Thus, people with lower incomes spend more on cigarettes than do people with higher incomes. The cigarette taxes paid by low-income people represent a larger share of their income than do the cigarette taxes paid by high-income people.

Proportional Tax. A **proportional tax** is one that takes a fixed percentage of income. Total taxes rise as income rises, but taxes are equal to the same percentage no matter what the level of income. Some people argue that the U.S. income tax system should be changed into a so-called flat tax system, a tax that would take the same percentage of income from all taxpayers. Such a tax would be a proportional tax.

Progressive Tax. A **progressive tax** is one that takes a higher percentage of income as income rises. President Clinton's deficit reduction plan, passed in 1993, attempted to make the federal income tax more progressive. A family of four earning less than $15,600 doesn't pay federal income taxes at all; it receives an earned income credit. A family with an income between $15,600 and $36,900, pays taxes at a rate of 15 percent. The rate jumps to 28 percent for incomes over $39,900, 36 percent for incomes over $140,000, and 39.6 percent for incomes over $250,000. The personal income tax is thus a progressive tax.

Benefits Received

An alternative criterion for establishing a tax structure is the **benefits received principle.** It suggests that taxes be based on the benefits received from the government services funded by the tax.

Local governments rely heavily on taxes on property, in large part because the benefits of many local services, including schools, streets, and the provision of drainage for wastewater, are reflected in higher property values. Suppose, for example, that public schools in a particular area are especially good. People are willing to pay more for houses served by those schools, so property values are higher; property owners benefit from better schools. The greater their benefit, the greater the property tax they pay. The property tax can thus be viewed as a tax on benefits received from some local services.

Fees charged for government services apply the benefits received principle directly. A student paying tuition, a visitor paying an entrance fee at a national park, and a motorist paying a highway toll are all paying to consume a publicly provided service; they are thus paying directly for something from which they expect to benefit. Such fees can be used only for goods for which exclusion is possible; a user fee could not be applied to a service such as national defense.

Taxes to finance public goods may satisfy both the ability-to-pay and benefits received principles. The demand for public goods generally rises with income. Thus, people with higher incomes receive more benefit from public goods. The benefits received principle thus suggests that taxes should rise with income, just as the ability-to-pay principle does. Consider, for example, an effort financed through income taxes by the federal government to clean up the environment. People with higher incomes will pay more for the cleanup than people with lower incomes, consistent with the ability-to-pay principle. But people with higher incomes have a greater demand for environmental improvement than do people with lower incomes—a clean environment is a normal good. Requiring people with higher incomes to pay more for the cleanup can thus be justified on the benefits received principle as well.

- A **proportional tax** takes a fixed percentage of income as taxes, regardless of the level of income.
- A **progressive tax** is one that takes a higher percentage of income as income rises.
- The **benefits received principle** of taxation holds that taxes should be based on the benefits received from public sector services.

Types of Taxes

It's hard to imagine anything that hasn't been taxed at one time or another. Windows, closets, buttons, junk food, salt, death—all have been singled out for special taxes. In general, taxes fall into one of four primary categories. *Income taxes* are imposed on the income earned by a person or firm; *property taxes* are imposed on assets; *sales taxes* are imposed on the value of goods sold; and *excise taxes* are imposed on specific goods or services.

Personal Income Taxes

The federal personal income tax is the largest single source of tax revenue in the United States; most states and many cities tax income as well (see Exhibit 15-4). All income tax systems apply a variety of exclusions to a taxpayer's total income before arriving at *taxable income,* the amount of income that is actually subject to the tax. In the U.S. federal income tax system, for example, a family deducted $2,450 from total income earned in 1994 for each member of the family as part of its computation of taxable income.

EXHIBIT 15-4

Sources of Government Revenue, 1992

The chart shows sources of revenue for federal, state, and local governments in the United States. The data omit revenues from government-owned utilities and liquor stores (all figures in billions of dollars).

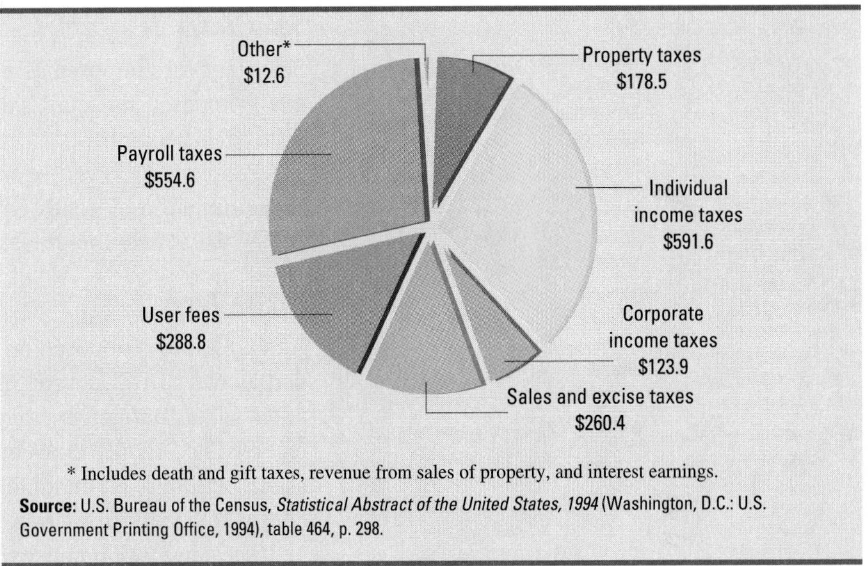

* Includes death and gift taxes, revenue from sales of property, and interest earnings.

Source: U.S. Bureau of the Census, *Statistical Abstract of the United States, 1994* (Washington, D.C.: U.S. Government Printing Office, 1994), table 464, p. 298.

Income taxes can be structured to be regressive, proportional, or progressive, but most income tax systems are progressive. We've already seen that the U.S. income tax system is sharply progressive.

In analyzing the impact of a progressive tax system on taxpayer choice, economists focus on the **marginal tax rate.** This is the tax rate that would apply to an additional $1 of taxable income received by the household. A single taxpayer with a 1994 taxable income of $60,000 per year, for example, paid federal income tax of $13,997, or 23.3 percent of taxable income. If the taxpayer were to receive $1 more of taxable income, however, that $1 would be taxed at a rate of 31 percent, the rate that applied in 1994 to taxable incomes between $55,100 and $115,000 for single taxpayers.

Economists argue that choices are made at the margin; it is thus the marginal tax rate that is most likely to affect decisions. Say that our single taxpayer is considering moonlighting—taking a second job. The job would require working evenings and would increase the person's income to $70,000 per year. With a marginal tax rate of 31 percent, the worker would keep $6,900 of the additional $10,000 earned. It is that benefit that the taxpayer will weigh against the cost in forgone leisure in deciding whether to take the second job.

The **marginal tax rate** is the rate that would apply to an additional $1 of taxable income received by a taxpayer.

Early in the 1980s, the top marginal tax rate was reduced to 28 percent from 70 percent. The primary justification was the argument that the 70 percent rate discouraged wealthy taxpayers from seeking additional income through harder work or through saving.

Property Taxes

Property taxes are imposed on assets. Local governments, for example, generally impose a property tax on business and personal property. The property's value is determined by a government official, and a proportional tax rate is then applied to that value.

Property ownership tends to be concentrated among higher income groups; economists generally view property taxes as progressive. That conclusion, however, rests on assumptions about who actually pays the tax, an issue examined later in this chapter.

Sales Taxes

Sales taxes are imposed as a fixed percentage of firms' sales. Sales taxes are generally imposed on retail sales. Some items, such as food, are often exempted from sales taxation.

People with lower incomes generally devote a larger share of their incomes to consumption of goods covered by sales taxes than do people with higher incomes. Sales taxes are thus likely to be regressive.

Excise Taxes

An excise tax is imposed on specific items. In some cases, excise taxes are justified as ways of discouraging the consumption of demerit goods, such as cigarettes and alcoholic beverages. In other cases, an excise tax is a kind of benefits received tax. Excise taxes on gasoline, for example, are typically earmarked for use in building and maintaining highways, so that those who pay the tax are the ones who benefit from the service provided.

The most important excise tax in the United States is the payroll tax imposed on workers' earnings. In 1995, the payroll tax was 15.30 percent and was levied on incomes up to $61,200. The Medicare portion of the payroll tax, 2.9 percent, was levied on all earned wages without limit. Half this tax is charged to employers, half to employees. The proceeds of this excise on payrolls finances Social Security and Medicare benefits. Most U.S. households pay more in payroll taxes than for any other tax.

Exhibit 15-4 shows the contribution of each of these major categories of taxes to total federal, state, and local government revenues.

Tax Incidence Analysis

Next time you purchase an item at a store, notice the sales tax imposed by your state, county, and city. The clerk rings up the total, then adds up the tax. The store is the entity that "pays" the sales tax, in the sense that it sends the money to the government agencies that imposed it, but you are the one who actually foots the bill—or are you? Is it possible that the sales tax affects the price of the item itself?

Tax incidence analysis seeks to determine whether the burden of a tax falls on consumers, workers, or owners of other factors of production.

These questions relate to the problem of **tax incidence analysis,** which seeks to determine where the actual burden of a tax rests. Does the burden fall on consumers, workers, owners of capital, owners of natural resources, or owners

Case in Point — Who Pays the Payroll Tax?

If you work for pay, you've noticed that part of your wage—7.65 percent of it as of 1995—is sent by your employer to the government as your Social Security and Medicare contribution. In addition to sending the government "your" payroll tax, your employer must send in an additional 7.65 percent, for a total of 15.3 percent. The 6.2 percent Social Security portion of tax is imposed on the first $61,200 in annual earnings for any one worker; both the firm and the worker continue to pay the 1.45 percent Medicare tax on earnings above that amount. But who actually bears the burden of the tax?

Economic analysis suggests that the elaborate charade of having the firm pay half the tax and the worker the other half has no effect on who really bears the burden of the tax. The payroll tax introduces a 15.3 percent gap between the cost of labor to the firm and the wage received by the worker. Whether firms or workers bear the primary burden of the tax depends on the relative slopes of the demand and supply curves.

In the absence of a tax, the wage would be determined by supply and demand. The wage is *W* in Panels (a) through (c). The tax, shown by the grey vertical line, drives a gap between the wage paid by the employer (W_E) and the wage received by the worker (W_W). In Panel (a), the absolute values of the slopes of the demand and supply curves for labor are equal, and the burden of the tax is shared equally by employers and workers. In Panel (b), the supply curve is much steeper than the demand curve, and workers bear most of the burden of the tax.

Some economists argue that because the substitution and income effects of a wage change work in opposite directions, the supply curve for labor is vertical, as shown in Panel (c). If this is true, workers bear the entire burden of the payroll tax. In general, the steeper the supply curve and the flatter the demand curve, the greater the burden of the tax on workers.

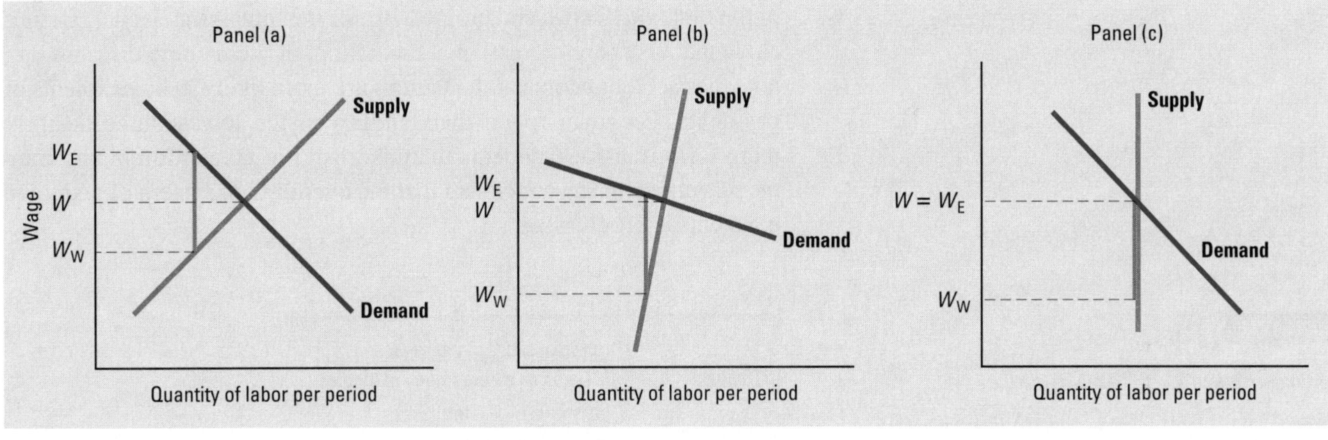

of other assets in the economy? When a tax imposed on a good or service increases the price, the burden of the tax falls on consumers. If instead it lowers wages or lowers prices for some of the natural resources (such as land) used in the production of the good or service taxed, the burden of the tax falls on owners of these factors. If the tax doesn't change the product's price or factor prices, the burden falls on the owner of the firm—the owner of capital.

We've already examined questions of tax incidence as part of our work in the models presented in previous chapters. A tax imposed on firms producing a good or service in a perfectly competitive market will be partially shifted to consumers in the short run and fully shifted to them in the long run (Chapter 8). The short-run shifting happens because firms cut back on their production, thus boosting prices. The long-run shifting happens because firms leave the industry. A tax imposed on a resource such as land, whose supply curve is perfectly inelastic, isn't shifted anywhere; the price of the resource falls by the present value of expected future tax payments. A per unit tax imposed on a monopoly good is shifted partly to consumers (through reduced output). Assuming the per unit tax does not force the monopoly firm to go out of business, the tax isn't fully shifted to consumers because the firm is able to continue to earn some monopoly profits—resources don't leave the taxed activity to the extent they do in a competitive market.

These examples suggest that to the extent that resources are free to leave the taxed activity, the burden of the tax will be shifted to consumers. To the extent they aren't, the burden will be borne by the owners of those resources.

Clearly, it's the final burden that matters in evaluating whether a tax is progressive, proportional, or regressive. The late Joseph Pechman made an attempt to sort out the ultimate burden of all taxes imposed in the United States. He ranked the U.S. population according to income and then divided the population into deciles (percentage groups containing 10 percent of the population). Then, given the tax burden on each decile and the income earned by people in that decile, he computed the average tax rate facing that group. Pechman's results are reported in Exhibit 15-5.

In a regressive tax system, people in the lowest deciles face the highest tax rates. A proportional system imposes the same rates on everyone; a progressive system imposes higher rates on people in higher deciles. Pechman's estimate for 1988 suggests that taxes in the United States are mildly regressive over the range of the first two deciles and progressive for the remaining deciles. Before we conclude that taxes are regressive at the bottom of the income distribution, we must note the fact that people at the bottom are more likely to be recipients of transfer payments. Pechman found that families in the lowest three deciles received more from transfer payments than they paid in taxes. Combining transfer payments with taxes, he concluded that the overall U.S. system of taxes and transfer payments is progressive.

EXHIBIT 15-5

Assessing the U.S. Tax Structure

Based on his estimate of how tax burdens were distributed in 1988, Joseph Pechman estimated the degree of progressivity of the U.S. tax system. Each decile represents 10 percent of the population, with deciles ranked from lowest to highest in terms of income. His conclusion is that taxes in the United States are generally progressive.

Decile	Effective Federal, State, and Local Taxes as a Percentage of Income
1	16.4
2	15.8
3	18.0
4	21.5
5	23.9
6	24.3
7	25.2
8	25.6
9	26.8
10	27.7

Source: Joseph A. Pechman, "The Future of the Income Tax," *American Economic Review* 80(1) (March 1990): 1–20.

Checklist

- The primary principles of taxation are the ability-to-pay and benefits received principles.
- The fraction of income taken by a regressive tax falls as income rises. A proportional tax takes a constant fraction of income; a progressive tax takes a fraction that rises as income rises.
- The main types of taxes are income, property, sales, and excise taxes.
- Tax incidence analysis seeks to determine who ultimately bears the burden of taxes. Overall, the tax burden in the United States appears to be generally progressive.

Choices in the Public Sector

How are choices in the public sector made? This section examines two perspectives on public sector choice. The first is driven by our examination of market failure. Choices in the public sector are a matter of locating problems of market failure, determining the efficient solution, and finding ways to achieve it. This approach, called the **public interest theory** of government, assumes that the goal of government is to maximize welfare by seeking an efficient allocation of resources. An alternative approach treats public sector choices in the same way as private sector choices. **Public choice theory** argues that individuals in the public sector make choices that maximize their utility—whether as voters, politicians, or bureaucrats, people seek solutions consistent with their self-interest.

Public Interest Theory

In the public interest approach to the analysis of public sector choices, decision-making is a technical matter. The task of government officials is to locate the efficient solution and find a way to move the economy to that point.

For a public good, the efficient solution occurs where demand intersects the marginal cost curve for producing the good. Because the demand for the public good isn't revealed in the market, the task for government officials is to find a way to estimate these curves and then to arrange for the production of the optimum quantity. Economists have developed an approach to such tasks. **Cost-benefit analysis** seeks to quantify the costs and benefits of an activity in an effort to locate the efficient solution. In general, the efficient solution occurs where the net benefit of the activity is maximized.

Public sector intervention to correct market failure presumes that market prices do not correctly convey the benefits and costs of a particular activity. If those prices are generated by a market that we may regard as perfectly competitive, then the failure of prices to convey information about costs or benefits suggests that there is a free rider problem on the demand side or an external cost problem on the supply side. In either case, it is necessary to estimate costs or benefits that are not revealed in the marketplace.

Economists estimate benefits and costs that aren't revealed in the marketplace in two ways. The first is to infer such benefits and costs from the demand or supply for other goods for which a market failure problem does not exist. The second is to employ surveys.

Estimating Benefits and Costs: Market Evidence

Suppose we wish to estimate the demand for cleaner air, which is a public good. Free riders are a problem; no one reveals a willingness to pay for clean air in the marketplace. But a market approach can be used to estimate the demand for clean air nonetheless. The key is to find a complement for clean air whose demand is revealed in the market.

One of the most common complements to clean air used in cost-benefit analysis is residential housing. The demand for housing should be greater where air quality is relatively good than where air quality is poorer. Prices for otherwise identical houses will thus be higher in areas with clean air than in areas with dirty air. Because average air quality typically varies substantially in different parts of a given metropolitan area, we can observe the relationship between house prices and air quality statistically. That, in turn, allows us to estimate the demand curve for cleaner air.

- **Public interest theory** assumes that the goal of government is to maximize welfare by seeking an efficient allocation of resources.
- **Public choice theory** assumes that individuals in the public sector make choices that maximize their own utility.
- **Cost-benefit analysis** quantifies the benefits and costs of an activity in an effort to locate the efficient solution.

EXHIBIT **15-6**

Estimating Demand for a Public Good from the Market for a Complement

Houses command higher prices in areas where the air is relatively clean than where the air is dirty. Suppose a typical house in a metropolitan area sells for prices that vary with air quality as shown in the table.

If there are 100,000 houses in the area, we can infer a demand curve for cleaner air (as shown in the diagram, air quality is measured as the concentration of pollution; it improves as we travel to the right on the horizontal axis and concentration falls). If it costs $300 million for each 1-unit reduction in pollution, the efficient solution quality is a pollution level of 3 ppm.

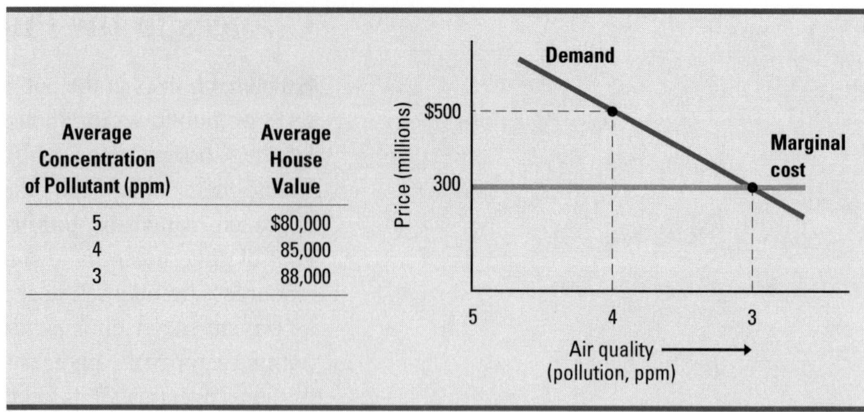

Average Concentration of Pollutant (ppm)	Average House Value
5	$80,000
4	85,000
3	88,000

The process of estimating the demand curve for cleaner air from housing market information is illustrated in Exhibit 15-6. Suppose that in an area where the average concentration of a particular atmospheric pollutant is 5 parts per million (ppm), a typical house costs $80,000. In a district in the same city where the average concentration is 4 ppm, the same house sells for $85,000, and in areas where the average pollution level is 3 ppm, the house sells for $88,000. Assuming that all other factors that affect house values have been considered in the analysis, we can conclude that the value of improving average air quality from a pollution level of 5 ppm to 4 ppm is $5,000 per house and that the value of improving air quality from 4 ppm to 3 ppm is $3,000 per house. Multiplying by the number of houses gives the marginal benefit of this improvement in air quality. We could infer that in a metropolitan area with 100,000 houses, people would be willing to pay $500 million to reduce pollution from 5 ppm to 4 ppm and another $300 million to reduce it from 4 ppm to 3 ppm. These values give us a demand curve for cleaner air. If each 1-ppm reduction in pollution costs $300 million, as suggested by the horizontal marginal cost curve in Exhibit 15-6, a reduction to 3 ppm is the efficient solution.

Estimating the demand for a public good based on market information for a related private good has an important advantage: people have an incentive to reveal their preferences in the private market. The method, however, is far from perfect. It's often difficult to sort out the impact of cleaner air on house prices. To the extent that economists are able to determine it, information from private markets is often a useful guide in the analysis of public goods.

Survey Approaches in Estimating Benefits and Costs

When there is no private market from which to obtain information about the benefits or costs of an activity, a survey approach is often used. Economists elicit information from respondents about their demand for public goods and about the impacts of external costs.

Suppose, for example, that the federal government is considering preserving a particular area as wilderness. A survey might ask questions such as "Would you be willing to pay $20 per year to preserve the area in its natural state?" A respondent who answers "No" might then be asked if he or she would pay $15, or $10, and so on. By asking the same series of questions of a large sample of people, the survey can infer the demand curve for the wilderness area and thus estimate the benefit of its preservation.

The Public Choice Perspective

Public choice theory discards the notion that people in the public sector seek to maximize social welfare. Rather, it assumes that each participant in the public sector seeks only to maximize his or her own utility. This section introduces the flavor of the public choice approach by examining two of its more important conclusions: that many people will rationally abstain from voting and that legislative choices are likely to serve special interests.

Economics and Voting: The Rational Abstention Problem

Public choice theory argues that individuals don't leave their utility functions behind when they enter the voting booth—or even when they're thinking about whether to go to the voting booth. The assumption of utility maximization by voters helps us to understand why most people don't vote in most elections.

Suppose your state is about to hold a referendum on expanded support for state recreation areas, to be financed by an increase in the state sales tax. Given your own likely use of these areas and the way in which you expect to be affected by the tax, you estimate that you will be better off if the program passes. In fact, you've calculated that the present value of your net benefits from the program is $1,000. Will you vote?

As a utility maximizer, you will vote if the benefits to you of voting exceed the costs. One benefit of voting is the possibility that your vote will cause the measure to be passed. That would be worth $1,000 to you. But $1,000 is a benefit to you of voting *only* if it is your vote that determines the outcome.

The probability that any statewide election will be decided by a single vote is, effectively, zero. State elections that are decided by as many as a few hundred votes are likely to be subject to several recounts, each of which is likely to produce a different result. The outcomes of extremely close elections are ordinarily decided in the courts or in legislative bodies; there is virtually no chance that one vote would, in fact, determine the outcome. Thus, the $1,000 benefit that you expect to receive may not be a factor in your decision about whether to vote. The other likely benefit of voting is the satisfaction you receive from performing your duty as a citizen in a free society. There may be additional social benefits as well from the chance to visit with other people in your precinct. The cost of voting would be the value of the best alternative use of your time, together with possible transportation costs.

The fact that no one vote is likely to determine the outcome means that a decision about whether to vote is likely to rest on individual assessments of the satisfactions versus the costs of voting. Most people, in making such decisions, find the costs are greater. In most elections, most people who are eligible to vote don't vote. Public choice analysis suggests that such a choice is rational; a decision not to vote because the costs outweigh the benefits is called **rational abstention.**

Rational abstention suggests there is a public sector externality problem. Elections are a way of assessing voter preferences regarding alternative outcomes. An election is likely to do a better job reflecting voter preferences when more people vote. But the benefits of an outcome that reflects the preferences of the electorate do not accrue directly to any one voter; a voter faces only some of the benefits of voting and essentially all of the costs. Voter turnouts are thus likely to be lower than is economically efficient.

Rational abstention is a decision not to vote on grounds that the costs of voting exceed the benefits.

In the 1992 presidential election, for example, slightly more than half of the voting-age population actually cast votes. President Clinton won 43 percent of the votes cast, so it follows that he was elected president through the expressed support of less than one-fourth of the adult population. State and local elections have even lower turnouts.

Legislative Choice and Special Interests

One alternative to having the general public vote on issues is to elect representatives who will make choices. Public choice theory suggests there are some difficulties with this alternative as well.

Suppose legislators seek to maximize the probability that they will be reelected. That requires that a legislator appeal to a majority of voters in his or her district. Suppose that each legislator can, at zero cost, learn the preferences of every voter in his or her district. Further, suppose that every voter knows, at zero cost, precisely how he or she will be affected by every government program.

In this imaginary world of costless information and ambitious legislators, each representative would support programs designed to appeal to a majority of voters. Organized groups would play no special role. Each legislator would already know how every voter feels about every issue, and every voter would already know how every program will affect him or her. A world of costless information would have no lobbyists, no pressure groups seeking a particular legislative agenda. No voter would be more important than any other.

Now let us drop the assumption that information is costless but retain the assumption that each legislator's goal is to be reelected. Legislators no longer know how people in the district feel about each issue. Furthermore, voters may not be sure how they will be affected by particular programs. People can obtain this information, but it is costly.

In this more realistic world of costly information, special-interest groups suddenly play an important role. A legislator who doesn't know how elderly voters in his or her district feel about a certain issue may find a conversation with a representative of the American Association of Retired Persons (AARP) to be a useful source of information. A chat with a lobbyist for the AFL-CIO may reveal something about the views of workers in the district. These groups may be also able to influence voter preferences through speeches and through public information and political action efforts.

A legislator in a world of costly information thus relies on special-interest groups for information and for support. To ensure his or her reelection, the legislator might try to fashion a program that appeals not to a majority of individuals but to a coalition of special-interest groups capable of delivering the support of a majority of voters. These groups are likely to demand something in exchange for their support of a particular candidate; they are likely to seek special programs to benefit their members. The role of special-interest groups is thus inevitable, given the cost of information and the desire of politicians to win elections. In the real world, it is not individual voters who count but well-organized groups that can deliver the support of voters to a candidate.

Public choice theorists argue that the inevitable importance of special-interest groups explains many choices the public sector makes. Consider, for example, the fact noted earlier in this chapter that the bulk of U.S. transfer payments go to groups who are, on average, richer than the population as a whole. In the public choice perspective, the creation of a federal transfer program, even one that is originally intended to help poor people, will lead to competition among interest groups to be at the receiving end of the transfers. To win at this competition, a group needs money and organization—things poor people are not likely to have. In the competition for federal transfers, it is the nonpoor who are likely to win.

The growing power of special-interest groups in the United States has led to two types of reform efforts. The first is the imposition of term limits, which restrict the number of terms a legislator can serve. Term limits were first established in Colorado in 1990; nearly half the states had imposed such limits by 1995. One argument for term limits is that over time, incumbent legislators establish such close relationships with interest groups that they are virtually assured reelection; limiting terms may weaken these relationships and weaken special interests. The Supreme Court ruled in 1995 that individual states could not impose term limits on members of Congress. If such limits are to prevail, a constitutional amendment will be required.

The second type of reform effort is a proposal that campaigns for seats in Congress be federally funded. If candidates do not need to seek funding from special interests, it is argued, the influence of these groups will wane. President Clinton declared such a change to be a high priority, but at the time this text went to press no such effort had been passed.

Checklist

- Public interest theory examines government as an institution that seeks to maximize public welfare. It assumes government will seek the efficient solution in market failure problems.
- Nonmarket benefits and costs can sometimes be estimated using information in related markets for goods and services.
- Public choice theory assumes that individuals pursue their self-interest in their dealings with the public sector; they continue to try to maximize utility or profit.
- It may be rational for eligible voters to abstain from voting.
- Politicians seeking reelection are likely to try to appeal to coalitions of special-interest groups.

A Look Back—And a Look Ahead

In this chapter we examined the role of the public sector in the market economy. That role has grown considerably in the United States since 1929. Both the size and scope of government activities in the market have expanded.

People demand government participation in three areas of economic activity. First, people want correction of market failure involving public goods, external costs, and inefficient allocation created by imperfect competition. In each case of market failure, the shift from an inefficient allocation to an efficient one generates benefits in excess of costs. Second, people seek government intervention to expand consumption of merit goods and to reduce consumption of demerit goods. Third, people want government to participate in the transfer of income. Programs to transfer income have expanded dramatically in the United States within the past few decades. The bulk of transfer payment spending is not means-tested.

Government activity is financed primarily by taxes. Two principles of taxation are the ability-to-pay principle, which holds that tax payments should rise with income, and the benefits received principle, which holds that tax payments should be based on the benefits each taxpayer receives. Taxes may be regressive, proportional, or progressive. The major types of taxes in the United States are income taxes, sales and excise taxes, and property taxes. Economists seek to determine who bears the burden of a tax by examining its incidence. Taxes may be borne by consumers or by owners of capital, labor, or natural resources.

Two broad perspectives are used to examine choices in the public sector. One is the public interest approach, which uses cost-benefit analysis to find the efficient solution to resource allocation problems. It assumes that the goal of the public sector is to maximize welfare. Cost-benefit analysis requires the estimation of demand and marginal cost curves when these curves are not revealed in the marketplace. Economists may use surveys or evidence from related markets to estimate the curves. The second approach to the analysis of the public sector is public choice theory, which assumes utility-maximizing behavior on the part of participants in the public sector. We examined two conclusions of public choice theory, the problem of rational abstention and the role of special interests.

This chapter concludes our investigation of microeconomic theory. In Part Five, we shall apply this theory to a series of specific topics. The next five chapters examine problems of agriculture, antitrust policy and regulation, environmental issues, discrimination and poverty, and health care.

Terms and Concepts for Review

Ability-to-pay principle
Benefits received principle
Cost-benefit analysis
Demerit goods
Government expenditures
Government purchases
Marginal tax rate
Means-tested transfer payment
Merit goods
Non-means-tested transfer payment
Progressive tax
Proportional tax
Public choice theory
Public finance
Public interest theory
Rational abstention
Regressive tax
Tax incidence analysis
Transfer payments
User fees

For Discussion

1. Identify each of the following government programs as efforts to correct market failure, to promote or discourage the consumption of merit or demerit goods, or to transfer income.
   - **a.** Head Start, a preschool program for low-income children
   - **b.** Sports leagues for children sponsored by local governments
   - **c.** A program to limit air pollution generated by power plants
   - **d.** Species preservation efforts by the government
2. Public Broadcasting System (PBS) stations regularly solicit contributions from viewers. Yet only about 11 percent of these viewers, who on average have much higher incomes than the rest of the population, ever contribute. Why?
3. Do you expect to benefit from the research efforts sponsored by the American Cancer Society? Do you contribute? If you answered "Yes," then "No," does this make you a free rider?
4. Suppose the population of the United States increases. What will happen to the demand curve for national defense? What will happen to the efficient quantity of defense?
5. How could a program that redistributes income from rich to poor be considered to be a public good?
6. We noted that local governments typically supply tennis courts but not bowling alleys. Can you give a public choice explanation for this phenomenon?

7. Find out the turnout at the most recent election for student body president at your school. Does the turnout indicate student apathy?
8. Federal welfare programs reduce benefits by $1 for every $1 that recipients earn; in effect, this is a tax of 100 percent on recipient earnings. Who pays the tax?
9. Suppose elementary education is a public good. How can we infer the demand for elementary school quality from residential property values?

Problems

1. In an effort to beautify their neighborhood, four households are considering leasing a small section of vacant land for a park. For a monthly leasing fee, the owner of the vacant land is willing to arrange for some of the maintenance, and to make the park available only to the four households. The demand curves for the four households (D_A, D_B, D_C, and D_D) wanting parkland are as follows (all demand curves are linear):

	Acres per Month of Parkland Demanded			
Price per Month	D_A	D_B	D_C	D_D
$100	0			
75	1	0		
50	2	1⅓	0	
25	3	2⅔	2	0
0	4	4	4	4

Draw the demand curves for the four neighbors, and show the neighborhood demand curve for parkland.

2. Suppose the owner of the vacant land will provide for and maintain a neighborhood park at a fee of $125 per acre; the neighbors may lease up to 5 acres of land per month. Add this information to the graph you drew in Problem 1, and show the efficient solution. Are the neighbors likely to achieve this solution? Explain the problems involved in achieving it.
3. The perfectly competitive compact disc industry is in long-run equilibrium, selling discs for $5 a piece. Now the government imposes an excise tax of $2 per disc produced. Show what happens to the price and output of discs in the short run and in the long run. Who pays the tax? (*Note:* Show quantities as Q_1, Q_2, etc.)
4. Zounds! A monopoly firm has just taken over the compact disc industry. There have been technological advances that have lowered cost, but the monopoly firm charges a price greater than average total cost, even in the long run. As it turns out, the firm is still selling compact discs for $5. The government imposes an excise tax of $2 per disc produced. What happens to price and output? Compare your results to your answer in Problem 3 and explain.
5. The following hypothetical data give annual spending on various goods and services for households at different income levels. Assume that an excise tax on any of these would, in the long run, be shifted fully to consumers. Determine whether a tax on any of these goods would be progressive, proportional, or regressive.

Income Range	Average Income	Food	Clothing	Entertainment
$0–25,000	$20,000	$5,000	$1,000	$500
25,000–50,000	40,000	8,000	2,000	2,000
50,000–75,000	65,000	9,750	3,250	5,200
75,000–100,000	80,000	10,000	4,000	8,000
> 100,000	200,000	16,000	10,000	30,000

Part Five Microeconomic Applications

16

Agriculture: Government in a Competitive Market

Chapter Objectives

After mastering the material in this chapter, you will be able to:

1. Discuss recent trends in productivity, farm prices, and farm incomes.
2. Explain why productivity increases and economies of scale have caused the size of the average farm to rise.
3. Outline the major agricultural policies of the federal government and explain their impact on prices and output.
4. Explain why government subsidies aren't likely to increase farm profits in the long run.
5. Discuss alternatives to current U.S. farm policy.

Farmers should raise less corn and more Hell.

Mary E. Lease, Kansas, 1890

What's Ahead

Good morning! It's time for breakfast. How about some cereal and orange juice?

Your cereal probably contains wheat, oats, corn, or rice. Each of these grains is made more expensive by federal programs that induce farmers to keep much of their land idle—60 million acres of farmland were kept out of production as a result of such programs in 1992. The government subsidizes farmers who agree to reduce their production of food.

Want some milk? The federal government buys billions of pounds of milk each year just to prop up the price dairy farmers receive. Some sugar? The Department of Agriculture is charged by law with limiting sugar imports enough to hold the price of sugar in the United States well above the world price. Care for some orange juice? When the Department of Agriculture fears citrus prices are falling too low, it issues marketing orders to growers requiring them to let a fraction of their crop rot in the trees. Your juice is thus more costly than it might have been.

Markets for agricultural goods present us with something of a paradox. Economists argue that a perfectly competitive market would allocate goods and services more efficiently than an imperfectly competitive one. Agricultural markets generally match the conditions of a perfectly competitive market, yet the government regularly intervenes in such markets to push up prices and to push down output—precisely the effects predicted by models of imperfect competition. The government does so in an effort to create higher and more stable incomes for farmers.

This chapter examines agricultural markets and explores the ways in which U.S. farm programs affect farmers and consumers. We'll investigate farm incomes and learn that, despite all the help farmers receive, many of them don't earn very high incomes.

Productivity and Income in U.S. Agriculture

Farming has changed dramatically in the last 200 years. Farmers have enjoyed sharp gains in productivity as they have introduced new technologies, new equipment, and new crops. Although these changes have made farmers more productive, farm incomes have generally fallen in recent years. We shall survey these trends in this section. Another major development, the rise of government intervention, will be explored later in this chapter.

Productivity Gains

Agriculture is one of the most rapidly advancing sectors of the economy in terms of the application of scientific research to the production process. U.S. agricultural productivity has increased phenomenally. In 1800, production of 100 bushels of wheat took 373 labor-hours; by 1985, it took less than 5. The number of labor-hours required to produce a bale of cotton fell from 601 to 4 over the same period.

The increased productivity of farm labor is largely the result of improved technology and more capital-intensive production. The use of mechanical power and machinery on U.S. farms has risen more than 30 percent since 1947; the quantity of labor employed has fallen by nearly 75 percent. The quantity of agricultural fertilizers, herbicides, and insecticides used in 1990 was 8 times greater than in 1947. Hybrid strains of seeds that increase crop yields and resist disease and pests have been widely adopted.

Indexes of Productivity Gain

Exhibit 16-1 shows two measures of the increase in productivity: an index of crop production per acre and an index of farm output per hour of labor. These indexes can fluctuate dramatically from year to year as weather and other factors affect agricultural production, but the general trend in productivity has been

EXHIBIT 16-1

Crop and Labor Productivity

Crop production per acre and farm output per hour of labor have increased substantially since 1947.

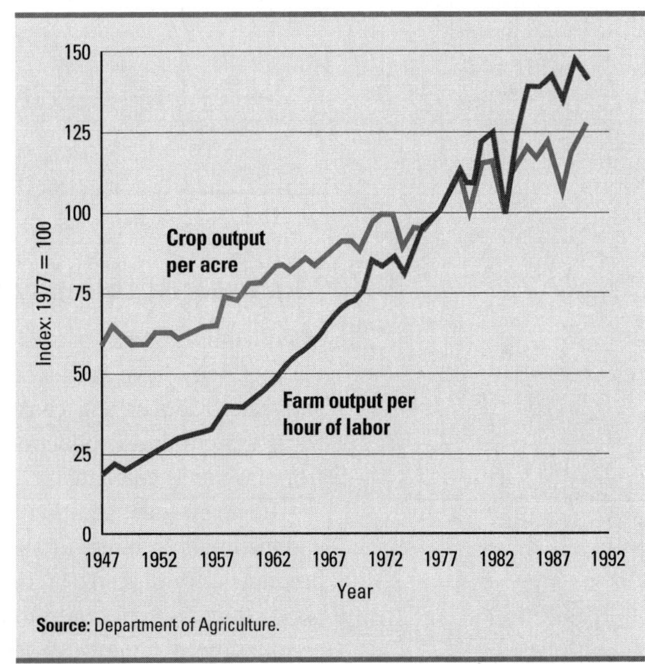

Source: Department of Agriculture.

sharply upward. Crop production per acre more than doubled between 1950 and 1991. Farm output per labor-hour was more than 6 times greater in 1991 than it was in 1950—a productivity gain 3 times greater than that in the rest of the economy. When all inputs to the production process are considered, agricultural output more than doubled between 1950 and 1991.

Productivity Gain and Economies of Scale

Increases in factor productivity reduce production costs. That means that long-run average cost (LRAC) curves in agriculture have been shifting downward. But there has been another change as well. As farmers have adopted new, more capital-intensive technologies, they have achieved economies of scale over larger and larger operations, and average farm size has steadily increased.

We learned in Chapter 7 that producers in a perfectly competitive market will, in the long run, move to the lowest point on their LRAC curves. A change in technology that gives economies of scale over a larger range of output will therefore cause farmers to expand their output—and farms will become larger.

Exhibit 16-2 shows the effect of technological change, both in theory and in fact. In Panel (a), we see a shift in the long-run average cost curve to $LRAC_2$ so the lowest average cost is achieved at a higher output Q_2. In Panel (b), we see the effect on farm size. In 1900, the size of the average farm was 146 acres. By 1991, it had increased to 467 acres. The total number of farms dropped from 5.2 million in 1950 to 2.1 million in 1991.

EXHIBIT 16-2

Falling Costs and Increasing Scale in Agriculture

Changes in technology have lowered the cost of agricultural production and have expanded the range over which farmers experience economies of scale. That has shifted long-run average cost curves in the manner shown here, from $LRAC_1$ to $LRAC_2$. The size of the average farm increased from 146 acres in 1900 to 467 acres in 1991.

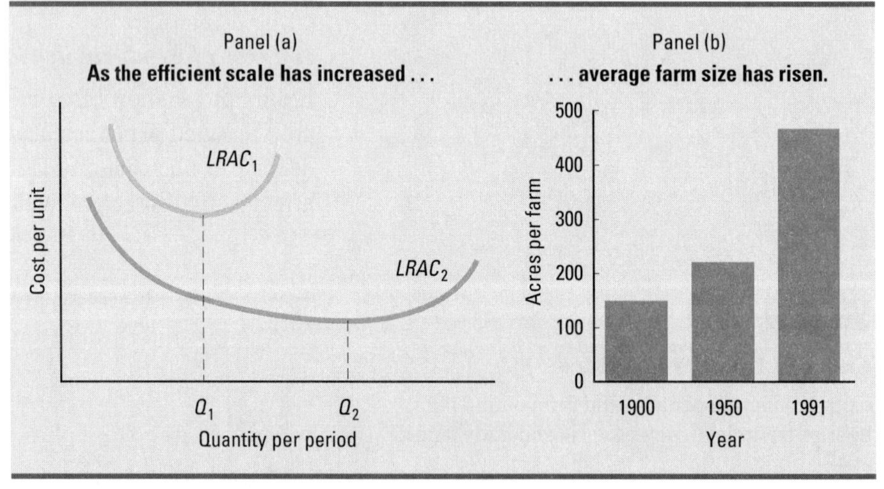

Market Institutions

Many communities sponsor occasional farmers' markets at which farmers sell the food they have produced directly to consumers. But these direct exchanges between producer and consumer involve only a tiny fraction of farm output. Most agricultural production passes through several transactions on the way from farmer to consumer.

In general, the addition of layers of exchange between the primary producer and the final consumer of a good lowers costs to consumers and raises returns to producers. Two kinds of intermediate transactions take place as agricultural goods flow from the farm to the consumer. The first kind alters the agricultural commodity in some way—by transporting it, processing it, or packaging it for final consumption. The second is purely financial, changing only the ownership of the commodity.

Intermediate Producers in Agriculture

Intermediate producers, those who use the output of other firms as inputs, are often among the least loved characters in the economy. Advertisers trumpet the virtues of avoiding the middleman and thus reducing cost. Farmers complain, often bitterly, of the wedge that intermediate producers drive between the prices farmers receive and the prices consumers ultimately pay for food. For every $1 U.S. consumers spend on food, U.S. farmers receive only about 25 cents.

Do intermediate producers get in the way of efficient exchanges between the farmer and the consumer? Suppose a farmer, Martin Olsen, has sold his produce in farmers' markets; no intermediate producers were involved. But now another producer proposes to buy Mr. Olsen's crops. The intermediate producer will arrange for the shipping and marketing of Mr. Olsen's crops. Mr. Olsen will receive a lower price for his produce at the farm than at a farmers' market, but his costs will be lower as well. In fact, he won't agree to the transaction unless his savings in cost are greater than his reduction in revenue in selling his crop. His profits will increase as a result of the transaction. Because the intermediate producer can transport and market Mr. Olsen's produce at a lower cost, and because prices in perfectly competitive markets are ultimately driven down to long-run average cost, we can expect prices to consumers to fall. In the marketplace we will observe that consumers pay higher prices than those received by farmers, but the impact of the intermediate producer has been to increase profits for the farmer and to lower prices to the consumer.

What about intermediate producers whose efforts raise prices to consumers? Suppose, for example, that a firm purchases Mr. Olsen's produce, adds some other ingredients, does a bit of cooking, freezes the result, and sells the final product as a frozen dish than can be popped in a microwave and then eaten. The price of that frozen dish will be quite high relative to the prices of the ingredients that went into it; this intermediate producer has added to the price of food. But what about the overall cost? Consumers buy already prepared foods because they've judged that the cost of those foods is lower than the cost of the alternative—preparing the foods from scratch at home or eating at a restaurant. Once again, the intermediate producer has lowered cost to consumers.

Speculators in Agriculture

Farmers take on two kinds of risk when they plant their crops. The first risk is inherent to farming; crop yields are subject to what nature offers in the way of weather, insects, and diseases. The second risk involves the farmer's role as a price taker. A farmer planting corn in May can't know what the price will be at harvest in September.

The theory of supply suggests that a price-taking firm calculates the profit-maximizing output for a market-determined price and produces that output. Producers who don't know what that price will be must predict it. A farmer who guesses wrong could suffer big losses, either by producing a large crop in the incorrect expectation that the price will be high or by holding back on planting in the incorrect expectation that prices will be low.

Markets for agricultural goods have responded to the risks associated with fluctuations in prices in a variety of ways. One of the most important is the role played by speculators.

Suppose a speculator observes farmers planting a large quantity of grain in response to an expectation of a high price. The large planting is likely to drive prices down, so the speculator can profit by purchasing grain at a low price, storing it, and selling it in a subsequent period when prices are high. The actions of such speculators tend to stabilize prices over time. By withholding grain from the market when its price is falling, speculators keep the price higher than it would otherwise be, and by selling when the price begins to rise, they keep the price lower. Speculators who guess correctly about future price swings tend to stabilize markets.

If speculators guess incorrectly, however, they can destabilize the market. Speculators who expect farm prices to rise will buy grain, hoping to sell it when its price rises. That boosts current prices. If grain prices in fact start falling, speculators may be forced to sell, causing prices to fall even further.

Speculators obviously have a strong incentive not to make incorrect price forecasts. Guessing wrong has a price: the speculators lose money. Economists generally agree that speculative behavior contributes to stability in agricultural markets.

Avoiding Market Risk

Speculation can limit the volatility of farm prices. Still, unexpected events can cause sharp fluctuations in farm prices. Market institutions allow farmers to insulate themselves from the risks of such fluctuations.

Suppose farmers are planting a crop of corn, and the price of corn is $3 per bushel. Farmers can't know what the price will be when the crop is ready to harvest—it could rise, fall, or remain unchanged.

From the point of view of farmers, of course, the worst possibility is that corn prices will fall. To avoid that possibility, farmers can sell their corn long before it's harvested. A farmer can sell a contract to deliver a certain quantity of corn in the future; the buyer of that contract holds the farmer's commitment for the delivery of the corn, say 100,000 bushels in September. A contract that commits the issuer to deliver a certain quantity of a commodity on some future date for a given price is called a **futures contract.**

The advantage to the farmer is that the futures contract locks in the current price. If the price of corn plunges to $1 per bushel by September, the farmer won't be hurt. The speculator who bought the contract, of course, will take a beating—corn purchased at $3 per bushel is now worth only one-third as much.

Futures contracts are typically bought and sold in organized commodity markets like the Chicago Board of Trade. Dealers at these markets represent buyers and sellers from all over the world. Some buyers purchase contracts to ensure they will have a particular commodity at a guaranteed price; others buy and sell on a purely speculative basis, hoping to profit from price swings. Futures contracts and other financial instruments available in these markets allow farmers to insulate themselves from the risks of fluctuating prices.

Institutions like the Chicago Board of Trade give farmers easy access to buyers. Because the prices at which commodities are exchanged at the Board of Trade are broadcast instantaneously throughout the world, such markets enable the free flow of information—a necessary condition for a perfectly competitive market. Advances in communications technology have made it easier for farmers to gain access to such markets, further reducing their costs.

A **futures contract** is a commitment by the issuer to deliver a certain quantity of a commodity on a certain date for a given price.

Product	Price Elasticity of Demand
Beef	−0.58
Pork	−0.78
Broilers (chicken)	−0.14
Fresh vegetables	−0.20
Canned vegetables	−0.20
Frozen vegetables	−0.67
Cereals and bakery products	−0.70
Eggs	−0.23
Milk used for cheese	−0.54
Milk used for ice cream	−0.11
Wheat	−0.80
Potatoes	−0.11

Sources: For meats, William F. Hahn, "Effect of Income Distribution on Meat Demand," *Journal of Agricultural Economics Research* 40(2) (Spring 1988): 19–24; for vegetables and cereal and bakery products, Laura Blanciforti and Richard Green, "The Almost Ideal Demand System: A Comparison and Application to Food Groups," *Journal of Agricultural Economics Research* 35(3) (July 1983): 1–10; for vegetables, Thomas L. Cox and Michael K. Wohlgenant, "Prices and Quantity Effects in Cross-Sectional Demand Analysis," *American Journal of Agricultural Economics* 68(4) (November 1986): 908–919; for all other estimates, G. E. Brandow, "Interrelations Among Demands for Farm Products and Implications for Control of Market Supply," Bulletin 680, University Park: Pennsylvania State University Agricultural Experiment Station, 1961.

EXHIBIT 16-3

Price Elasticities of Demand for Selected Foods

The demand for most of the goods farmers produce is inelastic.

Farm Markets and Farm Incomes

Gains in productivity, and the increasing ease with which farmers can take advantage of intermediate producers and financial services, have lowered farmers' production costs. The prices farmers receive for their products, relative to the prices of all goods in the economy, have fallen 50 percent since 1950. In this section we'll examine how these price reductions have affected farm incomes.

Demand and Supply in Agriculture

The demand for most food products is inelastic, as shown in Exhibit 16-3. Given inelastic demand, a reduction in price lowers total expenditures—and the total revenues received by farmers. Farmers thus face the problem of all price-taking producers of goods and services for which demand is inelastic. As individual farmers find ways to produce more efficiently and thus lower their costs, their combined efforts expand production and force down the prices they face, so their total revenues fall.

Increases in supply generated by productivity gains have not been the only factor affecting agricultural markets. Production capacity in the rest of the world has expanded dramatically, pushing food prices down further. On the demand side, increases in population and income have boosted the demands for agricultural goods.

The tendency for rising incomes to boost demand is expressed by the income elasticity of demand. Farm products are, for the most part, normal goods—increases in income produce increases in demand. But even though the income elasticity of demand for these goods is positive, it is generally less than 1. A 10 percent increase in income, for example, will boost the demand for food by less than 10 percent, so as incomes go up, people spend a smaller percentage of their incomes on food. In 1929, for example, consumers in the United States spent an average of 23 percent of their income on food. By 1991, expenditures on food represented just 11 percent of income.

In the United States, then, the demand for food has gone up. Higher productivity and an expansion in foreign production have increased supply. We know that the relative price of food has fallen and that the quantity has increased. This must mean that the net effect of all these changes has been an increase in supply that exceeds the increase in demand, as illustrated in Exhibit 16-4.

EXHIBIT 16-4

Supply and Demand Shifts in Agriculture

A relatively large increase in the supply of farm products from S_1 to S_2, accompanied by a relatively small increase in the demand for farm products from D_1 to D_2, has reduced the price and increased the output of agricultural goods.

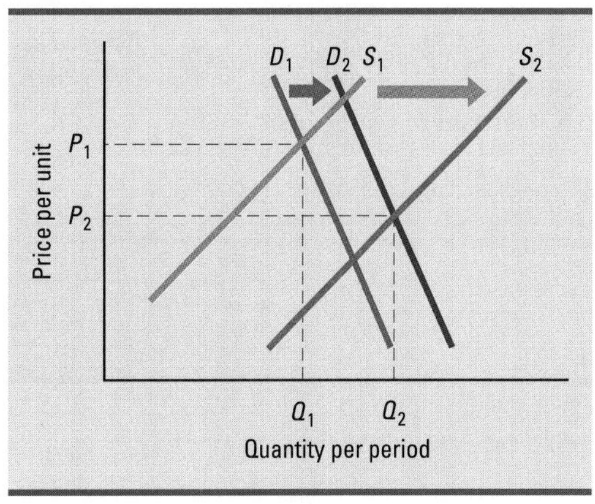

Case in Point: A Boom Goes Bust

Everything from anchovies to the weather clicked for American farmers in the early 1970s. The period stands out in Exhibit 16-5 as a dramatic leap in net farm incomes. In 1973, at the height of the boom, inflation-adjusted net farm income was more than double its level in 1971.

A Missouri farmer watches as truckloads of his equipment are hauled away after being sold to pay off debts.

The boom was fueled by several factors. Anchovies are harvested for animal feed; the bulk of the catch is taken off the coast of Peru. But in 1972, the anchovies seemed to disappear. Anchovies became more expensive, and producers of livestock feed shifted to mixes with heavier concentrations of soybeans, corn, and cottonseed. The result was rising grain prices—and higher profits for farmers.

Weather contributed as well. Two years of drought in the former Soviet Union, combined with a thaw in U.S.-Soviet relations, led the U.S. government to permit American farmers to sell grain to the Soviet Union, giving demand for grain a further boost. Drought in Africa reduced production there, further increasing the demand faced by U.S. farmers.

But the high profits of 1972 and 1973 stimulated sharp increases in output, both in the United States and abroad. High profits, of course, attracted new entry. The entry of new firms shifted the supply curve to the right. New firms also bid up the price of farmland, shifting average total cost curves for farmers upward. In addition to these normal adjustments to high profits, the Organization of Petroleum Exporting Countries (OPEC) raised oil prices sharply in 1974, increasing costs to farmers. By 1976, net farm incomes, adjusted for inflation, stood at their lowest level in more than a decade.

Farm Profits

The profitability of U.S. farms fluctuates as world and domestic market conditions change. Exhibit 16-5 shows the accounting profits—net farm income—earned by U.S. farmers since 1950, adjusted for inflation. The chart also shows net farm income as a percentage of farm assets—the rate of return earned by

EXHIBIT 16-5

Net Farm Income, 1950–1993

The chart shows net income, adjusted for inflation, and the rate of return earned by U.S. farmers.

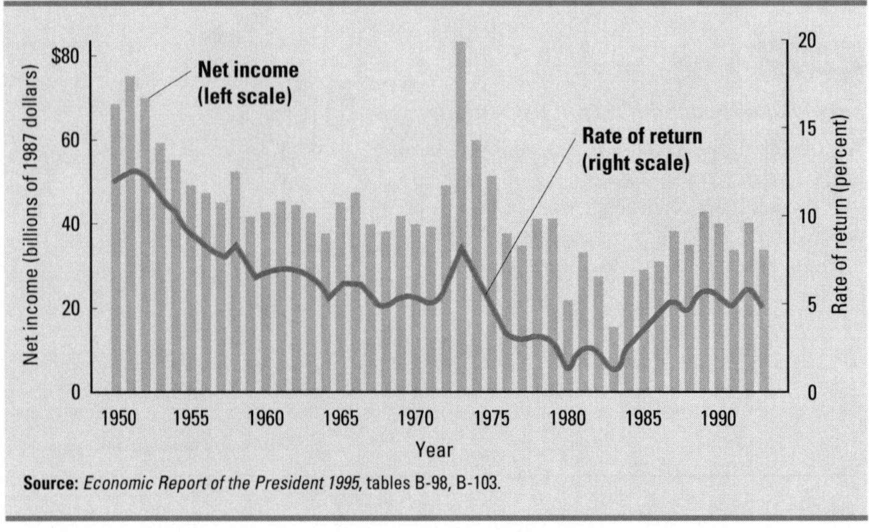

Source: *Economic Report of the President 1995*, tables B-98, B-103.

farmers. We see that net farm income and the rate of return declined throughout the 1950s. U.S. farm profits were very high during and immediately after World War II; they fell as other countries expanded their production capacity. Farmers' net income then stabilized at about 5 percent of assets during the 1960s. Profits soared early in the 1970s; they plunged when oil prices shot up in 1974 and in 1979. The rate of return has hovered near 5 percent for the past decade.

We would never expect farming to be an unusually profitable activity. An increase in profits would, after all, attract new entry. Because farming is a land-intensive activity, efforts by new firms to enter the industry bid up land prices. The higher rents generated by agricultural land would soak up much of any potential increase in profits; lower prices brought by increased supply eliminate the rest.

EXHIBIT 16-6

Entry Erases Profits for Farmers

In Panel (a) the initial price of wheat P_1 is determined by the intersection of the demand and supply curves D_1 and S_1. In Panel (b), an individual farmer responds by producing q_1 bushels of wheat. Price equals average total cost ATC_1, so profits equal zero. The initial price per acre of a fixed quantity of farmland F_1, is determined by the intersection of demand D_1 and supply S in Panel (c); it is R_1. An increase in demand for wheat to D_2 in Panel (a) boosts the price of wheat to P_2; the farmer in Panel (b) increases output to q_2 and is now earning a profit. In the long run, new firms will enter the activity. The supply curve in Panel (a) will begin shifting to the right, pushing the price of wheat down. The demand for farmland in Panel (c) will increase, boosting the price per acre of farmland to R_2. Panel (b) shows that average total costs rise to ATC_2 and prices fall to P_3 until wheat farmers are again earning zero profit. The long-run equilibrium price and quantity in Panel (a) are given by P_3 and Q_3. The individual farmer produces q_3, in Panel (b), and the price of farmland is R_2 in Panel (c).

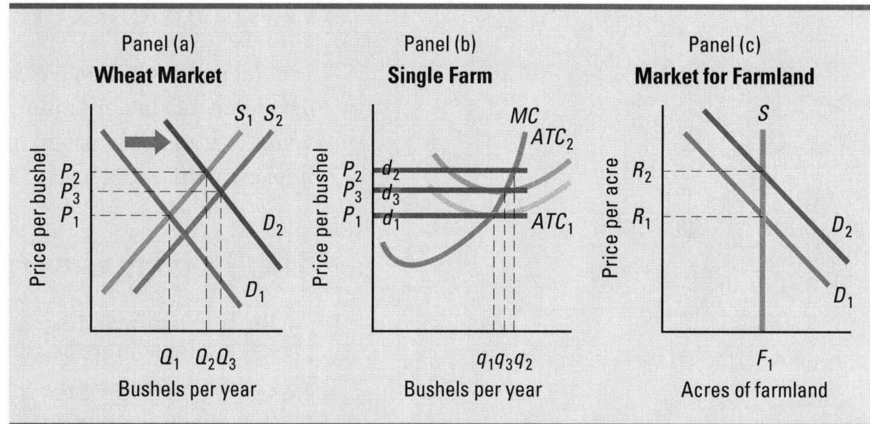

Exhibit 16-6 shows what happens to farmers in the wake of a good year. In Panel (a), the initial price and output of wheat, P_1 and Q_1, are determined by the intersection of the demand and supply curves D_1 and S_1, and wheat farmers are in long-run equilibrium. The case of a single farmer is illustrated in Panel (b). The farmer responds to the market price P_1 by producing q_1 bushels of wheat; because price equals average total cost ATC_1, profits equal zero. Panel (c) shows the market for farmland—a fixed quantity of land is available for farming, and its initial price per acre is R_1.

Now suppose there is an increase in the demand for wheat; the market demand curve shifts to D_2 in Panel (a). The price rises to P_2 and quantity rises to Q_2. Individual farmers respond to the higher price by increasing their output; the farmer in Panel (b) increases production to q_2. Because price is now greater than ATC_1, the farmer now earns a profit.

In the long run, new firms will enter the activity. Two things happen as a result. First, the supply curve in Panel (a) shifts to the right. Land that had been used to produce other crops is now shifted into wheat, so a greater quantity can be produced. Second, the demand for farmland rises, increasing the price. In Panel (c), an increase in demand to D_2 raises the price of land to R_2. The increase in the price of land boosts the average total cost curve for farmers; in Panel (b), ATC_1 shifts up to ATC_2. Equilibrium in the long run is achieved at a price P_3 in Panel (a). The farmer has reduced output to q_3 in Panel (b) and is again earning zero profits. New entry has forced wheat prices down and land prices up, wiping out the profits produced by the initial increase in demand.

Checklist

- Increases in agricultural productivity have caused relatively rapid increases in the supply of agricultural commodities.
- Intermediate producers and easy access to futures markets reduce costs to farmers and to consumers.
- Demand for agricultural goods tends to be price inelastic and to have low income elasticity.
- Increases in the supply of agricultural commodities have tended to outpace increases in demand, thereby putting downward pressure on agricultural prices.
- Lacking barriers to entry, farmers find that prosperity is short-lived as entry pushes prices down and drives up land rents. In the long run, the best farmers can expect is to break even, as predicted by the model of perfect competition.

Government Intervention in Agriculture

Federal programs aimed at helping farmers have been among the most important developments in agriculture in the twentieth century. This section traces the development of those programs and examines current federal policy, assessing its impact on the economy.

The Evolving Government Role in Agriculture

Prior to the passage of the Agricultural Adjustment Act of 1933, government played a rather limited and indirect role aimed at improving the ability of markets to work. For example, the federal government subsidized the development of railroads in the nineteenth century in order to improve the transportation network throughout the country. Before that, government agencies at all levels had helped in the construction of roads, canals, and ports that made transportation of agricultural and other goods cheaper.

The extension of the transportation system opened up vast territories in the West and was a boon to the growth of agriculture. The Homestead Act of 1862 allowed settlers in the West to acquire tracts of land at no charge, provided they worked the land for at least 5 years. Beginning in the 1860s, the federal government gave the states large tracts of federal land they could sell to support the creation of state universities and research centers (land grant institutions). Much of the work done at these universities involved the scientific and technological improvement of agriculture. By the turn of the century, the federal government was in the business of creating massive water projects that subsidized irrigation throughout the West. But beyond such indirect attempts to help U.S. farmers, the federal government tended to let the agricultural markets operate under the broad forces of supply and demand. Market developments beginning during World War I and culminating in the Great Depression of the 1930s, however, brought the federal government into direct manipulation of the markets.

World War I and the 1920s

World War I was a particularly prosperous time for U.S. farmers. Preparation for the war in Europe and the beginning of the war itself in 1914 spurred demand, and the prices of U.S. agricultural products reached an all-time high relative to other prices in the economy. With the end of the war in 1919, however, the European market for U.S. agricultural goods dried up as European soldiers returned to their farms and production facilities destroyed by the war were repaired and reopened. A further blow came as European nations imposed tariffs and other trade barriers. The demand for U.S. farm goods collapsed, and prices received by farmers fell by over half from 1920 to 1921.

The farm sector recovered, and farmers as a group enjoyed an increase in incomes, adjusted for inflation, during the 1920s. But the picture was not so rosy for some. As the analysis of Exhibit 16-6 predicts, farmland prices had risen sharply during World War I, and many farmers had borrowed heavily to acquire acreage. While farm prices recovered slowly from their 1921 plunge, farmers who had committed to fixed mortgage payments during the boom years of World War I found themselves in trouble. Farm foreclosures, which soared in 1920 and 1921, remained high throughout the decade. Farmers pressured Washington to do something about their plight.

In 1922, the Capper-Volstead Act was passed. It gave farmers the right to organize cooperatives in order to obtain a degree of monopoly power in selling their goods. High tariffs were imposed in 1929, aimed in part at protecting farmers from foreign competition. The Agricultural Marketing Act of 1929 committed the federal government for the first time to the role of stabilizing farm prices. This legislation had little impact, however, because it did not give the government power to limit output.

Farm prices are determined by demand and supply. With no ability to control shifts in either curve, the passage of federal legislation calling for more stable prices was akin to passing a law calling for more rain. The government could call for stable prices, but it was powerless to bring them about.

The Great Depression and the New Deal

The Great Depression proved a turning point in defining the federal government's role in agriculture. The Depression affected the entire economy, but it hit farmers particularly hard. Prices received by farmers plunged nearly two-thirds from 1930 to 1933.

The average price of corn fell from $0.77 per bushel in 1930 to $0.19 in 1933. Wheat dropped from $1.08 to $0.33 per bushel over the same period. Although farmers' costs fell at the same time, the drop in their revenues was far greater. Federal efforts to slow the collapse in prices failed, in large part because of the government's inability to restrict supply.

Those farmers who had a tough time keeping up mortgage payments in the 1920s faced disaster in the 1930s. By 1932, more than half of all farm loans were in default.

The Agricultural Adjustment Act (AAA) of 1933 was a response to the crises of the first years of the Great Depression and to the difficulties faced by some farmers during the 1920s. It established a framework for agricultural policy that remains in effect today. The AAA authorized the Secretary of Agriculture to determine the total acreage that would be planted in major crops such as wheat and corn each year. Farmers who agreed to limit their output received a subsidy. Wheat farmers, for example, were paid a bonus of about 30 cents per bushel for the crop they actually produced.

Farm prices began rising almost immediately after the AAA was passed; they continued to rise until 1937. The recession of 1937–1938 sent prices down again, although they remained much higher than their 1933 level. At the end of the decade, fighting in Europe that would give way to World War II boosted the demand for U.S. farm products, and the debacle of the Great Depression was over. But the massive role for the federal government has remained.

A **target price** is a price the government guarantees farmers will receive for a particular crop.

A **deficiency payment** is made to farmers when the market price of a particular crop falls below the target price.

The effort to boost farm prices has been at the heart of U.S. agricultural policy for the past half century. In the next section, we shall review the operation of major U.S. farm programs and examine their impact on farmers and on the economy.

Farm Income Support Programs

Farm legislation passed during the Great Depression sought to boost farm incomes in two ways. First, it guaranteed a minimum price to farmers. A price floor greater than the equilibrium price produces a surplus in a competitive market; price guarantees were backed by government programs to purchase any surplus. The second approach, often combined with the first, imposes limits on agricultural production. In both kinds of programs, the goals are to increase farm incomes and insulate farmers from market fluctuations.

Target Prices

A **target price** is a price the government guarantees to farmers. In the event the market price falls below the target price, farmers can collect a **deficiency payment.** The deficiency payment rate is the difference between the target price and the market price.

The impact of a target price is illustrated in Exhibit 16-7. The graph shows a market with an equilibrium price of P_E. A target price is imposed above this equilibrium at P_T. The government agrees to pay farmers a deficiency payment equal to the difference between the price they receive in the market and the target price. The target price is similar to a price floor in that it induces farmers to supply a quantity Q_T in excess of the equilibrium quantity Q_E.

A support program that relied solely on target prices would induce farmers to produce a greater output and would therefore lower the market price. In Exhibit 16-7, Q_T units of output clear the market at a price P'_T. The government would be obliged to make up the difference between the target and market prices ($P_T - P'_T$) for each of the Q_T units produced. Such a program would benefit consumers by lowering food prices and would benefit farmers by raising the prices they receive, but it would be enormously costly and result in an excessive shift of resources to the farming sector. (Mexico has relied on programs similar to this one, although it is now phasing out its farm subsidy programs.)

EXHIBIT 16-7

Target Prices

In the absence of government intervention, the price would equal P_E and the quantity would be Q_E. A target price at P_T is established by the federal government; it agrees to pay farmers participating in a price support program a deficiency payment per unit of output equal to the difference between the target price and the price farmers receive in the market. If that were the only provision of the program, output would rise to Q_T, requiring a deficiency payment of $Q_T(P_T - P'_T)$. By requiring farmers to restrict their output to Q_R, the government reduces deficiency payments as shown in the shaded area $Q_R(P_T - P_R)$.

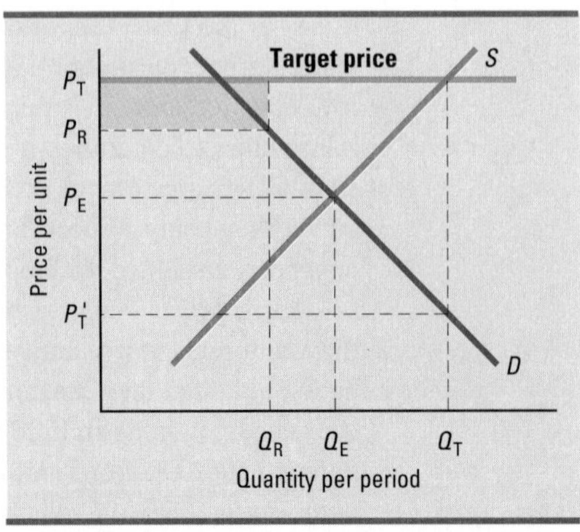

Case in Point — Discouraging Smoking and Helping Tobacco Growers

In some respects, federal policy toward tobacco growers is no different than it is for other major crops. The government seeks to boost the prices tobacco growers receive.

Critics of tobacco support programs often note the apparent inconsistency of a government that actively discourages smoking on grounds that it is harmful to health yet encourages it by aiding tobacco growers. One might be critical of federal efforts to cut down smoking, and one might complain about assistance to tobacco growers; the two sets of policies are not, however, inconsistent.

Prior to 1982, the government carried out a typical farm price support program for tobacco growers. Farmers could borrow money on their crops at a loan rate set by the government. If the market price fell below that level, farmers could simply forfeit the loans and turn their crops over to the government. In exchange for receiving this guarantee of a minimum price, growers had to agree to government restrictions on their crops. Taxpayers had to pay to support the guaranteed purchases of growers' crops.

The old program was completely consistent with the government's efforts to discourage smoking. After all, it reduced the quantity of tobacco planted and thus raised its price. But still, the fact that taxpayers were subsidizing growers was upsetting.

With passage of the No-Net-Cost Tobacco Program Act of 1982, Congress eliminated taxpayer subsidies of growers. Quotas and loans remained in effect, but the cost of the program was shifted to growers through fees imposed on them. Subsequent legislation in 1986 shifted to a more market-based approach. The Department of Agriculture estimates tobacco demand each season and adjusts crop quotas so that tobacco prices will be close to a certain level. If prices drop, the department reduces the quota.

The program now boosts tobacco prices in two ways. First, it restricts planting, and second, it imposes fees on growers. Both factors boost cigarette prices. Smokers, not taxpayers, are therefore coughing up the funds for the program.

Target price programs in the United States have always had another component. To qualify to receive deficiency payments, farmers must agree to reduce the acreage they plant by a percentage determined by the Department of Agriculture. In 1992, farmers held 60 million acres of land out of production in order to qualify for government support programs. The greater the reduction in production required, the higher the market-clearing price paid by consumers and the lower the required government deficiency payment.

Suppose farmers set aside enough acreage to reduce production to Q_R in Exhibit 16-7. The market-clearing price is P_R, and the deficiency payment per unit is $P_T - P_R$. The program thus reduces government spending for farm programs but boosts prices to consumers. In 1993–1994, for example, the target price for wheat was $4 per bushel, the average price of wheat was $2.95, and the average deficiency payment was $1.05.

Guaranteed Loans

Another income support program allows producers to place any portion of their production in approved storage and receive a loan from a federal agency, the Commodity Credit Corporation (CCC), at a specified rate per unit of output. Typically the loan rate or **market price support** is below the target price established for the commodity. If the actual market price goes above the loan rate, the

A **market price support** is a specified loan rate for selected crops. The farmer may repay the loan at interest or forfeit the commodity at the end of the loan period as full payment of the loan.

farmer sells the stored commodity and repays the loan. If the price falls below the market price support, the farmer can simply forfeit his or her crop to the government as full payment for the loan. In effect, the government buys the crop. Alternatively, the farmer can sell at the market price and turn the revenue over to the Department of Agriculture, which accepts the proceeds as payment of the loan. Regardless of the option chosen, the farmer still receives a deficiency payment equal to the difference between the price farmers receive and the target price.

Not all farmers choose to participate in price support programs. After all, the cost of their participation is that they must agree to limit their production. For some farmers, it makes more sense to forgo the offer of price supports and deficiency payments in order to sell a greater quantity. Most production, however, is subject to federal price guarantees and the crop restrictions attached to them.

Other Programs

Target price and support mechanisms are the primary means through which the federal government seeks to aid farmers. Other kinds of programs also aim to raise the prices farmers receive.

To boost prices received by dairy farmers, the CCC buys dry milk and cheese from the nation's dairies—enough to hold the price of fresh milk at a level specified by Congress. In 1992, the CCC purchased 10.2 billion pounds of dairy products to bolster dairy prices. The program is funded by fees imposed on dairy farmers by the federal government. Both the fees and the government's purchases of dairy products boost the prices of these goods.

Imports of sugar from other countries are restricted in order to keep sugar prices high. The Department of Agriculture limits imports each year in order to hold the U.S. price above 24 cents per pound.

The prices of citrus fruits are propped up through a program of marketing orders issued by the Department of Agriculture. If the department determines that a good harvest is likely to depress fruit prices, it may order growers not to harvest a portion of their crop. By forcing a reduction in supply, the Department raises prices to consumers.

For many agricultural products, no government price support programs exist. Vegetables, eggs, beef, and pork are all produced without price supports.

In addition to carrying out policies designed to reduce the supply of agricultural commodities, the government conducts programs aimed at increasing demand; perhaps the most widely known program is the nationwide school lunch program. The surplus commodities purchased by the government under the programs described earlier are distributed to local school districts.

The government has actively supported research on alternative uses for the nation's agricultural commodities. One program aims to convert corn and grain into methanol, which is then used as an alternative to gasoline as a fuel. While typically justified for their effect on air quality, federal measures requiring the use of gasoline containing methanol have served to increase the demand for corn.

Other government programs ship surplus commodities to developing nations as grants-in-aid or sell them in international markets at a fraction of the price paid for them in the United States. The government also subsidizes U.S. farmers who export their commodities, thereby increasing effective demand and reducing domestic supply.

Agricultural Policy: A Critique and an Examination of Reform Alternatives

It's hard to find anything very good to say about U.S. agricultural policy. It raises prices to consumers, and it forces farmers to leave resources idle in order to qualify for farm aid. Federal programs to boost farm incomes are also expensive; they cost taxpayers $7 billion in 1995.

Although government programs do boost the incomes of farmers who receive payments, it's doubtful that they increase the profitability of U.S. farmers in the long run. To the extent that these programs boost farm profits above a normal rate of return, they succeed only in attracting entry and bidding up land prices.

Help to farmers is sometimes justified on grounds it boosts "small" farmers. But almost all the assistance provided by the U.S. government goes to the largest farms. In 1990, for example, the largest 15 percent of farms received 72 percent of all federal farm subsidies.

Can U.S. agricultural policy be reformed? Proposals for change abound. They include scrapping the system of farm subsidies altogether, modifying current programs, and shifting farm aid so that it becomes more like a welfare program, with help targeted to the poorest farmers.

Eliminating all price support programs would increase the quantities supplied of products, such as wheat and corn, which carry restrictions on their output under current programs. It would also reduce, in the short run, the incomes of farmers receiving the aid. In the long run, we would expect these farmers to earn a normal rate of return, but that would be achieved by forcing many farmers out of the market. A further problem lies in farmland prices. If one result of current programs is a bidding up of these prices, then some farmers will have purchased land at prices which reflected their expectations of continued price supports. Would it be fair now to remove these supports?

An alternative to simply abolishing federal price support programs is to begin phasing them out. Such an approach would allow farmers more time to adjust to changes in the rules of farming. The federal government could, for example, reduce target prices on crops such as wheat and corn by a certain percentage each year. The Congressional Budget Office in 1995 estimated that reducing target prices for wheat, corn, rice and cotton by 3 percent per year would save about $12 billion over the next five years.

A more radical approach than simply beginning a phaseout of agricultural programs would be to change their focus so that they target help to the poorest farmers. Farm aid could be designed so that it puts a floor under incomes rather than prices. By establishing a minimum income for the nation's farmers, poverty among farmers would be alleviated. At the same time, prices for agricultural commodities would no longer be artificially high, thereby helping consumers throughout the rest of the economy.

Congress was considering a new farm bill at the time this book went to press in 1995. It seemed likely that the bill would introduce changes designed to reduce the degree to which the government seeks to prop up farm prices and farm incomes.

Checklist ✓

- The federal government began income support programs for farmers in 1933. Most of the provisions of current programs were born in the Great Depression.
- Current government programs aimed at supporting farm income include the establishment of target prices and deficiency payments, government-guaranteed loans, supply restrictions and import quotas, and demand enhancement.
- U.S. farm programs aren't likely to increase farm incomes in the long run; they reduce total output and increase prices to consumers.
- Alternatives for reform include eliminating farm subsidy programs, phasing them out, or restructuring them so that help is targeted to the poorest farmers.

A Look Back—And A Look Ahead

Agriculture is particularly intriguing to economists because it provides a real-world example of the model of perfect competition. There is also extensive government involvement in agriculture, so it is an important area for public policy.

Two fundamental factors have led to falling net income in agriculture. Rapid improvements in technology and productivity have led to widespread increases in supply while demand for agricultural products has not kept pace. Given the price inelasticity of demand and a low income elasticity, shifts of supply and demand have caused farm prices to fall relative to other prices in the economy.

Government programs aimed at boosting farm income have encouraged farmers to reduce their output. These programs block U.S. farmers from fully exploiting their comparative advantage in agricultural production and reduce the quantities of goods and services the overall economy can consume. Many economists believe that alternative programs supporting income rather than prices would better serve the interests of farmers and consumers and society at large.

In the next chapter, we shall examine government involvement in the economy in sectors other than agriculture. Chapter 17 examines government efforts to make the economy more competitive, as well as regulations imposed on the economy for other purposes, such as consumer protection.

Terms and Concepts for Review

Deficiency payment

Futures contract

Market price support

Target price

For Discussion

1. "During most of the past 50 years the U.S. has had a surplus of farmers, and this has been the root of the farm problem." Comment.
2. Does the farm problem—falling relative prices, rising productivity, and the decline in the number of small farms—present a difficulty to consumers?
3. If farmers in the long run can expect to do no better than break even, making zero profit, why do they stay in business?
4. "Farm prices are unstable from year to year because demand is price inelastic. If farmers decide what crops to produce this year based on last year's price, the price of the commodity will be even more unstable." Explain.
5. "The fact that farmers receive just 25 cents of each dollar consumers spend on food suggests a simple answer to the farm problem. We could eliminate intermediate producers, and farmers could receive a fourfold increase in their income without raising prices to consumers." Comment.
6. Suppose the Department of Agriculture ordered all farmers to reduce the acreage they plant by 10 percent. Would you expect a 10 percent reduction in food production? Why or why not?
7. The federal government keeps U.S. sugar prices high by restricting imports of sugar. What would happen if these restrictions were removed?
8. In the absence of government purchases of surplus commodities, what do you predict will happen to the market-clearing price if the government increases its target price for a particular farm commodity? How will this affect the total amount of government deficiency payments? Explain.
9. Small farms in the United States are considerably less profitable than larger farms, suggesting that the smaller farms are not taking advantage of potential economies of scale. What difficulties does this suggest for a policy of changing farm aid so that it subsidizes only poor farmers?
10. The Department of Agriculture supports tobacco prices through a loan program for tobacco growers. To participate in the program, growers must reduce the acreage they plant. Such programs are often criticized on grounds the government is seeking to reduce smoking at the same time it subsidizes growers. Are the two efforts inconsistent?

Problems

Problems 1–4 are based on the following demand and supply schedules for wheat (all quantities are in millions of bushels per year).

Price per Bushel	Quantity Demanded	Quantity Supplied
$0	6	0
1	5	1
2	4	2
3	3	3
4	2	4
5	1	5
6	0	6

1. Draw the demand and supply curves for wheat. What is the equilibrium price? The equilibrium quantity?
2. Suppose the government now imposes a price floor at $4 per bushel. Show the effect of this program graphically.
3. Suppose the government, given the demand and supply curves in Problem 1, imposes a target price of $4 per bushel and promises growers a deficiency payment equal to the difference between the target price and the market price. Show graphically what happens to the price and output of wheat; and show, using a shaded area on your graph, the total amount of the deficiency payment.
4. Refer to Exhibit 16-3 and use the price elasticities of demand for selected foods to predict the impact on the price of a 10 percent reduction in the quantity of each of the following foods:
   a. beef
   b. eggs
   c. wheat
   d. What conclusion do your results suggest about the relationship between the price elasticity of demand and the change in price?

17

Antitrust Policy and Business Regulation

Chapter Objectives

After mastering the material in this chapter, you will be able to:

1. Discuss what is meant by antitrust policy and trace the evolution of this policy over the past century.
2. Explain the difference between business actions that are always illegal and those that require analysis according to the rule of reason.
3. Contrast a horizontal merger with a vertical merger.
4. Show how a joint venture can improve social welfare.
5. Discuss the relationship between antitrust policy and the competitiveness of U.S. firms in the global economy.
6. Compare and contrast the competing theories of regulation.
7. Summarize the alternative approaches to regulating the price of a natural monopoly and explain the problems associated with each approach.
8. Discuss the pros and cons of consumer protection.

"Microsoft may not have matured to the position where it understands how it should act with respect to the public interest and the ethics of the marketplace."
Federal Judge Stanley Sporkin

"Yes, we are aggressive; yes, we are competitive. I didn't realize that was a sin."
Microsoft executive vice president Steven Ballmer

What's Ahead

There aren't many areas of the computer software market in which Microsoft Corporation doesn't have a large share. The company successfully extended its leadership in the operating systems market to dominate most software applications.

The market for personal-finance software has been a painful exception to the company's general rule of industrial triumph. Microsoft's contender in that market, a program called Money, ranks a distant second behind Quicken, a product of Intuit, Inc., which has an estimated 70 to 90 percent of the market.

Microsoft came up with a simple solution to its lackluster performance: in 1994, it proposed to purchase Intuit. The Justice Department filed suit in an effort to block the $2.1 billion acquisition. In a complaint filed in federal court, the government charged that the combination "would substantially increase concentration and substantially reduce competition" in the market.

This action wasn't the Justice Department's first attempt to curb Microsoft. We'll examine the government's ongoing battle with the giant firm later in this chapter.

Should Microsoft's effort to dominate another market be curtailed? Or should one firm be allowed to buy another whenever both parties agree? Would Microsoft's acquisition of Intuit and its likely use of that software product to offer personal banking services be good for consumers or harmful to them? The company decided not to wait for a court verdict. In May 1995, Microsoft called off the proposed merger with Intuit. Microsoft announced in July 1995 that it would launch an alternative ploy—it was to begin distributing free copies of its Money software.

In this chapter we'll examine some of the limits government imposes on the actions of private firms. The first part of the chapter considers antitrust policy, an effort to maintain a competitive marketplace. The second part considers other regulation of business firms, including regulations that seek to enhance worker and consumer safety.

Antitrust: Protecting Competition Versus Protecting Competitors

In the decades after the Civil War, giant corporations began to dominate railroads, oil, banking, and a dozen other industries. These businesses were led by entrepreneurs who gained, rightly or wrongly, the image of being "robber barons" out to crush their competitors, monopolize markets, and gouge their customers. They gained their market power by forming *trusts,* the nineteenth-century name given to cartels and other business agreements aimed at restricting competition. It was in response to the rise of these giant firms that antitrust policy was created in the United States.

A Brief History of Antitrust Policy

The final third of the nineteenth century saw two major economic transitions. The first was industrialization—a period in which U.S. firms became far more capital intensive. The second was the emergence of huge firms able to dominate whole industries. In the oil industry, for example, Standard Oil of New Jersey began acquiring smaller firms, eventually controlling 90 percent of U.S. oil-refining capacity. In tobacco, American Tobacco gained control of up to 90 percent of the market for tobacco products.

Concern about the monopoly power of these giants led to a major shift in U.S. policy toward business. What had been an economic environment in which the government rarely intervened in the affairs of private firms was transformed into an environment in which government agencies took a much more vigorous role. The first arena of intervention was antitrust policy, in which the federal government challenged the monopoly power of some firms head-on. **Antitrust policy** refers to government attempts to prevent the acquisition and exercise of monopoly power and to encourage competition in the marketplace. It gets its name from the abuse of market power through trust and cartel agreements that were commonplace in the late nineteenth century.

The Sherman Antitrust Act of 1890

The Sherman Antitrust Act of 1890, the first U.S. antitrust policy, remains the cornerstone of our antitrust laws. The Sherman Act outlaws contracts, combinations, and conspiracies in restraint of trade. The act aimed, in part, to prevent **price-fixing,** in which two or more firms agree to set prices or to coordinate their pricing policies. For example, in the 1950s General Electric, Westinghouse, and several other manufacturers colluded to fix prices. They agreed to assign market segments in which one firm would sell at a lower price than the others. In 1961, the General Electric–Westinghouse agreement was declared to be illegal. The companies paid a multimillion-dollar fine, and their officers served brief jail sentences.

The Sherman Act also outlaws the acquisition of one firm by another, or the merger of two firms in an industry, when such an acquisition or merger is likely to produce substantial monopoly power. The interpretation of this part of the Sherman Act has been subject to a great deal of debate among legal scholars, economists, and policymakers. Early interpretations suggested that any action in restraint of trade, including price-fixing or the merger of large firms, was **illegal per se.** An action is illegal per se if it is illegal in and of itself without regard to the circumstances under which it occurs. The Latin phrase *per se* means "on its

- **Antitrust policy** refers to government attempts to prevent the acquisition and exercise of monopoly power and to encourage competition in the marketplace.
- **Price-fixing** is an agreement between two or more firms to collude in order to establish a price and not to compete on the basis of price.
- A business practice is **illegal per se** if it violates the law and if no consideration is given to the circumstances under which it occurs.

Case in Point: The Government, Microsoft, and the Rule of Reason

There isn't much doubt that Microsoft, whose operating system is at the heart of 85 percent of the nation's personal computers, has huge clout in the software market. But does it exercise that clout reasonably?

Microsoft thinks it does. A lot of competitors disagree. The company, which was once an upstart developer of software products, suddenly emerged as a dominant firm when IBM chose Microsoft's Disk Operating System, DOS, for IBM's personal computers. That quickly led to DOS becoming virtually the industry standard. As the manufacturer of the system on which computers operate, Microsoft has been able to extend its power over the software applications that use its operating system.

Microsoft has been aggressive in maintaining and expanding its competitive advantage. In selling its operating systems to computer manufacturers, it offers a pricing scheme that encourages manufacturers to use Microsoft systems exclusively. Developers of applications software require the technical details of Microsoft's operating systems; Microsoft has been accused of making these details available only to companies that don't pose a challenge to Microsoft's dominance. Finally, Microsoft often announces that it will release new software long before it is ready for the market. The purpose of such announcements is to deter consumers from buying rival products.

Bill Gates.

These tactics are standard. There's nothing unusual about a company giving buyers an incentive to make exclusive use of its products. There's nothing unusual about a company being willing to share secrets with friends and not with enemies. It's commonplace for software developers to announce new products before they're ready. The policy question is whether Microsoft should, because it's so big, be held to a different standard.

The Federal Trade Commission launched an investigation of Microsoft in 1991 to determine whether the company had violated antitrust laws. It dropped its inquiry in 1993. The same day the FTC dropped out, the Justice Department launched an investigation of its own.

After nearly a year of investigation, the Justice Department and Microsoft announced a settlement in which Microsoft agreed to make details of its operating systems more readily available to rivals and to modify the pricing of these systems to computer manufacturers. Federal Judge Stanley Sporkin rejected that settlement early in 1995, charging that the government had been far too lenient and that the terms of the settlement didn't end what he regarded as an abuse of monopoly power. The quote from Judge Sporkin at the beginning of this chapter is taken from his ruling. The rejection of the settlement will force the government to seek tougher action or to drop its suit against Microsoft entirely.

Judge Sporkin's ruling was overturned on appeal in the summer of 1995. Meanwhile, the Justice Department reopened its investigation of Microsoft to see if the company's strategies in marketing its Windows 95 software violated the antitrust laws.

Microsoft has been the world leader in software development. Its actions have brought consumers expanded services and sharply lower prices. Those same actions have given the company enormous power in a critically important industry. The determination of whether Microsoft's actions should be applauded or banned will be a major question for public policy in the nineties.

Source: Viveca Novak and Don Clark, "Microsoft Antitrust Pact Rejected by Federal Judge," *The Wall Street Journal*, February 15, 1995, p. A3.

face." Shoplifting, for example, is illegal per se; courts don't inquire whether shoplifters have a good reason for stealing something in determining whether their acts are illegal.

The Sherman Act was first successfully applied in 1911 against Standard Oil and American Tobacco. Standard Oil had gained control of about 90 percent of the oil-refining industry; American Tobacco had gained control of between 70 and 90 percent of the market for tobacco products, excluding cigars. The Supreme Court found that such dominant market shares constituted violations per se of the Sherman Act.

But the Supreme Court quickly moved away from the notion that clear-cut standards could be established to define per se violations of the Sherman Act. In the next 10 years, the Court threw out antitrust suits brought by government prosecutors against Eastman Kodak, International Harvester, United Shoe Machinery, and United States Steel. The Court determined that none of them had used unreasonable means to achieve their dominant positions in the industry. Rather, they had successfully exploited economies of scale to reduce costs below competitors' costs and had used reasonable means of competition to reap the rewards of efficiency. The Court argued that a **rule of reason** should be applied, wherein the Court would look at the specific behavior of the firm and take into consideration the circumstances surrounding business practices. Emphasis was placed on the conduct, not the structure or size, of the firms.

The rule of reason suggested that "bigness" is no offense if it has been achieved through legitimate business practices. This precedent was challenged in 1945 when the U.S. Court of Appeals ruled against the Aluminum Company of America (Alcoa). The court acknowledged that Alcoa had been able to capture over 90 percent of the aluminum industry through reasonable business practices, good management, and production efficiency. Nevertheless, the court held that by sheer size alone, Alcoa was in violation of the prohibition against monopoly.

In a landmark 1962 court case involving a proposed merger between Brown Shoe Company and one of its competitors, the Supreme Court blocked the merger because the resulting firm would have been so efficient that it could have undersold all of its competitors. The Court recognized that lower shoe prices would have benefited consumers but chose to protect competitors instead.

The Alcoa case and the Brown Shoe case, along with many other antitrust cases in the 1950s and 1960s, added confusion and uncertainty to the antitrust environment. That confusion persists today, as suggested in the accompanying Case in Point.

Other Antitrust Legislation

Concerned about the continued growth of monopoly power, in 1914 Congress created the Federal Trade Commission (FTC), a five-member commission that, along with the antitrust division of the Justice Department, was given the power to prosecute firms that used illegal business practices. The FTC continues to play an important role in antitrust enforcement.

In addition to establishing a new agency to enforce antitrust laws, Congress has created new laws. Some of the most important are the Clayton Act, the Robinson-Patman Act, and the Celler-Kefauver Act.

The Clayton Act of 1914. The Clayton Act of 1914 attempted to spell out what actions were illegal per se. The act made it illegal to buy a rival firm or to have common members sitting on the boards of directors of competing firms. These provisions, however, were ineffective; firms found it relatively easy to get around them. More successful was the act's prohibition against price discrimination that lessened competition or tended to create a monopoly. The act also outlawed **tying agreements.** In one form of tying agreement, a manufacturer refuses to sell to dealers unless they agree not to handle its competitors' products. In another form of tying agreement, a manufacturer requires a dealer to purchase or distribute one product in order to purchase or distribute another.

- The **rule of reason** holds that whether or not a particular business practice is illegal depends upon the circumstances surrounding the action.

- A **tying agreement** requires buyers to meet conditions placed on them by sellers in order to be able to purchase or distribute the manufacturers' products.

The Robinson-Patman Act. Unlike other antitrust legislation aimed at enhancing competition, the Robinson-Patman Act, passed in 1935, restrained competition in order to protect small firms (typically distributors) from larger ones (typically producers). The Robinson-Patman Act prohibited firms from granting discounts or special concessions such as advertising subsidies to favored distributors unless these favors were granted to all buyers or distributors. The act made it illegal to sell the same product to different distributors at different prices if those price differences did not reflect differences in cost. It also prohibited paying brokerage fees or rebates to selected dealers who did not provide a service in exchange (this was simply another form of illegal discount).

The Celler-Kefauver Antimerger Act. Early antitrust policy was aimed at preventing **horizontal mergers.** A horizontal merger is one that combines two or more producers of the same good or service. Horizontal mergers, by reducing the number of firms in a single industry, increase concentration and, therefore, the likelihood of collusion among the remaining firms.

The Celler-Kefauver Act extended the antitrust provisions of earlier legislation by blocking **vertical mergers** where a reduction in competition could be shown. A vertical merger is one that involves firms at different stages in the production and distribution of a product. For example, the acquisition by Ford Motor Company of a firm that supplies it with steel would be a vertical merger.

U.S. Antitrust Policy Today

The "bigness is badness" doctrine dominated antitrust policy from 1945 to the 1970s. But it always had its critics. If a firm is more efficient than its competitors, why should it be punished? Critics of the antitrust laws point to the fact that of the 500 largest companies in the United States in 1950, over 100 no longer exist. New firms, including such giants as IBM, Microsoft, and Federal Express, have taken their place. The critics argue that the emergence of these new firms is evidence of the dynamism and competitive nature of the modern corporate scene. There is little evidence to suggest, for example, that the degree of concentration across all industries has increased over the past 20 years. Moreover, they argue, it is not necessary that an industry be perfectly competitive to achieve the benefits of competition. It need merely be contestable. A large firm may be able to prevent small firms from competing, but other equally large firms may enter the industry in pursuit of extraordinary profits earned by the firm.

Justice Department Merger Guidelines

Prior to 1984, the Justice Department defined a highly concentrated industry as one having a 4-firm concentration ratio (the share of total output produced by an industry's 4 largest firms) of 75 percent or higher. It would not allow even relatively small firms in such industries to merge. This strict interpretation of market concentration kept the number of mergers and acquisitions very low.

Under the Reagan administration, however, a new set of much less restrictive guidelines emerged. These were based on the Herfindahl index, introduced in Chapter 13, which is calculated by summing the squared percentage market shares of all firms in an industry. The higher the value of the index, the greater the degree of concentration. Possible values of the index range from 0 in the case of perfect competition to 10,000 (= 100^2) in the case of monopoly.

- A **horizontal merger** is the consolidation of firms that compete in the same industry or product line.
- A **vertical merger** is the consolidation of firms that participate in the production of a given product line, but at different stages of the production process.
- **Joint ventures** are cooperative projects carried out by two or more firms. In the context of antitrust, joint ventures involve collusion that otherwise would be prohibited.

If the post-merger Herfindahl index is found to be . . .	then the Justice Department will likely take the following action:
Unconcentrated (< 1,000)	No challenge
Moderately concentrated (1,000–1,800)	Challenge if post-merger index changes by more than 100 points
Concentrated (> 1,800)	Challenge if post-merger index changes by more than 50 points

Source: *U.S. Department of Justice Merger Guidelines* (1984).

EXHIBIT 17-1

Department of Justice Merger Guidelines

In 1984, the Justice Department announced that it considered any industry with a Herfindahl index under 1,000 to be unconcentrated. Except in unusual circumstances, mergers of firms with a post-merger index under 1,000 would not be challenged. The Justice Department said it would challenge proposed mergers with a post-merger Herfindahl index between 1,000 and 1,800 if the index increased by more than 100 points. The Justice Department declared that industries with an index greater than 1,800 were highly concentrated and said it would seek to block mergers in these industries when the post-merger index increased by 50 points or more. Exhibit 17-1 summarizes the use of the Herfindahl index by the Justice Department. These guidelines have continued to be in effect under the Clinton administration.

EXHIBIT 17-2

Mergers and Acquisitions Over $1 Billion, 1982–1989

Year	Number of Deals	Value (millions)
1982	10	$19,440.3
1983	6	9,110.5
1984	19	55,178.5
1985	26	61,458.6
1986	31	67,932.4
1987	30	62,175.9
1988	42	96,399.4
1989	35	117,477.4

Source: Murray Weidenbaum and Mark Jensen, "Introduction to The Modern Corporation and Private Property," Working Paper 134 (St. Louis: Center for the Study of American Business, Washington University 1990), p. 3. Reprinted with permission.

Mega-Mergers in the 1980s

In the 1980s both the courts and the Justice Department held that bigness did not necessarily translate into badness, and corporate mergers proliferated. As shown in Exhibit 17-2, in the period 1982–1989 there were almost 200 mergers and acquisitions of firms whose value exceeded $1 billion. Thousands of horizontal and vertical mergers of smaller firms also took place during the period.

Checklist ✓

- The government uses antitrust policies to maintain competitive markets in the economy.
- The Sherman Antitrust Act of 1890 and subsequent legislation attempted to define what business practices were illegal, but these acts left a great deal to be settled by agency and court interpretation.
- Although price-fixing and tying contracts are illegal per se, most business practices that may lessen competition are interpreted under the rule of reason.
- The Justice Department uses the Herfindahl index to determine which industries are so concentrated that antitrust efforts should prevent mergers and acquisitions.

Antitrust and Competitiveness in a Global Economy

In the early 1980s U.S. imports from foreign firms rose faster than U.S. exports, and the trade deficit reached record levels. Antitrust laws had a relatively minor role to play, but business interests and politicians have argued that the United States should overhaul its antitrust laws in order to make U.S. firms more competitive against multinational companies headquartered in places such as Japan, Korea, Singapore, Taiwan, Hong Kong, and Europe.

Antitrust enforcement was altered in the late 1980s so that horizontally competitive U.S. firms could cooperate in joint ventures in research and development (R & D) aimed at innovation, cost-cutting technological advances, and new product development. In an antitrust context, **joint ventures** refer to cooperative arrangements between two or more firms that would not be allowed under the antitrust laws. Proponents of change argued that foreign multinational firms were not subject to stringent antitrust restrictions and therefore had a competitive advantage over U.S. firms.

Cooperative Ventures Abroad

Policymakers who altered U.S. antitrust restrictions on joint ventures pointed out that Japanese and European firms are encouraged to cooperate and to collude not only in basic research and development projects, but in production and marketing as well.

The evidence is difficult to interpret, but at least one U.S. study suggests that nearly 20 percent of research projects in Japan are sponsored jointly by firms in the same market. Moreover, the evidence is fairly clear that Japan allows horizontal consolidations and mergers in moderately concentrated markets where antitrust policy would be applied in the United States. Mergers that create substantial monopoly power in Japan are not typically prosecuted by the government.

In Europe, the potential competitive threat to U.S. firms is twofold. First, as the European Community (EC) moved toward economic unification in 1992, it relaxed antitrust enforcement for mergers between firms in different nations even though they would become a single transnational firm in the near future. In 1984, for example, the EC adopted a regulation that provided blanket exemptions from antitrust provisions against collusion in R & D for firms whose total market share did not exceed 20 percent. This exemption included horizontal R & D and extended to include production and distribution, to the point of final sale. Moreover, firms that had a market share greater than 20 percent could apply to the EC for an exemption based on a case-by-case examination.

The U.S. government has, in some cases, relaxed some antitrust restrictions in an effort to make domestic firms more competitive in global competition. In particular, it has begun to permit joint ventures that would once have been prohibited.

Antitrust Policy and U.S. Competitiveness

In the early 1980s Congress passed several laws that relaxed the antitrust prohibition against cooperation among U.S. firms.

The Export Trading Company Act of 1982 (ETCA) required cooperating firms applying for a certificate that would "immunize" them against antitrust rules to show that their joint activities would not reduce competition. ETCA certification simply meant that the venture would not have been prosecuted under existing antitrust laws in any event, so it did not serve as much of a stimulant to joint ventures.

The National Cooperative Research Act of 1984 (NCRA) provided a simple registration procedure for joint ventures in R & D. The NCRA protected members of registered joint ventures from punitive antitrust penalties if the venture was later found to illegally reduce competition or otherwise act in restraint of trade. Between 1984 and 1990 over 200 research joint ventures were registered, substantially more than were formed over the same period within the EC.

In 1988, Congress passed the Omnibus Trade and Competitiveness Act (OTCA). The OTCA declared that unfair methods of competition by foreign firms and importers are punishable under the U.S. antitrust laws. It also changed the wording of existing laws concerning "dumping" (selling below cost) by foreign firms. In the past, a domestic firm that claimed injury from a foreign competitor had to prove that the foreign firm was "undercutting" the U.S. market prices. The OTCA changed this provision to the much less restrictive term "underselling" and specifically stated that the domestic firm did not have to prove that the act involved predatory intent. This legislation opened the door to U.S. competitors to use the antitrust laws to *prevent* competition from foreigners, quite the opposite of the original intent of the antitrust laws.

The Justice Department announced in 1988 that the rule of reason would replace per se illegality in analysis of joint ventures that would increase U.S. competitiveness. The Justice Department uses the 1984 domestic guidelines and the Herfindahl index of concentration to determine whether a proposed cooperation would increase concentration and thereby lessen competition. In making that assessment, the Justice Department also looks at (1) whether the firms directly compete in other markets, (2) the possible impact on vertical markets, and (3) whether any offsetting efficiency benefits outweigh the anticompetitiveness of the joint venture. Although mergers between two firms in a moderately or highly concentrated industry are prohibited, joint ventures between them may be allowed.

The major antitrust issues to be resolved in the 1990s go beyond joint R & D ventures. Using the potential threat posed by the economic unification of Europe in 1992, some economists have called for a relaxation of U.S. antitrust policies so that firms can engage in joint ventures that involve production and marketing. The issue remains unresolved, and this area of antitrust practice and policy will be closely watched and studied by economists.

Checklist ✓

- A rising trade deficit in the 1980s and concerns about U.S. competitiveness led to relaxation of antitrust enforcement against firms that cooperated in joint ventures, particularly in research and development projects.
- A joint venture, in the context of antitrust, is a cooperative project between firms that otherwise would not be allowed to merge or collude under existing antitrust guidelines.
- Foreign firms in Japan and Europe are subject to less stringent antitrust enforcement than U.S. firms; the evidence is not clear, but many people claim that this fact explains why U.S. firms have lost a competitive edge to foreign firms.
- In 1988, the Justice Department announced that it would apply the Herfindahl index and the rule of reason in determining what mergers and joint ventures would be allowed among U.S. firms threatened by competition from foreign firms.

Regulation: Protecting People from the Market

Antitrust policies are primarily concerned with preventing the accumulation and use of market power. Government **regulation** is used to control the choices of private firms or individuals. Regulation may constrain the freedom of firms to enter or exit markets, to establish prices, to determine product design and safety, and to make other business decisions.

Regulation is an effort by government agencies to control the choices of private firms or individuals.

In general terms, there are two types of regulatory agencies. One group of regulatory agencies attempts to protect consumers by limiting the abuse of market power by firms. Another attempts to influence business decisions that affect consumer and worker safety. Regulation is carried out by over 50 federal government agencies that must interpret the applicable laws and apply them in the specific situations they find in real-world markets. Exhibit 17-3 lists some of the major federal regulatory agencies, many of which are duplicated at the state level.

Theories of Regulation

Competing explanations for why there is so much regulation range from theories that suggest regulation protects the public interest to those that argue regulation protects the producers or serves the interests of the regulators.

The Public Interest Theory of Regulation

The public interest theory of regulation holds that regulators seek to find market solutions that are economically efficient. It argues that the market power of firms in imperfectly competitive markets must be controlled. In the case of natural monopolies, regulation is viewed as necessary to lower prices and increase output. In the case of oligopolistic industries, regulation is often advocated to prevent cutthroat competition.

Agency	Mission
Financial Markets	
Federal Reserve Board	Regulates banks and other financial institutions
Federal Deposit Insurance Corporation	Regulates and insures banks and other financial institutions
Securities and Exchange Commission	Regulates and requires full disclosure in the securities (stock) markets
Commodity Futures Trading Commission	Regulates trading in futures markets
Product Markets	
Department of Justice, Antitrust Division	Enforces antitrust laws
Federal Communications Commission	Regulates broadcasting and telephone industries
Federal Trade Commission	Focuses efforts on consumer protection, false advertising, and unfair trade practices
Federal Maritime Commission	Regulates international shipping
Interstate Commerce Commission	Regulates railroads, pipelines, trucking, and domestic water transportation
Health and Safety	
Occupational Health and Safety Administration	Regulates health and safety in the workplace
National Highway Traffic Safety Administration	Regulates and sets standards for motor vehicles
Federal Aviation Administration	Regulates air traffic and aviation safety
Food and Drug Administration	Regulates food and drug producers; emphasis on purity, labeling, and product safety
Consumer Product Safety Commission	Regulates product design and labeling to reduce risk of consumer injury
Energy and the Environment	
Environmental Protection Agency	Sets standards for air, water, toxic waste, and noise pollution
Department of Energy	Sets national energy policy
Nuclear Regulatory Commission	Regulates nuclear power plants
Corps of Engineers	Sets policies on construction near rivers, harbors, and waterways
Labor Markets	
Equal Employment Opportunity Commission	Enforces antidiscrimination laws in the workplace
National Labor Relations Board	Enforces rules and regulations governing contract bargaining and labor relations between companies and unions

EXHIBIT 17-3

Selected Federal Regulatory Agencies and Their Missions

The public interest theory of regulation also holds that firms may have to be regulated in order to guarantee that certain goods and services—such as electricity, medical facilities, and telephone service—are available to communities that otherwise would not prove profitable for unregulated firms to enter. Firms providing such goods and services are often granted licenses and franchises that prevent other firms from entering the industry. The regulatory authority allows the firm to set prices above average cost in the protected market in order to cover losses in the target community.

Proponents of the public interest theory also justify regulation of firms by pointing to externalities, such as pollution, that are not taken into consideration when unregulated firms make their decisions. As we saw in Chapter 5, in the absence of property rights that force the firms to consider all of the costs and benefits of their decisions, the market fails to allocate resources efficiently.

The Capture Theory of Regulation

The public interest theory of regulation assumes that regulations serve the interests of consumers by restricting the harmful actions of business firms. That assumption, however, is now widely challenged. Advocates of the capture theory of regulation hold that government regulations, regardless of their original intent, often end up serving the regulated firms rather than their customers.

Competing firms always have an incentive to collude or operate as a cartel. The public is protected from such collusion by a pervasive incentive of firms to cheat. Capture theory asserts that firms seek licensing and other regulatory provisions to prevent other firms from entering the market. Firms seek price regulation to prevent price competition. In this view, the regulators take over the role of policing cartel pricing schemes; individual firms in a cartel would be incapable of doing so themselves.

Because it is practically impossible for the regulatory authorities to have as much information as the firms they are regulating, and because these authorities often rely on information provided by those firms, the firms find ways to get the regulators to enforce regulations that protect profits. The regulators get captured by the very firms they are supposed to be regulating.

The Public Choice Theory of Regulation

The public choice theory of regulation rests on the basic premise that all individuals are driven by self-interest. Public servants in regulatory agencies are no exception. They maximize their own satisfaction, not the public interest. This insight suggests that regulatory agencies seek to expand their bureaucratic structure in order to serve the interests of the bureaucrats. As the people in control of providing government protection from the rigors of the market, bureaucrats respond favorably to lobbyists and special interests. Murray Weidenbaum, Director of the Center for the Study of American Business, argues, for example, that the budget of the Environmental Protection Agency (EPA)

> is more tied to dramatic news events than to public health risks or shortcomings in the marketplace. Thus, EPA spending rises with reports of leaking dump sites. The Coast Guard Budget benefits from oil spills. Food and Drug Administration outlays rise in response to shortcomings in approving generic drugs. The Securities and Exchange Commission grows following insider trading abuses and other Wall Street scandals.[1]

Public choice theory views the regulatory process as one in which various groups jockey to pursue their respective interests. Firms may exploit regulation to limit competition. Consumers may seek lower prices or changes in products. Regulators themselves may pursue their own interests in expanding their prestige or incomes. The abstract goal of economic efficiency is unlikely to serve the interest of any one group; public choice theory does not predict that efficiency will be a goal of the regulatory process. Regulation may improve on inefficient outcomes, but it may not.

Consumer Protection

Every day we come into contact with a seemingly endless array of regulations designed to protect us consumers from unsafe products, unscrupulous sellers, or our own carelessness. Seat belts are mandated in cars and airplanes; drivers must provide proof of liability insurance; deceptive advertising is illegal; firms cannot run "going out of business" sales forever; electrical and plumbing systems in new construction must be inspected and approved; packaged and prepared foods must carry ever-increasing amounts of information on ingredient labels; cigarette packages must warn users of the dangers involved in smoking; doctors must warn their patients about side effects of drugs and prescribed treatments;

[1] Murray Weidenbaum, "The New Wave of Business Regulation," Contemporary Issues Series 40, December 1990 (St. Louis: Center for the Study of American Business, Washington University), p. 3. Reprinted with permission.

gasoline stations must prevent gas spillage and gasoline fume emissions; used car odometers must be certified as accurate. The list of regulations is seemingly endless.

There are very good reasons behind consumer protection regulation, and most economists accept such regulation as a legitimate role and function of government agencies. But there are costs as well as benefits to consumer protection.

The Benefits of Consumer Protection

Consumer protection laws are generally based on one of two conceptual arguments. The first holds that consumers don't always know what's best for them. The second suggests that consumers simply don't have sufficient information to make appropriate choices.

Laws prohibiting the use of certain products are generally based on the presumption that not all consumers make appropriate choices. Drugs such as cocaine and heroin are illegal for this reason. Children are barred from using products such as cigarettes and alcohol on grounds they are incapable of making choices in their own best interest.

Other regulations presume that consumers are rational but hold that people may not have adequate information to make choices. Rather than expect consumers to determine whether a particular prescription drug is safe and effective, for example, federal regulations require the Food and Drug Administration to make that determination for them.

The benefit of consumer protection occurs when consumers are prevented from making choices they'd regret if they had more information. A consumer who purchases a drug that proves ineffective will presumably stop using it. By preventing the purchase in the first place, the government saves the consumer the cost of learning that lesson.

One problem in assessing the benefits of consumer protection is that the laws themselves often induce behavioral changes that work against the intent of the legislation. For example, requirements for greater safety in cars appear to have induced drivers to drive more recklessly. Requirements for child-proof medicine containers appear to have made people more careless with medicines. Requirements that mattresses be flame-resistant appear to have made people more careless about smoking in bed. In some cases, the behavioral changes induced by consumer protection laws may actually worsen the problem the laws seek to correct. In any event, these behavioral changes certainly reduce the benefits achieved by these laws.[2]

The Cost of Consumer Protection

Regulation aimed at protecting consumers may benefit them, but it can also impose costs. It adds to the cost of producing goods and services and thus boosts prices. It restricts the freedom of choice of individuals, some of whom are willing to take more risks than others.

Those who demand, and are willing to pay the price for, high-quality, safe, warranted products can do so. But some argue that people who demand and prefer to pay (presumably) lower prices for lower-quality products that may have risks associated with their use should also be allowed to exercise this preference. By increasing the costs of goods, consumer protection laws may adversely affect

[2] See, for example, Kip Viscusi, "The Lulling Effect: The Impact of Protective Bottlecaps on Aspirin and Analgesic Poisonings," *American Economic Review* 74(2) 1984: 324–327.

Case in Point: Putting Out a Contract on Regulation

Most Republican candidates for the House of Representatives endorsed a "Contract with America" as part of their 1994 campaigns. The contract called for a scaling back of government in general and regulatory effort in particular.

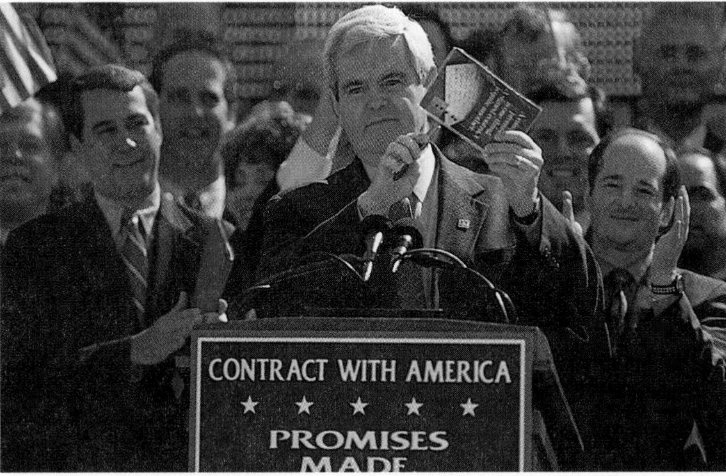

House Speaker Newt Gingrich holding a copy of the Republican party's "Contract with America."

The Republican party's dramatic victory in the 1994 election left it in control of both the House and the Senate—and in a position to implement some of the provisions of the contract. The House quickly passed the contract's regulatory provisions; action by the Senate was pending when *Economics* went to press. The new measures impose a moratorium on new regulation, tighten the requirement for benefit-cost analyses, and impose a compensation requirement for "regulatory takings." The moratorium is of little consequence, but the other changes promise a major shift in the regulatory landscape.

In 1981 the Reagan administration began requiring benefit-cost analyses of all regulations that would impose a cost greater than $100 million; the requirement has remained in effect under the Bush and Clinton administrations. The new provision extends the requirement to regulations with a cost of $25 million.

The most important regulatory change is the provision that property owners be compensated whenever an environmental regulation reduces the value of property by 20 percent or more. The provision is intended to make it harder for agencies to impose restrictions for such efforts as species or wetlands preservation. The Clinton administration has joined environmentalists in opposing the Republican proposal. The measure was still being considered by Congress when this book went to press.

the poor in society, who are forced to purchase higher-quality products; the rich would presumably buy higher-quality products in the first place.

To assess whether a particular piece of consumer protection is desirable requires a careful look at costs as well as benefits. Economists generally recommend that regulations whose cost exceeds their benefits should be dropped.

Deregulating the Economy

Concern that regulation might sometimes fail to serve the public interest prompted a push to deregulate some industries, beginning in the late 1970s and continuing today.

In 1978, for example, Congress passed the Airline Deregulation Act, which removed many of the regulations that had prevented competition in the airline industry. Safety regulations were not affected. The results of deregulation included a substantial reduction in airfares, the merger and consolidation of airlines, and the emergence of frequent flier plans and other marketing schemes designed to increase passenger miles. Not all the results of deregulation were applauded, however. Many airlines, unused to the demands of a competitive, unprotected, and unregulated environment, went bankrupt or were taken over by other airlines. Large airlines abandoned service to small and mid-sized cities. Although most of these routes were picked up by smaller regional airlines, some consumers complained about the lack of adequate service. Nevertheless, the more competitive airline system today is probably an improvement over the highly regulated industry that existed in the 1970s. It is certainly cheaper.

Checklist

- Federal, state, and local governments regulate business practices. The rationale for such regulation is to protect consumers by (1) limiting the exercise of monopoly power and (2) influencing business decisions that affect consumer and worker safety.
- The idea that business regulations serve the public interest is now widely challenged. One school of thought suggests that regulations are imposed because firms seek protection from competitors. Another suggests that bureaucratic interests, not the interests of the public, are served by regulation.
- Consumer protection laws may be necessary, but the added cost of such protection is high. Economists search for the most efficient way to achieve the objective of consumer protection and emphasize market incentives rather than bureaucratic mandates and regulations.

The record of deregulation in other industries has been mixed. Airline and trucking prices have fallen. Banking services have expanded, but deregulation probably contributed to the huge wave of failures of saving and loan institutions and of some banks in the late 1980s and early 1990s. The deregulation of cable television prices in 1984 ushered in a series of very rapid price boosts, which led to the reregulation of the industry in 1992.

Congressional Republicans, who won control of the House and Senate in the 1994 elections, have vowed to expand the deregulation effort, as suggested in the accompanying Case in Point. They seek to cut down on government regulation of private firms.

But there are forces working in the opposite direction as well. Many businesses continue to turn to the government for protection from competition. Public choice theory suggests that more, not less, regulation is often demanded by firms threatened with competition at home and abroad. More and more people seem to demand environmental protection, including clear air, clean water, and regulation of hazardous waste and toxic waste. There is little reason to expect less demand for regulations in the areas of civil rights, handicapped rights, gay rights, medical care, and elderly care.

Perhaps the best economists can hope for is that obsolete regulations will be removed, competition will be encouraged, institutional arrangements will increase the competitiveness of markets, and whenever possible, economic incentives will be used to encourage efficient compliance. If and when it is determined that regulation is appropriate for achieving a desired objective, the government should use the most efficient mechanism possible. The basic test of rationality—that benefits exceed costs—should guide the formulation of regulations.

A Look Back—And a Look Ahead

This chapter has shown that government intervention in markets takes the form of antitrust action to prevent the abuse of market power and regulations aimed at achieving socially desired objectives that are not or cannot be provided by an unregulated market system.

We saw that antitrust policy has evolved from a simplistic view that big business was bad business to a more sophisticated attempt to assess how the behavior of firms and the structure of markets affects social welfare and the public interest. The rule of reason rather than per se illegality guides most antitrust policy today, but because there is considerable debate concerning the appropriate role of government antitrust policy and regulation, application of the rule of reason in specific cases is uneven.

The emergence of a global economy in the last half of the nineteenth century increased the contestability of markets and altered the degree of market power held by domestic firms. Policy makers are reconsidering antitrust policy and what types of joint ventures and cooperation among competing firms should be allowed. Antitrust policy has not been abandoned, but since the early 1980s it has been applied with greater consideration of its implications for the competitiveness of U.S. businesses against Japanese, European, and other multinational firms.

We saw that there are many different schools of thought concerning regulation. One group believes that regulation serves the public interest. Another be-

lieves that much current regulation protects regulated firms from competitive market forces and that the regulators get captured by the firms they are supposed to regulate. Yet another group points out that the regulators may do little more than serve their own interests, which include increasing the bureaucratic reach of their agencies.

Finally, the chapter looked at the complex issues surrounding consumer protection regulations. Consumer protection legislation has costs, borne by consumers and taxpayers. Economists are not in agreement concerning which, if any, consumer protection regulations are warranted. They do agree, however, that market incentives ought to be used when appropriate and that the most cost-effective policies should be pursued.

Chapter 18 turns to an examination of the economics of environmental issues. This is an area in which government regulation is often justified by externality and public goods arguments.

Terms and Concepts for Review

Antitrust policy
Horizontal merger
Illegal per se
Joint ventures
Price-fixing
Regulation
Rule of reason
Tying agreement
Vertical merger

For Discussion

1. Apex Manufacturing charges Zenith Manufacturing with predatory pricing (i.e., selling below cost). What do you think the antitrust authorities will want to consider before they determine whether to prosecute Zenith for unfair practices in restraint of trade?
2. Many states and localities require firms to close on Sunday. What types of firms support these laws? Why? What types of firms do not support these laws? Why?
3. Taxicabs in New York and Chicago must be licensed, but there are only a fixed number of licenses. Who benefits from such a regulation?
4. What do you predict is the impact on workers' wages of safety regulations in the workplace if the labor market is competitive?
5. Many states require barbers and beauticians to be licensed. Using the public interest theory of regulation as a base, what, if any, arguments could you make to support such a regulation? Do you think consumers gain from such regulations? Why not just allow anyone to open up a barber shop or beauty salon?
6. Suppose a landowner is required to refrain from developing his or her land in order to preserve the habitat of an endangered species. The restriction reduces the value of the land by 50 percent, to $1 million. Under present law, the landowner does not have to be compensated. The proposal described in the Case in Point on page 385 would require that this landowner be compensated. How does this affect the cost of the regulation?
7. A study by the Federal Trade Commission compared the prices of legal services in cities that allowed advertising by lawyers to prices of those same services in cities that didn't. It found that the prices of simple wills with trust provisions were 11 percent higher in cities that did not allow advertising than they were in cities that did.[3] This, presumably, suggests the cost of such regulation. What might be the benefits? Do you think that such advertising should be restricted?
8. Economist Kip Viscusi studied the effects of federal regulations that require certain medicines be sold in child-proof containers. He found that such requirements tended to increase the number of deaths from children ingesting these medications. How could this be? (*Hint*: Think in terms of the effect of the requirement on the cost of closing aspirin and other medicines, and then apply the law of demand.)[4]
9. Explain how licensing requirements for providers of particular services result in higher prices for such services. Are such requirements justified? Why or why not.
10. What's so bad about price fixing? Why does the government prohibit it?

[3] See Carolyn Cox and Susan Foster, "The Costs and Benefits of Occupational Regulation," Federal Trade Commission, October 1990, p. 31.

[4] Viscusi, *op. cit.* (see footnote 2).

18

The Economics of Pollution

Chapter Objectives

After mastering the material in this chapter, you will be able to:

1. Explain the nature of the benefits and costs associated with pollution.
2. Describe the approaches economists use to determine the efficient level of a particular type of pollution.
3. Summarize the issues involved in choosing between pollution control strategies based on market incentives versus those based on direct controls or on persuasion.
4. Review briefly the major accomplishments and shortcomings of public sector efforts to deal with the problems of air and water pollution and the dumping of solid wastes.

The twenty-first century is going to be about using markets to solve social and environmental problems.
Richard L. Sandor, Economist

What's Ahead

Wisconsin Power and Light, a Madison utility company, wrote a new page in the history of environmental policy in 1992 when it sold rights to dump 15,000 tons of airborne sulfur dioxide to Duquesne Light, a Pittsburgh utility.

Federal legislation passed in 1990 set tough new standards for the dumping of sulfur dioxide, a pollutant associated with acid rain. The standards, which went into effect in 1995, impose ceilings specifying the maximum quantity of sulfur dioxide each utility can dump per year. Utilities that dump less than that quantity are permitted to sell rights to other firms, which can then dump more. Duquesne Light calculated that it would be cheaper for it to buy additional rights than to cut its emissions further. Wisconsin Power and Light, for its part, had an aggressive program in place to cut its emissions well below its ceiling; it could boost its profits by selling some of its rights.

Wisconsin Power and Light's sale was the first under the new program. Today, rights to dump sulfur dioxide are traded at the Chicago Board of Trade, where commodities such as pork bellies and gold are exchanged. The effort represents a major new thrust in environmental policy—the use of markets to solve environmental problems.

The development of a market for pollution rights puts market forces to work in an effort to reduce the problem of acid rain. A much broader program of pollution rights exchanges is being introduced in Southern California. Indeed, we'll find that pollution control policy is beginning to unleash market forces to solve a wide range of pollution problems.

In this chapter we shall put the analytical tools we've already developed to work on the problems of air and water pollution. We'll look particularly at alternative regulatory approaches to such problems. Direct controls, in which government agencies tell polluters what they must do to reduce pollution, remain the primary means of government regulation. Persuasion, seeking voluntary compliance with pollution reduction efforts, is also used. Two alternatives that economists advocate are taxes imposed on pollutants and marketable pollution rights; such systems are gaining in importance.

We all pollute the environment. We do so not because we get some perverse satisfaction from polluting, but because by polluting we can produce other activities that give us utility. We do not drive our cars in order to dump carbon monoxide into the air but because we gain utility from the transportation and convenience cars provide. Firms pollute the environment if doing so allows them to produce goods and services at lower cost.

The benefits we derive from pollution are indirect. We obtain them from the other activities that generate pollution. But that's not unusual—there are lots of things we do because of the other benefits they produce. Firms benefit from hiring labor not because their owners enjoy hiring workers but because those workers produce greater profits. We purchase electricity not because we enjoy the feeling of having the stuff racing through wires in the house but because the electricity produces light, heat, and other services more cheaply than would alternatives such as candles or fires. We pollute in the process of obtaining more of other goods and services we enjoy. We thus benefit from our pollution.

Of course, we suffer from our pollution as well. Smog-choked air robs us of views and damages our health. We may not be able to fish or swim in polluted rivers. Just as the generation of pollution makes many of the activities we pursue less expensive, the fact that we have pollution increases many costs. Polluted rivers increase the cost of producing drinking water. Polluted air requires us to paint our buildings more often and to spend more on health care. Polluted soils produce less food.

Like any other activity, then, pollution has benefits as well as costs. The difficulty in pollution problems is that decisionmakers experience the benefits of their own choices to pollute the environment, but the costs spill over to everyone who breathes the air or consumes the water. The environment presents us with an allocation problem in which decisionmakers aren't faced with all the benefits and costs of their choices. Environmental resources will not, in such cases, be allocated efficiently. Economists who examine and analyze environmental problems try to determine what an efficient allocation of the environment would most likely be—one that maximizes the difference between the benefits and costs of our pollution.

A second task of environmental economics is to find ways to get from where we are, which typically is far more pollution than would be efficient, to the efficient solution. We learned in Chapter 5 that private markets often fail to achieve efficient solutions to environmental problems because property rights are difficult to define and to exchange. We'll see, however, that environmental economists have devised innovative ways to introduce property rights to environmental policy and to harness market forces to improve rather than degrade environmental quality.

Maximizing the Net Benefits of Pollution

Pollution exists whenever human activity generates a sufficient concentration of a substance in the environment to cause harm to people or to resources valued by people. Many potentially harmful substances are natural features of the environment, but they are not generally regarded as pollutants. Pollutants are the products of people, not nature.

Pollution exists when human activity produces a sufficient concentration of a substance in the environment to cause harm to people or to resources valued by people.

Pollution implies scarcity. If an activity emits harmless by-products into the environment, then the emission of the by-products isn't an alternative to some other activity. A scarcity problem exists at the point where harm occurs. A campfire in the wilderness whose smoke goes unnoticed doesn't suggest a scarcity problem. But when there are enough campfires generating smoke, or other campers who will be harmed by the smoke, then one person's enjoyment of a campfire becomes an alternative to another person's enjoyment of fresh air. Fresh air has become scarce, and pollution has become an economic problem.

What about pollution that harms plants or animals? Economists generally argue that such pollution imposes a cost *if* the plants or animals are valued by people. When a farmer uses a pesticide that damages another farmer's crop, for example, a pollution problem occurs. If an oil spill in the ocean damages sea animals that people care about, there is a pollution problem. It is, after all, people who make the choices that lead to pollution. It is people who can choose to limit their pollution. Economists therefore examine pollution problems from the perspective of the preferences of people.

The Efficient Level of Pollution

Pollution has benefits as well as costs. The efficient level of pollution is the quantity at which its total benefits exceed its total costs by the greatest possible amount. This occurs where the marginal benefit of an additional unit of pollution equals its marginal cost.

Exhibit 18-1 shows how we can determine an efficient quantity of pollution. Suppose two individuals, Mary and John, generate air pollution that harms two other individuals, Sarah and Richard, who live downwind. We shall assume that Mary and John are the only polluters and that Sarah and Richard are the only people harmed by the pollution.

Mary's and John's demand curves for pollution are shown in Panel (a). These demand curves, D_M and D_J, show the quantities of emissions each generates at each possible price. At a price of $13 per unit, for example, Mary will emit 20 units of pollutant per period, and John will emit 14. Total emissions at a price of $13 would be 34 units per period. If the price of emissions were zero, total emissions would be 60 units per period. Whatever the price they face, Mary and John will emit additional units of the pollutant up to the point that their marginal benefit equals that price. We may therefore interpret their demand curves as their marginal benefit curves for emissions. Their combined demand curve D_T gives the marginal benefit to society (that is, to Mary and John) of pollution.

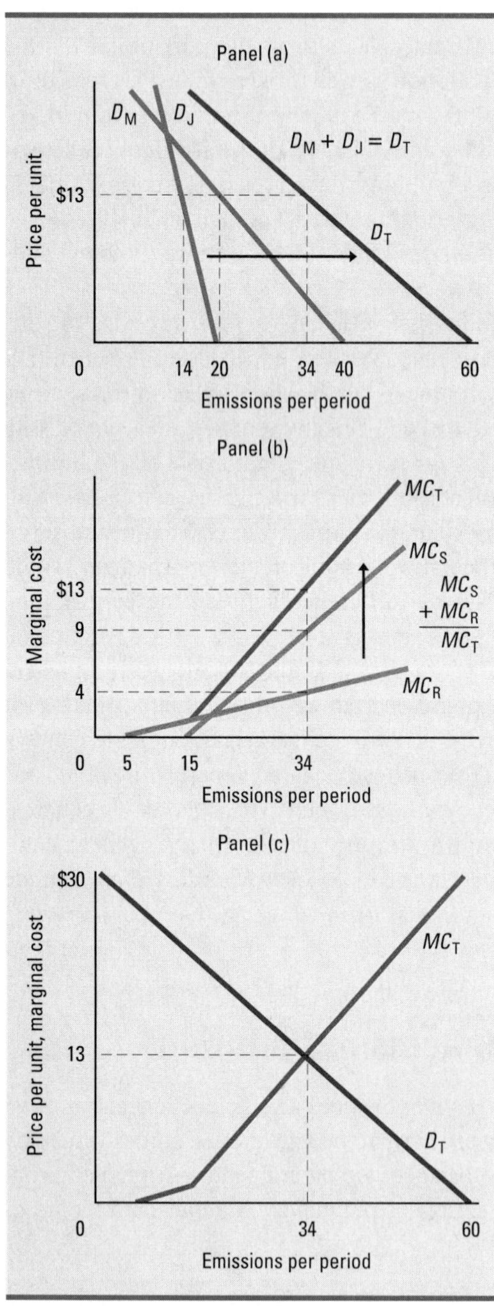

EXHIBIT 18-1

Determining the Efficient Level of Pollution

In Panel (a), we add the demand curves for emissions for Mary (D_M) and John (D_J) to get the total demand D_T for emitting the pollutant. At a price of $13 per unit, the quantity of emissions per period equals 34; at a price of zero, it is 60. In Panel (b), we see the effects of the pollution on Sarah and Richard; we add their marginal cost curves MC_S and MC_R vertically to obtain total marginal cost MC_T. The curves for total demand and total marginal cost are shown in Panel (c); the efficient solution is 34 units of pollutant emitted per period.

In Panel (b) we see how much Sarah and Richard are harmed; the marginal cost curves MC_S and MC_R show their respective valuations of the harm imposed on them by each additional unit of emissions. Notice that over a limited range, some emissions generate no harm. At very low levels, neither Sarah nor Richard are even aware of the emissions. Richard begins to experience harm as the quantity of emissions goes above 5; it is here that pollution begins to occur. As emissions increase, the additional harm each unit creates becomes larger and larger—the marginal cost curves are upward-sloping. The first traces of pollution may be only a minor inconvenience, but as pollution goes up, the problems it creates become more serious—and its marginal cost rises.

Because the same emissions affect both Sarah and Richard, we add their marginal cost curves vertically to obtain their combined marginal cost curve MC_T. The 34th unit of emissions, for example, imposes an additional cost of $9 on Sarah and $4 on Richard. It thus imposes a total marginal cost of $13.

The efficient quantity of emissions is found at the intersection of the demand (D_T) and marginal cost (MC_T) curves in Panel (c) of Exhibit 18-1, with 34 units of the pollutant emitted. The marginal benefit of the 34th unit of emissions, as measured by the demand curve D_T, equals its marginal cost MC_T. The solution at which marginal benefit equals marginal cost maximizes the net benefit of an activity.

Suppose no mechanism exists to charge Mary and John for their emissions; they face a price of zero and emit 60 units of pollutant per period. The marginal benefit of the 60th unit of pollution equals zero. We see in Panel (c), however, that the 60th unit of pollutant imposes a high cost on Sarah and Richard. It is clearly inefficient. Indeed, as long as the marginal cost of an additional unit of pollution exceeds its marginal benefit, as measured by the demand curve, there is too much pollution; the net benefit of emissions would be greater with a lower level of the activity.

Just as too much pollution is inefficient, so is too little. Suppose Mary and John aren't allowed to pollute; emissions equal zero. We see in Panel (c) that the marginal benefit of dumping the first unit of pollution is quite high; the marginal cost it imposes on Sarah and Richard is zero. Because the benefit of additional pollution exceeds its cost, the net benefit to society would be increased by increasing the level of pollution. That's true at any level of pollution below 34 units, the efficient solution.

The notion that too little pollution could be inefficient may strike you as strange. To see the logic of this idea, imagine that the pollutant involved is carbon monoxide, a pollutant emitted whenever combustion occurs. It is, for example, emitted when you drive a car. Now suppose that no emissions of carbon monoxide are allowed. Among other things, this would require a ban on driving. Surely the benefits of some driving would exceed the cost of the pollution created. The problem in pollution policy is to find the quantity of pollution at which total benefits exceed total costs by the greatest possible amount—the solution at which marginal benefit equals marginal cost.

The Measurement of Benefits and Costs

Saying that the efficient level of pollution occurs at a certain rate of emissions, as we have done so far, is one thing. Determining the actual positions of the demand and marginal cost curves that define that efficient solution is quite another. Economists have devised a variety of methods for measuring these curves.

Benefits: The Demand for Dumping

A demand curve for emitting pollutants shows the quantity of emissions at each price. It can, as we've seen, be taken as a marginal benefit curve for emitting pollutants.

The general approach to estimating demand curves involves observing quantities demanded at various prices, together with the values of other determinants of demand. In most pollution problems, however, the price charged for emitting pollutants has always been zero—we simply don't know how the quantity of emissions demanded will vary with price.

One approach to estimating the demand curve for pollution utilizes the fact that this demand occurs because pollution makes other activities cheaper. If we know how much the emission of 1 more unit of a pollutant saves, then we can infer how much consumers or firms would pay to dump it.

Suppose, for example, that there is no program to control automobile emissions—motorists face a price of zero for each unit of pollution their cars emit. Suppose that a particular motorist's car emits an average of 10 pounds of carbon monoxide per week. Its owner could reduce emissions to 9 pounds per week at a cost of $1. This $1 is the marginal cost of reducing emissions from 10 to 9 pounds per week. It's also the price the motorist would pay to increase emissions from 9 to 10 pounds per week—it's the marginal benefit of the 10th pound of pollution.

Now suppose that emissions have been reduced to 9 pounds per week and that the motorist could reduce them to 8 at an additional cost of $3 per week. The marginal cost of reducing emissions from 9 to 8 pounds per week is $3. Alternatively, this is the price the motorist would be willing to pay to increase emissions from 8 to 9 pounds; it is the marginal benefit of the 9th pound of pollution.

We can thus think of the marginal benefit of an additional unit of pollution as the added cost of not emitting it. It is the saving a polluter enjoys by dumping additional pollution rather than going to the cost of preventing its emission. Exhibit 18-2 shows this dual interpretation of cost and benefit. Initially, our motorist emits 10 pounds of carbon monoxide per week. Reading from right to left, the curve measures the marginal costs of pollution abatement (MC_A). We see that the marginal cost of abatement rises as emissions are reduced. That makes sense; the first reductions in emissions will be achieved through relatively sim-

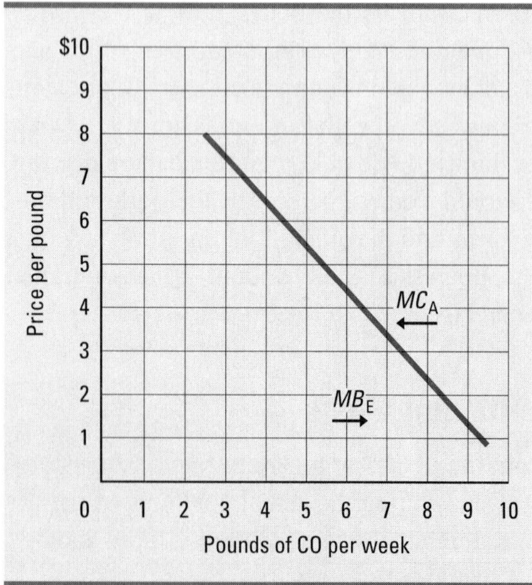

EXHIBIT 18-2

Abatement Costs and Demand

A car emits an average of 10 pounds of carbon monoxide per week when no restrictions are imposed—when the price of emissions is zero. The marginal cost of abatement (MC_A) is the cost of eliminating a unit of emissions. The same curve can be read from left to right as the marginal benefit of emissions (MB_E).

ple measures such as getting more frequent tune-ups. Further reductions, however, might require burning more expensive fuels or installing more expensive pollution control equipment.

Read from left to right, the curve in Exhibit 18-2 shows the marginal benefit of additional emissions (MB_E). Its negative slope suggests that the first units of pollution emitted have very high marginal benefits, because the cost of not emitting them would be very high. As more of a pollutant is emitted, however, its marginal benefit falls—the cost of preventing these units of pollution becomes quite low.

Economists have also measured demand curves for emissions by using surveys in which polluters are asked to report the costs to them of reducing their emissions. In cases in which polluters are charged for the emissions they create, the marginal benefit curve can be observed directly.

As we saw in Exhibit 18-1, the marginal benefit curves of individual polluters are added horizontally to obtain a market demand curve for pollution. This curve measures the additional benefit to society of each additional unit of pollution.

The Marginal Cost of Emissions

Pollutants harm people and the resources they value. The marginal cost curve for a pollutant shows the additional cost imposed by each unit of the pollutant. As we saw in Exhibit 18-1, the marginal cost curves for all the individuals harmed by a particular pollutant are added vertically to obtain the marginal cost curve for the pollutant.

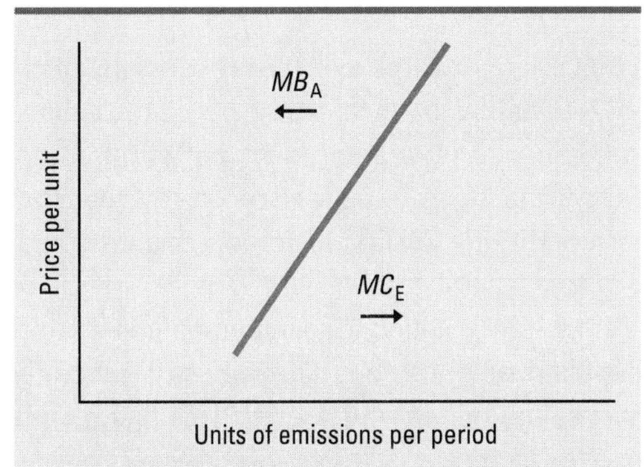

EXHIBIT 18-3

The Marginal Cost of Emissions

The marginal cost curve for emissions (MC_E) is found by adding individual marginal cost curves vertically. It can be read from right to left as the marginal benefit curve for obtaining emissions (MB_A), or the demand curve for cleaner air.

Like the marginal benefit curve for emissions, the marginal cost curve can be interpreted in two ways, as suggested in Exhibit 18-3. Read from left to right, the curve measures the marginal cost of additional units of emissions (MC_E). If one more unit of pollutant imposes a cost of $1,000, though, the marginal benefit of not being exposed to that unit of pollutant must have a marginal benefit of $1,000. The marginal cost curve can thus be read from right to left as a marginal benefit curve for abating emissions (MB_A). This marginal benefit curve is, in effect, the demand curve for cleaner air.

Economists estimate the marginal cost curve of pollution in several ways. One is to infer it from the demand for goods for which environmental quality is a complement. Another is to survey people, asking them what pollution costs—or what they would pay to reduce it. Still another is to determine the costs of damages created by pollution directly.

Environmental quality is a complement of housing. The demand for houses in areas with cleaner air is greater than the demand for houses in areas that are more polluted. By observing the relationship between house prices and air quality, economists can learn the value people place on cleaner air—and thus the cost of dirtier air. Studies have been conducted in cities all over the United States to determine the relationship between air quality and house prices so that a measure of the demand for cleaner air can be made. They show that increased pollution levels result in lower house values.[1]

Surveys are also used to assess the marginal cost of emissions. The fact that the marginal cost of an additional unit of emissions is the marginal benefit of avoiding the emissions suggests that surveys can be designed in two ways.

[1] For a summary of studies of house values and pollution levels, see Barry C. Field, *Environmental Economics* (New York: McGraw Hill, 1994).

Respondents can be asked how much they would be harmed by an increase in emissions, or they can be asked what they would pay for a reduction in emissions. Economists often use both kinds of questions in surveys designed to determine marginal costs.

A third kind of cost estimate is based on objects damaged by pollution. Increases in pollution, for example, require buildings to be painted more often; the increased cost of painting is one measure of the cost of added pollution. In a study of the effects of air pollutants on agriculture in the Ohio River basin, it was found that air pollution in the region would destroy about $7 billion worth of soybeans, wheat, and corn during the final quarter of this century.[2]

Checklist

- Pollution is related to the concept of scarcity. The existence of pollution implies that an environmental resource has alternative uses.
- Pollution has benefits as well as costs; the emission of pollutants benefits people by allowing other activities to be pursued at lower costs.
- The efficient rate of emissions occurs where the marginal benefit of additional emissions equals the marginal cost they impose.
- The marginal benefit curve for emitting pollutants can also be read from right to left as the marginal cost of abating pollution. The marginal cost curve for increased pollution levels can also be read from right to left as the demand curve for improved environmental quality, a public good.
- Surveys are sometimes used to measure the marginal benefit curves for emissions and the marginal cost curves for increased pollution levels.
- Marginal cost curves may also be inferred from other relationships. Two that are commonly used are the demand for houses and the relationship between pollution and production.

Alternatives in Pollution Control

Suppose that the present level of emissions exceeds the efficient level and that the goal of public policy is to reduce the level of emissions. Three types of policy alternatives could be applied. The first is persuasion—people can be exhorted to reduce their emissions. The second relies on direct controls, and the third uses incentives to induce reductions in emissions.

Moral Suasion

Smokey the Bear asks us to be careful with fire. Signs everywhere remind us not to litter. Some communities have mounted campaigns that admonish us to "Give a hoot—don't pollute."

These efforts to influence our choices are examples of **moral suasion,** an effort to change people's behavior by appealing to their sense of moral values. Moral suasion is widely used as a tactic in attempting to reduce pollution. Many cities, for example, ask that people refrain from unnecessary driving or from using their fireplaces when weather conditions are likely to contribute to high levels of pollution.

Moral suasion is an effort to change people's behavior by appealing to their sense of moral values.

Moral suasion appears to have been fairly successful in campaigns against littering, which can be considered a kind of pollution. They are not generally successful in reducing activities that pollute the air and water. Pleas that people refrain from driving on certain days, for example, achieve virtually no compliance.

Moral suasion appears to be most effective in altering behaviors that are not already widespread and for which the cost of compliance is low. It's easy to be careful with one's fires or to avoid littering. Most people probably refrain from littering or from being careless with fires even in the absence of campaigns asking them to do so.

Moral suasion does not, however, appear to lead to significant changes in behavior when compliance costs are high or when the activity is already widely practiced. It is therefore not likely to be an effective tool for reducing most forms of pollution.[3]

[2] Walter P. Page et al., "Estimation of Economic Losses to the Agricultural Sector from Airborne Residuals in the Ohio River Basin," *Journal of the Air Pollution Control Association* 32(2) (February 1982): 151–154.

[3] In the author's hometown, a citizen's group has a vigorous campaign discouraging driving and fireplace burning on days pollution is likely to be high. Surveys taken on such days suggest no significant changes in driving and roughly a 15 percent reduction in fireplace burning.

Command and Control

In the most widely used regulatory approach to environmental pollution, a government agency tells a polluting agent how much pollution it can emit or requires the agent to use a particular production method aimed at reducing emissions. This method, in which the government agency tells a firm how much or by what method it must adjust its emissions, is called the **command-and-control approach.**

In the United States, pollution control agencies issue regulations specifying how polluting agents must alter their behavior. In many areas, car owners are required to show that their cars emit less than a certain quantity of pollutants per mile driven. Firms that dump pollutants are told to reduce their emissions to a specific level.

Economists are generally critical of the command-and-control approach for two reasons. First, it achieves a given level of emissions reduction at an unnecessarily high cost. Second, it gives polluters no incentive to explore technological and other changes that might reduce the demand for emissions.

Suppose two firms, A and B, each dump 500 tons of a certain pollutant per month, and that the price for their emissions equals zero. Total emissions for the two firms thus equal 1,000 tons per month. The EPA decides to cut this in half and orders each firm to reduce its emissions to 250 tons per month, for a total reduction of 500 tons. This is a command-and-control regulation because it specifies the amount of reduction each firm must make. Although it may seem fair to require equal reductions by the two firms, this approach is likely to generate excessive costs.

Suppose that Firm A is quite old and that the reduction in emissions to 250 tons per period would be extremely costly. Suppose that removing the 251st ton costs this firm $1,000 per month. Put another way, the marginal benefit to Firm A of emitting the 251st ton would be $1,000.

Suppose Firm B, a much newer firm, already has some pollution control equipment in place. Reducing its emissions to 250 tons imposes a cost, but a much lower cost than to Firm A. Indeed, suppose Firm B could reduce its emissions to 249 tons at an additional cost of $100; the marginal benefit to firm B of emitting the 250th ton is $100.

If two firms have different marginal benefits of emissions, the allocation of resources is inefficient. The same level of emissions could be achieved at a lower cost. Suppose, for example, Firm A is permitted to increase its emissions to 251 tons while Firm B reduces emissions to 249. Firm A saves $1,000, while the cost to Firm B is just $100. Society achieves a net gain of $900, and the level of emissions remains at 500 tons per month.

As long as Firm A's marginal benefit of emissions exceeds Firm B's, a saving is realized by shifting emissions from B to A. At the point at which their marginal benefits are equal, no further reduction in the cost of achieving a given level of emissions is possible, and the allocation of emissions is efficient. When a given reduction in emissions is achieved so that the marginal benefit of an additional unit of emissions is the same for all polluters, it is a **least-cost reduction in emissions.** A command-and-control approach is unlikely to achieve a least-cost reduction in emissions.

How inefficient are command-and-control regulations? Exhibit 18-4 compares the costs of regulating air pollution using existing command-and-control methods to the least-cost way of achieving the same air quality. The ratio of 6 for

- In the **command-and-control approach,** a government agency specifies how much or by what method a polluting agent must adjust its emissions.
- A **least-cost reduction in emissions** is one in which emissions are reduced so that the marginal benefit of an additional unit of pollution is the same for all polluters.

Pollution Problem	Ratio of CAC Cost to Least Cost
Particulates, St. Louis, 1974	6.00
Sulfur dioxide, Four Corners region (Utah, Colorado, Arizona, and New Mexico), 1981	4.25
Sulfates, Los Angeles, 1982	1.07
Nitrogen oxide, Baltimore, 1983	5.96
Sulfur dioxide, Delaware Valley, 1984	1.78
Particulates, Delaware Valley, 1984	22.00
Hydrocarbons, Du Pont plants, 1984	4.15
Chlorofluorocarbon (CFC) emissions, U.S. (nonaerosol), 1980	1.96

Source: Thomas H. Tietenberg, *Emissions Trading: An Exercise in Reforming Pollution Control* (Washington, D.C.: Resources for the Future, 1985), pp. 42–43. ©1985 Resources for the Future.

EXHIBIT 18-4

Comparison of Pollution Control Costs: Command-and-Control Versus Least-Cost Programs

The table shows ratios of the cost of various command-and-control (CAC) regulatory programs to estimates of the lowest cost of achieving the same goals.

St. Louis's program of reducing airborne particulate matter, for example, means that the command-and-control approach achieved its goal for a cost *6 times* greater than the lowest-cost solution. In only one case studied, sulfate reduction in Los Angeles, is the command-and-control approach close to achieving its goals in an efficient way; that's because marginal abatement costs were similar for various sources.

The inefficiency of command-and-control regulation is important for two reasons. First, of course, it wastes scarce resources. If the same level of air or water quality could be achieved at a far lower cost, then surely it makes sense to use the cheaper method. Perhaps even more significant, reliance on command-and-control regulation makes environmental quality far more expensive than it needs to be—and that's likely to result in an unwillingness to achieve the improvements that would be economically efficient.

Incentive Approaches

Markets allocate resources efficiently when the price system confronts decisionmakers with the costs and benefits of their decisions. Prices create incentives—they give producers an incentive to produce more and consumers an incentive to economize. Regulatory efforts that seek to create market-like incentives to encourage reductions in pollution, but that allow individual decisionmakers to determine how much to pollute, are called **incentive approaches.**

An **incentive approach** to pollution regulation creates market-like incentives to encourage reductions in pollution but allows individual decisionmakers to decide how much to pollute.

Emissions Taxes

One incentive approach to pollution control relies on taxes. If a tax is imposed on each unit of emissions, polluters will reduce their emissions until the marginal benefit of emissions equals the tax, and a least-cost reduction in emissions is achieved.

Emissions taxes are widely used in Europe. France, for example, has enacted taxes on the sulfur dioxide and nitrous oxide emissions of power plants and other industrial firms. Spain has recently imposed taxes on the dumping of pollutants into the country's waterways. Emissions taxes have long been imposed on firms that dump pollutants into some river systems in Europe. Such taxes have not been widely used in the United States. President Richard Nixon proposed an emissions tax on U.S. utilities of 10 cents per pound of sulfur dioxide, but the proposal was rejected by Congress in 1972.

An emissions tax requires, of course, that a polluter's emissions be monitored. The polluter is then charged a tax equal to the tax per unit times the quantity of emissions. The tax clearly gives the polluter an incentive to reduce emissions. It also ensures that reductions will be accomplished by those polluters that can achieve them at the lowest cost. Polluters for whom reductions are most costly will generally find it cheaper to pay the emissions tax.

In cases where it is difficult to monitor emissions, a tax could be imposed indirectly. Consider, for example, farmers' use of fertilizers and pesticides. Rain may wash some of these materials into local rivers, polluting the water. Clearly, it would be virtually impossible to monitor this runoff and assess responsible farmers a charge for their emissions. But it would be possible to levy a tax on these materials when they are sold, confronting farmers with a rough measure of the cost of the pollution their use of these materials imposes.

Case in Point: Incentives to Reduce Global Warming

Some gases, when emitted into the atmosphere, trap heat energy from the sun, thus warming the earth. Carbon dioxide, the most important of these so-called greenhouse gases, is a by-product of the combustion of fossil fuels.

Some scientists believe that increasing emissions of carbon dioxide will trap more of the sun's energy and make the planet warmer. The results, they say, could include flooding of coastal areas, losses in agricultural production, and the elimination of many species. If this global warming hypothesis is correct, then carbon dioxide is a pollutant with global implications, one that calls for a global solution. The United Nations Conference on Development and the Environment called in 1992 for a reduction in carbon dioxide emissions by the year 2000 to the 1990 level. The Clinton administration has endorsed this proposal.

Rain forests such as this one in Costa Rica are among the areas being protected by new economic incentives.

Economists Dale W. Jorgenson of Harvard University and Daniel T. Slesnick and Peter J. Wilcoxen of the University of Texas at Austin have estimated that a $2 per ton tax on the carbon content of fossil fuels would achieve the required reduction. They note, however, that as demand increases over time, higher taxes will be necessary to hold the dumping of carbon dioxide at the 1990 level. By 2020, for example, the required tax would be $17.65 per ton (in 1990 dollars). Such a tax would boost the price of coal by 40 percent and thus raise the price of electricity, which is generated from coal, by 5.6 percent. The prices of other fossil fuels would rise much less; gasoline, fuel oil, and natural gas would cost about 2 percent more.

Another alternative would be to issue carbon emissions rights that could be traded internationally. Such a system could exploit an important feature of carbon. Trees remove carbon from the atmosphere; the world's forests thus act to prevent global warming. Under a system of carbon rights, countries that preserve their forests could be given carbon credits. These credits would be valuable, so countries would have a greater incentive to preserve forests. Discussions of global rights exchange in carbon emissions are under way as part of the ongoing effort to address the concerns raised by the global warming hypothesis.

Source: Dale W. Jorgenson, Daniel T. Slesnick, and Peter J. Wilcoxen, "Carbon Taxes and Economic Welfare," *Brookings Papers on Economic Activity,* (Microeconomics, 1992): 393–341.

Marketable Pollution Permits

An alternative to emissions taxes is marketable pollution permits, which allow their owners to emit a certain quantity of pollution during a particular period. The introduction to this chapter dealt with an example of marketable pollution permits; each of the permits that Duquesne Light purchased from Wisconsin Power and Light allowed the owner to dump 1 ton of sulfur dioxide per year.

To see how this works, suppose that firms A and B are again told that they must reduce their emissions to 250 tons per month. This time, however, they are given 250 permits each—1 permit allows the emission of 1 ton per month. They can trade their permits; a firm that emits less than its allotted 250 tons can sell some of its permits to another firm that wants to emit more.

We saw that firm B can reduce its emissions below 250 tons for a much lower cost than firm A. For example, it could reduce its emissions to 249 tons for $100. Firm A would be willing to pay $1,000 for the right to emit the 251st ton of emissions. Clearly, a mutually profitable exchange is possible. In fact, as long as their marginal benefits of pollution differ, the firms can profit from exchange. Equilibrium will be achieved at the least-cost solution at which the marginal benefits for both firms are equal.

Wisconsin Power and Light sold rights to dump 15,000 tons of sulfur dioxide to Duquesne Light, applying the concept of marketable pollution permits. The sulfur dioxide emitted from coal-burning power plants is thought to be a major cause of acid rain. The EPA regards acid rain as an international problem and a reduction in sulfur dioxide emissions as a national goal, hence its willingness to allow emissions rights to be traded across state lines.

One virtue of using marketable permits is that this approach represents only a modest departure from traditional command-and-control regulation. Once a polluter has been told to reduce its emissions to a certain quantity, it has a right to emit that quantity. Polluters will exchange rights only if doing so increases their utility or profits—allowing rights to be exchanged can only make them better off. The greatest benefit, of course, is that such exchanges allow a shift from the inefficient allocation created by command-and-control regulation to an efficient allocation in which pollution is reduced at the lowest possible cost.

Merits of Incentive Approaches

Incentive systems, either emissions taxes or tradable permits, can achieve reductions in emissions at a far lower cost than command-and-control regulation. Even more important, however, are the long-run incentives they create for technological change. A firm that is ordered to reduce its emissions to a certain level has no incentive to do better, whereas a firm facing an emissions tax has a constant incentive to seek out new ways to lower its emissions and thus lower its taxes. Similarly, a firm faces a cost for using an emissions permit—the price that could be obtained from selling the permit—so it will seek ways to reduce emissions. As firms discover new ways to lower their costs of reducing emissions, the demand for emissions permits will fall, lowering the efficient quantity of emissions—and improving environmental quality even further.

Checklist

- Public sector intervention is generally needed to move the economy toward the efficient solution in pollution problems.
- Command-and-control approaches are the most widely used methods of public sector intervention, but they are inefficient.
- The exchange of pollution rights can achieve a given reduction in emissions at the lowest cost possible. It also creates incentives to reduce pollution demand through technological change. Tax policy can also achieve a least-cost reduction in emissions.
- Pollution control policy in the United States has achieved gains in air quality, but water quality has shown little improvement.
- Public policy has stressed command-and-control regulation; however, it is beginning to shift to incentive approaches, especially to systems of marketable pollution permits.

Public Policy and Pollution: The Record

Federal efforts to control air and water pollution in the United States have produced mixed results. Air quality has generally improved; water quality has improved in some respects but deteriorated in other ways.

Exhibit 18-5 shows how annual average concentrations of airborne pollutants in major U.S. cities have declined since 1975. Lead concentrations have dropped most dramatically, largely because of the increased use of unleaded gasoline.

Public policy has generally stressed command-and-control approaches to air and water pollution. To reduce air pollution, the EPA sets air quality standards that regions must achieve, then tells polluters what adjustments they must make in order to meet the standards. For water pollution, the EPA has set emissions limits based on the technologies it considers reasonable to require of polluters. If the implementation of a particular technology will reduce a polluter's emissions by 20 percent, for example, the EPA will require a 20 percent reduction in emissions. National standards have been imposed; no effort has been made to consider the benefits and costs of pollution in individual streams. Further, the EPA's technology-based approach pays little attention to actual water quality—and

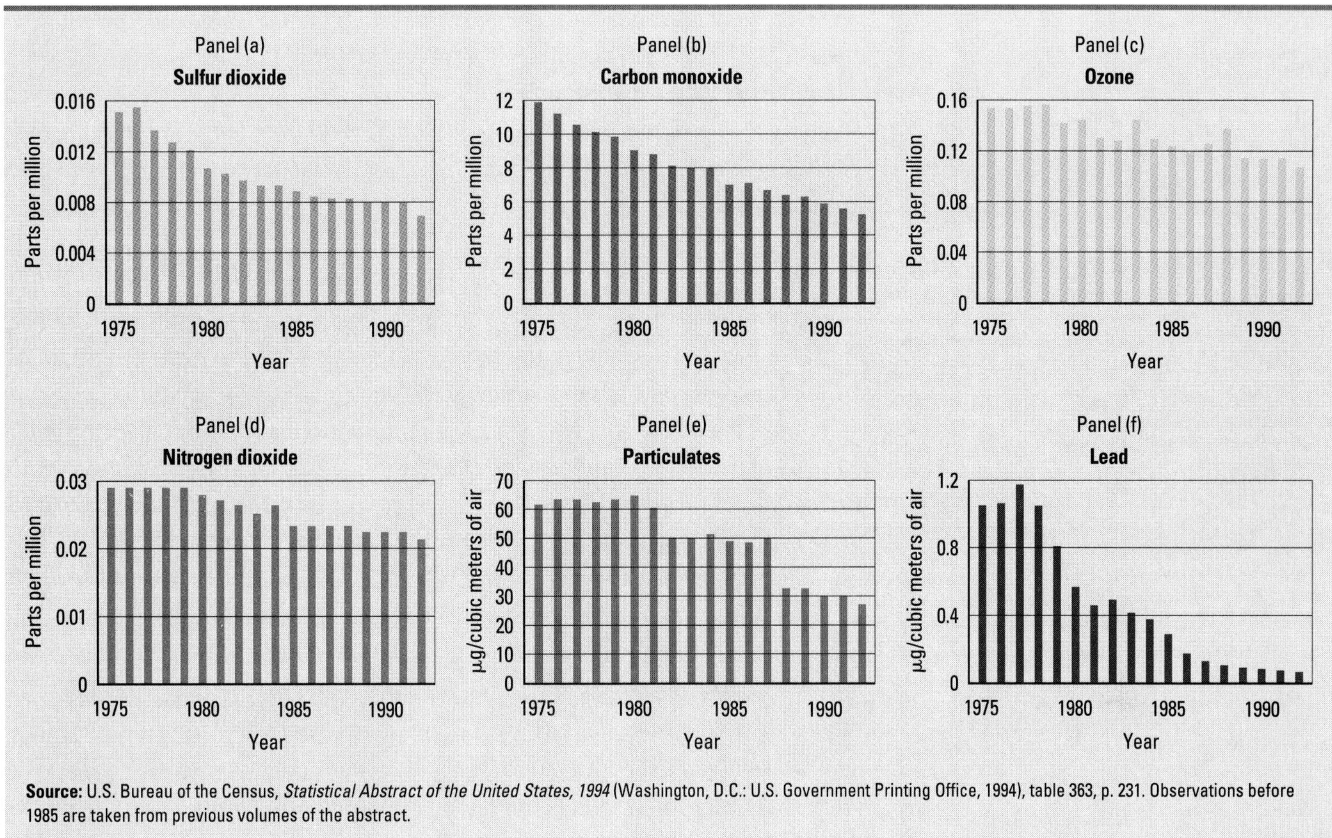

Source: U.S. Bureau of the Census, *Statistical Abstract of the United States, 1994* (Washington, D.C.: U.S. Government Printing Office, 1994), table 363, p. 231. Observations before 1985 are taken from previous volumes of the abstract.

EXHIBIT 18-5

Progress Against Pollution

Panels (a) through (f) give average concentration levels of major pollutants in U.S. cities from 1975 to 1992. Levels have generally fallen over that period.

has produced few gains. A survey of U.S. streams showed virtually no improvement in water quality from 1978 to 1987.[4]

The conventional command-and-control approach to pollution has produced some gains, but at enormous cost. Economists have demonstrated convincingly that incentive approaches would be far superior, and their work has begun to affect policy. Some states have introduced pollution rights exchange along local waterways. We've already noted the EPA's creation of a market in rights to emit sulfur dioxide. Southern California is beginning to introduce opportunities to exchange pollution rights.

These changes in the approach to regulation of environmental pollution demonstrate the power of economic analysis. As pollution control authorities replace command-and-control strategies with incentive approaches, society will reap huge savings. In the long run, we will enjoy a much cleaner environment.

A Look Back—And a Look Ahead

Pollution is a by-product of human activity. It occurs when the environment becomes scarce—when dumping garbage imposes a cost. There are benefits as well as costs to pollution; the efficient quantity of pollution occurs where the difference between total benefits and costs is maximized. This solution is also

[4] Dennis P. Lettenmaier, Eric R. Hooper, Colin Wagoner, and Kathleen B. Faris, "Trends in Stream Water Quality in the Continental United States, 1978–1987," *Water Resources Research* 27(3) (March 1991): 327–339.

achieved where the marginal benefit of additional pollution equals the marginal cost.

Economists measure the benefits of pollution in terms of the costs of not dumping the pollution. The same curve can be read from left to right as the marginal benefit curve for emissions and from right to left as the marginal cost curve for abatement.

The costs of pollution are measured in two ways. One is through direct surveys. Respondents can be asked how much compensation they would be willing to accept in exchange for a reduction in environmental pollution; alternatively, they can be asked how much they would pay for an improvement in environmental quality. A second approach infers the marginal cost of increased pollution from other relationships. The effects of pollution on house prices, for example, allow economists to estimate the value people place on environmental quality. Pollution costs can also be estimated on the basis of the costs they impose on firms in production.

Three types of policies are available to reduce pollution. Moral suasion is sometimes used, but it is effective only under limited conditions. Command-and-control regulation is used most commonly, but it is likely to be inefficient. It also fails to provide incentives for technological change in the long run. The most promising policies are the incentive approaches, which include emissions taxes and marketable pollution permits. Both can be designed to reduce emissions at the lowest cost possible, and both create an incentive for firms to search out new and cheaper ways to reduce emissions.

Although public policy has stressed command-and-control methods in the past, pollution rights exchanges are now being introduced. Past policies may have been inefficient, but they have succeeded in improving air quality, at least in the nation's cities.

In the next chapter, we'll turn to another set of public policy issues that can be assessed using economic analysis: the problems of poverty and discrimination. We'll look at the sources of poverty and discrimination and examine alternative public sector responses to these problems.

Terms and Concepts for Review

Command-and-control approach

Incentive approach

Least-cost reduction in emissions

Moral suasion

Pollution

For Discussion

1. We noted that economists consider the benefits and costs of pollution from the perspective of people's preferences. Some critics argue, however, that the interests of plants and animals should be considered: for example, if pollution is harming trees, the trees have a right to protection. Do you think that's a good idea? How would it be implemented?
2. List five choices you make that result in pollution. What price do you pay to pollute the environment? Does that price affect your choices?
3. In any urban area, what group is likely to be exposed to a greater level of pollution—rich people or poor people? (*Hint:* Utilize the findings of economists concerning the relationship between house prices and pollution levels.)
4. Suppose the accompanying graph shows the demand and marginal cost curves, *D* and *MC*, for a pollutant in a particular area. How do you think future economic and population growth will affect the efficient rate of emissions per period, *Q*, and thus the level of pollution?

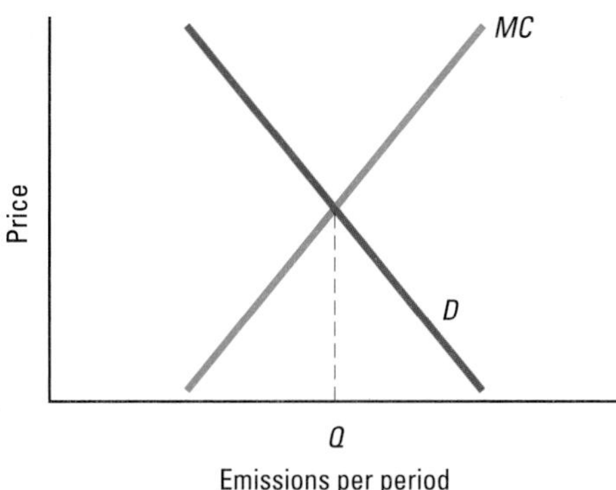

5. "Environmental quality is not just a matter of technical efficiency; it's about how people relate to nature. Economists are completely off base in their analysis of the benefits and costs of pollution." Comment.

6. Campaigns that exhort us to "Give a hoot—don't pollute" imply that anyone who pollutes the environment is uncaring—that people who are concerned about environmental quality would not be dumping garbage into the environment. Is that true?

7. We've seen that a system of marketable pollution permits achieves the same solution as a system of emissions taxes. Which do you think would be more fair? Why?

8. Many environmentalists are horrified by the notion of marketable pollution permits advocated by economists. These environmentalists insist that pollution is wrong, and that no one should be able to buy the right to pollute the environment. What do you think?

9. Some people object that charging firms for their emissions will do no good—firms will simply raise their prices and go on doing what they were doing before. Comment on this objection to emissions taxes.

10. Suppose firms in a perfectly competitive industry generate water pollution as a by-product of their production, and they aren't charged for this. Who benefits from their free use of the environment as a dumping ground? If an emissions tax is imposed, costs to these firms increase and emissions drop. Who will bear the burden of this tax? Is that fair?

Problems

1. Suppose the dry-cleaning industry is perfectly competitive. The process of dry cleaning generates emissions that pollute the air, and firms now emit this pollution at no cost. If the long-run equilibrium price for dry-cleaning a typical item is $3 and a pollution control program increases the marginal cost by $1 per item, how will the pollution control program affect the price and output of dry-cleaning services in the short run and in the long run? Explain and illustrate graphically. Who pays for pollution control in the industry? Explain.

2. Suppose local government regulations allow only a single firm to provide dry-cleaning services to a local community, and this firm generates pollution as in Problem 1. The firm initially charges a price of $4 per item. Now a pollution control program is imposed, increasing the firm's marginal and average total costs by $1 per item. Explain and illustrate graphically how the program will affect the firm's price and output. Who pays for the pollution control program?

3. Suppose the marginal benefit (*MB*) and marginal cost (*MC*) curves for emitting particulate matter are given by the following schedules, where *E* is the quantity of emissions per period:

E	*MB*	*MC*
0	$230	$−10
200	190	10
400	150	30
600	110	50
800	70	70
1,000	30	90

   a. Plot the marginal benefit and marginal cost curves and state the efficient quantity of emissions per period.
   b. What quantity of emissions will occur when the price of emissions is zero?
   c. What tax rate would achieve the efficient rate of emissions?

4. Now suppose that rising incomes increase marginal cost as follows:

E	New *MC*
0	$−10
200	30
400	70
600	110
800	150
1,000	190

   a. Plot the new marginal cost curve in the graph you drew in Problem 3. What is the new efficient quantity of emissions per period?
   b. What quantity of emissions will occur when the price of emissions is zero?
   c. What tax rate would achieve the efficient rate of emissions?

19

Poverty and Discrimination

Chapter Objectives

After mastering the material in this chapter, you will be able to:

1. State the difference between relative and absolute measures of poverty.
2. Discuss the reasons the United States has made relatively little apparent progress in the War on Poverty.
3. Describe the characteristics that seem to be concentrated among poor people in the United States.
4. Explain how federal programs to deal with poverty affect labor force participation among the poor.
5. Evaluate proposals to reform welfare.
6. Summarize the evidence concerning the degree of discrimination in the labor market and show how racial preferences produce such discrimination.
7. Describe federal policies designed to deal with discrimination and assess their effects.

Money is not the root of all evil. A lack of money is the root of all evil.

George Bernard Shaw

What's Ahead

It was January 8, 1964. President Lyndon B. Johnson stood before the Congress of the United States to make his first State of the Union address and to declare a new kind of war, a War on Poverty. "This administration today here and now declares unconditional war on poverty in America," the president said. "Our aim is not only to relieve the symptoms of poverty but to cure it; and, above all, to prevent it." In the United States that year, 35.1 million people were, by the official definition, poor.

The president's plan included stepped-up federal aid to low-income people, an expanded health care program for the poor, new housing subsidies, expanded federal aid to education, and job training programs. The proposal became law later that same year.

Three decades and more than $3 trillion in federal antipoverty spending later, the nation seems to have made little progress toward the president's goal. The number of people defined as poor by the federal government is greater than it was when the president launched his program to eliminate poverty. By 1993, 39.3 million people in the United States were, by the official definition, poor.

In this chapter we will analyze the problem of U.S. poverty. We will examine government programs designed to alleviate poverty and explore why so little progress appears to have been made toward eliminating it three decades after the War on Poverty began. We will see that part of the problem is one of measurement, but the larger part is the result of more fundamental issues.

We shall also explore a related problem: discrimination. Poverty is more prevalent among racial minorities and among women than it is among white males. To a degree, this reflects discrimination. We shall investigate the economics of discrimination and its consequences for the victims and for the economy. We shall also assess efforts by the public sector to eliminate discrimination.

- An **absolute income test** defines a person as poor if his or her income falls below a specific level.
- A **relative income test** defines people as poor if their incomes fall at the bottom of the distribution of income.
- The **poverty line** is an annual income level that marks the dividing line between poor households and those that are not poor.

The Economics of Poverty

Poverty in the United States is something of a paradox. Per capita incomes in this country are the highest on earth. How can a nation that is so rich have so many people who are so poor?

There is no single answer to the question of why so many people are poor. But we shall see that there are economic factors at work that help to explain poverty. We will also examine the nature of the government's response to poverty and the impact that response has. First, however, we shall examine the definition of poverty and look at some characteristics of the poor in the United States.

Defining Poverty

Suppose you were asked to determine whether a particular family was poor or not poor. How would you do it?

You might begin by listing the goods and services that would be needed to provide a minimum standard of living and then finding out if the family's income was enough to purchase those items. If it wasn't, you might conclude that the family was poor. Alternatively, you might examine the family's income relative to the incomes of other families in the community or in the nation. If the family was on the low end of the income scale, you might classify it as poor.

These two approaches represent two bases on which poverty is defined. The first is an **absolute income test,** which sets a specific income level and defines a person as poor if his or her income falls below that level. The second is a **relative income test,** in which people whose incomes fall at the bottom of the income distribution are considered poor. Both approaches are used in discussions of the poverty problem. When we speak of the number of poor people, we are typically using an absolute income test of poverty. When we speak of the problems of those at the bottom of the income distribution, we are speaking in terms of a relative income test.

Number of People in Household	Poverty Line
1	$7,363
2	9,414
3	11,522
4	14,763
5	17,449
6	19,718
7	22,383
8	24,838
9 or more	29,529

Source: U.S. Bureau of the Census, *Income, Poverty, and Valuation of Noncash Benefits: 1993* (Washington, D.C.: U.S. Government Printing Office, 1995), table 7, p. 21.

EXHIBIT 19-1

The Poverty Line and Household Size in the United States, 1993

The poverty line varies with household size. Figures are adjusted each year by the rate of inflation.

The Poverty Line

The federal government has a straightforward answer to the question of whether the members of a particular household are poor. They are poor if the household's annual income falls below a dollar figure called the **poverty line.** If household income is equal to or greater than the poverty line, the household is not considered poor. In 1993, the poverty line for a family of four was an income of $14,763. Exhibit 19-1 shows the poverty line for various family sizes. The use of a poverty line to define poverty is an example of an absolute income approach to poverty definition.

The concept of a poverty line grew out of a Department of Agriculture study in 1955 that found low-income families spending one-third of their incomes on food. With the one-third figure as a guide, the Department then selected four food plans that met the minimum daily nutritional requirements established by the federal government. The cost of the least expensive plan for each household size was multiplied by 3 to determine the income below which a household would be considered poor. The government used this method to count the number of poor people from 1959 to 1969. The poverty line was adjusted each year as food prices changed. Beginning in 1969, the poverty line was adjusted

The **poverty rate** is the percentage of the population living in households whose income falls below the poverty line.

annually by the average percentage price change for all consumer goods, not just changes in the price of food.

There is little to be said for the methodology by which poverty in the United States is defined. No attempt is made to establish an income at which a household could purchase basic necessities. Indeed, no attempt is made in the definition to establish what such necessities might be. The day has long passed when the average household devoted one-third of its income to food purchases; today such purchases account for less than one-fifth of household income. Still, it's useful to have some threshold that is consistent from one year to the next so that progress—or the lack thereof—in the fight against poverty may be assessed.

Exhibit 19-2 shows the percentage of the population that fell below the poverty line in each year since 1959. This percentage is called the **poverty rate.** Notice that the poverty rate has generally fallen during periods of economic growth, highlighted in the chart. It has risen during periods in which the economy was not growing.

Economic growth tends to reduce the poverty rate, but such reductions have become less dramatic. The economic expansion of the 1980s, the longest peacetime expansion in U.S. history, brought a reduction in the poverty rate of just 2.2 percentage points. The expansion of the 1960s reduced the rate by nearly 10 percentage points. Economic growth does not appear to pack the antipoverty wallop it once did. We'll examine possible explanations for this fact later in this chapter.

EXHIBIT 19-2

The Poverty Rate

The poverty rate has generally fallen during periods of economic expansion (shown as shaded areas in the chart).

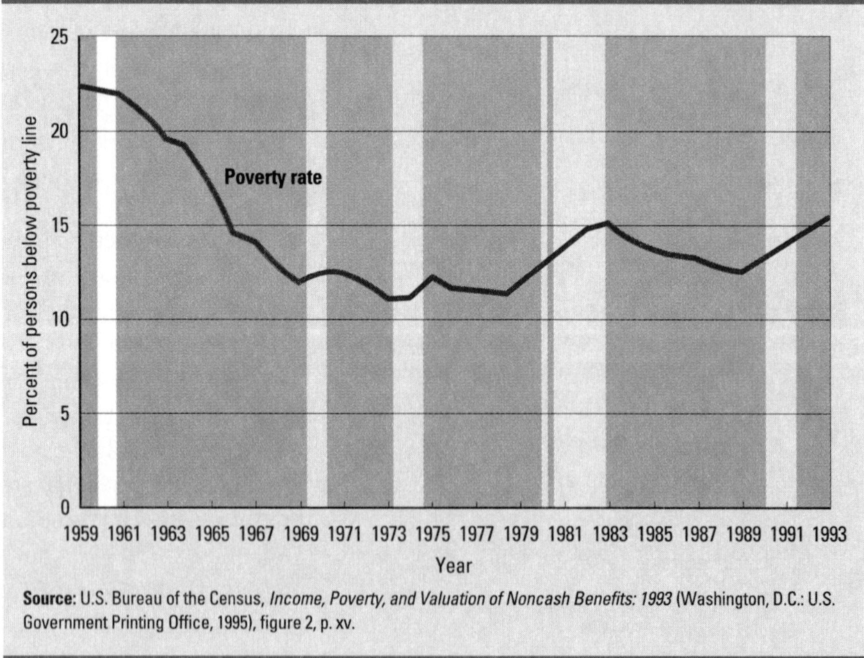

Source: U.S. Bureau of the Census, *Income, Poverty, and Valuation of Noncash Benefits: 1993* (Washington, D.C.: U.S. Government Printing Office, 1995), figure 2, p. xv.

Overstating Poverty?

It can be argued that the nation has made somewhat more progress against poverty than the official poverty rate suggests. Economists generally agree that the methodology used to calculate the inflation rate in the 1970s tended to overstate inflation significantly. Because the poverty line is adjusted according to the inflation rate, any overstatement of inflation overstates the poverty line and thus overstates the number of people who fall below it. Housing costs, for example, which are one factor in computing the inflation rate, were once measured in terms of the average mortgage payment for a newly purchased home. As interest rates and house prices rose dramatically during the 1970s, new mortgage payments soared and drove up the reported rate of inflation. But most people weren't living in newly purchased homes; their housing costs had not risen.

The government's methodology for computing inflation was revised in 1983 to reflect a broader measure of housing costs, eliminating the source of the earlier error. Since then, the poverty line has been adjusted by a more accurate gauge of inflation. But the upward bias introduced between 1969 and 1983 remains.

The Census Bureau also reports the poverty line and poverty rate that would apply if the current approach to estimating inflation had been used in the 1970s. Under that method, the poverty line for a family of four in 1992 would be $13,190, not $14,335. The lower poverty line would produce a poverty rate of 13.1 percent rather than the official rate of 14.8 percent. That figure suggests somewhat more progress, but significant poverty remains.

Another objection to the methodology by which poverty is measured is that no adjustment is made for regional differences in living costs. The same income tests are applied in Connecticut, where living costs are high, and Mississippi, where costs are relatively low. That doesn't affect the poverty rate nationwide, because the overstatement of poverty in states with low living costs is canceled by the understatement of poverty in states with high living costs. It does, however, affect the funding of poverty programs. States with higher percentages of people below the poverty line receive more federal funds, so that federal help may be somewhat misallocated.

The use of a poverty line suggests a way to determine what it would cost to eliminate poverty. The Census Bureau does this by estimating the amount by which poor households would have to increase their incomes in order to rise above the poverty line. The **income deficit,** the amount that would bring every U.S. household above the poverty line, was $79.7 billion in 1993—and total government aid to the poor that year was more than twice that amount.

How could spending on poverty programs be more than twice as great as the sum that would be required to lift everyone in the United States out of poverty? One explanation could be that the income deficit implies that current spending simply falls short. Poverty programs lift people partway out of poverty, and the income deficit suggests how much more spending it would take to eliminate poverty entirely. An alternative explanation focuses on shortcomings in poverty programs and asserts that they aren't really focused on lifting anyone out of poverty. The fact that it would be relatively cheap to raise everyone above the poverty line may suggest not that more needs to be spent but that existing programs need radical reform. We'll examine these alternative perspectives later in this chapter.

A Relative Definition of Poverty

An alternative to the poverty threshold approach is to define poverty in relative terms. We could, for example, rank households according to income and define the lowest one-fifth of households as poor. In 1992, any household with an annual income below $16,960 fell in this category.

Using a relative measure of poverty does not allow any "progress" against poverty—there will always be a lowest one-fifth of the population. But it does make an important point: poverty is in large measure a relative concept. In the

The **income deficit** is the amount that would be required to bring every family in the United States above the poverty line.

United States, poor people have much higher incomes than most of the world's people. By international standards, poor people in the United States are rich! But people judge their incomes relative to incomes of people around them, not relative to people everywhere on the planet. A family of four in a Los Angeles slum with an annual income of $13,000 surely does not feel rich because its income is several times higher than the average family income in Ethiopia. But a family in Ethiopia with an income equivalent in purchasing power to $13,000 per year would feel quite wealthy. What we think of as poverty clearly depends more on what people around us are earning than on some absolute measure of income.

The Demographics of Poverty

There is no iron law of poverty that dictates that a household with certain characteristics will be poor. Nonetheless, poverty is much more highly concentrated among some socioeconomic groups than among others.

The characteristic most dramatically associated with poverty is family structure. In 1992, just 6.2 percent of the families headed by married couples fell below the poverty line. The poverty rate was 34.9 percent for households headed by unmarried women. Indeed, an important factor accounting for the persistence of poverty in the wake of economic growth has been the sharp rise in female-headed families during this period, from 10.8 percent of all families in 1970, to 16.5 percent by 1990.

One by-product of the rise in female-headed households that are poor has been the emergence of a poverty problem among children. Fully 37 percent of the nation's poor people in 1992 were under the age of 15. The poverty rate among children under 15 in 1992 was 22.7 percent.

Another characteristic closely associated with poverty is the amount of education completed by adults in a household. The more education the adults have, the less likely the household is to be poor. In 1992, the poverty rate among adults age 25 or over who had not completed high school was 25.6 percent. Those with a high school education and no college had a much lower rate of 9.6 percent. A college education is an even surer ticket out of poverty; the rate for college graduates was 3.0 percent.

When we combine family structure with education, we see an even more powerful effect. The poverty rate in 1992 for households headed by married couples with at least a high school education was 5.7 percent. The rate for households headed by women with children but without a high school education was 49.9 percent.

As one would expect, employment plays a role in poverty. The poverty rate in 1992 among those people age 16 and over who did not work during the year was 23.4 percent. It was 2.6 percent for those who worked full-time throughout the year.

Race plays a role in poverty as well. The poverty rate in 1992 for whites was 11.6 percent, for blacks 33.3 percent, and for Hispanics, 29.3 percent.

Finally, geography is a factor in poverty. Poverty rates vary significantly by region. The highest poverty rate in the United States in 1992 was in the South, where 16.9 percent of the population fell below the poverty line. The lowest rate was in the Northeast, which had a poverty rate of 12.3 percent.

Exhibit 19-3 shows poverty rates for various groups and for the population as a whole in 1992.

EXHIBIT 19-3

Demographic Characteristics Affecting Poverty Rates, 1992

Panels (a) through (e) compare poverty rates among different groups of the U.S. population.

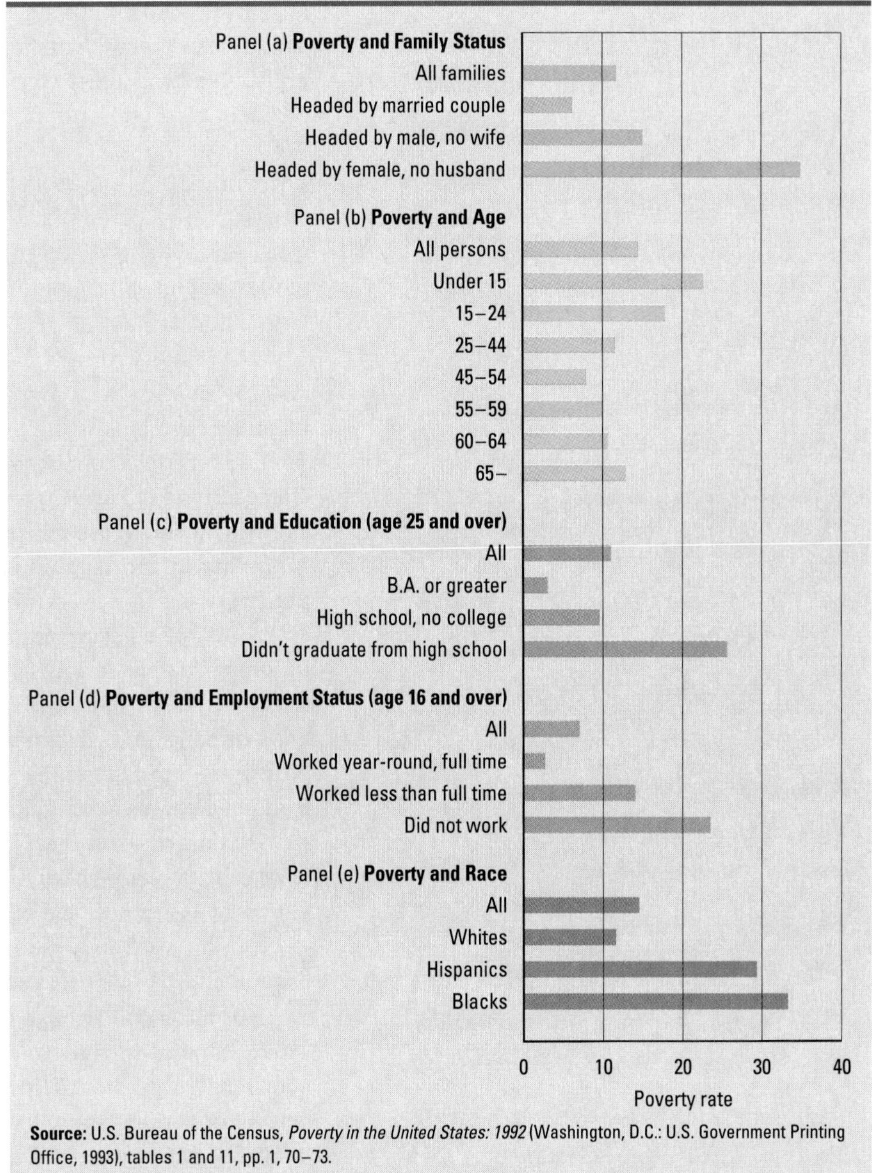

Source: U.S. Bureau of the Census, *Poverty in the United States: 1992* (Washington, D.C.: U.S. Government Printing Office, 1993), tables 1 and 11, pp. 1, 70–73.

Checklist

- Poverty can be defined in both absolute and relative terms. The standard definition of poverty is based on the concept of the poverty line, an absolute test.
- The U.S. government's measure of poverty overstates the poverty rate because the consumer price index overstated inflation in the 1970s.
- Poverty is concentrated among households headed by women, households in which the adults have little education and/or do not participate in the labor force, the young, and racial minorities. The poverty rate is higher in the South than in other regions.
- Only a small fraction of the nation's poverty population participates in the labor market.

The fact that poverty is concentrated among children and adults who do not work suggests one explanation for the weak relationship between poverty and economic growth in recent years. A growing economy reduces poverty by creating more jobs and higher incomes. Neither of those will reach those who, for various reasons, are not in the labor force.

Of the nation's 36.9 million poor people in 1992, 14.6 million were under the age of 16. Another 4.0 million were retired. That means that half of the nation's poor were too young or too old to participate in the labor force. Of the remaining 18.3 million, 3.6 million were sick or disabled. Another 4.0 million were students. The Census Bureau reports that 5.6 million were unavailable for work because of their family situations, such as responsibility for caring for disabled family members. That leaves just 5.1 million poor people who could be considered available to participate in the labor market. Of those, 2.6 million worked full time throughout 1992. There were thus only 2.5 million poor people

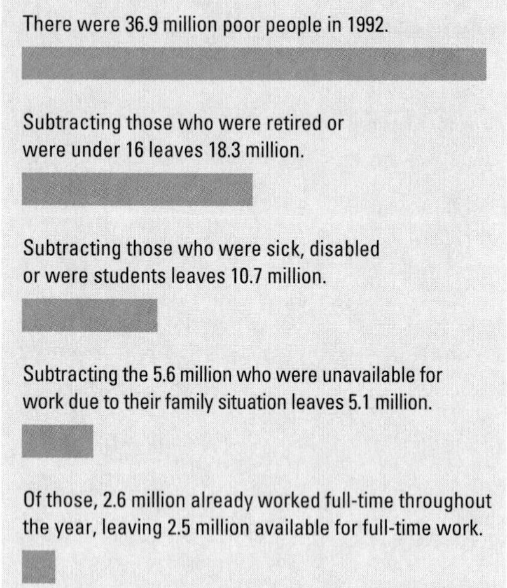

There were 36.9 million poor people in 1992.

Subtracting those who were retired or were under 16 leaves 18.3 million.

Subtracting those who were sick, disabled or were students leaves 10.7 million.

Subtracting the 5.6 million who were unavailable for work due to their family situation leaves 5.1 million.

Of those, 2.6 million already worked full-time throughout the year, leaving 2.5 million available for full-time work.

Source: U.S. Bureau of the Census, *Poverty in the United States: 1992* (Washington, D.C.: U.S. Government Printing Office, 1993), table 1, p. 1.

EXHIBIT 19-4

Employment Status of the Nation's Poor

Most poor people are, for reasons of age, physical condition, or family or school status, unavailable for work at any one time.

available for work in 1992 who weren't already working full time. Exhibit 19-4 summarizes this information; it shows that most of the nation's poor people are unlikely to be available for work in an expanding economy.

Government Policy and Poverty

Consider a young single parent with three small children. The parent is not employed and has no support from other relatives. What does the government provide for the family?

The primary form of cash assistance is likely to come from a program called Aid to Families with Dependent Children (AFDC), a program that provides monthly payments to low-income families. In addition to this assistance, the family is likely to qualify for food stamps, which are vouchers that can be exchanged for food at the grocery store. The family may also receive rent vouchers, which can be used as payment for private housing. The family may qualify for Medicaid, a program that pays for physician and hospital care as well as for prescription drugs.

A host of other programs provide help ranging from counseling in nutrition to job placement services. The parent may qualify for federal assistance in attending college. The children may participate in the Head Start program, a program of preschool education designed primarily for low-income children. If the poverty rate in the area is unusually high, local public schools the children attend may receive extra federal aid.

In addition to all this public sector support, a wide range of help is available from private sector charities. These may provide scholarships for education, employment assistance, and other aid.

Exhibit 19-5 lists the major federal programs to help the poor and shows how much was spent for each in 1993.

Not all people whose incomes fall below the poverty line receive aid. In 1992, 73 percent of those counted as poor received some form of aid. But the percentages who were helped by individual programs were much lower. Only 43 percent of people below the poverty line received some form of cash assistance in 1992. Slightly over half received food stamps or lived in a household in which one or more people received medical services through Medicaid. Only about one-fifth of the people living in poverty received some form of housing aid.

Although for the most part poverty programs are federally funded, individual states set eligibility standards and administer the programs. As state budgets have come under greater pressure, many states have tightened standards. In 1972, a single mother earning wages equal to 75 percent of the poverty line would have received AFDC payments in 49 states. By 1992, that same woman would have received AFDC money in only 5 states.

Cash Versus Noncash Assistance

- **Cash assistance** is a money payment that a recipient may spend as he or she deems appropriate.
- **Noncash assistance** is the provision of specific goods and services rather than cash.

Aid provided to people falls into two broad categories: cash and noncash assistance. **Cash assistance** is a money payment that a recipient can spend as he or she wishes. **Noncash assistance** is the provision of specific goods and services, such as food or medical services, rather than cash.

Exhibit 19-6 shows the total volume of spending by federal, state, and local governments for cash and noncash assistance to poor people since 1980. The

EXHIBIT 19-5

Public Sector Programs to Aid the Poor

The chart shows spending in various categories of government aid provided to low-income people. Some of the major programs include these benefits:

Cash The primary source of money payments to families comes from the Aid to Families with Dependent Children (AFDC) program. In addition, disabled people and the dependents of deceased workers receive money from Social Security.

Medical Care Medicaid acts as a kind of government insurance program that pays for health care for many low-income people.

Food Benefits Food stamps, vouchers distributed to low-income people, can be exchanged for food at grocery stores. Low-income children also qualify for subsidized meals at school.

Housing The federal government owns housing and provides it at a fraction of cost to low-income people. It also has a program that provides rent vouchers, which can be used as payment for rent.

Education The federal government provides funds to school districts with a high percentage of people below the poverty line. Other educational programs include Head Start for preschool children and Pell Grants, Stafford Loans, and work-study grants for college aid.

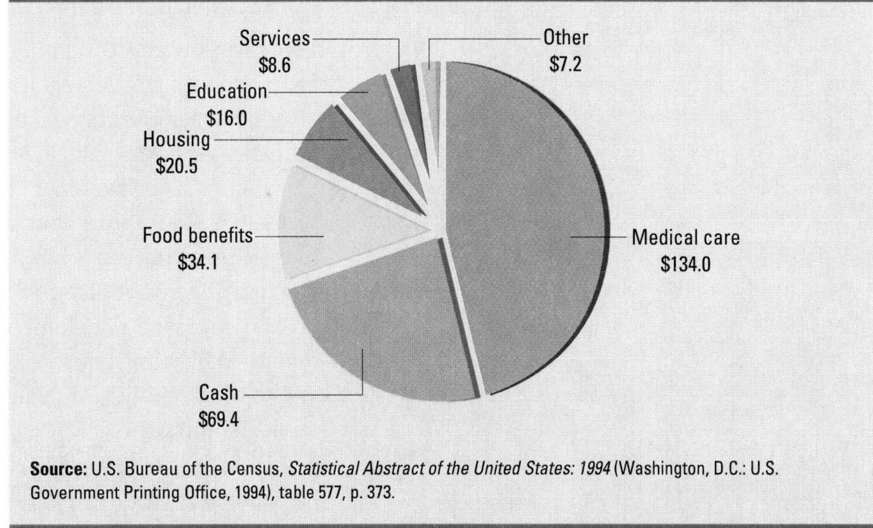

Source: U.S. Bureau of the Census, *Statistical Abstract of the United States: 1994* (Washington, D.C.: U.S. Government Printing Office, 1994), table 577, p. 373.

amounts are expressed in dollars of equivalent purchasing power to correct for the effects of inflation. Notice that noncash assistance is the most important form of aid to the poor and that it has been rising in importance during the past decade.

The increasing share of noncash relative to cash assistance raises two issues. First, the theory of consumer behavior implies that the poor would be better off with cash rather than noncash assistance. Second, the importance of noncash assistance raises an important issue concerning the methodology by which the poverty rate is measured in the United States. Each of these issues is examined below.

EXHIBIT 19-6

Cash Versus Noncash Assistance

The chart shows total state, local, and federal cash and noncash assistance to the poor from 1978 to 1990. Noncash aid rose in relative importance during the period. All figures are given in dollars of equivalent purchasing power over the period 1982–1984 to correct for the impact of inflation.

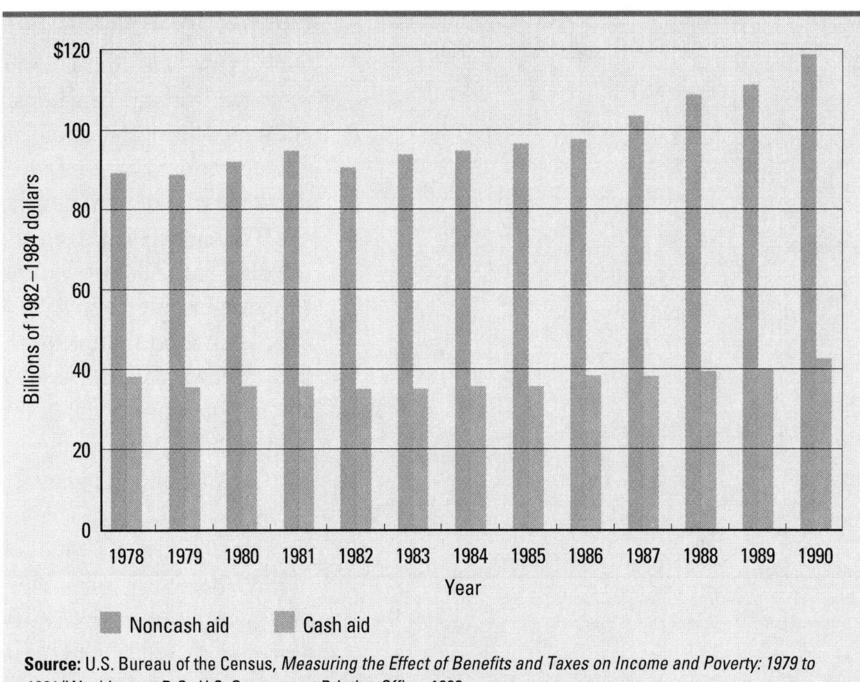

Source: U.S. Bureau of the Census, *Measuring the Effect of Benefits and Taxes on Income and Poverty: 1979 to 1991* (Washington, D.C.: U.S. Government Printing Office, 1992).

Consumer Choice Theory and Cash Versus Noncash Aid

Suppose you had a choice between receiving $515 or a television set worth $515. Neither gift is taxable. Which would you take?

Given a choice between cash and an equivalent value in merchandise, you'd probably take the cash. Unless the television set happened to be exactly what you'd purchase with the $515, you could find some other set of goods and services that would give you greater utility than the TV set. The same is true of money that you can spend on anything versus money whose spending is restricted. Given a choice of $515 that you could spend on anything and $515 that you could spend only on food, which would you choose? A given amount of money allows a greater degree of satisfaction than does a specific set of goods and services, because consumers with money can choose their own utility-maximizing combinations.

We can conclude, then, that poor people who receive government aid would be better off with money grants than with noncash aid. Why, then, is most government aid given as noncash benefits?

Economists have suggested two explanations. The first is based on the preferences of donors. Recipients might prefer cash, but the preferences of donors matter also. The donors, in this case, are taxpayers. Suppose they want poor people to have specific things—perhaps food, housing, and medical care. Given such donor preferences, it's not surprising to find aid targeted at providing these basic goods and services. The second explanation for the rise of noncash aid comes from public choice theory. We saw in Chapter 15 that the poor are not likely to be successful competitors in the contest to be at the receiving end of public sector income redistribution efforts; most redistribution goes to people who are not poor. But firms that provide services such as housing or medical care might be highly effective lobbyists for programs that increase the demand for their products. They could be expected to seek more help for the poor in the form of noncash aid that increases their own demand and profits.

Poverty Measurement and Noncash Aid

Only money income is counted in determining the poverty rate. The value of food, medical care, or housing through various noncash assistance programs is not included in household income. That's an important omission, because most government aid is noncash aid. Data for the official poverty rate thus do not reflect the full extent to which government programs act to reduce poverty.

The Census Bureau estimates the impact of noncash assistance on poverty, calculating the dollar value of the aid. This adjustment is based on the utility argument presented above. If a typical household would prefer, say, $515 in cash to $515 in food stamps, then $515 worth of food stamps is not valued at $515 in cash. Economists at the Census Bureau adjust the value of noncash aid to an amount they think yields the same total utility to households. Suppose, for example, that given the choice between $515 in food stamps and $475 in cash, a household reports that it is indifferent between the two—either would be equally satisfactory. That implies that $515 in food stamps generates utility equal to $475 in cash; the food stamps are thus "worth" $475 to the household.

We have now examined two reasons the Census Bureau's official measure may overstate actual poverty. First, the adjustment of the poverty line for inflation tended to overstate the actual poverty rate during the 1970s, and those errors remain imbedded in current figures for the poverty line. Second, the official rate

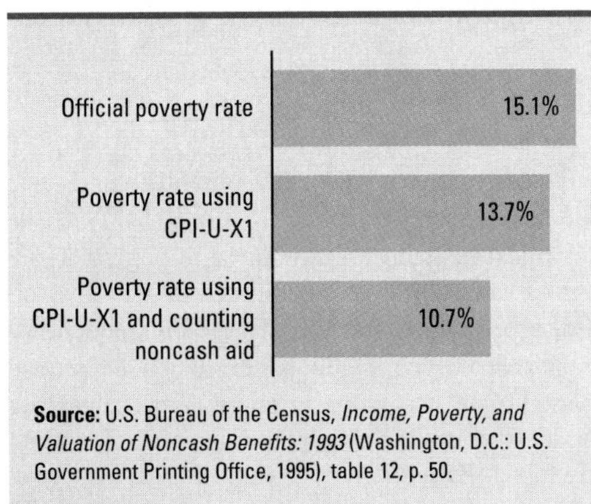

Source: U.S. Bureau of the Census, *Income, Poverty, and Valuation of Noncash Benefits: 1993* (Washington, D.C.: U.S. Government Printing Office, 1995), table 12, p. 50.

EXHIBIT 19-7

Alternative Measures of the Poverty Rate

Using a measure of prices that doesn't tend to overstate inflation during the 1970s, called the CPI-U-X1, reduces the poverty rate from the official level of 15.1 percent in 1993 to 13.7 percent. Adding an estimate of the value of noncash assistance reduces it further to 10.7 percent.

doesn't adjust for the value of the noncash assistance programs that have become so important during the past 25 years.

Each year, the Census Bureau reports alternative estimates of the poverty rate that correct for these two problems. Exhibit 19-7 shows the official poverty rate for 1993, 15.1 percent. Recalculating the poverty line using a corrected measure of inflation reduces this to 13.7 percent. Incorporating the value of noncash assistance reduces it to 10.7 percent.

Proposals for Reform

The welfare system in the United States has come under increasing attack in recent years. It is expensive, and it has clearly failed to eliminate poverty. Many observers worry that welfare is becoming a way of life for people who have withdrawn from the labor force. President Clinton made welfare reform one of the key issues in the 1992 presidential campaign. Reform proposals range from building on the successes of past efforts within the context of existing programs to more radical attempts to scrap the present system altogether.

Building on Successes

Some welfare experts point to successes in the vast array of programs spawned in the War on Poverty effort President Lyndon Johnson launched three decades ago. They say the War on Poverty can be won if the nation commits adequate resources to the battle.

Some Head Start programs, for example, have achieved dramatic gains. Head Start attempts to give disadvantaged children, who could otherwise be expected to do poorly in school, a head start in learning and an orientation for academic success. Perhaps the best-known Head Start program is the Perry Preschool in Ypsilanti, Michigan. A study of children 16 years after they completed the program concluded that each $1 spent saved $6 in subsequent expense for remedial education, criminal justice, and social programs.[1]

Supporters of the present antipoverty system would spend more on it, beefing up such programs as Head Start, counseling services for parents, job training, health care, and education. Critics of this idea stress that the present system has had only isolated successes that probably cannot be duplicated throughout the nation.

Limiting Eligibility

President Bill Clinton has proposed a shift in the emphasis of welfare programs to job training efforts for able-bodied adults whose children are over 6 years of age. Recipients would be required to participate in training—and would face a 2-year limit to their eligibility for welfare payments. If they didn't find work, their aid would be cut off.

The Clinton plan would have a backup—those who couldn't find work would be guaranteed jobs in the public sector. Under the plan, recipients would be guaranteed health care benefits and would be provided with child care. Administration officials estimate that the program would require about 1.5 million jobs per year to be created for welfare recipients.

[1] Jason DeParle and Peter Applebome, "Ideas to Aid the Poor Abound, but Consensus Is Wanting," *New York Times*, 29 January 1991, A1.

Case in Point Pushing Jobs in Hamilton County

Ohio has been one of the success stories in implementing the kind of job training programs anticipated by the Clinton administration. Its job training programs have been credited with achieving a modest 11 percent reduction in the number of people receiving welfare. The experience in Hamilton County, which includes Cincinnati, points out some difficulties involved in the effort to put welfare recipients to work.

Welfare recipients receiving job training in electronics.

Under Ohio's rules, recipients are required to participate in job training programs unless they have children under age 3 or are caring for a disabled family member. Hamilton County has 23,000 families that receive welfare, but the exclusion leaves just 8,900 participants who are, in theory, required to participate in job training. Those who don't participate have their monthly AFDC benefits reduced. Benefits for a family of three with one parent, for example, are reduced to $274 per month from $334 if the parent chooses not to participate.

Despite this incentive, only about 2,000 recipients participate in job training efforts (the remainder accept the benefit reduction). Of these, about half lack even minimal job skills and are sent to remedial educational programs. Program officials report good luck placing those who remain in the program and attend classes regularly—but few do. At the end of 1993, only 100 of the county's 23,000 welfare recipients were working 20 hours a week or more under the program.

Source: Paulette Thomas, "Getting Families Off Welfare and Into Jobs Isn't as Easy as AFDC," *The Wall Street Journal,* 25 October 1993, A1.

Experiments that contain some features of the Clinton plan are under way throughout the United States. A welfare reform measure, the 1988 Family Support Act, requires states to enroll at least 20 percent of the eligible welfare population in job training programs by 1995. This measure, sponsored by Senator Daniel Patrick Moynihan, a New York Democrat, has spawned a host of experiments in finding ways to get people working and off welfare rolls. All these programs extend Medicaid coverage and provide child care for the first year a recipient works. Some programs allow recipients who find jobs to keep some of their welfare benefits for up to a year, temporarily cutting the benefit reduction rate.

The Center for Law and Social Policy in Washington, D.C. estimated in 1993 that 10 percent of the nation's welfare recipients were enrolled in job training and placement programs, and that one-fourth of those participants found jobs. Of course, those programs didn't apply the stern medicine anticipated by the Clinton program of cutting off benefits entirely after 2 years. But the reluctance of welfare recipients to participate in existing programs suggests the difficulties of weaning them off welfare by offering job training.

Market-Oriented Reform

Many people argue that the current welfare system, together with other tax and regulatory policies, is the main obstacle to advancing the poor. They propose other reforms that would rely more heavily on market forces to reduce welfare.

Jack Kemp, a former secretary of Housing and Urban Development and Republican congressman, has championed the concept of "enterprise zones" in low-income areas. Firms locating in an enterprise zone receive special tax breaks. Such zones, in theory, attract business investment and thus create employment opportunities in impoverished areas. Mr. Kemp has also advocated conversion of public housing projects to private ownership by their tenants, as well as programs that would allow parents to choose the schools their children attend. Mr. Kemp contends that his policies would "empower" poor families. Once they can choose their children's schools, own their homes, and find jobs encouraged by enterprise zones, he argues, they will work their way out of poverty.

Advocates of market-based reforms also stress the need to cut the benefit reduction rate for welfare recipients who work. If recipients can keep more of every dollar they earn, advocates argue, more of them will be motivated to find work.

Critics of the market approach to reform question whether poor people in the nation's inner cities, who would be the primary targets of such efforts, would flourish in quite the way advocates such as Mr. Kemp anticipate. They argue that the nation's poor people need more than market incentives—they need programs that will give them the skills to take advantage of these incentives.

What's ahead for welfare reform? Republican candidates for Congress in 1994 pledged their support of a plan that would, like President Clinton's proposal, put a 2-year limit on receipt of welfare assistance for persons capable of working. The Republican plan would not, however, guarantee public sector employment as a backup. As this book went to press in 1995, approval of some version of a 2-year welfare limit seemed likely.

Checklist

- Most welfare aid is given in the form of noncash assistance. This form of aid is rising in importance relative to cash benefits despite the fact that noncash benefits provide less utility to recipients than an equal level of cash benefits.
- The dominance of noncash benefits may reflect donor preferences. The rising relative role of noncash benefits may also reflect the lobbying efforts of firms that supply the goods and services that make up noncash assistance.
- The official poverty rate is based on estimates of household money income only; it does not count the value of noncash benefits. A calculation of the rate incorporating a better measure of inflation and the value of noncash benefits suggests a much lower poverty rate than the official measure.
- Reform proposals discussed here include expansion of the present system, limitations on eligibility for welfare, and reforms designed to stimulate economies in poor areas.

The Economics of Discrimination

In our analysis of market outcomes thus far, people with the same economic characteristics have been treated alike. Workers with the same marginal revenue product receive the same wage. Consumers are all charged the same prices. There is, in short, no discrimination.

In the real world, however, we know that women and members of racial minorities receive different wages than white male workers, even though they all may have similar qualifications and backgrounds. They may be charged different prices or denied employment opportunities. This section examines the economic forces that create such discrimination, as well as the measures that can be used to address it.

Economists define **discrimination** as occurring when people with similar economic characteristics experience different economic outcomes because of their race, sex, or other noneconomic characteristics. A black worker whose skills and experience are identical to those of a white worker but who receives a lower wage is a victim of discrimination. A woman denied a job opportunity solely on the basis of her sex is the victim of discrimination.

Discrimination occurs when people with similar economic characteristics experience different economic outcomes because of their race, sex, or other noneconomic characteristics.

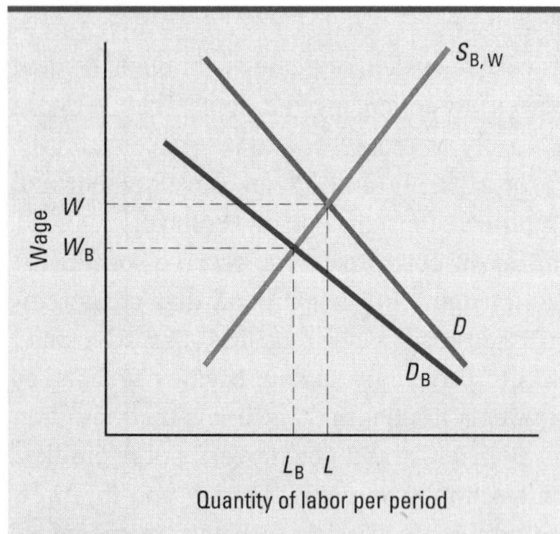

EXHIBIT 19-8

A Model of Discrimination

Assume that black and white workers have the same supply curve S, these two groups have identical marginal products, and employers have no discriminatory preferences. Both black and white workers face the same demand curve D. Both groups earn the same wage W and experience the same level of employment L. If discriminatory preferences or attitudes confront blacks with a lower demand D_B, they will receive a lower wage W_B. Employment among black workers will fall to L_B.

Discrimination in the Marketplace: A Model

Pioneering work on the economics of discrimination was done by Gary S. Becker, an economist at the University of Chicago who won the Nobel Prize in Economics in 1992. Becker suggested that discrimination occurs because of people's preferences or attitudes. If enough people have prejudices against certain racial groups, or against women, or against people with any particular characteristic, the market will respond to those preferences.

In Becker's model, discriminatory preferences drive a wedge between the outcomes experienced by different groups. Discriminatory preferences may make salespeople less willing to sell to one group than to another or make consumers less willing to buy from the members of one group than from another.

Let's explore Becker's model by examining discrimination against black workers. We begin by assuming that no discriminatory preferences or attitudes exist. For simplicity, suppose that the supply curves of black and white workers are identical; they are shown as a single curve in Exhibit 19-8. Suppose further that all workers have identical marginal products. In the absence of racial preferences, the demand for workers of both races would be D. Black and white workers would each receive a wage W per unit of labor. A total of L black workers and L white workers would be employed.

Now suppose that employers have discriminatory attitudes that cause them to assume that the marginal product of a black worker is less than the marginal product of an otherwise similar white worker. Now employers have a lower demand, D_B, for black than for white workers. Employers pay black workers a lower wage, W_B, and employ fewer of them, L_B instead of L, than they would in the absence of discrimination.

Sources of Discrimination

As illustrated in Exhibit 19-8, racial prejudices on the part of employers produce discrimination against black male workers, who receive lower wages and have fewer employment opportunities than white men. Discrimination can result from prejudices among other groups in the economy as well.

One source of discriminatory prejudices is other workers. Suppose, for example, that white workers prefer not to work with black workers and require a wage premium for doing so. Such preferences would, in effect, raise the marginal factor cost to the firm of hiring black workers. Firms would respond by demanding fewer of them, and wages for black workers would fall.

Another source of discrimination against black workers could come from customers. If the buyers of a firm's product prefer not to deal with black employees, the firm might respond by demanding fewer of them. In effect, prejudice on the part of consumers would lower the marginal revenue product of black workers.

Whether discriminatory preferences exist among employers, employees, or consumers, the impact on the group discriminated against will be the same. Fewer members of that group will be employed, and their wages will be lower than the wages of other workers whose skills and experience are otherwise similar. Economists have found, for example, that Hispanics, blacks, and women receive consistently lower wages for the same work than white men, even if their backgrounds and other characteristics are similar.

Race and sex aren't the only characteristics that affect hiring and wages. Some studies have found that people who are short, overweight, or physically unattractive also suffer from discrimination, and charges of discrimination have been voiced by disabled people and by homosexuals. Whenever discrimination occurs, it implies that employers, workers, or firms have discriminatory preferences. For the effects of such preferences to be felt in the marketplace, they must be widely shared.

Discrimination and Public Policy

The federal government has waged a long and vigorous battle against discrimination. As we shall see, however, government programs have had little effect on the wages and employment opportunities of people against whom discrimination is practiced.

The Fight Against Discrimination

In 1954, the U.S. Supreme Court rendered its decision that so-called separate but equal schools for black and white children were inherently unequal, and the court ordered that racially segregated schools be integrated.

Federal legislation was passed in 1962 and in 1965 to ensure that minorities were not denied the right to vote. The Equal Pay Act of 1963 requires employers to pay the same wages to men and women who do substantially the same work.

Congress passed the most important federal legislation against discrimination in 1964. The Civil Rights Act barred discrimination on the basis of race, sex, or ethnicity in pay, promotion, hiring, firing, and training. An Executive Order issued by President Lyndon Johnson in 1967 required federal contractors to implement affirmative action programs to ensure that members of minority groups and women were given equal opportunities in employment. The practical effect of the order was to require that these employers increase the percentage of women and minorities in their work forces.

The Impact of Antidiscrimination Laws

Despite the federal government's efforts to stamp it out, discrimination persists. Pay gaps for minority groups and for women have been little affected by legislation against discrimination. For example, although it's true that the incomes of nonwhite males relative to white males have increased, this effect is largely the result of greater gains in education among nonwhite workers. (These gains may be the result of efforts to end discrimination in education.) The wage gap between white and nonwhite workers with similar human capital has shown no sign of diminishing.

A look at the ratio of earnings of nonwhite to white full-time male workers shows improvement since federal civil rights efforts were launched in 1954; see Panel (a) of Exhibit 19-9. If we look at this gap by region, we see that there were significant gains in the South but virtually no gains in other regions of the country. John J. Donohue III, a professor of law at Northwestern University, and James Heckman, an economist at the University of Chicago, argue that the civil rights effort in the South shattered an entire way of life that had subjugated black Americans and had separated them from mainstream life. But legislation aimed at the economic effects of discrimination appears to have had virtually no impact on wages in the rest of the country.

EXHIBIT 19-9

Changing Ratios of Wages of Nonwhite Versus White Male Workers, 1955–1989

While the ratio of the wages of nonwhite males to white males has risen, virtually all of the gains have been achieved in the South.

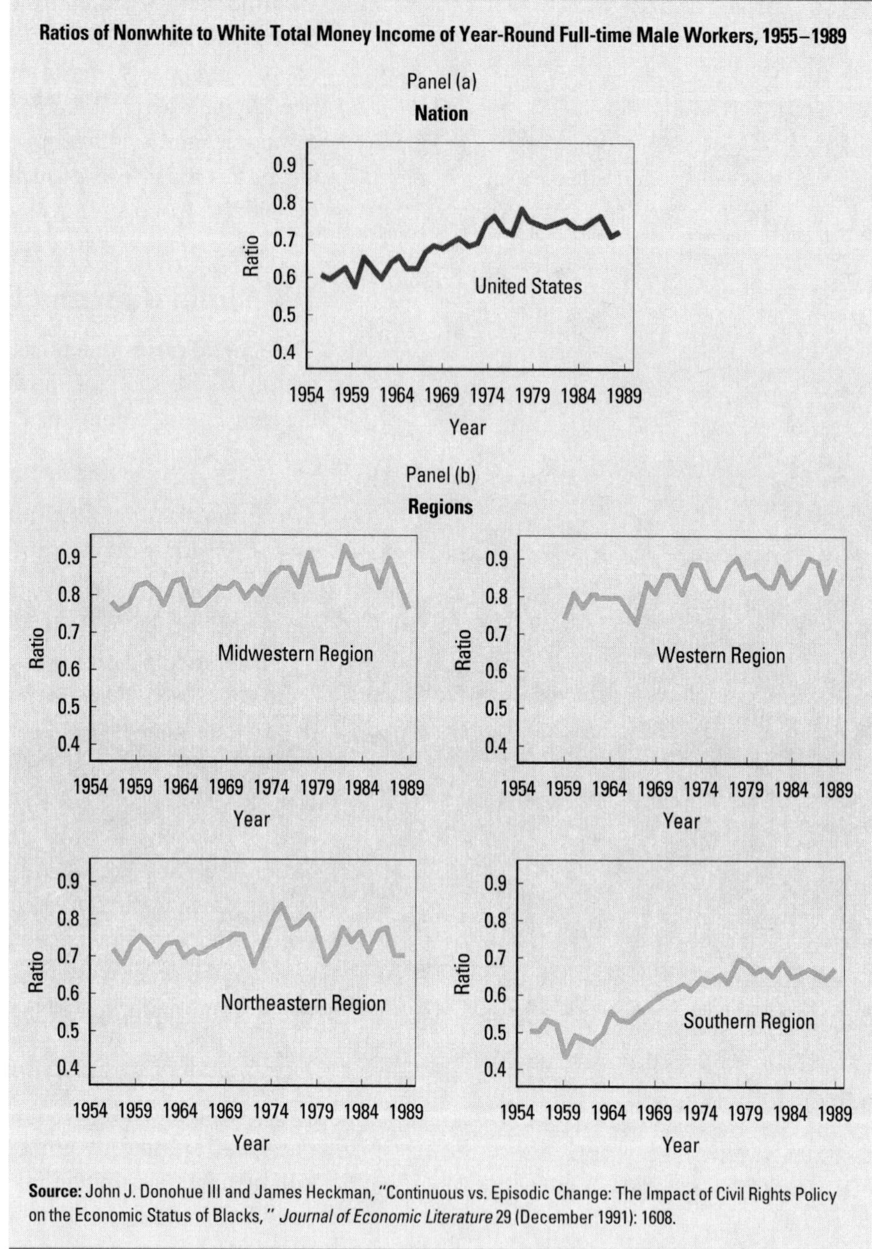

Studies of discrimination against women suggest much the same story. Women have made gains relative to men because they have invested more heavily in their human capital. But adjusted for differences in human capital, wage gaps between men and women have not declined since federal efforts to eliminate them began.

The discouraging lack of progress against discrimination may reflect the widespread persistence of discriminatory preferences. The model proposed by Professor Becker (see Exhibit 19-9) suggests that discrimination will be persistent only if discriminatory preferences are widely shared. And if they are, the market forces that respond to these preferences will be powerful indeed.

Checklist

- Discrimination occurs when people with similar economic characteristics experience dissimilar economic outcomes because of a characteristic such as race or sex.
- An economic model suggests that discrimination is a response to discriminatory preferences on the part of individual employers, consumers, or employees.
- Discriminatory preferences cause some groups to experience lower wages and fewer employment opportunities and to pay higher prices than others.
- Although market competition reduces some forms of discrimination, it actually rewards discrimination based on discriminatory preferences among consumers.
- Federal legislation bans discrimination. It is not clear, however, that women and minority groups have done better as a result of federal enforcement efforts. One region that appears to be an exception to this conclusion is the South.

A Look Back—And a Look Ahead

Poverty can be measured using an absolute or a relative income standard. The official measure of poverty in the United States relies on an absolute standard. This measure tends to overstate the poverty rate because it overstates inflation and because it does not count most welfare aid as income. An assessment of poverty by the relative income standard shows a great deal of movement among income groups.

Poverty is concentrated among female-headed households, minorities, people with relatively little education, and people who are not in the labor force. Children have a particularly high poverty rate.

Proposals to reform welfare have focused on efforts to induce recipients to work. President Clinton has called for a 2-year limit on welfare benefits. After that, a recipient would be dropped from welfare and required to work.

Discrimination occurs if people who have similar characteristics experience dissimilar economic outcomes because of factors such as race or sex. Discrimination appears to reflect discriminatory preferences, particularly among consumers. Empirical analyses suggest that discrimination against women is greater than discrimination against nonwhite males. The federal government has sought to end discrimination, but the data suggest that little progress has been made.

In the next chapter, we'll turn to another application of microeconomic theory and study the health care issue. We'll look at the economic forces at work in the market for health care, explain why many people perceive that there is a problem with the U.S. health care system, and examine proposals for reform.

Terms and Concepts for Review

Absolute income test
Cash assistance
Discrimination
Income deficit
Noncash assistance
Poverty line
Poverty rate
Relative income test

For Discussion

1. How would you define poverty? How would you determine whether a particular family is poor? Is the test you have proposed an absolute or a relative test?
2. Why does the failure to adjust the poverty line for differences in living costs lead to an understatement of poverty in some states and an overstatement of poverty in others?
3. The text argues that welfare recipients could achieve higher levels of utility if they received cash rather than in-kind aid. Use the same argument to make a case that gifts given at Christmas should be in cash rather than specific items. Why do you suppose they usually are not?
4. Suppose a welfare program provides a basic grant of $10,000 per year to poor families but reduces the grant by $1 for every $1 of income earned. How would such a program affect a household's incentive to work?
5. The Clinton program calls for a 2-year limit on welfare payments, after which recipients must go to work. Suppose a recipient with children declines work offers. Should aid be cut? What about the children?
6. How would you tackle the welfare problem? State the goals you would seek, and explain how the measures you propose would work to meet those goals.
7. Suppose a common but unfounded belief held that people with blue eyes were not as smart as people with brown eyes. What would we expect to happen to the relative wages of the two groups? Suppose you were an entrepreneur who knew that the common belief was wrong. What could you do to enhance your profits?
8. Suppose black workers are receiving a wage of W_B as in Exhibit 19-8, while white workers receive W. Now suppose a regulation is imposed that requires that black workers be paid W also. How does this affect the employment, wages, and total incomes of black workers?

20

Chapter Objectives

After mastering the material in this chapter, you will be able to:

1. Discuss the primary shortcomings of the U.S. health care system.
2. Describe the role of insurance in the market for health care.
3. Explain how insurance works and discuss the market problems facing all health insurance plans.
4. Assess the importance of the combination of insurance and technological change on health care costs in the long run.
5. Explain why many observers advocate government intervention in the health care market.
6. Compare and assess major plans for reform in the health care market.

The Economics of Health Care

All of our efforts to strengthen the economy will fail unless we take bold steps to reform our health care system.

President Bill Clinton, State of the Union Address, 1993

What's Ahead

Here's a quick quiz: Among Hong Kong, Japan, and the United States, which nation has the longest life expectancy? The lowest infant mortality rate? The most physicians per 1,000 population?

The United States leads in just one of those categories: physicians per 1,000 population. In 1990, the United States had 50 percent more physicians per 1,000 people than Japan and more than twice as many as Hong Kong.

But having all those doctors doesn't seem to improve U.S. health statistics. Among the three countries, Japan leads in life expectancy and has the lowest infant mortality rate. Hong Kong has the next-best record; the United States ranks third. Among all developed nations, 5 nations rank above the United States in life expectancy. Nineteen have lower rates of infant mortality. The poor U.S. showing is particularly troubling in light of the fact that this country spends more per person on health care than does any other nation. Given that we spend so much, why aren't we healthier?

The answers to this question lie partly in cultural factors and partly in the economics of the health care market. This chapter focuses on the economic forces at work in this key market. It also examines alternative health care delivery systems.

The Market for Health Care Services

The phrase "health care" is often used as an adjective for "problem" or even for "crisis." But why is that? What is it about health care that poses a problem for society?

In selecting health care as a major area of policy concern in 1993, the Clinton administration focused on two elements: first, it argued that the cost of health care in the United States was too high and that ordinary market forces were insufficient to restrain these costs; second, it pointed to the large number of people (then, about 37 million Americans) who lacked health care insurance.

EXHIBIT 20-1

Per Capita GDP and Health Care Spending in 22 Nations

The points show gross domestic product (GDP) per capita and health care spending per capita in 1989 in 22 member nations of the Organization for Economic Cooperation and Development (Iceland and Luxembourg are omitted). All values are expressed in units of equivalent purchasing power in each country. The heavy straight line suggests the positive relationship between per capita income and health care spending. The United States spends far more on health care than other industrial nations.

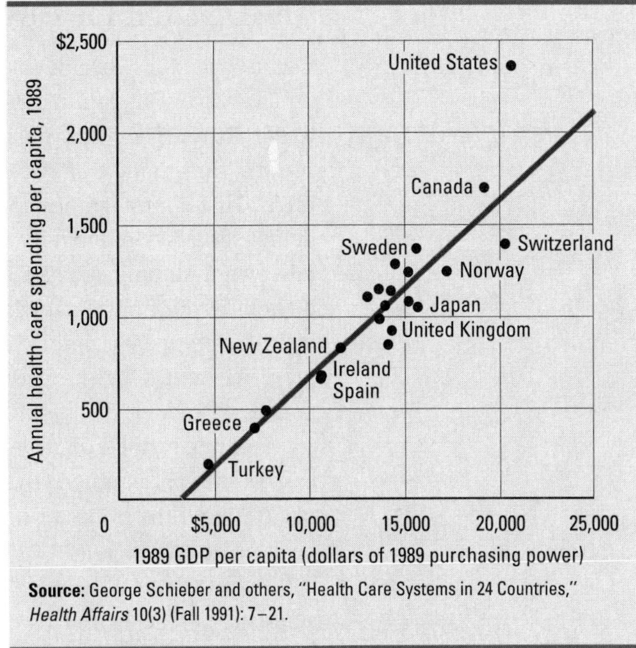

Source: George Schieber and others, "Health Care Systems in 24 Countries," *Health Affairs* 10(3) (Fall 1991): 7–21.

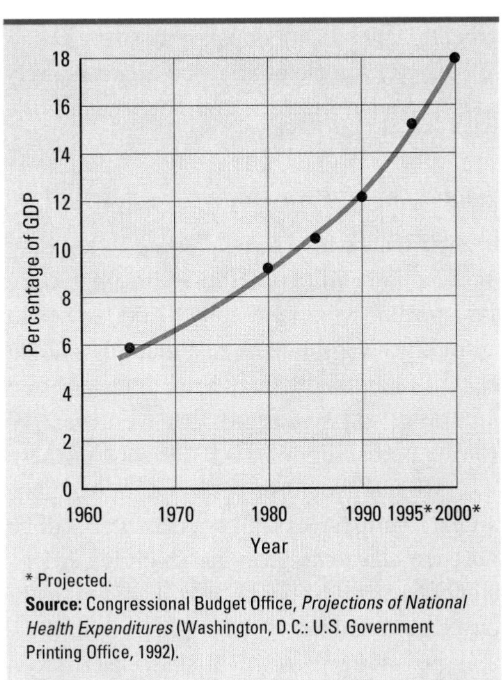

* Projected.

Source: Congressional Budget Office, *Projections of National Health Expenditures* (Washington, D.C.: U.S. Government Printing Office, 1992).

EXHIBIT 20-2

Health Care Spending as a Percentage of GDP

Health care's share of total gross domestic product (GDP) in the United States has risen sharply since 1960. The Congressional Budget Office projects that this share will increase through the remainder of the century.

The fact that many people are uninsured raises problems both of equity and of efficiency. Many argue that a system in which some people can't afford health insurance or are denied it because of their medical situation is unfair. Furthermore, we'll find as we analyze the market that individuals who simply choose not to have coverage can impose costs on other consumers. That implies an externality problem that may create an inefficient outcome.

The other element cited by the president, that health care costs too much, presents a difficult conceptual problem. How much is too much? People who charge that U.S. health care spending is too high often support their argument through international comparisons. As we noted, the United States spends more on health care than any other country. But remember that health care is a normal good, and people in the United States enjoy the highest incomes in the world. With higher incomes, people in the United States will spend more on health care. The data suggest, however, that income alone can't account for the high level of U.S. spending. Exhibit 20-1 shows gross domestic product (GDP) per capita, which is a measure of income, and annual health care spending per capita for the United States and for 21 other industrialized nations in 1989. The heavy line suggests the positive relationship that appears to exist between per capita income and per capita health care spending among countries other than the United States. U.S. spending is far higher than would be expected based on income alone.

Not only is spending for health care in the United States high—it is rising, both in absolute terms and as a percentage of total output. Exhibit 20-2 shows the percentage of U.S. output accounted for by health care services in various years since 1960, together with Congressional Budget Office projections for 1995 and for 2000. Clearly, health care is gobbling up an ever larger share of our total output.

In our analysis of health care we must explain its high—and rising—total cost. We'll do that as part of our investigation of the economics of health care in this section. In the next section, we'll examine alternatives for reform of the health care system.

The Demand for Health Care

One might expect health care services to be an exception to the law of demand, on the basis of an argument that has, perhaps, some intuitive appeal: People go to the doctor when they get sick and follow the course of action the doctor prescribes; the quantity of health care services they buy has nothing to do with the price. That argument, however, is wrong. Extensive research by economists has demonstrated convincingly that the demand curve for health care services is downward sloping. People do, after all, have choices. Whether they see their doctors in the first place will depend partly on the price they must pay for the visit. Whether they purchase the drugs and follow the procedures that doctors prescribe will depend on the price of those drugs and procedures. Prices do matter.

But prices don't matter very much. The price elasticity of demand for health care services is estimated to be −0.2. This quite inelastic demand for health care means that if the prices of health care services are rising, then total spending on health care will increase.

Any analysis of health care demand is greatly complicated by a special characteristic of the health care market: insurance. Most consumer purchases of health care services are compensated by insurance. This lowers the price consumers pay to a level well below the market price and increases the quantity demanded. U.S. consumers of health care services pay directly for only one-fifth of their health care costs; the remainder comes from private insurance and from government payments. This arrangement, in which individuals choose the health care services they consume while others pay for them, is called a **third-party payer system.** As we shall see, this structure has dramatic consequences for the operation of the health care market.

Insurance and Health Care Demand

Insurance allows individuals to pool their risks with a large group of other people. Suppose each of 10,000 skiers faces a probability of 0.001 of breaking a leg during any one year and that such a misfortune would consume $1,000 in health care costs for X rays and the services of physicians, nurses, and therapists. Each person in this group of 10,000 skiers thus individually faces a small chance of a substantial loss. For the entire group, however, we can say that we *expect* 10 broken legs a year (10,000 skiers times a probability of 0.001). If each of these 10,000 skiers were to pay $1 per year, $10,000 would be collected in insurance premiums each year—just enough to fix 10 broken legs. Of course, there will be some years in which more legs are broken and some years in which fewer legs are broken. But on average, a payment of $1 per year per skier will cover the annual cost of mending broken legs for the group.

An insurance program could thus be arranged in which skiers pay into a fund that will cover the health care costs of fixing broken legs. There will also be a cost in administering such a program—someone must collect the money, arrange payment of medical expenses, determine that the claims submitted are legitimate, and undertake the risk that there will be an occasional bad year in which more than 10 legs will be broken. The insurer will need to charge an additional amount to cover these other costs.

A **third-party payer system** is one in which consumers select their health care services while other institutions pay a share of the cost of those services.

Health insurance works in much the same manner as our hypothetical group plan for broken legs. An insurer determines the expected loss in any one year for a particular group of people, adds the costs of administering the program, and offers the insurance. The price charged for the insurance per period is called a premium. This premium covers the amount of expected claims plus other costs the insurer will have.

Insurance is a mechanism through which risk is transferred from individuals to the insurer. Individual skiers in our example face 1 chance in 1,000 of a large financial cost; they have traded this for the certainty of an annual premium. It is the insurer that now confronts the risk of loss. The insurer is able to do that because it has pooled the risks of a large number of individuals into a group for which annual outcomes can be predicted with a high degree of confidence.

Insurance creates a win-win situation typical of market exchange. Subscribers to insurance are better off because they have transferred risk, which they don't like, to the insurer. The owners of the insurance firm are better off because they are making at least an accounting profit. There are, however, problems inherent in the provision of insurance, problems that affect health care costs. We shall examine these problems in the context of our hypothetical problem of insuring skiers against broken legs.

Insurance and Adverse Selection In our skier problem, we assumed that the probability of any one skier breaking a leg in any year was 0.001. But in reality, someone who skis every day of the season has a higher probability of breaking a leg than someone who skis two or three times, and a reckless skier or one who uses inferior equipment has a higher chance of breaking a leg than a more conservative skier who uses the best equipment. Each skier, then, has a different probability of breaking a leg. More important, those probabilities will vary with factors that the insurer can't determine. An insurer can't know how fast or how recklessly a particular skier will ski. A potential subscriber knows, but the insurer does not.

Suppose that the average probability of breaking a leg in any one season is still 0.001 and that the insurer charges a premium of $1.20 per year to cover its expected payout plus other costs of business operation. What can we say about people who will purchase the insurance? On average, they are likely to be those who have the greatest probabilities of breaking a leg. Those who are least likely to break a leg may forgo the insurance. As skiers with higher-than-average probabilities of accidents subscribe and skiers with lower-than-average probabilities pass up the plan, the average probability of accidents for those insured will rise above the average probability for the population of skiers as a whole. The process through which the selection of subscribers raises the probability those subscribers will experience the outcome for which insurance is provided is called **adverse selection.**

The insurer will have to charge a higher premium to compensate for adverse selection. But as the premium rises, more people with lower probabilities of having an accident will forgo insurance, making the problem even worse. All insurance plans face the problem of adverse selection to some degree. Probabilities of loss always differ among individuals, and each individual always knows more about his or her own situation than the insurer can know.

Insurers can seek to limit adverse selection. Health and life insurance plans companies, for example, may require subscribers to receive a physical examination prior to enrolling, excluding applicants with a high risk of imposing costs on the system. Similarly, insurers often refuse to accept people who engage in particularly risky activities. Our skiing insurer may cancel the policies of people who have frequent claims—just as real-world insurers sometimes cancel the coverage of people whose histories reveal they are likely to incur unusually high health care costs.

Adverse selection means the selection o subscribers to an insurance plan raises the probability of the event insured against.

Moral hazard is the tendency for insurance protection to increase the rate at which the insured outcome occurs by changing the behavior of those protected by the insurance.

In health care, however, attempts by insurers to solve adverse selection problems are generally regarded as part of the public policy problem. Insurers may, for example, reject applicants who are HIV positive and thus likely to develop AIDS, or applicants with a history of heart disease. But then people whose need for insurance protection is greatest are least likely to be able to get it. Adverse selection is a problem for insurers and for their customers; attempts to resolve it can create severe hardship for some people.

Moral Hazard Suppose you had obtained the skiers' insurance described above. Because you have it, the cost of breaking your leg is now lower. Of course, there will still be pain and inconvenience, but you won't have to pay the $1,000 for medical care a broken leg would require. Because the cost of suffering a broken leg has been reduced, some people will make less of an effort to avoid one, skiing more often or more recklessly and increasing the probability that an accident will occur. The tendency of insurance to change behavior in a way that causes more frequent occurrence of the outcome against which the insurance protects is called **moral hazard.** Like adverse selection, moral hazard raises the cost of providing insurance and is an inevitable problem in any insurance plan.

Moral hazard is an implication of the law of demand. Because insurance reduces the cost of an event, that event will occur more often. People whose cars are insured against theft are less likely to make an effort to avoid having their cars stolen than people who don't have theft insurance. People with insurance against natural disasters such as floods are more likely to build homes in areas prone to flood damage. People with health insurance may be less careful to avoid accidents. Health insurance may even cause people to get sick more often by reducing the incentive to prevent illness.

Still another implication of moral hazard can be seen once the loss occurs. Suppose a skier has broken a leg. The insurance policy pays the health care costs, reducing the price of those services to the subscriber to zero. But the lower price will increase the quantity of health care services demanded by the skier. The skier may choose more physical therapy or more X rays, so the total cost will be more than the $1,000 average cost of treating a broken leg. Insurers commonly seek to limit moral hazard through devices such as requiring subscribers to obtain a second medical opinion prior to surgery or restricting payments for some types of services. For example, insurers typically set much higher copayment rates for services with a high potential for moral hazard to boost costs, such as mental health care.

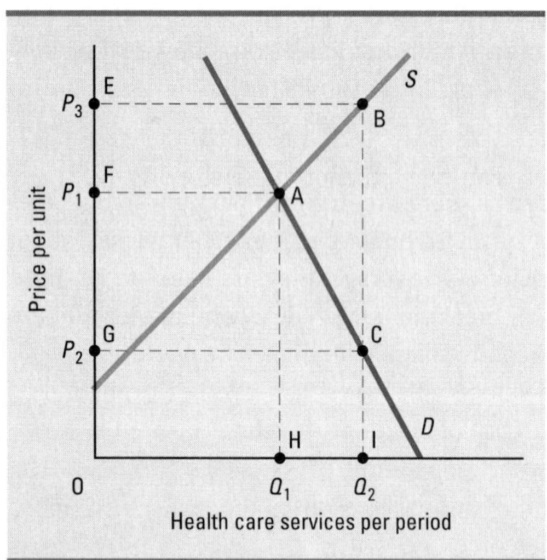

EXHIBIT 20-3

Moral Hazard and the Market for Health Care

Moral hazard increases the quantity of health care services demanded by lowering the price people pay. In the absence of insurance, the market reaches equilibrium at point A, at a price P_1 and a quantity Q_1 per period. Total spending is OFAH. Insurance lowers the price consumers pay to P_2, increasing the quantity demanded to Q_2. Inducing the production of Q_2 units of health care service requires a price of P_3. Total health care costs rise to OEBI, with GEBC paid by insurers and OGCI paid by consumers.

Exhibit 20-3 illustrates the impact of moral hazard on health care costs. The demand curve *D* shows the quantity of health care services demanded at each price; the supply curve *S* shows the quantity supplied. In the absence of insurance, the price per unit of health care services is P_1 and the quantity demanded and supplied is Q_1. The total cost of health care is given by the rectangle OFAH. Suppose that insurance lowers the price to P_2. This increases the quantity demanded to Q_2. That quantity will be available in the market at a price of P_3. The total cost of health care thus rises to OEBI. Consumers pay a quantity OGCI of this cost, and insurers pay GEBC.

Information Problems in the Demand for Health Care

Insurance is a device through which people insulate themselves from prices that would otherwise signal the costs of their health care choices. It is thus a source

Physician-induced demand occurs when doctors prescribe treatments that are not medically justified in order to increase their own incomes.

of inefficiency in the market for health care services. Another source of market inefficiency is lack of information.

To a much greater degree than is the case in other markets, consumers rely on health care suppliers—primarily physicians—for information about the health care choices they should make. But physicians have a financial interest in the quantity of health care services their patients demand; they may therefore prescribe procedures that serve primarily to increase their own income. The tendency for doctors to prescribe treatments that are not medically justified in order to increase their own incomes is called **physician-induced demand.**

It is difficult to determine the extent of physician-induced demand. Physicians are likely to have legitimately different views about the best treatment for a particular patient, so a doctor who prescribes more costly treatments than another is not necessarily seeking to increase his or her own profit. There is, however, considerable evidence consistent with the hypothesis that physician-induced demand occurs. An increase in the number of surgeons per capita, for example, is associated with a greater number of operations per capita. If two cities are similar in other respects but one has more surgeons, it will have more operations. Attempts to limit health care costs by reducing payments for certain procedures are known to increase the quantity of procedures prescribed as physicians seek to maintain their incomes. A study of health care claims for 65,000 patients showed that doctors who had diagnostic imaging equipment in their offices ordered 4 times more imaging exams than did doctors who referred patients elsewhere for the same tests. The phenomenon of physician-induced demand suggests that many health care providers can manipulate the demand curve for their services in order to increase their profits.

We thus see that several features on the demand side of the health care market affect outcomes in that market. The phenomenon of third-party payers in health care increases the quantity of health care demanded. Adverse selection increases the cost of insurance. And the problems of moral hazard and physician-induced demand all increase the demand for health care.

We turn next to an examination of special characteristics that affect the supply of health care services.

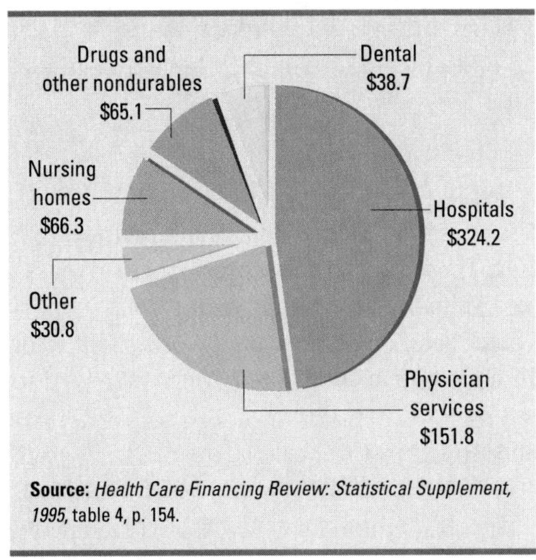

EXHIBIT 20-4

Suppliers of Health Care Services, 1992

The chart shows how health care spending was distributed among major suppliers in 1992.

The Supply of Health Care

Health care services are supplied by a wide range of providers, ranging from physicians in private practice to huge health maintenance organizations (HMOs). Exhibit 20-4 shows how health care spending is distributed among major groups of providers. Hospitals account for the largest share, followed by physicians and nursing homes. The "other" category includes chiropractors, physical therapists, psychologists, and a host of other providers.

Competition in the Health Care Market

Competitive structures vary throughout the health care market. A single doctor in a small town operates as a monopoly firm. We saw in Chapter 12 that some suppliers of prescription drugs enjoy monopoly power because of government regulations. In most cities, a few hospitals dominate the market as an oligopoly. Physicians generally operate under conditions that are closest to the model of monopolistic competition, although restrictions on entry exist.

While there is a degree of competition in most health care markets, the fact that consumers generally pay less than one-fourth of the cost of the health care services they consume limits the degree of price competition. With an insurance company or the government footing the lion's share of the bill, consumers are less responsive to price than they would be if they directly paid a greater share.

The lack of price competition among health care providers produces some unusual market twists. Economists have found, for example, that an increase in the supply of hospitals in a metropolitan area can actually increase prices. Hospitals compete to attract doctors to their staffs; it is the doctors who generate most patient admissions. Physicians, in turn, are attracted to hospitals that offer equipment embodying the latest technology—equipment that is costly to provide. Adding equipment attracts doctors, and doctors associated with a hospital boost demand for the hospital's services. The fact that this raises hospital costs may have little effect on patient choices of hospitals, given that insurers will pay most of the bill. Thus, competition among hospitals can increase health care costs rather than reduce them.

Government and Health Care Supply

Government policy has powerful effects on the supply of health care services. In general, government participation in the health care market has tended to restrict supply and thus to increase health care prices.

Probably the most important supply restriction occurs in the market for physicians' services. State licensing requirements limit the supply of physicians in each market. These physicians are further protected by regulations that limit competition from other health care providers. Nurses, for example, are generally barred from offering health care services except under the supervision of a physician. Most states do not allow midwives to deliver babies, and the ones that do generally require a doctor's supervision.

Restrictions on physician supply are one reason physician incomes are so high in this country. Exhibit 20-5 compares physician incomes, measured in dollars of U.S. purchasing power, in 14 industrialized countries in 1986. All salaries are reported net of malpractice insurance premiums physicians must pay. The table also shows the ratio of physician income to average income in each country—physician incomes exceed other incomes to a much greater degree in the United States than in other countries.

Country	Physician income	Ratio of physician income to average income in country
Australia	$34,191	2.26
Canada	70,144	3.47
Denmark	39,061	2.01
Finland	35,558	1.82
France	N.A.	3.27 (1979)
West Germany	91,244	4.28
Ireland	17,830	1.08
Italy	N.A.	1.10 (1981)
Japan	56,437	2.46
Norway	31,664	1.38
Sweden	N.A.	1.80 (1983)
Switzerland	118,501	4.10
United Kingdom	33,615	2.39
United States	119,500	5.12

N.A.: Not available.
Source: J. Paul Leigh, "International Comparisons of Physicians' Salaries," *International Journal of Health Services* 22(2) (1992):218. With permission of Baywood Publishing Co., Inc.

EXHIBIT 20-5

An International Comparison of Physician Salaries, 1986

Annual incomes of physicians in 14 countries are reported in dollars of 1986 purchasing power. The third column shows the ratio of physician income to the average income in each country. Income is adjusted by the amount of malpractice insurance premiums paid by physicians.

Health Maintenance Organizations and Other Health Care Organizations

A rising share of the health care market is accounted for by health maintenance organizations, popularly called HMOs. These firms offer subscribers a full package of health care services for a fixed annual fee, together with a small copayment for each visit. Physicians and other health care providers work directly for the HMO. In 1993, roughly 41 million people in the United States belonged to HMOs.

An HMO turns the ordinary incentives in the health care market upside down. The provider, the HMO, receives a fixed amount each year for each patient who subscribes to the service. The HMO thus can't increase its income by prescribing more services—unnecessary care raises costs and reduces the firm's profits. While there may be a temptation in the short run to err in the opposite direction, trying to save money by not performing needed procedures, such a policy would surely cause the HMO to lose subscribers in the long run.

HMOs and traditional health insurance plans also differ in their attitude toward preventive medicine. When patients receive regular physical exams, their medical problems may be detected earlier and thus treated at far lower cost.

That's in the interest of the HMO, and HMOs thus emphasize preventive medicine. For the traditional insurer, however, preventive medicine poses a problem. It has the potential to lower costs, but preventive medicine is also subject to a high degree of moral hazard, since patients could easily have more exams. Traditional insurers often do not cover the cost of physical exams; those that do typically impose restrictions on their coverage.

In theory, then, an HMO should both lower the cost of health care and deliver services that leave its subscribers satisfied with their care. The evidence suggests that HMOs succeed. They deliver health care at a much lower cost than traditional insurance plans. Their cost advantage has attracted customers, either by appealing to subscribers directly or by appealing to the employers who buy coverage for their employees; enrollment in HMOs increased fourfold between 1982 and 1992.

HMOs reduce costs by changing incentives. An alternative approach exploits the potential monopsony power of large insurers. Ordinary health insurance plans allow consumers to choose their physicians, but most plans now offer the option of signing up for coverage under a preferred provider organization (PPO). A PPO is a network of physicians and other providers that have agreed to charge fees established by the insurer. Subscribers who choose providers in the PPO network pay lower coinsurance rates and have lower deductibles. In effect, a PPO allows the insurer to impose lower prices than would otherwise prevail in the marketplace.

As the United States struggles to reduce its health care bill, increased reliance on HMOs and PPOs seems likely. Such reliance, of course, comes at a cost. These organizations reduce choices to consumers. An HMO allows subscribers the choice of only those doctors on its staff. A PPO allows a choice only among doctors on its list. But if one source of high health care spending is physician-advised consumer choice backed by third-party payers, then one way to solve the problem is to limit that choice.

Although HMOs and PPOs can deliver health care at lower cost than traditional systems, the rate of increase in cost is about the same as in all these systems. A switch to greater use of HMOs and PPOs would be likely to lower costs in the short run but would do little to solve the problem of escalating total costs in the long run.

Health Care and Technological Change

Probably the single most important factor behind the rapid increase in U.S. health care spending has been technological change. As new procedures are developed to treat illness, health care providers can offer a wider range of services. The costs of those services contribute to rising health care costs.

Consider, for example, the problem of kidney failure. Before the invention of dialysis machines, victims of kidney failure could expect to die. Now these patients can survive with dialysis, but the treatments can cost as much as $60,000 per year. Another new development, the kidney transplant, frees patients from reliance on dialysis, at a cost of as much as $100,000.

Although technological advances can save lives, many economists suggest that expensive treatments are not always justified. In other segments of the economy, a technological advance is subject to a market test that weighs its benefits and costs. But in the health care market, consumers aren't confronted with the costs of their choices and may thus demand new technologies whose cost exceeds their benefit.

Checklist

- U.S. health care spending exceeds that of any other country on a per capita basis, in total and as a percentage of GDP.
- The U.S. system is dominated by third-party payers, principally private insurance companies.
- Insurance allows subscribers to reduce their risk, but also invites problems of adverse selection and moral hazard.
- Health care markets range from monopolistically competitive to monopoly market structures.
- Government intervention in the United States has tended to restrict the supply of health care providers, especially of physicians.
- Two new ways of supplying health care, the HMO and the PPO, tend to reduce the cost of health care provision. They do, however, limit consumer choice.
- Technological change interacts with insurance coverage to produce sharply rising health care costs.

Burton Weisbrod, an economist at Northwestern University, has suggested a simple model of the dynamics of health care costs. The model stresses the positive feedback between technological change and health insurance coverage. The rate of technological change increases when insurance coverage pays for new procedures—and then demand for insurance coverage increases as technology advances because there are greater, and costlier, benefits to be had. Technological change thus boosts the insurance coverage people hold, which boosts the rate of technological change—and makes it even more desirable to obtain insurance.

Technological change has been the dominant factor driving health care costs upward—economists generally agree that it has accounted for about half the increase in U.S. health care spending over the past decade. The remainder has been a result of inflation and increased population.

Public Policy and Health Care

We have already seen that government plays a major role in the health care market. It is a regulator of private suppliers, a consumer of their services, and a supplier of health care. This section examines the role of government in the health care market and explores alternatives for health care reform.

Government's Role Today

The expanding government role in the health care market is illustrated in Exhibit 20-6, which shows the shares of health care spending coming from the private sector and from government at the federal, state, and local levels in 1960 and in 1992. The government share has increased most dramatically at the federal level because of the expansion of the two largest health care programs, Medicaid and Medicare. Taken at all levels, government spending accounts for close to one-half of all the health care spending in the United States today.

This sketch of health care spending understates the importance of government in the health care market. We have already seen that the government plays

EXHIBIT 20-6

Sources of Health Care Spending in the United States

The federal government's share of health care spending has increased sharply since 1960. We also see that private third-party payments, which are primarily made by insurance companies, have become a much more important source of health care spending in the United States.

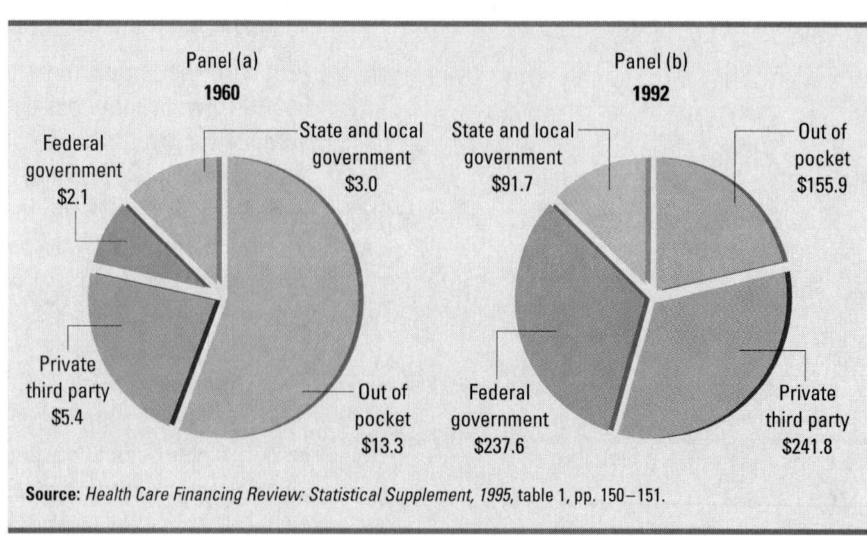

Source: *Health Care Financing Review: Statistical Supplement, 1995,* table 1, pp. 150–151.

an important role in regulating the market. Perhaps the most important role of government, however, is one that does not appear in the federal budget and that involves no direct regulation. It lies in government tax policy.

Tax Policy

We've already seen that most health care consumption is financed through insurance. A curious feature of this insurance is that most of it is purchased not by consumers but by employers.

At first glance, it seems odd that virtually all private purchases of health care insurance are carried out under employer sponsorship. Employers don't pay for their employees' food, housing, or clothing. Why do they pay for health care? The answer appears to be that one of the most important features of the U.S. health care system was more a historical accident than a conscious choice.

Prior to World War II, only 11 percent of the U.S. population had health insurance of any kind; most of this was purchased by individuals. During World War II, the federal government imposed wage and price controls throughout the economy in an effort to avoid inflation. The war effort used a substantial share of the labor force; unemployment fell almost to zero. There were severe labor shortages in many sectors of the economy. That would ordinarily have produced higher wages, but wage controls prevented this. Employers competed for scarce labor by offering more nonwage benefits, including health insurance. The federal government ruled that these benefits did not constitute wages and thus did not violate the wage and price control program. The Internal Revenue Service maintained the fiction that provision of health care benefits did not constitute wages by ruling that such benefits were exempt from taxation.

As income tax and payroll tax rates have risen since the war, the tax-exempt status of health care benefits has become more important to workers and to firms. Suppose the employer of a worker earning $40,000 per year wants to add $1 in pay. The worker falls in the 28 percent bracket of the federal income tax, and payroll taxes take an additional 15.3 percent. If state and local income taxes take another 4 percent, our worker will be able to keep 53 cents out of the extra $1 in pay. But if the employer chooses to put $1 into health care instead, none of that benefit will be taxed. Given a choice between 53 cents in spendable income and an extra $1 worth of health care insurance, many workers and their employers choose the insurance. Tax policy has thus contributed to another change suggested by Exhibit 20-6—the rising importance of third-party payers, principally insurance companies, in the health care market.

The impact of a choice that was made in the midst of a national battle for survival in World War II has been staggering. Workers now generally assume that it is the responsibility of their employers to provide their health insurance, and they presume this benefit will go untaxed. The exemption of health care benefits reduced the amount of federal taxes collected by $65 billion in 1992. If these lost taxes were included in spending for health care, the federal government alone would account for more than half the total.

Regulation

Government's regulatory role in the health care market has generally focused on consumer protection—ensuring that health care providers meet certain standards and regulating new drugs. Such regulations have tended to limit competition and thus to boost health care costs. Increasingly, however, government's regulatory efforts are aimed at reducing health care costs.

The Federal Trade Commission (FTC), an enforcer of antitrust laws, has prodded states to ease some of their restrictions on competition in the health care industry. We saw in Chapter 13 that many states once banned advertising of prescription eyeglasses. Lack of information greatly increased prices to consumers and thus increased health care costs. FTC officials have urged states to drop such bans; virtually all have done so.

Still another innovation aims to reduce health care costs by changing federal antitrust policy. Hospitals would slow the race to have the best equipment if they could specialize, say with one having equipment to treat heart disease, another to treat cancer. Such collusion would allow fuller utilization of equipment and would reduce the quantity of equipment acquired. But it would also run afoul of antitrust laws, which prohibit collusion among competing firms. The Clinton administration, as part of its health care reform package, introduced legislation in 1993 that would allow hospitals to collude in an effort to economize on purchases of equipment. It had not been approved when this book went to press.

Another regulation that plays a key role in health care provision in the United States is the requirement in most states that hospital emergency rooms provide treatment for all comers, regardless of ability to pay. People who lack insurance coverage often obtain care for common ailments by going to the hospital, knowing that they will be able to see a doctor and that they are not likely to have to pay for the service provided. Hospitals typically receive payments for only about half the services they provide. This drives up prices for those who do pay.

Government Health Care Programs

The federal and state governments act as insurers of health care. The federal Medicare program is a health insurance program for the elderly; it is financed through payroll taxes. Medicaid is a joint federal and state health insurance program for low-income people. The federal government also provides health care through Veteran's Administration hospitals. In addition, the U.S. military operates base hospitals. With the rapid expansion of Medicare and Medicaid in the past three decades, government has emerged as an important source of payment for health care services. Roughly one-third of all health care spending in the United States is financed by these two programs.

Alternatives in Health Care Reform

There appears to be widespread agreement that the U.S. health care system needs reform. Current discussions of health care reform in the United States focus on three groups of proposals. One approach relies extensively on market mechanisms. A second would still rely on a market but would change the ground rules to give buyers more clout. A third would have the federal government become the sole payer for health care services with a system of national health insurance similar to the program in Canada. All of these would incorporate mechanisms for extending health care coverage to everyone. All would make it illegal for insurers to deny coverage to a person based on his or her medical history.

As you read about the various alternatives, recall that the essential problem with the U.S. system is that decisionmakers are confronted with only a small fraction of the costs of their choices. That increases the quantity of health care services demanded and stimulates technological changes that have driven health care costs up. To succeed in limiting cost, any reform proposal must address this problem.

Market-Based Health Care Reforms

Proposals based on reforms in the health care market call for continued reliance on private markets to provide services. Indeed, they generally call for a sharply reduced role for government, save for provisions that ensure health insurance is available to all.

A key element in market-based reforms would be a requirement that all individuals purchase at least a basic health care insurance package. This basic plan could be offered by any private insurer. Most market-based reforms anticipate a basic package that would require subscribers to pay a larger share of their health care bills than do most current plans.

Another feature of all market-based plans is that low-income individuals would be given funds to purchase insurance. Most market-based reform proposals would permit employers to offer health insurance coverage as a benefit, but they would generally tax the value of such plans as ordinary income. People could, under market-based plans, opt to purchase more generous insurance coverage if they wished.

Market-based proposals typically call for extensive deregulation of health care services. Individuals buying their own insurance, or paying taxes on the insurance provided by their employers, would be likely to pay more attention to cost. That could make price competition more effective, and then removing governmental restrictions against competition, such as the regulations that prevent nurses from competing with doctors for the provision of minor medical services, would have a greater payoff.

Managed Competition

Alain Enthoven, an economist at Stanford University, has proposed a system aimed at giving buyers of health care a degree of monopsony power. He argues that such power would drive down the prices of health care services.

In a **managed competition** system, private health insurance purchasing cooperatives (HIPCs) would negotiate with insurers and HMOs for coverage; consumers could select an HIPC. The HIPCs most successful in driving health care costs down would presumably gain the most customers; the market would reward their success.

An HIPC could offer a variety of insurance plans and a list of providers who agree to meet its prices. Individuals could compare the services offered by different HIPCs and pick the package most to their liking. Under Mr. Enthoven's plan, individuals could bypass the HIPC and purchase care directly from a physician or purchase insurance directly from an individual company.

Managed competition would change the present system by very little. In fact, many large insurance companies are already acting very much like HIPCs, offering potential subscribers a wide range of plans and lists of providers who have agreed to offer services at low prices. The HIPCs anticipated under a system of managed competition would encompass several of these packages. Their greater share of the marketplace would give them a greater degree of monopsony power and thus give them the ability to force costs down.

One difficulty is that it's not clear that the HIPC concept would slow the rate of increase in health care costs. HIPCs could force costs down to a degree, but they don't appear to provide any new mechanism to check the tendency for

In a **managed competition** system, private health insurance purchasing cooperatives (HIPCs) would negotiate prices with insurers and health care providers, and consumers could select their HIPCs.

Case in Point: The Oregon Plan

Like all other states, Oregon has wrestled with the problem of soaring Medicaid costs. Its solution to the problem illustrates some of the choices a single-payer system might make in seeking to reduce health care costs.

Oregon used to have a plan similar to plans in many other states. Households whose incomes were lower than 50 percent of the poverty line qualified for Medicaid. In 1987, the state began an effort to manage its Medicaid costs. It decided that it would no longer fund organ transplants and that it would use the money saved to give better care to pregnant women. The decision turned out to be a painful one; the first year, a 7-year-old boy with leukemia, who might have been saved with a bone marrow transplant, died. But state officials argued that the shift of expenditures to pregnant women would ultimately save more lives.

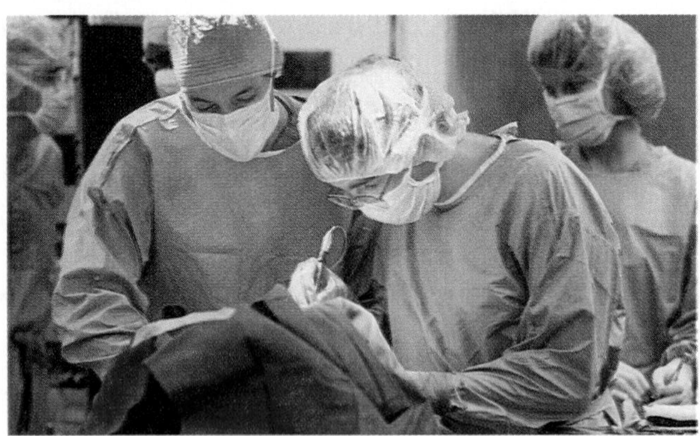

The state gradually expanded its concept of determining what services to fund and what services not to fund. It collapsed a list of 10,000 different diagnoses that had been submitted to its Medicare program in the past into a list of 709 condition-treatment pairs. One such pair, for example, is appendicitis-appendectomy. Health care officials then ranked these pairs in order of priority. The rankings were based on such factors as the seriousness of a particular condition and the cost and efficacy of treatments. The state announced that it would provide Medicaid to all households below the poverty line, but that it would not fund any procedure ranked below 588 on its list. Among the treatments no longer funded are surgery for low back pain, treatment for extremely premature babies, liver transplants for alcoholic cirrhosis, and treatment of viral warts. The plan also sets a budget limit for any one year; if spending rises above that limit, the legislature must appropriate additional money or drop additional procedures from the list of those covered by the plan.

While Oregon serves as a single payer only for households below the poverty line that are not covered by other programs, its plan suggests some of the choices necessary in rationing health care under a single-payer plan. Clearly, if part of the health care problem is excessive provision of services, a single-payer system designed to cut services must determine what treatments not to fund.

Subscribers to the plan lose because they have a less generous range of covered services than people under other Medicaid programs. The population as a whole, however, is assured coverage over a much wider range of incomes.

technological changes to boost costs. It thus seems unlikely that the HIPC would, by itself, solve the problem of escalating health care costs.

The Single-Payer Alternative

The most radical proposal is a **single-payer plan** in which the federal government would replace all private insurers. Individuals might still pay a deductible and copayment, but the government would provide the rest. Most proposals calling for the single-payer alternative assume that no one would pay premiums, general taxes would pay for health insurance.

In a single-payer plan, a program such as Medicaid or Medicare would simply be extended to everyone. By paying most of the bills, it is argued, the government could exert its monopsony power to push down prices charged by providers. It could also act to limit care it regards as unnecessary.

Canada now has a single-payer plan. The system has proved successful in limiting health care expenditures, but it achieves this in part by restricting the availability of many forms of high-tech care commonly available in the United States. For example, a study comparing treatment of heart attack patients found that doctors in the United States are much more likely to use aggressive—and expensive—measures than are doctors in Canada. Coronary bypass surgery, for

- In a **single-payer plan,** the federal government would replace all private insurers.

Checklist

- The federal government is a major health insurer through its Medicare and Medicaid programs; the latter are operated in conjunction with individual states. The federal government also supplies health care through various military programs.
- The chief impact of the federal government on health care has been to create a system of employer-paid health insurance. This is a response to federal tax policy.
- Proposals for health care reform include market-based plans that would stress lower coinsurance rates and higher deductibles, managed competition that would seek to give buyers of health care services a greater degree of monopsony power, and single-payer plans that would make the federal government or some other agency the sole party responsible for paying for health care services.

example, is far more common in the United States, which has 3 times as many facilities equipped for the procedure per 1 million people as does Canada. The study found that survival rates in the two countries are similar but that U.S. patients report less discomfort and are able to go back to work sooner than Canadian patients.

A single-payer system can force costs down by rationing health care. As the sole purchaser of services, the government can determine what kinds of services will be purchased and for whom they will be made available. The National Health Service in Great Britain, for example, has determined that people over the age of 65 are not eligible for government-provided heart surgery. The British system also limits access to hospitals; in 1993 more than 100,000 people were on waiting lists for nonemergency hospital admissions.

Of the three reform alternatives, the market-based and single-payer plans appear to have the greatest potential for limiting health care costs. They represent a sharp philosophical choice. Market-based plans allow individuals to choose the health care they want, which means that people with higher incomes will have access to more and better care. While market-based proposals provide a basic level of coverage to all, there would be sharp disparities in treatment according to income. Single-payer plans would provide the same care to everyone and would substitute government edict for individual choice as the primary mechanism for holding down health care costs. Exhibit 20-7 summarizes the three basic reform alternatives.

Plan	Universal Coverage?	Cost Control?	Pros	Cons
Market based	Yes, through tax credits and purchase requirements.	Most plans would increase deductible and coinsurance rate, giving subscribers an incentive to economize.	Gives greater choice.	Unless deductibles and coinsurance rates are very high, plans retain incentives to increase health care spending.
Managed competition	Not a central feature, but could be accommodated in a plan.	Health insurance purchasing cooperatives (HIPCs) would exert monopsony power to force prices down.	Involves only a modest change from the existing system; preserves considerable freedom of choice.	Unlikely to solve the problem of the costs imposed by technological change, and thus unlikely to slow the rate of increase in health care costs.
Single payer	Yes, through taxes.	Government exploits monopsony power; determines what services to cover.	Allows high degree of cost containment; simplifies payment system.	Reduces choice; involves more extensive government regulation.

EXHIBIT 20-7

Health Care Options

A Look Back—And a Look Ahead

Our health care system poses two problems. First, under the present system, many people lack health care coverage. Second, health care costs appear to be excessive in the United States. Costs are not only high but are rising rapidly. People in the United States spend far more than citizens of other countries on health care, yet they aren't clearly healthier.

Insurance makes people better off by insulating them from cost risks, but it also exacerbates problems in the health care market. Because people face only a fraction of the costs they incur, they choose an excessive amount of health care services. Further, insurance coverage encourages the rapid technological change that has forced health care costs up—and at the same time provided much more effective health care.

The health care market ranges from monopolistically competitive to monopoly segments. Two important market innovations are health maintenance organizations (HMOs) and preferred provider organizations (PPOs).

Government's role as a provider, consumer, and regulator in the health care market has expanded greatly in recent years. One key result of government policy is the phenomenon of employer-provided health insurance.

Reform proposals for health care include market-based plans, managed competition, and single-payer plans. Of these, market-based reforms and single-payer plans seem most likely to control costs. They represent a choice between a system in which individuals make choices that will limit costs and one in which a government agency makes those choices. The latter would result in more uniform care; the former allows greater freedom.

Terms and Concepts for Review

Adverse selection
Managed competition
Moral hazard
Physician-induced demand
Single-payer plan
Third-party payer system

For Discussion

1. Given that people pay premiums for their health insurance, how can we say that insurance lowers the prices people pay for health care services?
2. Some market-based reform plans would allow individuals to set up a health care savings account that would be exempt from taxation provided the money were used for health care. Money would be drawn from the account to pay health care bills. Any money left over in the account could be used for other purposes but would be subject to income tax. Suppose an individual opens such an account and deposits $2,000 per year; part of the account pays for an insurance policy that pays all health care costs over $2,000 per year. The individual faces a marginal income tax rate of 30 percent and has spent $1,000 on health care services so far this year. What is the effective cost to this individual of purchasing an additional $1 worth of health care services?
3. We hear that people can't afford health care, and we hear many complaints that health care spending takes up too large a share of GDP. Yet families spend, on average, more for housing and for food than they do for health care. Why do we hear of a health care crisis but not a housing or a food crisis?
4. Suppose that physicians now charge $30 for an office visit and insurance policies require a copayment of 33⅓ percent, so the out-of-pocket cost to consumers is $10 per visit. In an effort to control costs, the government imposes a price ceiling of $27 per office visit. Using a demand and supply model similar to that in Exhibit 20-3, show how this policy would affect the market for health care.
5. Suppose health insurance purchasing cooperatives are created, and each HIPC enjoys monopsony power. Using the monopsony model, show what the market will look like. What do you think is a likely market response to such a situation?
6. Do you think the U.S. health care system requires reform? Why or why not? If you think reform is in order, explain the approach to reform you advocate.

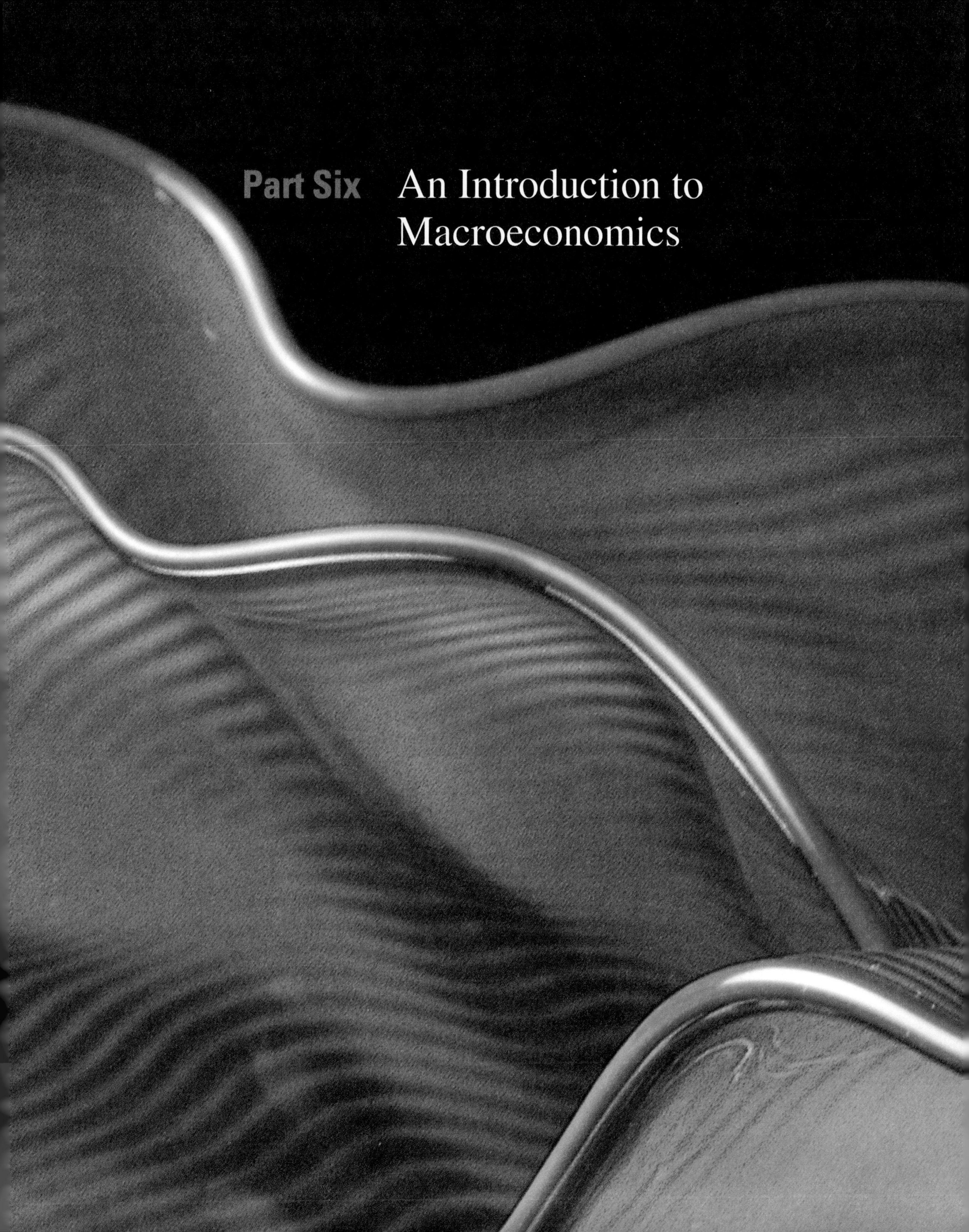

Part Six An Introduction to Macroeconomics

21

The Measurement of Economic Activity

Chapter Objectives

After mastering the material in this chapter, you will be able to:

1. Use the circular flow model to explain how the production of goods and services generates income to households, and explain why an economy's total output equals total income.
2. Discuss the potential for overcounting the nation's output and the ways in which such overcounting is avoided.
3. Explain the difference between nominal and real measures of macroeconomic activity.
4. Discuss the conceptual difficulties in measuring output in today's economy.
5. Comment on the use of macroeconomic measures to compare economic performance among countries.

. . . the age of chivalry is gone. That of sophisters, economists, and calculators, has succeeded; and the glory of Europe is extinguished for ever.
Edmund Burke

What's Ahead

It's still early when the half-dozen senior officials enter the lockup—a room at the Commerce Department in Washington. Once inside, they'll have no communication with the outside world until they've completed their work later that day. They'll have no telephone, no computer links. They'll be able to slip out to an adjoining restroom, but only in pairs.

When they've finished their computations, they'll put their results in a sealed envelope and sign it. A government messenger will hand-carry the sealed parcel to the Executive Office Building and give it to a senior adviser to the president of the United States. The adviser will examine its contents, then carry it across the street to the White House and give it to the president.

The envelope contains the government's estimate of the economy's total output, called gross domestic product (GDP). The senior officials who meet in secret to compute GDP aren't spies, they're economists. The adviser who will deliver the estimate to the president is the chair of the Council of Economic Advisers.

The elaborate precautions for secrecy won't end there. At 7:30 the next morning, journalists from all over the world will gather in an electronically sealed auditorium at the Commerce Department building in Washington. They'll be given the GDP figure and an explanation of what it means. The reporters will have an hour to prepare their reports on the number, but they won't be able to communicate with anyone else until an official throws the switch at 8:30. At that instant their computers will connect to their respective news services, and they'll be able to file their stories. These will be major stories in the next editions of the nation's newspapers; the estimate of the previous quarter's GDP will be the lead item on television and radio news broadcasts that day.

The clandestine proceedings for the release of GDP figures reflect the importance of this indicator. The estimate of GDP provides the best "read" available on what's happening to the economy. It will affect government policy, and it will influence millions of decisions in the private sector. Prior knowledge of the

GDP estimate could be used to anticipate the response in the stock and bond markets, so great care is taken that only a handful of trusted officials have access to the information until it's officially released. In a country that churns out millions of numbers each year, the estimate of GDP is one of the most important.

In this chapter, we'll examine the computation of real and nominal GDP. We'll learn what these estimates mean and why they're so important. We'll also explore some conceptual difficulties in estimating these variables.

This chapter begins our investigation of macroeconomic analysis. As we've already learned, macroeconomics focuses on the determination of aggregate values in the economy. (One of those aggregates is GDP, the economy's total output.) We'll be using measures of output throughout our exploration of macroeconomic analysis; this chapter will equip you with an understanding of such measures.

In 1994, Domino's Pizza produced 230 million pizzas. USX Corporation produced 11.7 million tons of steel. The University of Nebraska football team drew 453,401 fans to its six home games—and won the national championship. Leesa Mahaffey, a detective for the Long Beach, California police department, responded to 564 calls, made 93 arrests, and filled out 966 pages of police reports.

What kind of year was 1994 for the economy? Clearly we aren't going to get very far trying to wade through a list of all the goods and services that were produced that year. Instead, economists use a summary statistic of total output called **gross domestic product (GDP),** which is the total value, at current market prices, of all final goods and services produced during a particular period. Each item produced, whether a bran muffin or a battleship, is valued at its current market price and added to GDP, which is the primary measure of the economy's performance. We shall investigate the computation of this key macroeconomic indicator and, in the process, learn something about important relationships in macroeconomics.

Notice that only "final" goods and services are included in GDP. Many goods and services are purchased for use as inputs in producing something else. A pizza parlor buys flour to make pizzas. If we counted the value of the flour and the value of the pizza, we'd end up counting the flour twice and thus overstating the value of actual production. **Final goods and services** are those that are sold or are ready for sale to buyers who will use them for consumption, investment, government purchases, or net exports—components of GDP that we will discuss in this chapter.

An important identity underlies the estimation of GDP: The production of a given value of goods and services generates an equal value of income. The necessary equality between GDP and gross domestic income suggests that GDP can be measured both as the total value of output produced and as the income generated in producing that output.

Consider a $4 box of Cheerios. It's part of the total output of the economy and thus is part of GDP. Who gets the $4?

Part of the answer to that question can be found by a glance at the cereal box. Cheerios are made from oat flour, wheat starch, sugar, salt, and a variety of vitamins and minerals. That means that part of the $4 goes to the farmers who grew the oats, the wheat, and the beets or cane from which the sugar was

- An economy's **gross domestic product (GDP)** is the value, at current market prices, of the final goods and services produced during a particular period.

- **Final goods and services** are those that are sold or are ready for sale to buyers who will use them for consumption, investment, government purchases, or net exports.

extracted. Workers at General Mills combined the ingredients, crafted all those little O's, toasted them, and put them in a box. The workers were paid part of the $4 as wages. The owners of General Mills received part of the $4 as profit. The box containing the Cheerios was made from a tree, so a lumber company somewhere received part of the $4. The truck driver who brought the box of cereal to the grocery store got part of the $4, as did the owner of the truck itself and the owner of the oil that fueled the truck. The clerk who rang up the sale at the grocery store was paid part of the $4. And so on.

How much of the $4 was income generated by owners of the factors of production that produced the Cheerios? The answer is simple: all of it. Some of the money went to workers as wages. Some went to owners of the capital and natural resources used to produce it. Surpluses, or profits, generated along the way went to the owners of the firms involved. The total value of the *output* of the box of Cheerios—the $4—was *income* generated by the owners of the productive factors that produced the Cheerios.

As it is with Cheerios, so it is with everything else. The value of output equals the income generated as the output is produced. One way to measure GDP, then, is to measure output. Another is to measure the income generated in producing that output. We shall begin our examination of GDP by considering it as a measure of output.

GDP: A Measure of Output

The goods and services that make up GDP can be divided into four categories: personal consumption, investment, government purchases, and net exports. These categories represent different buyers. Consumers purchase the goods and services included in personal consumption. Firms engage in investment, which adds to the capital stock. Government agencies also purchase goods and services. Finally, the net impact of foreign buying and selling of goods is included in the category of net exports.

We shall examine the components of GDP using the **circular flow model,** a model that traces aggregate flows of spending and income through the economy. The model divides the economy into two broad groups: firms and households. Firms produce goods and services using factors of production—labor, capital, and natural resources—owned by households. As we consider each component of GDP, we'll add it to the circular flow diagram.

Personal Consumption

The **personal consumption** component of GDP measures the money value of goods and services that are purchased by households during a time period. Purchases by households of groceries, health care services, clothing, automobiles—all are counted as consumption.

Production of consumer goods and services equals more than two-thirds of total output. Because consumption is such a large part of GDP, economists seeking to understand the determinants of GDP must pay special attention to the determinants of consumption. In Chapter 27 we'll explore the determinants of consumption and the impact of consumption on economic activity.

To put consumption into the context of the circular flow model, we shall imagine that firms produce *only* consumer goods and services. We'll disregard

A **circular flow model** is a pictorial representation of aggregate flows of spending and income through the economy.

Personal consumption measures the value of goods and services purchased by households during a particular period.

production of goods and services for other firms, for government agencies, or for foreign buyers. Indeed, we'll assume for now that there is no government or foreign sector. We shall also assume that households spend all their income on consumption—there is no saving.

Exhibit 21-1 shows the circular flow model as it would exist in such an economy. Households purchase goods and services from firms; their spending for personal consumption is shown as the blue arrow labeled "Personal consumption." Personal consumption becomes the demand for individual goods and services, as suggested by the individual demand and supply graphs for blue jeans, haircuts, and apartments embedded within the red arrow. Just as there is a flow of spending from households to firms, there is a return flow of goods and services—such as blue jeans and haircuts—from firms to households. We will be focusing on the spending flows, so the return flow of goods and services is not shown.

EXHIBIT 21-1

Consumption in the Circular Flow Model
This simplified version of the circular flow model illustrates an economy in which firms produce only consumer goods and services and there is no government and no foreign sector. Personal consumption flows from households to firms; factor incomes flow from firms to households. These flows, in turn, represent the aggregates of individual markets for consumer goods and services and of individual markets for factors of production.

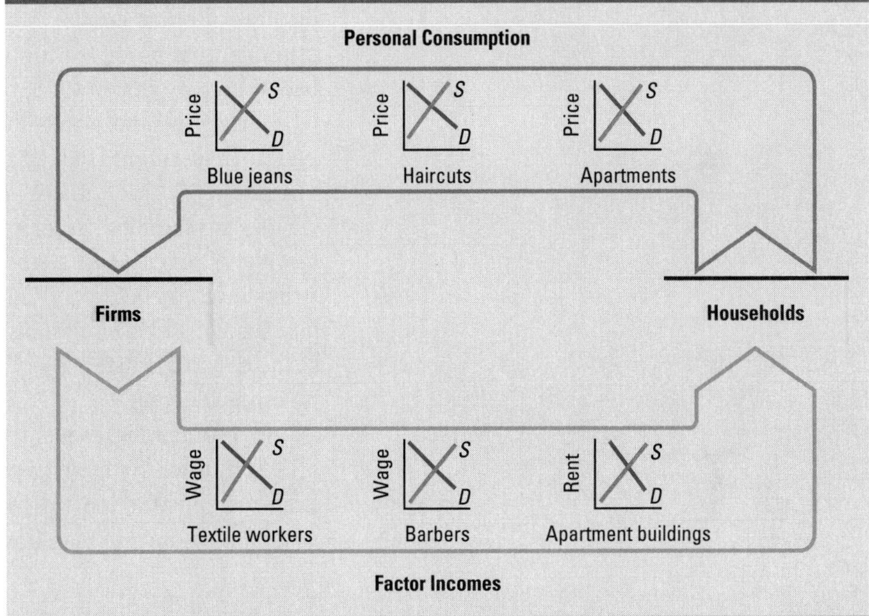

Exhibit 21-1 reminds us of the distinction between macroeconomic and microeconomic analysis. In microeconomic analysis, we focus on individual markets. We might, for example, examine the market for haircuts or for apartments. In macroeconomic analysis, we aggregate the activity of all those markets. Instead of speaking of the market for haircuts and the market for apartments, we aggregate the spending for those goods and speak of personal consumption.

The lower arrow in Exhibit 21-1 shows payments by firms for the factors of production that households supply. An economy's resources are owned by people, and those people live in households. Accordingly, as firms use factors of production, their spending for these factors flows to individual households. This spending, labeled "Factor incomes," represents all the income generated as firms produce goods and services in response to the demands placed on them. The household spending for blue jeans, haircuts, and apartments in the personal consumption flow creates a demand by firms for textile workers, barbers, and apartment buildings, which creates income for the owners of those factors in the factor income flow.

Once again, we can compare the microeconomic and macroeconomic perspectives as we look at firms' spending on factors of production. In microeconomics, we focus on individual markets. In macroeconomics, we aggregate those markets and speak of the sum of all factor incomes flowing from firms to households.

Because we are assuming for now that the economy produces only consumer goods and services, GDP equals the total production of consumer goods and services, C.

$$\text{GDP} = C \tag{1}$$

GDP is thus equal to the total value of the personal consumption flow and the total value of the factor incomes.

Investment

Investment includes the value of all goods produced by firms for use in the production of other goods. A hammer produced for a carpenter is investment. A printing press produced for a magazine publisher is investment, as is a conveyor belt system produced for a manufacturing firm. Recall from Chapter 2 that capital includes all the goods that have been produced for use in producing other goods. **Investment** is an addition to the stock of capital during a period.

The term "investment" can generate confusion. In everyday conversation, we use "investment" to refer to uses of money aimed at earning more money. We say we've invested in a stock or invested in a bond. Economists, however, restrict "investment" to activities that increase the economy's stock of capital. The purchase of a share of stock doesn't add to the capital stock; it isn't investment in the economic meaning of the word. Only when new capital is produced does investment occur.

Investment represents a flow of spending from firms to firms. The purchase of a Ford truck by a construction firm, for example, creates a flow of spending from the construction firm to the Ford Motor Company. Exhibit 21-2 adds investment to our circular flow model. The picture no longer depicts individual

EXHIBIT 21-2

Adding Investment to the Circular Flow Model

Saving by households flows into the financial markets, from which investment funds are made available to firms. Firms use these funds together with other funds they may have available to purchase capital goods and services—that is, to engage in investment. The flow labeled "Investment" goes from firms to firms. GDP equals the sum of investment plus consumption. It also equals the sum of factor incomes, which now include incomes earned by households in the production of consumption and of investment goods. Here, investment is shown in blue and the flows of funds to and from financial markets are shown in green. Factor incomes are shown in red.

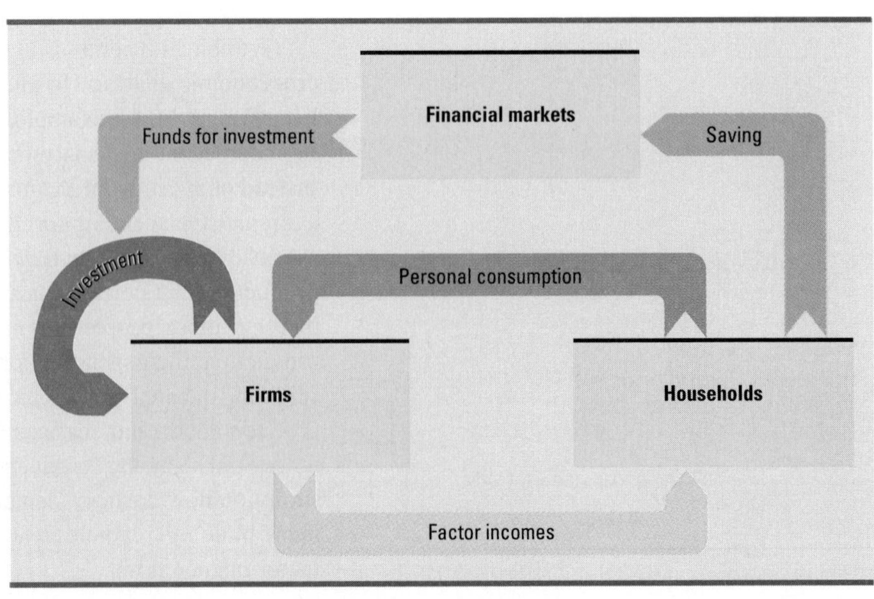

markets, but the flow labeled "Funds for investment" comprises markets for such investment goods as trucks, drill presses, and cranes. When firms produce these goods, they employ factor services supplied by households; the value of investment goods produced thus generates an equal value of income for households. With investment added to the circular flow, GDP now equals the sum of production for personal consumption, C, plus investment, I.

$$\text{GDP} = C + I \quad \textbf{(2)}$$

Exhibit 21-2 adds two other flows to the analysis of Exhibit 21-1. First, it shows that households save some of their income. Household saving flows to the **financial markets,** markets in which funds accumulated by savers are distributed to borrowers. The financial markets include institutions such as banks and pension funds as well as the stock market and the bond market. The financial markets make funds available to firms to finance their investment activities. A manufacturer planning to add a new assembly plant, for example, borrows the funds for the plant from a bank.

The blue arrows in Exhibit 21-2 show spending flows that occur in exchange for goods and services, such as personal consumption and investment. The red arrow shows the flow of factor incomes. The green arrows show other flows, such as saving and the flow of funds for investment. We'll follow these color conventions throughout our development of this model. As we add new flows to the model, they will be shown with dark shades; flows previously introduced are shown in lighter shades of the corresponding colors.

The official measure of investment in the economy is called **gross private domestic investment.** It includes three flows that add to the nation's capital stock: expenditures by business firms on new buildings, plants, tools, and equipment that will be used in production of goods and services; expenditures on new residential housing; and changes in business inventories.

Residential housing may seem a surprising component in investment, since houses are purchased primarily by consumers. In the national income and product accounts, however, houses are treated as part of the nation's capital stock. Each year houses "produce" the service of shelter. Owners of houses are treated as firms that supply houses to themselves; the value of this housing each period is counted in GDP.

Inventory is the value of the stock of goods firms have on hand at any one time. Inventories have, of course, been produced and are available to "produce" subsequent sales. They are thus counted as part of the capital stock. Changes in inventories are counted as part of investment. Suppose, for example, that a pocket video game is produced during 1996 but not sold. Because no one bought it, it won't be counted in consumption. It will be treated instead as an addition to inventory and thus counted as investment in 1996. If it's sold in 1997, it will be counted as part of consumption in that period. It will also be deleted from inventory and will thus be represented as a negative change in inventory, so the two entries cancel out in 1997. Production of the video game will affect GDP only in 1996—the year it was produced.

Despite investment's relatively small share of total economic activity, it plays a crucial role in the macroeconomy for two reasons:

1. Investment represents a choice to forgo current consumption in order to add to the capital stock of the economy. Investment therefore adds to the economy's capacity and shifts its production possibilities curve outward. Investment is thus a key determinant of economic growth.

- **Investment** is an addition to the stock of capital during a period.
- The **financial markets** are markets in which funds accumulated by savers are distributed to borrowers.
- **Gross private domestic investment** is the official measure of investment in computing GDP.
- **Inventory** is the value of the stock of goods firms have on hand at any one time.

2. Investment is a relatively volatile component of GDP; it can change dramatically from one year to the next. That means fluctuations in GDP are often driven by fluctuations in investment. We'll examine the determinants of investment in Chapter 28.

Government Purchases

Government agencies at all levels purchase goods and services from firms. They purchase office equipment, vehicles, buildings, janitorial services, and so on. Many government agencies also produce goods and services. Police departments produce police protection, public schools produce education, the Postal Service produces mail delivery services. **Government purchases** are the sum of purchases of goods and services from firms by government agencies plus the total value of output produced by government agencies themselves during a time period. Government purchases make up about 20 percent of GDP.

When a government agency produces a good or service, it is treated as a firm in the national income and product accounts. This "firm" is then thought of as supplying a good or service to the appropriate government agency. A public school that produces first-grade education, for example, is treated as a firm that supplies education to a local school district. All government purchases thus represent flows of spending from government agencies to firms, as shown in Exhibit 21-3. This spending generates factor incomes, which flow from firms to households.

EXHIBIT 21-3

Adding Government Purchases to the Circular Flow Model

Government purchases represent another source of spending flowing into firms. Other flows in the model include tax payments from households to government agencies and transfer payments from government agencies to households. When government agencies incur a deficit, they borrow the funds in the financial markets; this flow is labeled "Lending to government."

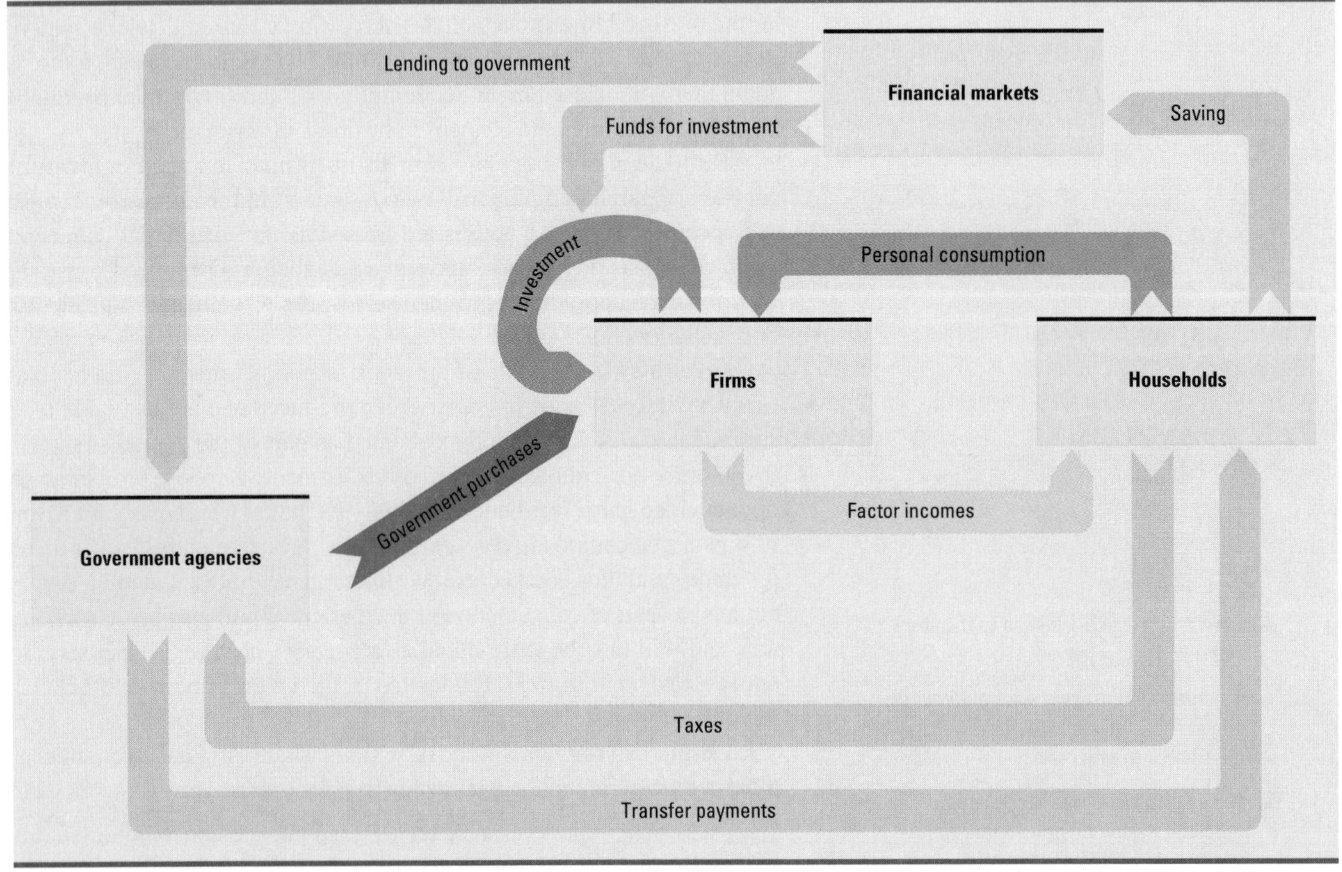

Government agencies take funds from households through taxes and provide funds to households through other programs. **Transfer payments,** payments that do not require a good or service in exchange, include welfare payments, food stamps, and Social Security. Exhibit 21-3 thus shows taxes flowing from households to government agencies and transfer payments flowing from government agencies to households.

Finally, there is a flow of funds between the government sector and the financial markets. When the government incurs a deficit, it borrows the amount of the deficit through the financial markets. This is the flow labeled "Lending to government" in Exhibit 21-3. In order to simplify the picture, we omit flows of tax payments from firms to government agencies and saving by firms.

Services produced by government agencies pose a special problem for economists estimating GDP. What's the value of a day of work put in by a police officer? How about the services of a U.S. senator? The economists who estimate GDP have chosen a simple answer to such questions; they value government services based on their cost of production. The services of the police officer and the senator are thus valued according to their respective salaries.

It's easy to see why such a simple method of valuation has been chosen; trying to determine what the services of government agencies are worth would be an enormously difficult and controversial task. But the valuation of government services based on production costs does introduce a problem. The production of most goods and services generates a profit. Those goods are worth more than the cost of the inputs that produced them. To the extent that government services are also worth more than the cost of their production, their value is understated in GDP figures. Of course, some government services may be worth less than their cost of production; their value is overstated in GDP!

Note that only government purchases of goods and services are counted as part of GDP. Taxes, transfer payments, and government borrowing are not part of GDP because no good or service is produced directly as a result of these payments. Only when a tax payment or government borrowing is spent by a government agency is it counted as a government purchase. Only when a transfer payment is spent by a household is it counted as consumption.

The incorporation of the government sector in the circular flow model adds the total value of goods and services purchased by government agencies, G, to GDP. We can thus write

$$\text{GDP} = C + I + G \qquad \textbf{(3)}$$

In estimating GDP, no effort is made to distinguish government purchases for current consumption from those made for capital investment. The purchase of a pad of paper is treated in the same fashion as the purchase of a new prison. The prison facility is new capital; it should therefore be counted as a form of investment. But the U.S. accounts treat all government purchases as if they were a form of current consumption. There is no justification for failing to distinguish current government consumption from government investment. It is inconsistent with the accounting systems used in other countries and gives a misleading picture of investment in the United States. The Bureau of Economic Analysis plans to correct this practice and to distinguish government consumption and government investment. This reform of the U.S. accounting system is expected to be introduced within a few years.

Government purchases include purchases by federal, state, and local government agencies as well as the total value of output produced by government agencies.

Transfer payments are payments that do not require the recipients to produce a good or service in exchange.

- **Exports** represent sales of goods and services to foreign buyers during a period.
- **Imports** represent purchases of foreign-produced goods and services during a period.
- **Net exports** are a country's exports minus its imports during a period.
- Negative net exports imply a **trade deficit.**

Net Exports

Sales of a country's goods and services to foreigners during a particular time period represent its **exports.** A purchase by a Japanese buyer of a Ford Taurus produced in the United States is an export. Exports also include such transactions as the purchase of accounting services from a New York accounting firm by a shipping line based in Hong Kong, or the purchase of a ticket to Disney World by a tourist from Argentina. Purchases of foreign-produced goods and services by a country's residents during a period constitute its **imports.** U.S. imports include such transactions as the purchase by Americans of cars produced in Japan or tomatoes grown in Mexico, or a stay in a French hotel by a tourist from the United States. Subtracting imports from exports yields **net exports.**

In 1994, foreign buyers purchased $718.7 billion worth of goods and services from the United States. In the same year, U.S. citizens, firms, and government agencies purchased $816.9 billion worth of goods and services from foreign countries. The difference between these two figures, −$98.2 billion, represented the net exports of the U.S. economy in 1994. Net exports were negative because imports exceeded exports. Negative net exports constitute a **trade deficit.** The magnitude of the deficit is the amount by which imports exceed ex-

EXHIBIT 21-4

Adding Exports and Imports to the Circular Flow Model

Export demand represents export spending flowing from the rest of the world to firms. Imports are shown as a flow of spending from firms to the rest of the world.

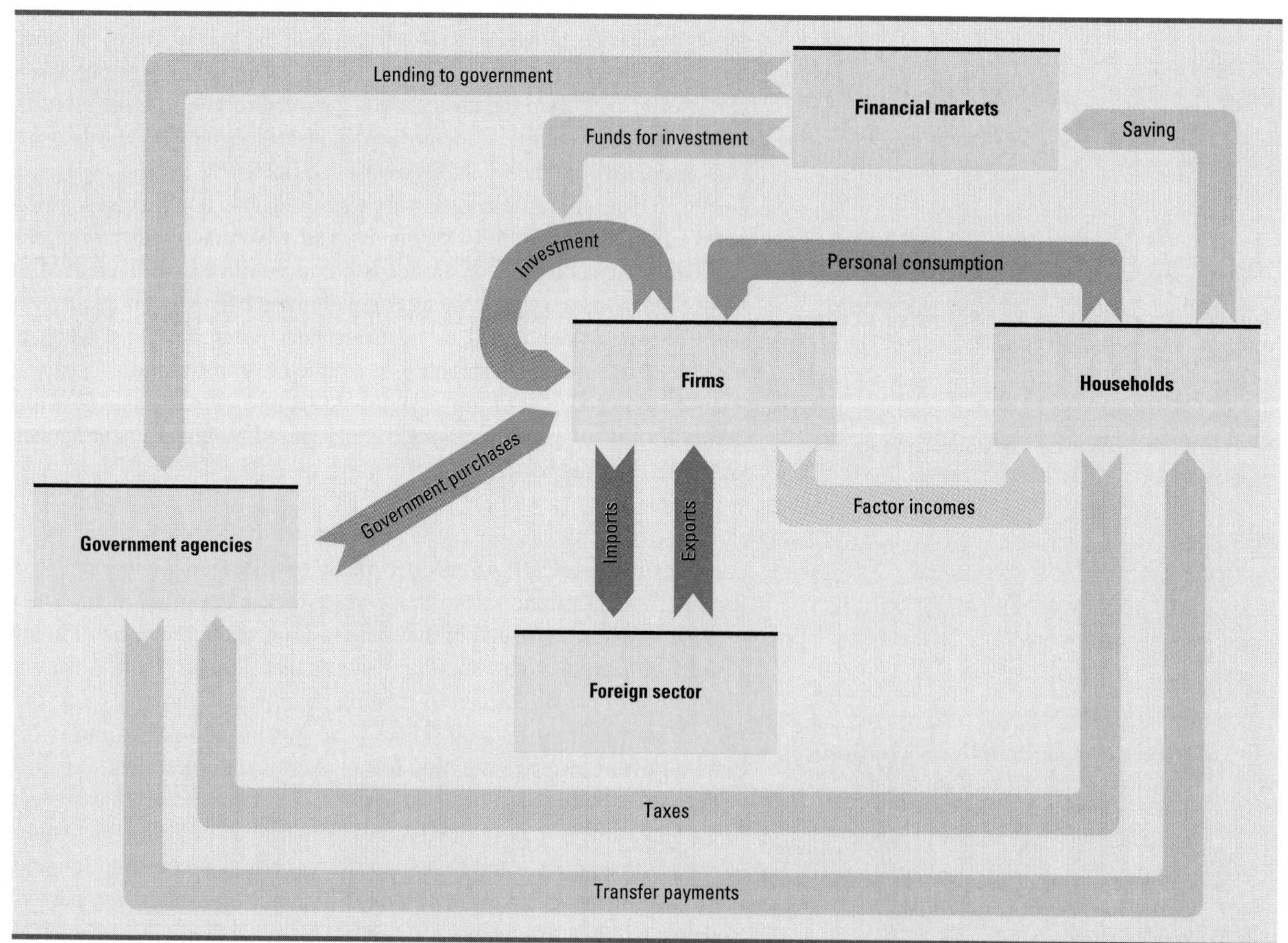

Positive net exports imply a **trade surplus.**

ports. When exports exceed imports there is a **trade surplus.** The magnitude of the surplus is the amount by which exports exceed imports.

Exhibit 21-4 adds exports and imports to the circular flow diagram. Exports are represented as a flow of spending from the rest of the world to firms in the economy. Imports are shown as a flow of spending from firms in the economy to the rest of the world. In computing GDP, we add exports X and subtract imports M to obtain net exports X_n, which are counted as part of total output. Thus, the equation

$$GDP = C + I + G + (X - M)$$

is rewritten as

$$GDP = C + I + G + X_n \quad (4)$$

The United States has recorded more deficits than surpluses since World War II, but the amounts have typically been relatively small—a few billion dollars. The trade deficit began to soar, however, in the 1980s, reaching $143.1 billion in 1987, the largest trade deficit ever recorded. We shall examine the reasons for persistent deficits in Chapter 29. Even when the trade deficit is small, however, the foreign sector plays a key role in the economy. Goods and services produced for export represent roughly 11 percent of GDP, and the goods and services the United States imports add significantly to our standard of living.

Exhibit 21-5 shows the share of GDP of each component that we've discussed. Consumption makes up the largest share of GDP, followed by government purchases and investment. Net exports represent a much smaller share.

EXHIBIT 21-5

Components of GDP, 1994

Consumption makes up the largest share of GDP. Net exports were small and negative in 1994.

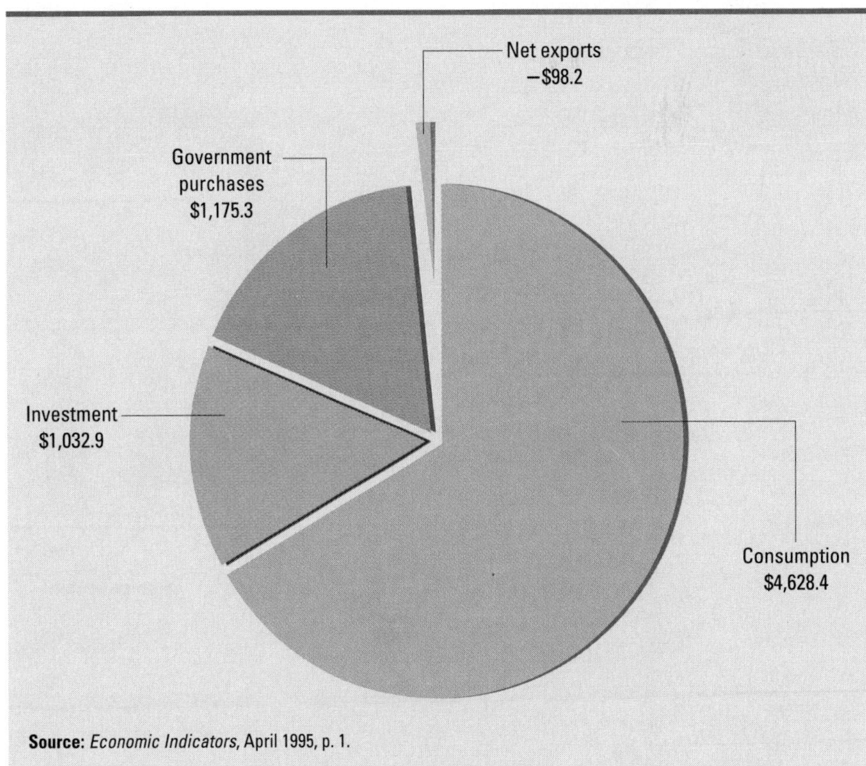

Source: *Economic Indicators,* April 1995, p. 1.

The Circular Flow Model and Economic Activity

Exhibit 21-6 shows the complete circular flow diagram for an economy. The blue flows illustrate the demands placed on firms by households for personal consumption, by firms for investment, by government agencies for government purchases, and by the rest of the world for exports. Import spending flows from firms to the rest of the world. Factor incomes flow from firms to households and are shown in red. The dollar value associated with this arrow equals GDP, which, in turn, equals the sum of the four spending flows. The flows of funds shown in green include the flow of saving from households to the financial markets, the flow of investment funds from the financial markets to firms, and the flow of lending from the financial markets to government agencies. In addition, taxes flow from households to government agencies, and transfer payments flow from government agencies to households.

To see how the circular flow relates to the nation's GDP, let's consider some typical transactions that make up part of GDP and identify the corresponding flows involved. Remember that the flows shown in Exhibit 21-6 represent money payments for each transaction.

A consumer's purchase of a haircut is personal consumption. The production of an Apple computer sold in Great Britain is part of exports. A purchase by

EXHIBIT 21-6

The Complete Circular Flow Diagram

This diagram incorporates the interactions among all the sectors in the circular flow model.

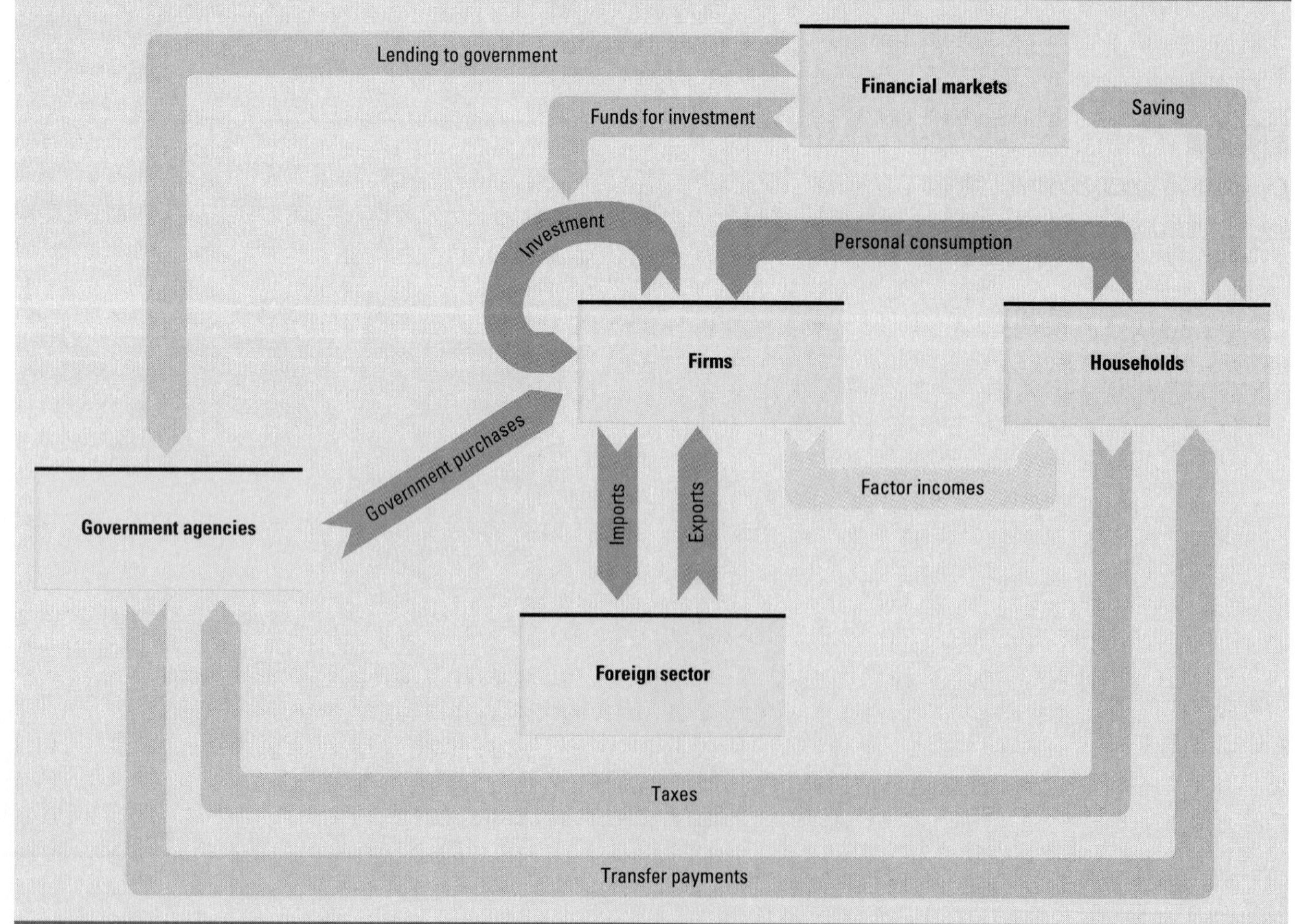

Case in Point: President Clinton's Nonstarting Jump Start

President Clinton, faced with unemployment rates hovering at around 7 percent and weak job growth in his first months in office in 1993, called for a $16 billion stimulus package that would, he said, "jump-start" the economy.

The measure called for increased government purchases of goods and services, together with tax cuts designed to stimulate investment spending by firms. The president's chief economic adviser, Laura Tyson, said that the measure would generate 250,000 jobs immediately, and an equal number later on. She explained that the additional consumer income would boost consumption, thus boosting income further, creating more consumption, and so on. She said that this "multiplier effect" would create an additional 250,000 jobs, so the measure would create half a million jobs in all.

Critics of the measure insisted that the economy was recovering on its own, fueled by rising investment. Further, they argued that the measure would increase government borrowing and thus reduce funds available for investment—an effect that would offset some or all of any positive effect on employment the measure might have.

The critics won in Congress—the president's jump-start plan was defeated. Unemployment fell to 6 percent the following year, about the rate generally associated with full employment.

Laura Tyson, President Clinton's economic advisor, with her boss.

the city of Miami of a new Chrysler sedan is a government purchase. The purchase by a logging company of a new chainsaw is an investment. Each of these spending flows generates an equal amount of factor income.

The flows of funds shown in green don't enter GDP directly, but they do affect it. Household saving can affect GDP in two ways. First, money saved isn't spent for consumption, so saving can reduce GDP. But the funds saved flow to the financial markets, from which investment funds can be made available. Increased investment tends to increase GDP. Taxes provide the revenues from which the government makes purchases and transfer payments. Governments often run deficits, however, thus borrowing from the financial markets; there is no simple rule linking government purchases to tax revenues.

The circular flow model suggests a taste of the macroeconomic phenomena we'll be discussing in future chapters. Suppose, for example, that a plunge in incomes in the rest of the world leads to a reduction in exports. Firms respond by cutting their production—and thus their use of factors of production. That reduces factor incomes to households, so households reduce their consumption—which could induce firms to reduce their spending still further!

Or suppose managers of firms throughout the economy decide that demand for their respective goods and services is about to increase, so they increase their investment spending so that they'll have the capacity to meet this demand. The increase in investment spending causes firms that produce investment goods to increase their production, which will boost factor incomes. Then households will increase their consumption spending—which will boost incomes, and thus consumption, still further. The expectation of greater consumption will thus lead to greater consumption!

Checklist

- GDP can be measured as the flow of total output produced or of total income generated during a particular period.
- GDP as a flow of output includes personal consumption, investment, government purchases, and net exports.
- The relationship between the flows of spending, output, and income is suggested by the circular flow model.

Or, finally, suppose that the economy is slumping and that unemployment is high. The circular flow model suggests that government action may be able to give the economy a boost. The government could, for example, increase its purchases of goods and services. That would create additional income for households, which would boost their consumption, creating still more demand for firms, still more income, and so on. Alternatively, the government could cut taxes, which would give households more income that they could use for consumption, which would boost incomes—and consumption—still more.

One could raise objections to government efforts to stimulate the economy. If spending is increased or taxes are reduced, the deficit will rise. That will mean the government must borrow more money from the financial markets, a source of investment funds. If the government borrows more, there may be a reduction in the funds available for investment. That's an issue to which we'll return in subsequent chapters.

GDP: A Measure of Income

Our analysis thus far has demonstrated that the total value of output equals the total of factor incomes. In this section we'll discuss the measurement of GDP using income data and examine more carefully just how the production of goods and services generates income to households.

The Dual Computation of GDP

In the introduction to this chapter we spoke of the lockup where economists estimate GDP each quarter. The procedures they go through illustrate the fact that GDP can be estimated in terms of either output or total income.

Some of the staffers at the lockup represent the team of economists at the Bureau of Economic Analysis who have estimated total output in the economy. Some have worked on the estimate of personal consumption; others have worked on the estimate of government purchases; and others have worked on other output components of GDP. The data from which these estimates are made come from surveys that ask individual firms how much they produced during a period. The economists who work on output data combine estimates of the various components of output into a single estimate of GDP.

Other staffers work on income data. The Census Bureau does monthly surveys of individual households to determine their income from supplying factors of production such as labor to firms. By adding up all the incomes households generate, staffers estimate GDP from the income side of the ledger.

After the two groups compile their GDP estimates, they compare their numbers. In theory, the numbers should add to the same total. If the totals don't match, the economists pore over the estimates to find and resolve any discrepancies between the two sets of numbers. The important thing to see, however, is that the process through which GDP estimates are made is based on the identity between the value of output and the value of income generated in producing that output.

Just as the output estimate of GDP doesn't include government transfer payments, the income estimate of GDP doesn't include income received by households unless it is *earned* in the production of the GDP. A household's income from welfare or Social Security payments, for example, is not part of the income counted in the GDP estimate because it isn't income that was earned for producing goods and services.

The Components of Factor Income

Employee compensation looms largest among the components of factor income. Other components include profit, rent, and interest. Two others, however, don't sound as if they should be income: depreciation and indirect business taxes.

These latter two components of the income side of GDP don't really represent income to households in the sense described in the circular flow model. They are part of the cost of producing goods and services, however, and must therefore be accounted for in estimating GDP on an income basis.

Employee Compensation

Compensation of employees in the form of wages, salaries, and benefits makes up the largest single component of income generated in the production of GDP. In 1994 employee compensation represented 59.4 percent of GDP.

The structure of employee compensation has changed dramatically in the last 45 years. In 1950, virtually all employee compensation—95 percent of it—came in the form of wages and salaries. The remainder came in the form of additional benefits such as employer contributions to retirement programs and health insurance. By 1994, benefits had more than tripled as a share of total compensation.

The nation's soaring health care bill has had a dramatic impact on the nature of employee compensation. Employers pay the bulk of health insurance premiums for their employees, and this benefit is an increasingly important form of employee compensation. In 1970, health care benefits made up 2 percent of the average employee's compensation package, according to the Employee Benefits Research Institute. By 1989, this share had tripled to 6 percent. The Institute reports that wages and salaries, adjusted for inflation, increased by just 0.5 percent between 1970 and 1989. Health care benefits paid by employers soared 163 percent over the same period.

Profits

The profit component of income earned by households equals total revenues of firms less direct accounting costs. Profits equaled 15.3 percent of GDP, or $1,028.0 billion, in 1994, down sharply from four decades earlier, when profits represented 25.6 percent of the income generated in GDP.

Profits are the reward the owners of firms receive for being in business.[1] The opportunity to earn profits is the driving force behind production in a market economy. Profits are driven down by competition among firms; the falling share of profits in the economy reflects, in part, the impact of competitive forces.

Rent

Rental income, such as the income earned by owners of rental housing, is the smallest source of income in GDP; it is the smallest of the income flows to households. The meaning of rent in the national income accounts is the same as

[1] The concept of profit used in macroeconomics corresponds to profits as defined in conventional accounting statements.

- **Depreciation** measures the degree to which capital wears out or becomes obsolete during a period.
- **Indirect business taxes** are taxes imposed on firms in the course of their production of goods and services.

its meaning in conventional usage; it is a charge for the temporary use of some capital asset.[2]

Interest

Households both receive and pay interest. GDP includes net interest, which subtracts interest paid by households from interest income earned by them. It accounted for 6.1 percent of GDP in 1994.

When households borrow money, they pay interest—on credit cards, installment loans, and home mortgage loans, for example. When they lend money to firms, households receive interest payments. People who purchase bonds issued by firms, for example, are lending money to the firms and receive interest payments for these loans.

Depreciation

When goods and services are produced, the machinery and buildings that are used to produce them wear out or become obsolete. A farmer's tractor, for example, wears out as it is used. A technological change may make some equipment obsolete. The introduction of personal computers, for example, made the electric typewriters used by many firms obsolete. **Depreciation** is a measure of the degree to which capital wears out or becomes obsolete during a period.

The total of depreciation for each period is computed by economists at the Bureau of Economic Analysis. They estimate the total value of capital at the beginning of each period and then estimate to what degree that capital wore out or became obsolete. Depreciation is referred to in official reports as the *capital consumption allowance.*

Depreciation is a cost of production, so it represents part of the price charged for goods and services. It is therefore counted as part of the income generated in the production of those goods and services. Depreciation represented 11 percent of GDP in 1994.

Indirect Business Taxes

The final component of the income measure of GDP is **indirect business taxes.**[3] These are taxes imposed on the production or sale of goods and services or on other business activity. (By contrast, a direct tax is a tax imposed directly on income; the personal income and corporate income taxes are direct taxes.) Indirect business taxes, which include sales and excise taxes, payroll taxes, and property taxes, make up part of the cost to firms of producing goods and services. Like depreciation, they are part of the price of those goods and services and are therefore treated as part of the income generated in their production. Indirect business taxes amounted to 8.2 percent of GDP in 1994.

Indirect business taxes are assuming an increasingly important role in the United States. Payroll taxes, used to finance Social Security, have risen sharply in the last several decades. The payroll tax is the largest single tax most Americans pay.

Exhibit 21-7 shows the share of GDP represented by each source of income in 1994. Employee compensation represented the largest share of GDP.

Checklist

- The output measure of GDP is based on survey data on individual firms.
- The income measure of GDP is based on survey data on individual households. The income and output estimates of GDP must agree.
- The components of GDP measured as a flow of income include employee compensation, profits, rents, net interest, depreciation, and indirect business taxes.

[2] If you've studied microeconomics, you know that the term "rent" in economics has a quite different meaning. The national income and product accounts use the accounting, not the economic, meaning of "rent."

[3] The adjustment for indirect business taxes includes two other minor elements: transfer payments made by business firms and surpluses or deficits of government enterprises.

EXHIBIT 21-7

GDP and Income Shares, 1994

The chart shows the relative magnitudes of employee compensation, profits, rents, interest, depreciation, and indirect business taxes in GDP in 1994.

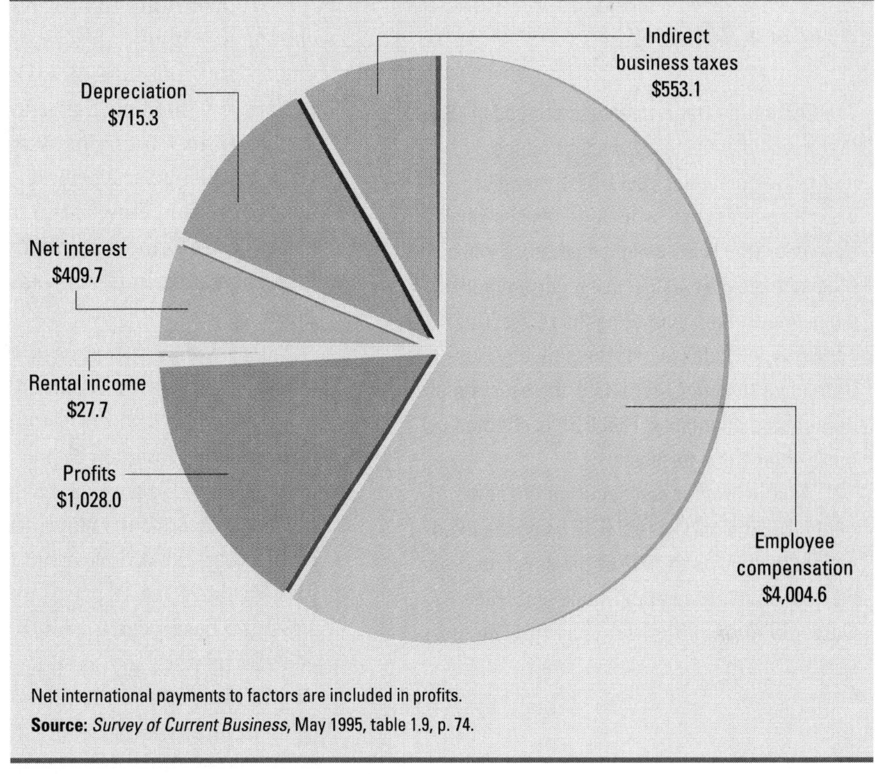

Net international payments to factors are included in profits.
Source: *Survey of Current Business*, May 1995, table 1.9, p. 74.

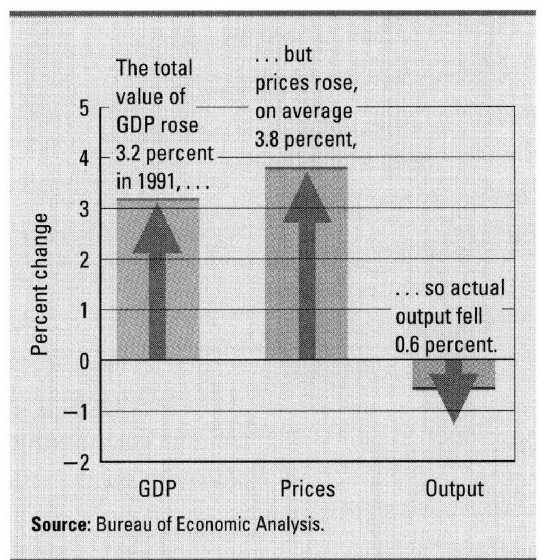

Source: Bureau of Economic Analysis.

EXHIBIT 21-8

GDP Changes: Output Versus Prices

The chart shows percentage changes in total output and prices between 1990 and 1991. The value of output can be thought of as the number of units produced times the average price per unit. The average price increased by more than the total value of output; it follows that actual output fell.

Putting GDP Estimates to Work

We use GDP estimates to assess economic performance. Is the economy expanding or contracting? How fast is the economy growing—or shrinking?

To answer such questions, we must distinguish changes in prices from changes in output. We shall examine this critical distinction in the next section.

Real Versus Nominal GDP

Price changes can distort the meaning of GDP.

Consider what happened to U.S. GDP in 1991. It was up by $179 billion over the year before, a gain of 3.2 percent. But total employment was down in 1991 by nearly 1 million workers. With fewer people working in 1991 than in 1990, it seems reasonable to expect that less was produced in 1991, not more. And that's what happened in 1991; output fell.

How could less output have been produced while GDP was going up? The answer lies in a changing price level. The prices of the goods and services produced in 1991 were, on average, 3.8 percent higher than prices in 1990. Since reported GDP was up only 3.2 percent, the volume of production actually fell in 1991, just as the falling employment numbers implied. While fewer goods and services were produced in 1991, their prices had risen enough that GDP, which measures the dollar value of total output, rose. The reduction in output is shown in Exhibit 21-8. Changing prices can create misleading impressions. We need a way to know whether a change in GDP is a result of a change in output or a change in prices—or both.

Reader's Advisory 

The Commerce Department announced in 1995 that it would, late in that year, introduce a new method of computing real GDP. Instead of weighting quantities by their prices in a single base year (the fixed-weight method), it will compute indexes of real GDP using current and previous prices, then averaging the result. This "chain-type" index avoids the difficulty illustrated by Problem 4 (page 459): the estimate of percentage changes in real GDP is affected by one's choice of a base year.

Your instructor has details of the new method. Estimates of real GDP using the fixed-weight method, with 1992 as the new base year, were to be released at the same time. (See *Survey of Current Business,* July 1995, for details.)

To determine the degree to which a change in GDP reflects an underlying change in output or prices, the Commerce Department reports GDP in two ways. One is the measure of GDP that we've been discussing, in which individual items are valued at their current prices. When the GDP for a particular period is valued in terms of prices for that period, it is called **nominal GDP.** Nominal GDP in 1995, for example, values 1995 output at 1995 prices. Because prices change from one period to the next, nominal GDP may rise in response to rising prices, even if the volume of production hasn't increased. Nominal GDP has, in fact, increased in every year since 1949, while levels of production have fallen often.

To obtain a measure of production that does not rise if prices alone increase, we must hold prices constant. If we measure the value of basketball output using a fixed price for valuing the basketballs, then only an increase in the number of basketballs produced could increase the value of basketball output. That is the strategy the Bureau of Economic Analysis employs in its calculation of **real GDP,** a measure in which the output of a particular period is valued at the price levels that existed in a base year. The base year can be any year; choosing it gives a fixed set of prices for use in valuing production in subsequent years. In 1995 the base year for GDP was 1987, so real GDP equaled 1995 output valued at 1987 prices.

Exhibit 21-9 illustrates the computation of real and nominal GDP for a hypothetical economy that produces two goods, apples and bulldozers. Nominal GDP values the output for a period at its price in that period. The nominal value of bulldozer output in year 2, for example, is \$28.6 million (130 bulldozers × \$220,000). Taking year 1 as the base year, however, we value the contribution of bulldozers produced in year 2 to real GDP by calculating the output in year 2 valued at its price in year 1, or \$23.4 million (130 bulldozers × \$180,000).

EXHIBIT 21-9

Calculating Real and Nominal GDP

Assume that an economy produces two goods, apples and bulldozers. Using the hypothetical data shown for prices and output in years 1 and 2, we calculate real and nominal GDP for each year. The real GDP calculation uses year 1 as a base year.

	Year 1		Year 2		Contribution to Nominal GDP ($ millions)		Contribution to Real GDP ($ millions)	
Good	Price	Quantity	Price	Quantity	Year 1	Year 2	Year 1	Year 2
Apples	$1	100,000,000	$1.20	90,000,000	$100.0	$108.0	$100.0	$90.0
Bulldozers	180,000	150	220,000	130	27.0	28.6	27.0	23.4
				Total	$127.0	$136.6	$127.0	$113.4

The table gives nominal and real GDP. Nominal GDP rose in year 2 while real GDP fell. Nominal GDP rose because of higher prices for both goods; real GDP fell because actual output fell. The real GDP figure gives us a better assessment of economic performance than does the figure for nominal GDP.

Real GDP is the gauge we use to determine whether the economy is expanding or contracting. A period in which real GDP is rising is called an **expansion.** A period in which real GDP falls for two or more consecutive quarters is called a **recession.** When people speak of the 1980s as the longest peacetime expansion in U.S. history, for example, they are referring to gains in real, not nominal, GDP that occurred from 1982 to 1990. That expansion came to an end when real GDP turned down in the third quarter of 1990. The ensuing recession lasted from the third quarter of 1990 to the second quarter of 1991, when another expansion began. As *Economics* went to press that expansion was continuing. We'll discuss expansions and recessions in the next chapter.

Problems in the Interpretation of Real GDP

Although real GDP is intended solely as a measure of production in an economy, it is often used in a normative sense to determine how well an economy is performing. An increase in real GDP is generally taken as a sign the economy is doing well; a reduction is interpreted as a sign the economy is doing badly. Are such conclusions justified?

In this section we examine some problems underlying the use of GDP to measure domestic economic performance. We also note how GDP is used to measure such performance and how it is used to make international comparisons of economic performance.

Measurement Problems in Real GDP

Although real GDP is probably the best single indicator we have of macroeconomic performance, there are problems in its measurement that many economists view as quite serious. They may mislead us in our thinking about an economy.

Revisions. The first estimate of real GDP for a calendar quarter is called the *advance estimate.* It is issued about a month after the quarter ends. To produce a measure that quickly, officials at the Bureau of Economic Analysis must rely on information from relatively few firms and households. One month later it issues a *revised estimate,* and a month after that it issues its *final estimate.* Often the advance estimate will paint a picture of economic performance that differs sharply from that of the final estimate.

But the revision story does not end there. Every summer, the Bureau issues revised figures for the previous 2 or 3 years. Once every 5 years, the Bureau conducts an extensive analysis that traces flows of inputs and outputs throughout the economy. It focuses on the outputs of some firms that are inputs to other firms. In the process of conducting this analysis, the Bureau revises real GDP estimates over the previous 5 years. Sometimes the revisions can paint a picture of economic activity that is quite different from what the initial estimates of GDP suggested, as the Case in Point on the next page shows.

The Service Sector. Real GDP is current output valued at base-year prices. In sectors such as agriculture, output is relatively easy to compute. There are so many bushels of corn, so many pounds of beef. But what is the output of a bank? Of a hospital? It's easy to record the dollar value of output to enter in nominal GDP, but estimating the quantity of output to use in real GDP is quite another matter.

The Bureau of Economic Analysis solves this problem by estimating output based on inputs used. If a bank increases its number of employees by 10 percent, for example, the Bureau assumes the bank produces 10 percent more services. A bank with the same number of employees as in a previous period is assumed to have the same output at before. But this approach incorrectly assumes that worker productivity in services is constant. For example, a single bank worker could process 265 checks per hour in 1971, but by 1986 the worker could process 825 checks per hour. Economists who have studied productivity in the service sector generally conclude that it's growing rapidly, and that the Bureau's implicit assumption of constant productivity understates economic growth by perhaps 1 percentage point per year. That is a huge error; an economy growing at a 3 percent annual rate would be two times as large after 72 years as an economy that started at the same level but grew at a 2 percent rate.

- **Nominal GDP** is the GDP for a period valued at prices in that period.
- **Real GDP** is the total value, calculated at base-year prices, of the final goods and services produced during a given time period.
- An **expansion** is a period of rising real GDP.
- A **recession** is a period in which real GDP falls for two or more consecutive quarters.

Case in Point GDP Estimates and the 1992 Election

In its annual revision of GDP estimates released in August 1993, the Bureau of Economic Analysis rewrote the history of the early 1990s. The revision suggested that the Bureau had overestimated the severity of the 1990–1991 recession and underestimated the strength of the expansion that followed.

The accompanying table gives the Bureau's estimates of quarter-to-quarter changes in real GDP expressed at annual rates. This is the standard way of presenting such changes—it shows the percentage by which real GDP would rise if a percentage change from one quarter to the next persisted for a year. The table also shows the revised figures released in 1993. The figures show that in virtually every quarter from 1990 through 1992, the Bureau understated the rate of expansion or overstated the severity of recession.

	Percentage Change in Real GDP: Quarterly Values at Annual Rates	
Year and Quarter	Previous Estimates	1993 Revisions
1990-1	2.8	3.5
1990-2	1.0	1.5
1990-3	−1.6	−0.9
1990-4	−3.9	−3.2
1991-1	−3.0	−2.4
1991-2	1.7	1.5
1991-3	1.2	1.4
1991-4	0.6	0.6
1992-1	2.9	3.5
1992-2	1.5	2.8
1992-3	3.4	3.4
1992-4	4.7	5.7

The earlier figures painted a picture of an economy that had plunged into a recession, followed by growth that was quite weak. The Bureau's early estimates showed the economy was growing at a 2.6 percent rate during 1992—a poor performance when unemployment was high. The revisions showed the economy growing at 3.2 percent, a much more impressive rate of growth.

The Bureau's early characterization of recession followed by weak recovery was reported over and over in the press. Many articles, including several by me, discussed the sluggish economy. All of that helped to create an impression of poor economic performance under President George Bush—and that perception contributed to his defeat by Bill Clinton in the 1992 election.

The revision was the biggest change ever reported based on annual revisions. The largest errors had occurred in three areas: personal consumption (especially of durable goods), producers' durable equipment (one component of investment), and state and local government purchases.

Whether more accurate reporting of economic activity in 1991 and 1992 would have produced a different outcome in the election will never be known. What is clear is that initial estimates created a distorted picture of actual economic performance.

Source: "Annual Revisions of the U.S. National Income and Product Accounts," *Survey of Current Business* (August 1993): table 5, p. 25.

Quality Changes and New Goods. Consider the problem the Bureau faced in the early 1980s in estimating the nation's output of personal computers. The base year for real GDP then was 1972. But there weren't any personal computers in 1972; Steven Jobs and Stephen Wozniak, who would introduce the personal computer later in that decade, were in junior high school at the time.

The Bureau solved this problem by assuming that personal computers were like electric typewriters. It then examined price changes for electric typewriters since 1972, assumed that personal computer prices would have behaved the same way, and came up with a price for 1972. That method seriously overstated price rises in the industry and thus understated real output. A revision in 1985 showed far more real output of personal computers than had previously been reported, and roughly $2 billion in real GDP was added to the previous estimates. The Bureau then changed its base year to 1982, and the problem was largely solved.

The Bureau faces a similar problem with quality changes. Suppose a 1995 model car gets better mileage, is safer, and requires less maintenance than its 1987 version. The new model also costs 40 percent more. Should the 1995 model car be counted as the equivalent of the 1987 car and valued at the 1987 price in computing real GDP? Or should it be considered "more car" because its quality has increased? The Bureau does make quality adjustments, but most economists who study its procedures have concluded that it understates quality changes and thus understates gains in output.

Conceptual Problems in Real GDP

Another set of limitations of real GDP is caused not by problems of measurement but by problems inherent in the indicator itself. Real GDP measures market-oriented activity. Goods and services that are produced and exchanged in a market are counted; goods and services that are produced but that are not exchanged in markets are not.[4]

Household Production. Suppose you're considering whether to go home for dinner tonight or to eat out. You could cook dinner for yourself at a cost of $4 for the ingredients plus an hour or so of your time. Alternatively, you could buy an equivalent meal at a restaurant for $12. Your decision to eat out rather than cook would add $8 to the GDP.

But that $8 addition would be misleading. After all, if you had stayed home you would have produced an equivalent meal. The only difference is that the value of your time would not have been counted. But that surely does not mean that your time is worthless—only that it is not counted. Similarly, GDP does not count the value of your efforts to clean your own house, to wash your own car, or to grow your own vegetables. In general, GDP omits the entire value added by members of a household who do household work themselves.

There is reason to believe this omission is serious. Some economists estimate that the total value of household-produced goods and services is as much as 25 percent of reported GDP. Even more important, the share of GDP made up of household production has been changing. As more women enter the work force, more of what they used to produce at home is purchased in the market. Households in which both husband and wife are working are more likely to hire out housekeeping, child care, and yard maintenance tasks. They are likely to buy more prepared (and thus more expensive) meals at the grocery store. They are likely to eat out more often. All that will show up in the GDP. But it may not reflect an actual increase in production; it may simply reflect a shift in production from a category that isn't counted (household production) to a category that is.

Underground and Illegal Production. Some production goes unreported in order to evade taxes or the law. It's not likely to be counted in GDP either. Legal production for which income is unreported in order to evade taxes is generally said to take place in the "underground economy." For example, a carpenter

[4] There are two exceptions to this rule. The value of food produced and consumed by farm households is counted in GDP. More important, an estimate of the rental values of owner-occupied homes is included. If a family rents a house, the rental payments are included in GDP. If a family lives in a house it owns, the Department of Commerce estimates what the house would rent for and then includes that rent in the GDP estimate, even though the house's services weren't exchanged in the marketplace.

might build a small addition to a dentist's house in exchange for orthodontic work for the carpenter's children. Although income has been earned and output generated, the transaction is unlikely to be reported for income tax or other purposes and thus is not counted in GDP.

Another kind of production that is not reported in the GDP accounts is illegal production. Illegal drugs, for example, are a very big business; many experts estimate that the nation's marijuana crop is one of its largest. But such production isn't reported for income tax or survey purposes, for obvious reasons; it is thus not counted as part of GDP.

Leisure. Leisure is an economic good. All other things equal, more leisure is better than less leisure.

But all other things are not likely to be equal when it comes to consuming leisure. Consuming more leisure means supplying less work effort. And that means producing less GDP. If everyone decided to work 10 percent less, the GDP would fall. But that would not mean that people were worse off. In fact, their choice of more leisure would suggest they prefer the extra leisure to the goods and services they give up by consuming it. That means that a reduction in GDP would be accompanied by an increase in utility, not a reduction.

The GDP Accounts Ignore "Bads." Suppose a wave of burglaries were to break out across the United States. One would expect people to respond by buying more and louder burglar alarms, better locks, fiercer German shepherds, and more guard services than they had before. To the extent that they pay for these by dipping into savings rather than replacing other consumption, GDP is increased. An epidemic might have much the same effect on GDP by driving up health care spending. But that doesn't mean that crime and disease are good things; it means only that crime and disease may force an increase in the production of goods and services counted in the GDP.

Similarly, the GDP accounts ignore the impact of pollution on the environment. We might produce an additional $200 billion in goods and services but create pollution that makes us feel worse off by, say, $300 billion. The GDP accounts simply report the $200 billion in increased production. Indeed, some of the environmental degradation might itself boost GDP. Dirtier air may force us to wash clothes more often, to paint buildings more often, and to see the doctor more often—all of which would be good for GDP! The Green GDP project, discussed in the following Case in Point, plans to generate within a few years an estimate of environmental degradation that includes problems such as air pollution.

Conclusion: GDP and Human Happiness

The simple conclusion is that more GDP cannot be equated with more human happiness. But more GDP does mean more of the goods and services we measure. It means more jobs. It means more income. And most people seem to place a high value on those things. Commentators who say that more GDP is better may not be far off the mark. For all its faults, GDP does measure the production of most goods and services. And goods and services get produced, for the most part, because we want them. We might thus be safe in giving two cheers for GDP—and holding back the third in recognition of the conceptual difficulties that are inherent in using a single number to summarize the state of an entire nation's economic health.

Case in Point: A Green Approach to NDP

The Bureau of Economic Analysis went "green" in 1994. It introduced a set of estimates of net domestic product (NDP) adjusted for environmental damage.

One criticism of GDP estimates has always been that they don't adjust for environmental damage. President Clinton ordered the Bureau to develop a set of so-called green accounts that would reflect such damage. In addition to subtracting depreciation of capital goods from GDP to compute NDP, the Bureau subtracted damage to environmental resources. Its first estimate subtracted the value of oil and other minerals that had been extracted during 1993 and thus removed from the nation's stock of natural resources.

A paper mill creating air and water pollution.

The new "satellite accounts" don't replace the traditional system of estimating GDP; they are reported as a different set of accounts. "It's important to preserve continuity in the traditional accounts for purposes of historical comparison," says Carol S. Carson, the Bureau's director. "The new accounts will give a different picture of economic activity; they won't replace the old picture."

Over the next few years, the Bureau will begin adjusting for changes in the stock of renewable natural resources such as forests, soils, water aquifers, and fish stocks. It will seek also to make adjustments for changes in air and water quality.

"Ultimately, we'd like to have a complete measure of capital, both manufactured and natural," says Ms. Carson. "We can then show what's happened to that capital over time."

Source: Personal interview and "Integrated Economic and Environmental Satellite Accounts," *Survey of Current Business* (April 1993): 33–72.

Net Domestic Product

While GDP is the principal measure of economic activity, several other measures are computed in the process of estimating the value of total output. One that is particularly important is net domestic product.

Some capital wears out or becomes obsolete; depreciation measures the extent to which the capital stock is diminished in any one period. Subtracting depreciation from GDP yields **net domestic product (NDP).**

NDP can provide important clues to understanding economic performance during a particular period that would not be available from a look at GDP alone. Suppose, for example, that a country managed to increase its GDP dramatically during a period of several years but that it was rapidly exhausting its capital stock in the process. That problem would appear as a widening gap between GDP and NDP, one that would signal trouble ahead for production.

Subtracting depreciation from gross private domestic investment yields **net private domestic investment.** Because investment is an addition to the capital stock during a period and depreciation a reduction of the capital stock, net private domestic investment gives the net change in capital during a particular period. Net private domestic investment would be negative—the capital stock would fall—if depreciation in a particular period were greater than investment.

- **Net domestic product (NDP)** equals GDP minus depreciation.
- **Net private domestic investment** is gross private domestic investment minus depreciation.

Per capita real GDP is real GDP divided by population.

International Comparisons of Real GDP

Real GDP estimates are often used in making comparisons of economic performance among countries. In making such comparisons, it's important to keep in mind the general limitations to real GDP as a measure of economic performance that we noted above. Further, countries use different methodologies for collecting and compiling data. Three other issues are important in comparing GDP for different countries: the adjustment of GDP figures for population, adjusting to a common currency, and the incorporation of nonmarket production.

Per Capita Real GDP

In international comparisons of real GDP, economists generally make comparisons not of real GDP but of **per capita real GDP,** which equals a country's real GDP divided by its population. Japan, for example, had a GDP of $2,596 billion in 1993, and Switzerland had a real GDP of $168.0 billion that year. We can conclude that Japan's economy produced far more goods and services than did Switzerland's. But Japan had almost 18 times as many people in 1991 as did Switzerland. Japan's per capita real GDP in 1993 was $19,390; Switzerland's was $21,780, the second-highest in the world (the United States ranked first).

The Unit of Account

Switzerland's real GDP is measured in Swiss francs; Japan's is measured in yen. To compare them, we must convert the GDP numbers to a common unit of account. The World Bank, which provides extensive economic and other data for the world's nations, uses a measure it calls *current international dollars.* This is $1 of equivalent purchasing power in each country.

Exhibit 21-10 compares per capita real GDP for 10 countries in 1993. The disparities in income are striking; the United States, the country with the highest per capita GDP, had an income 43 times greater than Mozambique, the country with the lowest per capita GDP.

Nonmarket Production

We've already noted that much of production involves goods and services that aren't exchanged in markets, so aren't counted in GDP figures. In low-income countries with poorly developed communications and transportation networks, a much greater share of goods and services isn't exchanged in a market, so it can be even more difficult to estimate GDP.

EXHIBIT 21-10

Comparing Per Capita Real Output, 1993

There is a huge gap between per capita income in one of the poorest countries in the world, Mozambique, and wealthier nations such as France and the United States. The output measure here is gross national product (GNP), which is almost the same as GDP.

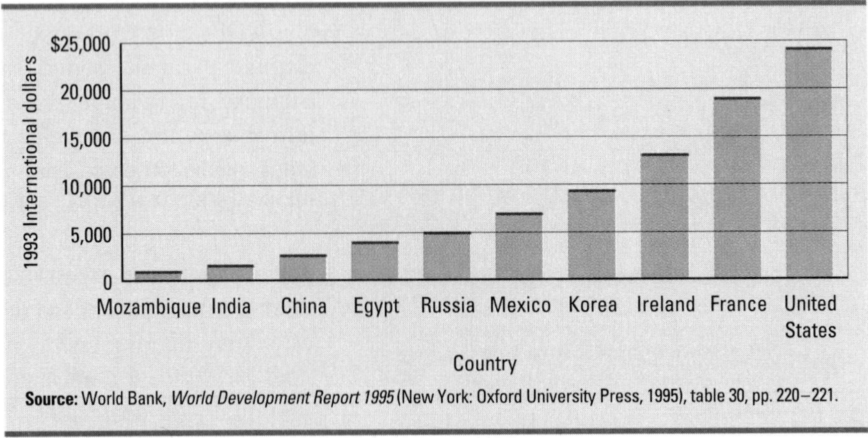

Source: World Bank, *World Development Report 1995* (New York: Oxford University Press, 1995), table 30, pp. 220–221.

Case in Point — Russia's GDP: How Sharp a Fall?

Russia's Goskomstat, the state agency that measures GDP, uses some of the world's most sophisticated computers to grind out some of the world's gloomiest numbers. By Goskomstat's tally, real GDP plunged a breathtaking 50 percent between 1991, when market reforms were introduced, and 1994. But it's not clear that a collapse of that magnitude really occurred.

Yuri Yurkov, president of Goskomstat, estimates that the official number could understate actual production by 40 percent.

Tee shirts for sale in Moscow.

High taxes and an economic system that still imposes extensive regulations have induced many new businesses to remain "off the books"— operating outside the legal system. These operations, technically illegal, don't pay taxes and don't report their sales to government statisticians.

State-run firms, too, may report inaccurate production data. Plant managers, who still may be rewarded for high levels of production, often falsify the figures. Further, the prices of these goods are typically an invention of government planners, not market-determined prices that reflect the value of these goods.

Mr. Yurkov recognizes the problems and is trying to find ways to fill the statistical gaps. He knows, for example, that state companies often report false production figures. "We are not naive, and what our companies tell us, we do not consider to be final," he told *The Wall Street Journal.* But knowing that state firms' production reports are inaccurate and that many private firms don't report at all still doesn't solve the problem of coming up with reliable numbers. "There are more problems than achievements," Mr. Yurkov says.

The lack of reliable numbers to measure economic performance makes it impossible to judge with any confidence how the reform process is proceeding. Are Russian incomes rising or falling? We can't use the official estimates to answer this basic question of economic policy.

Source: Claudia Rosett, "Figures Never Lie, But They Seldom Tell the Truth About Russian Economy," *The Wall Street Journal,* 1 July 1994, A6.

The World Bank's per capita GDP estimates attempt to adjust for nonmarket production (such as that of rural families that grow their own food, make their own clothing, and produce other household goods and services themselves), but the reliability of such adjustments is suspect.

Checklist

- Nominal GDP measures output at current prices; real GDP measures output at base-year prices.
- Problems in the measurement of real GDP stem from revisions in the data, the difficulty of measuring output in some sectors, and the problem of new goods and quality change.
- Real GDP does not include nonmarket production, nor does it adjust for "bads" produced in the economy.
- Real GDP is used to indicate whether the economy is expanding or contracting.
- Per capita real GDP is used to compare economic performance in different countries.

A Look Back—And a Look Ahead

This chapter focused on the measurement of GDP, which reports the money value of an economy's output.

The calculation of GDP is based on a fundamental identity: The total value of output equals the total value of income generated in producing that output. GDP is estimated using two types of data: (1) data that show the total value of output and (2) data that show the total value of income generated by that output.

The components of GDP measured in terms of output include consumption, investment, government purchases, and net exports. The components of GDP measured in terms of input are employee compensation, profits, rental income, net interest, depreciation, and indirect business taxes.

A measure of GDP for any period based on prices of that period is called nominal GDP. Because nominal GDP can be influenced by price changes, another measure of GDP, called real GDP, is more often used. It reflects the same goods and services, but it values that output in terms of the prices of a base year rather than the prices that prevail at the time GDP is being calculated. Real GDP is thus a more reliable measure of actual changes in production than is nominal GDP.

There are problems with our estimate of real GDP. Revisions in the data are frequently undertaken, and these revisions sometimes change our picture of the economy considerably. Many economists believe that procedures the Bureau of Economic Analysis uses for dealing with new goods and with quality changes for existing ones systematically understate output. Conceptual problems suggest that GDP may not be an adequate indicator of how well the economy is doing. It omits nonmarket production and several other factors, including the value of leisure and the negative aspects of economic life. We cannot assert with confidence that more GDP is a good thing and that less is bad. However, real GDP remains our best single indicator of economic performance. It is used not only to indicate how any one economy is performing over time but to compare the economic performance of different countries.

In the next chapter we'll look at three major economic problems: inflation, unemployment, and the business cycle. We'll examine the causes of each and their impacts on the economy.

Terms and Concepts for Review

Circular flow model
Depreciation
Expansion
Exports
Final goods and services
Financial markets
Government purchases
Gross domestic product (GDP)
Gross private domestic investment
Imports
Indirect business taxes
Inventory
Investment
Net domestic product (NDP)
Net exports
Net private domestic investment
Nominal GDP
Per capita real GDP
Personal consumption
Real GDP
Recession
Trade deficit
Trade surplus
Transfer payments

For Discussion

1. GDP is used as a measure of macroeconomic performance. What, precisely, does it measure?
2. Many economists have attempted to create a set of social accounts that would come closer to measuring the economic well-being of the society than does GDP. What considerations or alterations in the current approach would you recommend to them?
3. Every good produced creates income to the owners of the factors of production that created the product or service. For a recent purchase you made, try to list all of the types of factors of production involved in making the product available, and try to determine who received income.
4. Explain how the sale of used textbooks in your campus bookstore affects the GDP calculation.
5. Look again at the circular flow diagram in Exhibit 21-6 and assume it's drawn for the United States. State the flows in which each of the following transactions would be entered.
   - **a.** A consumer purchases fresh fish at a local fish market.
   - **b.** A grocery store acquires 1,000 rolls of paper towels for later resale.
   - **c.** NASA purchases a new Saturn rocket.
   - **d.** People in France flock to see the latest Woody Allen movie.
   - **e.** A construction firm builds a new house.
   - **f.** A couple from Seattle visit Guadalajara and stay in a hotel there.
   - **g.** The city of Dallas purchases computer paper from a local firm.
6. Under what circumstances might the real GDP for a given year be greater than the nominal GDP for that same year?
7. Suggest an argument for and an argument against counting in GDP all household-produced goods and services that aren't sold, such as the value of child care or home-cooked meals.
8. How would each of the following affect a "green" version of net domestic product?
   - **a.** A country pumps 500 billion barrels of oil out of the ground.
   - **b.** A country develops a process to extract oil from deposits previously considered uneconomic to drill.
   - **c.** A country develops a more efficient program to recycle aluminum.
9. Suppose that virtually everyone in the United States decides to take life a little easier, and the length of the average work week falls by 25 percent. How will that affect GDP? Per capita GDP? How will it affect economic welfare?
10. Comment on the following statement: "It doesn't matter that the value of the labor people devote to producing things for themselves isn't counted in GDP; because we make the same "mistake" every year, relative values are unaffected.

Problems

1. Given the following nominal data, construct the corresponding GDP and NDP accounts.

Nominal data for GDP and NDP	$ billions
Consumption	2,799.8
Depreciation	481.6
Exports	376.2
Net private domestic investment	189.4
Indirect business taxes	331.4
Government purchases	869.7
Government transfer payments	947.8
Imports	481.7

2. Using the data provided in the endpapers of this book, prepare a chart showing real GNP per capita among any 10 nations you select.
3. Assume that an economy produced only two goods, computers and television sets, in 1995 and 1996. It produced 100 computers in 1995 at a price of $1,000 and 200 computers in 1996 at a price of $500. It produced 1,000 television sets in 1995 at a price of $500 and 800 television sets in 1996 at a price of $600. Compute nominal and real GDP for each year, using 1995 as the base year.
4. Using year 2 as the base year, compute real GDP in year 1 and year 2 for the economy in Exhibit 21-9. Does the use of a different base year change your conclusion about whether real GDP rises or falls?

22

Inflation, Unemployment, and the Business Cycle

Chapter Objectives

After mastering the material in this chapter, you will be able to:

1. Show how inflation is measured.
2. Discuss the ways in which inflation affects individuals in the economy.
3. Explain the conceptual difficulties in measuring inflation and discuss the reasons the measured rate may overstate the true rate.
4. Show how unemployment is measured.
5. Distinguish among the different categories of unemployment.
6. Explain the concept of a natural level of employment and show how it is achieved.
7. Discuss the concept of the business cycle.

Inflation is like sin; every government denounces it and every government practices it.

Sir Frederick Leith-Ross, 1957

What's Ahead

Tihomir Nikolic barred the door of his boutique with a mop to keep shoppers away while he changed his prices in 1993. He didn't want his customers to get in and claim a bargain.

The potential saving for someone who got in ahead of the price changes would have been impressive. One day early in August 1993, Mr. Nikolic boosted the prices of a Snickers bar to 11,940,000 dinars from yesterday's price of 6,000,000 dinars. A video cassette recorder fetched 20,391,560,223 dinars, up from 10,247,015,187 the day before.

With prices rising so fast, no one wanted to hold dinars. Upon being paid, people would race to a money changer to swap dinars for dollars. When they needed to buy something, they'd swap dollars for dinars, then sprint to a store to try to get in ahead of the next round of price hikes.

Denis Celebic, the manager of a construction-supply company, dashed into a store and handed over 152 million dinars for diapers for his 7-day-old daughter—just ahead of a price hike. "If you stop to have a coffee, you lose money," he said.

The Yugoslav nightmare was brought on by the government's rapid printing of money. By the summer of 1993, the government mint was running 24 hours per day, and contracts had been given to private printers to print even more. Early in 1994 the government decreed an end to the madness. It issued a new dinar worth $0.61 and pledged not to increase the money supply so rapidly as to cause more inflation. The inflation came to a halt. A Snickers bar cost 1 new dinar in May 1994, and it still cost 1 new dinar in January 1995.[1]

[1] Roger Thurow, "Special, Today Only: Six Million Dinars For a Snickers Bar," *The Wall Street Journal,* 4 August 1993, A1+, and "Yugoslavia Devalues the Dinar," *The Wall Street Journal,* 19 August 1993, A6. I am grateful to Radmila Diklic of the U.S. Embassy in Belgrade for providing an update on Snickers prices.

Yugoslavia's bout with inflation was spectacular, but by no means unprecedented. Russia struggled with inflation rates of about 1,000 percent at about the same time Yugoslavia was having its troubles. Brazil's rate reached 2,567 percent that year. Bolivia's inflation rate soared past 20,000 percent late in the 1980s. Germany saw its price level rise a dizzying 750-billion-fold between 1920 and 1923.

What causes such inflation? What are its effects? What are the effects of the relatively mild inflation rates—in the neighborhood of 2 to 4 percent per year—that the United States has experienced in recent years?

In this chapter we'll examine the nature of inflation and look at its impact on the economy. Our investigation of the cause of inflation will have to await our investigation of money in Chapters 24 and 25.

Inflation is one major macroeconomic problem. We'll also look at two others in this chapter: unemployment and the business cycle—the cycle of expansion and recession that marks economic activity. This chapter will provide a preliminary sketch of these three macroeconomic phenomena. We'll be grappling with inflation, unemployment, and the ups and downs of economic activity throughout our exploration of macroeconomic analysis.

Inflation

We often hear news reports about inflation; sometimes we hear people complaining about it. But just what is it? How is it measured? And most important, how does it affect us? These are some of the questions we'll explore in this section.

Inflation means persistent increases in the average level of prices. In an economy experiencing inflation, most prices are likely to be rising.

There are three key elements in the definition of inflation:

1. Inflation refers to what is happening to the average level of prices, not to what is happening to particular prices. An increase in medical costs is not inflation. An increase in gasoline prices is not inflation. Inflation means the average level of prices is rising.
2. Inflation refers to *rising* prices; therefore, it does not have anything to do with the *level* of prices at any one time. "High" prices do not imply the presence of inflation, nor do "low" prices imply its absence. Inflation means a positive rate of change in prices.
3. Inflation refers to *persistent* increases in prices. If all prices were to rise 5 percent tomorrow and then fall back 5 percent the next day, we would not generally refer to that event as inflation. Inflation implies that price increases are continuing over a period of time.

Price Indexes

Inflation is measured as the percentage rate of change in the level of prices. But how do we find a price level?

Economists measure the price level with a **price index,** a number whose movement reflects movement in the average level of prices. If a price index rises 10 percent, it means the average level of prices has risen 10 percent.

- **Inflation** means persistent increases in the average level of prices.
- A **price index** is a number whose movement reflects movement in the average level of prices.

A **base period** is a time period against which costs of the market basket in other periods will be compared in computing a price index.

Economists go through four steps in computing a price index:

1. Select the kinds and quantities of goods and services to be included in the index. A list of these goods and services, and the quantities of each, is the "market basket" for the index.
2. Determine what it would cost to buy the goods and services in the market basket in some period that is the base period for the index. A **base period** is a time period against which costs of the market basket in other periods will be compared. If, for example, a price index had a base period of 1990, costs of the basket in other periods would be compared to the cost of the basket in 1990. Most often, the base period for an index is a single year. We'll encounter one index, however, whose base period stretches over 3 years.
3. Compute the cost of the market basket in the current period.
4. Compute the price index. It equals the current cost divided by the base-period cost of the market basket.[2]

$$\text{Price index} = \frac{\text{current cost of basket}}{\text{base-period cost of basket}} \qquad \textbf{(1)}$$

Suppose that we want to compute a price index for movie fans, and a survey of movie watchers tells us that a typical fan rents 4 movies on videocassette and sees 3 movies in theaters each month. At the theater, the average viewer consumes a medium-sized soft drink and a medium-sized box of popcorn. Our market basket might thus include 4 video rentals, 3 movie admissions, 3 medium soft drinks, and 3 medium servings of popcorn.

Our next step in computing the movie price index is to determine the cost of the market basket. Suppose we surveyed movie theaters and video rental stores in 1995 to determine the average prices of these items, finding the values given in Exhibit 22-1. At those prices, the total monthly cost of our movie market basket in 1995 was $44. Now suppose that in 1996 the prices of movie admissions, video rentals, and soft drinks at movies rise while popcorn prices fall. The combined effect of these changes pushes the 1996 cost of the basket to $47.25.

EXHIBIT 22-1

Pricing a Market Basket for a Price Index

To compute a price index, we need to define a market basket and determine its price. The table gives the composition of the movie market basket and prices for 1995 and 1996. The cost of the entire basket rises from $44 in 1995 to $47.25 in 1996.

Item	Quantity in basket	1995 price	Cost in 1995 basket	1996 price	Cost in 1996 basket
Video rental	4	$2.00	$ 8.00	$2.25	$ 9.00
Movie admission	3	7.50	22.50	7.75	23.25
Popcorn	3	2.50	7.50	2.25	6.75
Soft drink	3	2.00	6.00	2.75	8.25
Total cost of basket			1995 = $ 44.00		1996 = $ 47.25

Using the data in Exhibit 22-1, we could compute price indexes for each year. Recall that a price index is the ratio of the current cost of the basket to the base year cost. We can select any year we wish as the base year; let's take 1995. The 1996 movie price index (MPI) is thus

$$MPI_{96} = \frac{\$47.25}{\$44} = 1.07$$

[2] Published price indexes are typically multiplied by 100 to express them as a percentage. Our work with the index will be simplified by omitting this step.

Case in Point — Buy Me Some Peanuts and Cracker Jack . . .

The cost of a trip to the old ball game jumped 9 percent in 1994, according to *Team Marketing Report,* a Chicago-based newsletter. The report bases its estimate on its fan price index, whose market basket includes 4 average-priced tickets, 2 small beers, 2 small sodas, 4 hot dogs, parking for 1 car, 2 game programs, and 2 twill baseball caps. The average price of the market basket was $96.48 in 1994.

Team Marketing compiles the cost of the basket for each of major league baseball's 28 teams. According to this compilation, the New York Yankees were the most expensive team to watch in 1994; the Cincinnati Reds were the cheapest. The table shows the cost of the fan price index market basket.

Team	1994 Basket Cost	Team	1994 Basket Cost
New York Yankees	$115.15	Pittsburgh Pirates	$93.40
Toronto Blue Jays	113.53	Florida Marlins	92.18
Atlanta Braves	112.98	St. Louis Cardinals	91.72
Chicago Cubs	108.97	New York Mets	91.06
Chicago White Sox	106.13	Philadelphia Phillies	91.00
Baltimore Orioles	104.96	Los Angeles Dodgers	90.73
Cleveland Indians	103.75	Minnesota Twins	90.61
Detroit Tigers	103.45	California Angels	90.24
Boston Red Sox	102.55	Houston Astros	89.26
San Francisco Giants	100.80	Milwaukee Brewers	87.53
Oakland Athletics	100.47	San Diego Padres	83.34
Texas Rangers	99.26	Montreal Expos	82.89
Kansas City Royals	98.79	Colorado Rockies	82.08
Seattle Mariners	95.42	Cincinnati Reds	79.31

Source: John Helyar, "Going Out to the Ballpark Costs More This Season, Especially for the Best Fans," *The Wall Street Journal,* 5 April 1994, B1.

The value of any price index in the base period is always 1. In the case of our movie price index, the 1995 index would be the current (1995) cost of the basket, $44, divided by the base-period cost, which is the same thing: $44/$44 = 1.

The Consumer Price Index (CPI)

One widely used price index is the **consumer price index (CPI),** a price index whose movement reflects changes in the prices of goods and services typically purchased by consumers. When you hear news reports that refer to the U.S. inflation rate, it's usually a rate computed using the CPI. The CPI is also used to determine whether people's incomes are keeping up with the costs of the things they buy.

The market basket for the CPI contains hundreds of goods and services. The composition of the basket is determined by the Bureau of Labor Statistics (BLS), an agency of the Labor Department, based on Census Bureau surveys of household buying behavior. Surveyors tally the prices of the goods and services in the basket each month in cities all over the United States to determine the current cost of the basket.

The **consumer price index (CPI)** is a price index whose movement reflects changes in the prices of goods and services typically purchased by consumers.

The current cost of the basket of consumer goods and services is then compared to the base-period cost of that same basket. The base period for the CPI is 1982–1984; the base-period cost of the basket is its average cost over this period. Each month's CPI thus reflects the ratio of the current cost of the basket divided by its base-period cost.

$$\text{CPI} = \frac{\text{current cost of basket}}{\text{1982–1984 cost of basket}} \tag{2}$$

Like most other price indexes, the CPI is computed with a fixed market basket. The composition of the basket generally remains unchanged from one period to the next. Because buying patterns change, however, the basket is revised roughly once each decade. After a revision, the basket retains its fixed nature for the next decade.

The Implicit Price Deflator

The computation of nominal and real GDP, described in the last chapter, provides us with the information to calculate the broadest-based price index available. The **implicit price deflator,** a price index for all goods and services produced, is computed from the ratio of nominal GDP to real GDP.

In computing the implicit price deflator for a particular period, economists define the market basket quite simply: It is all the final goods and services produced during that period. The nominal GDP gives the current cost of that basket; the real GDP gives the base-period cost. The implicit price deflator is thus given by

$$\text{Implicit price deflator} = \frac{\text{nominal GDP}}{\text{real GDP}} \tag{3}$$

As we develop our analysis of the determination of output and the price level in subsequent chapters, we will use the implicit price deflator as the measure of the price level in the economy.

Computing the Inflation Rate

The inflation rate is measured as the percentage rate of change in a price index between two periods. Given price index values for two periods, we can calculate the inflation rate as the change in the index divided by the initial value of the index, stated as a percentage:

$$\text{Inflation rate} = \frac{\text{change in index}}{\text{initial value of index}} \tag{4}$$

To calculate inflation in movie prices over the period 1995–1996, for example, we could apply Equation (4) to the price indexes we computed for those two years as follows:

$$\text{Movie inflation rate in 1996} = \frac{1.07 - 1.00}{100} = 0.07 = 7\%$$

The **implicit price deflator** is a price index that reflects the prices of all goods and services. It is computed from the ratio of nominal GDP to real GDP.

The CPI is the index most often used for calculating inflation for the economy. Economists generally determine the rate of inflation by computing the percentage change in the CPI from December of the previous year to December of the year in question. For example, the rate of inflation in 1993 can be computed from the December 1992 level (1.424) and the December 1993 level (1.463):

$$\text{Inflation rate} = \frac{1.463 - 1.424}{1.424} = 0.027 = 2.7\%$$

The market basket for the implicit price deflator changes every quarter; it doesn't have an upward bias resulting from fixed weights, whereas the CPI does. Of course, it also covers a much wider range of goods and services than the CPI. When we use the implicit price deflator, we get a somewhat lower estimate of the inflation rate between 1992 and 1993 than we get with the CPI. Because the implicit price deflator is available only on a quarterly basis, we use the fourth quarter values for 1993 and 1992 to compute the 1993 inflation rate:

$$\text{Inflation rate} = \frac{1.241 - 1.219}{1.219} = 0.018 = 1.8\%$$

Computing Real Values Using Price Indexes

Suppose you have a friend who started college in 1984 and had a job busing dishes that paid $3.50 per hour. In 1994 you had the same job; it paid $5 per hour. Which job paid more?

At first glance, the answer is straightforward: $5 is a higher wage than $3.50. But $1 had greater purchasing power in 1984 than in 1994, because prices were lower in 1984 than in 1994. To obtain a valid comparison of the two wages, we must use dollars of equivalent purchasing power. A value expressed in units of constant purchasing power is a **real value.** A value expressed in dollars of the current period is called a **nominal value.** The $3.50 wage in 1984 and the $5 wage in 1994 are nominal wages. The contrast between real and nominal values is the same as the contrast between real and nominal GDP. Real GDP gives output measured in dollars of equal purchasing power; nominal GDP gives output measured in current prices.

To convert nominal values to real values, we divide by a price index. The real value for a given period is the nominal value for that period divided by the price index for that period. This procedure gives us a value that is expressed in dollars that have the purchasing power of the base period for the price index used. Using the CPI, for example, yields values expressed in dollars of 1982–1984 purchasing power, the base period for the CPI. The real value of a nominal amount X at time t, X_t, is found using the price index for time t, P_t:

$$\text{Real value of } X_t = \frac{X_t}{P_t} \tag{5}$$

Let's compute the real value of the $5 wage for busing dishes in 1994 versus the $3.50 wage paid to your friend in 1984. The CPI in 1984 was 1.096; in 1994 it was 1.482. Real wages for the two years were thus

$$\text{Real wage in 1984} = \frac{\$3.50}{1.096} = \$3.19$$

$$\text{Real wage in 1994} = \frac{\$5.00}{1.482} = \$3.37$$

Given the nominal wages in our example, you earned more in real terms in 1994 than your friend did in 1984; your real wage rose.

A **real value** is a value measured in dollars of constant purchasing power.

A **nominal value** is a value measured in dollars of current purchasing power.

EXHIBIT 22-2

Changing Real and Nominal Prices, 1975 to 1995

Here are the nominal prices of several items in 1975 and 1995. All prices are then converted to real values to determine whether the real price of each item has risen.

Item	1975 price	1995 price	Real 1975 price	Real 1995 price
First class stamp	$ 0.10	$ 0.32	$ 0.32	$ 0.21
One gallon of regular gasoline	.57	1.19	1.05	.78
General admission ticket to an L.A. Dodgers game	1.50	6.00	2.79	3.93
Minimum wage	2.10	4.25	3.90	2.79
Honda Civic	2,799.00	11,970.00	5,203.00	7,849.00

Exhibit 22-2 shows the nominal prices for several items in 1975 and in 1995. The nominal prices of all the items rose. To compare real prices, we need to state all prices in terms of dollars of equivalent purchasing power. Applying Equation 5, we can measure the price of each item in dollars of 1982–1984 purchasing power. In real terms, we see that the minimum wage and the price of gasoline have fallen. The prices of postage stamps, Dodger games, and Honda Civics have, in real terms, risen.

Price indexes are useful in a wide range of contexts. They allow us to summarize what is happening to the general level of prices. They allow us to estimate the rate of change in prices, which we report as the rate of inflation. And they give us a tool for converting nominal values to real values so we can check whether those nominal values are "keeping up" with the inflation rate.

Inflation: Friend or Foe?

Inflation is very much like a bad habit. Most people would prefer not to have it around, but we can't quite seem to get rid of it. Exhibit 22-3 shows how persistent inflation has been over the past three decades, measured as the annual rate of change in the CPI. Inflation worsened in the 1960s and became dramatically worse in the 1970s. The inflation rate plunged in the 1980s and continued to ease downward in the 1990s.

EXHIBIT 22-3

Inflation, 1960–1995

The inflation rate, measured as the annual rate of change in the CPI, varied dramatically over the period 1960–first half of 1995.

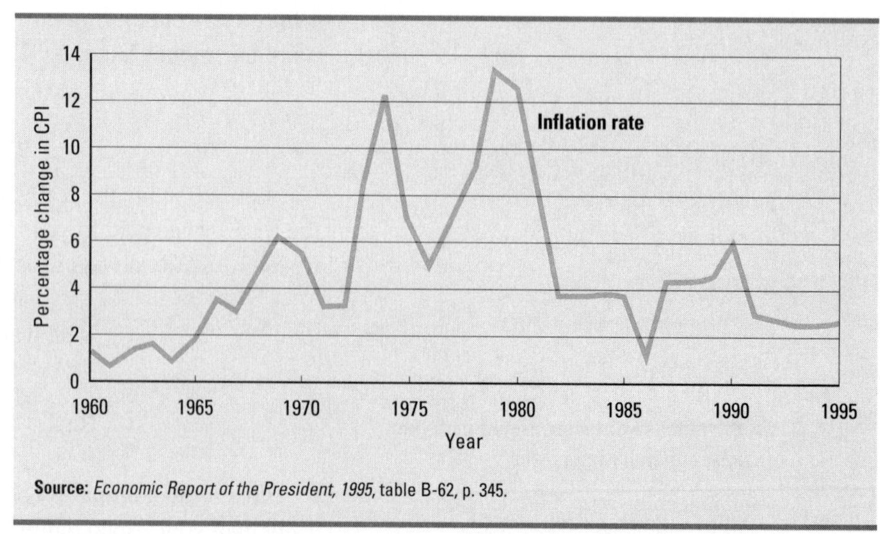

Source: *Economic Report of the President, 1995,* table B-62, p. 345.

Case in Point: The Real Value of Presidential Pay

Who was the best-paid president? The worst-paid? In nominal terms, the answer is easy to figure out.

Presidential pay was last increased in 1969 when Richard Nixon took office. Every president since has earned the same salary: $200,000 plus expenses. That's a far cry from George Washington's paltry $25,000. But George Washington didn't pay income taxes—and he faced much lower prices than those of today. Presidential pay stayed at $25,000 for the next 84 years, when Congress raised it to $50,000 at the start of Ulysses S. Grant's second term. Pay was bumped up again in 1909—William Howard Taft earned $75,000, plus, for the first time, a travel allowance.

Harry Truman got the next-to-last pay increase in 1949. His salary went up to $100,000, plus a $40,000 travel allowance. He was the first president to receive a living allowance—of $50,000.

Economists Michael J. Ahearn and Paul E. Greenberg of Cambridge, Massachusetts calculated after-tax presidential salaries and adjusted these to dollars of equal purchasing power. Using the CPI for years since 1929 and estimating CPI values based on census data for earlier years, they stated presidential salaries in dollars of 1993 purchasing power. To do that, they converted nominal values to base-year values as indicated by Equation 5, then multiplied by the price index for 1993.

Washington's $25,000 would have been worth $550,000 in dollars of 1993 purchasing power. William Howard Taft was our best-paid president—the real value of his salary was $1.5 million.

Our lowest-paid president has been Bill Clinton. Does historical parity suggest that a raise is in order?

Source: Michael T. Ahearn, "High Office, Low Pay," *The Wall Street Journal*, 7 April 1994, A14.

George Washington

Ulysses S. Grant

William Howard Taft

Harry Truman

Richard Nixon

Bill Clinton

We will examine the causes of inflation and the measures that can reduce or increase it in the later chapters. Here we examine the impact of inflation on the economy. As we shall see, whether one regards inflation as a "good" thing or a "bad" thing depends very much on one's economic situation. Whatever that situation may be, inflation always produces the following effects on the economy: it reduces the value of money, it reduces the value of future obligations, and it creates uncertainty about the future.

Suppose that you've just found a little cache of $10 you stashed away in 1979. Prices have more than doubled since then; your money will buy less than half what it would have purchased when you put it away. Your money has thus lost value.

Money loses value when its real value falls. Since inflation implies a rising price index, the real value of a given amount of money falls with inflation.

Just as inflation reduces the value of money, it reduces the value of future claims on money. Suppose you've borrowed $100 and have agreed to pay it back in one year. During the year, however, prices double; the inflation rate is 100 percent. That means the real value of the money you pay back at the end of the year is $50—only half of what you originally borrowed. That's good for you but tough on the person who lent you the money. Of course, if you and your friend had anticipated such rapid inflation, you might have agreed to pay back a larger sum to adjust for it. When people anticipate inflation, they can adjust for its consequences in determining future obligations. But unanticipated inflation helps debtors and hurts creditors.

Inflation's impact on future claims can be particularly hard on people who must live on a fixed stream of such claims. The value of a **fixed income** is predetermined through some contractual arrangement and does not change with economic conditions. An annuity, for example, provides a fixed stream of money payments. Retirement pensions sometimes generate fixed income. Inflation erodes the value of such fixed payments.

A useful rule for gauging the impact of inflation on fixed incomes is the **rule of 72.** When something grows at a given percentage rate, it approximately doubles over fixed periods of time, equal to 72 divided by the interest rate, with the interest rate stated as a whole number.

Suppose the inflation rate is 4 percent per year. At that rate, the price level will double in about 18 years (72/4). A couple retiring at age 62 on a fixed pension of $30,000 per year will find that the purchasing power of their income has fallen by half by the time they're 80.

Given the danger posed by inflation for people on fixed incomes, many retirement plans arrange for indexed payments. An **indexed payment** is one whose nominal value rises with the inflation rate. If a nominal value rises at the same rate as the inflation rate, the real value of the payment remains constant. Social Security payments, for example, are indexed to the inflation rate to maintain their purchasing power.

Because inflation reduces the purchasing power of money, the threat of future inflation can make people reluctant to lend money for long periods. From a lender's point of view, the danger of a long-term commitment of funds is that future inflation will wipe out the value of the money eventually paid back. Lenders are reluctant to make such commitments, so it can be difficult for firms to obtain the funds they need to finance their investments. Uncertainty about inflation can thus reduce investment and economic growth.

- A **fixed income** is one whose value is determined through some contractual arrangement and that does not change with economic conditions.
- The **rule of 72** states that a value growing at a given percentage rate will double over a fixed interval approximated by 72 divided by the interest rate, stated as a whole number.
- An **indexed payment** is one whose nominal value is adjusted for the inflation rate.

Case in Point: Hyperinflation in Germany Clobbers Ferdinand Porsche

It was Germany, 1923, and times were hard. Inflation over the past 3 years had driven prices to very high levels. Ferdinand Porsche, the carmaker, needed cash.

Porsche had received three luxury cars as partial compensation when he left Austro-Daimler. The three cars, called City Coaches, were elaborate creations. In front they offered open seats for the chauffeur and passengers. Behind these were two more open seats with a movable cover in case of rain, and at the rear was a closed compartment for passengers to use in case of severe weather. The manufacturer boasted that the City Coach combined the best features of an open car, a convertible, and a limousine. Porsche approached a friend in Stuttgart, business executive Alfred Neubauer, and said, "Help me turn my City Coach into money, Herr Neubauer. I don't know half as much about financial matters as you."

Neubauer found a buyer in Backnang for one of the cars. He recalled later that Mr. Porsche was delighted with the price, which was in the millions of marks.

The car was delivered to the buyer. One week later the money reached Stuttgart. During that week, however, the pace of inflation had accelerated. Porsche had sold one of the grandest vehicles in the world—but by the time he got the money, it was just enough to pay for six rides on the local streetcar line.

Source: Alfred Neubauer and Harvey T. Rowe, *Männer, Frauen und Motoren* (Stuttgart: Motorbuch Verlag, 1978). Translation courtesy of Curtis Poulton. Neubauer recalled that at the beginning of 1923, he had spent his entire week's salary to buy a pair of socks and a small bottle of cologne—and at that same time a small band of men, marching in brown shirts and calling themselves Nazis, had proclaimed a "Day of the Germans."

Ferdinand Porsche, behind engine, far right.

Uncertainty can be particularly pronounced in countries where extremely high inflation is a threat. **Hyperinflation** is generally defined as an inflation rate in excess of 200 percent per year. Inflation of that magnitude erodes the value of money very fast. With inflation of 200 percent per year, prices triple each year.

Hyperinflation is an inflation rate in excess of 200 percent per year.

Do Price Indexes Overstate Inflation?

Price indexes that employ fixed market baskets are likely to overstate the inflation rate for three reasons: First, the fixed nature of the market basket means it can't adjust to reflect consumer responses to changing relative prices. Second, a fixed basket excludes new goods and services. Third, quality changes may be understated in computing the inflation rate.

Suppose the price of gasoline rises and the price of beef falls. The law of demand tells us that people will respond by consuming less gasoline and more beef. But if we use a fixed market basket of goods and services in computing a price index, we won't be able to make these adjustments. The market basket holds constant the quantities of gasoline and beef consumed. The importance in consumer budgets of the higher gasoline price is thus overstated, while the importance of the lower beef price is understated. More generally, a fixed market basket will overstate the importance of items that rise in price and understate the importance of items that fall. Fixing quantities in the market basket thus lends an upward bias to price index changes and to the inflation rate. The implicit price deflator solves this problem by introducing an entirely new basket every quarter, but that creates a new problem, a lack of comparability. Indeed, for that reason the implicit price deflator isn't generally used as a measure of inflation.

A second source of bias in price indexes comes from their omission of new goods. A good introduced after a market basket has been defined won't, of course, be included in it. But a new good, once successfully introduced, is likely to fall in price. When VCRs were first introduced, for example, they generally cost more than $1,000. An equivalent machine cost less than $200 within a few years. But when VCRs were introduced, the Bureau of Labor Statistics (BLS) was computing the CPI based on a market basket that had been defined in the early 1970s. There was no VCR in the basket, so the impact of this falling price was omitted from the index.

A third problem with price indexes comes when firms improve the quality of the goods and services they provide. Suppose, for example, that IBM introduces a new personal computer with twice the memory, twice the hard disk capacity, and twice the speed of its previous model. Suppose the old model cost $2,000 and the new model costs $2,400, a 20 percent increase in price. Should economists at the BLS simply record the new model as being 20 percent more expensive than the old one?

Clearly, the new model isn't the same product as the old model. Indeed, one could argue that the new model represents twice the computing capacity of the old model; the price per unit of computing capacity has actually fallen. BLS economists faced with such changes try to adjust for quality. They might, for example, conclude that the gains offered with the new computer make it the equivalent of 50 percent more computer than the old model. With a 50 percent gain in quality and only a 20 percent increase in price, the new model would actually be recorded as having fallen in price.

Other economists who study the measurement of inflation generally agree that the adjustments made by the BLS don't fully reflect quality gains. To the extent that such adjustments understate quality change, they overstate inflation. If, for example, the BLS concluded that the new IBM computer was only 10 percent "more computer" than the old model, it would still record a price increase for the computer.

It's fairly easy to quantify quality change in the case of a computer. Indeed, the BLS uses a formula based on such factors as memory, hard disk storage capacity, and speed. But how should it measure the quality change of a new car that offers a quieter, smoother ride? A grocery store that offers 24-hour service? A CD player with better sound?

Economists differ on the degree to which the problems of a fixed market basket, new goods, and quality change result in overstating the true rate of inflation, but there is broad agreement that the reported rate is between 0.5 and 2 percentage points higher than the actual rate. That finding has enormous practical significance. It means that if inflation is brought down to a 2 percent rate, a feat that had almost been achieved when *Economics* went to press, the United States will have won—or nearly won—the fight against inflation.

Further, if the computation of price indexes overstates the rate of inflation, then the use of price indexes to correct nominal values results in an understatement of gains in real incomes. Suppose nominal incomes are rising at a 3 percent rate while the inflation rate is also measured at 3 percent, so that the official statistics record no gain in real incomes. If the true inflation rate is only 1 percent, then real incomes are actually rising 2 percent per year. Using the rule of 72, we would find that real incomes double every 36 years. Over a long period, the understatement of improvement in real incomes that results from an overstatement in inflation could become very large.

Checklist ✓

- Inflation implies continuing increases in the price level. It is measured as the percentage rate of change in a price index.
- A price index shows the cost of a particular basket of goods and services relative to its base-period cost. The consumer price index (CPI) is the most widely used price index in the United States. Another important price index is the implicit price deflator.
- Nominal values can be converted to real values by dividing by a price index.
- Economists generally agree that inflation rates measured by conventional price indexes significantly overstate the true inflation rate.
- The threat of inflation increases the degree of uncertainty about future incomes, a problem that can be especially severe when hyperinflation is a likely threat.
- Inflation reduces the real values of money, of future obligations measured in money, and of fixed incomes.

Unemployment

For an economy to produce all it can, to achieve a solution on the production possibilities curve, the resources in the economy must be fully employed. Failure to fully employ resources leads to a solution inside the production possibilities curve, where society is not achieving the output it's capable of producing.

In thinking about the employment of society's resources, we place special emphasis on labor. Labor accounts for the bulk of value added in the economy. Furthermore, the loss of a job can wipe out a household's entire income; it's a more compelling human problem than, say, a vacant apartment. In measuring unemployment, we thus focus on labor rather than on capital and natural resources.

Measuring Unemployment

- **Unemployment** is measured as the number of people not working who are looking and available for work at any one time.
- The **labor force** is the number of people working plus the number of people unemployed.
- The **unemployment rate** is the percentage of the labor force who are unemployed.

When is a worker unemployed? The BLS defines **unemployment** as the number of people who are not working but are looking and available for work. The **labor force** is the total number of people working or unemployed. The **unemployment rate** is the number of people unemployed expressed as a percentage of the labor force.

To estimate the unemployment rate, government surveyors fan out across the country each month to pay calls on roughly 65,000 households. At each household, which has been randomly selected for survey purposes, the surveyor asks about each adult (everyone age 16 or over) who lives there. Many households include more than one adult; the survey reveals information about roughly 100,000 adults. The surveyor asks if each adult is working. If the answer is yes, that person is counted as employed. If the answer is no, the surveyor asks if that person has looked for work at some time during the previous 4 weeks and is available for work at the time of the survey. If the answer to that question is yes, that person is counted as unemployed. If the answer is no, that person is not counted as a member of the labor force. Exhibit 22-4 shows the survey's results for the civilian (nonmilitary) population for 1994. The unemployment rate is then computed as the number of people unemployed divided by the labor force—the sum of the number of people looking for work plus the number of people working. In 1994, the unemployment rate was 6.1 percent.

EXHIBIT 22-4

Computing the Unemployment Rate, 1994

A monthly survey of households divides the civilian adult population into three groups. Those who have jobs are counted as employed. Those who don't have jobs but are looking for them and are available for work are counted as unemployed. Those who aren't working and aren't looking for work are not counted as members of the labor force. The unemployment rate equals the number of people looking divided by the sum of the number of people looking and the number of people employed. Values given are for 1994. All numbers are in thousands.

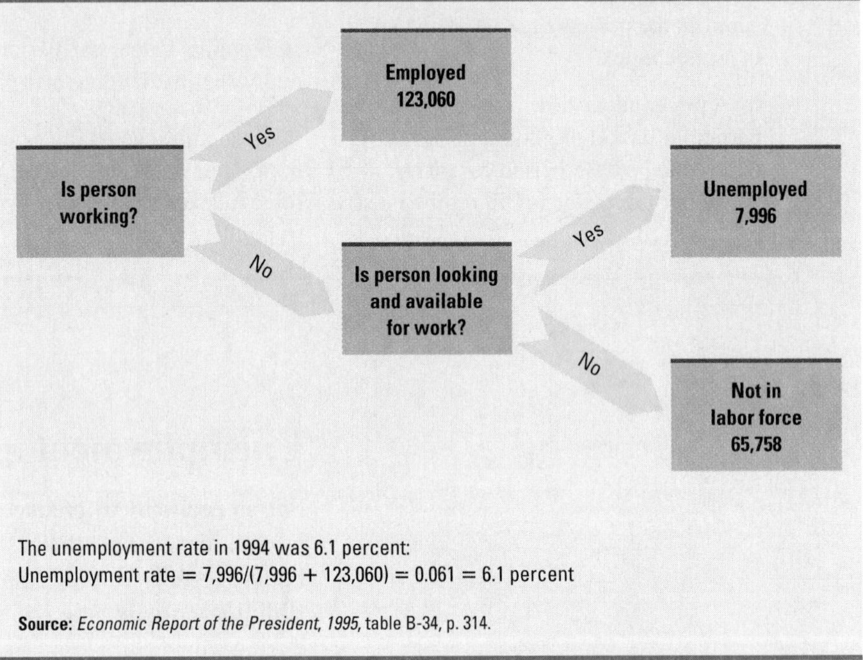

The unemployment rate in 1994 was 6.1 percent:
Unemployment rate = 7,996/(7,996 + 123,060) = 0.061 = 6.1 percent

Source: *Economic Report of the President, 1995,* table B-34, p. 314.

There are several difficulties with the survey. The old survey, designed during the 1930s, put the "Are you working?" question differently depending on whether the respondent was a man or woman. A man was asked, "Last week, did you do any work for pay or profit?" A woman was asked, "What were you doing for work last week, keeping house or something else?" Because of that approach to the question, many women looking for work stated that they were "keeping house"; those women weren't counted as unemployed. The BLS didn't get around to fixing the survey—asking women the same question it asked men—until 1994. When the new survey was used, the unemployment rate among women rose by 0.5 percentage point. More than 50 million women are in the labor force; the change added more than a quarter of a million workers to the official count of the unemployed.[3]

[3] For a description of the new survey and other changes introduced in the method of counting unemployment, see Janet L. Norwood and Judith M. Tanur, "Unemployment Measures for the Nineties," *Public Opinion Quarterly* 58(2)(Summer 1994): 277–294.

A **discouraged worker** is one who is not working and would like to work but who has given up looking for work and is thus not counted as unemployed.

The **natural level of employment** is the level of employment at which the quantity of labor demanded equals the quantity supplied.

The problem of understating unemployment among women has been fixed, but others remain. A worker who has been cut back to part-time work is still counted as employed, even if that worker would prefer to work full time. A person who is out of work, would like to work, and is available for work, but who has given up looking, is considered a **discouraged worker.**[4] Discouraged workers are not counted as unemployed, but a tally is kept each month of the number of discouraged workers.[5] Further, the test for whether a person is "looking" is not very stringent. If a person has done anything to seek information about the job market—looking once at the "Help Wanted" ads, asking a friend whether jobs are available—that person is considered to be looking for work.

The official measures of employment and unemployment can yield anomalous results. When economic activity rises, for example, firms will expand output, but they may be reluctant to hire additional workers until they can be sure the demand for increased output will be sustained. They may respond first by extending the hours of employees previously reduced to part-time work or by asking full-time personnel to work overtime. None of that will increase employment, because people are simply counted as "employed" if they are working, regardless of how much or how little they are working. Further, an increase in economic activity may make discouraged workers more optimistic about job prospects, and they may resume their job searches. Engaging in a search makes them unemployed again—which increases unemployment. Thus, an upturn in economic activity may have little effect initially on employment and may even increase unemployment.

Types of Unemployment

Workers may find themselves unemployed for different reasons. Each source of unemployment has quite different implications, not only for the workers it affects but for public policy.

Exhibit 22-5 applies the demand and supply model to the analysis of the labor market. The price of labor is taken as the real wage ω, which is the nominal wage divided by the CPI. The supply curve is drawn as a vertical line because we shall assume that the quantity of labor supplied is, at any one time, fixed. The demand curve shows the quantity of labor demanded at each real wage. The lower the real wage, the greater the quantity of labor firms will demand. In the case shown here, the initial real wage, ω_1, equals the equilibrium solution defined by the intersection of the demand curve D_1 and the supply curve S_1. The quantity of labor demanded L_1 equals the quantity supplied. The employment level at which the quantity of labor demanded equals the quantity supplied is called the **natural level of employment.** It is sometimes referred to as full employment.

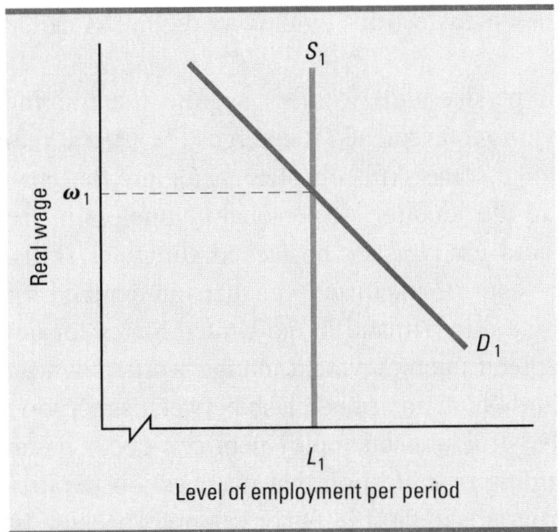

EXHIBIT 22-5

The Natural Level of Employment

The employment level at which the quantity of labor demanded equals the quantity supplied is called the natural level of employment. Here, the natural level of employment is L_1, which is achieved at a real wage ω_1.

Frictional and Structural Unemployment

Even if the economy is operating at its natural level of employment, there will still be some unemployment, because information in the labor market is costly and because worker skills and job requirements may not match.

[4] An additional requirement for being counted as a discouraged worker was added in 1994: the person must have looked for a job sometime within the past year.

[5] The Bureau of Labor Statistics does estimate the number of discouraged workers and workers who are working fewer hours than they would like. This information is reported each month in the *Monthly Labor Review.*

Even when the quantity of labor demanded equals the quantity of labor supplied, not all employers and potential workers have found each other. Some workers are looking for jobs, and some employers are looking for workers. During the time it takes to match them up, the workers are unemployed. Unemployment that occurs because it takes time for employers and workers to find each other is called **frictional unemployment.**

The case of college graduates engaged in job searches is a good example of frictional unemployment. Those who didn't land a job while still in school will seek work. Most of them will find jobs, but this will take time. During that time, new graduates will be unemployed. If information about the labor market were costless, firms and potential workers would instantly know everything they needed to know about each other and there would be no need for searches on the part of workers and firms. There would be no frictional unemployment. But information is costly. Job searches are needed to produce this information, and frictional unemployment exists while the searches continue.

Another reason there can be unemployment even if employment equals its natural level stems from potential mismatches between the skills employers seek and the skills potential workers offer. When we draw the demand and supply curves for labor, we assume that labor and employment are homogeneous. In the world of the graph, one worker is exactly like another, one job exactly like another. But the real world is not so tidy. Every worker is different; every job has its special characteristics and requirements. In such a world, the qualifications workers offer in the job market may not match those that firms require. Even though the number of employees firms demand equals the number of workers available, people whose qualifications don't satisfy what firms are seeking will find themselves without work. Unemployment that results from a mismatch between worker qualifications and the characteristics employers require is called **structural unemployment.**

Structural unemployment will persist until workers acquire the training firms demand or firms adjust their job requirements. It emerges for several reasons. Technological change may make some skills obsolete or require that new ones be developed. The widespread introduction of personal computers in the 1980s, for example, lowered demand for typists who lacked computer skills. Structural unemployment can also occur in response to changes in demand for goods and services. The huge reduction in demand in the United States for defense protection has created widespread unemployment among workers whose old skills aren't needed in a world in which an armed clash between superpowers no longer seems likely. Finally, structural unemployment can occur if too many or too few workers seek training or education that matches job requirements. Students flocked to MBA programs in the 1980s, for example, because of high salaries—and the result was what many observers called a "glut" in the MBA market. Students can't predict precisely how many jobs there will be in a particular category when they graduate, and they aren't likely to know how many of their fellow students are training for these jobs. Structural unemployment can easily occur if students guess wrong about how many workers will be needed or how many will be supplied.

Structural employment can also result from geographical mismatches. Economic activity may be booming in one region and slumping in another. It will take time for unemployed workers to relocate and find new jobs. And poor transportation may block some urban residents from obtaining jobs only a few miles away.

Frictional unemployment is unemployment that occurs because it takes time for employers looking for workers and workers looking for work to find each other.

Structural unemployment is unemployment that results from a mismatch between worker qualifications and employer requirements.

- The **natural rate of unemployment** is the unemployment rate consistent with employment at the natural level.
- **Cyclical unemployment** occurs when the quantity of labor supplied exceeds the quantity of labor demanded.
- A **sticky price** is one that is slow to adjust to its equilibrium level.

Public policy responses to structural unemployment generally focus on job training and education to equip workers with the skills firms demand. The government publishes regional labor market information, helping to inform unemployed workers of where jobs can be found. The North American Free Trade Agreement (NAFTA), which created a free trade region encompassing Mexico, the United States, and Canada, is expected to create structural unemployment in the United States. The legislation authorizing the pact in 1994 included provisions for job training programs for displaced U.S. workers.

Public policies directed at frictional unemployment focus on its source: information costs. Many state agencies, for example, serve as clearinghouses for job market information. They encourage firms seeking workers and workers seeking jobs to register with them. To the extent that such efforts make labor market information more readily available, they may reduce frictional unemployment.

Although public sector efforts may reduce frictional and structural unemployment, they can't eliminate it. Information in the labor market will always have a cost, and that cost creates frictional unemployment. An economy with changing demands for goods and services, changing technology, and changing production costs will always have some sectors expanding and others contracting—structural unemployment is inevitable. An economy operating at its natural level of employment will therefore have frictional and structural unemployment. The rate of unemployment consistent with the natural level of employment is called the **natural rate of unemployment.** It is generally thought to be an unemployment rate of about 6 percent. We'll examine the issues involved in computing the natural rate of unemployment later in this book.

Of course, the economy may not be operating at its natural level of employment, so unemployment may be above or below its natural level In the next chapter we'll explore what happens when the economy generates employment greater than the natural level. In the next section we examine the unemployment that results when employment falls below the natural level. In such cases, unemployment will exceed the natural rate.

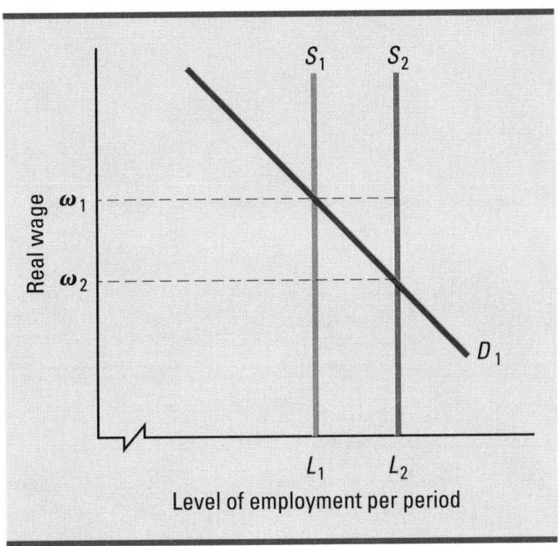

EXHIBIT 22-6

Price Stickiness and Disequilibrium in the Labor Market

An increase in the supply of labor to S_2 increases the natural level of employment to L_2 and reduces the equilibrium real wage to ω_2. Sticky nominal wages and prices, however, may slow such an adjustment and cause cyclical unemployment to persist. If the real wage remains at ω_1, for example, cyclical unemployment equals $L_2 - L_1$.

Cyclical Unemployment

Cyclical unemployment occurs when the quantity of labor supplied exceeds the quantity demanded. It represents a surplus in the labor market.

Exhibit 22-6 shows the same demand and supply curves for labor D_1 and S_1 given in Exhibit 22-5. Initially, employment is at its natural level. Notice that the horizontal axis is drawn with a break. That's because actual values of employment are far greater than zero; we don't really know what might happen to the demand and supply curves for labor if employment were to approach zero. The real wage is ω_1, and the level of employment is L_1. Now suppose there is an increase in the supply of labor to S_2, perhaps because of an increase in population or because more people decide to join the labor force. The natural level of employment is now L_2; it would be achieved if the real wage fell to ω_2.

A reduction in the real wage, however, requires either a reduction in nominal wages or an increase in the price level. There are several reasons to expect a reduction in nominal wages to be slow in coming. First, many wages are set by long-term contracts. Union wages, for example, are typically established for 3-year periods. Other wages are likely to be fixed for periods of at least 1 year. Furthermore, workers are likely to resist a cut in their nominal wages, even if the result is rising unemployment. Nominal wages are an example of a **sticky price,**

Checklist

- Unemployment is measured as the number of people looking and available for work at any one time.
- The unemployment rate shows unemployment as a percentage of the labor force.
- Discouraged workers are not counted as unemployed.
- When the labor market is in equilibrium, employment is at the natural level and the unemployment rate equals the natural rate of unemployment, thought to be roughly 6 percent.
- Even if employment is at the natural level, the economy will experience frictional and structural unemployment.
- If the real wage exceeds the equilibrium real wage, the economy will have a surplus of labor, or cyclical unemployment. Sticky prices and wages can cause cyclical unemployment to persist.
- If real wages are sticky, cyclical unemployment may persist.

a price that is slow to adjust to its equilibrium level, creating sustained periods of shortage or surplus. We can expect a surplus of labor to produce downward adjustments in nominal wages eventually, but the process will be a slow one.

Of course, real wages could also fall as a result of an increase in other prices. But with a surplus of labor, the pressure on wages is downward. There's not likely to be upward pressure on other prices. Moreover, we'll see as we continue our investigation of macroeconomic phenomena that other prices in the economy may show stickiness as well. Stickiness both in wages and in other prices is thus likely to retard the adjustment of the real wage to its equilibrium level. A surplus in the labor market may thus persist. If the real wage remains at ω_1 in the face of an increase in the supply of labor to S_2, there will be a surplus of labor equal to $L_2 - L_1$. This surplus is cyclical unemployment.

The problem of price stickiness presents a central issue for macroeconomic analysis. The greater the degree of stickiness, the more difficult it is for markets to achieve equilibrium. In the labor market, stickiness of the real wage can cause persistent cyclical unemployment. If real wages are flexible, however, the labor market will adjust relatively quickly to its natural level of employment, and cyclical unemployment will be a minor problem.

Exhibit 22-7 shows the unemployment rate in the United States, as well as an estimate of the natural rate, for the period 1960–1995. We see that the actual rate has fluctuated around the natural rate, sometimes exceeding it and sometimes falling below it. The analysis of the reasons for such fluctuations, and the public sector responses to them, will occupy center stage in much of the remainder of this book.

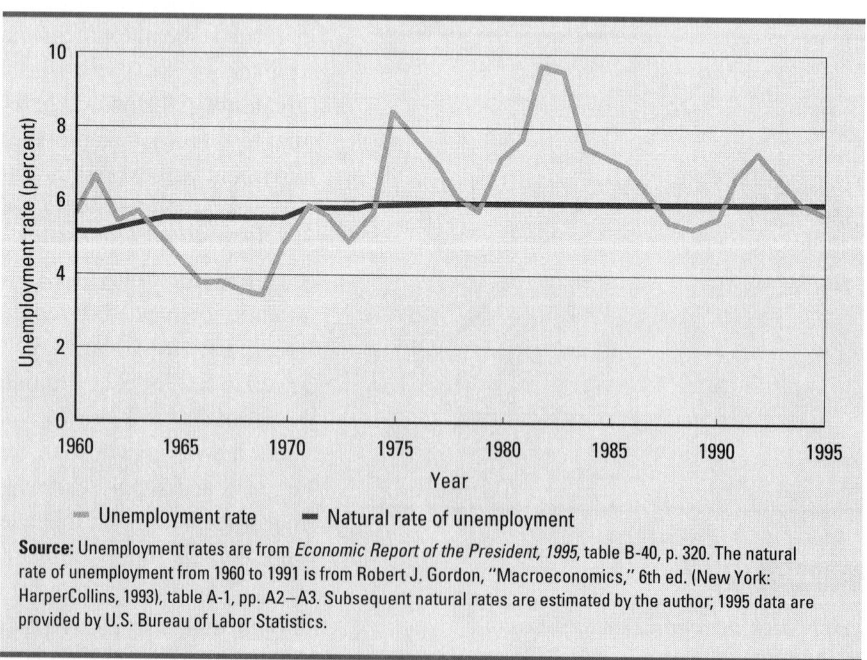

Source: Unemployment rates are from *Economic Report of the President, 1995,* table B-40, p. 320. The natural rate of unemployment from 1960 to 1991 is from Robert J. Gordon, "Macroeconomics," 6th ed. (New York: HarperCollins, 1993), table A-1, pp. A2–A3. Subsequent natural rates are estimated by the author; 1995 data are provided by U.S. Bureau of Labor Statistics.

EXHIBIT 22-7

Actual Versus Natural Unemployment, 1960–1995

The chart compares the actual unemployment rate to an estimate of the natural rate for each year from 1960 to 1995. Notice that the natural rate stays close to 6 percent.

The Business Cycle

- The **business cycle** is a pattern of expansion, then recession, then expansion again.
- The **trend rate of real GDP growth** is the average annual growth rate of real GDP over some period.

Inflation and unemployment aren't the economic equivalents of, say, flooding and drought. They aren't disasters that come to us as natural forces like the winds and the tides. They are phenomena produced by the behavior of people, and it is in understanding the behavior of people that we can gain an understanding of macroeconomic phenomena such as inflation and unemployment.

Changes in unemployment and inflation are related to changes in the level of economic activity. An increase in real GDP, for example, means that firms are producing more goods and services. That will require them to hire more workers, reducing unemployment. It may also put upward pressure on prices, increasing inflation. Conversely, a reduction in real GDP means there is a slump in production. That's likely to cause firms to reduce the number of workers they employ and increase unemployment. It will put downward pressure on prices, reducing inflation.

A period in which real GDP is rising is called an expansion. A period in which real GDP falls for at least two consecutive quarters is called a recession. The economy's pattern of expansion, then recession, then expansion again is called the **business cycle.**

Exhibit 22-8 shows movements in real GDP from 1960 to the first half of 1995. During that period the economy experienced six recessions, shown by the shaded areas in the chart. Although periods of expansion have been more prolonged than periods of recession, we see the cycle of expansion, then contraction, then expansion that characterizes economic life.

EXHIBIT 22-8

Expansions and Recessions, 1960–1995

The chart shows movements in real GDP since 1960. Recessions—periods of falling GDP—are shown as shaded areas. The trend rate of real GDP over the period showed an average annual rate of growth of 3.1 percent per year.

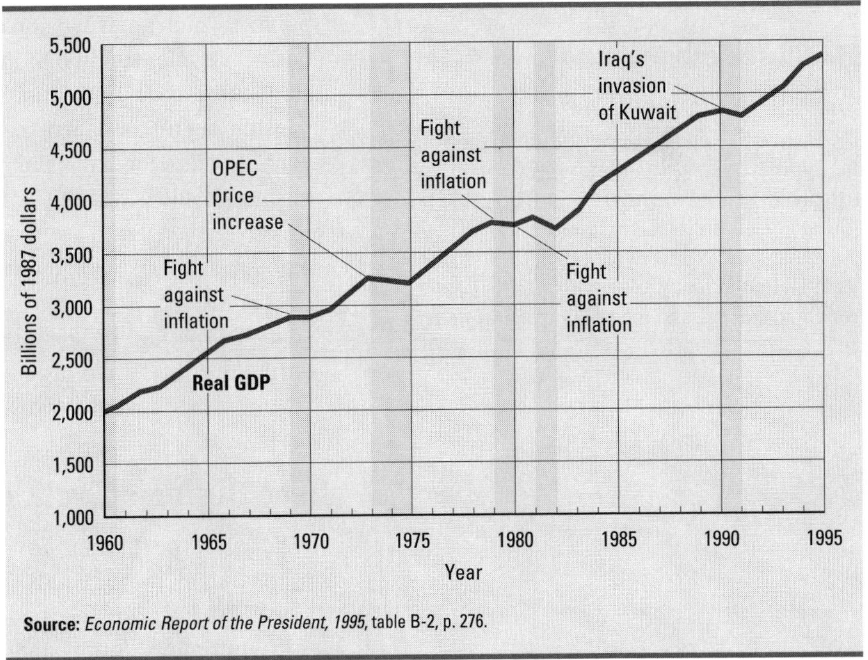

Real GDP clearly grew between 1960 and 1995; the average rate of increase over the period was 3.1 percent per year. The average annual rate at which real GDP grows over some period is called the **trend rate of real GDP growth.** The actual value of real GDP fluctuated about this trend.

Generally speaking, we expect expansions to be periods of falling unemployment—provided real GDP is rising fast enough to keep up with growth in the labor force and growth in productivity. Periods of recession are likely to be marked by rising unemployment. The link between the business cycle and inflation is not so simple—inflation may rise or fall during any phase of the business cycle. An understanding of the relationship between the business cycle, unemployment, and inflation will be something that we'll accomplish in subsequent chapters.

Phases of the Business Cycle

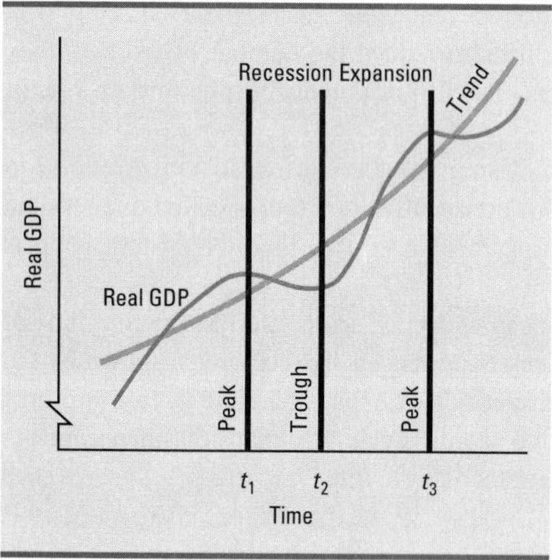

EXHIBIT 22-9

Phases of the Business Cycle

The business cycle is a series of fluctuations about the economy's long-run trend of economic growth, shown by the heavy line. The cycle begins at a peak, followed by a recession, trough, and expansion. A new cycle begins at the next peak. Here, the first peak occurs at time t_1, the trough at time t_2, and the next peak at time t_3.

The cycles of expansion and recession shown in Exhibit 22-8 vary in terms of length of expansions and recessions, severity of recessions, and vigor of expansions, but there are common elements to every business cycle. To understand these common elements, we shall construct an idealized picture of a business cycle and examine its phases.

Exhibit 22-9 shows the phases of a typical business cycle. The orange line shows the economy's long-term trend of economic growth—it shows what GDP would be if it increased each year at the same rate. From 1960 to 1995, for example, we saw that real GDP grew at an average rate of 3.1 percent per year; growth at such a rate would be the trend rate of growth. The business cycle occurs as fluctuations about this trend. That's the pattern we saw in Exhibit 22-8—the economy experienced expansions and recessions, but its general trend during the period was one of rising GDP. The red line, labeled "Real GDP," shows the movement of GDP about this trend.

At time t_1, the previous expansion ends and real GDP turns downward. The point at which an expansion ends and a recession begins is called the **peak** of the business cycle. Real GDP then falls during a period of recession. Eventually it starts upward again (at time t_2). The point at which a recession ends and an expansion begins is called the **trough** of the business cycle. The economy then continues into an expansion until another peak is reached at time t_3. A complete business cycle is defined by the passage from one peak to the next.

Over the period from 1960 to 1991, the average expansion has lasted 61 months, and the average recession has lasted 11 months. The longest expansion in U.S. history, which came during the 1960s, lasted almost 8 years; that expansion was marked by the Vietnam War. The longest peacetime expansion came during the 1980s and lasted almost as long. The expansion that was under way when this book went to press began in March 1991.

- The **peak** of a business cycle is reached when real GDP stops rising and begins falling.
- The **trough** of a business cycle is reached when real GDP stops falling and begins rising.

The Business Cycle and the Circular Flow

We can use the circular flow model introduced in Chapter 21 to interpret what's happening as the economy passes through the phases of the business cycle. As we've already seen, the model suggests how swings in economic activity can be self-reinforcing. An expanding economy generates more income, which generates more demand for goods and services, which generates more production—and thus more income. The circular flow model also suggests some factors that could cause turning points in the business cycle.

Exhibit 22-10 repeats the circular flow diagram we developed in Chapter 21. The blue arrows flowing into firms represent the four sources of demand placed on firms: personal consumption, investment, government purchases, and

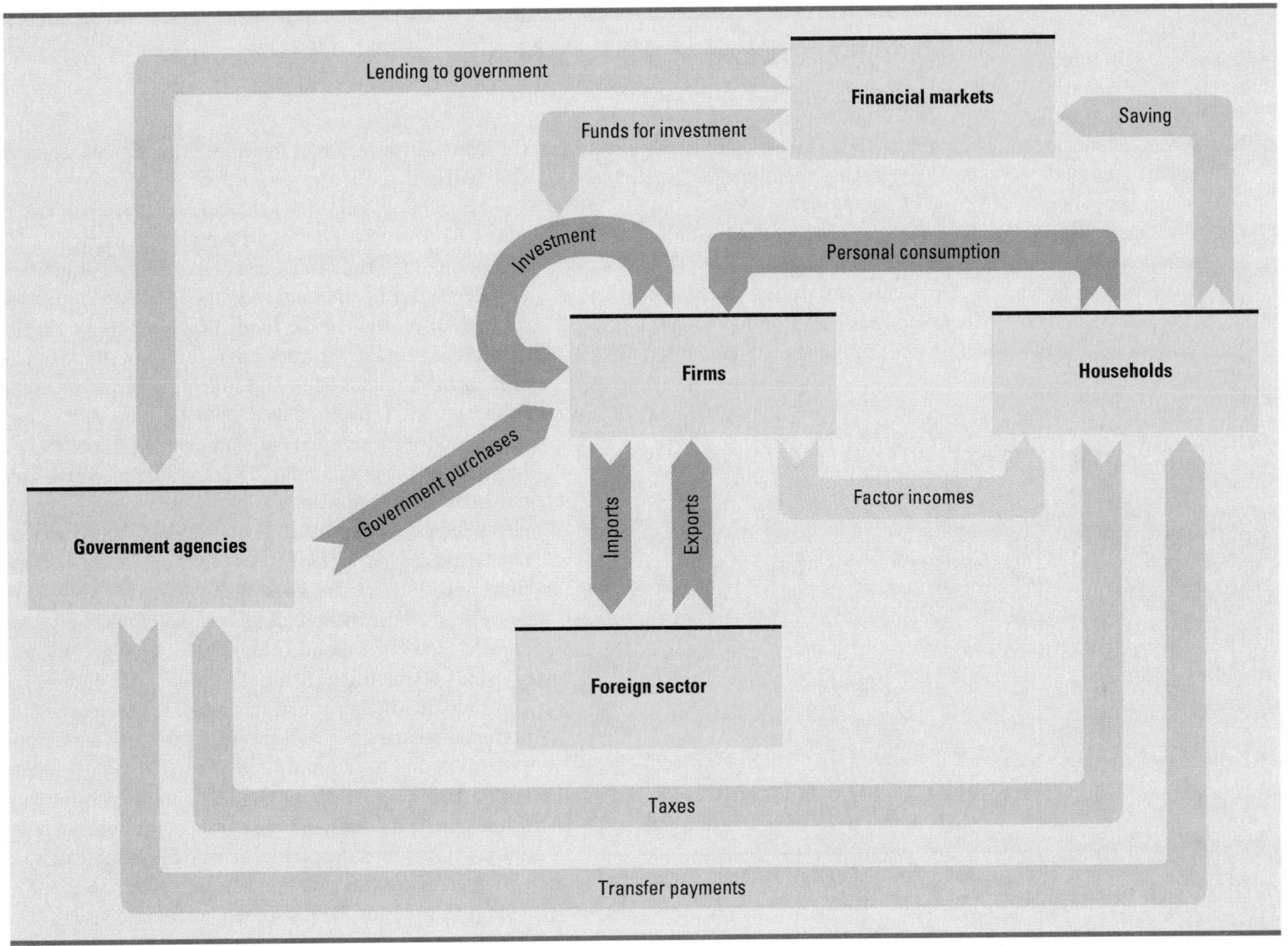

EXHIBIT 22-10

The Circular Flow Model

We can use the circular flow model to interpret the factors that contribute to the business cycle.

exports and imports. As firms produce goods and services in response to these demands, they generate income to households. Those households use that income to finance their consumption.

Suppose the economy is now experiencing an expansion. Rising production generates rising incomes, which generate demand for still more production. What would cause this happy state of self-reinforcing growth to come to an end, bringing the economy into recession?

The circular flow model suggests several potential sources of trouble. One set of problems could come from the demand arrows in the circular flow diagram. A weakening in one of those sources of demand could cause firms to cut back their output, initiating a recession.

Demand could weaken for several reasons. Economic problems in other countries could reduce export demand. The expansion may have boosted inflation, and the federal government might try to cool the economy off by cutting back government purchases. It could also cut transfer payments or increase taxes; either action would reduce household incomes and thus reduce consumption demand. Still another source of a possible downturn would be a reduction in investment. As firms increase production during an expansion, they demand more factors of production: more labor, more capital, and more natural

Case in Point: Predicting the End of the Expansion

Every expansion in history has come to an end. It therefore seems reasonable to expect the one that began in 1991 to do the same. But when?

One rule for predicting the length of an expansion was developed by Geoffrey Moore, an economist at Columbia University who directs the Center for International Business Cycle Research. Mr. Moore's rule is based on movement in the prime rate, the base interest rate that banks charge corporations for loans. An increase in the prime rate signals when the expansion will end.

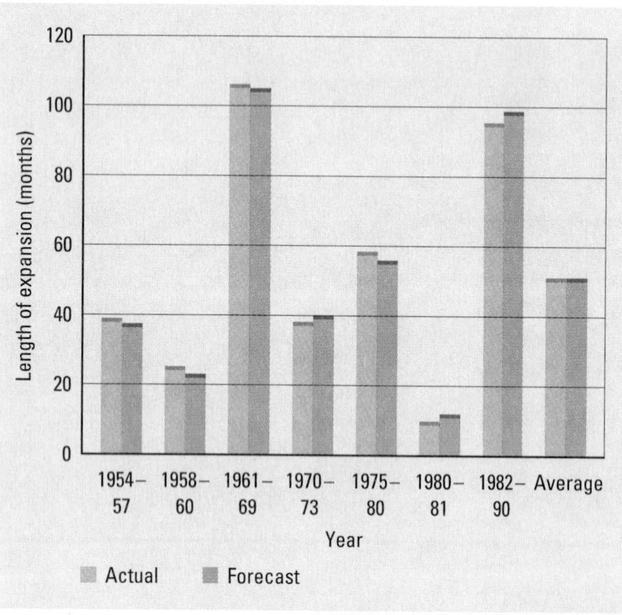

Mr. Moore's rule states that an expansion will last 15 months plus 1.57 times the number of months the expansion has continued before the prime rate heads up. A higher prime rate is likely to reflect a rise in other interest rates, which will increase the cost to firms of borrowing the funds they need to finance investment projects. Eventually, higher interest rates in the financial market will lead to a reduction in investment. Reduced spending for new capital goods forces reduced output by the firms that produce those goods. Those firms cut back on their use of labor and other factors of production, reducing household incomes. That leads to reduced consumption and still more reductions in output. If these negative effects are strong enough to offset any increases in demands placed on firms from other components of the circular flow model, the expansion will end.

The accompanying chart suggests that the length of past expansions has corresponded to the rule. Fitting a rule to past relationships is one thing; using it to predict the future, however, is quite another. In any event, readers of this book will have an opportunity to see how well the rule forecasts the duration of the expansion that began in March 1991. The prime rate started rising in March 1994, 36 months after the expansion began. (The prime rate rose largely because of Federal Reserve policies we'll discuss in the next chapter.) The rule thus predicts the expansion will last 6 years and will end in March 1997 ($36 \times 1.57 = 56.52$; adding 15 gives us 71.52 months, or about 6 years).

Source: Lindley H. Clark, Jr., "A Slump Predictor Clinton Should Love," *The Wall Street Journal,* 28 December 1994, A1.

resources. Increases in demand will boost factor prices, but that will reduce firm profits. At first, rising demands for goods and services could offset this effect. But eventually, the economy will strain against the limits of its resources, and factor prices will rise quickly. As profits fall, firms may cut back on their investment. Alternatively, potential lenders in the financial market, seeing profits falling, might reduce their lending, drying up the funds firms need for increased investment. Finally, consumers may begin to sense trouble ahead and cut back on their purchases, especially of major items such as cars or household furnishings. Reductions in any of these sources of demand facing firms could cause output to fall. The economy reaches a peak and turns down, and a recession begins.

Once output starts falling, the same reinforcing mechanism that worked on the way up will operate on the way down. As firms cut back their output, households will have less income. They'll cut back their consumption, prompting still more cuts in output.

To see how a recession might end, we can look again to the sources of demand facing firms. Other economies may be expanding, prompting an increase in exports. The federal government might seek to end the recession by boosting its purchases of goods and services, increasing transfer payments, or cutting taxes. A recession means firms are cutting back on their use of labor, capital, and natural resources; the prices of these factors of production will begin falling. That could boost profitability, prompting an increase in investment. After a period of reducing their consumption, consumers might begin making purchases they had been postponing. As they do so, they could prompt a recovery.

These explanations of the business cycle focus on the demands for goods and services. Cycles could also be generated by changes on the supply side. A technological change might stimulate new investment and produce an expansion. A reduction in the availability of natural resources could force an increase in production costs that causes a recession.

Economists have sought for centuries to explain the forces at work in a business cycle. Not only are the currents that move the economy up or down intellectually fascinating; an understanding of them is of tremendous practical importance. A business cycle isn't just a movement along a curve in a textbook. It's new jobs for people, or the loss of them. It's new income, or the loss of it. It's the money to build new schools, reduce the federal deficit, or provide better health care—or the lack of money to do all those things. The story of the business cycle is the story of progress and plenty, of failure and sacrifice.

As we continue our investigation of macroeconomics, we'll learn more about the various components in the circular flow diagram, and we'll thus gain an understanding of the forces at work in the business cycle. We'll also explore policies through which the public sector might act to make recessions less severe and, perhaps, to prolong expansions.

Checklist

- The economy follows a path of expansion and then recession that fluctuates about its long-run trend. These fluctuations are called the business cycle.
- The point at which an expansion becomes a recession is called the peak of a business cycle; the point at which a recession becomes an expansion is called the trough.
- We can use the circular flow model to interpret the forces at work in generating the business cycle.

A Look Back—And a Look Ahead

In this chapter we examined inflation, unemployment, and the business cycle. We saw how these phenomena are defined and looked at their consequences.

Inflation is a persistent series of increases in the general price level. It is measured as the percentage rate of change in a price index. We looked at the calculation of the consumer price index (CPI) and the implicit price deflator. The CPI is widely used in the calculation of inflation. It may overstate the inflation rate because it holds quantities in the market basket fixed, because it tends to omit new goods, and because economists computing the index may fail to adjust adequately for quality change.

Inflation affects economic activity in several ways. It reduces the value of money and of claims on money. Unexpected inflation benefits debtors and hurts creditors. The threat of inflation creates uncertainty, which reduces investment and slows the economy's growth in the long run.

The unemployment rate is measured as the percentage of the labor force seeking work. Cyclical unemployment occurs when there is a surplus of labor. Such unemployment may persist if real wages are sticky, preventing the economy from achieving its natural level of employment. Frictional unemployment occurs because information about the labor market is costly; it takes time for firms seeking workers and workers seeking firms to find each other. Structural unemployment occurs when there is a mismatch between the skills offered by potential workers and the skills sought by firms. Structural unemployment has become a more important element of unemployment in today's economy because of rapid changes in technology and in international competition. Both frictional and structural unemployment occur even if employment and the unemployment rate are at their natural levels.

A look at real GDP shows a long upward trend, but with the economy going through phases of expansion and recession around that trend. These phases make up the business cycle. An expansion reaches a peak, and the economy falls into a recession. The recession reaches a trough and becomes an expansion again. We saw how the circular flow model can be used to interpret these swings in economic activity.

In the next chapter, we'll develop a new model that will guide us in our analysis of macroeconomic events through the following 14 chapters. We'll also have a look at some key markets in the economy, markets that have powerful effects on real GDP, the price level, and unemployment.

Terms and Concepts for Review

Base period
Business cycle
Consumer price index (CPI)
Cyclical unemployment
Discouraged worker
Fixed income
Frictional unemployment
Hyperinflation
Implicit price deflator
Indexed payment
Inflation
Labor force
Natural level of employment
Natural rate of unemployment
Nominal value
Peak
Price index
Real value
Rule of 72
Sticky price
Structural unemployment
Trend rate of real GDP growth
Trough
Unemployment
Unemployment rate

For Discussion

1. During the late 1970s, when the inflation rate was a major news story, some television networks sent correspondents to purchase a fixed collection of groceries each month and report on the prices. Explain how you might use the data from these reports to compute a grocery price index.
2. Suppose you calculate a grocery price inflation rate based on the data in Problem 1. Using the arguments presented in the chapter, explain three possible sources of upward bias in the rate you calculate, relative to the actual trend of food prices.
3. Name three items you have purchased during the past year that have increased in quality during the year. What kind of adjustment would you make in assessing their prices for the CPI?
4. Exhibit 22-2 showed that the real price of a Honda Civic rose between 1975 and 1995. The 1995 model, though, had several features the 1975 model lacked, including disc brakes, dual airbags, 5-speed transmission (instead of

4-speed), and a rear window defroster. The 1995 model got better mileage, had a more powerful engine and generated less pollution than the 1975 model. How do these changes affect your interpretation of what happened to the price of the car?

5. A recent local newspaper editorial lamented that many high school and college graduates were leaving the state to obtain jobs in other regions. Even if nothing is done to stem the tide of out-migration, what do you predict will happen to the unemployment rate in that state if the trend continues? What might happen to the unemployment rates in the more prosperous states if people keep moving to them?

6. Minority teenagers have the highest unemployment rates observed for any group. One reason for this phenomenon is high transportation costs for many minority teens. What form of unemployment (cyclical, frictional, or structural) do high transportation costs suggest?

7. Suppose a law is passed requiring all welfare recipients to look for work and accept a job if it is offered. How would this affect the unemployment rate?

8. We noted that there isn't a systematic relationship between inflation and the phase of the business cycle. Use your knowledge of demand and supply analysis to explain what's likely to happen to the prices of individual goods and services during the expansion phase. Can you think of any reason prices might rise during the recession phase?

9. On the basis of recent news reports, what phase of the business cycle do you think the economy is in now? What's the inflation rate? The unemployment rate?

Problems

1. Suppose that in 1997, the items in the market basket for our movie price index cost $49.60. Use the information in the chapter to compute the price index for that year. How does the rate of movie price inflation from 1996 to 1997 compare with the rate from 1995 to 1996?

2. Recompute the movie price indexes for 1995 and 1996 using 1996 as the base year. Now compute the rate of inflation for the period 1995–1996. Compare your result to the inflation rate calculated for that same period using 1995 as the base year.

3. Here are some employment statistics for 1990. Compute the unemployment rate for that year (all figures are in thousands).

Population	249,924
Employment	117,914
Unemployment	6,874

4. Suppose an economy has 10,000 people looking and available for work and 90,000 people working. What is its unemployment rate? Now suppose 4,000 of the people looking for work get discouraged and give up their searches. What happens to the unemployment rate? Would you interpret this as good news for the economy or bad news? Explain.

5. Yale University economist William Nordhaus has compared official measures of lightbulb, candle, and lantern prices over the past two centuries to changes in the cost per lumen of light. He found that the official measures don't reflect quality gains, which he measured as increases in the amount of light produced. The results, he claims, is that the government's statistics have overstated lighting costs by 3.6 percent per year since 1800.[6] At that rate, by how much do current indices overstate the true cost of light?

6. Plot the quarterly data for real GDP for the last 2 years. (You can find the data in the *Survey of Current Business* or in *Current Economic Indicators* in the current periodicals section of your library. Alternatively, your instructor may be able to make the data available to you.) Relate what's happening to the concept of the phases of the business cycle.

7. The average price of going to a baseball game, based on the observations in the Case in Point on page 463, was $96.48. Using this average as the equivalent of a base year, compute Fan Price Indexes for the Yankees and for the Reds.

[6] William Nordhaus, Cowles Foundation Discussion Paper 1078, 1994, forthcoming as an NBER working paper.

23

Demand and Supply in the Macroeconomy

Chapter Objectives

After mastering the material in this chapter, you will be able to:

1. Interpret the aggregate demand and short-run aggregate supply curves and identify the factors that shift each curve.
2. Show how the intersection of the aggregate demand and short-run aggregate supply curves determines the equilibrium level of real GDP and the price level.
3. Relate shifts in aggregate demand or short-run aggregate supply to changes in equilibrium real GDP and the price level.
4. Relate the natural level of employment to the natural level of real GDP and explain how the economy adjusts to its natural level.
5. Contrast the main ideas of the three major schools of macroeconomic thought.
6. Show how the demand and supply for bonds determines both the price of bonds and the interest rate.
7. Define the exchange rate and explain how the demand and supply for dollars determines the exchange rate.
8. Use the model of aggregate demand and aggregate supply to illustrate how events in the bond and currency markets affect real GDP and the price level.

What's Ahead

Iraq's 1990 invasion of Kuwait sent oil prices soaring and shifted demand and supply curves in a wide range of related markets. But those microeconomic effects weren't the only story.

Economists who forecast macroeconomic events were scrambling in the wake of the invasion to adjust their estimates of economic performance downward. Most said a recession was imminent. Forecasters adjusted their predictions of unemployment and inflation upward.

Markets that are closely tied to macroeconomic performance reacted immediately. Interest rates rose. Real GDP plunged.

In this chapter we introduce a new model of macroeconomic activity that we can use to analyze problems such as the impact of higher oil prices on the economy: the model of aggregate demand and aggregate supply. In Chapter 26 we will discuss the model in much more detail. We'll be using this model throughout our exploration of macroeconomics. In this chapter we also apply demand and supply analysis to the markets for bonds and for currencies. Together with the labor market that we investigated in the last chapter, these markets play key roles in macroeconomic analysis.

Finally, we'll examine three major schools of macroeconomic thought. We'll be contrasting the views of economists in each of these three schools throughout the remainder of this book.

Aggregate Demand and Short-Run Aggregate Supply

In Chapter 22 we learned how changes in spending by households, firms, government agencies, and foreign buyers could affect macroeconomic phenomena such as unemployment, inflation, and the business cycle. We built that analysis in the context of the circular flow model, which gives us a schematic view of flows of spending and of goods and services in the economy. We now turn to a demand and supply model that seeks to explain how equilibrium real GDP and the price level are determined. We'll find that this model is similar in many ways to the model of demand and supply for an individual market. But there are important differences as well.

Aggregate demand is the relationship between the total quantity of goods and services demanded and the price level, all other determinants of spending unchanged.

The **aggregate demand curve** is a graphical representation of aggregate demand.

Aggregate Demand

The circular flow model shows the four sources of demand that firms in the economy face: households (personal consumption), other firms (investment), government agencies (government purchases), and foreigners (net exports). In this section we shall lump these four sources of demand together. Economists define **aggregate demand** as the relationship between the total quantity of goods and services demanded and the price level, all other determinants of spending unchanged. The **aggregate demand curve** is a graphical representation of aggregate demand.

The Slope of the Aggregate Demand Curve

We shall use the implicit price deflator as our measure of the price level; the aggregate quantity of goods and services demanded is measured as real GDP. A typical aggregate demand curve is illustrated in Exhibit 23-1. At point A, at a price level of 1.34, $4,800 billion worth of goods and services will be demanded. At point B, a reduction in the price level to 1.30 increases the quantity of goods and services demanded to $5,000 billion, and at point C, at a price level of 1.26, $5,200 billion will be demanded.

EXHIBIT **23-1**

Aggregate Demand

An aggregate demand curve *AD* shows the relationship between the quantity of aggregate output demanded (measured as real GDP) and the price level (measured as the implicit price deflator). At a price level of 1.34, the aggregate quantity of goods and services demanded is $4,800 billion (point A). A reduction in the price level to 1.30 increases the aggregate quantity of goods and services demanded to $5,000 billion (point B). A further reduction to a price level of 1.26 increases the aggregate quantity of goods and services demanded to $5,200 billion (point C). The break shown in the vertical and horizontal axes reminds us that we are dealing with only a limited range of price levels and outputs.

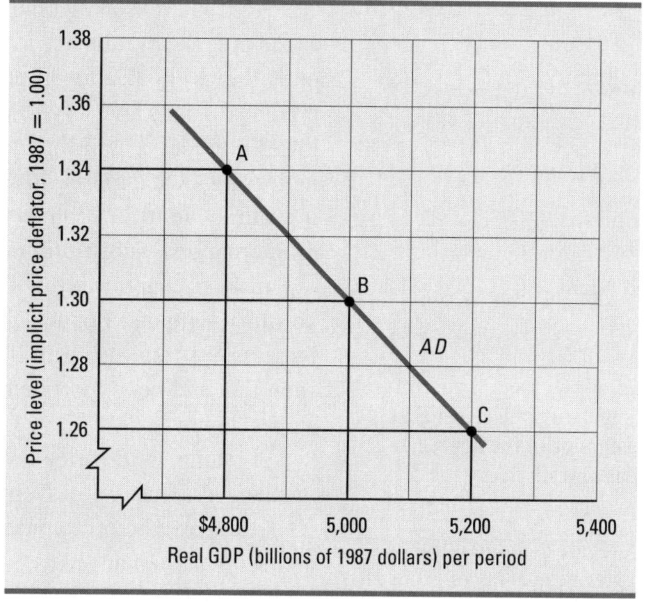

The negative slope of the aggregate demand curve suggests that it behaves in the same way as an ordinary demand curve. But we can't rely on the reasoning we use to explain downward-sloping demand in individual markets to explain downward-sloping aggregate demand. There are two reasons for a negative relationship between price and quantity demanded in individual markets. First, a lower price induces people to substitute more of the good whose price has fallen, increasing the quantity demanded. Second, the lower price creates a higher real income. For a normal good, this increases quantity demanded further. These are the substitution and income effects of a price change.

Neither of these effects is likely to be relevant to a change in prices in the aggregate. When we are dealing with the average of all prices—the price level—we are no longer in a position to say that a fall in prices will induce a change in relative prices. The price of corn may have fallen, but the prices of wheat, sugar, tractors, steel, and every other good or service produced in the economy are likely to have fallen as well. There is no reason for consumers to substitute among goods and services.

Furthermore, a reduction in the average of all prices means that it isn't just the prices consumers pay that are falling. It means the prices people receive—their wages, the rents they may charge as landlords, the interest rates they earn—are likely to be falling as well. A falling price level means that goods and services are cheaper, but incomes are lower, too. There is no reason to expect that a change in real income will boost the quantity of goods and services demanded—indeed, no change in real income would occur. If nominal incomes and prices all rise by 10 percent, for example, real incomes don't change.

Why, then, does the aggregate demand curve slope downward? One reason for the downward slope of the aggregate demand curve lies in the relationship between money, prices, wealth, and consumption. People hold some of their wealth as money. When the price level falls, the real value of their money increases—it packs more purchasing power. The real wealth of the public increases. An increase in wealth will induce people to increase their consumption. The consumption component of aggregate demand will thus be greater at lower than at higher price levels.

A second reason that the total quantity of goods and services demanded rises as the price level falls lies in the net export component of aggregate demand. All other things equal, a lower price level in the economy reduces the prices of U.S.-produced goods and services relative to foreign-produced goods and services. A lower price level will thus make U.S. goods more attractive to foreign buyers, increasing U.S. exports. It will also make foreign-produced goods and services less attractive to U.S. buyers, reducing our imports. The result, which is a kind of international substitution effect, will be an increase in net exports.

In later chapters we will see that a lower price level will also increase investment demand. For now, however, we may conclude that lower price levels increase the total quantity of goods and services demanded by increasing consumption and net export demand. The result is that the aggregate demand curve slopes downward.

A change in the price level, with all other determinants of aggregate demand unchanged, causes a movement *along* the aggregate demand curve. In Exhibit 23-1, suppose the initial price level is 1.34 and the aggregate quantity of goods and services demanded is $4,800 billion, shown by point A. Now suppose the price level drops to 1.30 but other determinants of aggregate demand remain unchanged. The schedule given suggests that the aggregate quantity of goods and services demanded rises to $5,000 billion, shown by point B. A movement along an aggregate demand curve is a **change in the aggregate quantity of goods and services demanded.** Such a change is a response to a change in the price level.

Notice that the axes of the aggregate demand curve graph are drawn with a break near the origin. That construction reminds us that the values reflected in the graph are for a relatively narrow range of changes in real GDP and the price level. We don't know what might happen if the output for an entire economy approached zero. Happily, such a phenomenon has never been observed.

Changes in Aggregate Demand

Aggregate demand changes in response to a change in any of its components. An increase in the total quantity of consumer goods and services demanded at every

- A movement along the aggregate demand curve is called a **change in the aggregate quantity of goods and services demanded.**
- A **change in aggregate demand** is a change in the aggregate quantity of goods and services demanded at each price level.
- **Aggregate supply** is the relationship between the total output produced and the price level, all other things unchanged.
- The **short run** in macroeconomic analysis is a period in which real wages are sticky.
- The **long run** in macroeconomic analysis is a period in which real wages are flexible.
- The **short-run aggregate supply (SRAS) curve** is a graphical representation of the relationship between the price level and the total output that will be produced in the short run, assuming all other factors that affect output remain unchanged.

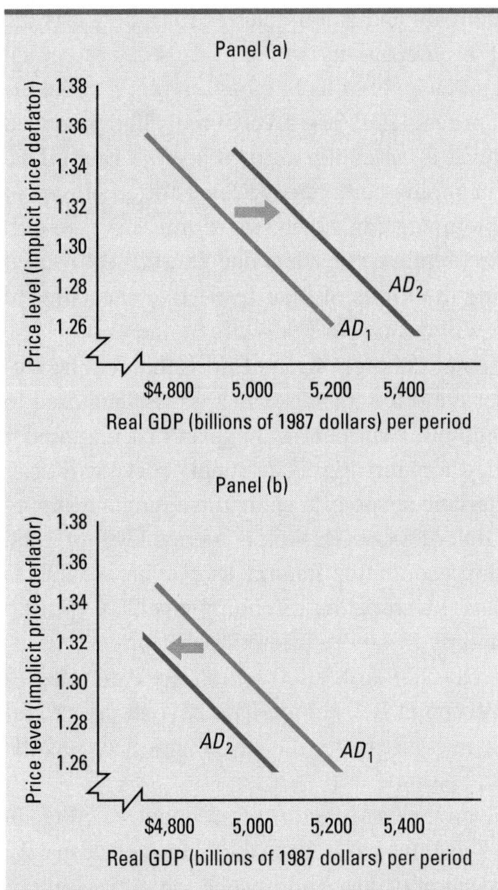

EXHIBIT 23-2

Changes in Aggregate Demand

An increase in consumption, investment, government purchases, or net exports shifts the aggregate demand curve AD_1 to the right, as shown in Panel (a). A reduction in one of the components of aggregate demand shifts the curve to the left, as shown in Panel (b).

price level, for example, would shift the aggregate demand curve to the right. Such a change might occur because people feel more confident about the future and thus more willing to spend today. An increase in government purchases, investment demand, or net exports would also shift aggregate demand to the right. Similarly, a reduction in consumption demand, government purchases, investment demand, or net exports would shift the aggregate demand curve to the left. A change in the aggregate quantity of goods and services demanded at every price level is a **change in aggregate demand.** A change in aggregate demand shifts the aggregate demand curve. Increases and decreases in aggregate demand are shown in Exhibit 23-2.

Short-Run Aggregate Supply

Just as the concept of demand can be extended to the aggregate of economic activity, so can the concept of supply. We can use aggregate supply curves in individual markets to develop a supply curve for the total economy, one that relates total output to the price level. The relationship between the total output produced and the price level, all other things unchanged, is called **aggregate supply.**

Time Periods and Aggregate Supply

Economists distinguish two types of aggregate supply relationships according to whether real wages are sticky or flexible during the time period considered. We saw in Chapter 22 that nominal wages can be sticky. We'll find other examples of sticky prices as we continue our exploration of macroeconomic theory. Sticky wages and prices make the real wage, which is the ratio of the nominal wages to the price level, sticky as well.

Sticky real wages affect the economy's production of goods and services. If sticky wages limit firms' hiring of workers, for example, production will be limited. Stickiness in real wages also affects the economy's ability to adjust to changes in demand and supply in individual markets.

Time periods in macroeconomic analysis are defined according to the degree of stickiness that prevails. The **short run** in macroeconomic analysis is a period in which real wages are sticky and may prevent the economy from achieving its natural level of employment. The **long run** in macroeconomic analysis is a period over which real wages are flexible and adjust fully to achieve the natural level of employment.

The analysis in this section focuses on aggregate supply in the short run. We will explore aggregate supply in the long run later in this chapter.

The **short-run aggregate supply (SRAS) curve** is a graphical representation of the relationship between production and the price level in the short run, assuming all other factors that affect output remain unchanged. Among the factors held constant in drawing a short-run aggregate supply curve are the economy's labor force, the capital stock, the stock of natural resources, the level of technology, and the prices of factors of production.

In our examination of demand and supply curves in Chapter 3, we saw that a higher price is necessary to induce a greater level of output in a particular market. Similarly, a higher price level is necessary to induce a higher level of output in the economy. The short-run aggregate supply curve will thus be upward sloping.

A key concept in aggregate supply relates to the economy's natural level of employment. We saw in the last chapter that the natural level of employment is

- The **natural level of real GDP** is the level of real GDP produced when the economy is operating at its natural level of employment.
- A **change in the aggregate quantity of goods and services supplied** is a movement along the short-run aggregate supply curve in response to a change in the price level.
- A **change in short-run aggregate supply** is a change in the aggregate quantity of goods and services supplied at every price level in the short run.

defined by the intersection of the demand and supply curves for labor; it is the equilibrium level of employment. For an economy with a given stock of capital and of natural resources and with a given level of technology, employment at the natural level produces a given level of real GDP. The level of real GDP produced when employment is at its natural level is called the **natural level of real GDP.**

We saw in Chapter 22 that an economy can generate levels of employment above the natural level. Just as employment can exceed its natural level, so output can exceed its natural level. As output approaches and exceeds its natural level, however, firms will be pushing the limits of their respective capacities to produce goods and services, which will put upward pressure on their costs. The greater the level of real GDP, the greater the proportion of firms that will be facing such constraints, and the greater the price increases that will be required to induce firms to produce still more output. We therefore expect that the greater the level of real GDP, the steeper the short-run aggregate supply curve will be.

Exhibit 23-3 shows the characteristic shape of a short-run aggregate supply curve. Firms are producing a real GDP of $4,800 billion at a price level of 1.28, as shown by point A′. Suppose this economy's natural level of real GDP is $5,000 billion; output at point A′ puts it well below its natural level.

Firms will increase their output only if they're offered higher prices. An increase in production to the natural real GDP of $5,000 billion, for example, requires that the price level rise to 1.30 (point B′). An increase beyond the natural level, say to $5,200 billion, requires an even greater increase in the price level to 1.36 (point C′).

Ultimately, an economy with given levels of factors of production will reach a limit as to what can be produced. This physical limit to the economy's capacity explains why the short-run aggregate supply curve approaches an upper limit to real GDP. The *SRAS* curve in Exhibit 23-3, for example, appears to reach this limit at a level of output slightly above $5,200 billion.

A change in the price level produces a movement along the short-run aggregate supply curve. Such a change is called a **change in the aggregate quantity of goods and services supplied.** Suppose, for example, that the current price

EXHIBIT 23-3

The Aggregate Supply Curve

The short-run aggregate supply curve *SRAS* shows the aggregate quantity of goods and services supplied at each price level. At a price level of 1.28, real GDP equals $4,800 billion (point A′). To induce firms to increase output to $5,000 billion, an increase in the price level to 1.30 is required (point B′). An increase in output to $5,200 billion requires an increase in the price level to 1.36 (point C′). The greater the level of output, the greater the proportion of firms that are approaching the limits of their respective capacities to produce goods and services, and the greater the increase in price required to induce additional output.

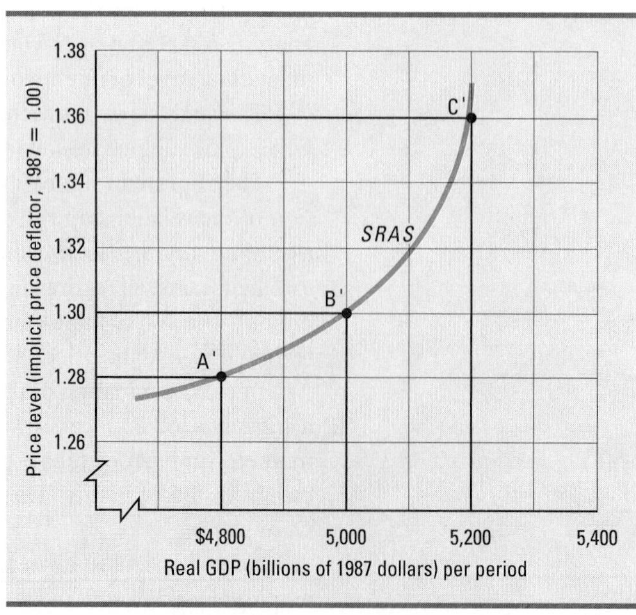

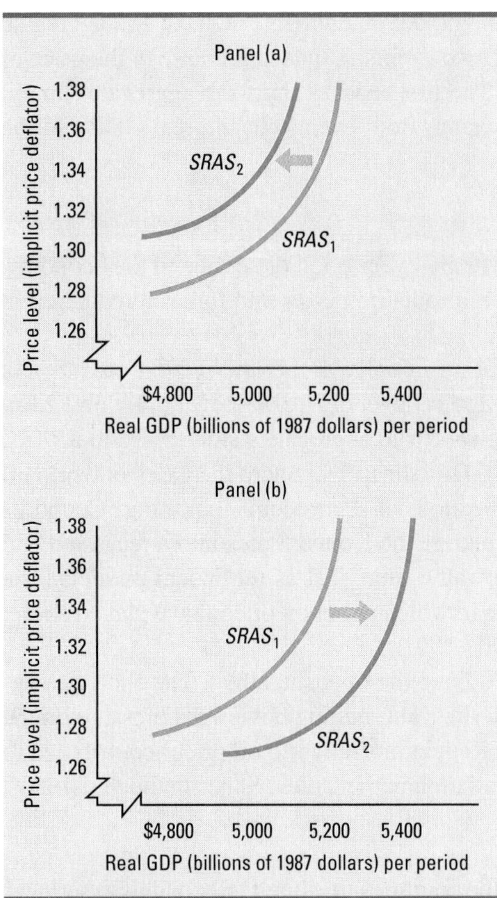

EXHIBIT 23-4

Changes in Short-Run Aggregate Supply

A reduction in short-run aggregate supply shifts the curve from $SRAS_1$ to $SRAS_2$ in Panel (a). An increase shifts it to the right to $SRAS_2$ as shown in Panel (b).

level is 1.28 and the aggregate quantity of goods and services supplied is $4,800 billion, as shown by point A′. An increase in the price level to 1.30 would produce a change in the aggregate quantity of goods and services supplied to $5,000 billion, as shown by point B′.

A change in the quantity of goods and services supplied at every price level in the short run is a **change in short-run aggregate supply.** Changes in the factors held constant in drawing the short-run aggregate supply curve shift the curve. Changes in the prices of factors of production, the labor force, the capital stock, the stock of natural resources, and technology will shift the short-run aggregate supply curve.

One type of event that would shift the short-run aggregate supply curve is a reduction in the availability of natural resources. Prices for natural resources will rise, and there will be a reduction in short-run aggregate supply. In Panel (a) of Exhibit 23-4, $SRAS_1$ shifts leftward to $SRAS_2$. An improvement in technology would allow greater production from the economy's stock of resources and would shift the short-run aggregate supply curve to the right; such a shift is shown in Panel (b) by a shift from $SRAS_1$ to $SRAS_2$.

Equilibrium Price and Output in the Short Run

The aggregate demand curve shows the total quantity of goods and services that consumers, firms, government agencies, and foreign buyers will purchase at every price level. The short-run aggregate supply curve shows the total quantity of goods and services that firms will supply at every price level. The intersection of the two curves defines the price level and total output at which the macroeconomic system reaches equilibrium in the short run.

Exhibit 23-5 combines the aggregate demand and short-run aggregate supply curves we have already introduced. They intersect at point B, with a real GDP of $5,000 billion per year and a price level, the implicit price deflator, of 1.30. At this price level, producers will produce, in the aggregate, the same quantity of goods and services that buyers will buy.

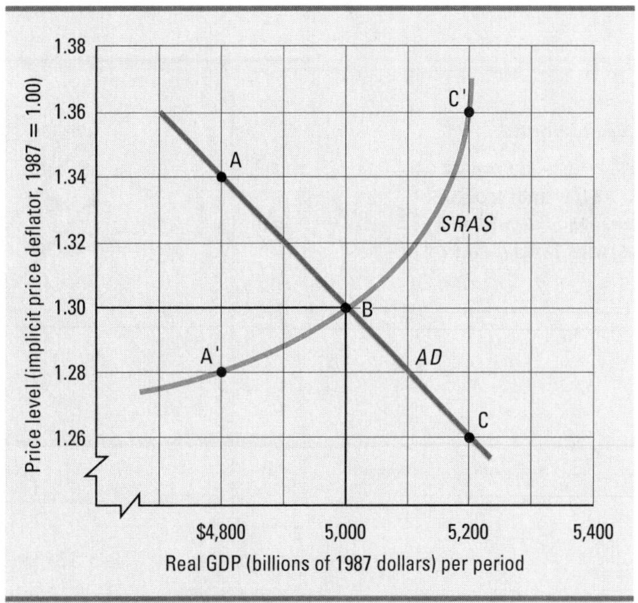

EXHIBIT 23-5

Macroeconomic Equilibrium in the Short Run

The equilibrium level of both real GDP and the price level in the short run is determined by the intersection of the aggregate demand (*AD*) and short-run aggregate supply (*SRAS*) curves. Here, equilibrium occurs at a price level of 1.30 and a real GDP of $5,000 billion. Real GDP equals its natural level.

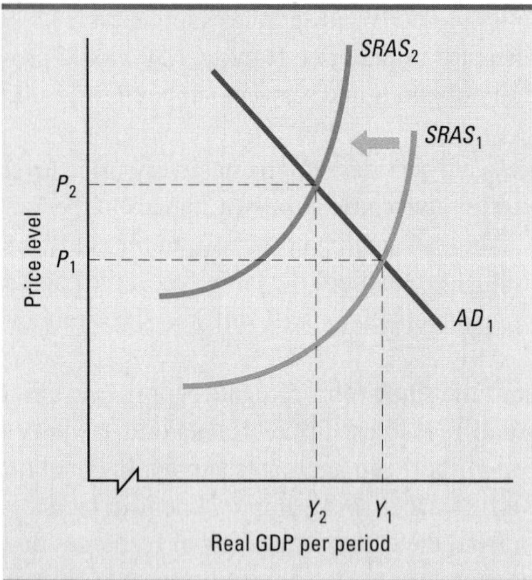

EXHIBIT 23-6

A Shift in Short-Run Aggregate Supply

An increase in the price of oil pushes up production costs, reducing short-run aggregate supply from $SRAS_1$ to $SRAS_2$. The price level rises and output falls. Here, the price level rises from P_1 to P_2 and real GDP falls from Y_1 to Y_2.

To illustrate how we will use the model of aggregate demand and aggregate supply, let's examine the impact of two events: a sudden increase in the price of oil and an increase in net exports. The first reduces short-run aggregate supply; the second increases aggregate demand. Both events change real GDP and the price level.

A Change in Oil Prices

Oil is used in the production of virtually every good or service in the economy. An increase in the price of oil raises production costs and forces a reduction in short-run aggregate supply.

Suppose the economy is operating initially at the intersection of AD_1 and $SRAS_1$, with a real GDP of Y_1 and a price level of P_1, as shown in Exhibit 23-6. The increase in oil prices shifts the short-run aggregate supply curve to $SRAS_2$. The price level rises to P_2 and real GDP falls to Y_2. Sharp increases in world oil prices engineered by the Organization of Petroleum Exporting Countries (OPEC) in 1973 and 1974 helped plunge the United States into a recession and set off sharp price increases at the same time, just as the model predicts. The 1974 recession was the first of three in which rising oil prices have played a role; others followed in 1980 and in 1990–1991.

A reduction in oil prices would have the opposite effect. The short-run aggregate supply curve would shift to the right, putting downward pressure on the price level and boosting real GDP. Reductions in world oil prices contributed to growth in real GDP and to falling inflation in the United States in the mid-1980s.

A Change in Net Exports

Suppose income gains in many of the countries that buy U.S. goods and services lead to more imports from the United States. That translates into an increase in U.S. net exports and in aggregate demand.

Assuming no other changes affect aggregate demand, the increase in net exports shifts the aggregate demand curve to the right to AD_2 in Exhibit 23-7. Real GDP rises from Y_1 to Y_2, while the price level rises from P_1 to P_2.

In the short run, real GDP and the price level are determined by the intersection of the aggregate demand and short-run aggregate supply curves. Recall,

EXHIBIT 23-7

An Increase in Aggregate Demand

An increase in net exports boosts aggregate demand from AD_1 to AD_2. At the intersection of AD_2 and the short-run aggregate supply curve $SRAS_1$, the price level rises to P_2 and real GDP rises to Y_2.

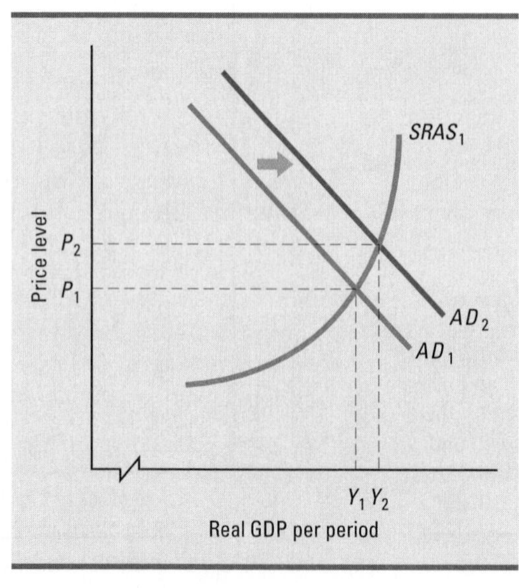

Case in Point: The Recession of 1990–1991

Shifts in aggregate demand and in short-run aggregate supply dealt the U.S. economy a double whammy in the summer of 1990, leading to the first recession since the economy had begun expanding 8 years earlier. Indeed, the 1990 downturn ended the longest peacetime expansion in U.S history.

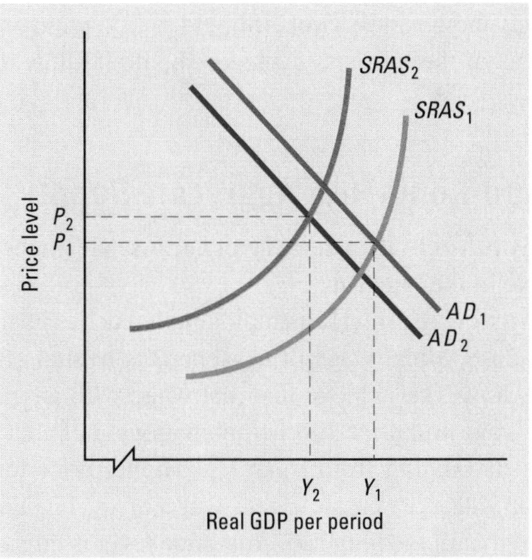

Investment, government purchases, and net exports all fell in the third quarter. Consumption rose slightly, but reductions in the other components swamped that gain.

At the same time as aggregate demand was shifting leftward, trouble in the Middle East bumped the short-run aggregate supply curve upward and to the left. Iraq invaded Kuwait in August. Iraq's leader, Saddam Hussein, threatened to destroy oil-production facilities throughout the Middle East. That set off some understandable jitters in world oil markets; the price of crude oil soared nearly 50 percent in the next few weeks. The increase in oil prices forced a reduction in short-run aggregate supply.

The reduction in aggregate demand and in short-run aggregate supply produced a reduction in real GDP and an increase in the price level in the third quarter. As firms scaled back their production, households found themselves with less income. They cut their consumption in the fourth quarter, making the economy's downward plunge all the worse.

The accompanying graph shows the reduction in aggregate demand from AD_1 to AD_2 and the reduction in short-run aggregate supply from $SRAS_1$ to $SRAS_2$. Notice that the price level rises from P_1 to P_2.

The recession came to an end with the allies' swift victory over Iraq in February 1991. Oil prices quickly plunged, increasing short-run aggregate supply. Real GDP resumed its upward march in the next quarter.

however, that the short run is a period in which sticky prices may prevent the economy from reaching its natural level of employment. In the next section, we'll see how the model adjusts as changes in real wages move the labor market to equilibrium in the long run.

Checklist

- The aggregate demand curve is a downward-sloping curve that relates the quantity of total output that will be purchased to the price level.
- An increase in consumption demand, investment demand, government purchases, or net exports shifts the aggregate demand curve to the right; a reduction in any of these sources of demand shifts it to the left.
- The short run is a period over which stickiness in wages and prices prevents the real wage from reaching the equilibrium solution in the labor market. Real GDP may fall short of or exceed its natural level.
- The short-run aggregate supply curve is an upward-sloping curve that shows the quantity of total output that will be produced at each price level in the short run. The curve becomes steeper as real GDP rises.
- The equilibrium price level and the equilibrium level of total output are determined by the intersection of the aggregate demand and short-run aggregate supply curves.
- The price level and real GDP change in response to changes in aggregate demand and short-run aggregate supply.

The **long-run aggregate supply (LRAS) curve** relates the level of output produced by firms to the price level in the long run.

The Long Run and Public Policy

The model of aggregate demand and aggregate supply offers some startling conclusions for the long run. Because wage flexibility eliminates cyclical unemployment, the economy moves to its natural level. It achieves this output regardless of what may have happened to aggregate demand or short-run aggregate supply, and regardless of the price level. The long run puts a nation's macroeconomic house in order: only frictional and structural unemployment remain, and the price level is stabilized, eliminating inflation.

The notion that the economy can adjust on its own to its natural level is at the heart of a fundamental disagreement among economists about the role of public policy vis-à-vis the business cycle. Should public policy seek to smooth out the ups and downs of the business cycle, or should it allow the economy to adjust on its own?

Natural GDP and Long-Run Aggregate Supply

Real GDP eventually moves to its natural level because all wages and prices are assumed to be flexible in the long run.

There is a single real wage at which employment reaches its natural level. In Panel (a) of Exhibit 23-8, a real wage of ω_n generates natural employment L_n. The economy could, however, achieve this real wage with any of an infinitely large set of nominal wage and price-level combinations. In Panel (b), for example, we see price levels ranging from P_1 to P_4. Higher price levels would require higher nominal wages to create a real wage of ω_n but flexible nominal wages would achieve that in the long run. Any price level is thus consistent with production of the economy's natural level of real GDP in the long run, so the long-run aggregate supply curve *LRAS* is a vertical line at the natural level of output.

Suppose, for example, that the equilibrium real wage (the ratio of wages to the price level) is 1.5. We could have that with a wage level of 1.5 and a price level of 1.0, a wage level of 1.65 and a price level of 1.1, a wage level of 3.0 and a price level of 2.0, and so on. In the long run, then, the economy can achieve its natural levels of employment and output at *any* price level. This conclusion gives us our **long-run aggregate supply curve,** a curve that relates the level of

EXHIBIT 23-8

Natural Employment and Long-Run Aggregate Supply

When the economy achieves its natural level of employment, it produces its natural level of real GDP. In Panel (a), the intersection of the demand and supply curves for labor, *D* and *S*, determine the natural level of employment, L_n, and the equilibrium real wage, ω_n. In Panel (b), the natural level of employment produces the natural level of output, Y_n, and the long-run aggregate supply curve *LRAS* is a vertical line at Y_n. At any price level, flexible nominal wages will adjust to achieve the equilibrium real wage ω_n. For example, production of Y_n could occur at price levels P_1, P_2, P_3, and P_4.

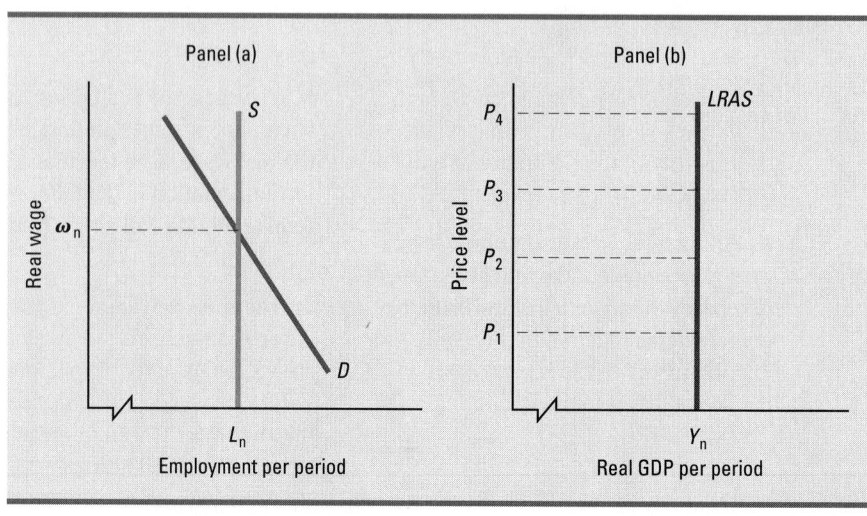

When the economy is producing an output below the natural level, it has a **recessionary gap** equal to the difference between the natural and actual levels of real GDP.

output produced by firms to the price level in the long run. With only one level of output and any price level, the long-run aggregate supply curve is a vertical line, as shown in Panel (b) of Exhibit 23-8. The economy's natural level of real GDP is designated Y_n. We'll see in Chapter 26 precisely how the natural level of employment determines a specific level of natural real GDP.

A Recessionary Gap

In the long run, the economy reaches its natural level of output. In the short run, however, sticky wages and other prices can prevent output from achieving this natural level. Actual output may exceed or fall short of its natural level.

Again, real GDP and the price level are determined by the intersection of the aggregate demand and short-run aggregate supply curves. If employment is below the natural level of employment, real GDP will be below natural real GDP. The aggregate demand and short-run aggregate supply curves will intersect to the left of the long-run aggregate supply curve.

Suppose an economy's natural level of employment is L_n, shown in Panel (a) of Exhibit 23-9. This level of employment is achieved at a real wage of ω_n. Suppose, however, that the initial real wage ω_1 exceeds this equilibrium value. Employment at L_1 falls short of the natural level; there is a surplus of labor. A lower level of employment produces a lower level of output; the aggregate demand and short-run aggregate supply curves, AD_1 and $SRAS_1$, intersect to the left of the long-run aggregate supply curve $LRAS_1$ in Panel (b). The gap between the actual level of output Y_1 and the natural level Y_n is called a **recessionary gap.**

How can we determine that the economy has a recessionary gap? A recessionary gap implies that employment falls below the natural level, so the unemployment rate exceeds the natural rate. The natural rate of unemployment is about 6 percent. As a rough guide, then, we may conclude that an economy with an unemployment rate in excess of 6 percent is operating with a recessionary gap.

EXHIBIT 23-9

A Recessionary Gap

Suppose that the natural level of employment is L_n, as shown in Panel (a), and the natural level of real GDP is Y_n, as shown in Panel (b). However, the real wage ω_1 exceeds the equilibrium real wage ω_n, so employment L_1 falls below the natural level L_n. If employment is below the natural level, then output must be below the natural level. In Panel (b), we see that real GDP, Y_1, falls below the natural level at Y_n. The recessionary gap equals $Y_n - Y_1$. The aggregate demand curve AD_1 and the short-run aggregate supply curve $SRAS_1$ intersect to the left of the long-run aggregate supply curve $LRAS_1$.

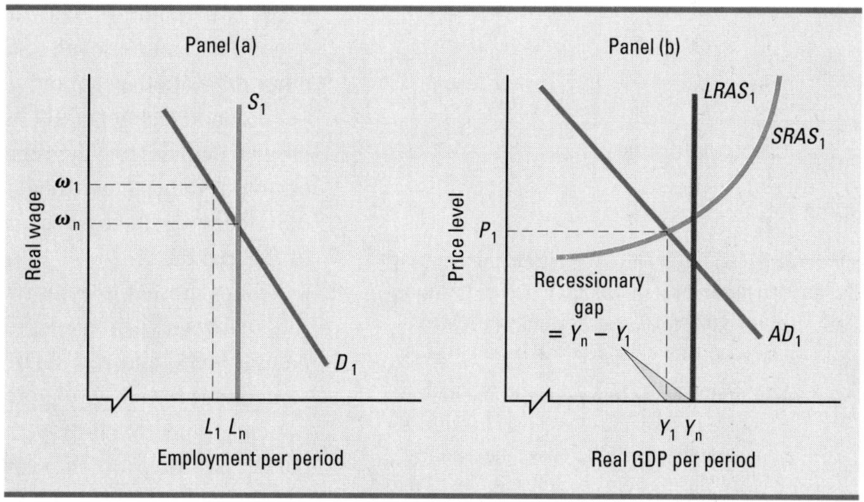

An Inflationary Gap

Just as employment can fall short of its natural level, it can exceed it. If employment is greater than its natural level, real GDP will also be greater than the natural level.

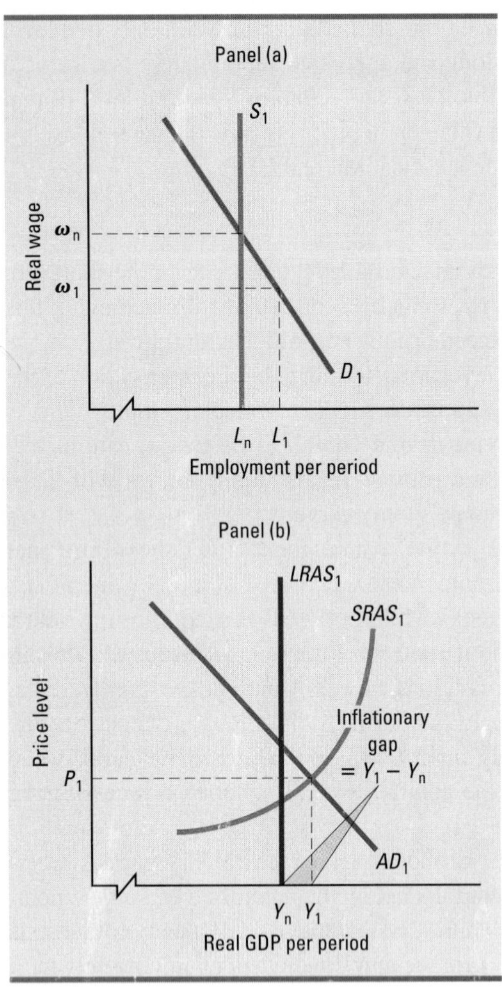

EXHIBIT 23-10

An Inflationary Gap

Suppose L_n is the natural level of employment in Panel (a); Y_n is the corresponding natural level of real GDP in Panel (b). If the real wage ω_1 is below the equilibrium real wage ω_n, then employment L_1 will exceed its natural level L_n. That implies output exceeds its natural level, as is the case in Panel (b) when the aggregate demand curve AD_1 and short-run aggregate supply curve $SRAS_1$ intersect to the right of the long-run aggregate supply curve $LRAS_1$ at Y_1. The inflationary gap equals $Y_1 - Y_n$.

Exhibit 23-10 shows an economy with a natural level of employment of L_n in Panel (a) and a natural level of real GDP of Y_n in Panel (b). If the real wage ω_1 is less than the equilibrium real wage ω_n, then employment L_1 will exceed the natural level. As a result, real GDP, Y_1, exceeds its natural level. A situation in which real GDP exceeds its natural level is called an **inflationary gap;** it equals the difference between actual and natural real GDP.

Just as we can conclude that the economy has a recessionary gap when the unemployment rate is greater than the natural rate of unemployment, we can conclude that it has an inflationary gap when the unemployment rate is less than the natural rate. Assuming the natural rate is 6 percent, then, there is an inflationary gap whenever the unemployment rate falls below 6 percent.

Gaps and Public Policy

Recessionary and inflationary gaps are generally regarded as undesirable. A recessionary gap means the economy has cyclical unemployment and isn't producing as many goods and services as it could be. It means unemployment exceeds its natural level. An inflationary gap means the economy is operating beyond its natural level, and that's likely to put upward pressure on wages and other prices in the economy.

Economists generally agree that the preferred solution in the model of aggregate demand and aggregate supply is to have the economy at its natural level of output rather than to have a recessionary or an inflationary gap. If the economy faces a gap, however, how do we get from that solution to the natural level of real GDP?

Gaps present us with two alternatives. First, we can do nothing. In the long run, real wages will adjust to the equilibrium level, employment will move to its natural level, and real GDP will move to its natural level. Second, we can do something. Faced with a recessionary or an inflationary gap, we can undertake policies aimed at shifting the aggregate demand or short-run aggregate supply curves in a way that moves the economy to its natural level. A policy choice to take no action to try to shift aggregate demand or short-run aggregate supply to close a recessionary or an inflationary gap, but to allow the economy to adjust on its own to its natural level of real GDP, is a **nonintervention policy.** A policy in which some action by the public sector seeks to shift either the aggregate demand or short-run aggregate supply curve and thus to move the economy to its natural level is called a **stabilization policy.**

- When the economy is producing above its natural level of output, it has an **inflationary gap** equal to the difference between the actual and natural levels of real GDP.
- A **nonintervention policy** is a policy choice to take no action to try to correct a recessionary or inflationary gap and to allow the economy to adjust on its own to its natural level.
- **Stabilization policy** involves some action by the public sector to shift aggregate demand or short-run aggregate supply to move the economy toward its natural level of real GDP.

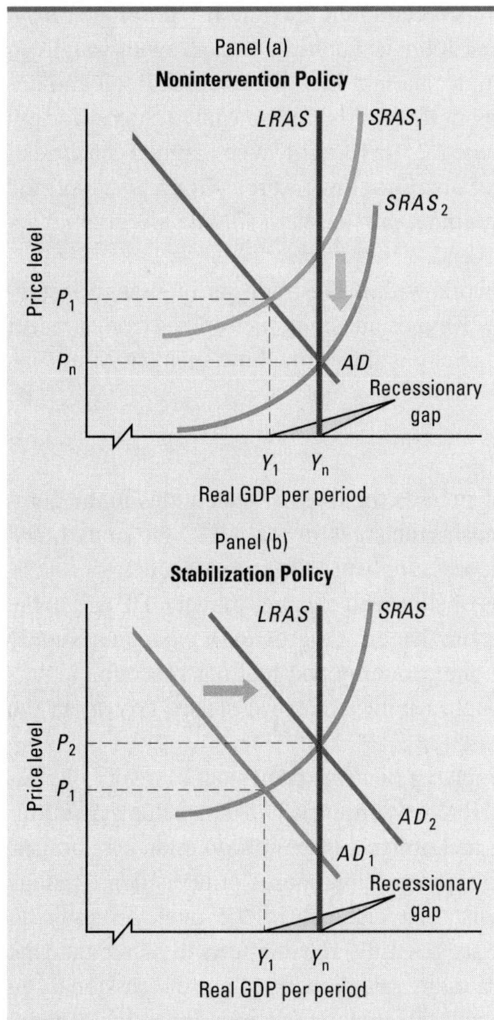

EXHIBIT 23-11

Alternatives in Closing a Recessionary Gap

Panel (a) illustrates a gradual closing of a recessionary gap. Under a nonintervention policy, short-run aggregate supply shifts downward toward equilibrium at a price level of P_n and the natural level of output Y_n. Panel (b) shows the effects of a stabilization policy acting on aggregate demand to close the gap.

Exhibit 23-11 illustrates the alternatives in closing a recessionary gap. In both panels, the economy starts with a real GDP of Y_1 and a price level of P_1. In Panel (a), the economy is permitted to close the gap through a process of self-correction. Real wages will fall as long as employment remains below the natural level. Lower wages shift the short-run aggregate supply curve. The process is a gradual one, however, given the stickiness of wages. A series of downward shifts in the short-run aggregate supply curve move the economy toward equilibrium at a price level of P_n and the natural level of out-put Y_n.

Panel (b) illustrates the stabilization alternative. Faced with an economy operating below its natural level, public officials act to stimulate aggregate demand, for example, by boosting government purchases of goods and services or by cutting taxes. Tax cuts give people more money to spend, boost their consumption, and increase aggregate demand. As AD_1 shifts to AD_2 in Exhibit 23-11, the economy achieves its natural level of output Y_n.

Some economists argue that stabilization policy can and should be used when recessionary or inflationary gaps exist. Others urge reliance on the economy's own ability to correct itself. They may believe that the tools available to the public sector to influence aggregate demand aren't likely to shift the curve, or they may believe that the tools would shift the curve in a way that could do more harm than good. These differing perspectives on policy come from three broad schools of macroeconomic thought. We'll be revisiting these schools repeatedly as we continue our exploration of macroeconomic theory and policy.

Major Schools of Macroeconomic Thought

Individual economists have individual differences in their views on particular aspects of macroeconomic theory on policy. We can, however, identify three broad schools of macroeconomic analysis: the new Keynesian school, the monetarist school, and the new classical school. Each is introduced below. A fuller discussion of the evolution of these schools of thought is offered in Chapter 33.

The New Keynesian School

The **new Keynesian school** stresses the stickiness of wages and other prices and the economy's resultant inability to adjust to its natural level quickly. Indeed, some new Keynesians doubt the economy can adjust to its natural level at all. New Keynesian economists have traditionally emphasized the role that fluctuations in aggregate demand play in creating inflationary or recessionary gaps. They argue that public policy can be used to shift aggregate demand back to a level consistent with the economy's natural level of output.

The **new Keynesian school** emphasizes the stickiness of prices and the resultant inability of the economy to achieve its natural level of employment on its own.

The new Keynesian school of macroeconomic thought has developed from the work of the late British economist John Maynard Keynes. Keynes sought an explanation of the Great Depression, a calamity in which real GDP fell and unemployment soared in many nations in the 1930s. In the United States, for example, the unemployment rate reached 25 percent. Keynes argued that sticky prices would block the attainment of a natural level of real GDP; he advocated policies such as an increase in government purchases to stimulate economic activity and bring the Depression to an end.

New Keynesians continue to work within the tradition of thought established by Keynes. The "new" in new Keynesian economics comes from a recent effort to explain just why prices are sticky and to show how such stickiness can affect economic activity.

The Monetarist School

Whereas the new Keynesian school stresses the role of fluctuations in the components of aggregate demand in causing changes in real GDP, the **monetarist school** argues that changes in the money supply are the primary source of fluctuations in aggregate demand and thus of short-run changes in real GDP and in the price level. Monetarists generally argue that erratic growth in the money supply is a primary source of instability in the economy and that macroeconomic performance would be improved through a policy of slow, steady growth in the money supply.

As we'll see in Chapter 25, monetarist doctrine grows out of a very old tradition in macroeconomic analysis. Recently, however, it has achieved prominence as an alternative to the ideas and policies of new Keynesian economists. Monetarists argue that changes in government purchases or taxes don't change aggregate demand. While they insist that changes in the money supply do change aggregate demand, monetarists generally reject efforts to manipulate the money supply in order to manipulate aggregate demand to close recessionary or inflationary gaps. They argue that such efforts to stabilize a dynamic economy are as likely to exaggerate the ups and downs of the business cycle as to smooth them out.

The New Classical School

A third school of macroeconomic thought emerged in the 1970s. It grew out of the work of economists who believe that macroeconomic analysis should be built explicitly on microeconomic foundations. These economists argue that economic models should be based on the maximizing behavior of consumers and firms, not on the observations about economic aggregates that characterize Keynesian and monetarist thought. These economists stress the flexibility of wages and prices and the ability of the economy to move quickly to its natural level of employment.

This branch of economic analysis, which emphasizes wage and price flexibility and the microeconomic foundations of economic behavior, is called the **new classical school.** Its emphasis on the economy's ability to achieve equilibrium through price adjustments is reminiscent of the classical school, a tradition that was very influential in the nineteenth century. The modern version adds the term "new" because it is based on mathematical models of maximizing behavior.

Two basic notions characterize the new classical school. One is that people are rational, not just in the sense of making choices that maximize the value of

- The **monetarist school** argues that changes in the money supply are the primary source of fluctuations in aggregate demand and thus of short-run changes in real GDP and in the price level.
- The **new classical school** emphasizes wage and price flexibility and the microeconomic foundations of economic behavior.

Case in Point — Clashing Philosophies in Washington

As the U.S. economy slipped into recession in 1990, President George Bush's chief economic adviser, Michael Boskin, had some straightforward advice: Do nothing.

Mr. Boskin argued that the economy would correct itself on its own. Furthermore, he said that an attempt to stimulate the economy with more government spending and lower taxes would be harmful. The manipulation of spending and taxes, he said, would create uncertainty and thus reduce investment. That, in the long run, would cut economic growth. Mr. Bush agreed, and he proposed no policy changes while the recession was in progress. A recovery began the following spring.

Michael Boskin.

The recovery gradually gained steam, and the economy experienced strong growth in 1992. But the gains were not sufficient to close the recessionary gap left by the downturn. President Bill Clinton took office in 1993 with a new philosophy and a new chief economic adviser, Laura Tyson. Ms. Tyson, a new Keynesian economist, recommended a stimulus package that included increased government purchases and tax cuts designed to stimulate investment. The package was rejected by Congress, but the fact that Mr. Clinton had proposed it suggested a major shift in economic philosophies. Mr. Clinton was unwilling to wait for the economy to recover; he wanted to boost aggregate demand immediately.

After 12 years dominated by the monetarist and new classical economists advising President Bush and President Ronald Reagan, the new Keynesians were back in power—at least in the White House.

some objective but in forming their expectations. An economic theory based on the view that people form their expectations making the best possible use of all available information is called **rational expectations.** New classical economists explore the implications of rational expectations for macroeconomic performance and for macroeconomic policy. The new classical school's emphasis on the ability of the economy to achieve its natural level of output has produced a second major idea central to this school's approach: the theory holds that changes in long-run aggregate supply are the main source of fluctuations in economic activity. The view that changes in long-run aggregate supply are the main source of macroeconomic fluctuation is called **real business cycle theory.**

Many new classical economists support the monetarist argument that the money supply should be allowed to grow at a slow, steady rate. They also tend to agree that changes in government purchases or taxes will not affect economic activity, although their explanations for this assertion differ from those of the monetarist school.

A Comparison of the Three Schools of Macroeconomic Thought

New Keynesians believe that recessionary and inflationary gaps are a problem but that the economy's own adjustment to its natural level is too slow a process because of sticky prices. They believe that stabilization policy should be used to correct such gaps.

Monetarists believe that erratic fluctuations in the money supply are a primary cause of inflationary and recessionary gaps. Changes in the quantity of money could be used to fix the gaps, but monetarists argue that the cure could be worse than the disease. Monetarists advocate slow, steady growth in the money supply and reject other public sector efforts to stabilize the economy.

- **Rational expectations** is an approach to macroeconomic analysis that assumes that individuals make the best possible use of all available information in forming their expectations.
- **Real business cycle theory** asserts that changes in long-run aggregate supply are the primary source of fluctuations in real GDP.

New classical economists stress the flexibility of prices and the economy's ability to adjust to its natural level. Like the monetarist school, they generally reject public sector stabilization efforts to close recessionary or inflationary gaps. Indeed, they question whether such gaps are really a problem.

Which approach is most useful? This book will give you the understanding you'll need to make your own choice. More important, it will help you identify the sources of disagreement among economists who advocate different policies for dealing with the economy.

Checklist

- The economy produces its natural level of real GDP when employment is at its natural level.
- The long-run aggregate supply (LRAS) curve is a vertical line at the natural level of real GDP.
- When the aggregate demand and short-run aggregate supply curves intersect below natural real GDP, the economy has a recessionary gap. When they intersect above natural real GDP, it has an inflationary gap.
- Inflationary and recessionary gaps are closed as the real wage changes. Because of wage and price stickiness, however, such an adjustment takes time.
- New Keynesians generally advocate policy intervention to shift the aggregate demand curve to close a recessionary or inflationary gap. Monetarists stress slow, steady growth in the money supply. Monetarists and new classical economists generally prefer to allow the economy to correct itself.

The Bond and Foreign Exchange Markets

Some markets play such important roles in the economy that a change in one will have substantial effects on aggregate demand and aggregate supply. We've already seen how developments in the labor market affect the economy. We'll explore two other key markets in this section: the bond market and the market for foreign exchange. Events in these markets can affect price and output for the entire economy.

The Bond Market

As institutions conduct their daily business operations, they often borrow money. They may seek funds from a bank. Many institutions, however, obtain credit by selling bonds. A **bond** is a written promise by the issuer of a bond to pay the owner of the bond a series of payments on specific dates.

When an institution sells a bond, it obtains the price paid for the bond as a kind of loan. A local school district might sell bonds to finance the construction of a new school. Your college or university has probably sold bonds to finance new buildings on campus. Firms often sell bonds to finance expansion. The institution that issues the bond is obligated to make payments on the bond in the future.

Bond Prices and Interest Rates

Suppose you are the manager of a company and you need to borrow some money to expand your production facility. You could do so in the following way: You print, say, 500 pieces of paper, each bearing the company's promise to pay the bearer $1,000 in a year. These pieces of paper are bonds, and your company, as the issuer, promises to make a single payment. You then offer these bonds for sale, announcing that you will issue them to the buyers who offer the highest prices. Suppose the highest price you're offered is $950, and you sell all the bonds at that price. Each bond is, in effect, your IOU for $1,000.

Let's examine what you've done. You've sold a promise to pay the holder of each piece of paper $1,000 in a year. Buyers bought your promise for $950. The buyer of the each bond will be lending you $950; you'll pay each bond holder back $1,000 in a year. The buyers of the bonds are being paid $50 for the service of lending you $950 for a year.

The $1,000 printed on the bonds you sold is their **face value;** it is the amount you as the issuer will have to pay when the loan matures, or "comes due." The $950 at which you sold them is their price. The difference between the face value and the price is the premium you'll pay for the use of the money you get from selling the bond.

A **bond** is a promise by the issuer of the bond to make a series of payments to the owner of the bond on specific dates.

The **face value** of a bond is the amount that will be paid to the holder of the bond when it matures.

An **interest rate** is a premium paid for the use of money, expressed as a percentage of the amount of money involved.

An **interest rate** is the premium paid for the use of money, expressed as a percentage of the amount of money involved. The bonds you sold command an interest rate equal to the difference between the face value and the price, divided by the price. At a price of $950, the interest rate is thus 5.3 percent ($50/$950).

The interest rate on any bond is determined by its price. As the price falls, the interest rate rises. Suppose, for example, that the best price you can get for your bonds is $900. Now the interest rate is equal to $100 (the difference between the face value and the price) divided by $900, or 11.1 percent. A price of $800 would mean an interest rate of 25 percent; $750 would mean an interest rate of 33.3 percent; a price of $500 translates into an interest rate of 100 percent. The lower the price of a bond relative to its face value, the higher the interest rate.

Bonds in the real world are more complicated than the piece of paper in our example, but their structure is basically the same. They have a face value (usually an amount between $1,000 and $100,000) and a maturity date. That maturity date might be 3 months from the date of issue; it might be 30 years. In many cases, an interest rate or "coupon rate" is stated on the bond. Bondholders then receive an amount equal to the interest rate times the face value each year they hold the bond. The lower the price paid for the bond, the higher the interest return. Bondholders also receive the entire face value when the bond matures.

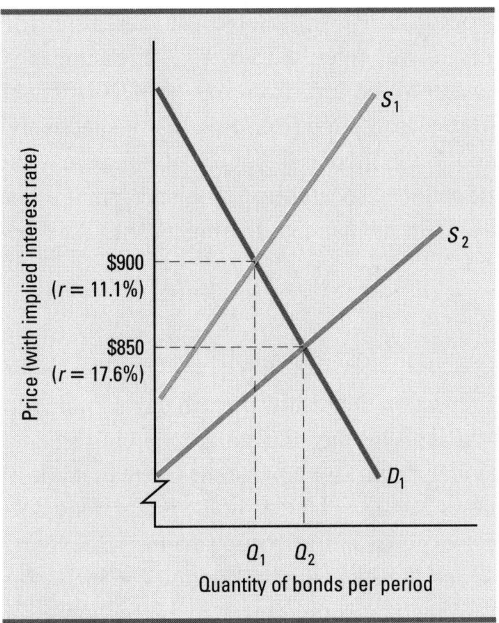

EXHIBIT 23-12

The Bond Market

The equilibrium price for bonds is determined where the demand and supply curves intersect. The initial solution here is a price of $900, implying an interest rate of 11.1 percent. An increase in federal government borrowing, all other things equal, increases the supply of bonds to S_2 and forces the price of bonds down to $850. The interest rate rises to 17.6 percent [($1,000 − $850)/$850]. This example assumes that all bonds have a face value of $1,000 and mature in 1 year.

Exhibit 23-12 illustrates the market for bonds. Their price is determined by demand and supply. Buyers of newly issued bonds are, in effect, lenders. Sellers of newly issued bonds are borrowers—recall that corporations and other institutions sell bonds when they want to borrow money. Once a newly issued bond has been sold, its owner can resell it; a bond may change hands several times before it matures.

Bonds aren't exactly the same sort of beast as, say, broccoli or some other good or service. Can we expect bonds to have the same kind of downward-sloping demand curves and upward-sloping supply curves we encounter for ordinary goods and services? Consider demand. At lower prices, bonds pay higher interest. That makes them more attractive to buyers of bonds and thus increases the quantity demanded. On the other hand, lower prices mean higher costs to borrowers—suppliers of bonds—and should reduce the quantity supplied. Thus, the negative relationship between price and quantity demanded and the positive relationship between price and quantity supplied suggested by conventional demand and supply curves holds true in the market for bonds.

If the quantity of bonds demanded is not equal to the quantity of bonds supplied, the price will adjust almost instantaneously to balance the two. Bond prices are perfectly flexible in that they change immediately to balance demand and supply. Suppose, for example, that the initial price of bonds is $900, as shown by the intersection of the demand and supply curves in Exhibit 23-12. We will assume that all bonds have equal risk and a face value of $1,000 and that they mature in 1 year. Now suppose that borrowers increase their borrowing by offering to sell more bonds at every interest rate. This increases the supply of bonds: the supply curve shifts to the right from S_1 to S_2. That, in turn, lowers the equilibrium price of bonds—to $850 in Exhibit 23-12. The lower price for bonds means a higher interest rate.

The Bond Market and Economic Activity

Changes in bond prices change the interest rates bonds provide. These changes immediately translate into changes in other interest rates throughout the economy. When bonds yield high rates, for example, lenders are less willing to supply funds for mortgages or for new car loans, so the interest rates on these loans will rise. Interest rates in the bond market influence every other interest rate in the economy. Indeed, we can think of interest rates in the economy as being determined in the bond market. Changes in bond market interest rates affect not just other interest rates but the entire economy.

The connection between the bond market and the economy derives from the way interest rates affect aggregate demand. Investment is one component of aggregate demand, and interest rates affect investment. Firms are less likely to acquire new capital if interest rates are high; they're more likely to add capital if interest rates are low.

If the price of bonds falls, the interest rate goes up. Higher interest rates tend to discourage investment, so aggregate demand will fall. A fall in aggregate demand, other things unchanged, will mean fewer jobs and less total output than would have been the case with lower rates of interest. In contrast, an increase in the price of bonds lowers interest rates and makes investment cheaper. That may boost investment and thus boost aggregate demand. Exhibit 23-13 shows how an event in the bond market can stimulate changes in the economy's output and prices. In Panel (a), an increase in demand for bonds raises bond prices. Interest rates thus fall. Lower interest rates stimulate investment demand, shifting the aggregate demand curve to the right, from AD_1 to AD_2 in Panel (b). Real GDP rises from Y_1 to Y_2; the price level rises from P_1 to P_2. In Panel (c), an increase in the supply of bonds pushes bond prices down. Interest rates rise. Investment is likely to fall, shifting aggregate demand to the left, from AD_1 to AD_2 in Panel (d). Output and the price level fall from Y_1 to Y_2 and from P_1 to P_2, respectively. Of course, the money borrowed through the increased supply of bonds may be spent.[1] If it is, that spending will tend to increase aggregate demand. But if other determinants of aggregate demand remain unchanged, the higher interest rates will tend to reduce aggregate demand.

Currency Markets

Network news broadcasts generally report on the results of each day's trading in the market for dollars and other currencies. One day, the dollar might fall against the Japanese yen. Another day, the dollar might rise against the German mark.

Such developments are major news because changes in the price of the dollar relative to other currencies affect exports and imports. Changes in exports and imports affect aggregate demand and thus the entire economy. The market in which currencies are traded thus has tremendous importance in the economy.

Foreigners wishing to purchase goods and services or assets in the United States must typically pay for them with dollars. U.S. purchasers of foreign goods must generally make the purchase in a foreign currency. These transactions are accomplished in the **foreign exchange market,** a market in which currencies are traded for one another. An Egyptian family, for example, exchanges Egyptian pounds for dollars in order to pay for admission to Disney World. A German investor purchases dollars to buy U.S. government bonds. A family from the United States visiting India, on the other hand, needs to obtain rupees in order to make purchases there. A U.S. bank wanting to invest in Mexico City first purchases pesos.

The **foreign exchange market** is a market in which currencies from different countries are traded for one another.

[1] In most cases, the money will be spent. But we'll learn in the next chapter of a mechanism through which an increased supply of bonds doesn't translate into additional spending.

EXHIBIT 23-13

Bond Prices and Macroeconomic Activity

An increase in the demand for bonds to D_2 in Panel (a) raises the price of bonds to P_2, which lowers interest rates and boosts investment. That increases aggregate demand to AD_2 in Panel (b); real GDP rises to Y_2 and the price level rises to P_2.

An increase in the supply of bonds to S_2 lowers bond prices to P_2 in Panel (c) and raises interest rates. The higher interest rate, taken by itself, is likely to cause a reduction in investment and aggregate demand. AD_1 falls to AD_2, real GDP falls to Y_2, and the price level falls to P_2 in Panel (d).

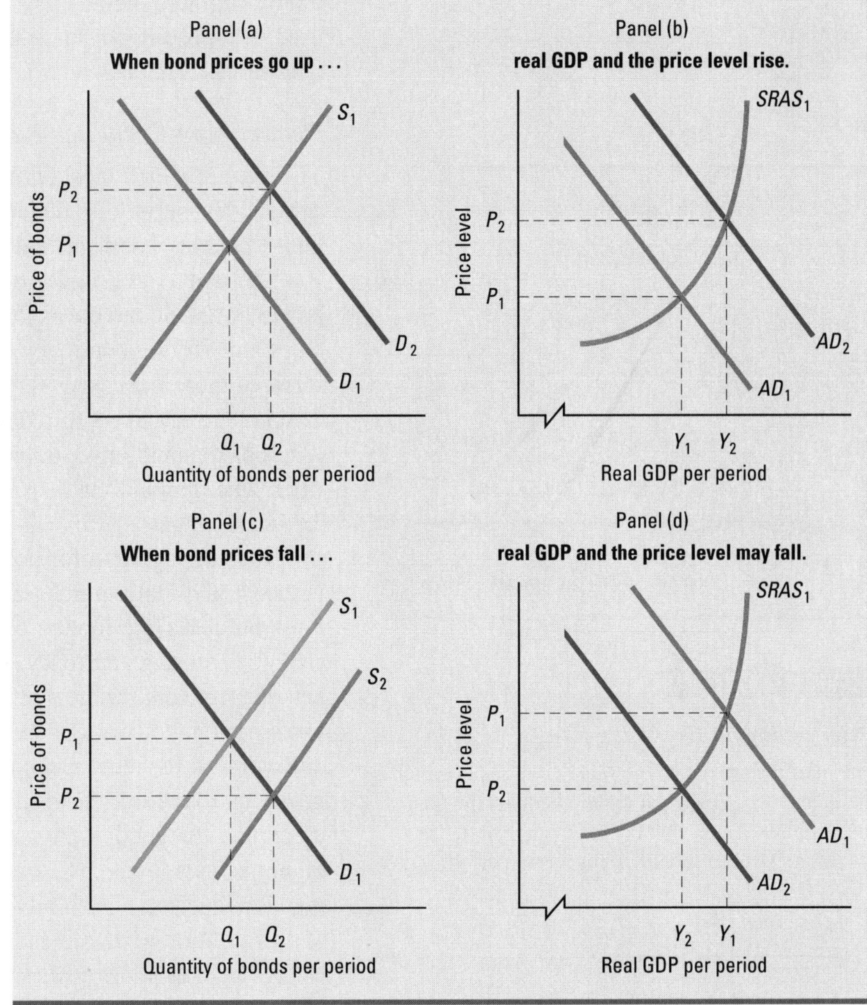

The foreign exchange market isn't a single location in which currencies are traded. The term refers instead to the entire array of institutions through which people buy and sell currencies. It includes a hotel desk clerk who provides currency exchange as a service to hotel guests, brokers who arrange currency exchanges worth billions of dollars, and governments and central banks that exchange currencies. Major currency dealers are linked by computers so that they can track currency exchanges all over the world.

The Exchange Rate

A country's **exchange rate** is the price of its currency in terms of another currency or currencies. On May 22, 1995, for example, the dollar traded for 87.34 Japanese yen, 1.44 German marks, 30.89 Pakistani rupees, 5.88 Mexican pesos, and so on. There are as many exchange rates for the dollar as there are countries whose currencies exchange for the dollar—roughly 200 of them.

Economists summarize the movement of exchange rates with a **trade-weighted exchange rate,** which is an index of exchange rates. A trade-weighted exchange rate index for the U.S. dollar selects a group of countries, weights the price of the dollar in each country's currency by the amount of trade that country does with the United States, and then reports the price of the dollar based on that

- A country's **exchange rate** is the price of its currency in terms of another currency or currencies.
- The **trade-weighted exchange rate** is an index of exchange rates.

trade-weighted average. Because trade-weighted exchange rates are so widely used in reporting currency values, they are often referred to as exchange rates themselves. That convention will be used in this text.

Determining Exchange Rates

The rates at which most currencies exchange for one another are determined by demand and supply. To understand the determination of exchange rates, we must understand how demand and supply operate in the foreign exchange market.

The demand curve for dollars relates the number of dollars buyers want to buy in any period to the exchange rate. An increase in the exchange rate means it takes more foreign currency to buy a dollar. That, in turn, makes U.S. goods and services more expensive for foreign buyers and reduces the quantity they will demand. That's likely to reduce the quantity of dollars they demand. Foreigners will thus demand fewer dollars as the price of the dollar—the exchange rate—rises. The demand curve for dollars is thus downward sloping, as in Exhibit 23-14.

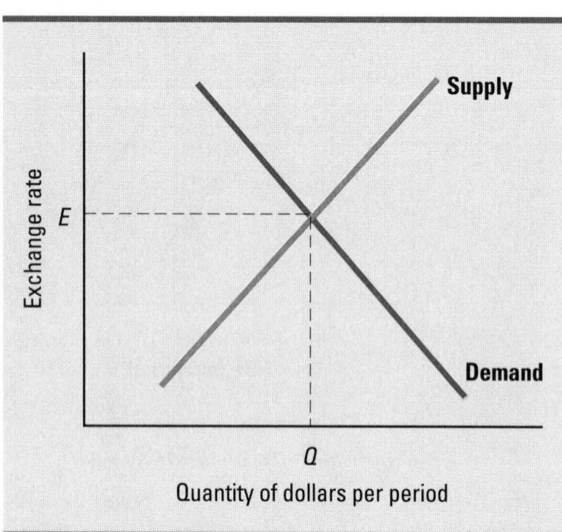

EXHIBIT 23-14

Determining an Exchange Rate

The equilibrium exchange rate is the rate at which the quantity of dollars demanded equals the quantity supplied. Here, that occurs at exchange rate *E*, at which *Q* dollars are exchanged per period.

The supply curve for dollars emerges from a similar process. When people in the United States purchase goods, services, or assets in foreign countries, they must purchase the money of those countries first. They supply dollars in exchange for foreign currency. The supply of dollars on the foreign exchange market thus reflects the degree to which people in the United States are buying foreign money at various exchange rates. A higher exchange rate means that a dollar trades for more foreign currency. In effect, the higher rate makes foreign goods and services cheaper to U.S. buyers, so U.S. consumers will purchase more foreign goods and services. People will thus supply more dollars at a higher exchange rate; we expect the supply curve for dollars to be upward sloping, as suggested in Exhibit 23-14.

In addition to private individuals and firms that participate in the foreign exchange market, most governments participate as well. A government might seek to lower its exchange rate by selling its currency; it might seek to raise the rate by buying its currency. We'll consider the role of government in foreign exchange rates in Chapter 29. Although governments often participate in foreign exchange markets, they generally represent a very small share of these markets. The most important traders are private buyers and sellers of currencies.

Exchange Rates and Economic Activity

People purchase a country's currency for two quite different reasons: to purchase goods or services in that country, or to purchase the assets of that country—its money, its capital, its stocks, its bonds, or its real estate. These two motives are at work whenever the factors that determine demand and supply change.

One thing that can cause the price of the dollar to rise, for example, is a reduction in bond prices in American markets. Exhibit 23-15 illustrates this phenomenon. Suppose the supply of bonds on the U.S. bond market increases from S_1 to S_2 in Panel (a). Bond prices will drop. Lower bond prices mean higher interest rates. Foreign investors attracted by the opportunity to earn higher returns in the United States will increase their demand for dollars on the foreign exchange market in order to purchase U.S. bonds. Panel (b) shows that the demand curve for dollars shifts from D_1 to D_2. Simultaneously, U.S. investors, attracted by the higher interest rates at home, become less likely to invest abroad and thus supply fewer dollars to exchange markets. The fall in the price of U.S. bonds

EXHIBIT 23-15

Shifts in Demand and Supply for Dollars on the Foreign Exchange Market

In Panel (a), an increase in the supply of bonds lowers bond prices to P_2 (and thus raises interest rates). Higher interest rates boost the demand and reduce the supply for dollars, increasing the exchange rate in Panel (b) to E_2. These developments in the bond and foreign exchange markets are likely to lead to a reduction in net exports and in investment, reducing aggregate demand from AD_1 to AD_2 in Panel (c). The price level in the economy falls to P_2 and real GDP falls to Y_2.

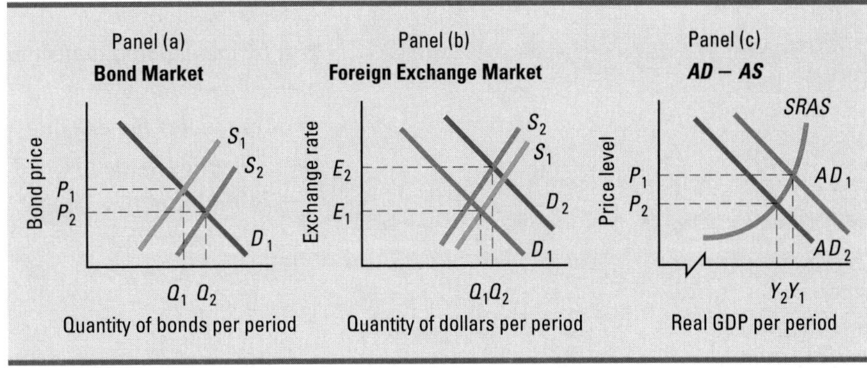

shifts the supply curve for dollars on the foreign exchange market from S_1 to S_2 and the exchange rate rises from E_1 to E_2.

The higher exchange rate makes U.S. goods and services more expensive to foreigners, so it reduces exports. It makes foreign goods cheaper for U.S. buyers, so it increases imports. Net exports thus fall, reducing aggregate demand. Panel (c) shows that output falls from Y_1 to Y_2; the price level falls from P_1 to P_2. This development in the foreign exchange market reinforces the impact of higher interest rates we observed in Exhibit 23-13. They not only reduce investment—they reduce net exports as well.

Checklist

- A bond represents an IOU of a borrower; bond prices are determined by demand and supply.
- The interest rate on a bond is inversely related to the price of the bond. As the price of a bond increases, the interest rate falls.
- An increase in the interest rate tends to reduce investment and aggregate demand.
- The foreign exchange market is where people exchange foreign currency for dollars and dollars for foreign currency in order to finance transactions between citizens of different countries.
- The demand for dollars represents foreign demand for U.S. goods, services, and assets. The supply of dollars represents U.S. demand for foreign goods, services, and assets. The demand for and the supply of dollars determine the exchange rate.
- A rise in U.S. interest rates will increase the demand for dollars and reduce the supply. As a result, the exchange rate will increase, reducing aggregate demand. A fall in U.S. interest rates will have the opposite effect.

A Look Back—And a Look Ahead

In this chapter, we took a first look at the model of aggregate demand and aggregate supply. Aggregate demand is the relationship between the quantities of total output that will be purchased and the price level. Aggregate supply is the relationship between the quantities of total output that will be produced and the price level.

Economists distinguish between short-run and long-run aggregate supply. In the short run, the stickiness of real wages may prevent the economy from reaching its natural level of employment. Real GDP, which is determined by the intersection of the aggregate demand and short-run aggregate supply curves, may be above or below its natural level—there may be an inflationary or recessionary gap. In the long run, the real wage is flexible. Employment reaches its natural level, and real GDP reaches its natural level. The long-run aggregate supply curve is thus a vertical line at the natural level of real GDP.

Recessionary or inflationary gaps close by themselves in the long run. New Keynesian economists generally argue, however, that relying on the economy to close these gaps through changes in the real wage will take too long; they prefer to close such gaps through measures designed to shift the aggregate demand curve. Monetarists and new classical economists generally prefer to allow the economy to close recessionary or inflationary gaps by itself.

Bonds are IOUs; their interest rate is determined by the relationship between their face value and their price. That price is determined by the demand and supply for bonds. An increase in bond prices means interest rates are lower. A reduction in bond prices means interest rates are higher.

The price of the dollar is determined in international foreign exchange markets by the demand and supply for dollars. The demand for dollars is based ultimately on foreign demand for U.S. goods, services, and assets. The supply of dollars reflects the demand by U.S. residents for foreign goods, services, and assets. Changes in the price of the dollar reflect changes in these demand curves.

In the next two chapters we'll turn to the role of money in the economy. We'll examine what money is, how it's created, and how it affects the economy. We'll also study the role of the Federal Reserve System, the central bank in the United States.

Terms and Concepts for Review

Aggregate demand
Aggregate demand curve
Aggregate supply
Bond
Change in aggregate demand
Change in short-run aggregate supply
Change in the aggregate quantity of goods and services demanded
Change in the aggregate quantity of goods and services supplied
Exchange rate
Face value
Foreign exchange market
Inflationary gap
Interest rate
Long run
Long-run aggregate supply (LRAS) curve
Monetarist school
Natural level of real GDP
New classical school
New Keynesian school
Nonintervention policy
Rational expectations
Real business cycle theory
Recessionary gap
Short run
Short-run aggregate supply (SRAS) curve
Stabilization policy
Trade-weighted exchange rate

For Discussion

1. Explain how the following changes in aggregate demand or short-run aggregate supply, other things held unchanged, are likely to affect the level of total output and the price level in the short run.
   - **a.** An increase in aggregate demand
   - **b.** A decrease in aggregate demand
   - **c.** An increase in short-run aggregate supply
   - **d.** A reduction in short-run aggregate supply
2. Use the model of aggregate demand and short-run aggregate supply to explain how each of the following would affect real GDP and the price level.
   - **a.** An increase in government purchases
   - **b.** A reduction in wages
   - **c.** A major improvement in technology
   - **d.** A reduction in net exports
3. How would an increase in the supply of labor affect the natural levels of employment and real GDP? How would it affect the real wage, the level of real GDP, and the price level in the short run? How would it affect long-run aggregate supply? What kind of gaps would be created?
4. What factors might increase the demand for bonds? The supply?
5. What would happen to the market for bonds if a law were passed that set a minimum price on bonds that was above the equilibrium price?
6. When the price of bonds decreases, the interest rate rises. Explain.
7. One journalist writing about the complex interactions between various markets in the economy stated: "When the government spends more than it takes in taxes it must sell bonds to finance its excess expenditures. But selling bonds drives interest rates down and thus stimulates the economy by encouraging more investment and decreasing the foreign exchange rate, which helps our export industries. Therefore, the deficit can't be all that bad." Carefully analyze the statement. Do you agree? Why or why not?
8. What do you predict will happen to the foreign exchange rate if interest rates in the United States increase dramatically over the next year? Explain, using a graph of the foreign exchange market.
9. How would the event in Question 8 affect the price level and real GDP?
10. Suppose the government were to increase its purchases, issuing bonds to finance these purchases. Use your knowledge of the bond and foreign exchange markets to explain how this would affect investment and net exports.

Problems

1. Suppose the aggregate demand and short-run aggregate supply curves for an economy whose natural level of real GDP equals $2,700 are given by the following table:

	Aggregate quantity of goods and services:	
Price level	Demanded	Supplied
0.50	$3,500	$1,000
0.75	3,000	2,000
1.00	2,500	2,500
1.25	2,000	2,700
1.50	1,500	2,800

   a. Draw the aggregate demand, short-run aggregate supply, and long-run aggregate supply curves.

   b. State the short-run equilibrium level of real GDP and the price level.

   c. Characterize the current economic situation. Is there an inflationary or a recessionary gap? If so, how large is it?

   d. Now suppose aggregate demand increases by $700 at each price level; for example, the aggregate quantity of goods and services demanded at a price level of 0.50 now equals $4,200. Show the new aggregate demand curve, state the new short-run equilibrium price level and real GDP, and state whether there is an inflationary or a recessionary gap and give its size.

2. An economy is characterized by the following values for aggregate demand and short-run aggregate supply; its natural level of real GDP is $1,500:

	Aggregate quantity of goods and services:	
Price level	Demanded	Supplied
0.50	$2,500	$1,500
0.75	2,000	2,000
1.00	1,500	2,300
1.25	1,000	2,500
1.50	500	2,600

   a. Draw the aggregate demand, short-run aggregate supply, and long-run aggregate supply curves.

   b. State the equilibrium level of real GDP and the price level.

   c. Characterize the current economic situation. Is there an inflationary or a recessionary gap? If so, how large is it?

   d. Now suppose that nominal wages rise and that the price level required to induce a particular level of total output rises by 0.50. For example, a price level of 1.00 is now required to induce producers to produce a real GDP of $1,500. Show the new short-run aggregate supply curve, state the new equilibrium price level and real GDP, and state whether there is an inflationary or a recessionary gap and give its size. Why might such a change occur?

3. Suppose that the demand and supply schedules for bonds which have a face value of $100, but which have no coupon rate, are as follows:

Price	Quantity demanded	Quantity supplied
$100	0	600
95	100	500
90	200	400
85	300	300
80	400	200
75	500	100
70	600	0

   a. Draw the demand and supply curves for these bonds, find the equilibrium price, and determine the interest rate.

   b. Now suppose the quantity demanded increases by 200 bonds at each price. Draw the new demand curve and find the new equilibrium price. What has happened to the interest rate?

4. Suppose there are two countries, Germany and Japan. The demand and supply curves for Germany's currency, the mark, are given by the following table (prices for the German mark are given in Japanese yen; quantities of marks are in millions):

Price (in yen)	Marks demanded	Marks supplied
¥75	0	600
70	100	500
65	200	400
60	300	300
55	400	200
50	500	100
45	600	0

   a. Draw the demand and supply curves for German marks and state the equilibrium exchange rate (in yen) for the mark. How many marks are required to purchase one yen?

   b. Suppose an increase in interest rates in Germany increases the demand for marks by 100 million at each price. At the same time, it reduces the supply by 100 million at each price. Draw the new demand and supply curves and state the new equilibrium exchange rate for the mark. How many marks are now required to purchase one yen?

   c. How will the event in (b) affect net exports in Germany? How will it affect aggregate demand in Germany. How will the event in (b) affect net exports in Japan? How will it affect aggregate demand in Japan?

24

Money, the Banking System, and the Fed

Chapter Objectives

After mastering the material in this chapter, you will be able to:

1. Define money and explain the alternative definitions of money used in the United States today.
2. Explain the role of reserves in the banking system.
3. Describe the main regulations imposed on banks and explain their purpose and effects.
4. Trace the processes through which money is created and destroyed.
5. Describe the operation of the Federal Reserve System and its relationship to banks in the United States.
6. Trace the process through which a central bank influences the quantity of money in an economy.
7. Explain how the Fed's choices of a discount rate and reserve requirements for banks affect the economy.

Money, n. A blessing that is of no advantage to us excepting when we part with it.
Ambrose Bierce, *The Devil's Dictionary*

What's Ahead

You had to bring your Kent cigarettes with you if you wanted to buy gas, or just about anything else. People with ordinary money found empty shelves or "Closed" signs.

The time was January 1990, the place, Romania. The communist government had been toppled the previous month, and there was enormous uncertainty about what lay ahead. Faced with this situation, merchants were reluctant to accept the leu, the official Romanian currency.

Merchants were, however, willing to accept Kent cigarettes. A pack of Kents would buy a few liters of gas, a pair of nylons kept under the counter at the clothing store, a visit to a local doctor. A fistful of lei would generally elicit little more than a shrug.[1]

The emergence of Kents as an unofficial form of money in Romania says a lot about Romania's chaotic political situation then. But it says even more about the importance of money. When the currency Romanians had been accustomed to using no longer functioned as money, they quickly adopted a new kind of money. Every society finds something to serve as money in order to facilitate exchange. Laundry detergent, gold, cognac, ivory, seashells, salt, horses—all have served at some time and in some place as money.

In this chapter and the next we examine money and the role it plays in the economy. In this chapter, we'll focus on the nature of money and the process through which it is created.

This chapter also introduces the largest financial institution in the world, the Federal Reserve System of the United States. The Fed, as it is commonly called, plays a key role in determining the quantity of money in the United States. We'll see how the Fed operates and examine the policy tools at its disposal.

[1] This example is taken from *The Wall Street Journal.* Professor Henry McCarl of the University of Alabama at Birmingham notes that this was not the first time Romanians had resorted to the use of Kents as money. He recalls that while on a sabbatical there in 1977–1978, he was able to purchase virtually anything using packs of Kent 100s as currency. He still has the "caicula" he bought for 10 packs of Kents.

Defining Money

If cigarettes, horses, salt, and seashells have all served as money, then just what *is* it? It turns out that money is quite easy to define. **Money** is anything that serves as a medium of exchange. A **medium of exchange** is anything that is widely accepted as a means of payment. In Romania, for example, Kent cigarettes served as a medium of exchange; that made them money.

Money, ultimately, is defined by people. When people use something as a medium of exchange, it becomes money. If people were to begin accepting basketballs as payment for most goods and services, basketballs would be money. We'll learn in this chapter that changes in the way people use money over the past three decades have created new types of money and have changed the way money is measured.

The Functions of Money

Money serves three basic functions. By definition, it is a medium of exchange. It also serves as a unit of account and as a store of value.

A Medium of Exchange

The exchange of goods and services in markets is among the most universal features of human life. To facilitate these exchanges, people settle on something that will serve as a medium of exchange—they select something that will serve as money.

We can best understand the significance of a medium of exchange by considering its absence. A **barter system** is an economy that lacks a medium of exchange. Because no one item serves as a medium of exchange, potential buyers must find things that individual sellers will accept. A buyer might find a seller who will trade a pair of shoes for two chickens. Another seller might be willing to provide a haircut in exchange for a garden hose. Suppose you were visiting a grocery store in a barter economy. You would need to load up a truckful of items the grocer might accept in exchange for groceries. That would be a chancy affair; you couldn't know when you headed for the store which items the grocer might agree to trade. Indeed, the complexity—and cost—of a visit to a grocery store in a barter economy would be so great that there probably wouldn't *be* any grocery stores!

A moment's contemplation of the difficulty of life in a barter economy will demonstrate why human societies always select something—sometimes more than one thing—to serve as a medium of exchange. If a barter economy were to exist, people would quickly settle on a medium of exchange to free themselves from the enormous costs of arranging exchanges that such an economy would entail.

A Unit of Account

Ask someone in the United States what he or she paid for something, and that person will respond by quoting a price stated in dollars: "I paid $50 for this radio," or "I paid $10 for this pizza." People don't say, "I paid 5 pizzas for this radio." That statement might, of course, be literally true in the sense of the opportunity cost of the transaction, but we don't report prices that way for two reasons. One is that people don't arrive at places like Radio Shack with 5 pizzas and

- **Money** is anything that serves as a medium of exchange.
- A **medium of exchange** is anything that is widely accepted as a means of payment.
- A **barter system** is an economy that lacks a medium of exchange.

expect to purchase a radio. The other is that the information wouldn't be very useful. Other people may not think of values in pizza terms, so they might not know what we meant. Instead, we report the value of things in terms of money.

Money serves as a **unit of account,** which is a consistent means of measuring the value of things. We use money in this fashion because it's also a medium of exchange. When we report the value of a good or service in units of money, we are reporting what another person is likely to have to pay to obtain that good or service.

A Store of Value

The third function of money is to serve as a store of value. Consider a $10 bill that you left in a coat pocket a year ago. When you find it, you'll be pleased. That's because you know the bill still has value. Value has, in effect, been "stored" in that little piece of paper.

Money, of course, is not the only commodity that can store value. Houses, buildings, land, works of art, and many other commodities serve as a means of storing wealth and value. Money differs from these other stores of value by being readily exchangeable into other commodities. Its role as a medium of exchange makes it a convenient store of value.

Because money acts as a store of value, it can be used as a standard for future payments. When you borrow money, for example, you typically sign a contract pledging to make a series of future payments to pay off the debt. These payments will be made using money, because money acts as a store of value.

Money is not, however, a risk-free store of value. We saw in Chapter 22 that inflation reduces the value of money. In periods of rapid inflation, people may not wish to rely on money as a store of value, and they may turn to commodities such as land or gold instead.

Types of Money

While money can take an extraordinary variety of forms, there are four basic types of money. These include commodity money, convertible paper money, fiat money, and debt money.

Commodity Money

Kent cigarettes in Romania were an example of commodity money. **Commodity money** is money that has a value apart from its use as money. Kent cigarettes could be used to buy gas in Romania; they could also be smoked.

Gold and silver have been the most widely used forms of commodity money. The first known use of coins, for example, was in the Greek city-state of Lydia in the beginning of the seventh century B.C. The coins were fashioned from electrum, a natural mixture of gold and silver. Gold and silver can be used as jewelry and for some industrial and medicinal purposes, so they have value apart from their use as money.

One disadvantage of commodity money is that its quantity can fluctuate erratically. Gold, for example, was one form of money in the United States in the nineteenth century. Gold discoveries in California and later in Alaska sent the quantity of money soaring. Some of this nation's worst bouts of inflation were set off by increases in the quantity of gold in circulation during the nineteenth century. The newly discovered gold was quickly converted to money, and the resultant increase in the money supply forced prices upward.

- A **unit of account** is a consistent means of measuring the value of things.
- **Commodity money** is money that has a value apart from its use as money.

The quantities of gold and silver in circulation are limited by the quantities of these metals that can be extracted from the earth. Gold and silver are valuable in large part because people know their quantities aren't going to increase suddenly. A much greater problem exists with commodity money that can be produced. In the southern part of colonial America, for example, tobacco served as money. There was a continuing problem of farmers increasing the money supply by growing too much money. The problem was sufficiently serious that vigilante squads were organized to roam the countryside and burn tobacco fields in an effort to keep the money supply under control.

Another problem is that commodity money may vary in quality. Given that variability, there is a tendency for lower-quality commodities to drive higher-quality commodities out of circulation. Horses, for example, served as money in the New England region during the colonial period. It was common for loan obligations to be stated in terms of a quantity of horses to be paid back. Given such obligations, there was a tendency to use lower-quality horses to pay back debts; higher-quality horses were kept out of circulation for other uses. Laws were passed forbidding the use of lame horses in the payment of debts. Unless a means can be found to control the quality of commodity money, the tendency for that quality to decline can threaten its acceptability as a medium of exchange.

Convertible Paper Money

Convertible paper money is paper money that can be redeemed for a specific commodity at a rate specified on the money. While convertible paper money isn't common today, it was once the primary form of money. The United States, for example, has had convertible paper money for most of its history.

Before 1879, most money in the United States consisted of convertible paper issued by private banks. U.S. banks accepted deposits of gold and issued bank notes in exchange. A bank note was a piece of paper printed in a specific denomination ($1, $10, etc.) that had a promise by the bank to pay to the bearer a specific amount of gold on demand. These bank notes were a form of convertible paper money.

The United States government began issuing currency on a regular basis in 1879. **Currency** is paper money and coin issued by a government. The first U.S. currency was a form of convertible paper money. A $1 bill, for example, contained a promise by the U.S. Treasury to pay to the bearer on demand $1 in gold. The Treasury would exchange gold for currency at a rate of one ounce for $21.

The practice of exchanging dollars for gold was largely eliminated in 1933, when the official rate was changed to $35 per ounce of gold. In an effort to prevent speculative behavior, the United States at the same time made it illegal for its citizens to hold gold coins or gold ingots. The promise on a dollar was changed to a promise to pay to the bearer on demand $1 in "lawful money."[2] The U.S. government did, however, continue to redeem U.S. currency to foreign central banks or governments at a rate of $35 per ounce of gold. Richard Nixon ordered an end to that practice in 1971 as part of a radical shift in U.S. policy concerning international finance. We'll study that shift in Chapter 29. The action removed the last promise to exchange a commodity for U.S. currency; our currency has no commodity backing today.

- **Convertible paper money** is paper money that may be redeemed for a specific commodity at a rate specified on the currency.
- **Currency** is paper money and coin issued by a government.

[2] Legend has it that in 1947, a Mr. A. F. Downs of Cleveland, Ohio, tested this promise by sending a $10 bill to the Treasury and demanding payment in lawful money. He received two $5 bills. The promise to redeem currency with lawful money was subsequently replaced with the phrase "In God We Trust."

Fiat Money

Fiat is Latin for "by order of the authority." **Fiat money** is money that some authority, generally a government, has ordered to be accepted as a medium of exchange. The money itself has virtually no intrinsic value. The U.S. government issued currency—called "greenbacks"—to help finance the Civil War. Despite the federal government's order that it be accepted as a medium of exchange at its full face value, this first currency didn't win wide acceptance. It traded at a discount for bank notes that could be converted into gold. At one point, a greenback exchanged for as little as 35 cents in gold-backed notes. Our currency today is fiat money. You'll notice the order on each bill: "This note is legal tender for all debts, public and private."

The danger of fiat money is that it can be printed so fast that it causes inflation. That has happened within the past few years in Russia, in Yugoslavia, and in many other countries. If the quantity of money is not increased too fast, however, there is no reason that the issue of fiat money should cause inflation.

Debt Money

Private debt money is a loan that the borrower promises to repay on demand. A checking account, for example, is private debt money. The owner of a checking account has, in effect, loaned the money he or she deposits to the bank; the bank can use the proceeds in any way it wishes. But the bank promises to pay the depositor, in currency, on demand—whenever the depositor decides to cash a check.

Balances in checking accounts are called **checkable deposits**—deposits whose ownership can be transferred with a check. A **check** is a written order to a bank to transfer ownership of a checkable deposit. Suppose, for example, that you have $100 in your checking account and you write a check to your campus bookstore for $30. The $30 will be transferred from your checking account to the bookstore's checking account.

Another form of private debt money is a traveler's check. When you buy a traveler's check, you are lending money to the issuer of the check. The issuer agrees to pay upon demand the amount designated on the check to you or to anyone to whom you give the check. In the meantime, the issuer is free to make use of your funds.

Credit cards are not considered money. A credit card identifies you as a person who has a special arrangement with the card issuer in which the issuer will lend you money and transfer the proceeds to another party whenever you want. Thus, if you present a MasterCard to a jeweler as payment for a $200 ring, the firm that issued you the card will lend you the $200 and send that money, less a service charge, to the jeweler. You, of course, will be required to repay the loan later. But a card that says you have such a relationship is not money.

- **Fiat money** is money that some authority has ordered be accepted as money.
- **Private debt money** is a loan that the borrower promises to repay on demand.
- A **checkable deposit** is a bank deposit whose ownership can be transferred with a check.
- A **check** is a legal document used to transfer the ownership of a checkable deposit.
- The **money supply** is the total quantity of money in the economy at any one time.

Measuring Money

The total quantity of money in the economy at any one time is called the **money supply.** Economists measure the money supply because they know that it affects the level of economic activity. Change in the money supply is one of the factors economists use in predicting future changes in nominal and real GDP.

One criterion for selecting a measure of the money supply is its correspondence to nominal GDP. What we measure as money should give us a good gauge with which to assess what's happening to the economy. The measure of the

Case in Point — Coming Soon: The Electronic Purse

An electronic alternative to carrying currency may be available to you quite soon. The electronic purse would be a prepaid card that would look like a credit card, but it would function precisely like currency.

Many colleges and universities already have prepaid cards students can use to make purchases on campus. A student takes his or her card to the campus finance office and, in effect, deposits money in it. When the card is inserted in a campus pop machine, a can of pop comes out, and the machine subtracts the price of the pop from the student's card. Once the money in the card is spent, more money may be deposited in it.

A similar arrangement is available on many transit systems. Instead of using cash, commuters buy prepaid cards. A $10 card, for example, is good for $10 worth of rides. Suppose each ride costs $1.25. Each time the card is inserted to allow a rider to board the system, $1.25 is subtracted from the card. Once eight rides have been taken, the card loses its value and the commuter must buy another. Such systems are commonly used for telephone calls in Europe and in some parts of the United States.

An electronic purse will function the same way, except that it could be used everywhere. You could transfer money from a checking account to your electronic purse at an automatic teller machine. You could then pay for goods and services by presenting your card; a machine would read your card and instantly transfer money from your card to the vendor's card. The cards would make money transfers quite easy. A person in Atlanta could insert an electronic purse into a special pay phone and punch a few buttons to transfer money instantly to a person at a pay phone in San Francisco.

Electronic purses are already in use in Denmark and in Finland. In Denmark, the DANMONT card can be used in vending machines, phones, trains, buses and parking meters. Finland's Avant card is in use in several cities and is being phased in for use throughout the country.

One important issue is whether purchases with the cards should be tracked. Unlike credit cards, electronic purses allow money to be transferred from one card to another without having the issuing institution recording the transfer. It would, however, be possible to develop an electronic system in which the issuer did record the transfers. Law enforcement officials are likely to prefer that transactions be recorded. Users of the card, though, may prefer that transactions be as anonymous as a cash transfer.

Another big question is who should issue the cards. The European Community is already studying this issue; an advisory panel has recommended that only banks be permitted to issue the cards.

The technology for the electronic purse already exists. Such "purses" will almost certainly be available soon. The days of fumbling for a quarter for a vending machine or a parking meter are numbered.

Source: John Wenninger and David Laster, "The Electronic Purse," Federal Reserve Bank of New York, *Current Issues in Economics and Finance* (April 1995) 1(1): 1–5.

money supply used until 1980 was closely related to our definition of money. The money supply was measured as the sum of currency in circulation and checkable deposits held at commercial banks. This measure of the money supply once seemed to correspond closely to nominal GDP, but the relationship between the two started to unravel in the 1970s.

The 1970s were a period of high interest rates and high inflation. Commercial banks weren't allowed to pay interest on checkable deposits, so customers tried to find ways to hold funds that would earn more interest but still allow them to spend their money when they needed it. Savings and loan institutions developed NOW accounts—negotiable orders of withdrawal—that worked like checkable deposits but paid interest. Credit unions offered share draft accounts that did the same thing. Because only checkable deposits at commercial banks were counted as money, transfers of funds from conventional checking accounts to NOW and share draft accounts appeared in the statistics as reductions in the money supply, despite the fact that the new deposits were still used to finance consumption.

Banks, which weren't permitted to offer NOW or share draft accounts, responded to the increased competition by making it easier to shift funds in other kinds of deposits into checkable deposits. For example, depositors once had to visit the bank to transfer funds from a savings account to a checking account. The procedure was modified so that all it took was a telephone call. Banks also developed new types of accounts that paid even higher interest than savings deposits but were still easy to transfer into checking accounts. Savings deposits and other interest-earning accounts weren't measured as part of the money supply.

As people began keeping more funds in NOW accounts, share draft accounts, and interest-earning accounts at commercial banks, the old measure of the money supply became a less reliable gauge of future economic activity. To attain a measure of money that corresponded closely to economic activity, money funds in NOW and share draft accounts had to be included, along with assets that didn't serve as media of exchange but could easily be converted into currency or checkable deposits.

Economists refer to the ease with which an asset can be converted into currency as the asset's **liquidity.** Currency itself is perfectly liquid; you can always change two $5 bills for a $10 bill. Checkable deposits are almost perfectly liquid; you can easily cash a check. An office building, however, is highly illiquid. It can be converted to money only by selling it, a time-consuming and costly process.

As financial assets other than checkable deposits have become more liquid, economists have had to develop broader measures of money that would correspond to economic activity. In the United States, the final arbiter of what is and what isn't measured as money is the Federal Reserve System—the Fed. Because it's difficult to determine what (and what not) to measure as money, the Fed uses three different measures of money, called M1, M2, and M3.

M1 is the narrowest of the Fed's money supply definitions. It includes currency in circulation, checkable deposits, and traveler's checks. Until 1980, M1 served as the Fed's basic measure of the money supply, and the checkable deposits it included were only those at commercial banks. After 1980, NOW and share draft accounts were also included in M1. Traveler's checks were also added at that time.

M2 is a broader measure of the money supply than M1. It includes M1 and other deposits such as small time deposits (less than $100,000) and savings accounts, as well as accounts such as money market mutual funds (MMMFs) on which limited checks can be written.[3]

M2 is sometimes called the broadly defined money supply, while M1 is the narrowly defined money supply. The assets in M1 may be regarded as perfectly

- The **liquidity** of an asset reflects the ease with which it can be converted to money.
- **M1** includes currency in circulation plus checkable deposits plus traveler's checks.
- **M2** includes M1 as well as other deposits, such as small time deposits, savings accounts, and money market mutual funds, that are easily converted to checkable deposits.
- **M3** includes M2, large time deposits, money market mutual funds held by institutions, and other assets that are somewhat less liquid than those in M2.

[3] The deposits included in M2 that are not a part of M1 include **savings deposits; small time deposits** (a time deposit is one that matures on a certain date, such as a certificate of deposit); **money market deposit accounts** (MMDAs—banks use the funds deposited in these accounts to purchase short-term securities, and allow a limited number of checks to be written on them); **money market mutual funds** (MMMFs—mutual funds that combine funds from many individuals and firms and purchase short-term securities; these funds operate in a manner similar to the MMDAs offered by banks; and limited check writing is generally permitted); **overnight Eurodollar deposits** (dollar-denominated deposits kept in foreign banks); and **overnight repurchase agreements** (arrangements in which a corporation purchases Treasury securities from a bank, and the bank agrees to buy them back the next day at a slightly higher price).

Case in Point The Case of the Missing M2

Roughly $70 billion in M2 turned up missing in the early 1990s. Economist John V. Duca of the Federal Reserve Bank of Dallas thinks he's found it. His discovery could lead to yet another change in the definition of M2.

Economists say money is "missing" when the ratio of nominal GDP to a money measure changes in ways that can't be accounted for by standard economic models. By that test, M2 was $70 billion less than it "should" have been in 1993.

The missing money was not just a frustration for economists. The Fed had been seeking throughout the 1990s to boost M2 growth to try to stimulate the economy. Despite the Fed's efforts, M2 barely grew at all. Critics howled that the Fed wasn't doing enough to stimulate the economy. Fed officials responded that the slow M2 growth reflected not their own policies but some underlying change in the economy. They weren't sure what had happened, but they were pretty sure *something* had happened. They were pushing harder on the accelerator, but the car wasn't responding.

Mr. Duca's analysis may have solved the problem. He notes that late in the 1980s, banks and other institutions began developing yet another type of deposit for their customers. They created funds that pool money from many people and use the funds to purchase longer-term bonds. Such bonds generally command higher interest rates than the short-term securities purchased by money market funds. The new bond funds offer a high degree of liquidity; banks permit customers to switch their money between the funds and checkable deposits.

During the 1990s, the spread between rates on long- versus short-term securities increased dramatically. That boosted the attractiveness of the bond funds, which aren't part of M2. People started taking funds out of lower-interest M2 accounts and putting them in the bond funds.

Mr. Duca says that by redefining M2 to include bond funds held by individuals (except for those funds held in special retirement accounts), he was able to obtain a measure that continued to track economic activity closely in the 1990s. It's time, he says, for yet another redefinition of M2.

Source: John V. Duca, "Regulation, Bank Competitiveness, and Episodes of Missing Money," *Federal Reserve Bank of Dallas Economic Review* (Second Quarter 1993):1–23 and personal interview.

liquid; the assets in M2 are highly liquid, but somewhat less liquid than the assets in M1. An even broader measure of the money supply, **M3**, includes M2, large time deposits, money market mutual funds held by institutions, and other assets that are somewhat less liquid than those in M2. M3 is used less frequently as a measure of the money supply than are M1 and M2. Exhibit 24-1 shows the composition of M1, M2, and M3 in April 1995.

EXHIBIT 24-1

The Three M's: April 1995

M1, the narrowest definition of the money supply, includes assets that are perfectly liquid. M2 and M3 provide successively broader measures of the money supply and include somewhat less liquid assets. Amounts are in billions of dollars and represent money supply data for April 1995.

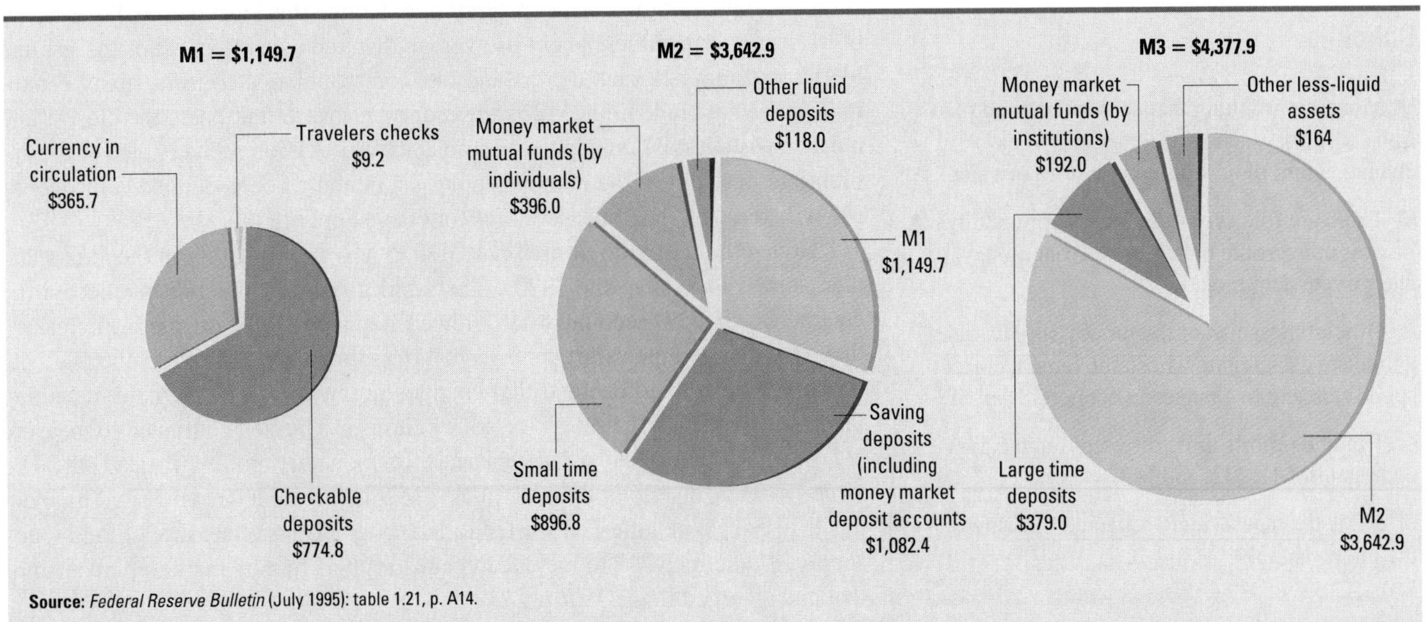

Source: *Federal Reserve Bulletin* (July 1995): table 1.21, p. A14.

EXHIBIT 24-2

Money Measures and Economic Activity

Each panel shows quarterly values of the ratio of nominal GDP to one of the Fed's three monetary measures since 1960. The horizontal gray lines give the average ratio for each of the money measures. Over the entire period, M2 appears to have had the most stable relationship to nominal GDP.

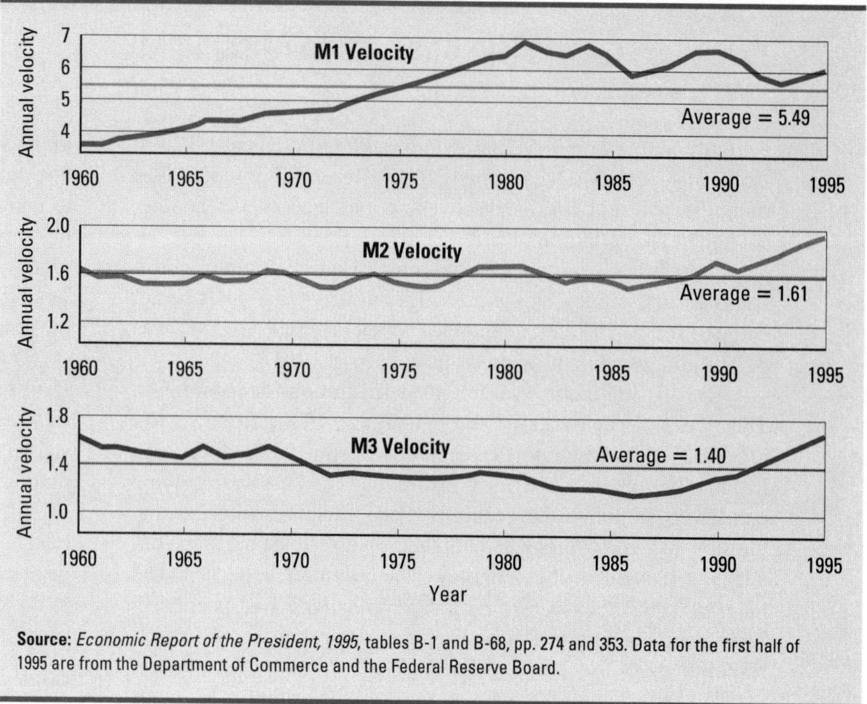

Source: *Economic Report of the President, 1995,* tables B-1 and B-68, pp. 274 and 353. Data for the first half of 1995 are from the Department of Commerce and the Federal Reserve Board.

Which M?

With all the operational definitions of money available, which one should we use? Economists generally answer that question by asking another: Which measure of money is most closely related to the level of economic activity?

Exhibit 24-2 presents a simple test of the degree to which the three alternative money measures correspond to changes in economic activity. It gives the ratio of nominal GDP to each money measure annually since 1960 (we'll find in the next chapter that this ratio plays a key role in the analysis of money and economic activity). The average value of each of these three ratios over the period shown is given by the horizontal gray line. Notice that nominal GDP per dollar of M2 has fluctuated less about its average than the equivalent ratios for M1 and M3. Based on tests such as this and on more sophisticated tests, many economists have concluded that M2 is the money measure that bears the closest and most consistent relationship to economic activity. Although the choice of the appropriate measure of the money supply is a matter of considerable controversy, M2 will serve as "the" measure of the money supply in this text.

Notice that the ratio of nominal GDP to M1 grew steadily in the 1960s and then started to soar in the 1970s. The rapid growth in the 1970s reflected the emergence of new accounts that allowed depositors to earn more interest on their deposits and then shift deposits to M1 as they needed to write checks.

In 1980, the Fed decided that changes in the ways people were managing their money made M1 useless for policy choices. The Fed continued to measure M1 but no longer used it as a measure of monetary policy. Instead, the Fed turned to M2. In simpler monetary days, M2 merely added savings and time deposits to M1. When the Fed shifted to M2 as its primary measure of the money supply, it redefined M2 to include deposits such as money market mutual funds that had emerged in the 1970s.

- Money is anything that serves the three functions of money, acting as a medium of exchange, a unit of account, and a store of value.
- There are four types of money: commodity money, convertible paper money, fiat money, and private debt money.
- Official measures of the money supply seek a monetary aggregate whose movement corresponds closely to changes in economic activity.
- The Fed reports three different monetary aggregates: M1, M2, and M3.
- M2 is the most widely accepted measure of the money supply.

The Banking System and Money Creation

Where does money come from? How is its quantity increased or decreased? We'll find in this section that the answers to these questions have an almost magical quality. Money is created by banks when they issue loans. In effect, money is created by the stroke of a pen or a click of a computer key.

We'll begin by examining the operation of banks and the banking system. We'll find that, like money itself, the nature of banking has undergone, and is continuing to undergo, rapid change.

Banks and Other Financial Intermediaries

An institution that collects funds from lenders and distributes these funds to borrowers is called a **financial intermediary.** Financial intermediaries operate within the financial markets in the circular flow model we developed in Chapter 21. A pension fund is an example of a financial intermediary. Workers and firms place money in the fund for their retirement; the fund earns income by lending money to firms or by investing in their stock. The fund thus makes retirement saving available for other spending.

Banks play a particularly important role as financial intermediaries.

Types of Banks

Banks take in their depositors' money and lend it to borrowers—they thus function as financial intermediaries. With the interest they earn on their loans, banks are able to pay interest to their depositors, cover their own operating costs, and earn a profit, all the while maintaining the ability of the original depositors to spend the funds when they desire to do so. One key characteristic of banks is that they offer their customers the opportunity to open checking accounts, thus creating checkable deposits. These functions define a **bank,** which is a financial institution that accepts deposits, makes loans, and offers checking accounts.

There were once important distinctions among types of banks. These distinctions have blurred during the past three decades, but some differences remain.

Commercial Banks. Commercial banks account for the bulk of checkable deposits. They specialize in commercial loans but also make consumer and mortgage loans. Commercial banks usually have the word "bank" in their names. There were roughly 12,000 commercial banks in the United States in 1994.

Savings and Loan Associations. Savings and loan associations (S&Ls, for short) were originally established to finance home building. Although they still tend to specialize in home mortgage financing, they also offer most of the services offered by commercial banks. They cannot, however, use the word "bank" in their names. S&Ls have been a source of considerable difficulty, as we shall see later in this chapter. There were approximately 2,000 S&Ls in the United States in 1994.

Mutual Savings Banks. Savings banks were created in the nineteenth century to encourage saving by the "common people." These banks are owned by their depositors; they thus operate as cooperatives. There were about 500 mutual savings banks in 1994; most operated in the northeastern United States.

- A **financial intermediary** is an institution that collects funds from lenders and distributes these funds to borrowers.
- A **bank** is a financial institution that accepts deposits, makes loans, and offers checking accounts.

Case in Point: Competition Forces a Banking Transformation

The Whitney Group, an executive search firm in New York, has a new banker: Merrill Lynch. Whitney turned to the huge securities firm when banks turned down its request for a $1 million line of credit. Merrill Lynch not only came up with the credit banks wouldn't offer—it took over the management of the firm's term loans and its retirement business, and it established money market accounts for Whitney's executives. "They really grab you with everything. Merrill has become a traditional banker for us," Whitney's president, Gary Goldstein, told *The Wall Street Journal.*

Merrill manages a whopping $642 billion in client assets—2.5 percent of all the financial assets in the United States. The firm has moved aggressively to provide banking services in an effort to entice firms and individuals to let Merrill manage their financial assets. Jerome P. Kenney, Merrill's corporate strategy chief, put it bluntly in a statement to *The Wall Street Journal:* "We're not looking just to have loan accounts. We're interested in it as a way to capture money of wealthy people and have access to their working capital and the securities-related services they need."

The aggressive efforts of firms like Merrill Lynch, which aren't banks and don't face the regulatory structure with which banks must contend, are making a dent in traditional banking services. And banks are beginning to respond.

The shift in strategy by two longtime banking competitors in the South, First Union Corporation and NationsBank Corporation, illustrates the new path banks are beginning to follow. Faced with tough competition from mutual funds and other nonbank financial intermediaries, the two rivals are focusing less on competing with each other as bankers and more on taking on nonbank rivals in stock brokerage services, mutual funds, and other financial services. Edward E. Crutchfield, chairman and chief executive officer of First Union, explained the banks' motivation for their new thrust to *The Wall Street Journal:* "We bankers are throwing snowballs (at each other), and there's someone out there with an Uzi."

As competitors grab a larger share of banking services, more banks will move to offer the kinds of financial services other financial intermediaries have offered. Not only are different types of banks becoming more alike; banks in general are becoming more like other financial intermediaries. Those other financial intermediaries are, in turn, becoming more like banks.

Sources: Michael Siconolfi, "Merrill Lynch, Pushing into Many New Lines, Expands Bank Services," *The Wall Street Journal,* 7 July 1993, A1; Martha Brannigan and Eleena de Lisser, "Two Big Rival Banks In Southeast Take On New-Age Competitors," *The Wall Street Journal,* 8 July 1993, A1.

Credit Unions. Credit unions are cooperatives that generally serve specific employee or community groups. They specialize in small consumer loans. They also maintain checkable deposits and savings deposit accounts. There were about 13,000 credit unions in the United States in 1994.

All these institutions have more similarities than differences. They all function as banks, taking in deposits, making loans, and offering checking accounts. Given these similarities, we'll refer to them henceforth as banks, except when it's important to highlight specific differences.

Other Financial Intermediaries

Banks aren't the only financial intermediaries in the economy. A host of institutions act to amass funds from one group and make them available to others. Insurance companies, for example, use some of the premiums paid by their customers to lend to firms for investment. Mutual funds make money available to firms and other institutions by purchasing their stocks or bonds. Brokerage firms such as Merrill Lynch offer customers interest-earning accounts and make loans. All these institutions act as financial intermediaries; they stop short of acting as banks because they don't offer checking accounts. Even that distinction, however, is blurring. Many mutual funds allow their customers to write a limited number of checks on their accounts, although the minimum denomination of such checks is typically constrained. They may, for example, require that checks be written for no less than $500.

As the importance of nonbank financial intermediaries has grown, in large part as a response to regulatory changes discussed below, banks' share of the nation's total financial assets has diminished. In the early 1970s, banks accounted for nearly 40 percent of U.S. financial assets. By 1993, that share had dropped to less than 25 percent.

The fact that banks account for a declining share of U.S. financial assets alarms some observers. We'll see that banks are tightly regulated; one reason for that regulation is to maintain control over the money supply. Other financial intermediaries, however, don't face the same regulatory restrictions as banks. Indeed, their freedom from regulation is one reason they have grown so rapidly. As other financial intermediaries become more important, central authorities begin to lose control over the money supply. We'll examine the implications of that lack of control later in this book.

Bank Finance and a Fractional Reserve System

Although their share of total financial assets is declining, banks continue to play a critical role in the economy. Bank finance, in particular, lies at the heart of the process through which money is created. To understand money, we need to understand some of the basics of bank finance.

The best way to grasp the essential features of bank finance is to examine the first banks, which economic historians think emerged in the Middle Ages. These banks were operated by goldsmiths.

Money in the Middle Ages consisted primarily of gold coins. The coins were bulky to carry around, and theft was common. Goldsmiths, who had secure safes to protect their own inventories of gold, began renting out space in their safes to others who wanted to leave their gold for safekeeping. A goldsmith would give a receipt to a customer who left gold in the safe.

Receipts issued by goldsmiths represented claims on gold. Some customers began using their receipts to buy goods and services or to pay debts. Whoever got the receipts now owned claims on gold at the goldsmith's safe. Because the receipts were easier to handle and to keep than coins, they often circulated as money for a long time, with no one bothering to go in to claim the coins.

Goldsmiths thus operated as banks. They took in deposits, the gold coins, and issued receipts that functioned very much like checks today. As receipts changed hands, they transferred ownership of the coins in the safe, just as checks transfer ownership of money in a checking account.

- A **T-account** is a form of financial statement showing assets, liabilities, and net worth.
- An **asset** is anything that is of value.
- A **liability** is an obligation to another party.
- **Net worth** equals assets less liabilities.

The goldsmith's financial situation can be depicted using a **T-account,** which is a form of financial statement showing assets, liabilities, and net worth. **Assets** are anything that is of value. **Liabilities** are obligations to other parties. **Net worth** equals assets less liabilities. All these are given dollar values in a firm's T-account. If an asset held by a firm is owned by that firm, it represents net worth. If the asset is owned by someone else, it's a liability. The sum of liabilities plus net worth must therefore equal the sum of all assets.

Assets		Liabilities Plus Net Worth	
Gold	$500	Net worth	$500

EXHIBIT 24-3

A Goldsmith's T-Account

A T-account lists assets, liabilities, and net worth. Shown above is the T-account for a goldsmith who owns $500 in gold; that is the firm's only asset.

A T-account for a goldsmith is shown in Exhibit 24-3. Assets are listed on the left, liabilities and net worth on the right. Suppose the goldsmith owns $500 worth of gold. Initially, there are no liabilities. For simplicity, we shall assume that the gold is the goldsmith's only asset. Because the goldsmith owns the gold, it is net worth. The T-account shows the goldsmith's initial situation.

Now suppose a customer brings $100 in gold to deposit in the safe. The goldsmith now has $600 in gold. This gold is an asset, so the goldsmith's assets rise to $600. But the gold is owned by someone else, so there must be a corresponding entry as a liability. The receipt for $100 is the corresponding liability; the goldsmith must surrender the gold when the receipt is presented. The goldsmith still owns the initial $500 in gold and retains that as net worth.

Goldsmith's T-Account

Assets		Liabilities Plus Net Worth	
Gold	$600	Gold receipts	$100
		Net worth	$500

The deposit of $100 in gold coins and the corresponding issue of $100 in gold receipts doesn't change the money supply. The gold coins are no longer in circulation; they've been replaced by the receipts.

The convenience and security of gold receipts presented goldsmiths with an opportunity to make more money. Because people rarely claimed the gold for which they had receipts, and because receipts were widely accepted as a medium of exchange, a goldsmith could simply write up receipts and issue them as loans.

Suppose, for example, that our goldsmith writes up an additional $1,100 in receipts and offers them as loans. The loans are an asset for the goldsmith because the borrowers sign IOUs promising to pay back the loans. The loans are therefore listed as an asset, along with the $600 in gold. The additional $1,100 in receipts are liabilities to the goldsmith. After all, the receipts carry the goldsmith's guarantee to exchange gold if they're brought in. Together with the $100 receipt the goldsmith has already issued, the goldsmith now has $1,200 in liabilities outstanding.

Assets		Liabilities Plus Net Worth	
Gold	$ 600	Gold receipts	$1,200
Loans	$1,100	Net worth	$ 500

The goldsmith's loans of $1,100 change the money supply. An additional $1,100 in receipts are now circulating as money in the economy. This illustrates a key fact about banks: *Banks create money when they issue loans.* We'll explore the process of money creation in greater detail later in this chapter.

Our goldsmith is taking a risk. If all the customers claim their gold at once, there won't be enough to make good on the goldsmith's promise to return gold for receipts. For the venture to succeed, people must have faith in the goldsmith. As long as people are confident the goldsmith will be able to return gold for receipts, they aren't likely to bring in their receipts. If they begin to lose confidence in the goldsmith, however, they'll try to claim their gold, and our goldsmith may end up dangling by his neck from a nearby oak tree! In general, the system of banks operated by goldsmiths worked well. It worked because people believed in it. As long as customers maintained their faith in the system, banks could continue to generate receipt liabilities that greatly exceeded the stock of gold coins held in reserve. The arrangement allowed goldsmiths to earn additional income—they could charge interest on the loans.

A system in which banks hold reserves whose value is less than the sum of claims outstanding on those reserves is called a **fractional reserve banking system.** By issuing receipts in excess of their gold reserves, goldsmiths were able to issue more loans and thus earn more interest income. Because goldsmiths issued a larger supply of loans, borrowers must have paid lower interest rates than they otherwise would have.

The medieval penchant for fractional reserve banking wasn't an aberration. Banks have continued to hold reserves equal to only a fraction of their deposit liabilities ever since.

Exhibit 24-4 provides a consolidated T-account for commercial banks in the United States for April 26, 1995. Just as the goldsmiths held gold as reserves against the liabilities represented by receipts, so modern banks hold reserves against the liabilities represented by their checkable deposits.

EXHIBIT 24-4

The T-Account for U.S. Commercial Banks, April 26, 1995

This T-account for all commercial banks in the United States shows their financial situation on April 26, 1995.

Assets		Liabilities and Net Worth		
Reserves	$ 218.4	Checkable deposits		$ 795.0
Other assets	253.0	Other deposits		1,773.1
Loans	2,612.9	Borrowings		695.3
Securities	952.8	Other liabilities		455.0
Total assets	4,037.1	Total liabilities	3,718.4	
		Net worth	318.7	

Source: *Federal Reserve Bulletin* (July 1995): p. A-18.

Today, the **reserves** banks hold against their deposit liabilities must take one of two forms: cash in the vault or deposits the bank keeps with the Fed. Notice that these reserves were less than one-tenth of checkable deposit liabilities in 1995.

In the next section, we'll learn about the regulatory structure that determines what fraction of their deposit liabilities banks must hold as reserves. We'll see later in this chapter that such requirements play an important role in money creation.

- A **fractional reserve banking system** is one in which banks hold reserves whose value is less than the sum of claims on those reserves.
- **Reserves** equal the cash a bank has in its vault plus deposits the bank maintains with the Fed.

The Regulation of Banks

Banks are among the most heavily regulated of commercial institutions. They are regulated in part to protect individual depositors against corrupt business practices. Banks are also susceptible to crises of confidence. Because their reserves equal only a fraction of their deposit liabilities, an effort by customers to get all their cash out of a bank could force it to fail. A few poorly managed banks could create such a crisis, leading people to try to withdraw their funds from well-managed banks. Another reason for the high degree of regulation is that variations in the quantity of money have important effects on the level of economic activity, and banks are the institutions that create money.

Deposit Insurance and Moral Hazard

From a customer's point of view, the most important form of regulation comes in the form of deposit insurance. For commercial banks, this insurance is provided by the Federal Deposit Insurance Corporation (FDIC). The FDIC maintains two different insurance funds, the Bank Insurance Fund for commercial banks and the Saving Association Insurance Fund for S&Ls. These funds are maintained through a premium assessed on banks for every $100 of bank deposits.

If a commercial bank or S&L fails, the FDIC guarantees to reimburse depositors up to at least $100,000 per account. In practice, the FDIC has made good on all deposits in failed banks and S&Ls, regardless of the size of the account. From a depositor's point of view, therefore, it isn't necessary to worry about a bank's safety.

One difficulty this insurance creates, however, is that it may induce the officers of a bank to take more risks. With a federal agency on hand to bail them out if they fail, the costs of failure are reduced. Bank officers can thus be expected to take more risks than they would otherwise—which, in turn, makes failure more likely. Insuring against failure could thus make failure more likely to occur. The tendency for insurance protection to increase the frequency of the event against which the insurance is provided is called **moral hazard.** Insurance against any calamity—whether car accidents or bank failures—has a tendency to increase the frequency with which the calamity occurs.

Banks present us with a fundamental dilemma. A fractional reserve system means that banks can operate only if their customers maintain their confidence in them. Once bank customers lose confidence, they're likely to try to withdraw their funds. But with a fractional reserve system, a bank actually holds funds in reserve equal to only a small fraction of its deposit liabilities. If its customers think a bank will fail and try to withdraw their cash, the bank is likely to fail. Bank panics, in which frightened customers rushed to withdraw their deposits, contributed to the failure of one-third of the nation's banks between 1929 and 1933. Deposit insurance was introduced in large part to give people confidence in their banks and to prevent failure. But moral hazard suggests that the deposit insurance that seeks to prevent bank failures may lead to less careful management—and thus encourage bank failure.

Regulation to Prevent Bank Failure

To counter the possibility that deposit insurance could encourage bankers to take undue risks, banks are severely limited in what they can do. They are barred from certain types of investments and from some activities viewed as too risky. They are required to keep reserves equal to 3 percent of their checkable deposits up to about $50 million and 10 percent of any deposits over that (the cutoff figure is adjusted each year based on changes in the total volume of checkable deposits; it was $54 million in 1995). There is no reserve requirement for savings deposits, time deposits, or money market mutual funds. Banks are also required to maintain a minimum level of net worth as a fraction of total assets. Regulators from the FDIC regularly perform audits and other checks of individual banks to ensure they are operating safely.

Moral hazard is the tendency for insurance protection to increase the frequency of the event against which the insurance is provided.

Case in Point — Silverado: The Collapse of a High-Flying S&L

The Rocky Mountain region enjoyed an economic boom in the 1970s and early 1980s as the region's rich oil, gas, and mineral deposits came into high demand. Denver emerged as the financial capital of this boom. Skyscrapers started popping up throughout the city, and the business community foresaw little but good times ahead.

The boom coincided with bank legislation passed early in the 1980s that allowed S&Ls to join in the financing of commercial ventures. Silverado Savings and Loan was aggressive in exploiting this new opportunity. Headquartered in Denver, with branches all over Colorado, Silverado quickly rose to be one of the state's largest S&Ls.

But in 1982–1983 came a drastic slump in world oil prices. With prices down and foreign production up, domestic producers had to cut back production. Mines and new exploration ventures closed all over the region. In addition to that local calamity, in 1981–1982 the United States suffered the worst recession since the Great Depression.

Workers dismantling a Silverado Banking sign.

Denver was especially hard hit by the recession and by plunging oil prices. Vacancy rates for commercial office space in Denver approached 40 percent. Some building owners offered as many as 3 years of free rent to anyone willing to sign a 5-year lease for office space. Investors who had bet on a continuing boom lost, and lost big.

Silverado had financed many of those failed ventures. As one commercial loan after another failed, the bank had to transfer assets from loans outstanding to what bankers bitterly called OREOs—Other Real Estate Owned. Silverado suddenly found itself the owner of a great deal of commercial real estate, real estate whose value was plunging. Forced by regulators to reflect those falling values on its balance sheet, Silverado took a $198 million write-down on its books in the summer of 1988, which pushed it into insolvency.

Government regulators, strapped for cash themselves, took no action. Silverado continued to operate through the fall, offering depositors much higher rates—some of the highest in the state—in a desperate bid to attract cash.

Finally, in December 1988, government regulators ordered Silverado shut down. The shutdown was a matter of little note to Silverado's depositors. Silverado reopened under new ownership the following Monday as Mile High Federal Savings and Loan. Silverado's depositors continued to get their money—the automatic teller machines even continued to operate overnight. Mile High agreed to take over the institution, but our government was left holding the bag for the institution's lack of funds to meet depositor claims. The estimated cost to the government of the takeover was $1 billion—a cost made greater because of its failure to move in on the institution sooner. Ultimately, these claims, along with several hundred billion dollars more from other S&Ls and commercial banks that became insolvent throughout the nation, were passed on to taxpayers who will continue to pay the bills for years to come.

The FDIC has the power to close a bank whose net worth has fallen below the required level. In practice, it typically acts to close a bank when it becomes insolvent. A bank is insolvent when its net worth becomes negative. That, in turn, implies that the bank's liabilities exceed its assets.

Insolvency typically strikes a bank when firms and individuals that have borrowed from it get into financial trouble themselves and are unable to make payments on their loans. The bank then forecloses, canceling the loans and taking over assets pledged as collateral. In the S&L crisis that struck the nation in the 1980s, most of the problems came when loans to finance residential or commercial real estate had to be foreclosed. A bank then reduced the value of its loans outstanding on the asset side of its T-account and it added the office buildings, shopping malls, homes, or other real estate it acquired in foreclosing on the loans. This typically didn't cause immediate trouble for the bank; the value of the real estate generally equaled the value of the loans foreclosed. But the difficulties facing borrowers generally reflected more widespread economic problems in a bank's region. Those problems pushed real estate values down sharply. When the market value of its assets falls, the bank is required to reduce the value of its assets on its balance sheet. When it reduces the value of its assets, the bank records an equal reduction in its net worth. This "writing down" of assets often pushed net worth below zero, and many banks became insolvent.

When the FDIC closes a bank, it arranges for depositors to receive their funds. When the bank has insufficient funds, the FDIC uses money from the appropriate insurance fund. The FDIC then turns the institution over to the Resolution Trust Corporation (RTC), a government agency created in response to the S&L crisis of the 1980s and 1990s. The RTC sells the bank's assets and uses the proceeds to pay other bank liabilities. Alternatively, the FDIC may arrange for another bank to purchase the failed bank. The FDIC, however, continues to guarantee that depositors won't lose any money. So many S&Ls and commercial banks failed in the 1980s and 1990s that the insurance funds maintained to guarantee deposits ran out of money, and the federal government had to make up the difference.

Money Creation

We saw in our analysis of the first banks, operated by goldsmiths, that money was created when the goldsmiths made loans. We'll see in this section that the money creation process hasn't changed: money is created when banks issue loans.

To understand the process of money creation, let's create a hypothetical system of banks. We'll focus on three banks in this system: Acme Bank, Bellville Bank, and Clarkston Bank. Assume that all banks are required to hold reserves equal to 10 percent of their checkable deposits. The quantity of reserves banks are required to hold is called **required reserves.** The reserve requirement is expressed as a **required reserve ratio;** it specifies the ratio of reserves to checkable deposits a bank must maintain. Banks may hold reserves in excess of the required level; such reserves are called **excess reserves.** Excess reserves plus required reserves equal total reserves.

Because banks don't earn interest on their holdings of reserves, we shall assume that they seek to hold no excess reserves. When a bank's excess reserves equal zero, it is **loaned up.** Finally, we shall ignore assets other than reserves and loans and deposits other than checkable deposits. To simplify the analysis further, we shall suppose that banks have no net worth.

- The quantity of reserves banks are required to hold is called **required reserves.**
- The **required reserve ratio** is the ratio of reserves to checkable deposits banks are required to maintain.
- Any reserves banks hold in excess of required reserves are called **excess reserves.**
- A bank is **loaned up** if it holds no excess reserves.

Money Creation in the Banking System

Let us suppose that every bank in our imaginary system begins with $1,000 in reserves, $9,000 in loans outstanding, and $10,000 in checkable deposit balances held by customers. The T-account for one of these banks, which is shown as AnyBank, is given in Exhibit 24-5. The required reserve ratio is 0.1: each bank must have reserves equal to 10 percent of its checkable deposits. Because reserves equal required reserves, excess reserves equal zero. Each bank is loaned up.

EXHIBIT 24-5

A T-Account for AnyBank

We assume that all banks in a hypothetical system of banks have $1,000 in reserves, $10,000 in checkable deposits, and $9,000 in loans. With a 10 percent reserve requirement, each bank is loaned up; it has zero excess reserves.

Any Bank, USA			
Assets		**Liabilities**	
Reserves	$1,000	Deposits	$10,000
Loans	$9,000		

Acme Bank, like every other bank in our system, starts out with the T-account balances given in Exhibit 24-5. Now suppose one of Acme Bank's customers deposits $1,000 in cash in a checking account. The money goes into the bank's vault and thus adds to reserves. The customer now has an additional $1,000 in his or her account. Two versions of Acme's T-account are given here. The first shows the changes brought by the customer's deposit: reserves and checkable deposits rise by $1,000. The second shows how these changes affect Acme's T-account balances. Reserves now equal $2,000 and checkable deposits equal $11,000. With checkable deposits of $11,000 and a 10 percent reserve requirement, Acme is required to hold reserves of $1,100. With reserves equaling $2,000, Acme has $900 in excess reserves.

At this stage, there has been no change in the money supply. When the customer brought in the $1,000 and Acme put the money in the vault, currency in circulation fell by $1,000. At the same time, the $1,000 was added to the customer's checking account balance, so the money supply did not change.

Acme Bank, Changes in T-Account				Acme Bank, T-Account to Date			
Assets		**Liabilities**		**Assets**		**Liabilities**	
Reserves	+ $1,000	Deposits	+ $1,000	Reserves	$2,000	Deposits	$11,000
				Loans	$9,000		
				(Excess reserves = $900)			

Acme earns no interest on its excess reserves; we assume it will try to loan them out. Suppose Acme lends the $900 to one of its customers. It will make the loan by crediting the customer's checking account with $900. Acme's loans outstanding and checkable deposits rise by $900. The $900 in checkable deposits is new money; Acme created it when it issued the $900 loan. Now you know where money comes from—it's created with a stroke of a pen, or a click of a computer key, when a bank issues a loan.

Acme Bank, Changes in T-Account				Acme Bank, T-Account to Date			
Assets		**Liabilities**		**Assets**		**Liabilities**	
Loans	+ $900	Deposits	+ $900	Reserves	$2,000	Deposits	$11,900
				Loans	$9,900		

Presumably, the customer who borrowed the $900 did so in order to spend it. That customer will write a check to someone else, who is likely to bank at some other bank. Suppose that Acme's borrower writes a check to a firm with an account at Bellville Bank. In this set of transactions, Acme's checkable deposits fall by $900. The firm that receives the check deposits it in its account at

Bellville Bank, increasing that bank's checkable deposits by $900. Bellville Bank now has a check written on an Acme account. Bellville will submit the check to the Fed, which will reduce Acme's deposits with the Fed—its reserves—by $900 and increase Bellville's by $900.

Acme Bank, Changes in T-Account				Acme Bank, T-Account to Date			
Assets		Liabilities		Assets		Liabilities	
Reserves	− $900	Deposits	− $900	Reserves	$1,100	Deposits	$11,000
				Loans	$9,900		

Bellville Bank, Changes in T-Account				Bellville Bank, T-Account to Date			
Assets		Liabilities		Assets		Liabilities	
Reserves	+ $900	Deposits	+ $900	Reserves	$1,900	Deposits	$10,900
				Loans	$9,000		
				(Excess reserves = $810)			

Notice that Acme Bank emerges from this round of transactions with $11,000 in checkable deposits and $1,100 in reserves. It has eliminated its excess reserves by issuing the loan for $900; Acme is now loaned up. Notice also that from Acme's point of view, it hasn't created any money! It merely took in a $1,000 deposit and emerged from the process with $1,000 in additional checkable deposits.

The $900 in new money Acme created when it issued a loan hasn't vanished—it's now in an account in Bellville Bank. Like the magician who shows the audience that the hat from which the rabbit appeared was empty, Acme can report that it hasn't created any money. That's because money is created within the banking system—not by a single bank.

The process of money creation won't end there. Let's go back to Bellville bank. Its deposits and reserves rose by $900 when the Acme check was deposited in a Bellville account. The $900 deposit required an increase in required reserves of $90. Because Bellville's reserves shot up by $900, it now has $810 in excess reserves. Just as Acme lent the amount of its excess reserves, we can expect Bellville to lend this $810. The next set of T-accounts shows the transaction. Bellville's loans and checkable deposits rise by $810.

Bellville Bank, Changes in T-Account				Bellville Bank, T-Account to Date			
Assets		Liabilities		Assets		Liabilities	
Loans	+ $810	Deposits	+ $810	Reserves	$1,900	Deposits	$11,710
				Loans	$9,810		

The $810 that Bellville lent will be spent. Let's suppose it ends up with a customer who banks at Clarkston Bank. Bellville's checkable deposits fall by $810; Clarkston's rise by the same amount. Clarkston submits the check to the Fed, which transfers the money from Bellville's reserve account to Clarkston's. Notice that Clarkston's deposits rise by $810; that requires an increase of $81 in its reserves. But its reserves have risen by $810, so it has excess reserves of $729.

Bellville Bank, Changes in T-Account				Bellville Bank, T-Account to Date			
Assets		**Liabilities**		**Assets**		**Liabilities**	
Reserves	− $810	Deposits	− $810	Reserves	$1,090	Deposits	$10,900
$10,900				Loans	$9,810		

Clarkston Bank, Changes in T-Account				Clarkston Bank, T-Account to Date			
Assets		**Liabilities**		**Assets**		**Liabilities**	
Reserves	+ $810	Deposits	+ $810	Reserves	$1,810	Deposits	$10,810
				Loans	$9,000		
				(Excess reserves = $729)			

Notice that Bellville is now loaned up. And notice that it hasn't created any money either! It took in a $900 deposit, and its checkable deposits have risen by that same $900. The $810 it created when it issued a loan is now at Clarkston Bank. There is a wonderful irony in the magic of money creation: banks create money when they issue loans, but no one bank ever seems to keep the money it creates. Money creation happens in the banking system, not in a single bank.

The process won't end there. Clarkston will lend the $729 it now has in excess reserves, and the money that's been created will end up at some other bank, which will then have excess reserves—and create still more money. How much will be created? With a 10 percent reserve requirement, each dollar in reserves backs up $10 in checkable deposits. The $1,000 in cash that Acme's customer brought in adds $1,000 in reserves to the banking system. It can therefore back up an additional $10,000! In just the three banks we've shown, checkable deposits have risen by $2,710 ($1,000 at Acme, $900 at Bellville, and $810 at Clarkston). Subtracting the original $1,000 that had been a part of currency in circulation, we have a net increase in the money supply of $9,000.

The Deposit Multiplier

We can relate the potential increase in the money supply to the change in reserves that created it using the **deposit multiplier (m_d)**, which equals the ratio of the maximum possible change in checkable deposits to the change in reserves. In our example, the deposit multiplier was 10.

$$m_d = \frac{\text{change in deposits}}{\text{change in reserves}} = \frac{\$10{,}000}{\$1{,}000} = 10 \qquad \textbf{(1)}$$

We can solve for the deposit multiplier using the required reserve ratio r. If banks in the economy are loaned up, then reserves R equal the required reserve ratio times checkable deposits D:

$$R = rD \qquad \textbf{(2)}$$

A change in reserves produces a change in loans and a change in checkable deposits. We shall use the Greek letter Δ (delta) to denote "change in." Once banks are fully loaned, the change in reserves, ΔR, will equal the required reserve ratio times the change in deposits, ΔD:

The **deposit multiplier (m_d)** equals the ratio of the maximum possible change in checkable deposits divided by the change in reserves that created it.

$$\Delta R = r\Delta D \qquad \textbf{(3)}$$

Solving for ΔD, we have

$$\Delta D = \frac{1}{r}\Delta R \tag{4}$$

The deposit multiplier is $1/r$; it is thus given by the reciprocal of the required reserve ratio. With a required reserve ratio of 0.1, the deposit multiplier is 10. A required reserve ratio of 0.2 would produce a deposit multiplier of 5. The higher the required reserve ratio, the lower the deposit multiplier.

Actual increases in checkable deposits won't be nearly as great as suggested by the deposit multiplier. That's because the artificial conditions of our example aren't met in the real world. Some banks hold excess reserves, customers withdraw cash, and some loan proceeds aren't spent. Each of these factors reduces the degree to which checkable deposits are affected by an increase in reserves. The basic mechanism, however, is the one described in our example, and it remains the case that checkable deposits increase by a multiple of an increase in reserves.

The entire process of money creation can work in reverse. When you withdraw cash from your bank, you reduce the bank's reserves. Just as a deposit at Acme Bank increases the money supply by a multiple of the original deposit, your withdrawal reduces the money supply by a multiple of the amount you withdraw. And just as money is created when banks issue loans, it is destroyed as the loans are repaid. A loan payment reduces checkable deposits; it thus reduces the money supply.

Suppose, for example, that the Acme Bank customer who borrowed the \$900 makes a \$100 payment on the loan. Only part of the payment will reduce the loan balance; part will be interest. Suppose \$30 of the payment is for interest, while the remaining \$70 reduces the loan balance. The effect of the payment on Acme's T-account is shown below. Checkable deposits fall by \$100, loans fall by \$70, and net worth rises by the amount of the interest payment, \$30.

Changes in Acme Bank's T-Account

Assets		Liabilities Plus Net Worth	
Loans	− \$70	Deposits	− \$100
		Net worth	+ \$ 30

Checklist

- Banks are financial intermediaries that also provide checking accounts for their customers.
- Banks include commercial banks, savings and loan institutions, mutual savings banks, and credit unions.
- The most important forms of bank regulation include the provision of deposit insurance, the requirement that banks maintain a given degree of net worth, and requirements for the reserves they must hold.
- Deposit insurance creates a potential moral hazard problem; this is one reason banks are so heavily regulated.
- Money is created within the banking system as banks issue loans; it is destroyed as the loans are repaid.
- An increase in reserves in the banking system can increase the money supply. The maximum amount of the increase is equal to the deposit multiplier times the change in reserves; the deposit multiplier equals the reciprocal of the required reserve ratio.

The Federal Reserve System

The Federal Reserve System of the United States, or Fed, is this country's central bank. A **central bank** performs four primary functions:

1. It acts as a banker to the central government.
2. It acts as a banker to banks.
3. It acts as a regulator of banks.
4. It sets monetary policy.

For the first 137 years of its history, the United States did not have a true central bank. While a central bank was often proposed, there was resistance to creating an institution with such enormous power. A series of bank panics, in which depositors lost confidence in their banks and rushed to withdraw their funds, slowly increased support for the idea that a central bank would be desirable. The bank panic of 1907 proved to be the final straw. Bank failures were so widespread, and depositor losses so heavy, that concerns about centralization of power gave way to a desire to create an institution that would be perceived to be a stabilizing force in the banking industry.

Congress passed the Federal Reserve Act in 1913, creating the Fed and giving it all the powers of a central bank.

Structure of the Fed

In creating the Fed, Congress determined that a central bank should be as independent of the government as possible. It also sought to avoid too much centralization of power in a single institution. These potentially contradictory goals of independence and decentralized power are evident in the Fed's structure and in the continuing struggles between Congress and the Fed over possible changes in that structure.

In an effort to decentralize power, the Fed was created as a system of 12 regional banks. Each of these banks operates as a kind of bankers' cooperative; the regional banks are owned by the commercial banks in their districts that have chosen to be members of the Fed. The owners of each Federal Reserve bank select the board of directors of that bank; the board selects the bank's president.

Several provisions of the Federal Reserve Act seek to maintain the Fed's independence. The board of directors for the entire Federal Reserve System is called the Board of Governors. The seven members of the Board are appointed by the president of the United States and confirmed by the Senate. To ensure a large measure of independence from any one president, the members of the Board of Governors serve 14-year terms. One member of the board is selected by the president of the United States to serve as chairperson for a 4-year term.

As a further means of ensuring the independence of the Fed, Congress authorized it to buy and sell federal government bonds. The expectation was that this would be a profitable activity, one that would allow the Fed to pay its own bills. The Fed wouldn't be dependent on a Congress tempted to force a particular set of policies on it.

It's important to recognize that the Fed is technically not part of the federal government. Members of the Board of Governors do not legally have to answer to Congress, the president, or anyone else. The president and members of Congress can certainly try to influence the Fed, but they can't order it to do anything.

A **central bank** oversees the banking system in a nation by acting as a banker to the central government and to other banks, by regulating banks, and by setting monetary policy.

Congress, however, created the Fed. It could, by passing another law, abolish the Fed's independence. The Fed can maintain its independence only by maintaining the support of Congress—and that sometimes requires being responsive to the wishes of Congress.

In recent years, Congress has sought to increase its own oversight of the Fed. The chairperson of the Federal Reserve Board is required to report to Congress twice each year on its **monetary policy,** the set of actions that manipulate the money supply and other variables that the central bank can influence.

Powers of the Fed

The Fed's principal powers stem from its role in conducting monetary policy. It can do this using three policy tools: setting reserve requirements, operating the discount window, and conducting open-market operations.

Reserve Requirements

It is the Fed that sets the required ratio of reserves to deposit liabilities. In theory, the Fed could use this power as an instrument of monetary policy. It could lower reserve requirements when it wished to increase the money supply and raise them when it wished to reduce the money supply. In practice, however, the Fed does not use its power to set reserve requirements in this way. That's because frequent manipulation of reserve requirements would make life difficult for bankers, who would have to adjust their lending policies to changing requirements.

The Fed's reluctance to tamper with reserve requirements has minimized changes in the required reserve ratio in recent years. The reserve requirement for checkable deposits was set at 3 and 12 percent in 1980; the requirement was reduced to 3 and 10 percent in 1992. The reduction wasn't announced as a stimulative measure. Instead, it was aimed at boosting bank profits. The 1992 reduction moved $9 billion in bank reserves from the required to the excess category, allowing banks to increase their lending and earn more profits. The Fed anticipated that bank profits would rise by between $300 million and $600 million as a result of the change. The Fed announced when it made the change that it wasn't attempting to increase the money supply, and that it would sell bonds if needed to prevent any increase in the money supply beyond its target range.

The Fed's power to set reserve requirements was expanded by the Monetary Control Act of 1980. Before that, the Fed set reserve requirements only for commercial banks that were members of the Federal Reserve System. Most banks aren't members of the Fed; the Fed's control of reserve requirements thus extended to only a minority of banks. The 1980 act required virtually all banks to satisfy the Fed's reserve requirements.

The Discount Window

One Fed responsibility is to act as a lender of last resort to banks. When banks fall short on reserves, they can borrow reserves from the Fed through its discount window. The **discount rate** is the interest rate charged by the Fed when it lends reserves to banks. It is set by the Board of Governors.

By lowering the discount rate, the Fed makes funds cheaper to banks; this could place downward pressure on interest rates in the economy. However, banks rarely borrow from the Fed, reserving use of the discount window for emergencies. A typical bank borrows only about once or twice per year.

- **Monetary policy** is the set of actions that manipulate the money supply and other variables that the central bank can influence.
- The **discount rate** is the interest rate the Fed charges to banks when it lends reserves to them.

Case in Point Making Money at the Fed

When the light flashes on Richard Kelly's Fed phone, he drops everything and listens. He's likely to hear something like this: "We're taking offerings of bills. Regular delivery. Click."

The message is from one of the traders at the New York Fed's trading desk. It means that the Fed is buying short-term federal securities such as 3-month Treasury bills.

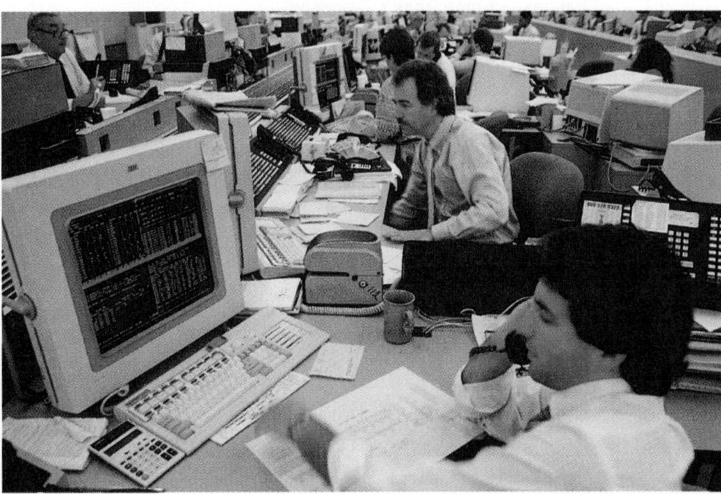

Mr. Kelly is a bond dealer at Aubrey Lanston & Company in New York. Lanston is one of about four dozen primary dealers who will receive the call. The New York Fed tries to reach all of them in the space of a minute to avoid giving any one dealer an advantage in responding to the Fed's call for offers.

Once he gets the message, Mr. Kelly will let his fellow dealers at Lanston know what happened: "The Fed's in!" he'll shout. Dealers at Lanston will quickly get on the phone and canvass the firm's major customers to see if anyone wants to sell federal government securities to the Fed. Those interested in selling will list the securities they have to sell and the prices they'll accept. Lanston will have only a couple of hours to assemble a list of offers to sell; then the firm submits it to the Fed. Traders at the Open Market Desk compare offers submitted by the primary dealers and take the best ones. When the Fed is "in," it typically purchases about $8 billion in federal securities. The transactions will be completed, and money deposited in the sellers' accounts, by the end of the day.

Source: Timothy Tregarthen, "Making Money at the Fed," *The Margin* 2(3) (March 1987): 10–11.

Instead of borrowing from the Fed when they need reserves, banks typically rely on the federal funds market to obtain reserves. The **federal funds market** is a market in which banks lend reserves to one another. The **federal funds rate** is the interest rate charged for such loans; it is determined by demand and supply in the market. As the federal funds market has grown in importance, the Fed has tended to adjust the discount rate to the federal funds rate. The ability to set the discount rate is no longer an important tool of Federal Reserve policy.

Open-Market Operations

The Fed's ability to buy and sell federal government securities has proved to be its most important policy tool. Such transactions are called **open-market operations.** When the Fed buys or sells government bonds, it adds or subtracts reserves from the banking system. Such changes affect the money supply and interest rates.

Suppose the Fed buys a government bond in the open market. It writes a check on its own account to the seller of the bond. When the seller deposits the check at a bank, the bank submits the check to the Fed for payment. The Fed "pays" the check by crediting the bank's account at the Fed, so the bank has more reserves.

The Fed's purchase of a bond can be illustrated using a T-account. Suppose the Fed buys a bond for $1,000 from one of Acme Bank's customers. When that customer deposits the check at Acme, checkable deposits will rise by $1,000.

- The **federal funds market** is a market in which banks lend reserves to one another.
- The **federal funds rate** is the rate of interest charged for reserves in the federal funds market.
- **Open-market operations** are transactions in which the Fed buys or sells federal government securities.

The check is written on the Federal Reserve System; the Fed will credit Acme's account. Acme's reserves thus rise by $1,000. With a 10 percent reserve requirement, that will create $900 in excess reserves and set off the same process of money expansion as did the cash deposit we've already examined. The difference is that the Fed's purchase of a bond created new reserves with the stroke of a pen, where the cash deposit created them by removing $1,000 from currency in circulation. The purchase of the $1,000 bond by the Fed could thus increase the money supply by as much as $10,000, the maximum expansion suggested by the deposit multiplier.

Changes in Acme Bank's T-Account

Assets		Liabilities Plus Net Worth	
Reserves	+$1,000	Deposits	+$1,000

Where does the Fed get the $1,000 to purchase the bond? It simply creates the money when it writes the check to purchase the bond. On the Fed's T-account, assets increase by $1,000 because the Fed now has the bond; bank deposits with the Fed, which represent a liability to the Fed, rise by $1,000 as well.

When the Fed sells a bond, it gives the buyer a federal government bond it had previously purchased and accepts a check in exchange. The bank on which the check was written will find its deposit with the Fed reduced by the amount of the check. That bank's reserves and checkable deposits will fall by equal amounts; the reserves, in effect, disappear. The result is a reduction in the money supply.

Exhibit 24-6 suggests how the Fed influences the flow of money in the economy. Funds flow from the public—individuals and firms—to banks as deposits. Banks use those funds to make loans to the public—to individuals and firms. The Fed can influence the volume of bank lending by buying bonds and thus injecting reserves into the system. With new reserves, banks will increase their lending, which creates still more deposits and still more lending as the deposit multiplier goes to work. Alternatively, the Fed can sell bonds. When it does that, reserves flow out of the system, reducing bank lending and reducing deposits.

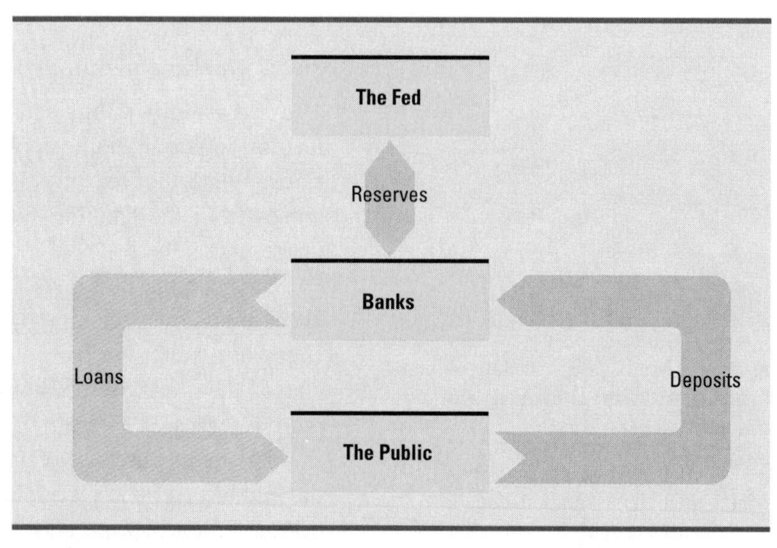

EXHIBIT 24-6

The Fed and the Flow of Money in the Economy

Individuals and firms (the public) make deposits in banks; banks make loans to individuals and firms. The Fed can buy bonds to inject new reserves into the system, thus increasing bank lending, which creates new deposits, and creating still more lending as the deposit multiplier goes to work. Alternatively, the Fed can sell bonds, withdrawing reserves from the system, thus reducing bank lending and reducing total deposits.

The Fed's purchase or sale of bonds is conducted by the Open Market Desk at the Federal Reserve Bank of New York, one of the 12 district banks. Traders at the Open Market Desk are guided by policy directives issued by the Federal Open Market Committee (FOMC). The FOMC consists of the 7 members of the Board of Governors plus 5 regional bank presidents. The president of the New York Federal Reserve Bank serves as a member of the FOMC; the other 11 bank presidents take turns filling the remaining 4 seats.

The FOMC meets 8 times per year to chart the Fed's monetary policies. Traditionally, FOMC meetings have been closed, with no report of the committee's action until the release of the minutes 6 weeks after the meeting. Faced with pressure to open its proceedings, the Fed began in 1994 issuing a report of the decisions of the FOMC immediately after each meeting.

Checklist

- The Fed, the central bank of the United States, acts as a bank for other banks and for the federal government. It also regulates banks and sets monetary policy.
- The Fed is largely independent of the president and Congress, but the political reality is that it must be sensitive to their wishes.
- The Fed sets reserve requirements and the discount rate and conducts open-market operations. Of these tools of monetary policy, open-market operations are the most important.
- The Fed creates new reserves and new money when it purchases bonds. It destroys reserves and thus reduces the money supply when it sells bonds.

A Look Back—And a Look Ahead

In this chapter we investigated the money supply and looked at how it is determined. We began by noting that a change in the quantity of money can be expected to shift the aggregate demand curve. It could thus affect real GDP and the price level.

Money is anything that serves as a medium of exchange. Whatever serves as money also functions as a unit of account and as a store of value. There are four types of money: commodity money, convertible paper money, fiat money, and debt money.

In the United States, currency in circulation, traveler's checks, and checkable deposits serve as media of exchange. The total of currency in circulation, traveler's checks, and checkable deposits equals M1. Another measure of the money supply, M2, adds most savings accounts, small time deposits, and other assets that are highly liquid but less liquid than those in M1. M2 is the measure of the money supply used in this text.

Banks are institutions that accept deposits, provide checking services, and issue loans. Banks create money when they issue loans. The ability of banks to issue loans is controlled by their reserves. Reserves comprise cash in bank vaults and bank deposits with the Fed. Historically, banks have always operated in a fractional reserve system; that is, they maintain reserves equal to only a small fraction of their deposit liabilities.

The 1980s was a decade of tremendous change in the structure of banking, changes that made different types of banks much more alike—and more directly competitive for the funds on which they base their operations. Unfortunately, many of these regulatory changes produced a situation that led to widespread bank failures, mostly among savings and loan institutions. Many of these failures were encouraged by the moral hazard problem created by deposit insurance. One reason for bank regulation is to offset the tendency of moral hazard to create more bank failures.

A bank that serves as a bank for banks, a regulator of banks, a manager of the money supply, and a bank for a nation's government is known as a central bank. The Federal Reserve System was created in 1913 as a central bank for the

United States. The Fed is a privately owned bank governed by a Board of Governors whose members are appointed by the president of the United States, subject to confirmation by the Senate.

The Fed can lend reserves to banks through the discount window, change reserve requirements, and engage in purchases and sales of federal government bonds in the open market. Decisions about those latter actions are made by the Federal Open Market Committee (FOMC); the Fed's open-market operations represent its primary tool for influencing the money supply. Fed purchases of bonds initially increase the reserves of banks by an amount equal to the value of the bonds purchased. The overall economic impact of the purchase, however, is greater. With excess reserves on hand, banks will attempt to increase their loans, and in the process the money supply will change by an amount equal to the money multiplier times the change in reserves. Similarly, the Fed can reduce the money supply by selling bonds.

This chapter has established the basic mechanics of the monetary system. It has also suggested that what happens to the money supply will have important macroeconomic effects. In the next chapter we'll use the model of aggregate demand and aggregate supply to explore in greater detail how changes in the money supply affect the economy.

Terms and Concepts for Review

Assets
Bank
Barter system
Central bank
Check
Checkable deposit
Commodity money
Convertible paper money
Currency
Deposit multiplier
Discount rate
Excess reserves
Federal funds market
Federal funds rate
Fiat money
Financial intermediary
Fractional reserve banking system
Liabilities
Liquidity
Loaned up
M1
M2
M3
Medium of exchange
Monetary policy
Money
Money supply
Moral hazard
Net worth
Open-market operations
Private debt money
Required reserve ratio
Required reserves
Reserves
T-account
Unit of account

For Discussion

1. Airlines have "frequent flier" clubs in which customers accumulate miles according to the number of miles they have flown with the airline. Frequent flier miles can then be used to purchase other flights, to rent cars, or to stay in some hotels. Are frequent flier miles money?

2. Consider the following example of bartering:

1 10-ounce T-bone steak can be traded for 5 soft drinks.

1 soft drink can be traded for 10 apples.

100 apples can be traded for a T-shirt.

5 T-shirts can be exchanged for 1 textbook.

It takes 4 textbooks to get 1 VCR.

a. How many 10-ounce T-bone steaks could you exchange for 1 textbook? How many soft drinks? How many apples?

b. State the price of T-shirts in terms of apples, textbooks, and soft drinks.

c. Why do you think we use money as a unit of account?

3. Debit cards allow an individual to directly transfer funds in a checkable account to a merchant without writing a check. How is this different from the way credit cards work? Are either credit cards or debit cards money? Explain.

4. Many colleges now have special cards students can use to purchase everything from textbooks or meals in the cafeteria to use of washing machines in the dorm. Students deposit money in their cards; as they use their cards for purchases, electronic scanners remove money from the cards. To replenish a card's money, a student makes a cash deposit that is credited to the card. Would these cards count as part of the money supply?

5. The Case in Point on page 511 describes a new financial instrument, the electronic purse. Suppose such purses come into widespread use. Present your views on the following issues:

a. Would you count balances in the purses as part of the money supply? If so, would they be part of M1? M2? M3?

b. Should any institution be permitted to issue electronic purses, or should they be restricted to banks?

c. Should the issuers of electronic purses be subject to reserve requirements?

d. Suppose electronic purses are issued by banks. How do you think the use of such purses would affect the money supply? Explain your answer carefully.

e. What's your position on the anonymity issue raised in the essay? Should the issuers of electronic purses record the transactions as credit card transactions are recorded, or should the transactions go unrecorded, as cash transactions?

6. When the Fed enters the bond market to purchase bonds, what do you predict will happen to the interest rate in the bond market? Beyond the impact on the money supply itself and based on your reading of Chapter 23, what other changes in the economy do you predict might be caused as a result of this action?

7. When the Fed reduced the maximum required reserve ratio on checkable deposits from 0.12 to 0.10, it indicated that it would undertake open-market operations as needed to ensure that the money supply would not be affected by this measure. Bond prices fell when this announcement was made. Why do you suppose that happened?

8. Which of the following items is part of M1? M2?

a. 27 cents that has accumulated under a couch cushion

b. Your $2,000 line of credit with your Visa account

c. The $210 balance in your checking account

d. $417 in your savings account

e. 10 shares of stock your uncle gave you on your eighteenth birthday, which are now worth $520

f. $200 in traveler's checks you have purchased for your spring break trip

g. A $5,000 certificate of deposit that will mature in time to make your tuition payment next fall

9. The text claims that car insurance increases the number of accidents. Can that be true? Why?

10. The goldsmith in the example in the text seemed to be pulling something of a fast one in issuing receipts for nonexistent gold. Who benefited from the goldsmith's action?

Problems

1. Assume that the banking system is fully loaned up and that any open-market purchase by the Fed directly increases reserves in the banks. If the required reserve ratio is 0.2, by how much could the money supply expand if the Fed purchased $2 billion worth of bonds?

2. Suppose the Fed sells $5 million worth of bonds to Econobank.

a. What happens to the reserves of the bank?

b. What happens to the money supply in the economy as a whole if the reserve requirement is 10 percent, all payments are made by check, and there is no net drain into currency?

c. How would your answer in part (b) be affected if you knew that some people involved in the money creation process kept some of their funds as cash?

3. A $1,000 deposit in Acme Bank has increased reserves by $1,000. A loan officer at Acme reasons as follows: "The reserve requirement is 10 percent. That means that the $1,000 in new reserves can back $10,000 in checkable deposits. Therefore I'll loan an additional $10,000." Is there any problem with the loan officer's reasoning?

4. If half the banks in the nation borrow additional reserves totaling $10 million at the Fed discount window, and at the same time the other half of the banks reduce their excess reserves by a total of $10 million, what is likely to happen to the money supply? Explain.

5. Suppose a bank with a 10 percent reserve requirement has $10 million in reserves and $100 million in checkable deposits, and a major corporation makes a deposit of $1 million. Explain how the deposit affects the bank's reserves and checkable deposits. By how much will the bank increase its lending?

25

Money and the Economy

Chapter Objectives

After mastering the material in this chapter, you will be able to:

1. Explain the meaning of the equation of exchange—the equation that relates the supply of money to the level of nominal GDP.
2. Explain the concept of the demand for money and how this demand affects the relationship between money and the economy.
3. Explain the motives for holding money.
4. Explain why the quantity of money demanded varies negatively with the interest rate and discuss other determinants of the demand for money.
5. Relate changes in the money supply to changes in the equilibrium interest rate.
6. Relate changes in the money supply to changes in aggregate demand, the price level, and real GDP.

But it is pretty to see what money can do.

Samuel Pepys, *Diary,* 1667

What's Ahead

It's July 1979. With inflation approaching 14 percent and interest rates on 3-month Treasury bills soaring past 10 percent, a desperate President Jimmy Carter takes action. He appoints Paul Volcker, the president of the New York Federal Reserve Bank, as chairman of the Fed's Board of Governors. Mr. Volcker makes clear that his objective as chairman will be to bring down the inflation rate—no matter what the consequences for the economy. Mr. Carter gives this effort his full support.

Mr. Volcker wastes no time in putting his policies to work. He slows the rate of money growth immediately. The economy's response is swift; the United States slips into a brief recession in 1980, followed by a crushing recession in 1981–1982. In terms of their goal of reducing inflation, Mr. Volcker's monetary policies are a dazzling success: inflation plunges below a 4 percent rate within 3 years; by 1986 the inflation rate falls to 1.1 percent. The tall, bald, cigar-smoking Mr. Volcker emerges as a folk hero in the fight against inflation. Mr. Carter is not so lucky; he emerges as a former president, losing the 1980 presidential election to Ronald Reagan.

The Fed's 7-year fight against inflation illustrates an important point: changes in the money supply can have powerful effects on the economy. In this chapter we'll see why.

The chapter begins with an overview of the relationship between money and nominal GDP. We'll find that the ability of changes in the money supply to influence economic activity depends on what factors determine the demand for money—the quantity of money people and firms wish to hold. We'll examine in detail the factors that influence money demand, paying particular attention to the role of interest rates.

We'll then turn to an examination of the interaction of demand and supply in the market for money. We'll utilize our model of aggregate demand and aggregate supply to explore the impact that changes in this market have on the economy. We'll see that changes in the market for money can affect aggregate demand—which can lead to changes in real GDP and the price level.

Money and Economic Activity

Money, the song says, makes the world go around. The world would probably continue to revolve without it, but money certainly helps the economy to function. Changes in the quantity of money can also affect real GDP and the price level. This section presents an overview of the link between money and economic activity.

We shall explore the relationship between money and the economy in the context of an equation that relates the money supply to nominal GDP. We'll use this equation to develop a framework for understanding the concept of the demand for money. We'll use that framework to see the ways in which the demand for money affects the relationship between money and economic activity.

The Equation of Exchange

We can relate the money supply to economic activity by using the **equation of exchange.** It states that the money supply M times its velocity V equals nominal GDP. **Velocity** is the number of times the money supply is spent to obtain the goods and services that make up GDP during a particular time period.

We saw in Chapter 22 that the implicit price deflator P equals nominal GDP divided by real GDP (Y). It follows that nominal GDP equals the price level (the implicit price deflator) times real GDP. Letting P equal the price level and Y equal real GDP, we can write the equation of exchange as

$$MV = PY \quad \textbf{(1)}$$

Let's apply the concept of the equation of exchange to a hypothetical economy that consists of 50 people, each of whom has a car. Each person has \$10 in cash and no other money. The money supply of this economy is thus \$500. Now suppose that the sole economic activity in this economy is car washing. Each person in the economy washes one other person's car once a month, and the price of a car wash is \$10. In one month, then, a total of 50 car washes are produced at a price of \$10 each. During that month, the money supply is spent once.

Applying the equation of exchange to this economy, we have a money supply M of \$500 and a velocity V of 1. Because the only good or service produced is car washing, we can measure real GDP as the number of car washes. Thus Y equals 50 car washes. The price level P is the price of a car wash: \$10. The equation of exchange for a period of 1 month is

$$\$500(1) = (\$10)50 \quad \textbf{(2)}$$

Now suppose that in the second month everyone washes someone else's car again. Over the full 2-month period, the money supply has been spent twice—the velocity over a period of 2 months is 2. The total output in the economy is \$1,000—100 car washes have been produced over a 2-month period at a price of \$10 each. Inserting these values into the equation of exchange, we have

$$\$500(2) = (\$10)100 \quad \textbf{(3)}$$

Let's suppose this process continues for 1 more month. For the 3-month period, the money supply of \$500 has been spent 3 times, for a velocity of 3. We have

$$\$500(3) = (\$10)150 \quad \textbf{(4)}$$

- The **equation of exchange** states that the money supply times its velocity equals nominal GDP.
- The **velocity** of money is the number of times the money supply is spent for the goods and services that make up GDP during a particular period.

The essential thing to see about the equation of exchange is that it *always* holds. That should come as no surprise. The left side, MV, gives the money supply times the number of times that money is spent during a period. It thus measures total spending. The right side gives nominal GDP. But that is a measure of total spending as well. Nominal GDP is the value of all goods and services produced during a particular period. Those goods and services are either sold or added to inventory. If they're sold, then they must be part of total spending. If they're added to inventory, then some firm must have either purchased them or paid for their production; they thus represent a portion of total spending. In effect, the equation of exchange says simply that total spending measured as MV equals total spending, measured as PY (or nominal GDP). The equation of exchange is thus an identity, a mathematical expression that is true by definition.

The equation of exchange provides us with an extremely useful framework for thinking about the relationship between the money supply and economic activity. We've applied the equation to a hypothetical economy that produces only car washes; let's see how the equation applies to the U.S. economy.

To apply the equation of exchange to a real economy, we need measures of each of the variables in it. Three of these variables are readily available. The Department of Commerce reports the implicit price deflator and real GDP. The Federal Reserve Board reports M2, the money supply. For 1994, the values of these variables were

$$M = \$3{,}600.0 \text{ billion}$$

$$P = 1.261$$

$$Y = \$5{,}344.0 \text{ billion}$$

To solve for the velocity of money V, we divide both sides of equation (1) by M:

$$V = \frac{PY}{M} \tag{5}$$

Using the data for 1994 to compute velocity, we get

$$V = \frac{1.261 \times \$5{,}344.0}{\$3{,}600.0}$$

$$V = 1.87$$

A velocity of 1.87 means that the money supply was spent 1.87 times in the purchase of goods and services in 1994.

You may recall that you've already seen estimates of velocity in the previous chapter. As a test for the measure of money that most closely corresponds to nominal GDP, we compared the ratio of GDP to each of the three measures of the money supply: M1, M2, and M3. We found that ratio to be most stable for M2. That ratio is velocity. One reason for using M2 as the measure of the money supply, then, is that in the past its velocity has been relatively stable. Between 1960 and 1995, it averaged 1.61.

We'll see in the next section that the velocity of money plays a crucial role in linking the money supply to the level of economic activity. We'll find that it's not the level of velocity that's so important; it's the way velocity changes over time. Changes in velocity affect the way in which money and other factors influence economic activity.

Velocity and the Demand for Money

We can recast the equation of exchange as an equation for the demand for money. The **demand for money** is the relationship between the quantity of money people want to hold and the factors that determine that quantity. These factors include the interest rate, preferences, expectations, and the liquidity of nonmoney assets.

At first glance, the concept of the demand for money may seem rather odd; the amount of money people want to hold is, surely, *more*. When economists speak of the demand for money, however, they are examining money as one means of holding wealth. There are lots of other ways to hold wealth—it can be held as stocks, bonds, gold, real estate, collections of rare objects, or any of a variety of other things. In examining the demand for money, economists explore how much of their wealth people choose to hold as money. The demand for money thus represents a choice concerning how much money to hold, given the level of wealth people have. In general, people hold money because it's useful for purchasing goods and services. Money may also be considered safer than other assets; its nominal value doesn't fluctuate as do the values of such things as stocks, bonds, or gold.

The quantity of money people hold varies significantly from one day to the next. Each time you make a purchase or are paid for something, the quantity of money you hold changes. For that reason, economists think of the demand for money as representing the *average* quantity of money people wish to hold over a particular time period.

We can gain some insight about the demand for money and its significance by rearranging terms in the equation of exchange. If we multiply both sides of Equation 1 by the reciprocal of velocity, $1/V$, we have this equation for money demand:

$$M = \frac{1}{V}(PY) \tag{6}$$

The equation of exchange can thus be rewritten as an equation that expresses the demand for money as a fraction, $1/V$, of nominal GDP. With a velocity of 1.87, for example, people wish to hold a quantity of money equal to 53 percent (1/1.87) of nominal GDP.

If people wished to hold a quantity of money equal to a larger fraction of nominal GDP, velocity would be a smaller number. Suppose, for example, that people held a quantity of money equal to 80 percent of nominal GDP. That would imply a velocity of 1.25. If people held a quantity of money equal to a smaller fraction of nominal GDP, velocity would be a larger number. If people held a quantity of money equal to 25 percent of nominal GDP, for example, the velocity would be 4.

Money, Velocity, and Nominal GDP

The equation of exchange and the money demand equation we derived from it suggest the importance of an investigation of the demand for money. To see that, let's make an assumption that will turn out to be false. Suppose the quantity of money people demand is a constant fraction, $1/V$, of nominal GDP. People will demand more or less money in response to an increase or a decrease in nominal GDP, but nothing else will change the quantity of money demanded. If $1/V$ were

The **demand for money** is the relationship between the quantity of money people want to hold and the factors that determine that quantity.

a constant, then V, the velocity, would be a constant. We shall express a constant velocity as $\overline{V}$. Our equation of exchange is now written as

$$M\overline{V} = PY \tag{7}$$

A constant value for velocity would have two important implications:

1. Nominal GDP could change *only* if there were a change in the money supply. Other kinds of changes, such as a change in government purchases or a change in investment, could have no effect on nominal GDP.
2. A change in M2 would always change nominal GDP, and by an equal percentage.

In short, if velocity were constant, a course in macroeconomics would be quite simple. The quantity of money would determine nominal GDP; nothing else would matter. As it turns out, velocity isn't constant; it varies significantly from one period to the next. Exhibit 25-1 shows annual values of the velocity of M2 from 1960 through the first half of 1995. Velocity is not constant, so other factors must affect economic activity. We've learned that any change in velocity implies a change in the demand for money. In the next section we'll explore the demand for money in more detail.

EXHIBIT 25-1

The Velocity of M2, 1960–1995

The annual velocity of M2 varied about an average of 1.61 between 1960 and the first half of 1995.

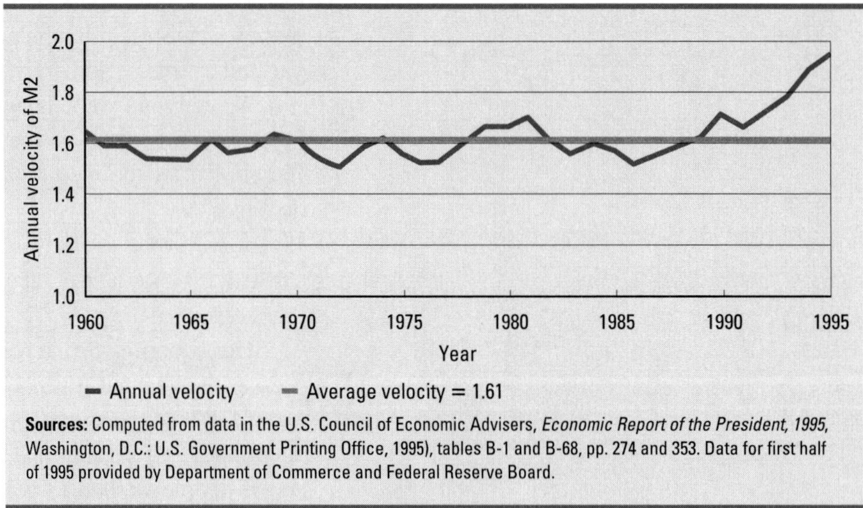

Sources: Computed from data in the U.S. Council of Economic Advisers, *Economic Report of the President, 1995,* Washington, D.C.: U.S. Government Printing Office, 1995), tables B-1 and B-68, pp. 274 and 353. Data for first half of 1995 provided by Department of Commerce and Federal Reserve Board.

Checklist

- The quantity of money times its velocity equals nominal GDP.
- Money is one form in which people can hold wealth; the demand for money relates the quantity of wealth people will hold as money to factors that determine that demand.
- The quantity of money people hold can be expressed as a fraction of nominal GDP. That fraction is the reciprocal of velocity.
- If velocity were constant, nominal GDP could change only if the quantity of money changed, and changes in the quantity of money would necessarily produce changes in nominal GDP.
- Velocity is variable if the quantity of money people demand, expressed as a fraction of nominal GDP, is variable.

Determinants of the Demand for Money

We've seen that the velocity of M2 varies, and that changes in velocity imply changes in the demand for money. In this section we'll examine the demand for money more carefully. As we learn what factors influence the demand for money, we'll be learning what factors influence velocity.

In deciding how much money to hold, people make a choice about how to hold their wealth. How much wealth shall be held as money and how much as other assets? For a given amount of wealth, the answer to this question will depend on the relative costs and benefits of holding money versus other assets.

To simplify our analysis, we will assume there are only two ways to hold wealth: as money in an M2 account (such as a checking account or savings account) or in a bond market mutual fund that purchases long-term bonds on behalf of its subscribers. Most M2 accounts earn interest, but the return on these accounts is generally lower than what could be obtained in a bond fund. The advantage of M2 accounts is that they are highly liquid and can thus be easily spent. We shall think of the demand for money as a curve that represents the outcomes of choices between the greater liquidity of an M2 account and the higher interest rates that can be earned by holding a bond fund. The difference between the interest rates paid on M2 deposits and the interest return available from bonds is the cost of holding money.

Motives for Holding Money

One reason people hold their assets as money is so that they can purchase goods and services. The money held for the purchase of goods and services may be for everyday transactions such as buying groceries or paying the rent, or it may be kept on hand for contingencies such as having the funds available to pay to have the car fixed or to pay for a trip to the doctor. Still another reason people hold money was suggested by John Maynard Keynes; he noted that people may hold money because they expect other assets to decline in value.

Transactions Demand

The **transactions demand** for money is money people hold to make anticipated purchases of goods and services. When you carry money in your purse or wallet to go to a movie, you are holding the money as part of your transactions demand for money.

Precautionary Demand

The money people hold for contingencies represents their **precautionary demand** for money. Money held for precautionary purposes may include money kept for possible home repairs or health care needs. People don't know precisely when the need for such expenditures will occur, but they can prepare for them by holding money so that they'll have it available when the need arises.

- The **transactions demand** for money is the money households and firms hold in order to pay for goods and services they buy.
- The **precautionary demand** for money is the money people and firms hold for contingencies that people expect will occur, but at an uncertain time and in an uncertain amount.

Speculative Demand

Bond prices fluctuate constantly. As a result, holders of bonds not only earn interest but experience gains or losses in the value of their assets. Bondholders enjoy gains when bond prices are rising and suffer losses when bond prices fall. Because of this, expectations play an important role as a determinant of the

Case in Point: Betting on a Plunge

Managers of some of the world's largest investment funds shifted from bonds to money in 1993. Betting that interest rates on long-term bonds were headed up—that is, that bond prices were headed down—they sold bonds.

William Gross, a managing director of Pacific Investment Managing Co., which manages $45 billion in Treasury bonds, told *The Wall Street Journal* that his firm had sold roughly $500 million in long-term bonds over a 3-day period. The sale represented about 5 percent of the firm's holdings of long-term Treasury bonds. Mr. Gross said it was the first time in several years that his firm had sold such a large amount of securities. The proceeds of the sales, he said, were being held in cash.

Mr. Gross wasn't the only fund manager betting on a plunge in long-term bond prices. John Templeton, who directs the management of several funds with a total of $23 billion in assets, said his firm was unloading long-term bonds as well: "For many months we have not held as many long bonds as usual. In general, we have felt that this very long bull market in bonds must be somewhere near its end." (A bull market is one in which prices are rising.)

These money managers expected bond prices to fall and responded by shifting the funds they manage toward greater holdings of money and less of bonds. They were sacrificing the higher returns available from bonds for the greater safety of money. With billions of dollars involved, the gamble was a huge one.

Did the gamble pay off? Bond prices continued to rise during the remainder of 1993, and it began to appear that selling bonds had been a bad mistake. But then bond prices plunged sharply early in 1994–and the sudden drop left many bondholders, and holders of assets linked to bonds, in dire straits. Orange County, California, had invested its funds in bonds and derivatives whose values would rise or fall with bond prices—and the county declared bankruptcy. The decision to convert assets to money was looking like a very smart move, indeed.

Source: Warren Getler and Thomas T. Vogel, Jr., "Some Heavy Hitters Go Light on Bonds," *The Wall Street Journal*, 5 May 1993, C1.

demand for bonds, as we saw in Chapter 23. Holding bonds is one alternative to holding money, so these same expectations can affect the demand for money.

Keynes, who was an enormously successful speculator in bond markets himself, suggested that bondholders who anticipate a drop in bond prices will try to sell their bonds ahead of the price drop in order to avoid this loss in asset value. Selling a bond means converting it to money. Keynes called money held in response to concern that bond prices and the prices of other financial assets might fall the **speculative demand** for money.

Of course, money is money. One can't sort through someone's checking account and find what funds are held for transactions and what funds are there because the owner of the account is worried about a drop in bond prices. We distinguish money held for different motives in order to understand how the quantity of money demanded will be affected by a key determinant of the demand for money: the interest rate.

Interest Rates and the Demand for Money

The quantity of money people hold to pay for transactions and to satisfy precautionary and speculative demand is likely to vary with the interest rates they can earn from alternative assets such as bonds. When interest rates rise relative to the rates that can be earned in M2 accounts, people hold less money. When interest rates fall, people hold more money. The logic underlying these conclusions about the money people hold and interest rates depends on the people's motives for holding money.

The **speculative demand** for money is the money households and firms hold because of a concern that bond prices and the prices of other financial assets might fall.

Transactions and Precautionary Demand and Interest Rates

Money held as part of the transactions and precautionary demand is money households intend to spend. The quantity they hold will therefore vary with the level of spending they anticipate. It will also vary with the interest rate.

The essential thing to see about the relationship between the transactions and precautionary demands for money is that a given level of spending can be maintained while holding different average quantities of money.

Suppose, for example, that a household earns and spends $3,000 per month. It spends an equal amount of money each day. For a month with 30 days, that's $100 per day. One way the household could manage this spending, would be to leave the money in a checking account, which we'll assume pays zero interest. The household would thus have $3,000 in the checking account when the month begins, $2,900 at the end of the first day, $1,500 halfway through the month, and zero at the end of the last day of the month. Averaging the daily balances, we find that the quantity of money the household demands equals $1,500. This approach to money management, which we'll call the "cash approach," has the virtue of simplicity, but the household will earn no interest on its funds.

Consider an alternative money management approach that permits the same pattern of spending. At the beginning of the month, the household deposits $1,000 in its checking account and the other $2,000 in a bond fund. Assume the bond fund pays 1 percent interest per month, or an annual interest rate of 12.7 percent. After 10 days, the money in the checking account is exhausted, and the household withdraws another $1,000 for the next 10 days. On the 20th day, the final $1,000 from the bond fund goes into the checking account. With this strategy, the household has an average daily balance of $500, which is the quantity of money it demands. Let's call this money management strategy the "bond fund" approach.

Remember that both money management strategies allow the household to spend $3,000 per month, $100 per day. The cash approach requires a quantity of money demanded of $1,500, while the bond fund approach lowers this quantity to $500.

The bond fund approach generates some interest income. The household has $1,000 in the fund for 10 days (1/3 of a month) and $1,000 for 20 days (2/3 of a month). With an interest rate of 1 percent per month, the household earns $10 in interest each month [($1,000 × 0.01 × 1/3) + ($1,000 × 0.01 × 2/3)]. The disadvantage of the bond fund, of course, is that it requires more attention—$1,000 must be transferred from the fund twice each month. There may also be fees associated with the transfers.

Of course, the bond fund strategy we've examined here is just one of many. The household could begin each month with $1,500 in the checking account and $1,500 in the bond fund, transferring $1,500 to the checking account midway through the month. This strategy requires one less transfer, but it also generates less interest—$7.50 (= $1,500 × 0.01 × 1/2). With this strategy, the household demands a quantity of money of $750. The household could also maintain a much smaller average quantity of money in its checking account and keep more in its bond fund. For simplicity, we can think of any strategy that involves transferring money in and out of a bond fund or another interest-earning asset as a bond fund strategy.

Which approach should the household use? That's a choice each household must make—it's a question of weighing the interest a bond fund strategy creates against the hassle and possible fees associated with the transfers it requires. Our example doesn't yield a clear-cut choice for any one household, but we can make some generalizations about its implications. First, a household is more likely to adopt a bond fund strategy when the interest rate is higher. At low interest rates, a household doesn't sacrifice much income by pursuing the simpler cash strategy. As the interest rate rises, a bond fund strategy becomes more attractive. That means that the higher the interest rate, the lower the quantity of money demanded. Second, people are more likely to use a bond strategy when the cost of transferring funds is lower. The creation in the 1970s and 1980s of savings plans that allowed easy transfer of funds between interest-earning assets and checkable deposits tended to reduce the demand for money. We saw in Chapter 24 that the creation of bond funds that allow easy transfer of funds into checking accounts has reduced the quantity of M2 demanded.

Some M2 accounts, such as savings accounts and money market deposit accounts, pay interest. In evaluating the choice between holding assets as M2 or in other forms such as bonds, households will look at the differential between what those funds pay and what they could earn in the bond market. A higher interest rate in the bond market is likely to increase this differential; a lower interest rate will reduce it. An increase in the spread between rates on M2 accounts and the interest rate in the bond market reduces the quantity of money demanded; a reduction in the spread increases the quantity of money demanded.

An illustration of the impact of a change in the spread between rates on non-M2 assets and assets that are part of M2 is provided by the experience of 1994. Early in 1994, interest rates on long-term bonds rose sharply while interest rates on very short-term bonds hardly changed. Funds in money market deposit accounts and money market mutual funds, which are part of M2, are typically invested in short-term bonds. But bond funds, which aren't counted as part of M2, are typically invested in longer-term securities. As interest rates in bond funds rose relative to those in money market deposit accounts and money market mutual funds, the quantity of money demanded fell.

Speculative Demand and Interest Rates

When investors believe that the prices of bonds and other assets will fall, their speculative demand for money goes up. The speculative demand for money thus depends on expectations about future changes in asset prices. Will this demand also be affected by present interest rates?

If interest rates are low, bond prices are high. It seems likely that as bond prices rise, investors will become concerned that bond prices might fall. That suggests that high bond prices—low interest rates—would increase the quantity of money held for speculative purposes. Conversely, if bond prices are already relatively low, it's likely that fewer investors will expect them to fall still further. They'll hold smaller speculative balances. Economists thus expect that the quantity of money demanded for speculative reasons will vary negatively with the interest rate.

The Demand Curve for Money

We have seen that the transactions, precautionary, and speculative demands for money vary negatively with the interest rate. Putting those three sources of demand together, we can draw a demand curve for money to show how the interest rate affects the total quantity of money people hold. The **demand curve for money** shows the quantity of money demanded at each interest rate, all other de-

The **demand curve for money** shows the quantity of money demanded at each interest rate, all other determinants of demand unchanged.

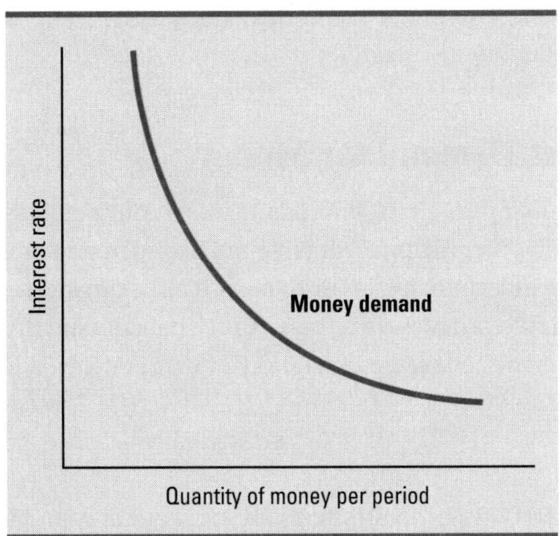

EXHIBIT 25-2

The Demand Curve for Money

The demand curve for money shows the quantity of money demanded at each interest rate. Its downward slope expresses the negative relationship between the quantity of money demanded and the interest rate.

terminants of demand unchanged. Such a curve is shown in Exhibit 25-2. An increase in the interest rate reduces the quantity of money demanded. A reduction in the interest rate increases the quantity of money demanded.

The relationship between interest rates and the quantity of money demanded is an application of the law of demand. If we think of the alternative to holding money as holding bonds, then the interest rate—or the differential between the interest rate in the bond market and the interest paid on M2 deposits—represents the price of holding money. As is the case with all goods and services, an increase in price reduces the quantity demanded.

Velocity and the Demand for Money

We've established that the reciprocal of velocity, $1/V$, measures the fraction of nominal GDP that people will hold as money. We've also established that the quantity of money people demand varies negatively with the interest rate. At higher interest rates, people choose money management strategies that keep more of their funds in nonmoney assets and less in assets such as checking accounts that are part of the money supply. It follows that for a given level of nominal GDP, the fraction people will hold as money will vary negatively with the interest rate. At low interest rates people will hold a quantity of money equal to a relatively large fraction of nominal GDP—that implies a relatively low value for velocity. At high interest rates, they will hold a quantity of money equal to a relatively small fraction of nominal GDP—that implies a relatively high value for velocity. Given the negative relationship between the quantity of money demanded and the interest rate, the relationship between velocity and interest rates should be a positive one.

Exhibit 25-3 shows the annual velocity of M2 and interest rates over the period from 1960 to 1995. The interest rate shown is the average rate on 3-month Treasury bills. When this interest rate has risen, velocity has generally risen. When it has fallen, velocity has generally fallen. Although correlation does not

EXHIBIT 25-3

Velocity and Interest Rates

If increases in interest rates reduce the quantity of M2 demanded, they will increase the velocity of M2 and vice versa. There should therefore be a direct relationship between interest rates and velocity. The chart shows that data for M2 velocity and the interest rate on 3-month Treasury bills are consistent with the theory.

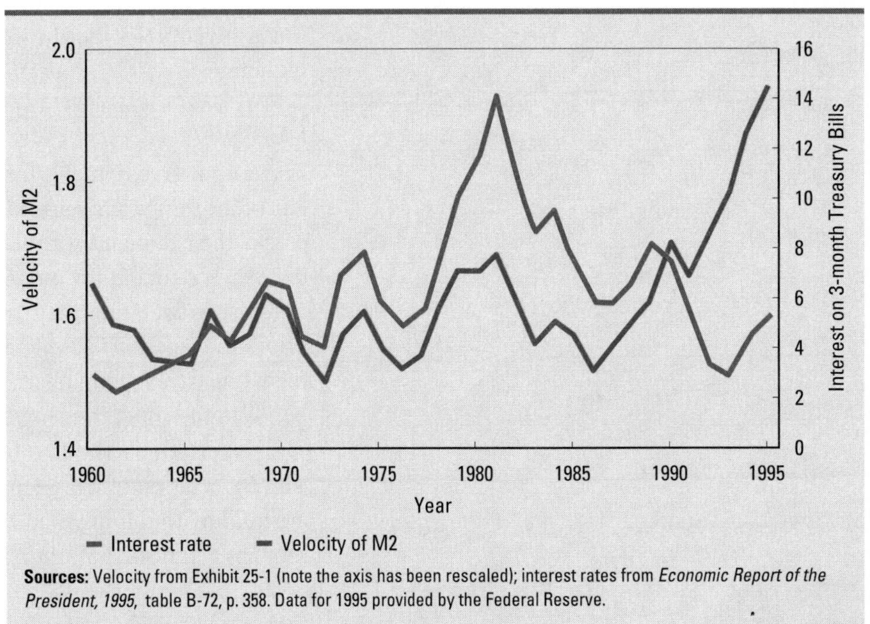

Sources: Velocity from Exhibit 25-1 (note the axis has been rescaled); interest rates from *Economic Report of the President, 1995,* table B-72, p. 358. Data for 1995 provided by the Federal Reserve.

prove causation, this result is consistent with our theoretical analysis of the relationship between interest rates and money demand.

Other Determinants of the Demand for Money

We draw the demand curve for money to show the quantity of money people will hold at each interest rate, all other determinants of money demand unchanged. A change in those "other determinants" will thus shift the demand for money. Among the most important variables that may shift the demand for money are the level of real GDP, the price level, expectations, transfer costs, and preferences.

Income and Real GDP

A household with an income of $10,000 per month is likely to demand a larger quantity of money than a household with an income of $1,000 per month. That suggests that money is a normal good: as income increases, people demand more money, and as income falls, they demand less.

An increase in real GDP increases incomes throughout the economy. The demand for money in the economy is therefore likely to be greater when real GDP is greater.

The Price Level

The higher the price level, the more money is required to purchase a given quantity of goods and services. All other things unchanged, the higher the price level, the greater the demand for money.

Together with the positive relationship between the level of real GDP and the demand for money, the positive relationship between the demand for money and the price level suggests a positive relationship between the demand for money and nominal GDP. That is what the relationship between money demand, nominal GDP, and velocity implies:

$$M = \frac{1}{V} PY$$

For a given velocity, the demand for money is greater when nominal GDP is higher.

Expectations

The speculative demand for money is based on expectations about bond prices. All other things unchanged, if people expect bond prices to fall, they will increase their demand for money. If they expect bond prices to rise, they will reduce their demand for money.

The expectation that bond prices are about to change actually causes bond prices to change. If people expect bond prices to fall, for example, they will sell their bonds, exchanging them for money. That will shift the supply curve for bonds to the right, thus lowering their price.

Expectations about future price levels also affect the demand for money. The expectation of a higher price level means that people expect the money they are holding to fall in value. Given that expectation, they are likely to hold less of it in anticipation of a jump in prices.

Case in Point — Velocity in the Confederacy

The Union and the Confederacy financed their respective efforts during the Civil War largely through the issue of paper money. The Union roughly doubled its money supply through this process—and the Confederacy printed enough "Confederates" to increase the money supply in the South 20-fold from 1861 to 1865. That huge increase in the money supply boosted the price level in the Confederacy dramatically. It rose from an index of 100 in 1861 to 9,200 in 1865.

Estimates of real GDP in the South during the Civil War are unavailable, but it could hardly have increased very much. Although production undoubtedly rose early in the period, the South lost considerable capital and an appalling toll of men killed in battle. Let us suppose that real GDP over the entire period remained constant. For the price level to rise 92-fold with a 20-fold increase in the money supply, there must have been a 4.6-fold increase in velocity. People in the South must have reduced their demand for Confederates.

An account of an exchange for eggs in 1864 from the diary of Mary Chestnut illustrates how eager people in the South were to part with their Confederate money. It also suggests that other commodities had assumed much greater relative value.

> She asked me 20 dollars for five dozen eggs and then said she would take it in "Confederate." Then I would have given her 100 dollars as easily. But if she had taken my offer of yarn! I haggle in yarn for the million the part of a thread! . . . When they ask for Confederate money, I never stop to chafer [bargain or argue]. I give them 20 or 50 dollars cheerfully for anything.

Mary Boykin Chestnut.

Sources: C. Vann Woodward, ed., *Mary Chestnut's Civil War* (New Haven: Yale University Press, 1981), p. 749. Money and price data from E. M. Lerner, "Money, Prices, and Wages in the Confederacy, 1861–1865," *Journal of Political Economy* 63 (February 1955): 20–40.

Expectations about future price levels play a particularly important role during periods of hyperinflation. If prices rise very rapidly and people expect them to continue rising, people are likely to try to reduce the amount of money they hold, knowing that it will fall in value as it sits in their wallets or their bank accounts. Toward the end of the great German hyperinflation of the early 1920s, prices were doubling as often as 3 times a day. Under those circumstances, people tried not to hold money even for a few minutes—within the space of 8 hours money would lose half its value!

The expectation of higher prices can be self-fulfilling. If people expect prices to rise, they will reduce their demand for money. A lower demand for money means a higher velocity. A higher velocity, in turn, means a higher nominal GDP. To the extent that an increase in nominal GDP comes as a result of higher prices, the expectation of higher prices contributes to higher prices.

Transfer Costs

For a given level of expenditures, reducing the quantity of money demanded requires more frequent transfers between nonmoney and money deposits. As the cost of such transfers rises, some consumers will choose to make fewer of them. They will therefore increase the quantity of money they demand. In general, the demand for money will increase as it becomes more expensive to transfer between money and nonmoney accounts.

Preferences

Preferences also play a role in determining the demand for money. Some people place a high value on having a considerable amount of money on hand. For others, this may not be important.

Household attitudes toward risk are another aspect of preferences that affect money demand. As we have seen, bonds pay higher interest rates than M2 deposits, but holding bonds entails a risk that bond prices might fall. There is also a chance that the issuer of a bond will default. An M2 account such as a savings deposit might earn a lower yield, but it's a safe yield. People's attitudes about the tradeoff between risk and yields affect the degree to which they hold their wealth as money.

Exhibit 25-4 shows an increase in the demand for money. Such an increase could result from a higher nominal GDP, a change in expectations, an increase in transfer costs, or a change in preferences. As always when dealing with a demand curve, a movement along the curve shows a change in quantity demanded, and a shift in the curve reflects a change in demand.

EXHIBIT 25-4

An Increase in Money Demand

An increase in nominal GDP or in transfer costs will increase the quantity of money demanded at any interest rate r, increasing the demand for money from D_1 to D_2. The quantity of money demanded at interest rate r rises from $M2_1$ to $M2_2$. The demand for money will also rise if people become more concerned about the risk associated with holding bonds or if they revise their price-level expectations downward. The reverse of any of these events would reduce the quantity of money demanded at every interest rate, shifting the demand curve to the left.

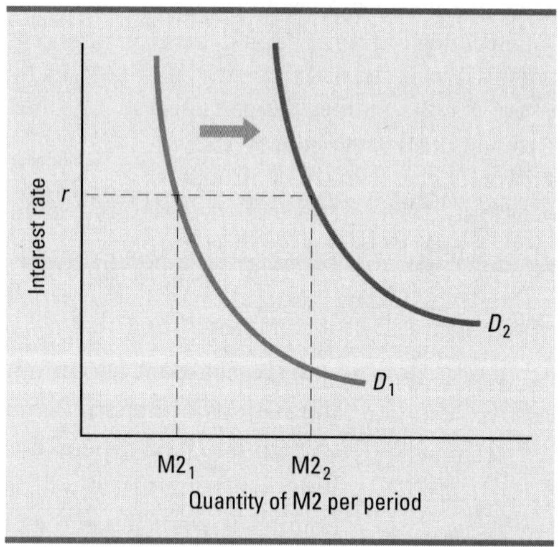

Checklist

- People hold money in order to buy goods and services (transactions demand), to have it available for contingencies (precautionary demand), and in order to avoid possible drops in the value of other assets such as bonds (speculative demand).
- The higher the interest rate, the lower the quantities of money demanded for transactions, for precautionary, and for speculative purposes.
- The negative relationship between the interest rate and the quantity of money demanded implies a positive relationship between the interest rate and velocity.
- The demand for money will change as a result of a change in nominal GDP, transfer costs, expectations, or preferences.

- The **supply curve of money** relates the quantity of money that banks supply in the economy to the interest rate.
- The **money market** is the interaction among institutions through which money is supplied to individuals, firms, and other institutions that demand money.
- **Money market equilibrium** occurs at the interest rate at which the quantity of money demanded is equal to the quantity of money supplied.

Demand, Supply, and Equilibrium in the Money Market

We've examined the demand curve for money. There is a supply curve for money as well. To understand what determines the quantity of money people will hold, we must combine the demand and supply curves for money.

The Supply of Money

The **supply curve of money** shows the relationship between the quantity of money supplied and the market interest rate, all other determinants of supply unchanged. We saw in Chapter 24 that the Fed, through its open-market operations, is able to determine the total quantity of reserves in the banking system. We shall assume that banks increase the money supply in fixed proportion to their reserves. Because the quantity of reserves is determined by Federal Reserve policy, we draw the supply curve of money in Exhibit 25-5 as a vertical line, determined by the Fed's monetary policies.

Equilibrium in the Market for Money

The **money market** is the interaction among institutions through which money is supplied to individuals, firms, and other institutions that demand money. **Money market equilibrium** occurs if the quantity of M2 that people demand is equal to the quantity of M2 supplied. Exhibit 25-6 combines demand and supply curves for M2 to illustrate the achievement of equilibrium in the market for money. With a stock of money M2, the equilibrium interest rate is *r*.

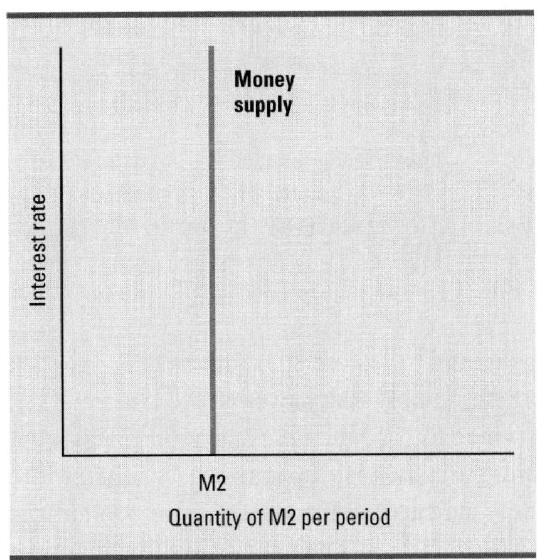

EXHIBIT 25-5

The Supply Curve of Money

We assume that the quantity of money supplied in the economy is determined as a fixed multiple of the quantity of bank reserves, which is determined by the Fed. Suppose the quantity of money (M2) is $3,200 billion. The supply curve of money is a vertical line at that quantity.

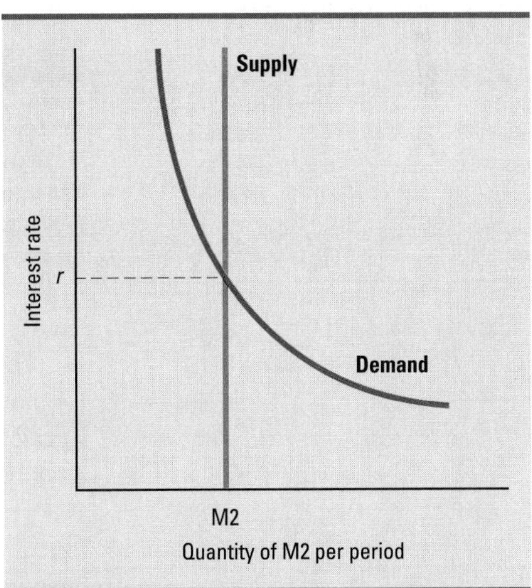

EXHIBIT 25-6

Money Market Equilibrium

The market for money is in equilibrium if the quantity of money demanded is equal to the quantity of money supplied. Here, that occurs at interest rate *r*.

Changes in the Money Supply

Suppose the market for money is in equilibrium and the Fed changes the money supply. How will this change affect the equilibrium solution?

Panel (a) of Exhibit 25-7 shows an economy with a money supply of $M2_1$, which is in equilibrium at an interest rate of r_1. Now suppose the Fed increases the money supply to $M2_2$; that shifts the supply curve for money to the right to S_2. At the original interest rate r_1, people do not wish to hold the newly supplied money; they would prefer to hold nonmoney assets. To reestablish equilibrium in the money market, the interest rate must fall to increase the quantity of money demanded. In the economy shown, the interest rate must fall to r_2 to increase the quantity of money demanded to $M2_2$.

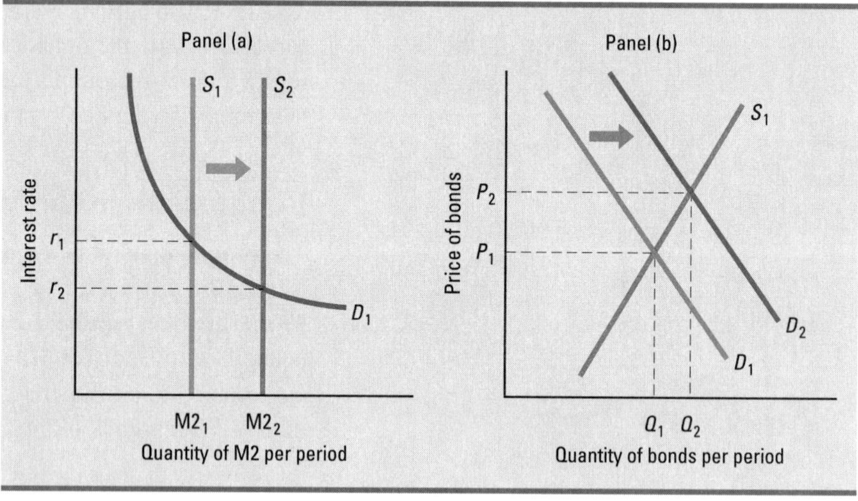

EXHIBIT 25-7

An Increase in the Money Supply

If the money supply increases to $M2_2$ in Panel (a), the interest rate must fall to r_2 to achieve equilibrium. The Fed increases the money supply by buying bonds, increasing the demand for bonds in Panel (b) to D_2 and the price of bonds to P_2. When bond prices go up, the interest rate falls.

The reduction in interest rates required to restore equilibrium to the market for money after an increase in the money supply is achieved in the bond market. Recall the primary method through which the Fed increases the money supply: it buys bonds. The impact of Fed bond purchases is illustrated in Panel (b). The Fed's purchase of bonds shifts the demand curve to the right, raising bond prices to P_2. The increase in bond prices lowers interest rates, which will increase the quantity of money people demand. If the Fed's purchase of bonds still leaves people holding more money than they would prefer, people will buy bonds. That will further increase the demand for bonds, which will raise bond prices and reduce interest rates still further. The result will be a sufficient reduction in interest rates to achieve equilibrium in the market for money.

A reduction in the money supply shifts its supply curve to the left, as shown in Panel (a) of Exhibit 25-8. At the initial equilibrium interest rate r_1, the quantity of money demanded exceeds the quantity of money supplied. In order to re-

EXHIBIT 25-8

A Reduction in the Money Supply

After a reduction in the money supply to $M2_2$ in Panel (a), the interest rate must rise to r_2 to achieve equilibrium in the money market. Such an increase is achieved by the action that reduces the money supply—the Fed's sale of bonds. That sale shifts the supply curve for bonds to S_2, lowering the price of bonds to P_2 in Panel (b). The lower price for bonds implies a higher interest rate.

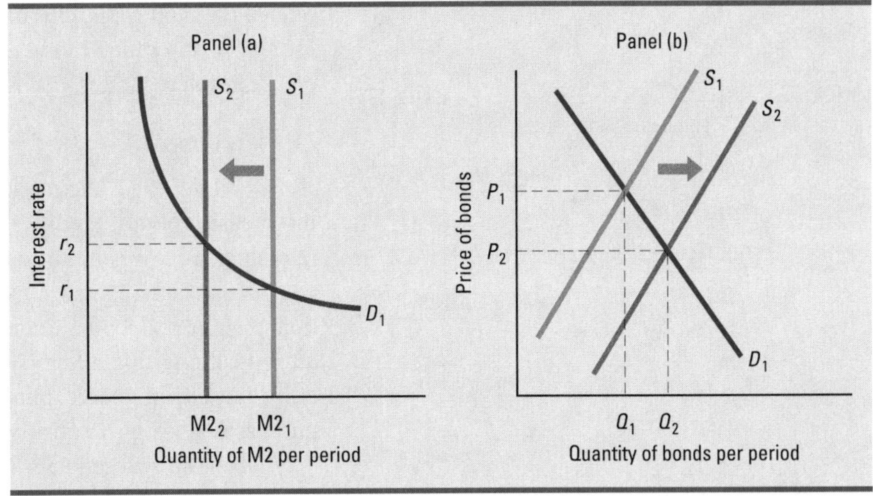

store equilibrium in the market for money, the interest rate must rise to r_2. An increase in the interest rate is achieved through the action the Fed takes to reduce the supply of money in the first place: it sells bonds. As shown in Panel (b), this shifts the supply curve for bonds to the right, lowering the price of bonds and thus raising the interest rate. If people still demand a larger quantity of money than is available, they will sell bonds in an effort to obtain more money. That will shift the supply curve for bonds further to the right, putting additional upward pressure on the interest rate until the money market is in equilibrium.

The process of achieving equilibrium in the money market thus works in tandem with the achievement of equilibrium in the bond market. The interest rate consistent with money market equilibrium is the same as the interest rate achieved in the bond market.

- We assume that the supply of money is determined by the Fed. The supply curve for money is thus a vertical line.
- Money market equilibrium occurs at the interest rate at which the quantity of money demanded equals the quantity of money supplied.
- An increase in the supply of money lowers the equilibrium interest rate.
- A reduction in the supply of money raises the equilibrium interest rate.

The Money Market, Interest Rates, and Economic Activity

We've seen that the velocity of money forges a crucial link between money and nominal GDP. Velocity, in turn, varies with the interest rate. The interest rate is simultaneously determined in the market for money and in the bond market. The interest rate, in turn, affects the equilibrium level of real GDP and the price level.

Money Supply Changes and Aggregate Demand

The aggregate demand curve combines the total demand for goods and services at each price level. It includes consumption, investment, government purchases, and net exports. If a change in the money supply is to affect the product market through a change in aggregate demand, it must affect one or more of the components of aggregate demand. As we shall see, a change in the money supply is likely to have an effect on all the components of aggregate demand except government purchases.

Suppose the Fed acts to change the money supply. To increase the money supply it will buy bonds, driving bond prices up and interest rates down. To reduce the money supply it will sell bonds, driving bond prices down and interest rates up. A reduction in interest rates will increase aggregate demand; an increase in interest rates will reduce it.

Consumption

If the Fed increases the money supply, interest rates will fall, and consumers can more easily obtain credit. They can get loans to purchase new cars and other durable goods. When the cost of financing such purchases drops, the demand for consumer goods goes up, increasing aggregate demand. Increases in consumption that helped boost economic activity in 1993, for example, were widely attributed to falling interest rates that year. Virtually all of the gains in consumption reflected increased purchases of durable goods such as automobiles; such purchases are highly sensitive to interest rate changes.

When the Fed reduces the money supply and interest rates rise, the demand for goods typically financed on credit will drop. Higher interest rates can thus reduce the consumption component of aggregate demand.

There is, however, a mechanism through which interest rate changes can affect consumption in a manner that is opposite to the effects described here. When interest rates fall, people who receive incomes from interest-earning assets experience a reduction in income. For them, lower interest rates are likely to reduce consumption. We can, however, argue that a reduction in interest rates, given the level of income, will tend to increase consumption.

Investment

When the Fed increases the money supply, interest rates fall. Because firms typically borrow the funds to purchase new capital—whether buildings, equipment, or inventory—a reduction in interest rates will increase these purchases. Households also borrow to purchase new homes; a lower interest rate will increase new house purchases as well. Purchases of new capital and homes are investment; investment will thus rise with an increase in the money supply, all other things unchanged.

Similarly, an action by the Fed to reduce the money supply will tend, ceteris paribus, to reduce investment. To reduce the money supply, the Fed will sell bonds. That will push bond prices down and interest rates up. At higher interest rates, firms will be less likely to purchase new capital. Households will be less likely to purchase new homes.

Net Exports

The link between a change in the interest rate and a change in net exports is indirect; it is mediated through the international market for dollars that we examined in Chapter 23. Recall that the demand for dollars in the market for foreign exchange is driven by foreign purchases of U.S. goods, services, and assets. Dollars are supplied—sold to buy foreign currencies—to finance U.S. purchases of foreign goods, services, and assets.

When the Fed acts to increase the U.S. money supply, interest rates fall, and foreign buyers are less enthusiastic about purchasing U.S. interest-earning assets. They demand fewer dollars, so the demand curve for dollars shifts to the left, as shown in Panel (a) of Exhibit 25-9. At the same time, individuals in the United States are more likely to purchase foreign interest-earning assets now that U.S. yields are lower. They thus supply more dollars as they buy the foreign currency necessary to purchase those foreign assets. With reduced demand and

EXHIBIT 25-9

Interest Rates and the Dollar

In Panel (a), a lower interest rate reduces the demand for dollars to D_2 and increases the supply to S_2, thus lowering the exchange rate to E_2. In Panel (b), a higher interest rate increases the demand for dollars to D_2 and reduces the supply to S_2, increasing the exchange rate to E_2.

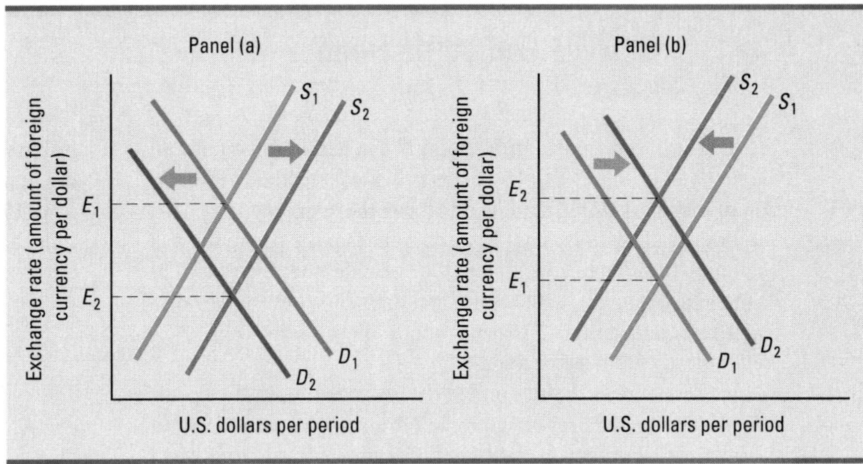

increased supply, the price of the dollar falls. A cheaper dollar stimulates U.S. export sales because it makes U.S. goods and services cheaper for foreigners. But if the dollar is cheaper, foreign currency is more expensive. That reduces U.S. demand for foreign goods and services, reducing U.S. imports. With exports up and imports down, net exports rise, increasing aggregate demand.

A move by the Fed to reduce the U.S. money supply causes interest rates to rise. Foreign buyers, attracted by the higher rates on U.S. interest-earning assets, demand more dollars. People in the United States are less attracted by foreign interest-earning assets, so the supply of dollars falls. With rising demand and falling supply, the price of the dollar rises, as shown in Panel (b). Net exports and aggregate demand will fall.

An increase in the money supply thus produces lower interest rates, which stimulate consumption, investment, and net export demand. The increase in the money supply thus shifts the aggregate demand curve to the right, as shown in Panel (a) of Exhibit 25-10. The price level rises to P_2, and real GDP to Y_2.

A reduction in the money supply raises interest rates and lowers consumption, investment, and net export demand. A reduced money supply thus reduces aggregate demand, as shown in Panel (b). The price level falls to P_2, real GDP to Y_2.

EXHIBIT 25-10

Changes in the Money Supply Affect Aggregate Demand

In Panel (a), an increase in the money supply lowers interest rates and encourages consumption, investment, and net exports, thus increasing aggregate demand from AD_1 to AD_2. The price level rises to P_2 and real GDP rises to Y_2. In Panel (b), reduction in the money supply raises interest rates and reduces consumption, investment, and net exports. It thus tends to reduce aggregate demand. Here, the price level falls to P_2 and real GDP falls to Y_2.

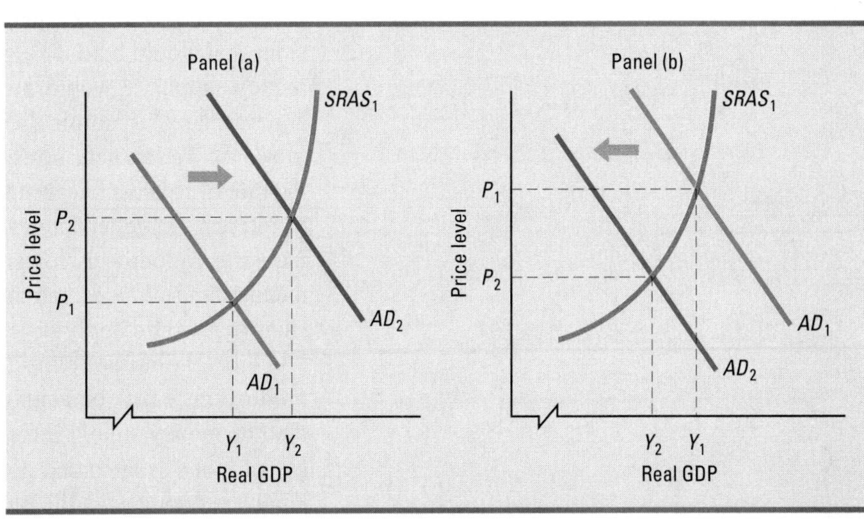

Case in Point Fed at the Helm

The Fed was very much at the helm of the nation's economy in the first half of the 1990s. Its efforts provided a textbook illustration of monetary policy and its effects on the economy.

In the fall of 1990, as it became clear that the economy was beginning to slip into a recession, the Fed unleashed every tool in its monetary arsenal. It cut reserve requirements, lowered the discount rate, and bought Treasury bonds. The results were . . . well, not very impressive at first.

Interest rates fell quite quickly in response to the Fed's action. The prime rate, for example, fell from 10 percent in 1990 to 6 percent in 1992. Interest rates on both short-term and long-term bonds dropped throughout the fall and continued to decline in 1991. Consumption and investment began to rise in 1991, but their growth was weak. Unemployment continued to rise because growth in output was too slow to keep up with growth in the labor force. It was not until the fall of 1992, two years after the Fed's action, that the economy started to pick up steam. Investment, consumption, and net exports all surged, increasing aggregate demand to AD_2 in the accompanying figure. The episode demonstrated an important difficulty with stabilization policy: attempts to manipulate aggregate demand achieve shifts in the curve, but only with a lag. The 1990 effort to boost aggregate demand didn't score solid gains until 1992.

Those gains did, however, promote recovery. By the first part of 1994, the economy was close to closing its recessionary gap, and the Fed started worrying about inflation. It moved several times during 1994 to push interest rates up, selling bonds to take reserves out of the money supply. Interest rates rose sharply; the prime rate began shooting up in March, and other rates were rising as well. The Fed's action achieved a slowing in growth early in 1995, and the economy was operating close to its natural level. Indeed, by the summer of 1995 the Fed determined that the economy had slowed enough, and moved to push interest rates down.

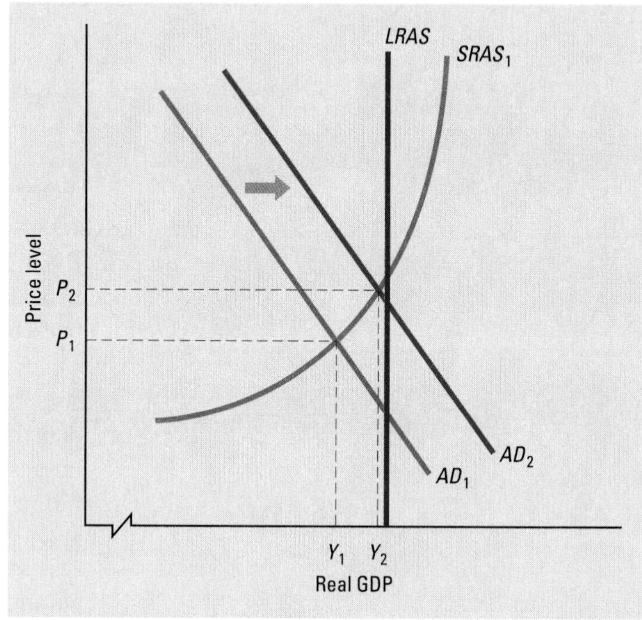

Velocity, the Money Market, and the Equation of Exchange

In our first look at the equation of exchange, we noted some remarkable conclusions that would hold if velocity were constant: a given percentage change in the money supply M would produce an equal percentage change in nominal GDP, and no change in nominal GDP could occur without an equal percentage change in M. We've learned, however, that velocity is a variable. Velocity varies with the rate of interest because the quantity of money demanded varies with the rate of interest. A higher interest rate reduces the quantity of money demanded and increases velocity. A lower interest rate increases the quantity of money demanded and reduces velocity. These relationships completely alter the conclusions that would apply if velocity were constant.

First, we do not expect a given percentage change in the money supply to produce an equal percentage change in nominal GDP. Suppose, for example, that the money supply increases by 10 percent. Interest rates drop and the quantity of money demanded goes up. Velocity is likely to decline, though not by as large a percentage as the money supply increases. The result will be a reduction in the degree to which a given percentage increase in the money supply boosts nominal GDP.

Second, nominal GDP could change even when there is no change in the money supply. Suppose government purchases increase. We learned in Chapter 23 that such an increase shifts the aggregate demand curve to the right, increasing real GDP and the price level. That effect would be impossible if velocity were constant. The fact that velocity varies, and varies positively with the interest rate, suggests that an increase in government purchases could easily boost aggregate demand and nominal GDP. To finance increased spending, the government will borrow money by selling bonds. An increased supply of bonds lowers their price, and that means higher interest rates. The higher interest rates produce the increase in velocity that must happen if increased government purchases are to boost the price level and real GDP.

Our analysis of macroeconomic events must always consider two elements of the economy: the product market and the money market. Events in the product market, represented by the model of aggregate demand and aggregate supply, affect the money market. The money market, represented by the demand and supply curves for money, affects the product market. In thinking about the role of money in the economy, we must keep this web of relationships firmly in mind.

Checklist

- An increase in the money supply lowers interest rates. That increases consumption, investment, and net exports, shifting the aggregate demand curve to the right and increasing the price level and real GDP.
- A reduction in the money supply raises interest rates. That reduces consumption, investment, and net exports, shifting the aggregate demand curve to the left and reducing the price level and real GDP.
- Velocity changes in a direction opposite to that of money supply changes, weakening the impact of a money supply change on nominal GDP.
- Because velocity is variable, nominal GDP may change in the absence of a change in the money supply.

A Look Back—And a Look Ahead

We saw in this chapter that the money supply is related to the level of nominal GDP by the equation of exchange. A crucial issue in that relationship is the stability of the velocity of money. If the velocity of money were constant, nominal GDP could change only if the money supply changed, and a change in the money supply would produce an equal percentage change in nominal GDP. But velocity is variable, so other factors can affect nominal GDP, and a change in the money supply does not necessarily alter nominal GDP. It's therefore important to understand the determinants of velocity so we can understand the role of money in the economy.

Velocity and the demand for money are related; the reciprocal of velocity gives the fraction of nominal GDP that equals the quantity of money people demand. We saw that the demand for money varies inversely with the interest rate (so velocity varies positively with the interest rate). We confirmed this theoretical conclusion by looking at the relationship between the velocity of M2 and interest rates. We also saw that other factors affect the demand for money, including real GDP; the price level; expectations; the cost of transferring funds between money and nonmoney accounts; and preferences, especially preferences concerning risk.

Equilibrium in the market for money is achieved at the interest rate at which the quantity of money demanded equals the quantity of money supplied. We assumed that the supply of money is determined by the Fed. An increase in the money supply lowers the equilibrium interest rate; a reduction in the money supply raises the equilibrium interest rate.

Finally, we returned to the question of the relationship between the money supply and economic activity. We saw that when the Fed increases the money supply, interest rates drop, stimulating consumption, investment, and net exports and thus increasing aggregate demand. A shift to the right in aggregate demand increases the price level and real GDP. When the Fed reduces the money supply, interest rates rise. Consumption, investment, and real GDP fall, reducing aggregate demand. A shift to the left in aggregate demand reduces the price level and real GDP.

This chapter completes our introduction to macroeconomics. In the next part we shall more carefully explore the forces that determine the level of economic activity. We shall begin with a detailed investigation of the model of aggregate demand and aggregate supply.

Terms and Concepts for Review

Demand curve for money	Precautionary demand
Demand for money	Speculative demand
Equation of exchange	Supply curve of money
Money market	Transactions demand
Money market equilibrium	Velocity

For Discussion

1. How would each of the following affect the demand for money?
   a. A tax on bonds held by individuals
   b. A forecast by the Fed that interest rates will rise sharply in the next quarter
   c. A wave of muggings
   d. An announcement of an agreement between Congress and the president that, beginning in the next fiscal year, government spending will be reduced by an amount sufficient to eliminate all future borrowing
2. Most low-income countries do not have a bond market. In such countries, what substitutes for money do you think people would hold?
3. Explain what is meant by the statement that people are holding more money than they want to hold.
4. Explain how the Fed's sale of government bonds shifts the supply curve for money.
5. Suppose a 10-percent tax were imposed on all transfers of funds into and out of nonmoney accounts. How would that affect the demand for money?
6. Trace the impact of a sale of government bonds by the Fed on bond prices, interest rates, consumption, investment, net exports, aggregate demand, real GDP, and the price level.
7. Suppose we observed an economy in which changes in the money supply produce no changes whatever in nominal GDP. What could we conclude about velocity?
8. Suppose the price level were falling 10 percent per day. How would this affect the demand for money? How would it affect velocity? What can you conclude about the role of velocity during periods of rapid price change?
9. Suppose investment increases and the money supply does not change. Use the model of aggregate demand and aggregate supply to predict the impact of such an increase on nominal GDP. Now what happens in terms of the variables in the equation of exchange?

Problems

1. We know that the U.S. economy faced a recessionary gap in the Fall of 1990 and that the Fed responded with an expansionary monetary policy. You will present the results of the Fed's action in a 4-panel graph. In Panel (a), show the initial situation, using the model of aggregate demand and aggregate supply. In Panel (b), show how the Fed's policy affects the bond market and bond prices. In Panel (c), show how the market for U.S. dollars and the exchange rate will be affected. In Panel (d), incorporate these developments into your analysis of aggregate demand and aggregate supply, and show how the Fed's policy will affect real GDP and the price level in the short run.

2. We know that the Fed was concerned in 1994 about the possibility that the United States was moving into an inflationary gap and that it adopted a contractionary monetary policy as a result. Draw a 4-panel graph showing this policy and its expected results. In Panel (a), use the model of aggregate demand and aggregate supply to illustrate an economy with an inflationary gap. In Panel (b), show how the Fed's policy will affect the market for bonds. In Panel (c), show how it will affect the exchange rate. Finally, in Panel (d), incorporate these developments into your analysis of aggregate demand and aggregate supply, and show how the Fed's policy will affect real GDP and the price level in the short run.
3. For this problem, you'll present a two-panel graph. Suppose the market for money is in equilibrium at an interest rate of 6 percent with a quantity of M2 of $3,000 billion. Now suppose the Fed acts to increase the money supply to $4,000 billion and that the new equilibrium interest rate equals 4 percent. Show this change with a graph of the money market in Panel (a). Assuming that all bonds have a face value of $100, no coupon rate, and that they mature in one year, calculate the price of bonds at each interest rate and show this change in the bond market in Panel (b). To calculate the interest rate, use the relationship between the price of bonds, *P*, and the interest rate given in Chapter 23, p. 499.
4. Here are data for the U.S. economy in 1993. Determine where each number fits in the equation of exchange, and compute the velocity for that year. What percentage of nominal GDP did people choose to hold in the form of M2 that year?

   Real GDP: $5,134.5 billion

   Implicit price deflator: 1.235

   M2: $3,567.9 billion

Part Seven Modeling the Macroeconomy

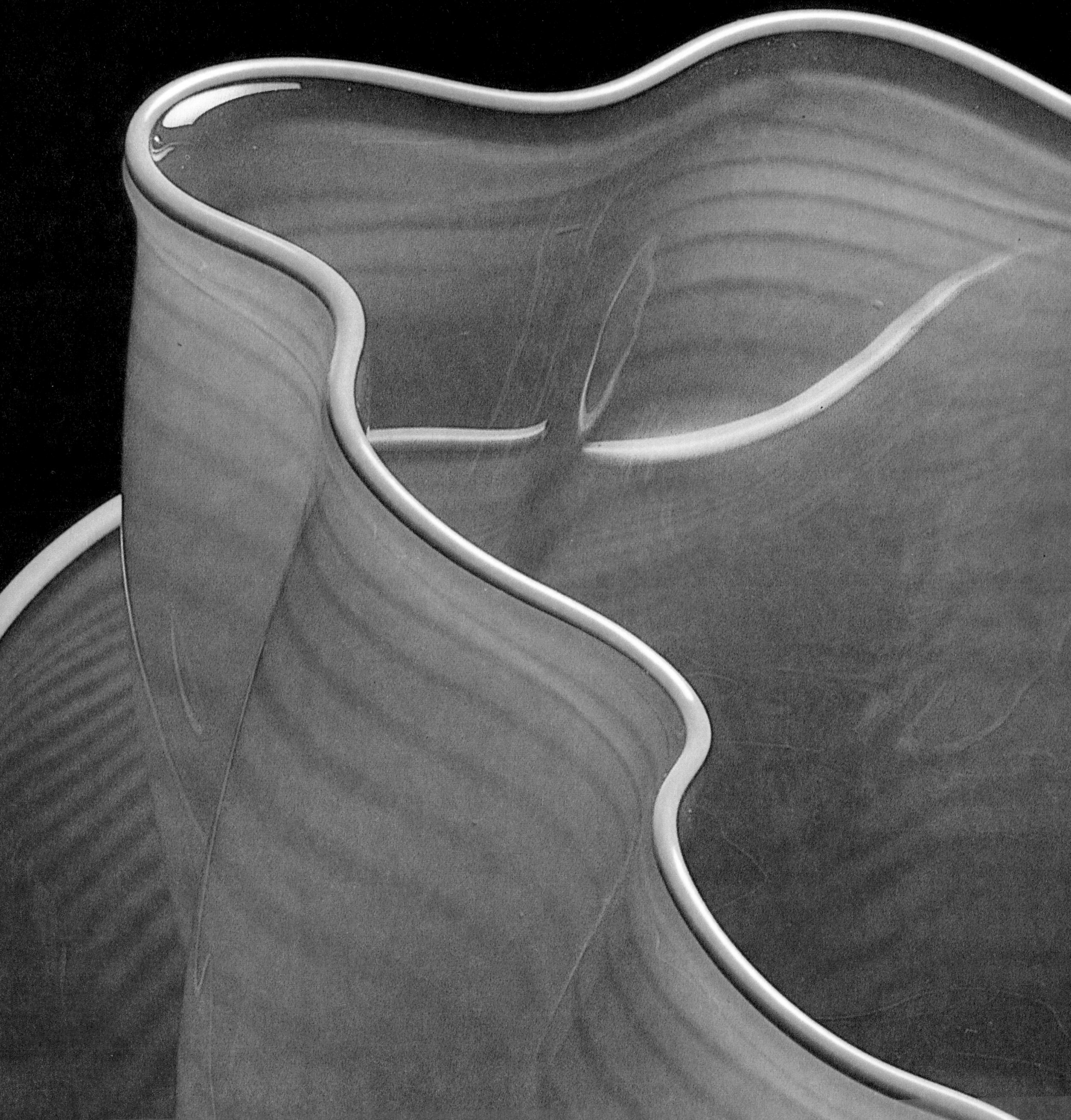

26

Aggregate Demand and Aggregate Supply

Chapter Objectives

After mastering the material in this chapter, you will be able to:

1. Explain the derivation of the aggregate demand, short-run aggregate supply, and long-run aggregate supply curves.
2. Identify the events that can shift the aggregate demand, short-run aggregate supply, and long-run aggregate supply curves and trace the short-run and long-run consequences of shifts in these curves.
3. Explain the process through which the economy may adjust to its natural level of output given a recessionary or inflationary gap.
4. Discuss the pros and cons of using monetary or fiscal policy to close a recessionary or inflationary gap versus letting the economy adjust on its own.
5. Discuss the differences between the three major schools of macroeconomic thought—new Keynesian, monetarist, and new classical—in using the model of aggregate demand and aggregate supply to explain outcomes in the economy.

Let us beware of this dangerous theory of equilibrium which is supposed to be automatically established. A certain kind of equilibrium, it is true, is re-established in the long run, but it is only after a frightful amount of suffering.

Simonde de Sismondi
Nouveaux Principes d'Economie politique, 1827

What's Ahead

The first warning came from the Harvard Economic Society, an association of Harvard economics professors, early in 1929. The Society predicted in its weekly newsletter that the 7-year-old expansion was coming to an end. Recession was ahead.

Almost no one took the warning seriously. The economy, fueled by soaring investment, had enjoyed stunning growth. The decade that had seen the emergence of whole new industries—automobiles, public power, home appliances, synthetic fabrics, radio and motion pictures—seemed to have acquired a momentum all its own. Prosperity was not about to end, no matter what a few economists might say.

Summer came, and no recession was apparent. The Harvard economists withdrew their forecast. As it turned out, they lost their nerve too soon. Industrial production fell that summer. The worst downturn in our history, the Great Depression, had begun.

The collapse was swift. The stock market crashed in October 1929. Real GDP plunged nearly 10 percent by 1930. By the time the economy hit bottom in 1933, real GDP had fallen 30 percent, unemployment had increased from 3.2 percent in 1929 to 25 percent in 1933, and prices, measured by the implicit price deflator, had plunged 23 percent from their 1929 level. The depression held the economy in its cruel grip for a decade; it was not until World War II that full employment was restored.

The model of aggregate demand and aggregate supply that was introduced in Chapter 23 helps us to understand the forces that brought on the Great Depression and those that brought recovery. In this chapter we develop that model in more detail. We'll examine the derivation of the aggregate demand curve and the short- and long-run aggregate supply curves. We'll investigate the forces that cause these curves to shift. We'll also explore conditions under which an economy achieves an equilibrium level of real GDP that is consistent with full employment in the labor market. When an economy fails to achieve such a solution, there may be measures that the government or the central bank can take to push the economy toward its natural level of real GDP.

Deriving the Aggregate Demand Curve

Economists use the model of aggregate demand and aggregate supply to show the factors that influence real GDP and the price level. Exhibit 26-1 shows typical aggregate demand, short-run aggregate supply, and long-run aggregate supply curves that make up the graphic formulation of the model. At any one time, we assume that the economy operates at the intersection of its aggregate demand and short-run aggregate supply curves. In Panel (a), the economy is operating below its natural level of output, Y_n. There is a recessionary gap equal to $Y_n - Y$. In Panel (b), the economy is producing a level of real GDP that exceeds the natural level; there is an inflationary gap equal to $Y - Y_n$. Panel (c) shows an economy that is operating at its natural level.

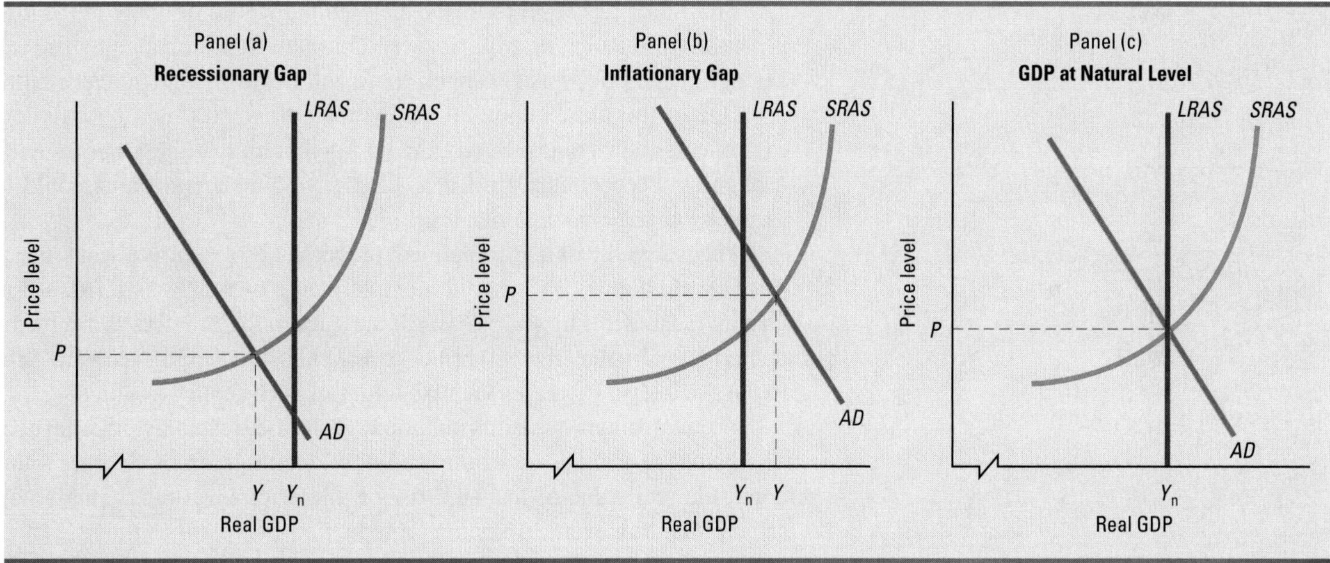

EXHIBIT 26-1

The Model of Aggregate Demand and Aggregate Supply

In the short run, the equilibrium levels of real GDP and the price level are determined by the intersection of the aggregate demand (*AD*) and short-run aggregate supply (*SRAS*) curves. In Panel (a), the equilibrium real GDP, *Y*, falls short of the natural level, Y_n—there is a recessionary gap equal to $Y_n - Y$. In Panel (b), the equilibrium real GDP exceeds the natural level; there is an inflationary gap $Y - Y_n$. Finally, Panel (c) shows an economy in which GDP equals its natural level.

We've already completed a considerable amount of work on the model of aggregate demand and aggregate supply. The model itself was introduced in Chapter 23. After learning how money is created in Chapter 24, we saw in Chapter 25 how changes in the quantity of money can influence aggregate demand. In this section we'll examine in greater detail the derivation of the aggregate demand, short-run aggregate supply, and long-run aggregate supply curves. Later in this chapter we'll explore the policy issues that confront an economy faced with either a recessionary or inflationary gap.

Aggregate Demand

The aggregate demand curve shows the total quantity of goods and services demanded, measured as real GDP, at each price level. Its downward slope tells us that when the price level falls, the total quantity of goods and services demanded will go up, and that when the price level rises, the total quantity of goods and services demanded will drop. Aggregate demand comprises consumption, investment, government purchases, and net exports. A change in any of these components at each price level will shift the aggregate demand curve.

The Slope of the Aggregate Demand Curve

We saw in Chapter 23 that the aggregate demand curve slopes downward because a lower price level is likely to increase the real volume of consumption and of net exports. We'll see in this section that a lower price level also stimulates investment. The relationship between each component of aggregate demand and the price level is reviewed below.

Consumption. A change in the price level affects real wealth, so it also affects consumption. An increase in the price level reduces real wealth and thus reduces consumption. A reduction in the price level increases real wealth and thus increases consumption.

At first glance, the relationship between the price level and real wealth may seem obvious. Real wealth equals the nominal value of wealth divided by the price level. For a given nominal value of total wealth, a higher price level reduces real wealth, and a lower price level increases it.

But if the price level changes, the nominal values of many of the assets people hold will change as well. If these nominal values change by the same percentage as the price level changes, there will be no change in real wealth.

One of the most important components of wealth held by individuals, for example, is their homes. Surely the nominal values of these homes will tend to change as the economy's price level changes; their real value could be unaffected by changes in the price level.

The real value of one component of wealth, however, is always affected by a price level change. Because the nominal value of money is fixed, a price level change must affect its real value. An increase in the price level, for example, reduces the real value of a $10 bill or of $1,000 in a checking account. A reduction in the price level increases the real values of such money holdings.

The real values of claims on money are also affected by price-level changes. The owner of a bond, for example, owns a claim given by the face value of the bond; the real value of that sum rises if the price level falls. The issuer of that same bond, however, experiences a reduction in wealth as the real value of the liability rises. For privately issued debt, the gains of creditors balance the losses of debtors. But individuals and firms also hold government bonds—debt issued by the government. The real value of those bonds rises with a reduction in the price level, increasing the real wealth of the public. The government's real wealth then falls, of course, but such a reduction is unlikely to affect its purchases of goods and services.

A reduction in the price level thus boosts the real value of money and, on balance, of claims on money, so it increases real wealth; similarly, an increase in the price level reduces real wealth. An increase in real wealth tends to boost consumption; a reduction in real wealth tends to lower it. The tendency for a change in the price level to affect real wealth and thus alter consumption is called the **real balance effect;** it suggests a negative relationship between the price level and the real value of consumption spending.

The **real balance effect** is the tendency of a price level change to affect the real value of wealth and thus to alter consumption.

Investment. All other determinants of investment unchanged, investment will rise if the interest rate falls and fall if the interest rate rises. A lower price level

The **Keynes effect** is the tendency for a change in the price level to affect the interest rate and thus to alter the real level of investment.

tends to reduce the interest rate, a higher level to increase it. There is therefore a relationship between the price level and the level of investment.

Exhibit 26-2 shows the demand and supply curves for money in an economy. With a supply curve S and a demand curve D_1, the equilibrium interest rate is r_1. Now suppose the price level falls. That will reduce nominal GDP and the demand for money, shifting D_1 to D_2. The interest rate falls to r_2. A reduction in interest rates tends to increase investment. Lower interest rates, for example, stimulate purchases of new homes and thus tend to increase investment in residential housing. The tendency for a change in the price level to affect the interest rate and thus change the real volume of investment is called the **Keynes effect.** The Keynes effect is a second reason the aggregate demand curve slopes downward.

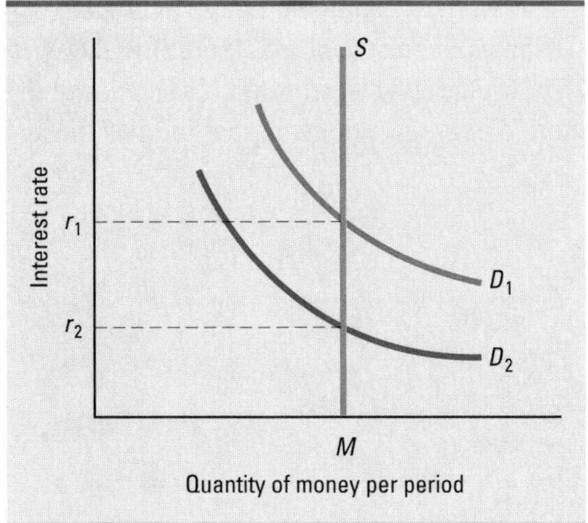

EXHIBIT 26-2

The Price Level and the Interest Rate

A reduction in the price level reduces the demand for money from D_1 to D_2, reducing the interest rate to r_2.

Government Purchases. Government purchases are determined through a political process. We shall assume that there's no causal link between the price level and the real volume of government purchases. This component of aggregate demand therefore does not contribute to the downward slope of the curve.

Net Exports. A reduction in the U.S. price level leads foreign buyers to purchase more U.S. goods and services, so U.S. exports rise. It also makes foreign goods and services relatively more expensive, so U.S. buyers purchase fewer of them and imports fall. A lower price level thus increases net exports.

Deriving the Aggregate Demand Curve

Aggregate demand is the sum of demands stemming from consumption, investment, government purchases, and net exports. The negative relationship between three of those components and the price level produces the negative relationship between the aggregate quantity of goods and services demanded and the price level. The table in Exhibit 26-3 gives values for each component of aggregate demand at each price level for a hypothetical economy. The aggregate demand curve AD_1 is the sum of those components. The forces that determine consumption, investment, and net exports are discussed further in the next three chapters.

EXHIBIT 26-3

The Aggregate Demand Curve

The schedule gives hypothetical values of consumption C, investment I, government purchases G, and net exports X_n at each price level. The sum of these demands at each price level equals aggregate demand AD_1. All figures are in billions of real dollars.

The aggregate demand curve AD_1 in the graph is the sum of the demands for consumption, investment, government purchases, and net exports given in the table. Note that government purchases are shown as a vertical line; this component of aggregate demand is determined by public policy.

Point on AD_1 curve	Price level	C +	I +	G +	X_n =	AD_1
A	0.8	$632	$70	$100	$42	$844
B	1.0	600	60	100	40	800
C	1.2	568	50	100	38	756
D	1.4	536	40	100	36	712

$X_n + I + G$ + C = AD_1

Price level (implicit price deflator): 1.4, 1.2, 1.0, 0.8

Real GDP (billions): $100, 200, 300, 400, 500, 600, 700, 800, 900

D, C, B, A

Changes in Aggregate Demand

A change in the quantity of real GDP demanded at each price level shifts the aggregate demand curve. An increase in aggregate demand is a shift to the right, a reduction a shift to the left.

Column (1) of the table in Exhibit 26-4 lists the values that determined the aggregate demand curve in Exhibit 26-3. If the values at each price level of one of the components of aggregate demand were to change, then the aggregate demand curve would shift. Column (2) shows the result of a $200 billion increase in aggregate demand that produces a new curve, AD_2. Column (3) shows values resulting from a $200 billion reduction in aggregate demand that implies the aggregate demand curve AD_3.

EXHIBIT 26-4

Shifts in the Aggregate Demand Curve

The same price levels and quantities of real GDP demanded that defined AD_1 in Exhibit 26-3 are given in columns (1) and (2). When the quantity of real GDP demanded changes at each price level, a new aggregate demand curve is generated. Column (3) shows the result of a $200 billion increase in aggregate demand that produces curve AD_2. Column (4) shows how a $200 billion reduction in aggregate demand shifts the curve to AD_3. All figures are in billions of real dollars.

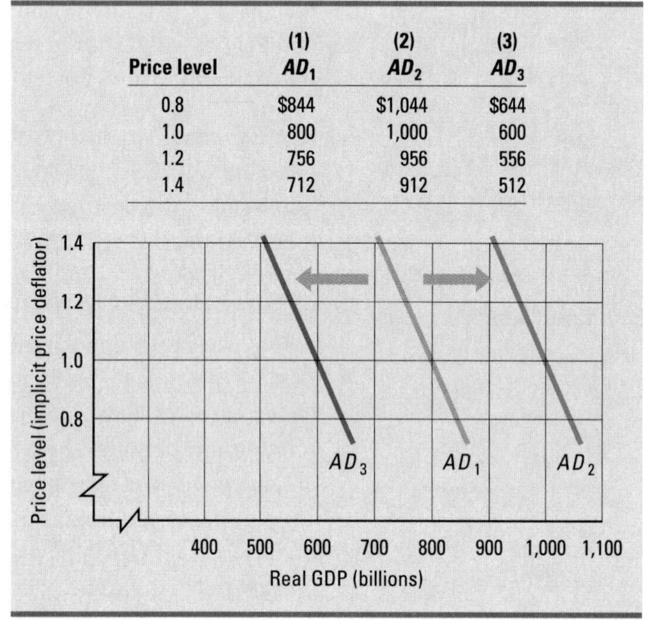

Price level	(1) AD_1	(2) AD_2	(3) AD_3
0.8	$844	$1,044	$644
1.0	800	1,000	600
1.2	756	956	556
1.4	712	912	512

Whenever a component of aggregate demand increases, firms will increase their production in response to it. Increased investment, for example, boosts production of capital goods. That increase in production generates more income and thus stimulates consumption. The increased consumption generates still more production, which of course creates more income—and still more consumption. This positive feedback between the components of aggregate demand and consumption means that an increase in any of the components will shift the aggregate demand curve by a larger amount than the initial increase. We'll study that relationship in detail in Chapter 27.

Changes in Consumption. Several events could change the real quantity of consumption at each price level and thus shift aggregate demand. One factor in consumption is consumer confidence. If consumers are more optimistic about their economic prospects, they're more likely to buy major items such as cars or furniture. That would increase the real value of consumption at each price level and increase aggregate demand.

Iraq's invasion of Kuwait in 1990, for example, created widespread fears that war in the Middle East would disrupt oil supplies, force prices up, and depress economic activity. Surveys showed that consumers became sharply more pessimistic in the months following the invasion and cut their consumption of durable goods. The reduction in consumption decreased aggregate demand.

Another factor that can change consumption and shift aggregate demand is tax policy. A cut in personal income taxes leaves people with more after-tax income, which may induce them to increase their consumption. The federal government cut taxes in 1964, in 1975, and in 1982; each of those tax cuts tended to increase consumption and aggregate demand. Those efforts are discussed in detail in Chapter 27.

Transfer payments such as welfare or Social Security also affect the income people have available to spend. An increase in transfer payments increases consumption and aggregate demand and a reduction lowers consumption and aggregate demand.

Changes in Investment. Investment is the production of new capital that will be used for future production of goods and services. Firms make choices for investment based on what they think they'll be producing in the future. The expectations of firms thus play a critical role in determining investment. If firms expect their sales to go up, they're likely to increase their investment so they can increase their production and meet consumer demand. Such an increase in investment raises the aggregate quantity of goods and services demanded at each price level; it increases aggregate demand.

Changes in interest rates also affect investment. Chapter 25 showed that an increase in the money supply can lower interest rates and stimulate investment. That would raise aggregate demand. A reduction in the money supply can raise interest rates and reduce investment, thus lowering aggregate demand. We must be careful to distinguish such changes from the Keynes effect, which causes a movement *along* the aggregate demand curve. A change in interest rates that results from a change in the price level affects investment in a way that's already captured in the downward slope of the aggregate demand curve; it causes a movement along the curve. A change in interest rates for some other reason shifts the curve.

Investment can also be affected by tax policy. Special tax provisions introduced in 1962 and 1981 allowed firms to reduce their tax payments by increasing their investment. These programs were designed to promote investment and to increase aggregate demand; the tax changes in those years helped usher in the longest expansions in U.S. economic history. The Tax Reform Act of 1986 sharply increased taxes on investment income; many economists argue that the tax increase played a role in reducing investment in the late 1980s and early 1990s. Other factors that can affect investment are discussed in Chapter 28.

Changes in Government Purchases. Any change in government purchases will, all other things equal, change aggregate demand. An increase in government purchases increases aggregate demand; a decrease in government purchases decreases aggregate demand.

Increased defense spending in the early 1980s, for example, was credited by some economists with increasing aggregate demand and boosting economic activity. Reductions in defense spending in the wake of the collapse of the Soviet Union in 1991 tended to reduce aggregate demand. Indeed, falling defense

Case in Point: Firms Lose Confidence, Cut Investment

Clark Johnson, chairman of the board of Pier 1 Imports, a national chain specializing in imported consumer goods, says that the store's customers didn't take long to respond to Iraq's 1990 invasion of Kuwait. "We track sales on a daily basis. They were pretty steady for several weeks before the invasion. The first day after the invasion they fell 7 percent. A month later they fell another 5 percent. I think that reflects consumer concern and apprehension about the economy."

An uncertain international situation wasn't the only thing Mr. Johnson saw affecting aggregate demand late in the summer of 1990. "Federal gas, liquor, and tobacco taxes are up. Payroll taxes are up. Income taxes are up, state taxes are up. All that will affect consumption demand."

Mr. Johnson's firm was quick to act on its expectation of continued weak consumer demand. Pier 1 had planned to open 84 stores late in 1990 and early in 1991; it put 18 of those on hold.

Other firms scaled back their investment plans as well. The Marriott Corporation in Washington, D.C., announced it was shelving construction of a new hotel that had been scheduled to start in the fall of 1990. Tim Comby, the chief executive officer of National Graphics Company in Atlanta, told *The Wall Street Journal* that he had postponed plans to install a new million-dollar printing press "until the economy has some predictability to it."

Firms' expectations that consumption would fall proved correct; the real value of consumption expenditures fell in the fourth quarter of 1990. Anticipating that fall, firms reduced their investment even more sharply. The combination of falling consumption and investment sent real GDP down sharply in the fourth quarter as the recession of 1990–1991 got under way, ending an expansion that had begun 8 years earlier.

An abandoned construction project in Washington, D.C.

Source: Timothy Tregarthen, "Rising Oil Prices Choke Already Gasping U.S. Economy," *The Margin* 6(3) (January/February 1991): 34–35.

purchases are one factor cited by economists in explaining weak gains in real GDP in the early 1990s.

Changes in Net Exports. A change in the real value of net exports at each price level shifts the aggregate demand curve. A major determinant of net exports is foreign demand for a country's goods and services; that demand will vary with foreign incomes. An increase in foreign incomes increases a country's net exports and aggregate demand; a slump in foreign incomes reduces net exports and aggregate demand. For example, several major U.S. trading partners, including Japan and Germany, suffered recessions in 1993. That reduced U.S. exports and tended to reduce aggregate demand. Weakness in the economies of U.S. trading partners pushed U.S. exports, and net exports, down that year.

Foreign exchange rates also influence net exports, ceteris paribus. A rise in the U.S. exchange rate, for example, increases prices paid by foreigners for goods and services produced in the United States, thus reducing exports; it reduces the cost of foreign-produced goods and services for U.S. consumers, thus increasing imports. A higher exchange rate tends to reduce net exports, reducing aggregate demand. A lower exchange rate tends to increase net exports, increasing aggregate demand.

Foreign price levels can affect aggregate demand in the same way as exchange rates. For example, when foreign price levels fall relative to the price level in the United States, U.S. goods and services become relatively more expensive. That will cut exports and boost imports in the United States. Such a reduction in net exports reduces aggregate demand. An increase in foreign prices relative to U.S. prices would have the opposite effect.

The trade policies of various countries can also affect net exports. A policy by Japan to increase its imports of U.S. goods, for example, would increase net exports in the United States. Indeed, the United States has applied considerable pressure on Japan to buy more U.S. goods and services; that policy has been aimed at increasing aggregate demand in the United States.

Stabilization Policy and Aggregate Demand

We've already explored the possibility that aggregate demand and short-run aggregate supply will intersect at a level of real GDP other than the natural level—there may be a recessionary or an inflationary gap. In such cases, policymakers may undertake stabilization policies aimed at shifting the aggregate demand curve in an effort to close such a gap. Stabilization policy may involve fiscal or monetary changes.

Fiscal policy is the use of government purchases, taxes, and transfer payments to influence the level of economic activity. An **expansionary fiscal policy** is one that seeks to increase the level of economic activity. In 1981, for example, the Reagan administration faced a large recessionary gap. It introduced tax cuts that encouraged consumption and investment, and at the same time it increased defense spending. The combined effect of these expansionary fiscal policies was to increase aggregate demand. A **contractionary fiscal policy** is one that seeks to reduce the level of economic activity. Such a policy could include cuts in government purchases or transfer payments or increases in taxes. Facing an inflationary gap when he took office in 1969, for example, President Richard Nixon ordered immediate cuts in government spending. This contractionary fiscal policy sought to shift the aggregate demand curve to the left.

We saw in the last chapter that a central bank such as the Fed can influence aggregate demand through its policies. The choices of a central bank concerning open-market operations, the discount rate, and reserve requirements comprise monetary policy. An **expansionary monetary policy** is a set of monetary policies intended to increase the level of economic activity; a **contractionary monetary policy** is a set of monetary policies intended to reduce it. In the fall of 1990, for example, the Fed adopted an expansionary monetary policy in an effort to close a recessionary gap that had emerged as the economy slipped into recession. The Fed reduced the discount rate and purchased government bonds to increase the money supply. These measures reduced interest rates and led to expanded investment that helped end the recession. A reduction in interest rates, ceteris paribus, leads to an increase in investment, which increases aggregate demand. Fearing the opening of an inflationary gap in 1994, the Fed shifted to a contractionary monetary policy. It sold government bonds to reduce the money supply, and it raised the discount rate. These policies tended to increase interest rates—the Fed was seeking to force a reduction in investment and a reduction in aggregate demand.

- **Fiscal policy** is the use of government purchases, transfer payments, and taxes to influence the level of economic activity.
- An **expansionary fiscal policy** is a fiscal policy aimed at increasing the level of economic activity.
- A **contractionary fiscal policy** is a fiscal policy aimed at reducing the level of economic activity.
- An **expansionary monetary policy** is a set of monetary policy choices aimed at increasing the level of economic activity.
- A **contractionary monetary policy** is a set of monetary policy choices aimed at reducing the level of economic activity.

Checklist

- The aggregate demand curve represents the total of consumption, investment, government purchases, and net exports in any period.
- Consumption and the price level are negatively related because of the real balance effect.
- Investment and the price level are negatively related because of the Keynes effect.
- Net exports and the price level are negatively related because a higher price level discourages exports and encourages imports, while a lower price level encourages exports and discourages imports.
- The aggregate demand curve shifts when the quantity of real GDP demanded at each price level changes.
- Stabilization policy can be used to influence the level of economic activity. Expansionary fiscal or monetary policies seek to increase the level of economic activity; contractionary fiscal or monetary policies seek to reduce it.

Deriving the Aggregate Supply Curve

We learned in Chapter 23 that there are two versions of the aggregate supply curve: the long-run aggregate supply curve and the short-run aggregate supply curve. Over the long run, the real wage adjusts to achieve equilibrium in the market for labor. In the short run, however, the stickiness of the nominal wage and of other prices prevents full adjustment of the real wage and may leave the economy with either a surplus or a shortage of labor. A surplus of labor implies there is a recessionary gap; a shortage implies an inflationary gap.

The long- and short-run aggregate supply curves show how the price level is related to the level of real GDP. Real GDP, in turn, is a measure of the total output of firms. The aggregate supply curves thus show the output of all firms at each price level. To achieve an understanding of the aggregate supply of all firms, we will first look at the supply curve of a single firm, then turn to the entire economy to derive the long- and short-run aggregate supply curves.

The Supply Curve for a Single Firm

A firm's willingness to supply goods and services depends crucially on the relationship between its use of inputs and its production. This section examines that relationship for a single firm. The supply curve we derive for this hypothetical firm is typical of supply curves of firms throughout the economy.

Consider a small auto service shop that provides oil changes. It has a given stock of capital, which includes its building, machinery, and tools. With this stock of capital, the shop can service more cars per day by hiring more workers. The relationship between the number of workers the firm employs each day and the number of cars the firm can service is given by the table in Exhibit 26-5. The same information is plotted graphically using a **total product curve** that relates the firm's total output per period to the quantity of a variable input, with the quantities of other inputs and the technology available to the firm unchanged.[1]

A **total product curve** relates the output of a firm per period to the quantity of a variable input used, with quantities of other inputs and technology unchanged.

[1] Total product curves are often drawn with a region in which the slope of the curve increases with output, then declines. No firm would produce in the range of the curve over which the slope increases; it is therefore ignored here.

EXHIBIT **26-5**

The Total Product Curve

A total product curve relates a firm's use of a variable factor of production in any period to its output in that period. The total product curve shown here gives the number of cars serviced each day with varying quantities of labor for a firm with a given capital stock and technology.

Point on curve	A	B	C	D	E	F	G
Labor per day	0	1	2	3	4	5	6
Output per day	0	30	55	75	90	100	105

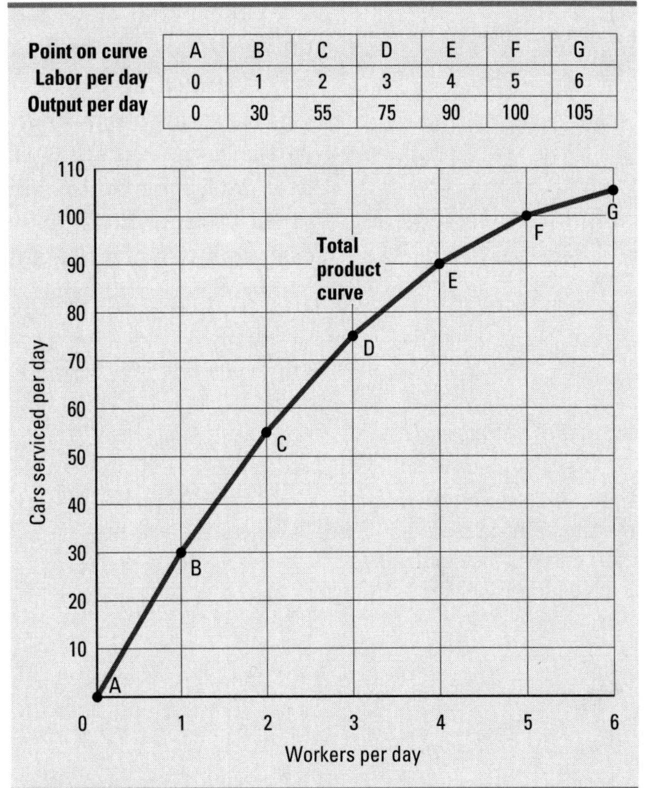

In the total product curve in Exhibit 26-5, labor is the variable input. We assume that other factors, such as the firm's capital stock and the technology with which it produces oil changes, are fixed.

The Marginal Product of Labor

The values given in Exhibit 26-5 for output and the quantity of labor employed suggest an important characteristic of total product curves. We see that increasing the quantity of labor raises the firm's output of oil changes, but by smaller and smaller amounts. The first worker, for example, increases output from zero to 30 oil changes. The second boosts output by 25, the sixth by only 5. Output tends to rise by decreasing amounts because the firm's capital stock remains constant as it adds workers. All the workers use the same set of equipment and work in a limited space, so output rises by less and less. The tendency for output to increase by decreasing amounts as labor is added accounts for the characteristic shape of the total product curve. Its slope is positive, but that slope diminishes as labor increases.

The change in output with an additional unit of labor, holding constant the technology and the quantities of capital and other inputs, is called the **marginal product of labor.** Equation 1 shows how the marginal product of labor MP_L is computed; it equals the ratio of the change in output ΔQ to the change in the use of labor ΔL. We shall consider 1-unit changes in the quantity of labor, so that ΔL equals 1.

The **marginal product of labor** is the change in output resulting from an additional unit of labor, given technology and the quantities of all other inputs.

$$MP_L = \frac{\Delta Q}{\Delta L} \qquad (1)$$

Exhibit 26-6 shows how the marginal product of labor is calculated. Panel (a) gives the total product curve introduced in Exhibit 26-5. The slope of the curve between any two points equals the vertical change in the curve divided by the horizontal change. The vertical change is the increase in output; the horizontal change reflects the employment of an additional worker. The slope of the total product curve thus gives us the marginal product of labor. The slope between points B and C, for example, equals 25, or the increase in the number of cars serviced as a result of the addition of the second worker—slope equals the marginal product of labor.

EXHIBIT 26-6

The Total Product Curve and the Marginal Product of Labor

The total product curve in Panel (a) shows the relationship between the quantity of labor used and total output; the slope of this curve is the marginal product of labor, which is plotted in Panel (b).

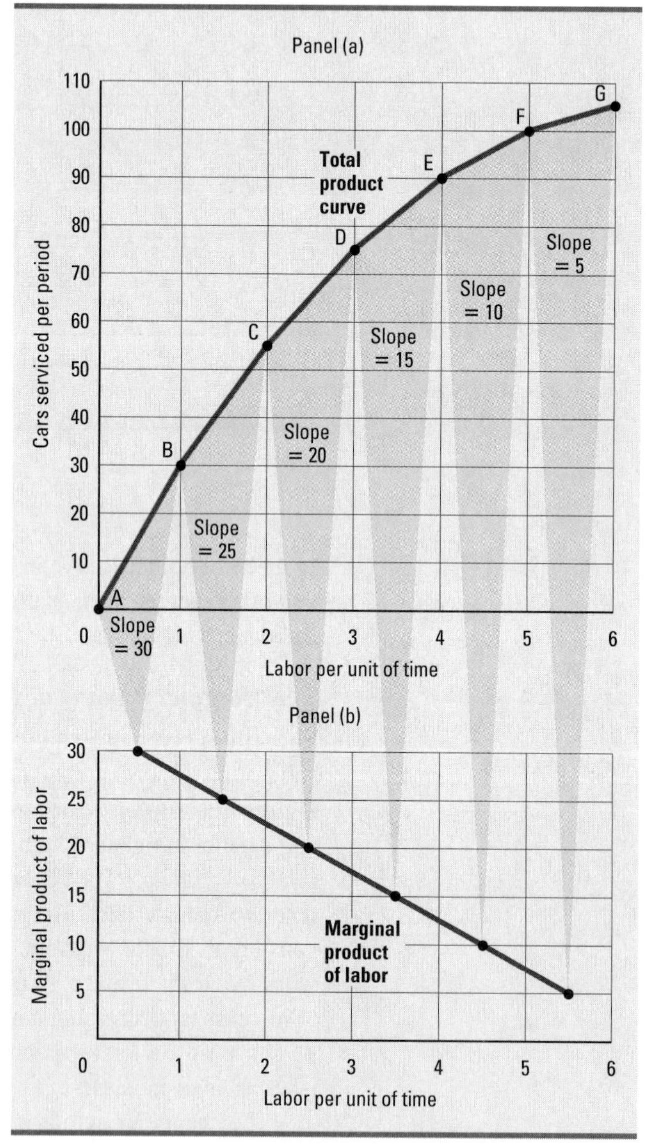

The marginal product of labor is plotted in Panel (b) of Exhibit 26-6. Because marginal product shows the slope of the total product curve between two points, each of the marginal products in Panel (b) is plotted midway between the respective quantities of labor. The marginal product of adding the first worker, for example, is plotted midway between 0 and 1 units of labor on the curve.

A **production function** relates total employment to total output in the economy, all other determinants of production unchanged.

The Production Function and the Demand for Labor

A firm's total product curve relates its output to its use of labor, assuming the quantities of other inputs and the level of technology are unchanged. We can extend this analysis to the entire economy by drawing a **production function,** a curve that relates the total output of an economy to the total amount of labor employed in the economy, all other determinants of production (which include capital, natural resources, and technology) unchanged.

Panel (a) of Exhibit 26-7 shows a production function for an economy. Notice that it shows output levels for a range of employment between 90 million and 110 million workers. When the level of employment is 90 million, the economy produces a real GDP of $3,500 billion (point A). A level of employment of 100 million produces a real GDP of $4,000 billion (point B), and when 110 million workers are employed, a real GDP of $4,300 billion is produced (point C).

The production function in Panel (a) has the same shape as the total product curve for a firm; the slope of the curve declines as total employment rises. That slope is the marginal product of labor; the marginal product of labor thus falls as employment rises.

Panel (b) shows the marginal product of labor curve for the production function given in Panel (a). For each unit of labor, we compute the amount by which real GDP increases. A segment of the production function around point B in Panel (a) is magnified in the graph; it shows that the 100-millionth worker adds $40,000 in real GDP to total output. Suppose that a similar process of magnification reveals that the 90-millionth worker adds $60,000 (point A′) and the 110-millionth worker adds $20,000 to real GDP (point C′). Each of these values is a marginal product. Like the marginal product of labor curve derived for a firm in Exhibit 26-6, the marginal product of labor curve for the economy is a downward-sloping line.[2]

[2] In their analyses of production functions for an economy, economists don't actually take out magnifying glasses to compute marginal products. Instead, they write an equation for the production function and solve for the marginal product of labor mathematically. With large numbers of workers, the convention of plotting values at the midpoints of intervals no longer affects the graph.

EXHIBIT 26-7

The Production Function and the Demand for Labor

The production function in Panel (a) shows the real GDP produced at every level of employment. The slope of the production function is the marginal product of labor, plotted in Panel (b). This curve is the demand curve for labor in the economy. As shown in the blown-up segment of the curve, the 100-millionth worker adds $40,000 to real GDP per year; that is the marginal product of the 100-millionth worker. If the real wage were $40,000, then 100 million workers would be employed.

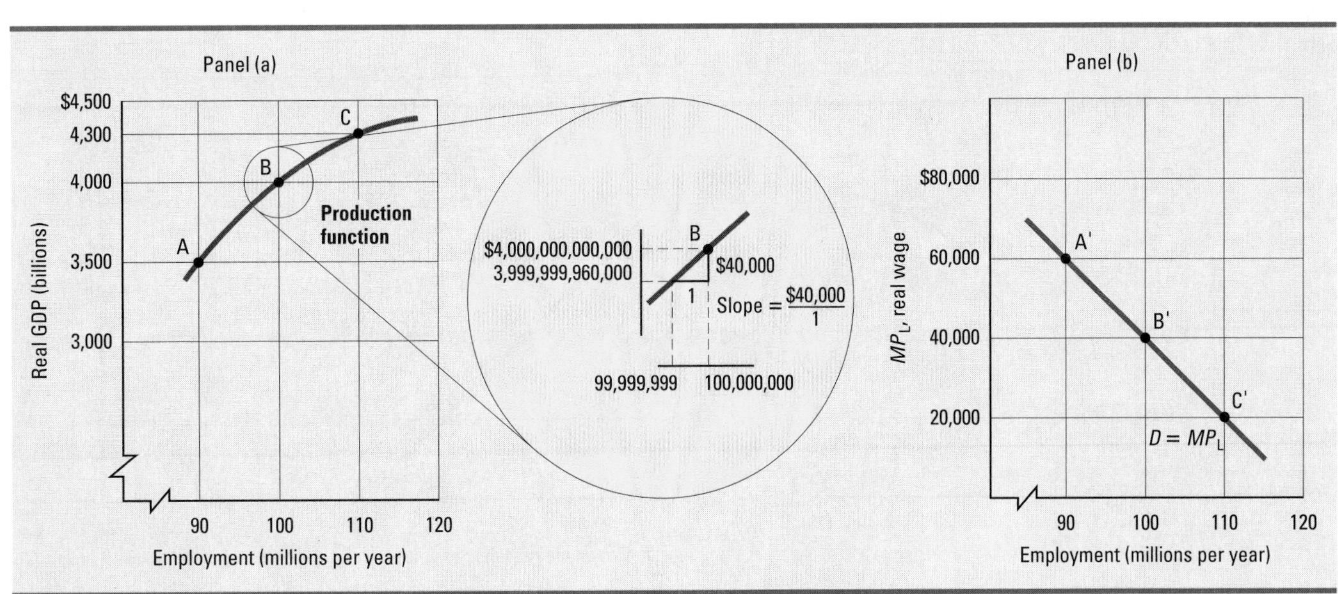

We can interpret the economy's marginal product curve as a demand curve for labor. Suppose, for example, that the real wage is $40,000. At this real wage, how many workers will be demanded in the economy? Firms will hire additional workers if their marginal product, their contribution to total output, exceeds their real wage. Thus, a worker who adds $50,000 to real GDP but commands a real wage of $40,000 will certainly be hired by some firm—hiring such a worker would increase that firm's profits by $10,000. Indeed, with the marginal product curve in Panel (b) of Exhibit 26-7, profit-maximizing firms will hire additional workers up to the 100-millionth worker, because each one of those workers has a marginal product greater than $40,000. The model predicts, though, that the 100,000,001st worker won't be hired; that worker has a marginal product below $40,000. Thus, workers will be employed up to the point that the real wage equals the marginal product of labor. That implies that the marginal product of labor curve is the demand curve for labor in the economy. Given any real wage, the total number of workers demanded by firms will be found as a point on the marginal product of labor curve.

The Production Function, the Market for Labor, and Long-Run Aggregate Supply

To derive the long-run aggregate supply curve, we must add one more piece to the story told in Exhibit 26-7: we need a supply curve for labor. We assume the economy has a fixed quantity of 100 million workers available, so we draw the supply curve for labor, *S*, as a vertical line at 100 million in Panel (b) of Exhibit 26-8.

The labor market is in equilibrium at the natural level of employment. The demand and supply curves for labor intersect at the real wage at which the economy achieves its natural level of employment. We see in Panel (b) that the equilibrium real wage is $40,000 per year and the natural level of employment is 100 million workers. Panel (a) shows that with 100 million workers, the economy can produce a real GDP of $4,000 billion. That output equals the economy's natural level of output.

The long-run aggregate supply curve in Panel (c) shows price levels at which production in the economy will equal natural real GDP. We know that this

EXHIBIT 26-8

Deriving the Long-Run Aggregate Supply Curve

To find the long-run aggregate supply curve, shown here in Panel (c), we begin with the production function PF_1 for the economy in Panel (a). The marginal product of labor MP_L, which is the demand curve for labor in Panel (b), is found by computing the slope of the production function at each quantity of labor. The natural level of employment, determined by the intersection of the demand and supply for labor, is 100 million workers. The production function tells us that at this level of employment, real GDP equals $4,000 billion—the natural level of real GDP. The long-run aggregate supply curve *LRAS* in Panel (c) is a vertical line at the natural level of real GDP.

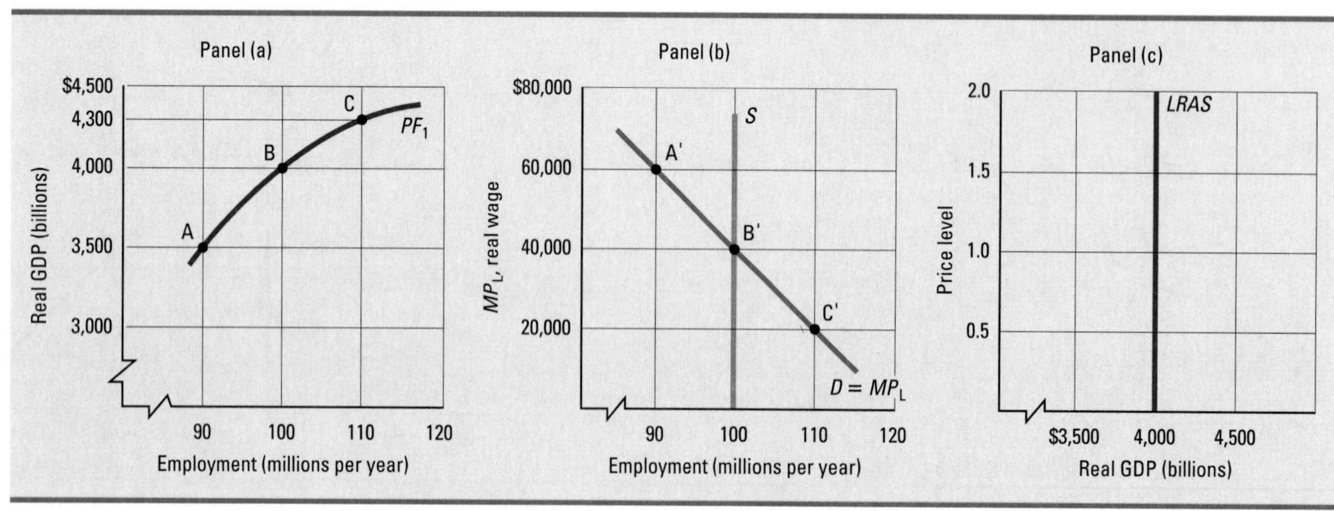

happens in the economy in Exhibit 26-8 at a real wage of $40,000 per year. The real wage is the ratio of the nominal wage to the price level; we thus need price levels at which the real wage equals $40,000. But for *every* price level there is a nominal wage at which the real wage equals $40,000. For example, the economy could achieve its natural level of real GDP at price level–nominal wage combinations of 1.0 and $40,000, 0.5 and $20,000, and 1.5 and $60,000. Because the nominal wage is perfectly flexible in the long run, *any* price level is consistent with a real wage of $40,000. In Panel (c), the long-run aggregate supply curve *LRAS* is therefore a vertical line at the natural level of real GDP, at $4,000 billion.

Changes in Long-Run Aggregate Supply

The position of the long-run aggregate supply curve is determined by two curves: the production function and the supply curve for labor. A change in either will shift the long-run aggregate supply curve.

Exhibit 26-9 shows one possible shifter of long-run aggregate supply: a change in the production function. Suppose, for example, that an improvement in technology shifts the production function in Panel (a) from PF_1 to PF_2. Other developments that could produce an upward shift in the curve include an increase in the capital stock or in the availability of natural resources. The new curve is steeper at each level of employment than the old one; the demand for labor in Panel (b) shifts from D_1 to D_2. With a fixed supply of labor, the natural level of employment remains unchanged. But the real GDP produced at that level of employment rises—labor has become more productive as a result of the technological advance. The real wage rises to $50,000 per year at point E′.

The output the economy can now produce at its natural level of employment is the new natural level of real GDP. We see in Panel (a) that the natural level of real GDP is now $4,300 billion (point E). That output, in turn, defines the new long-run aggregate supply curve. It shifts from $LRAS_1$ to $LRAS_2$ in Panel (c).

A downward shift in the production function reduces the natural level of real GDP. As the production function curve becomes flatter, the marginal product of labor drops, and thus the demand for labor falls. The equilibrium real wage therefore falls. The reduction in the natural level of real GDP causes the long-run aggregate supply curve to shift to the left.

EXHIBIT 26-9

An Increase in the Production Function Increases Long-Run Aggregate Supply

An upward shift in the production function from PF_1 to PF_2 in Panel (a) causes a shift in the demand for labor from D_1 to D_2 in Panel (b). The natural level of output increases from $4,000 billion to $4,300 billion, shifting the long-run aggregate supply curve from $LRAS_1$ to $LRAS_2$ in Panel (c). The equilibrium real wage rises to $50,000 per year at point E′ in Panel (b).

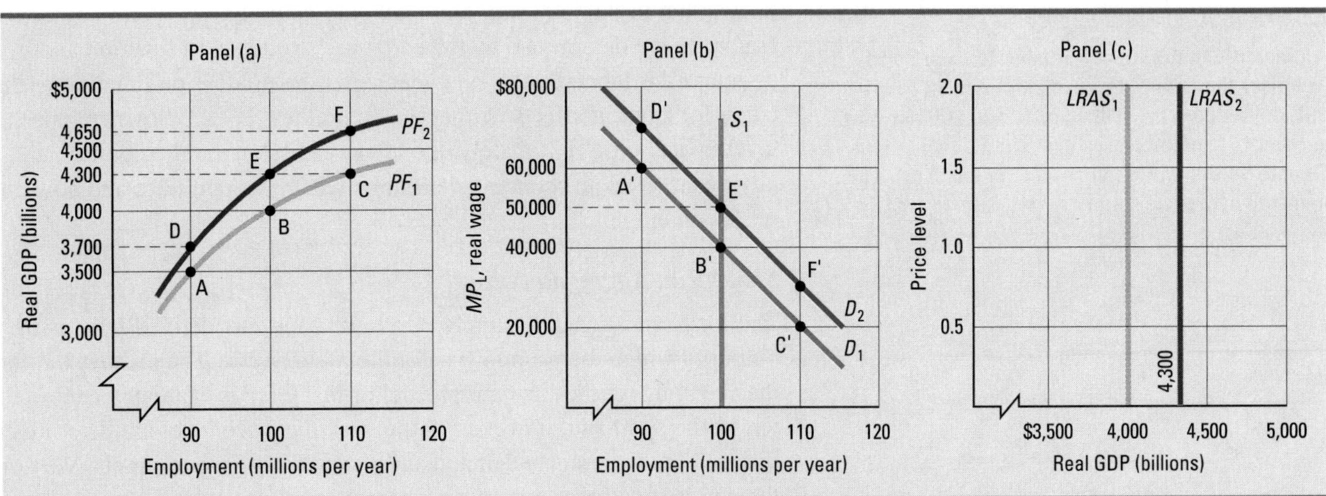

Exhibit 26-10 shows the effects of an increase in the supply of labor, perhaps because of immigration or natural increases in the population or because of increased participation in the labor force by the adult population. Increased participation by women, for example, has tended to increase the supply curve for labor during the past several decades.

In Panel (b), an increase in the labor supply shifts the supply curve to S_2. The increase in the supply of labor doesn't change the stock of capital or natural resources, nor does it change technology—it therefore doesn't shift the production function. Because there is no change in the production function, there is no shift in the demand for labor. The real wage falls to $20,000 per year at point C′ in Panel (b). The natural level of employment has risen to 110 million and the natural level of real GDP has risen to $4,300 billion at point C in Panel (a). The long-run aggregate supply curve in Panel (c) thus shifts to $LRAS_2$. Notice that this is the same shift that was produced by the upward shift in the production function in Exhibit 26-9. The increased supply of labor, however, raises the natural level of employment and reduces the real wage.

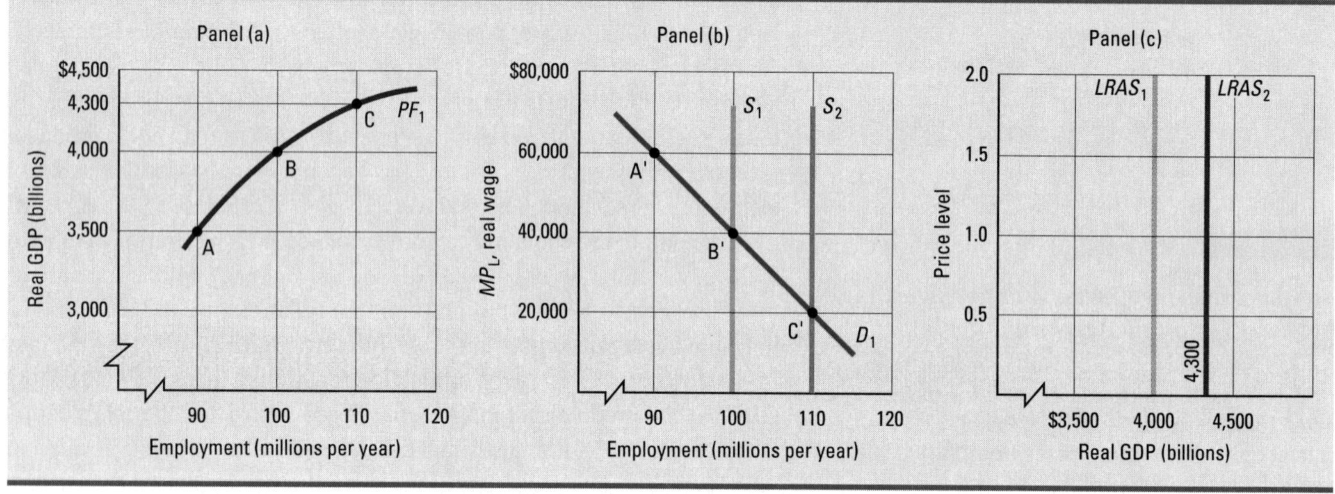

EXHIBIT 26-10

An Increase in the Supply of Labor Increases Long-Run Aggregate Supply

An increase in the supply of labor to S_2 in Panel (b) raises the natural level of employment to 110 million, reduces the real wage to $20,000 per year at point C′, and increases the natural level of real GDP to $4,300 billion at point C in Panel (a). The long-run aggregate supply curve shifts to $LRAS_2$ in Panel (c).

The story told by our model of long-run aggregate supply is a powerful one. It says that in the long run, real GDP, the natural level of employment, and the real wage are determined by the economy's production function and by the supply curve for labor. Unless an event shifts the production function or the supply curve for labor, it affects neither the natural level of employment nor the natural level of real GDP. Ultimately, the labor, capital, natural resources, and technology available to an economy determine what it can produce and how many people it will employ.

Short-Run Aggregate Supply

The long-run aggregate supply curve we have just derived tells us the level of output to which the economy will ultimately adjust. The process through which the economy reaches its natural level of real GDP is examined later in this chapter. In the short run, however, output and the price level are determined by the interaction of aggregate demand and short-run aggregate supply. We turn now to the derivation of the short-run aggregate supply curve.

Case in Point

Technological Change, Employment, and Real Wages During the Industrial Revolution

Technological change and the capital investment that typically comes with it are often criticized on grounds that they replace labor with machines, reducing employment. Such changes, critics argue, hurt workers. The model of aggregate demand and aggregate supply, however, suggests a quite different conclusion. It predicts that improved technology will increase the demand for labor and boost real wages. The natural level of employment changes only if the supply of labor changes.

The period of industrialization, generally taken as encompassing the period between the Civil War and World War I, was a good test of these competing theories. Technological changes were dramatic as firms shifted toward mass production and automation. Capital investment soared. Immigration increased the supply of labor. What happened to workers?

Employment more than doubled during this period, consistent with the prediction of our model. It's harder to predict, from a theoretical point of view, the consequences for real wages. The latter third of the nineteenth century was a period of massive immigration to the United States. Between 1865 and 1880 more than 5 million people immigrated here; most were of working age. The pace accelerated after that. Between 1880 and 1923 more than 23 million people moved to the United States from other countries. Immigration increased the supply of labor, which would reduce the real wage. There were thus two competing forces: technological change and capital investment tended to increase real wages, while immigration tended to reduce them.

The evidence suggests that the forces of technological change and capital investment proved far more powerful than increases in labor supply. Real wages soared 60 percent between 1860 and 1890. They continued to increase after that. Real wages in manufacturing, for example, rose 37 percent from 1890 to 1914.

Technological change and capital investment displace workers in some industries. But for the economy as a whole, they increase worker productivity, increase the demand for labor, and increase real wages.

Sources: Wage data taken from Clarence D. Long, *Wages and Earnings in the United States, 1860–1990* (Princeton, New Jersey: Princeton University Press, 1960), p. 109, and from Albert Rees, *Wages in Manufacturing, 1890–1914* (Princeton, New Jersey: Princeton University Press, 1961), pp. 3–5. Immigration figures taken from Gary M. Walton, and Hugh Rockoff, *History of the American Economy,* 6th ed. (New York: Harcourt Brace Jovanovich, 1990), p. 371.

An early brick factory.

We derive the short-run aggregate supply curve from the production function and from the labor market in much the same way as we derived the long-run aggregate supply curve. The difference is that in the short run, the nominal wage and some other prices are sticky. That stickiness could generate a real wage at which there is a surplus or a shortage in the labor market. Indeed, because the real wage isn't free to adjust in the short run, the assumptions on which a supply curve are typically based are violated. In drawing a conventional supply curve, we show how sellers react to market-determined prices. But in the short run, the real wage isn't market determined; it is determined instead by a combination of changes in the price level and by nominal wages held in place by agreements between workers and their employers. In the short run, then, the supply curve for labor isn't relevant—it's a concept we shall apply only in our analysis of the long run.

Exhibit 26-11 illustrates the framework from which the short-run aggregate supply curve is derived. Panel (a) shows the same production function we used in our analysis of the long-run aggregate supply curve. We thus have the same marginal product of labor—the demand curve for labor—in Panel (b).

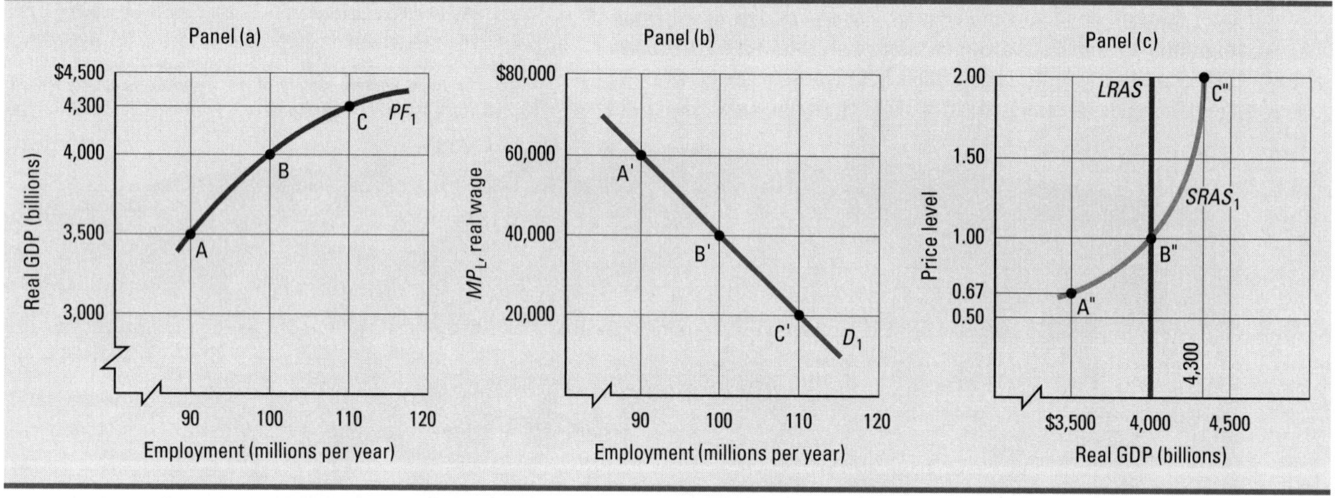

EXHIBIT 26-11

Deriving the Short-Run Aggregate Supply Curve

The slope of the production function PF_1 in Panel (a) gives us the demand curve for labor D_1 in Panel (b). We assume the nominal wage is given; here, it equals $40,000 per year. We select different price levels, compute the real wage, and then determine the quantity of labor demanded in Panel (b). We then determine the quantity of real GDP produced in Panel (a). The resulting combination of price level and real GDP give us a point on the short-run aggregate supply curve $SRAS_1$ in Panel (c).

Suppose the annual nominal wage is $40,000. Nominal wages are sticky in the short run, so we shall suppose the nominal wage is fixed at $40,000. Suppose the price level is 1.00. The real wage is thus $40,000. At that real wage, firms employ 100 million workers and output is $4,000 billion. Recall from our analysis in Exhibit 26-8 that these employment and output levels correspond to the economy's natural levels of employment and output. This output, together with the price level of 1.0, give us point B″ on the short-run aggregate supply curve shown in Panel (c).

Our strategy for deriving other points on the short-run aggregate supply curve is as follows: We select other price levels and calculate the real wage, assuming the nominal wage remains at $40,000. We then check the demand curve for labor to see how many workers will be employed, and we read up to the production function to determine the real GDP produced at that level of employment. We now have a price level and the corresponding real GDP level that lie on the short-run aggregate supply curve.

Let's take, for example, a price level of 0.67. (This is rounded off; the actual value is ⅔. To obtain accurate results, we need to use the fraction in our calculation.) The nominal wage is sticky; it remains at $40,000. With a lower price level and a constant nominal wage, the real wage rises to $60,000 (=$40,000/⅔). At that real wage, firms reduce the number of workers they employ to 90 million, at point A′ in Panel (b). That level of employment generates a real GDP of $3,500 billion, at point A in Panel (a). We now have a second point on our short-run aggregate supply curve in Panel (c); point A″ corresponds to an output of $3,500 billion and a price level of 0.67.

Now suppose the price level rises to 2.00. At the higher price level, with a nominal wage of $40,000, the real wage falls to $20,000 in Panel (b). At that real wage, firms increase the quantity of labor they demand to 110 million at point C′. With the higher level of employment, output rises to $4,300 billion, at point C in Panel (a). A price level of 2.00 thus produces an output of $4,300 billion at point C″ in Panel (c).

The short-run aggregate supply curve is drawn for a given nominal wage. We derive it by selecting different price levels for the economy, then computing the real wage and determining from the demand curve for labor how many workers would be employed at each real wage. Once we determine employment, we can determine real GDP from the production function. Price levels and corresponding levels of real GDP give points on the short-run aggregate supply curve.

We see now that the shape of the short-run aggregate supply curve is related to the shape of the production function. When we first encountered the short-run aggregate supply curve in Chapter 23, we saw that the curve becomes steeper and is almost vertical where the economy approaches its capacity constraint. That idea of capacity is also reflected in the production function for the economy; the production function in Panel (a) approaches an upward limit in the neighborhood of $4,500 billion. As a result, the short-run aggregate supply curve $SRAS_1$ approaches the same capacity constraint in Panel (c).

Changes in Short-Run Aggregate Supply

We can derive the short-run aggregate supply curve from the production function and an assumed value for the nominal wage. It follows that a change in the production function or the nominal wage will shift the short-run aggregate supply curve. The production function will shift if there is a change in the quantity of capital or natural resources available to firms or if there is a change in technology. The nominal wage will be affected by changes in labor markets throughout the economy.

It will be important to distinguish between two kinds of shifts in the short-run aggregate supply curve: those that are produced by shifts in the production function and those that are produced by changes in nominal wages. The reason is that changes in the production function also shift the long-run aggregate supply curve and therefore change the economy's natural level of real GDP. Changes in nominal wages shift only the short-run aggregate supply curve and therefore have no long-run effects.

Consider first a shift in short-run aggregate supply resulting from a shift in the production function. Let's examine the effects of the same technological change we investigated in Exhibit 26-9. The technological advance moves the production function upward to PF_2 in Panel (a) of Exhibit 26-12 and increases the demand for labor in Panel (b) to D_2. Suppose the nominal wage is $40,000

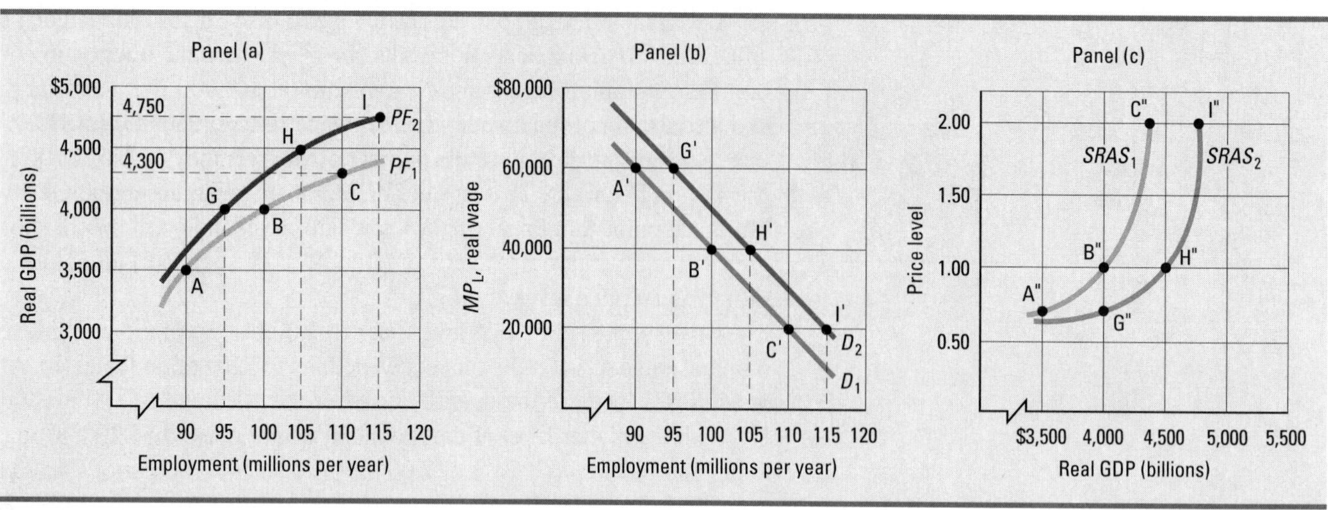

EXHIBIT 26-12

A Shift in the Production Function Shifts the Short-Run Aggregate Supply Curve

An upward shift in the production function to PF_2 in Panel (a) increases the demand for labor to D_2 in Panel (b). That increases the quantity of labor demanded at each real wage in Panel (b). The nominal wage remains at $40,000 in the short run. At a price level of 1.00 the real wage equals $40,000 and the quantity of labor demanded rises to 105 million [point H′ in Panel (b)]. These workers produce a real GDP of $4,500 [point H in Panel (a)]. We thus obtain point H″ on the new short-run aggregate supply curve $SRAS_2$, with a real GDP of $4,500 billion and a price level of 1.00.

and the price level is 1.00. The quantity of labor demanded at a real wage of $40,000 increases to 105 million at point H′ in Panel (b). As before, we assume that in the short run, firms will be able to employ these additional workers. The real GDP produced at this level of employment is found from PF_2 in Panel (a); it is $4,500 billion at point H. The real GDP associated with a price level of 1.00 thus rises to $4,500 billion at point H″ in Panel (c).

Similar increases in production occur at price levels of 0.67 and 2.00, as shown in Panel (c). The quantity of labor demanded at each real wage rises, increasing output. The short-run aggregate supply curve $SRAS_1$ thus shifts to the right to $SRAS_2$. The upward shift in the production function has increased the economy's capacity to produce real GDP. The new short-run aggregate supply curve $SRAS_2$ thus approaches being a vertical line at a higher level of output than before.

Now consider the impact of a change in the nominal wage. We derived the short-run aggregate supply curve from the production function in Exhibit 26-11 based on an arbitrary assumption that the nominal wage was $40,000. We then computed the real wage at different price levels in order to derive combinations of price levels, employment levels, and then real GDP levels to plot on the short-run aggregate supply curve. If the nominal wage were to fall, then the price level consistent with a particular real wage would be lower.

In the analysis of Exhibit 26-11, a nominal wage of $40,000 and a price level of 1.00 implied a real wage of $40,000, employment of 100 million, and production at its natural level of $4,000 billion. But suppose that the nominal wage falls to $30,000 with the production function unchanged. The economy will produce the same level of output only if the real wage remains at $40,000. That, in turn, would require a price level of 0.75 ($30,000/0.75 = $40,000). The level of real GDP produced at that real wage, $4,000 billion, would thus require a price level of 0.75, not 1.00, and the aggregate supply curve would shift downward. This shift is shown in Panel (c) of Exhibit 26-13.

The change in the nominal wage has not shifted the production function; it has not changed the economy's capacity to produce real GDP. The new short-run aggregate supply curve thus approaches the economy's capacity constraint at the same range of real GDP as before. We thus say that the new short-run aggregate supply curve has shifted downward.

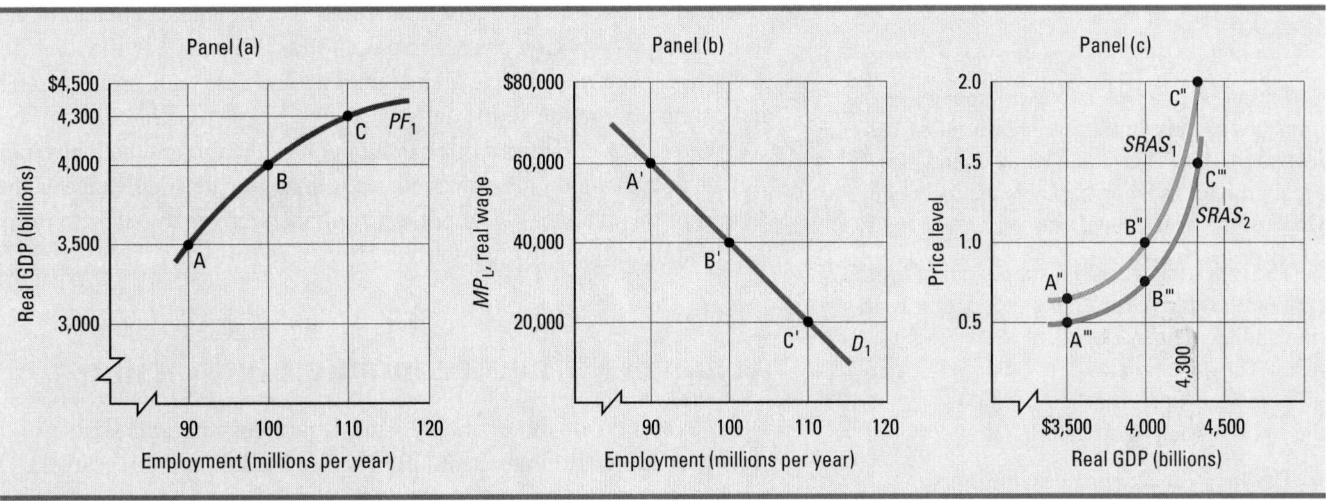

EXHIBIT 26-13

A Reduction in the Nominal Wage Shifts the Aggregate Supply Curve Downward

Suppose the economy faces the same production function PF_1, but now the nominal wage falls from $40,000 to $30,000. That means the price level consistent with each level of output falls. At point B′ in Panel (b), 100 million workers are demanded at a real wage of $40,000; Panel (a) shows that those workers produce a real GDP of $4,000 billion. A price level of 0.75 would achieve a real wage of $40,000 ($30,000/0.75 = $40,000). We thus have a new point B‴ in Panel (c) corresponding to a price level of 0.75 and a real GDP of $4,000 billion.

A reduction in the nominal wage thus shifts the short-run aggregate supply curve downward. An increase in the nominal wage shifts it upward. Such changes don't affect the economy's capacity to produce goods and services; therefore, they do not move the capacity constraint that limits the range of the short-run aggregate supply curve.

In Exhibit 26-14, Panel (a) contrasts the left-right shifts produced by changes in the production function with Panel (b) showing the up-down shifts generated by changes in the nominal wage. A change in the production function alters the economy's capacity constraint; it therefore changes the range of the short-run aggregate supply curve—the curve approaches a capacity constraint at a different level of output. A change in the nominal wage leaves this constraint unchanged; the short-run aggregate supply curves shifts up or down but approaches the same capacity constraint.

There are two reasons it's important to distinguish between left-right and up-down shifts in short-run aggregate supply. First, the effects are caused by different events. Left-right shifts reflect a shift in the production function while up-down shifts reflect a change in nominal wages. Second, the two kinds of shifts have very different implications for the long run. A left-right shift, which results

EXHIBIT 26-14

Distinguishing Shifts in the Short-Run Aggregate Supply Curve

Shifts in the production function change the economy's capacity constraint and thus change the range of the short-run aggregate supply curve. We can think of such changes as shifts of the curve to the left or right as shown in Panel (a). Changes in nominal wages leave the capacity constraint unaffected but change the price level associated with each level of real GDP. Such changes can be thought of as up-down shifts in the short-run aggregate supply curve, as shown in Panel (b).

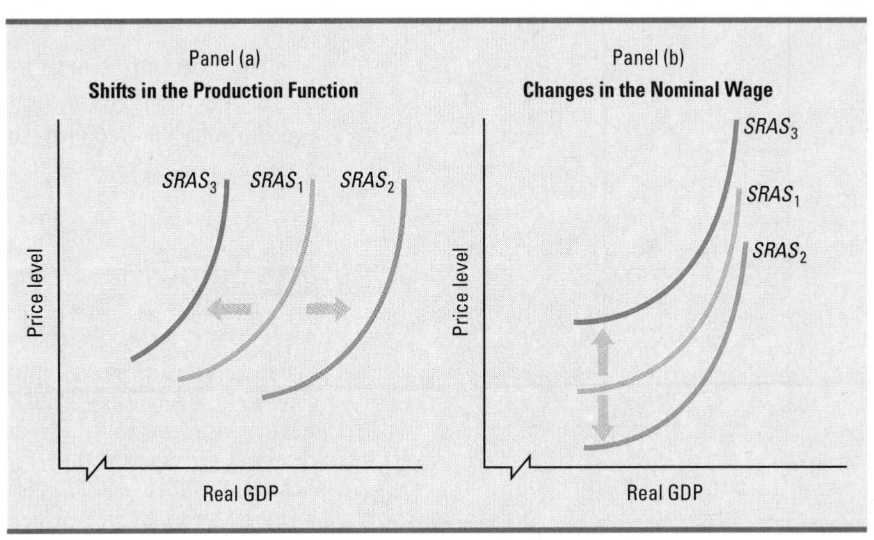

Checklist

- The slope of a firm's total product curve diminishes as the quantity of labor used by the firm increases. This slope, which is the marginal product of labor, explains the increasing slope of the firm's supply curve.
- The long-run aggregate supply curve for the economy is derived from the production function and the demand and supply curves for labor. The demand curve for labor is the marginal product curve for labor, which is a plot of the slope of the production function.
- The long-run aggregate supply curve is a vertical line at the natural level of real GDP. The curve shifts in response to changes in the economy's production function or in the supply curve for labor. Shifts in the production function can be caused by changes in the economy's stock of natural resources or capital or by changes in technology.
- The derivation of the short-run aggregate supply curve requires the specification of a value for the nominal wage.
- The short-run aggregate supply curve shifts to the right or left with shifts in the production function. It shifts up or down with changes in the nominal wage. The curve also shifts up or down when other changes affect firms' production costs.

from a change in the production function, accompanies a change in natural real GDP and thus implies a change in output that will persist in the long run. An up-down shift does not involve a change in natural real GDP and thus affects price and output only in the short run.

We've now completed our examination of the factors that determine the aggregate demand and long-run and short-run aggregate supply curves. In the final section of this chapter, we'll put the combined curves together to examine how the economy adjusts to changes that affect these curves.

Achieving Macroeconomic Equilibrium

The intersection of the economy's aggregate demand and short-run aggregate supply curves determines its equilibrium real GDP and price level in the short run. The intersection of aggregate demand and long-run aggregate supply determines its long-run equilibrium. In this section we'll examine the process through which an economy achieves equilibrium and learn how it responds to changes in the equilibrium solution.

Changes in Aggregate Demand

We've already seen that the aggregate demand curve shifts in response to a change in consumption, investment, government purchases, or net exports. Now we'll see how the economy responds to such shifts.

An Increase in Aggregate Demand

Suppose an economy is initially in equilibrium at its natural level of output Y_n in Exhibit 26-15. Because the economy is operating at its natural level, the labor market must be in equilibrium; the quantities of labor demanded and supplied are equal.

Now suppose aggregate demand increases because one or more of its components (consumption, investment, government purchases, and/or net exports) has increased at each price level. The aggregate demand curve shifts from AD_1 to AD_2. That will increase real GDP to Y_2 and force the price level up to P_2 in the short run. The higher price level, combined with a fixed nominal wage, results in a lower real wage. Firms employ more workers to supply the increased output.

The economy's new production level Y_2 exceeds the natural level. Employment exceeds its natural level. The solution at Y_2 and P_2 is only a short-run equilibrium; the economy has an inflationary gap equal to the difference between Y_2 and Y_n.

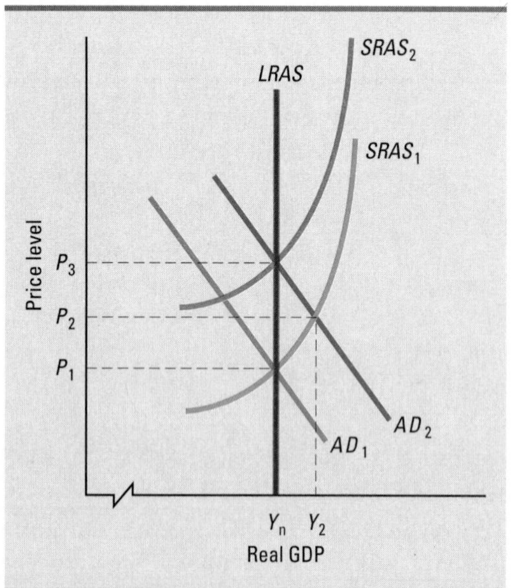

EXHIBIT 26-15

An Increase in Aggregate Demand

In the short run, an increase in aggregate demand to AD_2 boosts real GDP to Y_2 and the price level to P_2, creating an inflationary gap equal to $Y_2 - Y_n$. The increase in the price level lowers the real wage and increases employment past the natural level. In the long run, increases in the nominal wage shift the short-run aggregate supply curve upward to equilibrium at $SRAS_2$. The price level rises to P_3, and real GDP returns to Y_n. Employment returns to its natural level.

Ultimately, the nominal wage will rise as workers seek to restore their lost purchasing power. As the nominal wage rises, the short-run aggregate supply curve will begin shifting upward. It will continue to shift upward as long as the nominal wage rises, and the nominal wage will rise as long as there is an inflationary gap. Upward shifts in short-run aggregate supply, however, will reduce real GDP and thus begin to close this gap. When the short-run aggregate supply curve reaches $SRAS_2$, the economy will have returned to its natural level of output, and employment will have returned to its natural level.

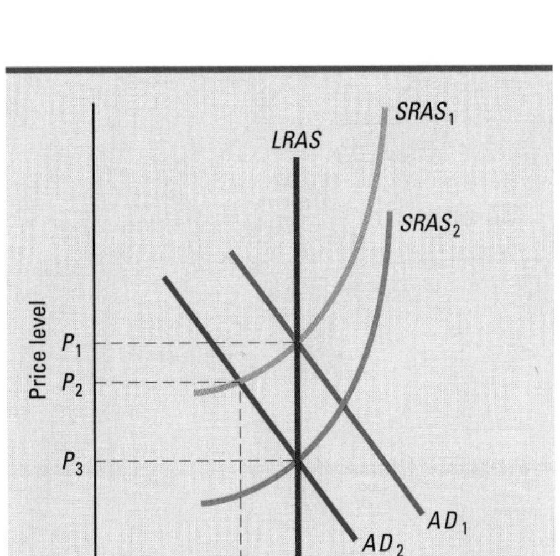

EXHIBIT 26-16

A Reduction in Aggregate Demand

The economy shown here is in equilibrium at its natural level of output Y_n, and there is full employment. A reduction in aggregate demand shifts the aggregate demand curve AD_2, reducing real GDP and the price level to Y_2 and P_2, respectively. There is a recessionary gap with a surplus of labor. Eventually, the nominal wage will start to fall, pushing the short-run aggregate supply curve downward. Long-run equilibrium is achieved when the curve reaches $SRAS_2$. The economy returns to its natural level of output, and real wages return to a level that achieves equilibrium in the labor market.

A Decrease in Aggregate Demand

A decrease in aggregate demand produces a reduction in real GDP in the short run. In the long run, however, the economy returns to its natural level of output as the real wage adjusts to its equilibrium level.

Suppose the economy is in equilibrium at its natural level, as shown in Exhibit 26-16. Real GDP equals Y_n and the price level is P_1. The labor market is in equilibrium with employment at its natural level. If a reduction in consumption, investment, government purchases, or net exports shifts the aggregate demand curve to AD_2, the price level falls to P_2 and real GDP drops to Y_2. With the nominal wage fixed in the short run, the real wage rises, reducing employment. There is a surplus of labor, and the economy has a recessionary gap equal to $Y_n - Y_2$.

The recessionary gap can last only as long as stickiness prevents wages and prices from adjusting so that the real wage returns to its original level. Because there will be continued downward pressure on prices when the economy has a recessionary gap, the nominal wage must fall by even more than the price level to produce the required reduction in the real wage. That adjustment occurs in the long run. As the nominal wage falls, the short-run aggregate supply curve shifts downward. It will continue to do so as long as a recessionary gap remains. Long-run equilibrium is achieved when the short-run aggregate supply curve shifts to $SRAS_2$. Real GDP returns to its natural level, the price level falls to P_3, and employment returns to the natural level.

Our analysis of increases and reductions in aggregate demand demonstrates an important implication of the model: Changes in aggregate demand affect employment and real GDP only in the short run. They do not change employment or real GDP in the long run. That's because real GDP ultimately returns to its natural level. Only changes in long-run aggregate supply can produce changes in real GDP in the long run. We turn now to an examination of changes in aggregate supply.

Changes in Aggregate Supply

We have distinguished between two categories of change in aggregate supply. The first type shifts the long-run and short-run aggregate supply curves to the right or left, because of a change in the production function or in the supply of labor. Because such changes produce a new level of natural real GDP, their impact on the economy is sustained in the long run. A second category of change involves an up-down shift in short-run aggregate supply with no change in the long-run aggregate supply curve. Such changes are caused by changes in nominal wages. They create an inflationary or a recessionary gap in the short run, but no change in natural real GDP.

Case in Point: Aggregate Demand and the Great Depression

What brought on the Great Depression of the 1930s? The accompanying figure suggests it was set off by a series of reductions in aggregate demand.

Planned investment and consumption began falling late in 1929. Those reductions were reinforced by plunges in net exports and in government purchases. By 1933, aggregate demand had fallen all the way to AD_{33}.

Reductions in aggregate demand in the 1930s forced the economy into a recessionary gap. Nominal wages began falling, shifting the short-run aggregate supply curve downward. Nominal wages plunged 26 percent between 1929 and 1933. The downward shifts in short-run aggregate supply tended to increase real GDP, but those effects were swamped by continued reductions in aggregate demand. We'll examine the reasons for subsequent reductions in aggregate demand—and for the economy's eventual recovery from the Great Depression—in subsequent chapters.

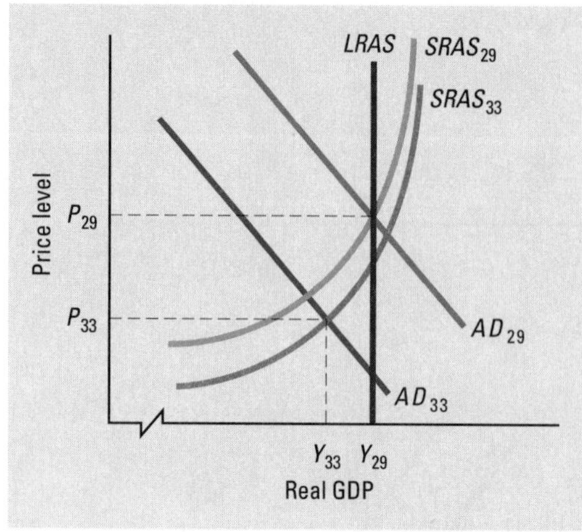

Changes in Natural Real GDP

Exhibit 26-17 illustrates a change in the economy's natural level of real GDP. Suppose, for example, that the economy's production function shifts upward, perhaps because of an increase in the stock of capital or natural resources or a technological advance. The upward shift in the production function shifts the long-run aggregate supply curve to the right to $LRAS_2$, increasing the economy's natural level of real GDP to Y_n'. The change in the production function shifts the short-run aggregate supply curve to $SRAS_2$. Real GDP rises to Y_2 and the price level falls to P_2. This is the economy's short-run response to the change.

Notice that the short-run solution at Y_2 lies to the left of the economy's new natural level of real GDP, Y_n'. Despite the fact that real GDP has risen, the economy now faces a recessionary gap. In the short run, the economy hasn't fully taken advantage of its increased ability to produce goods and services. In the long run, the recessionary gap produces the same kind of adjustment mechanism we traced above. Nominal wages fall, shifting the short-run aggregate supply curve down to $SRAS_3$. The price level falls to P_3, and output achieves its new natural level Y_n'.

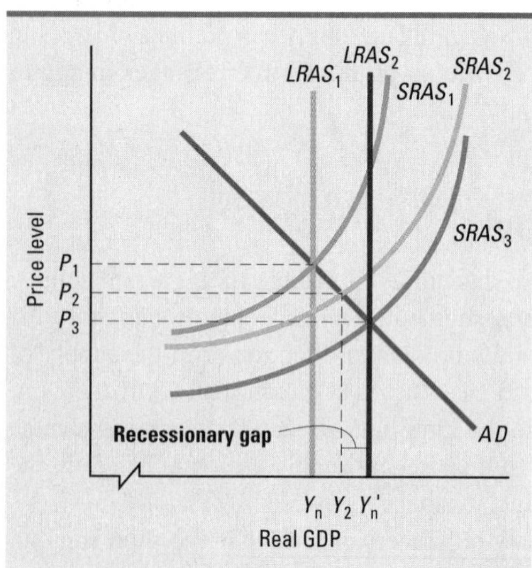

EXHIBIT 26-17

An Increase in Short- and Long-Run Aggregate

An upward shift in the production function or a rightward shift in the supply curve for labor shifts the long- and short-run aggregate supply curves to the right. The natural level of real GDP rises to Y_n'. In the short run, real GDP rises to Y_2, leaving the economy with a recessionary gap. As nominal wages fall, short-run aggregate supply begins shifting down. Long-run equilibrium is achieved when the curve reaches $SRAS_3$, real GDP equals its new natural level, and the price level drops to P_3.

Short-Run Changes in Aggregate Supply

Changes in nominal wages can shift the economy's short-run aggregate supply curve up or down without affecting the long-run curve. We'll see in subsequent chapters that government policies can change wage costs to firms in a way that shifts the short-run aggregate supply curve, creating an inflationary or a recessionary gap. Such changes do not, however, affect the natural level of real GDP.

Gap Closing: Nonintervention Versus Stabilization Policies

As we saw in Chapter 23, the model of aggregate demand and aggregate supply confronts us with a choice in dealing with recessionary or inflationary gaps. Policymakers faced with such gaps can elect to allow the economy to correct itself on its own, simply waiting until nominal wages and other prices adjust and equilibrium is achieved at the natural level of output. Such a policy is a nonintervention policy. Alternatively, policymakers might choose to use a stabilization policy, employing fiscal or monetary policy to shift the aggregate demand curve.

Panel (a) of Exhibit 26-18 shows an economy with a recessionary gap. By definition, employment in such an economy falls short of its natural level—the supply of labor in the long run exceeds the quantity demanded. A nonintervention policy means waiting until a falling nominal wage shifts the short-run aggregate supply curve down to $SRAS_2$. Alternatively, an expansionary stabilization policy could be used in an effort to shift aggregate demand to AD_2 to close the gap.

Panel (b) shows an economy with an inflationary gap. Employment in an economy with an inflationary gap exceeds its natural level—the quantity of labor demanded exceeds long-run supply. A nonintervention policy would rely on nominal wages to rise in response to the shortage of labor. As wages rise, the short-run aggregate supply curve begins to shift upward, bringing the economy to its natural level when it reaches $SRAS_2$. The alternative to a nonintervention policy that permits the economy to close the gap on its own is a contractionary stabilization policy. Such a policy would aim at shifting the aggregate demand curve to AD_2 to close the gap.

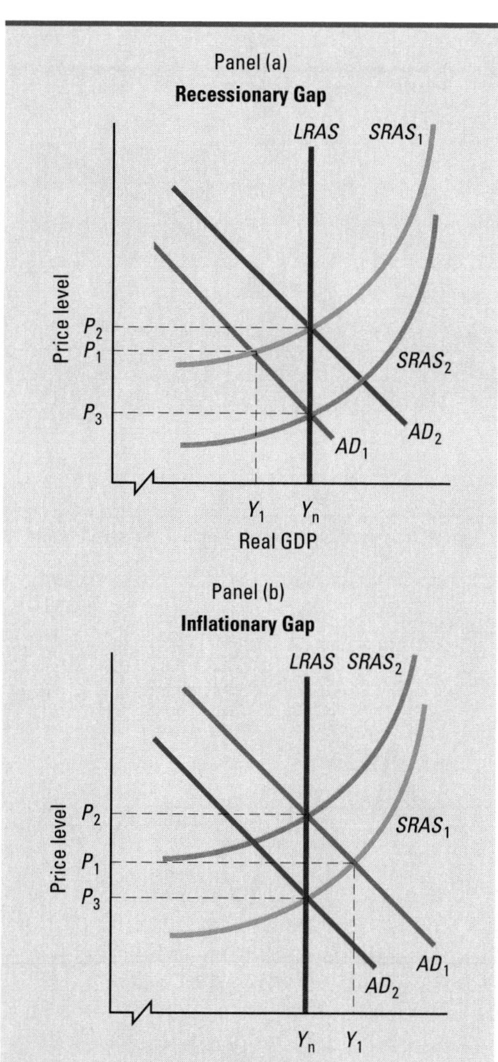

EXHIBIT 26-18

Alternatives in Gap Closing

Panel (a) shows an economy with a recessionary gap. Such an economy has a surplus of labor and thus an unemployment rate that exceeds the natural rate. A nonintervention policy would rely on reductions in the nominal wage to shift the short-run aggregate supply curve downward to $SRAS_2$, where the economy reaches its natural real GDP of Y_n at a price level of P_3. Alternatively, an expansionary fiscal or monetary policy could be used in an effort to increase aggregate demand to AD_2, returning the economy to its natural level at a price level of P_2. Panel (b) shows an economy with an inflationary gap. There is thus a shortage of labor. A nonintervention policy would allow nominal wages to rise, shifting the short-run aggregate supply curve to $SRAS_2$ and returning the economy to its natural level at a price level of P_2. Alternatively, contractionary fiscal or monetary policies could be used to shift the aggregate demand curve to AD_2 and return the economy to its natural level at a price level of P_3.

How large are inflationary and recessionary gaps? Panel (a) of Exhibit 26-19 shows the economy's natural versus its actual level of real GDP since 1950. We see that economic activity has fluctuated about its natural level, but that there have been periods in which inflationary or recessionary gaps have been sustained for several years. Panel (b) shows the sizes of these gaps expressed as percentages of natural GDP. The percentage gap is positive during periods of inflationary gaps and negative during periods of recessionary gaps. The economy seldom departs by more than 5 percent from its natural level.

Economists differ on the relative merits of stabilization versus nonintervention responses to recessionary and inflationary gaps. Those who advocate stabilization policies argue that prices are sufficiently sticky that the economy's own adjustment to its natural level will be a slow process—and a painful one. For an economy with a recessionary gap, unacceptably high levels of unemployment will persist for too long a time. For an economy with an inflationary gap, the increased prices that occur as the short-run aggregate supply curve shifts upward impose too high an inflation rate in the short run. These economists believe it is far preferable to use stabilization policy to shift the aggregate demand curve in an effort to shorten the time the economy is subject to a gap.

EXHIBIT 26-19

Real GDP and Natural GDP, 1950–1995

Panel (a) shows natural GDP (the red line) and actual real GDP (the black line) since 1950. Panel (b) shows the gap between natural and actual real GDP expressed as a percentage of natural GDP since 1950. The percentage gap is positive in periods in which the economy had an inflationary gap and negative during periods of a recessionary gap. The gap has generally been less than 5 percent of real GDP.

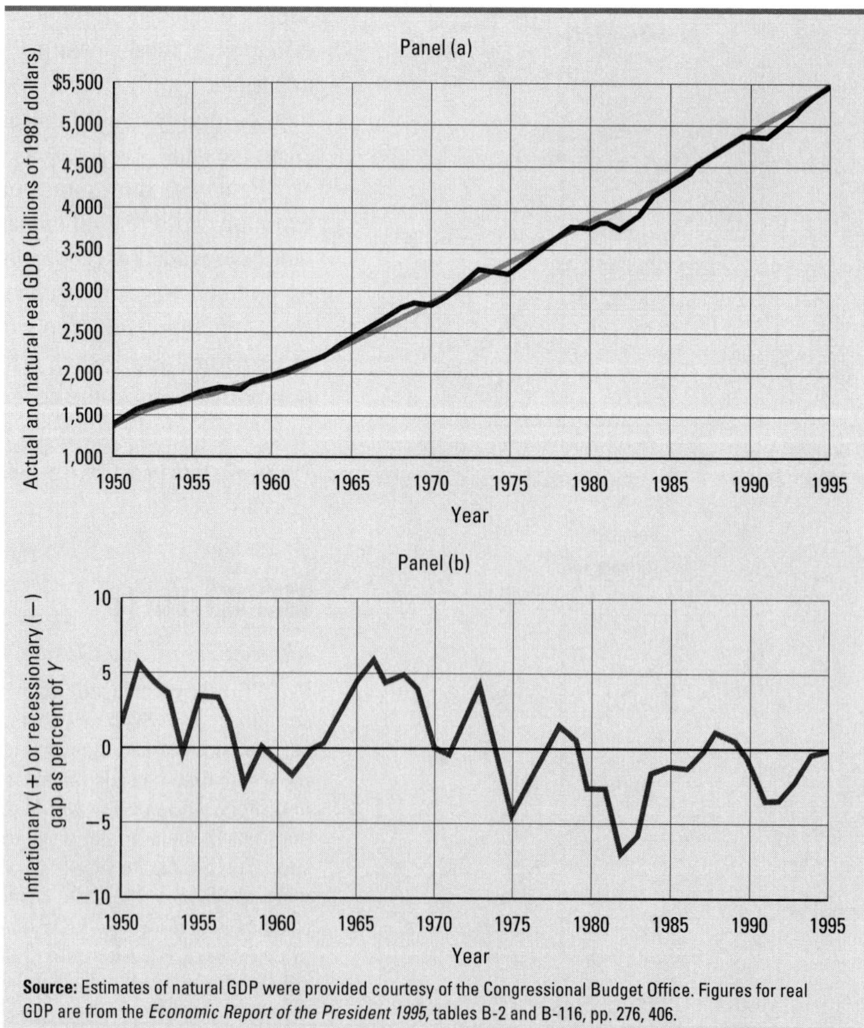

Source: Estimates of natural GDP were provided courtesy of the Congressional Budget Office. Figures for real GDP are from the *Economic Report of the President 1995*, tables B-2 and B-116, pp. 276, 406.

New Keynesian economists, who emphasize the stickiness of prices, are most likely to advocate the use of stabilization policy. They argue that policy intervention has the potential to improve on economic performance. Their view is nicely anticipated in the quotation from the Swiss economist Simonde de Sismondi that opens this chapter. Equilibrium may ultimately be achieved at the economy's natural level, but the suffering required to get there is too high a cost to pay, given the ability of policymakers to close a gap quickly through policies that shift aggregate demand.

Economists who favor a nonintervention approach are likely to do so for different reasons. Some accept the notion that stabilization policy can be used to shift the aggregate demand curve. They argue, however, that such efforts are not nearly as simple in the real world as they may appear in a textbook. They note that policies undertaken to change real GDP are not likely to affect economic activity for months, or even years, after they are undertaken. Stabilization policy must thus respond to gaps we expect in the future—not gaps that we may be able to assess today. That means that policymakers could end up guessing wrong about what kind of stabilization policy should be undertaken. They may choose an expansionary policy when a contractionary one is needed or a contractionary policy when an expansionary one is needed, so their efforts to stabilize the economy could be destabilizing. Another line of objection comes from economists who question whether serious gaps even exist. If prices are sufficiently flexible to keep the economy close to its natural level, then observed fluctuations in real GDP may reflect swings in natural GDP, not the emergence of recessionary or expansionary gaps. In this view, there may be no macroeconomic problem to fix!

Monetarist and new classical economists are most likely to adhere to the nonintervention view. First, these economists stress the economy's own ability to correct itself. Second, they question whether stabilization policies can stabilize. Monetarists note the potential of stabilization policy to be destabilizing. New classical economists question whether such policies can work—and whether they're needed.

The debate over how policymakers should respond to recessionary versus inflationary gaps will emerge over and over as we continue our investigation of macroeconomics. We must remember that this is a debate over policy alternatives in the short run. A separate set of issues is involved in assessing how public policy can influence the determination of the economy's natural level of real GDP. We'll examine those issues in subsequent chapters as well.

These issues of nonintervention versus stabilization policies lie at the heart of the macroeconomic policy debate. We'll return to them as we continue our analysis of the determination of income and the price level in the next seven chapters.

Checklist ✓

- An increase in consumption, investment, government purchases, or net exports shifts the aggregate demand curve to the right. A reduction in any of these variables shifts it to the left.
- Changes in the production function or in the supply of labor shift the long- and short-run aggregate supply curves. Changes in nominal wages shift the short-run but not the long-run aggregate supply curve.
- New Keynesian economists generally favor the use of stabilization policy to close inflationary or recessionary gaps. Monetarists and new classical economists generally prefer a nonintervention approach.

A Look Back—And a Look Ahead

In this chapter we derived the aggregate demand and aggregate supply curves introduced in Chapter 23. We examined the factors that can shift the curves, and we traced the economy's response to shifts in those curves.

The aggregate demand curve slopes downward, reflecting the tendency for the aggregate quantity of goods and services demanded to rise as the price level falls and to fall as the price level rises. The negative relationship between the price level and the quantity of goods and services demanded results from the real balance effect for consumption, the Keynes effect for investment, and the impact of a changing price level on net exports.

Aggregate supply is derived from the economy's production function, from which the demand curve for labor may be obtained, and the supply curve for labor. The intersection of the demand and supply for labor determine the natural level of employment. Applying the natural level of employment to the production function, we obtain the natural level of output. Given flexibility of prices and the nominal wage in the long run, the long-run aggregate supply curve is a vertical line at the natural level of output. The short-run aggregate supply curve is found by taking the initial nominal wage as given, then determining the real wage at different price levels. Each real wage determines a level of employment, which determines a level of output. Combining price levels and their resultant levels of output gives us the short-run aggregate supply curve. The curve will shift in response to a shift in the production function or a change in the nominal wage.

For an economy operating at its natural level, a change in aggregate demand or aggregate supply will induce a recessionary or inflationary gap. Such a gap will be closed in the long run by changes in the nominal wage, which will shift the short-run aggregate supply curve upward (to close an inflationary gap) or downward (to close a recessionary gap).

Policymakers may respond to a recessionary or inflationary gap with a nonintervention policy, one that allows the economy to adjust to its natural level on its own. The alternative is the use of stabilization policy, which relies on changes in government spending, taxes, or the money supply to close the gap. A nonintervention policy may require several years before the economy closes a gap, particularly a recessionary one. It avoids, however, the danger of policy intervention that may misjudge the size of the gap and replace one gap with another. Stabilization policy may allow a gap to be closed more quickly, but it risks moving the economy even further from its natural level if policymakers err in administering economic medicine. In general, new Keynesian economists tend to lean toward greater reliance on stabilization policies, while monetarist and new classical economists rely on a nonintervention approach.

In the next three chapters we'll explore the components of aggregate demand that are affected by the price level: consumption, investment, and net exports. In examining consumption in the next chapter, we'll gain a better understanding of the forces at work in shifting the aggregate demand curve.

Terms and Concepts for Review

Contractionary fiscal policy
Contractionary monetary policy
Expansionary fiscal policy
Expansionary monetary policy
Fiscal policy
Keynes effect
Marginal product of labor
Production function
Real balance effect
Total product curve

For Discussion

1. Give three reasons for the downward slope of the aggregate demand curve.
2. What's the difference between the short run and the long run in the model of aggregate demand and aggregate supply?
3. Distinguish between the short-run and long-run aggregate supply curves.

4. "When prices decrease, the wealth of people holding money increases. When wealth increases, the real volume of consumption increases. Therefore, a decrease in prices will cause the aggregate demand curve to shift to the right." Do you agree? Explain.

5. What are the major forces that can cause the short-run aggregate supply curve to shift? What makes the curve shift up and down? What makes it shift left and right? What is the important difference between these two types of shifts in the aggregate supply curve?

6. Suppose the economy has a recessionary gap. We know that if we do nothing, the economy will close the gap on its own. Alternatively, we could arrange for an increase in aggregate demand (say, by increasing government spending) to close the gap. How would your views about the degree of price stickiness in the economy influence your views on whether such a policy would be desirable?

7. The nominal wage includes not only payments made directly to workers but payments made on behalf of workers as well, such as contributions by employers to pension plans and to health care insurance for employees. How would an increase in the cost of employer-provided health insurance affect the economy?

8. Suppose nominal wages never change. What would be the significance of such a characteristic?

9. Suppose minimum wages were increased sharply. How would this affect the solution in the model of aggregate demand and aggregate supply?

10. "Supply-side" economic policies attempt to increase the ability of firms to produce goods and services by encouraging technological change and the acquisition of new capital. How would the successful implementation of such policies affect the equilibrium solution in the short run? In the long run?

11. Explain the short-run impact of each of the following.

a. A discovery that makes cold fusion a reality, greatly increasing the economy's ability to produce energy

b. A decision by a significant number of workers to cut back on their work hours in order to have more leisure

c. An increase in the payroll tax

d. An increase in human capital that increases the productivity of the labor force

12. Discuss how the changes in Question 11 will affect the economy as it moves toward long-run equilibrium in the model of aggregate demand and aggregate supply.

Problems

1. Suppose the price level in a particular economy equals 1.3 and the components of aggregate demand at this price level equal the following:

Consumption	$700
Investment	200
Government purchases	200
Net exports	100

An increase of 0.1 point in the price level reduces consumption by $80 (the real balance effect), investment by $70 (the Keynes effect), and net exports by $70. A reduction of 0.1 point would produce increases in each of the components of aggregate demand by the same respective amounts. Compute the quantity of real GDP demanded at price levels of 1.40, 1.30, and 1.20, and draw the aggregate demand curve.

2. An economy has the production function and demand curve for labor shown below. Assume that there is a fixed supply of 125 workers. Using a copy of the grid in Panel (c), show the long-run aggregate supply curve.

3. Now assume that the nominal wage equals $1,000 per period. Derive the short-run aggregate supply curve, and use a copy of the grid in Panel (c) to plot it.

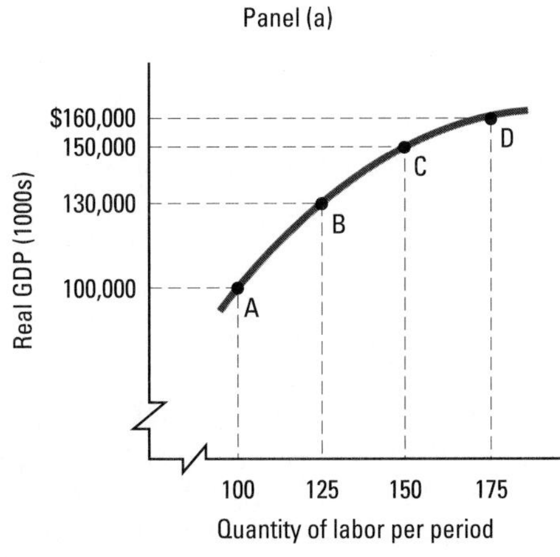

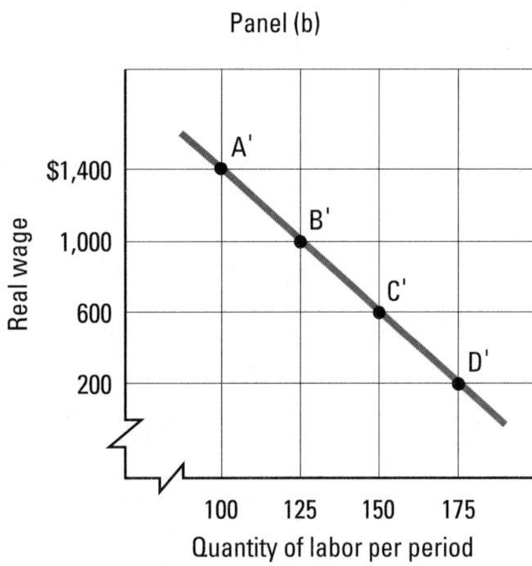

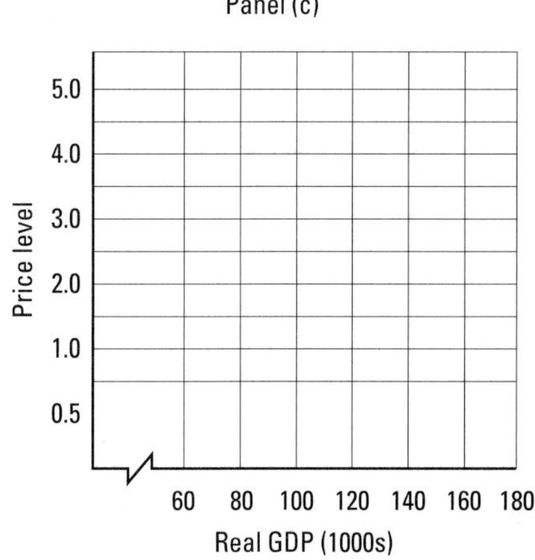

27

Consumption

Chapter Objectives

After mastering the material in this chapter, you will be able to:

1. Explain the factors that determine consumption.
2. Explain the relationship between saving and consumption.
3. Explain how consumption can be a determinant of real GDP and be determined by real GDP at the same time.
4. Explain how changes in consumption, investment, government purchases, or net exports can produce additional changes in consumption, amplifying the impact of these changes on aggregate demand.
5. Explain how tax policy can be used to change consumption and explain how such changes affect economic activity.

Consumption . . . is, in fact, the great end and object of industry.

J. R. McCulloch, 1825

What's Ahead

Stability in the Middle East wasn't the only thing that was undone by Iraq's 1990 invasion of Kuwait. As oil prices soared, consumer confidence plunged to its lowest level in more than a decade. That plunge in confidence, according to Federal Reserve Chairman Alan Greenspan, played an important role in bringing on the recession of 1990–1991.

Consumers, uncertain about their economic prospects, scaled back their consumption, especially their purchases of durable goods. Sales of automobiles and new homes plunged dramatically in the months following the invasion.

The plunge in consumption reduced aggregate demand and thus tended to reduce real GDP. The reduction in real GDP gave consumers less income and produced further reductions in consumption. We'll discover in this chapter that this pattern is typical: changes in consumption can change real GDP, and changes in real GDP can change consumption. We will discuss that two-way relationship in the context of a new model, the aggregate expenditures model. This model will give us a fuller understanding of the nature of shifts in the aggregate demand curve as well as the forces that determine its slope.

Consumer choices help shape the economy's allocation of resources. How much lettuce shall be produced? How many haircuts? The model of demand and supply tells us that consumer demands play a key role in a market economy's answer to these questions of microeconomics. What consumers do is important also for macroeconomics. The choices consumers make can determine whether the economy is growing or slumping, whether unemployment will be high or low, whether inflation will be severe or mild.

In this chapter we examine the macroeconomic aspects of consumer choices. We'll discuss the forces that determine consumption as well as the ways in which consumption affects economic activity.

Determining the Level of Consumption

It's important to understand how the level of consumption is determined, for several reasons. First, as suggested by the statement of nineteenth-century economist J. R. McCulloch at the beginning of this chapter, the ultimate purpose of

Disposable personal income is the income households receive less the taxes they pay.

economic activity *is* consumption. Goods and services are produced so that people can use them. The factors that determine consumption thus determine how successful an economy is in fulfilling its ultimate purpose: providing goods and services for people. Second, we must understand how consumption is determined if we are to understand the forces that determine GDP. Consumption, after all, accounts for two-thirds of GDP; changes in consumption loom large as factors that influence changes in economic activity.

We saw another reason for the importance of consumption in Chapter 21, when we began our examination of macroeconomics. In looking at the circular flow model, we saw that an increase in any of the components of aggregate demand—consumption, investment, government purchases, and net exports—induces firms to produce additional goods and services. That production, in turn, generates additional income for households. And that additional income stimulates still more consumption, thus more production, thus more income—and still more consumption. That series of feedback effects determines the impact of changes in every component of aggregate demand. We'll see in this chapter how these feedback effects work and develop a measure of how important they are.

Consumption and Disposable Personal Income

It seems intuitively reasonable to expect that consumption spending by households will be closely related to their **disposable personal income,** which equals the income households receive less the taxes they pay. Disposable personal income is the income available for consumption, so it should come as no surprise that consumption and disposable personal income are closely related.

Note that disposable personal income and GDP aren't the same thing. GDP is a measure of total income; disposable personal income is the income households have available to spend. We'll look at the relationship between disposable personal income and GDP more closely later in this chapter. In the United States, disposable personal income is a little over 60 percent of GDP.

Exhibit 27-1 shows quarterly real values of consumption and disposable personal income from 1993 through the first half of 1995. A straight line has been added that corresponds to the observations of these variables; notice that

EXHIBIT 27-1

The Relationship Between Consumption and Disposable Income in the 1990s

Plots of consumption and disposable personal income suggest that a linear relationship exists between the two variables. The points plotted here are quarterly values at annual rates for the period from 1993 through the first half of 1995. All figures are in billions of 1987 dollars.

Source: U.S. Council of Economic Advisers, *Economic Report of the President 1995* (Washington, D.C.: U.S. Government Printing Office, 1995), table B-28, p. 307. Data for the first half of 1995 provided by the Commerce Department.

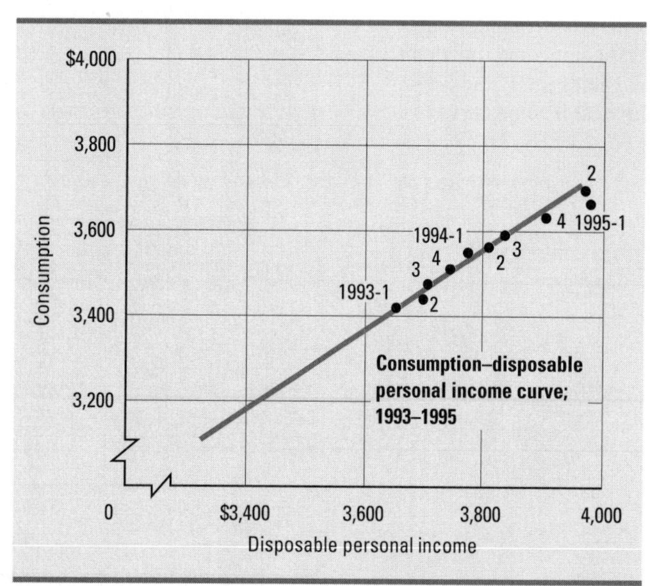

the data fit the straight line quite closely. The fact that the relationship between consumption and disposable personal income can be described by a straight line plays a key role in the theory of consumption.

- A **consumption–disposable personal income function** is an equation that relates consumption to the level of disposable personal income.
- A **consumption–disposable personal income schedule** is a table that shows levels of consumption at various levels of disposable personal income.

The Consumption Function and the Consumption–Disposable Personal Income Curve

The close relationship between consumption and disposable personal income suggests that we can write a **consumption–disposable personal income function,** an equation relating consumption to the level of disposable personal income. Equation (1) gives an example of a consumption function for an economy. Consumption C equals a constant term ($300 billion) plus a fraction (0.75) times disposable income Y_d:

$$C = \$300 + 0.75Y_d \tag{1}$$

We can use the consumption function to derive a **consumption–disposable personal income schedule,** a table that shows values of consumption at various levels of income. A consumption–disposable personal income schedule is given in Exhibit 27-2. To derive the schedule, we select values for disposable personal income and insert those values in place of the Y_d term in Equation (1). Suppose, for example, we select a value of $800 billion (in dollars of 1987 purchasing power) for disposable personal income. Inserting this value in Equation (1), we have

$$C = \$300 \text{ billion} + 0.75(\$800 \text{ billion})$$
$$C = \$300 \text{ billion} + \$600 \text{ billion} = \$900 \text{ billion}$$

Notice that at a disposable personal income of $800 billion, consumption exceeds income. That means people are either borrowing or using money they had previously saved. The schedule even shows consumption for a level of dis-

EXHIBIT 27-2

Plotting a Consumption–Disposable Personal Income Curve

The consumption–disposable personal income schedule gives hypothetical values (in billions of 1987 dollars) for consumption C and disposable personal income Y_d; it is derived from the consumption–disposable personal income function $C = \$300 + 0.75Y_d$. These values imply the consumption–disposable personal income curve shown here.

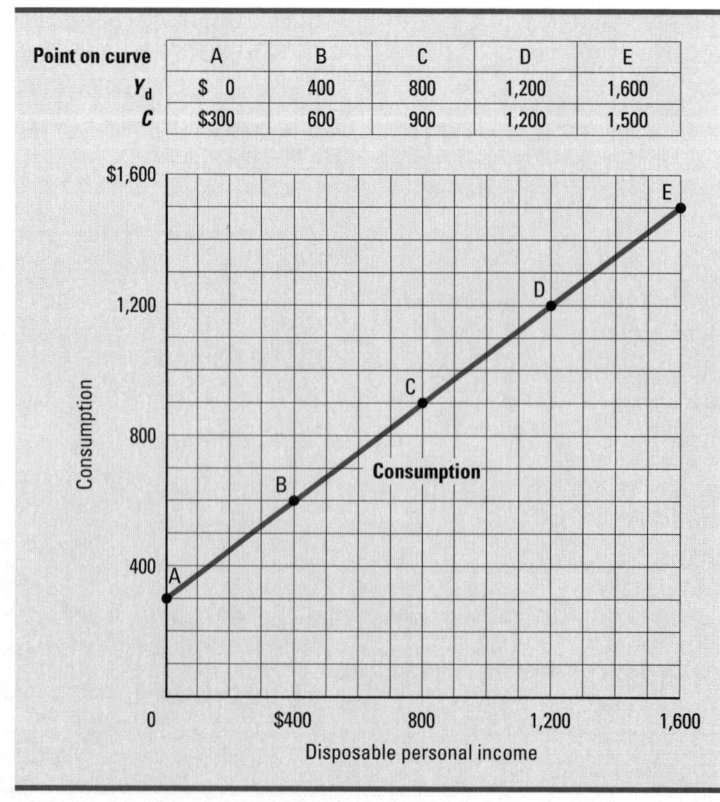

Point on curve	A	B	C	D	E
Y_d	$ 0	400	800	1,200	1,600
C	$300	600	900	1,200	1,500

Case in Point: The Marginal Propensity to Consume and the 1964 Tax Cut

The late Walter W. Heller, the Chairman of the Council of Economic Advisers under President John F. Kennedy, was instrumental in applying the ideas of the consumption–disposable personal income curve and the marginal propensity to consume out of disposable personal income to the economic policies of the administration. The most dramatic element of those policies was the 1964 tax cut.

When the tax cut was still in the proposal stage. Mr. Heller discussed its likely impact with members of Congress. Testifying before the Senate Subcommittee on Employment and Manpower on October 28, 1963 (less than a month before President Kennedy was to be assassinated), he said that the economy faced a recessionary gap of about $30 billion. The tax cut was designed to increase aggregate demand and eliminate this gap—it was to be the nation's first use of an expansionary fiscal policy aimed at closing a recessionary gap.

The proposal called for a cut in personal income taxes of $8.8 billion and a cut in corporate income taxes of $2.3 billion. Heller estimated that the cut in corporate taxes, which would increase corporate after-tax profits by an equal amount, would generate additional dividend payments by corporations. Such payments are part of personal income; after the tax cuts, Heller said, disposable personal income would increase by $10 billion.

To determine the impact of the increased disposable personal income on consumption, Heller used the marginal propensity to consume out of disposable personal income MPC_d. He told the Subcommittee that the MPC_d had been 0.93 in recent years. Applying that figure to the income change, he said that "one can safely project that consumer spending would rise by about 93 percent of the rise in disposable personal income, or by over $9 billion."

The tax cut would, Mr. Heller said, generate other spending to close the gap. But the primary component of the total change was to be that $9 billion boost in consumption, an increase calculated by applying the marginal propensity to consume out of disposable personal income.

John F. Kennedy and his economic advisor Walter Heller.

Did the experiment work? The tax cut, passed early in 1964, increased disposable personal income that year by $10 billion. In 1965, the Council of Economic Advisers reported that the initial impact of the tax cut had been consistent with its earlier projections: the tax cut had increased consumption by about $9 billion in 1964. To the administration's economists, the experience represented important confirmation of the theoretical ideas that had been used in designing the tax cut.

Sources: Heller's testimony is reprinted in the *Economic Report of the President 1964,* pp. 166–190. See also the *Economic Report of the President 1965* p. 65.

posable personal income of zero. (This time the "billions" are omitted; we shall assume that all values in the function are in billions of 1987 dollars.)

$$C = \$300 + 0.75(0) = \$300$$

Even with a disposable personal income of zero, $300 billion in consumption still occurs. After all, people must eat; they must acquire clothing. No one has ever observed what actually happens in an economy with no disposable personal income, but there have been times in the United States when consumption exceeded the total of disposable personal income in the economy.

We've now shown the relationship between consumption and disposable personal income algebraically and with a table. We can also show it graphically with a **consumption–disposable personal income curve,** a line that shows the relationship between consumption and disposable personal income, all other determinants of consumption unchanged. The consumption–disposable income curve in Exhibit 27-2 shows the combinations of consumption and disposable personal income given in the schedule.

A **consumption–disposable personal income curve** shows the value of consumption at each level of disposable personal income, all other determinants of consumption unchanged.

The **marginal propensity to consume out of disposable personal income** (**MPC_d**) is the change in consumption ΔC divided by the change in disposable personal income ΔY_d; it is the slope of the consumption–disposable personal income curve.

The Marginal Propensity to Consume

Suppose you were given an extra \$1,000—tax free. Your disposable personal income has risen by \$1,000. Would you increase your consumption? Probably. Would you increase your consumption by the full \$1,000? Probably not. Most people increase their consumption when their disposable personal income rises, but only by a fraction of the increase in income.

The relationship between an increase in disposable personal income and the increase in consumption that results from it plays a key role in macroeconomic analysis. The slope of the consumption–disposable personal income curve provides the key to understanding this relationship; the slope equals the change in consumption divided by the change in disposable personal income between any two points on the curve. The ratio of these changes is the **marginal propensity to consume out of disposable personal income** (**MPC_d**). (The Greek letter Δ is used to denote "change in.")

$$MPC_d = \frac{\Delta C}{\Delta Y_d} \qquad \textbf{(2)}$$

Exhibit 27-3 shows the consumption–disposable personal income curve plotted in Exhibit 27-2. The slope of this curve is computed between points C and D. The change in consumption between those points is \$300 billion; the change in disposable personal income is \$400 billion. The slope, 0.75 (= \$300/\$400), is the marginal propensity to consume out of disposable personal income. It can be interpreted as the fraction of an extra \$1 of disposable personal income that people spend on consumption. Thus, if your marginal propensity to consume out of disposable personal income were 0.75 and you received \$1,000, your consumption would rise by \$0.75 for each extra \$1 of disposable personal income, or \$750.

Consumption, Personal Saving, and Disposable Personal Income

Personal saving is disposable personal income not spent on consumption during a particular period; the value of personal saving for any period is found by

EXHIBIT 27-3

The Consumption–Disposable Income Curve and the Marginal Propensity to Consume

The slope of the consumption–disposable personal income curve, which is the marginal propensity to consume out of disposable personal income, can be computed between any two points on the curve. Here the slope computed between points C and D equals 0.75. All values are in billions of 1987 dollars.

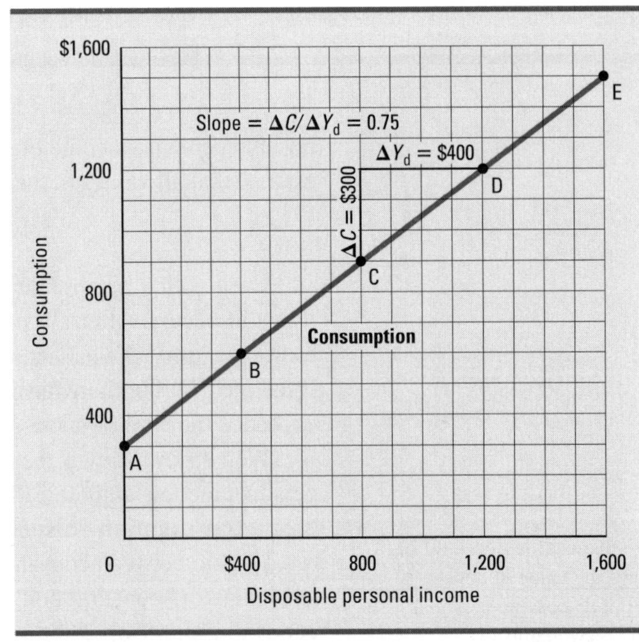

subtracting consumption from disposable personal income for that period. The consumption–disposable personal income curve, which shows the relationship between consumption and disposable personal income, can thus be used to determine the relationship between saving and disposable personal income.

We'll learn in subsequent chapters that personal saving isn't the only form of saving—firms and government agencies may save as well. In this chapter, however, our focus is on the choice consumers make between using disposable personal income for consumption or for saving.

A **saving–disposable personal income curve** relates personal saving in any period to the level of disposable personal income in that period. The derivation of the curve is illustrated in Exhibit 27-4. The values for consumption and disposable personal income that we encountered in the last two exhibits are repeated in the table; personal saving is calculated by subtracting values for consumption from values for disposable personal income. Notice that a 45-degree line has been added to the graph. At every point on the 45-degree line, the value on the vertical axis equals that on the horizontal axis. The consumption–disposable personal income curve intersects the 45-degree line at an income of $1,200 billion (point D). At this point, consumption equals disposable personal income and personal saving equals zero (point D′). To find personal saving at other levels of disposable personal income, we subtract consumption, given by the consumption–disposable personal income curve, from disposable personal income, given by the 45-degree line.

- **Personal saving** is disposable personal income not spent on consumption during a particular period.
- A **saving–disposable personal income curve** relates saving to the level of disposable personal income.

EXHIBIT 27-4

Consumption and Personal Saving

Personal saving equals disposable income minus consumption. The schedule gives the same values for disposable income and consumption that were used in Exhibit 27-2. Personal saving *S* is computed by subtracting values in the consumption row from the disposable income row. All values are in billions of 1987 dollars.

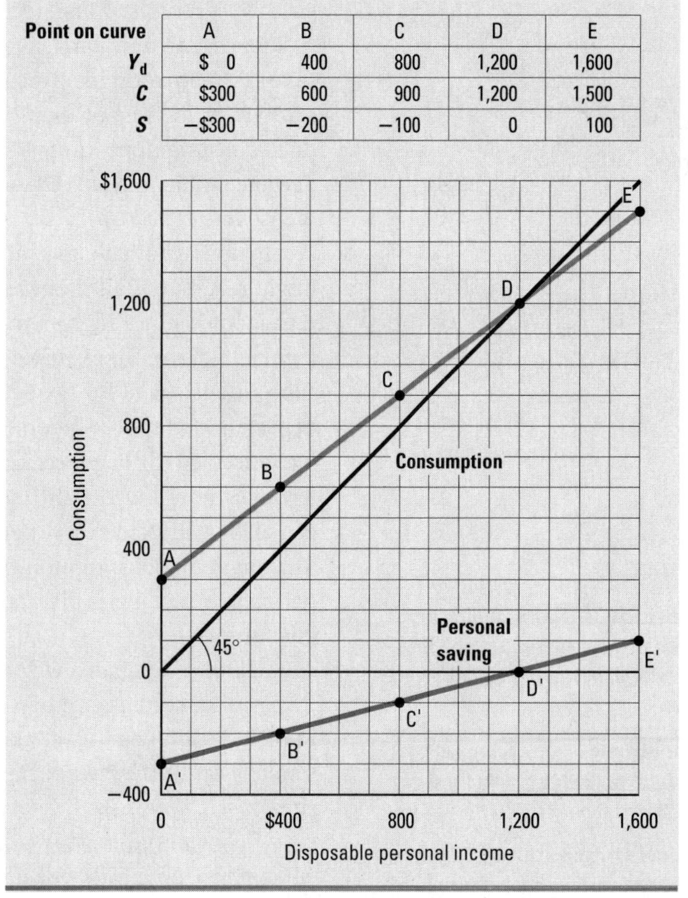

Point on curve	A	B	C	D	E
Y_d	$ 0	400	800	1,200	1,600
C	$300	600	900	1,200	1,500
S	−$300	−200	−100	0	100

At a disposable personal income of \$1,600 billion, for example, consumption is \$1,500 billion (point E). Personal saving equals \$100 billion—the vertical distance between the 45-degree line and the consumption–disposable personal income curve (point E′). At an income of \$400 billion, consumption totals \$600 billion (point B). The consumption–disposable personal income curve lies above the 45-degree line at this point; personal saving is −\$200 billion (point B′). A negative value for saving means that consumption exceeds disposable personal income; it must have been financed out of saving accumulated in the past or through borrowing.

Current Versus Permanent Income

The discussion so far has related consumption in a particular period to income in that same period. This approach, the **current income theory of consumption,** asserts that consumption in any one period depends on income during that period, or current income.

Although it seems obvious that consumption should be related to income, it isn't so obvious that consumers base their consumption in any one period on the income they receive during that period. In buying a new car, for example, consumers might base their decision not only on their current income but on the income they expect to receive during the 4 or 5 years they expect to be making payments on the car. Parents who purchase a college education for their children might base their decision on their expected lifetime income.

Indeed, it seems likely that virtually all consumption choices could be affected by expectations of income over a very long period. One reason people save is to provide funds to live on during their retirement years. Another is to build an estate they can leave to their heirs through bequests. The amount people save for their retirement or for bequests depends on the income they expect to receive for the rest of their lives. For these and other reasons, then, saving (and thus consumption) in any one year is influenced by **permanent income.** Permanent income is the average income people expect to receive for the rest of their lives.

People who have the same current income but different permanent incomes might reach very different saving decisions. Someone with a relatively low current income but a high permanent income (a college student planning to go to medical school, for example) might save little or nothing now, expecting to save for retirement and for bequests later. A person with the same low income but no expectation of higher income later might try to save some money now to provide for retirement or bequests later. Because a decision to save a certain amount determines how much will be available for consumption, consumption decisions can also be affected by expected lifetime income. Thus, an alternative approach to explaining consumption behavior is to assume that consumption depends on permanent income. This approach is called the **permanent income theory of consumption.**

- The **current income theory of consumption** assumes that consumption spending in any one period is determined by income in that period.
- **Permanent income** is the average annual income people expect to receive for the remainder of their lives.
- The **permanent income theory of consumption** asserts that current consumption spending depends on permanent income.

Milton Friedman and Franco Modigliani, both of whom have won the Nobel Prize in Economics, are two economists who have made important contributions in the development of the permanent income theory of consumption. A primary implication of their work lies in the analysis of the marginal propensity to consume.

If consumption is based on current income, then any increase in disposable personal income will boost consumption by an amount equal to the marginal propensity to consume out of disposable personal income times the change in

Case in Point President Ford's Quick Fix

Faced with the severe recession brought on by oil price increases in 1973 and 1974, President Gerald Ford in 1975 tried introducing a quick dose of economic stimulus to the economy. He ordered up an $8.1 billion bonus for taxpayers.

The Ford measure was designed as a temporary rebate of income taxes. Households would be sent checks equal to 10 percent of their 1974 tax bills, up to a maximum of $200 per household. Mr. Ford proposed the measure in January of 1975, the House of Representatives passed it in February, and the Senate passed it the following month. The Treasury sent checks totaling $8.1 billion to U.S. households over the next 2 months.

Here was a classic test of the current and permanent income theories. Unlike the 1964 tax cut, the 1975 rebate was temporary, providing households with a onetime windfall. Current income theory predicted consumption would rise by the marginal propensity to consume out of disposable personal income times $8.1 billion. The permanent income theory predicted consumption would rise hardly at all.

An analysis of actual consumption during the period by economist James M. Poterba of the Massachusetts Institute of Technology suggested that the truth lay, as it often does, somewhere in between. He calculated that the rebate increased consumption by $0.12 to $0.24 for each $1 returned to taxpayers, so a household with a $200 tax rebate increased its consumption by $24 to $48. That was far less than the current income theory predicted, but somewhat more than the permanent income theory anticipated. The experience led many economists who had subscribed to the current income theory of consumption to give greater weight to the role of permanent income in consumption decisions.

Source: James M. Poterba, "Are Consumers Forward Looking? Evidence from Fiscal Experiments," *American Economic Review* 78(2)(May 1988): 413–418.

disposable personal income. But if consumption is based on permanent income, then a change in current income that is perceived as temporary will have little impact on permanent income and thus will have little impact on consumption.

The question of whether permanent versus current income is a determinant of consumption came to the center of discussion in 1992 when President Bush ordered a change in the withholding rate for personal income taxes. Workers have a fraction of their paychecks withheld for taxes each pay period; Mr. Bush directed that this fraction be reduced. The change didn't change income tax rates; by withholding less in 1992, taxpayers would either receive smaller refund checks in 1993 or owe more taxes. The change thus left taxpayers' permanent income unaffected. Economists who subscribed to the permanent income theory of consumption predicted that the change wouldn't have any effect. Those who subscribed to the current income theory of consumption predicted that the measure would boost consumption and thus aggregate demand in 1992 and reduce it in 1993. Consumption rose sharply in the second half of 1992 and then slowed in the first half of 1993. Determining the extent to which these changes resulted from the tax policy will require careful statistical analysis.

Consumption and Real GDP

The consumption–disposable personal income curve relates consumption to disposable personal income. In investigating the determination of GDP, however, we will need to relate consumption to GDP. That relationship follows directly from the relationship we've already explored between consumption and disposable personal income.

The argument is as follows. We know there is a stable relationship between GDP and disposable personal income, which in turn is closely related to consumption, so there should be a close relationship between consumption and GDP.

GDP measures the total income generated in the economy in any one period. Disposable income is income received by households minus the direct taxes they pay. The two measures differ largely because much of the income generated in the economy is not actually received by households (for example, depreciation, indirect business taxes, and corporate profits not distributed to shareholders as dividends) and because households receive income that isn't generated in the production of GDP (mainly transfer payments from government programs such as welfare and Social Security). Another gap between real GDP and disposable personal income comes from the fact that taxes paid by households are subtracted from personal income in computing disposable personal income. Despite these differences, real GDP and real disposable personal income tend to move closely together. An increase in production tends to increase incomes generally, and that increases disposable personal income.

The relationship between disposable personal income and GDP in the United States is illustrated in Exhibit 27-5. A rise in GDP increases disposable personal income; a drop reduces it. Notice, however, that changes in GDP have been somewhat sharper than changes in disposable income. That's because taxes and transfer payments "smooth out" disposable personal income as GDP changes. When GDP rises, tax collections rise. Fewer people are poor, so welfare payments fall. Disposable personal income rises, but by less than the increase in GDP. Similarly, a fall in GDP produces a reduction in taxes collected and an increase in transfer payments. Disposable income falls, but by less than the reduction in GDP. Disposable personal income thus changes in the same direction as GDP, but it is somewhat more stable than GDP.

If consumption is related to disposable personal income, and if disposable personal income is related to GDP, then it follows that consumption should be related to GDP. The degree to which an additional $1 of GDP boosts consump-

EXHIBIT 27-5

Disposable Personal Income and GDP

Real values of disposable personal income (Y_d) and GDP (Y) are plotted for the period from 1960 through the first half of 1995. Notice that disposable personal income generally changes in the same direction as does real GDP, but changes in disposable personal income are smaller than changes in GDP. All values are in billions of 1987 dollars.

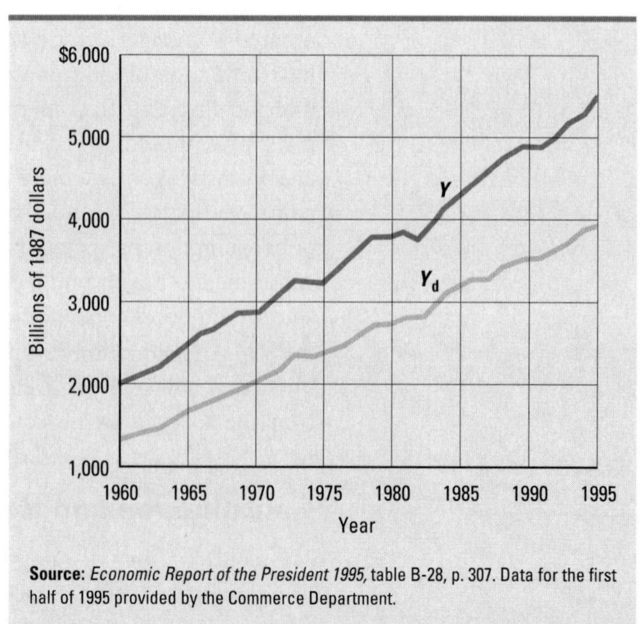

Source: *Economic Report of the President 1995,* table B-28, p. 307. Data for the first half of 1995 provided by the Commerce Department.

- A **consumption–GDP function** is an equation that relates consumption to GDP.
- A **consumption–GDP schedule** is a table that relates consumption to GDP.
- A **consumption–GDP curve** shows the value of consumption at each level of GDP, all other determinants of consumption unchanged.
- The **marginal propensity to consume out of GDP (MPC_Y)** is the change in consumption divided by the change in GDP when moving along the consumption–GDP curve; it is the slope of the consumption–GDP curve.

tion, however, will be smaller than the degree to which an additional $1 of disposable personal income boosts consumption.

Suppose that a $1 increase in real GDP increases household income by $0.90. If taxes take, on average, 1/3 of household income, $0.60 cents of each $1 in household income will be left as disposable personal income. Say that the marginal propensity to consume out of disposable personal income is 5/6; this means that consumption will rise by $0.50 for each additional $1 of GDP generated (5/6 of $0.60).

The relationship between consumption and GDP can be shown algebraically, with a table, or graphically. A **consumption–GDP function** is an equation relating the level of consumption to the level of GDP. A **consumption–GDP schedule** is a table that shows levels of consumption at various levels of income. Finally, a **consumption–GDP curve** is a graph that shows the value of consumption at each level of GDP. In all of these depictions of the relationship between consumption and GDP, we assume that all other determinants of consumption are unchanged. Like the consumption–disposable personal income curve, the consumption–GDP curve is an upward-sloping straight line. In general, however, the consumption–GDP curve is flatter than a consumption–disposable personal income curve.

Exhibit 27-6 shows a consumption–GDP schedule and curve based on the following consumption function, where C equals consumption and Y equals real GDP. As before, all values are in billions of 1987 dollars.

$$C = 100 + 0.5Y \qquad \textbf{(3)}$$

The slope of the consumption–GDP curve equals the change in consumption divided by the change in GDP; this slope is the **marginal propensity to consume out of GDP (MPC_Y).** Because the consumption–GDP curve is flatter

EXHIBIT 27-6

The Consumption–GDP Curve

The consumption–GDP schedule gives values for real GDP (Y) and consumption (C) based on the consumption–GDP function $C = \$100 + 0.5Y$. The slope of the consumption–GDP curve is the marginal propensity to consume out of GDP; computed between points C and D, the slope equals 0.5. All values are in billions of 1987 dollars.

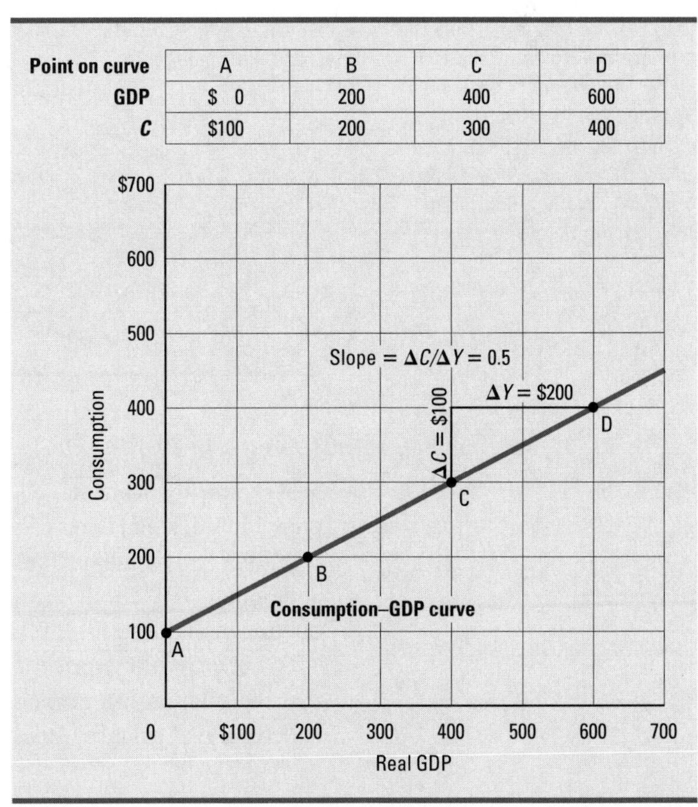

Point on curve	A	B	C	D
GDP	$ 0	200	400	600
C	$100	200	300	400

than the consumption–disposable personal income curve, the marginal propensity to consume out of GDP is less than the marginal propensity to consume out of disposable personal income. The marginal propensity to consume out of GDP can be thought of as the amount by which consumption increases in response to an additional \$1 of GDP. A marginal propensity to consume out of GDP of 0.5, for example, implies that an additional \$1 of GDP will induce an additional \$0.50 of consumption.

$$MPC_Y = \frac{\Delta C}{\Delta Y} \tag{4}$$

The value of the marginal propensity to consume out of GDP is calculated between points C and D on the consumption–GDP curve shown in Exhibit 27-6. The change in consumption is \$100 billion, the change in GDP is \$200 billion, and the marginal propensity to consume out of GDP is 0.5.

Shifts in the Consumption–GDP Curve

The consumption–GDP curve relates consumption spending to the level of GDP. Changes in GDP cause movements *along* the consumption–GDP curve; they do not shift the curve. The consumption–GDP curve shifts when other determinants of consumption change. Listed below are some examples of changes that could shift the consumption–GDP curve; illustrations of possible shifts in the curve are presented in Exhibit 27-7.

EXHIBIT 27-7

Shifts in the Consumption–GDP Curve

An increase in the level of consumption at each level of real GDP shifts the consumption–GDP curve upward in Panel (a). Among the events that would shift the curve upward are an increase in real wealth, an increase in consumer confidence, and a cut in taxes. A reduction in the level of consumption shifts the curve downward in Panel (b). The events that could shift the curve downward include a reduction in real wealth, a decline in consumer confidence, and an increase in taxes.

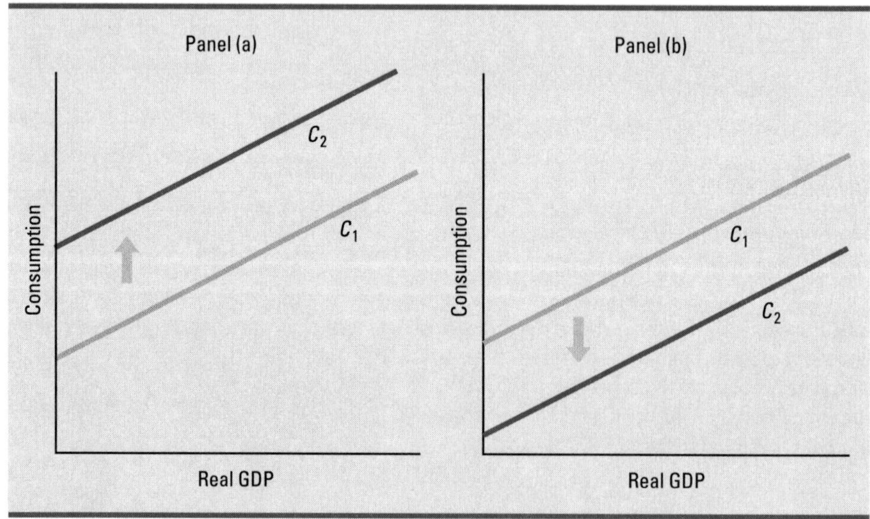

Changes in Real Wealth

We've already seen that a change in real wealth affects consumption. An increase in stock and bond prices, for example, would make holders of these assets wealthier and would be likely to increase their consumption. That shifts the consumption–GDP curve upward, as illustrated in Panel (a) of Exhibit 27-7. A reduction in real wealth shifts it downward, as shown in Panel (b).

A change in the price level changes real wealth. We learned in Chapter 26 that the relationship between the price level, real wealth, and consumption is called the real balance effect. A reduction in the price level increases real wealth and shifts the consumption–GDP curve upward in Panel (a). An increase in the price level shifts the curve downward in Panel (b).

Changes in Expectations

Consumers are likely to be more willing to spend money when they are optimistic about the future. Surveyors attempt to gauge this optimism using "consumer confidence" surveys that ask respondents to report whether they are optimistic or pessimistic about their own economic situation and about the prospects for the economy as a whole.

One of the most famous surveys of consumer confidence is conducted each month by the Survey Research Center (SRC) at the University of Michigan. Here are the questions asked in the survey:

1. Now looking ahead—do you think that a year from now you (and your family living there) will be better off financially, or worse off, or just about the same as now?
2. Now turning to business conditions in the country as a whole—do you think that during the next twelve months we'll have good times financially, or bad times, or what?
3. Looking ahead, which would you say is more likely—that in the country as a whole we'll have continuous good times during the next five years or so, or that we will have periods of widespread unemployment or depression, or what?

The SRC computes an Index of Consumer Expectations from the responses to these three questions by subtracting the percentage of people giving a pessimistic response to each question from the percentage giving an optimistic response, then averaging for the three questions. Results of the Michigan survey are widely reported in the press, and the index is included in the Commerce Department's Index of Leading Economic Indicators. In general, we expect an increase in consumer confidence to lead to an upward shift in the consumption–GDP curve in Panel (a) of Exhibit 27-7, while a reduction in confidence should lead to a downward shift in Panel (b).

Consumer expectations concerning unemployment are also related to consumption spending. In general, when people are worried about losing their jobs, they are likely to cut back their consumption, shifting the consumption–GDP curve downward. When they're less concerned, the schedule should shift upward, increasing consumption at every level of real GDP.

The relationship between consumption and consumer expectations concerning future economic conditions tends to be a form of self-fulfilling prophecy. If consumers expect economic conditions to worsen, they'll cut their consumption—and economic conditions will worsen! Political leaders often try to persuade people that economic prospects are good. In part, such efforts are an attempt to increase economic activity by boosting consumption.

Income Tax Changes

Changes in income tax rates alter the amount of disposable personal income available from a given level of total GDP. They thus change consumption at each level of GDP, shifting the consumption–GDP curve. A tax cut tends to shift the consumption–GDP curve upward in Panel (a) of Exhibit 27-7; a tax increase tends to shift it downward in Panel (b).

Checklist

- Consumption is closely related to disposable personal income. The consumption–disposable personal income curve describes this relationship.
- The marginal propensity to consume out of disposable personal income is measured as the slope of the consumption–disposable personal income curve; it shows the amount by which consumption changes in response to a change in disposable personal income.
- Disposable income not spent on consumption is saved; a curve showing the level of saving at each level of disposable personal income can be derived from the consumption–disposable personal income curve.
- The current income theory of consumption relates consumption in a period to income in the same period; the permanent income theory relates consumption to permanent income. The permanent income theory predicts that the marginal propensity to consume out of a temporary change in income will be much lower than the marginal propensity to consume out of a change in income that is expected to be permanent.
- The relationship between consumption and GDP is given by the consumption–GDP curve; its slope is the marginal propensity to consume out of GDP.
- A change in consumption at each level of GDP shifts the consumption–GDP curve. Factors that could shift the consumption–GDP curve include changes in real wealth, changes in consumer expectations, and changes in income tax rates.

- The **aggregate expenditures model** relates the sum of consumption, investment, government purchases, and net exports to the level of GDP, all at a given level of prices.
- **Aggregate expenditures** equal the sum of consumption, investment, government purchases, and net exports, all computed for a given price level.
- **Autonomous expenditures** are expenditures that do not vary with the level of GDP.
- **Induced expenditures** are expenditures that vary with the level of GDP.

The Aggregate Expenditures Model

The consumption–GDP curve relates the level of consumption to the level of GDP. In this section we extend that concept to the other components of aggregate demand: investment, government purchases, and net exports. In doing so we shall develop a new model of the determination of equilibrium GDP, the **aggregate expenditures model.** This model relates **aggregate expenditures,** which equal the sum of consumption, investment, government expenditures, and net exports at a given level of prices, to the level of GDP.

One purpose of examining the aggregate expenditures model is to gain a deeper understanding of the "ripple effects" from a change in aggregate demand. An initial change in aggregate expenditures leads to greater production; this means additional GDP, which induces additional consumption, leading to still more production, more GDP, and more consumption. The aggregate expenditures model provides a context within which this series of ripple effects can be understood. A second reason for introducing the model is that we can use it to derive the aggregate demand curve for the model of aggregate demand and aggregate supply.

We can gain useful insights from an exploration of the aggregate expenditures model, but the model of aggregate demand and aggregate supply will remain our primary tool for analyzing macroeconomic events. That model gives us a tool for showing how the price level is determined. It also gives us a much better perspective on aggregate supply, both in the long run and in the short run.

The Aggregate Expenditures Curve

The aggregate expenditures model can be presented algebraically or graphically. The model is developed graphically in this chapter; an algebraic treatment is given in the Appendix to this chapter.

Autonomous and Induced Aggregate Expenditures

Economists distinguish two types of expenditures. Those that do not vary with the level of GDP are called **autonomous expenditures.** Government purchases are one example; the volume of such purchases is determined through the political process and has no necessary relationship to GDP. Expenditures that vary with GDP are called **induced expenditures.** Consumption spending rises with GDP; it is an example of an induced expenditure. Exhibit 27-8 illustrates the difference between autonomous and induced expenditures. With GDP on the horizontal axis and aggregate expenditures on the vertical axis, autonomous expenditures are shown as a horizontal line in Panel (a). A curve showing induced expenditures is sloped; its value changes with changes in GDP. Panel (b) shows induced expenditures that are positively related to GDP.

EXHIBIT 27-8

Autonomous and Induced Expenditures

Autonomous expenditures don't vary with the level of real GDP; induced expenditures do. Autonomous expenditures are shown by the horizontal line in Panel (a). Induced expenditures vary with GDP, as in Panel (b).

Autonomous and Induced Consumption

The concept of the marginal propensity to consume out of GDP suggests that consumption contains induced expenditures; an increase in GDP raises consumption. But consumption contains an autonomous component as well. The level of consumption at the intersection of the consumption–GDP curve and the vertical axis is regarded as autonomous consumption; this level of spending would occur regardless of the level of GDP.

Consider the consumption–GDP function we used in deriving the consumption–GDP schedule and curve illustrated in Exhibit 27-6:

$$C = \$100 + 0.5Y$$

At every level of real GDP, consumption includes \$100 billion in autonomous expenditures. It will also contain expenditures "induced" by the level of real GDP. At a level of real GDP of \$400 billion, for example, consumption equals \$300 billion: \$100 billion in autonomous expenditures and \$200 billion in consumption induced by the \$300 billion level of real GDP. Exhibit 27-9 illustrates these two components of consumption. Autonomous consumption C_A, which is always \$100 billion, is shown in Panel (a); its equation is

$$C_A = \$100 \text{ billion} \qquad (5)$$

Induced consumption C_I is shown in Panel (b); its equation is

$$C_I = 0.5Y \qquad (6)$$

The consumption–GDP curve is given by the sum of Equations (5) and (6); it is shown in Panel (c) of Exhibit 27-9.

Other Components of Aggregate Expenditures

To simplify the analysis that follows, let us assume that the other components of aggregate expenditures are autonomous. We thus assume that investment, government purchases, and net exports are unaffected by the level of GDP. (We'll examine the determinants of investment and net exports in the next two chapters.) Suppose that we are given the following values for these variables:

$$\text{Investment } I = \$160 \text{ billion} \qquad (7)$$

$$\text{Government purchases } G = \$30 \text{ billion} \qquad (8)$$

$$\text{Net exports } X_n = \$10 \text{ billion} \qquad (9)$$

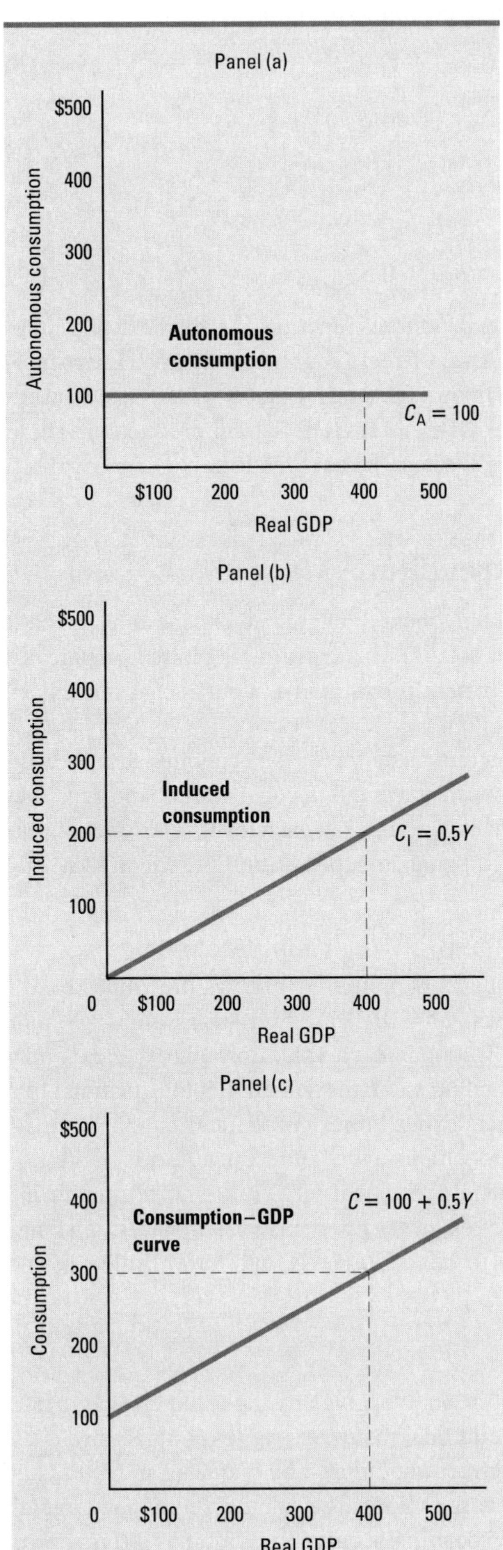

EXHIBIT 27-9

Autonomous and Induced Consumption

Consumption has an autonomous and an induced component. In Panel (a), autonomous consumption C_A equals \$100 billion at every level of real GDP. Panel (b) shows induced consumption C_I. At a real GDP of \$400 billion, for example, C_I equals \$200 billion. Total consumption C is shown in Panel (c); at a real GDP of \$400 billion, C equals \$300 billion. All figures are in billions of 1987 dollars.

Aggregate expenditures equal the sum of consumption C, investment, government purchases, and net exports. Given the consumption–GDP function in Equation (3) and Equations (7) to (9), we can derive an **aggregate expenditures function,** which is an equation relating aggregate expenditures to the value of real GDP.

We begin with the definition of aggregate expenditures:

$$AE = C + I + G + X_n \qquad \textbf{(10)}$$

Substituting the information from the equations above yields

$$AE = 100 + 0.5Y + 160 + 30 + 10$$

or

$$AE = 300 + 0.5Y \qquad \textbf{(11)}$$

Equation (11) is the aggregate expenditures function. We shall use this equation to determine the equilibrium level of real GDP in the aggregate expenditures model. It's important to keep in mind that aggregate expenditures measure total spending at each level of real GDP. Real GDP is total production. These two values need not be equal, as we'll see in the next section.

Plotting the Aggregate Expenditures Curve

In Equation (11), the autonomous component of aggregate expenditures is $300 billion, and the induced component is $0.5Y$. This equation is plotted graphically in Exhibit 27-10 as an **aggregate expenditures curve,** a curve that relates aggregate expenditures to the level of GDP.

To compute the aggregate expenditures curve for the economy described by the equations above, we arbitrarily select various levels of GDP and then use Equation (11) to compute aggregate expenditures at each level. At a level of real GDP of $300 billion, for example, aggregate expenditures AE equal $450 billion:

$$AE = 300 + 0.5(300) = 450$$

The aggregate expenditures schedule in Exhibit 27-10 shows the values of aggregate expenditures at various levels of GDP. Based on these values, we plot the aggregate expenditures curve. To obtain each value for aggregate expenditures, we simply insert the corresponding value for real GDP into Equation (11).

The value at which the aggregate expenditures curve intersects the vertical axis corresponds to the level of autonomous aggregate expenditures. In our example, autonomous aggregate expenditures equal $300 billion. That figure includes $200 billion in planned investment, government purchases, and net exports, all of which are assumed to be autonomous, and $100 billion in autonomous consumption.

- An **aggregate expenditures function** is an equation relating aggregate expenditures to the level of real GDP.
- The **aggregate expenditures curve** shows the relationship between aggregate expenditures and GDP.
- The **marginal expenditure rate (*MER*)** is the rate at which aggregate expenditures increase as GDP increases; it is the slope of the aggregate expenditures curve.

The Marginal Expenditure Rate

The slope of the aggregate expenditures curve, given by the change in aggregate expenditures divided by the change in GDP between any two points, measures the rate at which additional expenditures are induced by increases in GDP. This slope is the **marginal expenditure rate (*MER*).** The calculation of the marginal expenditure rate for the aggregate expenditures curve in Exhibit 27-10 is shown for points B and C: it is 0.5.

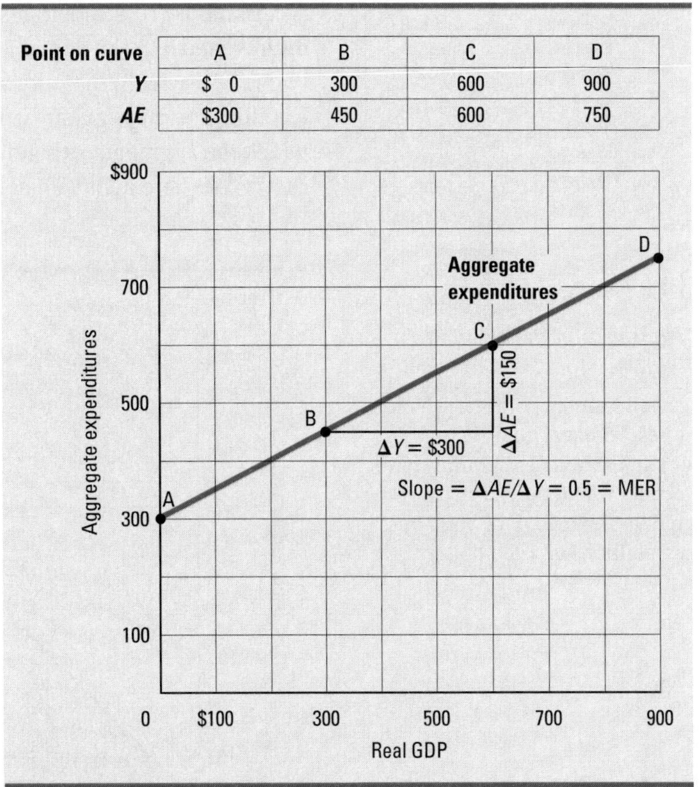

Point on curve	A	B	C	D
Y	$ 0	300	600	900
AE	$300	450	600	750

EXHIBIT 27-10

Plotting the Aggregate Expenditures Curve

Values for aggregate expenditures *AE* are computed by inserting values for real GDP into Equation (11); these are given in the aggregate expenditures schedule. The point at which the aggregate expenditures curve intersects the vertical axis is the value of autonomous aggregate expenditures, here $300 billion. The slope of this aggregate expenditures curve, which is called the marginal expenditure rate (*MER*), is 0.5. All values are in billions of 1987 dollars.

In the aggregate expenditures curve illustrated in Exhibit 27-10, the marginal expenditure rate equals the marginal propensity to consume out of GDP. That's because we have assumed that the values of planned investment, government purchases, and net exports are autonomous; changes in GDP thus affect only consumption. As we investigate these other sources of aggregate demand in subsequent chapters, we'll find that some of them, too, will change with GDP and thus affect the marginal expenditure rate.

Equilibrium in the Aggregate Expenditures Model

Real GDP is a measure of the total output of firms. Aggregate expenditures equal total spending on that output. Equilibrium in the model occurs where aggregate expenditures equal real GDP. One way to think about equilibrium is to recognize that firms produce goods and services with the intention of selling them. Aggregate expenditures consist of what people and firms spend and therefore equal what firms sell. If the economy is at its equilibrium GDP, then firms are selling what they produce.

Exhibit 27-11 illustrates the concept of equilibrium in the aggregate expenditures model. A 45-degree line connects all the points at which the values of the two axes, which measure aggregate expenditures and real GDP, are equal. Equilibrium must occur at some point along this 45-degree line. The point at which the aggregate expenditures curve crosses the 45-degree line is the equilibrium GDP, here achieved at a real GDP of $600 billion.

EXHIBIT 27-11

Determining the Equilibrium in the Aggregate Expenditures Model

The 45-degree line shows all the points at which aggregate expenditures *AE* equal GDP, which is what is required for equilibrium. The equilibrium solution therefore occurs where the *AE* curve crosses the 45-degree line, at a GDP of $600 billion. All figures are in billions of 1987 dollars.

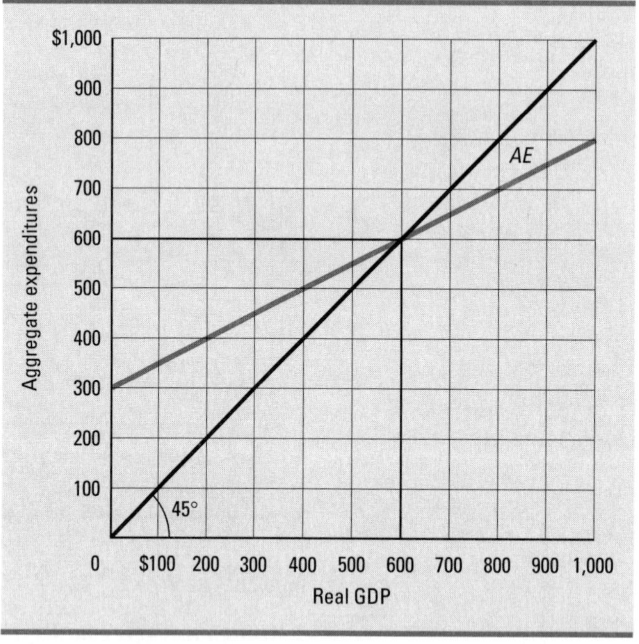

Equation (10) tells us that at a real GDP of $600 billion, the sum of consumption, investment, government purchases, and net exports is $600 billion—precisely the level of output firms produced. A real GDP of $600 billion represents equilibrium in the sense that it generates an equal level of aggregate expenditures.

If firms were to produce a real GDP greater than $600 billion, aggregate expenditures would fall short of real GDP. At a level of real GDP of $800 billion, for example, aggregate expenditures equal $700 billion. Firms would be left with $100 billion worth of goods they intended to sell and didn't. With those unsold goods on hand, firms would be likely to cut their output, moving the economy toward its equilibrium GDP of $600 billion. If firms were to produce $400 billion, aggregate expenditures would be $500 billion. Consumers, firms, government agencies, and foreign buyers would demand more than was produced; firms would respond by increasing their output, again moving the economy toward its equilibrium real GDP of $600 billion.

Changes in Aggregate Expenditures: The Multiplier

In the aggregate expenditures model, equilibrium is found at the level of real GDP at which the aggregate expenditures curve crosses the 45-degree line. It follows that a shift in the curve will change equilibrium real GDP. This section examines the nature of such changes.

Exhibit 27-12 begins with the aggregate expenditures curve shown in Exhibit 27-11. Now suppose that planned investment increases from the original value of $60 billion to a new value of $210 billion—an increase of $150 billion. This increase in investment shifts the aggregate expenditures curve upward by $150 billion. Notice, however, that the new aggregate expenditures curve intersects the 45-degree line at a GDP of $900 billion. The $150 billion increase in investment has produced an increase in equilibrium real GDP of $300 billion.

EXHIBIT 27-12

A Change in Aggregate Expenditures Changes Equilibrium GDP

An increase of $150 billion in investment raises aggregate expenditures *AE* by an equal amount. Equilibrium real GDP thus rises from $600 to $900 billion. All figures are in billions of 1987 dollars.

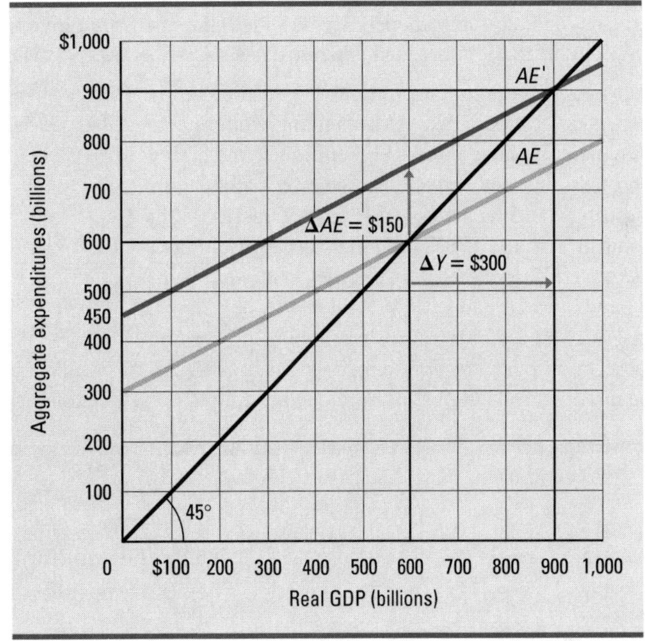

How could an increase in aggregate expenditures of $150 billion produce an increase in equilibrium GDP of $300 billion? The initial increase is a change in autonomous expenditures. Because firms have increased their demand for investment goods by $150 billion, the firms that produce those goods will have $150 billion in additional orders. They will produce $150 billion in additional GDP. But in this economy, each $1 of additional GDP induces $0.50 in additional consumption. The $150 billion increase in autonomous aggregate expenditures induces $75 billion in additional consumption.

The $75 billion in additional consumption boosts production, creating another $75 billion in GDP. But that induces $37.5 billion in additional consumption, creating still more production and still more GDP. Eventually, the $150 billion increase in aggregate expenditures will result in a $300 billion increase in equilibrium GDP.

- A change in aggregate expenditures produces a larger change in equilibrium GDP in the aggregate expenditures model. This phenomenon is called the **multiplier effect.**
- The **multiplier** is given by the ratio of the change in equilibrium GDP to the change in aggregate expenditures that produced it.

The Multiplier

The ability of a change in aggregate expenditures to produce an even larger change in equilibrium GDP is called the **multiplier effect.** The **multiplier** is the ratio of the change in equilibrium GDP to the change in aggregate expenditures that produced it.

Case in Point: The Multiplier Effect of the 1964 Tax Cut

The Case in Point on page 589 reported on Walter W. Heller's 1963 testimony to the Senate Subcommittee on Employment and Manpower. Mr. Heller expected a \$10 billion cut in personal income taxes to boost consumption "by over \$9 billion." He applied a marginal propensity to consume out of disposable personal income of 0.93 to make this prediction.

To assess the ultimate impact of the tax cut, Mr. Heller applied the aggregate expenditures model. He rounded the increased consumption off to \$9 billion and explained:

> This is far from the end of the matter. The higher production of consumer goods to meet this extra spending would mean extra employment, higher payrolls, higher profits, and higher farm and professional and service incomes. This added purchasing power would generate still further increases in spending and incomes. . . . The initial rise of \$9 billion, plus this extra consumption spending and extra output of consumer goods would add over \$18 billion to our annual GDP. . . . We can summarize this continuing process by saying that a "multiplier" of approximately 2 has been applied to the direct increment of consumption spending.

Mr. Heller also predicted that the bill's cuts in corporate income tax rates would increase investment by about \$6 billion. The total change in aggregate expenditures would thus be \$15 billion: \$9 billion in consumption and \$6 billion in investment. He predicted that the total increase in equilibrium GDP would be \$30 billion, the amount the Council of Economic Advisers had estimated would be necessary to bring the economy to full employment.

What really happened? The tax cuts recommended by the Council of Economic Advisers were approved later in 1964; the Council reported in 1965 that their impacts were approximately what it had projected. Monetarists, however, argued that observed increases in consumption, investment, and GDP were the result of monetary policies undertaken at the same time, not tax policy.

Source: *Economic Report of the President 1964,* pp. 172–173.

Let Y^* be the equilibrium level of real GDP in the aggregate expenditures model. Then the multiplier is

$$\text{Multiplier} = \frac{\Delta Y^*}{\Delta AE} \tag{12}$$

In the example we have just discussed, a change in aggregate expenditures of \$150 billion produced a change in equilibrium real GDP of \$300 billion. The value of the multiplier is therefore 2.

The multiplier effect works because a change in aggregate expenditures causes a change in real GDP, inducing a further change in the level of aggregate expenditures, which creates still more GDP and thus an even higher level of aggregate expenditures. The degree to which a given change in real GDP induces a change in aggregate expenditures is given by the marginal expenditure rate. That rate is thus linked to the size of the multiplier. We turn now to an investigation of the relationship between the marginal expenditure rate and the multiplier.

The Marginal Expenditure Rate and the Multiplier

We can compute the multiplier from the marginal expenditure rate. We know that the amount by which equilibrium real GDP will change as a result of a change in aggregate expenditures consists of two parts: the change in aggregate expenditures itself, ΔAE, and the induced change in spending. That induced change equals the marginal expenditure rate MER times the change in equilibrium GDP, ΔY^*. Thus

$$\Delta Y^* = \Delta AE + MER\Delta Y^* \tag{13}$$

Subtract the $MER\Delta Y^*$ term from both sides of the equation:

$$\Delta Y^* - MER\Delta Y^* = \Delta AE$$

Factor out the ΔY^* term on the left:

$$\Delta Y^*(1 - MER) = \Delta AE$$

Finally, solve for the multiplier $\Delta Y^*/\Delta AE$:

$$\frac{\Delta Y^*}{\Delta AE} = \frac{1}{(1 - MER)} \tag{14}$$

We thus compute the multiplier by taking 1 minus the marginal expenditure rate, then dividing the result into 1. In our example, the marginal expenditure rate is 0.5; the multiplier is 2, as we have already seen [multiplier = $1/(1 - MER) = 1/(1 - 0.5) = 1/0.5 = 2$].

Exhibit 27-13 illustrates the multiplier effect of a change in aggregate expenditures at various marginal expenditure rates. In each case, the initial equilibrium GDP is $200 billion and the increase in aggregate expenditures is $100 billion. That change in aggregate expenditures produces very different results, however, depending on the marginal expenditure rate and the multiplier. In Panel (a), the marginal expenditure rate is zero, and an increase in aggregate expenditures of $100 billion increases equilibrium GDP by $100 billion. The multiplier equals 1 [$=1/(1 - 0)$]. In an economy with a zero marginal expenditure rate, increases in GDP induce no additional spending, so the impact of an increase in aggregate expenditures is limited to the increase itself—it induces no additional income. In Panel (b), the marginal expenditure rate is 0.5, and the increase in aggregate expenditures boosts equilibrium GDP by $200 billion. In Panel (c), the marginal expenditure rate is 0.75. The increase in aggregate expenditures increases equilibrium GDP by $400 billion. The multiplier equals 4 [$=1/(1 - 0.75)$].

EXHIBIT 27-13

Marginal Expenditure Rates and the Multiplier

Each panel shows a $100 billion increase in aggregate expenditures with an initial equilibrium GDP of $1,000 billion. In Panel (a), the marginal expenditure rate equals zero, and the multiplier equals 1. An increase of $100 billion in aggregate expenditures increases real GDP by that amount; it induces no additional spending. In Panel (b), the marginal expenditure rate equals 0.5, and the increase in aggregate expenditures boosts equilibrium real GDP by $200 billion—the multiplier equals 2. In Panel (c), the marginal expenditure rate equals 0.75, the multiplier equals 4, and equilibrium real GDP rises by $400 billion. The greater the marginal expenditure rate, the greater the multiplier. All figures are in billions of 1987 dollars.

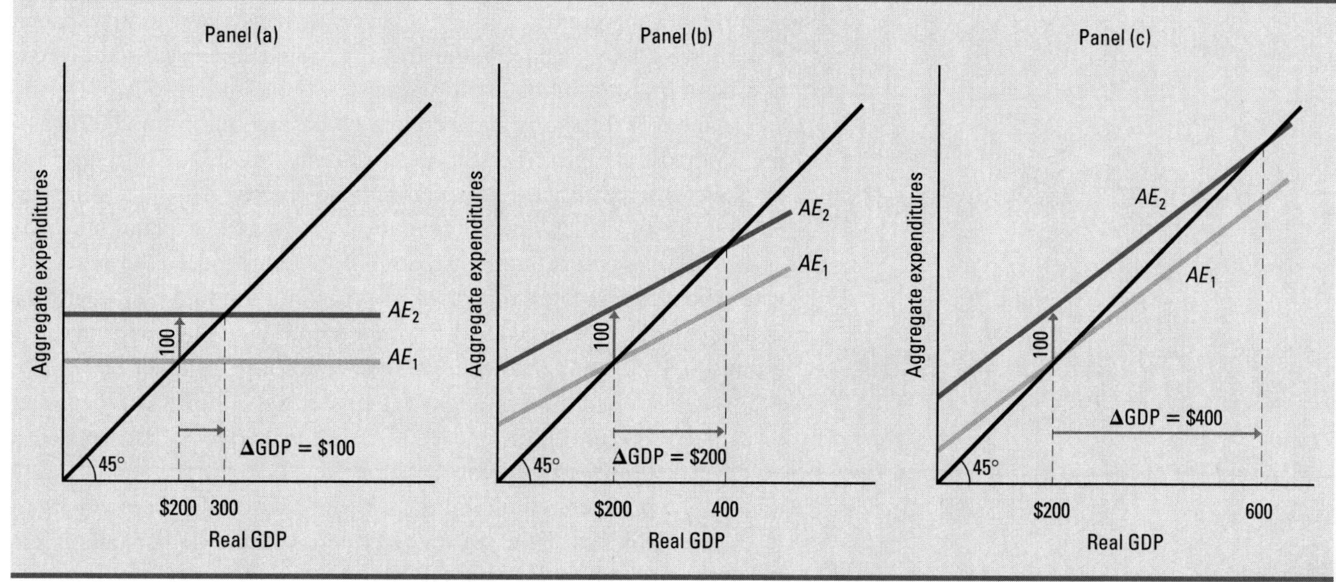

The greater the marginal expenditure rate, the greater the effect of increases in real GDP on additional expenditures. The greater the marginal expenditure rate, then, the greater the multiplier.

Checklist

- The aggregate expenditures curve shows the volume of aggregate expenditures at each level of GDP.
- The marginal expenditure rate gives the rate at which the level of aggregate expenditures rises with each additional dollar of GDP; it is the slope of the aggregate expenditures curve.
- Equilibrium in the aggregate expenditures model is achieved where aggregate expenditures equal GDP; it is found graphically at the intersection of the aggregate expenditures curve and the 45-degree line.
- Changes in aggregate expenditures produce larger changes in equilibrium GDP due to the multiplier effect. The change in equilibrium GDP equals the change in aggregate expenditures times the multiplier.
- The higher the marginal expenditure rate, the greater the multiplier. The multiplier is given by $1/(1 - MER)$.

Aggregate Expenditures and Aggregate Demand

We can use the aggregate expenditures model to gain greater insight into the nature of the aggregate demand curve. In this section we shall see how to derive the aggregate demand curve from the aggregate expenditures model. We shall also see how to apply the analysis of multiplier effects in the aggregate expenditures model to the aggregate demand–aggregate supply model.

Aggregate Expenditure Curves and Price Levels

The aggregate expenditures curve in Exhibit 27-11 was based on a consumption-GDP curve and autonomous values for investment, government purchases, and net exports. Such an aggregate expenditures curve assumes a fixed price level. If the price level were to change, the levels of consumption, investment, and net exports would all change, producing a new aggregate expenditures curve and a new equilibrium solution in the aggregate expenditures model.

Exhibit 27-11 showed an economy whose equilibrium GDP was $600 billion. Suppose the price level in that economy was 1.0. The aggregate expenditures curve from that analysis can thus be labeled $AE_{P=1.0}$, as in Panel (a) of Exhibit 27-14. At a lower price level, aggregate expenditures would rise. Assume that at every level of real GDP, a reduction in the price level to 0.5 would boost aggregate expenditures by $200 billion to $AE_{P=0.5}$, and an increase in the price level from 1.0 to 1.5 would reduce aggregate expenditures by $200 billion. The aggregate expenditures curve for a price level of 1.5 is shown as $AE_{P=1.5}$. There is thus a different aggregate expenditures curve, and a different level of equilibrium GDP, for each of these three price levels. A price level of 1.5 produces equilibrium at point A, a price level of 1.0 does so at B, and a price level of 0.5 produces equilibrium at C. More generally, there will be a different level of equilibrium GDP for *every* price level; the higher the price level, the lower the equilibrium value of GDP.

EXHIBIT 27-14

From Aggregate Expenditures to Aggregate Demand

Because there is a different aggregate expenditures curve for each price level, there is a different equilibrium real GDP for each price level. Panel (a) shows aggregate expenditures curves for three different price levels. Panel (b) shows that the aggregate demand curve, which shows the quantity of goods and services demanded at each price level, can thus be derived from the aggregate expenditures model. The aggregate expenditures curve for a price level of 1.0, for example, intersects the 45-degree line in Panel (a) at point B, producing an equilibrium real GDP of $600 billion. We can thus plot point B′ on the aggregate demand curve in Panel (b), which shows that at a price level of 1.0, a real GDP of $600 billion is demanded. All figures are in billions of 1987 dollars.

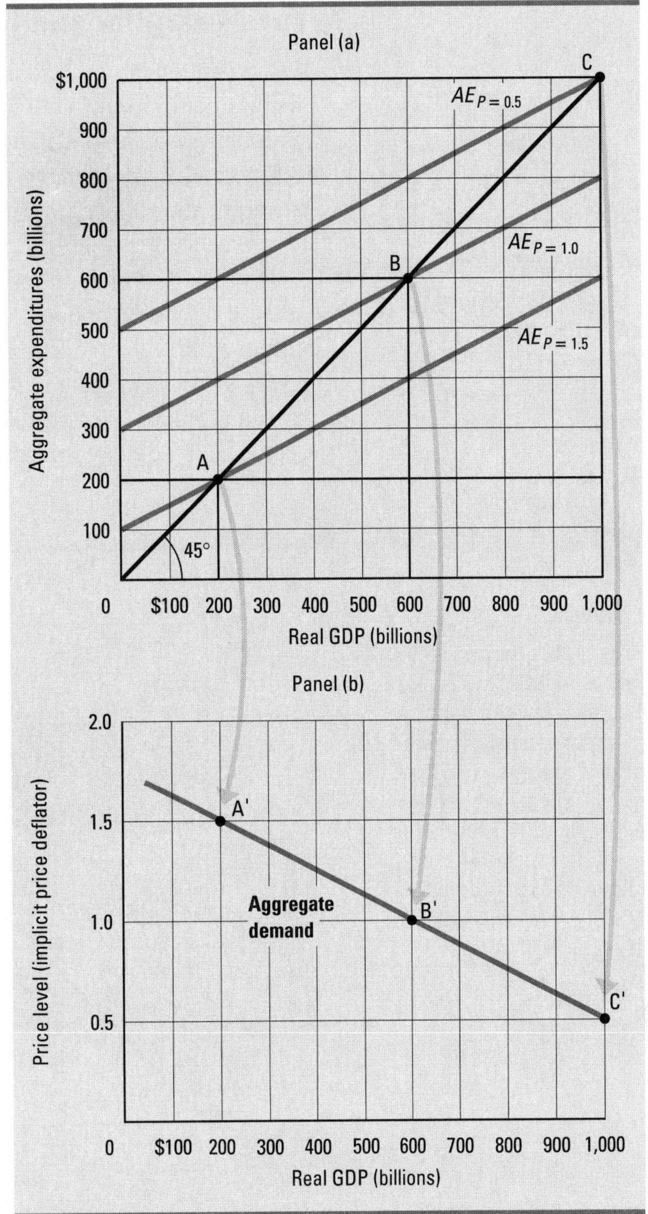

Panel (b) of Exhibit 27-14 shows how an aggregate demand curve can be derived from the aggregate expenditures curves for different price levels. The equilibrium real GDP associated with each price level in the aggregate expenditures model is plotted as a point showing the price level and the quantity of goods and services demanded (measured as real GDP). At a price level of 1.0 for example, the equilibrium level of real GDP in the aggregate expenditures model in Panel (a) is $600 billion at point B. That means $600 billion worth of goods and services is demanded; point B′ on the aggregate demand curve in Panel (b) corresponds to a real GDP demanded of $600 billion and a price level of 1.0. At a price level of 0.5 the equilibrium GDP demanded is $1,000 billion at point C′, and at a price level of 1.5 the equilibrium real GDP demanded is $200 billion at point A′. The aggregate demand curve thus shows the equilibrium real GDP from the aggregate expenditures model at each price level.

The Multiplier and Changes in Aggregate Demand

In the aggregate expenditures model, a change in aggregate expenditures changes equilibrium real GDP by the multiplier times the change in aggregate expenditures. That model, however, assumes a constant price level. How can we incorporate the concept of the multiplier into the model of aggregate demand and aggregate supply?

Consider the aggregate expenditures curves given in Panel (a) of Exhibit 27-15, each of which correspond to a particular price level. Suppose there is an increase in one component of aggregate expenditures: net exports rise by $100 billion. Such a change increases aggregate expenditures by $100 billion. But we have a set of aggregate expenditures curves, each corresponding to a different price level. How do we deal with changes in aggregate expenditures curves when we already have an entire set of such curves?

EXHIBIT 27-15

Changes in Aggregate Demand

The aggregate expenditures curves for price levels of 1.0 and 1.5 are the same as in Exhibit 27-14, as is the aggregate demand curve *AD*. Now suppose a $100 billion increase in net exports shifts each of the aggregate expenditures curves up; $AE_{P=1.0}$, for example, rises to $AE'_{P=1.0}$. The aggregate demand curve thus shifts to the right by $200 billion, the change in aggregate expenditures times the multiplier. All figures are in billions of 1987 dollars.

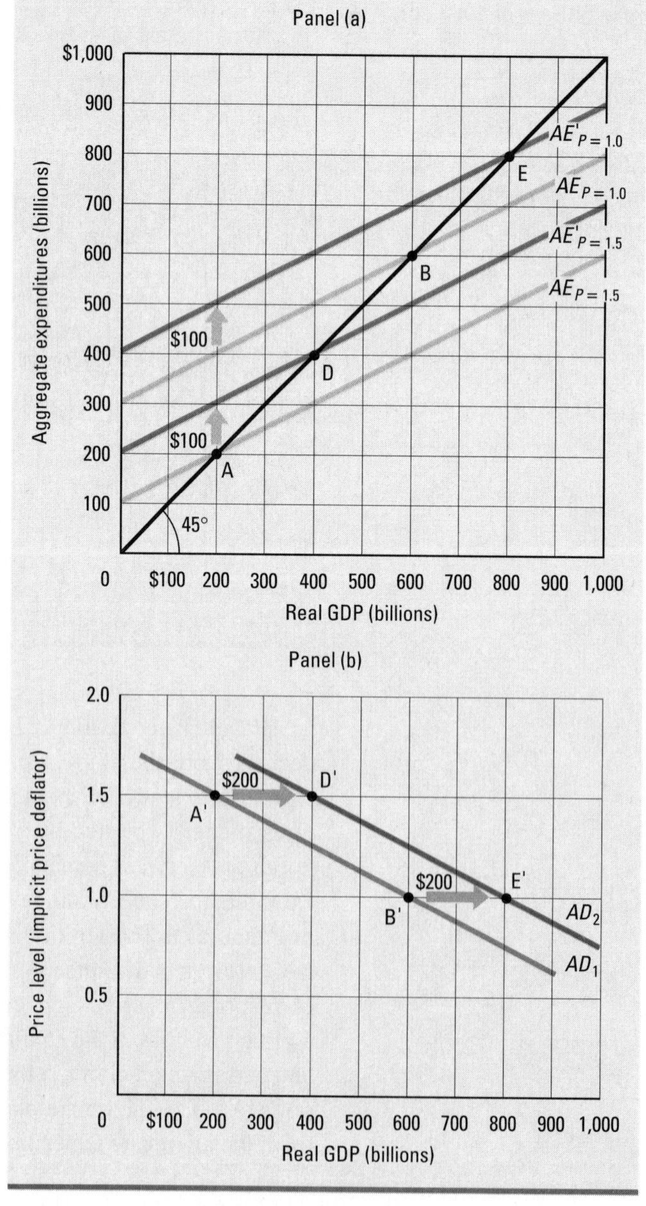

Checklist

- There is a different aggregate expenditures curve, and a different equilibrium GDP, for every price level; the higher the price level, the lower the aggregate expenditures curve and the lower the equilibrium level of GDP.
- The aggregate demand curve is derived from the family of aggregate expenditures curves and their respective equilibrium solutions.
- An increase in aggregate expenditures shifts the aggregate expenditures curve for each price level upward. That shifts the aggregate demand curve to the right by an amount equal to the change in aggregate expenditures times the multiplier. A decrease in aggregate expenditures shifts the aggregate expenditures curve for each price level downward. That shifts the aggregate demand curve to the left by an amount equal to the change in aggregate expenditures times the multiplier.

The answer lies in the assumption in the aggregate expenditures model that the price level is constant. Our analysis of shifts in a single aggregate expenditures curve was thus *based on a single price level.* Now that we recognize that the price level is a variable, and that there is a different aggregate expenditures curve for each price level, we must shift the aggregate expenditures curve for each price level to show the impact of the change in net exports. Exhibit 27-15 illustrates this procedure for aggregate expenditures curves drawn for price levels of 1.0 and 1.5, $AE_{P=1.0}$ and $AE_{P=1.5}$, respectively. The aggregate expenditures curves $AE_{P=1.0}$ and $AE_{P=1.5}$ shown in Panel (a) are the same ones shown in Panel (a) of Exhibit 27-14, and the aggregate demand curve AD_1 in Panel (b) of Exhibit 27-15 is the same curve as in Panel (b) of Exhibit 27-14. A $100 billion increase in net exports shifts each of the aggregate expenditures curves up by $100 billion, to $AE'_{P=1.0}$ and $AE'_{P=1.5}$. That changes the equilibrium real GDP associated with each price level; it thus shifts the aggregate demand curve to AD_2 in Panel (b). In the aggregate expenditures model equilibrium GDP changes by an amount equal to the change in aggregate expenditures times the multiplier, so the aggregate demand curve shifts by the same amount. The aggregate demand curve thus shifts to the right by $200 billion, 2 times the $100 billion change in aggregate expenditures.

In general, any change in aggregate expenditures shifts the aggregate demand curve. The amount of the shift is always equal to the change in aggregate expenditures times the multiplier. An increase in aggregate expenditures shifts the aggregate demand curve to the right; a reduction shifts it to the left.

A Look Back—And a Look Ahead

This chapter related consumption to income and showed the significance of that relationship for the aggregate demand curve and for shifts in aggregate demand. The model that linked consumption to aggregate demand was the aggregate expenditures model.

We began by observing the close relationship between consumption and disposable personal income. A consumption–disposable personal income curve shows this relationship. The slope of this curve is the marginal propensity to consume out of disposable personal income. The saving–disposable personal income curve can be derived from the consumption–disposable personal income curve and the 45-degree line.

The time period over which income is considered as a determinant of consumption is important. The current income theory holds that consumption in one period is a function of income in that same period. The permanent income theory holds that consumption is a function of permanent income. An important implication of this theory is that the marginal propensity to consume out of disposable personal income will be smaller for temporary than for permanent changes in disposable personal income.

We then turned to the relationship between consumption and real GDP, which is illustrated with the consumption–GDP curve. The slope of the consumption–GDP curve is the marginal propensity to consume out of GDP.

Several factors could cause the consumption–GDP curve to shift, including changes in income tax rates, transfer payments, real wealth (including the real value of money holdings), the availability of credit, consumer preferences, and consumer expectations. Such changes shift the consumption–GDP curve; changes in GDP do not shift the curve but cause movements along it.

We used the consumption–GDP curve to derive an aggregate expenditures curve, which shows the total of consumption, planned investment, government purchases, and net exports at each level of GDP. This curve is used in the aggregate expenditures model to determine the equilibrium real GDP; the slope of the curve is the marginal expenditure rate MER. A change in aggregate expenditures produces a multiplier effect that leads to a larger change in equilibrium GDP. The multiplier equals 1/(1 − MER).

Finally we derived the aggregate demand curve from the aggregate expenditures model. The downward slope of the aggregate demand curve reflects the real balance effect. A change in aggregate expenditures shifts the aggregate demand curve by an amount equal to the change in aggregate expenditures times the multiplier.

We shall continue our analysis of the components of aggregate demand in the next two chapters. Chapter 28 examines investment, and Chapter 29 discusses net exports. That discussion will conclude our basic analysis of models of macroeconomic activity; we'll put all this theory to work in Part Eight with an analysis of policy issues. An algebraic treatment of the aggregate expenditures model is given in the appendix to this chapter.

Terms and Concepts for Review

Aggregate expenditures
Aggregate expenditures curve
Aggregate expenditures function
Aggregate expenditures model
Autonomous expenditures
Consumption–disposable personal income curve
Consumption–disposable personal income function
Consumption–disposable personal income schedule
Consumption–GDP curve
Consumption–GDP function
Consumption–GDP schedule
Current income theory of consumption
Disposable personal income
Induced expenditures
Marginal expenditure rate (*MER*)
Marginal propensity to consume out of disposable personal income (MPC_d)
Marginal propensity to consume out of GDP (MPC_y)
Multiplier
Multiplier effect
Permanent income
Permanent income theory of consumption
Personal saving
Saving–disposable personal income curve

For Discussion

1. Distinguish between consumption–personal disposable income functions, schedules, and curves.
2. The consumption function we studied in the chapter predicted that consumption would sometimes exceed disposable personal income. How could this be?
3. Explain why the marginal propensity to consume out of GDP is likely to be less than the marginal propensity to consume out of disposable personal income.
4. Explain the role played by the 45-degree line in the aggregate expenditures model.
5. Your college or university, if it does what many others do, occasionally releases a news story claiming that its impact on the total employment in the local economy is understated by its own employment statistics. If the institution keeps accurate statistics, is that possible?
6. Explain and illustrate graphically how each of the following events affects aggregate expenditures and equilibrium real GDP. In each case, state the nature of the change in aggregate expenditures and state the relationship between the change in *AE* and the change in equilibrium GDP.

a. Investment falls.

b. Government purchases go up.

c. The government sends \$1,000 to every person in the United States.

d. Real GDP rises by \$500 billion.

7. Mary Smith, whose marginal propensity to consume out of disposable personal income is 0.75, is faced with an unexpected increase in taxes of \$1,000. Will she cut back her consumption expenditures by the full \$1,000? How will she pay for the higher tax? Explain.

8. Suppose the level of investment in a certain economy automatically adjusts to changes in the level of GDP; an increase in real GDP induces an increase in investment, while a reduction in real GDP causes investment to fall. How do you think such behavior would affect the marginal expenditure rate? The multiplier?

9. Suppose the marginal expenditure rate in economy A is 0.9, while in economy B it is 0.5. Both economies experience an increase in investment of \$100 billion. Compare the shifts in aggregate demand this will produce in the two economies.

10. Give an intuitive explanation for how the multiplier works on a reduction in aggregate expenditures. Why does equilibrium GDP fall by more than the change in aggregate expenditures?

Problems

1. For the purpose of this exercise assume that the consumption function is given by $C = \$500$ billion $+ 0.8Y_d$. Construct a consumption and saving table showing how income is divided between consumption and saving when real disposable personal income (in billions) is \$0, \$500, \$1,000, \$1,500, \$2,000, \$2,500, \$3,000, and \$3,500. Graph your results, placing real disposable personal income on the horizontal axis and consumption on the vertical axis.

2. Assume an economy in which people would spend \$200 billion on consumption even if GDP were zero and, in addition, increase their consumption by \$0.60 for each additional \$1 of GDP. Assume further that the sum of investment plus government purchases plus net exports is \$200 billion. What is the equilibrium level of income in this economy? If the economy is currently operating at an output level of \$1,200 billion, what do you predict will happen to GDP in the future?

3. The equations below give consumption–GDP functions for economies in which investment, government purchases, and net exports are all autonomous. Compute the marginal expenditure rate and multiplier for each economy.

a. $C = \$650 + 0.33Y$

b. $C = \$180 + 0.9Y$

c. $C = \$1{,}500$

d. $C = \$700 + 0.8Y$

4. Suppose the first aggregate expenditures curve in Problem 2 is drawn for a price level of 1.2. A reduction in the price level to 1 increases aggregate expenditures by \$400 billion at each level of real GDP. Draw the implied aggregate demand curve.

27 Appendix The Algebra of Equilibrium

The aggregate expenditures model was presented in the main chapter using text, tables, and graphs. The model can also be expressed in algebraic form as well.

Suppose, for example, that we are given a consumption–disposable personal income function, a tax equation that gives tax revenues T as a fraction of real GDP Y, and equations that give autonomous values for investment I, government purchases G, and net exports X_n. All figures are in billions of 1987 dollars.

$$C = \$300 + 0.75(Y_d)$$

$$T = 0.2Y$$

$$I = \$200$$

$$G = \$400$$

$$X_n = -\$100$$

Notice that net exports in this economy are negative. The tax equation tells us that 20 percent of GDP is collected in income taxes. We shall assume for simplicity that income taxes make up the only difference between GDP and disposable personal income, so that $Y - T = Y_d$.

Equations such as these represent a specific model of a hypothetical economy. Together, they specify what we need to know about the economy in order to determine the equilibrium level of income.

Aggregate Expenditures and Income

At equilibrium, aggregate income is equal to aggregate expenditures. In the chapter we found the equilibrium solution by using a graph. Our strategy was to look for the level of output (income) at which aggregate expenditures would be equal to that level of output. Another way of solving such problems is to state the equilibrium condition algebraically, add whatever details are given to us in the problem, and solve. We first write the equilibrium condition that real GDP equals aggregate expenditures:

$$Y = AE = C + I + G + X_n \qquad \textbf{(1A)}$$

We write down the information we are given about each of the terms on the right-hand side of the equation and get

$$Y = \$300 + 0.75(Y_d) + 200 + 400 - 100$$

In the equation above, the autonomous values are understood to be expressed in billions of 1987 dollars. We now have a single equation with two unknowns, Y and Y_d. We need to replace the Y_d term on the right-hand side of the equation with a Y term. We do so by noting that

$$Y_d = Y - T = Y - 0.2Y = 0.8Y$$

We thus write

$$Y = \$300 + 0.75(0.8Y) + 200 + 400 - 100$$

or

$$Y = \$300 + 0.6Y + 200 + 400 - 100$$

Collecting the autonomous terms, we have

$$Y = \$800 + 0.6Y$$

We can now solve for Y:

$$Y - 0.6Y = \$800$$

$$0.4Y = \$800$$

$$Y = \$2{,}000$$

Equilibrium real GDP is \$2,000 billion. It is wise to check such solutions to confirm that at a level of GDP of \$2,000 billion, aggregate expenditures equal \$2,000 billion. Taxes take \$400 billion, leaving \$1,600 billion of disposable personal income. Inserting that amount into the consumption equation, we find that consumption would be \$1,500 billion. Adding the given values for investment, government purchases, and net exports, we confirm that the total of aggregate expenditures would be \$2,000 billion.

The General Solution

The general form of the algebraic approach can be derived as well. We use the same strategy of stating the equilibrium condition and then solving. In the general case we are given,

$$C = A + MPC_d(Y_d) \qquad \textbf{(2A)}$$

where A is autonomous consumption and MPC_d is the marginal propensity to consume out of disposable personal income. In addition,

$$T = tY \qquad \textbf{(3A)}$$

where t is the tax rate, stated as a fraction of real GDP. We know that

$$Y_d = Y - T \qquad \textbf{(4A)}$$

We assume that the values of investment, government purchases, and net exports are given, as before.

Notice that Equations (2A) through (4A) are equivalent to the specific equations that defined the problem we worked above.

Solving for Equilibrium

The equilibrium condition in the aggregate expenditures model requires that aggregate expenditures equal GDP. We specify that condition algebraically:

$$Y = AE \tag{5A}$$

But aggregate expenditures AE consist of consumption plus investment plus government purchases plus net exports. We thus replace the right-hand side of Equation (5A) with those terms to get

$$Y = C + I + G + X_n \tag{6A}$$

Consumption is given by Equation (2A). Inserting Equation (2A) into Equation (6A), we have

$$Y = A + MPC_d(Y_d) + I + G + X_n \tag{7A}$$

We have one equation with two unknowns, Y and Y_d. We therefore need to express Y_d in terms of Y. From Equations (3A) and (4A) we can write

$$Y_d = Y - tY \tag{8A}$$

We then factor the Y term and get

$$Y_d = (1 - t)Y \tag{9A}$$

We now substitute this expression for Y_d in Equation (7A) to get

$$Y = A + MPC_d(1 - t)Y + I + G + X_n \tag{10A}$$

The coefficient of GDP, $MPC_d(1 - t)$, gives the fraction of an additional dollar of GDP that will be spent for consumption; it is the marginal propensity to consume out of GDP. It is also the marginal expenditure rate, MER. We can thus rewrite Equation (10A) as

$$Y = A + MER(Y) + I + G + X_n \tag{11A}$$

Combining the autonomous terms in Equation (11A) in parentheses, we have

$$Y = (A + I + G + X_n) + MER(Y) \tag{12A}$$

We solve Equation (12A) for Y:

$$Y - MER(Y) = (A + I + G + X_n)$$

$$Y(1 - MER) = (A + I + G + X_n)$$

$$Y = \frac{1}{1 - MER}(A + I + G + X_n) \tag{13A}$$

In Equation (13A), $1/(1 - MER)$ is the multiplier. Equilibrium is achieved at a level of income equal to the multiplier times the volume of autonomous spending.

Problems

1. Suppose an economy is characterized by the following equations. All figures are in billions of 1987 dollars.

$$C = 200 + 2/3(Y_d)$$

$$T = 1/4(Y)$$

$$G = 400$$

$$I = 200$$

$$X_n = 100$$

Solve for the equilibrium level of income. (You will find it easier to retain the marginal propensity to consume and the tax rate in the form of fractions.) Now let G rise to 500. What happens to the solution? What is the multiplier?

2. Consider the following economy. All figures are in billions of 1987 dollars.

$$C = 100 + 0.8(Y_d)$$

$$T = 0.25Y$$

$$I = 300$$

$$G = 400$$

$$X_n = 200$$

Solve for the equilibrium level of real GDP. Now suppose investment falls to $200 billion. What happens to equilibrium real GDP? What is the multiplier?

28

Investment and Economic Activity

Chapter Objectives

After mastering the material in this chapter, you will be able to:

1. Explain the factors that determine the quantity of capital firms want to hold.
2. Interpret investment as postponed consumption.
3. Explain the factors that determine the level of investment.
4. Show the ways in which public policy affects investment.
5. Show how investment affects aggregate demand and long-run aggregate supply.

Investment . . . equips workers with more and better capital; workers so equipped are more productive.

—U.S. Council of Economic Advisers, 1995

What's Ahead

Andrew S. Grove, the head of Intel Corporation, remembers how his colleagues' eyes got pretty big as they looked at a chart showing what Intel would need to invest over the next few years to install facilities required for its planned Pentium chip.[1]

The chart would have made anyone's eyes pretty big. It projected spending $5 billion in new capital for the production facilities to make the new chip. A chip is a semiconductor that serves as the brain of a computer. The new chip would replace Intel's 486 chip, which had itself required $1 billion worth of new facilities.

Betting $5 billion on anything is a daunting prospect. But in 1991, the mission to build an entirely new chip seemed especially risky. Big increases in world supplies of computer chips had sent prices plunging in the mid-1980s, cutting the profits of companies such as Intel sharply. With the United States in a recession and countries such as Japan and Germany heading into one, it wasn't clear the market for chips would recover.

Intel's Senior Vice President, Gerhard H. Parker, told fellow board members it would. He argued that the huge gains in computing efficiency offered by the Pentium chip would translate into sharply lower prices for computers and sharp increases in the number of computers purchased. The board agreed, and Intel took the $5 billion plunge.

By 1995, the bet seemed to have paid off. New, more powerful chips allowed sharp reductions in prices for computers that were more powerful than ever, and the quantity of computers demanded soared. In May of 1995, the Semiconductor Industry Association upped its 1995 forecast to a whopping 39 percent increase in the quantity of chips sold worldwide—the organization's previous forecast had anticipated a 15 percent gain. Intel's expansion put the company in position

[1] This example is drawn from Don Clark, "A Big Bet Made Intel What It Is Today; Now, It Wagers Again," *The Wall Street Journal*, 7 June 1995, A1.

to take advantage of the huge surge in the quantity of computers demanded—most of those computers came in boxes with a bright "Intel Inside" label, designating them as computers powered by Intel's new chip. The company's profits in 1995 were expected to reach $3.5 billion; some analysts were predicting that Intel, within a few years, will become the world's most profitable company—provided a calamity such as a worldwide recession doesn't come along to derail the boom.

Whatever Intel's future may hold, the 1991 decision was a classic choice by a firm to invest in its future by expanding its production capacity now. Such choices must always be made in the face of uncertainty—firms can't know what the marketplace has in store. Investment is a gamble; firms that make the gamble hope for a profitable payoff.

Investments made by firms play an important role in the long run, for they influence the rate at which an economy grows, thus determining a country's future standard of living. Investment is important in the short run as well. Increases in investment boost aggregate demand, while reductions in investment lower it.

In this chapter we'll examine factors that determine investment, and we'll study investment's relationship to output in the short run and in the long run. We'll also explore the role public policy plays in determining investment.

The Role and Nature of Investment

How important is investment? Consider any job you've ever performed. Your productivity in that job was largely determined by the investment choices that had been made before you began to work. If you worked as a clerk in a store, your productivity was affected by the equipment used in collecting money from customers. It may have been a simple cash register, or a sophisticated computer that scanned purchases and computed the store's inventory and did an analysis of the store's sales as you entered each sale. If you've worked for a lawn maintenance firm, your productivity was influenced by the kind of equipment you had to work with. You were more productive if you had the latest mulching power lawn mowers than if you struggled with a push mower. In both tasks, your ability to do the work depended on the skills you brought to the job—the human capital you have—and on the technology available. Whatever the work you might have done, your productivity was strongly influenced by the kind and quality of physical, human, and intellectual capital you had to work with. And that capital was available because investment choices had provided it.

Investment is important because it adds to the nation's capital stock. We saw in Chapter 26 that an increase in capital shifts the production function upward, increases the demand for labor, and shifts the long-run aggregate supply curve to the right. Investment therefore affects the economy's natural level of real GDP and thus its standard of living in the long run.

Investment plays an important role in the short run as well. Investment is a component of aggregate demand. Changes in investment shift the aggregate demand curve and thus change real GDP and the price level in the short run. An increase in investment shifts the aggregate demand curve to the right; a reduction shifts it to the left.

Components of Investment

The components of investment correspond to the forms of capital to which they add. Economists distinguish three forms of capital: physical capital, human capital, and intellectual capital. Physical capital includes all the goods that have been produced for the production of other goods and services; it includes buildings, equipment, and transportation facilities. Human capital is the set of skills and talents people have acquired through education and training. Intellectual capital is our technology, our stock of knowledge about how goods and services can be produced. The production of new capital is called investment. Investment thus adds to the stock of physical, human, or intellectual capital.

Investment can take a wide range of forms. In reading this book, you're adding to your human capital—you're engaging in investment. The construction of a new street or factory adds to the stock of physical capital and is part of investment. The development of computer software to increase the efficiency of accounting systems adds to the intellectual capital available for the production of goods and services and is thus part of investment. Investment occurs when we do anything to add to our stock of capital.

As we saw in Chapter 21, there is a gap between the economic concept of investment and the national income accounting measure of investment. The measure of investment included in GDP is gross private domestic investment (GPDI), which is the production of physical capital for use by private firms. This measure of investment does not include the production of public sector capital such as roads or new public schools, the production of human capital, or additions to intellectual capital. But the gap between theory and measurement is closing. Within a few years, the Commerce Department will begin to include additions to public sector capital and some forms of intellectual capital as investment. Because the economic concept of investment differs from the way it is measured, and because the measurement of gross investment is changing, there is necessarily some confusion in any discussion of investment. Much of our discussion will focus on gross private domestic investment, but factors that affect it are likely to affect the broader concept of investment as well.

Gross Private Domestic Investment

GPDI includes four categories of investment: business structures, equipment, residential investment, and changes in business inventories.

Business Structures. This category of investment includes the construction of private office buildings, warehouses, factories, private hospitals and universities, and other structures in which the production of goods and services is to take place. A structure is counted as investment only during the period in which it is built. It may be sold several times after being built, but such sales are not counted as investment. Recall that investment is part of GDP, and GDP is the value of *production* in any period, not total sales.

Equipment. Producers' durable equipment includes things such as machinery, computers, trucks, cars, desks—any business equipment that is expected to last more than a year. A telephone company's installation of telephone lines will be an investment in equipment. Equipment is counted as investment only in the period in which it is produced.

Residential Investment. Housing construction is counted as part of gross private domestic investment. This measure includes all forms of residential construction, whether apartment houses or single-family homes.

Change in Business Inventories. Business inventories are considered part of the nation's capital stock because those inventories are used to produce other goods. All inventories are capital; additions to inventories are thus investment. When inventories fall, that's recorded as negative investment.

Exhibit 28-1 shows the components of gross private domestic investment from 1975 to 1995. We see that producers' durable equipment is the largest component of investment in the United States, followed by residential structures.

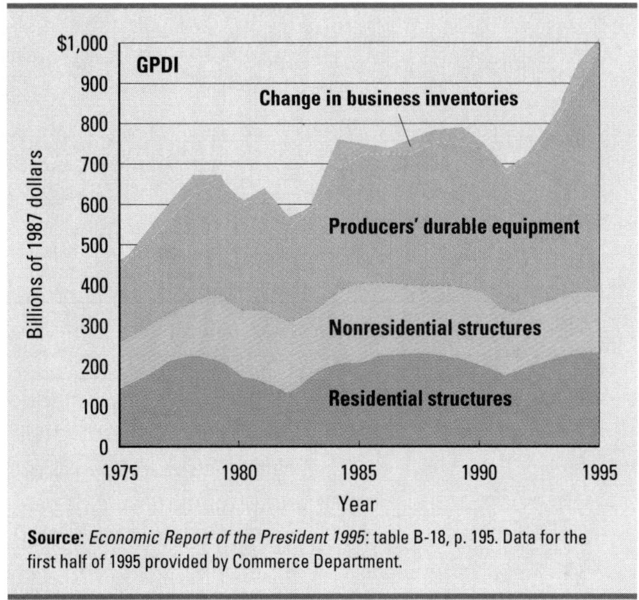

Source: *Economic Report of the President 1995*: table B-18, p. 195. Data for the first half of 1995 provided by Commerce Department.

EXHIBIT 28-1

Components of Gross Private Domestic Investment, 1975–1995

This chart shows the levels of each of the four components of gross private domestic investment from 1975 through the first half of 1995. Producers' durable equipment is the largest component of GPDI and has shown the most substantial growth over the past 20 years. All figures are in billions of 1987 dollars.

Gross and Net Investment

As capital is used, some of it wears out or becomes obsolete; it undergoes depreciation. Investment adds to the capital stock, and depreciation reduces it. Investment minus depreciation is net investment. If investment is greater than depreciation in any period, then net investment is positive and the capital stock increases. If investment is less than depreciation in any period, net investment is negative and the capital stock declines.

In the official estimates of total output, investment (GPDI) minus depreciation equals net private domestic investment (NPDI). The value for NPDI in any period gives the amount by which the privately held capital stock increased during that period.

Case in Point

Reducing Private Capital in the Depression

Net private domestic investment (NPDI) has been negative during only two periods in the last 60 years. One was World War II, during which massive defense spending forced cutbacks in private sector spending. (Recall that government investment isn't counted as investment in the official accounts; production of defense capital thus isn't reflected in these figures.) The other period in which NPDI was negative was the Great Depression.

Aggregate demand plunged during the first 4 years of the Depression. As firms cut their output in response to reductions in demand, their need for capital fell as well. They reduced their capital by holding gross private domestic investment below depreciation beginning in 1931. That produced negative net private domestic investment; it continued to be negative through 1935 and became negative again in 1938. In all, firms reduced the private capital stock by more than $150 billion (in 1987 dollars) during the period.

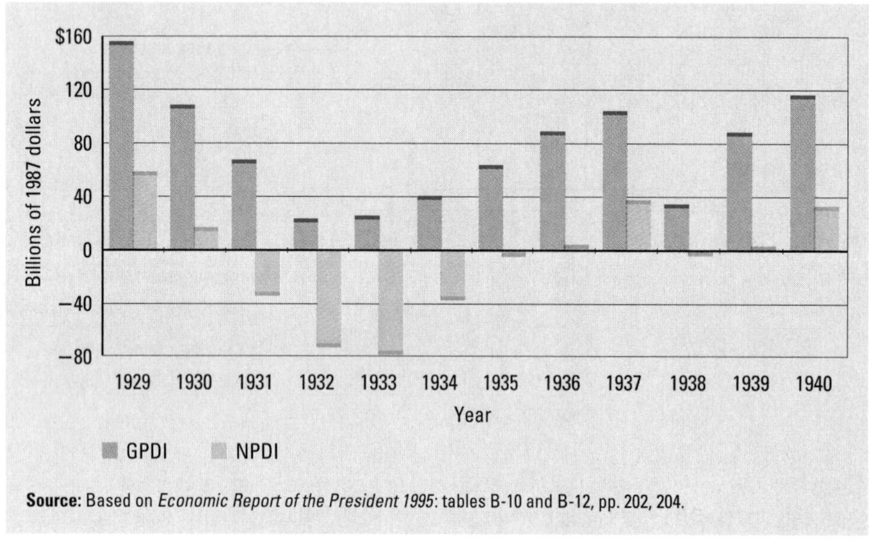

Source: Based on *Economic Report of the President 1995*: tables B-10 and B-12, pp. 202, 204.

Exhibit 28-2 reports the real values of GPDI, depreciation, and NPDI from 1975 to 1995. We see that the bulk of GPDI replaces capital that has been depreciated. Notice the sharp reductions in NPDI during the recessions of 1981–1982 and 1990–1991.

We don't have estimates of the degree to which a broader conception of investment—one that included additions to public sector, human, and intellectual capital—would reflect replacement of depreciated capital versus being a net addition to the capital stock. The wearing out of roads represents depreciation; public sector expenditures for road maintenance are a form of investment that replaces depreciated capital. Human capital depreciates as we forget things we've learned or skills we had acquired. Certainly a good deal of investment in human capital replaces capital that has depreciated. If you take an intermediate-level course in macroeconomic theory, for example, you will cover some of the same material you're learning now. That reflects a presumption that some of the human capital gained in an introductory course needs replacement in an intermediate course.

EXHIBIT 28-2

Gross Private Domestic Investment, Depreciation, and Net Private Domestic Investment, 1975–1995

The bulk of gross private domestic investment goes to the replacement of capital that has depreciated, as shown by the experience of the past two decades. All figures here are in billions of 1987 dollars.

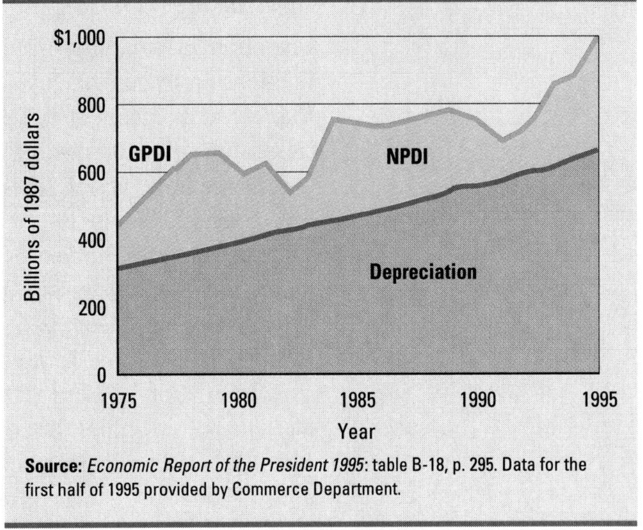

Source: *Economic Report of the President 1995*: table B-18, p. 295. Data for the first half of 1995 provided by Commerce Department.

The Volatility of Investment

Investment, measured as GPDI, is among the most volatile components of GDP. In percentage terms, year-to-year changes in investment are far greater than the year-to-year changes in consumption or government purchases. Net exports are also quite volatile, but they represent a much smaller share of GDP. Exhibit 28-3 compares annual percentage changes in investment, personal consumption, and government purchases.

Given that the aggregate demand curve shifts by an amount equal to the multiplier times a change in investment, the volatility of investment is an important factor in economic activity in the short run. One reason for this volatility is that investment is the mechanism through which the capital stock is adjusted.

EXHIBIT 28-3

Changes in Components of GDP, 1975–1995

Annual percentage changes in real GPDI have been much greater than annual percentage changes in the real values of personal consumption or government purchases.

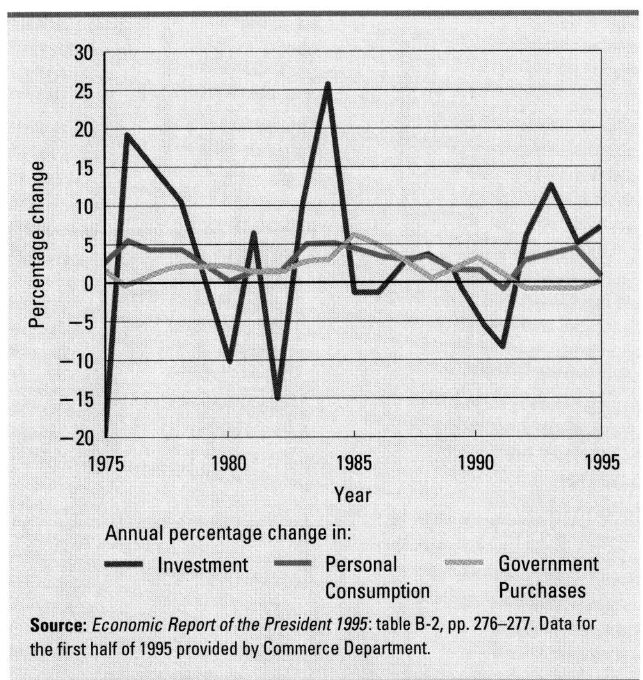

Source: *Economic Report of the President 1995*: table B-2, pp. 276–277. Data for the first half of 1995 provided by Commerce Department.

Investment As an Adjustment of the Capital Stock

The observed volatility of investment results in large part from the nature of its relationship to capital. Investment is undertaken to change the stock of capital. The act of investment therefore implies that the current stock of capital falls short of the quantity desired.

To see how the relationship of investment to capital affects the volatility of investment, let's imagine an economy in which there is no depreciation—all investment therefore increases the capital stock. Suppose that the capital stock in this economy has been $1,000 for several years. There has been no change in the capital stock in recent years, so investment has equaled zero during that period. If in 1995 this capital is increased by 5 percent to $1,050, that means investment rises from $0 in 1994 to $50 in 1995. Now suppose that in 1996 there is no further change in capital. That means investment falls back to zero—a plunge of 100 percent! Small percentage changes in the stock of capital—or a decision not to change the stock of capital—imply huge percentage changes in investment.

Investment, Consumption, and Saving

We used the production possibilities curve in Chapter 2 to illustrate the choice between investment, consumption, and saving. Because that choice is crucial to understanding the nature and role of investment, it will be useful to reexamine it here.

Exhibit 28-4 shows a production possibilities curve for an economy that can produce two kinds of goods: consumption goods and investment goods. Think of investment goods in the broadest economic sense, including additions to physical, human, and intellectual capital. An economy operating at point A on PCC_1 is using its factors of production fully and efficiently. It is producing C_A units of consumption goods and I_A units of investment each period. Suppose that depreciation equals I_A, so that the quantity of investment each period is just sufficient to replace depreciated capital; net investment equals zero. Absent population growth or a change in natural resources, the production possibilities curve will remain fixed at PPC_1.

Now suppose a decision is made to sacrifice the production of some consumption goods in favor of greater investment. The economy moves to point B

EXHIBIT 28-4

The Choice Between Consumption and Investment

A society with production possibilities curve PPC_1 could choose to produce at point A, producing C_A consumption goods and investment of I_A. If depreciation equals I_A, then net investment is zero and the production possibilities curve won't shift. By cutting its production of consumption goods and increasing investment to I_B, however, the society can, over time, shift its production possibilities curve out to PPC_2, making it possible to enjoy greater production of consumption goods in the future.

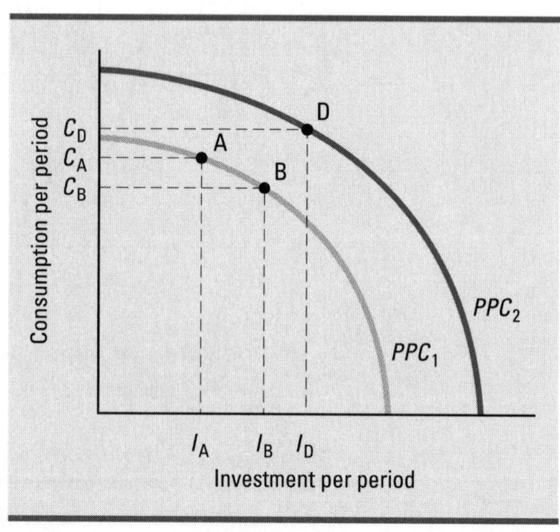

Checklist

- Investment adds to the stock of capital, which includes publicly and privately owned physical capital, human capital, and intellectual capital.
- Gross private domestic investment includes the construction of nonresidential structures, the production of producers' durable equipment, residential construction, and changes in business inventories.
- The bulk of gross private domestic investment goes to the replacement of capital.
- The volatility of investment is explained in large part by the fact that small changes in the desired stock of capital can lead to big changes in the flow of investment.
- Investment represents a choice to postpone consumption—it requires saving. The United States has a relatively low saving rate and devotes a relatively small share of its GDP to investment.

on PPC_1. Production of consumption goods falls to C_B, and investment rises to I_B. Assuming depreciation remains I_A, net investment is now positive. As the nation's capital increases, the production possibilities curve shifts outward to PPC_2. Once that shift occurs, it will be possible to select a point such as D on the new production possibilities curve. At this point, consumption equals C_D and investment equals I_D. By sacrificing consumption early on, the society is able to increase its consumption in the future.

We see that a movement along the production possibilities curve in the direction of the production of more investment goods and fewer consumption goods allows the production of more of both types of goods in the future. We might therefore wonder why the United States devotes such a small fraction of its GDP to investment. Investment averaged 22 percent of GDP for the world as a whole in 1992; the U.S. share that year was 16 percent. We'll examine another element of investment's role in determining future living standards, the relationship between investment and economic growth, later in this chapter.

Determinants of Investment

We shall see in this section that interest rates play a key role in the determination of the desired stock of capital and thus of investment. Because investment is a process through which capital is increased in one period for use in future periods, expectations play an important role in investment as well.

Capital is one factor of production, along with labor and natural resources. A decision to invest is a decision to use more capital in producing goods and services. Factors that affect firms' choices in the mix of capital, labor, and natural resources will affect investment as well.

We'll also see in this section that public policy affects investment. Some investment is undertaken by government agencies as they add to the public stock of capital. In addition, the tax and regulatory policies chosen by the public sector can affect the investment choices of private firms and individuals.

Interest Rates and Investment

You've probably heard news reports that spell out the relationship between investment and interest rates. We often hear, for example, that low interest rates have stimulated housing construction or that high rates have reduced it. Such reports imply a negative relationship between interest rates and investment in residential structures. This relationship applies to all forms of investment: higher interest rates tend to reduce the quantity of investment, while lower interest rates increase it.

To see the relationship between interest rates and investment, let's suppose you own a small factory and are considering the installation of a solar energy collection system to heat your building. You have determined that the cost of installing the system would be \$10,000 and that the system would lower your energy bills by \$1,000 per year. To simplify the example, we shall suppose that these savings will continue forever and that the system will never need repair or maintenance. Given these assumptions, we need to consider only the \$10,000 purchase price and the \$1,000 annual savings.

If the system is installed, it will be an addition to the capital stock and will therefore be counted as investment. Should you purchase the system?

Reader's Advisory !

To make sense of the discussion of the relationship between interest rates and investment, you must remember that investment is an addition to capital, and that capital is something that has been produced in order to produce other goods and services. A bond is *not* capital. The purchase of a bond is *not* an investment. We can thus think of purchasing bonds as an alternative to investment. The more attractive bonds are (i.e., the greater their interest rate), the less attractive investment becomes.

If we forget that investment is an addition to the capital stock and that the purchase of a bond is not investment, we can fall into the following kind of error: "Higher interest rates mean a greater return on bonds, so more people will purchase them. Higher interest rates will therefore lead to greater investment." That's a mistake, of course, because the purchase of a bond is not an investment.

Higher interest rates increase the cost of using funds for investment. They do not encourage greater investment.

Suppose that your business already has the $10,000 on hand. You're considering whether to use the money for the solar energy system or for the purchase of a bond. Your decision to purchase the system or the bond will depend on the interest rate available on the bond.

Putting $10,000 into the solar energy system generates an effective income of $1,000 per year—the saving the system will produce. That's a return of 10 percent per year. Suppose the bond pays 12 percent per year. It thus generates interest income of $1,200 per year—enough to pay the $1,000 in heating bills and have $200 left over. At an interest rate of 12 percent, the bond is the better purchase. If, however, the interest rate on bonds were 8 percent, then the solar energy system would yield a higher income than the bond. At interest rates below 10 percent, you'll invest in the solar energy system. At interest rates above 10 percent, you'll buy a bond instead. At an interest rate of precisely 10 percent, it's a toss-up.

If you don't have the $10,000 on hand and would need to borrow the money to purchase the solar energy system, the interest rate still governs your decision. At interest rates below 10 percent, it makes sense to borrow the money and invest in the system. At interest rates above 10 percent, it doesn't.

In effect, the interest rate represents the cost of putting funds into the solar energy system rather than into a bond. The cost of putting the $10,000 into the system is the interest return that could be obtained from a bond.

At any one time, millions of investment choices hinge on the interest rate. Each decision to invest will make sense at some interest rates but not at others. The higher the interest rate, the fewer potential investments will be justified; the lower the interest rate, the greater the number that will be justified. There is thus a negative relationship between the interest rate and the level of investment.

Exhibit 28-5 shows an **investment demand curve** for the economy—a curve that shows the level of investment at each interest rate, with all other determinants of investment held constant. At an interest rate of 8 percent, the level of investment is $700 billion at point A. At a lower interest rate of 6 percent, the investment demand curve shows that investment will rise to $750 billion at point B. A reduction in the interest rate thus causes a movement along the investment demand curve.

EXHIBIT 28-5

The Investment Demand Curve

The investment demand curve shows the volume of investment spending at each interest rate, assuming all other determinants of investment are constant. The curve shows that as the interest rate falls, the level of investment rises. A reduction in the interest rate from 8 percent to 6 percent, for example, would increase investment from $700 billion to $750 billion, all other determinants of investment unchanged.

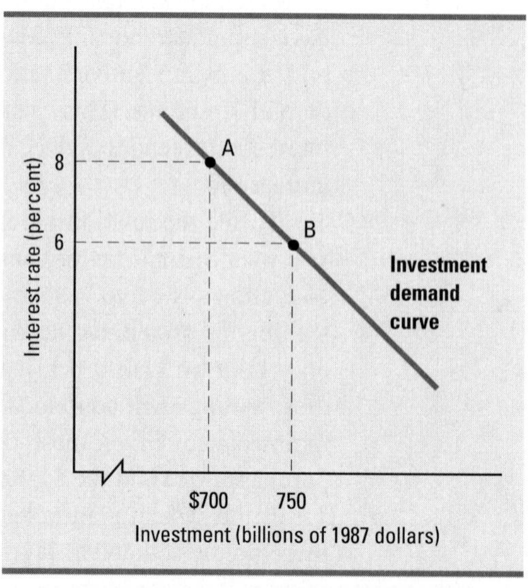

Other Determinants of Investment Demand

Perhaps the most important feature of the investment demand curve is not its negative slope, but rather the fact that it shifts often. Although investment certainly responds to changes in interest rates, changes in other factors appear to play the more important role in driving investment choices.

This section examines seven additional determinants of investment demand: expectations, the level of economic activity, the stock of capital, the cost of capital goods, other factor costs, technological change, and public policy. A change in any of these can shift the investment demand curve.

Expectations

A plan to change the capital stock is a plan to change future production capacity. It therefore depends crucially on expectations about the future. A firm considers likely future sales; a student weighs prospects in different fields and their required educational and training levels; a government agency considers likely demands on road capacity or water treatment facilities. As expectations change in a way that increases the expected return from investment, the investment demand curve shifts to the right.

A university that is operating close to capacity may decide to construct new classroom facilities. Why would it do that? The most likely explanation is that it anticipates increased enrollment. Its expectation of greater demand causes it to increase investment now.

Intel's investment in a huge expansion in its production capacity, described in the introduction to this chapter, was based on an expectation that production of personal computers, and thus the demand for semiconductors, would expand dramatically in the 1990s. Clearly, Intel expected to profit from having the capacity to meet the expected increase in demand.

The Level of Economic Activity

Firms need capital to produce goods and services. An increase in the level of production is likely to boost demand for capital and thus lead to greater investment. We thus have some of the same circularity that exists with consumption demand. An increase in investment boosts real GDP, and an increase in real GDP is likely to stimulate investment. The relationship between investment and real GDP is not nearly as close as the relationship between consumption and real GDP. That's because other determinants of investment are so important. Nonetheless, increases in real GDP do, all other things unchanged, tend to increase investment.

To the extent that increases in GDP boost investment, the marginal expenditure rate is increased. To the extent that an increase in real GDP induces not only additional consumption but additional investment, it increases the value of the multiplier. Suppose, for example, that the marginal propensity to consume out of GDP equals 0.5 and that all other components of aggregate expenditures are autonomous. That would imply a multiplier of 2. Now suppose each additional $1 of real GDP induces not only $0.50 in additional consumption but $0.10 in additional investment. That would make the marginal expenditure rate equal to 0.6 and boost the value of the multiplier to 2.5 [$=1/(1-0.6)$].

An **investment demand curve** is a curve that shows the level of investment at each interest rate, with all other determinants of investment held constant.

The Stock of Capital

The quantity of capital already in use affects the level of investment in two ways. First, because most investment replaces capital that has depreciated, a greater capital stock is likely to lead to more investment—there will be more capital to replace. But second, a greater capital stock can tend to reduce investment. That's because investment occurs to adjust the stock of capital to its desired level. Given that desired level, the amount of investment needed to reach it will be lower when the current capital stock is higher.

Suppose, for example, that real estate analysts expect that 100,000 homes will be needed in a particular community by 1998. That will create a boom in construction—and thus in investment—if the current number of houses is 50,000. But it will create hardly a ripple if there are now 99,980 homes.

How will these conflicting effects of a larger capital stock sort themselves out? Because most investment occurs to replace existing capital, a larger capital stock is likely to increase investment. But that larger capital stock will certainly act to reduce net investment. The more capital already in place, the less new capital will be required to reach a given level of capital that may be desired.

The Cost of Capital Goods

As the cost of acquiring capital goods rises relative to other prices, the demand for capital will fall. An increase in the construction cost of new buildings, for example, will reduce the number of new buildings demanded, all other factors unchanged. Conversely, a reduction in the cost of capital will increase the demand for capital. A reduction in construction cost will increase demand for new buildings.

The $10,000 cost of the solar energy system in the example above certainly affects a decision to purchase it. We saw that buying the system makes sense at interest rates below 10 percent and does not make sense at interest rates above 10 percent. If the system cost $5,000, then the interest return on the investment would be 20 percent (the annual saving of $1,000 divided by the $5,000 initial cost), and the investment would be undertaken at any interest rate below 20 percent.

Other Factor Costs

Firms and government agencies have a range of choices concerning how particular goods can be produced. A factory, for example, might use a sophisticated capital facility and relatively few workers, or it might use more workers and relatively less capital. A school might try to use more computers and software—capital—and reduce the number of teachers—labor. The choice to use capital will be affected by the cost of the capital goods and the interest rate, but it will also be affected by the cost of labor. As labor costs rise, the demand for capital is likely to increase.

Our solar collector example suggests that energy costs influence the demand for capital as well. The assumption that the system would save $1,000 per year in energy costs must have been based on the prices of fuel oil, natural gas, and/or electricity. If these prices were higher, the savings from the solar collector system would be greater, increasing the demand for this form of capital.

Technological Change

The implementation of new technology often requires new capital. Changes in technology can thus increase the demand for capital. Advances in computer technology have encouraged massive investments in computers. The development of fiber optics, a new technology for transmitting signals, has stimulated huge investments by telephone and cable television companies.

Case in Point: Tax Policies Affect Investment

After accelerated depreciation and the investment tax credit were introduced by the Kennedy administration early in the 1960s, investment soared. These measures to encourage investment were scaled back in the 1970s. The Reagan administration then expanded them as part of its 1981 tax cut package; it also slashed the capital gains tax. The purpose of the tax provisions introduced under both the Reagan and Kennedy administrations, was to encourage firms to increase their capital stocks through greater investment.

Real gross private domestic investment took off in the wake of the Reagan tax cuts. From 1982 to 1985, it rose at an annual rate of 11.2 percent, more than double the annual rate of increase for the previous 15 years. The United States enjoyed more rapid growth in gross private domestic investment during this period than did any other major industrialized country; growth in U.S. investment was almost six times the rate of growth in investment in Japan.

One difficulty with offering special tax rates on capital income, however, is that many people think it makes the tax code unfair. People who earn income from investment tend to be wealthy; tax measures that encourage investment are often attacked as a benefit to the rich. Such tax policies require that tax rates on other forms of income be increased. The Tax Reform Act of 1986 sought to be more evenhanded in its treatment of various forms of income. It eliminated special treatment of capital gains and investment in favor of lowering taxes overall. The result was sharply higher taxes on income from capital.

The table below compares effective tax rates on capital income from equipment, structures, and inventories before and after passage of the Tax Reform Act (TRA). Rates increased dramatically, particularly on equipment, the category of capital that had been most heavily favored by accelerated depreciation and the investment tax credit.

Effective Tax Rate on Capital Owned by Corporations (percent)

	Prior to TRA	After TRA
Equipment	10.0	39.6
Structures		
Nonresidential	34.4	43.1
Residential	49.5	52.5
Public utility	32.6	44.5
Inventories	48.8	45.8

Growth in investment slowed sharply in the wake of the Tax Reform Act. After rising at an annual rate of 11.2 percent from 1982 to 1985, investment growth slowed to a rate of 1.3 percent from 1985 to 1990. Many economists argue that the higher taxes imposed on capital income by the Tax Reform Act contributed to the slowing in investment growth in the second half of the decade.

Sources: *Economic Report of the President 1989:* p. 93; *Economic Report of the President 1995, p. 276.*

One technology that might be developed in the next century is a cold fusion process to generate energy. Such a method would mean that energy could be produced at low cost and virtually without limit—and without pollution. A technological change that dramatic would create massive investment needs for new forms of power plants. It would also be likely to revolutionize the applications of energy, extending such applications to products and services undreamed of today. The expansion of those applications would spawn whole new industries, creating still greater demands for investment in the economy.

Public Policy

Public policy can have significant effects on the demand for capital. Such policies typically seek to affect the cost of capital to firms. The Kennedy administration introduced two such strategies in the early 1960s. One, accelerated depreciation, allowed firms to depreciate capital assets over a very short period of time. They could report artificially high production costs in the first years of an asset's life and thus report lower profits and pay lower taxes. Accelerated depreciation didn't change the actual rate at which assets depreciated, of course, but it cut tax payments during the early years of the asset's use and thus reduced the cost of holding capital.

The second strategy was the **investment tax credit,** which permitted a firm to reduce its tax liability by a percentage of its investment during a period. A firm acquiring new capital could subtract a fraction of its cost—10 percent under the Kennedy administration's plan—from the taxes it owed the government. In effect, the government "paid" 10 percent of the cost of any new capital; the investment tax credit thus reduced the cost of capital for firms.

A third measure to encourage greater capital accumulation is a **capital gains tax** that allows gains on assets held during a certain period to be taxed at a different rate than other income. When an asset such as a building is sold for more than its purchase price, the seller of the asset is said to have realized a capital gain. Such a gain could be taxed as income under the personal income tax. Alternatively, it could be taxed at a lower rate reserved exclusively for such gains. A capital gains tax makes assets subject to the tax more attractive. It thus increases the demand for capital.

Accelerated depreciation, the investment tax credit, and a capital gains tax all increase the demand for private physical capital. Public policy can also affect the demands for other forms of capital. The federal government subsidizes state and local government production of many transportation, educational, and other facilities to encourage greater investment in public sector capital. For example, the federal government pays 90 percent of the cost of local government investment in new buses for public transportation systems. Government subsidies for education act to increase the stock of human capital. The federal government funds research, and it also grants firms a tax credit for their expenditures on research and development of new products, thus expanding the nation's stock of intellectual capital. Of course, public policy also affects the level of investment by spending on capital goods such as highways and public buildings.

Checklist

- The quantity of investment in any period is negatively related to the interest rate. This relationship is illustrated by the investment demand curve.
- A change in the interest rate causes a movement along the investment demand curve. A change in any other determinant of investment causes a shift of the curve.
- The other determinants of investment include expectations, the level of economic activity, the stock of capital, the cost of capital goods, other factor costs, technological change, and public policy.

An **investment tax credit** reduces a firm's tax liability by a fraction of its investment during a period.

A **capital gains tax** taxes income realized from the sale of assets at a different rate than that applied to other income.

Investment and the Economy

We shall examine the impact of investment on the economy in the context of the aggregate demand–aggregate supply model. Investment is a component of aggregate demand; changes in investment shift the aggregate demand curve by the amount of the change times the multiplier. Investment changes the capital stock; changes in the capital stock shift the production possibilities curve and thus shift the long- and short-run aggregate supply curves to the right or to the left.

Investment and Aggregate Demand

In the short run, changes in investment have an important impact on aggregate demand. We've already seen that investment is a highly volatile component of aggregate demand; changes in investment shift the aggregate demand curve.

Consider, for example, the impact of a reduction in the interest rate, given the investment demand curve (ID). In Exhibit 28-6, which uses the same investment demand curve introduced in Exhibit 28-5, a reduction in the interest rate from 8 percent to 6 percent increases investment by $50 billion in Panel (a). Assume that the multiplier is 2. With an increase in investment of $50 billion and a multiplier of 2, the aggregate demand curve shifts to the right by $100 billion to AD_2 in Panel (b). The quantity of real GDP demanded at each price level thus increases. At a price level of 1.0, for example, the quantity of real GDP demanded rises from $4,000 billion to $4,100 billion.

A reduction in investment would shift the aggregate demand curve to the left by an amount equal to the multiplier times the change in investment.

The relationship between investment and interest rates is the key to the application of monetary policy to the economy. When the Fed seeks to increase aggregate demand to close a recessionary gap, it purchases bonds. That raises bond prices, reduces interest rates, and stimulates investment and aggregate demand as illustrated in Exhibit 28-6. Similarly, a contractionary policy by the Fed would seek to raise interest rates, cut investment, and reduce aggregate demand. Such a policy might be undertaken to close an inflationary gap.

EXHIBIT 28-6

A Change in Investment and Aggregate Demand

A reduction in the interest rate from 8 percent to 6 percent increases the level of investment by $50 billion in Panel (a). With a multiplier of 2, the aggregate demand curve shifts to the right by $100 billion in Panel (b). The total quantity of real GDP demanded increases at each price level. Here, for example, the quantity of real GDP demanded at a price level of 1.0 rises from $4,000 billion at point C to $4,100 billion at point D.

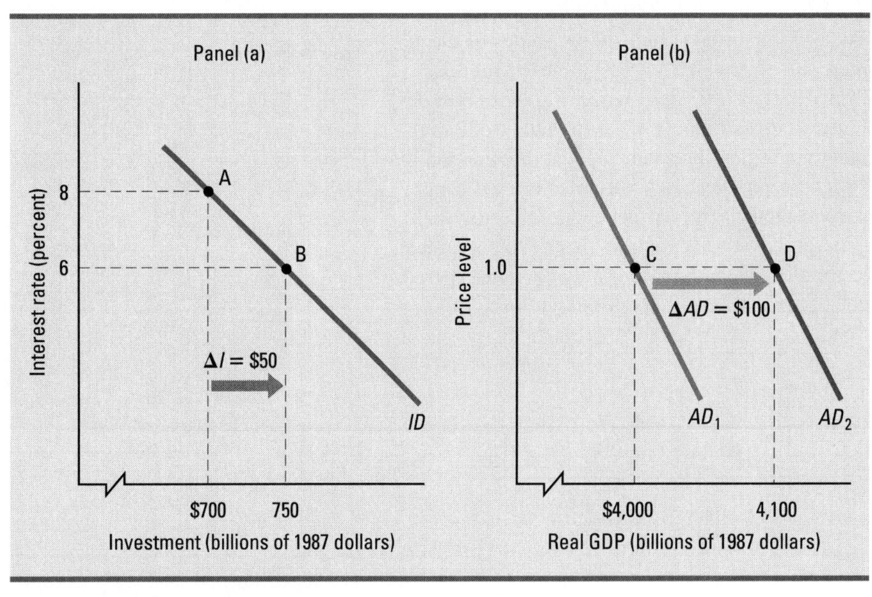

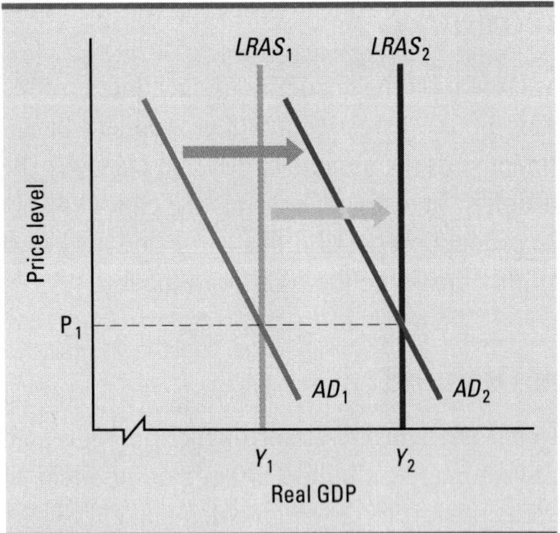

EXHIBIT 28-7

Investment and Long-Run Aggregate Supply

Suppose increased investment shifts the aggregate demand curve to the right to AD_2, and at the same time increased capital shifts the long-run aggregate supply curve to the right to $LRAS_2$. If both curves shift by the same amount, the price level will be unchanged at P_1 while real GDP rises to Y_2.

Investment and Economic Growth

Investment adds to the stock of capital, and the quantity of capital available to an economy is a crucial determinant of its productivity. Investment thus contributes to economic growth. We saw in Exhibit 28-4 that an increase in an economy's stock of capital shifts its production possibilities curve outward. That also shifts its long-run aggregate supply curve to the right. At the same time, of course, an increase in investment affects aggregate demand, as we saw in Exhibit 28-6.

Investment and Long-Run Aggregate Supply

Exhibit 28-7 illustrates how an increase in investment affects aggregate demand and long-run aggregate supply. Here an increase in investment shifts aggregate demand to AD_2 and shifts the long-run aggregate supply curve to $LRAS_2$. Given these shifts, the price level remains at P_1. A rightward shift in long-run aggregate supply shifts the short-run aggregate supply curve as well; this curve is not shown in Exhibit 28-7 in order to keep the graph simple.

Depending on the relative magnitudes of shifts in long-run aggregate supply and aggregate demand, the price level may rise or fall as the capital stock and aggregate demand increase. The shifts in aggregate demand and long-run aggregate supply shown in Exhibit 28-7 suggest the possibility that economic growth could occur without increasing the price level.

The relationship between increases in the capital stock and economic growth suggests that the greater the share of investment in a country's total output, the greater its rate of economic growth will be. Exhibit 28-8 shows gross domestic investment as a fraction of 1993 GDP and shows average annual growth in GDP from 1980 to 1993 for 22 high-income countries, as computed by the World Bank. We see that the share of GDP devoted to investment is lower in the United States than in most other countries.

The relationship between investment shares and economic growth is not a precise one; many other factors also affect economic growth. But in general, we

EXHIBIT 28-8

Investment Shares and Growth: An International Comparison

The accompanying chart shows values of the annual rate of growth in gross domestic product from 1980 to 1993 and shares of total output devoted to investment in 1993 for each of 22 high-income nations. The data suggest that the relationship between these two variables is a loose one; several other factors affect economic growth. In general, however, countries that devote a larger share of their total output to investment experienced higher rates of economic growth.

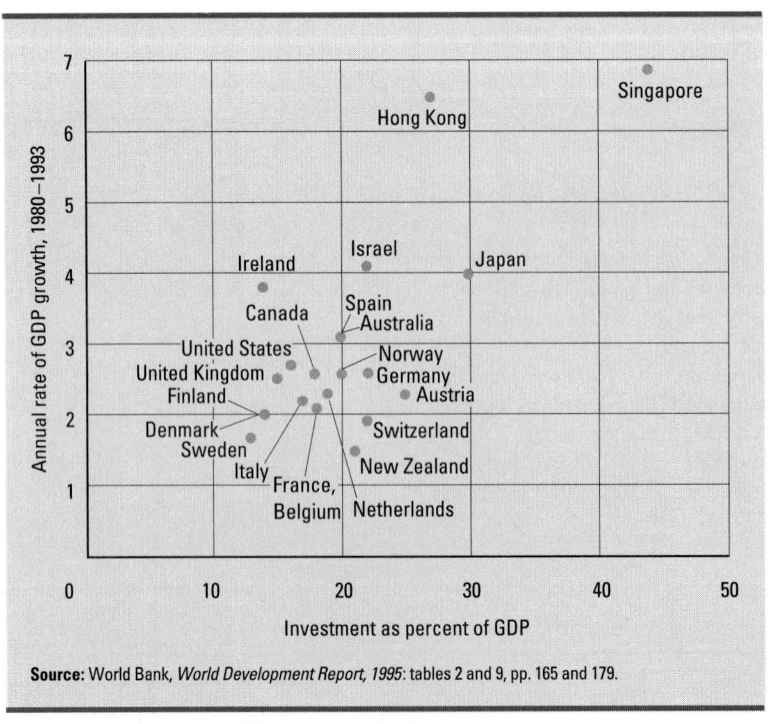

Source: World Bank, *World Development Report, 1995*: tables 2 and 9, pp. 165 and 179.

Case in Point: Seeking Saving to Boost Growth

Three tax reform proposals under consideration in 1995 sought to boost saving and investment in the United States. All three measures were based on a presumption that Americans save too little, that more savings would ultimately translate into a higher standard of living, and that a change in the tax code could encourage saving. The measures would either exempt saving from taxation or end the taxation of interest income. They would thus increase the return on saving.

A joint proposal by Senator Peter Domenici (R–New Mexico) and Senator Samuel Nunn (D–Tennessee) would have allowed taxpayers to exempt their saving from taxation. For example, if a family with an annual income of $60,000 put $15,000 into saving during a particular year, it would be taxed only on the $45,000 it hadn't saved.

A second proposal by Representative William Archer (R–Texas) would shift taxation from income to consumption. Mr. Archer has suggested achieving this goal with either a national sales tax or a tax on total consumption by households. Like the Nunn-Domenici plan, a consumption-based tax would allow families to reduce their taxes by saving more.

House Majority Leader Richard Armey (R–Texas), a former economist, has called for the most radical reform. He would replace the current system, which imposes higher rates on people with higher incomes, with a flat tax of 17 percent. The Armey plan would not tax interest earned on saving.

The three plans clearly seek to shift the long-run aggregate supply curve rightward by rewarding investment. "Higher levels of savings lead to higher levels of investment," Mr. Nunn says. "High levels of investment lead to higher productivity. It is only through higher productivity that we can improve our . . . capacity to create more and better jobs . . . and ultimately a higher standard of living for our people."

Whether tax incentives would lead to more saving is an open question. Economist Joel Slemrod of the University of Michigan told *The Wall Street Journal* that past experience in tinkering with the tax code hasn't affected saving behavior very much: "The evidence generated by the major tax changes of the 1980s is that saving and investment have proved to be less responsive to taxation than many economists believed."

Still, the government has not tried a reform as dramatic as one that would allow taxpayers to achieve unlimited reductions in their tax liability by increasing their saving. Some economists have long advocated consumption-based taxes. Politicians who aim at a higher saving rate seem increasingly likely to give such taxes a try.

Source: David Wessel, "Talk of Tax Reform Is Gaining Momentum, But Plans Vary Widely," *The Wall Street Journal*, 21 January 1995, A1.

see that there appears to be a positive relationship between the two variables. Countries with higher investment shares have had generally higher growth rates than countries with lower investment shares.

Another way to assess the role of investment in economic growth is to examine its contribution directly. The late Edward F. Denison estimated the degree to which increases in labor, natural resources, and capital influenced economic growth in the United States during the postwar period. His results are shown in Exhibit 28-9. Real GDP increased from $1,300.0 billion in 1948 to $4,897.3 billion in 1990. Denison calculated that increases in the labor force accounted for 28 percent of this growth, increases in capital for the remainder. Increases in physical capital accounted for 28 percent of U.S. economic growth, human capital for 13 percent, and intellectual capital for 31 percent. That means human and

EXHIBIT 28-9

The Sources of Growth, 1948–1990

The late Edward F. Denison estimated the degree to which increases in various factors of production contributed to U.S. economic growth from 1948 to 1990.

	Billions of 1987 dollars	Percentage of total
Total increase in real GDP	$3,597.3	100%
Contribution of:		
Labor	1,007.2	28
Land	0	0
Physical capital	1,007.2	28
Human capital	467.7	13
Intellectual capital	1,115.2	31

Source: Based on estimates in Edward Denison, *Trends in American Economic Growth 1929–1982* (Washington, D.C.: Brookings Institution, 1985).

intellectual capital together accounted for nearly half the increase in output the nation enjoyed during the postwar period. Increases in all forms of capital accounted for 72 percent of growth in the period, according to Denison's estimate.

Checklist

- Changes in investment shift the aggregate demand curve to the right or left by an amount equal to the change in investment times the multiplier.
- Investment adds to the capital stock; it therefore contributes to economic growth.
- It's possible for aggregate demand to increase at the same time as economic growth is increasing long-run aggregate supply; this could lead to growth without increases in the price level.
- The share of total output accounted for by investment appears to be positively related to the rate of economic growth.
- Investment has accounted for 72 percent of U.S. growth since 1948; the most important contribution came from investment in intellectual capital.

A Look Back—And a Look Ahead

Investment is an addition to the capital stock, which includes physical capital, human capital, and intellectual capital. Investment may occur as a net addition to capital or as a replacement of depreciated capital. The bulk of investment spending for physical capital in the United States falls in the latter category.

Investment is a flow that adjusts the stock of capital. Small changes in the stock of capital can imply large percentage changes in investment; investment is the most volatile component of gross domestic product (GDP).

The decision to save is linked directly to the decision to invest. If a nation is to devote a larger share of its production to investment, it must devote a smaller share to consumption. And that requires people to save more. The United States, compared to other nations, has a relatively low saving rate.

Investment is affected by the interest rate; the negative relationship between investment and the interest rate is illustrated by the investment demand curve. The position of this curve is also affected by expectations, the level of economic activity, the stock of capital, the price of capital, the prices of other factors, technology, and public policy.

Because investment is a component of aggregate demand, a change in investment shifts the aggregate demand curve to the right or left. The amount of the shift will equal the change in investment times the multiplier. Changes in investment caused by a change in the price level are an exception to this statement.

In addition to its impact on aggregate demand, investment can also affect economic growth. To the extent that investment increases the economy's stock of physical, intellectual, and human capital, it shifts the production possibilities curve outward and shifts the long- and short-run aggregate supply curves to the right.

In the next chapter we'll take up another component of aggregate demand—net exports.

Terms and Concepts for Review

Capital gains tax
Investment demand curve
Investment tax credit

For Discussion

1. Which of the following would be counted as gross private domestic investment?
   a. Millie builds a new garage.
   b. Millie buys a new car.

c. Grandpa buys Tommy a savings bond.

d. General Motors issues 1 million shares of stock.

e. General Motors builds a new automobile assembly plant.

f. Consolidated Construction purchases 1,000 acres of land for a regional shopping center it plans to build in a few years.

g. K-Mart adds 1,000 T-shirts to its inventory.

2. If saving dropped sharply in the economy, what would be likely to happen to investment? Why?

3. Suppose local governments throughout the United States increase their tax on business inventories. What would you expect to happen to U.S. investment? Why?

4. Suppose the government announces it will pay for half of any new investment undertaken by firms. How will this affect the investment demand curve?

5. White House officials often exude more confidence than they actually feel about future prospects for the economy. Why might this be a good strategy? Are there any dangers inherent in it?

6. Suppose everyone expects investment to rise sharply in 3 months. How would this expectation be likely to affect bond prices?

7. Suppose that every increase of $1 in real GDP automatically stimulates $0.20 in additional investment spending. How would this affect the marginal expenditure rate? How would it affect the multiplier?

8. If environmental resources were counted as part of the capital stock, how would environmental pollution affect net investment?

9. Suppose that a program is launched that successfully trains high school dropouts to work as computer operators. How would such a program affect aggregate demand, long-run aggregate supply, and the production possibilities curve?

10. In the Case in Point on reducing private capital in the Great Depression, we saw that net investment had become negative during that period. Could gross investment ever be negative? Explain.

Problems

1. Suppose real GDP in an economy equals its natural level of $2,000 billion, the marginal expenditure rate is 0.8, investment is raised by $200 billion, and the increased investment does not affect the economy's natural level of real GDP. Show the short- and long-run effects of the change upon real GDP and the price level, using the graphical framework for the model of aggregate demand and aggregate supply. Would real GDP rise by the multiplier times the change in investment in the short run? In the long run? Explain.

2. Look at former Senator Nunn's statement quoted in the Case in Point on tax policies. Use the model of aggregate demand and aggregate supply to evaluate his argument that an increase in investment would raise the standard of living.

3. These 1993 data drawn from the *Economic Report of the President 1994* are in billions of 1987 dollars. Use the information to compute the levels of gross and net private domestic investment for 1993.

Change in business inventories	$ 15.4
Residential construction	214.2
Producers' durable equipment	439.9
Nonresidential structures	151.4
Depreciation	598.6

29

Net Exports and International Finance

Chapter Objectives

After mastering the material in this chapter, you will be able to:

1. Explain why international trade raises the standard of living in nations that participate in it.
2. List the determinants of exports and imports.
3. Relate changes in exports and imports to shifts in aggregate demand, and explain how the relationship of imports to GDP affects the multiplier.
4. Explain the relationship between net exports and the flows of investment into and out of a country.
5. Explain how changes in the exchange rate affect net exports and aggregate demand.
6. Discuss the alternative systems in which exchange rates are determined and their implications for economic performance.

No nation was ever ruined by trade.
Benjamin Franklin

What's Ahead

For Eric Weissgarber, the world of international finance turned upside down in December 1994.

Mexico's central bank gave up its commitment to hold the exchange rate at 3.5 pesos to the dollar. Within a few weeks, the market exchange rate was 6 pesos to the dollar. That hurt sales for Mr. Weissgarber's firm, Custom Forest Products of San Antonio, Texas. The firm sells hardwoods grown in the United States to manufacturers of furniture, flooring, and cabinetry.

"Over the previous 18 months, we'd gone from having no sales to Mexico to sales of over $300,000 per month," Mr. Weissgarber says. "That was about 15 percent of our total sales. Then the devaluation came, and our sales to Mexico fell by half the following month."

Mr. Weissgarber, who is director of international marketing for the firm, recalls the impact of the devaluation on one major customer. "We had a guy in Mexico that was buying one trailer load a week of red oak. Our price was $10,000 per load, so he was writing checks to his bank for 35,000 pesos at the old exchange rate. His bank then paid us in dollars.

"After the devaluation, those same loads still cost $10,000 in U.S. currency, but they cost him 60,000 pesos. He's stopped buying."

Custom Forest Products will have a rough time making up the loss of its Mexican sales. "We've tried developing markets in Hong Kong, and we've just gotten our first order," said Mr. Weissgarber in February 1995. "But now there's talk of a trade war, and our buyers may face duties on goods they buy from the United States and sell in China. Right now I'm looking at possible new markets here in Texas."[1]

[1] Source: Personal interview.

Mr. Weissgarber's experience illustrates how changes in exchange rates can affect domestic economic activity. We looked briefly at the determination of exchange rates in Chapter 23. In this chapter we'll examine in more detail the forces that determine exchange rates, and we'll see how changes in exchange rates can affect the level of economic activity.

We'll look at the reasons the United States went from running a trade surplus in most of the 1950s, 1960s, and 1970s to running a trade deficit in the 1980s and 1990s. We'll find out how this country became a "debtor nation" and examine what that label means. Finally, we'll examine alternative regimes for determining exchange rates between international currencies. In today's market-based system, exchange rates are for the most part free to change with fluctuations in demand and supply. This system replaced one with fixed exchange rates between currencies. We'll evaluate these systems as well as others in which exchange rates between some countries are fixed while they float in relation to the rest of the world.

The International Sector: An Introduction

How important is international trade?

Take a look at the labels on some of your clothing. You're likely to find that what you're wearing came from all over the globe. Look around any parking lot. You may find cars from Japan, Korea, Sweden, Britain, Germany, France, Italy, Yugoslavia—and even the United States! Do you use a computer? Even if it's an American computer, its components are likely to have been assembled in Indonesia or in some other country. Visit the grocery store. Much of the produce probably comes from Latin America and Asia.

The international market is important not just in terms of the goods and services it provides to a country, but as a market for that country's goods and services. The United States is the world's largest exporter. Although foreign demand for U.S. exports doesn't loom large as a component of aggregate demand, it can be very important in terms of growth. The increase in exports from 1988 to 1992, for example, accounted for almost three-fourths of the gain in U.S. real GDP during that period.

In this chapter we'll examine the impact of international trade on the macroeconomic variables we've been studying. We'll be engaged in a study of **international finance,** the field that examines the macroeconomic consequences of the monetary flows associated with international trade.

Before turning to the investigation of the macroeconomic implications of financing international trade, we need to review what international trade can accomplish in terms of a nation's living standards.

The Case for Trade

International trade increases the quantity of goods and services available to the world's consumers. We saw in Chapter 2 that by allocating resources according to the principle of comparative advantage, trade allows nations to consume combinations of goods and services they would be unable to produce on their own, combinations that lie outside each country's production possibilities curve. That argument is critical to the case for trade.

International finance is the study of the economic implications of the monetary flows associated with international trade.

A country has a comparative advantage in the production of a good if it can produce that good at a lower opportunity cost than can other countries. If each country specializes in the production of goods in which it has a comparative advantage and trades those goods for things in which other countries have a comparative advantage, global production of all goods and services will be increased. The result can be higher levels of consumption for all.

To see the argument, let's consider a highly simplified example. Suppose the world consists of two countries, the United States and Mexico, and that these countries do not trade with one another. Each produces only two goods, brooms and vacuum cleaners. The two countries have the production possibilities curves given in Panels (a) and (b) of Exhibit 29-1. Recall from Chapter 2 that the slope of a production possibilities curve gives the opportunity cost of 1 additional unit of the good on the horizontal axis. Given the production possibilities curves here, the opportunity cost of 1 vacuum cleaner in the United States is 10 brooms. In Mexico it equals 40 brooms. Put another way, the opportunity cost of 1 broom is 1/10 of a vacuum cleaner in the United States, 1/40 of a vacuum cleaner in Mexico. The United States has a comparative advantage in vacuum cleaners; Mexico has a comparative advantage in brooms. These opportunity costs give the rates at which one good exchanges for another. In the United States, 10 brooms exchange for 1 vacuum cleaner. In Mexico, it takes 40 brooms to purchase 1 vacuum cleaner.

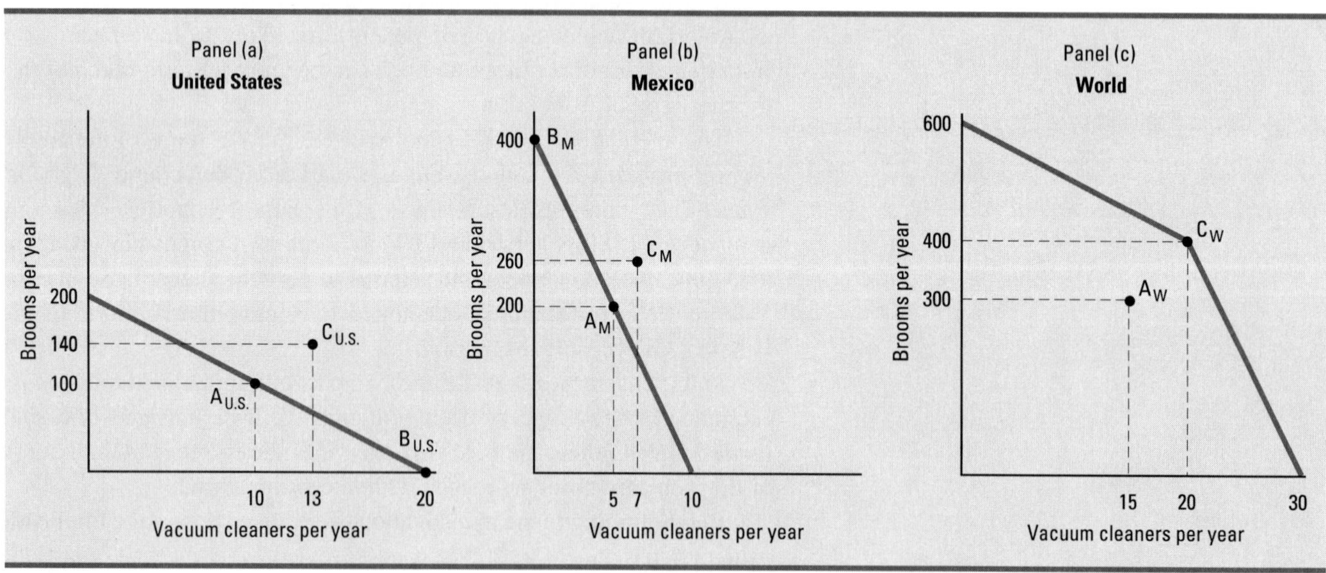

EXHIBIT 29-1

Production Possibilities, Comparative Advantage, and Trade

Hypothetical production possibilities curves are given for the United States in Panel (a) and for Mexico in Panel (b). All units represent annual production levels. Before trade, the United States produces at point $A_{U.S.}$, manufacturing 100 brooms and 10 vacuum cleaners per year. Mexico produces at point A_M, manufacturing 200 brooms and 5 vacuum cleaners per year. That leaves world production within the combined production possibilities curve for the two countries in Panel (c). When the countries specialize according to comparative advantage (the United States moves to $B_{U.S.}$ while Mexico moves to B_M), production moves to the world production possibilities curve. Both countries increase their consumption of both goods.

Assume that each country operates at the midpoint of its production possibilities curve. The United States thus produces 100 brooms and 10 vacuum cleaners per period, operating at point $A_{U.S.}$ in Panel (a), and Mexico produces 200 brooms and 5 vacuum cleaners at point A_M in Panel (b). World production totals 300 brooms and 15 vacuum cleaners per period at point A_W in Panel (c).

Now suppose the two countries engage in trade. Because vacuum cleaners sell for such a high price in Mexico (equal to 40 brooms), U.S. producers will expand their vacuum production to take advantage of the opportunity. Given the linear production possibilities curve in Panel (a), the United States will move to point $B_{U.S.}$, producing 20 vacuum cleaners and no brooms per year. Mexico will specialize in broom production at point B_M, in Panel (b), producing 400 brooms and no vacuums each year. The two goods will exchange for one another at a rate that lies between the rates that prevailed in the absence of trade. Suppose the rate turns out to be 20 brooms for 1 vacuum cleaner. One possible solution would be for the United States to export 7 of its 20 vacuum cleaners to Mexico in exchange for 140 brooms. That would leave U.S. consumers with 13 vacuum cleaners and 140 brooms, a combination shown by point $C_{U.S.}$ in Panel (a). Mexican consumers would have 260 brooms (400 less the 140 exported to the United States) and 7 vacuum cleaners—point C_M in Panel (b). Consumers in both countries enjoy consumption levels that lie outside their production possibilities curves.

We can see the gains from international trade in another way by combining production possibilities curves for the two countries to obtain a world production possibilities curve in Panel (c). This is the strategy we used in Chapter 2. Notice that the pretrade production levels lie inside the world curve at point A_W, even though both countries were operating on their respective production possibilities curves. Only with trade does the world achieve point C_W on the world production possibilities curve.

If international trade allows expanded world production of goods and services, it follows that restrictions on trade will reduce world production. That, in a nutshell, is the economic case for free trade. It suggests that restrictions on trade, such as a **tariff,** a tax imposed on imported goods and services, or a **quota,** a ceiling on the quantity of specific goods and services that can be imported, reduce world living standards.

The conceptual argument for free trade is a compelling one; virtually all economists support policies that reduce barriers to trade. Economists were among the most important advocates for the 1993 ratification of the North American Free Trade Agreement (NAFTA), which virtually eliminated trade restrictions between Mexico, the United States, and Canada, and for the 1994 ratification of the General Agreement on Tariffs and Trade (GATT), a pact slashing tariffs and easing quotas among 117 nations, including the United States.

Despite the strong economic case for free trade, it remains a controversial topic. One source of opposition to free trade will be the owners of factors of production used in industries in which a nation lacks a comparative advantage. In the case illustrated in Exhibit 29-1, for example, broom producers in the United States and vacuum producers in Mexico will be forced by trade to move to other activities; they can be expected to oppose any attempt to remove restrictions on trade.

A related argument is that trade not only reduces employment in some sectors but reduces employment in the economy as a whole. In the long run, this argument is clearly wrong. The economy's natural level of employment is

- A **tariff** is a tax imposed by a country on an imported good or service.
- A **quota** is a ceiling imposed by a country on the quantity of a good or service it will import.

Case in Point NAFTA and the Gigantic Sucking Sound

H. Ross Perot, the Texas billionaire who ran for president of the United States in 1992, provided the most colorful metaphor in the intense U.S. debate over whether to approve the North American Free Trade Agreement (NAFTA). If NAFTA were approved, Mr. Perot warned, "a gigantic sucking sound" would be heard throughout the nation as U.S. jobs were sucked out of the United States and into Mexico.

Cast in terms of the model of aggregate demand and aggregate supply, Mr. Perot's argument boiled down to the claim that the elimination of trade barriers with Mexico would shift aggregate demand to the left, reducing real GDP and employment in the short run. The leftward shift in aggregate demand would be caused by a reduction in net exports. But we've already seen that trade agreements don't affect long-run aggregate supply and therefore do not affect employment in the long run.

Ross Perot campaigning against NAFTA.

Certainly the agreement will boost U.S. imports from Mexico. NAFTA removes many of the restrictions that have limited imports of agricultural goods, and it removes tariffs on virtually all goods and services. For example, workers at the France Broom Company, Paxton, Illinois, a firm that manufactures brooms, worried that removal of the 32 percent tariff that the United States had imposed on brooms imported from Mexico would mean that their firm could no longer compete. Mr. Perot predicted that passage of NAFTA would lead to the loss of 5 million U.S. jobs.

Economists were quick to reject the Perot argument. They pointed out that before NAFTA, U.S. tariffs on Mexican-produced goods and services averaged just 3 percent. Eliminating them wouldn't make much difference. Mexico's tariffs on goods and services produced in the United States averaged about 10 percent. The economists argued that the elimination of those tariffs will generate a larger increase in Mexican purchases of U.S. goods and services than in U.S. purchases of Mexican goods and services. Exports should thus rise more than imports, producing a net increase in aggregate demand and increased employment in the short run.

Economists predicted that NAFTA's short-run impact on U.S. employment would be positive but small. Mexico's economy in 1993 was about a twentieth the size of the U.S. economy; any increase in its purchases of U.S. goods and services wasn't likely to be huge. The real gains, the economists said, would lie in greater availability of goods and services to consumers in both countries. They noted also that the agreement would contribute to Mexico's conversion from a command capitalist to a market capitalist economy (see Chapter 2).

Economists are virtually unanimous in advocating free trade; there was overwhelming support for NAFTA among leading economists. Every living American winner of the Nobel Prize in Economics endorsed the agreement. In the end their argument prevailed, and the agreement was ratified. NAFTA took effect January 1, 1994; its provisions will be phased in over the remainder of the decade.

determined by forces unrelated to trade policy, and employment moves to its natural level in the long run. In the long run, trade affects consumption, not employment.

In the short run, trade does affect aggregate demand. Net exports are one component of aggregate demand; a change in net exports shifts the aggregate demand curve and affects real GDP in the short run. We'll discuss the link between net exports and aggregate demand in greater detail later in this chapter.

As we examine the macroeconomic implications of international trade, we should keep in mind the reason it occurs. Individuals engage in international trade because it makes them better off by increasing the quantities of goods and services available to them.

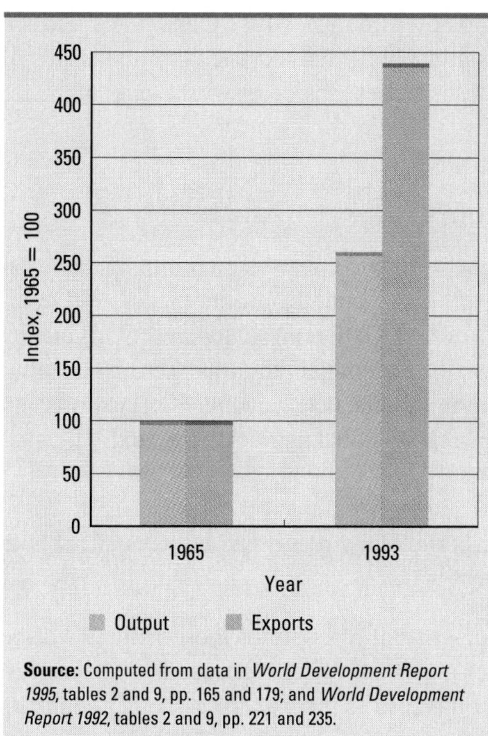

Source: Computed from data in *World Development Report 1995,* tables 2 and 9, pp. 165 and 179; and *World Development Report 1992,* tables 2 and 9, pp. 221 and 235.

EXHIBIT 29-2

World Output and World Exports, 1965–1993

While the real level of world output rose by 161 percent between 1965 and 1993, the level of world exports increased by 336 percent.

The Rising Importance of International Trade

One of the most dramatic developments of the last several decades has been the tremendous growth of world trade. Exhibit 29-2 presents indexes of the real values of world output and world exports from 1965 to 1993. The chart shows that output rose by 161 percent during the period. But the gains in total exports were even more spectacular; they soared by 336 percent!

While international trade was rising around the world, it was playing a more important role in the United States as well. In 1960, exports represented just 5 percent of GDP; by 1994, exports accounted for 11 percent of real GDP. Exhibit 29-3 shows the growth in exports and imports as a percentage of nominal GDP in the United States from 1960 to 1995. Notice that exports generally exceeded imports in the 1960s; imports have exceeded exports in the 1980s and 1990s. We'll examine the reasons for the emergence of a trade deficit later in this chapter.

Why has world trade risen so spectacularly? Two factors account for the boom. First, advances in transportation and communication have dramatically reduced the costs of moving goods around the globe. Second, trade barriers between countries have fallen. Average tariff rates have been cut dramatically over the past few decades. The removal of virtually all barriers to trade within the

EXHIBIT 29-3

Exports and Imports Relative to U.S. GDP, 1960–1995

The chart shows exports and imports as a percentage of GDP from 1960 through the first half of 1995. We see that exports generally exceeded imports in the 1960s; the two variables were about equal in the 1970s, and a trade deficit emerged in the 1980s and 1990s.

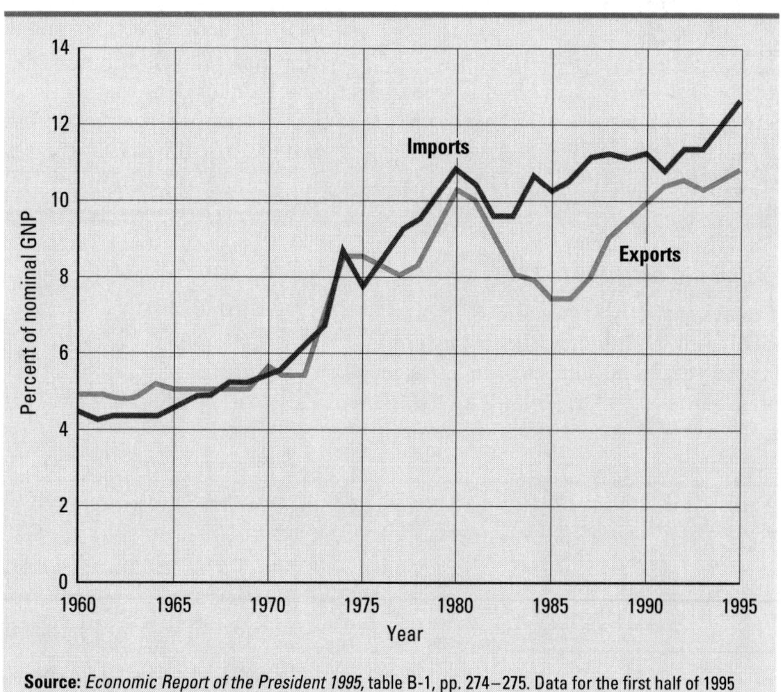

Source: *Economic Report of the President 1995,* table B-1, pp. 274–275. Data for the first half of 1995 provided by Commerce Department.

European Community and within North America will expand trade further. More important, the 1994 ratification of GATT slashed tariffs on thousands of goods and services and promises substantial expansion of world trade in the remainder of this decade.

Net Exports and the Economy

As trade has become more important worldwide, exports and imports have assumed increased importance in nearly every country on the planet. We've already discussed the increased shares of U.S. GDP represented by exports and by imports. We'll find in this section that the economy both influences, and is influenced by, net exports. This section examines the determinants of net exports and then discusses the ways in which net exports affect aggregate demand.

Determinants of Net Exports

Net exports equal exports minus imports. Many of the same forces affect both exports and imports, albeit in different ways.

Income. As incomes in other nations rise, the people of those nations will be able to buy more goods and services—including foreign goods and services. Any one country's exports thus will increase as incomes rise in other countries and will fall as incomes drop in other countries. U.S. exports fell in 1993, for example, as the economies of Japan, Germany, and several other major U.S. trading partners slipped into recession.

A nation's own level of income affects its imports the same way it affects consumption. As consumers have more income, they'll buy more goods and services. Because some of those goods and services are produced in other nations, imports will rise. An increase in GDP thus boosts imports; a reduction in GDP reduces imports. Exhibit 29-4 shows the relationship between real GDP and the real level of import spending in the United States from 1991 through the first half of 1995. Notice that the observations lie close to the straight line drawn through them in the exhibit.

EXHIBIT 29-4

U.S. GDP and Imports, 1991–1995

The chart shows quarterly values of U.S. imports and real GDP from 1991 through the first half of 1995. The observations lie quite close to a straight line.

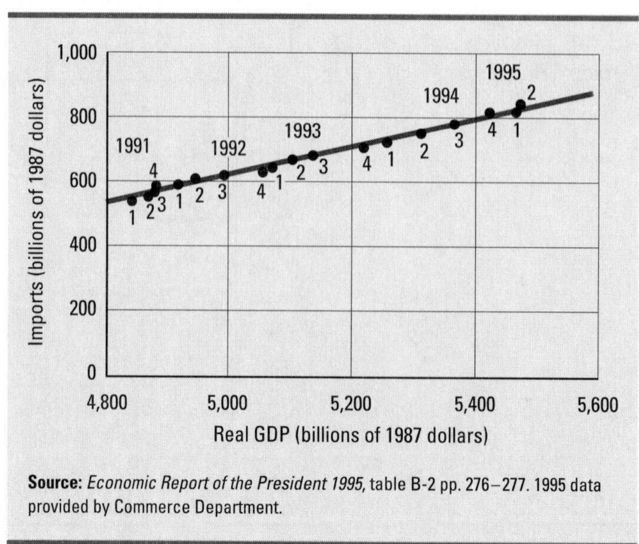

Source: *Economic Report of the President 1995,* table B-2 pp. 276–277. 1995 data provided by Commerce Department.

Case in Point — Higher Yen Boosts U.S. Auto Sales

It took a lot fewer yen to buy $1 in 1993 than in 1992. The exchange rate averaged 126.8 yen to $1 in 1992; it fell to 111.1 yen in 1993, roughly a 12 percent plunge. That change produced a dramatic shift in the U.S. auto market.

A cheaper dollar, of course, meant a more expensive yen. Importers had to pay more for the cars they brought in from Japan. And that meant higher prices for cars built in Japan. That gave U.S. producers a competitive advantage. Their share of U.S. auto sales rose to 74 percent in the 1993 model year, while the share of the U.S. market captured by Japanese car makers fell to 23 percent. The Ford Taurus toppled the Honda Accord as the number one passenger car in the United States for the 1993 model year. The Accord had held the top spot for the previous 3 years.

A Ford dealership in Tokyo.

The higher yen also produced changes in strategies for Japanese plants in the United States, which traditionally relied heavily on parts produced in Japan. When Toyota began manufacturing some of its Camrys at its plant in Georgetown, Kentucky, in 1985, 60 percent of the parts came from U.S. manufacturers. By 1993, the U.S. share had risen to 75 percent. Similarly, the percentage of U.S. parts in Honda Accords manufactured in Marysville, Ohio, rose to 80 percent in 1993—it had been 75 percent at the start of the year. That increase in U.S. parts included sunroofs, passenger-side air bags, and antilock brake assemblies. According to *The Wall Street Journal,* Honda was considering shifting production of the Acura to the United States. "The yen is killing us," Richard B. Thomas, head of Honda's U.S. Acura division, told the *Journal.*

Although the U.S. share of the market for parts in Japanese cars rose in 1993, Japan retained its huge trade surplus in this category. Indeed, 20 percent of Japan's surplus in trade with the United States results from its surplus in auto parts. The higher yen, however, reduced that surplus. It thus tended to reduce net exports in Japan while putting upward pressure on net exports in the United States.

Sources: Based on Krystal Miller and Jacqueline Mitchell, "Big Three Won Car-Sales Race in Latest Year," *The Wall Street Journal,* 6 October 1993, A2, A12, and Neal Templin, "Japan Auto Makers Buy More U.S. Parts," *The Wall Street Journal,* 24 August 1993, A2.

Relative Prices. A change in the price level within a nation simultaneously affects exports and imports. A higher price level in the United States, for example, makes U.S. exports more expensive for foreigners and thus tends to reduce exports. At the same time, a higher price level in the United States makes foreign goods and services relatively more attractive to U.S. buyers and thus increases imports. A higher price level therefore reduces net exports. A lower price level encourages exports and reduces imports, increasing net exports. As we've seen, the negative relationship between net exports and the price level is one reason for the negative slope of the aggregate demand curve.

The Exchange Rate. Foreigners must generally buy dollars in order to buy U.S. goods and services. U.S. consumers must generally purchase foreign currencies to buy foreign goods and services. An increase in the exchange rate means foreigners must pay more for dollars, and must thus pay more for U.S. goods and services. It therefore reduces U.S. exports. At the same time, a higher exchange rate means that a dollar buys more foreign currency. That makes foreign goods and services cheaper for U.S. buyers, so imports are likely to rise. An increase in the exchange rate should thus tend to reduce net exports. A reduction in the exchange rate should increase net exports.

When the value of the Mexican peso plunged in December 1994, Mexican goods and services suddenly were cheaper for foreign buyers to acquire—and foreign goods and services suddenly were far more expensive for Mexicans to purchase. That's why Custom Forest Products, the San Antonio firm whose story is told in the introduction to this chapter, experienced a plunge in sales in the wake of the devaluation.

Trade Policies. A country's exports depend on its own trade policies as well as the trade policies of other countries. A country may be able to increase its exports by providing some form of government assistance (such as special tax considerations for companies that export goods and services, government promotional efforts, assistance with research, or subsidies). A country's exports are also affected by the degree to which other countries restrict or encourage imports. The United States, for example, has sought changes in Japanese policies toward products such as U.S.-grown rice. Japan banned rice imports in the past, arguing it needed to protect its own producers. That's been a costly strategy; consumers in Japan typically pay as much as 10 times the price consumers in the United States pay for rice. Japan has given in to pressure from the United States and other nations to end its ban on foreign rice as part of the GATT accord. That will increase U.S. exports and lower rice prices in Japan.

Similarly, a country's imports are affected by its trade policies and by the policies of its trading partners. A country can limit its imports of some goods and services by imposing tariffs or quotas on them—it may even ban the importation of some items. If foreign governments subsidize the manufacture of a particular good, that may increase domestic imports of the good. For example, if the governments of countries trading with the United States were to subsidize the production of steel, then U.S. companies would find it cheaper to purchase steel from abroad than at home, increasing U.S. imports of steel. The United States has long complained that Europe subsidizes production of the Airbus, a wide-body passenger plane. Manufacturers of the Airbus plead guilty, but they charge that the United States subsidizes its aircraft industry through its military procurement policies.

Preferences and Technology. Consumer preferences are one determinant of the consumption of any good or service; a shift in preferences affecting a foreign-produced good will affect the level of imports of that good. The preference among the French for movies and music produced in the United States has boosted French imports of these services. Indeed, the shift in French preferences has been so strong that the government of France, claiming a threat to its cultural heritage, has cracked down. It has restricted the showing of films produced in the United States. French radio stations are fined if more than 40 percent of the music they play is from "foreign" (in most cases, U.S.) rock groups.

Changes in technology affect the kinds of capital firms import. Technological changes have emphasized the application of computers to manufacturing processes, for example, leading to increased demand for high-tech capital equipment, a sector in which the United States dominates world production. That has boosted net exports in the United States.

Exhibit 29-5 shows the composition of U.S. exports and imports in 1994. The United States is a net exporter of capital goods, food, and services. It is a net importer of consumer goods, automotive products, and industrial supplies and materials (oil is the principal U.S. import in this category).

EXHIBIT 29-5

The Composition of U.S. Exports and Imports, 1994

The chart shows the composition of U.S. exports and imports in 1994. The United States had a surplus in foods, capital goods, and services. It recorded deficits in automotive vehicles, parts and engines, consumer goods, and industrial supplies.

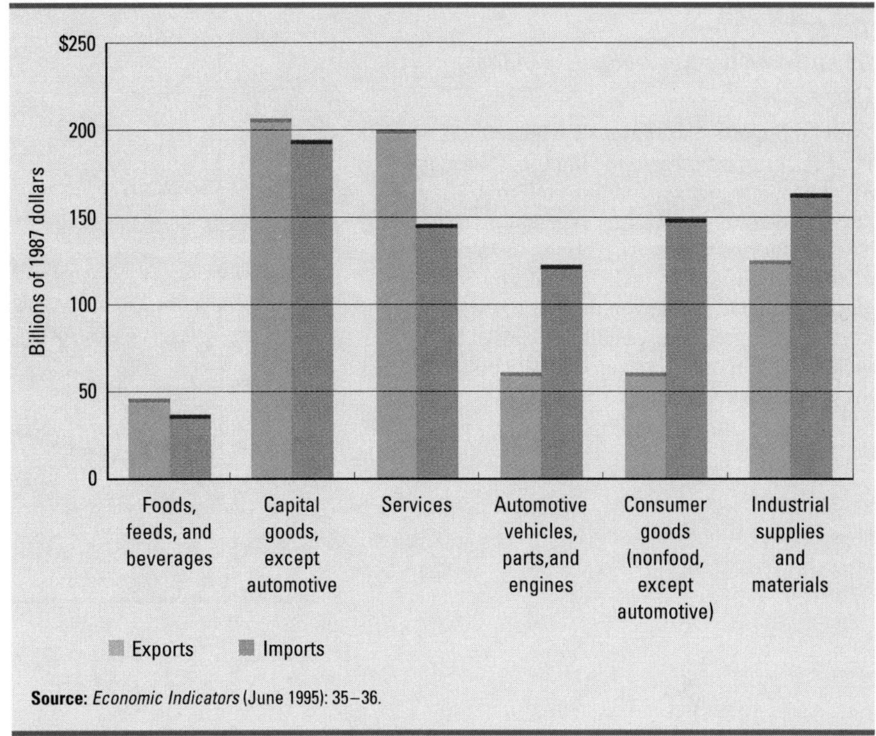

Source: *Economic Indicators* (June 1995): 35–36.

Net Exports and Aggregate Demand

Net exports affect aggregate demand in three ways: First, the relationship between net exports and the price level is one reason the aggregate demand curve is a downward-sloping curve. Second, the relationship between imports and GDP affects the value of the multiplier. Third, a change in the autonomous component of net exports shifts the aggregate demand curve.

Net Exports and the Slope of the Aggregate Demand Curve. We've already seen that net exports vary with the price level. The fact that a higher price level reduces net exports and a lower price level increases net exports is one reason for the downward slope in the aggregate demand curve. Because the impact of a price-level change on net exports is already reflected in the construction of the aggregate demand curve, a change in net exports caused by a price-level change does not shift the curve. Instead, it represents one more reason, along with the Keynes and real balance effects, for a change in the price level to cause a movement along the aggregate demand curve.

Imports and the Multiplier. We saw in Exhibit 29-4 that the level of import spending is closely related to GDP. This fact affects the slope of the aggregate expenditures curve—the marginal expenditure rate—and thus affects the value of the multiplier. To the extent that increases in income are used to purchase foreign rather than domestic goods and services, the multiplier effect of a change in aggregate expenditures is reduced.

To see the impact of imports on the multiplier, we'll work through an example of an aggregate expenditures model in which imports initially are zero. Then we'll explore the impact of having a positive level of imports.

EXHIBIT 29-6

Imports and the Aggregate Expenditures Curve

With no imports, the aggregate expenditures curve is AE_1. If imports rise to the imports-GDP curve M, then aggregate expenditures fall to AE_2, a curve with a lower marginal expenditure rate and a lower multiplier than AE_1. Here, the new multiplier is 2. Equilibrium real GDP falls by an amount equal to the new multiplier times the reduction in aggregate expenditures caused by the increase in imports from zero to $125 billion at the original level of income.

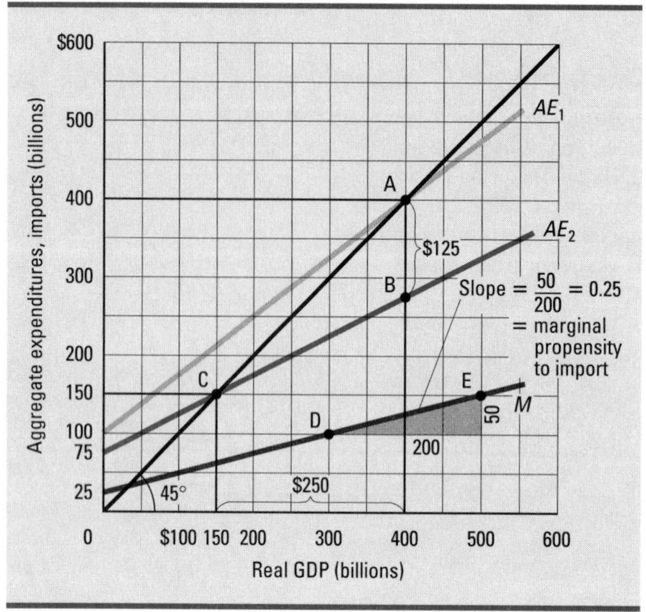

The aggregate expenditure curve AE_1 in Exhibit 29-6 is drawn for a hypothetical economy in which imports equal zero because all imports have been forbidden. We'll assume that the rest of the world has been remarkably patient with this policy, and that no restrictions have been imposed by other countries on this economy's exports. Aggregate expenditures thus include consumption, investment, government purchases, and exports. The equation for aggregate expenditures in this economy is

$$AE_1 = \$100 + 0.75Y \qquad \textbf{(1)}$$

AE_1 intersects the 45-degree line at a real GDP of $400; that is the equilibrium solution in the aggregate expenditures model. The slope of the aggregate expenditures curve, the marginal expenditure rate, is 0.75. The multiplier equals 4 [= (1/1 − 0.75)].

Now suppose that the restriction on imports is abolished and imports rise to the level shown by curve M in Exhibit 29-6. This **imports-GDP curve** shows the level of imports at each level of real GDP, all other determinants of imports unchanged.

The equation for the imports-GDP curve M in Exhibit 29-6 is

$$M = \$25 + 0.25Y \qquad \textbf{(2)}$$

This curve intersects the vertical axis at a positive level of import spending, $25. We saw in Chapter 27 that consumption is positive at a zero level of real GDP. Some consumption is of imported goods and services; we thus expect imports to be positive at a zero level of real GDP as well.

- The **imports-GDP curve** shows the level of imports at each level of real GDP, all other determinants of imports unchanged.
- The **marginal propensity to import** gives the rate at which imports increase with increases in real GDP.

The slope of the imports-GDP curve M shows the rate at which imports increase as real GDP rises; it is the **marginal propensity to import.** The slope of the curve can be computed between any two points. At point D, for example, imports equal $100 and real GDP equals $300. At point E, imports equal $150 and real GDP equals $500. The slope between those two points is 0.25; it is the marginal propensity to import.

Imports are a negative component of aggregate expenditures. We thus subtract Equation (2) from Equation (1) to obtain the new level of aggregate expenditures, AE_2:

$$AE_2 = \$75 + 0.5Y \qquad \textbf{(3)}$$

The new aggregate expenditures curve, AE_2, is also presented in Exhibit 29-6. Notice that the addition of imports shifts the curve down and reduces its slope. The marginal expenditure rate for AE_2 is 0.5. That lower marginal expenditure rate suggests a reduced value for the multiplier; it now equals 2 [= (1/1 − 0.5)]. The positive relationship between imports and real GDP thus suggests a lower value of the multiplier than would otherwise exist.

The increase in imports reduces net exports and aggregate expenditures. At the original level of real GDP, \$400 billion, net exports have fallen by \$125 billion, shifting the aggregate expenditures curve to AE_2. Equilibrium real GDP in the aggregate expenditures model falls by the multiplier, now 2, times the \$125 billion change in aggregate expenditures. The new equilibrium GDP is thus \$150 billion, \$250 billion below the old level.

Changes in Net Exports and Aggregate Demand. With two exceptions, a change in net exports shifts the aggregate demand curve. The exceptions involve factors that are already incorporated in constructing the curve. For other changes in net exports, the aggregate demand curve shifts by a horizontal distance equal to the multiplier times the change in net exports, as shown in Exhibit 29-7.

A change in net exports caused by a change in real GDP or in the price level won't shift the aggregate demand curve. A change in real GDP causes a movement along the imports-GDP curve. It doesn't shift the imports-GDP curve, and it doesn't shift the aggregate expenditures curve from which aggregate demand is derived. A change in the price level affects exports and imports, but this effect is already incorporated in the aggregate demand curve—it's one reason the curve slopes downward. As we've noted before, a price level change doesn't shift aggregate demand.

A change in net exports that is not simply a response to a change in GDP or the price level does shift the aggregate demand curve. Changes in net exports resulting from changes in exchange rates, preferences, technology, or foreign price levels all shift the curve.

- International trade allows the world's resources to be allocated on the basis of comparative advantage and thus allows the production of a larger quantity of goods and services than would be available without trade.
- Growth in international trade has outpaced growth in total output in the United States and the rest of the world over the past four decades.
- The chief determinants of net exports are domestic and foreign incomes, relative price levels, exchange rates, domestic and foreign trade policies, preferences, and technology.
- Imports vary with real GDP; this relationship is shown by the imports-GDP curve. The slope of the curve is the marginal propensity to import. The greater the marginal propensity to import, the lower the marginal expenditure rate and the lower the multiplier.
- A change in net exports shifts the aggregate demand curve by an amount equal to the change in net exports times the multiplier. Changes in net exports caused by changes in real GDP or the price level, however, do not shift the aggregate demand curve.

EXHIBIT 29-7

Changes in Net Exports and Aggregate Demand

In Panel (a), an increase in net exports shifts the aggregate demand curve to the right by an amount equal to the multiplier times the change in net exports ΔX_n. In Panel (b), a reduction shifts the aggregate demand curve to the left by the same amount.

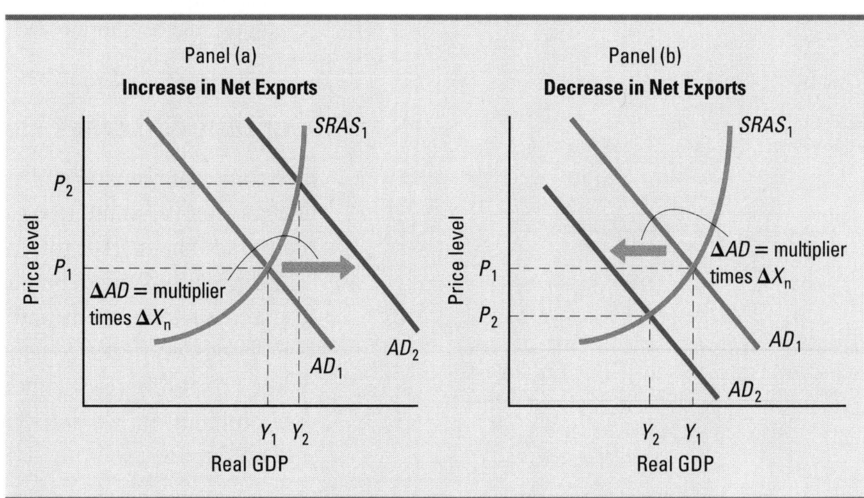

The Balance of Payments

This section examines the relationship between spending that flows into a country and spending that flows out of it. These spending flows include not only spending for a nation's exports and imports, but payments to owners of assets in other countries, international transfer payments, and purchases of foreign assets.

The relationship between spending that flows into an economy and spending that flows out of it is constrained by the nature of equilibrium in the market for a country's currency. We'll therefore begin by reviewing the determination of the equilibrium exchange rate. Exhibit 29-8 shows the demand and supply curves for a nation's currency that were introduced in Chapter 23. Given the demand and supply curves shown, the equilibrium exchange rate, determined by the intersection of the curves at point A, is E_1. The equilibrium quantity of currency exchanged is Q_1.

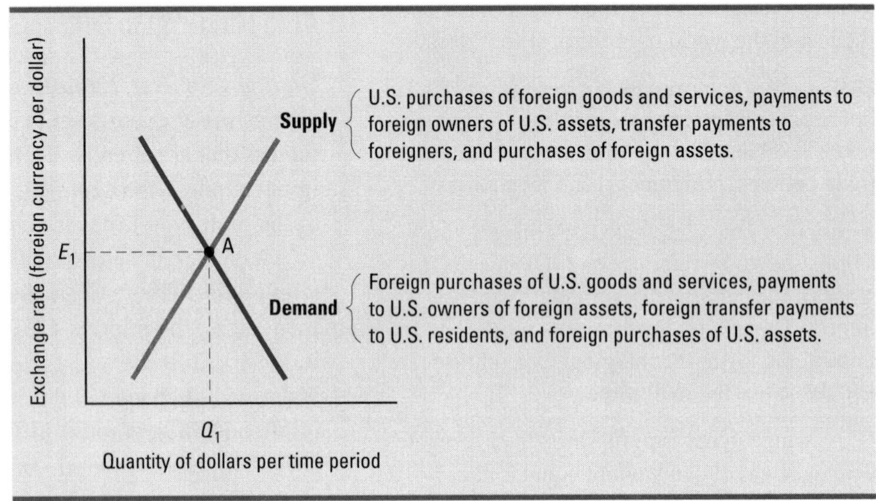

EXHIBIT 29-8

The Currency Market and Exchange Rate Determination

A nation's equilibrium exchange rate is determined by the intersection of the demand and supply curves for its currency. At point A, the equilibrium exchange rate is E_1 and a quantity Q_1 of the nation's currency is traded in international currency markets.

Currency Market Demand and Supply

The forces of demand and supply affect the value of any currency. To make the analysis more straightforward, let us focus on a single country, the United States, and the market for dollars.

U.S. dollars are demanded for four reasons. First, foreign buyers may wish to purchase U.S. goods and services. Purchases of the dollar for use in buying U.S. goods and services equal U.S. exports. Second, income earned by U.S. owners of foreign assets generates a demand for dollars. The U.S. owner of a condominium in Mexico, for example, converts the pesos earned by that asset into dollars for use in the United States. A third source of demand for dollars is transfer payments from foreigners to people in the United States. A family in Canada, for example, might send money to relatives living in the United States. This gift will require the purchase of U.S. dollars. Finally, foreign buyers may wish to purchase U.S. assets. Those assets include items such as stocks in U.S. companies, bonds, real estate, and the dollar itself. The total quantity of dollars demanded during any period represents spending flowing into the United States from other countries.

U.S. dollars are supplied to purchase foreign currencies. Just as dollars are demanded for four reasons, there are four reasons for their supply. Dollars supplied for the purchase of foreign goods and services equal U.S. imports during a particular period. Dollars are also supplied when foreign owners receive income on their U.S. assets. The French owner of a U.S.-government bond, for example, will be paid interest in dollars. He or she is likely to sell those dollars for francs, the French currency. Third, dollars are supplied when transfer payments flow from the United States to other countries. Foreign aid programs, for example, typically involve the supply of dollars that will be used to purchase other currencies. Finally, U.S. dollars are supplied when people in the United States purchase assets in other countries. The supply curve for dollars shown in Exhibit 29-8 represents spending flowing out of the economy.

The price of the dollar—the exchange rate—fluctuates constantly in the global market for currencies. More than $200 billion exchanges hands in this market each day. Because the price is free to fluctuate in the market, it moves almost instantaneously to the equilibrium level at which the quantity of dollars demanded equals the quantity supplied.

The fact that the quantity of dollars demanded will be the same as the quantity supplied means that spending flowing into a country *must* equal spending flowing out of it. This relationship is crucially important to an understanding of the relationship between net exports and international purchases of assets.

Accounting for International Payments

In the next two sections we'll build a set of accounts to track international payments. To do this, we'll establish a balance sheet for such payments. Those payments that require the purchase (demand) of dollars will be entered as credits on the balance sheet—they represent spending flowing into the United States. Transactions that require the sale (supply) of dollars will be entered as debits on the balance sheet—they represent spending flowing out of the United States. Credit items are recorded as positive entries; debits are recorded as negative entries.

The balance between spending flowing into a country and spending flowing out of it is called the **balance of payments.** We've seen that equilibrium in the currency market ensures that spending flowing in equals spending flowing out. Because transactions that result in spending flowing in are recorded as positive entries and those that result in spending flowing out are recorded as negative entries, the balance of payments should equal zero— the two sets of entries should cancel each other.

The **balance of payments** is the balance between spending flowing into a country from other countries and spending flowing out of that country to other countries.

Two separate accounts are maintained for a nation's balance of payments. One, the current account, includes debits and credits involved in the exchange of goods and services, the payment of income earned from assets held in foreign countries, and the flow of transfer payments. The other account is the capital account, which shows debits and credits in the purchases of assets. The relationship between these two accounts plays a central role in international finance.

The Current Account

The **current account** is an accounting statement of spending flows into and out of the country during a particular period for exports and imports, together with the flow of payments to owners of foreign assets and transfer payments that flow across international borders. A nation's current account is one component of a statement of its balance of payments. It includes all spending flows across a nation's border except those that represent purchases of assets. A nation's **balance on current account** is the balance between debit and credit entries in its current account.

Because the current account represents one component of a statement of a nation's balance of payments, the same conventions apply in listing credits and debits. Any transaction that results in spending flowing into a country from other countries is listed as a credit, a positive entry. Credit items thus reflect demand for a nation's currency. A transaction that results in spending flowing out of a country is listed as a debit, a negative entry. Such transactions reflect the supply of a nation's currency.

The major component of a country's current account is likely to be its net exports. To compute net exports, imports are subtracted from exports. Exports are listed as positive entries and imports as negative entries in a country's current account; its balance on current account differs from its net exports only because the current account also includes payments to owners of foreign assets and transfer payments.

Payments to U.S. owners of foreign assets generally exceed payments to foreign owners of U.S. assets; this component of the U.S. current account has shown a surplus in every year since World War II except 1994. But the United States makes more transfer payments abroad than it receives; this component of the current account generally shows a deficit. In fact, the United States has had a deficit in net transfer payments in every year since World War II, with one exception. In 1991, U.S. allies in the Persian Gulf War made payments to the United States to compensate for the costs of conducting that war. Those payments were treated as transfer payments.

If a country's balance on current account is negative, it has a **current account deficit.** That means the total of debits exceeds the total of credits. A current account deficit is likely to imply a trade deficit; that is, it is likely to imply that net exports are negative. If a country's balance on current account is positive, it has a **current account surplus**—credits on current account exceed debits. A country with a current account surplus during a particular period is likely to have positive net exports for that period—a trade surplus.

Exhibit 29-9 shows the current account for the United States in 1994. We see that the United States had a deficit on current account in 1994. Notice also that net exports were the primary component of the U.S. current account balance; the United States had a trade deficit that year as well.

A nation's current account records the transactions that make up part of the demand and supply for its currency. Credit entries in the account contribute to the demand for its currency, and debit entries contribute to the supply. The current account does not, however, incorporate all the sources of demand and supply. It does not include purchases of assets. Part of the demand for a country's currency comes when foreigners acquire its assets. Part of the supply comes

- A nation's **current account** is a statement of spending flows into and out of the nation during a particular period for exports and imports, together with the flow of payments to owners of foreign assets and transfer payments that flow across international borders.
- A nation's **balance on current account** is the sum of credit and debit items in its current account.
- A **current account deficit** exists if the balance on current account is negative.
- A **current account surplus** exists if the balance on current account is positive.
- A nation's **capital account** is a statement of spending flows into and out of the country during a particular period for purchases of assets.
- The **balance on capital account** is the sum of credits and debits in the capital account.
- A country has a **capital account surplus** if its balance on capital account is positive.
- A country has a **capital account deficit** if its balance on capital account is negative.

EXHIBIT 29-9

The U.S. Current Account Balance, 1994 (Billions)

The United States had a deficit on current account in 1994.

Credit items		
Merchandise exports	$502.5	
Exports of services	198.7	
Receipts on U.S. assets abroad	137.6	
Total credits on goods and services and receipts		$838.8
Debit items		
Merchandise imports	−$668.6	
Imports of services	−138.8	
Payments on foreign assets in U.S.	−146.9	
Total debits on goods and services and payments		−$954.3
Net transfer payments		−$35.8
Balance on current account		−$151.3

Source: *Economic Indicators* (June 1995): 35–36.

when people in the country acquire assets in other countries. A nation's balance of payments includes transactions in assets as well.

The Capital Account

A country's **capital account** is a statement of spending flows into and out of the country during a particular period for purchases of assets. A purchase by a foreigner of assets in the United States is entered as a credit on the U.S. capital account. For example, in 1990 Sony Corporation, a Japanese company, purchased Columbia Pictures, a U.S. company; the transaction was listed as a credit on the U.S. capital account that year. A purchase by a resident of the United States of an asset in another country is entered as a debit on current account. Examples of debit transactions include U.S. purchases of foreign stocks, bonds, and real estate. As in the current account, credit items are recorded as positive flows and debit items as negative flows. The sum of credits and debits in a nation's capital account is the **balance on capital account.**

If credits exceed debits in a country's capital account, the balance on capital account will be positive; there is a **capital account surplus.** That means that during the period recorded in the capital account, foreigners spent more acquiring that country's assets than people in that country spent acquiring foreign assets. If a country's balance on capital account is negative, there is a **capital account deficit.** The country's residents spent more on foreign assets than foreigners spent on that country's assets.

Exhibit 29-10 shows the U.S. capital account for 1994. It shows that foreign buyers purchased assets in the United States totaling $291.4 billion. Those purchases are recorded as credit entries in the capital account. U.S. buyers purchased $125.9 billion worth of foreign assets—those purchases are recorded as debit items. The United States had a capital account surplus in 1994. That means foreigners spent more acquiring U.S. assets than people in the United States spent acquiring foreign assets.

Foreign purchases of U.S. assets (credits)	$291.4
U.S. purchases of foreign assets (debits)	−125.9
Balance on capital account	$165.5

Source: *Economic Indicators* (June 1995): 35–36.

EXHIBIT 29-10

The U.S. Balance on Capital Account, 1994 (Billions)

A statistic related to the capital account for any one period reports the total value of a country's assets held by foreigners versus the total value of foreign assets held by that country's residents. A country's **net foreign investment position** equals the value of assets its residents hold in other countries minus the value of assets held in that country by people in other countries. A country whose net foreign investment position is positive is called a **creditor nation.** One whose net foreign investment position is negative is called a **debtor nation.**

The "debtor nation" terminology is something of a misnomer; being a debtor nation doesn't mean that a nation is actually in debt. It simply means that the value of the nation's assets owned by foreigners exceeds the value of foreign assets owned by residents of that nation.

Until 1989, the value of foreign assets held by U.S. residents exceeded the value of U.S. assets owned by foreigners. The United States was, therefore, a creditor nation. Heavy foreign purchases of U.S. assets in the late 1980s tipped this balance, and in 1989 the United States became a debtor nation.

Reconciling the Current and Capital Accounts

The credit items on current and capital account make up the demand for dollars. The debit items make up the supply. Equilibrium in the currency market ensures that the quantity of dollars demanded equals the quantity supplied. These facts imply a relationship between the balances on current and capital account in a country's balance of payments.

First, we simply note the equilibrium condition in the currency market. For the market for U.S. dollars, for example, equilibrium requires that

$$\text{Dollars demanded} = \text{dollars supplied} \tag{4}$$

Dollars demanded are credit items in the current and capital accounts, and dollars supplied are debit items, so we can rewrite Equation (4) as

$$\text{Credit items} = \text{debit items} \tag{5}$$

A purchase by a foreign buyer of a $1,000 computer produced in the United States would be reported as a credit item on the left-hand side of Equation (5). A purchase by a U.S. resident of a $70 sweater made in Britain would be added to the total of debit items on the right-hand side of Equation (5). Credits and debits can be accumulated on current and capital account, so Equation (5) can be rewritten as

$$\begin{matrix}\text{Current} & & \text{capital} & & \text{current} & & \text{capital} \\ \text{account} & + & \text{account} & = & \text{account} & + & \text{account} \\ \text{credits} & & \text{credits} & & \text{debits} & & \text{debits}\end{matrix} \tag{6}$$

If we rearrange Equation (6) so that current account items are on the left and capital account items are on the right, we have

$$\begin{matrix}\text{Current} & & \text{current} & & \text{capital} & & \text{capital} \\ \text{account} & - & \text{account} & = & \text{account} & - & \text{account} \\ \text{credits} & & \text{debits} & & \text{debits} & & \text{credits}\end{matrix} \tag{7}$$

We factor out the minus sign on the right-hand side of Equation (7) to obtain

$$\begin{matrix}\text{Current} & & \text{current} \\ \text{account} & - & \text{account} \\ \text{credits} & & \text{debits}\end{matrix} = -1 \times \begin{bmatrix}\text{capital} & & \text{capital} \\ \text{account} & - & \text{account} \\ \text{credits} & & \text{debits}\end{bmatrix} \tag{8}$$

The term on the left-hand side of Equation (8) is the balance on current account.

A country's **net foreign investment position** equals the value of foreign assets held by its residents minus the value of its assets held by foreign residents.

A **creditor nation** is a nation with a positive net foreign investment position.

A **debtor nation** is a nation with a negative net foreign investment position.

The term in brackets on the right-hand side is the balance on capital account. Equation (8) can thus be simplified:

$$\text{Balance on current account} = -(\text{balance on capital account}) \qquad \textbf{(9)}$$

Equation (9) is an extremely important result: the balance on current account equals the negative of the balance on capital account. An imbalance in one account *necessarily* implies an opposite imbalance in the other. A nation with a capital account surplus must therefore have a current account deficit. A capital account deficit implies a current account surplus. Exhibit 29-11 combines the current and capital accounts for 1994.

Current account balance	−$151.3
Capital account balance	165.5
Statistical discrepancy	−14.2
Balance of payments	$0.0

Source: *Economic Indicators* (June 1995): 35–36.

EXHIBIT 29-11

Reconciling the Current and Capital Accounts for the United States, 1994 (Billions)

The current and capital account balances for the United States are reported for 1994. The imbalance between the two is reported as a statistical discrepancy. All values are in billions of dollars.

Official measures of international spending flows inevitably miss many transactions. U.S. imports of illegal drugs, for example, aren't counted in the government's statistics on imports, but they clearly make up part of the supply curve for dollars. The ease with which goods and services can cross most international borders means that many legitimate transactions are missed in official estimates of the current and capital accounts as well. Incomplete data on international transactions can create statistical imbalances between official estimates of the current and capital accounts. These measurement errors are listed in the accounts as statistical discrepancies. Notice that the statistical discrepancy in 1994 was $14.2 billion. Given the huge flows of international spending, that's a remarkably small error; over $800 billion in total spending flowed into the United States that year.

Exhibit 29-12 shows current and capital account balances for the United States since 1981. In 1981 there was a current account surplus—exports exceeded imports. The current account balance shifted to a deficit in 1982 and has remained in deficit since. That means the United States has had a capital account surplus since 1982.

Why did the United States shift from a position of generally having surpluses in its current account to always having deficits? The primary reasons for the emergence of a current account deficit in the early 1980s appear to have been fiscal and monetary policy in the United States. Sharply increased government

EXHIBIT 29-12

U.S. Current and Capital Account Balances: 1981–1994

The United States had a small surplus on current account and a deficit on capital account in 1981. Since then, it has had a current account deficit and a capital account surplus. The difference between the absolute value of the current and capital account balances in any year is a statistical discrepancy.

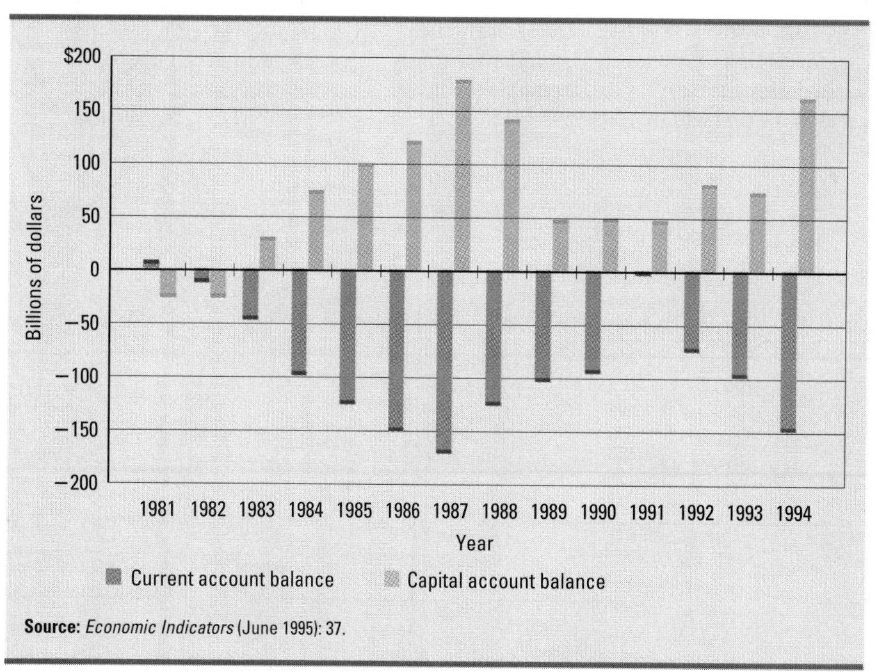

Source: *Economic Indicators* (June 1995): 37.

spending and a cut in taxes in the early 1980s produced a large budget deficit. To finance the deficit, the federal government sold bonds. The increased supply of bonds boosted U.S. interest rates. Higher interest rates increased the demand and reduced the supply of dollars, as explained in Chapter 23. That increased the exchange rate, which increased the cost of U.S. exports and reduced the cost of U.S. imports. Net exports fell as a result. The Fed's effort to bring down inflation in the early 1980s meant a tighter monetary policy at the same time, placing even greater upward pressure on U.S. interest rates. Exhibit 29-13 shows the sharp increase in the U.S. exchange rate from 1980 to 1985.

Exhibit 29-13 suggests two additional puzzles. First, why did the U.S. exchange rate drop after 1985? Second, if the increase in the exchange rate was a factor in creating the trade deficit, why hasn't the reduction in the U.S. exchange rate eliminated it?

The reduction in the price of the dollar after 1985 reflects two forces. First, U.S. interest rates have generally fallen since 1985, in part because the federal deficit has fallen relative to GDP. Second, the United States has, since 1985, experienced considerably more inflation than many of its major trading partners. Recall that one determinant of the exchange rate of a currency is its relative buying power. As inflation erodes the buying power of the dollar, its value in terms of other currencies falls. From 1985 to 1994, consumer prices in the United States rose at an annual rate of 3.6 percent. Over that same period, prices in Japan rose at an annual rate of just 1.5 percent. Germany's inflation rate over the

EXHIBIT 29-13

The U.S. Exchange Rate, 1975–1995

The chart shows exchange rates for the dollar in terms of the Canadian dollar, the German mark, and the Japanese yen. It also shows movement of the dollar against a broader exchange rate (the blue line), which reflects the price of the dollar in terms of 20 leading industrial nations. That broader exchange rate rose during the first half of the 1980s; by the end of the decade it had fallen back to about its 1980 level. The dollar was fairly stable during the early 1990s, then plunged in value in the first half of 1995.

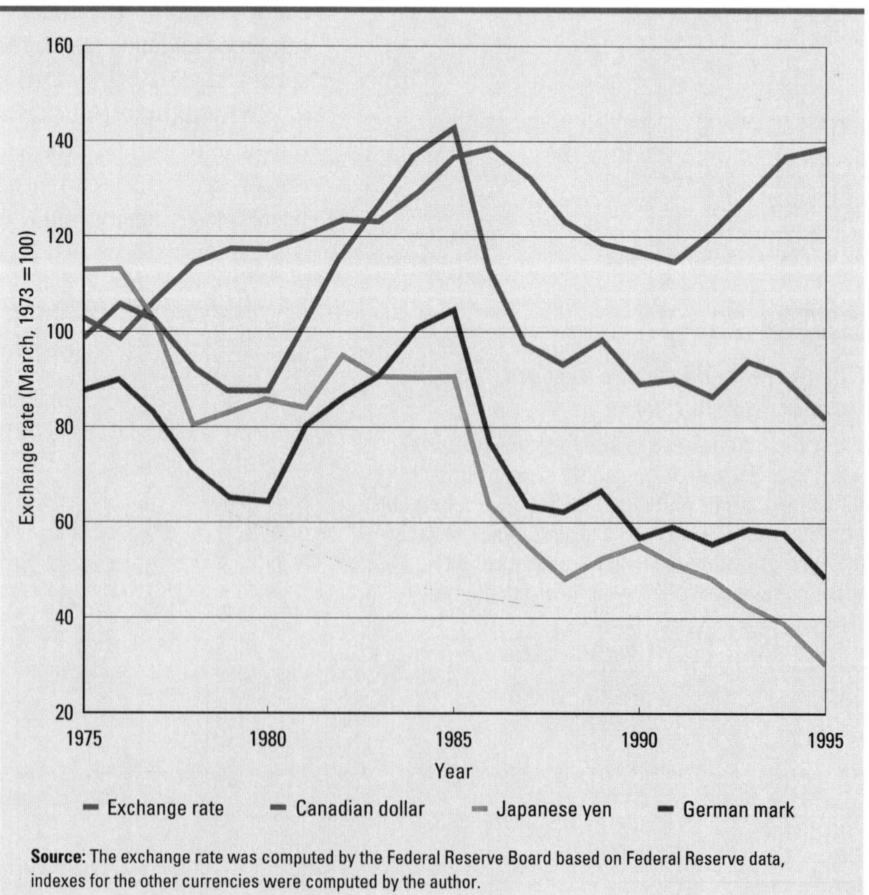

Source: The exchange rate was computed by the Federal Reserve Board based on Federal Reserve data, indexes for the other currencies were computed by the author.

same period was 2.4 percent. Of course, a host of factors affects the demand and supply for any currency, but the relatively high rate of U.S. inflation clearly played a role in bringing down the dollar.

All other things equal, a higher exchange rate reduces net exports; a lower exchange rate increases them. A higher exchange rate certainly reduced net exports between 1980 and 1985—why hasn't the subsequent reduction in the exchange rate boosted net exports? Why has the trade deficit been so persistent?

Strong economic performance has been one factor contributing to the U.S. trade deficit in recent years. As we've already seen, an increase in GDP produces an increase in imports, which reduces net exports. The United States has, in recent years, scored sharper gains in GDP than many of its trading partners. Indeed, many U.S. trading partners were mired in recessions during the early 1990s. While the United States had a recession of its own in 1990 to 1991, Japan and Germany suffered sharper and longer-lasting recessions between 1992 and 1994. Notice in Exhibit 29-3 that U.S. net exports rose sharply in 1991, when the U.S. had a recession, and that they have fallen sharply since.

Perhaps the most important source of a persistent trade deficit has been a persistent federal deficit. We'll examine the reasons for that linkage in Chapter 34.

Deficits and Surpluses: Good or Bad?

The United States has a current account deficit and a capital account surplus. Is that good or bad?

Viewed from the perspective of consumers, neither phenomenon seems to pose a problem. A current account deficit is likely to imply a trade deficit. That means more goods and services are flowing into the country than are flowing out. A capital account surplus means more spending is flowing into the country for the purchase of assets than is flowing out. It's hard to see the harm in any of that.

Public opinion, however, appears to regard a current account deficit and capital account surplus as highly undesirable, perhaps because people associate a trade deficit with a loss of jobs. But that is erroneous; employment in the long run is determined by forces that have nothing to do with a trade deficit. An increase in the trade deficit (i.e., a reduction in net exports) reduces aggregate demand in the short run, but net exports are only one component of aggregate demand. Other factors—consumption, investment, and government purchases—affect aggregate demand as well. There is no reason a trade deficit should imply a loss of jobs. Perhaps the best way to see the lack of a relationship between the trade deficit and job creation is to note that in the period since 1981, the United States has created more jobs than any other industrialized nation—while it piled up huge trade deficits. Indeed, more jobs were created in the 1980s than in any other decade in U.S. history.

What about foreign purchases of U.S. assets? One objection to such purchases is that if foreigners own U.S. assets, they will receive the income from those assets—spending will flow out of the country. But it's hard to see the harm in paying income to an investor. When someone buys a bond issued by General Motors, interest payments will flow from GM to the bondholder. Does GM view the purchase of its bond as a bad thing? Of course not. Despite the fact that GM's payment of interest on the bond and the ultimate repayment of the face value of the bond will exceed what the company originally received from the bond purchaser, GM is surely not unhappy with the arrangement. It expects to put that money to more productive use; that's the reason it issued the bond in the first place.

A second concern about foreign asset purchases is that the United States in some sense loses sovereignty when foreigners buy its assets. But why should this be a problem? Foreign-owned firms competing in U.S. markets are at the mercy of those markets just like firms owned by U.S. nationals. Foreign owners of U.S. real estate have no special power. What about foreign buyers of bonds issued by the U.S. government? Foreigners own slightly less than 20 percent of these bonds; they are thus the creditors for slightly less than 20 percent of the national debt. But this position gives them no special power. They hold an obligation of the U.S. government to pay them a certain amount of money on a certain date, nothing more. A foreign owner could sell his or her bonds, but more than $100 billion worth of these bonds are sold every day. The resale of U.S. bonds by a foreign owner is unlikely to have any effect on the U.S. government.

In short, there's no apparent reason to be concerned about having a current account deficit and a capital account surplus—nor would there be any reason to be concerned about the opposite state of affairs. The important feature of international trade is its ability to improve living standards for people. It's not a game in which current account figures are the scorecard.

Checklist ✓

- Exchange rates are determined by demand and supply; the flexibility of exchange rates ensures that currency markets are in equilibrium.
- Exports, imports, payments to owners of foreign assets, and transfer payments are recorded in a nation's current account balance.
- International purchases of assets are reported in a nation's capital account balance.
- The balance on current account equals the negative of the balance on capital account.
- A debtor nation is one in which foreign ownership of its assets exceeds its ownership of foreign assets. A creditor nation is one in which foreign ownership of its assets is less than its ownership of foreign assets.

Exchange Rate Systems

Exchange rates are determined by demand and supply. But governments can influence those exchange rates in various ways. The extent and nature of government involvement in currency markets defines alternative systems of exchange rates. In this section we'll examine alternative exchange rate systems and explore some of their macroeconomic implications.

There are three broad categories of exchange rate systems. In one system, exchange rates are set purely by private market forces with no government involvement. Values change constantly as the demand and supply for currencies fluctuate. In another system, currency values are allowed to change, but governments participate in currency markets in an effort to influence those values. Finally, governments may seek to fix the values of their currencies, either through participation in the market or through regulatory policy.

Free-Floating Systems

In a **free-floating exchange rate system,** governments and central banks do not participate in the market for foreign exchange. The relationship between governments and central banks on the one hand and currency markets on the other is much the same as the relationship between these institutions and stock markets. Governments may regulate stock markets to prevent fraud, but stock values themselves are left to float in the market. The U.S. government, for example, does not intervene in the stock market to influence stock prices.

The concept of a completely free-floating exchange rate system is a theoretical one. In practice, all governments or central banks intervene in currency markets in an effort to influence exchange rates. Some countries, such as the United States, intervene to only a small degree, so that the notion of a free-floating exchange rate system comes close to what actually exists in this country.

A **free-floating exchange rate system** is one in which governments and central banks do not participate in the currency market.

A free-floating system has the advantage of being self-regulating. There's no need for government intervention if the exchange rate is left to the market. Market forces also restrain large swings in demand or supply. Suppose, for example, that a dramatic shift in world preferences led to a sharply increased demand for goods and services produced in Canada. That would increase the demand for Canadian dollars, raise Canada's exchange rate, and make Canadian goods and services more expensive for foreigners to buy. Some of the impact of the swing in foreign demand would thus be absorbed in a rising exchange rate. That would tend to reduce the degree to which events in the rest of the world would affect the prices and output of goods and services in Canada. In effect, a free-floating exchange rate acts as a kind of buffer to insulate an economy from the impact of international events.

The primary difficulty with free-floating exchange rates lies in their unpredictability. Contracts between buyers and sellers in different countries must not only reckon with possible changes in prices and other factors during the lives of those contracts; they must consider the possibility of exchange rate changes as well. An agreement by a U.S. distributor to purchase a certain quantity of French wine each year, for example, will be affected by the possibility that the exchange rate between the French franc and the U.S. dollar will change while the contract is in effect. Fluctuating exchange rates make international transactions riskier and thus increase the cost of doing business with other countries.

Managed Float Systems

Governments and central banks often seek to increase or decrease their exchange rates by buying or selling their own currencies. Exchange rates are still free to float, but governments try to influence their values. Government or central bank participation in a floating exchange rate system is called a **managed float.**

Most governments that have a floating exchange rate system intervene from time to time in the currency market in an effort to raise or lower the price of their own currency. Typically, the purpose of such intervention is to prevent sudden large swings in the value of a nation's currency. Such intervention is likely to have only a small impact, if any, on exchange rates. Roughly $200 billion worth of currencies changes hands every day in the world market; it's difficult for any one agency—even an agency the size of the U.S. government or the Fed—to force significant changes in exchange rates.

Still, governments or central banks can sometimes influence their exchange rates. Suppose the price of a country's currency is rising very rapidly. The country's government or central bank might seek to hold off further increases in order to prevent a major reduction in net exports. An announcement that a further increase in its exchange rate is unacceptable, followed by sales of that country's currency by the central bank in order to bring its exchange rate down, can sometimes convince other participants in the currency market that the exchange rate won't rise further. That change in expectations could reduce demand and increase supply for the currency, thus achieving the goal of holding the exchange rate down. Massive efforts by the federal government and by many other countries to shore up the dollar in 1994 and 1995 failed, however, to prevent the slide shown in Exhibit 29-13. More fundamental forces, such as a U.S. inflation rate that exceeded the inflation rate for many other nations, proved more powerful than the efforts of governments.

A **managed float** is a system of floating exchange rates in which some governments or central banks seek to manipulate their exchange rates by buying or selling currency in the open market.

Fixed Exchange Rates

In a system of **fixed exchange rates,** the exchange rate between two currencies is determined by government policy. There are several mechanisms through which fixed exchange rates may be maintained. Whatever the system for maintaining these rates, however, all fixed exchange rate systems share some important features.

A Commodity Standard

In a **commodity standard system,** countries fix the value of their respective currencies relative to a certain commodity or group of commodities. With each currency's value fixed in terms of the commodity, currencies are fixed relative to one another.

For centuries, the values of many currencies were fixed relative to gold. Suppose, for example, that the price of gold were fixed at $20 per ounce in the United States. That would mean that the government of the United States was committed to exchanging 1 ounce of gold to anyone who handed over $20. (That was the case in the United States—and $20 was roughly the price—up to 1933.) Now suppose that the exchange rate between the British pound and gold was £5 per ounce of gold. With £5 and $20 both trading for 1 ounce of gold, £1 would exchange for $4. No one would pay more than $4 for £1 because $4 could always be exchanged for 1/5 ounce of gold, and that gold could be exchanged for £1. And no one would sell £1 for less than $4, because the owner of £1 could always exchange it for 1/5 ounce of gold, which could be exchanged for $4. In practice, actual currency values could vary slightly from the levels implied by their commodity values because of the costs involved in exchanging currencies for gold, but these variations were slight.

Under the gold standard, the quantity of money was regulated by the quantity of gold in a country. If, for example, the United States guaranteed to exchange dollars for gold at the rate of $20 per ounce, it couldn't issue more money than it could back up with the gold it owned.

The gold standard was a self-regulating system. Suppose that at the fixed exchange rate implied by the gold standard, a country's balance of payments was in deficit. That would imply that spending flowing out of the country exceeded spending flowing in. As residents supplied their currency to make foreign purchases, foreigners acquiring that currency could redeem it for gold. Gold would thus flow out of the country running a deficit. Given an obligation to exchange the country's currency for gold, a reduction in a country's gold holdings would force it to reduce its money supply. That would reduce aggregate demand in the country, lowering income and the price level. But both of those events would increase net exports in the country, eliminating the deficit in the balance of payments. Balance would be achieved, but at the cost of a recession. A country with a surplus in its balance of payments would experience an inflow of gold. That would boost its money supply and increase aggregate demand. That, in turn, would generate higher prices, and higher real GDP, and ultimately an inflationary gap. Those events would reduce net exports and correct the surplus in the balance of payments, but again at the cost of wrenching changes in the domestic economy.

Because of this tendency for imbalances in a country's balance of payments to be corrected only through massive changes in the entire economy, nations

- A system of **fixed exchange rates** is one in which exchange rates are set by government policy.
- A **commodity standard system** is a fixed exchange rate system in which the prices of various currencies are fixed relative to a given quantity of some commodity.

began abandoning the gold standard in the 1930s. That was the period of the Great Depression, during which world trade virtually ground to a halt. World War II made the shipment of goods an extremely risky proposition, so trade remained minimal during the war. As the war seemed to be nearing an end, representatives of the United States and its allies met in 1944 at Bretton Woods, New Hampshire, to fashion a new mechanism through which international trade could be financed. The system was to be one of fixed exchange rates, but with much less emphasis on gold as a backing for the system.

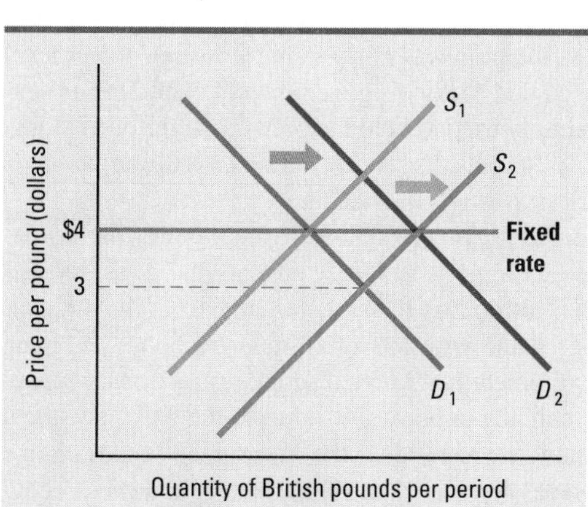

EXHIBIT 29-14

Maintaining a Fixed Exchange Rate Through Intervention

Initially, the equilibrium price of the British pound equals $4, the fixed rate between the pound and the dollar. Now suppose an increased supply of British pounds lowers the equilibrium price of the pound to $3. The Bank of England could purchase pounds by selling dollars in order to shift the demand curve for pounds to D_2. Alternatively, the Fed could shift the demand curve to D_2 by buying pounds.

Fixed Exchange Rates Through Intervention

The Bretton Woods Agreement called for each currency's value to be fixed relative to other currencies. The mechanism for maintaining these rates, however, was to be intervention by governments and central banks in the currency market.

Again suppose that the exchange rate between the dollar and the British pound is fixed at $4 per £1. Suppose further that this rate is an equilibrium rate, as illustrated in Exhibit 29-14. As long as the fixed rate coincides with the equilibrium rate, the fixed exchange rate operates in the same fashion as a free-floating rate.

Now suppose that the British choose to purchase more U.S. goods and services. The supply curve for pounds increases, and the equilibrium exchange rate for the pound (in terms of dollars) falls to, say, $3. Under terms of the Bretton Woods Agreement, Britain and the United States would be required to intervene in the market to bring the exchange rate back to the rate fixed in the agreement, $4. If that's done by the British central bank, the Bank of England, it would have to purchase pounds. It would do that by exchanging dollars it had previously acquired in other transactions for pounds. As it sold dollars, it would take in checks written in pounds. When a central bank sells an asset, the checks that come into the central bank reduce the money supply and reserves of that country. We saw in Chapter 24, for example, that the sale of bonds by the Fed reduces the U.S. money supply. Similarly, the sale of dollars by the Bank of England would reduce the British money supply. In order to bring its exchange rate back to the agreed-to level, Britain would have to carry out a contractionary monetary policy.

Alternatively, the Fed could intervene. It could purchase pounds, writing checks in dollars. But when a central bank purchases assets, it adds reserves to the system and increases the money supply. The United States would thus be forced to carry out an expansionary monetary policy.

Domestic disturbances were created by efforts to maintain fixed exchange rates; this brought the demise of the Bretton Woods system. Japan and West Germany gave up the effort to maintain the fixed values of their currencies in the spring of 1971 and announced they were withdrawing from the Bretton Woods system. President Richard Nixon pulled the United States out of the system in August of that year, and the system collapsed. An attempt to revive fixed exchange rates in 1973 collapsed almost immediately, and the world has operated largely on a managed float ever since.

Under the Bretton Woods system, the United States had redeemed dollars held by other governments for gold; President Nixon terminated that policy as he withdrew the United States from the Bretton Woods system. The dollar is no longer backed by gold.

Case in Point: The Peso Plunges

The plunge rocked world markets. In the course of a few days of furious trading, the peso, which had held at a dollar price of between 28 and 33 cents for three years, lost almost half its value. The plunge hurt companies exporting to Mexico, whose goods suddenly cost Mexican buyers almost twice as much. It hurt Mexicans, who have now been told they must brace for a severe recession.

What happened? Mexico had fixed its exchange rate against the dollar. Its central bank, Banco de Mexico, allowed the rate to adjust, but it would announce in advance how low the peso would be permitted to fall. Through most of 1994, the central bank did not allow the price of the peso to fall below 28 cents. When market forces threatened to nudge the peso even lower, the bank stepped in to buy pesos.

With a huge current account deficit—equal to nearly 8 percent of GDP in 1994—the pressure downward on the peso was substantial. Of course, that current account deficit was matched by a capital account surplus; foreign investment was pouring into Mexico. But foreign investors were becoming increasingly skittish. A small-scale civil war had broken out in the southern state of Chiapas on the day NAFTA went into effect. The atmosphere of unrest was heightened by the assassination in 1994 of presidential candidate Donaldo Colosio.

Declining confidence led more and more speculators to sell pesos, shifting the supply curve for the peso to the right. That forced Banco de Mexico to buy them in order to shift the demand curve to the right to maintain the 28 cent price. That meant selling foreign currencies, and the bank was starting to run out. The bank started 1994 with $30 billion in foreign currency reserves; by November reserves had fallen to $16 billion. By mid-December continued selling had reduced reserves to $11 billion, and the bank gave up. The government announced on December 20th that it would no longer hold the peso to any particular level; the currency nose-dived immediately to about 16 cents. The United States and the International Monetary Fund, meanwhile, offered up a $40 billion package to shore up Mexico's reserves.

The fact that the peso was fairly stable at its new lower level in 1995 suggested that Mexico's government, which runs its central bank, had simply tried to hold the peso too high for too long. The new lower peso put Mexico in a stronger position vis-à-vis its North American partners in NAFTA.

For the short term, the peso's lower value spelled hard times in Mexico. Foreign imports suddenly cost a great deal more, as the example that introduces this chapter suggests. The $40 billion aid package came with lots of strings attached—the main one being a requirement that Mexico adopt contractionary monetary and fiscal policies to boost the value of the peso. President Zedillo predicted in 1995 that the measures would plunge Mexico into a recession that year. He predicted, however, recovery by 1996.

Sources: Based on "Putting Mexico Together Again," *The Economist* 334(7900) (Feb. 4, 1995): 65–67; and Craig Torres, "Mexico's Central Bank Struggles As Reserves Reach Lows," *The Wall Street Journal,* 3 February 1995, A8. Currency prices are from *International Financial Statistics,* various issues.

Ernesto Zedillo.

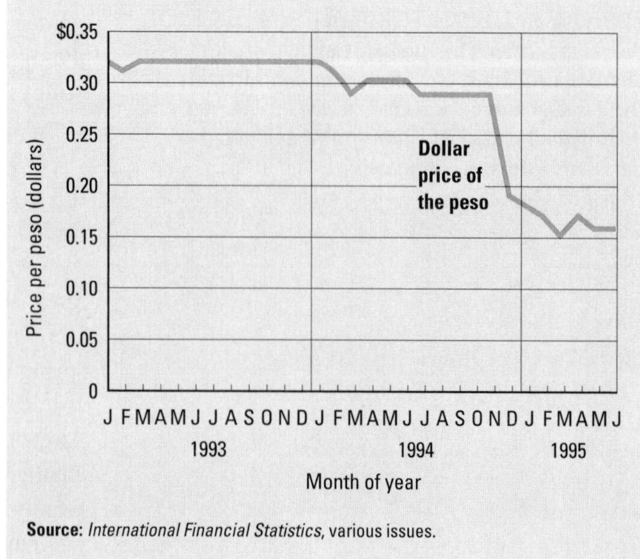

Source: *International Financial Statistics,* various issues.

The European Community (EC) established a variation on a fixed-rate theme in 1979. Eleven of the twelve members of the EC created a European Monetary System, in which exchange rates of the eleven participants (Greece did not participate) were fixed relative to one another, although each currency could fluctuate by as much as 2.25 percent on either side of the fixed rate. If an EMS participant's exchange rate diverged by more than 2.25 percent from the agreed-to level, the country was obliged to intervene in the currency market or take other measures to bring its currency in line.

Maintaining fixed exchange rates within the EMS has proved to be a daunting task. Italy and Britain dropped out of the system in 1992; they had not rejoined it as this book went to press.

Mexico maintained a fixed exchange rate between the peso and the dollar up to December 1994. When the central bank could no longer maintain that rate, it allowed the peso to float—and the peso fell in price from 28 cents to 16 cents 2 months later.

Fixed exchange rate systems offer the advantage of predictable currency values—when they're working. But for fixed exchange rates to work, the countries participating in them must maintain domestic economic conditions that will keep equilibrium currency values close to the fixed rates that have been set. Sovereign nations must be willing to coordinate their monetary and fiscal policies. Achieving that kind of coordination among independent countries can be a difficult task.

Once exchange rates start to diverge from the values at which they are supposed to be fixed, the effort to force currencies up or down through market intervention can be extremely disruptive. And when countries suddenly decide to give that effort up, exchange rates can swing sharply in one direction or another. When that happens, the main virtue of fixed exchange rates, their predictability, is lost.

Checklist ✓

- In a free-floating exchange rate system, exchange rates are determined by demand and supply.
- Exchange rates are determined by demand and supply in a managed float system, but governments intervene as buyers or sellers of currencies in an effort to influence exchange rates.
- In a fixed exchange rate system, exchange rates among currencies are not allowed to change. The gold standard and Bretton Woods were examples of fixed exchange rate systems.

A Look Back—And a Look Ahead

In this chapter we examined the role of net exports in the economy. We reviewed the benefits of international trade derived from the efficiency gains that come through allocating world resources on the basis of comparative advantage.

We found that export and import demand are influenced by many different factors, the most important being domestic and foreign income levels, changes in relative prices, the exchange rate, and consumer preferences.

In prior chapters we took net exports as autonomous; in this chapter we recognized that because imports rise as income increases, the total value of net exports is determined in part by the level of income achieved by the domestic economy. We found that when the induced component of imports is recognized in the aggregate expenditures model, the slope of the aggregate expenditures curve is reduced. The multiplier used to determine the shift in aggregate demand caused by a change in aggregate expenditures is reduced accordingly.

In the foreign exchange market, the equilibrium exchange rate is determined by the intersection of the demand and supply curves for a currency. Given the flexibility of exchange rates, we can assume this equilibrium is achieved.

That means that the quantity of a currency demanded equals the quantity supplied.

An economy can experience current account surpluses or deficits. The balance on current account equals the negative of the balance on capital account. We saw that one reason for the current account deficit in the United States is the U.S. capital account surplus; foreigners have found the United States an attractive place to invest. Corresponding to the balance on capital account is the historical accumulation of investment by U.S. citizens abroad and foreigners in the United States. In the 1980s, the United States shifted from being a creditor nation to being a debtor nation.

The chapter closed with an examination of floating and fixed exchange rate systems. Fixed exchange rate systems include commodity-based systems and fixed rates that are maintained through intervention. Exchange rate systems have moved from a gold standard, to a system of fixed rates with intervention, to a mixed set of arrangements of floating and fixed exchange rates. More and more countries are attempting to integrate their currencies into the world economy so they can take advantage of the opportunities offered by international trade.

This chapter completes our investigation of the private components of the aggregate demand curve. We'll turn in Part Nine to an investigation of monetary and fiscal policy. We'll find that the international market for goods and services, and the exchange rate system through which a country participates in that market, play important roles in determining how fiscal and monetary policy affect economic activity.

Terms and Concepts for Review

Balance of payments
Balance on capital account
Balance on current account
Capital account
Capital account deficit
Capital account surplus
Commodity standard system
Creditor nation
Current account
Current account deficit
Current account surplus
Debtor nation
Fixed exchange rates
Free-floating exchange rate system
Imports-GDP curve
International finance
Managed float
Marginal propensity to import
Net foreign investment position
Quota
Tariff

For Discussion

1. David Ricardo, a famous English economist of the nineteenth century, stressed that a nation has a comparative advantage in those products for which its efficiency relative to other nations is the highest. He argued in favor of specialization and trade based on comparative, not absolute, advantage. From a global perspective, what would be the "advantage" of that?
2. For several months prior to your vacation trip to Naples, Italy, you find that the exchange rate for the dollar has increased relative to the Italian lira. Are you pleased or sad? Explain.
3. Who might respond in a way different from your own to the falling value of the lira in Question 2?
4. When induced imports are included in the aggregate expenditures model, the marginal expenditure rate falls. Why?

5. Suppose people in the United States lost all interest in foreign goods and services, so they reduced the level of imports at each level of income and reduced the marginal propensity to import. Explain carefully how this would affect aggregate demand.
6. The following analysis appeared in a local newspaper editorial:

 If foreigners own our businesses and land, that's one thing, but when they own billions in U.S. bonds, that's another. We don't care who owns the businesses, but our grandchildren will have to put up with a lower standard of living because of the interest payments sent overseas. Therefore, we must reduce our trade deficit.

 Critically analyze this editorial view. Are the basic premises correct? The conclusion?
7. In the years prior to the abandonment of the gold standard, foreigners cashed in their dollars and the U.S. Treasury "lost gold" at unprecedented rates. Today, the dollar is no longer tied to gold and is free to float. What are the fundamental differences between a currency based on the gold standard and one that is allowed to float? What would the U.S. "lose" if foreigners decided to "cash in" their dollars today?
8. Can there be a deficit on current account and a deficit on capital account at the same time? Explain.
9. Suppose the people of a certain economy spend every cent of every additional dollar in GDP they generate on the goods and services of foreign countries. What is the marginal propensity to import? The marginal expenditure rate? The multiplier?
10. For the economy described in Question 9, what will be the impact on aggregate demand if planned investment rises by $100 billion? Explain.
11. The Case in Point on the yen and U.S. auto sales notes that U.S. carmakers had, by 1993, captured 74 percent of the U.S. market. Based on the information about exchange rates provided in Exhibit 29-13, what do you think has happened to the U.S. share since? Why?
12. Suppose you were a currency speculator in 1994, and you observed in November the reduction in foreign currency reserves noted in the Case in Point on the peso. How would observing a sharp reduction in reserves held by Banco de Mexico have affected your expectations about the peso? What might it have caused you to do? How would such behavior have affected Banco de Mexico?

Problems

1. Suppose a nation's aggregate expenditures function is given by

 $$AE = \$400 \text{ billion} + 0.5Y$$

 Included in aggregate expenditures are exports of $100 billion and an imports-GDP function given by

 $$M = 0.1Y$$

 What is the nation's trade balance? Now suppose government purchases rise by $100 billion. What happens to equilibrium GDP in the aggregate expenditures model? What happens to the trade balance?
2. Suppose Japan relaxes its restrictions on the import of foreign goods and services and begins importing more from the United States. Illustrate graphically how this will affect the U.S. exchange rate, price level, and level of real GDP in the short run and in the long run. How will it affect these same variables in Japan? (Assume both economies are initially operating at their natural levels.)
3. Suppose U.S. investors begin purchasing assets in Mexico. Illustrate graphically how this will affect the U.S. exchange rate, price level, and level of real GDP in the short run and in the long run. How will it affect these same variables in Mexico? (Assume both economies are initially operating at their natural levels.)
4. Suppose foreigners begin buying more assets in the United States. Illustrate graphically how this will affect the U.S. exchange rate, price level, and level of real GDP in the short run and in the long run. (Assume the economy is initially operating at its natural level.)
5. Given the following data for the United States in 1975, compute the balance on current account and the balance on capital account. What is the amount of the statistical discrepancy, if any? (All figures are in millions of dollars.)

Balance on goods and services	$12,404
Receipts from U.S.-owned assets abroad	25,351
Payments on foreign-owned assets in the U.S.	12,564
Transfer payments from foreigners, less transfers to foreigners	−7,075
U.S. purchases of foreign assets	39,703
Foreign purchases of U.S. assets	15,670

Part Eight Policy Choices in the Short Run

30

Monetary Policy and the Fed

Objectives

After mastering the material in this chapter, you will be able to

1. Review the goals of monetary policy and the tools the Fed has available in implementing these goals.
2. Discuss the problem of lags in the implementation of monetary policy.
3. Explain the issues involved in the Fed's selection of targets in conducting monetary policy: should it focus on interest rates, the money supply, prices, nominal GDP, or what?
4. Describe the ways in which political considerations affect monetary policy.

There is required for carrying on the trade of the nation, a determinate sum of specifick money, which varies, and is sometimes more, sometimes less as the circumstances we are in requires.

Sir Dudley North, 1691

What's Ahead

Some call it the Fed's finest hour. The stock market had just crashed. The Dow Jones Industrial Average, an index of the stock prices of 30 leading firms, plunged 508 points in a single day in October 1987—the so-called Monday massacre. More than $500 billion in wealth was erased in a few hours of frantic trading on the stock exchange. The response of the Fed was bold and unequivocal. Fed Chairman Alan Greenspan announced, "The Federal Reserve, consistent with its responsibilities as the nation's central bank, affirmed today its readiness to serve as a source of liquidity to support the economic and financial system."

Mr. Greenspan's words were backed with action. Traders at the New York Federal Reserve Bank went into high gear, buying bonds to inject reserves into a financial system that had just absorbed its worst blow ever. Economist Jerry Jordan, who was then chief economist at First Interstate Bank Corp. noted the significance of the move in a statement to The Wall Street Journal*: "I think Greenspan is the only candidate for restoring the confidence of the markets. It's the chairman of the Fed, when it comes down to it, who pulls the levers."*

It was memories of the 1929 crash that made the 1987 crash so scary and the Fed's response so important. The 1929 crash had helped to usher in the worst economic debacle in U.S. history. Could Americans expect the same from this one? Members of the Board of Governors in 1929 had met on the worst day of that crash, and they emerged late that day to say the Fed saw no need for action.[1] The Fed chose a much different response to the 1987 crash. It's willingness to take action helped to instill increased confidence. The market began to recover the next day. Over the next 7 years, it recorded the most dramatic gains in its history. More important, the economy barely skipped a beat in the wake of the 1987 crash. Real GDP growth slowed, but it remained strong. Unemployment fell *in the year following the crash.*

[1] Observations about Federal Reserve policy here are taken from Alan Murray, "Stock Market's Frenzy Puts Fed's Greenspan in a Crucial Position," *The Wall Street Journal,* 21 October 1987, A1, and "Reserve Board Finds Action Unnecessary," *The New York Times,* 30 October 1929, 1.

The Fed's response to the 1987 crisis illustrates two important points about monetary policy. First, it suggests the swiftness with which monetary authorities can act. Second, the episode suggests the importance of the Fed and of its choices in monetary policy. The chairman's pronouncement was treated as a major news story. It appeared on the front pages of the nation's newspapers that afternoon and the next morning. The Fed's willingness to act made a difference, and Mr. Greenspan's words made headlines.

This chapter examines questions of monetary policy and the roles of central banks in carrying out that policy. Our primary focus will be on the U.S. Federal Reserve System, but we'll compare the conduct of monetary policy in the United States and other countries. The basic tools used by central banks in many economies are similar, but their institutional structure and their roles in their respective economies can differ.

We saw in Chapter 24 how central banks can influence the money supply and in Chapter 25 how the money supply and interest rates affect the economy. In the last three chapters, we've examined three components of aggregate demand: consumption, investment, and net exports. In this chapter, we'll see how monetary policy can be used to influence aggregate demand and thus the level of economic activity. We'll find that monetary policy can be a powerful tool, but that there may be difficulties in using it to manipulate the economy. There is some controversy among economists about just how effective a tool it is.

The Goals and Tools of Monetary Policy

In many respects, the Fed is the most powerful maker of economic policy in the United States. Congress can pass laws, but the president must execute them; the president can propose laws, but only Congress can pass them. The Fed, however, both sets and carries out monetary policy. Deliberations concerning fiscal policy can drag on for months, even years, but the Federal Open Market Committee (FOMC) can, behind closed doors, set monetary policy in a day—and see that policy implemented within hours. The Board of Governors can change the discount rate or reserve requirements at any time. The impact of the Fed's policies on the economy can be quite dramatic. The Fed can push interest rates up or down. It can promote a recession or an expansion. It can cause the inflation rate to rise or fall. The Fed wields enormous power.

But to what ends should all this power be directed? With what tools shall Fed policies be carried out? And what problems exist in trying to achieve the Fed's goals? This section examines the goals of monetary policy, the tools available to the Fed in seeking those goals, and the problems the Fed faces in attempting to achieve them.

Goals

When we think of the goals of monetary policy, we naturally think of standards of macroeconomic performance that seem desirable. A low unemployment rate is desirable, given the costs imposed by unemployment. A stable price level is desirable, because inflation imposes high costs on the economy. Economic growth is desirable, because such growth raises living standards.

Case in Point China Faces Conflict in Goals

The problem of conflicts among the basic goals of macroeconomic policy confronts all economies. China faced such a conflict in the 1990s. Its resolution of the conflict made the priorities of its government quite clear.

China's economy enjoyed sensational growth in the 1980s. Real GDP soared at an annual rate of 9.5 percent, according to World Bank estimates. Inflation averaged 5.8 percent per year during the period. That's unusually low relative to most other nations; the World Bank estimates that inflation worldwide averaged 14.7 percent per year in the 1980s.

But China's inflation-growth picture tilted a bit in the 1990s. Output growth slowed slightly. Inflation, which had crept upward in 1991 and 1992, soared in 1993 to an annual rate of almost 15 percent. It accelerated again to a 23 percent rate in 1994.

Higher inflation in China would force a devaluation of the yuan, the Chinese currency. And that would increase costs to Chinese producers who import some of their supplies from abroad, because it would take more yuan to pay for these supplies. A devalued yuan would also mean that foreign investors in China would see their earnings plummet as they converted yuan to their own currencies. And that could make foreigners reluctant to provide the investment China relies on to finance much of its growth. AES China Generating Company, a U.S. firm that had planned to invest as much as $2 billion in building a power plant in China, put its investment on hold in 1994 until the Chinese would agree to absorb the company's exchange rate risks. AES demanded, in effect, that China's government protect the company's earnings on the operation from any devaluation that might occur.

An open-air market in China.

Worried about the consequences of increased inflation, Zhu Rongi, China's vice premier and head of its central bank, began slowing the rate of money growth in 1993. China's central bank subsidizes state-owned enterprises by writing checks to cover the losses of these enterprises. That increases the money supply, which can contribute to inflation. Mr. Zhu demanded that money-losing enterprises find a way to cut costs and get by on smaller subsidies. But that effort to control growth in the money supply threatened growth, so China's leader, Deng Xiaoping, said he wanted Mr. Zhu to ease up; the Chinese leader feared that a tightening of credit could threaten economic growth in China. Speaking for Mr. Deng, Chinese economist Fan Gang said, "If there are some problems, let there be problems—he's very clear about this."

China's central bank isn't independent of the government—it's part of it. When Mr. Deng said he wanted an easier monetary policy, he got it.

Mr. Deng's decision to promote growth regardless of the impact on inflation sent off shock waves in the United States. Many U.S. officials were concerned that this policy could actually threaten China's growth by scaring off more foreign investors. And they worried that high inflation and slower growth might cause China to slow its transition toward a market capitalist economy. Fed Chairman Alan Greenspan went to China and urged its leaders to slow the rate of money growth. China's leaders, however, made clear that growth remained their top priority. If a tightening of monetary policy threatened to slow growth, the tighter policy wouldn't happen—regardless of its impact on inflation.

Sources: Data for the 1980s are drawn from the World Bank's *World Development Report 1992* (Oxford: Oxford University Press, 1992), tables 1 and 2. Information for the 1990s is taken from Marcus W. Brauchli, "China Inflation Alarms U.S., Threatens Reform," *The Wall Street Journal,* 24 January 1994, A1; and Kathy Chen, "China Seems to Change Inflation Tune," *The Wall Street Journal,* 10 November 1994, A10.

It thus seems reasonable to conclude that the goals of monetary policy should include the maintenance of full employment, the avoidance of inflation, and the promotion of economic growth. But these goals, each of which is desirable in itself, may conflict with one another. A monetary policy that helps to close a recessionary gap may promote inflation. A monetary policy that seeks to reduce inflation may increase unemployment and weaken economic growth. One might expect that in such cases, monetary authorities would receive guidance from legislation spelling out goals for the Fed to pursue and specifying what to do when achieving one goal means missing another. But as we shall see, that kind of guidance wasn't provided in the initial legislation creating the Federal Reserve System. The federal government has since specified macroeconomic goals of very low unemployment and inflation. But these goals are wildly unrealistic, and it does not appear that anyone pays any attention to them. The Fed is free to define the goals it wishes to pursue.

The Federal Reserve Act

When Congress established the Federal Reserve System in 1913, it said little about the policy goals the Fed should seek. The closest it came to spelling out the goals of monetary policy was in the first paragraph of the Federal Reserve Act, the legislation that created the Fed:

> An Act To provide for the establishment of Federal reserve banks, to furnish an elastic currency, to afford means of rediscounting commercial paper, to establish a more effective supervision of banking in the United States, and for other purposes.

In short, nothing in the legislation creating the Fed anticipates that the institution will act to close recessionary or inflationary gaps, that it will seek to spur economic growth, or that it will strive to combat inflation. There is no guidance as to what the Fed should do when these goals conflict with one another.

The failure of the Federal Reserve Act to set forth goals of monetary policy can easily be explained. In the context of the times in which the Fed was created, monetary policy as it is understood today was unthinkable. The United States, like most nations at the time, was on a gold standard. Its money supply was thus tied to the quantity of gold. With Federal Reserve notes redeemable in gold at a fixed rate, any attempt by the Fed to expand the money supply beyond the limits of the gold available would quickly lead to depletion of U.S. gold reserves and force a reduction in the money supply.

The Fed was not created with the idea that it would play a central role in setting macroeconomic policy. No goals of macroeconomic performance were specified because no one expected that the Fed would ever be able to pursue such goals.

The Employment Act of 1946

The first official statement of goals for economic performance in the United States came with passage of the Employment Act of 1946. The Great Depression of the 1930s had instilled in people a deep desire to prevent similar calamities in the future. That desire, coupled with the 1936 publication of John Maynard Keynes's recipe for avoiding such problems through monetary and fiscal policy *(The General Theory of Employment, Interest and Money),* led to the passage of legislation declaring economic performance to be a federal responsibility. It declared that it would be:

> the continuing policy and responsibility of the Federal Government to use all practical means . . . to foster . . . the general conditions under which there will be afforded useful employment opportunities, including self-employment, for those able, willing and seeking to work, and to promote maximum employment, production and purchasing power.

The Employment Act thus appears to seek full employment; the objective of obtaining maximum production and purchasing power also implies that the government should seek to promote economic growth. But the Employment Act commits only the federal government, not the Fed, to the goals of full employment and maximum purchasing power. The Fed might be expected to be influenced by this specification of federal goals, but it isn't required to follow any particular path. Further, the legislation doesn't suggest what should be done if the goals of achieving full employment and maximum purchasing power conflict.

The Full Employment and Balanced Growth Act of 1978

The clearest, and most specific, statement of federal economic goals came in the Full Employment and Balanced Growth Act of 1978. This act, generally known as the Humphrey-Hawkins Act, specified that by 1983 the federal government would achieve an unemployment rate among adults of 3 percent or less, a civilian unemployment rate of 4 percent or less, and an inflation rate of 3 percent or less.[2] Although these goals have the virtue of specificity, they offer little in terms of practical policy guidance. The natural unemployment rate is generally thought to be about 6 percent. Trying to maintain the unemployment rate at 4 percent would imply maintaining a permanent inflationary gap—and that would hardly be consistent with the maintenance of an inflation rate of 3 percent or less. The last time the civilian unemployment rate in the United States fell below 4 percent was 1969, and the inflation rate that year was 6.2 percent.

The Humphrey-Hawkins Act requires that the chairperson of the Fed's Board of Governors report twice each year to Congress about the Fed's monetary policy. These sessions provide an opportunity for members of the House and Senate to express their views on monetary policy. As we shall see, there is some evidence that the views expressed at these sessions do influence the Fed's policies. Pleasing members of Congress appears to be one goal of monetary policy.

Federal Reserve Policy and Goals

Perhaps the clearest way to see the Fed's goals is to observe the policy choices it makes. Its actions over the past 15 years suggest that the Fed's primary goal is to keep inflation under control. Provided that the inflation rate falls within acceptable limits, however, the Fed will also undertake stimulative measures to close recessionary gaps.

In 1979, the Fed launched a deliberate program of bringing down the inflation rate. It stuck to that effort through the early 1980s, even in the face of the worst recession since the Great Depression. That effort achieved its goal; the annual inflation rate fell from 13.3 percent in 1979 to 3.8 percent in 1982. The cost, however, was great. Unemployment soared past 9 percent during the recession. With the inflation rate below 4 percent, the Fed shifted to a stimulative policy early in 1983.

In 1990, when the economy slipped into a recession, the Fed engaged in aggressive open-market operations to stimulate the economy, despite the fact that the inflation rate had jumped to 6.1 percent. Much of that increase in the inflation rate, however, resulted from an oil price boost that came in the wake of Iraq's invasion of Kuwait that year. A jump in prices that occurs at the same time as real GDP is slumping suggests an upward shift in short-run aggregate supply, a shift that creates a recessionary gap. Fed officials concluded that the upturn in

[2] Actual performance in 1983 didn't live up to the goals of the act. The unemployment rate among adults that year was 7.9 percent, total civilian unemployment was 9.6 percent, and the inflation rate was 3.8 percent.

inflation in 1990 was a temporary phenomenon and that an expansionary policy was an appropriate response to a weak economy. Once the recovery was clearly under way, the Fed shifted to a neutral policy, seeking neither to boost nor to reduce aggregate demand. Early in 1994, the Fed shifted to a contractionary policy, selling bonds to reduce the money supply and raise interest rates. Fed Chairman Greenspan indicated that the move was intended to head off any possible increase in inflation from its 1993 rate of 2.7 percent. Although the economy was still in a recessionary gap when the Fed acted, Mr. Greenspan indicated that any acceleration of the inflation rate would be unacceptable.

What can we infer from these three episodes? It seems clear that the Fed is determined not to allow the high inflation rates that dominated during the 1970s to occur again. When the inflation rate is within acceptable limits, the Fed will undertake stimulative measures in response to a recessionary gap. Those limits appear to be tightening. By 1994, it appeared that an inflation rate above 3 percent—or any indication that inflation would rise above 3 percent—would lead the Fed to adopt a contractionary policy. If inflation were expected to remain below a 3 percent rate, however, the Fed would undertake stimulative measures to close a recessionary gap.

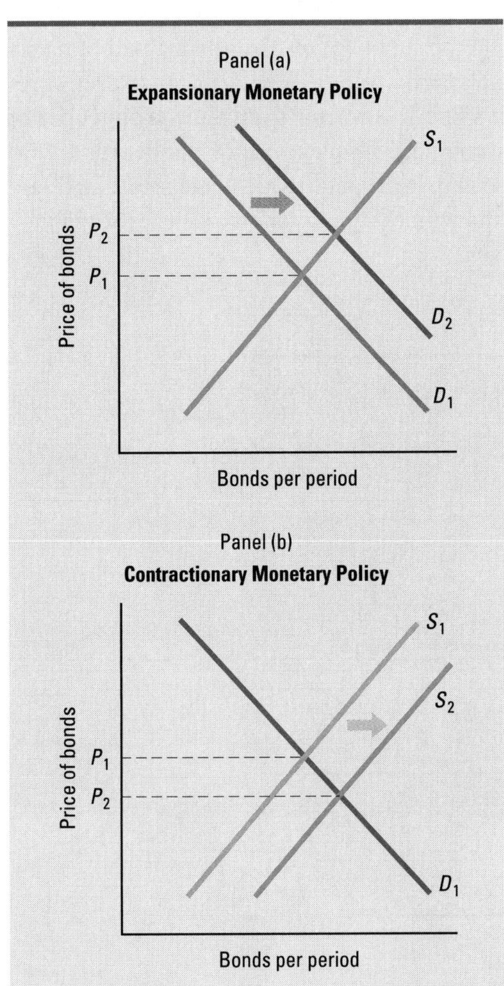

EXHIBIT 30-1

Open-Market Operations and Bond Prices

The Fed can change the money supply and interest rates through open-market operations. Panel (a) shows what happens under an expansionary monetary policy in which the Fed purchases bonds, boosting bond prices and thus lowering interest rates. Panel (b) illustrates a contractionary policy in which the Fed sells bonds, lowering bond prices and thus increasing interest rates.

The Tools of Monetary Policy

We saw in Chapter 24 that the Fed has three tools at its command to try to change aggregate demand and thus to influence the level of economic activity. It can buy or sell federal government securities, it can change the discount rate, or it can change reserve requirements. This section reviews these tools briefly.

Open-Market Operations

The Fed can participate in the bond market by buying or selling federal government securities. A purchase by the Fed of federal securities increases bank reserves. The purchase is made with a check written by the Fed. When the check is deposited in a bank, the bank will return the check to the Fed, which will then credit the bank's deposit account at the Fed. Recall that bank deposits at the Fed are one form of bank reserves. The sale of bonds by the Fed reduces bank reserves. The buyers pay for these bonds with checks written on their bank accounts. On receiving these checks, the Fed simply eliminates reserves in the amounts of the checks for the banks on which the checks are written.

Changes in reserves, in turn, may induce banks to change their volume of loans and thus to change the money supply. An increase in reserves is likely to induce an increase in bank lending and an increase in the money supply. A reduction in reserves will cause banks to reduce their volume of loans outstanding and thus to reduce the money supply. The Fed thus increases the money supply by buying bonds. It reduces the money supply by selling bonds.

Open-market operations affect interest rates as well as the money supply. When the Fed purchases bonds, it increases the demand for them, as illustrated in Panel (a) of Exhibit 30-1. The demand curve for bonds shifts to D_2, raising the price of bonds to P_2. A higher price for bonds lowers the interest rate. Panel (b) shows the impact of a sale of bonds. The supply curve shifts to the right to S_2, driving the price of bonds down to P_2. A lower price for bonds means a higher interest rate. An open-market operation aimed at increasing the money supply would thus tend to reduce interest rates, while a policy to reduce the money supply would increase them.

The Discount Rate

The discount rate is the interest rate the Fed charges on loans of reserves to banks. By lowering the discount rate, the Fed makes it cheaper for banks to borrow money from it. That could, in turn, induce banks to increase their lending and lower their interest rates. An increase in the discount rate raises costs to banks of borrowing from the Fed and could thus cause them to raise their interest rates.

As we saw in Chapter 24, however, changes in the discount rate aren't generally used as a tool of monetary policy. That's because banks have ready access to the federal funds market, a market in which banks lend reserves to one another. The interest rate at which these reserves are lent, typically overnight, is called the federal funds rate. It is determined by the demand for reserves on the part of banks that want to borrow and the supply of reserves on the part of banks that want to lend. A typical large bank participates as a lender or borrower of reserves several times each day, but it's likely to borrow from the Fed only once or twice per year. Indeed, the Fed discourages frequent use of the discount window—the name given to the mechanism through which loans to banks are made. It encourages banks to use "the window" only for emergencies when they have a temporary shortfall of reserves.

EXHIBIT 30-2

The Discount and Federal Funds Rate

The Fed has kept the discount rate close to the federal funds rate. The chart shows monthly averages of the federal funds rate (orange line) and values of the discount rate (black line) set by the Fed from 1990 to 1995.

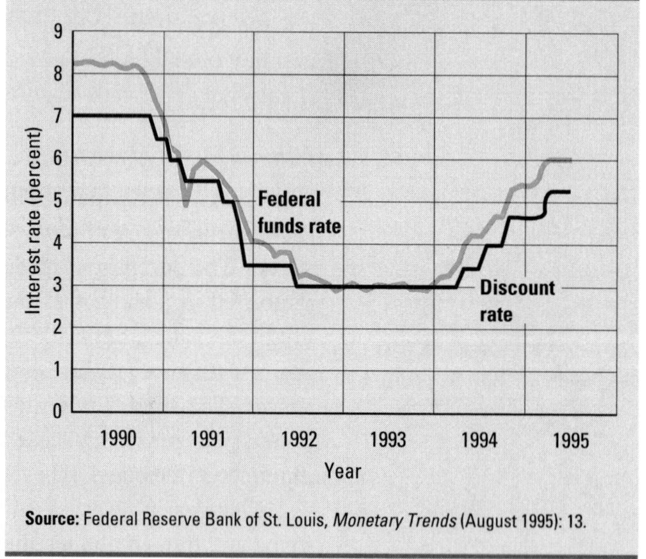

Source: Federal Reserve Bank of St. Louis, *Monetary Trends* (August 1995): 13.

Although the discount rate does not have a great deal of importance as a tool of monetary policy, the Fed does appear to use it to signal goals in open-market operations. These operations affect the federal funds rate directly. When the Fed buys bonds, it injects reserves into the banking system, increasing the supply of reserves in the federal funds market and lowering the federal funds rate. When the Fed sells bonds, it reduces the quantity of reserves and thus the supply of reserves in the federal funds market, pushing the rate up. Exhibit 30-2 shows monthly values of the discount and federal funds rates from 1990 through the first half of 1995. The Fed has often adjusted the discount rate and then used open-market operations to adjust the federal funds rate to a level close to the discount rate.

Case in Point — Fed Pulls Out Big Guns in Recession Battle

The Fed used every weapon in its command as it battled the 1990–1991 recession. It bought federal securities, made repeated cuts in the discount rate, and lowered reserve requirements. But the Fed's actions didn't suggest that all three tools have become regular instruments of monetary policy.

When it recognized in the fall of 1990 that the economy was slipping into a recession, the Fed acted immediately to inject new reserves into the system. Its purchase of federal securities helped to push the federal funds rate down. Only then did the Fed begin to lower the discount rate.

When the Fed announced in 1990 that it was changing reserve requirements, it made clear that the purpose of the change was to increase bank profits. With lower reserve requirements, a bank can shift its deposits at the Fed or its vault cash, neither of which earn interest, into interest-earning loans. The Fed stressed that it would take any measures necessary to prevent a change in reserve requirements from increasing the money supply beyond the Fed's own target.

The Fed may have pulled out all the weapons at its command, but open-market operations clearly took center stage. Cuts in the discount rate merely kept pace with falling interest rates generally. And cuts in reserve requirements were undertaken not to provide economic stimulus but to limit bank failure.

Alan Greenspan.

Reserve Requirements

The Fed's ability to set reserve requirements is a potentially powerful tool of monetary policy. A reduction in the reserve requirement instantly creates additional excess reserves, which could induce banks to increase their lending. An increase in reserve requirements could put banks in a position of having insufficient reserves and thus force them to reduce their volume of loans outstanding.

Although changes in reserve requirements would be a powerful tool, it's not one the Fed typically uses. Frequent changes in reserve requirements would make bank management more difficult. It would be like changing the size of a basketball court during a game. Recall that one reason the Fed was established was to facilitate commerce, not to make commerce more difficult.

Problems in the Implementation of Monetary Policy

The Fed has some obvious advantages in its conduct of monetary policy. The two policy-making bodies, the Board of Governors and the Federal Open Market Committee (FOMC), are small and largely independent from other political institutions. These panels can thus reach decisions quickly and implement them immediately. Their relative independence from the political process, together with the fact that they meet in secret, allows them to operate outside the glare of publicity that might otherwise be focused on bodies that wield such enormous power.

Despite the apparent ease with which the Fed can conduct monetary policy, it still faces difficulties in its efforts to stabilize the economy. These include the problems of lags in carrying out monetary policy, the choice of targets, and political pressures.

Lags

Perhaps the most important difficulty facing the Fed, or any other central bank, is the problem of lags. It's easy enough to show a recessionary gap on a graph and then to show how monetary policy can shift aggregate demand and close the gap. In the real world, however, it may take several months before anyone even realizes that a particular macroeconomic problem is occurring. When monetary authorities become aware of a problem, they can act quickly to inject reserves into the system or to withdraw reserves from it. Once that's done, however, it may be a year or more before the action affects aggregate demand.

The lag in realizing that a macroeconomic problem exists is called a **recognition lag.** It is a lag between the time something happens in the economy and the time at which policymakers become aware of it. The 1990–1991 recession, for example, began in July 1990. It was not until late October that members of the FOMC took note of a slowing in economic activity that required a stimulative monetary policy.

Recognition lags largely stem from problems of economic data. First, data are available only after the conclusion of a particular period. Preliminary estimates of real GDP, for example, are released about a month after the end of a quarter. Thus, a change that occurs early in a quarter won't be reflected in the data until several months later. Second, estimates of economic indicators are often subject to revision. The first estimates of real GDP in the third quarter of 1990, for example, showed it increasing. Not until several months had passed did revised estimates show that a recession had begun. And finally, different indicators can lead to different interpretations. Data on employment and retail sales might be pointing in one direction while data on housing starts and industrial production might be pointing in another. It's one thing to look back after a few years have elapsed and determine whether the economy was expanding or contracting. It's quite another to determine the course of economic activity when one is right in the middle of events. Even in a world brimming with computer-generated data on the economy, recognition lags can be substantial.

Only after a problem in the economy is recognized can action be taken to deal with it. The time required from the point at which a problem is recognized to the point at which a policy is put in place to deal with it is called the **implementation lag.** For monetary policy changes, the implementation lag is quite short. The FOMC meets eight times per year, and its members may confer between meetings through conference calls. Once the FOMC determines that a policy change is in order, the required open-market operations to buy or sell government bonds can be put into effect immediately.

Policymakers at the Fed still have to contend with the lag between the time at which a policy is put in place and the time that policy affects the economy. This lag is called the **impact lag.**

- A **recognition lag** is the delay between the time at which an event occurs and the time at which policymakers become aware of it.
- An **implementation lag** is the delay between the time at which a problem is recognized and the time at which a policy to deal with it is enacted.
- An **impact lag** is the lag between the time a policy goes into effect and the time the policy has its impact on the economy.

The impact lag for monetary policy occurs for several reasons. First, it takes some time for the money multiplier process to work itself out. The Fed can inject new reserves into the economy immediately, but the deposit expansion process of bank lending will need time to have its full effect on the money supply. Interest rates are affected immediately, but the money supply grows more slowly. Second, firms need some time to respond to the monetary policy with new investment—if they respond at all. A monetary change is likely to affect the exchange rate, but that translates into a change in net exports only after some delay. There will thus be a delay in the shift in aggregate expenditures that the

Case in Point

The Lag Outlasts George Bush

The slump that was to help turn George Bush into a one-term president began in July 1990. By October, the Fed had recognized the problem and had put an expansionary monetary policy in place. Interest rates had begun heading downward. All that was left was for the economy to respond.

The response came quickly enough. Economic activity turned upward, ending the recession, by the second quarter of 1991. But the upturn was extremely weak as business investment continued to fall. From the time the recovery began through the third quarter of 1992, the eve of the presidential election, real GDP increased at only a 2.3 percent annual rate. The economy was growing more slowly than its natural level, so the recessionary gap was widening even as economic activity was expanding; unemployment continued to rise during the first year of recovery. Although a recovery was under way by the official measure, it seemed to many that the economy was still in a recession. Poor economic performance under Mr. Bush became the central issue during the campaign. Promises by Bill Clinton to "grow this economy" struck a responsive chord.

Business investment finally began to respond to the Fed's expansionary monetary policy in the first quarter of 1992, more than a year after the Fed had begun to act. Investment increased slowly in 1992, then began to surge in 1993. Would Mr. Bush have won reelection if the lag had been shorter, if a recovery had been more obviously in place well before the 1992 election? It's a fascinating question, one that Mr. Bush probably ponders often.

President George Bush conceding defeat after the November 1992 elections.

monetary change produces. Third, the multiplier process of an expenditure change will require time to unfold.

Estimates of the length of time required for the impact lag to work itself out range from 6 months to 2 years. Worse, the length of the lag can vary—when they take action, policymakers can't know whether their choices will affect the economy within a few months or within a few years. Because of the uncertain length of the impact lag, efforts to stabilize the economy through monetary policy could be destabilizing. Suppose, for example, that the Fed responds to a recessionary gap with an expansionary policy, but that by the time the policy begins to affect aggregate demand the economy has already returned to its natural level. The policy designed to correct a recessionary gap could create an inflationary gap. Similarly, a shift to a contractionary policy in response to an inflationary gap might not affect aggregate demand until a self-correction process had already closed the gap. In that case, the policy could plunge the economy into a recession.

The problem of lags suggests that monetary policy should respond not to statistical reports of economic conditions in the recent past, but to conditions expected to exist in the future. In justifying the imposition of a contractionary monetary policy early in 1994, when the economy still had a recessionary gap, Mr. Greenspan indicated that the Fed expected a 1-year impact lag. The policy initiated in 1994 was a response not to the economic conditions thought to exist at the time, but to conditions expected to exist in 1995. The Fed expected the

Case in Point: The Fed Administers an Anticipatory Jolt to the Economy

It was a historic, if dry, press release: "Chairman Alan Greenspan announced today that the Federal Open Market Committee (FOMC) decided to increase slightly the degree of pressure on reserve positions." That meant that the Fed was selling bonds to reduce bank reserves and reduce the money supply. The announcement rocked world financial markets. Interest rates, which had been headed down, suddenly turned upward. The federal funds rate rose to 3.25 percent from its previous level of about 3 percent.

The announcement was historic for three reasons. The first was that it was made at all. Chairman Greenspan was quoting from the policy directive the FOMC had just approved. In the past, the results of an FOMC meeting weren't made public until about 6 weeks after the meeting. The decision to release the results immediately was made, Mr. Greenspan said, to "avoid any misunderstanding" of the reasons for the action.

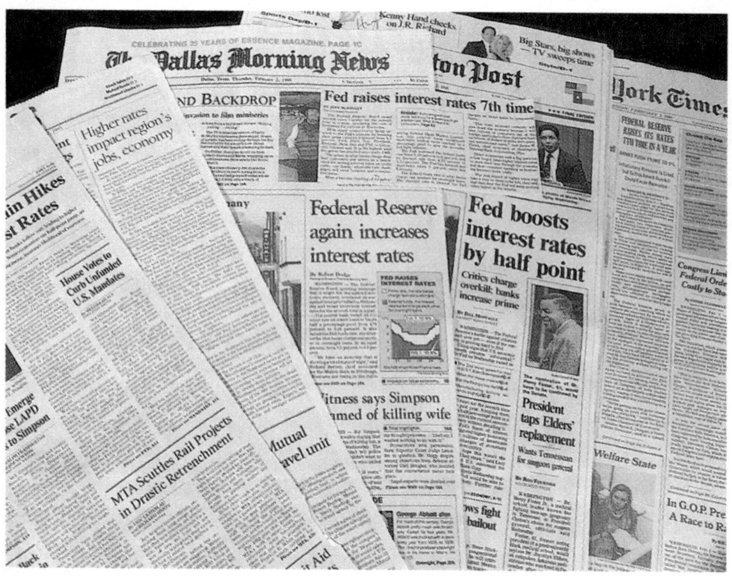

The announcement was also significant because it represented a reversal of earlier policy. Monetary policy had been sharply expansionary beginning the fall of 1990, when the Fed began an effort to close the recessionary gap that had been created by the 1990–1991 recession. Once the recovery was under way, the Fed had shifted into neutral—neither reducing nor increasing interest rates. The Fed's shift to a contractionary policy marked a major development.

But the most remarkable aspect of the Fed's action was its timing. It came as the economy was in a recessionary gap—the unemployment rate for the previous month had just been released as the FOMC began its deliberations. At 6.7 percent, it was well above the economy's natural rate.

Why would the Fed respond to a recessionary gap with a contractionary policy? In fact, the Fed expected strong growth in the remainder of 1994—growth at a rate that would exceed the rate at which the economy's natural level of real GDP would rise. That growth would close the recessionary gap, and it threatened to open an inflationary gap within a year. Mr. Greenspan noted in subsequent remarks that there was a lag of at least a year between the time the Fed took action and the time such actions began to affect economic activity. The measure was a response not to the economic conditions that prevailed when it was taken—but to conditions expected to prevail a year or more hence.

The Fed's action reduced the money supply—M2 fell by about $4 billion in February. It was the first of several interventions by the Fed during the next year. By the following February, the federal funds rate had been pushed up to 5.75 percent—and there were signs that the expansion was beginning to slow.

Sources: Federal Reserve press release, February 4, 1994; and Federal Reserve, "Minutes of the Federal Open Market Committee Meeting Held on February 3–4, 1994," mimeo, 25 March 1994.

economy to be nearly at its natural level by 1995, so inflation, not unemployment, was the central bank's chief concern.

The Fed's attempt to anticipate future conditions in designing monetary policy illustrates the difficulty lags create for macroeconomic policy. The track record of economists in forecasting future economic activity is mixed. Forecasts come reasonably close to what actually happens in the macroeconomy, but economists have a poor record at anticipating turning points in economic activity. And it is those turning points that the Fed would have to anticipate in order to design an appropriate macroeconomic policy.

Targeting Choices

In attempting to manage the economy, on what macroeconomic variables should the Fed base its policies? It must have some target, or set of targets, that it wants to achieve. The failure of the economy to achieve one of the Fed's targets would then trigger a shift in monetary policy. The choice of a target, or set of targets, is a crucial one for monetary policy.

Interest Rates. Interest rates, particularly the federal funds rate, play a key role in present Fed policy. The FOMC doesn't decide to increase or decrease the money supply. Rather, it instructs the trading desk at the New York Federal Reserve Bank to conduct open-market operations in a way that will either maintain, increase, or ease the current "degree of pressure" on the reserve positions of banks. That degree of pressure is reflected by the federal funds rate; if existing reserves are less than the amount banks would like to hold, then the bidding for the available supply will send the federal funds rate up. If reserves are plentiful, then the federal funds rate will tend to decline. When the Fed increases the degree of pressure on reserves, it sells bonds, thus reducing the supply of reserves and increasing the federal funds rate. The Fed decreases the degree of pressure on reserves by buying bonds, thus injecting new reserves into the system and reducing the federal funds rate.

The current operating procedures of the Fed, then, focus on interest rates. When the Fed wishes to stimulate economic activity, it buys bonds to push interest rates down. When it wishes to slow the pace of economic activity, it sells bonds to drive interest rates up.

Money Growth Rates. The Fed is required by law to announce to Congress at the beginning of each year its target for money growth that year. In announcing these targets, the Fed typically sets a broad range of growth rates. Having established broad targets, the Fed often fails to hit them. Exhibit 30-3 shows the Fed's targets and actual M2 growth in 1993, 1994, and 1995. When money growth slipped below the target in 1993, the Fed simply lowered the growth target to a range of 1 to 5 percent; that remained its target range in 1994 and 1995.

Officials at the Fed ascribe this consistent missing of targets to difficulties inherent in controlling the money supply itself. After all, the Fed controls only the quantity of reserves. The relationship between those reserves and what

EXHIBIT 30-3

Targets and Money Growth, 1993–1995

The cones (in color) give the Fed's target ranges for 1993, 1994, and the first half of 1995. The maroon line shows actual values of M2. The target range for any one year is for growth in M2 from its value in the fourth quarter of the previous year to the fourth quarter of that year. The Fed's target range in each of the last three years has been for M2 to grow at a rate between 1 and 5 percent. The original target for 1993 was a 2 to 6 percent range, shown by the lines labeled 2 and 6 in the graph. With M2 falling below that target, the Fed in July of 1993 announced that it was adjusting its target downward to the 1 to 5 percent range. M2 was close to the bottom of the target ranges in 1993 and 1994; it was near the upper limit of the range in the first half of 1995.

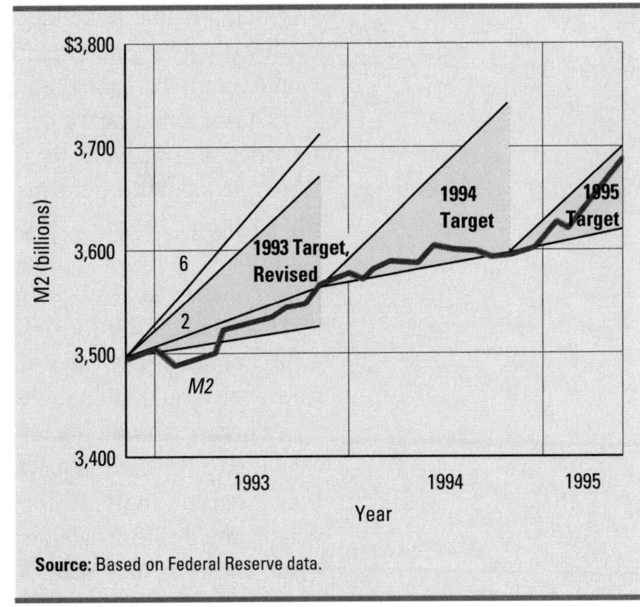

actually happens to the money supply depends on the choices made by banks and their customers. Critics of the Fed, especially monetarists, counter that the Fed could hit its targets if it wanted to; they say the fact that it has missed its targets is evidence that the Fed hasn't attached a high priority to achieving them.

An alternative approach would be for the Fed to target reserve growth. Monetarists generally argue that a stable rate of reserve growth would improve economic performance in the same way that a stable rate of money growth would.

Nominal GDP. Some economists argue that the Fed should target nominal GDP—current output valued at current prices. The Fed might, for example, seek a growth rate in nominal GDP consistent with the economy's long-run capacity to grow and with the Fed's goal for the rate of increase in the price level. If natural real GDP is growing at a rate of 2.5 percent per year and the Fed seeks an inflation rate of 2 percent per year, it could aim for a 4.5 percent growth rate in nominal GDP. If nominal GDP growth were to dip below this goal, the Fed could accelerate money growth. If GDP growth were to rise above this goal, the Fed could slow money growth.

The difficulty with using a nominal GDP target lies in the lags discussed above. The Fed's policies, reacting to a report of a prior change in nominal GDP, would affect the economy only after the impact lag. Adjusting money growth based on previous changes in nominal GDP could be destabilizing.

An alternative approach has been suggested by Northwestern University's Robert Gordon, a leading new Keynesian economist. Mr. Gordon suggests that the Fed could develop a four-quarter forecasting model of the economy. When the model pointed to trouble coming in a year, the Fed could take immediate action. If, for example, the model suggested that a slump in aggregate demand was ahead, the Fed could accelerate money growth. Such an approach could stabilize the economy, provided the model gave accurate signals of future economic change.

Prices. Many economists think the Fed should target a key price or set of prices. These economists argue that the Fed's primary goal should be price stability. If it is, though, what indicator of prices should the Fed target?

One possible price target would be gold. The Fed could seek to adjust the money supply so that the price of gold remained stable. In effect, such a policy would return the United States to a gold standard.

During inflationary periods the price of gold tends to rise sharply. Indeed, the price of gold typically rises if people *expect* inflation to increase. If the Fed were seeking to keep the price of gold constant, it would reduce the money supply whenever the price of gold was rising and increase the money supply when the price of gold was falling. Mr. Greenspan has indicated that the Fed does indeed consider gold prices in setting its policies. He cited rising gold prices in 1993 as one reason for the Fed's shift to a contractionary policy in 1994. The jump in gold prices, he said, suggested that inflation might accelerate in the future, even though inflation was falling when contractionary policy was imposed.

Another possible target is the price level itself. The Fed could target a particular price level, or a particular rate of change in the price level, and adjust its policies accordingly. If, for example, the Fed sought an inflation rate of 2 percent, it could shift to a contractionary policy whenever the rate rose above 2 percent. The difficulty with such a policy, of course, is that the Fed would be responding to past economic conditions with policies that aren't likely to affect the economy for a year or more.

Political Pressures

The institutional relationship between the leaders of the Fed and the executive and legislative branches of the federal government is structured to provide for the Fed's independence. Members of the Board of Governors are appointed by the president, with confirmation by the Senate, but the 14-year terms of office provide a considerable degree of insulation from political pressure. A president exercises greater influence in the choice of the chairman of the Board of Governors; that appointment carries a 4-year term. Neither the president nor Congress has any direct say over the selection of the presidents of Federal Reserve district banks. They're chosen by their individual boards of directors with approval of the Board of Governors.

While the Fed is formally insulated from the political process, the men and women who serve on the Board of Governors and the FOMC are human beings. They are thus not immune to the pressures that can be placed on them by members of Congress and by the president. The chairman of the Board of Governors meets regularly with the president and the executive staff and also reports to and meets with congressional committees that deal with economic matters.

The Fed was created by the Congress; its charter could be altered—or even revoked—by that same body. The Fed is in the somewhat paradoxical situation that to preserve its independence, it must cooperate with the legislative and executive branches. As economist Thomas Mayer of the University of California at Davis once said, "The Fed preserves its independence by running away from fights."

One theory of the way in which politics may affect Fed policies was proposed by Yale University economist William D. Nordhaus in 1975.[3] A president, he argued, is likely to pressure the Fed to accelerate money growth prior to a presidential election in order to stimulate growth in nominal GDP. That would, in turn, increase the reelection prospects of the incumbent—or the election prospects of a candidate from the president's own party. Nordhaus's theory seemed consistent with the Fed's policies in 1971 and 1972—the two years leading into President Richard Nixon's landslide reelection in November 1972. The Fed doubled the rate of money growth in those two years, then cut it by half in 1973. The Fed did the same thing at the end of President Gerald Ford's term in 1975 and 1976, but Mr. Ford failed in his reelection bid.

The Nordhaus theory seems to break down after that. The Fed didn't accelerate money growth at the end of Jimmy Carter's first term. It increased money growth in 1983, but then slowed it sharply in 1984, the year Ronald Reagan successfully sought reelection. There was no acceleration in money growth leading up to the presidential elections of 1988 (when George Bush won) or 1992 (when Bill Clinton defeated Mr. Bush). The evidence shows no consistent pattern of Fed policy as it relates to election years.

Another test of presidential influence on the Fed was developed by the Duke University economist Thomas Havrilesky, who analyzed press reports of

[3] William D. Nordhaus, "The Political Business Cycle," *Review of Economic Studies* 42(2) (April 1975): 169–190.

Checklist

- Congress has spelled out macroeconomic goals in various pieces of legislation, but it has not required the Fed to pursue these goals, nor has it specified what should be done when the pursuit of one goal conflicts with pursuit of another.
- In practice, the Fed's primary goal appears to be to hold the inflation rate down. Only when inflation is under control will the Fed act to stimulate the economy in the face of a recessionary gap.
- Although the Fed could use open-market operations, changes in the discount rate, and reserve requirement changes to influence aggregate demand, it generally relies only on open-market operations for this purpose. Changes in the discount rate or in reserve requirements are generally carried out for other reasons.
- Monetary policy is complicated by the existence of recognition, implementation, and impact lags.
- The Fed could target growth in nominal GDP, prices of specific commodities, interest rates, or money growth in conducting monetary policy. In practice, it appears to focus on interest rates, especially the federal funds rate.
- Although the Fed is nominally independent of the political process, some evidence suggests that it often bows to political pressure in selecting its monetary policies.

statements by administration officials concerning monetary policy.[4] He found that calls for a change in monetary policy by White House officials did affect money growth and the federal funds rate about 3 weeks later. Mr. Havrilesky also found that concerns expressed by senators to the chairman of the Federal Reserve Board at one of the biannual hearings on monetary policy tended to influence Fed policies in the month before the next hearing. He concluded that the Fed does pay attention to political pressure.

Interpreting the Impact of Monetary Policy

Most economists agree that monetary policy affects the level of economic activity, but they sometimes disagree on the precise mechanisms through which this occurs and on the ways in which monetary policy should be used. Before we address some of these issues, we shall review the ways in which monetary policy affects the economy in the context of the model we've developed.

Monetary Policy and Economic Activity

The model of aggregate demand and aggregate supply, together with demand and supply models for key sectors in the economy and the investment demand curve, gives us the parts of the monetary puzzle. This section reviews briefly how these parts fit together. Our focus will be on open-market operations, the purchase or sale by the Fed of federal securities.

Expansionary Monetary Policy

An expansionary monetary policy would be pursued in response to the initial situation shown in Panel (a) of Exhibit 30-4. An economy with a natural level of real GDP of Y_n is operating at Y_1; there is a recessionary gap. One possible policy response is to allow the economy to correct this gap on its own, waiting for reductions in nominal wages and other prices to shift the short-run aggregate supply curve $SRAS_1$ downward until it intersects the aggregate demand curve AD_1 at Y_n. An alternative is a stabilization policy that seeks to increase aggregate demand to AD_2 to close the gap. An expansionary monetary policy is one tool that could achieve such a shift.

To carry out an expansionary monetary policy, the Fed will buy bonds. That shifts the demand curve for bonds to D_2, as illustrated in Panel (b). Bond prices rise to P_2. The higher price for bonds reduces the interest rate to r_2, causing a movement along the investment demand curve and increasing investment to I_2 in Panel (c). Finally, the lower interest rate reduces the demand for and increases the supply of dollars in the currency market, reducing the exchange rate to E_2 in Panel (d). The lower exchange rate will stimulate net exports. The combined impact of greater net exports and greater investment will shift the aggregate demand curve to the right. The curve shifts by an amount equal to the multiplier times the sum of the change in net exports and the change in investment. In Panel (a), this is shown as a shift to AD_2, and the recessionary gap is closed.

We've seen that the Fed instituted an expansionary policy in response to the recession of 1990–1991. The policy succeeded in boosting investment and it

[4] Thomas Havrilesky, "Monetary Policy Signalling from the Administration to the Federal Reserve," *Journal of Money, Credit and Banking* 20(1)(February 1988):83–101. See also "Politicians Find Ways to Influence Fed Policy," *The Margin* 7 (Spring 1992): 18–19, by the same author.

EXHIBIT 30-4

An Expansionary Policy to Close a Recessionary Gap

In Panel (a), the economy has a recessionary gap $Y_n - Y_1$. An expansionary monetary policy could seek to close this gap by shifting the aggregate demand curve to AD_2. In Panel (b), the Fed buys bonds, shifting the demand curve for bonds to D_2 and increasing the price of bonds to P_2. The higher price of bonds means a lower interest rate, r_2, which increases investment to I_2 in Panel (c). The lower interest rate also reduces the demand and increases the supply of dollars, reducing the exchange rate to E_2 in Panel (d), which will increase net exports. The increase in investment and in net exports are responsible for increasing aggregate demand in Panel (a).

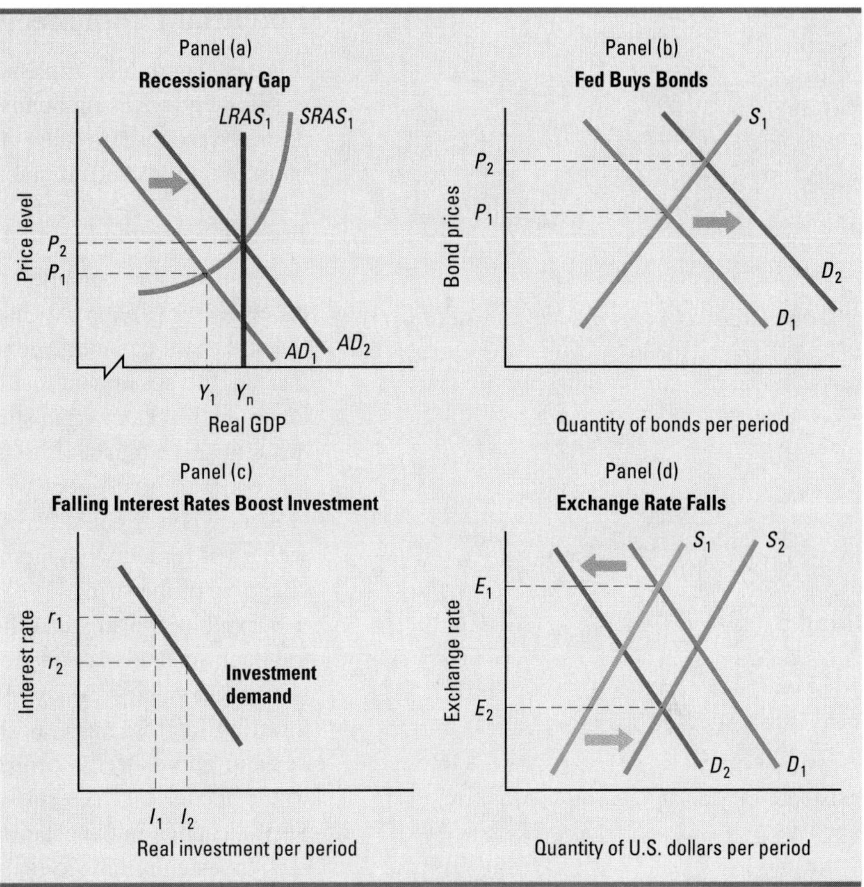

ultimately helped bring on a recovery. Investment began showing dramatic gains in 1993.

A Contractionary Monetary Policy

The Fed will generally select a contractionary monetary policy when it considers inflation a threat. Suppose, for example, that the economy faces an inflationary gap; the aggregate demand and short-run aggregate supply curves intersect to the right of the long-run aggregate supply curve.

To carry out a contractionary policy, the Fed sells bonds. The effects are the opposite of those illustrated in Exhibit 30-4. In the bond market, the supply curve shifts to the right, lowering the price of bonds and increasing the interest rate. That reduces the level of investment. The higher interest rate also induces a greater demand for dollars as foreigners seek to take advantage of higher interest rates in the United States. The supply of dollars falls; people in the United States are less likely to purchase foreign interest-earning assets now that U.S. assets are paying a higher rate. These changes boost the exchange rate, which reduces exports and increases imports and thus causes net exports to fall. The contractionary monetary policy thus reduces aggregate demand; the curve shifts to the left by an amount equal to the multiplier times the combined changes in net exports and investment.

The contractionary policy initiated by the Fed early in 1994 typifies this kind of policy. The Fed undertook the policy, fearing that the economy was close to heading into an inflationary gap. The result was higher interest rates, which the Fed hoped would weaken aggregate demand.

Potential Problems with Monetary Policy

It is easy enough to implement monetary policy: FOMC can order the purchase or sale of government bonds. There may, however, be problems in achieving the desired response to such policies. Expansionary monetary policies may not boost real GDP, and contractionary policies may not reduce it.

Investment Demand and Monetary Policy

We've noted the potentially volatile nature of investment demand. Investment depends crucially on expectations about the future; business leaders must be optimistic about economic conditions. That optimism may not exist in a recession. Instead, the pessimism that may prevail during an economic slump can prevent lower interest rates from stimulating an increase in investment. The investment demand curve may shift to the left by so much that even with a reduction in the interest rate, investment will fall. An effort to stimulate the economy through monetary policy could be like pushing on a string. The central bank could push with great force by buying bonds, but little might happen to the economy at the other end of the string.

Exhibit 30-5 suggests the possible problem with investment. Suppose a central bank such as the Fed seeks to increase aggregate demand through an expansionary monetary policy. It buys bonds, pushing up bond prices and thus lowering interest rates, as shown in Panel (a). Panel (b) shows the investment demand curve. If the original curve ID_1 remained in place, then investment would increase to I_2. But suppose business leaders become more pessimistic. Such a change in expectations shifts the investment demand curve to the left to ID_2. Investment falls to I_3, despite the lower interest rate.

EXHIBIT 30-5

A Change in Investment Demand Can Thwart Monetary Policy

Suppose a central bank wishes to expand aggregate demand. It purchases bonds, raising the price of bonds and thus lowering interest rates, as shown in Panel (a). A lower interest rate r_2 increases investment to I_2 if the investment demand curve stays put. In Panel (b), however, a shift of investment demand to the left to ID_2 reduces investment to I_3, even at the lower interest rate r_2.

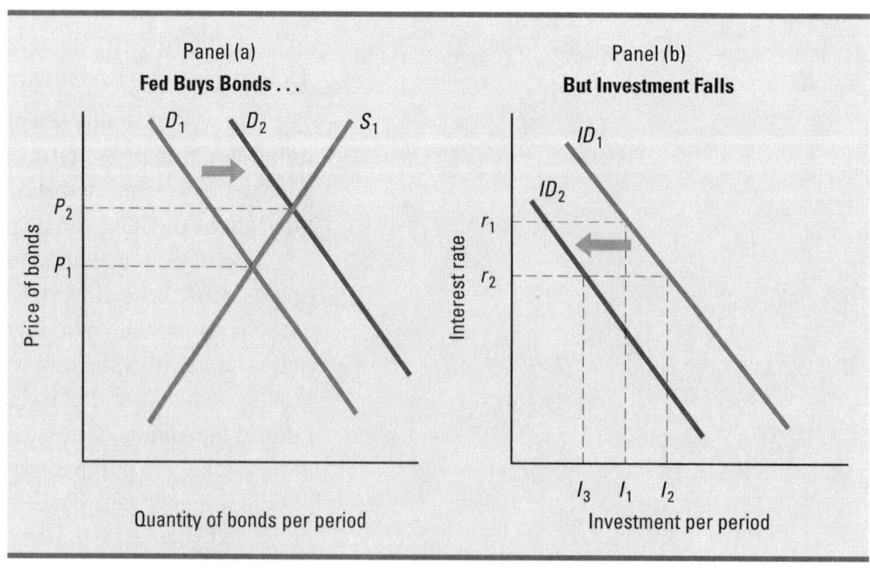

Similarly, an effort by the Fed to reduce aggregate demand in the face of an inflationary gap could be thwarted by rising investment demand. If the investment demand curve is shifting to the right at the same time as the Fed is boosting interest rates, higher rates could fail to reduce investment.

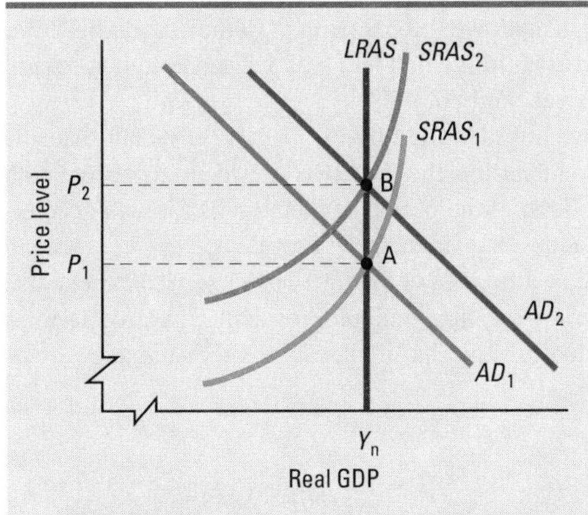

EXHIBIT 30-6

Monetary Policy and Rational Expectations

Suppose the economy is operating at point A and that individuals have rational expectations. They calculate that an expansionary monetary policy undertaken at price level P_1 will raise prices to P_2. They adjust their expectations—and wage demands—accordingly, shifting the short-run aggregate supply curve to $SRAS_2$ The result is a movement along the long-run aggregate supply curve *LRAS* to point B, with no change in real GDP.

Rational Expectations and Monetary Policy

The rational expectations hypothesis suggests an important problem for monetary policy. The hypothesis is that people use all available information to make forecasts about future economic activity and the price level, and that they adjust their behavior to these forecasts. We've seen that the rational expectations argument is one tenet of new classical economics; it suggests that monetary policy may affect the price level but not real GDP.

Exhibit 30-6 uses the model of aggregate demand and aggregate supply to suggest the implications of the rational expectations argument for monetary policy. Suppose the economy is at Y_n, as illustrated by point A. An increase in the money supply boosts aggregate demand to AD_2. In the analysis we have explored thus far, that would move the economy to a higher level of real GDP and create an inflationary gap. That, in turn, would put upward pressure on wages and other prices, shifting the short-run aggregate supply curve upward to $SRAS_2$ and moving the economy to point B, closing the inflationary gap. The rational expectations hypothesis, however, suggests a quite different interpretation.

Suppose people observe the initial monetary policy change undertaken when the economy is at point A and calculate that the increase in the money supply will ultimately drive the price level up to point B. Anticipating this change in prices, people adjust their behavior. For example, if the increase in the price level from P_1 to P_2 is a 10 percent change, workers will anticipate that the prices they pay will rise 10 percent and they will demand 10 percent higher wages. Their employers, anticipating that the prices they'll receive will also rise, will agree to pay those higher wages. As nominal wages increase, the short-run aggregate supply curve shifts upward to $SRAS_2$. The result is an upward movement along the long-run aggregate supply curve *LRAS.* There is no change in real GDP. The monetary policy has no effect, other than its impact on the price level. This rational expectations argument relies on another plank in the new classical platform: wages and prices must be sufficiently flexible that the change in expectations will allow the short-run aggregate supply curve to shift to $SRAS_2$.

One important implication of the rational expectations argument is that a contractionary monetary policy could be painless. Suppose the economy is at point B and the Fed reduces the money supply in order to shift the aggregate demand curve back to AD_1. In the model of aggregate demand and aggregate supply, the result would be a recession. But in a rational expectations world, people's expectations change, the short-run aggregate supply adjusts downward, and the economy moves painlessly down its long-run aggregate supply curve *LRAS* to point A.

Proponents of the rational expectations hypothesis argue that a change in monetary policy will affect real GDP only if it takes people by surprise. Suppose, for example, that the Fed carries out the expansionary monetary policy depicted in Exhibit 30-6, but that almost no one is aware of it. In that case, aggregate demand would shift to AD_2. Because no one knows the Fed has acted, there will be no change in price-level expectations. Short-run aggregate supply won't shift, and the real level of real GDP will rise, creating an inflationary gap. The gap will ultimately be closed as wages rise and short-run aggregate supply shifts upward to $SRAS_2$. But in the short run, the monetary policy will have affected real GDP. Some economists argue that such surprises are not unlikely. Federal reserve officials may, for example, announce that they are carrying out policies to maintain price stability while they actually increase the money supply quite rapidly. If people pay attention to public pronouncements rather than to

Case in Point: Presidential Elections and Monetary Surprises

Economists Jeffrey Sachs and Alberto Alesina, of Harvard and Carnegie-Mellon Universities, respectively, have proposed an intriguing test of two ideas: the notion that the Fed accommodates the policy preferences of presidents, and the rational expectations hypothesis.

An expected change in monetary policy would have no effect if rational expectations hold. People anticipate the effects of such policy and adjust their expectations accordingly, and the short-run aggregate supply curve shifts in a way that cancels the impact of the policy. But Professors Sachs and Alesina note that at the time of a presidential election, things will be different. During the year of the campaign itself, people won't know who will be elected. The next president will be either a Democrat, who is likely to seek—and get—a more stimulative monetary policy, or a Republican, who is likely to seek—and get—a more conservative policy. Many wage and price commitments will be made during the election year that will carry over to the following year. But people don't know what monetary policy will be because they don't know which candidate will be elected.

Suppose people resolve the difficulty by taking the average consequences of the two sets of possible monetary policies. Whichever candidate is elected, monetary policy will come as a surprise in the sense that it doesn't match the average policy to which people adjusted. Suppose in particular that a Democrat would shift aggregate demand to AD_{Dem} in the accompanying graph and that a Republican would leave aggregate demand unchanged at AD_{Rep}. If the aggregate supply curve shifts upward to $AS_{average}$ to capture the average impact of the two possible presidents, then real GDP will increase early in a Democrat's term and will tend to fall early in a Republican's term. Once the winner is known, people can adjust their expectations for decisions that affect the latter part of a president's term. The adjustment should reduce real GDP in the latter part of a Democratic president's term and increase it in the latter part of a Republican president's term.

Sachs and Alesina looked at real GDP growth in the first versus the second half of Democratic and Republican presidential terms from 1949 to 1984. They found that the pattern of real GDP growth was consistent with a rational expectations model. Annual growth in the first half of Democratic administrations was 5 percent, then slowed to 3.9 percent in the second half. For Republicans, growth in the first half was 1.2 percent, then rose to 4 percent in the second half.

The relationship identified by Professors Sachs and Alesina continued to hold during the first two presidential terms (both Republican) following the period of their study. Growth accelerated sharply in the second half of President Reagan's second term and in the second half of George Bush's term. Growth also accelerated during the first half of President Clinton's term—and was expected to slow sharply during the second half.

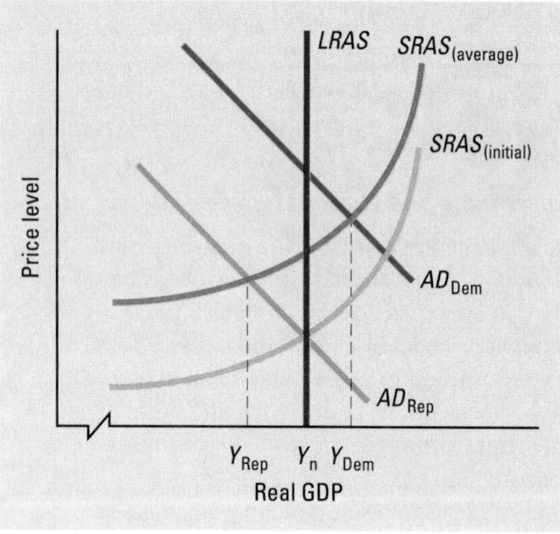

Source: Alberto Alesina and Jeffrey Sachs, "Political Parties and the Business Cycle in the United States, 1948–1984," *Journal of Money, Credit, and Banking* 20(1) (February 1988): 63–82.

actual money supply data, they might be fooled. Only if people are fooled will monetary policy affect real GDP. If changes in the money supply affect real GDP only when they take people by surprise, predicting the impact of monetary policy becomes all the more difficult. For new classical economists, that makes it all the more important that monetary policy not be used as a tool of stabilization policy.

Support for the rational expectations hypothesis was weakened by the Fed's effort to control inflation that began in 1979. As we've seen, President Jimmy Carter appointed Paul Volcker that year as chairman and pledged his full support for whatever the Fed might do to contain inflation. Mr. Volcker made clear that the Fed was going to slow money growth and boost interest rates. He acknowledged that this policy would have costs but said that the Fed would stick to it as long as necessary to control inflation. Here was a monetary policy that was clearly announced and carried out as advertised. It's hard to imagine it took any-

Checklist

- An expansionary monetary policy is one in which the central bank purchases bonds. That drives down interest rates, boosts investment, and increases net exports. A contractionary monetary policy does the opposite.
- Falling investment demand could prevent an expansionary monetary policy from stimulating economic activity in the face of a recessionary gap.
- Rising investment demand could prevent a contractionary policy from reducing aggregate demand in the face of an inflationary gap.
- The rational expectations hypothesis suggests that changes in monetary policy affect expectations in a way that prevents monetary policy from affecting real GDP. Only if a particular monetary policy takes people by surprise will it have any impact on the real level of economic activity.
- The Fed has consistently used monetary policy as a stabilization tool in recent years.

one by surprise. But the policy brought on the most severe recession since the Great Depression—a result that was inconsistent with the rational expectations argument that changing expectations would prevent such a policy from having a substantial effect on real GDP.[5]

The Fed has acknowledged the possibilities of both changing investment demand and changing expectations as factors that could pose difficulties with monetary policy, but its actual choices have been consistent with the model of aggregate demand and aggregate supply as we have developed it. As we've already noted, the Fed has responded to recessionary gaps with expansionary policies, provided it regards the inflation rate as falling within tolerable limits—apparently a 3 percent rate or less. When the economy has moved to an inflationary gap, the Fed has chosen contractionary policies. It may be hard to anticipate the effects of monetary policy, but the Fed has shown a determination to use such policy as a stabilization tool.

A Look Back—And a Look Ahead

Part of the Fed's power stems from the fact that it has no legislative mandate to seek particular goals. The legislation creating the Fed set no goals of macroeconomic performance for it to pursue. Subsequent legislation has spelled out macroeconomic goals for the United States, but these goals aren't achievable, so they're generally ignored. That leaves the Fed free to set its own goals. Its primary goal appears to be the maintenance of an inflation rate below 3 percent. Given success in meeting that goal, the Fed has acted to stimulate the economy to close a recessionary gap.

The tools available to the Fed to pursue these goals include open-market operations, the setting of the discount rate, and setting reserve requirements. Of these, open-market operations are the most important, and most used, tools of monetary policy. The Federal Open Market Committee (FOMC) can order a change in monetary policy and have it implemented immediately, but several problems in the implementation of monetary policy remain. These include the problem of lags, the issue of the choice of targets in conducting monetary policy, and political pressures placed on the process of policy setting.

Lags in the conduct of economic policy can occur for three reasons. First, there will be a lag between the time a problem emerges and the time policymakers recognize that it exists. This recognition lag can be particularly acute as the economy reaches a turning point. It may not be clear until several months after the fact that a recession or an expansion has begun. Once a problem has been recognized, there may be a delay in implementing a policy aimed at dealing with it. We'll see in the next chapter that this lag is particularly important in fiscal policy; implementation lags are not likely to be significant in the conduct of monetary policy. Finally, once an action is taken, there is a lag before the policy affects the economy. This lag, the impact lag, can be quite long, and it can be variable.

[5] One could, however, argue that people were aware of the Fed's pronouncements but skeptical about whether the anti-inflation effort would persist.

A second problem with the conduct of monetary policy is the choice of targets at which a central bank should aim. Should it seek to control interest rates, the quantity of money, some set of prices, nominal GDP, or what? The Fed's primary focus appears to be on interest rates.

A third complication in the conduct of monetary policy is politics. Although the Fed is largely independent of the executive and legislative branches in its conduct of monetary policy, it clearly is influenced by political forces. Research by economists suggests that the views of both administration officials and members of Congress affect policy choices of the Fed.

Once the Fed has made a choice to undertake an expansionary or contractionary policy, we can trace the impact of that policy. The Fed buys bonds to implement an expansionary policy. That action raises bond prices, lowers interest rates, boosts investment, lowers the exchange rate, and stimulates net exports. The result is an increase in aggregate expenditures and in aggregate demand. Real GDP and the price level rise. Under a contractionary policy, the Fed sells bonds. The price of bonds falls, interest rates increase, investment falls, the exchange rate rises, and net exports fall. Aggregate expenditures and aggregate demand fall, as do real GDP and the price level.

Shifting investment demand could prevent monetary policy from shifting aggregate demand in the desired direction. If people have rational expectations and respond to those expectations in their wage and price choices, then changes in monetary policy may have no effect on real GDP. Only a monetary policy that takes people by surprise will have any real impact on the economy. While members of the FOMC have acknowledged these possible difficulties, they have nonetheless continued to use monetary policy as a stabilization tool.

Terms and Concepts for Review

Impact lag

Implementation lag

Recognition lag

For Discussion

1. Suppose the Fed were required to conduct monetary policy so as to hold the unemployment rate below 4 percent, the goal specified in the Humphrey-Hawkins act. What implications for the economy would this have?
2. The legislative charter of the Bundesbank, Germany's central bank, requires it to seek price stability, period. How does this charter differ from that of the Fed? What significance does it have for monetary policy?
3. Do you think the Fed should be given a clearer legislative mandate concerning macroeconomic goals? If so, what should it be?
4. The Case in Point on China suggests that country's leaders have concluded that rapid money growth is essential to economic growth, despite its possible inflationary consequences. Do you agree?
5. Why isn't the power to set the discount rate a more effective tool of monetary policy? What would the Fed have to do to make it a more important tool?
6. One Case in Point indicates that when the Fed reduced reserve requirements during the recession of 1990–1991, it indicated that it would not allow the reduction to change its goals for monetary growth. Presumably, this meant that the Fed would not allow the reduction to affect the money supply. How could it prevent that? Interest rates rose when the Fed announced the reserve requirement reduction; explain this in light of your answer to this question.
7. The Case in Point on George Bush implies that Mr. Bush might have fared better in the 1992 election if the Fed had acted sooner to combat the 1990–1991 recession. Do you agree?

8. Some observers think that President Clinton sought in 1994 to influence Federal Reserve policy by appointing two economists to the Board of Governors who were "softer" on inflation than the FOMC had been. But we have seen that presidents can influence monetary policy simply by applying political pressure. Why didn't the president do that instead?

9. What does the Sachs-Alesina hypothesis described in the Case in Point predict about growth from the beginning of 1993 to the end of 1996? As the data become available, check to see whether the evidence is consistent with the hypothesis.

10. The text argues that the Fed's policies seem most consistent with the approach advocated by new Keynesian economists. Explain the basis for this conclusion.

11. In a speech in January 1995, Federal Reserve Chairman Alan Greenspan used a transportation metaphor to describe some of the difficulties of implementing monetary policy. He referred to the criticism levied against the Fed for shifting in 1994 to an antiinflation, contractionary policy when the inflation rate was still quite low:

> To successfully navigate a bend in the river, the barge must begin the turn well before the bend is reached. Even so, currents are always changing and even an experienced crew cannot foresee all the events that might occur as the river is being navigated. A year ago, the Fed began its turn, and we do not yet know if it has been successful.

Mr. Greenspan was referring, of course, to the problem of lags. What kind of lag do you think he had in mind? What do you suppose the reference to changing currents means?

Problems

1. Trace the impact of an expansionary monetary policy on bond prices, interest rates, investment, the exchange rate, net exports, real GDP, and the price level. Illustrate your analysis graphically.

2. Trace the impact of a contractionary monetary policy on bond prices, interest rates, investment, the exchange rate, net exports, real GDP, and the price level. Illustrate your analysis graphically.

3. The text notes that the FOMC adopts directives calling for the Open Market Desk at the New York Federal Reserve Bank to increase, decrease, or maintain the existing degree of pressure on reserve positions. Here are some meeting dates when the FOMC voted to decrease pressure on reserve positions (i.e., adopted a more expansionary policy):

   November 7, 1984

   December 17–18, 1985

   July 8–9, 1986

   July 5–6, 1989

   December 18–19, 1989

   November 13, 1990

   November 5, 1991

   Here are meeting dates on which the FOMC voted to increase reserve pressure:

   May 24, 1983

   May 19, 1987

   March 29, 1988

   June 29–30, 1988

   December 13–14, 1988

   February 3–4, 1994

   Pick one of these dates on which a decrease in reserve pressure was ordered and one on which an increase was ordered. Look up the minutes of that meeting in the *Federal Reserve Bulletin* in your library (the minutes are released about 6 weeks after a meeting and published in the next issue of the *Bulletin*) and find out why that particular policy was chosen.

4. Here are recent annual values for M2 and for nominal GDP (all figures are in billions of dollars). Compute the velocity for each year and the corresponding fraction of nominal GDP that was being held as money (see Chapter 25 if you need to review velocity). Monetarists argue that this fraction is stable in the long run. What is your conclusion?

	M2	Nominal GDP
1990	$3,345.5	$5,546.1
1991	3,445.8	5,722.9
1992	3,494.8	6,038.5
1993	3,551.7	6,374.0
1994	3,600.0	6,736.9

5. Discussion Question 4 asked whether you agree that rapid money growth, and the inflation that results from it, will promote growth in real GDP. Using data on money growth and inflation in a recent edition of the *World Development Report,* published by the World Bank, prepare a graph showing growth rates in real GDP on the vertical axis and inflation rates on the horizontal axis for the most recent period given (typically, the *Report* will give average annual rates of change for a 10-year period). Plot values for 20 countries that you select. What's your conclusion?

31

Fiscal Policy

Chapter Objectives

After mastering the material in this chapter, you will be able to:

1. Compare the ways in which government purchases, taxes, and transfer payments affect aggregate demand.
2. Explain how changes in fiscal policy can affect other components of aggregate demand—especially investment and net exports.
3. Discuss the ways in which fiscal policy can influence aggregate supply in the short run and explain why the burden of payroll taxes and other spending required of employers is ultimately borne by workers.
4. Show how fiscal policy is measured and relate that measure to whether policy is expansionary or contractionary.
5. Explain the ways in which taxes and some transfer payment programs reduce the value of the multiplier and thus act to stabilize the economy.

To tax and to please, no more than to love and be wise, is not given to men.
Edmund Burke, 1774

What's Ahead

The administrations of George Bush and Bill Clinton responded to the recession of 1990–1991 and its aftermath in sharply different ways. The contrast provides a clear illustration of the perspectives offered by new Keynesian economists on the one hand and monetarist and new classical economists on the other.

Mr. Bush, who was president during the recession itself, rejected the use of fiscal policy to stimulate the economy as the recession began. Six months into the recession, he agreed with Congress on a deficit reduction plan that increased taxes and cut government purchases—measures that, in the models we have developed, would reduce aggregate demand and worsen the recession. Such an approach was, he argued, consistent with long-run growth. Mr. Bush and his economic advisers, led by Stanford University's Michael Boskin, argued that an expansionary fiscal policy would not have any positive short-term impact on the economy, would reduce growth in the long run, and would be detrimental to the economy.[1]

President Clinton, faced in his first year in office with a weak recovery that left the economy with a recessionary gap, embraced the concept of an expansionary fiscal policy. Early in the term, he proposed a 5-year plan to bring down the deficit. That plan, like the Bush plan approved in 1990, called for higher taxes and reduced government purchases. But Mr. Clinton and his economic advisers called also for a dose of fiscal stimulus to be administered in 1993—his deficit reduction measures wouldn't begin until the following year. The stimulus package included increased government purchases and tax cuts designed to stimulate investment. Mr. Clinton's Council of Economic Advisers, led by Laura Tyson, calculated that passage of the measure would directly lead to the creation of 250,000 new jobs.[2] *With the multiplier, the plan would create 500,000 jobs. It was the kind of expansionary fiscal policy that had been rejected early on by the Bush administration.*

[1] Mr. Bush reversed himself early in 1992. Faced with a reelection effort and sagging popularity, he ordered an immediate reduction in income tax withholding rates in an attempt to increase disposable personal income and boost consumption (the plan is discussed in Chapter 27). He also called for a tax credit to assist people buying their first homes. The home purchase proposal was quickly rejected by the Congress.

[2] Like the Bush plan to stimulate home sales, the Clinton plan was rejected by Congress. One senator remarked that kicking off a deficit reduction plan with a measure that boosted spending and cut taxes was like having a chocolate fudge sundae the night before going on a diet.

How do government tax and expenditure policies affect economic activity? Why do economists differ so sharply in assessing the likely impact of such policies? Can fiscal policy be used as a stabilization device? We'll examine these issues and their implications for public policy in this chapter.

Chapter 30 reviewed the goals of macroeconomic policy as specified in the Employment Act of 1946 and in the 1978 Humphrey-Hawkins Act. The Employment Act declared it the responsibility of the federal government to conduct policy so as to maintain full employment and to maximize purchasing power. The Humphrey-Hawkins Act declared that the unemployment and inflation rates should be held below 4 and 3 percent per year, respectively. While neither act specifies a clear blueprint for economic policy, both make clear that macroeconomic performance is a federal responsibility. The tool through which the federal government seeks to influence such performance is fiscal policy—the use of the government's tax and expenditure policies for the manipulation of aggregate demand and aggregate supply. It is that tool of macroeconomic policy that we shall examine in this chapter.

Government and the Economy

The combined activities of local, state, and federal government agencies play a major role in the economy. Government purchases account for roughly one-fifth of GDP in the United States. Total spending, which includes transfer payments, is even larger. Taxes also have important economic effects. We shall begin our analysis of fiscal policy with an examination of government purchases, transfer payments, and taxes in the U.S. economy.

Government Purchases

The government purchases component of aggregate demand includes all purchases by government agencies of goods and services produced by firms, as well as direct production by government agencies themselves. When the federal government buys paper clips, the transaction is part of government purchases. The production of educational and research services by public colleges and universities is also counted in the government purchases component of GDP.

While we hear often of the growth of government, the government purchases component of aggregate demand has declined in relative importance in the past several years. In 1929, on the eve of the Great Depression, government purchases totaled 13.7 percent of real GDP. By 1933 this share had risen to 19.8 percent. Outside of wartime, government purchases remained close to 20 percent of GDP for the next several decades. In recent years they have fallen.

Exhibit 31-1 shows federal as well as state and local government purchases as a percentage of real GDP from 1960 to the first half of 1995. Notice the changes that have occurred within the past 35 years. In 1960, the federal government accounted for the lion's share of total purchases. Since then, however, federal purchases have fallen by almost half relative to GDP, from 11 percent to 6 percent. State and local purchases, meanwhile, have risen. They accounted for 9

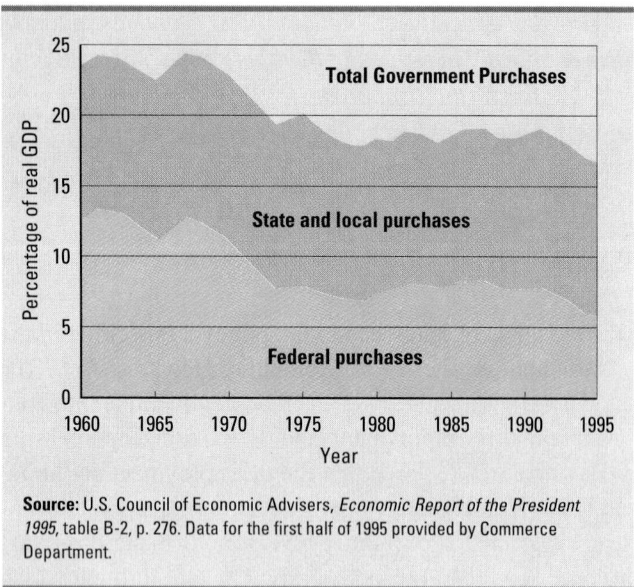

Source: U.S. Council of Economic Advisers, *Economic Report of the President 1995*, table B-2, p. 276. Data for the first half of 1995 provided by Commerce Department.

EXHIBIT 31-1

Federal and State and Local Purchases Relative to Real GDP, 1960–1995

Federal purchases have declined relative to GDP since 1960, while those of state and local governments have remained stable. Combining government purchases at all levels, we see that they have fallen relative to GDP.

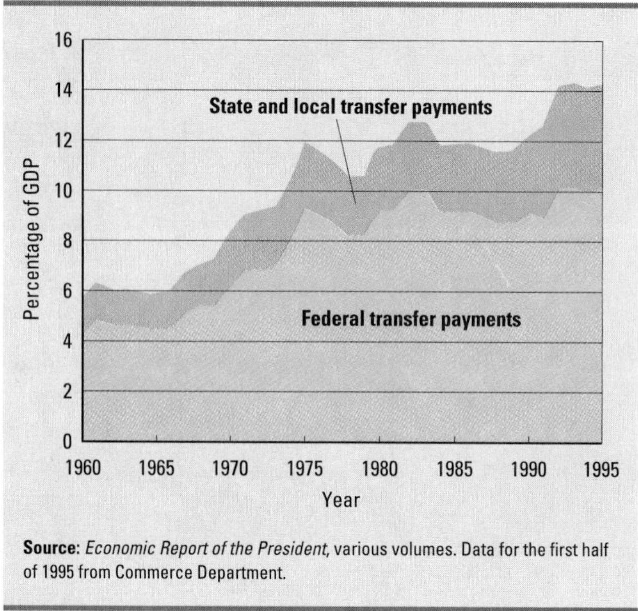

Source: *Economic Report of the President*, various volumes. Data for the first half of 1995 from Commerce Department.

EXHIBIT 31-2

Federal and State and Local Transfer Payments as a Percentage of Nominal GDP, 1960–1995

The chart shows transfer payment spending as a percentage of GDP from 1960 through the first half of 1995. This spending rose dramatically relative to GDP during the late 1960s and the 1970s as federal programs expanded. More recently, sharp increases in health care costs have driven spending for transfer payment programs such as Medicare and Medicaid upward. Transfer payments fluctuate with the business cycle, rising in times of recession and falling during times of expansion.

percent of GDP in 1960 and 11 percent in 1994. The reduction in federal purchases relative to GDP primarily reflects reductions in defense spending. The total of federal and state and local purchases has declined relative to GDP.

Transfer Payments

A transfer payment is the provision of aid or money to an individual who is not required to provide anything in exchange. Social Security and welfare benefits are examples of transfer payments. Transfer payments have become much more important in the past few decades.

Exhibit 31-2 shows that transfer payment spending by the federal government and by state and local governments has risen as a percentage of GDP. In 1960, such spending totaled less than 6 percent of GDP; by 1995, it had risen to more than 14 percent. The federal government accounts for the bulk of transfer payment spending in the United States.

Two kinds of changes have influenced transfer payments over the past several decades. First, they increased rapidly during the late 1960s and early 1970s. This was the period in which federal programs such as Medicare, Medicaid, and Aid to Families with Dependent Children (AFDC) were created and expanded.

In addition, sharp increases in health care costs have contributed to increases in spending for Medicare and Medicaid in recent years. Finally, transfer payment spending relative to GDP has fluctuated with the business cycle. Transfer payments fell during the late 1970s, a period of expansion, then rose as the economy slipped into a recessionary gap with the Fed's antiinflationary effort of 1979–1982. Transfer payments fell during the expansion that began late in 1982, then began rising in 1989 as the expansion began to slow. Transfer payments continued to rise relative to GDP during the recession of 1990–1991 and then began to edge down as the economy entered another expansionary phase.

The tendency of transfer payment spending to rise during recessions and fall during expansions results from the bases on which people qualify to receive these payments. People qualify to receive welfare programs such as AFDC, food stamps, or Medicaid (which provides health care), only if their income falls below a certain level. They qualify for unemployment compensation by losing their jobs. When the economy expands, incomes and employment rise, and fewer people qualify for welfare or unemployment benefits. Spending for those programs therefore tends to fall. When economic activity falls, incomes fall, people lose jobs, and more people qualify for aid, so spending for these programs rises.

In 1995, total transfer payments accounted for nearly half of all federal spending.

Exhibit 31-3 summarizes what we've just learned about trends in government spending since 1960. It shows three categories of government spending relative to GDP: government purchases, transfer payments, and net interest. Net interest includes payments of interest by governments at all levels on money borrowed, less interest earned on saving. As the federal government's debt has increased, interest payments on the debt have risen. We see that government purchases have declined slightly relative to GDP, while transfer payments and net interest have risen since 1960.

EXHIBIT 31-3

Government Spending as a Percentage of GDP, 1960–1995

This chart shows three major categories of government spending as percentages of GDP: government purchases, transfer payments, and net interest. Government purchases have fallen relative to GDP, while transfer payments and net interest have risen.

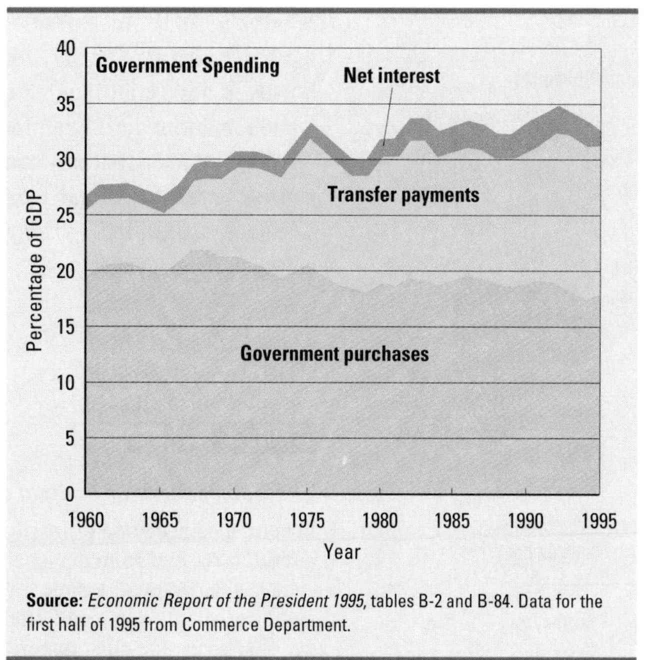

Source: *Economic Report of the President 1995,* tables B-2 and B-84. Data for the first half of 1995 from Commerce Department.

EXHIBIT 31-4

Government Revenue and Expenditure as a Percentage of GDP, 1960–1995

Government expenditures at the federal, state, and local levels have generally risen relative to GDP. Revenues, however, rose relative to GDP during the 1960s and have been fairly stable since. We see that expenditures have exceeded revenues in nearly all of the past 35 years.

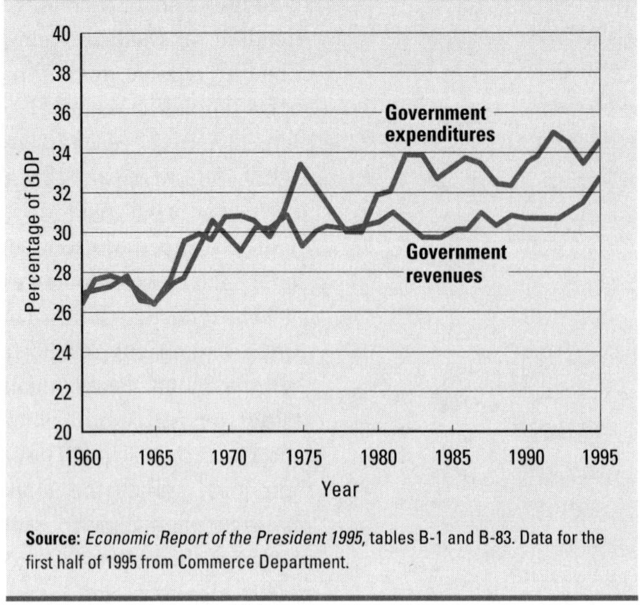

Source: *Economic Report of the President 1995,* tables B-1 and B-83. Data for the first half of 1995 from Commerce Department.

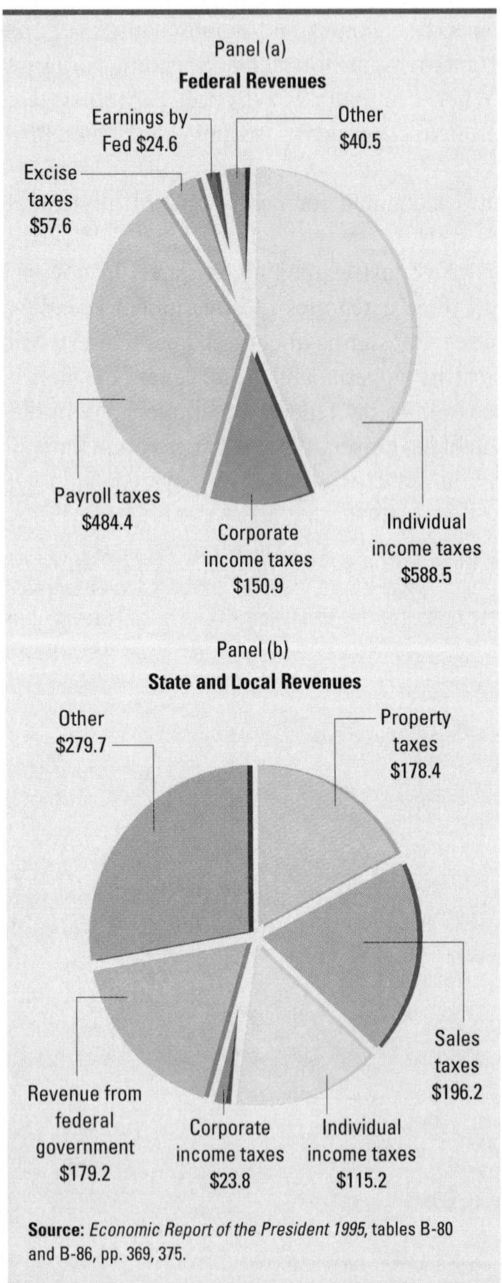

Source: *Economic Report of the President 1995,* tables B-80 and B-86, pp. 369, 375.

Taxes

Taxes affect the relationship between real GDP and personal disposable income; they therefore affect consumption expenditures. They also influence investment decisions. Taxes imposed on firms affect the profitability of investment decisions and therefore affect the levels of investment firms will choose. Payroll taxes imposed on firms affect the costs of hiring workers; they therefore have an impact on employment and on the real wages earned by workers.

Exhibit 31-4 compares government revenues to government expenditures relative to GDP since 1960. We see that revenues rose as a share of GDP during the 1960s and 1990s; they remained stable in the 1970s and 1980s. Expenditures, however, have continued to rise. Expenditures have generally exceeded revenue, a phenomenon we'll examine later in this chapter and in Chapter 34.

The bulk of federal receipts comes from the personal income tax and from payroll taxes. State and local tax receipts are dominated by property taxes and sales taxes. Exhibit 31-5 shows the composition of federal and state and local receipts in recent years.

EXHIBIT 31-5

The Composition of Federal and State and Local Revenues

Federal receipts come primarily from payroll taxes and from personal taxes such as the personal income tax. State and local tax receipts come from a variety of sources; the most important are property taxes, sales taxes, income taxes, and grants from the federal government. Revenue shares for the federal government are for fiscal 1995; shares for state and local governments are for fiscal 1991–1992.

Checklist ✓

- Government purchases are one component of GDP. The share of GDP represented by government purchases has declined slightly over the past three decades. Federal purchases have dropped while state and local purchases have risen.
- Spending for transfer payment programs has been the most rapidly rising form of government expenditure in the past several decades. Transfer payment programs now account for more than half of U.S. government expenditures.
- Government revenues have been fairly stable relative to GDP during the past two decades while expenditures have risen. Expenditures have exceeded revenues in nearly all of the past 35 years.
- The main types of federal taxes are income and payroll taxes. The main types of state and local taxes are sales and property taxes.

Fiscal Policy As a Stabilization Tool

Fiscal policy—the use of government expenditures and taxes to influence the level of economic activity—is the government counterpart to monetary policy. Like monetary policy, it can be used in an effort to close a recessionary or an inflationary gap. The use of fiscal policy to influence economic growth will be examined in Chapter 35.

Some tax and expenditure programs change automatically with the level of economic activity. We shall consider those in the next section. This section analyzes fiscal policies that seek to increase or decrease the equilibrium level of economic activity. Two examples of discretionary fiscal policy choices were the tax cut introduced by the Kennedy administration in the early 1960s, designed to stimulate aggregate demand and close a recessionary gap, and the increase in government purchases proposed by President Clinton in 1993.

Fiscal policies may be expansionary or contractionary. An expansionary fiscal policy tends to increase the equilibrium level of real GDP. Such a policy could be used to close a recessionary gap. A contractionary fiscal policy tends to reduce equilibrium real GDP. A contractionary policy could be used to close an inflationary gap.

In practice, expansionary and contractionary fiscal policies have focused on the manipulation of aggregate demand. In principle, however, fiscal policy could be used to manipulate aggregate supply as well. We shall examine both possibilities, beginning with the use of fiscal policy to shift the aggregate demand curve.

Fiscal Policy and Aggregate Demand

Government spending or tax policies may be used to shift aggregate demand. An expansionary fiscal policy features an increase in government purchases or transfer payments or a reduction in taxes; a contractionary fiscal policy uses a reduction in government purchases or transfer payments or an increase in taxes.

Exhibit 31-6 illustrates the use of fiscal policy to shift aggregate demand in response to a recessionary or inflationary gap. In Panel (a), the economy produces a real GDP of Y_1, which is below its natural level of Y_n. An expansionary

EXHIBIT 31-6

Expansionary and Contractionary Fiscal Policies to Shift Aggregate Demand

In Panel (a), the economy faces a recessionary gap ($Y_n - Y_1$). An expansionary fiscal policy seeks to shift aggregate demand to AD_2 to close the gap. In Panel (b), the economy faces an inflationary gap ($Y_1 - Y_n$). A contractionary fiscal policy seeks to reduce aggregate demand to AD_2 to close the gap.

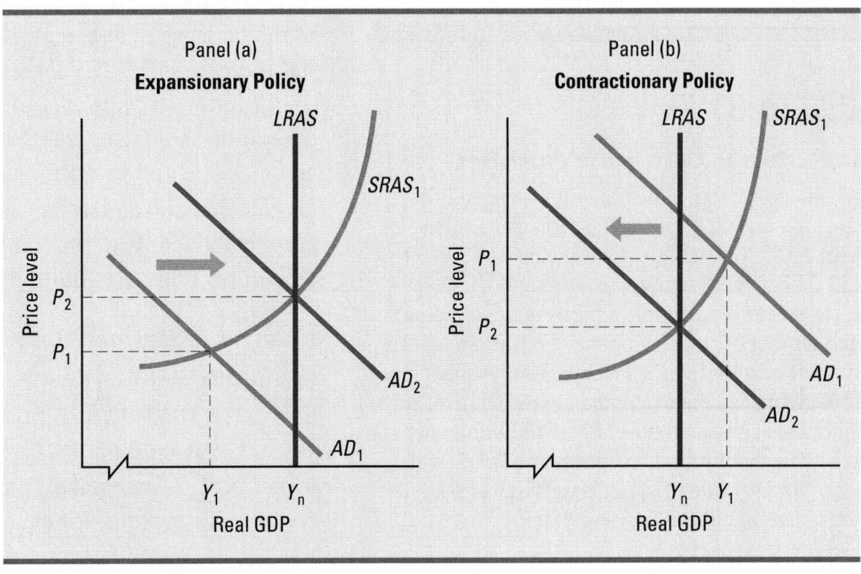

fiscal policy seeks to shift aggregate demand to AD_2, closing the gap. In Panel (b), the economy initially has an inflationary gap at Y_1. A contractionary fiscal policy seeks to reduce aggregate demand to AD_2 to close the gap.

Changes in Government Purchases

One policy through which the government could seek to shift the aggregate demand curve would be a change in government purchases. President Reagan, for example, increased defense spending in the early 1980s, boosting aggregate demand and shifting the aggregate demand curve to the right. Presidents Bush and Clinton presided over substantial reductions in defense spending. These reductions reduced government purchases and tended to shift the aggregate demand curve to the left.

Shifts in aggregate demand are related to shifts in aggregate expenditures. All other things equal, a change in government purchases shifts the aggregate expenditures curve by an amount equal to the change in government purchases. A $200 billion increase in government purchases, for example, shifts the aggregate expenditures curve upward by $200 billion. A $75 billion reduction in government purchases shifts the aggregate expenditures curve downward by that amount.

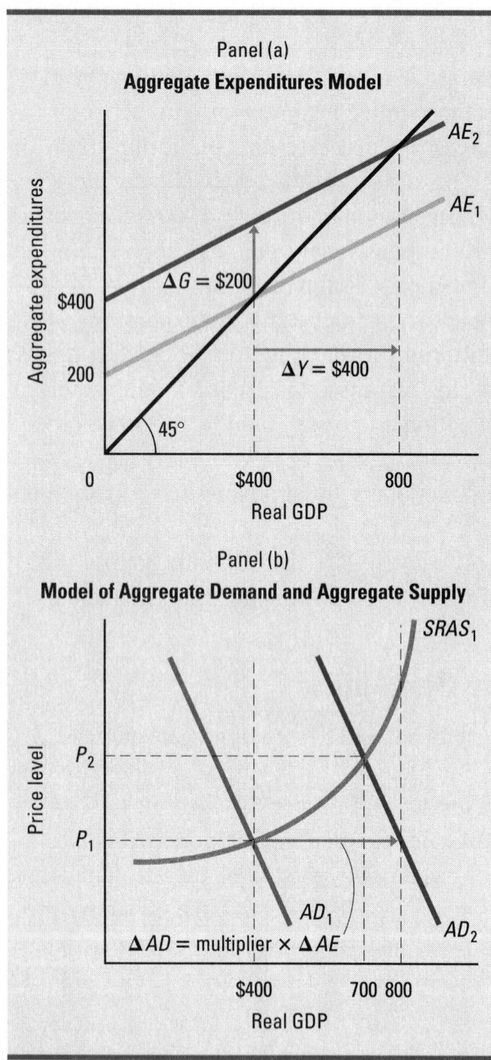

EXHIBIT 31-7

An Increase in Government Purchases

The economy shown here is initially in equilibrium at a real GDP of $400 billion and a price level of P_1. In Panel (a), an increase of $200 billion in the level of government purchases shifts the aggregate expenditures curve upward by that amount to AE_2, increasing the equilibrium level of income in the aggregate expenditures model by $400 billion. In Panel (b), the aggregate demand curve thus shifts to the right by $400 billion to AD_2. The equilibrium level of real GDP rises to $700 billion while the price level rises to P_2. All figures are in billions of 1987 dollars.

Panel (a) of Exhibit 31-7 shows an economy that is initially in equilibrium at an income of $400 billion. Suppose that the marginal expenditure rate is 0.5, so that the multiplier is 2. An increase of $200 billion in government purchases shifts the aggregate expenditures curve upward by that amount to AE_2. In the aggregate expenditures model, equilibrium real GDP increases by an amount equal to the multiplier times the change in aggregate expenditures. Real GDP in that model thus rises by $400 billion to a level of $800 billion.

The aggregate expenditures model, of course, assumes a constant price level. To get a more complete picture of what happens, we use the model of aggregate demand and aggregate supply. In that model, shown in Panel (b), the initial price level is P_1 and the initial equilibrium real GDP is $400 billion. That is the price level assumed to hold in the aggregate expenditures model. The $200 billion increase in government purchases increases the total quantity of goods and services demanded, at a price level of P_1, by $400 billion. The aggregate demand thus shifts to the right by that amount to AD_2. The equilibrium level of real GDP rises to $700 billion and the price level rises to P_2. Part of the impact of the increase in aggregate demand is absorbed by higher prices, preventing the full increase in real GDP predicted by the aggregate expenditures model.

A reduction in government purchases would have the opposite effect. All other things equal, aggregate expenditures in Panel (a) would shift downward by an amount equal to the reduction in government purchases. In the model of aggregate demand and aggregate supply, shown in Panel (b), the aggregate demand curve would shift to the left by an amount equal to the change in aggregate expenditures times the multiplier. Real GDP and the price level would fall.

Changes in Business Taxes

One of the first fiscal policy measures undertaken by the Kennedy administration in the 1960s was an investment tax credit. As we saw in Chapter 28, an investment tax credit allows a firm to reduce its tax liability by a percentage of the investment it undertakes during a particular period. With an investment tax credit of 10 percent, for example, a firm that engaged in $1 million worth of investment during a year could reduce its tax liability for that year by $100,000. The investment tax credit introduced by the Kennedy administration was later repealed. It was reintroduced during the Reagan administration in 1981, then abolished by the Tax Reform Act of 1986. President Clinton called for a new investment tax credit in 1993 as part of his job stimulus proposal, but that proposal was rejected by Congress.

An investment tax credit is intended, of course, to stimulate additional private sector investment. A reduction in the tax rate on corporate profits would be likely to have a similar effect. Conversely, an increase in the corporate tax rate or a reduction in an investment tax credit could be expected to reduce investment.

A change in investment affects the aggregate expenditures curve in precisely the same manner as a change in government purchases. It shifts aggregate expenditures by an amount equal to the change in investment, all other components of aggregate expenditures unchanged. That will shift the aggregate demand curve by an amount equal to the change in aggregate expenditures times the multiplier.

An increase in the investment tax credit, or a reduction in corporate income taxes, will increase investment and shift the aggregate demand curve to the right. Real GDP and the price level will rise. A reduction in the investment tax credit, or an increase in corporate income taxes, will reduce investment and shift the aggregate demand curve to the left. Real GDP and the price level will fall.[3]

Changes in Income Taxes

Income taxes affect the consumption component of aggregate demand. An increase in income taxes reduces disposable personal income and thus reduces consumption. That shifts the aggregate expenditures curve downward by an amount equal to the change in consumption. It shifts the aggregate demand curve to the left by an amount equal to the change in aggregate expenditures times the multiplier. A reduction in income taxes increases disposable personal income, increases consumption, and increases aggregate demand.

Changes in income tax rates produce an important complication. Recall from Chapter 27 that the marginal expenditure rate depends on the marginal propensity to consume out of disposable personal income and on the rate at which disposable personal income changes with a change in real GDP. That second rate, in turn, is affected by the income tax rate. An increase in income tax rates will reduce the marginal expenditure rate, so the aggregate expenditures curve will be flatter. A higher income tax rate thus shifts the aggregate expenditures curve downward *and* makes it flatter. Similarly, a lower income tax rate shifts the aggregate expenditures curve upward *and* makes it steeper.

Suppose that an economy whose initial equilibrium real GDP is $10,000 has an income tax rate of 0.25. Let T be the real value of income taxes collected, so that disposable personal income Y_d is 75 percent of real GDP:

$$T = 0.25Y \quad \textbf{(1)}$$

$$Y_d = Y - T = 0.75Y \quad \textbf{(2)}$$

[3] Investment also affects the long-run aggregate supply curve, since a change in the capital stock changes the natural level of real GDP. We shall examine that impact in Chapter 35.

Case in Point Sweden's Investment Fund

Sweden was one of the pioneers in implementing Keynes's ideas about the use of fiscal policy. Its investment fund was a bold attempt to use fiscal policy to manipulate aggregate demand.

Under the Swedish plan, the government subsidized investment whenever government officials determined that the economy needed additional stimulus. The system worked very much like an investment tax credit. When government officials determined that further stimulus wasn't necessary, they canceled the investment subsidy. The system thus encouraged firms to shift their investment to periods in which the economy had a recessionary gap.

As firms learned to adjust to the system, however, a difficulty soon appeared. Suppose firms calculate that a recessionary gap is likely to occur in, say, the next year. They know that once the government declares the existence of such a gap, it will subsidize investment. A firm contemplating an investment expenditure now might want to postpone it, expecting the government to subsidize it later.

Attempts by firms to manipulate the system could actually cause it to be destabilizing. If enough firms determined that a recession was imminent and those firms postponed investment projects in order to take advantage of the subsidy, the plan could actually cause the downturns it sought to avoid! Concern that firms were taking advantage of the system in precisely this manner was one of the reasons it was abandoned in the mid-1970s.

Source: John B. Taylor, "The Swedish Investment Funds System as a Stabilization Rule," *Brookings Papers on Economic Activity* 1 (1982): 57–106.

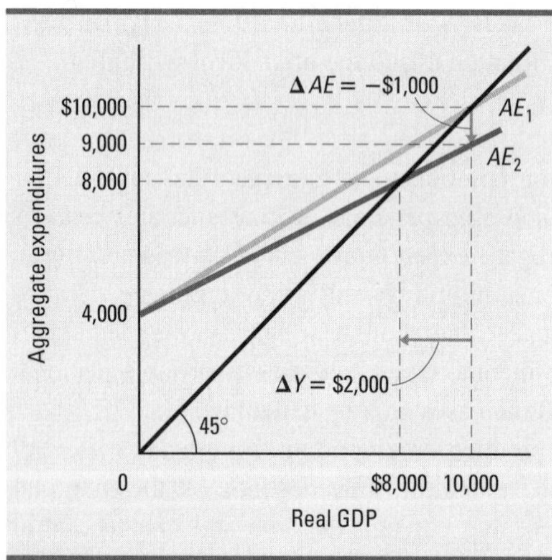

EXHIBIT 31-8

The Impact of an Increase in Income Tax Rates

An increase in the income tax rate shifts the aggregate expenditures curve downward by an amount equal to the change in consumption, \$1,000 in this case, assuming no other change in aggregate expenditures. It also reduces the slope of the aggregate expenditures curve and thus reduces the multiplier. Here, an increase in the income tax rate from 0.25 to 0.375 reduces the marginal expenditure rate from 0.6 to 0.5; it thus reduces the multiplier from 2.5 to 2. The higher tax reduces consumption by \$1,000 and reduces equilibrium real GDP in the aggregate expenditures model by \$2,000.

Suppose the marginal propensity to consume out of disposable personal income is 0.8. A \$1 change in real GDP produces an increase in personal disposable income of \$0.75, and that produces an increase in consumption of \$0.60 ($= 0.75 \times 0.8$). If the other components of aggregate expenditures are autonomous, then the marginal expenditure rate is 0.6. A marginal expenditure rate of 0.6 implies a multiplier of 2.5 [$= 1/(1 - 0.6)$].

Now suppose that the tax rate is increased to 0.375. The impact of such a tax change is illustrated in Exhibit 31-8. It shows the original aggregate expenditures curve AE_1 intersecting the 45-degree line at an income of \$10,000. The curve has a slope of 0.6, the marginal expenditure rate. The higher tax rate will shift this curve downward and make it flatter.

At the original level of income, \$10,000, tax collections equaled \$2,500. At the new tax rate, they equal \$3,750 ($= 0.375 \times \$10,000$). Disposable personal income at a real GDP of \$10,000 thus declines by \$1,250. With a marginal propensity to consume of 0.8, consumption drops by \$1,000 ($= 0.8 \times \$1,250$). The aggregate expenditures curve shifts down by this amount at the initial level of income of \$10,000, assuming no other changes in aggregate expenditures occur.

Before the tax increase, an additional \$1 of real GDP induced \$0.60 in additional consumption, implying a marginal expenditure rate of 0.6. At the new tax rate, the marginal expenditure rate falls to 0.5. An additional \$1 of real GDP creates \$0.625 in disposable personal income (\$1 in income minus \$0.375 in taxes). Given a marginal propensity to consume of 0.8, this \$1 increase in real GDP increases consumption by \$0.50 ($= 0.8 \times 0.625$). The new aggregate expenditures curve, AE_2 in Exhibit 31-8, shows the end result of the tax change in the aggregate expenditures model. The equilibrium level of real GDP falls to \$8,000 from its original level of \$10,000. The \$2,000 reduction in equilibrium real GDP is equal to the \$1,000 reduction in consumption times the new multiplier of 2. The tax increase has reduced aggregate expenditures and reduced the multiplier impact of this change (from 2.5 to 2). The aggregate demand curve will shift to the left by \$2,000, the multiplier times the change in aggregate expenditures.

In the model of aggregate demand and aggregate supply, a tax increase will shift the aggregate demand curve to the left by an amount equal to the change in aggregate expenditures induced by the tax boost times the new value of the multiplier. Similarly, a reduction in the income tax rate shifts the aggregate expenditures curve upward by an amount equal to the increase in consumption created by the lower tax rate. It also increases the marginal expenditure rate, increasing the value of the multiplier. Aggregate demand shifts to the right by an amount equal to the change in aggregate expenditures times the multiplier.

Changes in Transfer Payments

Transfer payments are not a component of aggregate expenditures or aggregate demand. However, changes in transfer payments alter the disposable personal income of households and thus affect their consumption. A change in transfer payments will thus shift the aggregate expenditures and aggregate demand curves.

Exhibit 31-9 shows the impact of a $1,000 increase in transfer payments in an economy in which the marginal propensity to consume out of disposable personal income is 0.8, the marginal expenditure rate is 0.5, and the equilibrium level of income is $8,000. We shall assume that the increase in transfer payments is autonomous; transfer payments rise at all levels of income by $1,000. Assuming the $1,000 increase in transfer payments is not subject to income taxes, the aggregate expenditures curve shifts upward by $800—the marginal propensity to consume out of disposable personal income times the change in disposable personal income. With a multiplier of 2, equilibrium income in the aggregate expenditures model rises by $1,600 to $9,600. The aggregate demand curve thus shifts to the right by $1,600, an amount equal to the multiplier times the change in aggregate expenditures.

EXHIBIT 31-9

A Change in Transfer Payments

An increase in transfer payments of $1,000 shifts the aggregate expenditures curve upward by an amount equal to the marginal propensity to consume out of disposable personal income times the change in transfer payments, or $800. In the aggregate expenditures model, equilibrium income rises by the multiplier times this amount, or $1,600.

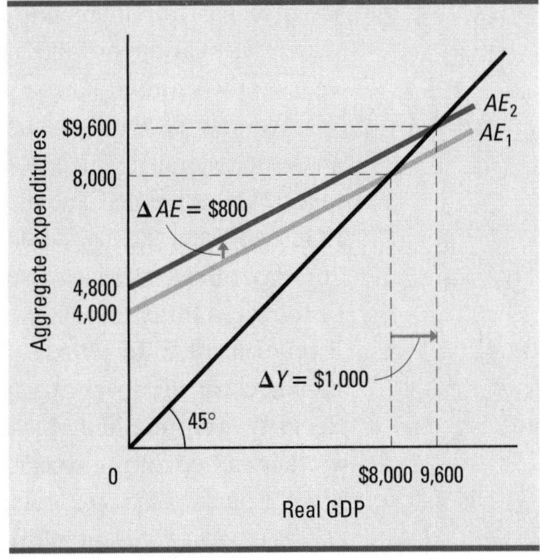

Exhibit 31-10 summarizes U.S. fiscal policies undertaken to shift aggregate demand since the 1964 tax cut. We see that expansionary policies have been chosen in response to recessionary gaps and that contractionary policies have been chosen in response to inflationary gaps. Changes in government purchases and in taxes have been the primary tools of fiscal policy in the United States.

EXHIBIT 31-10

Fiscal Policy in the United States After the 1964 Tax Cut

Year	Situation	Policy Response
1968	Inflationary gap	A temporary tax increase, first recommended by President Johnson's Council of Economic Advisers in 1965, goes into effect. This onetime surcharge of 10 percent is added to individual income tax liabilities.
1969	Inflationary gap	President Nixon, facing a continued inflationary gap, orders cuts in government purchases.
1975	Recessionary gap	President Ford, facing a recession induced by an OPEC oil price increase, proposes a temporary 10 percent tax cut. It is passed almost immediately and goes into effect within 2 months.
1981	Recessionary gap	President Reagan had campaigned on a platform of increased defense spending and a sharp cut in income taxes. The tax cuts are approved in 1981 and are implemented over a period of 3 years. The increased defense spending begins in 1981. While the Reagan administration rejects the use of fiscal policy as a stabilization tool, its policies tend to increase aggregate demand early in the 1980s.
1992	Recessionary gap	President Bush had rejected the use of expansionary fiscal policy during the recession of 1990–1991. Indeed, he agreed late in 1990 to a cut in government purchases and a tax increase. In a campaign year, however, he orders a cut in withholding rates designed to increase disposable personal income in 1992 and to boost consumption.
1993	Recessionary gap	President Clinton calls for a $16 billion jobs package consisting of increased government purchases and tax cuts aimed at stimulating investment. The president says the plan will create 500,000 new jobs. The measure is rejected by Congress.

Fiscal Policy and Aggregate Supply

Fiscal policies can also influence the level of economic activity through their impact on aggregate supply. We'll examine the impact of fiscal policy on long-run aggregate supply in Chapter 35, when we discuss economic growth. Fiscal policy also has important implications for the short-run aggregate supply curve, which we shall investigate in this section. Fiscal policy affects short-run aggregate supply primarily through the payroll tax.

We saw in Exhibit 31-5 that payroll taxes account for roughly the same share of federal revenue as income taxes. Indeed, for most Americans, payroll taxes, which finance Social Security, Medicare, and unemployment compensation, constitute the largest tax they pay.

Payroll taxes are assessed on wages and salaries earned. With the exception of the payroll tax that finances Medicare, the tax is applied only up to a certain level of income. In 1995, for example, a payroll tax of 1.45 percent was applied to wages at all levels to finance Medicare. Payroll taxes to finance Social Security were applied at a rate of 6.2 percent only up to the first $61,200 a worker earned during a year; no payroll tax was applied on earnings beyond that level. Equal taxes were levied against employers.

A payroll tax is an indirect business tax assessed on firms. To assess the impact of payroll taxes, we need to define a new term. **Cost per unit of labor** is the sum of all costs incurred by a firm as the result of employing 1 unit of labor. A worker's wage is part of this cost. If a firm must pay a payroll tax, that tax payment is part of the cost per unit of labor.

Cost per unit of labor is the sum of all costs incurred by a firm as a result of hiring a unit of labor.

Exhibit 31-11 shows how the imposition of a payroll tax affects the economy. The production function *PF* in Panel (a) gives the relationship between the quantity of real GDP produced and employment. In Panel (b), the slope of the production function, the marginal product of labor, is the demand curve for labor

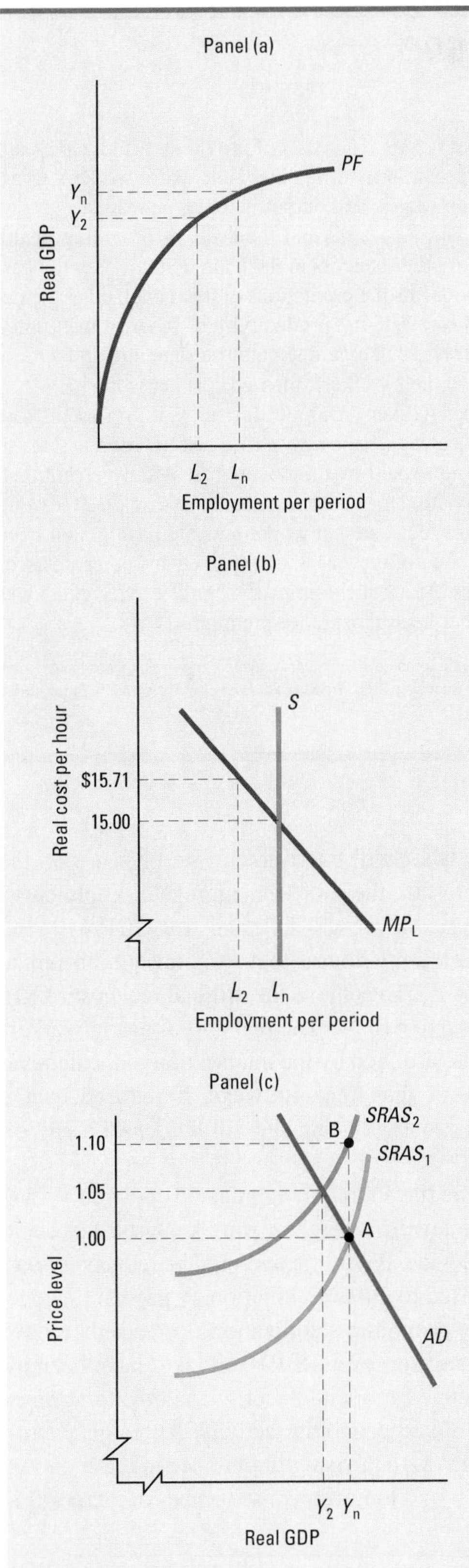

EXHIBIT 31-11

The Impact of a Payroll Tax

Suppose the economy is initially operating at its natural levels of output and employment. The real wage is $15 per hour in Panel (b) and the price level is 1.00 in Panel (c). The imposition on firms of a payroll tax of $1.50 per hour shifts the short-run aggregate supply curve in Panel (c) upward to $SRAS_2$, raising the price level to 1.05 and reducing real GDP to Y_2. The real wage cost facing firms rises to $15.71 in Panel (b), reducing employment to L_2. Real GDP thus falls to Y_2 in Panel (a). In the long run, nominal wages will fall, and wage costs to firms will fall back to a real wage and nominal wage of $15. Real GDP will return to its natural level Y_n, and the price level will return to 1.00. The equilibrium real and nominal wage of $15 will include, however, the $1.50 tax; workers will receive a real wage of $13.50.

MP_L. In the market for labor shown in Panel (b), the labor market is in equilibrium at the natural level of employment L_n and a real wage of $15 per hour. To obtain a point on the short-run aggregate supply curve in Panel (c), we assume that the initial value of the nominal wage, which is sticky, is given. Suppose it's $15, and that this wage equals the total cost per unit of labor. With a nominal wage of $15, the price level at which the nominal wage produces the equilibrium real wage is 1.00. That price level defines point A on the short-run aggregate supply curve, at which the economy's natural level of output Y_n is produced.

Now suppose a payroll tax of $1.50 per hour is imposed; the tax must be paid by firms. The cost per hour of labor thus includes the hourly wage plus this payroll tax. Initially, nominal wages are sticky; they remain at $15. The payroll tax adds $1.50, so firms now pay $16.50 to employ 1 hour of labor.

To determine the amount by which the higher cost of labor shifts the short-run aggregate supply curve, we compute the price level at which firms would continue to employ L_n units of labor despite the tax. They would employ this quantity *if the real cost per hour of labor remained at $15.* Because the cost per unit of labor has risen 10 percent, the price level would have to rise by 10 percent as well to maintain the real cost per hour at $15. A price level of 1.10 would thus be required—the real cost per hour at this price level would equal $15 ($16.50/1.10 = $15). The new short-run aggregate supply curve thus passes through point B, at which output equals Y_n and the price level equals 1.10; it shifts upward to $SRAS_2$. (It's important to remember that we use the computation of point B merely to place $SRAS_2$. We are not supposing that the price level will actually rise to 1.10.)

The new short-run equilibrium occurs at the intersection of $SRAS_2$ and the aggregate demand curve. The price level thus rises and real GDP falls. In the case shown, the price level rises to 1.05. (This number is estimated from the graph; we would need an equation for aggregate demand and short-run aggregate supply to compute it precisely.) The real cost per hour to firms is now $15.71 (= $16.50/1.05), and employment falls to L_2. There is a recessionary gap, and unemployment rises. Workers bear some of the burden of the tax in two ways. First, they suffer a reduced level of employment. Second, their real wage falls because of the higher price level. The $15.71 now paid by firms includes the $1.50 payroll tax. That means workers receive a real wage of $14.21. The real cost per hour of labor paid by firms has risen 71 cents while workers are receiving a real wage that has fallen by 79 cents.

Case in Point Health Care Costs, Employment, and Real GDP

Most health insurance in the United States is provided by firms for their employees. As the cost of health care has escalated over the last three decades, the cost of providing health insurance for workers has risen.

Because health insurance has become a standard part of most employment contracts, its cost affects the economy in precisely the same manner as a payroll tax. If we think of 1 unit of labor as 1 worker hired for 1 year, then the worker's annual health insurance premium is part of the cost per worker to firms. An increase in the cost of health insurance is thus equivalent to an increase in the payroll tax. With sticky nominal wages in the short run, the higher health insurance cost makes it more expensive to employ workers. Firms thus hire fewer workers. The short-run aggregate supply curve shifts upward, just as in Exhibit 31-11. Real GDP falls and the price level rises. In the long run, we would expect nominal wages to fall by an amount equal to the increase in health insurance costs. Thus, in the short run, higher health insurance costs reduce employment, reduce real GDP, and lead to a higher price level. In the long run, health insurance costs have no effect on real GDP or the price level; they result instead in lower nominal and real wages. The costs of providing health care, paying payroll taxes, and providing other benefits for workers all affect employment, wages, and output in the same way.

A look at data on wages and the costs of providing health care insurance or other benefits in the United States over the past three decades confirms the predictions of the model. Over the period from 1965 to 1991, the productivity of labor in the United States rose sharply; such a gain should translate into an increase in what firms pay their workers, the real cost per worker.

Real cost per worker did, indeed, rise by 17.8 percent from 1965 to 1991. Real wages, however, rose just 6.9 percent. Health insurance premiums paid by employers rose 452.6 percent, and the cost of providing for retirement benefits rose 76.3 percent. Most of the wage increase that workers would have gotten from their higher productivity was thus absorbed by other costs of labor, not wages. Most of the impact of productivity gains was taken up in higher health insurance premiums.

Source: Cathy Cowan and Patricia McDonnell, "Business, Households, and Governments: Health Spending 1991," *Health Care Financing Review* 14(3) (Spring 1993): 227–248.

In the long run, the surplus of labor will exert downward pressure on the nominal wage. As the wage begins to fall, the short-run aggregate supply curve will begin to shift downward, the price level will fall, and real GDP will rise. The process will continue until the economy returns to its original equilibrium at a price level of 1.00 and real GDP of Y_n. To achieve the original real cost of $15 per hour, the nominal wage must drop to $13.50. The real cost of hiring workers thus adjusts to an equilibrium level determined by the intersection of the demand and supply of labor. Labor's share of that total, its wage, is reduced by the amount of the payroll tax. Workers eventually bear the full burden of a payroll tax imposed on firms.

A change in the payroll tax shifts the short-run aggregate supply curve and thus affects real GDP and the price level in the short run. A payroll tax could therefore be used as a stabilization device. Payroll taxes could be reduced to correct for a recessionary gap or increased to close an inflationary gap. In practice, payroll taxes haven't been used for economic stabilization. Instead, they have been used solely for the purpose of raising revenue. Payroll taxes have been increased often to raise additional revenue for Social Security and other programs; they have not been reduced to stimulate economic activity. Although payroll taxes haven't been used for stabilization, their rising importance in the economy requires that we understand the short- and long-run consequences of increases in these taxes.

Crowding Out

Crowding out is the tendency for an expansionary fiscal policy to reduce other components of aggregate expenditures.

Because an expansionary fiscal policy either increases government spending or reduces revenues, it increases the deficit, which equals the difference between government expenditures and government revenues. When expenditures exceed

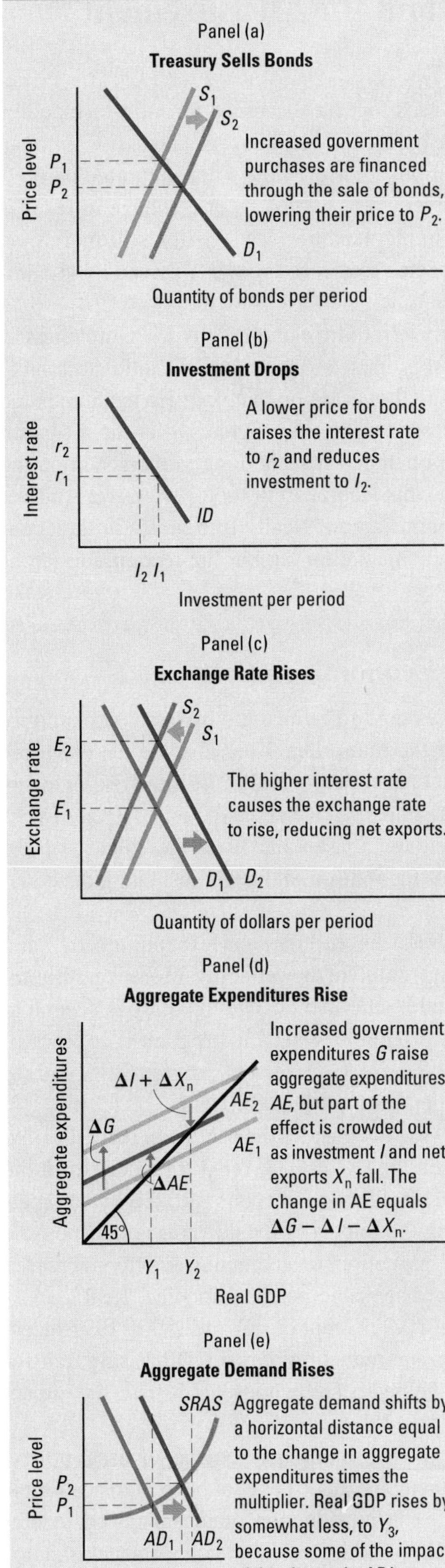
Panel (a)
Treasury Sells Bonds
Price level
P_1
P_2
S_1
S_2
D_1
Increased government purchases are financed through the sale of bonds, lowering their price to P_2.
Quantity of bonds per period
Panel (b)
Investment Drops
Interest rate
r_2
r_1
ID
A lower price for bonds raises the interest rate to r_2 and reduces investment to I_2.
I_2 I_1
Investment per period
Panel (c)
Exchange Rate Rises
Exchange rate
E_2
E_1
S_2
S_1
D_1 D_2
The higher interest rate causes the exchange rate to rise, reducing net exports.
Quantity of dollars per period
Panel (d)
Aggregate Expenditures Rise
Aggregate expenditures
$\Delta I + \Delta X_n$
ΔG
AE_2
AE_1
ΔAE
45°
Increased government expenditures G raise aggregate expenditures AE, but part of the effect is crowded out as investment I and net exports X_n fall. The change in AE equals $\Delta G - \Delta I - \Delta X_n$.
Y_1 Y_2
Real GDP
Panel (e)
Aggregate Demand Rises
Price level
P_2
P_1
SRAS
AD_1 AD_2
Aggregate demand shifts by a horizontal distance equal to the change in aggregate expenditures times the multiplier. Real GDP rises by somewhat less, to Y_3, because some of the impact of the change in AD is absorbed by rising prices.
Y_1 Y_3 Y_2
Real GDP

EXHIBIT 31-12

An Expansionary Fiscal Policy and Crowding Out

revenues, the government makes up the difference by borrowing money through the sale of bonds. A contractionary policy is likely to reduce the deficit and lower the quantity of bonds the government must sell. Fiscal policy thus has implications for the bond market. Our analysis of monetary policy has shown that developments in the bond market can affect investment and net exports. We shall find in this section that the same is true for fiscal policy.

Exhibit 31-12 shows the impact of an expansionary fiscal policy, an increase in government purchases. The increase in government purchases increases the deficit. To finance the increased borrowing, the Treasury will sell bonds, shifting the supply curve for bonds to the right in Panel (a). That reduces the price of bonds, raising the interest rate. The increase in the interest rate reduces investment in Panel (b). The higher interest rate increases the demand for and reduces the supply of dollars in the currency market, raising the exchange rate in Panel (c). A higher exchange rate reduces net exports. Panel (d) shows the effects of all these changes on the aggregate expenditures curve. Before the change in government purchases, the economy is in equilibrium at a real GDP of Y_1, determined by the intersection of AE_1 and the 45-degree line. The increase in government expenditures shifts the curve upward by an amount equal to the increase, ΔG. But the reduction in investment ΔI, together with reduced net exports ΔX_n, offsets this increase. The net change in aggregate expenditures ΔAE leaves the curve at AE_2. The tendency for an expansionary fiscal policy to reduce other components of aggregate expenditures is called **crowding out.**

Income in the aggregate expenditures model rises by an amount equal to the multiplier times the net change in aggregate expenditures; the aggregate demand curve shifts to the right by this same amount in Panel (e). In the short run, this policy leads to an increase in real GDP to Y_3 and a higher price level, P_2.

Crowding out weakens the impact of any expansionary fiscal policy, whether it be an increase in government purchases, an increase in transfer payments, or a reduction in income or payroll taxes. Each of these increases the deficit and thus increases government borrowing. The supply of bonds increases, interest rates rise, investment falls, the exchange rate rises, and net exports fall.

The reverse of crowding out occurs with a contractionary fiscal policy—a cut in government purchases or transfer payments, or an increase in taxes. Such policies reduce the deficit and thus reduce government borrowing, shifting the supply curve for bonds to the left. Interest rates drop, inducing more investment (provided there is no shift in the investment demand curve). Lower interest rates also reduce the demand for and increase the supply of dollars, lowering the exchange rate and boosting net exports.[4]

Crowding out and the reverse of crowding out clearly weaken the impact of fiscal policy. An expansionary fiscal policy has less punch; a contractionary policy puts less of a damper on economic activity. Indeed, we'll see later in this chapter that some economists argue that these forces are so powerful that a change in fiscal policy will have no effect on aggregate demand.

[4] There is no term used by economists for the reverse of crowding out. One of my students once suggested that it be called "inviting in."

Checklist ✓

- Discretionary fiscal policy may be either expansionary or contractionary.
- A change in government purchases shifts the aggregate expenditures curve by an amount equal to the change in government purchases. A change in government transfer payments shifts the aggregate expenditures curve by an amount equal to the change in transfer payments times the marginal propensity to consume. The aggregate demand curve shifts by an amount equal to the change in aggregate expenditures times the multiplier.
- A change in income taxes shifts the aggregate expenditures curve and changes the multiplier. An increase in income taxes reduces the multiplier; a reduction in taxes increases it. Aggregate demand shifts by an amount equal to the change in aggregate expenditures times the multiplier.
- A change in payroll taxes imposed on firms shifts the short-run aggregate supply curve. In the short run, an increase in such taxes reduces employment and real GDP. In the long run, employment and real GDP return to their natural level, and the burden of the payroll tax is shifted to workers.
- An expansionary fiscal policy increases the deficit, crowding out investment and net exports and reducing the expansionary impact of the policy. A contractionary fiscal policy reduces the deficit, increasing investment and net exports and thus lessening the degree to which the policy reduces real GDP.

Automatic Stabilizers and the Measurement of Fiscal Policy

Fiscal policy is subject to the same lags that we discussed for monetary policy. Policymakers will require some time before they realize that a recessionary or an inflationary gap exists—the recognition lag. More time will be required before a fiscal policy such as a change in government purchases or a change in taxes is agreed to and put into effect—the implementation lag. Finally, still more time will be required before the policy begins to affect aggregate demand—the impact lag.

Changes in fiscal policy are likely to require a particularly long implementation lag. The tax cut of 1964 was first proposed to presidential candidate John F. Kennedy in 1960 as a means of ending the recession that year. He recommended it to Congress in 1962. It was not passed until 1964, 3 years after the recession had ended. Some economists have concluded that the long implementation lag for discretionary fiscal policy makes this stabilization tool ineffective. Another form of fiscal policy, however, responds automatically to changes in the economy. It thus avoids not only the implementation lag but the recognition lag as well.

Automatic Stabilizers and Economic Activity

We've already seen that income taxes tend to reduce the marginal expenditure rate and thus to reduce the value of the multiplier. They insulate the economy from the impact of shocks that might raise or lower real GDP. Transfer payments have the same effect. They reduce the impact of a change in real GDP on disposable personal income and thus insulate households from the impact of the change. They also reduce the value of the multiplier, further insulating the economy from the impact of the shock.

Any government program that reduces the marginal expenditure rate and thereby reduces the multiplier tends to stabilize the economy. Moreover, the stabilizing effect of such programs is automatic. No change in policy is needed to initiate the stabilizing effect of such programs. Once the program is in place, it automatically acts to stabilize the economy. Government programs that reduce the marginal expenditure rate are called **automatic stabilizers.**

Automatic stabilizers are government programs that tend to reduce the marginal expenditure rate.

To see how automatic stabilizers work, consider the decline in real GDP that occurred during the 1990–1991 recession. Real GDP fell 1.6 percent from the peak to the trough of that recession. The reduction in economic activity automatically reduced tax payments, reducing the impact of the downturn on disposable personal income. Furthermore, the reduction in economic activity increased transfer payment spending, boosting disposable personal income. Real disposable personal income thus fell by only 0.9 percent during the 1990–1991 recession, a much smaller percentage than the reduction in real GDP. Rising transfer payments and falling tax collections helped cushion households from the impact of the recession.

Automatic stabilizers have emerged as important elements of fiscal policy. Increases in income tax rates and unemployment benefits have enhanced their importance as automatic stabilizers. The introduction of means-tested federal transfer payments in the 1960s and 1970s added to the nation's arsenal of automatic stabilizers. The advantage of automatic stabilizers is suggested by their name. As soon as income starts to change, they go to work. Because they affect disposable personal income directly, and because changes in disposable personal income are so closely linked to changes in consumption, automatic stabilizers act swiftly to dampen the impact of changes in autonomous expenditures on the level of economic activity.

Remember that the impact of automatic stabilizers is already reflected in the economy's aggregate expenditures curve. Changes in transfer payments or in tax collections that result from a change in real GDP don't shift the aggregate expenditures curve. They therefore do not shift aggregate demand. Only if there are changes in automatic stabilizer programs themselves will such programs shift the aggregate expenditures curve. Changes such as a change in income tax rates or a change in the level of compensation provided to unemployed workers will shift the aggregate expenditures curve. Changes in income tax collections or in unemployment compensation spending resulting from a change in real GDP do not.

The Measurement of Fiscal Policy

Federal expenditures and tax revenues remained roughly constant during the 1990–1991 recession. Does that mean fiscal policy had no effect? As the economy recovered between 1991 and 1994, federal expenditures and tax revenues rose. Was fiscal policy expansionary or contractionary?

The existence of automatic stabilizers means we can't simply look at real changes in expenditures or tax receipts and conclude such changes were expansionary or contractionary. Some changes in expenditures and revenues occur in response to changes in economic activity. They don't change the level of economic activity; they respond to it.

Suppose, for example, that real GDP is shrinking, as it was during the 1990–1991 recession. Spending for programs such as unemployment compensation and welfare will automatically go up. Real levels of tax revenues will fall because a reduced level of economic activity gives the government a smaller base from which to draw its revenues. Such automatic responses do not shift the aggregate expenditures or aggregate demand curves; they don't represent changes in fiscal policy.

How, then, are we to interpret data on federal expenditures and revenues? How can we tell whether a particular policy change will shift the aggregate demand curve? To see how economists resolve this difficulty, we'll examine the nature of federal budgets and then see how budget data can be used to determine whether fiscal policy is acting to change the level of economic activity.

The Federal Budget

We can think of the federal government's budget as being represented by two schedules, a **federal government expenditures curve** and a **federal government revenue curve.** A federal government expenditures curve shows the level of federal expenditures at each level of real GDP. A federal government revenue curve shows federal revenues at each level of real GDP. Because transfer payment spending tends to fall as real GDP rises, the expenditures curve is downward sloping. Because federal tax revenues rise as real GDP rises, the revenue curve slopes upward.

- The **federal government expenditures curve** shows the negative relationship between total nominal federal government expenditures and real GDP.
- The **federal government revenue curve** shows the positive relationship between total nominal federal revenues and real GDP.

EXHIBIT 31-13

The Federal Budget and Real GDP

The table shows hypothetical levels of federal expenditures and revenues at various levels of real GDP. The federal government's budget can be represented graphically with two curves, a government expenditures curve *(EXP)* and a government revenue curve *(REV)*. If expenditures exceed revenues, the government has a deficit. If revenues exceed expenditures, there is a surplus. We see that the federal government has a deficit at levels of real GDP below $4,400 billion and a surplus at levels of real GDP above $4,400 billion. There is a balanced budget at a real GDP of $4,400 billion. All figures are in billions of dollars.

Real GDP	Federal Revenues	Federal Expenditures	Surplus or deficit (−)
$3,500	$1,675	$2,125	−$450
3,600	1,700	2,100	−400
3,700	1,725	2,075	−350
3,800	1,750	2,050	−300
3,900	1,775	2,025	−250
4,000	1,800	2,000	−200
4,100	1,825	1,975	−150
4,200	1,850	1,950	−100
4,300	1,875	1,925	−50
4,400	1,900	1,900	0
4,500	1,925	1,875	50

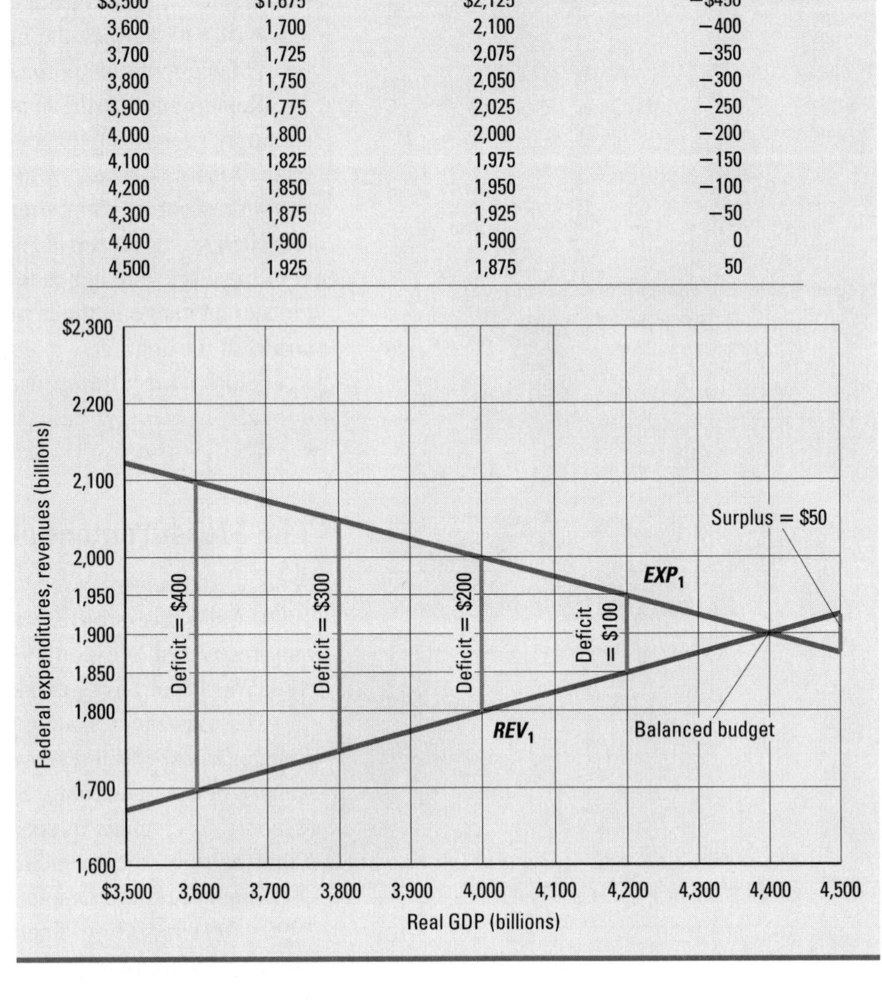

Exhibit 31-13 presents hypothetical values for federal expenditures and revenues at levels of real GDP ranging from $3,500 billion to $4,500 billion. The budget **surplus** equals revenues minus expenditures at any level of real GDP. In cases in which expenditures exceed revenues, the surplus is negative. A negative surplus is a **deficit.** In the case shown, the government has a deficit at levels of real GDP below $4,400 billion and a surplus at levels of real GDP above $4,400 billion. We can omit the minus sign in reporting a deficit. Thus, at a level of real GDP of $3,600 billion, we would say that the deficit equals $400 billion. Alternatively, we can say that the surplus equals −$400 billion. If the surplus equals zero, we say the government has a **balanced budget.** In Exhibit 31-13, the budget is balanced at a level of real GDP of $4,400 billion.

- The government **surplus** equals government revenue less government expenditures.
- A **deficit** is a negative surplus; it occurs if government expenditures exceed government revenue.
- The government has a **balanced budget** if the surplus equals zero.
- The **cyclically adjusted budget** shows what federal expenditures and revenues would be if the economy were operating at its natural level of output.

The Cyclically Adjusted Budget

There are three ways the federal government deficit or surplus can change. First, it can change because of a shift in the government expenditures curve. That would occur if Congress chose to alter the level of federal purchases or to change the structure of transfer payment programs. Second, the federal deficit can be affected by a change in federal tax rates that would shift the federal rev-

Reader's Advisory

Because the federal government revenue and expenditures curves intersect, it is tempting to interpret that intersection as an equilibrium level of real GDP. It isn't. The revenue and expenditures curves simply show levels of government revenue and spending at each level of real GDP; they do not determine equilibrium in the sense that the intersection of demand and supply curves determine equilibrium price and output. Equilibrium real GDP is determined by aggregate demand and aggregate supply. We then apply that level of real GDP to the federal government expenditures and revenue curves to determine the size of the deficit.

enue curve. Third, the federal deficit or surplus could change if real GDP changed, moving the government *along* the revenue and expenditures curves.

A change in the federal deficit or surplus that results from a change in real GDP does not shift the aggregate demand curve. The responses of expenditures and revenues to changes in the level of real GDP are already reflected in the aggregate expenditures curve and thus in the aggregate demand curve. Changes in the federal deficit or surplus that result from shifts in the government expenditures or revenue curves do shift the aggregate demand curve.

If we simply look at actual federal revenue and expenditures data for a particular period, we cannot say what was happening with fiscal policy. We can only determine whether fiscal policy is expansionary or contractionary by seeing whether the revenue and expenditure curves are shifted. But how are we to make such a determination?

We can determine whether the federal expenditures or revenue curves have shifted by examining the levels of federal expenditure and revenue that would occur *at a particular level* of real GDP. Those levels can change only if one or both of the curves shift. Economists use the economy's natural level of output to assess whether fiscal policy has changed. The **cyclically adjusted budget** shows what federal revenue and expenditures would be *if* the economy were operating at its natural level of real GDP. If government expenditures were to exceed revenues at the natural level of real GDP, there is a cyclically adjusted deficit. If revenue were to exceed expenditures, there is a cyclically adjusted surplus.

Exhibit 31-14 shows the cyclically adjusted budget for the government expenditures and revenue curves given in Exhibit 31-13, assuming the economy's natural level of real GDP is $4,200 billion. At that level of real GDP, federal expenditures would equal $1,950 billion and federal revenues would equal $1,850 billion, for a cyclically adjusted deficit of $100 billion.

EXHIBIT 31-14

The Cyclically Adjusted Budget

The cyclically adjusted budget shows the levels of government revenue and expenditures that would occur if the economy were operating at its natural level. Here, the natural level of real GDP is $4,200 billion and there is a cyclically adjusted deficit of $100 billion.

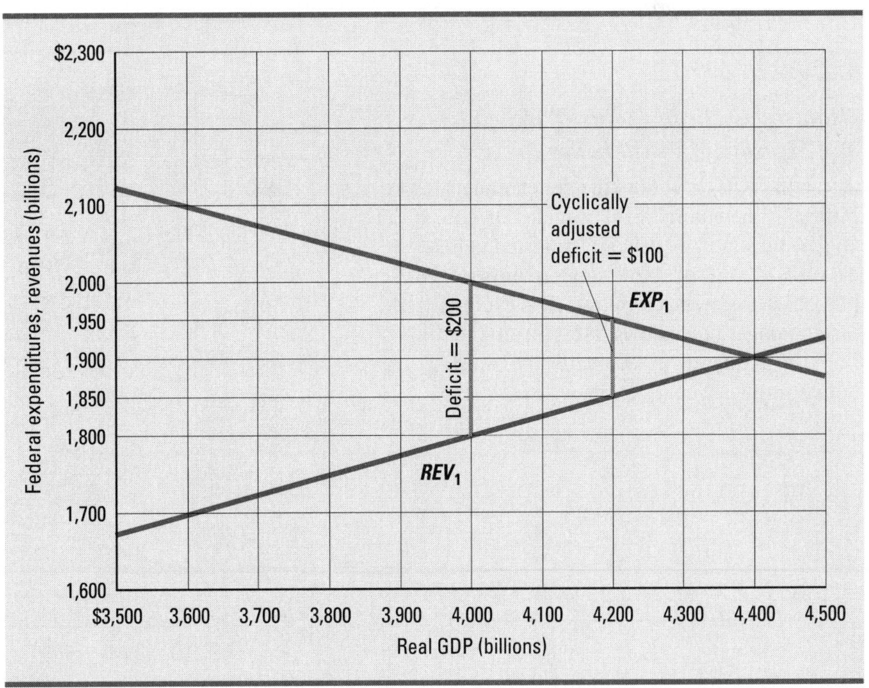

Suppose real GDP equals $4,000 billion, resulting in a deficit of $200 billion (note there is a recessionary gap). Now suppose real GDP falls to $3,800 billion. We see that federal expenditures rise to $2,050 billion while revenues fall to $1,750 billion, increasing the deficit to $300 billion. These changes in federal expenditures and revenue are responses to the reduction in real GDP; they do not shift aggregate demand. The test for whether a change in expenditures or revenues shifts the aggregate demand curve is to examine the cyclically adjusted budget. We see that the cyclically adjusted deficit has not changed; it remains $100 billion. When there is no change in the cyclically adjusted budget, there is no change in fiscal policy.

The cyclically adjusted deficit increases if the federal government expenditures curve shifts upward or if the federal government revenue curve shifts downward. An increase in the cyclically adjusted deficit is, therefore, generally taken as an indication that fiscal policy is expansionary. A reduction in the cyclically adjusted deficit, which implies a shift downward in the federal government expenditures curve or a shift upward in the federal government revenue curve, implies a contractionary fiscal policy.

Exhibit 31-15 shows the expenditures and revenue curves that we examined in the last two exhibits. Assume that the economy's natural level of real GDP remains at $4,200 billion and that real GDP now equals $4,000 billion—there is a recessionary gap. Now suppose government purchases are cut by $200 billion, shifting the government expenditures curve down to EXP_2. We can assess this policy first in terms of its effect on the cyclically adjusted budget. Cyclically adjusted expenditures fall by $200 billion, converting a cyclically adjusted deficit of $100 billion to a surplus of $100 billion. This change in the cyclically adjusted budget implies a contractionary fiscal policy.

A contractionary fiscal policy shifts the aggregate demand curve to the left and reduces real GDP. Suppose it falls to $3,700 billion. We consult EXP_2 and REV_1 and find that expenditures have fallen to $1,875 and revenue to $1,725, for

EXHIBIT 31-15

Using the Cyclically Adjusted Deficit as a Measure of Fiscal Policy

At a real GDP of $4,000, the deficit equals $200 billion. If the natural level of real GDP equals $4,200 billion, the cyclically adjusted deficit equals $100 billion. Now suppose government purchases fall by $200 billion. The cyclically adjusted budget now shows a surplus of $100 billion; this reduction in the cyclically adjusted deficit implies a contractionary fiscal policy.

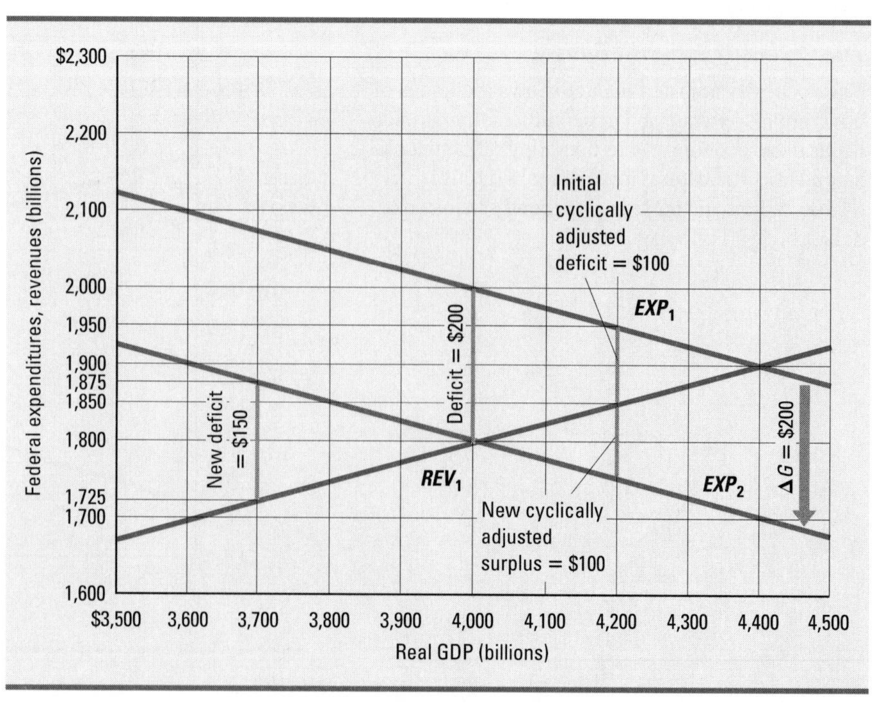

Case in Point — Fiscal Policy and the 1990–1991 Recession

We saw in the last chapter that the Fed responded vigorously to the 1990–1991 recession, launching an expansionary monetary policy to close a recessionary gap. What happened with fiscal policy?

At first glance, the fiscal policy might be regarded as expansionary. Federal revenues fell and federal spending rose. As we've seen, however, we can't determine whether fiscal policy is expansionary by looking at spending and revenue totals. A reduction in economic activity automatically cuts revenues as incomes fall. Those reductions in income will automatically boost transfer payment spending as people lose jobs. Such automatic responses to changes in economic activity don't shift the aggregate demand curve. They therefore do not constitute an expansionary fiscal policy.

To gauge whether fiscal policy is expansionary or contractionary, we must look at cyclically adjusted spending and revenue, not the simple totals. The accompanying table gives actual versus cyclically adjusted federal spending and revenue on a quarterly basis for 1990 and for the first half of 1991. The recession began in the third quarter of 1990 and continued through the first quarter of 1991. We see that on a cyclically adjusted basis, federal revenues rose. Expenditures followed a mixed pattern. They fell slightly as the recession began, rose in the fourth quarter, and then fell sharply again in the first quarter of 1991.

Using the criterion that an expansionary policy increases the cyclically adjusted deficit while a contractionary policy reduces it, we see that fiscal policy was contractionary as the recession began, became modestly expansionary in the fourth quarter, and then became sharply contractionary in the first quarter of 1991. That was the first quarter following a large tax increase in the fourth quarter of 1990. Clearly, the driving force for fiscal policy was concern about the deficit, not concern about stabilizing the economy. All figures are in billions of dollars and are seasonally adjusted at annual rates.

Quarters		Receipts		Expenditures		Surplus or Deficit (−)	
		Actual	Cyclically Adjusted	Actual	Cyclically Adjusted	Actual	Cyclically Adjusted
1990	1	$1,091.3	$1.061.7	$1,257.8	$1,252.2	−$166.4	−$190.5
	2	1,114.5	1,093.4	1,266.5	1,275.4	−152.0	−182.0
	3	1,123.7	1,116.0	1,268.3	1,273.6	−144.6	−157.6
	4	1,115.8	1,132.1	1,306.9	1,311.2	−191.0	−179.1
1991	1	1,120.1	1,160.1	1,264.5	1,257.9	−144.4	−97.8
	2	1,121.8	1,173.7	1,329.4	1,319.3	−207.6	−145.6

Source: Federal Reserve Bank of St. Louis, *National Economic Trends* (December 1994): 22. Figures may not add because of rounding.

a new deficit of $150 billion. The $200 billion cut in government purchases has reduced the deficit by $50 billion.

How could a $200 billion cut in government purchases produce only a $50 billion reduction in the deficit? The cut is a contractionary fiscal policy; it shifts aggregate demand to the left. That reduces real GDP. The changes in federal spending and revenue that we observe thus reflect two sets of changes. First, government purchases have fallen, reducing federal expenditures at every level of real GDP by $200 billion. Second, real GDP has fallen, inducing greater federal expenditures and lower revenue. We can untangle those effects and determine that the federal government has engaged in a contractionary policy by observing what has happened to the cyclically adjusted deficit.

Checklist

- Taxes and transfer payments reduce the multiplier and thus act as automatic stabilizers.
- Because tax collections and transfer payments respond automatically to changes in real GDP, we cannot conclude that a change in government expenditures or a change in tax collections implies an expansionary or a contractionary fiscal policy.
- An expansionary policy implies an increase in the cyclically adjusted deficit; a contractionary policy reduces the cyclically adjusted deficit.

A Look Back—And a Look Ahead

The government sector plays a major role in the economy. The spending, tax, and transfer policies of local, state, and federal agencies affect aggregate demand and aggregate supply and thus affect the level of real GDP and the price level.

Government purchases of goods and services have a direct impact on aggregate expenditures. All other things equal, a change in government purchases produces an equal vertical change in aggregate expenditures. That changes the equilibrium level of income in the aggregate expenditures model by an amount equal to the change in aggregate expenditures times the multiplier. The change in the equilibrium solution in the aggregate expenditures model gives the amount by which the aggregate demand curve shifts to the right or left. An increase in government purchases shifts the aggregate expenditures curve upward and shifts the aggregate demand curve to the right; a reduction in government purchases shifts the aggregate expenditures curve downward and shifts the aggregate demand curve to the left.

Changes in tax rates or in the level of transfer payments affect disposable personal income. They change consumption by an amount equal to the marginal propensity to consume times the change in taxes or transfer payments. They thus cause shifts in aggregate expenditures and in aggregate demand. Changes in income taxes also affect the slope of the aggregate demand curve and thus affect the multiplier. An increase in income tax rates makes the aggregate demand curve flatter and reduces the multiplier. A reduction in income tax rates makes the curve steeper and increases the multiplier.

Government policies also affect aggregate supply. Fiscal policy can affect the short-run aggregate supply curve by changing labor costs through payroll tax changes. Ultimately, however, payroll taxes are shifted fully to the worker; they have no long-run impact on the economy as a whole.

Fiscal policies generate some crowding out. An expansionary fiscal policy tends to reduce investment and net exports; a contractionary fiscal policy tends to increase investment and net exports.

We assess whether fiscal policy is expansionary or contractionary by examining changes in the cyclically adjusted deficit. An increase in the cyclically adjusted deficit implies an expansionary fiscal policy. A reduction in the cyclically adjusted deficit implies a contractionary policy.

We've now examined the two major areas of macroeconomic policy—fiscal policy and monetary policy. In the next chapter we'll turn to a key issue that affects policy choices in both arenas: the nature of the relationship between inflation and unemployment. Both are problems policymakers would like to avoid, but efforts to reduce one can sometimes increase the other. An expansionary policy that seeks to reduce unemployment, for example, may boost inflation.

Terms and Concepts for Review

Automatic stabilizers
Balanced budget
Cost per unit of labor
Crowding out
Cyclically adjusted budget
Deficit
Federal government expenditures curve
Federal government revenue curve
Surplus

For Discussion

1. What is the difference between government expenditures and government purchases? How do the two variables differ in terms of their effect on GDP?
2. Federally funded student aid programs generally reduce benefits by $1 for every $1 that recipients earn. Do such programs represent government purchases or transfer payments? Are they automatic stabilizers? Do they affect the multiplier? How?
3. Crowding out reduces the degree to which a change in government purchases influences the level of economic activity. Is it a form of automatic stabilizer?
4. Suppose unemployment compensation were reduced and income taxes were cut by an equal amount? How would the aggregate demand curve be affected?
5. Suppose a program of federally funded public works spending were introduced that was tied to the unemployment rate. Suppose the program were structured so that public works spending would be $200 billion per year if the economy were at full employment at the beginning of the fiscal year. Public works spending would be increased by $20 billion for each percentage point by which the unemployment rate exceeded 6 percent. It would be reduced by $20 billion for every percentage point by which unemployment fell below 6 percent. If the unemployment rate were 9 percent, for example, public works spending would be $260 billion. How would this program affect the aggregate expenditures curve?
6. Was the Swedish investment fund strategy described in the Case in Point a discretionary fiscal policy or an automatic stabilizer? Why do you think it was suspended?
7. Why is the actual deficit less than the cyclically adjusted deficit when there is an inflationary gap but greater than the cyclically adjusted deficit when there is a recessionary gap?
8. Suppose the president were given the authority to increase or decrease federal spending by as much as $50 billion in order to stabilize economic activity. Do you think this would tend to make the economy more or less stable?
9. When President Clinton proposed his jobs stimulus package in the spring of 1993, some new Keynesian economists opposed the measure. But the economy then was operating below its natural level. Why might a new Keynesian economist oppose an expansionary fiscal policy for an economy with a recessionary gap?
10. Why did the federal government adopt a contractionary fiscal policy in the midst of the 1990–1991 recession, as described in the Case in Point essay?
11. Compare the actual and cyclically adjusted deficit figures in the Case in Point on the 1990–1991 recession. What sort of gap (recessionary, inflationary, or none) existed in each quarter of the period shown? How can you tell?

Problems

1. Suppose the federal government required firms to pay for each employee's consumption of housing. Illustrate graphically the effect of such a requirement on real GDP and the price level in the short run and in the long run. (*Hint:* Use the analysis in the Case in Point essay on health care costs and employment.)
2. Suppose the government increases purchases in an economy with a recessionary gap. How would this policy affect bond prices, interest rates, planned investment, net exports, real GDP, and the price level? (Answer from a new Keynesian perspective, and show your results graphically.)
3. Suppose the government cuts transfer payments in an economy with an inflationary gap. How would this policy affect bond prices, interest rates, investment, the exchange rate, net exports, real GDP, and the price level? (Answer from a new Keynesian perspective.)
4. Suppose an economy has a consumption function $C = \$100 + 2/3Y_d$. The income tax rate is 10 percent, and $Y_d = 0.9Y$. Government purchases, investment, and net exports each equal $100. Solve the following problems. (*Hint:* Use the value 2/3 in your calculations—don't express it as 0.67.)
   a. Draw the aggregate expenditures curve, and find the equilibrium income for this economy in the aggregate expenditures model.
   b. Now suppose the tax rate rises to 25 percent, so $Y_d = 0.75Y$. Assume that government purchases, investments, and net exports are not affected by the change. Show the new aggregate expenditures curve and the new equilibrium level of income in the model. Relate your answer to the multiplier effect of the tax change. Compare your result in the aggregate expenditures model to what the aggregate demand–aggregate supply model would show.
5. Suppose a government's revenues R are related to real GDP as follows:

$$R = 0.2Y$$

   Its expenditures E are given by

$$E = \$2,600 - 0.2Y$$

   a. Draw the expenditures and revenue curves.
   b. Compute the deficit or surplus at a real GDP of $6,000.
   c. Compute the deficit or surplus at a real GDP of $8,000.
   d. Using your graph, determine the level of real GDP at which the budget would be balanced.
   e. Suppose the natural level of real GDP is $6,000. What is the cyclically adjusted deficit in this economy?

32

Inflation and Unemployment

Chapter Objectives

After mastering the material in this chapter, you will be able to:

1. Show graphically the concept of a tradeoff between unemployment and inflation and discuss the evidence concerning the relationship between these two variables.
2. Use the model of aggregate demand and aggregate supply to explain how a negative relationship could exist between inflation and unemployment in the short run. Use the same model to suggest how unemployment could rise with little change in inflation and how inflation and unemployment could fall at the same time.
3. Explain how expectations concerning inflation affect the relationship between inflation and unemployment.
4. Identify the major determinants of the rate of inflation and discuss the factors that affect the natural rate of unemployment.

". . . the experience of the past three decades has demonstrated that what appears to be a tradeoff between unemployment and inflation is quite ephemeral and misleading.

Alan Greenspan, 1994

What's Ahead

It was a classic confrontation over a fundamental issue. Federal Reserve Chairman Alan Greenspan, testifying before the Joint Economic Committee of Congress early in 1994, reported that the Fed would soon begin open-market operations to raise interest rates and to reduce the money supply. The Fed would continue to do so, he said, as long as there was any indication that inflation might accelerate.

While some members of the committee expressed support for the new policy, others were not so sure. Senator Paul Sarbanes (D–Maryland) charged that the Fed's action threatened employment.

Mr. Greenspan rejected the argument. He said that a policy that keeps inflation in check is the most likely to sustain a high level of employment in the long run. Trying to stimulate the economy in order to boost employment and reduce unemployment in the short run, he insisted, would only lead to higher inflation—and still higher unemployment.

Who's right? What is the relationship between inflation and unemployment? Can policymakers choose one or the other, as Mr. Sarbanes seemed to suggest, or would an effort to bring unemployment down be likely to produce more inflation and still more unemployment?

This chapter explores the answers to these and related questions. We'll find that there have been periods in which a clear tradeoff between inflation and unemployment seemed to exist. During such periods, the economy achieved reductions in unemployment at the expense of increased inflation. But there have also been periods in which inflation and unemployment rose together—and periods in which both variables fell together. We'll examine some alternative explanations for the sometimes perplexing relationship between the two variables.

Inflation and Unemployment: Is There a Tradeoff?

The introduction to this chapter noted a basic issue concerning inflation and unemployment: Is there a tradeoff between these two problems? Does progress against inflation come only at the expense of greater unemployment? Can we achieve reduced unemployment only at the expense of greater inflation?

Clearly, it would be desirable to reduce both variables. Unemployment represents a lost opportunity for workers to engage in productive effort. Inflation erodes the value of money people hold, and more important, the threat of inflation adds to uncertainty and makes people less willing to invest. If there is a tradeoff between the two, we can't make progress against both at the same time. We must pick our poison, choosing which malady to accept more of and which to avoid. But if no tradeoff exists, policymakers could seek gains against one problem without worrying about suffering setbacks against the other.

We'll begin our investigation of the relationship between inflation and unemployment by looking at the history of these two variables. We'll find that the answer to the question of whether there is a tradeoff is, "Sometimes." There have indeed been periods in which gains against unemployment were achieved at a cost of greater inflation. But there have also been times when both problems got worse—and times when both got better.

The fact that inflation and unemployment are related in a fashion that is more complex than that suggested by the notion of a tradeoff is suggested by the late Arthur Okun's "misery index," a number found by adding the inflation and unemployment rates for a particular period. Okun, who served as an economic adviser to Presidents John F. Kennedy and Lyndon B. Johnson, devised the index as a measure of economic unhappiness. He argued that if inflation is a bad thing and unemployment is a bad thing, then a higher misery index clearly indicates poor economic performance. The misery index also serves as a rough test of the tradeoff idea. If less unemployment implies more inflation, and vice versa, then misery index scores should be quite stable.

Exhibit 32-1 shows the misery index for the United States since 1950. The index has been anything but stable. After bouncing around after World War II,

EXHIBIT 32-1

The U.S. Misery Index, 1950–1995

The misery index is found by adding the inflation rate to the unemployment rate. Misery values in the United States reached their highest levels during the 1970s.

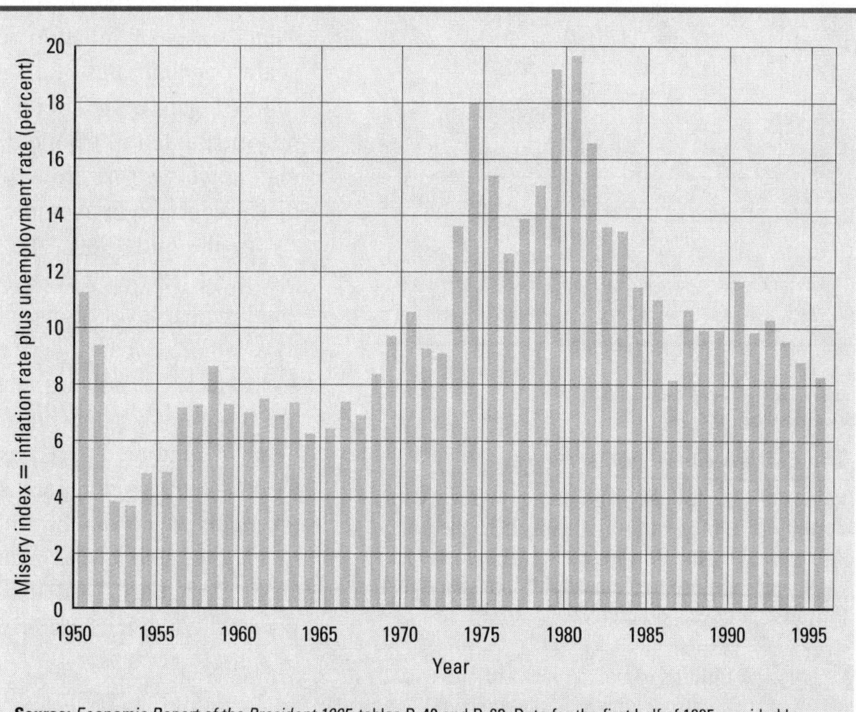

Source: *Economic Report of the President 1995,* tables B-40 and B-63. Data for the first half of 1995 provided by Labor Department.

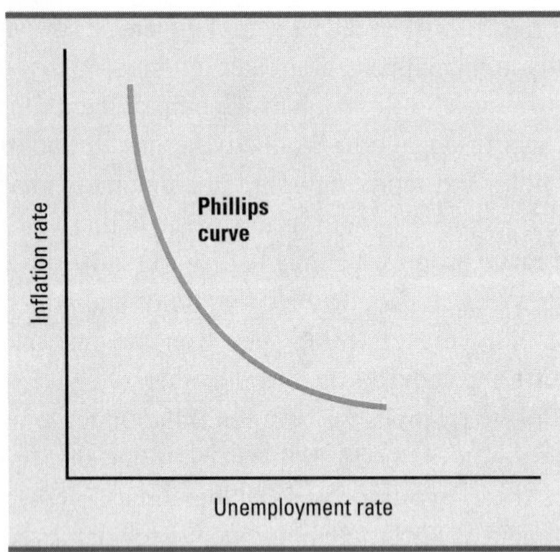

EXHIBIT 32-2

The Phillips Curve

The relationship between inflation and unemployment suggested by the work of Almarin Phillips is shown by a Phillips curve.

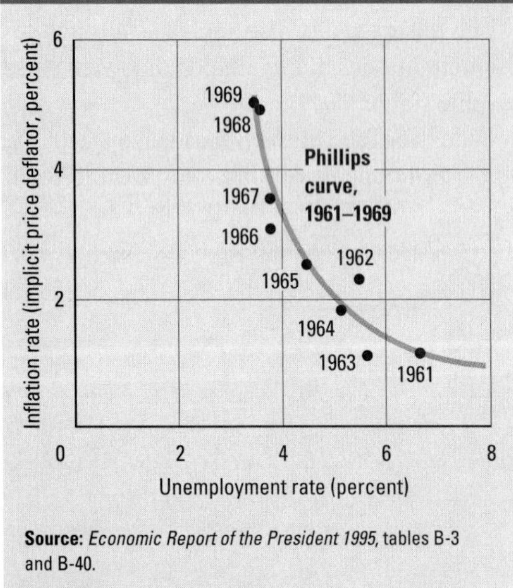

Source: *Economic Report of the President 1995*, tables B-3 and B-40.

EXHIBIT 32-3

The Phillips Curve in the 1960s

Values of U.S. inflation and unemployment rates during the 1960s conformed closely to the tradeoff implied by the Phillips curve. The points for each year lie close to a curve with the shape that Phillips's analysis predicted.

A **Phillips curve** implies a negative relationship between inflation and unemployment.

it stayed fairly low through the 1950s and 1960s and then soared in the 1970s. The index declined in the 1980s, but it has remained above the levels of the 1950s and 1960s.

The misery index suggests that there's more to the relationship between inflation and unemployment than a simple tradeoff. The next section examines the intellectual roots of the tradeoff argument and then looks at the evidence of inflation and unemployment rates in the United States.

The Phillips Curve

In 1958, New Zealand–born economist Almarin Phillips reported that his analysis of a century of British wage and unemployment data suggested that an inverse relationship existed between rates of increase in wages and British unemployment.[1] Economists were quick to incorporate this idea into their thinking, extending the relationship to the rate of price-level changes—inflation—and unemployment. The notion that there is a tradeoff between inflation and unemployment is expressed by a **Phillips curve,** a curve that suggests a negative relationship between the two. Exhibit 32-2 shows a Phillips curve.

The Phillips curve seemed to make good theoretical sense. Keynesian analysis, which was the dominant school of economic thought in the 1960s, suggested that the economy was likely to experience either a recessionary or inflationary gap. An economy with a recessionary gap would have high unemployment and little or no inflation. An economy with an inflationary gap would have very little unemployment and a higher rate of inflation. The Phillips curve suggested a smooth transition between the two. As expansionary policies were undertaken to move the economy out of a recessionary gap, unemployment would fall and inflation would rise. Policies to correct an inflationary gap would bring down the inflation rate, but at a cost of higher unemployment.

The experience of the 1960s suggested that precisely the kind of tradeoff the Phillips curve implied did, in fact, exist in the United States. Exhibit 32-3 shows annual rates of inflation (computed using the implicit price deflator) plotted against annual rates of unemployment from 1961 to 1969. The points appear to follow a path quite similar to a Phillips curve relationship. The civilian unemployment rate fell from 6.7 percent in 1961 to 3.5 percent in 1969. The inflation rate, however, rose from 1 percent in 1961 to 5.5 percent in 1969. It appeared that a reduction in unemployment had been "traded" for an increase in inflation.

In the mid-1960s, the economy moved into an inflationary gap as unemployment fell below its natural level. The economy had already reached its full employment level of output when the 1964 tax cut was passed. The Fed undertook a more expansionary monetary policy at the same time. The combined effect of the two policies was an increase in aggregate demand, one that pushed the economy beyond full employment and into an inflationary gap. Aggregate demand continued to rise as U.S. spending for the war in Vietnam expanded and as President Lyndon Johnson launched an ambitious program aimed at putting an end to poverty in the United States.

By the end of the decade, unemployment at 3.5 percent was substantially below its natural level, estimated by the Congressional Budget Office to be 5.6 percent. When Richard Nixon became president in 1969 it was widely believed

[1] Almarin W. Phillips, "The Relation between Unemployment and the Rate of Change of Money Wage Rates in the United Kingdom, 1861–1957," *Economica* 25 (November 1958): 283–299.

Case in Point Some Reflections on the 1970s

Looking back, we may find it difficult to appreciate how stunning the experience of 1970 and 1971 was. But those two years changed the face of macroeconomic thought.

Introductory textbooks of that time contained no mention of aggregate supply. The model of choice was the aggregate expenditures model. Students learned that the economy could be in equilibrium below full employment, in which case unemployment would be the primary macroeconomic problem. Alternatively, equilibrium could occur at an income greater than the full employment level, in which case inflation would be the main culprit to worry about.

These ideas could be summarized using a Phillips curve, a new analytical device. It suggested that economists could lay out for policymakers a menu of possibilities. Policymakers could then choose the mix of inflation and unemployment they were willing to accept. Economists would then show them how to attain that mix with the appropriate fiscal and monetary policies.

Then 1970 and 1971 came crashing in on this well-ordered fantasy. President Nixon had come to office with a pledge to bring down inflation. The consumer price index had risen 4.7 percent during 1968, the highest rate since 1951. Mr. Nixon cut government purchases in 1969, and the Fed produced a sharp slowing in money growth. The president's economic advisers predicted at the beginning of 1970 that inflation and unemployment would both fall. Appraising the 1970 debacle early in 1971, the president's economists said that the experience had not been consistent with what standard models would predict. The economists suggested, however, that this was probably due to a number of transitory factors. Their forecast that inflation and unemployment would improve in 1971 proved wide of the mark—both got worse that year.

As we'll see, the experience can be readily explained using the model of aggregate demand and aggregate supply. But this tool wasn't well developed then. The experience of the 1970s forced economists back to their analytical drawing boards and spawned dramatic advances in our understanding of macroeconomic events. We'll explore many of those advances in the next chapter.

Source: *Economic Report of the President 1971*, pp. 60–84.

that, with an economy operating with an inflationary gap, it was time to move back down the Phillips curve, trading a reduction in inflation for an increase in unemployment. President Nixon moved to do precisely that, serving up a contractionary fiscal policy and seeking—and getting—a contractionary monetary policy from the Fed.

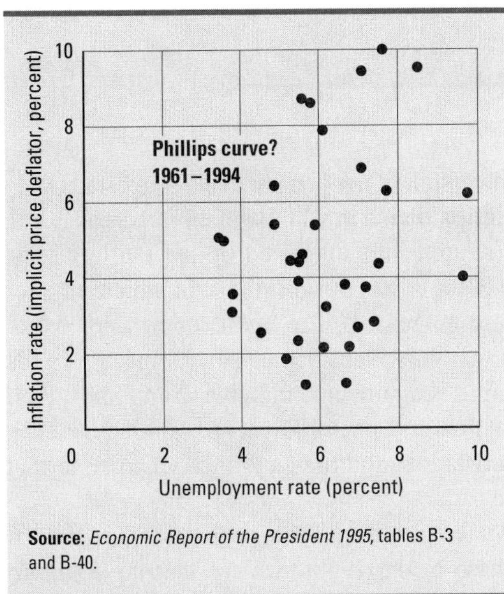

Source: *Economic Report of the President 1995*, tables B-3 and B-40.

EXHIBIT 32-4

Inflation and Unemployment, 1961–1994

Annual observations of inflation and unemployment from 1961 to 1994 do not seem consistent with a Phillips curve.

The Phillips Curve Goes Awry

The Nixon administration's plan to nudge the economy back down the Phillips curve to an unemployment rate closer to the natural level and a lower rate of inflation met with an unhappy surprise in 1970. Unemployment increased as expected. But inflation rose! The inflation rate, measured by the implicit price deflator, edged up to 5.4 percent from its 1969 level of 5 percent.

The tidy relationship between inflation and unemployment that had been suggested by the experience of the 1960s fell apart in the 1970s. Unemployment continued to rise in 1971—and the inflation rate held steady. In 1972, both rates fell. The economy seemed to fall back into the pattern described by the Phillips curve in 1973, as inflation rose while unemployment fell. But the next two years saw increases in both rates. The Phillips curve relationship between inflation and unemployment that had seemed to hold true in the 1960s no longer seemed to prevail.

Indeed, a look at annual rates of inflation and unemployment since 1961 suggests that the 1960s were quite atypical. Exhibit 32-4 shows the two variables over the period from 1961 through 1994. It's hard to see a Phillips curve lurking within that seemingly random scatter of points.

The Cycle of Inflation and Unemployment

Although the points plotted in Exhibit 32-4 aren't consistent with a Phillips curve, we can find a relationship. Suppose we connect the observations sequentially, as is done in Exhibit 32-5. This approach suggests a pattern of clockwise loops. We see periods in which inflation rises as unemployment falls, followed by periods in which unemployment rises while inflation remains high. And those periods are followed by periods in which inflation and unemployment both fall.

EXHIBIT 32-5

Inflation and Unemployment: Clockwise Loops

Connecting observed values for unemployment and inflation sequentially suggests a cyclical pattern of clockwise loops over the period 1961–1994.

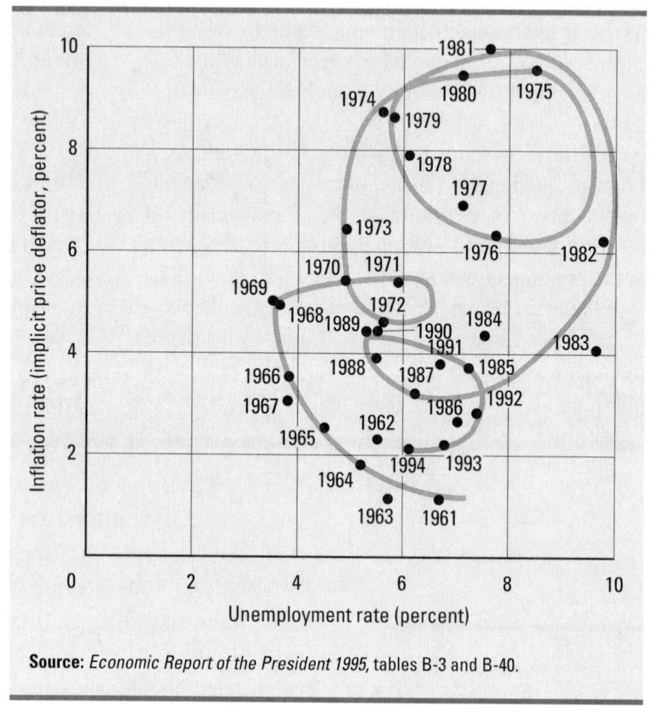

Source: *Economic Report of the President 1995*, tables B-3 and B-40.

Exhibit 32-6 gives an idealized version of the general cycle suggested by the data in Exhibit 32-5. There is a **Phillips phase** in which inflation rises as unemployment falls. In this phase, the relationship suggested by the Phillips curve holds. The Phillips phase is followed by a **stagflation phase** in which inflation remains high while unemployment increases. The term, coined by Massachusetts Institute of Technology economist Paul Samuelson during the 1970s, suggests a combination of a stagnating economy and inflation. And finally, there is a **recovery phase** in which inflation and unemployment both decline. This pattern of a Phillips phase, then stagflation, and then a recovery can be termed the **inflation-unemployment cycle.**

- The **Phillips phase** is a period in which the inflation rate rises and the unemployment rate falls.
- The **stagflation phase** is a period in which inflation remains high while unemployment increases.
- The **recovery phase** is a period in which inflation and unemployment decline.
- The **inflation-unemployment cycle** is the pattern of a Phillips phase, stagflation phase, and recovery phase observed in the relationship between inflation and unemployment.

Trace the path of the inflation-unemployment cycle as it unfolds in Exhibit 32-5. Starting with the Phillips phase in the 1960s, we see that the economy went through three inflation-unemployment cycles through the 1970s. Each took the United States to successively higher rates of inflation and unemployment. As the cycle that began in the late 1970s passed through the stagflation phase, however, something quite significant happened. The economy suffered its highest rate of unemployment during that period. It also achieved its most dramatic gains against inflation. Since then, the inflation-unemployment cycles have be-

EXHIBIT 32-6

Phases of the Inflation-Unemployment Cycle

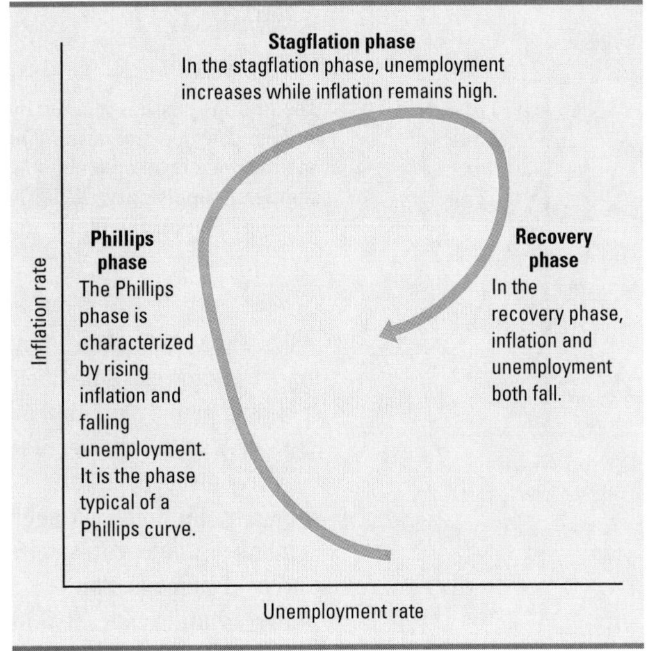
Stagflation phase
In the stagflation phase, unemployment increases while inflation remains high.
Phillips phase
The Phillips phase is characterized by rising inflation and falling unemployment. It is the phase typical of a Phillips curve.
Recovery phase
In the recovery phase, inflation and unemployment both fall.
Inflation rate
Unemployment rate

Checklist

- The notion that there is a negative relationship between inflation and unemployment is suggested by the Phillips curve.
- Although the experience of the 1960s was consistent with the Phillips curve, subsequent experience has not conformed to the hypothesis that a negative relationship exists between inflation and unemployment.
- The inflation-unemployment cycle follows three phases: a Phillips phase of rising inflation and falling unemployment, a stagflation phase in which unemployment rises while inflation remains high, and a recovery phase in which inflation and unemployment both fall.
- The data for inflation and unemployment for the period from 1961 to 1994 seem broadly consistent with the inflation-unemployment cycle described here.

come less dramatic. Fluctuations in inflation and unemployment have become less severe. Some of the explanation for that may simply be good luck. But one cause of that improved performance is the better understanding economists have gained from the policy mistakes of the 1970s. As our understanding of the relationship between inflation and unemployment has improved, so have the policies with which we address these two problems.

Explaining the Inflation-Unemployment Cycle

We've examined the cyclical pattern of inflation and unemployment suggested by the experience of the past three decades. Our task now is to explain it. We'll apply the model of aggregate demand and aggregate supply, along with material in the last two chapters on monetary and fiscal policy, to explain just why the economy performed as it did. We'll find that the relationship between inflation and unemployment depends crucially on macroeconomic policy and on expectations.

The next three sections illustrate the unfolding of the inflation-unemployment cycle using numbers for real GDP, the price level, inflation, and unemployment. Because equations for the curves that generate the numbers have not been given, you don't have enough information to solve for them. The purpose of these sections is to show how a typical cycle develops, not to suggest a way to compute actual values for the variables involved.

The Phillips Phase: Increasing Aggregate Demand

As we saw in the last section, the Phillips phase of the inflation-unemployment cycle conforms to the concept of a Phillips curve. It is a period in which inflation tends to rise and unemployment tends to fall.

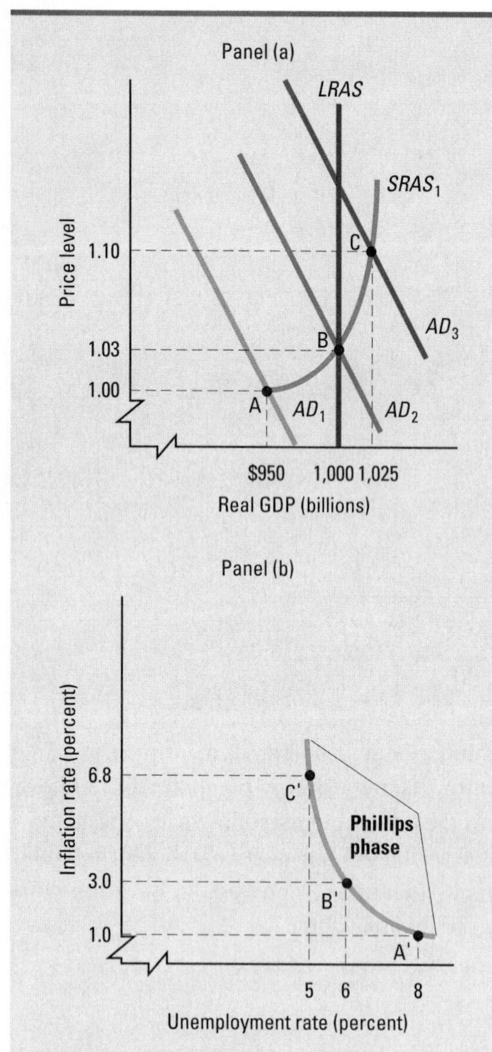

EXHIBIT 32-7

The Phillips Phase

The Phillips phase is marked by increases in aggregate demand pushing real GDP and the price level up along the short-run aggregate supply curve $SRAS_1$. The result is rising inflation and falling unemployment. The points labeled in Panels (a) and (b) correspond to one another; point A in Panel (a) corresponds to point A′ in Panel (b), and so on.

Exhibit 32-7 shows how a Phillips phase can unfold. Panel (a) shows the model of aggregate demand and aggregate supply; Panel (b) shows the corresponding path of inflation and unemployment. Suppose the economy is initially at point A, at the intersection of AD_1 and $SRAS_1$. The price level is 1.00, and real GDP equals $950 billion. The economy is operating below its natural level, shown by the long-run aggregate supply curve *LRAS*. Suppose the unemployment rate is 8 percent, and the current price level exceeds that of the previous period by 1 percent. Point A′ in Panel (b) corresponds to point A in Panel (a); it shows an initial rate of inflation of 1 percent and an unemployment rate of 8 percent.

Now suppose policymakers respond to the recessionary gap of the first period with an expansionary monetary or fiscal policy. Aggregate demand shifts to AD_2. In Panel (a), we see that the price level rises to 1.03, and the economy reaches its full-employment level of output at $1,000 billion at point B. Unemployment thus falls to its natural rate of 6 percent. The price increase from 1.00 to 1.03 gives us an inflation rate of 3 percent. Point B′ in Panel (b) shows the new combination of inflation and unemployment rates.

The economy reaches its natural level of output at point B, but Exhibit 32-7 suggests that aggregate demand continues to rise. That's quite plausible; policies that are initiated as a response to a recessionary gap may, as a result of implementation and impact lags, continue to affect aggregate demand long after the recessionary gap has been closed. As aggregate demand increases to AD_3, real GDP rises to $1,025 billion and the price level rises to 1.10 at point C in Panel (a). The increase in real GDP lowers the unemployment rate to 5 percent and the inflation rate rises to 6.8 percent at point C′ in Panel (b). Once again, unemployment has fallen at a cost of rising inflation.

The shifts from point A′ to point B′ to point C′ in Panel (b) are characteristic of the Phillips phase. It's crucial to note how these changes occurred. Inflation rose and unemployment fell because increasing aggregate demand moved along the original short-run aggregate supply curve $SRAS_1$. We saw in Chapter 26 that a short-run aggregate supply curve is drawn for a given level of the nominal wage and for a given set of expected prices. The Phillips phase, however, drives prices above what workers and firms expected when they agreed to a given set of nominal wages; real wages are thus driven below their expected level during this phase. Firms that have sticky prices are in the same situation. They set their prices based on some expected price level. As rising inflation drives the price level beyond their expectations, their prices will be too low relative to the rest of the economy. Because some firms and workers are committed to their present set of prices for some period of time, they'll be stuck with the wrong prices and wages for a while.

Case in Point

Oil Shocks and Stagflation

An increase in the expected price level isn't the only thing that can set off a stagflation phase. Two massive oil shocks in the 1970s helped turn that decade into a nightmare of rising inflation and unemployment.

The Organization of Petroleum Exporting Countries (OPEC), the world oil cartel, slapped an embargo on shipments of oil to the United States in 1973. It lifted the embargo the following year—with a fourfold increase in the price of oil. Those moves forced the long- and short-run aggregate supply curves to the left. The result was a sharp increase in the price level and a dramatic reduction in real GDP. More bad luck was in store for the U.S. economy in the next round of the inflation-unemployment cycle. In 1980, as the Fed was shifting to a contractionary policy aimed at curbing inflation, a war between Iran and Iraq sent oil prices soaring again. Notice in Exhibit 32-5 that the resulting stagflation phase roughly matched that of the previous cycle. As we saw in Exhibit 32-1, misery indexes for the period soared.

Just as oil-price pressures on aggregate supply worsened the inflation-unemployment cycles of the 1970s, they provided relief in the 1980s. Oil prices fell, boosting output at the same time as they put downward pressure on prices. A sharp increase in oil prices that came in the aftermath of Iraq's invasion of Kuwait in 1990 played a role in the recession of 1990–1991. The subsequent reduction in oil prices that came as the Persian Gulf War ended helped to generate a recovery.

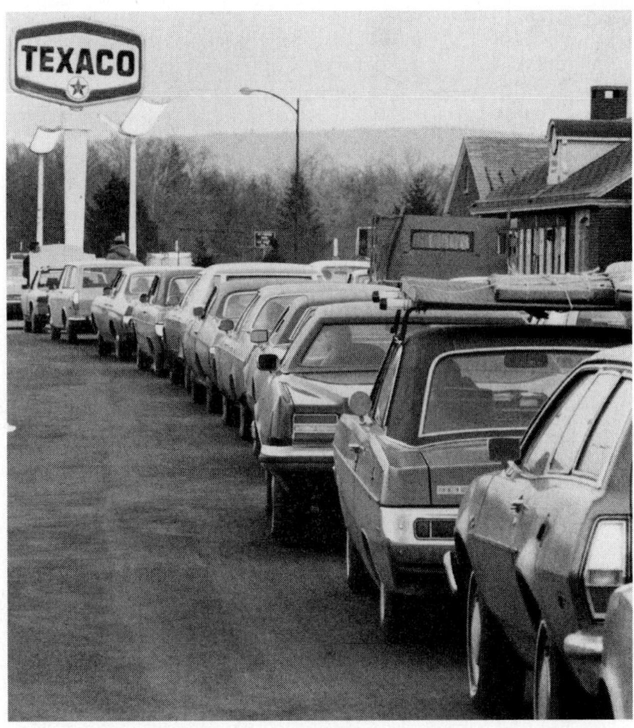

OPEC's 1973 embargo on oil to the United States, together with a price ceiling in effect at the time, produced long lines at gas stations.

The Phillips phase thus emerges for two reasons. First, people are surprised by the price increases produced by the rise in aggregate demand. Second, some prices and wages are sticky and are thus slow to adjust to correct for the surprise.

Ultimately, we should expect that workers and firms will begin adjusting nominal wages and other sticky prices to reflect the new, higher level of prices that emerges during the Phillips phase. It is this adjustment that leads to the next phase of the inflation-unemployment cycle.

Changes in Expectations and the Stagflation Phase

As workers and firms become aware that the general price level is rising, they will incorporate this fact into their expectations of future prices. In reaching new agreements on wages, they're likely to settle on higher nominal wages. Firms with sticky prices will adjust their prices upward as they anticipate higher prices throughout the economy.

As we saw in Chapter 26, changes in nominal wages and in sticky prices will shift the short-run aggregate supply curve upward. Such a shift is illustrated in Exhibit 32-8. In Panel (a), the curve shifts to $SRAS_2$. The result is a shift to

EXHIBIT 32-8

The Stagflation Phase

In the stagflation phase, workers and firms adjust their expectations in a higher price level. As they act on their expectations, the short-run aggregate supply curve shifts upward in Panel (a). The price level rises to 1.19 and real GDP falls to $983 billion. The inflation rate rises to 8.2 percent as unemployment rises to 6.7 percent at point D′ in Panel (b).

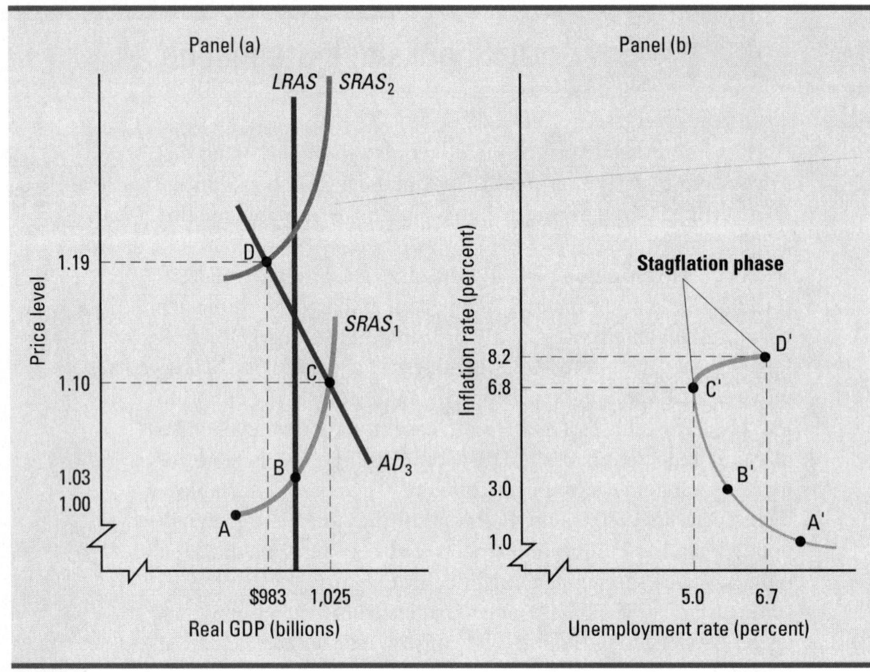

point D; the price level rises to 1.19 and real GDP falls to $983 billion. The increase in the price level from 1.10 to 1.19 implies an inflation rate of 8.2 percent; unemployment rises to 6.7 percent with the decrease in real GDP. The new combination of inflation and unemployment is given by point D′ in Panel (b).

The essential feature of the stagflation phase is a change in expectations. Workers and firms that were blindsided by rising prices during the Phillips phase ended up with lower real wages and lower relative price levels than they intended. In the stagflation phase, they catch up. But the catching up shifts short-run aggregate supply upward, producing a reduction in real GDP and an increase in the price level.

The Recovery Phase

The stagflation phase drawn in Exhibit 32-8 leaves the economy with a recessionary gap at point D in Panel (a). Aggregate demand is unchanged as the economy is bumped into a recession by changing expectations. Policymakers can be expected to respond to the recessionary gap by boosting aggregate demand. That increase in aggregate demand will lead the economy into the recovery phase of the inflation-unemployment cycle.

Exhibit 32-9 illustrates this phase. In Panel (a), aggregate demand increases to AD_4, boosting the price level to 1.24 and real GDP to $1,010. The new price level represents a 4.2 percent increase over the previous price level [(1.24 − 1.19)/1.19 = 4.2 percent]. The price level is higher, but the inflation rate has fallen sharply. Meanwhile, the increase in real GDP cuts the unemployment rate to 5.6 percent, shown by point E′ in Panel (b).

Policies that stimulate aggregate demand and changes in expected price levels are not the only forces that affect the values of inflation and unemployment. We shall examine some additional determinants of these two variables in the next section. But we can conclude that efforts to stimulate aggregate demand, together with changes in expectations, have played an important role in generating the inflation-unemployment cycles during the past three decades.

EXHIBIT 32-9

The Recovery Phase

Policymakers act to increase aggregate demand in order to move the economy out of the recessionary gap created during the stagflation phase. Here, aggregate demand shifts to AD_4, boosting the price level to 1.24 and real GDP to \$1,010 billion at point E in Panel (a). The increase in real GDP reduces unemployment. The price level has risen, but at a slower rate than in the previous period. The result is a reduction in inflation. The new combination of unemployment and inflation is shown by point E′ in Panel (b).

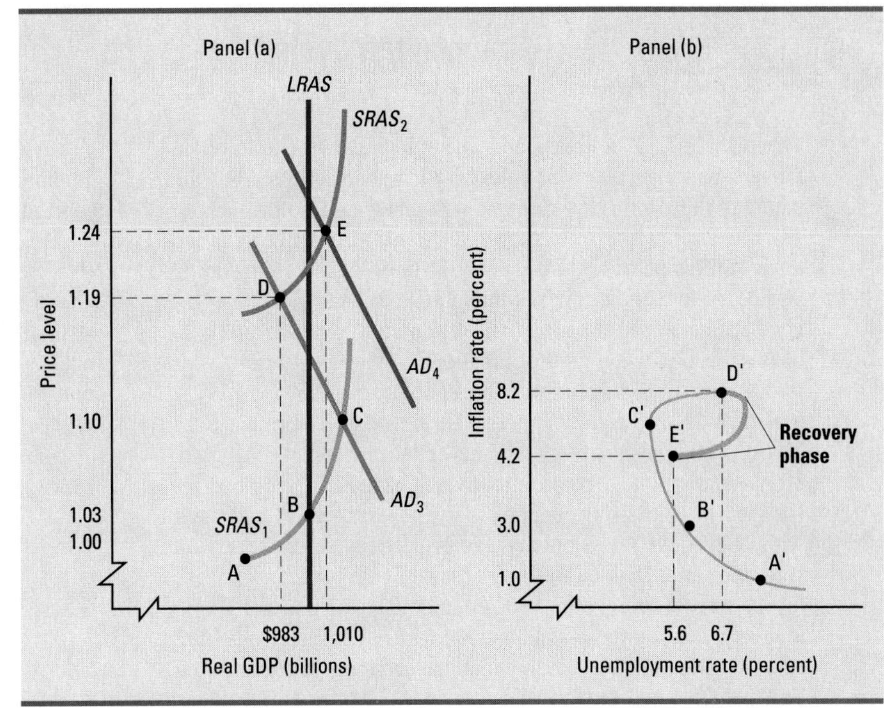

Checklist

- In the Phillips phase, aggregate demand increases and boosts real GDP. The price level rises at an increasing rate. Inflation rises and unemployment falls.
- The stagflation phase is marked by an upward shift in short-run aggregate supply as workers demand wage increases.
- In the recovery phase, policymakers boost aggregate demand. The price level rises at a much slower rate than in the previous period. Inflation and unemployment fall.

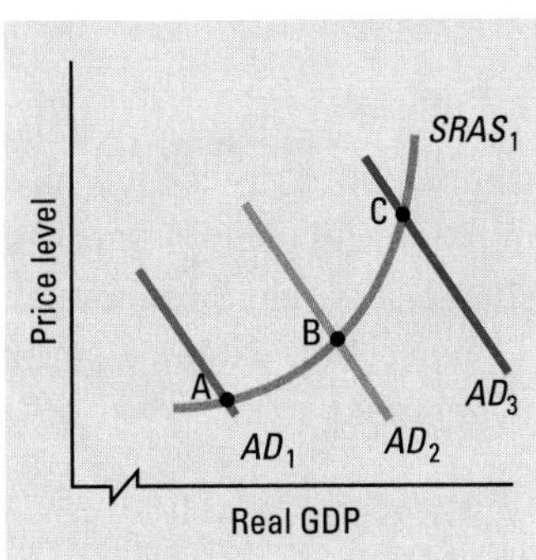

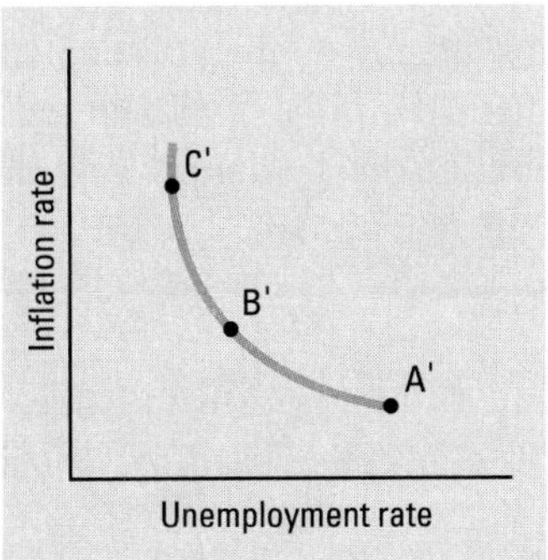

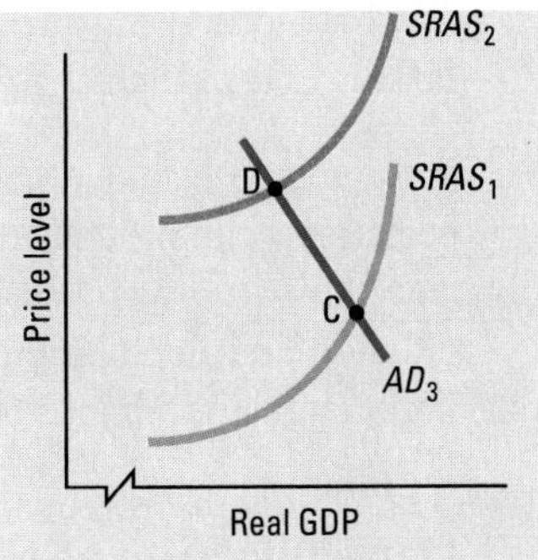

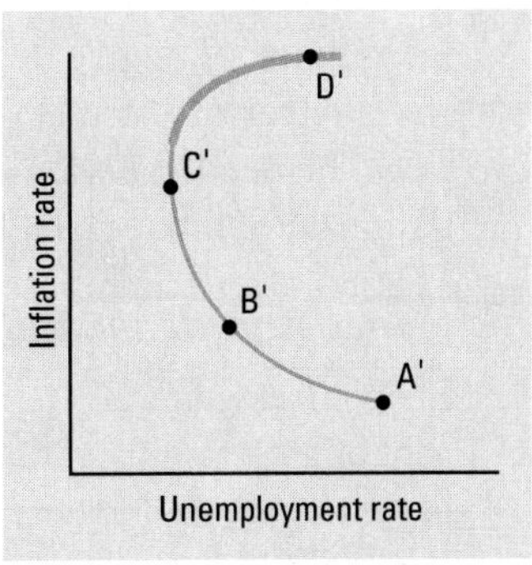

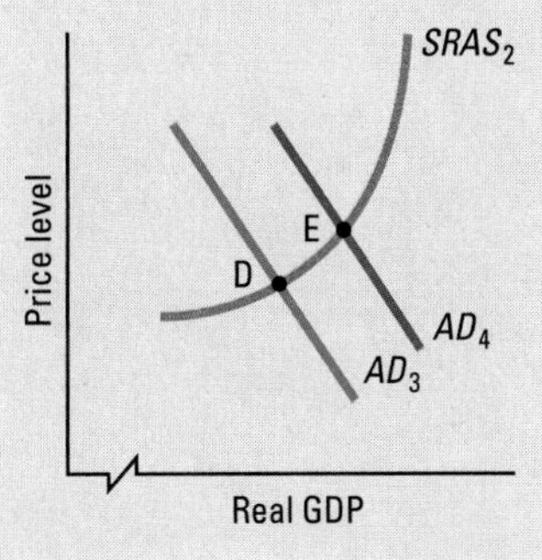

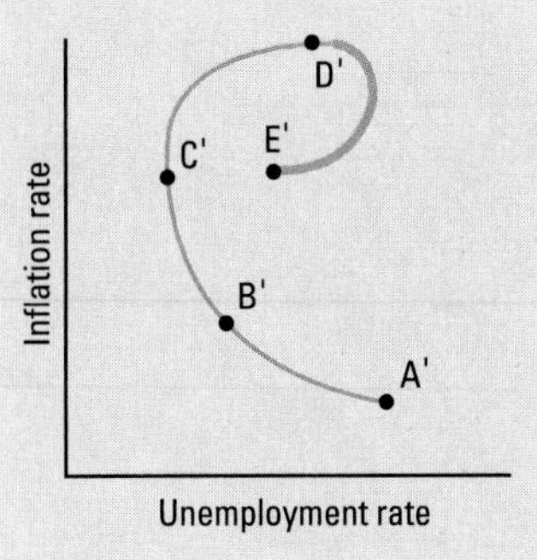

Case in Point Reining in the Cycle?

The path of U.S. inflation and unemployment has followed a fairly consistent pattern of clockwise loops since 1961, but the nature of these loops has changed with changes in policy.

If we follow the cycle shown in Exhibit 32-5, we see that the three Phillips phases that began in 1961, 1972, and 1976 started at successively higher rates of inflation. Fiscal and monetary policy became expansionary at the beginnings of each of these phases, despite rising rates of inflation.

As inflation soared into the double-digit range in 1979, President Jimmy Carter appointed a new Fed chairman, Paul Volcker. The president gave the new chairman a clear mandate: bring inflation under control, regardless of the cost. The Fed responded with a sharply contractionary monetary policy and stuck with it even as the economy experienced its worse recession since the Great Depression.

Falling oil prices after 1982 contributed to an unusually long recovery phase: inflation and unemployment both fell from 1982 to 1986. The inflation rate at which the economy started its next Phillips phase was the lowest since 1961.

The Fed's policies since then have clearly shown a reduced tolerance for inflation. The Fed shifted to a contractionary monetary policy in 1988, so that inflation during the 1986–1989 Phillips phase never exceeded 4 percent. When oil prices rose at the outset of the Persian Gulf War in 1990, the resultant swings in inflation and unemployment were much less pronounced than they had been in the 1970s.

The Fed continued its effort to restrain inflation in 1994 and 1995. It shifted to a contractionary policy early in 1994 when the economy was still in a recovery phase, with unemployment and inflation both falling. The Fed's announced intention was to prevent any future increase in inflation. If successful, the policy could spell an end to the cycles of inflation and unemployment that marked the past few decades. You can chart the recent record for yourself to see how the Fed's tougher line against inflation has worked.

Other Determinants of Inflation and Unemployment

In the last section, we saw how stabilization policy, together with changes in expectations, can produce the cycles of inflation and unemployment that characterized the past several decades. But other factors have influenced the levels of inflation and unemployment as well. This section examines some of the most important determinants of inflation and unemployment.

Determinants of the Inflation Rate

What factors determine the inflation rate? The price level is determined by the intersection of aggregate demand and short-run aggregate supply; anything that shifts either of these two curves changes the price level and thus the inflation rate. This section reviews some of these factors, beginning with the primary determinant of inflation in the long run, the rate of money growth.

Money Growth and Inflation

Economists generally agree that the rate of money growth is the main determinant of an economy's inflation rate. The conceptual basis for that conclusion lies in the equation of exchange: $MV = PY$. That is, the money supply times the velocity of money equals the price level times the value of real GDP.

There is a limit to how fast the economy's natural level of real GDP can grow. Economists generally agree that this natural level of output increases at only about a 2.5 percent annual rate in the United States. Velocity can vary, but there has been no long-term change in the velocity of M2.[2] These two facts suggest that very rapid increases in the quantity of money *M* will inevitably produce very rapid increases in the price level *P*.

Exhibit 32-10 gives annual rates of money growth and inflation (measured as the rate of change in the implicit price deflator for GDP) for 88 countries, as reported by the World Bank. The data suggest a positive relationship between money growth and the rate of inflation. The relationship is clearly not precise; some countries have relatively high rates of money growth with relatively low rates of inflation. There are no examples of high inflation rates that were not accompanied by high money growth rates.

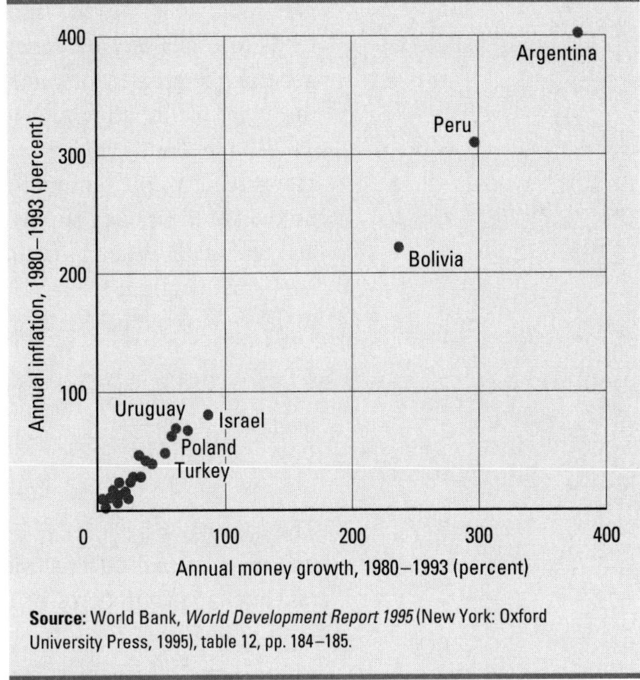

Source: World Bank, *World Development Report 1995* (New York: Oxford University Press, 1995), table 12, pp. 184–185.

EXHIBIT 32-10

Money Growth Rates and Inflation, 1980–1993

Data for 88 countries for the period 1980–1993 suggest a positive relationship between the rate of money growth and inflation. The World Bank uses a broad definition of the money supply, roughly consistent with M2. The United States had an average rate of money growth of 7.2 percent and an inflation rate of 3.8 percent during the period.

In the model of aggregate demand and aggregate supply, increases in the money supply shift the aggregate demand curve to the right and thus force the price level upward. As money growth occurs, it puts steady upward pressure on aggregate demand and thus creates the persistent increases in the price level we associate with inflation.

[2] We saw in Chapter 25 that the velocity of M2 increased in the early 1990s. If this increase proves permanent, it may be necessary to qualify our conclusion about the stability of velocity. Alternatively, the Fed may, once again, redefine M2.

Of course, other factors can shift the aggregate demand curve as well. An expansionary fiscal policy or an increase in autonomous consumption, investment, or net exports will shift aggregate demand. But these increases are not likely to be persistent. Factors other than money growth may influence the inflation rate from one year to the next, but they are not likely to cause changes in the inflation rate over long periods.

Inflation Rates and Aggregate Supply

A shift in the short-run aggregate supply curve will affect the price level and thus the inflation rate in any one year. Economic growth, which shifts the long- and short-run aggregate supply curves to the right, produces sustained changes in inflation rates.

An increase in the natural level of income, by shifting the short-run aggregate supply curve to the right, puts downward pressure on the price level. It thus tends to offset any tendency of rising aggregate demand to cause inflation. In general, the greater the rate of increase in the economy's natural level of output, the lower the inflation rate.

The tendency for an increasing level of natural GDP to lower the inflation rate is readily apparent in the equation of exchange. The equation shows that the product of the money supply and its velocity equals the product of the price level and real GDP. When two numbers are multiplied by one another and both numbers are changing, their product increases by a rate that is approximately equal to the sum of the percentage changes in the two numbers. Thus, if

$$MV = PY \tag{1}$$

then

$$\%\Delta M + \%\Delta V = \%\Delta P + \%\Delta Y \tag{2}$$

The value of Y, real GDP, converges in the long run on Y_n, the economy's natural level of real GDP. If velocity is stable in the long run, then its percentage rate of change will be zero. Thus, for the long run we can rewrite Equation (2) as

$$\%\Delta M = \%\Delta P + \%\Delta Y_n \tag{3}$$

or

$$\%\Delta P = \%\Delta M - \%\Delta Y_n \tag{4}$$

Equation (4) tells us that for a given rate of money growth, inflation in the long run will be lower when the rate of increase in the economy's potential level of real GDP is greater. Economic growth thus generates persistent changes in short-run aggregate supply that can cause persistent changes in the inflation rate associated with a given rate of money growth. But other changes in short-run aggregate supply will cause short-run changes in the price level and could thus affect the inflation rate in any one year.

We saw in the previous section that a change in the expected price level shifts short-run aggregate supply. An increase in the expected price level, for example, shifts the short-run aggregate supply curve upward—and raises the price level. A change in production costs can also shift the short-run aggregate supply curve and thus affect the inflation rate for any one year.

We saw earlier in this chapter that increases in world oil prices in 1973–1974, in 1980 and again in 1990 shifted short-run aggregate supply upward and to the left and thus boosted the price level at the same time as they acted to reduce real GDP. Similarly, reductions in oil prices in the 1980s tended to shift the short-run aggregate supply curve downward and to the right and thus put downward pressure on prices and on inflation. Changes in the cost of hiring workers, because of changes in nominal wages, payroll taxes, or other employment costs, also shift short-run aggregate supply and thus affect inflation in a particular year. Such changes in short-run aggregate supply are not, however, likely to cause persistent changes in inflation. In the long run, only a change in the rate of economic growth is likely to affect the inflation rate associated with a particular rate of growth in the money supply.

Determinants of Unemployment

Economists distinguish three types of unemployment: frictional unemployment, structural unemployment, and cyclical unemployment. The first two exist even when the economy has full employment. The third type suggests the existence of a recessionary gap; an economy operating at its natural level would have no cyclical unemployment.

In our work so far, we have focused on the problems of closing gaps; our focus has thus been on cyclical unemployment. In this section we'll turn to some policy issues raised by frictional and structural unemployment, and we'll look at some new research that challenges the very concept of an economy achieving its natural level of output.

Frictional Unemployment

Frictional unemployment occurs because it takes time for people seeking jobs and employers seeking workers to find each other. If the amount of time could be reduced, frictional unemployment would fall. The economy's natural rate of unemployment would drop, and its natural level of output would rise. This section presents a model of frictional unemployment and examines some issues in reducing the frictional unemployment rate.

A period of frictional unemployment ends with the individual getting a job. The process through which the job is obtained suggests some important clues to the nature of frictional unemployment.

By definition, a person who is unemployed is seeking work. At the outset of a job search, we presume that the individual has a particular wage in mind as he or she considers various job possibilities. The lowest wage that an unemployed worker would accept, if it were offered, is called the **reservation wage.** This is the wage an individual would accept; any offer below it would be rejected. Once a firm offers the reservation wage, however, the individual will take it and the job search will be terminated. Many people may hold out for more than just a wage—they may be seeking a certain set of working conditions, opportunities for advancement, or a job in a particular area. In practice, then, an unemployed worker might be willing to accept a variety of combinations of wages and other job characteristics. We shall simplify our analysis by lumping all these other characteristics into a single reservation wage.

The **reservation wage** is the lowest wage that, if offered, would be accepted by an unemployed worker.

A worker's reservation wage is likely to change as his or her search continues. One might initiate a job search with high expectations and thus have a high reservation wage. As the job search continues, however, this reservation wage might be adjusted downward as the worker obtains better information about what's likely to be available in the market and as the financial difficulties associated with unemployment mount. We can thus draw a reservation wage curve, as in Exhibit 32-11, that suggests a negative relationship between the reservation wage and the duration of a person's job search. Similarly, as a job search continues, the worker will accumulate better offers. The "best-offer-received" curve shows what its name implies; it is the best offer the individual has received so far in the job search.

EXHIBIT 32-11

A Model of Job Search

An individual begins a job search at time t_0 with a reservation wage W_0. As long as the reservation wage exceeds the best offer received, the individual will continue searching. A job is accepted, and the search is terminated, at time t_c, at which the reservation and "best-offer-received" curves intersect at wage W_c.

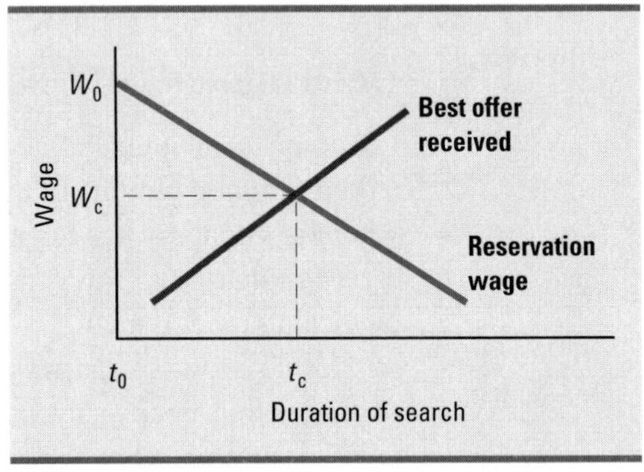

The search begins at time t_0, with the worker seeking wage W_0. Because the worker's reservation wage exceeds the best offer received, the worker continues the search. The worker reduces his or her reservation wage and accumulates better offers until the two curves intersect at time t_c. The worker accepts wage W_c, and the job search is terminated.

The job search model in Exhibit 32-11 doesn't determine an equilibrium duration of job search or an equilibrium initial wage. The reservation wage and best-offer-received curves will be unique to each individual's experience. We can, however, use the model to reach some conclusions about factors that affect frictional unemployment.

First, the duration of search will be shorter when more job market information is available. Suppose, for example, that the only way to determine what jobs and wages are available is to visit each firm separately. Such a situation would require a lengthy period of search before a given offer was received. Alternatively, suppose there are agencies that make such information readily available and that link unemployed workers to firms seeking to hire workers. In that second situation, the time required to obtain a given offer would be reduced, and the best-offer-received curves for individual workers would shift to the left. The lower the cost for obtaining job market information, the lower the average duration of unemployment. Government and private agencies that provide job information and placement services help to reduce information costs to unemployed workers and firms. They tend to lower frictional unemployment by shifting the best-offer-received (*BOR*) curves for individual workers to the left, as shown in Panel (a) of Exhibit 32-12. Workers obtain higher-paying jobs when they do find work; the wage at which searches are terminated rises to W_2.

EXHIBIT 32-12

Public Policy and Frictional Unemployment

Public policy can influence the time required for job-seeking workers and worker-seeking firms to find each other. Programs that provide labor market information tend to shift the best-offer received (*BOR*) curves of individual workers to the left, reducing the duration of job search and reducing unemployment, as in Panel (a). Note that the wage these workers obtain also rises to W_2. Unemployment compensation tends to increase the period over which a worker will hold out for a particular wage, shifting the reservation wage (*RW*) curve to the right, as in Panel (b). Unemployment compensation thus boosts the unemployment rate and increases the wage workers obtain when they find employment.

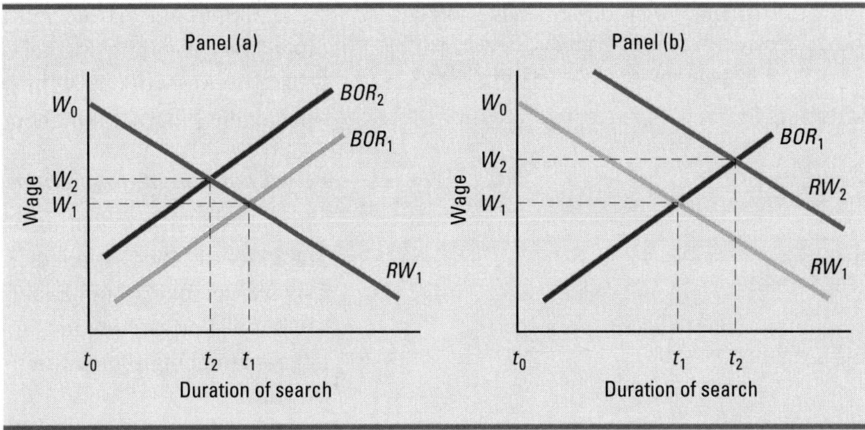

Unemployment compensation, which was introduced during the Great Depression to help workers who had lost jobs through unemployment, also affects frictional unemployment. Because unemployment compensation reduces the financial burden of being unemployed, it's likely to increase the amount of time people will wait for a given wage. It thus shifts the reservation wage curve to the right, raises the average duration of unemployment, and increases the wage at which searches end, as shown in Panel (b). An increase in the average duration of unemployment implies a higher unemployment rate. Unemployment compensation thus has a paradoxical effect—it tends to increase the problem against which it protects.[3]

Structural Unemployment

Structural unemployment occurs when a firm is looking for a worker and a worker is looking for a job, but the particular characteristics the firm seeks don't match up with the characteristics the worker offers. Technological change is one source of structural unemployment. New technologies are likely to require different skills than old technologies. Workers with training to equip them for the old technology may find themselves caught up in a structural mismatch. A skilled typist, for example, may find that his or her skills are no match for an office that relies extensively on computer networking and word processing. In general, the rate of structural unemployment is likely to rise with the rate of technological change.

Changes in demand can also produce structural unemployment. As consumers shift their demands to different products, firms that are expanding and seeking more workers may need different skills than firms for which demand has shrunk. Similarly, firms may shift their use of different types of jobs in response to changing market conditions, leaving some workers with the "wrong" set of skills. Regional shifts in demand can produce structural unemployment as well. The economy of one region may be expanding rapidly, creating job vacancies, while another region is in a slump, with many workers seeking jobs but not finding them.

[3] We saw in Chapter 24 that this phenomenon is known as *moral hazard.* That's the term economists use to describe the fact that the provision of insurance protection against any loss tends to increase the likelihood that loss will occur and the severity of the loss once it does occur.

Efficiency-wage theory holds that firms may try to increase productivity by paying a wage in excess of the market-clearing wage.

Public and private job training firms seek to reduce structural unemployment by providing workers with skills now in demand. Employment services that provide workers with information about jobs in other regions also reduce the extent of structural unemployment.

Cyclical Unemployment and Efficiency Wages

In our model, cyclical unemployment occurs if, at a given nominal wage, the quantity of labor supplied exceeds the quantity of labor demanded; in the analysis we've done so far, a labor market in equilibrium will experience an increase in supply or a reduction in demand. With sticky nominal wages, the resultant cyclical unemployment will persist until the economy moves back to its natural level.

Some new Keynesian economists, however, argue that a wage that achieves equilibrium in the labor market may *never* be reached. They suggest that some firms may intentionally pay a wage greater than the market equilibrium. Such firms could hire additional workers at a lower wage, but they choose not to do so.

Why would a firm pay higher wages than the market requires? Suppose that by paying higher wages, the firm is able to boost the productivity of its workers. Workers become more contented, more loyal, and more eager to perform in ways that boost the firm's profits. The idea that the wage level itself is tied to a worker's productivity and that firms may respond by paying a wage greater than the market-clearing wage is called **efficiency-wage theory.** This theory suggests that the labor market may divide into two segments. Workers with jobs will receive high wages. Workers without jobs, who would be willing to work at an even lower wage than the workers with jobs, find themselves closed out of the market.

Whether efficiency wages really exist remains a controversial issue, but the argument is an important one. If it is correct, then the wage rigidity that perpetuates a recessionary gap is transformed from a temporary phenomenon that will be overcome in the long run to a permanent feature of the market. The argument implies that a recessionary gap will *not* be eliminated by ordinary processes of self-correction. Instead, an increase in aggregate demand will be required. Efficiency-wage theory is an important example of new Keynesian economic thought. It suggests a theoretical argument, based on profit maximization, that prevents wages from adjusting to the market-clearing level.[4]

Checklist

- The two factors that can influence the rate of inflation in the long run are the rate of money growth and the rate of growth of natural GDP.
- Changes in aggregate demand and short-run aggregate supply can influence the inflation rate in a particular year.
- The rate of frictional unemployment is affected by information costs and by the existence of unemployment compensation.
- Policies to reduce structural unemployment include the provision of job training and information about labor market conditions in other regions.
- Efficiency-wage theory predicts that profit-maximizing firms will maintain the wage level at a rate too high to achieve full employment in the labor market.

A Look Back—And a Look Ahead

During the 1960s, it appeared that there was a stable tradeoff between the rate of unemployment and the rate of inflation. The Phillips curve, which describes such a tradeoff, suggests that lower rates of unemployment come with higher rates of inflation, and that lower rates of inflation come with higher rates of unemployment. But during the 1970s and 1980s, the actual values for unemployment and inflation did not follow the Phillips curve script. This is suggested by a

[4] For a discussion of the argument, see Janet Yellen, "Efficiency Wage Models of Unemployment," *American Economic Review, Papers and Proceedings* (May 1984):200–205.

look at misery index readings for the period. With a negative relationship between inflation and unemployment, misery index values should be relatively stable. Instead, they have fluctuated a great deal.

There has, however, been a relationship between unemployment and inflation over the past three decades. Periods of rising inflation and falling unemployment have been followed by periods of rising unemployment and continued inflation; those periods have, in turn, been followed by periods in which both the inflation rate and the unemployment rate fall. These periods are defined as the Phillips phase, the stagflation phase, and the recovery phase of the inflation-unemployment cycle.

The Phillips phase is a period in which aggregate demand increases, boosting output and the price level. Unemployment drops and inflation rises as prices increase rapidly. An essential feature of the Phillips phase is that the price increases that occur are unexpected. Workers thus experience lower real wages than they anticipated. Firms with sticky prices find that their prices are low relative to other prices. As workers and firms adjust to the higher inflation of the Phillips phase, they demand higher wages and post higher prices, so the short-run aggregate supply curve shifts upward. Inflation continues, but real GDP falls. This is the stagflation phase. Finally, aggregate demand begins to increase again, boosting both real GDP and the price level. The higher price level, however, is likely to represent a much smaller percentage increase than had occurred during the stagflation phase. This is the recovery phase: inflation and unemployment fall together.

There is nothing inherent in a market economy that would produce the inflation-unemployment cycle we have observed since 1961. The cycle requires expansionary policies launched to correct a recessionary gap. The Fed in 1994 undertook a contractionary monetary policy with the economy still in a recessionary gap. Whether the Fed's action will prevent a subsequent stagflation phase remains to be seen.

In the long run, inflation is essentially a monetary phenomenon. Assuming stable velocity of money over the long run, the inflation rate equals the money growth rate minus the rate of growth of real GDP. For a given money growth rate, inflation is thus reduced by faster economic growth.

The inflation rate for a given year can be affected by changes in aggregate demand or short-run aggregate supply. Events such as an increase in government purchases or a reduction in oil prices can thus affect inflation in the short run.

Frictional unemployment is affected by information costs in the labor market. A reduction in those costs would reduce frictional unemployment. Hastening the retraining of workers would reduce structural unemployment. Reductions in frictional or structural unemployment would lower the natural rate of unemployment and thus raise the natural level of real GDP. Unemployment compensation is likely to increase frictional unemployment.

Some new Keynesian economists believe that cyclical unemployment may persist because firms have an incentive to maintain real wages above the equilibrium level. This efficiency-wage argument implies that fiscal or monetary efforts are needed to increase aggregate demand in the face of a recessionary gap.

We've seen in this chapter how economic events that violate economists' expectations force changes in economic theories. Increases in unemployment with little change in inflation brought us not only a new term—stagflation—but the recognition of the role of changing expectations. In the next chapter we'll see other ways in which macroeconomic events have affected economic ideas, and we'll put the aggregate demand–aggregate supply model to work in interpreting these events.

Terms and Concepts for Review

Efficiency-wage theory

Inflation-unemployment cycle

Phillips curve

Phillips phase

Recovery phase

Reservation wage

Stagflation phase

For Discussion

1. The Case in Point on page 711 describes the changes in inflation and in unemployment in 1970 and 1971 as a watershed development for macroeconomic thought. Why was an increase in unemployment such a significant event?

2. As the economy slipped into recession in 1980 and 1981, the Fed was under enormous pressure to adopt an expansionary monetary policy. Suppose it had begun an expansionary policy early in 1981. What does the text's analysis of the inflation-unemployment cycle suggest about how the macroeconomic history of the 1980s might have been changed?

3. Here are some news reports covering events of the past 35 years. In each case, identify the stage of the inflation-unemployment cycle, and suggest what change in aggregate demand or aggregate supply might have caused it.

   a. "President Nixon expressed satisfaction with last year's economic performance. He said that with inflation and unemployment heading down, the nation is "is on the right course."

   b. "The nation's inflation rate rose to a record high last month, the government reported yesterday. The consumer price index jumped 0.3 percent in January. Coupled with the announcement earlier this month that unemployment was 0.5 percent, the reports suggested that the first month of President Nixon's second term had gotten off to a rocky start."

   c. "President Carter expressed concern about reports of rising inflation but insisted the economy is on the right course. He pointed to recent reductions in unemployment as evidence that his economic policies are working."

4. The Case in Point on page 715 suggests that oil-price changes played an important role in the inflation-unemployment cycles of the 1970s and 1980s. Shouldn't they be incorporated as part of the theory?

5. The Case in Point on page 718 suggests that the Fed may have been "successful" in reining in the inflation-unemployment cycle. What do you think this means? The statement itself suggests a normative judgment that the reining in was a good thing. Do you agree? Why or why not?

6. Suppose the full-employment level of real GDP is increasing at a rate of 3 percent per period and the money supply is growing at a 4 percent rate. What will happen to the long-run inflation rate?

7. Suppose that declining resource supplies reduce the full employment level of real GDP in each period by 4 percent. What kind of monetary policy would be needed to maintain a zero rate of inflation at full employment?

8. The Humphrey-Hawkins Act of 1978 required that the federal government maintain an unemployment rate of 4 percent and hold the inflation rate to less than 3 percent. What does the model of the inflation-unemployment cycle tell you about achieving such goals?

9. The American Economic Association publishes a monthly newsletter called *Job Openings for Economists* (JOE). Virtually all academic and many nonacademic positions for which applicants are being sought are listed in the newsletter, which is quite inexpensive. How do you think that the publication of this journal affects the unemployment rate among economists? What type of unemployment does it affect?

10. Many economists think that we are in the very early stages of putting computer technology to work, and that full incorporation of computers will cause a massive restructuring of virtually every institution of modern life. If they're right, what are the implications for unemployment? What kind of unemployment would be affected?

11. The natural unemployment rate in the United States has risen somewhat in the past 35 years. According to the Congressional Budget Office, the natural rate was 5.0 percent in 1958 and 5.5 percent in 1993. What do you think might have caused this increase?

12. Suppose the Fed begins carrying out an expansionary monetary policy in order to close a recessionary gap. Relate what happens during the next two phases of the inflation-unemployment cycle to the maxim "You can fool some of the people some of the time, but you can't fool all of the people all of the time."

Problems

1. Here are annual data for the inflation and unemployment rates for the United States for the period 1948–1961. Plot these observations and connect the points as in Exhibit 32-5. How does this period compare to the decades that followed? What do you think accounts for the difference?

Year	Unemployment Rate (percent)	Inflation rate (percent)
1948	8.0	3.0
1949	5.9	−2.1
1950	5.3	5.9
1951	3.3	6.0
1952	3.0	0.8
1953	2.9	0.7
1954	5.5	−0.7
1955	4.4	0.4
1956	4.1	3.0
1957	4.3	2.9
1958	6.8	1.8
1959	5.5	1.7
1960	5.5	1.4
1961	6.7	0.7

2. Here are hypothetical inflation and unemployment data for Econoland. Plot these points and identify which points correspond to the Phillips phase, which correspond to the stagflation phase, and which correspond to the recovery phase.

Time Period	Inflation Rate (percent)	Unemployment Rate (percent)
1	0	6
2	3	4
3	7	3
4	8	5
5	7	7
6	3	6

3. Relate the observations in Problem 2 to what must have been happening in the aggregate demand–aggregate supply model.

33

Interpreting Macroeconomic Change in the Twentieth Century

Chapter Objectives

After mastering the material in this chapter, you will be able to:

1. Explain the major economic developments of the 1930s, 1960s, 1970s, 1980s, and 1990s in the framework of the aggregate demand–aggregate supply model.
2. Provide a critique of macroeconomic policy for each of the decades examined in this chapter. What have we learned from these episodes?
3. Contrast the interpretations of each period from the perspectives of the new Keynesian, monetarist, and new classical schools of macroeconomic thought.
4. Summarize areas of agreement and areas of continuing disagreement among the schools of macroeconomic thought today.

No doubt in every age economic life has been a scene of conflict and compromise, defended by rationalizations that did not fit with experience.

Joan Robinson, *Economics: An Awkward Corner*

What's Ahead

As the disastrous decade of the 1930s wears on, many people begin to wonder if the United States will ever escape the Great Depression's cruel grip. Forecasts that prosperity lies just around the corner take on a hollow ring.

The collapse seems to defy the logic of classical economic thought—that economies should be able to reach their natural levels of output through a process of self-correction. The old ideas of macroeconomics don't seem to work—and it isn't clear what new ideas should replace them.

In Britain, Cambridge University economist John Maynard Keynes is struggling with ideas that he thinks will turn the conventional wisdom on its head. He is confident that he has found the key not only to understanding the Great Depression, but to correcting it.

. . .

It is the 1960s. The ideas of John Maynard Keynes dominate the economics profession. The tools Keynes suggested have won widespread acceptance among governments all over the world. But economist Milton Friedman of the University of Chicago continues to fight a lonely battle against what has become the Keynesian orthodoxy. He argues that money, not fiscal policy, is what matters in the determination of aggregate demand. He insists not only that fiscal policy can't work, but that monetary policy shouldn't be used to move the economy back to its natural level. He counsels a policy of steady money growth, leaving the economy to adjust to its natural level on its own

. . .

It is 1970. The economy has just taken a startling turn; real GDP has fallen, but inflation has remained high. A young economist at Carnegie-Mellon University, Robert E. Lucas, Jr., finds this a paradox, one that he thinks can't be explained by Keynes's theory. Along with several other economists, he begins work on a radically new approach to macroeconomic thought, one that will challenge Keynes's view head-on. Lucas and his colleagues suggest a world in which self-correction is swift, rational choices by individuals generally cancel the impact of fiscal and monetary policies, and stabilization efforts are likely to slow economic growth.

. . .

It is 1994. With recovery from the 1990–1991 recession under way, the Fed begins to tighten the money supply in an effort to ward off any acceleration of inflation. The Fed has, in classic Keynesian style, been fine-tuning the economy for over a decade. That effort has been focused primarily on bringing down inflation. President Clinton names two new members to the Fed's Board of Governors, Alan Blinder and Janet Yellen. The two are leading new Keynesian economists. Mr. Blinder, a professor at Princeton University, has served for the past year on President Clinton's Council of Economic Advisers. Ms. Yellen is a professor at the University of California at Berkeley. The appointments could shift the Fed toward an even more activist stance toward monetary policy, one that might move away from the Fed's recent hard line on inflation.

John Maynard Keynes, Milton Friedman, and Robert E. Lucas, Jr., each helped to establish a major school of macroeconomic thought. The work of Alan Blinder and Janet Yellen has contributed to molding an extensive revision of the Keynesian school of economic analysis, a revision significant enough to warrant renaming this body of thought the new Keynesian school.

The three primary intellectual traditions in the search for macroeconomic understanding are the new Keynesian, monetarist, and new classical schools. Each of these grew out of the attempts of economists to explain the world around them; each school was thus a product in part of economic events. The ideas represented by these schools of thought still contend with one another today.

In this chapter we'll examine closely the macroeconomic developments of five decades: the 1930s, 1960s, 1970s, 1980s, and 1990s. We'll use the aggregate demand–aggregate supply model to explain macroeconomic changes during these periods, and we'll see how the three major economic schools were affected by these events.

The Great Depression and the Emergence of Keynesian Economics

It's hard to imagine that anyone who lived during the Great Depression wasn't profoundly affected by it. From the beginning of the Depression in 1929 to the time the economy hit bottom in 1933, real GDP plunged nearly 30 percent. Real per capita disposable income sank nearly 40 percent. More than 12 million people were thrown out of work; the unemployment rate soared from 3 percent in 1929 to 25 percent in 1933. Some 85,000 businesses failed. Hundreds of thousands of families lost their homes.

The economy began to recover after 1933, but a huge recessionary gap persisted. Another downturn began in 1937, pushing the unemployment rate back up to 19 percent the following year.

The contraction in output that began in 1929 was not, of course, the first time the economy had slumped. But never had the economy fallen so far and for so long a period. Economic historians, who have gone back into the nineteenth century with their estimates of the economy's total output, estimate that in the 75 years before the Depression there had been 19 recessions. But those contractions had lasted an average of just 22 months. The Great Depression held the U.S. economy in its powerful grip for a decade. The severity and duration of the Great Depression distinguish it from other contractions; it is for that reason that it was given a much stronger name than "recession."

Exhibit 33-1 shows the course of real GDP compared to its natural level during the Great Depression. The economy did not regain its natural level of output until 1940, when the pressures of world war forced sharp increases in aggregate demand.

EXHIBIT 33-1

The Depression and the Recessionary Gap

The dark-shaded area shows real GDP from 1929 to 1942; the upper line shows natural GDP; and the light-shaded area shows the difference between the two—the recessionary gap. The gap nearly closed in 1941; an inflationary gap had opened by 1942. The chart suggests that the recessionary gap remained very large throughout the 1930s.

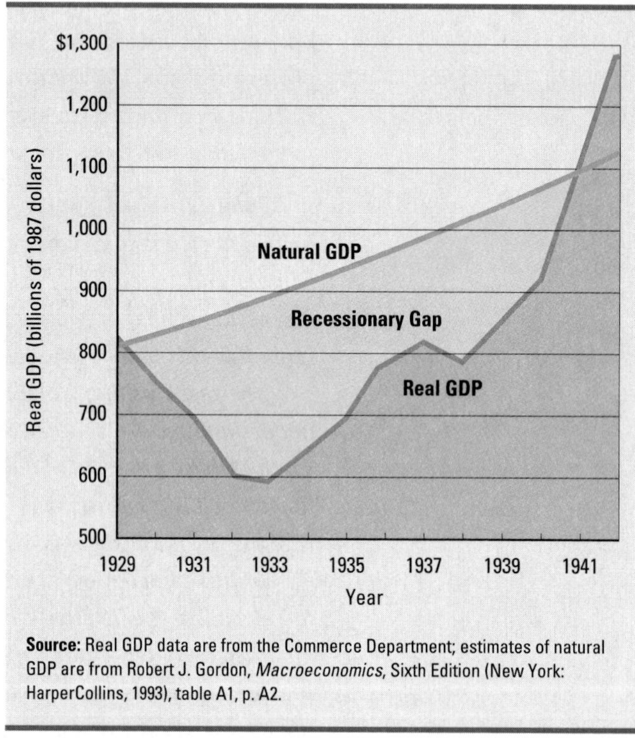

Source: Real GDP data are from the Commerce Department; estimates of natural GDP are from Robert J. Gordon, *Macroeconomics*, Sixth Edition (New York: HarperCollins, 1993), table A1, p. A2.

The Classical School and the Great Depression

The Great Depression came as a shock to what was then the conventional wisdom of economics. To see why, we must go back to the classical tradition of macroeconomic thought that dominated the profession when the Great Depression began.

Classical economics is the body of macroeconomic thought associated primarily with British economist David Ricardo. His *Principles of Political Economy and Taxation* established a tradition that dominated macroeconomic thought for over a century. Ricardo focused on the long run and on the forces that determine an economy's natural level of employment. He emphasized the ability of flexible wages and prices to keep the economy at or near its natural level of output.

Classical economics is the tradition of macroeconomic thought associated with the work of David Ricardo.

Malthus, Demand, and Say's Law

Not all economists of the classical period were confident of the economy's ability to achieve its natural level of output. A British economist of that period,

Case in Point Early Views on Stickiness

Although David Ricardo's focus on the long run emerged as the dominant approach to macroeconomic thought, not all of his contemporaries agreed with his perspective. Many eighteenth and nineteenth century economists developed theoretical arguments suggesting that changes in aggregate demand could affect the real level of economic activity in the short run. Like the new Keynesians, they based their arguments on the concept of price stickiness.

Henry Thornton's 1802 book, *An Enquiry into the Nature and Effects of the Paper Credit of Great Britain,* argued that a reduction in the money supply could, because of wage stickiness, produce a short-run slump in output:

> The tendency, however, of a very great and sudden reduction of the accustomed number of bank notes, is to create an unusual and temporary distress, and a fall of price arising from that distress. But a fall arising from temporary distress, will be attended probably with no correspondent fall in the rate of wages; for the fall of price, and the distress, will be understood to be temporary, and the rate of wages, we know, is not so variable as the price of goods. There is reason, therefore, to fear that the unnatural and extraordinary low price arising from the sort of distress of which we now speak, would occasion much discouragement of the fabrication of manufactures.

A half century earlier, David Hume noted that an increase in the quantity of money would boost output in the short run, again because of the stickiness of prices. In an essay titled "Of Money," published in 1752, Hume described the process through which an increased money supply could boost output:

> At first, no alteration is perceived; by degrees the price rises, first of one commodity, then of another, till the whole at least reaches a just proportion with the new quantity of (money) which is in the kingdom. In my opinion, it is only in this interval or intermediate situation . . . that the encreasing quantity of gold and silver is favourable to industry.

David Hume.

Hume's argument implies sticky prices; some prices are slower to respond to the increase in the money supply than others.

Eighteenth- and nineteenth-century economists are generally lumped together as adherents to the classical school, but their views were anything but uniform. Many developed an analytical framework that was quite similar to the essential elements of new Keynesian economists today. Economist Thomas Humphrey, a vice president of the Federal Reserve Bank of Richmond, marvels at the insights shown by early economists: "When you read these old guys, you find out first that they didn't speak with one voice. There was no single body of thought to which everyone subscribed. And second, you find out how much they *knew.* You could take Henry Thornton's 1802 book as a textbook in any money course today."

Source: Thomas M. Humphrey, "Nonneutrality of Money in Classical Monetary Thought," *Federal Reserve Bank of Richmond Economic Review* 77(2) (March/April 1991): 3–15, and personal interview.

Thomas Malthus, suggested the possibility that total demand might be insufficient to purchase all the goods and services produced. That, in turn, could cause firms to reduce their output, which would reduce income and thus reduce demand still further. Ricardo dismissed this view out of hand. In doing so he relied on an earlier argument by French economist Jean Baptiste Say, who had hit on the basic identity we noted in Chapter 21; the production of goods and services creates income equal to the value of that production.

Because income was generated in an amount equal to production, Ricardo argued, the demand for that production would necessarily be adequate to ensure its purchase. If households saved an increased share of their income, reducing consumption demand, then the increased savings would provide for increased investment. Whatever was saved, Ricardo said, would be invested.

In terms of the model of aggregate demand and aggregate supply, Ricardo's argument focused on the supply side. Whatever was produced—supplied—would create the income necessary to purchase that production. The assertion that the total value of goods and services produced will generate demand equal to that production is called **Say's law.** A shorthand version of Say's law can be stated thus: Supply creates its own demand.

Time Periods and Natural GDP

Say's law implies that equilibrium will be achieved; what is produced will be demanded. But the doctrine we associate with the classical school went further. It asserted that the equilibrium level of production would provide for the full employment of the economy's resources, with the economy operating at its natural level of output.

The essence of the argument was the presumption of flexible prices. If there were involuntary unemployment in the labor market—a surplus of labor—then wages would fall. The reduction in wages would increase the quantity of labor demanded and reduce the quantity supplied, returning the labor market to equilibrium. The same mechanism would ensure equilibrium in the markets for other factors of production.

The argument of the classical school suggests that achieving the natural level of output is not a problem; the economy can do that on its own. Classical economists recognized, however, that the process would take time. Ricardo admitted that there could be *temporary* periods in which employment would fall below the natural level. But his emphasis was on the long run, and in the long run all would be set right by the smooth functioning of the price system.

It was thus his long-run focus that produced Ricardo's cheery view that slumps weren't really a problem. His friend and colleague Malthus objected strongly that slumps *were* a serious problem, but Malthus wasn't able to overcome the ironclad rigor of Ricardo's logic. In a letter to his friend, Ricardo put his finger on the real source of their dispute:

> It appears to me that one great cause in our difference in opinion on the subjects which we have so often discussed is that you have always in your mind the immediate and temporary effects of particular changes, whereas I put these immediate and temporary effects quite aside, and fix my whole attention on the permanent state of things that will result from them. Perhaps you estimate these temporary effects too highly, whilst I am too much disposed to undervalue them. To manage the subject quite right, they should be carefully distinguished and mentioned, and due effects should be ascribed to each.[1]

Ricardo thus recognized that a key issue in the debate over whether slumps in economic activity could be a problem was the time period of the analysis. In the short run, such slumps could occur—as was painfully evident from the experience of the nineteenth century. But in the long run, the economy would correct these slumps and return to full employment.

In the context of the Great Depression, however, the classical counsel that all would be well in the long run hardly seemed helpful. How long was the long run to be? As the Depression ground on year after year after painful year, a theoretical framework that urged patience must have seemed a useless framework indeed.

Say's law is the assertion that the total value of goods and services produced will generate income—and therefore demand—equal to that production.

[1] As quoted in Henry W. Spiegel, *The Growth of Economic Thought* (Durham, N.C.: Duke University Press, 1983), p. 316.

Keynes's Challenge

In Britain, which had been plunged into a depression of its own, John Maynard Keynes had begun to develop a new framework of macroeconomic analysis, one that suggested that what for Ricardo were "temporary effects" could persist for a long time, and at terrible cost. Keynes's 1936 book, *The General Theory of Employment, Interest and Money,* was to transform the way many economists thought about macroeconomic problems.

In a nutshell, we can say that Keynes's book shifted the thrust of macroeconomic thought from the concept of aggregate supply to the concept of aggregate demand. Say's law and Ricardo's focus on the tendency of an economy to reach its natural level of output inevitably stressed the supply side—an economy tends to operate at a level of output given by the long-run aggregate supply curve. Keynes, in arguing that what we now call recessionary or inflationary gaps could be created by shifts in aggregate demand, shifted the theoretical argument back to the demand side. His insistence that such gaps were likely to be prolonged, together with his suggestion that monetary or fiscal policy could shift the aggregate demand curve to close such gaps, put the aggregate demand curve at the center of the policy debate as well.

Doubts About Self-Correction

Keynes argued that the economy could remain trapped in the bog of a recessionary gap for a very long time. He dismissed the classical school's confidence that the economy would correct itself in the long run as irrelevant. "In the long run," he wrote acidly, "we are all dead."

A key source of the difficulty in self-correction, Keynes argued, lay in the labor market. Workers might not accept a reduction in their wages, even in the face of slumping demand. Falling wages therefore could not be relied on to bring employment back to its natural level. Keynes believed that a leftward shift of the aggregate demand curve could push the economy below its natural level and leave it there. Keynes stressed the stickiness of prices, particularly wages. He insisted that workers would never accept the reduction in nominal wages required for the economy to correct a recessionary gap.

Keynesian Remedies: Fiscal and Monetary Policy

For Keynes, the remedy for a recessionary gap was straightforward. The problem was the economy's inability to recover from the slump in aggregate demand. The solution, then, was to boost that demand. Keynes suggested that the most direct way to do that would be to increase government purchases. The increase in such purchases would, he argued, boost household income and boost consumption. That would stimulate still more production, more income, and more consumption. Still another way the government could stimulate demand was by reducing taxes, thus giving consumers more disposable income to spend. An increase in the quantity of money could also stimulate spending, but Keynes worried that the additional money might not be spent and thus might not produce an increase in demand.

Keynes proposed expansionary fiscal and monetary policies in an open letter to U.S. President Franklin Roosevelt that was published in *The New York Times* in 1933. Keynes sailed to the United States the following year and met personally with Roosevelt. But the U.S. president was not persuaded; the combined impact of federal, state, and local government policy during the Great Depression generally failed to increase aggregate demand relative to natural GDP until increased government purchases were forced by the advent of war in Europe.

Monetary policy also failed to provide any stimulus to the economy during the Depression. The Fed took no action to prevent a wave of bank failures that swept across the country at the outset of the Depression. Between 1930 and 1933, 9,000 banks—one-third of all banks in the United States—failed. The money supply plunged 31 percent between 1929 and 1933.

The Fed could have prevented many of the failures by engaging in open-market operations to inject new reserves into the system and by lending reserves to troubled banks through the discount window. But it generally refused to do so; Fed officials sometimes even applauded bank failures as a desirable way to weed out bad management!

Real GDP started to rise after 1933. While the economy remained well below its full employment level, Federal Reserve officials began worrying about inflation. In 1937, the Fed announced a sharp increase in reserve requirements. The money supply fell sharply the following year, as did real GDP.

Keynes must have been appalled by the failure to use fiscal or monetary policy in an effective way to combat the Depression. It was not until the onset of World War II that the dramatic increases in aggregate demand that Keynes had called for were forced on the U.S. economy as firms stepped up their investment in capacity to produce weapons, the government increased its spending, and the Fed increased the money supply. These measures increased aggregate demand and brought a recovery—just as Keynes's new theory had predicted they would.

Clashing Interpretations of the Great Depression

The Great Depression was a watershed experience for macroeconomic analysis. It is important not just because it was the worst downturn in American economic history, but because it led to a radical revision of macroeconomic thought. For many economists, the episode demonstrates the relevance of Keynes's argument and the validity of his policy prescriptions. Others see the debacle in a quite different light. Monetarists and new classical economists argue that their policy prescriptions for steady growth in the money supply would have prevented the 1929 downturn from becoming the disaster that it did.

We shall assess these conflicting interpretations of the Great Depression in this section. First, however, it will be useful to examine the experience in the context of the model of aggregate demand and aggregate supply.

Aggregate Demand, Aggregate Supply, and the Great Depression

This chapter uses the model of aggregate demand and aggregate supply to interpret economic change during various periods. It suggests how changes in aggregate demand and in short-run aggregate supply cause actual changes in real GDP and in the price level.

One difficulty of trying to fit the data to the curves is that in the real world, long-run aggregate supply increases constantly as the labor force and the capital stock increase. As we saw in Chapter 26, an increase in long-run aggregate supply also increases short-run aggregate supply. With those curves shifting all the time, it's hard to pinpoint other macroeconomic forces that may be at work.

In order to isolate short-run changes from the background of increases in long-run aggregate supply, we'll use a modified version of the basic model. Instead of using a graph with real GDP on the horizontal axis, we'll measure real GDP as a percentage of natural GDP. That will allow us to focus on cyclical movements in real GDP. In this framework, the long-run aggregate supply curve is always a vertical line at 100 percent. A recessionary gap would imply a value of real GDP of less than 100 percent of its natural level; an inflationary gap would imply a value of greater than 100 percent.

In each period we study, we'll assume that the points plotted for each year correspond to the intersection of an aggregate demand curve and a short-run aggregate supply curve. We don't know the slopes of the actual curves, so we'll draw aggregate demand and short-run aggregate supply curves of the shape predicted by the theory in Chapter 26. We'll then shift the curves according to the actual values plotted for the price level and real GDP/natural real GDP and interpret the shifts that the graph suggests have occurred. For example, if real GDP and the price level rise during a particular period, the aggregate demand curve must have shifted to the right. An increase in the price level accompanied by a reduction in real GDP implies that the short-run aggregate supply curve has shifted up and to the left.

Exhibit 33-2 suggests an interpretation of the first years of the Great Depression. In 1929, the economy was in equilibrium at approximately its natural level. We see that aggregate demand began falling in 1930 and that it continued to decline each year until 1933. The biggest reduction in 1930 and in 1931 came in gross private domestic investment, which plunged by more than 60 percent during the 2-year period. Consumption took the biggest tumble in 1932. Government purchases began falling that year as well. Consumption and government purchases continued to decline in 1933. Net exports declined throughout the period, but they were such a tiny component of U.S. GDP that they had little impact on the price level or on output.

EXHIBIT 33-2

Aggregate Demand and Aggregate Supply: 1929–1933

Slumping aggregate demand brought the economy well below the full-employment level of output. By 1931, it appears that the aggregate supply curve had begun shifting downward as nominal wages fell.

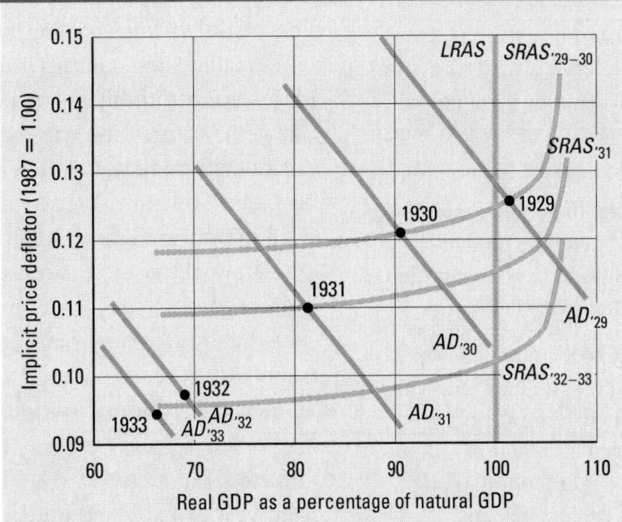

Source: Data for real GDP and the price level are from *Economic Report of the President 1995*, table B-116, p. 406. Estimates of natural GDP are from Robert J. Gordon, *Macroeconomics*, Sixth Edition (New York: HarperCollins, 1993), table A1, p. A2.

As aggregate demand shifted to the left, the economy fell into a recessionary gap. We saw in Chapters 23 and 26 that a recessionary gap implies a surplus of labor, which puts downward pressure on nominal wages. That certainly happened; nominal wages plunged roughly 20 percent from 1929 to 1933. According to our model, such a reduction should shift the short-run aggregate supply curve downward. Exhibit 33-2 suggests that the aggregate supply curve began shifting downward in 1931.

Could the economy's own self-correction mechanism have corrected the Great Depression? We'll never know. The Roosevelt administration, which took office in March 1933, interpreted the problem facing the economy as one of falling prices. It therefore imposed price restrictions aimed at blocking further reductions in wages and prices. Those price controls tended to block further downward shifts in short-run aggregate supply and thus acted to prevent the classical recovery mechanism of downward shifts in short-run aggregate supply that appears to have begun. The nation's price level, which had fallen 23 percent during the first 4 years of the Great Depression, rose during most of the rest of the period.

Checklist

- Classical economic thought stressed the ability of the economy to achieve its natural level of output in the long run.
- Say's law asserts that the total level of output will generate an equal volume of aggregate demand.
- The experience of the Great Depression convinced many economists that the self-correction mechanism of classical economics could not be relied upon.
- Aggregate demand fell sharply in the first 4 years of the Great Depression. As the recessionary gap widened, nominal wages began to fall and the short-run aggregate supply curve began shifting downward.
- Keynesians argued that the Great Depression showed that changes in aggregate demand could put the economy into a recessionary gap from which it could not recover on its own.
- Monetarists stress the role of monetary policy in bringing on the recession. New classical economists argue that underlying shifts in the production function forced a reduction in long-run aggregate supply and that federal intervention in the wage and price mechanism prevented the economy from adjusting to these changes.

Keynesian, Monetarist, and New Classical Perspectives on the Great Depression

For Keynesian economists, the experience of the Great Depression provided dramatic confirmation of the validity of Keynes's ideas. A sharp reduction in investment touched off the downturn. In the absence of any expansionary fiscal or monetary policy, the economy failed to correct itself. It was not until government purchases started rising sharply in 1940 and 1941 that the economy recovered. These expansionary policies, undertaken not for economic stimulus but in response to the threat of war, brought recovery—just as Keynes said they would.

Monetarists interpret the experience quite differently. For them, the key factor in bringing on the Depression was the monetary policies of the Fed. In allowing banks to fail and the money supply to fall, monetarists argue, the Fed in effect conducted contractionary policies on a massive scale. The Fed's doubling of reserve requirements in 1937 compounded its earlier errors. In the monetarist view, the Depression was a classic example of the power of money. Had the Fed conducted monetary policies that steadily increased the money supply, they insist, the downturn that began in 1929 would have ended quickly. The Great Depression need never have occurred.

New classical economists, who generally support the monetarist prescription of slow, steady growth in the money supply, agree with the view that the Fed undertook the wrong policies. Rather than point to the plunge in the money supply as the cause of the Depression, however, they point to developments that shifted the economy's production function downward and thus reduced long-run aggregate supply. Certainly the sudden failure of one-third of the nation's banks affected productivity. The Great Depression was marked by drought in the Midwest that affected productivity. In addition, New Deal policies aimed at preventing reductions in wages and prices tended to block the adjustment process through which new classical economists believe the economy maintains its natural level of output.

Case in Point — The Tax Policy Debate

The Kennedy tax cut of 1964 transformed the nation's approach to fiscal policy choices. The measure generated great controversy—both inside and outside the Kennedy administration.

Walter Heller, who headed President Kennedy's Council of Economic Advisers, believed from the outset that a tax cut was necessary. But in 1961, his colleagues on the Council, James Tobin (who would later win the Nobel Prize) and Kermit Gordon, disagreed, arguing that increased government purchases and investment were providing a sufficient stimulus to aggregate demand. Real GNP—which was then the primary gauge of economic activity—increased sharply in the fourth quarter of 1961, and Heller's insistence on a tax cut was set aside. He recalled the episode later:

> I thought we needed a tax cut but just at that point—mid-December 1961—we got the first estimate of the fourth quarter GNP in 1961 and dammit, it was a great big jump over the third quarter. You can see why I say 'dammit' about the good news—it strengthened the hand of [Tobin and Gordon].

Growth in real GNP fell below the administration's goal for 1962, however, and unemployment held stubbornly at 5.4 percent. President Kennedy wanted to bring the rate down to 4 percent. Heller, backed now by his colleagues on the Council, pressed again for a tax cut. The political difficulty of the Council's call for a tax cut was that it would increase the federal deficit, which reached $4.2 billion in 1962. Kennedy thought that the deficit required a tax increase; he feared that a tax cut would increase the deficit further. The Keynesian message, however, was that it was more important to bring the economy to full employment than to balance the government's books. President Kennedy was finally convinced by this argument and proposed a tax cut to Congress in 1963.

Kermit Gordon, Walter Heller, David Bell, and James Tobin (l. to r.). Bell was Budget Director; Gordon, Heller, and Tobin were members of the Council of Economics Advisors, which Heller chaired.

Approval of the proposal was slow in coming. Congress didn't pass it until 1964, after President Kennedy had been assassinated. But the tax cut had been passed—and it was the most dramatic implementation of a Keynesian fiscal policy ever undertaken in the United States.

Source: The quote from Heller is in Edwin Hargrove and Samuel Morley, eds., *The President and the Council of Economic Advisers: Interviews with CEA Chairmen (Boulder, CO: Westview Press, 1984).*

The 1960s and the Triumph of Keynes

The experience of the Great Depression led to the widespread acceptance of Keynesian theory among economists, but its acceptance as a conceptual framework for economic policy was slower. The notion that government spending and tax policy could or should be used to manipulate the equilibrium level of income was rejected by the administrations of Presidents Roosevelt, Truman, and Eisenhower. Truman vetoed a 1948 Republican-sponsored tax cut aimed at stimulating the economy after World War II (Congress, however, overrode the veto), and Eisenhower resisted stimulative measures to deal with the recessions of 1953, 1957, and 1960.

It was the administration of President John F. Kennedy that first used fiscal policy with the intent of manipulating aggregate demand to move the economy toward its natural level of output. Kennedy's willingness to embrace Keynes's ideas was to change the nation's approach to fiscal policy for the next two decades.

Expansionary Policy for a Recessionary Gap

The Kennedy administration was the first in the United States to use fiscal policy in an effort to close a recessionary gap. President Kennedy had appointed a team of economic advisers that believed in Keynesian economics, and they advocated an activist approach to fiscal and monetary policy.

The administration's fiscal policies were expansionary from the beginning. As a candidate, Kennedy had argued that the United States had fallen behind the Soviet Union in military preparedness. He won approval from Congress for sharp increases in defense spending. He also introduced accelerated depreciation to the tax code; we learned in Chapter 28 that this device can stimulate investment demand. Most dramatic, Kennedy proposed an income tax cut and an investment tax credit. These measures, which were passed in 1964, represented the first major application of a Keynesian fiscal policy.

The Fed followed the administration's lead. It, too, shifted to an expansionary policy in 1961. The Fed purchased government securities, boosting the rate of money growth and putting downward pressure on interest rates.

As shown in Exhibit 33-3, the expansionary policies of the early 1960s had pushed real GDP past its natural level by 1964. The expansionary policies, however, didn't stop there. Continued increases in federal spending for the newly expanded war in Vietnam and for President Lyndon Johnson's agenda of domestic programs, together with continued high rates of money growth, sent the aggregate demand curve further to the right. By 1966, the economy was operating well beyond the natural level of real GDP.

EXHIBIT 33-3

Boosting Aggregate Demand in the 1960s

Expansionary monetary and fiscal policies responded to a recessionary gap early in the 1960s, shifting the aggregate demand curve to the right. The gap had been closed, with the economy operating about at its natural level, by 1963.

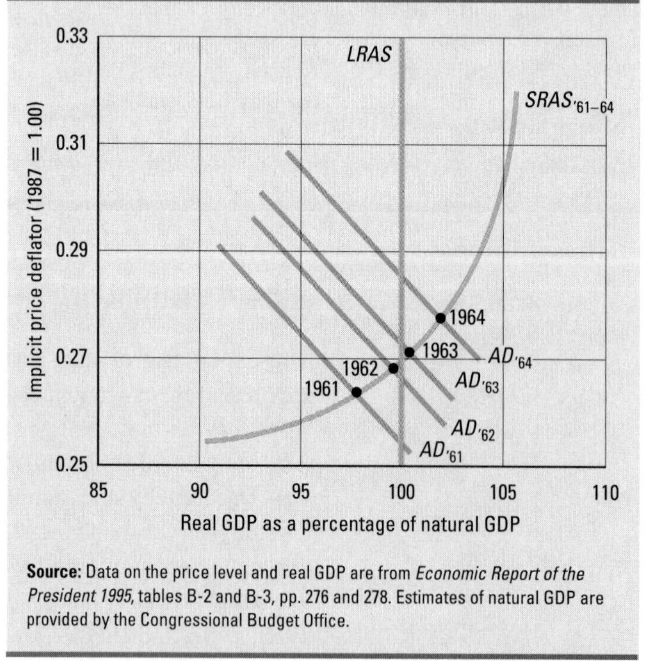

Source: Data on the price level and real GDP are from *Economic Report of the President 1995*, tables B-2 and B-3, pp. 276 and 278. Estimates of natural GDP are provided by the Congressional Budget Office.

Contractionary Policy for an Inflationary Gap

The Keynesian prescription for an economy operating below full employment called for policies to boost aggregate demand. On the fiscal side, that meant increasing government spending or cutting taxes. On the monetary side, it meant accelerating money growth. The Keynesian remedy for an economy that had moved *beyond* full employment, however, was the opposite: it called for reduced government spending, increased taxes, and/or slower money growth.

President Johnson's new chairman of the Council of Economic Advisers, Gardner Ackley, urged the president in 1965 to adopt fiscal policies aimed at nudging the aggregate demand curve back to the left. The president reluctantly agreed and called in the chairman of the House Ways and Means Committee, the committee that must initiate all revenue measures, to see what he thought of the idea. Wilbur Mills flatly told Johnson that he wouldn't even hold hearings to consider a tax increase. For the time being, the tax boost was dead.

The Federal Reserve System did slow the rate of money growth sharply in 1966. Mr. Ackley continued to press his case, and in 1967 President Johnson proposed a temporary 10 percent increase in personal income taxes. Mills now endorsed the measure. The temporary tax boost went into effect the following year. The Fed, concerned that the tax hike would be *too* contractionary, countered the administration's shift in fiscal policy with a policy of vigorous money growth in 1967 and 1968.

Exhibit 33-4 shows movements in aggregate demand and in aggregate supply in the second half of the 1960s. As we've already seen, increasing aggregate demand had opened up a large inflationary gap by 1964. The Fed's slowing of money growth in 1966 appears to have helped to put the brakes on the economy; aggregate demand does not appear to have risen in 1967. It rose in 1968, then held steady in 1969 and 1970 as fiscal and monetary policies continued to exert a contractionary influence on the economy.

EXHIBIT 33-4

Grappling with an Inflationary Gap: The Late 1960s

The Fed slowed money growth sharply in 1966 while fiscal policy remained expansionary. That combination of policies appeared to halt the outward shift in aggregate demand in 1967; the short-run aggregate supply curve shifted upward in the same year. Further slowing of money growth in 1969, together with contractionary fiscal policies, held aggregate demand steady after 1968. Those policies coincided with substantial upward shifts in aggregate supply in 1969 and 1970, closing the inflationary gap.

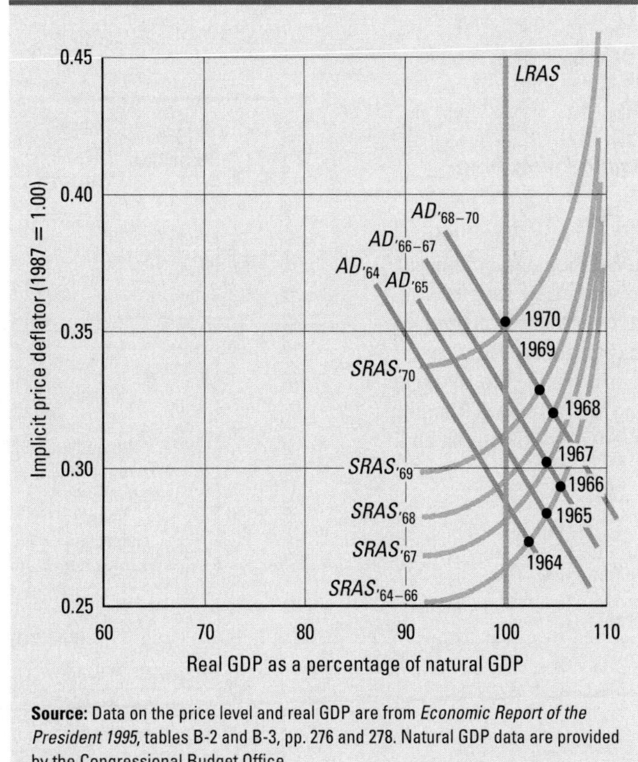

Source: Data on the price level and real GDP are from *Economic Report of the President 1995,* tables B-2 and B-3, pp. 276 and 278. Natural GDP data are provided by the Congressional Budget Office.

At the same time aggregate demand was being held back, however, the adjustments in aggregate supply that contribute to closing an inflationary gap were setting in. The aggregate supply curve began shifting upward in 1967 as workers demanded higher nominal wages to adjust for the higher prices they faced as consumers. The large upward shift in 1970, combined with a reduction in aggregate demand, produced a very large reduction in real GDP in 1970.

The late 1960s suggested a sobering reality about the new Keynesian orthodoxy. Stimulating the economy was politically more palatable than contracting it. President Kennedy, while he wasn't able to win approval of his tax cut during his lifetime, did manage to put the other expansionary aspects of his program into place early in his administration. His policies were reinforced by the Fed. Dealing with an inflationary gap proved to be quite another matter. President Johnson, a master of the legislative process, took three years to get even a mildly contractionary tax increase put into place, and the Fed acted to counter the impact of this measure by shifting to an expansionary policy.

The 1960s marked the beginning of an activist approach to fiscal and monetary policy, consistent with Keynesian economic doctrine. No longer were the government and the Fed content to allow the economy to achieve its own equilibrium in the short run. No longer was the economy treated like the weather —something people could complain about but could do nothing about. Policymakers proceeded as if they could tune the economy like a musical instrument, boosting it when it went flat and bringing it down when it soared too high. The artful application of Keynesian macroeconomic policies, many argued, spelled an end to the old problems of recession and inflation.

Exhibit 33-5 summarizes the major macroeconomic developments of the 1960s. The course of real GDP is shown, with periods of recession shaded. We see the shift to expansionary fiscal and monetary policies early in the 1960s,

EXHIBIT 33-5

Keynesian Macroeconomic Policy in the 1960s

Real GDP is shown by the red line. The 1960s marked a shift to the activist monetary and fiscal policies that had been prescribed by Keynes. Policymakers responded to the recessionary gap early in the 1960s with expansionary fiscal and monetary policies. Policies continued to be expansionary even after this gap was closed. Ultimately, contractionary policies were used to combat an inflationary gap.

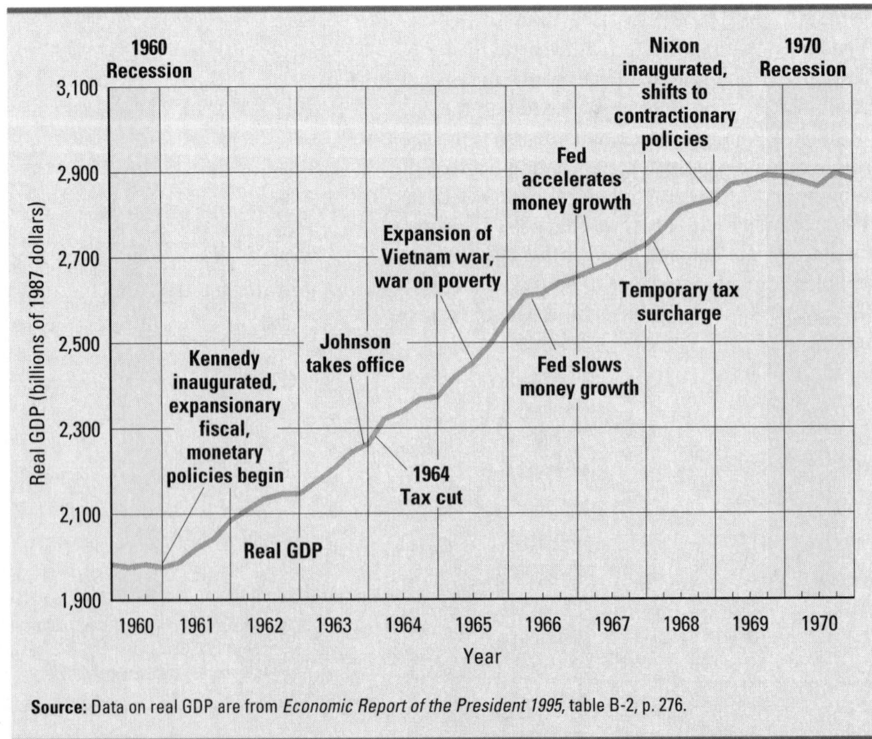

Source: Data on real GDP are from *Economic Report of the President 1995*, table B-2, p. 276.

halting attempts to shift to contractionary policies in the second half of the decade, and the final shift to contractionary monetary policies at the end of the decade.

As the 1960s came to an end, it was certainly possible to look back on a decade of triumph for macroeconomic policy. Real GDP had grown at an average annual rate of 3.8 percent. The price level had risen at only a 3 percent rate. The expansion that dominated the 1960s had lasted 116 months, longer than any other expansion recorded in U.S. history. Although the economy may have been overheated at the end of the period, most economists were confident that problem could be fixed with the appropriate contractionary policies. As we saw in the last chapter, the economy in 1969 seemed poised for a movement back down the Phillips curve. Policymakers would bring inflation back down with a modest increase in unemployment. Those who saw the 1960s as proof that Keynesian remedies could fix any macroeconomic ill would be in for a rude awakening. The 1970s were to bring new problems and new challenges to Keynesian thought.

Checklist

- Beginning in 1961, expansionary fiscal and monetary policies were used to close a recessionary gap; this was the first major U.S. application of Keynesian macroeconomic policy.
- The Kennedy-Johnson tax cut of 1964 is a classic illustration of an expansionary fiscal policy. It also suggests a difficulty of fiscal policy; it was passed 4 years after economists had first proposed it as a stabilization measure.
- As aggregate demand continued to rise through the mid-1960s, an inflationary gap opened; policymakers seemed reluctant to undertake fiscal or monetary measures to shift aggregate demand to the left. The gap produced upward shifts in aggregate supply.

The 1970s: Keynesians on the Defensive

In the United States, the first decade of Keynesian fiscal and monetary policies seemed a triumph. That triumph turned into a series of macroeconomic disasters in the 1970s as inflation and unemployment spiraled to ever higher levels. The fiscal and monetary medicine that had seemed to work so well in the 1960s seemed capable of producing only instability in the 1970s. The experience of the period shook the faith of many economists in Keynesian remedies and made them receptive to alternative approaches. Many turned to the monetarist ideas that had been refined over the past several decades; others turned to a radically different approach to macroeconomic theory, new classical economics.

This section reviews the major macroeconomic events of the 1970s. It then examines the emergence of the monetarist and new classical schools as major challengers to the Keynesian orthodoxy that had seemed so dominant a decade earlier.

Macroeconomic Policy: Coping with the Supply Side

The 1960s offered a familiar landscape for Keynesian economic policy. Aggregate demand at the beginning of the decade was too weak for the economy to reach its natural level. Macroeconomic policy could fix that; stimulative measures closed the recessionary gap by the middle of the decade. But the decade concluded with a surprise from the supply side. Trouble from aggregate supply would plague the economy throughout the next decade—and would prove far more difficult to manage than the demand-side weakness that had visited the economy a decade earlier.

The experience of 1970 and 1971 stunned economic policymakers. Unemployment rose in response to contractionary policies, as economists expected it would. But inflation remained stubbornly high. The implicit price deflator, which had risen at a 5 percent rate in 1969, recorded 5.4 percent increases in 1970 and again in 1971.

In retrospect, it's difficult to see what was so alarming. The economy in 1969 had had a huge inflationary gap; unemployment that year was just 3.5

percent. Such a gap means that workers and firms with sticky prices are taken by surprise by a rising price level. As workers adjust by demanding higher nominal wages and firms adjust by raising their prices, the short-run aggregate supply curve shifts upward. As it does, real GDP falls while prices continue to rise; inflation remains high. Unemployment rises as real GDP falls. That prediction of the aggregate demand–aggregate supply model was certainly consistent with experience; unemployment rose in 1970 to 4.9 percent and in 1971 to 5.9 percent. Inflation, meanwhile, rose in 1970 to 5.4 percent and remained at that rate in 1971.

With the benefit of hindsight, the experience of 1970 and 1971 seems perfectly normal. An inflationary gap in 1969 prompted workers and firms to seek higher wages and to boost sticky prices, shifting the short-run aggregate supply curve. That pushed inflation and unemployment up. The economy's correction of an inflationary gap had produced a stagflation phase in the inflation-unemployment cycle. By 1971, the unemployment rate had reached 5.9 percent—about equal to what the Congressional Budget Office now estimates was the natural rate for that year, 5.6 percent.

In 1971, however, the experience seemed anything but normal. The notion that an unemployment rate greater than 5 percent was consistent with macroeconomic equilibrium was rejected by policymakers of that time. The Kennedy administration had established a 4 percent rate of unemployment as a goal, and that remained the standard against which macroeconomic performance was judged.[2]

Faced with an economy that appeared to be out of control, President Richard Nixon imposed wage and price controls in August 1971. All wages and prices were frozen for 6 months; subsequent price increases required approval from the federal government. The Fed shifted to an expansionary monetary policy that year and continued to stimulate the economy in 1972. Fiscal policy, which in the first 2 years of the Nixon administration had been contractionary, also changed to become expansionary.

The economy enjoyed something of a breather in 1972 as it eased into the recovery phase of the inflation-unemployment cycle. Inflation and unemployment both fell. We see in Exhibit 33-6 that expansionary policies continued to push the economy past its natural level, opening an inflationary gap in 1973.

The model of aggregate demand and aggregate supply suggests that an inflationary gap will create a stagflation phase of rising inflation and rising unemployment. This time, however, the economy's natural adjustment was jolted by a dramatic boost in oil prices by OPEC nations, which shifted the short-run aggregate supply curve upward and to the left. The combination of a normal adjustment to an inflationary gap and an oil-price shock produced a dramatic shift in short-run aggregate supply, as illustrated in Exhibit 33-6.

The experience of the first half of the decade was repeated in the second half. Fiscal and monetary policy were sharply expansionary from 1975 to 1979. Unemployment fell as inflation rose. By 1979, real GDP had returned to its natural level, but the inflation rate had risen sharply.

If the 1960s had been a macroeconomic success story, the 1970s were a disappointment. Real GDP had grown much more slowly than in the 1960s, while inflation was far greater. Inflation averaged 7.4 percent—more than double the

[2] The Nixon administration tried to sell the idea that a 5 percent unemployment rate was a more reasonable goal, but this was widely ridiculed in the press as an admission of failure.

EXHIBIT 33-6

Expansionary Policy and an Oil Price Shock

Expansionary fiscal and monetary policies produced an inflationary gap in 1973, just as oil prices began rising. The economy's adjustment to this gap, together with the jump in oil prices in 1973 and 1974, produced upward shifts in short-run aggregate supply, creating another period of stagflation.

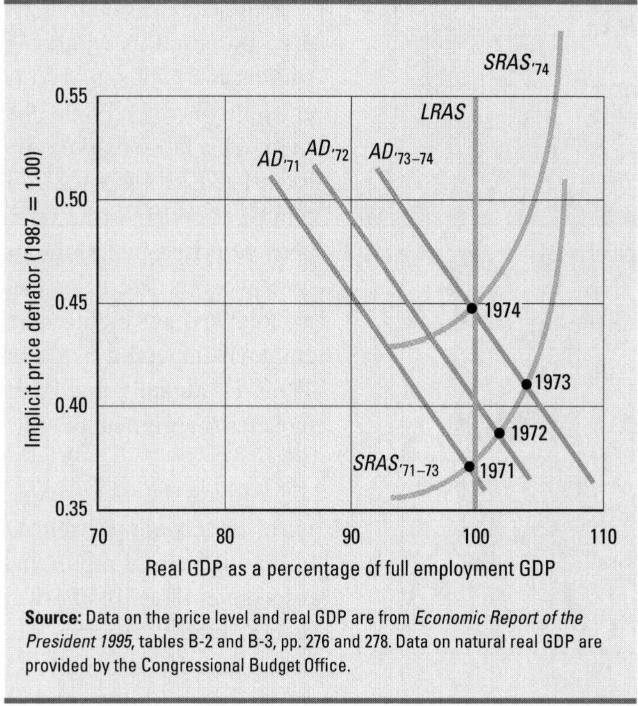

Source: Data on the price level and real GDP are from *Economic Report of the President 1995*, tables B-2 and B-3, pp. 276 and 278. Data on natural real GDP are provided by the Congressional Budget Office.

1960s rate. Unemployment averaged 7 percent; it exceeded the natural rate through much of the decade. We'll see in the next two chapters that other long-term changes were at work in that period: productivity growth was slowing down and a greater inequality in incomes was emerging.

The 1970s demonstrated that it was not just aggregate demand that could create problems for the economy; shifts in aggregate supply could cause problems as well. Keynesian economics, with its emphasis on the manipulation of aggregate demand, suddenly was a less sure guide to macroeconomic policy than it had seemed in the 1960s. The time was ripe for an intellectual counterattack, an attack that was provided by monetarists and new classical economists.

The Monetarist Challenge

The monetarist challenge to Keynesian macroeconomic thought was certainly not new. But monetarist ideas won wider acceptance as the Keynesian orthodoxy seemed to lose its relevance. Activist stabilization policies hadn't seemed particularly effective in the 1970s, and a framework of thought that counseled against the use of such policies gained in appeal.

While monetarists differ from Keynesians in their assessment of the impact of fiscal policy, the primary difference in the two schools lies in their degree of optimism about whether stabilization policy can, in fact, be counted on to bring the economy back to its natural level. For monetarists, the complexity of economic life and the uncertain nature of lags mean that efforts to use monetary policy to stabilize the economy can be destabilizing. Monetarists argued that the difficulties encountered by policymakers as they tried to deal with the dramatic events of the 1970s demonstrated the superiority of a policy that simply increased the money supply at a slow, steady rate.

Monetarists could also cite the apparent validity of an adjustment mechanism proposed by Milton Friedman in 1968. As the economy continued to expand in the 1960s, and as unemployment continued to fall, Friedman said that unemployment had fallen below its natural rate, the rate consistent with equilibrium in the labor market. Any divergence of unemployment from its natural rate, he insisted, would necessarily be temporary. He suggested that the low unemployment of 1968 (the rate was 3.6 percent that year) meant that workers had been surprised by rising prices. Higher prices had produced a real wage below what workers and firms had expected. Friedman predicted that as workers demanded and got higher nominal wages, the price level would shoot up and unemployment would rise. That, of course, is precisely what happened in 1970 and 1971. Friedman's notion of the natural rate of unemployment buttressed the monetarist argument that the economy moves to its natural level of output on its own.

Perhaps the most potent argument from the monetarist camp was the behavior of the economy itself. During the 1960s, monetarist and Keynesian economists alike could argue that economic performance was consistent with their respective views of the world. Keynesians could point to expansions in economic activity that they could ascribe to expansionary fiscal policy, but economic activity also moved closely with changes in the money supply, just as monetarists predicted. During the 1970s, however, it was difficult for Keynesians to argue that policies that affected aggregate demand were having the predicted impact on the economy. Changes in aggregate supply had repeatedly pushed the economy off a Keynesian course. But monetarists, once again, could point to a consistent relationship between changes in the money supply and changes in economic activity.

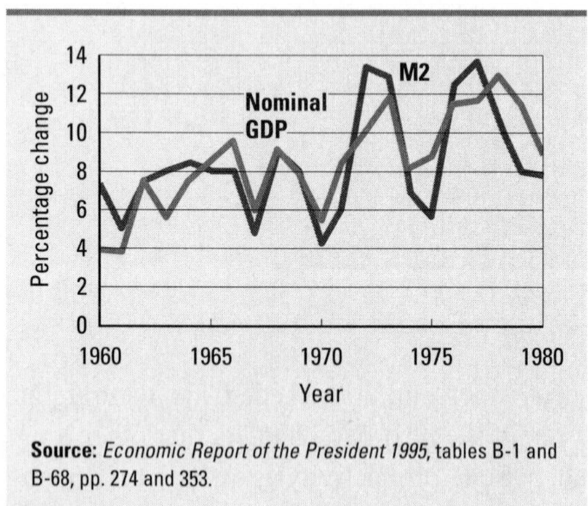

Source: *Economic Report of the President 1995*, tables B-1 and B-68, pp. 274 and 353.

EXHIBIT 33-7

Changes in Money and Nominal GDP, 1960–1980

Annual rates of change in nominal GDP (the green line) and M2 (the maroon line) are plotted, with M2 rates lagged a year. The observation for 1961, for example, shows that nominal GDP increased 3.6 percent and that M2 increased 4.9 percent in the previous year, 1960.

Exhibit 33-7 shows the movement of nominal GDP and M2 during the 1960s and 1970s. In the exhibit, annual percentage changes in nominal GDP are plotted against percentage changes in M2 a year earlier to account for the lagged effects of changes in the money supply. We see that there was a close relationship between changes in the quantity of money and subsequent changes in nominal GDP.

The New Classical School: A Focus on Aggregate Supply

Much of the difficulty policymakers encountered during the decade of the 1970s stemmed from shifts in aggregate supply. Keynesian economics and, to a lesser degree, monetarism had focused on aggregate demand. As it became clear that an analysis incorporating the supply side was an essential part of the puzzle, some economists turned to an entirely new way of looking at macroeconomic issues.

These economists started with what we identified in Chapter 1 as a distinguishing characteristic of economic thought: a focus on individuals and their decisions. Keynesian economics employed aggregate analysis and paid little attention to individual choices. Monetarist doctrine was based on the analysis of individuals' maximizing behavior with respect to money demand, but it did not extend that analysis to decisions that affect aggregate supply. The new approach aimed at an analysis of how individual choices would affect the entire spectrum of economic activity.

New classical economists rejected the entire framework of conventional macroeconomic analysis. Indeed, they rejected the very term. For new classical economists there is no macroeconomics, nor is there something called microeconomics. For them, there is only economics, which they regard as the analysis of behavior based on individual maximization. The analysis of the determination of the price level and real GDP becomes an application of basic economic theory, not a separate body of thought.

New classical economics is similar to the classical tradition in that it stresses the economy's ability to achieve its natural level of output. But there the similarity ends. Classical economic thought emerged in large part before economists had developed sophisticated mathematical models of maximizing behavior. The new classical economics puts mathematics to work in an extremely complex way to generalize from individual behavior to aggregate results.

Because the new classical approach suggests that the economy will remain at or near its natural level, it follows that the changes we observe in economic activity result not from changes in aggregate demand but from changes in long-run aggregate supply. New classical economics suggests that economic changes don't necessarily imply economic problems.

New classical economists pointed to the supply-side shocks of the 1970s, both from changes in oil prices and changes in expectations, as evidence that their emphasis on aggregate supply was on the mark. They argued that the large observed swings in real GDP reflected underlying changes in the economy's natural level of real GDP. The recessionary and inflationary gaps that so perplexed policymakers during the 1970s weren't gaps at all, the new classical economists insisted. Instead, they reflected changes in the economy's own natural level of output.

The 1970s put Keynesian economics and its prescription for activist policies on the defensive. The period lent considerable support to the monetarist argument that changes in the money supply were the primary determinant of changes in the nominal level of economic activity. A series of dramatic shifts in aggregate supply gave credence to the new classical emphasis on long-run aggregate supply as the primary determinant of real GDP. Events didn't create the new ideas, but they produced an environment in which those ideas could win greater support.

For economists, the period offered some important lessons. These lessons, as we'll see in the next section, forced a rethinking of some of the ideas that had dominated Keynesian thought. The experience of the 1970s suggested that:

1. The short-run aggregate supply curve couldn't be viewed as something that provided a passive path over which aggregate demand could roam. The curve could shift in ways that clearly affected real GDP, unemployment, and the price level.
2. Money mattered more than Keynesians had previously suspected. Keynes had expressed doubts about the effectiveness of monetary policy, particularly in the face of a recessionary gap. Work by monetarists suggested a close correspondence between changes in M2 and subsequent changes in nominal GDP, convincing many Keynesian economists that money was more important than they had thought.
3. Stabilization was a more difficult task than many economists had anticipated. Shifts in aggregate supply could frustrate the efforts of policymakers to achieve certain macroeconomic goals.

Checklist

- The 1970s were marked by shifts in aggregate supply resulting from changes in expectations and changes in oil prices.
- The experience of the 1960s and 1970s appeared to be broadly consistent with the monetarist argument that changes in the money supply are the primary determinant of changes in nominal GDP.
- The new classical school's argument that the economy operates at its natural level implies that real GDP is determined by long-run aggregate supply. The experience of the 1970s, in which changes in aggregate supply forced changes in real GDP and in the price level, seemed consistent with the new classical argument's focus on aggregate supply.
- The experience of the 1970s suggested that changes in the money supply were a more important determinant of economic activity than many Keynesians had previously thought and that stabilization policy was a more difficult task than it had seemed to be in the 1960s.

The 1980s and 1990s and the New Keynesian School

By 1979, 4 years of expansionary monetary and fiscal policies had returned the economy to its natural level of output. Increases in aggregate demand, however, had produced steady increases in inflation. In 1979, the implicit price deflator rose 8.6 percent. The consumer price index jumped even more sharply, rising 13.3 percent. According to public opinion polls, inflation had become Americans' number one concern.

Another concern was beginning to emerge as well. The federal government had run huge deficits to finance World War II, but deficits had subsequently been reduced. From 1950 to 1970, the federal deficit never exceeded 3 percent of GDP. In 5 years during the period, the federal budget had a surplus.

The last federal surplus came in 1969. There was a deficit during every year of the 1970s. And the deficits had risen relative to GDP. By 1976, the federal deficit had risen to $70.5 billion, the largest deficit recorded in U.S. history. It represented a larger percentage of GDP than any other federal deficit since 1950. As the 1980s began, the federal deficit had joined inflation as an important issue in public policy.

Inflation and deficit concerns have dominated the agenda of macroeconomic concerns during the last 15 years. They have had a profound effect on the conduct of monetary and fiscal policy. And our experience with policy during that period has affected macroeconomic thought as well.

Policy Constraints and Policy Choices

Monetary policy has taken center stage in U.S. stabilization efforts during the past 15 years. That's due in part to the fact that inflation worries have dominated the list of policy concerns during that period, and inflation is primarily a monetary phenomenon. Another reason for a greater reliance on monetary policy has been the deficit. As we'll see, concern about deficit spending has sharply constrained the use of fiscal policy, particularly in recent years. Finally, the 1980s brought an ideological tilt against the use of fiscal policy for stabilization.

The Battle Against Inflation

Faced with an inflation rate that had risen in every year he had been in office, President Jimmy Carter made a fateful decision near the end of his term. In 1979 he named Paul Volcker, who had been president of the Federal Reserve Bank of New York, to head the Fed's Board of Governors. Carter instructed Volcker to do whatever it took to bring down inflation and pledged his full support to the effort. The decision may have cost Carter the presidency.

The Volcker-led Fed proceeded immediately to tighten money growth. The next year, war broke out between Iran and Iraq, and world oil prices shot up. The Fed had responded to oil-price hikes in the mid-1970s, and the resultant recession, with an expansionary monetary policy that brought recovery but fueled inflation. This time, it was determined to bring down inflation—regardless of the impact on output and employment.

Higher oil prices, together with higher price-level expectations, forced the short-run aggregate supply curve upward. The combination of the shift in short-run aggregate supply and a contractionary monetary policy boosted inflation and unemployment. Interest rates soared as well; the prime rate (the interest rate banks use as a benchmark from which other rates are determined) averaged 15.3 percent in 1980. Stagflation played a key role in Ronald Reagan's defeat of Carter that year.

The Fed, meanwhile, stuck to its antiinflationary policy, despite soaring unemployment. It announced that it was targeting the rate of money growth and that it would no longer seek to achieve a particular interest rate. Inflation continued to edge upward, however, while the economy slipped into a recession. The prime rate soared above 20 percent. The Fed, with the support of the Reagan administration, maintained its antiinflation stance. Real GDP, which recovered briefly late in 1980, slipped again in 1981. The recession of 1981–1982 was the worst downturn since the Great Depression. The Fed finally succeeded in lowering the inflation rate in 1981; inflation plummeted in 1982. Unemployment, however, soared above 10 percent late in the year.

Fiscal Policy and Supply-Side Economics

As a presidential candidate in 1980, Ronald Reagan promised to boost defense spending, cut taxes, bring down inflation and interest rates, and cut the deficit. He would later joke that four out of five wasn't bad.

Reagan's economic policies present something of a paradox. Faced with an economy that had been in a brief recession in 1980 and was about to slip back into one in 1981, Reagan won quick congressional approval of a tax cut and sharp increases in defense spending. The tax cut slashed marginal income tax rates and reinstituted the investment tax credit for firms. It was standard Keynesian medicine. Indeed, the Reagan program seemed almost a carbon copy of the program John Kennedy had sought in the face of recession 20 years earlier. But Reagan rejected Keynesian theory. He surrounded himself with monetarist economic advisers—economists who didn't believe that fiscal policy could or should be used to manipulate aggregate demand in the short run and who favored stable money growth.

The Reagan program was justified not as a stabilization effort but as a program that would stimulate long-run economic growth. It was advertised as a program that would focus not on aggregate demand but on aggregate supply. By reducing marginal tax rates and encouraging investment, Reagan argued, the government would encourage individuals to work harder and invest more. In the model of aggregate demand and aggregate supply, the long-run aggregate supply curve would shift to the right because the supply of labor would increase and because the program would stimulate capital formation. The view that long-run aggregate supply could be increased through fiscal policy was known as **supply-side economics.**

A further element of the Reagan administration's supply-side program was deregulation. If regulation of business firms were eased, the administration argued, firms would become more productive. The long-run aggregate supply curve would thus shift further to the right. As we saw in Chapter 26, rightward shifts in long-run aggregate supply imply similar shifts in short-run aggregate supply, further increasing real GDP and putting downward pressure on prices. The Carter administration had put major deregulatory programs in place in the late 1970s; the Reagan administration continued that deregulatory effort.

Supply-side economics is the belief that fiscal policy can be used to stimulate long-run aggregate supply.

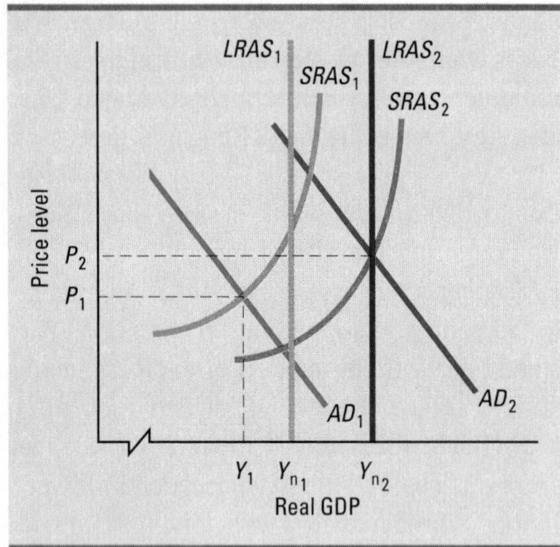

EXHIBIT 33-8

Supply-Side Policy

The economy begins with a recessionary gap at Y_1. In theory, supply-side policies such as deregulation and tax incentives to encourage greater work effort and investment shift the short- and long-run aggregate supply curves to $SRAS_2$ and $LRAS_2$. Lower taxes and greater investment also push aggregate demand to AD_2. Here, the policies return real GDP to its new natural level Y_{n2}.

Exhibit 33-8 shows the effects, in theory, of a supply-side fiscal policy. We begin with the economy operating with a recessionary gap at Y_1. Deregulation and tax cuts designed to encourage investment and work effort stimulate long-run and short-run aggregate supply, shifting these curves to $LRAS_2$ and $SRAS_2$, respectively. At the same time, the lower taxes and increased investment push aggregate demand to AD_2. The economy rises to its new natural level, Y_{n2}. The price level goes up, but by much less than it would have if long- and short-run aggregate supply had not increased.

Supply-side economics isn't an alternative school of macroeconomic thought; indeed, most of Mr. Reagan's economic advisers were monetarists. Instead, supply-side economics is an approach to fiscal policy that focuses on the long run. Its essential recommendation is that fiscal policy should attempt to establish a framework that encourages productive effort by limiting taxes, particularly taxes at the margin. Adherents of supply-side economics argue that when the government lowers the tax imposed on an additional dollar of income earned, individuals earn more dollars. The result should be greater economic growth.

Supply-side economics is thus consistent with both monetarist and new classical doctrine. Both schools reject the use of fiscal policy as a tool to manipulate aggregate demand. They argue, however, that fiscal policies should seek to encourage economic growth. The approach is even consistent with the views of many new Keynesian economists, who argue that lags and crowding out make fiscal policy ineffective as a tool for short-run stabilization. These economists also argue that fiscal policy should seek to establish a framework consistent with economic growth.

Did the Reagan policies represent a departure from the Keynesian approach, or were they simply the standard Keynesian medicine disguised in a supply-side bottle? The best answer is that they were both. Of course a cut in personal and business taxes encourages consumption and investment, thereby increasing aggregate demand. But the Reagan program also offered stimulus on the supply side. Increased investment boosted the capital stock and therefore increased long-run aggregate supply. Because an increase in long-run aggregate supply shifts the short-run aggregate supply curve to the right as well, it puts downward pressure on prices and thus reduces inflation. The Reagan years thus saw a modest acceleration of economic growth and a reduction in inflation. We will examine the relationship between the Reagan administration's fiscal policy and long-run economic growth more carefully in Chapter 35.

The other macroeconomic development of the Reagan years was a sharp increase in the federal deficit. Recall that a $70 billion deficit had been considered alarming in 1976. Ten years later the deficit soared past $200 billion. Federal deficits rung up during the 8 years of the Reagan administration totaled more than $1 trillion. This was more than the federal government had borrowed during the first two centuries of the nation's existence.

Did the explosion in federal borrowing matter? It certainly mattered for fiscal policy in the administrations of George Bush and Bill Clinton. As we'll see in the next section, the nation's primary fiscal priority in the years since the Reagan administration has been to reduce the deficit. Fiscal policy was, as a result, contractionary during the Bush and Clinton years. Massive deficits have had other macroeconomic consequences as well; we'll examine those in the next chapter.

Case in Point Ronald Reagan and the Recession

Murray Weidenbaum, who served as Ronald Reagan's first chief economic adviser, remembers when he delivered the bad news to the president.

"I told the president that we were headed for another recession, and that it would be a bad one. We were projecting that unemployment would rise above 9 percent, which would be the worst rate since the Great Depression," he recalls.

Murray Weidenbaum (l.) with Ronald Reagan and Don Regan.

Dr. Weidenbaum's advice? "I told Mr. Reagan to do nothing, that we should maintain the policies we had," he says.

That advice marked a rejection of the Keynesian approach to fiscal policy. With a contractionary monetary policy already in place, one might have expected the president's economist to recommend a stimulus package. But Mr. Reagan had appointed economists who rejected the use of fiscal policy to deal with recessions.

Of course, the president had already gotten approval from Congress for what amounted to an expansionary fiscal policy: tax cuts and increased government spending for defense were in place. As the text notes, however, those were put in place not to achieve economic stabilization but to promote economic growth and national security.

One may dispute whether the policies of the Reagan administration were Keynesian or not. In any case, they weren't justified by the administration as stabilization tools, nor has fiscal policy been used for stabilization purposes since that time. Just as the Kennedy administration's embrace was to make the use of fiscal policy a routine tool for stabilization policy for the next 20 years, the Reagan administration's rejection of it was to put an end, at least for the next decade and a half, to the use of fiscal policy to stabilize economic activity.

Source: Based on a personal interview with Murray Weidenbaum.

Fiscal and Monetary Policy in the 1990s: The Bush and Clinton Years

Concerns about the deficit and inflation have dominated the macroeconomic agenda of the last several years. Translated into macroeconomic policy, that has meant higher taxes, restraints on federal spending, and an often contractionary monetary policy.

The first major tax hike came in 1990, when Congress passed a budget bill that raised income taxes and gasoline taxes. The second wave of tax increases came two years later, with the passage of President Clinton's deficit reduction bill. Income tax hikes in both plans were concentrated on the rich. The result has been a sharp increase in the marginal tax rates that Ronald Reagan had sought to bring down. Under Reagan, the top marginal tax rate had been reduced to 28 percent; by 1995 it had increased to just over 40 percent.

The budget bills of 1990 and 1992 have also forced major reductions in federal purchases. The combination of reduced federal purchases and higher taxes has had a generally contractionary impact on the economy. As we saw in Chapter 31, fiscal policy remained contractionary even in the face of the 1990–1991 recession.

The Fed's monetary policies in the late 1980s were aimed at bringing down inflation. Policy became contractionary in 1988 as the economy returned to its natural level and inflation began to accelerate slightly. The Fed shifted to a sharply expansionary policy in 1990 as the economy slipped into a recession. But it maintained an expansionary policy only as long as inflation appeared to be under control. When Federal Reserve officials determined in 1994 that there was a possibility inflation might rise, the Fed shifted to a contractionary stance, despite the fact that unemployment remained above its natural level.

Exhibit 33-9 shows the movement of the aggregate demand and short-run aggregate supply curves during the 1990s. We see the economy operating close to its natural level in 1990. The oil price shock brought by Iraq's invasion of Kuwait shifts the short run aggregate supply curve upward; real GDP falls and the price level rises in 1991. The Fed's expansionary monetary policies boost aggregate demand early in the 1990s. Rising investment and consumption continued to fuel increasing aggregate demand in 1993 and 1994. At the same time aggregate demand was increasing, cost pressures continued to push the short run aggregate supply curve upward. These pressures included rising payroll taxes, increases in costs to firms for employee health care, and stricter environmental regulation. Higher expectations of inflation as the economy neared its natural level of output appeared to push the short run aggregate supply curve upward in 1995.

As we look back on the macroeconomic policy record since 1979, we see a period in which monetary policy has become the major tool of stabilization policy. While one can argue that the Reagan defense buildup and tax cuts of the

EXHIBIT 33-9

Aggregate Demand and Short-Run Aggregate Supply in the 1990s

An oil price shock in 1990 shifted the short-run aggregate supply curve upward; the economy had a recessionary gap by 1991. The Fed's expansionary monetary policies had brought the economy back to its natural level of real GDP by 1995.

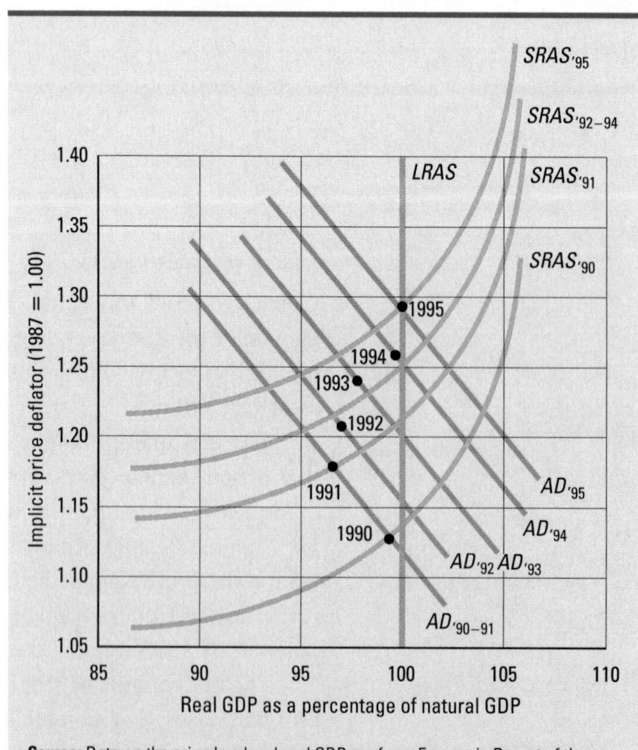

Source: Data on the price level and real GDP are from *Economic Report of the President 1995*, tables B-2 and B-3, pp. 276 and 278. Data on natural real GDP are provided by the Congressional Budget Office. Data for the first half of 1995 are provided by the Commerce Department.

early 1980s represented an expansionary policy, we also see that the behavior of inflation has been broadly consistent with the policy goals of supply-side economics. The unemployment rate has come down since 1983 without any substantial increases in inflation. The inflation rate has been below 3 percent in the early 1990's.

The Emergence of New Keynesian Economics

The experience of the 1970s boosted support among economists for the two primary challenges to the Keynesian approach: monetarism and new classical economics. Monetarists were able to make a convincing case that money was an important determinant of economic activity. And new classical economists demonstrated that changes in aggregate supply could have dramatic effects on the economy.

The 1980s, however, were to raise questions about the usefulness of the monetarist and new classical doctrines. At the same time, important developments were taking place within the Keynesian camp, developments that have forged the new Keynesian economics.

Monetary Change and the Monetarist School

Deregulation of the banking industry in the early 1980s produced sharp changes in the ways individuals dealt with money, thus changing the relationship of money to economic activity.

As deregulation efforts have continued, banks have been freed to offer a wide range of financial alternatives to their customers. One of the most important developments has been the introduction of bond funds offered by banks. These funds have allowed customers to earn the higher interest rates paid by long-term bonds while at the same time being able to transfer funds easily into checking accounts as needed. Because balances in these bond funds aren't counted as part of M2, the demand for M2 has dropped sharply.

We saw in Exhibit 33-7 that changes in M2 were closely related to subsequent changes in nominal GDP during the 1960s and 1970s. Exhibit 33-10 shows the same variables since 1980. The close relationship that once existed appears to have vanished.

EXHIBIT 33-10

Changes in M2 and in Nominal GDP, 1980–1995

A plot of changes in nominal GDP (the green line) against changes in M2 lagged 1 year (the maroon line), as was done in Exhibit 33-7, shows no apparent relationship between the two variables since 1980. The experience has cast doubt on the monetarist argument of a close relationship between the two variables in the long run.

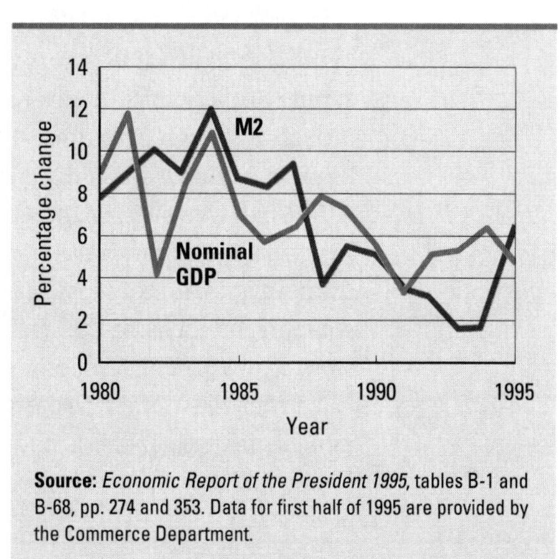

Source: *Economic Report of the President 1995,* tables B-1 and B-68, pp. 274 and 353. Data for first half of 1995 are provided by the Commerce Department.

Monetarists have argued that the experience of the 1980s reinforces their view that the instability of velocity in the short run makes monetary policy an inappropriate tool for short-run stabilization. They continue to insist, however, that the velocity of M2 remains stable in the long run. But the velocity of M2 appears to have diverged in recent years from its long-run path. Although it may return to its long-run level, the issue of the stability of velocity remains very much in doubt.

The New Classical School and Responses to Policy

New classical economics suggests that people should have responded to the fiscal and monetary policies of the 1980s in predictable ways. They didn't, and that has created new doubts among economists about the efficacy of the new classical argument.

Rational expectations theory predicts that if a shift in monetary policy by the Fed is anticipated, it will have no effect on real GDP. The slowing in the rate of growth of the money supply over the period from 1979 to 1982 was surely well known to the public. The Fed announced at the outset what it was going to do, then did it. It had the full support first of President Carter and then of President Reagan. But the policy plunged the economy into its worst recession since the Great Depression. The experience hardly seemed consistent with new classical logic.

The public's response to the huge deficits of the Reagan era also seemed to belie new classical ideas. One new classical argument predicts that people will increase their saving rate in response to an increase in public sector borrowing. The resultant reduction in consumption will cancel the impact of the increase in the deficit. But the private saving rate in the United States *fell* during the 1980s. New classical economists contend that standard measures of saving don't fully represent the actual saving rate, but the experience of the 1980s does not support the new classical argument.

The events of the 1980s don't suggest that either monetarist or new classical ideas should be abandoned, but those events certainly raise doubts about these approaches. As we'll see, doubts about Keynesian economics raised by the events of the 1970s led Keynesians to modify and strengthen their approach. Perhaps the events of the 1980s will produce similar progress within the monetarist and new classical camps.

The Rebirth of Keynesian Economics

While the main challengers to the Keynesian school were being buffeted by the events of the 1980s, many Keynesian economists were rethinking their own approach to macroeconomic theory. As they did so, they created the body of thought we have studied: new Keynesian economics.

What was new in new Keynesian economics? Fundamentally, what was new was the incorporation of ideas produced by monetarist and new classical economists. As Keynesian economists expanded their models to incorporate some of the ideas of the challengers, they produced a stronger, more believable story about how macroeconomic events unfold.

From the monetarists, new Keynesians have incorporated the notion that money matters. Indeed, new Keynesian economists often argue that monetary policy is likely to be a better tool than fiscal policy for macroeconomic stabilization.

Checklist

- Fiscal and monetary policy since 1980 have been dominated by concerns about the deficit and inflation.
- The Fed succeeded in bringing down the inflation rate in the early 1980s, but unemployment soared as the economy experienced the worst recession since the Great Depression.
- The Reagan administration's use of supply-side economics achieved a modest increase in economic growth, lowered inflation, and led to a huge increase in the federal deficit.
- The events of the 1980s and early 1990s do not appear to have been consistent with the hypotheses of either the monetarist or new classical schools.
- New Keynesian economists have incorporated major elements of the ideas of the monetarist and new classical schools in their formulation of macroeconomic theory.

From the ideas of the new classical schools, new Keynesians have accepted the challenge that macroeconomic ideas should be grounded in microeconomic foundations of maximizing behavior. Some of the most important work of the last decade has shown that profit-maximizing firms and utility-maximizing households may prefer sticky prices and sticky wages. New Keynesians have also incorporated changes in aggregate supply in their model. The model of aggregate demand and aggregate supply presented in this text is a product of that effort. The model shows clearly that changes from the supply side can affect real GDP and the price level.

Surveys of economists generally show that the new Keynesian approach has emerged as the preferred approach to macroeconomic analysis. Certainly it has become dominant in terms of macroeconomic policy. The Fed has long engaged in stabilization efforts consistent with new Keynesian prescriptions—and has been adamant about rejecting the policy rules proposed by monetarist and new classical economists. For the time being, at least, the new Keynesian school appears to have the upper hand in the effort to achieve understanding of macroeconomic theory and policy.

A Look Back—And a Look Ahead

We have surveyed the experience of the United States in light of the economic theories that prevailed or emerged during five decades. We have seen that events in the past century have had significant effects on the ways in which economists look at and interpret macroeconomic events.

Before the Great Depression, macroeconomic thought was dominated by the classical school. That body of theory stressed the economy's ability to reach full employment equilibrium on its own. The complacency of the classical school was shattered by the awesome power of the Depression. The severity and duration of that calamity caused many economists to rethink their acceptance of natural equilibrating forces in the economy.

John Maynard Keynes issued the most telling challenge. He argued that wage rigidities and other factors could prevent the economy from closing a recessionary gap on its own. Further, he showed that expansionary fiscal and monetary policies could be used to increase aggregate demand and move the economy to its natural level. Although these ideas did not immediately affect U.S. policy, the increases in aggregate demand brought by the onset of World War II did bring the economy to full employment. Many economists became convinced of the validity of Keynes's analysis and his prescriptions for macroeconomic policy.

Keynesian economists dominated economic policy in the United States in the 1960s. Fiscal and monetary policies increased aggregate demand and produced the longest expansion in U.S. history. But the economy pushed well beyond full employment in the latter part of the decade, and inflation increased.

While Keynesians were dominant, monetarist economists argued that it was monetary policy that accounted for the expansion of the 1960s and that fiscal policy could not affect aggregate demand.

Efforts by the Nixon administration in 1969 and 1970 to cool the economy ran afoul of shifts in the short-run aggregate supply curve. The ensuing decade saw a series of shifts in aggregate supply that contributed to three more recessions by 1982. As economists studied these shifts, they developed further the basic notions we now express in the aggregate demand–aggregate supply model: that changes in aggregate demand and aggregate supply affect income and the price level; that changes in fiscal and monetary policy can affect aggregate demand; and that in the long run, the economy moves to its natural level of real GDP.

The events of the 1980s and 1990s raised serious challenges for the monetarist and new classical schools. New Keynesian economists formulated revisions in their theories, incorporating many of the ideas suggested by monetarist and new classical economists. The new, more powerful theory of macroeconomic events has won widespread support among economists today.

This completes our examination of the macroeconomics of the short run. In Part Nine, we shall shift our focus to the long run. We'll begin with an examination of some contemporary issues that relate principally to the long run. We'll then examine the problems of economic growth and economic development.

Terms and Concepts for Review

Classical economics
Say's law
Supply-side economics

For Discussion

1. "For many years, the hands-off fiscal policies advocated by the classical economists held sway with American government. When times were hard, the prevailing response was to tough it out, awaiting the 'inevitable' turnaround. The lessons of the Great Depression and a booming wartime economy have since taught us, however, that government intervention is sometimes necessary and desirable—and that to an extent, we can take charge of our own economic lives." Evaluate the foregoing quotation based upon the discussion in this chapter. How would you classify the speaker in terms of a school of economic thought?
2. In his 1982 *Economic Report of the President,* Ronald Reagan said, "We simply *cannot* blame crop failures and oil price increases for our basic inflation problem. The continuous, underlying cause was poor government policy." What policies might he have been referring to?
3. Many journalists blamed poor economic policy of the Reagan administration for the extremely high levels of unemployment in 1982 and 1983. Given the record of the rest of the decade, do you agree that President Reagan's economic policies were a failure? Why or why not?
4. The day after the worst stock market crash in U.S. history —October 19, 1987—Federal Reserve Board Chairman Alan Greenspan issued the following statement: "The Federal Reserve, consistent with its responsibilities as the nation's central bank, affirmed today its readiness to serve as a source of liquidity to support the economic and financial system." Evaluate why the Fed chairman might have been prompted to make such a statement.
5. Compare the rationale of the Reagan administration for the 1981 tax reductions with the rationale expressed by Heller for the Kennedy-Johnson tax cut of 1964.
6. If the economy is operating below its natural level, what kind of gap exists? What kinds of fiscal or monetary policies might you use to close this gap? Can you think of any objection to the use of such policies?

7. If the economy is operating above its natural level, what kind of gap exists? What kinds of fiscal or monetary policies might you use to close this gap? Can you think of any objection to the use of such policies?

8. In the *General Theory,* Keynes wrote of the importance of ideas. The world, he said, is ruled by little else. How important do you think his ideas have been for economic policy today?

9. State whether each of the following events appears to be the result of a shift in short-run aggregate supply or aggregate demand, and state the direction of the shift involved.

a. The price level rises sharply while real GDP falls.

b. The price level and real GDP rise.

c. The price level falls while real GDP rises.

d. The price level and real GDP fall.

10. Explain whether each of the following events and policies will affect the aggregate demand curve or the short-run aggregate supply curve, and state what will happen to the price level and real GDP.

a. Oil prices rise.

b. The Fed sells bonds.

c. Government purchases increase.

d. Federal taxes increase.

e. The government slashes transfer payment spending.

f. Oil prices fall.

Problems

1. Using the model of aggregate demand and aggregate supply, illustrate an economy with a recessionary gap. Show how a policy of nonintervention would ultimately close the gap. Show the alternative of closing the gap through stabilization policy.

2. Using the model of aggregate demand and aggregate supply, illustrate an economy with an inflationary gap. Show how a policy of nonintervention would ultimately close the gap. Show the alternative of closing the gap through stabilization policy.

3. Here are hypothetical data for an economy. Use the same approach taken in the text: compute real GDP as a percentage of natural GDP for each period, then show the changes in aggregate demand or aggregate supply that appear to have taken place.

Period	Real GDP	Natural GDP	Price level
1	1,000	1,000	1.5
2	1,080	1,020	1.6

4. Here is another set of hypothetical data for an economy. Repeat the exercise in Problem (3).

Period	Real GDP	Natural GDP	Price level
1	1,000	1,000	1.3
2	950	1,020	1.5

Part Nine Long-Run Macroeconomic Problems

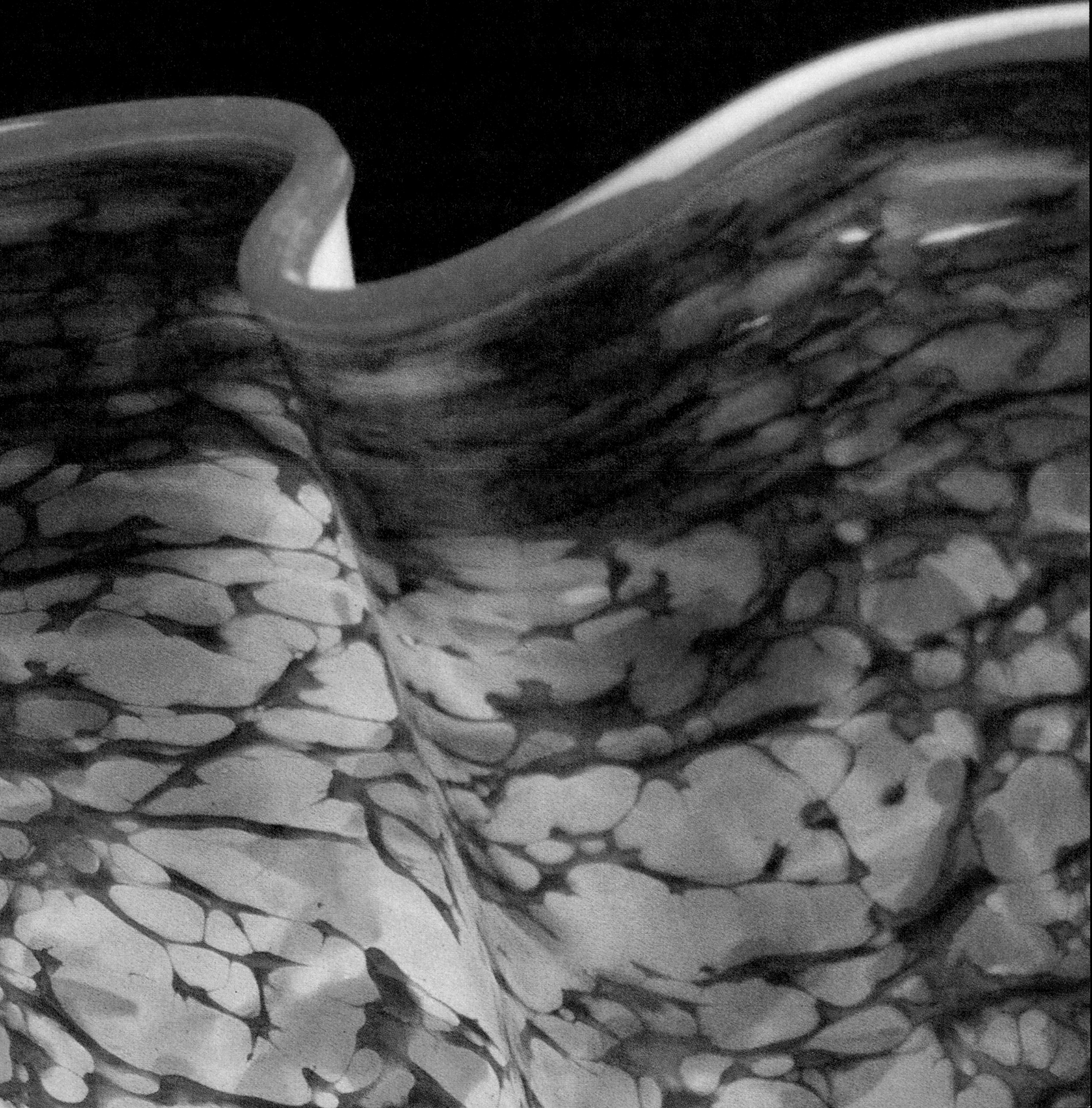

34

Contemporary Macroeconomic Issues

Chapter Objectives

After mastering the material in this chapter, you will be able to:

1. Show the relationship between federal deficits and the national debt, and explain the conceptual issues involved in measuring these two variables.
2. Identify the issues involved in the appropriate measurement of the deficit for any one period.
3. Discuss whether the burden of the national debt can be shifted from one generation to another and explain the concept of intergenerational accounting.
4. Examine the meaning of "competitiveness" as it is used by critics of U.S. international trade policy and list the objections traditionally suggested by economists in response to this argument.
5. Use national income accounting definitions to show how budget deficits are related to trade deficits.
6. Review the evidence concerning changes in the U.S. distribution of income over the past three decades and comment on the significance of that evidence.

The deficit is the radicalizing edge issue, but it's only part of the web of issues destroying the future of our generation.

Jon Cowan, co-founder of Lead or Leave, a lobbying organization representing the interests of Generation X

What's Ahead

Some members of Generation X, the generation born in the 1970s and 1980s, see the country they're going to inherit as headed for disaster. It's hopelessly in debt, it can't compete in world markets, and its society is brutally unfair—the rich are getting richer and the poor are getting poorer.

Others see a much rosier picture. True, the national debt is high, but it's manageable. Restructured U.S. firms are leaner and more competitive than ever, and that will usher in a wave of prosperity for those willing to work to attain it.

Which of these two pictures more fairly represents the United States in the 1990s? Certainly it's true that the national debt has soared—but expressed as a percentage of GDP, the debt doesn't loom so large. It was far higher in 1950 than it is today. By some standards, the United States doesn't appear to be very competitive; economists, however, argue that trade deficit figures mean little, and that the very notion of competitiveness has no application to an entire economy. Although many people bemoan the fact that the share of income going to the rich has risen while the share going to the poor has fallen during the last 25 years, others believe that the reasons for these shifts don't suggest a problem of fairness.

We can bring economic analysis to bear on the fierce debates over the issues of the debt, competitiveness, and fairness. This chapter presents the evidence and suggests a framework for the analysis of each issue. You will reach your own conclusions on these important issues, conclusions that will reflect some normative judgments that you choose to make as well as the positive contributions of economic analysis.

Deficits and the Debt

Does a rising national debt have any real economic significance? Can one generation shift the burden of its consumption of government-provided goods and services to another generation by borrowing? Can a national debt lead to national

The **national debt** is the sum of all past federal deficits.

bankruptcy? We'll examine these questions in this section. First, however, let's examine some issues related to the way in which the national debt and the deficits that add to it are measured.

Problems of Measurement

Two concerns dominate discussions of the impact of public sector borrowing. First, public sector borrowing may unfairly transfer the cost of public sector activities from one period to another. Second, it may reduce investment and thus reduce the capital stock available to workers in future periods. This section examines why the method by which deficits and the debt are measured makes these issues difficult to assess.

We've already learned that the federal government deficit is the difference between federal revenues and government expenditures during a particular period. The **national debt** is the sum of all past federal deficits.

Panel (a) of Exhibit 34-1 shows the size of the national debt in each year since 1929. The debt rises in years in which the federal government incurs a deficit; it falls in years of surplus. The debt rose dramatically during World War II

EXHIBIT 34-1

The National Debt and the Economy, 1929–1994

The size of the debt has increased during most of the period since 1929, as shown by Panel (a). Panel (b), however, shows that the debt relative to nominal GDP is much smaller today than it was during World War II.

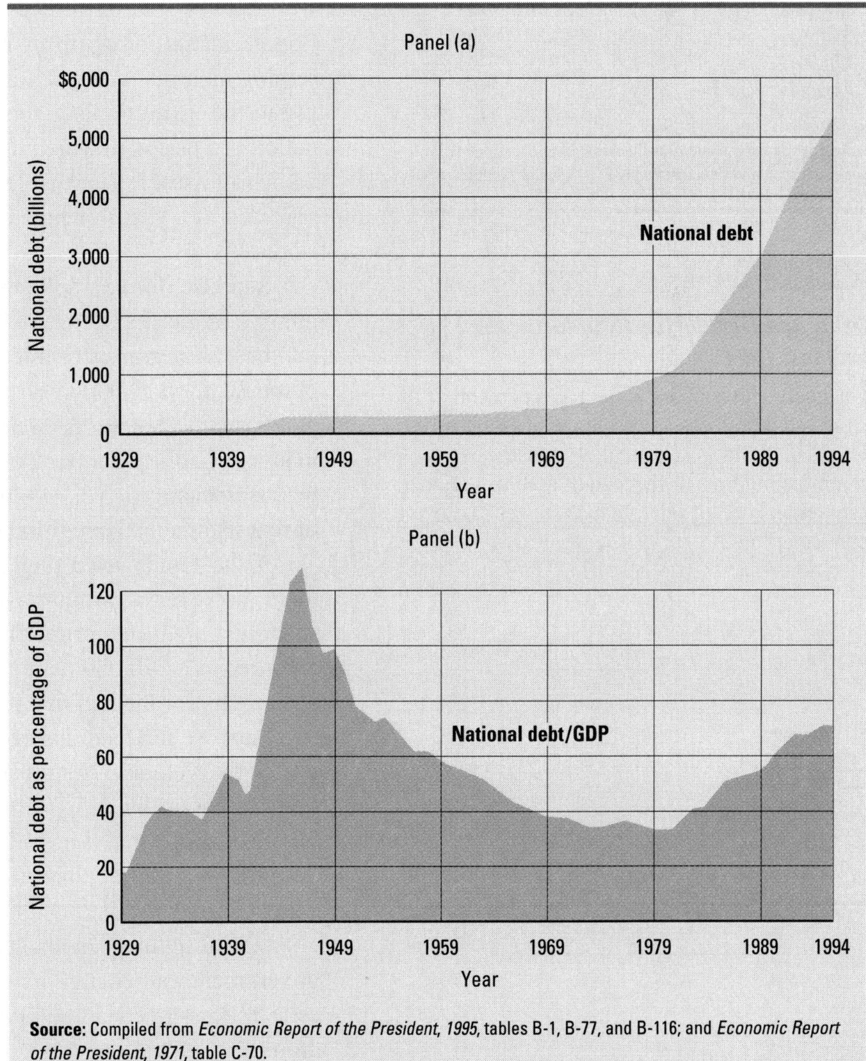

Source: Compiled from *Economic Report of the President, 1995,* tables B-1, B-77, and B-116; and *Economic Report of the President, 1971,* table C-70.

and again during the Korean War. Recent increases in the debt have come during peacetime and have dwarfed the scale of borrowing that financed the two major wars. Panel (b) shows the national debt as a percentage of nominal GDP. It suggests that, relative to the level of economic activity, the debt is well below the levels reached during World War II. The debt has, however, risen relative to nominal GDP during the past two decades.

Judged by international standards, the United States is about average among developed nations in terms of its national debt relative to its GDP. Exhibit 34-2 shows national debt as a percentage of GDP for 18 countries in 1994. It also shows deficits as a percentage of gross national product (GNP) for that year. As we saw in Chapter 21, GNP measures the value of total output produced using inputs owned by a nation's residents. For most nations, GNP and GDP are nearly the same.

Country	National Debt as Percentage of GDP	Deficit or Surplus (−) as Percentage of GNP
Belgium	141	5.4
Italy	116	10.0
Ireland	93	2.4
Greece	91	26.2
Canada	87	2.7
Netherlands	81	2.8
Sweden	76	−0.7
Denmark	68	0.3
Japan	66	1.6
United States	66	4.8
France	61	1.4
Spain	59	2.3
Austria	56	4.8
United Kingdom	52	−0.8
Finland	50	−0.1
Germany	50	2.5
Norway	50	−0.7
Australia	39	−0.6

Source: Based on data from the Organization for Economic Cooperation and Development (OECD) and the World Bank.

EXHIBIT 34-2

Debts and Deficits for 18 Industrialized Nations, 1994

The chart shows national debt as a percentage of GDP and deficits as a percentage of GNP in 1991. The United States is typical of industrialized countries in terms of the size of both its national debt and its deficit relative to the level of economic activity.

Standard government practice records expenditures and revenues without accounting for changes in assets and liabilities and fails to record the way in which inflation affects the real value of outstanding debt. Official measures of deficits and the debt therefore tell us very little about the economic impact of one year's budget on the future. We'll look at these problems in the next two sections.

Public Sector Assets and Liabilities

Private institutions—firms or families—track their financial positions by assessing their net worth at various points in time. Net worth is the difference between the institution's assets and its liabilities. We say the institution incurs a deficit in a period in which its net worth fell and a surplus in a period in which its net worth rises. A year that leaves the institution's net worth unchanged could be regarded as a year in which its budget is balanced between expenditures and receipts.

Suppose, for example, that a family purchases a $100,000 home at the beginning of the year. It uses $10,000 in savings plus a $90,000 loan to finance the purchase. The transaction leaves the family's net worth unchanged. Before the purchase, the $10,000 in savings was part of the household's net worth. After the purchase, the family has a $100,000 house as an asset and a $90,000 mortgage loan as a liability. Its net worth, the difference between its assets and its liabilities, is unchanged. We would not say the family has suddenly become a debtor or that its financial condition has worsened.

If the family used the same method of accounting as the federal government, however, it would have a huge deficit. It would record $100,000 in new spending, financed primarily through borrowing. The transaction would be recorded as a $90,000 deficit that added to the family's debt. There would be no accounting for the fact that the family had acquired an asset, its home.

Suppose the federal government borrows $25 million to build a new hospital for the Veterans Administration. In the government's accounts, the transaction increases the deficit and the national debt. The government's accounting ignores the fact that it has added an asset—the hospital. The government's budget fails to reflect the fact that its action this year has passed on to subsequent years not only a debt, but a hospital as well.

Deficit figures can also understate the degree to which actions taken by the government can change its situation in future years. Suppose the government sells Yellowstone National Park to a private corporation in 1999 for $1 billion in cash. The $1 billion would be treated on the government's books as ordinary

Case in Point

Generational Accounting

Washington policymakers are aware that their choices affect not only people today but people in the future. Legislation that promises future benefits will create benefits—and costs—for tomorrow's taxpayers. Legislation that provides more services today, financed by borrowing, means higher interest costs for future taxpayers. But how can we quantify the benefits and costs that are our legacy to tomorrow's taxpayers?

Laurence J. Kotlikoff, an economist at Boston University, thinks he has the answer: generational accounting. It is an approach to government budgeting that estimates how much generations now alive will pay during their lifetimes, minus the transfer payments they will receive, to service the government debt and to continue current government programs. Generational accounting also estimates the net costs of these services to generations yet unborn.

Generational accounting produces an estimate of each generation's lifetime income and its lifetime net taxes (taxes minus transfers) paid. The estimates of taxes and transfers include all levels of government.

The results for the United States are startling. According to Mr. Kotlikoff, future generations can expect to pay net taxes that add up to a whopping 71 percent of their lifetime incomes. The accompanying table shows his estimate of lifetime net taxes as a fraction of lifetime net earnings for various generations. It shows clearly how one generation can pile obligations on another. According to Mr. Kotlikoff, people face higher tax rates the younger they are.

Year of birth	Lifetime net taxes as percentage of lifetime earnings
1900	21
1930	28
1960	32
1990	50
Future	71

Mr. Kotlikoff says that incorporating the estimates of generational accounts could help governments to assess more accurately the consequences of current decisions for future taxpayers. His system was first incorporated in the United States as part of the last budget submitted by President Bush. Generational accounts are now estimated by the governments of Italy, Japan, and Norway.

"Current taxpayers face a simple choice," Mr. Kotlikoff writes. "They can continue to add to the tax burdens of future generations as they have in the past. Or they can agree to pay a bigger share of the government's bills and thus start to trim the enormous tax burdens that are our legacy to the future."

Source: Laurence J. Kotlikoff, "How Much Will Our Kids Pay?" *The Margin* 9 (Fall 1993): 31.

revenue. It would reduce the 1999 deficit and thus reduce the degree to which the national debt is increased that year. The fact that the transaction would leave future generations without a treasured national asset would not be reflected in the government's accounting of the transaction.

Alternatively, suppose that the government commits today to double all Social Security benefits beginning in 2010, but makes no provision to increase payroll taxes to finance this future burden. Such a measure would benefit today's workers by boosting their prospective retirement income. It would, however, impose enormous burdens on future workers, who could face sharp increases in *their* payroll taxes. None of this, though, would be reflected in the government's budget today. Despite the increase in the government's liability, neither the current deficit nor the national debt would be affected.

A better reflection of the economic status of the government would be achieved by accounting for its net worth in the same way as for private institutions. An increase in the government's net worth during a particular period would imply a surplus; a reduction would imply a deficit. Legislation to reform the government's accounting procedures has often been introduced, but it has never passed Congress.

Inflation and the Debt

A further difficulty with statements of the national debt results from the government's failure to reflect the impact of inflation. We saw in Chapter 22 that

The **inflation-adjusted deficit** for any period is the actual deficit for that period minus the amount by which inflation has reduced the real value of the national debt.

inflation reduces the real value of sums borrowed. It thus lowers the real value of the obligations of debtors. The federal government is a debtor; inflation reduces the real value of its debt. But the national debt is always reported in nominal, not real, terms.

Suppose the government owes $5 trillion in 1998 and has a balanced budget that year. It will end 1998 with the same debt with which it started the year, $5 trillion. But suppose the price level rises 10 percent during 1998. That reduces the real value of what the government owes. If the price index at the beginning of 1998 is 1.0, it will rise by the end of the year to 1.1. That means the real value of the debt will fall to $4.5 trillion by the end of the year ($5 trillion/1.1). The reduction in the real value of the debt implies that the government has, in real terms, operated at a surplus.

Inflation during any period reduces the real value of the government's outstanding debt. Letting ND equal the government's outstanding debt and π the rate of inflation, the change in the real value of the debt due to inflation is πND. The **inflation-adjusted deficit** for any period is the actual deficit for that period minus the amount by which inflation during that period has reduced the real value of the national debt.

If total government expenditures are given by E and government revenues are given by R, then the inflation-adjusted deficit D_π for any year is given by Equation (1):

$$D_\pi = E - R - \pi ND \tag{1}$$

This adjustment for inflation dramatically affects our perspective on the size of the deficit. In fiscal 1994, for example, the federal government's reported deficit was $172.5 billion. The national debt was $4,644 billion, and the inflation rate (implicit price deflator) was 2.1 percent. Inflation reduced the real value of the debt by $97.5 billion, so the inflation-adjusted deficit was $75 billion.

EXHIBIT 34-3

The Deficit and the Inflation-Adjusted Deficit, 1980–1994

The two curves show the values of the federal deficit as conventionally measured and the value of the inflation-adjusted deficit. Because inflation has been positive throughout the period, the inflation-adjusted deficit has been consistently lower than the deficit. Notice that in 1980, 1981, and 1989, the inflation-adjusted deficit has actually been negative, suggesting a surplus.

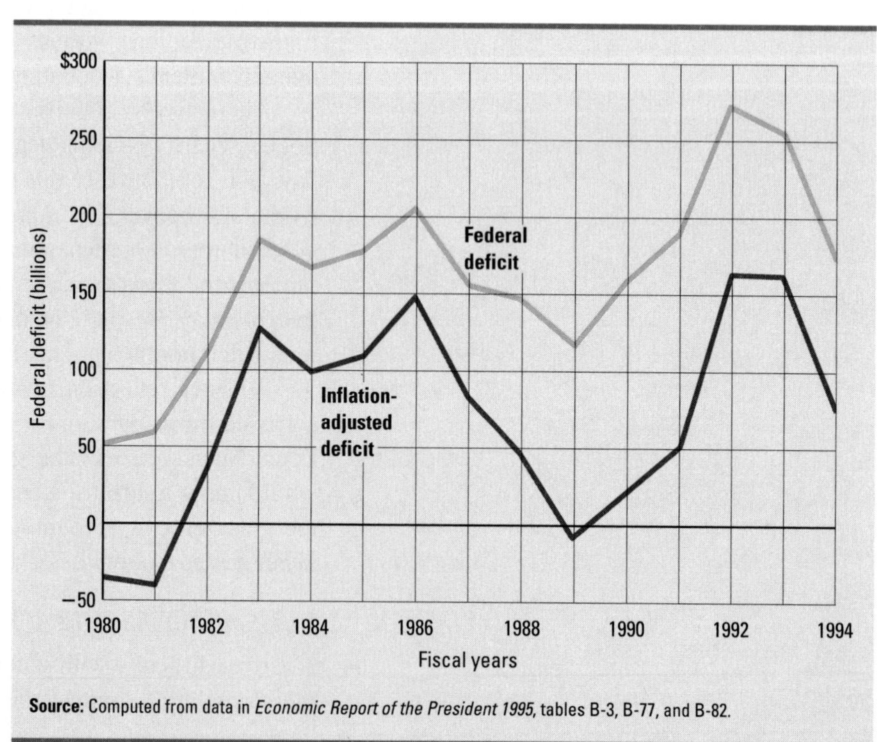

Source: Computed from data in *Economic Report of the President 1995,* tables B-3, B-77, and B-82.

Exhibit 34-3 shows the size of the deficit as conventionally measured and the size of the inflation-adjusted deficit in each year since 1980.

National Debt and National Bankruptcy

A common worry about the national debt is that it will somehow bankrupt the nation. Like a household, a nation that continues to live beyond its means will someday be unable to pay its bills. It will go bankrupt.[1]

The bankruptcy worry is easily dismissed. When it comes to paying off their debts, nations have three big advantages over individuals. First, they can order their citizens, through taxes, to make the required payments. Second, they can print the money to meet these obligations. And third, a nation that doesn't want to pay its debt can simply announce it isn't going to pay.

Paying Interest on the Debt

A government that has borrowed in the past must pay interest on its debt. Some people worry that interest payments could grow so large that the government would be unable to pay them.

The U.S. government spent $203 billion to pay interest on the national debt in fiscal 1994—an amount equal to 3 percent of nominal GDP that year. Levying taxes to pay such a charge does not impose the sort of burden that's likely to bring the economy to its knees.

One can imagine much more dire circumstances. Suppose the debt were so huge that the interest payments on it exceeded the economy's ability to generate income to pay them—that is, annual interest payments exceeded real GDP. For example, if the national debt in 1994 had been 33 times larger, with the same interest rate, interest on the debt would have exceeded nominal GDP. The actual debt, of course, was nowhere near that level. Moreover, we saw in Exhibit 34-1 that the debt is much smaller, relative to GDP, than it was 50 years ago. Although the ratio of debt to GDP has gone up in recent years, it hasn't risen in a way that suggests that disaster is looming. Indeed, the Congressional Budget Office projects that even without any further deficit reduction measures, interest payments on the debt will remain below 4 percent of GDP through 2010.

The Printing Press Option

Suppose a nation's debt does soar and its government decides it can't, or won't, raise taxes sufficient to make the interest payments. In that case, the government could simply print an amount of money equal to the interest payments. It could, if it wanted, print enough money to pay off the entire national debt!

Bonds issued by the United States government, for example, state that the government's obligation is to pay the bearers a certain number of dollars on certain dates. The federal government could simply print that money.

Such an approach would require a legislative change; present law doesn't allow the federal government to pay its bills by printing money. This sort of change would increase the money supply, since it would put new currency directly into circulation. It would be likely to boost the price level and thus to impose a kind of tax on all holders of money and money-denominated assets—including holders of the national debt. But the ability to take such a measure means that a government could always find a way to pay its bills.

[1] For a book that suggests that the national debt will produce, in the 1990s, "what may well be the greatest economic calamity of the millennium," see Larry Burkett, *The Coming Economic Earthquake* (Chicago: Moody Press, 1991).

Repudiation

The most extreme measure available to a government is **repudiation of the debt,** a declaration that the government won't honor its debt. A government can simply announce that all the securities it has issued are void: the government will no longer pay the interest and principal it promised to pay when it issued them.

Repudiation does not mean the same thing as bankruptcy. No international judge exists who can order a nation to turn over any of its assets to creditors. A country that repudiates its debt will find it difficult to issue new debt in the future, but the country has not, in a technical sense, gone bankrupt.

Deficits and the Issue of Burden Shifting

Certainly the greatest concern about public sector borrowing is that it shifts the burden of paying for one year's activities of the government to subsequent years. The degree to which borrowing actually shifts burdens to the future, however, is a matter of considerable controversy among economists.

We'll begin our assessment of burden shifting through public sector borrowing with a look at one mechanism through which all economists agree that borrowing in one year can impose a burden on future years: crowding out. To the extent that public sector borrowing reduces investment in one period, it reduces the capital stock available to subsequent periods. Future production falls, so future generations have fewer goods and services.

We'll then explore two sharply different perspectives on whether public sector borrowing can shift the cost of one year's activities to the future. One view holds that the burden of public sector activity is borne at the time the activity occurs, regardless of how the activity is financed. The other holds that borrowing to finance public sector activity unambiguously imposes burdens on future taxpayers.

Crowding Out and Investment

The government borrows money by selling bonds. More government borrowing means an increased supply of bonds, lower bond prices, and higher interest rates. Higher interest rates, in turn, lower the quantity of investment. Government borrowing can thus reduce investment.

To the extent that such borrowing crowds out investment, it generates a smaller capital stock than future generations would otherwise have available. That means a lower level of long-run aggregate supply and a lower standard of living than future generations would otherwise enjoy.

The fact that government deficits today may reduce the capital stock that would otherwise be available to future generations does not imply that such deficits are wrong. If, for example, the deficits are used to finance public sector investment, then the reduction in private capital provided to the future is offset by the increased provision of public sector capital. Future generations may have fewer office buildings, for example, but more schools.

The Interest Payment Controversy

Whatever the degree to which investment is crowded out by public sector borrowing, future taxpayers will have to make interest payments on the debt accumulated by earlier taxpayers. Do such interest payments constitute a burden on those taxpayers?

Repudiation of the debt is a declaration by a government that it will no longer honor its debt.

If future tax payments are a burden, it can be a large one. Consider, for example, the burden you face because of past federal borrowing, an amount that totaled roughly $4,600 billion in 1994. If you're 20 years old now, you can expect to live roughly another 60 years. At an interest rate of 7 percent, the total interest cost over your lifetime for federal borrowing up to 1994 will be over $19,000 billion. Assuming you form a household that pays an average share of taxes, your household's share of this interest cost will be about $150,000. That's a hefty sum.

Some economists, however, argue that the payment of interest on the national debt does not constitute a burden on the generation of taxpayers that pays it. They argue that the burden of public sector spending is borne at the time the spending occurs. Whether it is financed by taxes or by borrowing, this burden is borne by the generation that engages in the spending. Except for the possible impact of such spending on investment, the burden of this spending can't be transferred to the future.

The nontransfer argument is based first on the assertion that burdens are borne at the time the spending is done. This is an opportunity cost argument. Consider the case of defense spending. The production of defense services will transfer resources from other activities. The taxpayers that consume the defense will not be able to consume the goods and services that would have been produced had the resources not been used for defense. They bear the burden of the spending, even if they finance it by borrowing.

The second piece of the nontransfer argument is that the payment of interest does not constitute a burden; it is instead a transfer of income from one group of taxpayers to another. Taxpayers who own government bonds are at the receiving end of this transfer; taxpayers who don't are at the paying end. The benefit to one group of taxpayers cancels the cost to the other; taxpayers as a group bear no burden at all. The only case in which the payment of interest on the debt can be said to represent a burden occurs when government debt is owned by foreigners. In that instance, U.S. taxpayers transfer income to foreigners. Only about 10 percent of the U.S debt is owned by foreigners, so this burden is relatively minor.

Other economists reject both parts of the nontransfer argument. They base their analysis on an examination of whether the households of a particular generation experience an increase or a reduction in consumption opportunities as a result of government borrowing and subsequent interest payments.

Can the generation that consumes a government service be said to bear the burden of producing it? Of course, the resources used to produce the service are scarce; they could have been used to produce something else. But the owners of those resources are compensated for their use; the manufacturer who produces the service is paid for its production. The producer doesn't lose consumption opportunities. The people who consume the service, however, do so without paying for it. Consumers are thus better off while producers are no worse off. In this view, the generation that consumes a government service financed by borrowing bears none of the burden of its production.

What about subsequent generations of taxpayers who must pay interest on previous government borrowing? Taxpayers who pay the interest are clearly worse off; their opportunity to consume goods and services is reduced because they must pay taxes to pay interest. The individuals who receive these interest payments get them in return for a service they have provided—they lent the money to the government in the first place. They agreed to postpone consumption at the time they acquired the government-issued bonds in exchange for the

Case in Point: Is a Balanced Budget Amendment the Answer?

Efforts to bring down the federal deficit have not been very successful. In 1985, Congress passed the Gramm-Rudman Act, a bill that called for annual reductions that would cut the deficit to zero by 1991. When the government got behind on its deficit reduction schedule a few years later, Congress pushed the deadline for a balanced budget back 3 years. With the new deadline, the deficit was to reach zero by 1994.

As it turned out, of course, the deficit for 1994 wasn't zero. In fact, it was about the same as it had been when Congress passed the Gramm-Rudman Act in the first place. If legislation requiring a balanced budget has failed to tame the deficit, would a constitutional amendment succeed?

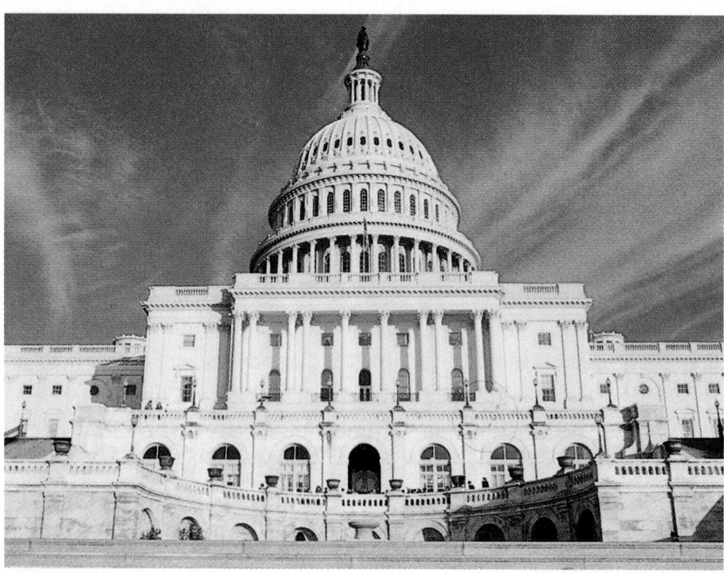

The U.S. Capitol, Washington D.C.

Calls for a constitutional amendment that would require the federal government to balance its budget have been floating about since the 1970s, when federal deficits began to mount. But the effort reached a head in 1995 when a new Republican majority in Congress, pledged to support such an amendment, brought it to a vote. The measure won the necessary two-thirds approval in the House of Representatives, but it fell one vote short in the Senate.

From the point of view of economic analysis, there is little to be said for a balanced budget amendment. The government's measure of its deficit makes no sense; a rule based on that measure seems silly. Critics argue that even if one accepts the notion that a balanced budget makes sense, it doesn't make sense to base the time period for that balancing on the number of days it takes the earth to orbit the sun. They suggest instead that Congress could balance the budget over longer periods, incurring deficits in times of recessionary gaps and surpluses in times of inflationary gaps. Holding to a balanced budget every year would require that government spending be reduced during recessions, when slumping economic activity would force incomes and tax revenues down. The result would be a contractionary fiscal policy for an economy that could be slipping into a recessionary gap.

Proponents of a balanced budget amendment counter that every attempt in the last quarter of a century to achieve a balanced budget has failed; every federal budget since 1969 has been in deficit. Although it might make sense in principle to have a deficit when the economy is slumping balanced by surpluses when the economy is expanding, the reality is that the budget has been in deficit regardless of underlying economic conditions. A balanced budget requirement might prove to be a clumsy tool, but it would force some sense of fiscal discipline on a federal government that has demonstrated that it cannot exercise such discipline on its own.

government's promise to pay interest on what it borrowed. They merely exchanged consumption in one period for consumption in another. Their consumption opportunities, viewed over time, haven't changed. Economists who reject the nontransfer argument insist that the payment of interest is not a transfer of income; recipients of interest payments are being compensated for a service. Taxpayers who pay interest are forced to reduce their consumption; taxpayers who receive it merely shift the time at which their wealth is consumed.

To economists who believe that the payment of interest does impose a burden on future generations, it doesn't matter whether bonds are held by foreigners or by residents of the United States. Payment of interest on the national debt always imposes a burden on the generations that make those payments.

Checklist

- The standard measure of deficits tells us little about the financial health of a government because it does not reflect the movement of other assets and liabilities the government may have.
- Adjusting a country's debt for the inflation of any period shows changes in the real value of the debt.
- A national debt cannot drive a country to bankruptcy. Private individuals or firms can go bankrupt; nations can't.
- One mechanism through which the accrual of debt by one generation can hurt another is the crowding out of investment.
- Economists have conflicting perspectives about whether the interest payments required by a debt constitute a mechanism through which the burden of one generation's consumption of government services can be transferred to another.

The issue of whether deficits transfer burdens to the future is essentially a normative question. How should we view the question? From the perspective of society as a whole, it's clearly true that the production of government goods and services has a cost in terms of giving up alternative goods and services. In that sense, one generation experiences the cost of its consumption of government services, whether it borrows the money to pay for them or not. If we choose to focus on individuals, however, it's clear that deficits transfer burdens to the future. And the evidence suggested by generational accounting suggests that burden will be very large indeed.

We'll see in the next section that not only do government deficits impose heavy financial burdens on future taxpayers—they contribute to another deficit as well: a deficit in the balance of trade. As we examine the relevant theory and evidence, we'll see that the emergence of large federal deficits in the last two decades has played a major role in inducing large trade deficits.

The Competitiveness Controversy

Does the United States have what it takes to compete in the global economy?

Many Americans believe that competitiveness is a core issue as the country faces a world in which potential rivals seem to crop up everywhere. For them, the words of President Bill Clinton sum up the challenge: "The American economy today is like a big corporation competing in the global marketplace." And many worry that this big corporation may not be up to the task.

Economists dismiss not only the worry but the entire context in which it is posed. For them, competitiveness is a meaningless concept. Individuals compete. Firms compete. But in matters of economics, nations don't.

Why do economists seem so diametrically opposed to what is emerging as mainstream thinking in the United States? Is this a case where everyone else is right and the economists are wrong? We'll examine these issues in this section. We'll also examine the primary policy issue in the competitiveness debate, strategic trade policy. First, however, we'll see what the two sides in the competitiveness debate have to say.

Those who think national competitiveness is a cause for concern generally base their concern on three propositions: First, the United States is competing in a newly emerged global economy, one that plays by a different set of economic rules. Second, it is losing this competition. Third, the United States can win only if it makes fundamental changes in its economic policies.

A Global Economy?

Of course there is a global economy. An economy, after all, is defined by production and exchange. People all over the world produce goods and services and exchange them with each other. But how significant is this global exchange? Does the recent pattern of such exchange represent a dramatic shift in the course of human affairs?

International trade is important. As we saw in Chapter 29, it accounts for a larger share of world economic activity than it did, say, 20 years ago. According to the World Bank, countries on average exported 21 percent of the goods and services they produced in 1993; that share was up from 14 percent in 1970. The

United States exported 10 percent of the goods and services it produced in 1993 (versus 6 percent in 1970).[2]

Although international trade has increased as a percentage of total economic activity in the last few decades, the emergence of a global economy is hardly a new phenomenon—nor does its significance represent a marked departure from the past.

International trade has occurred throughout recorded history. The United States has engaged in international trade since the colonial period. Indeed, the share of exports in U.S. GDP today is about the same as it was on the eve of the American Revolution.

Many historians date the emergence of a truly global economy to the nineteenth century and the creation of the British empire. With colonies all over the globe, Britain was able to base its economy on world trade. By the middle of the century, 40 percent of its output was exported—a substantially larger share than Britain exports today.

Certainly advances in transportation and communications have increased the importance of international trade within the past few decades. But viewed against the backdrop of world history, it's hard to see anything earthshaking in the current state of international trade.

Although the global economy is nothing new, it may still play by a different set of rules than those offered by the economic theory of comparative advantage and free trade. James Fallows, writing in *The Atlantic Monthly,* typifies the view that the United States must learn to play by different rules in order to compete:

> Americans persist in thinking that Adam Smith's rules for free trade are the only legitimate ones. But today's fastest-growing economies are using a very different set of rules.[3]

The argument that we need a new set of rules is really an argument for a greater degree of government intervention to assist domestic firms in international trade. We'll see below that economic theory suggests that some intervention may be desirable, but only under extremely limited conditions.

International Trade and Economic Performance

President Clinton's use of a corporate metaphor for the economy competing in the world marketplace captures perfectly the view many have of international trade. They see it as a contest in which one side—or country—wins while another loses. For them, the international economy is akin to World Cup soccer.

This view of international exchange contradicts one of the fundamental insights of economic analysis. Exchange, whether international or local, is an activity in which all parties gain. This mutual gain attribute explains why exchange is so ubiquitous. If exchange is a contest, it's a wonderful one—all participants win!

But suppose we set aside one of the most basic lessons of economics, that exchange benefits all who participate in it. Suppose we accept the notion that international exchange *is* a contest. Having taken that rather fanciful leap, how do we keep score? How do we know whether we're winning or losing?

[2] It may surprise you to learn that the United States devoted a larger share of its GDP to exports in 1993 than did Japan. Moreover, while the share of GDP devoted to exports rose in the United States from 1970 to 1993, the share in Japan fell slightly. (All data are taken from *World Development Report, 1995,* table 9.)

[3] James Fallows, "How the World Works," *The Atlantic Monthly* (December 1993): 61–87.

The next two sections explore two possible criteria we can use to judge an economy's performance in international trade: its trade balance and its ability to create high-paying jobs. We'll see that neither has anything to do with the ability of domestic firms to compete with foreign firms. Even if we take those who worry about U.S. competitiveness on their own terms, we'll find that their arguments make no sense.

Trade Balances and the Investment-Saving Identity

Trade balances are cited most often as the scorecard by which national performance should be judged. Only in the last decade and a half, a period in which the United States has rung up trade deficits every year, has competitiveness emerged as an issue. It's hard to imagine that anyone would be complaining about competitiveness if the United States were generating trade surpluses every year.

If trade balances are the criterion for success, then international competition must be a curious contest indeed. It's a game in which the loser gets most of the prizes!

A trade deficit means that more goods and services are flowing into a nation than out of it. During the last 15 years, the United States has received more goods and services from other nations than it has sent to them. Given that the ultimate purpose of economic activity is consumption, a net inflow of goods and services would seem to be a very good thing. Moreover, we saw in Chapter 29 that a trade deficit generally implies a capital account surplus. That means that the "winners"—the nations that are sending us all those goods and services—are also sending us capital.

There is, however, a more fundamental objection to the notion that trade balances reflect whether a nation is winning or losing at international trade. Such balances are determined in large part by domestic choices concerning saving. They have little or nothing to do with anything that could conceivably be related to "competitiveness." As we explore the relationship between trade balances and saving, we'll find that our previous issue, the government deficit, has a great deal to do with the trade deficit.

To see how public sector borrowing can affect trade balances, we can apply the accounting concepts we learned in Chapter 21. Real GDP Y equals the sum of consumption C, investment I, government purchases G, and net exports, $X - M$:

$$Y = C + I + G + X - M \tag{2}$$

Subtracting consumption from both sides, we have

$$Y - C = I + G + X - M \tag{3}$$

Recall from the circular flow model introduced in Chapter 21 that any income not devoted to consumption must go to private sector saving S_p or taxes T.[4] We can thus replace the $Y - C$ term on the left-hand side of Equation (3) with $S_p + T$:

$$S_p + T = I + G + X - M \tag{4}$$

Finally, we rearrange terms in Equation (4) so that investment is the only term on the right-hand side of Equation (5):

$$S_p + (T - G) + (M - X) = I \tag{5}$$

[4] In an economy with transfer payments, the tax term T equals the net value of tax collections from households minus transfer payments to them. The subscript p for private sector saving distinguishes this saving from other forms of saving introduced below.

Let's look at the terms in brackets on the left-hand side of Equation (5).

- S_p is private sector saving. It includes saving by households and saving done on their behalf by private firms. Most private saving in the United States is done by firms. Firms engage in saving on behalf of individuals when they accumulate pension funds and when they hold profits as retained earnings.
- $(T - G)$ is total tax receipts less transfer payments (the T term) minus government purchases. $(T - G)$ thus represents the government's income minus its outlays; it is public sector saving. When the public sector incurs a deficit, $(T - G)$ is negative. Because Equation (5) applies to the entire economy, public sector saving is the total saving of all levels of government: federal, state, and local.
- $(M - X)$ is the trade deficit—the amount by which the nation's imports exceed its exports. We can, however, view the trade deficit in another way. M is the rest of the world's earnings from its trade with the United States. X is what the rest of the world spends in the United States. The difference, $(M - X)$, is what the rest of the world saves in terms of its trade with the United States. The $(M - X)$ term is rest-of-world saving.[5]

Let government saving, $(T - G)$, be S_g. Let rest-of-world saving, $(M - X)$, be S_{row}. We can thus rewrite Equation (5) as

$$S_p + S_g + S_{row} = I \tag{6}$$

Equation 6 is the **investment–saving identity,** which states that the sum of private saving, government saving, and rest-of-world saving must equal investment. The relationship is an identity because it's derived from the definition of GDP. The two sides of the equation are always equal—*by definition.*

To see how the investment-saving identity suggests a potential relationship between government deficits and trade deficits, suppose that the public sector budget is balanced and there is no trade deficit: government saving and rest-of-world saving equal zero. In that case, private saving must equal investment. Now suppose that government purchases increase, so government saving becomes negative—the public sector incurs a deficit. The investment–saving identity tells us that one or a combination of three things *must* happen: private saving must rise (implying a reduction in consumption), rest-of-world saving must rise (implying in this case a trade deficit), or investment must fall. One or more of the other components of aggregate demand *must* be crowded out.

Exhibit 34-4 illustrates how these mechanisms have worked themselves out in recent U.S. history. It shows investment and each of the three components of saving as percentages of GDP in 3 years: 1978, 1986, and 1991.

In 1978, government and rest-of-world saving were each about zero. Although the federal government had a deficit that year, it was balanced by state and local government surpluses. With government and rest-of-world saving levels close to zero, private saving roughly matched private investment.

Soaring federal deficits in the 1980s pulled government saving down; it fell to −\$146.8 billion in 1986, the lowest level it reached during the 1980s. The investment–saving identity tells us that the reduction in government saving had to produce either an increase in private saving, an increase in rest-of-world saving,

The **investment–saving identity** states that the sum of private saving, government saving, and rest-of-world saving must equal investment.

[5] Recall that we showed in Chapter 29 that the trade deficit, which we can now interpret as rest-of-world saving, equals the negative of the capital account surplus. That means that rest-of-world saving remains in the United States; it equals net purchases by foreigners of U.S. assets.

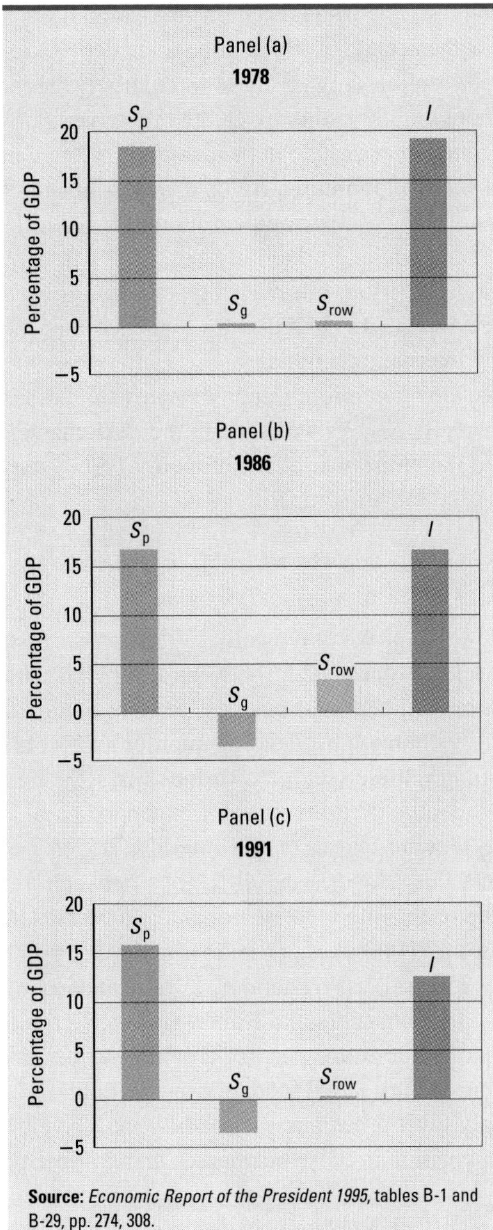

Source: *Economic Report of the President 1995*, tables B-1 and B-29, pp. 274, 308.

EXHIBIT 34-4

Components of the Investment–Saving Identity, 1978, 1986, and 1991

Government (S_g) and rest-of-world (S_{row}) saving were close to zero in 1978 so that private saving S_p equaled investment I as a percentage of GDP. Negative government saving was offset in 1986 by an increase in rest-of-world saving and in 1991 by sharply lower investment.

or a reduction in investment. We see that in 1986 the reduction in government saving was offset by an increase in rest-of-world saving. That jump in rest-of-world saving (i.e., the jump in the trade deficit) was the event that spawned concern about U.S. competitiveness.

An alternative to an increase in foreign saving as a response to reduced public sector saving emerged in 1991. Government saving fell again, but a U.S. recession lowered U.S. imports. As a result, the trade deficit nearly vanished. With plunging government saving, however, there had to be either an increase in private saving or a plunge in investment. Firms faced with falling sales slashed their acquisitions of new capital; it was investment that plunged to balance the reduction in government saving in 1991.

When public sector saving falls, one of three things must happen: private saving must rise, rest-of-world saving must rise, or investment must fall. Given the stability of the relationship between consumption and income, private saving is unlikely to rise. That leaves two possibilities: increased rest-of-world saving (a trade deficit) or a collapse in investment. Would those who worry about competitiveness say that the United States would have been more competitive in the 1980s if investment had collapsed? In retrospect, the soaring trade deficits of the 1980s were probably better for the economy—and for future generations—than the alternative of an investment collapse. One may question whether a choice to reduce government saving is desirable. But given that choice, a trade deficit may be the best of the available responses.

Jobs and Wages

Another standard against which a nation's economic performance is often judged is its ability to generate jobs—and high wages for those jobs. Although the generation of jobs is a desirable outcome of economic activity, and high real wages are also desirable, neither variable has anything to do with a nation's performance in international trade.

An economy moves in the long run to its natural level of employment and to the real wage that achieves equilibrium in the labor market. But as we saw in Chapter 26, the natural level of employment and the equilibrium real wage are determined by the economy's production function and the supply curve for labor—things that have nothing to do with international trade. Trade can affect aggregate demand and short-run aggregate supply. But the fact that the economy moves toward its natural level of output tells us that these effects are transitory. In the long run, it's the domestic economy that determines what the nation can produce. Trade affects the volume of goods and services a nation can consume, not what it's capable of producing.

The experience of the 1980s suggests the irrelevance of international trade for employment and wages. This was the decade in which huge trade deficits appeared. As the analysis in the previous section showed, these were largely the result of public sector deficits. The United States economy created more new jobs during this period than it had during any other decade in its history. It is true that real wage growth during this period was disappointing. But that was the result of slow productivity growth over the period. Total real compensation of U.S. workers during the 1980s rose 5.8 percent while productivity rose 5.1 percent.[6] Neither gain is impressive for a 10-year period, but real compensation moved with productivity, as economic theory predicts. There is no evidence that the course of real wages was affected by international trade.

One may be disappointed by the slowdown in productivity growth that has beset the U.S. economy since the early 1970s. As we'll see in the next chapter, however, the slowdown has affected the entire world. It can hardly be taken as an indication that the United States is no longer competitive.

Policies for Competitiveness

Those who argue that competitiveness is a problem typically say that in order to be competitive, a country must develop a partnership between the public and private sectors. In this partnership, government and business leaders work together to identify key sectors that the economy must develop in order to be competitive. The government then encourages these sectors in various ways.

How can these "key sectors" be identified? Proponents of expanded public-private cooperation have suggested they be chosen based on value added per worker. We saw in Chapter 21 that value added is the difference between the value of a firm's output and the value of the intermediate goods the firm uses in producing that output. A firm that uses $20,000 worth of lumber and other materials to produce a building worth $50,000 has generated a value added of $30,000. In an influential 1982 book, Ira Magaziner and Robert B. Reich termed industries with relatively high levels of value added per worker "high-value" industries. In the book they argue "Our country's real income can rise only if (1) its labor and capital flow increasingly toward businesses that add greater value per employee and (2) we maintain a position in those businesses that is superior to our international competitors."[7]

Competitiveness proponents argue that another way the government can choose industries it should help is by finding activities in which one nation can win at another's expense. This approach suggests that nations should adopt a strategic approach to trade just as they adopt a strategic approach to defense. We shall investigate this argument, which involves a recent reexamination of international trade theory, later in this section.

[6] The real compensation figure is calculated using a price index that excludes housing because this market is not affected by international trade. The productivity gain is measured in terms of consumption goods. See Robert Lawrence and Matthew Slaughter, "Trade and U.S. Wages: Great Sucking Sound or Small Hiccup?" *Brooking Papers on Economic Activity, Microeconomics* 2 (1993):161–210.

[7] *Minding America's Business* (New York: Harcourt Brace Jovanovich, 1982), p. 4. Another book with a similar theme is Lester Thurow's *Head to Head: The Coming Economic Battle Among Japan, Europe, and America* (New York: Morrow, 1992). These two books have been enormously important because of their influence in the Clinton administration. Reich was named Secretary of Labor, and Magaziner served as Hillary Rodham Clinton's chief of staff in designing the administration's health care proposal. Thurow took no post in the administration, but President Clinton has often commented approvingly on his book.

Seeking Higher Value Added

The notion that incomes and living standards could be increased by expanding activities with high value added per worker and contracting those with low value added per worker may have some intuitive appeal. But it assumes that government officials could do a better job of allocating resources than private decision-makers. Economic theory and the histories of countries that have tried such approaches quite strongly suggest otherwise.

In any event, following a prescription to encourage high-value-added sectors in the United States would have a simple policy implication: encourage the manufacture of tobacco products. The tobacco industry has by far the highest value added per worker of any major industry in the United States, as suggested in Exhibit 34-5. Petroleum refining ranks a distant second, with chemical production third. Another sector often cited as a candidate for government encouragement, electronics, is far down the list. Its value added per worker was only about average for all manufacturing industries.

The notion that the economy would be more productive if the government would assist the development of industries with high value added per worker is nonsensical. If it's possible to reallocate resources in a way that achieves greater productivity, the market will reward those who discover and exploit those opportunities. It hardly seems necessary to have a government agency undertake the task.

Strategic Trade Policy

Why do some countries specialize in and export the goods and services they do? Since David Ricardo explained the concept early in the nineteenth century, the standard answer to this question has been "Comparative advantage."

EXHIBIT 34-5

Value Added per Worker in U.S. Industry

Major industries are ranked here by value added per employee in 1990. The tobacco products industry tops this list.

Industry	Value Added per Employee
Tobacco products	$550,268
Petroleum and coal products	242,982
Chemicals and allied products	179,404
Instruments and related products	130,429
Food and kindred products	95,900
Paper and allied products	95,260
Leather and leather products	84,505
Transportation equipment	82,816
Primary metal industries	74,953
Electronics, other electric equipment	71,465
Industrial machinery and equipment	70,413
Printing and publishing	67,086
Stone, clay, and glass products	67,073
Rubber and miscellaneous plastic products	57,344
Fabricated metal products	55,561
Furniture and fixtures	43,377
Textile mill products	41,930
Lumber and wood products	41,870
Apparel and other textile products	33,267
Average, all manufacturing	$70,401

Source: U.S. Bureau of the Census, Statistical Abstract of the United States 1992, table 1244, pp. 733–737.

The comparative advantage argument works well enough to explain U.S. exports of wheat or Argentina's exports of beef, but it doesn't take us very far in assessing other specialization that we observe. Why should the United States be the world's primary manufacturer of airplanes? Why should Japan be the dominant producer of many consumer electronics products? These sets of goods require sophisticated capital and highly trained workers—both of which are abundant in both countries.

Still another problem for conventional trade theory is that it predicts that the direction of trade in individual goods and services will be one way: a country will export goods and services in which it has a comparative advantage and import those in which other countries have a comparative advantage. But the majority of the world's trade is two way: countries both export and import the same goods and services. The United States exports computers to Japan and imports computers from Japan. Chile exports wine to France and imports wine from France. The same goods flow in both directions.

Here's a related paradox: Comparative advantage theory suggests that the greatest gains from trade will be achieved through trade between dissimilar countries. A capital-intensive country will trade with a labor-intensive one. But the bulk of trade is between similar economies. The number one trading partner of the United States is Canada, not Mexico.

Economists examining these puzzles in international trade have developed a new approach to international trade theory.[8] It is still rooted in the doctrine of comparative advantage, but it asserts that comparative advantage can, in some cases, be acquired. The location of particular activities in particular countries results not from some iron law of comparative advantage but from a combination of circumstances in which countries have acquired advantages in the production of certain goods.

U.S. dominance of the aircraft industry, for example, appears to have resulted from heavy U.S. military spending during and after World War II. That spending prompted the development of several major U.S. firms, such as Boeing, McDonnell-Douglas, and Lockheed. As these firms expanded, other firms grew up to serve as suppliers to them. Ready access to the services of those support firms further solidified the advantages of the U.S. producers, and the United States emerged as the world's dominant producer of aircraft. In effect, the United States acquired a comparative advantage in aircraft production.

The recognition that comparative advantage could be acquired has spawned proposals that government support be offered to some industries. Such policies, which seek gains in international trade at the expense of other countries, are called **strategic trade policies.**

To see how a strategic trade policy could work, let's suppose that a powerful new personal computing device is invented. It's cheap, it's easily carried, and it will respond to any voice command, so it is expected to be enormously popular. But manufacturers can achieve cost advantages only if production of this device is undertaken at such extremely large volume that only a single producer can operate profitably. Production of the new machines will be an example of what economists call a natural monopoly.

Now suppose that two competing producers, General Electric and Sony, have access to this technology and are considering using it. It will require a huge investment and will be an extremely risky undertaking. If only one firm implements the technology, it will quickly dominate world production of the devices

Strategic trade policies are government policies that seek gains in international trade at the expense of other countries.

[8] This theory is examined in detail in the microeconomics half of this text, in Chapter 13.

and will be enormously profitable. But if both firms do so, then neither will be able to expand enough to produce the sets at the lowest cost possible. Use of the new technology by both firms is likely to mean both will lose money.

Exhibit 34-6 lays out the possibilities for using the new technology from the point of view of the two firms.[9] The two rows of the payoff matrix represent the alternatives available to General Electric: it may choose to invest in the new technology or not to invest. The two columns give the same choices for Sony. Each of the four cells gives a possible outcome for choices made by the two firms. The number in the shaded region of each cell is Sony's annual profit from the venture; the other number is General Electric's annual profit. If both firms enter the market, each firm loses $5 billion. If General Electric enters and Sony doesn't, General Electric will establish a global monopoly and make a profit of $30 billion. If GE doesn't enter, its profits will be zero—no matter what Sony does. Sony faces the same possibilities depending on whether General Electric enters.

EXHIBIT 34-6

A Strategic Trade Choice

The cells represent possible outcomes in a strategic game in which two firms, General Electric and Sony, are considering investing in a new technology. The entries in the dark-shaded portions in each cell show Sony's profit; the entries in the light-portions show General Electric's profit. Figures are in billions of dollars.

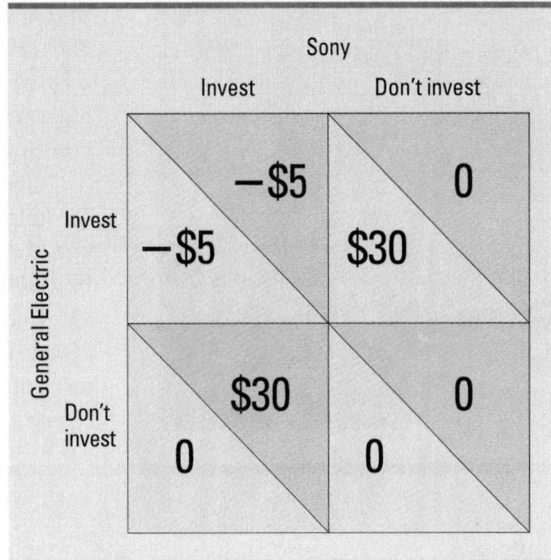

What will happen? Any of the cells is possible. If both firms play it safe, they will compare the worst outcomes under each strategy and pick the strategy with the best of these worst outcomes. If General Electric invests in the technology, for example, the worst thing that could happen would be a loss of $5 billion (which occurs if Sony invests also). If General Electric doesn't invest, the worst outcome is a profit of zero. General Electric will face the best of the worst outcomes by avoiding the technology altogether. Based on similar calculations, Sony might well do the same.

Suppose now that the U.S. government, aware that the technology is under consideration, offers General Electric a guaranteed subsidy of $10 billion if it invests and ends up losing money. In this case, the worst thing that could happen to General Electric is a net profit of $5 billion if it invests (equal to the $5 billion loss plus the $10 billion subsidy). Faced with the opportunity for a profit of either $30 billion or $5 billion, General Electric will clearly invest. Sony may well do the same, but its losses will soon force it out of the market (assuming Japan doesn't offer a similar subsidy). The government's guarantee wins the day for General Electric, and the United States becomes the home of the new industry.

[9] If you've studied microeconomics, you'll recognize this as a game theory problem (see Chapter 13). Firms contemplating choices based on a payoff matrix such as the one given in Exhibit 34-6 are said to be engaging in strategic behavior. It is from this perspective that strategic trade policy gets its name.

Case in Point

Strategic Trade: Do the Japanese Get It Right?

Advocates of a strategic trade policy cite Japan as an example of a country that is consistently successful in targeting promising industries and then lending government support to boost those industries to success in world competition. To many observers, the best hope for U.S. success lies in emulating the Japanese.

The most frequently cited Japanese success story is its support of its semiconductor industry in the 1970s. Semiconductors are the tiny chips of silicon that make up the "brains" of modern computers. As recently as the mid-1970s, Japan's semiconductor industry lagged behind that of the United States. U.S. firms held 90 percent of the market while Japanese firms struggled to hold on to a tiny share.

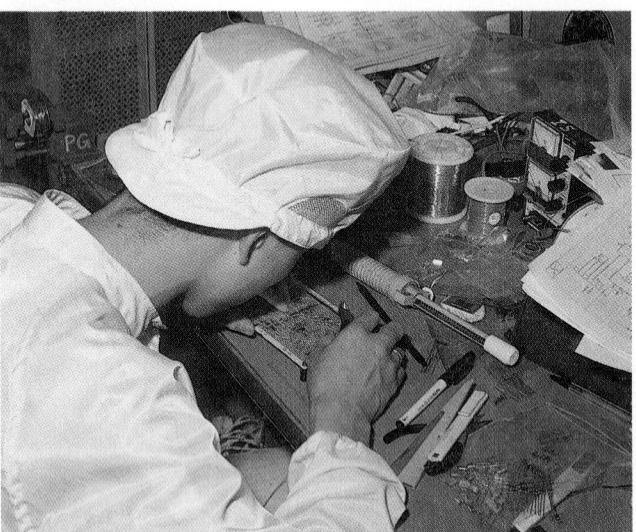

At that point, MITI, the Japanese Ministry for International Trade and Industry, decided to target semiconductors as an industry in which Japan would gain dominance. MITI lent research support and protection to Japanese firms from foreign competition. Japanese firms responded, and by the mid-1980s they dominated the world market with an 85 percent share.

MITI's efforts have not always been so successful. Its struggle to establish Japan as a major player in international shipping has failed—after investing billions, MITI gave up the effort. Other Japanese industries have succeeded with no help from MITI. When Japanese automakers approached MITI early in the 1960s with a plan to penetrate the U.S. market, agency officials scoffed at the idea and discouraged the firms from trying. Sony got a similar response when it proposed competing in the U.S. consumer electronics market.

One major study of 10 Japanese industries targeted by MITI for help found a *negative* correlation between the amount of aid and the success of Japanese industries—the more MITI has helped, the poorer the performance of the industry!

Even the semiconductor story has had an unhappy ending for Japan. Global competition has been fierce, turning semiconductors into a virtual commodity with razor-thin profits. U.S. and Korean firms have captured large shares of that market.

What's the payoff to the United States of "winning" the market for the new devices? General Electric's profits of $30 billion could be taxed; those taxes could benefit the entire population.

This conclusion, that a government boost to encourage an export industry might help the economy, is an important one. The boost needn't be a cash subsidy. It could involve help with research in developing the new product or a guarantee of protection for the new firm from potential competition from foreign firms such as Sony. Whatever the form of government aid, it has the potential for ensuring that the country granting it will capture the industry. For proponents of strategies aimed at boosting U.S. competitiveness, this potential offers a further justification for the idea of targeting industries for government help.

But economists argue that the opportunities for government intervention are quite limited. Remember that the fact that a successful firm will generate jobs is not a justification for government support—it will, after all, bid resources away from other firms. Some sectors will gain, but others will lose.

Under what conditions would the government's support of an industry increase domestic welfare? Here are some conditions that have been cited by the economists who developed the strategic trade model:

1. Government help must make a difference in the outcome. In the absence of the subsidy, a domestic firm will not succeed in the market. With it, it will.

2. The structure of the industry must be such that it will be a natural monopoly, so that profits realized by the firm will be sustained and will not be eroded by the entry of new firms. If this condition doesn't hold, new firms will enter and potential profits will be eliminated.
3. The expansion of a successful firm won't bid up factor prices in a way that reduces the profitability of other firms.

These conditions are quite restrictive. Indeed, the economists who have worked to develop the new theoretical approach generally argue that the combination of restrictive conditions and the likelihood that political pressures would distort the government's response make it unlikely that a strategic trade policy would enhance welfare.

Economic theory offers four major conclusions relevant to the competitiveness debate. First, a nation's policy with respect to international trade does not determine or even affect its natural level of employment or its average level of wages. Second, a trade deficit emerges in response to other choices about saving and investment. The existence of a trade deficit tells us nothing about how "competitive" a nation's firms might be. Third, a policy of government intervention to shift resources that offer higher average levels of value added per worker makes no sense in theory, nor is it likely to do anything to boost a nation's productivity. Finally, there is a theoretical case to be made for a strategic trade policy. Whether such a policy could be successfully implemented is an open question. The conditions under which such a policy might improve a nation's performance are quite narrow.

We shall turn next to the third issue considered in this chapter: the problem of the fairness of the income distribution, which presents society with one of the most difficult challenges it will face in the next century.

Checklist

- An economy's natural level of output and equilibrium level of real wages are determined by factors other than its policies for international trade.
- The investment–saving identity shows that a reduction in government saving must lead to an increase in private saving, an increase in rest-of-world saving, and/or a reduction in investment.
- Although some observers have advocated government efforts to expand industries with high value added per worker, there is no theoretical merit to the idea.
- Strategic trade theory suggests a conceptual justification for government support of a particular industry, but the circumstances required for such a policy to be effective are extremely limited.

The Fairness Issue

Economists and policymakers must always consider whether the distribution of incomes in an economy is fair. Changes in the U.S. distribution over the past quarter of a century have brought the issue of fairness to the forefront of public debate.

We'll learn in this section how the degree of inequality can be measured, and we'll see how inequality has risen in the United States since 1968. We'll examine the sources of rising inequality and consider what policy measures, if any, are suggested.

A Changing Distribution of Income

Many people test fairness by examining the distribution of income. The more equal the distribution, the fairer they perceive the society to be, and the more unequal, the less fair. This section describes a graphical approach to measuring the equality, or inequality, of the distribution of income.

Measuring Inequality

The primary evidence of growing inequality is provided by census data. Households are asked to report their income, and they are ranked from the household with the lowest income to the household with the highest income. The Census

Bureau then reports the percentage of total income earned by those households ranked among the bottom 20 percent, the next 20 percent, and so on, up to the the top 20 percent. Each 20 percent of families is called a quintile. The Bureau also reports the share of income going to the top 5 percent of households.

The census data clearly show growing inequality since 1968. The share of income going to the bottom quintile of families fell from 5.7 percent in 1968 to 5.2 percent in 1980 to 4.4 percent in 1992. The share of income going to those in the top quintile rose from 40.5 percent to 44.6 percent. This period has left the rich with a larger and the poor with a smaller share of income.

The table in Exhibit 34-7 reports income shares in 1968 and in 1992. We see that the shares going to the bottom 20 percent of families fell while the shares going to the top 20 percent rose. The shares received by the middle three quintiles fell slightly from 53.8 percent to 51.0 percent.

Income distribution data can be presented graphically using a **Lorenz curve,** a curve that shows cumulative shares of income received by individuals or groups. To plot the curve, we begin with the lowest quintile and mark a point to show the percentage of total income those families received. We then add the next quintile and its share and mark a point to show the share of the lowest 40 percent of families.

EXHIBIT 34-7

The Distribution of U.S. Income, 1968 and 1992

The distribution of income among families in the United States became more unequal from 1968 to 1992. The Lorenz curve for 1992 was more bowed out than the 1968 curve.

Quintile	1968 income share	1992 income share
Lowest 20%	5.7%	4.4%
Second 20%	12.4	10.5
Third 20%	17.7	16.5
Fourth 20%	23.7	24.0
Highest 20%	40.5	44.6
Top 5 percent	15.6	17.6

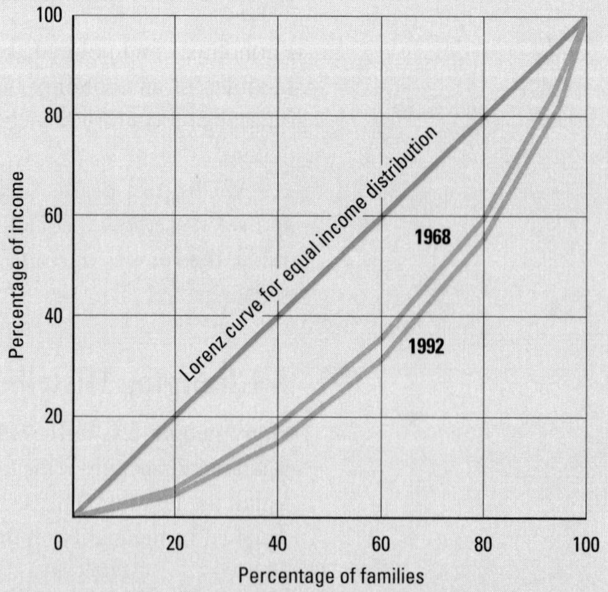

Source: U.S. Bureau of the Census, *Studies in the Distribution of Income 1992, Current Population Reports* pp. 60–183 (Washington, D.C.: U.S. Government Printing Office, 1992).

A **Lorenz curve** shows the cumulative shares of income received by individuals or groups.

If every family in the United States received the same income, the Lorenz curve would be the 45-degree line drawn in the exhibit. The bottom 20 percent of families would receive 20 percent of income, the bottom 40 percent would receive 40 percent, and so on. If the distribution of income were perfectly unequal, with one family receiving all the income and the rest zero, then the Lorenz curve would be shaped like a backwards L, with a horizontal line across the bottom of the graph at 0 percent of income and a vertical line up the right-hand side. The vertical line would show that, as always, 100 percent of families still receive 100 percent of income. Actual Lorenz curves lie between these extremes. The closer a Lorenz curve lies to the 45-degree line, the more equal the distribution. The more bowed out the curve, the less equal the distribution. We see that the Lorenz curve became more bowed out between 1968 and 1992.

Another way to examine the changing fortunes of different income groups is to see how the average incomes of each 20 percent of families changed. Exhibit 34-8 shows annual percentage rates of change in mean income for each quintile of families between 1950 and 1968 and between 1968 and 1992. The difference between the two periods is dramatic.

Panel (a) shows that families at all levels of income enjoyed substantial income growth from 1950 to 1968. Indeed, those at the bottom experienced somewhat more rapid gains than those at the top. The distribution of income became more equal.

The period from 1968 to 1992 differed from the earlier period in two ways. First, income changed at a much slower rate. Second, average incomes at the top of the income distribution rose more rapidly than did average incomes at the

EXHIBIT 34-8

Percentage Rates of Change in Mean Family Income, 1950–1968 and 1968–1992

The charts compare annual percentage gains in mean real family income for various income groups.

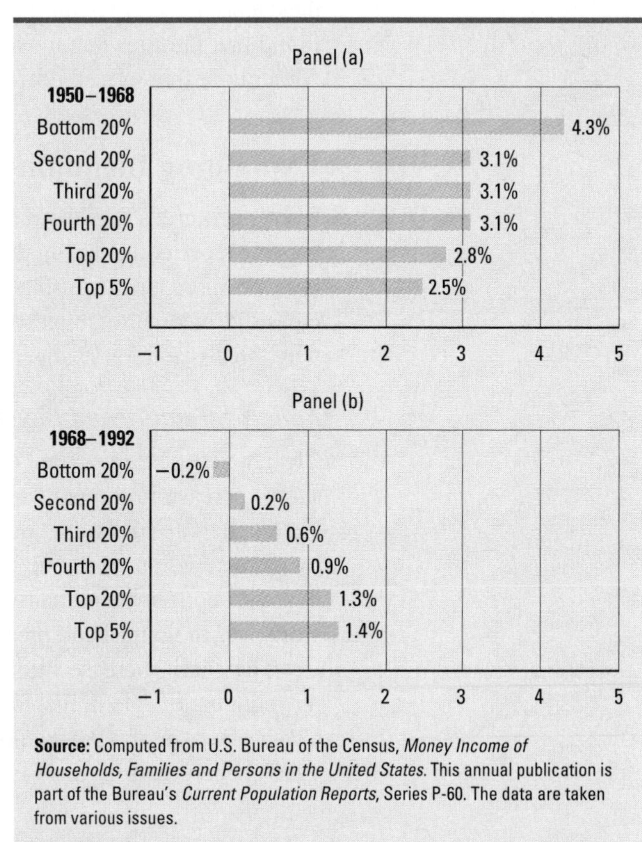

Source: Computed from U.S. Bureau of the Census, *Money Income of Households, Families and Persons in the United States.* This annual publication is part of the Bureau's *Current Population Reports*, Series P-60. The data are taken from various issues.

bottom. The bottom group of families saw reductions in their average income during the period. Income grew for each of the upper four quintiles, with the greatest gains going to the richest families. Even greater gains were recorded by the top 5 percent of families. The data show that the rich got somewhat richer while the poor got poorer.

Mobility of the Income Distribution

When we speak of the bottom 20 percent or the middle 20 percent of families, we aren't speaking of a static group. Some families who are in the bottom quintile one year move up to higher quintiles in subsequent years; some families move down. Indeed, an Urban Institute study by Isabel Sawhill and Mark Condon found that three out of five families moved to different quintiles of the income distribution between 1977 and 1986; similar mobility was found for the period from 1967 to 1976.[10]

The Urban Institute study found that about half of those starting one of the two periods in the top quintile had fallen to a lower quintile at the end of the period; almost half of those starting in the bottom quintile moved up. Because families move up and down the distribution, we get a quite different picture of income change when we look at the incomes of a fixed set of families rather than comparing average incomes for a particular quintile, as was done in Exhibit 34-8. Following the individual families who were in the bottom quintile in 1977, for example, the Urban Institute researchers found that they experienced a 77 percent increase in income by 1986. Those families who were in the top quintile in 1977 enjoyed only a 5 percent gain by 1986.

An important reason for the sharp gains in income for families at the bottom of the income distribution is that many who start out at the bottom are young; they tend to achieve substantial gains as they age. The Urban Institute study found that families that moved up the income distribution tended to be younger, while those that moved down or stayed put tended to be older.

Explaining Inequality

Everyone agrees that the distribution of income in the United States generally became more equal during the first two decades after World War II and that it has become more unequal since 1970. While some people conclude that this increase in inequality suggests the latter period was unfair, others want to know why the distribution changed. Let's examine some of the explanations.

Family Structure and Inequality

Clearly the most important source of rising inequality since 1970 has been the sharp increase in the percentage of families headed by women. These families are much more likely than others to be poor; the poverty rate for families headed by women with no husband present is about 5 times as great as the rate for families with both husband and wife present. The percentage of families headed by women with no husband present has nearly doubled since 1970.

The sharp increase in the proportion of households headed by women has played a major role in increasing income inequality. Indeed, a simulation by the Census Bureau of what would have happened to the distribution of income since 1970 if there had been no increase in the percentage of households headed by

[10] Isabel V. Sawhill and Mark Condon, "Is U.S. Income Inequality Really Growing?" *Policy Bites* 13(June 1992): 1–4.

women suggests that, instead of greater inequality, we would have observed a continuation in the trend toward greater equality.

Technological and Managerial Change

We've seen that technological change has affected the demand for labor. One of the most dramatic changes appeared in the late 1970s; the demand for skilled labor increased while the demand for unskilled labor appeared to fall.

The result has been an increase in the gap between the wages of skilled and unskilled workers. That has produced a widening gap between college- and high-school-trained workers. That gap more than doubled in percentage terms during the 1980s and thus contributed to rising inequality.

Technological change has meant the integration of computers into virtually every aspect of production. And that has increased the demand for workers with the knowledge to put new methods to work—and to adapt to the even more dramatic changes in production likely to come. At the same time, the demand for workers who don't have that knowledge has fallen.

Along with new technologies that require greater technical expertise, firms are adopting new management styles that require stronger communication skills. The use of production teams, for example, shifts decisionmaking authority to small groups of assembly-line workers. That means those workers need more than the manual dexterity that was required of them in the past. They need strong communication skills. They must write effectively, speak effectively, and interact effectively with other workers. Workers who can't do so simply aren't in demand to the degree they once were.

The "intellectual wage gap" seems likely to widen even further in the next century. That's likely to lead to an even higher degree of inequality and to pose a challenge to public policy for decades to come.

Public Policy

Did public policy contribute to rising inequality over the past quarter century? Two kinds of public choices have been identified as possible factors in rising inequality: welfare programs and tax changes.

Many states limit the assistance they give to households in which a husband is present. In the 1970s, most states refused to grant benefits under the Aid to Families with Dependent Children (AFDC) program, the largest program of cash transfers, if a husband was present. Such provisions may have contributed to the breakup of families and the increase in households headed by women. More generally, the fact that welfare aid is available may have increased the incidence of female-headed households.

Studies by economists have generally found that the degree to which welfare programs have affected family structure is small, if they have affected it at all. Although the percentage of families headed by women has increased in the past two decades, this trend began early in the century. It isn't clear that welfare programs have affected the trend in any significant way.

The tax changes most often cited in the fairness debate are the Reagan tax cuts introduced in 1981. When President Reagan came to office, the top tax rate for the rich was 70 percent. When he left, it was 28 percent. While the reductions in the top tax rate were most dramatic, taxes were reduced at all income levels. The Tax Reform Act of 1986, which lowered the top rate to 28 percent, also exempted millions of people at the bottom of the income distribution from paying any federal income tax.

Checklist

- The distribution of income has become more unequal since 1968. The share of total income going to the nation's richest families has increased while the share going to the poorest families has fallen.
- During the period from 1950 to 1968, all quintiles of the income distribution experienced substantial gains in income, with the greatest gains going to the lowest quintiles and the smallest gains going to those at the top of the income distribution. Income gains were much smaller between 1968 and 1992, with those at the top receiving the largest gains and those at the bottom losing income.
- There is considerable mobility among quintiles of the distribution of income, with many families moving from lower to higher quintiles and others moving from higher to lower quintiles.
- Among the factors contributing to increased inequality have been changes in family structure, the aging of the population, technological change, methods of measurement, and public policy.

As we have seen, the theory behind these reductions in marginal tax rates was to stimulate people to become more productive, earn more income, and thus in the end pay more taxes. The policy appears to have worked; taypayers at the top of the income distribution increased not only the amount of taxes they paid but their share of total income taxes. In 1980, the top 5 percent of income earners paid 37 percent of all federal income taxes. In 1991, their share had increased to 43 percent. Of course, this increase reflected the fact that the rich earned a larger share of total income. To the extent that this resulted from the stimulus offered by lower tax rates, tax policy contributed to rising inequality.

The policy issues we have examined—the deficit, competitiveness, and fairness—seem likely to remain near the top of the policy agenda for many years. In some respects, however, they may be overwhelmed by an even more fundamental challenge, the problem of economic growth. A faster rate of economic growth would make short work of the deficit by producing more rapid increases in government revenues. It would imply the rising productivity sought by people who worry about competitiveness. And though growth might not make the distribution of income more equal, it would generate the incomes that would allow society to address the problem of inequality more easily. We shall turn to the problem of economic growth in the next chapter.

A Look Back—And a Look Ahead

We've examined three issues of public policy in this chapter: the debt and the deficit, U.S. competitiveness, and the question of fairness.

Although federal deficits have increased sharply in recent years, the ratio of the national debt to GDP remains much lower than it was in the period after World War II. Furthermore, the ratio of debt relative to GDP in the United States is well within the range of the ratios for other developed countries. However, concern about the debt, and the deficits that add to it, has increased as the ratio of debt to GDP has once again begun to increase. No matter how high the debt rises, it can't force a nation into bankruptcy. At worst, a nation might choose to repudiate its debt.

We saw that one important issue involving deficits and the debt is measurement. Conceptually, the test of whether an institution incurs a deficit or a surplus in a particular period is whether its net worth rises or falls. But the U.S. government computes its deficit solely on the basis of revenues and expenditures. If expenditures exceed revenues, then there is a deficit. No accounting is made of changes in assets or of liabilities. Furthermore, no accounting is made of the degree to which inflation reduces the real value of outstanding debt. Our measures of deficits and the debt thus do a poor job of assessing the financial legacy one period of fiscal policy leaves to another.

Measurement issues aside, a question remains as to the degree to which increases in the national debt impose a burden on the future. To the degree that such increases crowd out investment, people in the future will have a smaller capital stock than would otherwise have been available. They will thus have a lower natural GDP and lower incomes. Whether interest payments on past borrowing allow people in one period to shift the burden of paying for their consumption of government services to people in subsequent periods is a controversial issue among economists. Some argue that the cost of government services is borne only by the generation that consumes them and that future payments of interest merely redistribute income. Others insist that the payment of interest does impose a burden on future generations, allowing one generation to shift some of the costs of its consumption to other generations.

We then turned to the question of competitiveness. Some people who worry about U.S. competitiveness vis-à-vis other nations are concerned about the nation's ability to generate high-paying jobs. But in the long run, employment and real wages are determined by the economy's production function and its supply of labor, neither of which is likely to be affected by international trade policies. Another competitiveness issue is the trade deficit. We saw that the investment–saving identity shows that a reduction in public sector saving must cause an increase in private saving, an increase in foreign saving, and/or a reduction in investment. Viewed in that light, the emergence of a trade deficit in the 1980s may have been a desirable result of a choice to reduce government saving.

Policies that have been advocated to increase competitiveness include the targeting of specific production sectors, on the basis of either value added per worker or strategic trade. We saw that the first criterion is nonsensical. A conceptual case can be made for the second on the basis of strategic trade theory, but the conditions under which such a policy could increase the welfare of one country at the expense of another are limited.

Finally, we examined the issue of fairness. More particularly, we looked at changes in the distribution of income in the United States since 1950. We saw that the income distribution became more equal between 1950 and 1968 and that it has become more unequal since. Among the factors contributing to increased inequality have been changes in family structure, the aging of the population, technological change, the method by which the income distribution is measured, and public policy. While rising inequality may be a concern, there is a good deal of movement of families up and down the distribution of income.

In the last two chapters of Part Nine, we'll turn to two of the most important macroeconomic issues facing us today: economic growth and economic development. Both chapters are about growth, but the first will focus on growth in developed economies such as the United States while the second will examine the challenge of growth for less developed economies.

Terms and Concepts for Review

Inflation-adjusted deficit
Investment–saving identity
Lorenz curve
National debt
Repudiation of the debt
Strategic trade policies

For Discussion

1. Suppose that the United States government developed a measure of its net worth and that a deficit was then defined as a negative change in net worth. Explain how each of the following would affect this new measure of the deficit, and compare that effect to its impact on the deficit as it is now measured.
   - **a.** Congress approves an increase in welfare benefits to begin next year.
   - **b.** The federal government sells an army base for $645 million.
   - **c.** The federal government borrows the money to build a new medical research center.
   - **d.** The federal government builds a new medical research center and pays for it out of current taxes.
   - **e.** The federal government borrows the money to provide a onetime bonus to working welfare recipients.
2. Suppose a country's price level is falling. How does its inflation-adjusted deficit compare to its actual deficit?
3. Suppose President Clinton were to announce that the federal government will henceforth use an inflation-adjusted measure of the deficit. How do you think the idea would fare politically?
4. Give and justify your view on whether government borrowing can shift the cost of providing public sector goods and services from one generation to the next.
5. Suppose the federal government printed an amount of paper money sufficient to pay off the entire national debt. How would this action affect the price level? Could the Fed offset this impact? How?
6. Explain carefully why economists argue that international trade has nothing to do with employment in the long run.
7. Could the United States increase its real GDP by shifting workers from apparel to tobacco products?
8. Strategic trade theory suggests that a nation may be better off if it becomes home to a firm that has a monopoly in the production of some internationally traded good. Why? What's so great about a monopoly? What if the only market for the good were domestic? Would it still make sense to subsidize the industry?
9. Explain how rising demand for college-educated workers and falling demand for high-school-educated workers contributes to increased inequality of the distribution of income.
10. Discuss the advantages and disadvantages of the following three alternatives for dealing with the rising inequality of wages.
    - **a.** Increase the minimum wage each year so that wages for unskilled workers rise as fast as wages for skilled workers.
    - **b.** Subsidize the wages of unskilled workers.
    - **c.** Do nothing.

Problems

1. Here are figures for federal expenditures E, revenues R, the national debt ND, and inflation π (measured by the implicit price deflator) during the 4 years of President Jimmy Carter's term. (Data are from *Economic Report of the President 1995,* tables B-77 and B-3.) Compute the deficit and the inflation-adjusted deficit for each year. Comment on your results.

	E (billions)	R (billions)	ND (billions)	π
1977	$409.2	$355.6	$706.4	6.9%
1978	458.7	399.6	776.6	7.9
1979	504.0	463.3	829.5	8.6
1980	590.9	517.1	909.1	9.5

2. Look up the table on Federal Receipts and Outlays, by Major Category, in the most recent *Economic Report of the President* available in your library, and complete the following table.

	Total Outlays	Percentage of Total Outlays
National defense		
International affairs		
Health		
Medicare		
Income security		
Social Security		
Net interest		
Other		

3. A nation's debt in year 1 is $1,000 billion, its deficit is $100 billion, and its inflation rate is 10 percent. What is the inflation-adjusted deficit in year 1?

4. From the following data for the United States, compute foreign saving for each year. Comment on your results. (Data are from *Economic Report of the President 1995,* table B-29. All figures are in billions.)

	Private Saving	Government Saving	Foreign Saving	Investment
1960	$81.5	$3.6		$78.7
1970	165.8	− 11.5		150.3
1980	499.6	− 35.3		467.6
1990	861.1	− 138.4		808.9

5. Here are income distribution data for three countries, from the *World Development Report 1994,* table 30. Plot the Lorenz curves for each in a single graph, and compare the degree of inequality for the three countries. (Don't forget to convert the data to cumulative shares; e.g., the lowest 40 percent of the population in Panama receives 8.3 percent of total income.) Compare your results to the Lorenz curve given in the text for the United States. Which country in your chart appears closest to the United States in terms of its income distribution?

	Quintiles				
	Lowest	2nd	3rd	4th	Highest 10%
Panama	2.0	6.3	11.6	20.3	42.1
Hungary	10.9	14.8	18.0	22.0	20.8
France	5.6	11.8	17.2	23.5	26.1

35

Economic Growth

Chapter Objectives

After mastering the material in this chapter, you will be able to:

1. Discuss the meaning and significance of economic growth.
2. Explain why small differences in growth rates lead to large differences in outcomes.
3. Evaluate the role of saving in generating economic growth.
4. Describe the relationship between population growth and economic growth.
5. Discuss how public policy affects economic growth.
6. Discuss the contribution of factors such as technology to U.S. economic growth.

We've got to grow this economy.
President Bill Clinton

What's Ahead

Is economic growth really all that important? The best way to answer that is to imagine life without growth—to imagine that we didn't have the gains growth brings.

For starters, try dividing your current income by 6 and imagining what your life would be like. Think about the kind of housing you could afford, the size of your entertainment budget, whether you could still afford school. That will give you an idea of life a century ago, when average incomes, adjusted for inflation, were about one-sixth what they are today—and when people had far smaller homes, they rarely had electricity in those homes, and only a tiny percentage of the population could even consider a college education.

To get a more recent perspective, consider how growth over the past half-century has changed living standards. When World War II came to an end in 1945, the United States was the world's richest nation. But if households then were rich, subsequent economic growth has made them far richer. Average per capita real disposable personal income has more than doubled since then. Indeed, the average household income in 1945, which must have seemed lofty then, was barely above what we now define as the poverty line for a household of four, even after adjusting for inflation. Economic growth during the last half-century has dramatically boosted our standard of living—and our standard of what it takes to get by.

One gauge of rising living standards is housing. A half-century ago, most families didn't own homes. Today, about two-thirds do. Those homes have gotten a lot bigger: new homes built today are about twice the size of new homes built 50 years ago. Some household appliances we now consider basic were luxuries in the period immediately after World War II. By 1950, just 12 percent of households had a television set. Today, there are far more television sets than households!

Economic growth has brought gains in other areas as well. We're able to afford more schooling. In 1950, the median number of years of school completed by adults age 25 or over was 6.8—today it's just over 12. We live longer. A baby born in 1950 had a life expectancy of 68 years. A baby born today has an expected life of 76 years.

Of course, economic growth is no panacea. Americans today worry about the rising level of violence in society, about environmental degradation, about what seems to be a loss of basic values. But while it's easy to be dismayed about many aspects of modern life, we can surely be grateful for our material wealth. Our affluence gives us the opportunity to grapple with some of our most difficult problems—and to enjoy a range of choices that people only a few decades ago could not have imagined.

In this chapter, we'll study the economic growth that has made our present standard of living possible. We'll explore the forces that determine a nation's growth rate and examine the prospects for growth in the future. This chapter considers growth in developed economies; the next chapter examines the problem of the economic development of poor countries.

The Nature and Significance of Economic Growth

Economic growth is certainly important. Politicians typically list it as among their main objectives. News reports regularly discuss how fast the economy is growing. But just what do we mean by "growth"? And how does economic growth translate into changes in standards of living?

Natural Real GDP and Economic Growth

We often hear that the economy grew at a certain rate in the last quarter, or that it is expected to grow at a particular rate during the next year. Such reports suggest that economic growth occurs whenever real GDP increases.

But economists define economic growth somewhat differently. To them, quarter-to-quarter or even year-to-year changes say little about growth. Such fluctuations are typically short run in nature; they are the stuff of the analysis of changes in aggregate demand and short-run aggregate supply. Such changes have no lasting impact on incomes. In the long run, economic activity moves toward its natural level, and it's that level that is the focus of the study of economic growth. Economists define **economic growth** as the process through which the economy's natural level of real GDP is increased.

There are three key elements in this definition of economic growth. First, growth is a *process.* It isn't a single event; rather, it's an unfolding series of events. Second, we define growth in terms of the economy's *ability* to produce goods and services, as indicated by its natural level of output. And third, of course, growth suggests that the ability to produce goods and services is rising. A discussion of economic growth is thus a discussion of the series of events that increase the economy's ability to produce goods and services.

Economic growth is the process through which the economy's natural level of real GDP is increased.

Exhibit 35-1 shows the record of economic growth for the U.S. economy since 1895. The graph shows annual levels of actual and natural real GDP. We

EXHIBIT 35-1

A Century of Economic Growth

Natural real GDP by 1995 was more than 22 times its level a century earlier. Over the past century, actual real GDP has fluctuated about that natural level.

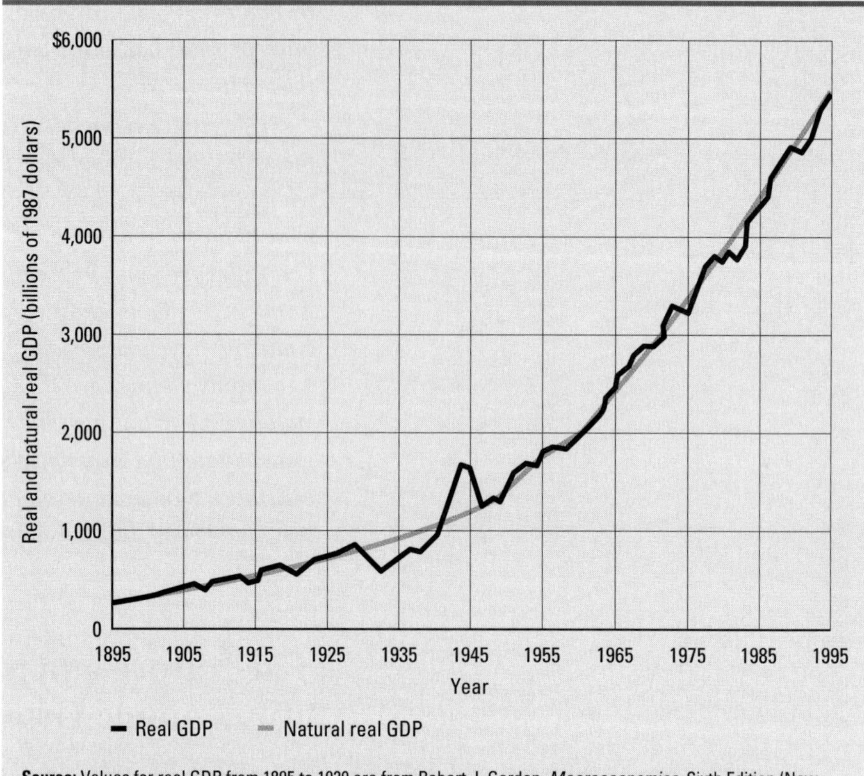

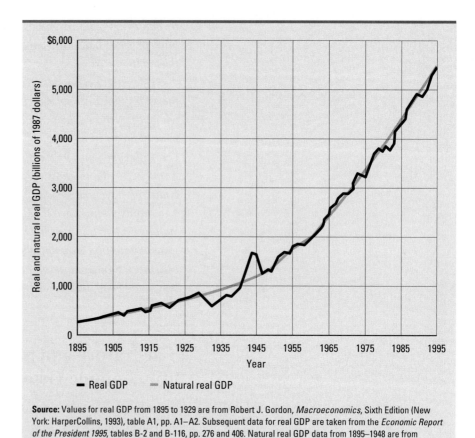

Source: Values for real GDP from 1895 to 1929 are from Robert J. Gordon, *Macroeconomics*, Sixth Edition (New York: HarperCollins, 1993), table A1, pp. A1–A2. Subsequent data for real GDP are taken from the *Economic Report of the President 1995*, tables B-2 and B-116, pp. 276 and 406. Natural real GDP data from 1895–1948 are from Gordon; subsequent observations are provided by the Congressional Budget Office.

see that the economy has experienced dramatic growth over the past century; natural GDP has soared more than 22-fold. The exhibit also reminds us of a central theme of our analysis of macroeconomics: real GDP fluctuates about its natural level.

Although real GDP fluctuates around its natural level, economists often measure the rate of economic growth by using actual values of real GDP. This approach is convenient, but it can lead to misleading interpretations of the record of economic growth. That's because actual values of real GDP are affected not just by changes in the natural level of output but by cyclical fluctuations about that level of output. Exhibit 35-2 suggests the difficulty. Suppose a hypothetical economy's natural level of real GDP is rising 2.5 percent per year. That path of growth over a 20-year period is shown by the heavy line; the lighter line shows a typical path of the cyclical ups and downs of actual real GDP.

Given our definition of economic growth, we would say that the economy depicted in Exhibit 35-2 grew at a 2.5 percent annual rate throughout the period. If we use actual values of real GDP, however, we may obtain quite different interpretations. Consider, for example, the first decade of this period: it began with a real GDP of $900 billion and a recessionary gap, and it ended in year 10 with a real GDP of $1,408 billion and an inflationary gap. If we record growth as the annual rate of change between these levels, we find an annual rate of growth of 3.5 percent—a rather impressive performance.

Now consider the second decade shown in Exhibit 35-2. It began in year 10, and it ended in year 20 with a recessionary gap. If we measure the growth rate over that period by looking at beginning and ending values of actual real GDP, we compute an annual growth rate of 0.5 percent. Viewed in this perspective, performance in the first decade is spectacular while performance in the second is dismal. But these figures depend on the starting and ending points we select; the actual growth rate was 2.5 percent throughout the period.

By measuring economic growth as the rate of increase in natural real GDP, we avoid such problems. One simple way to do this is to select years in which the economy was operating at full employment and then to compute the annual rate of change between those years. The result is an estimate of the rate at which natural real GDP increased over the period in question. For the economy shown in Exhibit 35-2, for example, we see that real GDP equaled its natural level in years 5 and 15. Real GDP in year 5 was $1,131, and real GDP in year 15 was $1,448. The annual rate of change between these two years was 2.5 percent. If we have estimates of natural levels of real GDP, of course, we can simply compute annual rates of change between any two years.

EXHIBIT 35-2

Cyclical Change Versus Growth

The use of actual values of real GDP to measure growth can give misleading results. Here, an economy's natural real GDP (shown by the green line) grows at a steady rate of 2.5 percent per year, with actual values of real GDP fluctuating about that trend. If we measure growth in the first 10 years as the annual rate of change between beginning and ending values of real GDP, we get a growth rate of 3.5 percent. The rate for the second decade is 0.5 percent. Growth estimates based on changes in real GDP are affected by cyclical changes that do not represent economic growth.

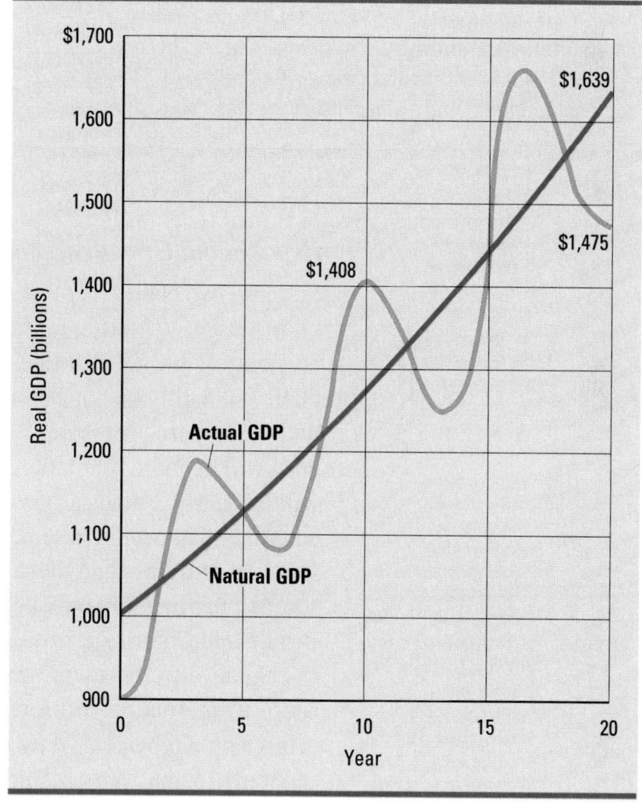

The Rule of 72 and Differences in Growth Rates

The Case in Point on the next page suggests a startling fact: the 3.5 percent growth rate that prevailed in the 1950s and 1960s began slowing in the 1970s, and natural real GDP has grown at only a 2.4 percent rate during the 1980s and 1990s. Does a 1.1 percentage point drop in the rate make much difference? It does; to see why, let's investigate what happens when a variable grows at a particular percentage rate.

Case in Point Presidents and Economic Growth

Presidents are often judged by the rate at which the economy grew while they were in office. This test is unfair on two counts. First, a president has little to do with the forces that determine growth. And second, such tests simply compute the annual rate of growth over the course of a presidential term. They can thus be affected by cyclical factors. A president who comes in when the economy is down and goes out with the economy up will look like an economic star; a president with the bad luck to reverse those circumstances will seem like a dud. Here are annual rates of change in real GDP for each of the postwar presidents, together with rates of economic growth, measured as the annual rate of change in natural GDP.

The presidents' economic records, measured as the rate at which real GDP rose during their terms, are clearly affected by luck. Presidents Truman, Kennedy, and Reagan, for example, began their terms when the economy had a recessionary gap and ended them with an inflationary gap. Real GDP thus rose much faster than natural GDP during their presidencies. The Eisenhower, Nixon, and Bush administrations each started with an inflationary gap and ended with a recessionary gap, thus recording rates of GDP increase below the rate of gain in natural GDP. Only Jimmy Carter, who came to office and left it with recessionary gaps, presided over equivalent rates of increase in actual versus natural real GDP.

The growth rates for natural GDP show a marked slowing in the 1970s and 1980s. That slowing, as we'll see, is important. We'll investigate the reasons for it later in this chapter.

President	Term	Annual increase in real GDP	Growth rate
Truman	1949–1952	5.7%	4.2%
Eisenhower	1953–1960	2.4	3.5
Kennedy-Johnson	1961–1968	4.5	3.5
Nixon-Ford	1969–1976	2.4	3.3
Carter	1977–1980	2.8	2.8
Reagan	1981–1988	2.8	2.4
Bush	1989–1992	1.5	2.4
Clinton	1993–	4.0*	2.4

* The figure for the Clinton administration records the annual rate of growth through the first half of 1995.

Exponential Growth and Natural GDP

Suppose two economies with equal populations start out at the same level of real GDP but grow at different rates. Economy A grows at a rate of 3.5 percent, and economy B grows at a rate of 2.4 percent. After a year, the difference in real GDP will hardly be noticeable. After a decade, however, real GDP in economy A will be 11 percent greater than in economy B. Over longer periods, the difference will be more dramatic. After 100 years, for example, income in economy A will be nearly 3 times as great as in economy B. If population growth in the two countries has been the same, the people of economy A will have a far higher standard of living than those in economy B. The difference in real GDP per person will be roughly equivalent to the difference that exists today between Great Britain and Colombia.

Small differences in growth rates create large differences in incomes because of the nature of growth. An economy growing at a 3.5 percent rate increases by 3.5 percent of its initial value in the first year. In the second year, the economy increases by 3.5 percent of that new, higher value. In the third year, it increases by 3.5 percent of a still higher value. When something grows at a given percentage rate, it experiences **exponential growth.** A variable that grows exponentially follows a path such as those given by the blue and green curves in Exhibits 35-1 and 35-2. These curves become steeper over time because the growth rate is applied to an ever larger base.

Inflation represents another form of exponential growth. As prices rise at a particular percentage rate, they grow exponentially. In Chapter 22, we saw that when a variable grows exponentially it doubles over fixed intervals of time. The doubling time is given by the rule of 72, which states that a variable's approximate doubling time equals 72 divided by the growth rate, stated as a whole num-

Exponential growth occurs when a variable grows at a given percentage rate.

ber. If the level of income were increasing at a 9 percent rate, for example, its doubling time would be roughly 72/9, or 8 years.[1]

Let's apply this concept of a doubling time to the reduction in the U.S. growth rate. Had the U.S. economy continued to grow at a 3.5 percent rate after 1970, then its natural level of real GDP would have doubled roughly every 20 years ($72/3.5) \cong 20$). That means natural GDP would have doubled by 1990, would double again by 2010, and would double again by 2030. Real GDP in 2030 would thus be 8 times as great as its 1970 level. Growing at a 2.4 percent rate, however, natural real GDP doubles only every 30 years ($72/2.4 = 30$). It would take until 2000 to double once from its 1970 level, and it would double once more by 2030. Natural real GDP in 2030 would thus be 4 times its 1970 level if the economy grew at a 2.4 percent rate (versus 8 times its 1970 level if it grew at a 3.5 percent rate). The 1.1 percent difference in growth rates produces a 100 percent difference in the natural level of real GDP by 2030. The different growth paths implied by these growth rates are illustrated in Exhibit 35-3.

EXHIBIT 35-3

Growth Rates and Growth Paths

The chart suggests the significance in the long run of a small change in the growth rate of real GDP. We begin in 1970, when real GDP equaled $2,873.9 billion. If real GDP grew at an annual rate of 3.5 percent from that year, it would double roughly every 20 years: in 1990, 2010, and 2030. Growth at a 2.4 percent rate, however, implies doubling every 30 years: in 2000 and 2030. By 2030, the 3.5 percent growth rate leaves real GDP at twice the level that would be achieved by 2.4 percent growth.

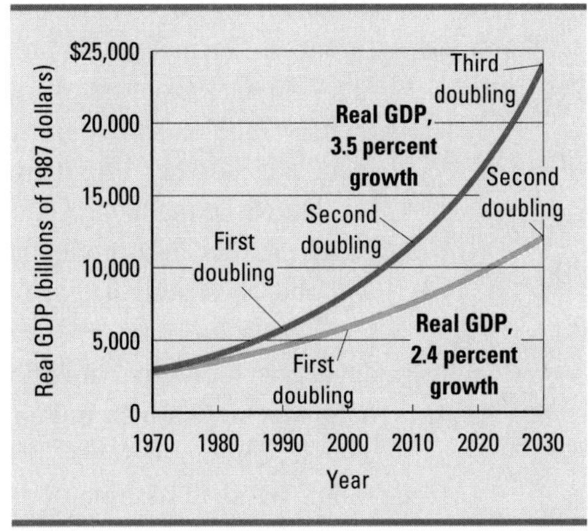

Growth and the Standard of Living

The model of aggregate demand and aggregate supply suggests two categories of forces that shift the economy's long-run aggregate supply curve to the right and thus produce economic growth. While both imply increases in the economy's natural level of real GDP, one improves living standards while the other may reduce them.

Increasing Productivity and Growth

Suppose something happens to increase the productivity of labor in an economy. The production function shifts upward; this is shown as a shift from PF_1 to PF_2 in Panel (a) of Exhibit 35-4. This could result from an increase in capital, whether physical capital such as new factories or intellectual capital such as new technology. It could also result from an increase in human capital or an increase in the availability of natural resources.

[1] Notice the use of the words "roughly" and "approximately." The actual value of an income of $1,000 growing at rate r for a period of n years is $\$1,000 \times (1 + r)^n$. After 8 years of growth at a 9 percent rate, income would thus be $\$1,000(1 + 0.09)^8 = \$1,992.56$. The rule of 72 predicts that its value will be $2,000. The rule of 72 gives an approximation, not an exact measure, of the impact of exponential growth.

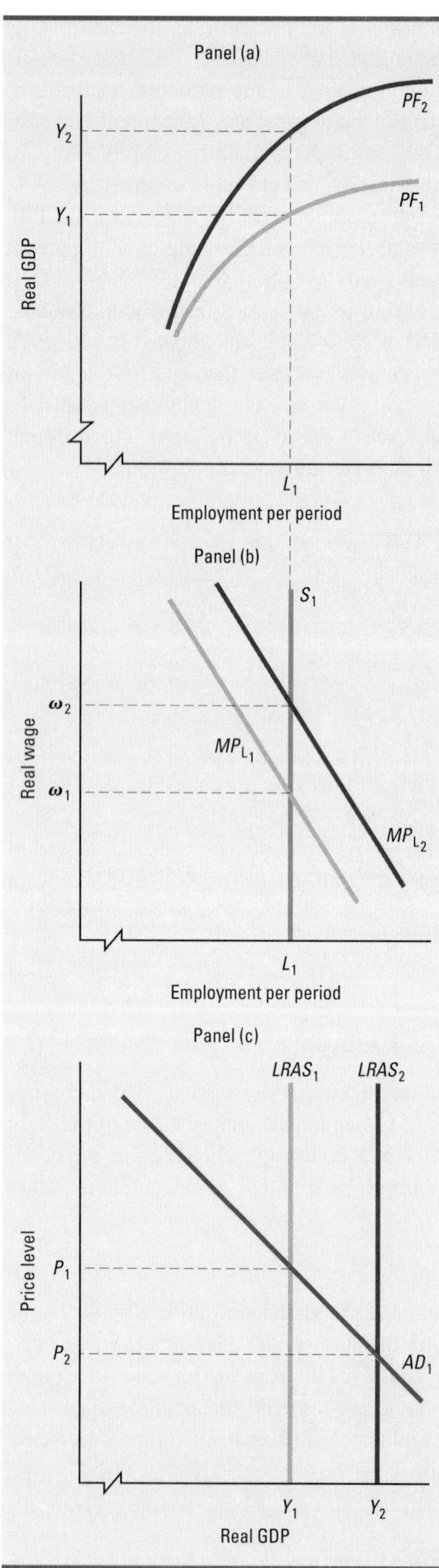

EXHIBIT 35-4

A Shift in the Production Function Produces Growth with a Higher Standard of Living

Economic growth implies a shift of the long-run aggregate supply curve to the right. If such a shift is caused by an upward shift in the production function, as in Panel (a), it improves living standards in the economy. The shift to PF_2 moves the marginal product of labor curve in Panel (b) to MP_{L_2} and thus boosts the real wage to ω_2. The economy's natural level of output rises to Y_2. The increase in long-run aggregate supply to $LRAS_2$ reduces the price level to P_2 in Panel (c).

The new production function PF_2 is steeper than PF_1, so the curve that shows its slope, the marginal product of labor curve, shifts as well. We see in Panel (b) that the curve shifts to the right to MP_{L_2}. We learned in Chapter 26 that the marginal product of labor curve can be interpreted as the demand curve for labor. The increase in the productivity of labor thus increases the demand for labor. Given a fixed supply of labor S_1, the increase in demand for labor to MP_{L_2} increases the real wage from ω_1 to ω_2. Notice that the natural level of employment does not increase; it remains at L_1.

Output at the natural level of employment rises from Y_1 to Y_2, as shown in Panel (a). Because production of this output requires that the real wage equal ω_2, and because that real wage is the ratio of the nominal wage to the price level, the equilibrium real wage can be achieved at any price level. The long-run aggregate supply curve is thus a vertical line at the economy's natural level of output, as determined in Panel (c). We see in Panel (c) that the long-run aggregate supply curve shifts to $LRAS_2$. Given the aggregate demand curve AD_1, which we shall assume does not shift, the price level falls to P_2 while output rises in the long run to the new natural level Y_2.

An upward shift in the production function thus boosts the real wage and increases the quantity of goods and services produced by a fixed number of workers. It thus improves living standards. Growth caused by a shift in the production function thus tends to enhance the material standard of living.

Growth and the Supply of Labor

Exhibit 35-5 shows growth that results from an increase in the supply of labor. An increase in the quantity of labor supplied also shifts the long-run aggregate supply curve to the right. This shift, however, could reduce living standards.

We begin in Panel (b) with an increase in the supply of labor to S_2. This increase could be caused by a rise in population or an increased desire to work; either more people would supply their efforts, or existing workers could supply a higher quantity of labor. The higher supply of labor lowers the real wage to ω_2 and raises the natural level of employment to L_2. The higher level of employment boosts the natural level of output to Y_2 in Panel (a). Notice, however, that the increase in real GDP achieved is relatively small. That's because each additional worker adds less to total output; the marginal product curve is downward sloping. Once again, we see in Panel (c) that the long-run aggregate supply curve shifts to $LRAS_2$, reducing the price level. Workers, however, emerge with lower real wages.

The increased supply of labor could reduce living standards. An increase in the population, taken by itself, would reduce the equilibrium real wage and tend

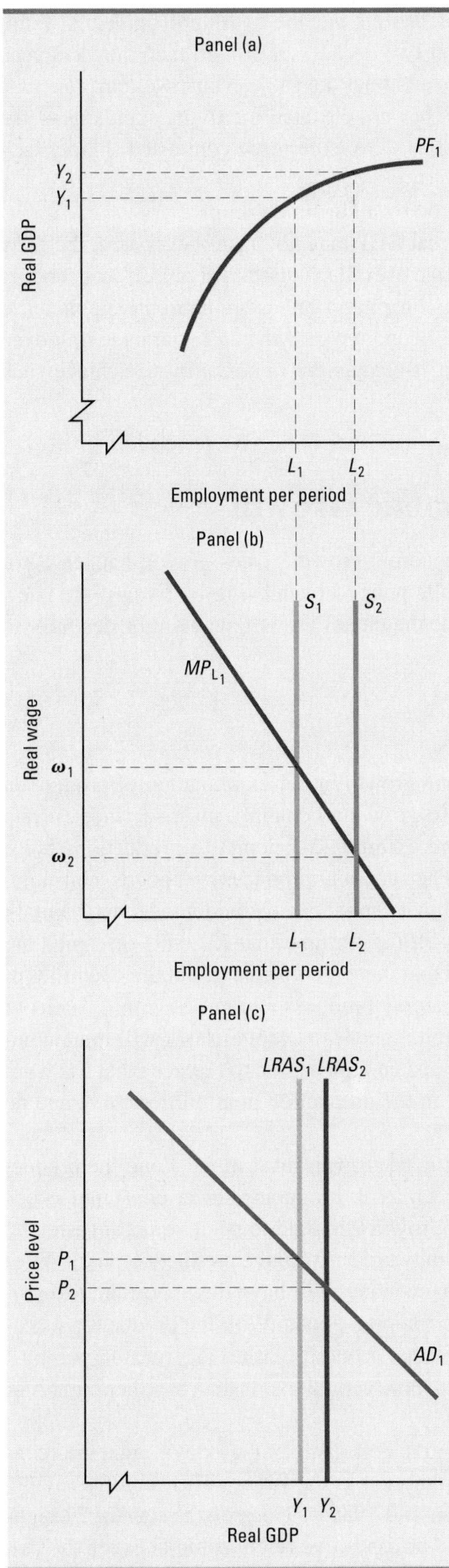

EXHIBIT 35-5

An Increase in the Supply of Labor Produces Economic Growth

An increase in the supply of labor to S_2 in Panel (b) lowers the real wage to ω_2. The natural level of employment rises to Y_2 in Panel (a), shifting the long-run aggregate supply curve to $LRAS_2$ in Panel (c).

to reduce per capita income. If the existing population supplies more labor, however, living standards could improve. Per capita output would rise despite the reduction in the real wage.

The simplest way to determine whether growth has tended to improve living standards is to examine data on growth in per capita real GDP. This growth rate is found by subtracting the population growth rate from the rate of GDP growth over a particular period. This calculation is done for Israel for the period 1980–1993 in Exhibit 35-6. Israel's GDP during the period grew at a 4.1 percent annual rate. Its population increased at a rate of 2.3 percent, reducing growth in per capita GDP to a rate of 1.8 percent.

Growth and the Distribution of Income

Another factor that influences the way in which economic growth affects living standards is the distribution of income. Suppose that an economy's per capita GDP grows quite rapidly, but only 10 percent of its people experience large gains in income while the other 90 percent suffer a small loss. The economy has achieved economic growth, but this growth has not improved living standards in the economy—for most people, the standard of living has fallen.

We saw in Chapter 34, for example, that changes in the distribution of income since 1968 have left the families at the bottom of the income distribution in the United States with a smaller share of total income. With slower growth in

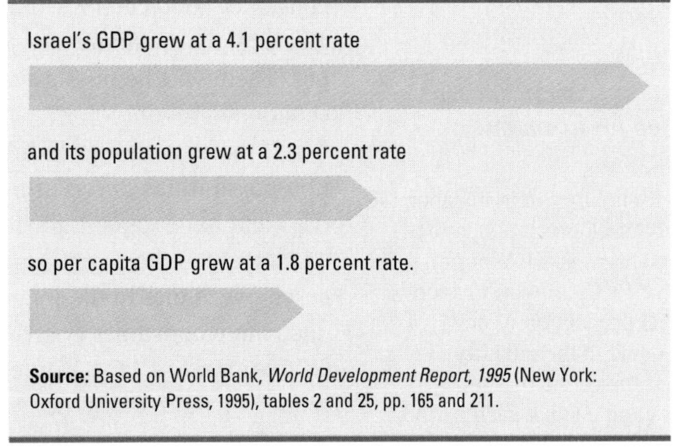

Israel's GDP grew at a 4.1 percent rate
and its population grew at a 2.3 percent rate
so per capita GDP grew at a 1.8 percent rate.

Source: Based on World Bank, *World Development Report, 1995* (New York: Oxford University Press, 1995), tables 2 and 25, pp. 165 and 211.

EXHIBIT 35-6

Growth in GDP Versus Growth in Per Capita GDP in Israel

The growth rate in per capita GDP equals the growth rate in GDP minus the rate of population growth. From 1980 to 1993, for example, Israel's real GDP grew at an annual rate of 4.1 percent while its population grew at a rate of 2.3 percent. The annual rate of increase in per capita real GDP was thus 1.8 percent.

Checklist

- Economic growth implies a shift to the right in long-run aggregate supply.
- The growth rate is measured as the rate of increase in the natural level of real GDP.
- Growth at a given percentage rate implies a doubling in output over fixed intervals of time.
- Economic growth can boost living standards if there is growth in per capita real GDP and if the gains are distributed among various income groups.

income and a smaller share of the economic pie, the bottom 40 percent of families actually emerged worse off after two decades of growth than they had been in 1968. The middle 20 percent stayed about the same. Thus, we may conclude that the growth of the last 25 years has not elevated the living standards of the majority of people in the United States. This experience contrasted sharply with the economic growth of the previous two decades, when growth occurred at a faster rate and its benefits were shared by all income groups.

Although growth in per capita real GDP may not benefit everyone, it clearly creates the opportunity to improve the overall standard of living. If an economy produces more goods and services per capita, it can use redistributive policies to ensure that benefits are widespread. Economic growth can't guarantee improved living standards for all people, but it creates the opportunity to achieve such gains.

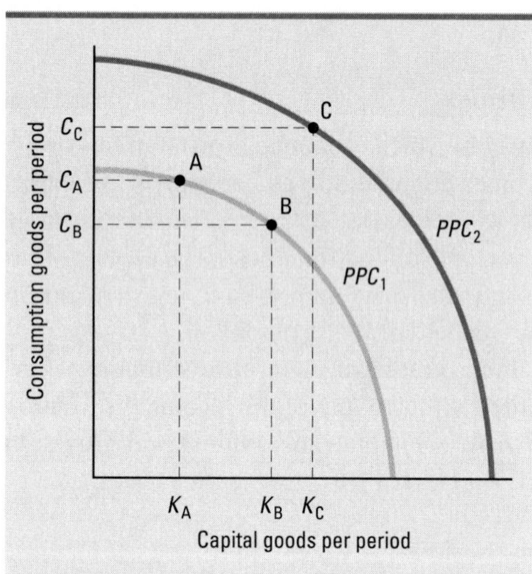

EXHIBIT 35-7

Sacrificing Consumption for Economic Growth

Consider an economy with no growth in its labor force or in natural resources. Depreciation equals K_A. If the economy produces at point A on production possibilities curve PPC_1, it won't experience economic growth; its production of new capital goods K_A is just equal to the quantity of capital that depreciates. If the economy moves to point B, it will add to its capital stock each period because its production of capital goods exceeds the quantity of capital that wears out. It will, however, sacrifice production of consumption goods. The gains in capital will shift the production possibilities curve outward. With the curve PPC_2, for example, the economy could operate at point C, producing more consumer goods and more capital goods than at point B.

Determinants of Economic Growth

How does an economy achieve economic growth? Does growth happen automatically, or is there a role for public policy in achieving it? Even if we knew how to achieve growth or to increase the rate of growth, would it be desirable to do so?

Saving and Growth

We saw one of the keys to economic growth in our examination of production possibilities curves in Chapter 2. To grow, an economy must sacrifice current consumption for future consumption. Exhibit 35-7 depicts a production choice we first encountered in Chapter 2. The economy produces two goods, consumption goods and capital goods (recall that capital can include intellectual capital). Its production possibilities curve is PPC_1. Assume that K_A units of capital are lost each period to depreciation and that there are no changes in the quantities of labor or natural resources. If the economy produces at point A, with C_A units of consumer goods and K_A units of capital goods, its capital stock will remain unchanged; the economy is producing just enough capital to replace what has worn out. There will be no outward shift in the production possibilities curve and no economic growth.

If the economy in Exhibit 35-7 is to grow, it must move along the production possibilities curve to a point such as B, producing fewer consumer goods (C_B) and more capital goods (K_B). Growth will lead to positive net investment, an increase in the capital stock, and outward shifts in the production possibilities curve over time. In the long run, the economy will have the opportunity to produce more consumer goods and more capital goods. With the production possibilities curve PPC_2, for example, the economy could operate at point C, producing more consumer goods and more capital goods than at either point A or point B.

For economic growth, we must give up consumption today so that the economy can achieve even greater consumption in the future. This requires saving. Exhibit 35-8 shows 1993 saving rates and 1980–1993 growth rates for 22 high-income economies. There appears to be a positive relationship between the two variables. Higher saving rates contribute to higher rates of capital formation and higher rates of economic growth.

EXHIBIT 35-8

Saving Rates and Growth Rates

The chart shows saving rates in 1993 versus growth rates in per capita GDP over the period 1980–1993 for 22 high-income economies. There appears to be a positive relationship between the two variables.

Source: *World Development Report 1995,* tables 2 and 9, pp. 165 and 179.

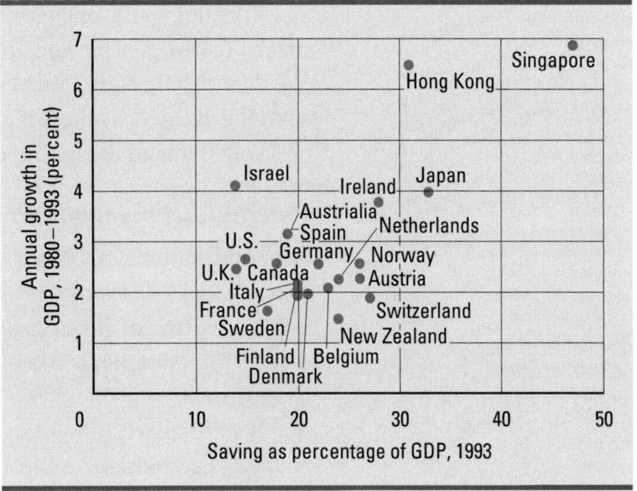

Other Determinants of Economic Growth

Although saving plays an important role in allowing the investment that promotes economic growth, other factors are crucial to the process of growth as well. The most important of these appear to be technological change and increases in human capital. This section examines these two factors as well as the roles of external economies in production, natural resources, and fiscal and monetary policy.

Technological Change

Technological change—the discovery and implementation of new ways to produce goods and services and the invention of new goods and services to produce—has always been a driving force in economic growth. The faster the pace of technological change, the greater the rate of growth.

Technological change is a kind of intellectual investment. It adds to intellectual capital and thus to the ability to produce goods and services. Like any production of capital goods, it requires that resources be devoted not to the production of goods for immediate consumption but to the ability to produce goods and services in the future—it requires saving.

What's ahead for technology? By its very nature, technological change is difficult to predict; it means doing things tomorrow that we don't know how to do today. Some economists argue that the pace of technological change is likely to slow. They suggest, in effect, that we've discovered most of the things we're likely to discover. Others see the opposite in store. They argue that in the next few decades, the development of more direct applications of computers in production processes will dramatically increase output. They see a wave of new advances analogous to the industrial revolution of the nineteenth century.

Human Capital

Investment in human capital shifts the production function upward by improving the skills of the work force. It is a way of increasing output by increasing not the quantity of labor but its quality. Investments in human capital thus affect real wages and living standards in the same way as an increase in physical capital. Indeed, recent research suggests that human capital is as important as physical capital in determining a nation's standard of living.

Technological change, by generating changes in the skills workers need, makes investment in human capital both more important and more productive. We saw in Chapter 23 that the wage gap between college-educated and high-school-educated workers almost tripled during the 1980s; this gap reflects the increasing demand technological change places on human capital.

External Economies in Production

Economists in recent years have focused on **external economies in production** as a source of economic growth. Such economies occur when expanded production in one sector lowers costs in another. The expansion of a local printing industry, for example, is likely to cut printing prices and thus lower costs for other local firms.

A particularly important aspect of external economies lies in technological change. Economists argue that the expansion of one sector, for example, the semiconductor industry, is likely to spawn technological developments in other sectors. Thus, public sector encouragement of an industry may stimulate economic growth.

Whether government policy can actually achieve such gains is, of course, an open question. But the potential for doing so opens up another area for consideration of government involvement in economic growth.

Natural Resources

A change in the availability of natural resources acts as an exogenous force that shifts the production function. We saw in Chapter 26 that an event such as an increase in the price of oil shifts the long-run aggregate supply curve to the left. Changes in natural resource prices can thus affect economic growth. The oil-price increases of the 1970s, for example, are cited by some economists as a major reason for the slowing in the rate of economic growth that began in that decade.

Fiscal and Monetary Policy

Fiscal and monetary policy can affect the level of economic activity in the short run. Do they have any impact in the long run?

One concern about the use of expansionary fiscal policy lies in the crowding out problem we discussed in Chapter 31. An expansionary fiscal policy tends to raise interest rates and thus tends to reduce investment. That reduces the capital stock and thus slows economic growth. Expansionary fiscal policy could stimulate economic activity by increasing aggregate demand, but it could also act to reduce gains in long-run aggregate supply.

Some economists argue that fiscal policy can be used to enhance growth. The Reagan administration's tax policies during the 1980s, for example, were intended to encourage investment and generate rightward shifts in long-run aggregate supply. Special tax subsidies for research and development spending by firms represent a similar attempt.

But do such incentives for growth-generating activities actually stimulate growth? The issue is controversial. Proponents note the acceleration in growth of real GDP during the 1980s, an acceleration that was stimulated by investment gains. Critics, however, cite the failure of the Reagan administration's policies to stimulate economic growth as defined in this chapter—the growth rate in natural real GDP continued to decline during the 1980s.

Many economists argue that government investment policy affects the rate of economic growth. They suggest that government spending for the develop-

External economies in production occur when expanded production in one sector leads to lower costs in another.

Case in Point: Daydreaming and Technological Change

Can an imaginary day at the beach boost the rate of technological change? Advocates of creativity training, an effort to teach workers to be more creative, argue that it can.

One in three U.S. firms now offers creativity training to its employees. The tactics range from brainstorming in small groups to encouraging workers to take some time to daydream—to take themselves mentally to a peaceful spot, perhaps a secluded beach or a quiet stream, and let their thoughts run free.

A recent experiment with creativity training at Federal Express targeted 350 systems analysts and computer programmers who design and maintain the complex computer system that tracks 1.5 million shipments every day. Employees were introduced to specific creativity techniques, then asked to put them to use and to track the gains they had made.

Brainstorming sessions produced new ways of searching through computer files for specific data, improvements to the system's security, and a much cheaper way of dealing with computer system failures. Employees using the daydreaming approach came up with a technique for integrating information about system changes into the system itself, replacing the costly printing of manuals. All in all, the experiment produced a threefold increase in the rate at which employees developed and implemented new approaches to managing the company's database system.

"Creativity training is a way of teaching people to put their intuition to work in new ways—ways that pay off for a company's bottom line. Companies have found that investment in creativity training has a rate of return many times as great as traditional research and development techniques. As more companies become better at using it, I think we'll see enormous gains," says J. Daniel Couger, a professor of information systems at the University of Colorado at Colorado Springs.

Sources: J. Daniel Couger, Patrick Flynn, and Doris Hellyer, "Enhancing the Creativity of Reengineering," *Information Systems Management* (Spring 1994): 24–29 and personal interviews.

ment of better highways and other transportation facilities—the nation's infrastructure—plays a key role in economic growth. They argue that the decline in public sector investment that began in the early 1970s played a role in the ensuing slowdown in economic growth. That's not a universal view; other economists insist that declining government investment had no role in the slowdown.

Another controversial issue raised by economists working on the theory of economic growth concerns stabilization policy. The model of aggregate demand and aggregate supply suggests that the economy moves to its natural level of GDP and that this level is not affected by changes in aggregate demand or in short-run aggregate supply. Some economists argue, however, that a recessionary gap robs unemployed workers of some of their skills and thus reduces their human capital and their productivity. **Hysteresis** is the tendency for temporary events to have long-lasting consequences. In the case of labor, if a period of unemployment permanently reduces a worker's skills, then a recessionary gap produces a downward shift in the production function.

The concept of hysteresis is quite plausible, but the issue of whether a recession significantly affects the economy's natural GDP is controversial. If economists who argue that recession has long-term effects are right, then stabilization policy is very important. If a recession imposes not just a temporary loss of income but a permanent loss in a nation's ability to produce goods and services, fiscal and monetary efforts to close recessionary gaps are an issue not just for the short run but for the long run as well.

Hysteresis is the tendency of temporary events to have long-lasting consequences.

Case in Point: Explaining the Great Slowdown

We saw earlier in this chapter that the rate of economic growth that held in the 1950s and 1960s slowed quite sharply in the 1970s and 1980s; there's been no indication of an acceleration of growth in the 1990s. We've also seen that the slowdown has had and will continue to have a dramatic impact on living standards. What caused it?

As we consider possible culprits, we must keep one thing in mind: the slowdown was a global phenomenon. Consider, for example, the fate of the Group of Seven, an organization of the world's leading industrialized economies. Growth in per capita output has slowed in every one.

Country	Growth in Per Capita Output (% per year)	
	1948–1972	1972–1993
Canada	2.9	2.0
France	4.3	2.0
Germany	5.7	1.9
Italy	4.9	2.6
Japan	8.2	3.2
United Kingdom	2.4	2.0
United States	2.2	1.9

The slowdown clearly can't be explained by events in any one country. Economists have identified a number of factors as possible causes of this slowdown, including the following:

- Higher oil prices. Sharp boosts in oil prices in 1973–1974 and again in 1979 depressed incomes in countries that weren't exporters of oil.
- The baby boom generation began to join the work force in the 1970s. This increased the size of the labor force, and because these workers were young, the average level of experience and thus of human capital of the labor force dropped.
- Government regulation and redistributive efforts have, in general, become more extensive. Such policies may be beneficial for other reasons, but they are likely to reduce the rate of increase in productivity and thus of economic growth.
- Higher inflation. The industrialized countries have generally experienced higher inflation since the early 1970s. If Mr. Greenspan's view that price stability contributes to growth is correct, these higher rates could have reduced growth rates.
- The world is running out of ideas. Growth rates will continue to drop as technological progress slows down.

With the exception of the running-out-of-ideas argument, none of these explanations suggests that the slowdown in growth will be sustained. Oil prices have, in real terms, fallen back below their levels at the beginning of the 1970s. The baby boom generation is no longer young and inexperienced. Most industrialized countries are seeking to scale back the scope of regulation and to limit their redistributive efforts. Finally, inflation rates are coming under control; they fell sharply in the 1980s and have continued to drop. If the slowdown continues through the rest of the century, the first four explanations will seem less plausible, and economists will give greater credence to suggestions that something has slowed the rate of technological change. If growth accelerates, then the first four explanations would be broadly consistent with experience, and the running-out-of ideas argument would be rejected. We'll have to wait and see.

Source: Angus Maddison, *Phases of Capitalist Development* (New York: Oxford University Press, 1982); World Development Report 1995, tables 2 and 25, pp. 165, 211.

Fed Chairman Alan Greenspan has suggested a contrary view, arguing that stabilization efforts—which, as we've seen, have become largely the province of the Fed in recent years—are unimportant in the long run. He asserts that the most effective contribution that stabilization policy can make to economic growth is to preserve price stability.

Checklist ✓

- Growth requires saving and thus the sacrifice of current consumption.
- Higher saving rates appear to generate higher growth rates.
- Other determinants of the growth rate for an economy include the rate of technological change, gains in human capital, the generation of external economies in production, changes in the stock of natural resources, and fiscal and monetary policy.

A Look Back—And a Look Ahead

We defined growth as an increase in the economy's ability to produce goods and services, measured by the rate of increase in natural GDP. We saw that measuring the rate of increase in actual real GDP can confuse growth statistics by introducing elements of cyclical variation.

Growth is an exponential process. A variable increasing at a fixed percentage rate doubles over fixed intervals. The doubling time is approximated by the rule of 72. The exponential nature of growth means that small differences in growth rates have large effects over long periods of time. Per capita rates of increase in real GDP are found by subtracting the growth rate of the population from the growth rate of GDP.

Saving plays an important role in economic growth. When a society saves more of its output, it has more capital available for future production, so the rate of economic growth can rise. Saving thus promotes growth.

Changes in technology also play a role in economic growth. Other factors include monetary and fiscal policy, human capital, and natural resources. Advances in these other factors increase growth and improve living standards. A new theory of economic growth seeks to explain the determination and role of these other factors in economic growth.

In the next chapter, we'll turn to problems of growth facing the world's poorest countries. While many of the principles we've examined in this chapter apply to those countries, additional challenges complicate their growth process.

Terms and Concepts for Review

Economic growth

Exponential growth

External economies in production

Hysteresis

For Discussion

1. Suppose the people in a certain economy decide to stop saving and instead use all their income for consumption. Discuss the prospects for growth of such an economy.
2. Japan has a saving rate that is roughly twice that of the United States. Largely because of its greater saving rate, the Japanese economy has grown faster than the U.S. economy. Presumably, if the United States increased its saving rate to twice the Japanese level, U.S. growth would surpass the Japanese rate. Would that be a good idea?
3. Suppose an increase in air pollution causes capital to wear out more rapidly, doubling the rate of depreciation. How would this affect economic growth?
4. Some people worry that increases in the capital stock will bring about an economy in which everything is done by machine, with no jobs left for people. What does the aggregate demand and aggregate supply model predict?
5. China's annual rate of population growth fell from 1.8 percent during the 1970s to 1.4 percent for the period 1980–1992. The World Bank predicts that China's rate of population growth will average 1 percent in the 1990s. How do you think this will affect the rate of increase in real GDP? How will it affect the rate of increase in per capita real GDP?
6. Suppose technology stops changing. Explain the impact on economic growth.
7. Suppose a series of terrorist attacks destroys half the capital in the United States but does not affect the population. What will happen to the natural level of real GDP and to the real wage?
8. "Given the rate at which scientists are making new discoveries, we will soon reach the point that no further discoveries can be made. Economic growth will come to a stop." Discuss.

Problems

1. The population of the world in 1992 was 5.438 billion. It grew between 1980 and 1992 at an annual rate of 1.7 percent. Assume that it continues to grow at this rate. Compute the doubling time and estimate the world population in 2075.
2. Per capita GDP in the United States grew at an annual rate of 1.9 percent during the 1980s, while per capita GDP in Japan grew at an annual rate of 3.7 percent. Compute the doubling times. Per capita GDP was $22,130 in the United States in 1992; it was $20,160 in Japan. Assuming the same growth rates continue, what will the respective levels of per capita GDP be in these countries in 2030?
3. Two countries, A and B, have identical levels of real GDP per capita. In Country A, an increase in the capital stock increases the natural level of real GDP by 10 percent. Country B also experiences a 10 percent increase in its natural level of real GDP, but this increase is the result of an increase in its labor force. Illustrate and explain, using production functions and labor market analyses for the two countries, how these events are likely to affect living standards in the two economies.

36

Chapter Objectives

After mastering the material in this chapter, you will be able to:

1. Discuss the primary economic problems facing poor nations today.
2. Explain what economic development is.
3. Show how population growth and economic development affect each other.
4. Contrast some of the characteristics of nations that have achieved success in their development efforts and nations that have not.

The Problem of Economic Development

'Twixt nations rich and nations poor
A widening gap doth grow.
A widening gap in a shrinking world
Doth grudge and envy sow.
Don Paarlberg

What's Ahead

You're four years old. You live with your family in Lagos, the capital of Nigeria. You're poor. Very poor.

You and your father, mother, four brothers and sisters, and grandmother live in a shack with a dirt floor. It commands a rather nice view of the Gulf of Guinea to the south, but the amenities end there. Drinking water, which you're learning to help fetch, is badly polluted—so you're sick much of the time. As for sanitation, there isn't any in your neighborhood. You're also hungry. You think of the gnawing feeling in your stomach, the slight dizziness you always feel, as normal.

Your newest brother, who was born last month, just died of cholera. Your mother tried to get him to the clinic, but it was closed when your brother needed it. Your father's usual optimism has vanished—he talks of going east to Abuja to find work. He's given up finding a job here.

Your father worked in the peanut fields in the eastern part of the country for several years, but he lost his job. After some very tough years marked by ethnic violence, your family came to the city. You were born shortly after that—you've never known your father to have a regular job. Your mother has had better luck finding work as a maid for some of the wealthy people, with real homes, across town.

You'll be old enough to start school next year, and you're looking forward to that. Your parents say you'll be fed there. But if you're like your older brothers and sisters, you won't go to school for more than a couple of years. Your family will need you to earn some money in the streets—begging, running errands, hustling.

You have no reason to think your life will ever get any better. Your own family's fortunes seem to have declined, not risen, all your life.

You can't know it, but you're not alone. Most of the world's population is poor. You're on the poor end even of that group, but there are billions who live pretty much the way you do. Poverty, desperate poverty, is the reality for most of the world's people.

In this chapter we'll take a look at the economies of poor countries like yours. We'll see that malnutrition, inadequate health care, high infant mortality, high unemployment, and low levels of education are the norm for a shockingly high fraction of the world's people.

The challenge of economic development is to find ways to achieve sustained economic growth in poor countries, to improve the living conditions of most of the world's people. It's an enormous task, one often marked by failure. But there have been successes. With those successes have come lessons that can guide us as we face what surely must be the most urgent of global tasks: economic development.

The Nature and Challenge of Economic Development

Throughout most of history, poverty has been the human condition. For most people life was and is, in the words of seventeenth-century English philosopher Thomas Hobbes, "nasty, brutish, and short." Only within the past 200 years have a handful of countries been able to break the chains of economic deprivation and poverty. Most nations have not.

Consider these facts:

- More than half of the world's people live in countries in which total per capita income is less than $695 per year.
- A baby born in a poor country is nine times more likely to die in its first year than is a baby born in a rich country.
- More than 40 percent of the people in low-income countries—and more than half of the women—are illiterate.
- Roughly one-fourth of the world's population does not have access to safe drinking water.[1]

Clearly, the high standards of living enjoyed by people in the world's developed economies are the global exception, not the rule. This chapter looks at the problem of improving the standard of living in poor countries.

Rich and Poor Nations

The World Bank classifies countries according to their levels of per capita GNP, an income measure similar to GDP. The categories in its 1995 report were as follows:

Low-income countries. These countries had per capita incomes of $695 or less in 1993. There were 45 countries in this category.

[1] Data on income, child mortality, and literacy are for 1993 and are taken from the World Bank, *World Development Report, 1995* (New York: Oxford University Press, 1995). The data on drinking water are from the United Nations Development Program, *Human Development Report 1992* (New York: Oxford University Press, 1992).

Middle-income countries. There were 62 countries with per capita incomes of more than $695 but less than $8,626.

High-income countries. There were 25 nations with per capita incomes of $8,626 or more.

Just 15 percent of the world's total population of more than 5.5 billion people lived in high-income countries in 1993. In the United States, per capita GNP totaled $24,740 in 1993. The average income of the other 85 percent of the world's people was less than one-twentieth the U.S. level. The World Bank converts GNP figures to dollars in two ways. One is to take GNP in a local currency

EXHIBIT 36-1

World Incomes

The table shows the World Bank's 1995 classifications for 132 nations. Nations whose per capita GNP in 1993 was $695 or less were classified as low income; those whose per capita GNP was from $696 to $8,626 were classified as middle income, and nations with higher levels of per capita GNP were classified as high income.

Low-Income Countries	GNP/Capita (1993 $s)	GNP/Capita (1993 International Dollars)
Mozambique	$ 90	$ 550
Tanzania	90	580
Ethiopia	100	—
Sierra Leone	150	750
Vietnam	170	—
Burundi	180	740
Uganda	180	900
Nepal	190	1,020
Malawi	200	690
Chad	210	720
Rwanda	210	740
Bangladesh	220	1,290
Madagascar	220	670
Guinea-Bissau	240	840
Kenya	270	1,290
Mali	270	520
Niger	270	780
Lao PDR	280	—
Burkina Faso	300	770
India	300	1,220
Nigeria	300	1,400
Albania	340	—
Nicaragua	340	1,900
Togo	340	1,000
Gambia	350	1,170
Zambia	380	1,040
Mongolia	390	2,020
Central African Republic	400	1,010
Benin	430	1,620
Ghana	430	1,970
Pakistan	430	2,170
Tajkikistan	470	1,380
China	490	2,330
Guinea	500	—
Mauritania	500	1,490
Zimbabwe	520	2,000
Georgia	580	1,750
Honduras	600	1,910
Sri Lanka	600	2,990
Cote d'Ivoire	630	1,400
Lesotho	650	1,620
Armenia	660	2,040
Egypt	660	3,780
Myanamar	—	—
Yemen	—	—
Average	$ 380	

Middle-Income Countries	GNP/Capita (1993 $s)	GNP/Capita (1993 International Dollars)
Azerbaijan	730	2,190
Indonesia	740	3,150
Senegal	750	1,650
Bolivia	760	2,420
Cameroon	820	2,100
Macedonia	820	—
Kyrgyz Republic	850	2,320
Philippines	850	2,670
Congo	950	2,440
Uzbekistan	970	2,510
Morocco	1,040	3,090
Moldova	1,060	2,870
Guatemala	1,100	3,350
Papua New Guinea	1,130	2,350
Bulgaria	1,140	4,100
Romania	1,140	2,800
Jordan	1,190	4,100
Ecuador	1,200	4,240
Dominican Republic	1,230	3,630
El Salvador	1,320	2,350
Lithuania	1,320	3,110
Colombia	1,400	5,490
Jamaica	1,440	3,000
Peru	1,490	3,220
Paraguay	1,510	3,390
Kazakhstan	1,560	3,710
Tunisia	1,720	4,780
Algeria	1,780	5,380
Namibia	1,820	3,790
Slovak Republic	1,950	6,290
Latvia	2,010	5,010
Thailand	2,110	6,260
Costa Rica	2,150	5,520
Ukraine	2,210	4,450
Poland	2,260	5,000
Russian Federation	2,340	5,050
Panama	2,600	5,840
Czech Republic	2,710	7,550
Botswana	2,790	5,160
Turkey	2,970	3,920
Iran	—	5,380
Venezuela	2,840	8,130
Belarus	2,870	6,240
Brazil	2,930	5,370

Less developed countries (LDCs) are those that are not among the high-income nations of the world.

and convert using the exchange rate. Another is to convert based on the purchasing power of the currencies; this is reported in "1993 International Dollars."

Nations in the low- and middle-income categories are often called **less developed countries (LDCs).** An LDC is thus a country that is not among the high-income nations of the world.

Exhibit 36-1 lists income levels for 132 nations in 1993. Per capita income levels of sparsely populated nations are not available, but rough estimates for them are incorporated in aggregate figures for low-, middle-, and high-income nations.

Middle-Income Countries	GNP/Capita (1993 $s)	GNP/Capita (1993 International Dollars)	High-Income Countries	GNP/Capita (1993 $s)	GNP/Capita (1993 International Dollars)
South Africa	$2,980	—	Portugal	9,130	10,710
Mauritius	3,030	12,420	New Zealand	12,600	16,040
Estonia	3,080	—	Ireland	13,000	13,490
Malaysia	3,140	7,930	Spain	13,590	13,510
Chile	3,170	8,400	Israel	13,920	14,940
Hungary	3,350	6,050	Australia	17,500	17,910
Mexico	3,610	6,810	Hong Kong	18,060	21,560
Trinidad and Tobago	3,830	8,080	United Kingdom	18,060	17,210
Uruguay	3,830	6,380	Finland	19,300	15,530
Oman	4,850	9,020	Kuwait	19,360	21,630
Gabon	4,960	—	Italy	19,840	17,830
Slovenia	6,490	—	Singapore	19,850	19,510
Puerto Rico	7,000	10,670	Canada	19,970	20,230
Argentina	7,220	8,250	Netherlands	20,950	17,330
Greece	7,390	9,000	United Arab Emirates	21,430	20,940
Korea	7,660	9,630	Belgium	21,650	19,640
Saudi Arabia	—	—	France	22,490	19,000
Turkmenistan	—	—	Austria	23,510	19,430
Average	$2,480		Germany	23,560	16,850
			Sweden	24,740	17,200
			United States	24,740	24,720
			Norway	25,970	19,780
			Denmark	26,730	19,560
			Japan	31,490	20,850
			Switzerland	35,760	23,660
			Average	$23,090	

Source: Data from *World Development Report 1995,* tables 1 and 30, pp. 162–163, 220–221.

Another way of thinking about the sharp disparity in incomes around the planet is to look at the global distribution of income. In 1989, the poorest 20 percent of the world's people received just 1.4 percent of its income, while the richest 20 percent received 82.7 percent of total income. That gap has increased in the last several decades. According to the United Nations, the share of income received by the poor has fallen since 1960 while the share going to the rich has risen. In 1960, the ratio of the share of income received by the top 20 percent to the share received by the bottom 20 percent was 30:1. By 1989 the ratio was 59:1. The equivalent figure for the United States is about 9:1. The distribution of world income is astonishingly unequal.

Characteristics of Low-Income Countries

Low incomes are often associated with other characteristics: severe inequality, poor health care and education, high unemployment, heavy reliance on agriculture, and rapid population growth. We'll examine most of these problems in this section. Population growth in low-income nations is examined later in the chapter. We'll begin with an assessment of incomes and living standards.

Incomes and Living Standards

The data listed for incomes so far in this chapter are for per capita GNP. While these are the data most universally available, they are a bit misleading. Each country's GNP is computed in terms of its own currency. These figures are then converted to dollars using the current exchange rate with the U.S. dollar. A country could have a relatively high standard of living but, for a variety of reasons, a low exchange rate. The per capita GNP figure would be quite low; the country would appear to be poorer than it is.

A better approach to comparing incomes converts currencies to dollars on the basis of purchasing power. The World Bank's International Comparison Programme (ICP) uses this approach. Thus, an ICP income of $1,000 in one country has half the purchasing power of an ICP income of $2,000 in another.

ICP estimates typically show higher incomes than estimates based on an exchange rate conversion. For example, in 1993 Mozambique's per capita GNP, based on exchange rates, was $90. Its per capita GNP based on the ICP estimate, was $550.

ICP estimates aren't available for all countries, so most comparisons are still done by converting to a common currency using existing exchange rates. For the 108 low- and middle-income nations for which ICP estimates have been made, the ICP numbers are consistently higher than estimates based on exchange rates.

The ICP figures yield particularly striking differences in reported levels of per capita income among rich countries. According to the per capita GNP figures in Exhibit 36-1, which convert data in domestic currencies to dollars using exchange rates, the United States ranked fifth in 1993. Its per capita GNP of $24,740 was far behind that of Switzerland, the world leader, which had a per capita GNP of $35,760. Converting incomes to a common currency based on a consistent measure of purchasing power, as is done in the ICP project, the World Bank obtained a quite different result. Switzerland's per capita GNP dropped to $23,660, putting it in second place behind the United States.

In still another approach to estimating world poverty, the United Nations converts local currency to dollars based on purchasing power, then uses a method similar to that used to gauge poverty in the United States. In the United States, a family is considered poor if its income falls below a certain threshold; the threshold for a family of four in 1994, for example was $15,141. The UN project defines the income needed to purchase the food, clothing, and shelter necessary for survival; it was less than $400 per person per year in 1989. By this test, 23 percent of the world's population was poor in 1989. That poverty was, of course, concentrated in poor countries. More than three-fifths of the people living in sub-Saharan Africa, for example, fell below this line.

Inequality

Not only are incomes in low-income countries quite low; income distribution is often highly unequal. Poverty is far more prevalent than per capita numbers suggest.

Consider Costa Rica and Panama, two Latin American countries with roughly equivalent levels of per capita GNP (Costa Rica's was $5,520 and Panama's $5,840 in 1993). Panama's income distribution was the most unequal of any reported by the World Bank; Costa Rica's was far more equal. Exhibit 36-2 compares the Lorenz curves for the two countries for 1989, the most recent year for which the information was available. The 20 percent of the households with the lowest incomes in Costa Rica had twice as large a share of their country's total income as did the bottom 20 percent of households in Panama. That means Costa Rica's poor were about twice as well off, in material terms, as Panama's poor that year. Costa Rica also generated a positive rate of growth in per capita GNP between 1980 and 1993, while Panama experienced negative growth.

In general, the greater the degree of inequality, the more desperate the condition of people at the bottom of an income distribution. We saw in Chapter 35 that figures for income growth in high-income nations must be judged against the record of distribution data. Given the high degree of inequality in low-

EXHIBIT 36-2

Poverty and the Distribution of Income: Costa Rica versus Panama

Costa Rica had about the same per capita GNP as Panama in 1992, but Panama's income distribution was far more unequal. Panama's poor had much lower living standards than Costa Rica's poor, as suggested by the Lorenz curves for the two nations.

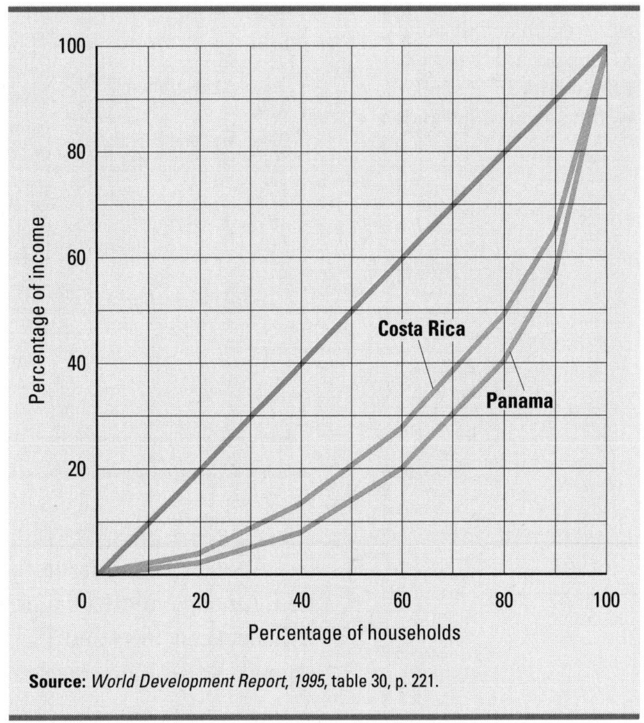

Source: *World Development Report, 1995,* table 30, p. 221.

income countries, it's even more important to look at income distributions when we compare living standards in different countries.

Health and Education

Poor nations are typically characterized by low levels of human capital. Where health care facilities are inadequate, that human capital can be reduced further by disease. Where educational resources are poor, there will be little progress in improving human capital.

One indicator of poor health care appears on the supply side. As might be expected, low-income countries have fewer doctors, relative to their populations, than high-income countries. In 1990, there were 6,760 people per physician in the world's low-income countries versus 420 in high-income countries. Virtually all births in high-income countries were attended by health care professionals in 1990; fewer than one-third of births in low-income countries were. The UN estimates that 1.45 billion people in 1990 had no access to health care services.

We can also see the results of poor health care in statistics on health. Among the world's low-income countries, the infant mortality rate, which reports deaths in the first year of life, was 64 per 1,000 live births in 1993. There were 7 infant deaths per 1,000 live births among the high-income countries that year. Another indicator of health care delivery is the disability-adjusted life-year (DALY). This shows the number of years of life lost to premature deaths or disability. Exhibit 36-3 shows DALYs per 1,000 population in various groups of countries in 1990.

EXHIBIT 36-3

Losses of Life Due to Premature Death and Disability, 1990

A DALY is a disability-adjusted life-year; it is the years of life lost to premature death and disability. The chart shows DALY values per 1,000 population in several regions of the world. In general, the higher the DALY, the lower the level of health in a country.

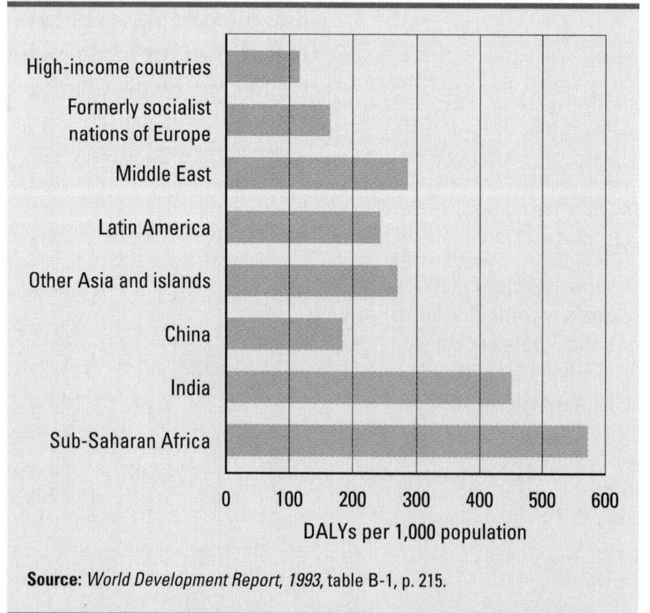

Source: *World Development Report, 1993,* table B-1, p. 215.

Another health issue facing the world's low-income countries is malnutrition. Among children under the age of 5, malnutrition rates in low-income countries between 1988 and 1993 ranged from 10 percent (Zimbabwe) to 67 percent (Bangladesh). Rates in excess of 30 percent are common.

Education in poor and middle-income nations is improving. Most children go to primary school, but education usually stops after that. Fewer than half the children in low-income nations attend high school, and only a tiny percentage get to college.

Although nearly all children in low- and middle-income countries attend at least some school, the quality of that education is often quite poor. Class sizes, particularly in low-income nations, are very large. Still, literacy rates are improving; more than half the adults in low-income countries can read.

Unemployment

Unemployment is pervasive in low-income nations. These nations, already faced with low levels of natural GDP, are producing well below natural levels.

Unemployment rates in low-income countries are typically about 10 to 15 percent. Those levels are not out of line with rates we observe among wealthy nations. European nations, for example, often have unemployment rates in the double digits. But if we count discouraged workers, people who have given up looking for work but who would take it if it were available, unemployment in low-income countries soars—typically to about 35 percent.

Migration within low-income countries often contributes to unemployment in urban areas. Factors such as ethnic violence, poverty, and drought often force people to move from rural areas to cities, where unemployment rates are already high.

Reliance on Agriculture

One of the dominant characteristics of poor nations is the concentration of employment in agriculture. Another is the very low productivity of that employment. Agriculture in low-income countries often employs a majority of the population but produces less than one-third of GDP.

One of the primary forces behind income growth in wealthy countries has been the shift of labor out of agriculture and into more productive sectors such as manufacturing. This shift has lagged far behind in low-income nations.

Low-income nations are, of course, plagued by low incomes. The living conditions these incomes imply are worsened, however, by inequality, inadequate health care, poor education, and high unemployment. A key contributor is the heavy concentration of the population of low-income nations in agriculture, where labor is not particularly productive and wages are low.

The solution to these problems is greater prosperity. With higher incomes, the majority of the world's people could afford the food, sanitation, health care, and education now enjoyed by a small minority. But how are those higher incomes to be achieved? The answer lies in economic development.

Economic Development: A Definition

If the problems of low-income nations are pervasive, the development that helps to solve those problems must transform the very nature of their societies. The late Austrian economist Joseph Schumpeter described economic development as a revolutionary process. Whereas economic growth implies quantitative change in production processes that are already familiar to the society, economic development requires qualitative change in virtually every aspect of life.

Case in Point: Growth Versus Development: Botswana and Hong Kong

The distinction between economic growth and economic development is powerfully illustrated by the cases of Botswana, a nation in southern Africa, and Hong Kong, a nation on the edge of China.

Both nations have achieved spectacular rates of economic growth during the past few decades. Botswana was the fastest-growing nation in the world throughout the 1970s and 1980s; its growth propelled it from the World Bank's list of low-income countries to a position near the top of the list of middle-income countries. Hong Kong also achieved substantial growth. It is now a high-income economy whose per capita GDP exceeds that of France.

Botswana's progress has not been widely shared. Its growth occurred primarily because of the success of its diamond industry. Most of Botswana's people work in its agricultural sector, where productivity and incomes are low. The World Bank reports the distribution of expenditures rather than incomes for Botswana; this distribution is among the most unequal the Bank measures. Unemployment rates are extremely high.

Botswana's poor remain desperately poor; the country cannot be said to be achieving economic development. It is certainly trying; its government is spending its diamond earnings on educational efforts, health care, and investment in transportation and communication facilities. Botswana is trying to do the "right" things to achieve economic development, but its efforts haven't yet brought higher standards of living to the great majority of its people.

Hong Kong's success, by contrast, has been widely shared. Its poorest 20 percent of households receive a larger share of income than do the poorest 20 percent of U.S. households. Hong Kong is a development success story. Botswana, despite its phenomenal growth, is not.

A home in Botswana.

Robert Heilbroner, an economist at the New School for Social Research in New York, has argued:

> Economic development is political and social change on a wrenching and tearing scale. . . . It is a process of institutional birth and institutional death. It is a time when power shifts, often violently and abruptly, a time when old regimes go under and new ones rise in their places. And these are not just the unpleasant side effects of development. They are part and parcel of the process, the very driving force of change itself.[2]

Economic development transforms a nation to its core. But what, precisely, is development? Many definitions follow Heilbroner in noting the massive institutional and cultural changes economic development involves. But whatever the requirements of development, its primary characteristics are rising incomes and improving standards of living. That means output must increase—and it must increase relative to population growth. And because inequality is so serious a problem in low-income nations, development must deliver widespread improvement in living conditions. It therefore seems useful to define **economic development** as a process that produces sustained and widely shared gains in per capita real GDP.

Economic development is a process that produces sustained and widely shared gains in per capita real GDP.

[2] Robert Heilbroner, *Between Capitalism and Socialism* (New York: Vintage Books, 1970), pp. 53–54.

Checklist

- The vast majority of the world's people live in low- and middle-income countries.
- Among the problems facing low- and middle-income nations are low living standards, inequality, inadequate health care and education, high unemployment, and the concentration of the labor force in low-productivity agricultural work.
- Economic development is a process that generates sustained and widely shared gains in per capita real GDP.

In the last chapter, we saw that economic growth is the process by which a nation's capacity to produce goods and services is increased. Economic development differs from economic growth because of the different challenges it confronts. First, poor countries typically operate well below their natural levels of output. Development must therefore do more than generate the promise of greater output; it must deliver. Development is therefore defined as gains in GDP, not the potential to produce GDP. Second, the fact that so many low-income nations have experienced population growth in excess of output growth in recent years suggests the need to stipulate gains in per capita output, not just in output. And third, because the goal of development is to improve living standards, the definition of development given here requires that gains in per capita GDP be widely shared, not concentrated in the hands of a few.

Population Growth and Economic Development

It is easy to see why some people have become alarmists when it comes to population growth rates in LDCs. Looking at the world's low-income countries, they see a population of more than 3 billion growing at a rate that suggests a doubling every 36 years. That would add over 3 billion more poor people by about 2030, and the population of low-income countries would quadruple two-thirds of the way through the twenty-first century. We can barely feed these populations now. How will we cope with a *quadrupling?* The following statement captures the essence of widely expressed concerns:

> At the end of each day, the world now has over two hundred thousand more mouths to feed than it had the day before; at the end of each week, one and one-half million more; at the close of each year, an additional eighty million. . . . Humankind, now doubling its numbers every thirty-five years, has fallen into an ambush of its own making; economists call it the "Malthusian trap," after the man who most forcefully stated our biological predicament: population growth tends to outstrip the supply of food.[3]

But what are we to make of such a statement? Certainly if the world's population continues to double at the rates that existed in the past 50 years, economic growth is less likely to be translated into an improvement in the average standard of living. But the rate of population growth isn't a constant; it is affected by other economic forces. This section begins with a discussion of the relationship between population growth and income growth, then turns to an explanation of the sources of population growth in low-income countries, and closes with a discussion of the Malthusian warning suggested in the quote above.

Population Growth and Income Growth

On a simplistic level, the relationship between population and growth in per capita income is clear. After all, per capita income equals total income divided by population. The growth rate of per capita income thus equals the difference between the growth rate of income and the growth rate of population. Kenya's annual growth rate in real GDP from 1980 to 1993, for example, was 3.8 percent. Its population growth rate during that period was 3.3 percent, leaving it a

[3] Phillip Appleman, ed., *Thomas Robert Malthus: An Essay on the Principle of Population—Text, Sources and Background, Criticism* (New York: Norton, 1976), p. xi.

Case in Point: China Curtails Population Growth

China is an example of a country that has achieved a very low rate of population growth and a very high rate of growth in per capita GNP.

China's low rate of population growth represents a dramatic shift. As recently as the early 1970s, China had a relatively high rate of population growth; its population expanded at an annual rate of 2.7 percent from 1965 to 1973. By the 1980s, that rate had plunged to 1.5 percent. The World Bank projects a growth rate in China's population of just 0.9 percent between 1993 and 2000.

This dramatic drop in the population growth rate was brought about by a strict government policy; couples are allowed to have only one child. If a woman who already has one child becomes pregnant, she will most likely be forced to have an abortion.

Although the policy has achieved its desired result—reduced population growth—it has had some horrible side effects. Given a strong cultural tradition favoring having a son, some couples resort to infanticide as a means of eliminating newborn daughters. When the sex of an unborn baby is determined to be female, abortion is common.

Another side effect is more comic. Some parents want fancy dresses for a daughter, but their only child is a son. It's common in China to see young boys wearing elaborate dresses. Some of the first babies born under China's plan are now of marrying age, and they're discovering another effect—potential brides are in short supply.

A Chinese family.

growth rate of per capita GDP of just 0.5 percent. A slower rate of population growth, together with the same rate of GDP increase, would have left Kenya with more impressive gains in per capita income. The implication is that if the developing countries want to increase their rate of growth of per capita GDP relative to the developed nations, they must limit their population growth.

Exhibit 36-4 plots growth rates in population versus growth rates in per capita GDP from 1980 to 1993 for 125 countries. We don't see a simple relationship. Many countries experienced both rapid population growth and negative changes in real per capita GDP. But still others had relatively rapid population growth, yet they had a rapid increase in per capita GDP. Clearly, there is more to achieving gains in per capita income than a simple slowing in population growth. But the challenge raised at the beginning of this section remains: can the world continue to feed a population that is growing exponentially—that is, doubling over fixed intervals?

The Malthusian Trap and the Demographic Transition

In 1798, Thomas Robert Malthus published his *Essay on the Principle of Population.* It proved to be one of the most enduring works of the time. Malthus's fundamental argument was that production is subject to the law of diminishing returns. (This idea was central to our derivation of the short- and long-run aggregate supply curves in Chapter 26: it is the reason the marginal product of labor curve slopes downward.)

A **Malthusian trap** is reached when population increases beyond the ability of the earth to feed it; starvation holds subsequent population in check.

Diminishing returns imply that adding more labor to a fixed quantity of land increases output, but by ever smaller amounts. Eventually, Malthus concluded,

EXHIBIT 36-4

Population and Income Growth, 1980–1993

A scatter chart of population growth rates versus GNP per capita growth rates for various countries for the period 1980–1993 suggests no systematic relationship between the rates of population and of income growth. The 5 countries who achieved growth rates in per capita GNP of 6 percent or greater during the period had population growth rates ranging from 1.1 percent (Korea) to 3.4 percent (Botswana).

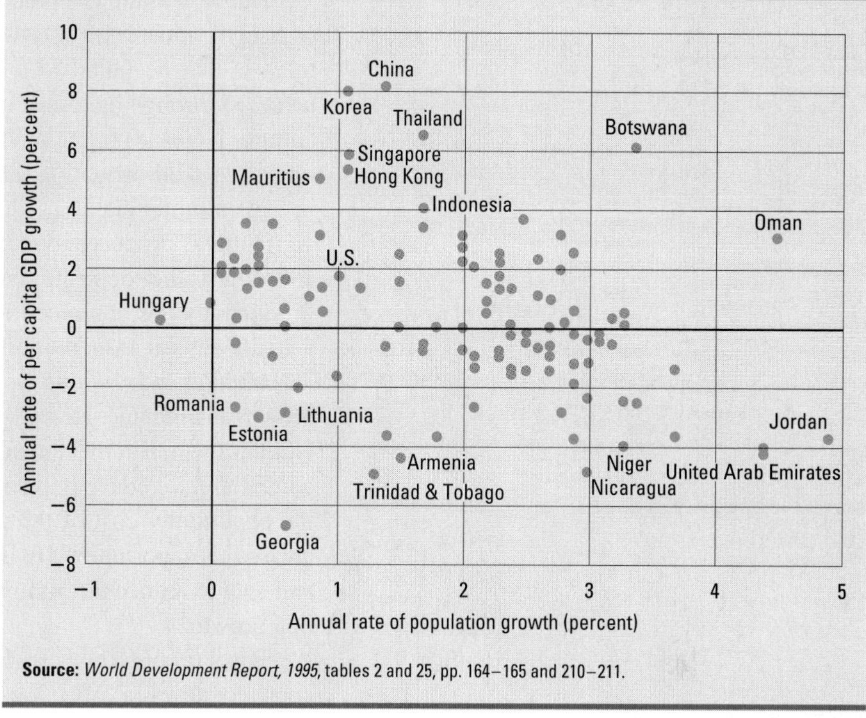

Source: *World Development Report, 1995,* tables 2 and 25, pp. 164–165 and 210–211.

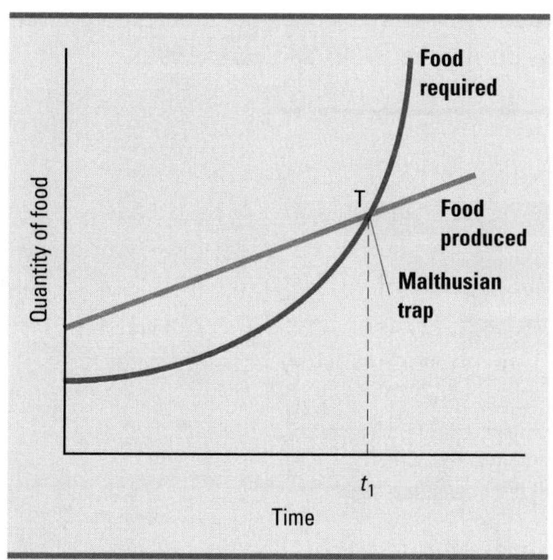

EXHIBIT 36-5

The Malthusian Population Trap

If population grows at a fixed exponential rate, the amount of food required will increase exponentially. But Malthus held that the output of food could increase only at a constant rate. Given these two different growth processes, food requirements would eventually catch up with food production. The population hits the subsistence level of food production at the Malthusian trap, shown here at point T. With inadequate food to support the rising population, gains in population are held in check beyond time t_1 by the inability to feed more people.

the percentage increases in output would be smaller than the percentage increases in human beings necessary to produce the output. As the population continued to grow unchecked, the number of people would eventually outstrip the ability of the land to generate enough food.

Malthus argued that population grows exponentially and thus doubles over fixed intervals that depend only on the percentage rate of growth. Agricultural output, he said, would at best increase by a constant amount each year. With population increasing exponentially and food production increasing by constant amounts, there would be an inevitable **Malthusian trap,** a point at which the world is no longer able to meet the food requirements of the population and starvation becomes the primary check to population growth.

A Malthusian trap is illustrated in Exhibit 36-5. We can determine the total amount of food required by multiplying the population in any period by the amount of food required to keep one person alive. Because population grows exponentially, food requirements rise at an increasing rate, as shown by the curve labeled "Food required." Food produced rises by a constant amount each period; its increase is shown by an upward-sloping straight line labeled "Food produced." Food required eventually exceeds food produced, and the Malthusian trap is reached at time t_1. The faster the rate of population growth, the sooner t_1 is reached.

What happens at the Malthusian trap? Clearly, there isn't enough food to support the population growth implied by the "Food required" curve. Instead, people starve, and population begins rising arithmetically, held in check by the "Food produced" curve. Starvation becomes the limiting force for population; the rest of the population lives at the margin of subsistence. For Malthus, the long-run fate of human beings was a standard of living barely sufficient to keep them alive. As he put it, "the view has a melancholy hue."

Happily, Malthus's predictions do not match the experience of Western societies in the nineteenth and twentieth centuries. One weakness of Malthus's argument is that he failed to take into account the gains in output that could be achieved through increased use of physical capital and new technologies in agriculture. Increases in the amount of capital per worker in the form of machines, improved seed, irrigation, and fertilization have made possible huge increases in agricultural output at the same time as the supply of labor was rising. Agricultural productivity rose rapidly in the United States between 1800 and 1995, just the opposite of the fall in productivity expected by Malthus. Productivity has continued to expand. In the United States, government policy actually aims at reducing food production, not increasing it.

Malthus was wrong as well about the relationship between population growth and income. He believed that any increase in income would boost population growth. But the law of demand tells us that the opposite is true: higher incomes tend to reduce population growth. The primary cost of having children is the opportunity cost of the parents' time in raising them—higher incomes increase this opportunity cost. Higher incomes increase the cost of having children and tend to reduce the number of children people want and thus to slow population growth.

Panel (a) of Exhibit 36-6 shows the birth rates of low-, middle-, and high-income countries in 1993. We see that, the higher the income level, the lower the birth rate. Fewer births translate into slower population growth. In Panel (b), we see that high-income nations had much slower rates of population growth than did middle- and low-income nations during the 1980s and early 1990s.

EXHIBIT 36-6

Income Levels and Population Growth

Panel (a) shows that low-income nations had much higher birth rates in 1993 than did high-income nations. In Panel (b), we see that low-income nations had a much higher rate of population growth from 1980 to 1993.

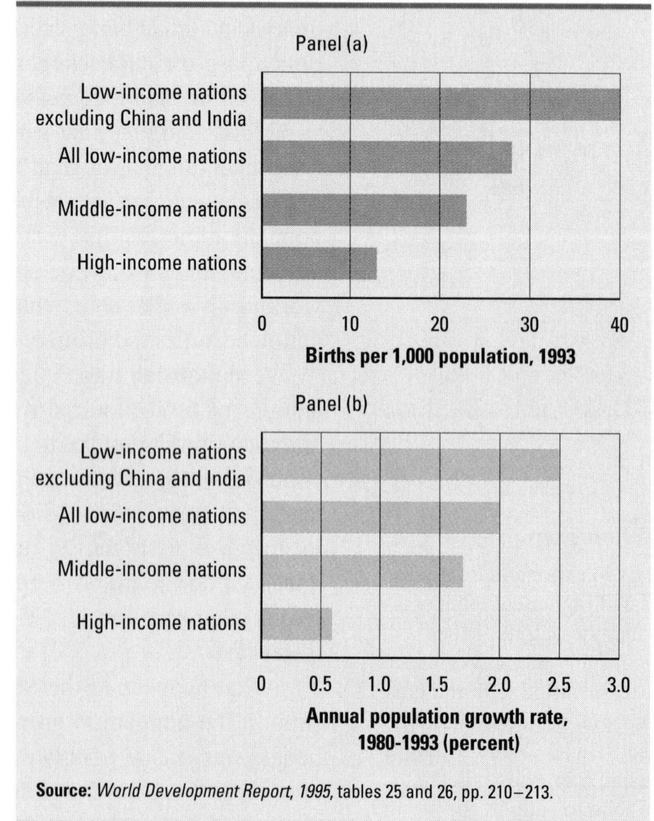

Source: *World Development Report, 1995,* tables 25 and 26, pp. 210–213.

Demographic transition is a process in which population growth rises with a fall in death rates and then falls with a reduction in birth rates.

Notice that the information for low-income nations in Exhibit 36-6 is reported in two ways. First, we see the birth rates and population growth rates of low-income nations excluding China and India; second, we see this same information for all low-income nations, including China and India. We've already seen that China has an aggressive program to limit its population growth. India does also; it provides incentives to encourage couples to have fewer children. Both nations have achieved birth rates more typical of middle- than of low-income nations.

An increase in a nation's income can be expected to slow its rate of population growth. Hong Kong, for example, has enjoyed dramatic gains in income since the 1960s. Its birth rate and rate of population growth have fallen by over half during that time. Indeed, Hong Kong's birth rate has fallen below that of the United States.

But if economic development can slow population growth, it can also increase it. One of the first gains a developing nation can achieve is improvements in such basics as the provision of clean drinking water, improved sanitation, and public health measures such as vaccination against childhood diseases. Such gains can dramatically reduce disease and death rates. As desirable as such gains can be, they also boost the rate of population growth. Nations are likely to enjoy sharp reductions in death rates before they achieve gains in per capita income. That can accelerate population growth early in the development process. Demographers have identified a process of **demographic transition** in which population growth rises with a fall in death rates and then falls with a reduction in birth rates.

The process of demographic transition has unfolded in a strikingly different manner in developed versus less developed nations over the past two centuries. In 1800, birth rates barely exceeded death rates in both developed and less developed countries. The result was a rate of population growth of only about 0.5 percent per year worldwide. By 1900, the death rate in developed nations had fallen by about 25 percent, with little change in the birth rate. Among developing nations, the birth rate was unchanged, while the death rate was down only slightly. The combined result was a modest increase in the rate of world population growth.

Changes have been much more rapid in this century. By 1965, the death rate among developed nations had plunged to about one-quarter of its 1800 level, while the birth rate had fallen by half. In developing nations, death rates took a similarly dramatic drop, while birth rates showed little change. The result was dramatic world population growth.

The world's high-income economies had completed the demographic transition by 1993, with sharp reductions in birth rates. Less developed nations have begun to make progress, with birth rates falling by a slightly greater percentage than death rates. The results have been a sharp slowing in the rate of population growth among high-income nations and a more modest slowing among low-income nations. The World Bank projects a continued slowing in population growth at all income levels, as suggested in Exhibit 36-7. For the world as a whole, the Bank predicts population growth will slow to a 1.1 percent rate during the first quarter of the next century, a rate that would imply a doubling time of 65 years. Between 1965 and 1980, the world population grew at an annual rate of 2 percent, suggesting a doubling time of 36 years.

Checklist

- The rate of increase in per capita income equals the rate of increase in income minus the rate of increase in population, but high rates of population growth do not necessarily imply low rates of growth in per capita income.
- Malthus's prediction of a world in which production would be barely sufficient to keep people alive has proven incorrect because of gains generated by increased physical, human, and intellectual capital and the tendency of higher incomes to slow population growth.
- A demographic transition is achieved when rising incomes begin to reduce birth rates and bring population growth in check.

EXHIBIT 36-7

The Demographic Transition at Work: Actual and Projected Population Growth

Population growth has slowed considerably in the past several decades, particularly within high-income nations.

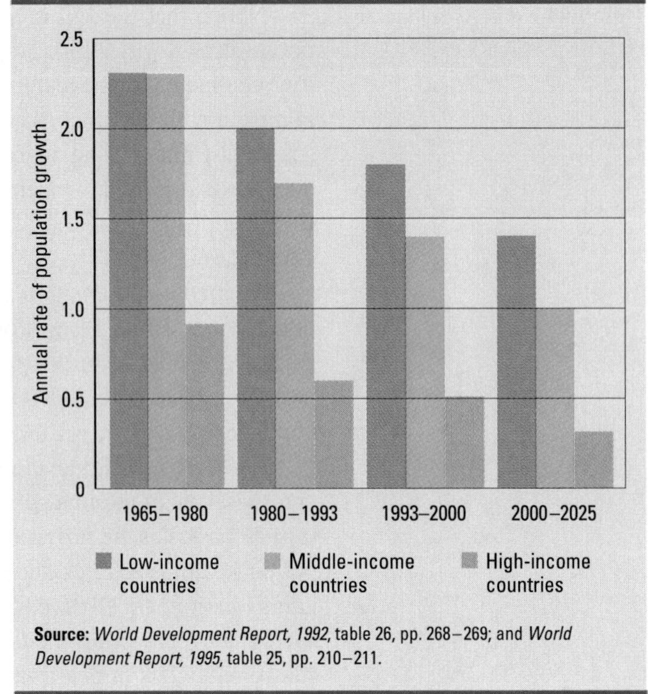

Source: *World Development Report, 1992,* table 26, pp. 268–269; and *World Development Report, 1995,* table 25, pp. 210–211.

Keys to Economic Development

What are the keys to economic development? Clearly, each nation's experience is unique; we can't isolate the sources of development success in the laboratory. We can, however, identify some factors that appear to have played an important role in successful economic development. We'll look separately at policies that relate to the domestic economy and at policies in international trade.

Domestic Policy and Economic Development

What domestic policies contribute to development? Looking at successful economies, those that have achieved high and sustained increases in per capita output, we can see some clear tendencies. They include a market economy, a high saving rate, and investment in infrastructure and in human capital.

Market Economies and Development

There can be no clearer lesson than that a market economy is a necessary condition for economic development. We saw in Chapter 2 that economic systems can be categorized according to whether capital is owned primarily by the private sector (capitalist systems) or by the public sector (socialist systems). These two systems can be delineated further according to whether choices about how factors of production will be used are made primarily by private individuals (market socialism or market capitalism) or by the public sector (command socialism or command capitalism). There are no examples of development success among command economic systems, whether command market or command socialist systems.

One of the most dramatic examples is provided by China. Its shift in the late 1970s to a more market-based economy has ushered in a period of phenomenal growth. China, which has shifted from a command socialist to what could most nearly be categorized as a market socialist economy, has been among the fastest-growing economies in the world for the past 15 years.

The experience of other economies reinforces the general observation that markets matter. South Korea, Hong Kong, Taiwan, Singapore—all have achieved gigantic gains with a market-based approach to economic growth.

We should not conclude, however, that growth has been independent of any public sector activity. China, for example, remains a nominally socialist state; its government continues to play a major role. The governments of South Korea, Taiwan, and Singapore all targeted specific sectors for growth and provided government help to those sectors. Even Hong Kong has a high degree of government involvement in the provision of housing, health care, and education.[4] As we saw in Chapter 2, a market economy is not a no-government economy. But those countries that have left the task of resource allocation primarily to the market have achieved dramatic gains. Hong Kong and Singapore, in fact, are now included in the World Bank's list of high-income economies.

The Rule of Law and Development

If a market is to thrive, individuals must be secure in their property. If crime or government corruption make it likely that individuals will regularly be subjected to a loss of property, then exchange will be difficult and little investment will occur.

We'll see in the next chapter, for example, that Russia's effort to achieve economic development through the adoption of a market economy has been hampered by widespread lawlessness. An important difficulty of command economies is that the power they grant to government officials inevitably results in widespread corruption that saps entrepreneurial effort and economic growth.

Investment and Saving

We've seen that saving is a key to growth and the achievement of high incomes. The 1995 *World Development Report* shows that high-growth LDCs (those with GDP growth rates of 7 percent or more during the 1980s) saved 30 percent or more of GDP. Saving rates for LDCs with lower growth rates were correspondingly lower. The relationship between saving rates and incomes confirms our expectation that high rates of saving are positively related to economic growth.

High saving rates accompany high levels of investment. The productivity of this investment, however, can be quite variable. Government efforts to invest in human capital by promoting education, for example, may or may not be successful in actually achieving education. Development projects sponsored by international relief agencies may or may not foster development.

Investment in infrastructure, however, clearly plays an important role in economic development. Transportation and communication facilities in LDCs are generally quite primitive. Investment in improved systems facilitates the exchange of goods and services and thus fosters development.

[4] Hong Kong, a colony of Great Britain, will become part of China in 1997.

International Economic Issues in Development

In 1974, the poorest nations among the LDCs introduced into the United Nations a *Declaration on the Establishment of a New International Economic Order.* The program called upon the rich nations to help the LDCs reduce the growing gap in real per capita income levels between the developed and developing nations. The declaration has come to be known as the New International Economic Order, or NIEO for short.

NIEO called for four fundamental changes in the relationships between the LDCs and the industrialized nations. It called for major but unspecified changes in the world pricing system, control over the multinational corporations that often dominate both internal production and international trade with the LDCs, changes in the international monetary system and the management of debt, and changes in tariffs and trade restrictions. In addition, NIEO called for increased development aid, transfer of labor-intensive industries from the rich to the poor nations, and acceptance by the rich nations of collusion and price-fixing among LDCs producing similar products. The proposal to provide different and special treatment to the LDCs in international trade reflected a widely held view of international relations known as dependency theory.

Dependency Theory and Trade Policy

Conventional economic theory concerning international trade is based on David Ricardo's idea of comparative advantage. As we have seen in Chapters 2, 11, and 29, the principle of comparative advantage suggests that free trade between two countries will benefit both, and, in general, the freer the trade the better. But some economists have proposed a doctrine that challenges this idea. **Dependency theory** concludes that poverty among developing nations is the result of their dependence on high-income nations.

Dependency theory holds that the industrialized nations control the destiny of the LDCs, particularly in terms of being the ultimate markets for their exports, serving as the source of capital required for development, and controlling the relative prices and exchange rates at which market transactions occur. At one extreme, dependency theory holds that a conspiracy exists among the former colonial powers of the world. A more moderate view holds that it is simply a matter of historical fact that the developing countries will need help from the rich countries if they are to achieve economic development.

Dependency theory, as developed by Swedish economist Gunnar Myrdal, winner of the Nobel Prize in Economics in 1974, holds that the benefits of trade between a rich country and a poor one will go almost entirely to the rich country, widening the gap between rich and poor. Myrdal argues that the factors that made the poor country poor in the first place will continue to work against it once trade is opened up. As exports from the rich country increase, firms spring up to provide support services to firms doing the exporting. Myrdal had in mind insurance, transportation, banking and finance, and marketing agents. These industries make export firms in the rich country even more efficient. But in the poor country, Myrdal said, limited transportation, a poorly developed financial sector, and an uneducated work force stand in the way of developing similar support services for their own exports. The poor country thus does not experience the kind of development and growth enjoyed by the rich country. Increased trade makes the poor country more dependent on the rich country and its export service firms. Myrdal suggested that the developing countries would need to become independent of the already developed nations if they were to achieve eco-

Dependency theory is a body of economic theory that concludes that the poverty found in the less developed nations is primarily caused by the inability of the developing nations to free themselves from dependence on the industrialized nations.

Case in Point Mexico Rejects Dependence

Mexico has long been a stronghold of dependency theory. For decades, to study economics in Mexico was to study dependency theory. For generations of Mexicans, the primary explanation of Mexican poverty was U.S. wealth.

President Lázaro Cárdenas, who served Mexico as president from 1934 to 1940, began to implement dependency theory ideas even before the theory itself evolved. He seized a host of foreign-owned firms in Mexico, transforming them to government ownership. His argument was that the foreign-owned firms were exploiting Mexico. Subsequent presidents slapped tight controls on imports and extended the government's ownership of private firms. Mexico's tariffs averaged 60 percent by 1985, with a top rate of 90 percent.

The dependency revolution was reversed in the 1980s, beginning with the term of President Miguel de la Madríd, who has a Ph.D. in economics. De la Madríd began to reduce Mexico's tariffs in 1985. He was followed by President Carlos Salinas de Gortari, another Harvard-trained economist, who engaged in extensive deregulation and negotiated NAFTA, the North American Free Trade Agreement that turned all of North America into a free trade zone.

Mexico scrapped dependency theory after falling into a terrible slump in the 1980s. Whether its shift to a market economy with free trade policies will produce greater growth remains to be seen. Civil war broke out in the southern state of Chiapas when NAFTA went into effect, and the Mexican economy was plunged into a recession in the wake of a currency crisis late in 1994. But the nation's commitment to free trade seems unshakeable. Its new president, Ernesto Zedillo—another economist—has made clear that Mexico won't go back to the old days of protectionism.

nomic development. In relative terms, free trade would leave the poor country poorer and the rich country richer. Some dependency theorists even argued that trade was likely to make poor countries poorer in absolute terms.

Tanzania's President Julius Nyerere, speaking before the United Nations in 1975, put it bluntly:

> "I am poor because you are rich."

Import Substitution Strategies and Export-Led Development

If free trade widens the gap between rich and poor nations and makes poor nations poorer, it follows that a poor country should avoid free trade. Many developing countries, particularly in Latin America, have attempted to overcome the implications of dependency theory by adopting a strategy of **import substitution,** a strategy of blocking most imports and substituting domestic production of those goods.

The import substitution strategy calls for rapidly increasing industrialization by mimicking the already industrialized nations. The intent is to reduce the dependence of the developing country on imports of consumer and capital goods from the industrialized countries by manufacturing these goods at home. But in order to protect these relatively high-cost industries at home, the developing country must establish very high protective tariffs. Tariff rates imposed by Latin American countries, for example, typically exceeded 100 percent. Moreover, the types of industries that produce the previously imported consumer goods and capital goods are unlikely to increase the demand for unskilled labor. Yet unskilled labor is the most abundant resource in the poor countries. Adopting the import substitution strategy raises the demand for expensive capital, managerial talent, and skilled labor—resources in short supply.

Import substitution refers to a developing nation's policy to restrict importation of consumer and capital goods, substituting domestically produced items.

High tariffs insulate domestic firms from competition, but that tends to increase their monopoly power. Recognizing that some imported goods, particularly spare parts for industrial equipment, will be needed, countries can establish complex permit systems through which firms can import vital parts and other equipment. But that leaves a company's fortunes in the hands of the government bureaucrats issuing the permits. A highly corrupt system quickly evolves in which a few firms bribe their way to easy access to foreign markets, reducing competition still further. Instead of the jobs expected to result from import substitution, countries implementing the ideas of dependency theorists get the high prices, reduced production, and poor quality that come from reduced competition.

No country that has relied on a dependency theory strategy of import substitution has been successful in its development efforts. It is an idea whose time has *not* come. In contrast, rapidly growing economies in Asia have kept their economies open to both imports and exports. They have shown the greatest ability to move the development process along.

Development and Debt

Successful development in the LDCs requires more than just redirecting labor and capital resources into newly emerging sectors of the economy. That could be accomplished by both domestic firms and international firms located within the economy. But to complement the reorientation of traditional production processes, economic infrastructure such as roads, schools, communication facilities, ports, warehouses, and many other prerequisites to growth must be put into place. Paying for the projects requires a high level of saving.

As we saw in Chapter 34, the sources of saving are private saving, government saving, and foreign saving. Grants in the form of foreign aid from the developed nations supplement these sources, but they form a relatively small part of the total.

Private domestic saving is an important source of funds. But even high *rates* of private saving cannot guarantee sufficient funds in a poor economy. Government saving in the form of tax revenues in excess of government expenditures is almost universally negative. If the required investments are to take place, the LDCs have to borrow the money from foreign savers.

The problem for developing nations borrowing funds from foreigners is the same potential difficulty any borrower faces: the debt can be difficult to repay. Unlike, say, the national debt of the United States government, whose obligations are in its own currency, LDCs typically commit to make loan payments in the currency of the lending institution. Money borrowed by Brazil from a U.S. bank, for example, must generally be paid back in U.S. dollars.

Many LDCs borrowed heavily during the 1970s, only to find themselves in trouble in the 1980s. Countries such as Brazil suspended payments on their debt when required payments exceeded net exports. Much foreign debt was simply written off as bad debt by lending institutions. While foreign debts created a major crisis in the 1980s, subsequent growth has made these payments more manageable, even for countries such as Brazil. Brazil's annual payments on its foreign borrowing, for example, represented just 9.2 percent of its export earnings by 1992, down from 33.7 percent in 1980. The so-called international debt crises of the 1980s appear, for the most part, to be over.

Development Successes

As we have seen throughout this chapter, the greatest success stories are found among the newly industrializing economies (NIEs) in East Asia. These economies, including Hong Kong, South Korea, Singapore, and Taiwan, share

Case in Point Democracy and Economic Development

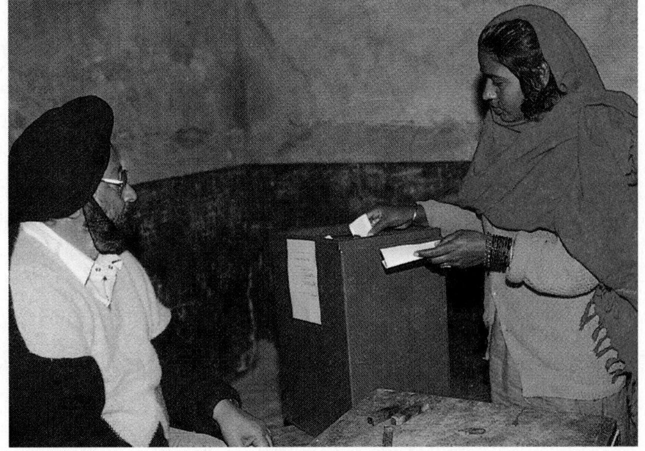

Democracy as an economic institution has typically received mixed notices from economists. While virtually all of the world's rich nations have democratic systems of government, it isn't clear that democracy is necessary for development.

India long provided the strongest counterexample to the idea that democracy promotes development. It has long been a democracy, yet its per capita income has kept it among the world's poor countries. India's government has traditionally opted for extensive regulation that has curtailed development. Countries such as China, with no democracy and a cruelly repressive government, have managed to generate very high levels of economic growth. China's per capita income now exceeds that of India by about 50 percent. Although the development success stories of Southeast Asia are generally democratic, political activity in those countries is sharply limited.

Many economists have reached the conclusion that countries are likely to become democratic once they achieve a high degree of economic development. Political freedom, they argue, is a normal good. The demand for freedom thus increases as incomes rise, making the creation of democratic institutions a product of economic growth, not a cause of it.

A recent study challenges the conventional view, arguing that democracy is not just a result of economic growth but a cause of it. Surjit Bhalla, a former World Bank economist, performed a statistical study of more than a century of evidence from all over the world to determine the relationship between democracy and growth. Using standard tests to sort out which is cause and which is effect, Mr. Bhalla found that democracy contributes to growth. He rated each of 90 countries on a political freedom scale of 1 (free) to 7 (not free). The United States, for example, scores a 1, whereas Iran scores a 7. He finds that, ceteris paribus, moving up 1 point on the political freedom scale adds a percentage point to a country's growth rate.

Mr. Bhalla suggests that clearly defined rights to property are essential to a market economy and to economic growth. Totalitarian as well as democratic nations can provide such rights, but rights in a democracy are likely to be more secure. A change in a few leaders at the top of a totalitarian state could topple a system of property rights. If property rights have emerged from democratic choice, however, it will be more difficult to unravel them. It follows, he says, that rights are more secure in democracies. It is for this reason, he says, that democracies have, other things equal, been able to enjoy somewhat more rapid rates of economic growth.

India may provide a counterexample of itself in support of Mr. Bhalla's argument. Its democratic government has, over the past few years, sought to transform its economy into one that has less government regulation and freer markets. The early results have been quite impressive; India has enjoyed very rapid growth in real GDP in recent years.

Source: Surjit Bhalla, "Free Societies, Free Markets and Social Welfare," presented at the Nobel Symposium on Democracy," Uppsala University, 1995.

two common traits. First, they have allowed their economies to develop through an emphasis on export-based, market capitalist strategies. The NIEs achieved higher per capita income and output by entering and competing in the global market for high-tech products such as computers, automobiles, plastics, chemicals, steel, shipbuilding, and sporting goods. These countries have succeeded largely by linking standardized production technologies with low-cost labor.

Second, the role of government was relatively limited in the NIEs, which made less use of regulation and bureaucratic controls. Apart from the promotion of shipbuilding and steel in Korea and a few strategic industries in Taiwan, the principal contribution of government in the Far Eastern NIEs has been to create a modern infrastructure (especially up-to-date communication facilities essential for the development of a strong financial sector), to provide a stable incentive system (including stable real effective exchange rates), and to ensure that

Checklist

- A market economy, perhaps with a substantial role for government, appears to be one key to economic growth. A system in which laws and property rights are well established and enforced also promotes growth.
- High rates of saving and investment can boost economic growth.
- Dependency theory suggests that poor countries should seek to insulate themselves from international trade.
- The import substitution strategies suggested by dependency theory have not been successful in generating economic growth.
- Countries that have grown rapidly in recent decades have achieved much of their growth through exports.

government bureaucracy will help rather than hinder exports (especially by not regulating export trade, labor markets, and capital markets).[5]

Chile adopted sweeping market reforms in the late 1970s, creating the freest economy in Latin America. Chile's growth has accelerated sharply, and the country has moved to the upper-middle-income group of nations. Perhaps more dramatic, the dictator who instituted market reforms, General Augusto Pinochet, agreed to democratic elections that removed him from power in 1989. Chile now has a greatly increased degree of political as well as economic freedom—and is emerging as one of the most prosperous countries in Latin America.

Although this development has been less heralded than the collapse of communism, it is surely significant. The nations of the less developed world, whose old, heavily regulated economies were generally command capitalist in structure, have begun to adopt sweeping market reforms. These reforms are examined in Chapter 37; they consist primarily of lowering trade barriers, selling government-owned firms to the private sector, and reducing government regulation.

Will market reforms translate into development success? The jury is still out. Market reform requires that many wealthy—and powerful—interests be swept aside. Whether that can be achieved, and whether poor people who lack human capital can be included in the development effort, remain open questions. But some dramatic success stories have shown that economic development can be achieved. The fate of billions of desperately poor people rests in the ability of their countries to match that success.

A Look Back—And a Look Ahead

Less developed countries (LDCs) face a host of problems: low incomes; unequal distributions of income; inadequate health care and education; high unemployment; and a concentration of workers in agriculture, where productivity is low. Economic development, the process that generates widely shared gains in income, can alleviate these problems.

The developing economies of the world face immense problems. This chapter offers no panaceas, no surefire formulas for steady improvement toward the standard of living shared by the already industrialized and developed nations.

The sources of economic growth in developing countries are not substantially different from those that apply to the developed countries. Saving and investment, particularly investment in appropriate technologies and human capital, appear to be critical. So too does the ability of LDCs to match their population growth rate with the ability of the economy to increase real output. Policies aimed at speeding the demographic transition, at which death and birth rates in an economy are equal, seem a necessary partner in any economic development strategy. Market economies with legal systems that provide for the reliable protection of property rights also tend to promote economic growth.

Dependency theory, the notion that developing countries are in the grip of the industrialized countries, led to import substitution schemes that proved

[5] Bela Balassa, "The Lessons of East Asian Development," *Economic Development and Cultural Change* 36(3) (April 1988; Supplement): S247–S290.

detrimental to the long-run growth prospects of LDCs. The movement of Latin American countries such as Mexico and Chile to market systems is a rejection of dependency theory.

There is a general movement toward market-based strategies to support economic development in the future. But even market-based strategies will work only if efforts are made to ensure an adequate infrastructure, including the development of financial and marketing institutions capable of providing the required signals to guide individual decisionmaking.

In the final two chapters of this book, we'll examine the economic systems of various countries. We'll examine first the problems of nations attempting the transition from socialism to market capitalism. We'll look at the economic systems of high-income economies and turn finally to the economic systems of low-income economies. In that investigation, we'll return to many of the themes of this chapter.

Terms and Concepts for Review

Demographic transition
Dependency theory
Economic development
Import substitution
Less developed countries (LDCs)
Malthusian trap

For Discussion

1. What is the difference between economic development and economic growth?
2. Look at the Case in Point comparing Botswana and Hong Kong (page 808). Do you agree with the assertion that Hong Kong has achieved economic development while Botswana has not? Why or why not?
3. What are the implications for the long-run development of a society that is unable to reduce its population growth rate below, say, 4 percent per year?
4. Explain how technological progress averts the Malthusian trap.
5. China reduced its rate of population growth by force (see the Case in Point on page 810). Given the likely effects of population growth on living standards, do you think such a policy is reasonable? Are there other ways a government might seek to limit population growth?
6. On what basis might a poor country argue that its poverty is a result of high incomes in another country? Do you think Mexico's poverty contributed to U.S. wealth?
7. The text argues that foreign aid efforts have little effect on development. Why might this be the case?
8. Given the arguments presented in the text, what do you think the United States should do to assist Mexico in its development efforts?

Problems

1. Consider two economies, one with an initial per capita income $16,000 (about the income of Finland) growing at a rate of 1.8 percent per year, the other with an initial per capita income of $600 (about the income of Tanzania) growing twice as fast (i.e., at a rate of 3.6 percent per year). Using the rule of 72 from Chapter 22, calculate how long it will take for the lower-income country to achieve the per capita income enjoyed by the richer one. How long will it take to literally "catch up" to the richer nation, assuming that the growth rates continue unchanged in the future?
2. Use the most recent copy of the *World Development Report* available in your library to determine the five poorest countries in the world. Look up data on the distribution of income, education, health and nutrition, and demography for each country (information on some of these variables will not be available for every country). Do you think that low incomes cause the observations you've made, or do you think that low levels of education, health, and nutrition and high rates of population growth tend to cause poverty?

Part Ten Alternative Economic Systems

37

Comparing Economic Systems

Chapter Objectives

After mastering the material in this chapter, you will be able to:

1. Distinguish economic systems as capitalist or socialist, market or command.
2. Discuss the rationale for command capitalist systems and the problems they create.
3. Discuss the major differences among market capitalist economies today.
4. Explain how the differing histories of the United States and of Japan led to quite different sets of economic institutions.
5. Comment on the ways in which the economic systems of France, Germany, the United Kingdom, and Sweden differ from that of the United States.
6. Describe the pressures on Western European nations to scale back the degree of government involvement in their economies.

A successful industrial nation—which means a nation with a future—doesn't allow itself to be organized as a collective amusement park.

German Chancellor Helmut Kohl, 1993

What's Ahead

Economic systems—the sets of rules that define how an economy's resources are owned and how choices about those resources are to be made—have been very much in the news over the past several years. Many countries are scrapping old economic systems and adopting new ones. Others are refining the systems they have in an effort to improve economic performance. The investigation of economic systems is important not only to help us understand other economies but to help us understand our own. Just as the study of a foreign language helps us to gain a better understanding of our own language, so a study of other economic systems sharpens our understanding of the forces at work in our economy.

In this chapter, we'll review the types of economic systems we find in the world today. These include market capitalism, command capitalism, market socialism, and command socialism.

Finally, we'll look carefully at the economies of Japan and four countries in Western Europe: France, Germany, the United Kingdom, and Sweden. Japan and Western Europe are emerging as economic superpowers along with the United States. They are also key U.S. trading partners. Each of the countries we'll examine is an intriguing variation on a market capitalist theme.

The Types and Characteristics of Alternative Economic Systems

We saw in Chapter 2 that economic systems can be distinguished according to two sets of institutional arrangements. The first is the ownership of capital. A system in which most capital is owned by the public sector is a socialist economic system. A system in which most capital is privately owned is a capitalist economic system. A second set of institutional arrangements defines how decisions concerning the use of capital and other factors of production will be made. A system in which those decisions are made, for the most part, by the public sector is a command system; a system in which those decisions are generally made by private individuals is a market system.

EXHIBIT 37-1

Classifying Economic Systems

Economic systems can be classified according to whether the ownership of capital and natural resources is primarily private or public and according to whether decisions concerning the use of those resources are made primarily by the private or the public sector.

	Allocative Decisions: Private Sector	Allocative Decisions: Public Sector
Ownership of Capital and Natural Resources: Private Sector	**Market Capitalism** The United States, Western Europe, Japan, and Hong Kong are market capitalist economies.	**Command Capitalism** Virtually every Latin American nation once fit this category, as did many nations in the Middle East and in Africa.
Ownership of Capital and Natural Resources: Public Sector	**Market Socialism** Yugoslavia was the primary example of a market socialist economy; some observers consider China to be such an economy today.	**Command Socialism** The Soviet Union was a command socialist economy. Cuba and North Korea continue to employ command socialist systems today.

Exhibit 37-1 uses a matrix to sort out these alternative arrangements. The two rows show public versus private ownership of capital and natural resources, and the two columns show public versus private decisions in the allocation of those resources.

The market capitalism cell in Exhibit 37-1 describes an economy in which resources are generally owned by private individuals rather than by government agencies. Decisions about how those resources will be used are made primarily by their owners. The capital employed by General Motors, for example, is owned by the shareholders of the firm; the management of the company decides how those resources will be used. Most resources in the United States fit a pattern of private ownership and private decisionmaking; it is a market capitalist economy.

In classifying economies, we must recognize that every system has elements of each of the four cells in Exhibit 37-1. In the United States, for example, the federal government owns the capital employed by the military; the government also determines how that capital will be used. In the classification system here, the military operates as a command socialist economic system. The government also controls many of the choices firms make with the capital they own privately. The Department of Agriculture may tell farmers how much wheat they can plant; it often controls the prices they will receive. Agriculture in the United States thus has elements of command capitalism. We can classify the United States as a market capitalist economy, even though not all resources are privately owned and not all allocative choices are made by private individuals, because for the most part, decisions and ownership are private.

Socialist Economic Systems

In socialist economies, the government owns most of the capital and natural resources. Private firms may exist, but most production is accomplished by state-owned firms.

The most important socialist system was the Union of Soviet Socialist Republics, or Soviet Union. This vast nation combined state ownership with state decisionmaking; it was thus a command socialist system. The Soviet Union was aggressive in spreading this economic system, imposing it in Eastern Europe after World War II. Other nations adopting the Soviet model included China, Cuba, and North Korea.

The Soviet Union collapsed in 1991, dissolving into 15 independent nations. Most of these nations have repudiated the command socialist systems under which they operated for decades. They are moving instead toward market capitalist systems. Similarly, the nations of Eastern Europe, such as Poland and Hungary, are replacing command socialist systems with market capitalist economic systems. Today, Cuba and North Korea are the only nations that seem wedded to the command socialist model.

An alternative to command socialism, market socialism, emerged in Yugoslavia after World War II. We'll examine the operation of Yugoslavia's experiment with market socialism, and the collapse of that system, in the next chapter.

Why did socialism fail? Fundamentally, the problem appeared to be one of incentives. Command socialist systems replace the invisible hand of the market system with government directives. There's no reason to expect those directives to send signals that reflect consumer preferences. In a socialist system, the people who make choices in the use of resources don't own them, so the decisionmakers have no incentive to seek out the most productive use of resources.

In Chapter 38, we'll look more carefully at the theory and practice of socialism, and the reasons so many nations have abandoned it. We'll also examine the problems involved in making a transition from a socialist to a capitalist economic system.

Capitalist Economic Systems

Capitalist economic systems leave the ownership of resources to the private sector. They differ in their definition of the role of government. In command capitalist systems, the government takes an active role in guiding the allocation of resources. It may control prices, specify how resources are to be used, or impose extensive regulations on how resources are to be used. Governments play a more passive role in market capitalist systems. They certainly influence the allocation of resources through their tax, spending, and regulatory policies, but they tend to leave the bulk of allocative choices to the private sector. In a market capitalist system, the market is the primary allocator of resources. In a command capitalist system, the government plays the central role.

Command Capitalist Economies

There are many ways a government can dominate the allocative choices of private owners of capital. It may require the permission of government officials before a firm introduces a new method of production or imports goods and services from another country. It may dictate which firms can and can't produce certain goods. It may control the prices that firms charge.

Command capitalist systems may emerge because of a lack of confidence in the ability of market forces to allocate goods and services in a way that matches perceived needs. In colonial America, for example, some colonies feared that the profitability of tobacco would lead to a market allocation in which no food was produced. To prevent this, laws were passed requiring farmers to plant a certain amount of grain each year.

Another motivation for a command system might be a concern that the resources created by a market economy would not be allocated equitably. The government may constrain the choices of large firms in order to protect small ones. Government officials may regard the very nature of market competition as an undesirable process and they may impose extensive regulations aimed at preventing it.

Still another motivation for a command capitalist system is self-interest. The owners of firms may bridle at the costs imposed on them by government through its tax and regulatory policies. But firms may be able to manipulate those policies to their own advantage. A firm might, for example, seek regulations whose effect would be the prevention of competition. The firm could then enjoy high profits without worrying about new firms coming along to whittle those profits down. A firm might seek controls on the import of key raw materials if it knows that it will still be able to import those materials but regulation will block some of its rivals.

The potential gains some firms can derive from the regulations of a command capitalist system suggest a primary drawback of such systems. When government officials dictate the choices of firms, those firms will have a powerful incentive to influence the officials. Suppose, for example, that an economy does not produce the hydraulic lifts used in auto repair shops and that the government requires approval before any foreign capital goods are imported. An auto repair firm that gains permission to import such a lift will gain an advantage over firms that don't; it will thus be tempting for some firm to bribe the official who passes out the permits to allow it to import the equipment and to prevent other firms from doing so.

Command capitalist systems are inevitably plagued by corruption. Of course, corruption occurs in any system, but it is particularly likely in a system in which government officials are in a position to hand out valuable favors or withhold them from private firms.

Another difficulty is that command capitalist systems may limit innovation. If approval is required before a firm introduces a new process or product, and if that approval is costly to acquire, then the rate at which innovation occurs will be slowed.

Are there any advantages to a command capitalist system? If government controls are administered in line with the public interest, a command capitalist system can be very successful. South Korea's heavily regulated capitalist economy has achieved rapid economic growth and dramatic gains in living standards. Whether regulation there is sufficiently extensive to put it in the command, rather than market, capitalist box is open to debate; some economists cite South Korea as a successful command capitalist economy, and others consider it a market capitalist economy. The South Korean government has imposed price controls, but it has not imposed regulations that limit the ability of new firms to compete in the marketplace or prevent existing firms from importing goods and services.

In the more typical case, command capitalist economies impose extensive regulations that lead to higher prices for consumers, limited competition in the marketplace, and low rates of economic growth. The countries of Latin America, for example, are very poor; and to a large degree, the blame for that poverty lies in the command capitalist economic system those countries have chosen. Recognition of that fact led Chile to launch a massive effort to move from command to market capitalism more than a decade ago. Similar efforts are under way today in Argentina, Bolivia, Brazil, Mexico, and Peru.

Checklist

- The economic systems of individual countries can be categorized according to whether the ownership of capital and natural resources and the authority over decisions about their use generally lie within the private or public sectors.
- Most command socialist systems have collapsed within the past few years. They suffered from an inability to develop incentives that would motivate decisionmakers to use resources efficiently.
- Command capitalist systems are likely to suffer from extensive corruption and from relatively low rates of economic growth.
- Market capitalist systems have delivered relatively high living standards for their people. The degree of public sector involvement in such economies varies.

Market Capitalist Economies

Market capitalist economies have emerged as the leading form of economic system in the twentieth century. Without exception, market capitalist economies enjoy high standards of living. The average income of market capitalist economies is several times greater than the average income of command capitalist or socialist economies.

Market capitalist systems are able to advance material living standards because markets harness the self-interest of people. An individual succeeds in a market economy by advancing someone else's interest. A firm succeeds by producing goods and services consumers want. A worker succeeds by making his or her firm more profitable. A consumer who purchases goods and services advances the interests of the producers of those items. In a market economy, firms have an incentive to produce the goods and services people demand and to do so as efficiently as possible.

Even in economies that leave the ownership of capital and labor and decisions concerning their use primarily to the private sector, there is a role for government. Governments in every market capitalist economy play an active role in assisting the poor and in producing such public goods as law enforcement, education, and environmental protection. The extent of public sector involvement in a market capitalist economy varies, but it is always much more limited than the government's role in a command capitalist economy.

Economic Systems in Action: A Comparison of Japan, France, Germany, Sweden, and the United Kingdom

In this section we'll look at market capitalist economies in Japan and Western Europe. We'll see that the role of government in a market capitalist economy is a central issue in each of these economies. Exhibit 37-2 compares per capita GNP

EXHIBIT 37-2

Per Capita GNP in France, Germany, Japan, Sweden, and the United States, 1993

France, Germany, Japan, Sweden, and the United States all had very high levels of per capita GNP in 1993.

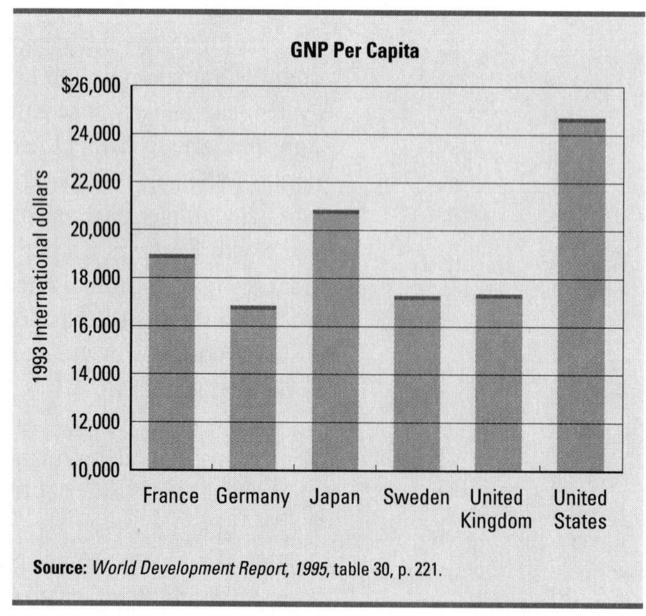

Source: *World Development Report, 1995,* table 30, p. 221.

in the five countries. All have very high levels of income—roughly 5 times as great as the average for the entire world.

Exhibit 37-3 compares the five economies in terms of other dimensions of economic performance. We see that Japan had the fastest rate of growth from 1980 to 1993, and Sweden had the highest rate of inflation and the highest level of government consumption of goods and services relative to GDP in 1993.

Finally, the Lorenz curves in Exhibit 37-4 compare income distributions in the six economies. As we saw in Chapter 34, the more unequal the distribution of income, the more the Lorenz curve bulges out from the 45-degree line. We see that of the five economies, the United States and the United Kingdom had the most unequal distributions; Japan's and Sweden's were the most equal.

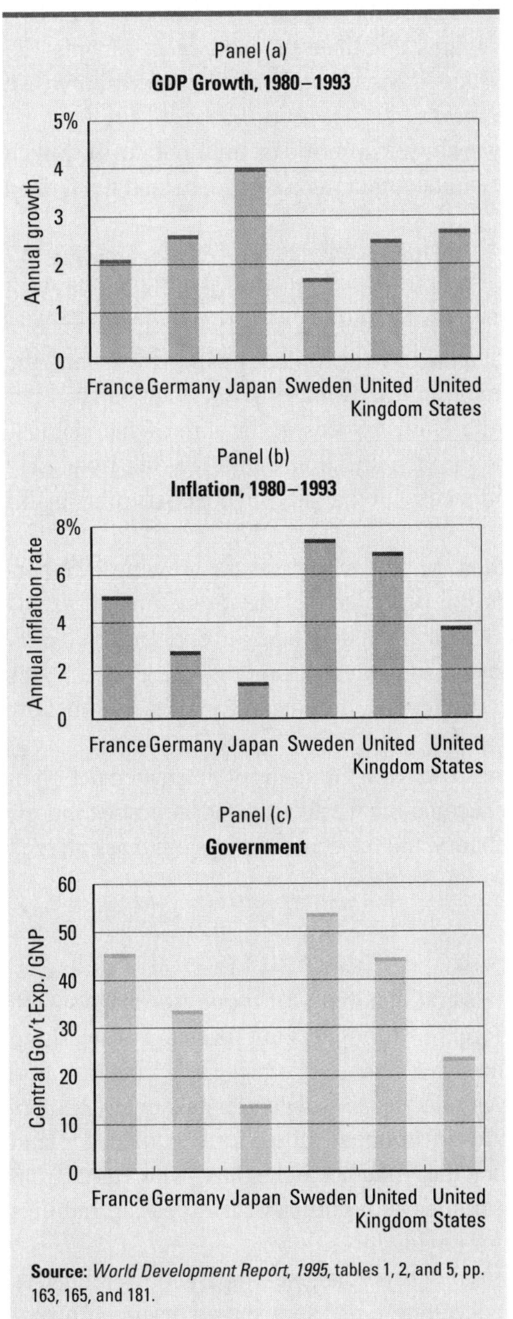

Source: *World Development Report, 1995*, tables 1, 2, and 5, pp. 163, 165, and 181.

EXHIBIT 37-3

Other Indicators of Economic Performance

Japan's was by far the fastest-growing economy among the five nations between 1980 and 1993, as shown in Panel (a). Japan also had the lowest rate of inflation, as shown in Panel (b). Central government expenditures as a percentage of GDP in 1993 were highest in Sweden and France among the nations shown in Panel (c).

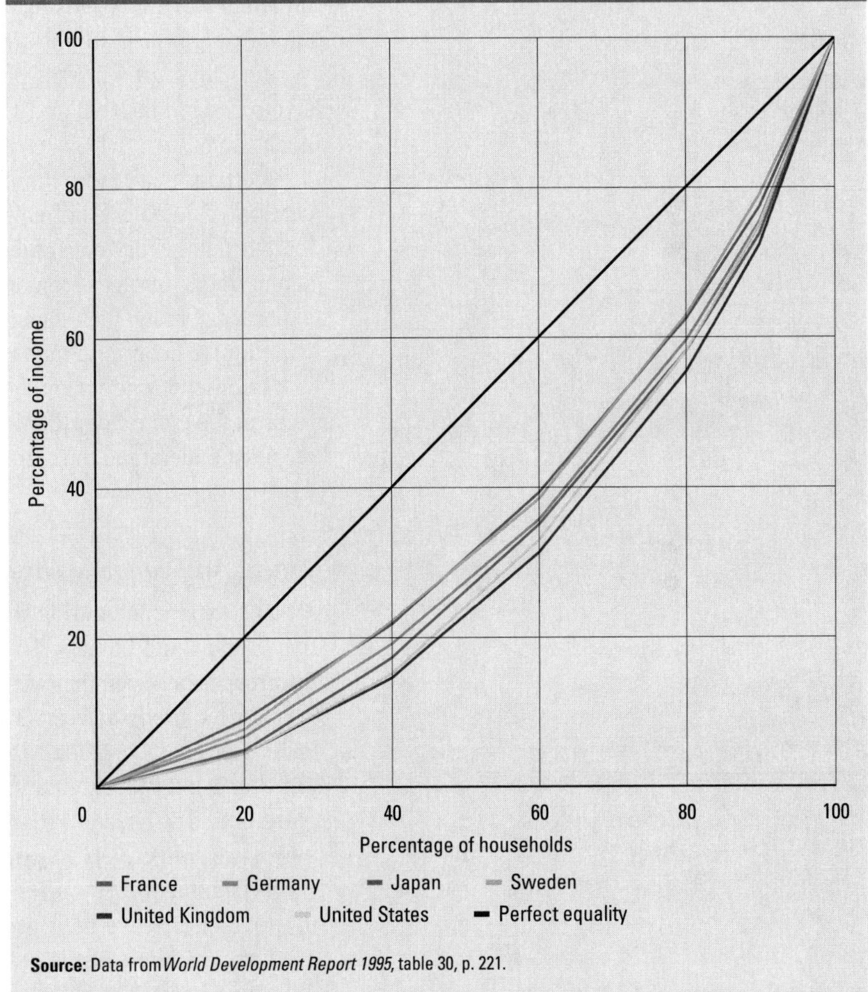

Source: Data from *World Development Report 1995*, table 30, p. 221.

EXHIBIT 37-4

Income Distribution

Lorenz curves reflect the distribution of household income in six countries. The data on which the curves are based are for different years: France, 1989; Germany, 1988; Japan, 1979; Sweden, 1981; United Kingdom, 1988; United States, 1985.

Japan

A look at its geography would not suggest that Japan has great promise. It is smaller in size than Montana. Mountains dominate the landscape; Japan's 125 million people live along its coasts. Japan has virtually no mineral resources. It must import nearly all of its raw materials.

But Japan is an economic powerhouse. In terms of total output, it ranked second in the world in 1993. Its per capita output ranked third, behind the United States and Switzerland.

Japan's rate of growth is the most impressive feature of its economy. As we saw in our survey of economic performance, Japan scored the most rapid growth of any major developed economy during the 1980s. It grew at a slightly faster rate in the 1970s. If Japan and the United States grow during the remainder of the 1990s at the rate they grew from 1980 to 1993, Japan's per capita output will surpass that of the United States at the turn of the century. Whether that growth will persist is an open question; Japan was hit by a massive recession in 1993 and 1994 and faces a potentially severe crisis in its banking system.

Perhaps even more important than the raw numbers is the growing U.S. perception of Japanese invincibility in the economic sphere. Sometimes it seems that virtually every consumer good we buy—and certainly every electronic consumer good—comes from a Japanese manufacturer. Although the United States exports far more than Japan does, the feeling that the Japanese are somehow winning the economic race runs deep.

In order to understand how Japan rose from the status of a defeated nation in ruins at the end of World War II to become the world's second-largest economy, we must understand the country's history and the economic system that emerged from it.

Japan: An Economic History

Japan's experience during the past several hundred years contrasts sharply with that of the United States. Those different histories account for many of the sharp differences between the two societies.

For hundreds of years Japan was ruled as an isolated feudal society. Rulers called shoguns controlled the central government. Local lords owned the land and ruled individual villages. Under the Tokugawa shoguns, who ruled from 1600 until 1867, each village was divided into groups of five peasant families who were collectively responsible for paying taxes.

Assignment of families to a group was permanent—peasants weren't free to move or to leave their group. Each group thus had a shared destiny. To succeed, the members of the group had to cooperate.

The forced cooperation under the Tokugawa shoguns contrasts sharply with the experience of the United States during the same period. The United States stressed individual freedom and fostered entrepreneurship. Americans who didn't like their jobs or their neighborhoods were free to move on. Japanese had to learn how to get along with their groups or accept a miserable life.

The Tokugawa shoguns were overthrown in 1867 by Emperor Meiji. The Meiji dynasty that he created sought to enhance Japanese ties with the West. It brought in U.S. experts to aid in economic development and to assist in public administration. The government also sought to encourage the development of private industry. It sponsored the development of large industrial organizations called *zaibatsu.*

The zaibatsu were families of firms with interlocking ownership structures. Each zaibatsu contained firms that handled the banking and commercial needs of other firms in the organization. Firms in a zaibatsu cooperated with one another and had little interaction with outside firms. The largest zaibatsu included Mitsui, Mitsubishi, Nissan, and Sumitomo. The zaibatsu were very much in character with the feudal groups that had dominated Japanese life for centuries.

Ownership of Japan's zaibatsu was highly concentrated, and the zaibatsu controlled the bulk of Japanese industrial capacity. By the time of World War II, just 4,000 families owned zaibatsu representing almost one-half of all corporate assets in Japan.

Japan's defeat by the Allies in World War II ushered in a new economic and political system. The Allies imposed a new constitution modeled after those of Western Europe and the United States. It established a parliamentary system in which an elected legislature, the Diet, has the power to pass laws. The majority party in the Diet selects a prime minister.

Anxious to avoid the reemergence of a military threat, the Allies included in the new constitution a provision barring Japan's right to wage war. That limitation proved advantageous to Japan's economic development; it didn't have to shoulder the burdens of national defense expenditure that were undertaken by the United States and its European allies.

The Allies also sought to create a more competitive economy in Japan. The zaibatsu were broken up. The constitution created an antitrust agency with the power to prevent the degree of concentration of economic power that had been represented by the zaibatsu.

The Japanese Economy Today

On paper, Japan's economic system is very much like that of any Western economy, save for the absence of a significant defense effort. The economic system that has emerged under a political system imposed by the West, however, retains a distinctly Japanese flavor.

To a large degree, Japan's economic institutions closely resemble the highly concentrated and tightly controlled zaibatsu the allies sought to abolish. Japan's government, while now democratically chosen, continues to play a key role in the development of Japanese industry. The vigorous antitrust enforcement envisioned by the Allies has not occurred. Japan's system continues to be a product of its own historical and cultural traditions.

Japanese political leaders have never had the enthusiasm for American-style antitrust policy that was anticipated in the constitution. The old zaibatsu quickly began to reorganize. The new organizations are called *keiretsu.* They are similar to the old organizations, although firms within them operate somewhat more independently than did the zaibatsu firms. The new organizations have been permitted to take on their old names; the names of the industrial giants that dominated the old Japan are almost household words in the United States today.

The ties among keiretsu firms have been the source of trade controversies with the United States. U.S. firms seeking to export to Japan have complained vehemently about the preference that Japan's firms show for other firms in their own keiretsu. U.S. firms say the practice makes it virtually impossible for them to penetrate the Japanese market.

Government officials and business leaders in Japan have a close and generally harmonious relationship. The relationship differs markedly from the often adversarial postures that characterize these relationships in the United States.

In part, the closer relationship between business and government in Japan is a product of the Meiji period. Government officials played a key role in helping the zaibatsu to form; a continuation of this relationship is a natural by-product of this history. Personnel policies in the Japanese government's bureaucracy also play a role.

Young people starting their careers in Japan's civil service compete for one of four levels of entry. The level of entry generally determines how far a bureaucrat will rise in the civil service. The highest entry level, Class A Elite, is the fast track to success in Japan. Those who qualify for this level are destined to rise to the top levels in Japan's government.

At about age 50, a Class A Elite civil servant can hope to reach the level of vice-minister. This is roughly equivalent to the post of a cabinet undersecretary in the United States. Failure to achieve vice-minister status is not a disgrace; only about 30 percent of those on Japan's fast track make it. Those who don't achieve the rank of vice-minister generally resign from the government. They go from there into careers in business or politics; many become members of the Diet. This process of going from a high-level civil service job to a high-level job in business or in politics is called *amakudari*—"descent from heaven."

Most top civil servants can thus expect to land in business or in politics when they turn 50. Those who go into business are likely to join industries they were involved with as government officials. They thus are likely to seek cordial relationships with firms while serving in the civil service. Once they go to work for a business firm, they're likely to maintain cordial relationships with their old colleagues in the civil service—many of whom will be planning an amakudari of their own.

The government ministries staffed by Japan's civil servants play a critical role in the country's economic development. The most important of these are the Ministry of International Trade and Industry (MITI) and the Ministry of Finance.

MITI acts as an adviser to and promoter of Japanese export products. If it determines that a particular industry has promise, it may assist the industry through such measures as providing protection from foreign competition or by organizing and even subsidizing joint research projects for firms in the industry. MITI is widely credited with helping the Japanese semiconductor industry to attain a dominant position in the world market. In the 1970s, when U.S. semiconductor firms dominated the market, MITI imposed protective tariffs to insulate Japanese firms from foreign competition and assisted in research efforts conducted jointly by Japanese manufacturers. By the mid-1980s, Japanese firms commanded 90 percent of the world market. Although U.S. firms have won back much of that market, MITI's intervention appears to have been helpful.

MITI has not always been so successful. When Japanese automakers approached MITI in the 1960s with a plan to take on the world market, MITI officials discouraged the effort, saying it would be impossible for Japanese firms to compete. When Sony approached MITI with a plan to expand in the world market for consumer electronics, it was similarly rebuffed. Sony and Japanese automakers have scored great successes, but without help from the Japanese government. MITI's efforts to turn Japan into a dominant force in markets such as shipbuilding have flopped, leaving the country with huge excess capacity.

MITI also arranges for the Ministry of Finance to encourage banks to make more credit available to targeted industries. The Ministry of Finance runs Japan's central bank, the Bank of Japan. Although the Bank of Japan can't direct the lending activities of private banks, it can provide what is called "window guidance" to these banks, encouraging them to increase their lending to certain industries.

Japan's system of extensive involvement of government agencies in the operation of business, together with the widespread practice of amakudari, serve as an invitation to corruption. Japan's government has been rocked by scandals in recent years. In 1993, Japan's Liberal Democratic party failed to win a majority of the Diet for the first time in 38 years. An unlikely coalition that included conservatives and socialists took power. United only by their opposition to corruption, however, the newly powerful parties seemed unlikely to create significant change in the Japanese system.

Europe: Scaling Back the Welfare State

A decade ago, a chapter on the economies of Europe would have noted sharp differences in the economic systems of European nations. A common thread, however, would have been the much greater degree to which government participated in the market economy. France had nationalized a high proportion of industrial firms. Germany required firms to provide workers with extensive benefits. Sweden engaged in redistribution of income, and the government provided many basic services.

Many of these features remain, but European governments are now scaling back their involvement in the economy. France and the United Kingdom have privatized many firms that had been nationalized; Germany is reducing its so-called social market economy; Sweden has slashed its social welfare spending.

Pressures to reduce government involvement have come from two sources. The first is the problem of government deficits. All the countries considered in this chapter have faced rising deficits. Second, all the nations suffered sharp reductions in growth, or recessions, in the early 1990s. Many officials saw slowing growth as a signal that in order for their countries to remain competitive in the world economy, their governments would have to scale back taxes and relax the labor laws imposed on firms in order to make them more competitive in world markets. In short, global competition appeared to be forcing a diminished role for government in the market economies of Western Europe.

In addition to global competition, another force shaping the economies of the three nations is regional competition. By the end of 1992, the nations of the European Community (EC) had removed virtually all artificial barriers to trade among member nations. Tariffs and quotas have been eliminated. Consumer protection laws and other regulations are now coordinated so that they don't constitute a barrier to trade.

France, Germany and the United Kingdom are members of the EC. Their destinies are thus shaped by it. Sweden is seeking to join. The expanded role of regional competition has thus become another force for change in the economic policies of these four nations.

France: Indicative Planning and Socialism

France has long had a market capitalist economy, but it also has a tradition of a strong central government. The French have for centuries retained a substantial role for government in their economy.

Indicative Planning. Perhaps the most striking feature of the French system has been its reliance on a system of indicative planning. Under this system, the General Planning Commissariat created a series of 5-year plans for the French economy. These plans were macroeconomic projections of growth. Groups of planning commissions operating under the direction of the Commissariat established goals for specific sectors, based on the national plan.

The French planning process was indicative, not a command system, in the sense that firms were not required to base their decisions on the growth targets specified by the plan. A plan projection that investment would increase by 15 percent in the steel industry, for example, did not require individual firms to increase their investment by this amount. Instead, there was a presumption that the economy would perform more successfully if firms did meet the plan's targets. Given this, planners expected firms to find it in their own interest to cooperate.

Whether indicative planning significantly affected the choices of private firms remains an open question. Plan projections for specific sectors were seldom met. Surveys showed, however, that firms did consider the plan in making their price and output choices. In general, larger firms were more likely to consider the plan than smaller firms.

French indicative planning played an important role up to the 1980s. François Mitterand, a socialist who was elected president in 1981, gave little emphasis to the planning process. He preferred to use traditional fiscal and monetary policy to manage the economy rather than to use indicative planning. Although planning continues, its importance in the French economy has diminished greatly.

Socialism and Nationalization. Mitterand sought to extend government control over industry through **nationalization,** a process whereby a government agency takes over the ownership and operation of a private firm.

Nationalization efforts were concentrated in basic industries and in banking. In the first years of Mitterand's administration, the government's share of the iron ore industry went from zero to 71 percent, its share of iron and steel production went from 1 to 79 percent, its share of basic chemical production went from 16 to 52 percent, and its share of synthetic fibers went from zero to 75 percent. By 1983, the French government controlled nearly one-third of total output.

In addition to pursuing nationalization, the new socialist government imposed a surtax on high incomes, sought to stimulate the economy with a massive infusion of public works spending, and increased taxes on energy. The program proved very unpopular, however, and the Socialist party suffered severe losses in local elections in 1983. Mitterand quickly reversed course, and France's push toward a socialist economy was ended. In a 1983 interview that has become known in France as the "The Confession," Mitterand said that his policies had been based on a "misconception." Further efforts at nationalization were abandoned.

Nationalization is a process through which a government agency assumes the ownership and operation of a previously private firm.

In 1993, the French government announced a major reversal of the early socialist policy. It would now engage in **privatization,** a process in which government-owned firms are transferred to the private sector. The government said that 21 of the largest state-owned companies, including Renault and Air France, would be shifted to private ownership. Perhaps even more dramatic from the French perspective was the announcement that the bidding for these firms would be open to foreigners as well. The election in 1995 of a new conservative president, Jacques Chirac, made it seem likely that the process of privatization would continue.

Germany: Social Policy in a Capitalist Economy

Like Japan, Germany has emerged from defeat in World War II to a position as an economic superpower. Its economy is the third largest in the world, behind the United States and Japan. It dominates the EC, the largest free trade area in the world. Germany has a long tradition of government involvement in seeking to enhance the social welfare of its citizens.

Germany's market capitalist economy was created by the stroke of a pen. The Allies divided the defeated nation into four zones, occupied respectively by the United States, England, France, and the Soviet Union. The United States, England, and France unified their zones in 1947 and established a single currency in 1948. That zone would become West Germany. The Soviet zone became East Germany and adopted a command socialist economic system.

The Allies imposed a command capitalist economy with extensive price controls. One Sunday in 1948, when the Allied generals who ruled the occupied nation were out of the office, the German leader they had appointed, Ludwig Erhard (who had a Ph.D. in economics), ordered that all price controls be repealed. The shortages that had plagued the economy disappeared almost instantly. Allied leaders, while furious, did not countermand Erhard's order, and what has become known as the German Miracle was born. Germany enjoyed spectacular growth in the 1950s and 1960s. Growth slowed in the 1970s and 1980s, as it did in many other nations, but Germany enjoys a very high standard of living. Its inflation rate has been the lowest in Europe.

Macroeconomic Policy. Germany does not employ the kind of planning process utilized in the past by the French. Like the United States, it relies on more traditional monetary and fiscal policies.

Fiscal policy in Germany—the use of government expenditure and tax policy to influence macroeconomic performance—differs from that of the United States in one important respect. In the United States, fiscal decisions by state and local governments are largely independent of federal policy. The federal government may seek to induce state and local spending changes through grants or matching aid to these jurisdictions, but it does not regulate their spending and tax choices. Germany's "stability law" establishes two commissions, a Business Cycle Commission and a Finance Policy Commission, to coordinate the budgets of the federal, state, and local governments in an effort to stabilize the economy.

Although Germany has had a tradition of low fiscal deficits, the collapse of East Germany in 1989 and its unification with Germany the following year created severe budget problems. Germany has subsidized its new citizens heavily and has experienced large deficits as a result.

Privatization is a process in which government-owned firms are transferred to the private sector.

The more important instrument of macroeconomic stabilization is monetary policy. Germany's central bank, the Bundesbank, is even more independent of elected officials than the U.S. Federal Reserve System. The Bundesbank has stressed price stability as its primary goal, and Germany has experienced one of the lowest inflation rates in the world over the past two decades.

The Social Market Economy. The most distinctive feature of the country's economy is a set of arrangements the Germans call the social market economy (*soziale Markwirtschaft*). These arrangements represent a major government effort to intervene in market processes in order to raise living standards.

Many government social welfare programs considered standard today, such as social security and unemployment compensation, originated in Germany in the nineteenth century under Otto von Bismarck. Contemporary German policy continues this tradition.

German redistribution efforts focus not on income but on capital formation. Low-income people receive premiums from the government that they can deposit in saving accounts. The money can't be withdrawn for 7 years. Saving for home purchases is encouraged through tax policy.

Workers receive special attention in the German social market economy. Under German law, firms with 2,000 or more workers must give half the seats on their corporate boards to labor representatives. In addition, any firm with 5 or more employees must have a worker-elected enterprise council. This council meets with management to determine wages, length of the workday, firings, and layoffs. No worker can be terminated without approval of the enterprise council.

Labor participation in firm decisions may account for Germany's unusually short workdays and long vacations. The average workweek in Germany, according to the Institute of the German Economy, was 37.6 hours in 1992, compared to 40 hours in the United States and 41.5 hours in Japan. German workers averaged 30 days of paid vacation per year, compared to 12 in the United States and 11 in Japan. Partly as a consequence, German labor costs per hour were almost twice the U.S. level and 40 percent higher than costs in Japan.

Whether the provisions of Germany's social market economy will survive the 1990s is an open question. Chancellor Helmut Kohl has fought for a scaling back of the system to allow German firms to cut their production costs and to compete more effectively in the world market.

Unification. The sudden collapse of East Germany in 1989 gave West Germany a monumental opportunity—and a huge headache. The 61 million people who lived in the West enjoyed high incomes and had a tradition of freedom and limited government. The 17 million people in the East had incomes only one-third as high and had lived for decades under a dictatorship.

Eager to welcome its new citizens as full partners in a new Germany, the German government decided to allow East Germans to exchange their currency, the ostmark, for German marks on a one-to-one basis. Given that 8 ostmarks had exchanged for 1 mark in the black market, this represented a significant overvaluation of the ostmark. The policy greatly increased the German money supply and contributed to inflationary pressures.

The productivity of workers in the East was only about one-fourth of the level in the West. There was, however, substantial union pressure to equalize wages for both groups of workers. This further attempt to create an equitable situation for all Germans meant that production costs in the East were suddenly increased. There has been little foreign investment in the former East Germany, and there is high unemployment among East German workers. Harsh economic conditions in the East, combined with Germany's generous benefits for unemployed workers, have created severe budgetary problems for the newly unified country.

Privatization of formerly state-owned firms in the East has moved fairly quickly. Each firm was reorganized as a joint stock company in which investors were permitted to purchase shares. Most industrial capacity in East Germany has been transferred to private ownership.

Absorption of East Germany into a unified Germany has been a more painful challenge than anyone in Germany seems to have anticipated. Still, the process is going forward, and the adjustments required in the East are being made.

Sweden: A Capitalist Welfare State

Sweden has long served as a model for a successful combination of market capitalism with extensive income redistribution and provision of social services. It achieved high growth rates and high incomes in the 1960s.

Sweden's welfare state provides a wide range of benefits. The government pays for health care, nursing home care, and day care for children. It provides housing, generous unemployment compensation, and income assistance. Sweden's social policies have achieved an income distribution among the most equal in Europe.

These benefits, however, come at a cost. Sweden's tax burden is among the highest in Europe. Partly as a result, Sweden's growth rate was the slowest in Europe in the 1980s. Inflation began to accelerate in the 1980s. Faced with a high tax burden, Sweden's firms had difficulty competing in world trade. Conditions did not improve in the early 1990s; from 1990 to 1993, Sweden was mired in its worst recession since the Great Depression.

The slumping economy exacerbated Sweden's deficit problems. With its citizens earning lower incomes, Sweden's government collected less in taxes. As unemployment and poverty increased, expenditures shot up. To bring down its deficit, Sweden launched an austerity program in 1991. It scaled back welfare benefits and turned over the operation of many government services, such as day-care centers, to private firms.

Whether Sweden's extensive provision of social services will last through the 1990s is an open question. Certainly the direction of change now is toward dismantling the system. Sweden is seeking membership in the EC, which would put its firms in a free trade area competing with others that have much lower tax burdens. EC membership would put further pressure on the Swedes to cut the size and scope of social welfare spending.

But the tradition in Sweden of equality achieved through social programs is a strong one. A government proposal to trim the allowance parents receive when they take a year off work to care for a new child to 75 percent—from the then current level of 80 percent—faced heated opposition in 1995. Supporters of the social welfare state in Sweden argue that poor economic performance is caused not by extensive income redistribution but by poor macroeconomic management by the government. Although opponents of the welfare state have had their way politically for the past few years, the pendulum in Sweden could easily swing back toward support of redistributive policies.

The United Kingdom: Fighting the British Disease

The United Kingdom led the world up the path of industrialization in the 18th century. It dominated world economic affairs through the 19th century as well. But by the end of the 1970s, the combination of slow growth, high unemployment, and high inflation had come to be called the "British disease." Was the British disease an inevitable malady facing mature market capitalist economies such as the United States?

The 1950s and 1960s: Malaise Sets In

In some respects, the British experience after World War II parallels that of France. Both countries suffered extensive damage during the war. Both engaged in extensive nationalization efforts during the post-War period.

But France enjoyed relatively rapid growth during this period. While the British economy grew, its rate lagged behind that of other industrial nations. The small island that had dominated the world began to slip behind.

Several factors may have contributed to Britain's weak performance. Its steeply progressive income tax system, with a top rate of 90 percent, caused many of its most productive citizens to flee the country. Those who support planning note that the French made extensive use of indicative planning during this period; the British rejected this approach. The British nationalized several key industries but never proceeded as far in this area as did the French. Some critics suggest that one explanation for poor economic performance was a strong class system that tended to distribute rewards and power based on ancestry rather than merit. Still another possible cause was the extensive use of fiscal policy to attempt to manage the economy. Called incomes policy by its adherents and stop-go management by its critics, efforts to stimulate the economy through greater government spending may have contributed to poor economic performance.

The 1970s: Responding to Shocks

The United Kingdom has always been highly dependent on international trade. It has few natural resources and little agricultural land, so it must rely on foreign suppliers for many basic commodities. Its imports as a share of gross domestic product account for more than twice as large a share of gross domestic product as is the case in the United States.

Given its reliance on international trade, it is not surprising that the United Kingdom was strongly affected by sharp increases in international oil prices during the 1970s. Those increases tended to push production costs and prices up and output down throughout the world.

But Britain, which had performed more poorly than most European nations in the previous two decades, seemed to suffer more. Its inflation rate during the 1970s was among the highest in Europe; its growth rate continued to be among the lowest. Productivity of labor languished, while powerful unions continued to achieve sharp wage gains. If there was such a thing as a British disease, it appeared to be worsening.

The Thatcher Era

Margaret Thatcher, the leader of the Conservative Party in Britain, became prime minister in 1979. Her diagnosis of the British disease was simple: It resulted from the excessive role of the public sector under a series of governments dominated by the Labor Party.

Mrs. Thatcher immediately launched a program to reverse the course of the British economy. She began privatizing industries nationalized under previous Labor governments. She sought to deregulate the economy, to weaken the power of national labor unions, and to lower marginal tax rates. She shifted British macroeconomic policy from an extensive use of fiscal policy to a reliance on monetary policy. That policy, in turn, sought to reduce inflation.

Thatcherism, as it came to be known, appears to have been a success. Among the countries covered in this chapter, the United Kingdom's growth rate ranked third during the 1980s. Although Britain's inflation rate remained relatively high, it was less than half the rate Britain suffered during the 1970s. Mrs. Thatcher became the first British prime minister in 160 years to be elected to three consecutive terms; she resigned in 1990.

It's not clear how much of Britain's turnaround can be attributed to Thatcherism and how much can be attributed to a fortuitous development of the late 1970s, the discovery of oil in Britain's North Sea. This discovery helped lift British production and put downward pressure on prices, moving the British economy in the same direction as did Mrs. Thatcher's policies. Untangling the contribution of each would be a difficult task.

In any event, the Thatcher era clearly changed the nature of the British economy. Mrs. Thatcher's successor, John Major, another Conservative, has generally continued her policies. Even the return to a Labor government would not be likely to return Britain to the policies it pursued so unsuccessfully in the postwar period.

The stories of four European nations—France, Germany, Sweden, and the United Kingdom—follow a consistent theme. All these economies are market capitalist in structure. All have achieved high levels of per capita income. All have featured much more extensive roles for the public sector than have prevailed in the United States. And all have begun an effort in the last several years to shrink the role of the public sector and to reduce the costs it imposes on the economy.

Checklist

- Among the developed economies discussed in this chapter, the United States has the highest level of per capita output, and Japan has the highest growth rate, the lowest inflation rate, the lowest share of government expenditures, and the most equal distribution of income.
- Three centuries of life under the Tokugawa shoguns fostered a collective mentality and a sense of shared destiny in Japan, in sharp contrast to the spirit of individualism that has predominated in the United States.
- Japan's amakudari tradition in its civil service fosters a close relationship between business and government.
- The governments of France, Germany, Sweden, and the United Kingdom have, in the last few years, sought to scale back the scope of government activity in the marketplace.

A Look Back—and a Look Ahead

Economies can be classified in terms of the ownership of capital and natural resources and the power over decisions in the use of those resources. An economy in which ownership is public is a socialist economy; one in which ownership of capital and natural resources is private is a capitalist economy. If decisions concerning the allocation of these resources are made primarily by the public sector, the economy is a command economy. If decisions are made primarily by the private sector, it is a market economy.

Command socialist and market socialist economies have almost disappeared. The only remaining command socialist economies are Cuba and North Korea; the others collapsed in the late 1980s and early 1990s. The primary difficulty of those economies appeared to be an inability to generate incentives to encourage the efficient use of resources.

Command capitalist economies suffer from extensive corruption and slow economic growth. These economies are typically quite poor. Many formerly command capitalist economies are slashing the scope of government regulation and moving in the direction of market capitalism.

Market capitalist economies provide powerful incentives for efficient resource use and have generated the highest living standards ever achieved. Such systems rely on government to redistribute income and to produce public goods.

We examined five market capitalist economies. They illustrate the varied roles governments may undertake within a market capitalist system. Japan has long had a close relationship between its government and private firms and has generated impressive economic growth. Germany, France, Sweden, and the United Kingdom have, in recent years, been scaling back the scope of government intervention in the economy. This effort appears to be a response to concerns about budget deficits and international competitiveness.

In Chapter 38, we'll examine another process of transition. Most command socialist nations are now undertaking transitions to a market capitalist system. We'll study the conceptual foundations of socialism and assess its performance as an economic system. Finally, we'll explore the transition process itself.

Terms and Concepts for Review

Nationalization

Privatization

For Discussion

1. How does market socialism differ from command socialism? From market capitalism? Would a market socialist firm have the same incentives and make the same choices as a market capitalist firm?
2. Distinguish between market capitalism and command capitalism.
3. Is the United States a market capitalist or a command capitalist economy? What about Canada?
4. Many people advocate a much stronger role for the government in the health care market. They argue that the government should set prices and determine which health care procedures should and should not be undertaken. What sort of economic system would this imply for the health care sector? If the United States were to adopt such a system, would that affect your answer to Question 3?
5. The text notes that many firms in France are owned and operated by the government. Does this make France a command socialist economy? Why or why not?
6. During the 1930s, the Roosevelt administration established controls over most prices charged in the United States. The Nixon administration did the same thing in 1971. What type of economic system did the United States have during those periods?
7. Vietnam, which has traditionally relied on a system of government ownership and government decisionmaking concerning the use of capital, has moved toward greater reliance on the market, letting the managers of government-owned firms make more of their own choices in determining prices to charge and quantities to produce. Toward what type of economic system does it appear to be moving?
8. Given the categories listed in the text, what form of economic system do you favor? Why?

38

Socialist Economies in Transition

Chapter Objectives

After mastering the material in this chapter, you will be able to:

1. Discuss the conceptual basis for Marx's prediction that capitalism would give way to socialism.
2. Trace the evolution of the system of command socialism in the Soviet Union.
3. Describe the operation of the command socialist system in the Soviet Union and note the problems it engendered.
4. Explain the operation of the market socialist system in Yugoslavia.
5. Discuss the problems faced by all countries engaged in the transition from command socialism to market capitalism.
6. Compare the approaches to transition chosen in China and Russia.

Socialism: The longest and most painful path from capitalism to capitalism.

A definition often offered in jest in formerly socialist countries

What's Ahead

It's hard, even in retrospect, to appreciate how swiftly the collapse came. Command socialism, which had reigned supreme in Russia for more than 70 years and in much of the rest of the world for more than 40, had come to seem a permanent institution. Indeed, many observers had expected its influence to increase by the end of the twentieth century. But in the span of 5 months in 1989, command socialist systems fell in six Eastern European nations. The Soviet Union broke up in 1991.

The start of the collapse can be dated to 1980. The government of Poland, a command socialist state that was part of the Soviet bloc, raised meat prices. The price boosts led to widespread protests and to the organization of Solidarity, the first independent labor union permitted in a Soviet bloc state. After 9 years of political clashes, Solidarity won an agreement from the Polish government for wide-ranging economic reforms and for free elections. Solidarity-backed candidates swept the elections in June 1989, and a new government, pledged to democracy and to market capitalism, came to power in August.

Command socialist governments in the rest of the Soviet bloc disappeared quickly in the wake of Poland's transformation. Hungary's government fell in October. East Germany opened the Berlin Wall in November, and the old regime, for which that wall had been a symbol, collapsed. Bulgaria and Czechoslovakia kicked out their command socialist leaders the same month. Romania's dictator, Nicolae Ceausescu, was executed after a bloody uprising in December. Ultimately, every nation in the Warsaw Pact, the bloc comprising the Soviet Union and its Eastern European satellite nations, announced its intention to discard the old system of command socialism. The collapse of the command socialist regimes of the former Soviet bloc precipitated an often painful process of transition as countries tried to put in place the institutions of a market capitalist economy.

Meanwhile, a very different process of transition has been under way in China. The Chinese began a gradual process of transition toward a market economy in 1979. It has been a process marked by spectacular economic gain and tragic political repression.

In this chapter we'll examine the rise of command and market socialist systems and explore their ideological roots. Then we'll see how these economic systems operated and trace the sources of their collapse. Finally, we'll investigate the problems and prospects for the transition from command socialism to market capitalism.

The Theory and Practice of Socialism

Socialism has a very long history. The earliest recorded socialist society is described in the Book of Acts in the Bible. Following the crucifixion of Christ, Christians in Jerusalem established a system in which all property was owned in common.

There have been other socialist experiments in which all property was held in common, effectively creating socialist societies. Early in the nineteenth century, such visionaries as Robert Owen, Count Claude-Henri de Rouvroy de Saint-Simon, and Charles Fourier established almost 200 communities in which workers shared in the proceeds of their labor. These visionaries, while operating independently, shared a common ideal—that in the appropriate economic environment, people will strive for the good of the community rather than for their own self-interest. Although some of these communities enjoyed a degree of early success, none survived.

Socialism as the organizing principle for a national economy is in large part the product of the revolutionary ideas of one man, Karl Marx. His analysis of what he saw as the inevitable collapse of market capitalist economies provided a rallying spark for the national socialist movements of this century. Another important contributor to socialist thought was Vladimir Ilyich Lenin, who modified many of Marx's theories for application to the Soviet Union. Lenin put his ideas into practice as dictator of that country from 1917 until his death in 1924. In the next two sections, we shall examine the ideas of Marx and Lenin and investigate the operation of the economic systems based upon them.

The Economics of Karl Marx

Marx is perhaps best known for the revolutionary ideas expressed in the ringing phrases of the *Communist Manifesto:* "Let the ruling classes tremble at a Communist revolution. The proletarians [workers] have nothing to lose but their chains. They have a world to win." Written with Friedrich Engels in 1848, the *Manifesto* was a call to arms. But it was Marx's exhaustive, detailed theoretical analysis of market capitalism, *Das Kapital ("Capital"),* that was his most important effort. This four-volume work, most of which was published after Marx's death, examines a theoretical economy that we would now describe as perfect competition. In this context, Marx outlined a dynamic process that would, he argued, inevitably result in the collapse of capitalism.

Marx stressed a historical approach to the analysis of economics. Indeed, he was sharply critical of his contemporaries, complaining that their work was wholly lacking in historical perspective. To Marx, capitalism was merely a stage in the development of economic systems. He explained how feudalism would tend to give way to capitalism and how capitalism would give way to socialism. Marx's conclusions stemmed from his labor theory of value and from his perception of the role of profit in a capitalist economy.

The Labor Theory of Value and Surplus Value

Adam Smith argued in *The Wealth of Nations* that the relative values of different goods were ultimately determined by the relative amounts of labor used in their production. This idea, which is called the **labor theory of value,** was widely accepted at the time Marx was writing. Economists recognized the roles of demand and supply but argued that these would affect prices only in the short run. In the long run, it was labor that determined value.

Marx attached normative implications to the ideas of the labor theory of value. Not only was labor the ultimate determinant of value; it was the only *legitimate* determinant of value. The price of a good in Marx's system equaled the sum of the labor and capital costs of its production, plus profit to the capitalist. Marx argued that capital costs were determined by the amount of labor used to produce the capital, so the price of a good equaled a return to labor plus profit. Marx defined profit as **surplus value,** the difference between the price of a good or service and the labor cost of producing it. Marx insisted that surplus value was unjustified and represented exploitation of workers.

Marx accepted another piece of conventional economic wisdom of the nineteenth century, the concept of subsistence wages. This idea held that wages would, in the long run, tend toward their subsistence level, a level just sufficient to keep workers alive. Any increase in wages above their subsistence level would simply attract more workers, forcing wages back down. Marx suggested that unemployed workers were important in this process; they represented a surplus of labor that acted to push wages down.

Capital Accumulation and Capitalist Crises

The concepts of surplus value and subsistence wages provide the essential dynamics of Marx's system. He said that capitalists, in an effort to increase surplus value, would seek to acquire more capital. But as they expanded capital, their profit rates, expressed as a percentage of the capital they held, would fall. In a desperate effort to push profit rates up, capitalists would acquire still more capital, which would only push their rate of return down further.

A further implication of Marx's scheme was that as capitalists increased their use of capital, the wages received by workers would become a smaller share of the total value of goods. Marx assumed that capitalists did not consume; they used all their funds to acquire more capital. Only workers, then, could be counted on for consumption. But their wages equaled only a fraction of the value of the output they produced—they could not possibly buy all of it. The result, Marx said, would be a series of crises in which capitalists throughout the economy, unable to sell their output, would cut back production. This would cause still more reductions in demand, exacerbating the downturn in economic activity. Crises would drive the weakest capitalists out of business; they would become unemployed and thus push wages down further. The economy could recover from such crises, but each one would weaken the capitalist system.

Faced with declining surplus values and reeling from occasional crises, capitalists would seek out markets in other countries. As they extended their reach throughout the world, Marx said, the scope of their exploitation of workers would expand. Although capitalists could make temporary gains by opening up international markets, their continuing acquisition of capital meant that profit rates would resume their downward trend. Capitalist crises would now become global affairs.

- The **labor theory of value** holds that the relative values of goods and services are ultimately determined by the quantities of labor required in their production.
- **Surplus value** is the difference between the price of a good or service and its labor cost.

According to Marx, another result of capitalists' doomed efforts to boost surplus value would be increased solidarity among the working class. At home, capitalist acquisition of capital meant workers would be crowded into factories, building their sense of class identity. As capitalists extended their exploitation worldwide, workers would gain a sense of solidarity with fellow workers all over the planet. Marx argued that workers would recognize that they were the victims of exploitation by capitalists.

Marx wasn't clear about precisely what forces would combine to bring about the downfall of capitalism. He suggested other theories of crisis in addition to the one based on insufficient demand for the goods and services produced by capitalists. Indeed, modern theories of the business cycle owe much to Marx's discussion of the possible sources of economic downturns. Although Marx spoke sometimes of bloody revolution, it isn't clear that this was the mechanism he thought would bring on the demise of capitalism. Whatever the precise mechanism, Marx was confident that capitalism would fall, that its collapse would be worldwide, and that socialism would replace it.

Marx's Theory: An Assessment

To a large degree, Marx's analysis of a capitalist economy was a logical outgrowth of widely accepted economic doctrines of his time. As we've seen, the labor theory of value was conventional wisdom, as was the notion that workers would receive only a subsistence wage. The notion that profit rates would fall over time was widely accepted. Doctrines similar to Marx's notion of recurring crises had been developed by several economists of the period.

What was different about Marx was his tracing of the dynamics of a system in which values would be determined by the quantity of labor, wages would tend toward the subsistence level, profit rates would fall and crises would occur from time to time. Marx saw these forces as leading inevitably to the fall of capitalism and its replacement with a socialist economic system. Other economists of the period generally argued that economies would stagnate; they did not anticipate the collapse predicted by Marx.

Marx's predictions have turned out to be wildly off the mark. Profit rates have not declined; they have remained relatively stable. Wages have not tended downward toward their subsistence level; they have risen. Labor's share of total income in market economies hasn't fallen; it has increased. Most important, the predicted collapse of capitalist economies hasn't occurred.

Revolutions aimed at establishing socialism have been rare. Perhaps most important, none has occurred in a market capitalist economy. In Cuba and Nicaragua, command capitalist systems were overthrown and socialist systems were established. In other cases where socialism has been established through revolution, it has replaced systems that could best be described as feudal. The Russian Revolution of 1917 that established the Soviet Union and the revolution that established the People's Republic of China in 1949 are the most important examples of this form of revolution. In the countries of Eastern Europe, socialism was imposed by the former Soviet Union in the wake of World War II.

Whatever the shortcomings of Marx's economic prognostications, his ideas have had enormous influence. Politically, his concept of the inevitable emergence of socialism promoted the proliferation of socialist governments during the middle third of this century. Before socialist systems began collapsing in 1989, fully one-third of the earth's population lived in countries that had adopted Marx's ideas. Ideologically, his vision of a market capitalist system in which one class exploits another has had enormous influence.

Socialist Systems in Action

The most important example of socialism was the economy of the Union of Soviet Socialist Republics, the Soviet Union. The Russian Revolution succeeded in 1917 in overthrowing the czarist regime that had ruled the Russian Empire for centuries. Leaders of the revolution created the Soviet Union in its place and sought to establish a socialist state based on the ideas of Karl Marx.

The leaders of the Soviet Union faced a difficulty in using Marx's writings as a foundation for a socialist system. He had sought to explain why capitalism would collapse; he had little to say about how the socialist system that would replace it would function. He did suggest the utopian notion that, over time, there would be less and less need for a government and the state would wither away. But his writings did not provide much of a blueprint for running a socialist economic system.

Lacking a guide for establishing a socialist economy, the leaders of the new regime in Russia struggled to invent one. The first government, set up by a freely elected Constituent Assembly, was overthrown in a coup led by Lenin in November 1917. Lenin, who then ruled as a dictator, attempted to establish what he called "war communism." The national government declared its ownership of most firms and forced peasants to turn over a share of their output to the government. The program sought to eliminate the market as an allocative mechanism; government would control production and distribution. The program of war communism devastated the economy. In 1921, Lenin declared a New Economic Policy. It returned private ownership to some sectors of the economy and reinstituted the market as an allocative mechanism.

Lenin's death in 1924 precipitated a power struggle from which Joseph Stalin emerged victorious. It was under Stalin that the Soviet economic system was created. Because that system served as a model for most of the other command socialist systems that emerged, we shall examine it in some detail. We shall also examine an intriguing alternative version of socialism, market socialism, that was created in Yugoslavia after World War II.

Command Socialism in the Soviet Union

Stalin began by seizing virtually all remaining privately owned capital and natural resources in the country. The seizure was a brutal affair; he eliminated opposition to his measures through mass executions, forced starvation of whole regions, and deportation of political opponents to prison camps. Estimates of the number of people killed during Stalin's centralization of power range in the tens of millions. With the state in control of the means of production, Stalin established a rigid system in which a central administration in Moscow determined what would be produced.

The justification for the brutality of Soviet rule lay in the quest to develop "socialist man." Leaders of the Soviet Union argued that the tendency of people to behave in their own self-interest was a by-product of capitalism, not an inherent characteristic of human beings. A successful socialist state required that the preferences of people be transformed so that they would be motivated by the collective interests of society, not their own self-interest. Propaganda was widely used to reinforce a collective identity. Those individuals who were deemed beyond reform were likely to be locked up or executed.

The political arm of command socialism was the Communist party. Party officials participated in every aspect of Soviet life in an effort to promote the concept of socialist man and to control individual behavior. Party leaders were represented in every firm and in every government agency. Party officials charted the general course for the economy as well.

A planning agency, the Gosplan, determined the quantities of output that key firms would produce each year and the prices that would be charged. Other government agencies set output levels for smaller firms. These determinations were made in a series of plans. A 1-year plan specified production targets for that year. Soviet planners also developed 5-year and 20-year plans.

Managers of state-owned firms were rewarded on the basis of their ability to meet the annual quotas set by the Gosplan. The system of quotas and rewards created inefficiency in several ways. First, no central planning agency could incorporate preferences of consumers and costs of factors of production in its decisions concerning the quantity of each good to produce. Decisions about what to produce were made by political leaders; they were not a response to market forces. Further, planners could not select prices at which quantities produced would clear their respective markets. In a market economy, prices adjust to changes in demand and supply. Given that demand and supply are always changing, it is inconceivable that central planners could ever select market-clearing prices. Soviet central planners typically selected prices for consumer goods that were below market-clearing levels, causing shortages throughout the economy. Changes in prices were rare.

Plant managers had a powerful incentive for meeting their quotas; they could expect bonuses equal to about 35 percent of their base salary for producing the quantities required of their firms. Those who exceeded their quotas could boost this to 50 percent. In addition, successful managers were given vacations, better apartments, better medical care, and a host of other perquisites. Quotas were set in terms of the gross value of production. Managers thus had a direct interest in meeting their quotas; they had no incentive to select efficient production techniques or to reduce costs.

Perhaps most important, there was no incentive for plant managers to adopt new technologies. A plant implementing a new technology risked start-up delays that could cause it to fall short of its quota. If a plant did succeed in boosting output, it was likely to be forced to accept even larger quotas in the future. A plant manager who introduced a successful technology would only be slapped with tougher quotas; if the technology failed he or she would lose a bonus. With little to gain and a great deal to lose, Soviet plant managers were extremely reluctant to adopt new technologies. Soviet production was, as a result, characterized by outdated technologies. When the system fell in 1991, Soviet manufacturers were using production methods that had been obsolete for decades in other countries.

Centrally controlled systems often generated impressive numbers for total output but failed in satisfying consumer demands. Gosplan officials, recognizing that Soviet capital was not very productive, ordered up a lot of it. The result was a heavy emphasis on relatively unproductive capital goods and relatively little production of consumer goods. On the eve of the collapse of the Soviet Union, Soviet economists estimated that per capita consumption was as low as one-tenth the U.S. level.

The Soviet system also generated severe environmental problems. In principle, a socialist system should have an advantage over a capitalist system in allocating environmental resources for which private property rights are difficult to define. Because a socialist government owns all capital and natural resources, the ownership problem is solved. The problem in the Soviet system, however, came from the labor theory of value. Since natural resources aren't produced by labor, the value assigned to them was zero. Soviet plant managers thus had no incentive to limit their exploitation of environmental resources, and terrible environmental tragedies were common. Russia's leaders today must grapple with the results of the environmental choices made under the Soviet system. The Lenin Steel Works exemplifies official unconcern for environmental resources. The plant, the world's largest, spews out so much pollution into the air in its home city of Magnitogorsk, a city 670 miles east of Moscow, that fewer than 1 percent of the children there are considered in good health.

Systems similar to that created in the Soviet Union were established in other Soviet bloc countries as well. The most important exceptions were Yugoslavia, which is discussed in the next section, and China, which started with a Soviet-style system and then moved away from it. The Chinese case is examined later in this chapter.

Yugoslavia: A Market Socialist Experiment

Although the Soviet Union was able to impose a system of command socialism on nearly all the Eastern European countries it controlled after World War II, Yugoslavia managed to forge its own path. Yugoslavia's communist leader, Marshal Tito, charted an independent course, accepting aid from Western nations such as the United States and establishing a unique form of market socialism. Most important, however, Tito quickly moved away from the centralized management style of the Soviet Union to a decentralized system in which workers exercised considerable autonomy.

In the Yugoslav system, firms with five or more employees were owned by the state but made their own decisions concerning what to produce and what prices to charge. Workers in these firms elected their managers and established their own systems for sharing revenues. Each firm paid a fee for the use of its state-owned capital. In effect, firms operated as labor cooperatives. Firms with fewer than five employees could be privately owned and operated.

Economic performance in Yugoslavia was impressive. Living standards there were generally higher than those in other Soviet bloc countries. The distribution of income was similar to that of command socialist economies; it was generally more equal than distributions achieved in market capitalist economies. The Yugoslav economy was plagued, however, by persistent unemployment, high inflation, and increasing disparities in regional income levels.

Yugoslavia began breaking up shortly after command socialist systems began falling in Eastern Europe. It had been a country of republics and provinces forced together through foreign domination and interrepublic conquest. Tito had been the glue that held them together. After his death, the groups began to move apart. In 1991, Croatia, Bosnia and Herzegovina, and Slovenia declared their independence from Yugoslavia; Macedonia followed suit in 1992. The country's intriguing experiment with market socialism was soon lost as a series of bloody ethnic struggles erupted.

Evaluating Economic Performance Under Socialism

Soviet leaders placed great emphasis on Marx's concept of the inevitable collapse of capitalism. While they downplayed the likelihood of a global revolution, they argued that the inherent superiority of socialism would gradually become apparent. Countries would adopt the socialist model in order to improve their living standards, and socialism would gradually assert itself as the dominant world system.

One key to achieving the goal of a socialist world was to outperform the United States economically. Stalin promised in the 1930s that the Soviet economy would surpass that of the United States within a few decades. The goal was clearly not achieved. Indeed, it was the gradual realization that the command socialist system could not deliver high living standards that led to the collapse of the old system.

Exhibit 38-1 shows the World Bank's estimates of per capita output, measured in dollars of 1993 purchasing power, for the republics that made up the Soviet Union, for the Warsaw Pact nations of Eastern Europe for which data are available, and for the United States in 1993. Nations that had operated within the old Soviet system had quite low levels of per capita output. Living standards were lower still, given that these nations devoted much higher shares of total output to investment and to defense than did the United States.

Ultimately, it was the failure of the Soviet system to deliver living standards on a par with those achieved by market capitalist economies that brought the system down. We saw in Chapter 2 that market capitalist economic systems create incentives to allocate resources efficiently; socialist systems do not. Of course, a society may decide that other attributes of a socialist system make it worth retaining. But the lesson of the 1980s was that few who had lived under command socialist systems wanted to continue to do so.

Checklist

- Marx's theory, based on the labor theory of value and the presumption that wages would approach their subsistence level, predicted the inevitable collapse of capitalism and its replacement by socialist regimes.
- Soviet leaders after the 1917 revolution had to develop their own version of socialism. The system installed by Stalin was a form of command socialism.
- In the Soviet Union a central planning agency, the Gosplan, set output quotas for enterprises and determined prices.
- Yugoslavia developed a system of market socialism in which firms were run by their workers as labor cooperatives.
- Command socialist systems generated very low standards of living relative to the United States and other industrialized nations.

EXHIBIT 38-1

Per Capita Output in Former Soviet Bloc States and in the United States, 1993

Per capita output was far lower in the former republics of the Soviet Union and in Warsaw Pact countries in 1993 than in the United States. All values are measured in units of equivalent purchasing power.

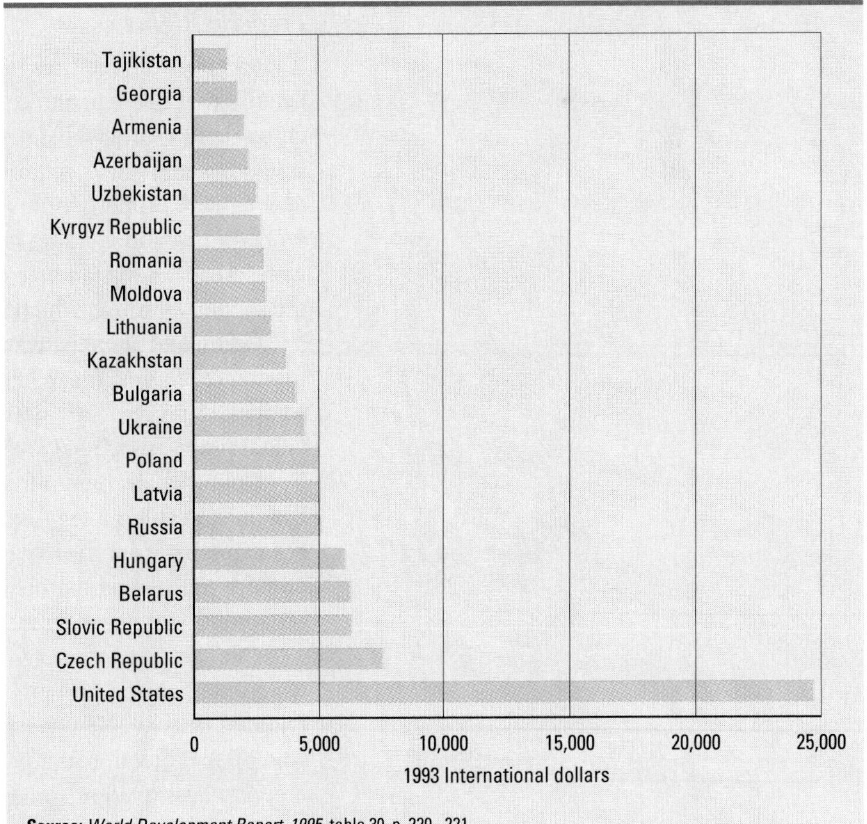

Source: *World Development Report, 1995,* table 30, p. 220–221.

Economies in Transition: China and Russia

Just as leaders of the Soviet Union had to create their own command socialist systems, so leaders of the economies making the transition to market capitalist economies must find their own paths to new economic systems. It is a task without historical precedent.

In this section we'll examine two countries and the strategies they have chosen for the transition. China was the first socialist nation to begin the process, and in many ways it has been the most successful. Russia was the dominant republic in the old Soviet Union; whether its transition is successful will be crucially important. Before turning to the transition process in these two countries, we shall consider some general problems common to all countries seeking to establish market capitalism in the wake of command socialism.

Problems in Transition

Establishing a system of market capitalism in a command socialist economy is a daunting task. It's also a task no nation has yet completed; the nations making the attempt must invent the process as they go along. Each of them, though, faces similar problems. Former command socialist economies must establish systems of property rights, establish banking systems, deal with the problem of inflation, and work through a long tradition of ideological antipathy toward the basic nature of a capitalist system.

Property Rights

A market system requires property rights before it can function. A property right details what one can and cannot do with a particular asset. A market system requires laws that specify the actions that are permitted and those that are proscribed, and it also requires institutions for the enforcement of agreements dealing with property rights. These include a court system and lawyers trained in property law and contract law. For the system to work effectively, there must be widespread understanding of the basic nature of private property and of the transactions through which it is allocated.

Command socialist economies possess virtually none of these prerequisites for market capitalism. When the state owned virtually all capital and natural resources, there was little need to develop a legal system that would spell out individual property rights. Governments were largely free to do as they wished.

Countries seeking a transition from command socialism to market capitalism must develop a legal system comparable to those that have evolved in market capitalist countries over centuries. The problem of creating a system of property rights and the institutions necessary to support it is a large hurdle for economies making the transition to a market economy.

One manifestation of the difficulties inherent in establishing clear and widely recognized property rights in formerly socialist countries is widespread criminal activity. Newly established private firms must contend with racketeers who offer protection at a price. Firms that refuse to pay the price may find their property destroyed or some of their managers killed. Criminal activity has been rampant in economies struggling toward a market capitalist system.

Banking

Banks in command socialist countries were operated by the state. There was no tradition of banking functions as they are understood in market capitalist countries.

In a market capitalist economy, a privately owned bank accepts deposits from customers and lends these deposits to borrowers. These borrowers are typically firms or consumers. Banks in command socialist economies generally accepted saving deposits, but checking accounts for private individuals were virtually unknown. Decisions to advance money to firms were made through the economic planning process, not by individual banks. Banks didn't have an opportunity to assess the profitability of individual enterprises; such considerations were irrelevant in the old command socialist systems. Bankers in these economies were thus unaccustomed to the roles that would be required of them in a market capitalist system.

Inflation

One particularly vexing problem facing transitional economies is inflation. Inflation in a market capitalist economy is caused when the money supply increases too rapidly, forcing up prices.

Under command socialist systems, the government set prices; it could abolish inflation by decree. But such systems were characterized by chronic shortages of consumer goods. Consumers, unable to find the goods they wanted to buy, simply accumulated money. As command socialist economies began their transitions, there was typically a very large quantity of money available for consumers to spend. A first step in transitions was the freeing of prices. Because the old state-determined prices were generally below equilibrium levels, prices typically surged in the early stages of transition. Prices in Poland, for example, shot up 400 percent within a few months of price decontrol. Prices in Russia went up 10-fold within 6 months.

One dilemma facing transitional economies has been the plight of bankrupt state enterprises. In a market capitalist economy, firms unable to generate revenues that exceed their costs go out of business. In command socialist economies, the central bank simply wrote checks to cover their deficits. As these economies have begun the transition toward market capitalism, they have generally declared their intention to end these bailouts and to let failing firms fail. But the phenomenon of money-losing state firms is so pervasive that allowing all of them to fail at once could cause massive disruption in economies in which output is already falling. Russian economics minister Andrei Nechayev estimated in 1992, for example, that half of all of Russia's state enterprises were on the verge of bankruptcy.

The practical alternative to allowing firms to fail has been continued bailouts. But in transitional economies, that has meant issuing money to failed firms. This practice increases the money supply and contributes to continuing inflation. Poland and Russia have managed to reduce their inflation rates somewhat, but prices continued to rise at a very rapid rate through the early 1990s.

Ideology

Soviet citizens, and their counterparts in other command socialist economies, have been told for decades that market capitalism is an evil institution, that it

Case in Point: Russia Erases Currency to Fight Inflation

Russian Finance Minister Boris Fyodorov did not mince words in describing the central bank's ploy to stem inflation. "Criminal," "nothing but fraud," "stupid and meaningless," and "economically illiterate" were among the terms he used to describe Central Bank Chairman Viktor Gerashchenko's sudden announcement. The bank chairman declared in July 1993 that two weeks later, rubles printed before 1993 would be invalid.

Russians waiting to change rubles at a bank.

Further, the bank official decreed that Russians could exchange no more than 35,000 old rubles—worth about $35—for new currency. If they had any more money than that, it would be erased.

The stated purpose of the new plan was to put a lid on inflation. Mikhail Gorbachev had instituted a similar policy in the last months of the old Soviet Union, declaring 50- and 100-ruble notes invalid in an effort to reduce the money supply and thus limit inflation. That policy failed, however, because the central bank continued to print new money. The 1993 declaration seemed certain to fail as well; Mr. Gerashchenko's decree did not include a plan to reduce the rate at which the bank would create new money.

The entire episode pointed up the uncertain nature of power in Russia's new government. Russia's president, Boris Yeltsin, denounced the central bank's policy. He ordered that the time limit for exchanging rubles be extended by 3 weeks and that the limit on the amount of currency Russians could exchange be increased. The Supreme Soviet, Russia's legislature, declared the central bank's order invalid. And the central bank insisted that it would carry out its policy as originally stated.

The episode illustrated the often chaotic nature of the new Russian government. Ultimately, the central bank, which is technically under the direction of the president, got its way, and the currency was abolished. And ultimately, the program failed to reduce inflation because the central bank continued to create new money to finance the deficits of state firms.

Source: Elisabeth Rubinfein, "Yeltsin Eases Terms of Program to Invalidate Pre-1993 Rubles," *The Wall Street Journal,* 27 July 1993, A12.

fosters greed and human misery. They've been told that some people become rich in the system, but that they do so only at the expense of others who become poorer.

In the context of a competitive market, this view of market processes as a zero-sum game—one in which the gains for one person come only as a result of losses for another—is wrong. In market transactions, one person gains only by making others better off. But the zero-sum view runs deep, and it is a source of potential hostility toward market forces.

Countries seeking to transform their economies from command socialist to more market-oriented systems face daunting challenges. Given these challenges, it is remarkable that they have persisted in the effort. There are a thousand reasons for economic reform to fail, but the reform effort has, in general, continued to move forward.

China: A Gradual Transition

China is a giant by virtually any standard. Larger than the continental United States, it is home to more than 1.4 billion people—more than one-fifth of the earth's population. Although China is desperately poor, its economy has been among the fastest growing in the world for the past 15 years. That rapid growth is the result of a gradual shift toward a market capitalist economy. The Chinese have pursued their transition in a manner quite different from the paths taken by former Soviet bloc nations.

Recent History

China was invaded by Japan during World War II. After Japan's defeat, civil war broke out between Chinese communists, led by Mao Zedong, and nationalists. The communists prevailed, and the People's Republic of China was proclaimed in 1949. The nationalists retreated to Taiwan, where they established a new country.

Mao set about immediately to create a socialist state in China. He nationalized firms and redistributed land to peasants. Many of those who had owned land under the old regime were executed. China's entry into the Korean War in 1950 led to much closer ties to the Soviet Union, which helped China to establish a centralized command socialist economy.

China's first 5-year plan, launched in 1953, followed the tradition of Soviet economic development. It stressed capital-intensive production and the development of heavy industry. But China had far less capital and a great many more people than did the Soviet Union. Capital-intensive development made little sense. In 1958, Mao declared a uniquely Chinese approach to development, which he dubbed the Great Leap Forward. It focused on labor-intensive development and the organization of small productive units. Indeed, households were encouraged to form their own productive units under the slogan "An iron and steel foundry in every backyard." The Great Leap repudiated the bonuses and other material incentives stressed by the Soviets; motivation was to come from revolutionary zeal, not self-interest.

In agriculture, the new plan placed greater emphasis on collectivization. Farmers were organized into communes containing several thousand households each. Small private plots of land, which had been permitted earlier, were abolished. China's adoption of the plan was a victory for radical leaders in the government.

The Great Leap was an economic disaster. Output plunged. Moderate leaders then took over, and the economy got back to its 1957 level of output by the mid-1960s.

Power shifted back and forth between radicals and moderates during the next 15 years. China remained a command socialist economy throughout this period; the two groups differed primarily on the nature of the incentives that the system would offer. Changes in economic policy at the center, however, contributed to greater autonomy at regional levels. Another factor promoting regional autonomy was Chinese geography. The country is vast, and transportation across it difficult. The eighth-century poet Li Bao once remarked that it was more difficult to get to Sichuan, a province in South Central China, than to get to heaven. Difficulty in travel and the lack of a good communications system contributed to a high degree of regional autonomy in China. That autonomy, in turn, played a key role in China's reform process.

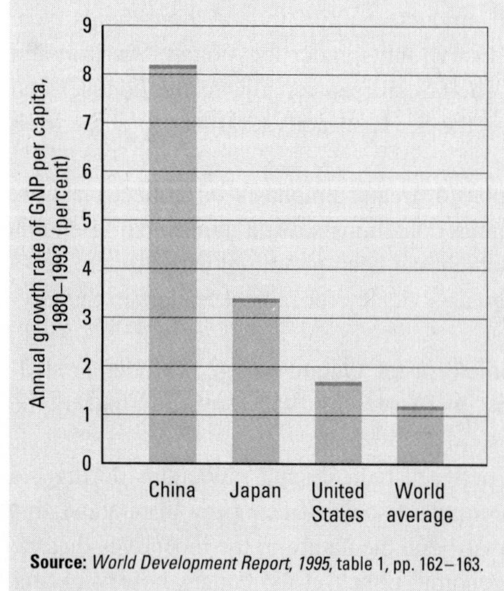

Source: *World Development Report, 1995,* table 1, pp. 162–163.

EXHIBIT 38-2

Soaring Output in China

China's growth in per capita output from 1980 to 1993 greatly exceeded rates recorded for Japan, the United States, or the average of all nations.

China's Reforms

In 1978 Zhao Ziyang, first secretary of the Communist party in Sichuan province, expressed his frustration with the Chinese economic system, likening China's economy to a silkworm locked in the cocoon of central planning. He issued an order freeing six state enterprises in Sichuan from control by the planning system and directed the firms to operate independently. They could determine their own output, set their own prices, and keep the profits they earned. Within 2 years, 6,600 firms had been unleashed. Zhao became China's head of state, and China was launched on a course that would take it closer to a market capitalist economy.

The initial impetus for reform thus came from a provincial leader. That was also true of agricultural reform, which has been the most impressive success story in the Chinese experience. Reform in China was thus a bottom-up process, one that began in the provinces and then became national policy. That's quite different from the top-down reform process of other transitional economies, in which the central government commits to reform and then orders local government officials to go along. Given the high level of autonomy of local leaders in China's system, a bottom-up approach to reform was probably the only one that could succeed.

Beginning in 1979, many Chinese provincial leaders instituted a system called *bao gan dao hu*—"contracting all decisions to the household." Under the system, provincial officials contracted the responsibility for operating collectively owned farmland to individual households. Government officials gave households production quotas they were required to meet and purchased that output at prices set by central planners. But farmers were free to sell any additional output they could produce at whatever prices they could get in the marketplace and to keep the profits for themselves.

The shift to household quotas from the old system of quotas that had been set for each collective was officially banned by China's central government in 1979. The ban, however, carried little weight. By 1984, 93 percent of China's agricultural land had been contracted to individual households.

The new system of household contracting was an immediate success. Crop output had increased at only a 2.5 percent rate between 1953 and 1978, a slower pace than the rate of population growth. From 1979 to 1984, it grew at a 6.8 percent rate. The central government finally withdrew its official opposition and sanctioned the program in 1984.

Urban industrial reform, which had been pursued on a limited basis since Zhao's directive in 1978, became national policy in 1984. State firms were told to meet their quotas and then were free to engage in additional production for sale in free markets.

In effect, China has two tiers of economic systems, a command system and a market system operating at the margin. By leaving the state system in place, the Chinese avoided the disruptions that have plagued the transition process in other countries. Chinese officials refer to the approach as "changing a big earthquake into a thousand tremors."

How well has the gradual approach to transition worked? Between 1980 and 1993, China had one of the fastest-growing economies in the world. Its per capita output, measured in dollars of constant purchasing power, more than doubled. The country, once one of the poorest in the world, now ranks eighth among low-income countries, according to the World Bank. Exhibit 38-2 compares

Case in Point — Production Goes into High Gear at China Bicycle

Shenzhen is a city that typifies the new China. It's a city with modern skyscrapers, luxury hotels, and new factories that manufacture virtually anything one might imagine.

The city is the jewel of Guandong province, which in turn is the showcase province for all of China. The province, which adjoins Hong Kong, has moved closer to market capitalism than any other in China. It has also had the fastest-growing economy. Output in the province soared at a stunning rate of 12 percent per year during the 1980s and early 1990s.

One of Shenzhen's many successful private ventures is China Bicycle Company. CBC was one of the first foreign-owned companies permitted to operate when China launched its economic reforms in 1979. Jerome Sze, a Hong Kong businessman, started the firm. Initially, it was permitted to manufacture bicycles only for sale abroad. Among CBC's early customers was Schwinn. As economic policies have continued to become more liberal, however, CBC has been given the green light to compete with state-owned bicycle firms.

The chance to compete in the vast Chinese market is a spoke-spinning prospect. CBC has built a new factory on the outskirts of Shenzhen that will allow it to make 2.5 million bicycles a year. The company expects continued increases in income in China to boost demand for its bikes, which are more sophisticated than those produced by other firms in China. The firm is also considering production of mopeds and motorcycles as Chinese incomes continue to rise.

A street in Beijing.

Source: George Melloan, "All Is Bustle on China's Capitalist Road," *The Wall Street Journal,* 15 March 1993, A13.

growth rates in China to those achieved by Japan and the United States and to the average annual growth rate of all world economies between 1980 and 1993.

Where will China's reforms lead? While the Chinese leadership has continued to be repressive politically, it has generally supported the reform process. The result has been continued expansion of the free economy and a relative shrinking of the state-run sector. Given the rapid progress China has achieved with its gradual approach to reform, it's hard to imagine that the country would reverse course. It now falls in the market socialist category of economic systems. Given the course it's on, China seems likely to become a market capitalist economy—and a prosperous one—within a few decades.

Russia: An Uncertain Path to Reform

Russia dominated the former Soviet Union. It contained more than half the Soviet people and more than three-fourths of the nation's land area. Russia's capital, Moscow, was the capital and center of power for the entire country.

Today, Russia retains control over the bulk of the military power that had been accumulated by the former Soviet Union. While it is now an ally of the United States, Russia still possesses the nuclear capability to destroy life on earth. Its success in making the transition to market capitalism and joining as a full partner in the world community thus has special significance for peace.

Recent History

Russia's shift toward market capitalism has its roots in a reform process initiated during the final years of existence of the Soviet Union. That effort presaged many of the difficulties that have continued to plague Russia.

The Soviet Union, as we have already seen, had a well-established system of command socialism. Leading Soviet economists, however, began arguing as early as the 1970s that the old system could never deliver living standards comparable to those achieved in market capitalist economies. The first political leader to embrace the idea of radical reform was Mikhail Gorbachev, who became General Secretary of the Communist party—the highest leadership post in the Soviet Union—in 1985.

Gorbachev instituted political reforms that allowed Soviet citizens to speak out, and even to demonstrate, against their government. Economically, he called for much greater autonomy for state enterprises and a system in which workers' wages would be tied to productivity. The new policy, dubbed *perestroika,* or "restructuring," appeared to be an effort to move the economy toward market socialism.

But Gorbachev's economic advisers wanted to go much further. A small group of economists, which included Gorbachev's top economic adviser, met in August 1990 to draft a radical plan to transform the economy to a market capitalist system—and to do it in 500 days. Stanislav Shatalin, a Soviet economist, led the group. Gorbachev endorsed the Shatalin plan the following month, and it appeared that the Soviet Union was on its way to a new system. The new plan, however, threatened the Soviet power elite. It called for sharply reduced funding for the military and for the Soviet Union's secret police force, the KGB. It would have stripped central planners, who were very powerful, of their authority. The new plan called for nothing less than the destruction of the old system—and the elimination of the power base of most government officials.

Top Soviet bureaucrats and military leaders reacted to the Shatalin plan with predictable rage. They delivered an ultimatum to Mr. Gorbachev: Dump the Shatalin plan or be kicked out.

Caught between advisers who had persuaded him of the necessity for radical reform and Communist party leaders who would have none of it, Mr. Gorbachev chose to leave the command system in place and to seek modest reforms. He announced a new plan that retained control over most prices but allowed prices for roughly 30 percent of Soviet output to be negotiated between firms that produced the goods and firms that purchased them. He left in place the state's ownership of enterprises. In an effort to deal with shortages of other goods, he ordered sharp price increases early in 1991.

These measures, however, accomplished little. Black market prices for basic consumer goods were typically 10 to 20 times the level of state prices. Those prices, which respond to demand and supply, may be taken as a rough gauge of equilibrium prices. People were willing to pay the higher black market prices because they simply couldn't find goods at the state-decreed prices. Gorbachev's order to double and even triple some state prices narrowed the gap between official and equilibrium prices, but did not close it. Exhibit 38-3 shows the price changes imposed and compares them to black market prices.

Perhaps the most important problem for Gorbachev's price hikes was that there was no reason for state-owned firms to respond to them by increasing their output. The managers and workers in these firms, after all, were government em-

Case in Point Economists as Revolutionaries

Soviet economists took center stage in the peaceful revolution that brought down the Soviet Union, a country that had been one of the world's superpowers. It was a revolution of ideas, not bullets. And the ideas of Soviet economists were among the most influential.

Perhaps the most important economist in bringing on the changes that stunned the world was Abel Aganbegyan (pronounced ah-gahn-by-YAHN). Mr. Aganbegyan, an economist from the former Soviet republic of Armenia, served as Mikhail Gorbachev's chief economic adviser when Mr. Gorbachev first took office. Mr. Aganbegyan had long been a critic of the Soviet system. Two decades before the Soviet Union collapsed, he described it as "the most technologically backward of all the industrially developed countries."

Shortly after Mr. Gorbachev took power, he had a long meeting with Mr. Aganbegyan, a meeting that would prove pivotal for the Soviet Union. It was the meeting at which Mr. Aganbegyan convinced his boss that command socialism couldn't work. The system, he told the Soviet leader, required a radical transformation. He recalled his talk with the Soviet leader in an interview in 1991:

"It was not so difficult to convince Gorbachev of the need for change," Mr. Aganbegyan said. "I simply put before him the statistics that showed how far behind the West we were and told him that we would never achieve prosperity under the present system. We had to move to a market."

Mr. Aganbegyan credits Mr. Gorbachev's political advisers with making the case for the political reforms that allowed Soviet citizens to express for the first time their frustration with the government. "I didn't deal with the political side of things. But clearly political freedom would be part of the process of achieving the economic freedom that a market would give us. The two worked together."

Abel Aganbegyan.

The economist whose ideas had so much to do with instituting the process of change that would bring an end to the old system expressed optimism for the reform process, but he recognized the difficulties that lay ahead. "We say in Armenia that a pessimist is someone who thinks things can't get any worse. An optimist is someone who thinks they can. I'm an optimist. Things could get worse, but ultimately they will improve."

Source: Personal interview.

ployees receiving government-determined salaries. There was no mechanism through which they would gain from higher prices. A private firm could be expected to increase its quantity supplied in response to a higher price. State-owned firms did not.

The Soviet people faced the worst of economic worlds in 1991. Soviet output plunged sharply, prices were up dramatically, and there was no relief from severe shortages. A small group of government officials opposed to economic reform staged a coup in the fall of 1991, putting Gorbachev under house arrest.

EXHIBIT 38-3

Official Versus Black Market Prices in the Soviet Union, 1991

Mikhail Gorbachev ordered sharp increases in the prices of most consumer goods early in 1991 in an effort to eliminate shortages. As the table shows, however, a large gap remained between official and black market prices.

Item	Old Price	New Price	Black Market Price
Children's shoes	2–10 rubles	10–50 rubles	50–300 rubles
Toilet paper	32–40 kopeks	60–75 kopeks	2–3 rubles
Compact car	7,000 rubles	35,000 rubles	70,000–100,000 rubles
Bottle of vodka	10.5 rubles	10.5 rubles	30–35 rubles

Note: 1 ruble = 100 kopeks = $0.60 at the official exchange rate in 1991.

Source: *Komsomolskaya Pravda.*

The coup produced massive protests throughout the country and failed within a few days. Chaos within the central government created an opportunity for the republics of the Soviet Union to declare their independence, and they did. As individual republics declared their independence, the Soviet Union collapsed late in 1991.

The Reform Effort

Boris Yeltsin, the president of Russia, had been a leading proponent of market capitalism even before the Soviet Union collapsed. He had supported the Shatalin plan and had been sharply critical of Gorbachev's failure to implement it. Once Russia became an independent republic, Yeltsin sought a rapid transition to market capitalism.

Yeltsin's reform efforts, however, have been slowed by Russian legislators, most of them former Communist officials who were appointed to their posts under the old regime. They fought reform and have repeatedly sought to impeach Yeltsin.

Despite the hurdles, Russian reformers have accomplished a great deal. Prices of most goods have been freed from state controls. Russians have won the freedom to start their own businesses. Most state-owned firms have been privatized, and most of Russia's GDP is now produced by the private sector.

To privatize state firms, Russian citizens were issued vouchers that could be used to purchase state enterprises. Under this plan, which was first used by Mongolia in implementing its own transition from command socialism, state enterprises were auctioned off. Individuals, or groups of individuals, could use their vouchers to bid on them. Russian officials auctioned 5 percent of state enterprises in the spring of 1993; by 1995 most state enterprises in Russia had been privatized and GDP was beginning to rise.

A Look Back—And a Look Ahead

Socialism, a system in which factors of production are owned in common or by the public sector, is a very old idea. The impetus for installing it as a national economic system came from the writings of Karl Marx.

Marx argued that capitalism would inevitably collapse and give way to socialism. He argued that under capitalism workers would receive only a subsistence wage. Capitalists would extract the difference between what workers receive and what they produce as surplus value, a concept roughly equivalent to profit. As capitalists struggled to maintain surplus value, the degree and extent of exploitation of workers would rise. Capitalist systems would suffer through a series of crises in which firms cut back their output. The suffering of workers would increase, and the capitalist class would be weakened. Ultimately, workers would overthrow the market capitalist system and establish socialism in its place.

Marx's predictions about capitalist development have not come to fruition, but his ideas have been enormously influential. By the 1980s, roughly one-third of the world's people lived in economies built on the basis of his ideas.

The most important command socialist economy was the Soviet Union. In this economy, central planners determined what would be produced and at what price. Quotas were given to each state-owned firm. The system, which was emulated in most socialist nations, failed to deliver living standards on a par with those achieved by market economies. This failure ultimately brought down the system.

A very different approach to socialism was pioneered by Yugoslavia. State-owned firms were managed by their workers, who shared in their profits. Yugoslavia's economic system fell apart as the country broke up and suffered from ethnic strife and civil war.

As the governments of command socialist nations fell in 1989 and early in the 1990s, new governments launched efforts to achieve transition to market capitalism. We examined two cases of transition. China's gradual strategy has produced rapid growth, but in a politically repressive regime. Russia's transition has met opposition from officials who held power under the old system and whose continued power is threatened by reforms. Russia had, however, begun to make progress in 1995. Real GDP and living standards appeared to be rising. As Economics *went to press, the majority of Russia's production capacity had been privatized.*

Terms and Concepts for Review

Labor theory of value

Surplus value

For Discussion

1. There is a gap between what workers receive and the value of what workers produce in a market capitalist system. Why? Does this constitute exploitation? Does it create the kinds of crises Marx anticipated? Why or why not?
2. What is meant by the labor theory of value? What are the shortcomings of the theory?
3. What would you say is the theory of value offered in this book? How does it differ from the labor theory of value?
4. In what ways does reliance on the labor theory of value create a problem for the allocation of natural resources?
5. What do you think would be the advantages of labor-managed firms of the kind that operated in Yugoslavia? The disadvantages?
6. Suppose you were the manager of a Soviet enterprise under the old command system. You've been given a quota and the promise of a big bonus if your firm meets it. How might your production choices differ from those of the management of a profit-maximizing firm in a market capitalist economy?
7. What are some government-operated enterprises in the United States? Do you see any parallels between the problems command economies faced with the production of goods and services and problems in the United States with state-run enterprises?
8. A Chinese firm operating in the two-tier system will have an incentive to produce the efficient level of output, even though some of its output is claimed by the state at state-determined prices. Why is that the case?
9. Given that market capitalist systems generate much higher standards of living than do command socialist systems, why do you think many Russian government officials have opposed the adoption of a market system?
10. How does widespread criminal activity sap economic growth?

Illustration Credits

Part One Opener

Opalescent Yellow Persian with Red Lip Wrap 1993. (Detail) Glass Sculpture by Dale Chihuly. 17 × 27 × 25″. Photo: Claire Garoutte

Part Two Opener

Cerulean Blue Persian Set with Red Lip Wraps 1990. (Detail) Glass Sculpture by Dale Chihuly. 11 × 19 × 19″. Photo: Roger Schreiber

Part Three Opener

Cerulean Persian with Chinese Red Lip Wrap 1989. (Detail) Glass Sculpture by Dale Chihuly. 18 × 32 × 36″. Photo: Terry Rishel

Part Four Opener

Burnt Sienna Persian Set with Cobalt Lip Wraps 1990. (Detail) Glass Sculpture by Dale Chihuly. 17 × 32 × 28″. Photo: Roger Schreiber

Part Five Opener

Glowing Violet Persian Set with Yellow Lip Wraps 1990. (Detail) Glass Sculpture by Dale Chihuly. 12 × 36 × 23″. Photo: Roger Schreiber

Part Six Opener

Cobalt Green Seaform Set with Purple Lake Lip Wraps 1987. (Detail) Glass Sculpture by Dale Chihuly. 7 × 14 × 14″. Photo: Terry Rishel

Part Seven Opener

Honeysuckle Blue Seaform Set with Yellow Lip Wraps 1993. (Detail) Glass Sculpture by Dale Chihuly. 13 × 26 × 15″. Photo: Terry Rishel

Part Eight Opener

Yellow Ochre Persian Single with Red Lip Wrap 1990. (Detail) Glass Sculpture by Dale Chihuly. 12 × 24 × 17″. Photo: Roger Schreiber

Part Nine Opener

Altrosa Pink Maccia Set #2 1990. (Detail) Glass Sculpture by Dale Chihuly. 13 × 30 × 22″. Photo: Roger Schreiber

Part Ten Opener

Cobalt Violet Persian Single with Yellow Lip Wrap 1990. (Detail) Glass Sculpture by Dale Chihuly. 17 × 34 × 27″. Photo: Roger Schreiber

Chapter 1

p. 6 Stephen J. Krasemann/DRK Photos; **p. 12** (top) Courtesy Sally Millar Reilly; **p. 12** (center) R. E. Ilg; **p. 12** (bottom) Courtesy Maria Muniagurria.

Chapter 2

p. 30 Reprinted with special permission of North America Syndicate; **p. 33** Tom and Pat Leeson/Photo Researchers, Inc.; **p. 38** National Archives/Photo Researchers, Inc.; **p. 40** (left) The Granger Collection; (right) Watercolor by Ludwig Gottfried von Redeken, 1787/The Granger Collection; **p. 42** Robert Trippett/Sipa Press; **p. 45** Alan McEwen/The Monterey County Herald.

Chapter 3

p. 62 Jim Noelker; **p. 66** David R. Frazier/Photo Researchers, Inc.

Chapter 4

p. 83 John Eastcott/Yva Momatiuk/The Image Works; **p. 87** Tony Stone Images.

Chapter 5

p. 100 Natalie Fobes/Tony Stone Images; **p. 104** Jeremy Woodhouse/DRK Photo; **p. 109** Dennis MacDonald/Photri; **p. 110** Colorado Historical Society.

Chapter 6

p. 116 Rob Gage/FPG International; **p. 127** Brian Bailey/Tony Stone Images.

Chapter 7

p. 146 Chris Harvey/Tony Stone Images; **p. 155** Mike Boroff/TexaStock; **p. 158** Will and Deni McIntyre/Photo Researchers, Inc.

Chapter 8

p. 180 Spencer Grant/Photo Researchers, Inc.: **p. 184** Treë.

Chapter 9

p. 203 George Goodwin/Monkmeyer Press; **p. 207** (left to right): Barry Talesnick/Retna; Bill Davila/Retna; Armondo Gallo/Retna; J. Cummings, All Action/Retna; John Chiasson/Gamma Liason Network; **p. 209** Ron Chapple/FPG International; **p. 213** Robert Burke/Gamma Liaison Network.

Chapter 10

p. 233 Elena Rooraid/PhotoEdit ; **p. 239** Bettmann Archive; **p. 243** Photri.

Chapter 11

p. 257 Photo Courtesy of Hewlett Packard Company and C-COR Electronics, Inc.; **p. 262** Renato Rotolo/Gamma Liaison Network; **p. 263** Susan McCartney/Photo Researchers, Inc.

Chapter 12

p. 274 Museo Delle Terme/Scala/Art Resource, NY; **p. 276** Hank Morgan/Rainbow; **p. 281** Rohan/Tony Stone Images.

Chapter 13

p. 300 Mark Cardwell, Reuter/Bettmann Archive; **p. 303** Treë; **p. 307** Archive Photos; **p. 310** Treë.

Chapter 14

p. 324 Greg Smith/SABA; **p. 326** Rhoda Sydney/PhotoEdit; **p. 330** Craig Schmittman/Tony Stone Images.

Chapter 15

p. 337 Jeffry W. Myers/The Stock Market; **p. 343** Alian Benainous/Gamma Liaison Network.

Chapter 16

p. 364 Jim Tucker, Farmland News AP/Wide World Photos; **p. 369** Susan Steinkamp/SABA.

Chapter 17

p. 376 Matthew McVay/SABA; **p. 385** Brad Markel/Gamma Liaison Network.

Chapter 18

p. 397 Michael Fogden/DRK Photo.

Chapter 19

p. 412 Brooks Kraft/Sygma.

Chapter 20

p. 430 Paul Kennedy/Gamma Liaison Network.

Chapter 21

p. 445 Dirck Halstead/Gamma Liaison Network; **p. 455** Dan Guravich/Photo Researchers, Inc.; **p. 457** Robert Wallis/SABA.

Chapter 22

p. 463 Daniel Sorine/Gamma Liaison Network; **p. 467** (top left) Bettmann Archive; (top right) National Portrait Gallery, Smithsonian Institution/Art Resource, NY; (center left & right) Bettmann Archive; (bottom left) Bettmann Archive; (bottom right) Diana Walker/Gamma Liaison Network; **p. 469** Verfugung gestellt von Frau Edith Nemegyei.

Chapter 23

p. 497 Dennis Brack/Black Star.

Chapter 24

p. 511 Luc Novovitch/Gamma Liaison Network; **p. 516** Courtesy of Merrill Lynch; **p. 521** Post File Photo; **p. 529** Perry Alan Werner/The Image Works.

Chapter 25

p. 545 National Portrait Gallery, Smithsonian Institution. On loan from Serena Williams Miles Van Ronsselach/Art Resource, NY.

Chapter 26

p. 564 Tony Freeman/PhotoEdit; **p. 573** Archive Photos.

Chapter 27

p. 589 AP/Wide World Photos; **p. 593** Dennis Brack/Black Star.

Chapter 28

p. 627 Guy Gillette/Photo Researchers, Inc.

Chapter 29

p. 638 Markel/Gamma Liaison Network; **p. 641** Caroline Parsons/Gamma Liaison Network; **p. 658** Dante Busquets-Sordo/Gamma Liaison Network.

Chapter 30

p. 666 J-P Laffont /Sygma; **p. 671** Bettmann Archive; **p. 673** Brooks Kraft/Sygma; **p. 674** Treë.

Chapter 32

p. 715 Patricia Hollander Gross/Stock, Boston.

Chapter 33

p. 731 Scottish National Portrait Gallery; **p. 737** Walter Bennett/TIME Magazine; **p. 749** O. Franken/Sygma.

Chapter 34

p. 766 Porter Gifford/Gamma Liaison Network; **p. 776** Jean Kugler/FPG International.

Chapter 35

p. 797 Donald Nausbaum/Tony Stone Images.

Chapter 36

p. 808 Gilles Martin/Gamma Liaison Network; **p. 810** Stan Ries/The Picture Cube; **p. 819** Robert Nickelsberg/Gamma Liaison Network.

Chapter 38

p. 852 Malcolm Linton/Black Star; **p. 855** Wolfgang Kaehler/Gamma Liaison Network; **p. 857** Sovfoto/Eastfoto.

Author Photo

Suzanne Tregarthen

Index

Note: Page numbers in boldface type indicate pages where terms are defined; those followed by n indicate notes.

Dictionary of Economic Terms

Dictionary of Economic Terms

Ability-to-pay principle suggests that people with more money should pay more taxes.

Absolute income test defines a person as poor if his or her income falls below a specific level.

Accounting profit is profit computed using explicit costs as the only measure of cost.

Adverse selection means the selection of subscribers to an insurance plan raises the probability of the event insured against.

Aggregate demand is the relationship between the total quantity of goods and services demanded and the price level, all other determinants of spending unchanged.

Aggregate demand curve is a graphical representation of aggregate demand.

Aggregate expenditures equal the sum of consumption, investment, government purchases, and net exports, all computed for a given price level.

Aggregate expenditures curve shows the relationship between aggregate expenditures and GDP.

Aggregate expenditures function is an equation relating aggregate expenditures to the level of real GDP.

Aggregate expenditures model relates the sum of consumption, investment, government purchases, and net exports to the level of GDP, all at a given level of prices.

Aggregate supply is the relationship between the total output produced and the price level, all other things unchanged.

Antitrust policy refers to government attempts to prevent the acquisition and exercise of monopoly power and to encourage competition in the marketplace.

Arc elasticity is computed by calculating percentage changes relative to the average value of each variable between two points.

Assets are anything that is of value.

Automatic stabilizers are government programs that tend to reduce the marginal expenditure rate.

Autonomous expenditures are expenditures that do not vary with the level of GDP.

Average total cost is total cost divided by the quantity of output produced.

Average variable cost is variable cost divided by the quantity of output produced.

Balanced budget occurs if the government has a surplus equal to zero.

Balance of payments is the balance between spending flowing into a country from other countries and spending flowing out of that country to other countries.

Balance on capital account is the sum of credits and debits in the capital account.

Balance on current account is the sum of credit and debit items in a nation's current account.

Bank is a financial institution that accepts deposits, makes loans, and offers checking accounts.

Barriers to entry are market conditions that prevent the entry of new firms in a monopoly market.

Barter system is an economy that lacks a medium of exchange.

Base period is a time period against which costs of the market basket in other periods will be compared in computing a price index.

Benefits received principle of taxation holds that taxes should be based on the benefits received from public sector services.

Bilateral monopoly is a situation in which a monopsony buyer faces a monopoly seller.

Bond is a promise to pay back a certain amount of money at a certain time.

Budget constraint restricts a consumer's spending to the total budget available to the consumer.

Budget line shows graphically the combinations of two goods a consumer can buy with a given budget.

Business cycle is a pattern of expansion, then recession, then expansion again.

Capital is a factor of production that has been produced for use in the production of other goods and services.

Capital account is a statement of spending flows into and out of a country during a particular period for purchases of assets.

Capital account deficit occurs if a country has a negative balance on its capital account.

Capital account surplus occurs if a country has a positive balance on its capital account.

Capital gains tax taxes income realized from the sale of assets at a different rate than that applied to other income.

Capital intensive describes a firm when it increases the ratio of capital to labor that it uses.

Carrying capacity of a resource is the quantity of its services that can be consumed in one period without reducing the stock of the resource in subsequent periods.

Cartel is a group of firms engaged in overt collusion.

Cash assistance is a money payment that a recipient may spend as he or she deems appropriate.

Central bank oversees the banking system in a nation by acting as a banker to the central government and to other banks, by regulating banks, and by setting monetary policy.

Ceteris paribus means "all other things unchanged."

Change in aggregate demand is a change in the aggregate quantity of goods and services demanded at each price level.

Change in the aggregate quantity of goods and services demanded is a movement along the aggregate demand curve.

Change in the aggregate quantity of goods and services supplied is a movement along the short-run aggregate supply curve in response to a change in the price level.

Change in quantity supplied is a movement along the supply curve; it results from a change in the price of a good or service.

Change in short-run aggregate supply is a change in the aggregate quantity of goods and services supplied at every price level in the short run.

Change in supply is a shift in the supply curve.

Check is a legal document used to transfer the ownership of a checkable deposit.

Checkable deposit is a bank deposit whose ownership can be transferred with a check.

Circular flow model is a pictorial representation of aggregate flows of spending and income through the economy.

Classical economics is the tradition of macroeconomic thought associated with the work of David Ricardo.

Closed shop is a firm in which workers must belong to a union before they can gain employment.

Collective bargaining is the representation of workers by a union during contract negotiations.

Command-and-control approach is one in which a government agency specifies how much or by what method a polluting agent must adjust its emissions.

Command capitalist economy is an economy in which resources are generally owned by private individuals, but the government exercises broad power to determine their use.

Command socialist economy is an economy in which the government owns most of the capital and natural resources and has broad power to determine how the economy's resources will be allocated.

Commodity money is money that has a value apart from its use as money.

Commodity standard system is a fixed exchange rate system in which the prices of various currencies are fixed relative to a given quantity of some commodity.

Common property resource is one for which no exclusive property rights exist.

Comparative advantage occurs when an economy producing a particular good has the lowest cost for producing that good.

Complementary factors of production are those in which an increase in the use of one increases the demand for the other.

Complements are two goods related in such a way that a reduction in the price of one increases the demand for the other.

Concentration ratio reports the percentage of total industry output accounted for by the largest firms in the industry.

Constant is something whose value does not change.

Constant price elasticity of demand curve is one whose price elasticity of demand is the same at every point on the curve.

Constant return to scale is experienced by firms when an increase in all factors by a given percentage results in an increase in output by the same percentage.

Constraint is a boundary that limits the range of choices an individual or a firm can make.

Consumer price index (CPI) is a price index whose movement reflects changes in the prices of goods and services typically purchased by consumers.

Consumer surplus is the difference between what a consumer would be willing to pay for a good or service and the price the consumer must pay to obtain that good or service.

Consumption–disposable personal income curve shows the value of consumption at each level of disposable personal income, all other determinants of consumption unchanged.

Consumption–disposable personal income function is an equation that relates consumption to the level of disposable personal income.

Consumption–disposable personal income schedule is a table that shows levels of consumption at various levels of disposable personal income.

Consumption–GDP curve shows the value of consumption at each level of GDP, all other determinants of consumption unchanged.

Consumption–GDP function is an equation that relates consumption to GDP.

Consumption–GDP schedule is a table that relates consumption to GDP.

Contractionary fiscal policy is a fiscal policy aimed at reducing the level of economic activity.

Contractionary monetary policy is a set of monetary policy choices aimed at reducing the level of economic activity.

Convertible paper money is paper money that may be redeemed for a specific commodity at a rate specified on the currency.

Cost of any choice is the value of the best opportunity forgone when the choice is made.

Cost-benefit analysis quantifies the benefits and costs of an activity in an effort to locate the efficient solution.

Cost per unit of labor is the sum of all costs incurred by a firm as a result of hiring a unit of labor.

Coupon rate is a percentage of the face value of a bond that will be paid periodically to its owner.

Creditor nation is a nation with a positive net foreign investment position.

Cross price elasticity of demand for one good or service equals the percentage change in quantity demanded for that good or service divided by the percentage change in price of a related good or service.

Crowding out is the tendency for an expansionary fiscal policy to reduce other components of aggregate expenditures.

Currency is paper money and coin issued by a government.

Current account is a statement of spending flows into and out of a nation during a particular period for exports and imports, together with the flow of payments to owners of foreign assets and transfer payments that flow across international borders.

Current account deficit exists if the balance on current account is negative.

Current account surplus exists if the balance on current account is positive.

Current income theory of consumption assumes that consumption spending in any one period is determined by income in that period.

Cyclically adjusted budget shows what federal expenditures and revenues would be if the economy were operating at its natural level of output.

Cyclical unemployment occurs when the quantity of labor supplied exceeds the quantity of labor demanded.

Debtor nation is a nation with a negative net foreign investment position.

Decreasing returns to scale, or **diseconomies of scale,** are experienced by a firm whose output rises by a smaller percentage than the increase in all its factors.

Deficiency payment is made to farmers when the market price of a particular crop falls below the target price.

Deficit is a negative surplus; it occurs if government expenditures exceed government revenue.

Demand curve is a graphical representation of a demand schedule. It shows the relationship between the price and quantity demanded of a good or service during a particular period, ceteris paribus.

Demand curve for capital shows the quantity of capital firms intend to hold at each interest rate.

Demand curve for money shows the quantity of money demanded at each interest rate, all other determinants of demand unchanged.

Demand for money is the relationship between the quantity of money people want to hold and the factors that determine that quantity.

Demand schedule is a table that shows the quantities of a good or service demanded at different prices during a particular period, ceteris paribus.

Demand shifter is a variable that can change the quantity of a good or service demanded at each price.

Demerit goods are goods whose consumption the public sector discourages on grounds that individuals don't adequately weigh their costs.

Demographic transition is a process in which population growth rises with a fall in death rates and then falls with a reduction in birth rates.

Dependency theory is a body of economic theory that concludes that the poverty found in the less developed nations is primarily caused by the inability of the developing nations to free themselves from dependence on the industrialized nations.

Dependent variable is one that changes in response to a change in another variable.

Deposit multiplier (M_d) equals the ratio of the maximum possible change in checkable deposits divided by the change in reserves that created it.

Depreciation is a reduction in the value of capital due to wearing out or to the passage of time.

Diminishing marginal returns occur when additional units of a variable factor add less and less to total output, given constant quantities of all other factors.

Discount rate is the interest rate the Fed charges to banks when it lends reserves to them.

Discouraged worker is one who is not working and would like to work but who has given up looking for work and is thus not counted as unemployed.

Discrimination occurs when people with similar economic characteristics experience different economic outcomes because of their race, sex, or other noneconomic characteristics.

Disposable personal income is the income households receive less the taxes they pay.

Dissaving is negative saving; it occurs when consumption during a period exceeds income during the period.

Dominant strategy is one that is the same regardless of the action of the other player in a game.

Dominant strategy equilibrium occurs if every player in a game has a dominant strategy.

Dumping occurs when an exporter sells a good to a country at a price below its own production cost.

Duopoly is an industry that consists of two firms.

Economic development is a process that produces sustained and widely shared gains in per capita real GDP.

Economic growth is the process through which the economy's natural level of real GDP is increased. It implies an outward shift in the production possibilities curve.

Economic rent is the amount by which the current price of a resource exceeds the minimum price necessary to make the resource available.

Economics is the study of how people choose among the alternatives available to them.

Economic system is the set of rules that define how an economy's resources are to be owned and how decisions about their use are to be made.

Economy is a system of institutions through which goods and services are produced and exchanged.

Efficiency condition requires that prices in the marketplace confront decisionmakers with the marginal benefits and marginal costs of their decisions. If the efficiency condition is met, the allocation of resources will be efficient.

Efficiency-wage theory holds that firms may try to increase productivity by paying a wage in excess of the market-clearing wage.

Efficient allocation of resources is one that achieves the maximum net benefit from all activities.

Efficient production is achieved when an economy operates on its production possibilities curve.

Elasticity is the ratio of the percentage change in a dependent variable to the percentage change in an independent variable, ceteris paribus.

Entrepreneurs are people who seek greater profits by finding new ways to combine capital, labor, and natural resources.

Equation of exchange states that the money supply times its velocity equals nominal GDP.

Equilibrium output is the output demanded and supplied at the equilibrium price.

Equilibrium price is the price at which the quantity demanded equals the quantity supplied.

Excess capacity exists when the profit-maximizing level of output is less than the output associated with the minimum possible average total cost of production.

Excess reserves are any reserves banks hold in excess of required reserves.

Exchange rate is the price of a country's currency in terms of another currency or currencies.

Exclusive property right is one that allows its owner to prevent others from using a resource.

Exhaustible natural resource is one for which consumption of its services necessarily reduces the stock of the resource.

Expansion is a period of rising real GDP.

Expansionary fiscal policy is a fiscal policy aimed at increasing the level of economic activity.

Expansionary monetary policy is a set of monetary policy choices aimed at increasing the level of economic activity.

Experimental economics employs controlled experiments using human or animal subjects to test economic hypotheses.

Explicit costs are charges that must be paid for the use of factors of production such as labor and capital, together with estimated depreciation costs.

Exponential growth occurs when a variable grows at a given percentage rate.

Exports represent sales of goods and services to foreign buyers during a period.

External cost is imposed when an action imposes costs on others outside the context of market exchange.

External economies in production occur when expanded production in one sector leads to lower costs in another.

Face value of a bond is the sum the issuer promises to pay when the bond matures.

Factor markets are markets in which households supply factors of production demanded by firms.

Factors of production are the resources the economy has available to produce goods and services.

Fallacy of false cause is the incorrect presumption that because two events tend to occur together, one must cause the other.

Federal funds market is a market in which banks lend reserves to one another.

Federal funds rate is the rate of interest charged for reserves in the federal funds market.

Federal government expenditures curve shows the negative relationship between total nominal federal government expenditures and real GDP.

Federal government revenue curve shows the positive relationship between total nominal federal revenues and real GDP.

Fiat money is money that some authority has ordered be accepted as money.

Final goods and services are those that are sold or are ready for sale to buyers who will use them for consumption, investment, government purchases, or net exports.

Financial intermediary is an institution that collects funds from lenders and distributes these funds to borrowers.

Financial market is a market in which funds accumulated by savers are distributed to borrowers.

Firms are organizations that produce goods and services.

Fiscal policy is the use of government purchases, transfer payments, and taxes to influence the level of economic activity.

Fixed costs are the costs associated with fixed factors of production.

Fixed exchange rates are exchange rates set by government policy.

Fixed factor of production is one whose quantity cannot be changed during a particular period.

Fixed income is one whose value is determined through some contractual arrangement and that does not change with economic conditions.

Foreign exchange market is a market in which currencies from different countries are traded for one another.

Fractional reserve banking system is one in which banks hold reserves whose value is less than the sum of claims on those reserves.

Free-floating exchange rate system is one in which governments and central banks do not participate in the currency market.

Free good is one that does not pose the problem of scarcity; one use of the good is not an alternative to another.

Free riders are people or firms that consume a public good without paying for it.

Frictional unemployment is unemployment that occurs because it takes time for employers looking for workers and workers looking for work to find each other.

Full employment means that all the factors of production that are available for use under current market conditions are being utilized.

Futures contract is a commitment by the issuer to deliver a certain quantity of a commodity on a certain date for a given price.

Game theory is an analytical framework used in the analysis of strategic choices.

Giffen good is a good for which the demand curve is upward sloping.

Good is a tangible commodity that people value.

Government expenditures include all spending by government agencies.

Government purchases occur when a government agency purchases or produces a good or service.

Graph is a pictorial representation of a relationship between two or more variables.

Gross domestic product (GDP) is the value, at current market prices, of the final goods and services produced by an economy during a particular period.

Gross private domestic investment is the official measure of investment in computing GDP.

Herfindahl index is an alternative measure of concentration, found by squaring the percentage share of each firm in an industry, then summing these squared market shares.

Horizontal merger is the consolidation of firms that compete in the same industry or product line.

Hotelling's principle asserts that the expected price of an exhaustible natural resource will rise at a rate equal to the market rate of interest.

Human capital is the set of acquired skills and abilities that workers bring to the production of goods and services.

Hyperinflation is an inflation rate in excess of 200 percent per year.

Hypothesis is a testable proposition about the relationship between two or more variables.

Hysteresis is the tendency of temporary events to have long-lasting consequences.

Illegal per se refers to an action that is illegal in and of itself without regard to the circumstances under which it occurs.

Impact lag is the lag between the time a policy goes into effect and the time the policy has its impact on the economy.

Imperfect competition exists in an industry with more than one firm and in which at least one firm is a price setter.

Implementation lag is the delay between the time at which a problem is recognized and the time at which a policy to deal with it is enacted.

Implicit cost is a cost that is included in the economic concept of cost but is not an explicit cost.

Implicit price deflator is a price index that reflects the prices of all goods and services. It is computed from the ratio of nominal GDP to real GDP.

Imports represent purchases of foreign-produced goods and services during a period.

Imports-GDP curve shows the level of imports at each level of real GDP, all other determinants of imports unchanged.

Import substitution refers to a developing nation's policy to restrict importation of consumer and capital goods, substituting domestically produced items.

Incentive approach to pollution regulation creates market-like incentives to encourage reductions in pollution but allows individual decisionmakers to decide how much to pollute.

Income-compensated price change is one in which we imagine that a consumer's income is adjusted at the same instant a price changes, so the consumer has just enough to buy the same goods and services at the new price.

Income deficit is the amount that would be required to bring every family in the United States above the poverty line.

Income effect of a price change is the amount by which a consumer changes his or her consumption of a good or service in response to the implicit change in income caused by a change in the good's price.

Income elasticity of demand (e_y) is the percentage change in quantity demanded divided by the percentage change in income, ceteris paribus.

Increasing marginal returns to a factor of production occur when the marginal product of the factor is rising as more of it is used, given a constant level of all other factors.

Increasing returns to scale (also called **economies of scale**) imply that when a firm increases all of its factors by a certain percentage, output increases by a larger percentage.

Independent variable is a variable that induces a change in a dependent variable.

Indexed payment is one whose nominal value is adjusted for the inflation rate.

Indifference curve shows combinations of two goods that yield the same level of utility.

Indirect business taxes are taxes imposed on firms in the course of their production of goods and services.

Induced expenditures are expenditures that vary with the level of GDP.

Inefficient allocation of resources is one that does not achieve the maximum net benefit from one or more activities.

Inefficient production results when an economy uses the resources it has available but produces at a point inside its production possibilities curve.

Infant industry is a new domestic industry with a potential for economies of scale.

Inferior good is one whose demand is reduced by increased income.

Inflation means persistent increases in the average level of prices.

Inflation-adjusted deficit for any period is the actual deficit for that period minus the amount by which inflation has reduced the real value of the national debt.

Inflationary gap results when the economy is producing above its natural level of output. It is equal to the difference between the actual and natural levels of real GDP.

Inflation-unemployment cycle is the pattern of a Phillips phase, stagflation phase, and recovery phase observed in the relationship between inflation and unemployment.

Interest is a premium paid to people who agree to postpone their use of wealth.

Interest rate is a premium paid for the use of money, expressed as a percentage of the amount of money involved.

International finance is the study of the economic implications of the monetary flows associated with international trade.

Inventory is the value of the stock of goods firms have on hand at any one time.

Investment is an addition to capital stock.

Investment demand curve is a curve that shows the level of investment at each interest rate, with all other determinants of investment held constant.

Investment–saving identity states that the sum of private saving, government saving, and rest-of-world saving must equal investment.

Investment tax credit reduces a firm's tax liability by a fraction of its investment during a period.

Isocost curve shows combinations of two factors that result in the same total cost for a firm.

Isoquant curve shows combinations of two factors that yield the same level of output.

Joint ventures are cooperative projects carried out by two or more firms. In the context of antitrust, joint ventures involve collusion that otherwise would be prohibited.

Keynes effect is the tendency for a change in the price level to affect the interest rate and thus to alter the real level of investment.

Kinked demand curve model assumes that rival firms will not change their prices if another firm raises its price but that they will match any price reduction.

Labor is the human effort applied to the production of goods and services.

Labor force is the number of people working plus the number of people unemployed.

Labor intensive describes a firm when it reduces the ratio of capital to labor that it uses.

Labor theory of value holds that the relative values of goods and services are ultimately determined by the quantities of labor required in their production.

Labor union is an association of workers that seeks to increase wages and to improve working conditions for its members.

Law is a theory that has won virtually universal acceptance.

Law of diminishing marginal returns holds that if the quantity of a variable factor of production is increased, with the quantities of all other factors given, the marginal product of the variable factor will eventually decline.

Law of diminishing marginal utility states that, beyond some level of consumption, the marginal utility of any good or service will decline as the quantity consumed increases during a given time period.

Law of increasing cost states that as output increases for one good in an economy that is on its production possibilities curve, the cost of additional units will be greater and greater.

Least-cost reduction in emissions is one in which emissions are reduced so that the marginal benefit of an additional unit of pollution is the same for all polluters.

Less developed countries (LDCs) are those that are not among the high-income nations of the world.

Liability is an obligation to another party.

Linear relationship implies a curve of constant slope—a straight line.

Liquidity of an asset reflects the ease with which it can be converted to money.

Loaned up describes a bank that holds no excess reserves.

Long run in microeconomics is a planning period during which all factors of production are variable. In macroeconomics it is a period in which real wages are flexible.

Long-run aggregate supply (LRAS) curve relates the level of output produced by firms to the price level in the long run.

Long-run average cost (LRAC) curve shows the lowest cost per unit at each level of output, assuming all factors of production are variable.

Long-run supply curve shows the quantity of a good or service supplied at various prices after all long-run adjustments to a price change have been completed.

Lorenz curve shows the cumulative shares of income received by individuals or groups.

M1 includes currency in circulation plus checkable deposits plus traveler's checks.

M2 includes M1 as well as other deposits, such as time deposits, small savings accounts, and money market mutual funds, that are easily converted to checkable deposits.

M3 includes M2, large time deposits, money market mutual funds held by institutions, and other assets that are somewhat less liquid than those in M2.

Macroeconomics is a branch of economics that examines the impact of choices on the total level of economic activity.

Managed competition describes the private health insurance system in which purchasing cooperatives (HIPCs) negotiate prices with insurers and health care providers, and consumers select their HIPCs.

Managed float is a system of floating exchange rates in which some governments or central banks seek to manipulate their exchange rates by buying or selling currency in the open market.

Malthusian trap is reached when population increases beyond the ability of the earth to feed it; starvation holds subsequent population in check.

Margin is a choice whether to do a little more or a little less of something.

Marginal benefit of an activity is the amount by which an additional unit of the activity increases total benefit.

Marginal cost of an activity is the amount by which an additional unit of the activity increases total cost.

Marginal decision rule: If the marginal benefit of an additional unit of an activity exceeds the marginal cost, the level of the activity should be increased. If the marginal benefit is less than the marginal cost, the level should be reduced. Net benefit is maximized at the quantity of the activity at which marginal benefit equals marginal cost.

Marginal expenditure rate (*MER*) is the rate at which aggregate expenditures increase as GDP increases; it is the slope of the aggregate expenditures curve.

Marginal factor cost (*MFC*) is the change in total cost when one more unit of a factor of production is added.

Marginal product of a factor of production is the change in total output resulting from a 1-unit increase in the quantity of the factor used, holding the quantities of all other factors constant.

Marginal product of labor is the change in output resulting from an additional unit of labor, given technology and the quantities of all other inputs.

Marginal propensity to consume out of disposable personal income (MPC_d) is the change in consumption ΔC divided by the change in disposable personal income ΔY_d; it is the slope of the consumption–disposable personal income curve.

Marginal propensity to consume out of GDP (MPC_Y) is the change in consumption divided by the change in GDP when moving along the consumption–GDP curve; it is the slope of the consumption–GDP curve.

Marginal propensity to import gives the rate at which imports increase with increases in real GDP.

Marginal rate of substitution is the maximum amount of one good that a consumer will give up to obtain an additional unit of another.

Marginal rate of technical substitution (MRTS) of capital for labor is the rate at which capital can be substituted for labor without affecting output; it is the negative of the slope of the isoquant curve.

Marginal revenue is the increase in a firm's total revenue when it sells an additional unit of output. It is measured as the slope of the total revenue curve ($\Delta TR/\Delta Q$).

Marginal revenue product (MRP) is the amount by which an additional unit of a factor increases a firm's total revenue during a period.

Marginal tax rate is the rate that would apply to an additional $1 of taxable income received by a taxpayer.

Marginal utility is the amount by which an additional unit of a good, service, or activity increases a consumer's total utility, ceteris paribus.

Market is a set of arrangements through which a particular good or service, or a group of goods or services, is produced and exchanged.

Market capitalist economy is one in which resources are generally owned by private individuals who have the power to make decisions concerning their use.

Market failure occurs when private decisions do not result in an efficient allocation of scarce resources.

Market price support is a specified loan rate for selected crops. The farmer may repay the loan at interest or forfeit the commodity at the end of the loan period as full payment of the loan.

Market socialist economy is one in which the government owns most of the capital and natural resources but allows the individuals who operate firms to make choices about the use of these factors.

Maturity date of a bond is the date on which the issuer promises to pay the face value.

Maximize is to make a choice that is expected to achieve the maximum value possible for some objective.

Means-tested transfer payment is a transfer payment for which recipients qualify on the basis of income.

Medium of exchange is anything that is widely accepted as a means of payment.

Merit goods are goods whose consumption the public sector encourages on grounds that individuals don't adequately weigh their benefits.

Microeconomics is a branch of economics that examines the choices of consumers and firms and the impacts of those choices on particular markets.

Model is a simplified representation of a particular problem.

Model of demand and supply combines demand and supply curves to explain the determination of price and output in a market.

Monetarist school argues that changes in the money supply are the primary source of fluctuations in aggregate demand and thus of short-run changes in real GDP and in the price level.

Monetary policy consists of a central bank's choices concerning open-market operations, a discount rate, and reserve requirements.

Money is anything that serves as a medium of exchange.

Money market is the interaction among institutions through which money is supplied to individuals, firms, and other institutions that demand money.

Money market equilibrium occurs at the interest rate at which the quantity of money demanded is equal to the quantity of money supplied.

Money supply is the total quantity of money in the economy at any one time.

Monopolistic competition is characterized by many firms producing differentiated products in a market with easy entry and exit.

Monopoly is a firm that is the only producer of a good or service for which there are no close substitutes and for which entry by potential rivals is prohibitively difficult.

Monopoly power is the power a firm has to sets its own price.

Monopsony is a market in which there is a single buyer of a good, service, or factor of production.

Monopsony power is held by a buyer facing an upward-sloping supply curve for a good, service, or factor of production.

Moral hazard is the tendency for insurance protection to increase the rate at which the insured outcome occurs by changing the behavior of those protected by the insurance.

Moral suasion is an effort to change people's behavior by appealing to their sense of moral values.

Multiplier is given by the ratio of the change in equilibrium GDP to the change in aggregate expenditures that produced it.

Multiplier effect is the phenomenon that occurs when a change in aggregate expenditures produces a larger change in equilibrium GDP in the aggregate expenditures model.

Nash equilibrium occurs when each player makes the best strategic choice, given the choice expected of the other player.

National debt is the sum of all past federal deficits.

Nationalization is a process through which a government agency assumes the ownership and operation of a previously private firm.

Natural level of employment is the level of employment at which the quantity of labor demanded equals the quantity supplied.

Natural level of real GDP is the level of real GDP produced when the economy is operating at its natural level of employment.

Natural monopoly exists whenever a single firm confronts economies of scale over the entire range of production that is relevant to its market.

Natural rate of unemployment is the unemployment rate consistent with employment at the natural level.

Natural resources are the resources of the natural environment that can be used for the production of goods and services.

Negative marginal returns occur when additional units of a variable factor of production reduce total output, given constant quantities of all other factors.

Negative relationship is one in which two variables move in opposite directions.

Net benefit of any activity is its total benefit minus its total cost.

Net domestic product (NDP) equals GDP minus depreciation.

Net exports are a country's exports minus its imports during a period.

Net foreign investment position of a country equals the value of foreign assets held by its residents minus the value of its assets held by foreign residents.

Net investment equals investment minus depreciation during a particular period.

Net present value (NPV) of an asset equals the present value of the revenues minus the present value of the costs associated with the asset.

Net private domestic investment is gross private domestic investment minus depreciation.

Net worth equals assets less liabilities.

New classical school emphasizes wage and price flexibility and the microeconomic foundations of economic behavior.

New international economics is a body of thought that applies theories of imperfect competition to the analysis of international trade.

New Keynesian school emphasizes the stickiness of prices and the resultant inability of the economy to achieve its natural level of employment on its own.

Nominal GDP is the GDP for a period valued at prices in that period.

Nominal value is a value measured in dollars of current purchasing power.

Noncash assistance is the provision of specific goods and services rather than cash.

Nonintervention policy is a policy choice to take no action to try to correct a recessionary or inflationary gap and to allow the economy to adjust on its own to its natural level.

Nonlinear relationship is shown by a curve whose slope is changing.

Non-means-tested transfer payment is one for which income is not a qualifying factor.

Nontariff barrier is a regulation that restricts imports without imposing a quota or tariff.

Normal good is one whose demand is increased by increased income.

Normative statement is one that makes a value judgment.

Oligopoly is a market dominated by a few firms; each of those firms recognizes that its own choices will affect the choices of its rivals and that its rivals' choices will affect it.

One-way trade occurs when a country is, in its trade with another country, either an importer or an exporter of the goods and services of a particular industry; it is not both.

Open-market operations are transactions in which the Fed buys or sells federal government securities.

Open shop is a firm that can hire and retain union as well as nonunion members.

Overt collusion means that firms agree openly on price, output, and other decisions aimed at achieving monopoly profits.

Payoff is the outcome of a strategic choice.

Peak of a business cycle is reached when real GDP stops rising and begins falling.

Per capita real GDP is real GDP divided by population.

Perfect competition is a model of the market that assumes that there are a large number of firms and buyers, that the firms produce identical products, that it is easy for new firms to enter and for existing firms to leave the market, and that buyers and sellers have complete information about market conditions.

Permanent income is the average annual income people expect to receive for the remainder of their lives.

Permanent income theory of consumption asserts that current consumption spending depends on permanent income.

Personal consumption measures the value of goods and services purchased by households during a particular period.

Personal saving is disposable personal income not spent on consumption during a particular period.

Phillips curve implies a negative relationship between inflation and unemployment.

Phillips phase is a period in which the inflation rate rises and the unemployment rate falls.

Physician-induced demand occurs when doctors prescribe treatments that are not medically justified in order to increase their own incomes.

Pollution exists when human activity produces a sufficient concentration of a substance in the environment to cause harm to people or to resources valued by people.

Positive relationship between two variables is one in which both variables move in the same direction.

Positive statement is a statement of fact or a hypothesis.

Poverty line is an annual income level that marks the dividing line between poor households and those that are not poor.

Poverty rate is the percentage of the population living in households whose income falls below the poverty line.

Precautionary demand for money is the money people and firms hold for contingencies that people expect will occur, but at an uncertain time and in an uncertain amount.

Present value of a specific future value is the amount that would, if deposited today at some interest rate, equal the future value.

Price ceiling is a maximum price set below the equilibrium price.

Price discrimination means charging different prices to different customers for the same good or service even though the cost of supplying those customers is the same.

Price elastic describes demand when the absolute value of the price elasticity of demand is greater than 1.

Price elasticity of demand (e_p) is the ratio of the percentage change in the quantity demanded to the percentage change in price, ceteris paribus.

Price-fixing is an agreement between two or more firms to collude in order to establish a price and not to compete on the basis of price.

Price floor is a minimum price set above the equilibrium price.

Price index is a number whose movement reflects movement in the average level of prices.

Price inelastic describes demand when the absolute value of the price elasticity of demand is less than 1.

Price setter is a firm that faces a downward-sloping demand curve.

Price takers are individuals in a market—buyers or sellers—who have no ability to affect the price of the good in the market.

Private debt money is a loan that the borrower promises to repay on demand.

Private good is one for which exclusion is possible and for which the marginal cost of an additional user is positive.

Privatization is a process in which government-owned firms are transferred to the private sector.

Production possibilities curve illustrates graphically the alternative combinations of goods and services an economy can produce with its scarce factors of production.

Product markets are markets in which firms supply goods and services demanded by households.

Profit is the difference between a firm's total revenue and its total economic costs.

Progressive tax is one that takes a higher percentage of income as income rises.

Property rights are a set of rules that specify the ways in which the resources for which they are defined may be used.

Proportional tax takes a fixed percentage of income as taxes, regardless of the level of income.

Protectionist policies are restrictions on free international trade designed to protect domestic industries from competitive market forces that originate beyond the borders of the country.

Public choice theory assumes that individuals in the public sector make choices that maximize their own utility.

Public finance is the study of government expenditure and tax policy and the impacts of these policies on the economy.

Public good is a good or service for which exclusion cannot be applied and for which the marginal cost of an additional user is zero.

Public interest theory assumes that the goal of government is to maximize welfare by seeking an efficient allocation of resources.

Quantity demanded of a good or service is the quantity consumers are willing to buy at a particular price during a particular period, ceteris paribus.

Quantity supplied of a good or service is the quantity sellers are willing to sell at a particular price during a particular period, ceteris paribus.

Quasi-public good is one for which some benefits are public while others are private.

Quota specifies the maximum amount of a good or service that may be imported during a specified period of time.

Rate of market substitution (RMS) is the rate at which units of one good can be exchanged for another in the marketplace.

Rate of product transformation (RPT) is the rate at which units of one good can be transformed into another.

Rational abstention is a decision not to vote on grounds that the costs of voting exceed the benefits.

Rational expectations is an approach to macroeconomic analysis that assumes that individuals make the best possible use of all available information in forming their expectations.

Real balance effect is the tendency of a price level change to affect the real value of wealth and thus to alter consumption.

Real business cycle theory asserts that changes in long-run aggregate supply are the primary source of fluctuations in real GDP.

Real GDP is the total value, calculated at base-year prices, of the final goods and services produced during a given time period.

Real value is a value measured in dollars of constant purchasing power.

Recession is a period in which real GDP falls for two or more consecutive quarters.

Recessionary gap occurs when the economy is producing an output below the natural level. It is equal to the difference between the natural and actual levels of real GDP.

Recognition lag is the delay between the time at which an event occurs and the time at which policymakers become aware of it.

Recovery phase is a period in which inflation and unemployment decline.

Regressive tax is one that takes a lower percentage of income as income rises.

Regulation is an effort by government agencies to control the choices of private firms or individuals.

Relative income test defines people as poor if their incomes fall at the bottom of the distribution of income.

Renewable natural resource is one whose services can be consumed without reducing the stock of the resource.

Repudiation of the debt is a declaration by a government that it will no longer honor its debt.

Required reserve ratio is the ratio of reserves to checkable deposits banks are required to maintain.

Required reserves are the quantity of reserves that banks are required to hold.

Reservation wage is the lowest wage that, if offered, would be accepted by an unemployed worker.

Reserves equal the cash a bank has in its vault plus deposits the bank maintains with the Fed.

Returns to scale examine how output will be affected by a given percentage change in the quantities of all factors used by a firm.

Rule of reason holds that whether or not a particular business practice is illegal depends upon the circumstances surrounding the action.

Rule of 72 states that a value growing at a given percentage rate will double over a fixed interval approximated by 72 divided by the interest rate, stated as a whole number.

Saving is income not spent on consumption.

Saving–disposable personal income curve relates saving to the level of disposable personal income.

Say's law is the assertion that the total value of goods and services produced will generate income—and therefore demand—equal to that production.

Scarce good is one for which the choice of one alternative requires that another be given up.

Scarcity is a situation in which we are forced to choose among alternatives.

Scientific method is a set of procedures through which knowledge is created.

Service is an intangible commodity that people value.

Shortage exists if the quantity of a good or service demanded exceeds the quantity supplied at the current price.

Short run in microeconomics is a planning period during which some factors of production are fixed in quantity. In macroeconomics it is a period in which real wages are sticky.

Short-run aggregate supply (SRAS) curve is a graphical representation of the relationship between the price level and the total output that will be produced in the short run, assuming all other factors that affect output remain unchanged.

Short-run supply curve is a supply curve found by summing the supply curves of individual firms in the short run.

Shutdown point is the minimum value of average variable cost for a firm.

Single-payer plan is one in which the federal government would replace all private insurers.

Slope of a curve is the ratio of the change in the variable on the vertical axis to the change in the variable on the horizontal axis, measured between two points on the curve.

Speculative demand for money is the money households and firms hold because of a concern that bond prices and the prices of other financial assets might fall.

Stabilization policy involves some action by the public sector to shift aggregate demand or short-run aggregate supply to move the economy toward its natural level of real GDP.

Stagflation phase is a period in which inflation remains high while unemployment increases.

Sticky price is one that is slow to adjust to its equilibrium level.

Stock market is the set of institutions in which shares of stock are bought and sold.

Strategic choice is based on the recognition that the actions of others will affect the outcome of the choice, and it takes these actions into account.

Strategic trade policy is the use of government intervention to promote the development of a particular industry that will increase domestic welfare through its trade with the rest of the world.

Structural unemployment is unemployment that results from a mismatch between worker qualifications and employer requirements.

Substitute factors of production are two goods related in such a way that the increased use of one lowers the demand for the other.

Substitutes are two goods related in such a way that a reduction in the price of one reduces the demand for the other.

Substitution effect of a price change is the amount by which the consumption of a good or service changes in response to an income-compensated change in its price.

Sunk cost is an expenditure that has already been made that cannot be recovered.

Supply curve is a graphical representation of a supply schedule. It shows the relationship between the price and quantity supplied of a good or service during a particular period, ceteris paribus.

Supply curve of money relates the quantity of money that banks supply in the economy to the interest rate.

Supply schedule is a table that shows the quantities of a good or service supplied at different prices during a particular period, ceteris paribus.

Supply shifter is a variable that can change the quantity of a good or service supplied at each price.

Supply-side economics is the belief that fiscal policy can be used to stimulate long-run aggregate supply.

Surplus exists if the quantity of a good or service supplied exceeds the quantity demanded at the current price.

Surplus (budget or government) equals government revenue less government expenditures.

Surplus value is the difference between the price of a good or service and its labor cost.

T-account is a form of financial statement showing assets, liabilities, and net worth.

Tacit collusion is an unwritten, unspoken agreement through which firms limit competition among themselves.

Target price is a price the government guarantees farmers will receive for a particular crop.

Tariff is a tax imposed by a government or country on imported goods or services.

Technology is knowledge that can be applied to the production of goods and services.

Terms of trade give the rate at which a country can trade domestic products for imported products.

Theory is a hypothesis that has been tested extensively without being rejected and that has won widespread acceptance.

Third-party payer system is one in which consumers select their health care services while other institutions pay a share of the cost of those services.

Time-series graph depicts how the value of a variable changes over time.

Tit-for-tat strategy is one in which a firm responds to cheating by a rival by cheating and to cooperation by a rival by cooperating.

Total cost is the sum of fixed and variable costs.

Total product curve relates the output of a firm per period to the quantity of a variable input used, with quantities of other inputs and technology unchanged.

Total revenue is equal to a firm's total output times the price at which it sells that output.

Total utility is a conceptual measure of the number of units of utility a person obtains by consuming a given quantity of a good, service, or activity during a given time period.

Trade deficit results from negative net exports.

Trade surplus results from positive net exports.

Trade-weighted exchange rate is an index of exchange rates.

Trading line is a line that shows all the combinations of two goods whose total monetary value equals some fixed amount.

Transactions demand for money is the money households and firms hold in order to pay for goods and services they buy.

Transferable property right is one that can be sold or leased to someone else.

Transfer payments are government payments to individuals in the form of grants rather than as payments for labor or other services.

Trend rate of real GDP growth is the average annual growth rate of real GDP over some period.

Trigger strategy is a threat to respond to a rival's cheating by permanently revoking an agreement.

Trough of a business cycle is reached when real GDP stops falling and begins rising.

Two-way trade occurs when a country both imports and exports the product of a particular industry.

Tying agreement requires buyers to meet conditions placed on them by sellers in order to be able to purchase or distribute the manufacturers' products.

Unemployment is measured as the number of people not working who are looking and available for work at any one time.

Unemployment rate is the percentage of the labor force who are unemployed.

Union shop is a firm that can hire union as well as nonunion workers, but nonunion workers are required to join the union within a specified period of time.

Unit of account is a consistent means of measuring the value of things.

Unit price elastic describes demand when the absolute value of the price elasticity of demand is equal to 1.

User fees are charges levied on consumers of government-provided services.

Utility is the satisfaction people receive from consuming goods and services or engaging in some activities.

Utility-maximizing condition requires that total outlays equal the budget and that the ratio of marginal utility to price is equal for all goods and services.

Variable is anything whose value can change.

Variable costs are the costs incurred by a firm in its use of variable factors of production.

Variable factor of production is one whose quantity can be changed during a particular period.

Velocity of money is the number of times the money supply is spent for the goods and services that make up GDP during a particular period.

Vertical merger is the consolidation of firms that participate in the production of a given product line, but at different stages of the production process.

Voluntary export restriction is a trade barrier by which foreign firms agree to limit the quantity of exports to a particular country.

Wealth is the total of assets less liabilities.

Zero-coupon bond is a bond that does not carry a coupon rate.